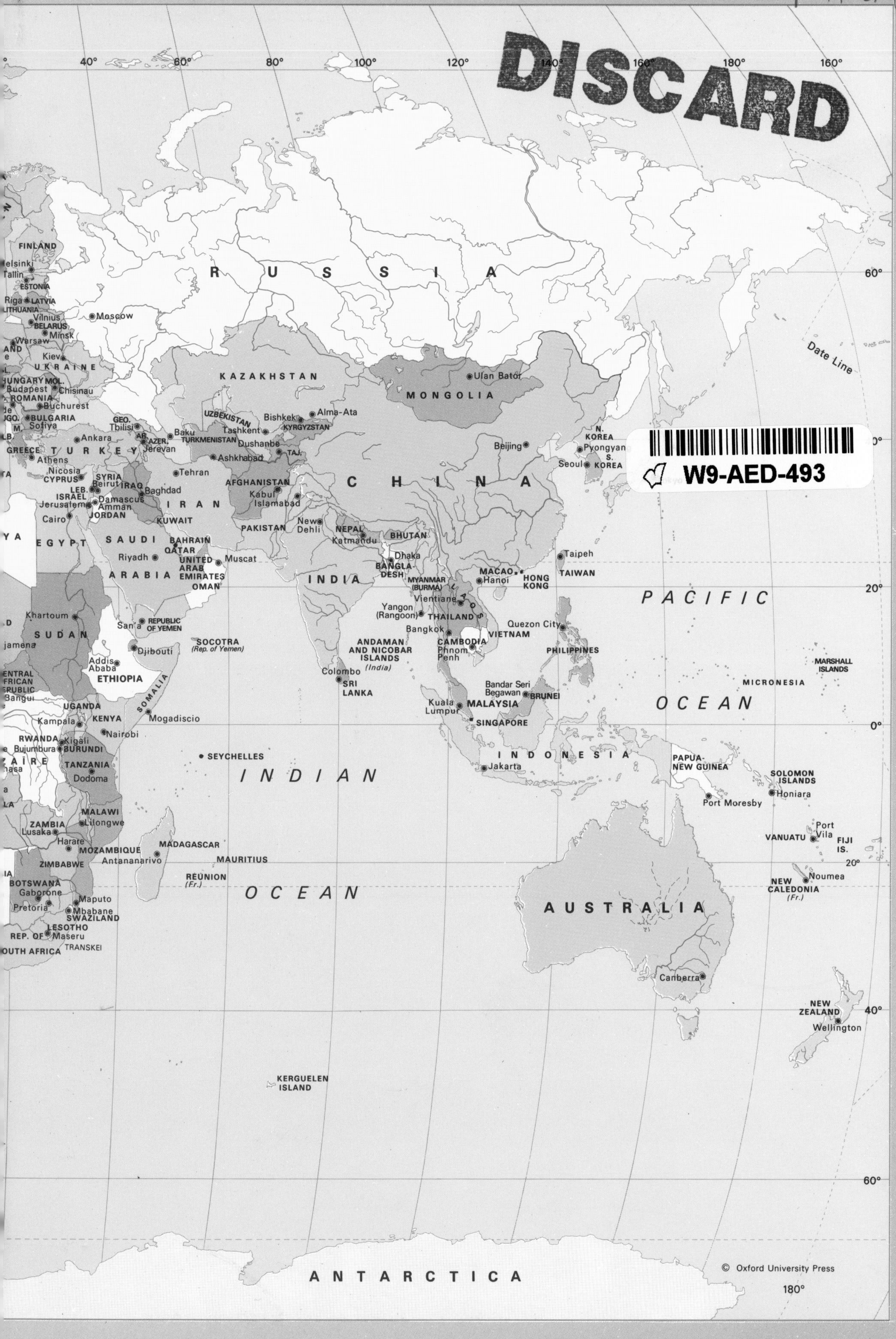
40°
60°
80°
100°
120°
140°
160°
180°
160°
R U S S I A
FINLAND
Tallinn
ESTONIA
Riga
LATVIA
Vilnius
BELARUS
Minsk
Moscow
Warsaw
Kiev
U K R A I N E
Budapest
MOL.
Chisinau
ROMANIA
Bucharest
BULGARIA
Sofiya
GEO.
Tbilisi
AR.
AZER.
Yerevan
Baku
GREECE
T U R K E Y
Ankara
Athens
Nicosia
CYPRUS
SYRIA
Beirut
LEB.
ISRAEL
Damascus
Jerusalem
Amman
JORDAN
IRAQ
Baghdad
Cairo
EGYPT
KAZAKHSTAN
UZBEKISTAN
Tashkent
TURKMENISTAN
Ashkhabad
Dushanbe
TAJ.
Bishkek
KYRGYZSTAN
Alma-Ata
Tehran
I R A N
KUWAIT
AFGHANISTAN
Kabul
Islamabad
PAKISTAN
S A U D I
A R A B I A
Riyadh
BAHRAIN
QATAR
UNITED ARAB EMIRATES
Muscat
OMAN
MONGOLIA
Ulan Bator
Beijing
C H I N A
N. KOREA
Pyongyang
S. KOREA
Seoul
New Dehli
NEPAL
Katmandu
BHUTAN
Dhaka
BANGLA-DESH
I N D I A
MYANMAR (BURMA)
Yangon (Rangoon)
Vientiane
THAILAND
Bangkok
CAMBODIA
Phnom Penh
VIETNAM
Hanoi
MACAO
HONG KONG
Taipeh
TAIWAN
Quezon City
PHILIPPINES
Date Line
60°
20°
0°
20°
40°
60°
Khartoum
SUDAN
San'a
REPUBLIC OF YEMEN
SOCOTRA
(Rep. of Yemen)
Djibouti
Addis Ababa
ETHIOPIA
SOMALIA
Mogadiscio
UGANDA
Kampala
KENYA
Nairobi
RWANDA
Kigali
Bujumbura
BURUNDI
TANZANIA
Dodoma
MALAWI
Lilongwe
ZAMBIA
Lusaka
Harare
MOZAMBIQUE
ZIMBABWE
BOTSWANA
Gaborone
Pretoria
Maputo
Mbabane
SWAZILAND
LESOTHO
Maseru
REP. OF SOUTH AFRICA
TRANSKEI
MADAGASCAR
Antananarivo
MAURITIUS
REUNION
(Fr.)
SEYCHELLES
I N D I A N
O C E A N
ANDAMAN AND NICOBAR ISLANDS
(India)
Colombo
SRI LANKA
Kuala Lumpur
MALAYSIA
SINGAPORE
Bandar Seri Begawan
BRUNEI
I N D O N E S I A
Jakarta
PAPUA-NEW GUINEA
Port Moresby
SOLOMON ISLANDS
Honiara
P A C I F I C
O C E A N
MICRONESIA
MARSHALL ISLANDS
VANUATU
Port Vila
FIJI IS.
NEW CALEDONIA
(Fr.)
Noumea
A U S T R A L I A
Canberra
NEW ZEALAND
Wellington
KERGUELEN ISLAND
A N T A R C T I C A
© Oxford University Press
180°

OXFORD
ILLUSTRATED
ENCYCLOPEDIA
of

PEOPLES AND CULTURES

OXFORD
ILLUSTRATED
ENCYCLOPEDIA

OXFORD
ILLUSTRATED
ENCYCLOPEDIA

of

PEOPLES AND CULTURES

Volume Editor
Richard Hoggart

OXFORD
OXFORD UNIVERSITY PRESS
NEW YORK   MELBOURNE
1992

Oxford University Press, Walton Street, Oxford OX2 6DP
Oxford New York Toronto
Delhi Bombay Calcutta Madras Karachi
Petaling Jaya Singapore Hong Kong Tokyo
Nairobi Dar es Salaam Cape Town
Melbourne Auckland
and associated companies in
Berlin Ibadan

Oxford is a trade mark of Oxford University Press

Published in the United States
by Oxford University Press, New York

© Oxford University Press 1992

British Library Cataloguing in Publication Data
Data is available from the British Library

Library of Congress Cataloging in Publication Data
Data applied for
ISBN 0-19-869139-4

Text processed by Oxford University Press
Printed in Hong Kong

Foreword

How often does each of us pause to consider what makes individuals or societies tick, what makes them so varied? Many of us follow current affairs on television or in a daily newspaper—but how far do we consider the concepts, beliefs, and ideas which underlie and give shape to the turmoil of daily affairs? The *Oxford Illustrated Encyclopedia of Peoples and Cultures* sets out to define and examine those ideas, in particular across the contemporary world. There has never been so great a need for understanding our own and other societies as in this era of mass communication and rapid scientific progress, when we are bombarded with information but do not always think through to the key underlying issues. In an age which has developed the potential for mutual mass destruction, it is more crucial than ever that we should try to understand other individuals and societies and to respect different systems of belief. My brief was to put together a book on all the different aspects of contemporary peoples and cultures. In planning this volume, we quickly realized that we would not have space to describe comprehensively each and every one of the many hundreds and thousands of peoples, tribes, nations, and societies in the world. Instead, we have illustrated different aspects of human cultural and social organization by including examples of certain regions, of certain 'exemplary' peoples who are famous through particular anthropological studies and interpretations, and of political minorities, peoples whose antagonistic relationships with the larger states in which they live have brought them wide attention. We also included a supplementary section on all countries of the world, which gives the current economic and political structure of each, together with a useful table of leading statistical and other indicators for each country.

The reader will not find history in this book. For that one must turn to the two earlier volumes of the *Oxford Illustrated Encyclopedia*, on world history. What we have put together here is a guide to the systems and ideas—economic, political, legal, religious, linguistic, philosophical, educational, demographic, psychological, and social—which have long been at work in creating the societies in which the people of the world live today. Although this book focuses on the contemporary world, there are many ideas and thought-systems whose origins date from antiquity and they have been included here because of their lasting influence on contemporary society. One thinks of the enduring impact of figures as diverse as Plato, Jesus Christ, St Augustine, Muhammed, Buddha, Confucius, Freud, and Marx. They are all here and rub shoulders with ideas and institutions more closely associated with the late 20th century: the debate between privatization and nationalization, for example, in economics; the demographic factors leading to ageing populations; the role of the welfare state in providing social security and health insurance; the belief and practice of the religions of the world and their responses to changing conditions; international organizations and their roles in today's world; legal and political systems, their differences and interactions. In the 20th century many technical languages have been coined by the social sciences, the new academic disciplines such as sociology, psychology, and anthropology, which seek systematically to describe and explain the activities of human beings and their relationships with one another. The reader will find here concise, clearly written entries which introduce the central terms and concepts.

In much of the work of compiling this book, we have been guided by the publications of the UN and its agencies, such as the World Bank. The reader who wishes to explore further cannot do better than consult the World Bank's *Investing in Development*, the UNDP's *Human Development Report*, UNICEF's *State of the World's Children*, and the World Resources Institute's *World Resources*. Our world's central dilemmas of poverty, hunger, and maldistribution of resources, and the attempts to alleviate them, are covered in much greater detail in these texts than has been possible here. This book will, I believe, provide the general reader as well as students, travellers, and businesspeople with a stimulating and informative guide to the world of social and cultural ideas, and at least introduce them to a wider understanding and tolerance of intellectual issues, traditions, and belief systems across the world.

I should like to thank very warmly all the authors who have contributed to the volume and the team of editors at Oxford University Press under Bridget Hadaway's direction: Molly Scott for her work at the early stages; Nancy Drucker for her advice and expertise in many areas; and most particularly Marian Ellingworth, whose wide knowledge and fluent editing have so clearly contributed to the breadth of information which this volume offers.

RICHARD HOGGART

CONTRIBUTORS

Timothy Allen

Timothy Andrewes

Michelle Aveline

Richard M. Bainbridge

Lionel Bently

Camilla Boodle

Jerome Booth

Dr J. Boyden

James Burch

Professor George Butterworth

Dr Margaret Chu

Dr Gordon S. Claridge

Professor Stephen R. L. Clark

Stephen C. Colvin

Mary Curtis

D. B. Curtis

Craig Dearden

Nancy Drucker

Professor Michael Dummett

David J. Dunn

Professor Eric Dunning

Pia Eekelaar

Dr O. Y. Elagab

Marian Ellingworth

Richard Ellingworth

Peter Ely

Dr Louise Fawcett

David Feldman

K. Gardner

Dr Sebastian Gardner

Miles Glen

Dr Alastair M. Gray

R. A. Hague

Dr Charles Hallisey

Bruce Hanlin

Dr Martin Harrop

Dr Bruce Henning

Deborah Duncan Honoré

Dr Gustaaf Houtman

Dr Eric James

Dr Eva Jaworska

Dr J. B. Jones

Stephen P. Jones

Dr Alexander Kalache

Adrian N. Keane

Dr Patrick Keeley

Dr Phillip Kreager

Roger Lamb

Michael Leitch

Dr Michael Lockwood

Dr Brian J. Longhurst

Dr Paul G. McGeown

W. H. S. MacKeith

Professor Peter J. Madgwick

Suzanne Mainzer

Roger Martyn

Kenneth Matthews

Dr Kevan Meethan

Dr David Miller

Brian R. Munday

Clare Palmer

Richard Parry

Dr Ram Prasad

R. A. Robinson

Molly Scott

Raymond Scott

Timothy Scott

Josephine Shaw

Michael Smith

Dr Jonathan Spencer

Dr Frances Stewart

Dr Peter M. Sullivan

Marianne Talbot

Dr Deborah Taylor

Dr Manuela Tecushan

Professor Trevor Watkins

M. J. Weait

Dr S. Wheeler

Dr Diana Woodhouse

Richard Wylie

General Preface

The *Oxford Illustrated Encyclopedia* is designed to be useful and to give pleasure to readers throughout the world. Particular care has been taken to ensure that it is not limited to one country or to one civilization, and that its many thousands of entries can be understood by any interested person who has no previous detailed knowledge of the subject.

Each volume has a clearly defined theme made plain in its title, and is for that reason self-sufficient: there is no jargon, and references to other volumes are avoided. Nevertheless, taken together, the eight thematic volumes (and the Index and Ready Reference volume which completes the series) provide a complete and reliable survey of human knowledge and achievement. Within each independent volume, the material is arranged in a large number of relatively brief articles in A–Z sequence, varying in length from fifty to one thousand words. This means that each volume is simple to consult, as valuable information is not buried in long and wide-ranging articles. Cross-references are provided whenever they will be helpful to the reader.

The team allocated to each volume is headed by a volume editor eminent in the field. Over four hundred scholars and teachers drawn from around the globe have contributed a total of 2.4 million words to the Encyclopedia. They have worked closely with a team of editors at Oxford whose job it was to ensure that the coverage and content of each entry form part of a coherent whole. Specially commissioned artwork, diagrams, maps, and photographs convey information to supplement the text and add a lively and colourful dimension to the subject portrayed.

Since publication of the first of its volumes in the mid-1980s, the *Oxford Illustrated Encyclopedia* has built up a reputation for usefulness throughout the world. The number of languages into which it has been translated continues to grow. In compiling the volumes, the editors have recognized the new internationalism of its readers who seek to understand the different technological, cultural, political, religious, and commercial factors which together shape the world-view of nations. Their aim has been to present a balanced picture of the forces that influence peoples in all corners of the globe.

I am grateful alike to the volume editors, contributors, consultants, editors, and illustrators whose common aim has been to provide, within the space available, an Encyclopedia that will enrich the reader's understanding of today's world.

HARRY JUDGE

A User's Guide

This book is designed for easy use, but the following notes may be helpful to the reader:

ALPHABETICAL ARRANGEMENT   The entries are arranged in simple letter-by-letter alphabetical order of their headings (ignoring the spaces between words) up to the first comma (thus **Keynes, John Maynard** comes before **Keynesianism**). When two entry headings are the same up to the first comma, then the entries are placed in alphabetical order according to what follows after the comma.

ENTRY HEADINGS   In order to help the reader locate entries quickly and easily, most entry headings have been given in the order in which they are naturally written: thus **academic freedom**, **communal conflict**, **political asylum**, and **social evolution**, for example, are to be found in letters 'A', 'C', 'P', and 'S'.

ABBREVIATIONS AND TRANSLITERATIONS   In the case of certain well-known international organizations, including the **EC**, **NATO**, **OECD**, **OPEC**, **UN**, **UNESCO**, and **UNCTAD**, the abbreviated initials by which the organization is commonly known are used throughout the text and as the entry heading, where they are followed by the organization's name in full. Similarly, indicators such as **GNP** and **GDP** have been quoted throughout in their abbreviated form. Chinese words and names are given in the pinyin romanization system, so that **Daoism**, for example, is used rather than Taoism. Arabic, Persian, Sanskrit, Hindi, and other foreign names and words have been transliterated as accurately as possible in order to reflect their original spelling. However, most place names, and some words or concepts such as **yoga**, **nirvana**, or **Sufi** which are sufficiently common in English usage, are given in their English form without diacritics.

CROSS-REFERENCES   An asterisk (*) in front of a word denotes a cross-reference and indicates the entry heading to which attention is being drawn. Cross-references in the text appear only in places where reference is likely to amplify or increase understanding of the entry being read. They are not given automatically in all cases where a separate entry can be found, so if you come across a name or term about which you would like to know more, it is worth looking for an entry in its alphabetical place even if no cross-reference is marked. The limited space available has meant that distinguished politicians and statesmen and women, for example, have no biographical entry, but are often covered in entries on the political theories or movements with which they are principally associated. Thus, for example, Mikhail Gorbachev is covered under **glasnost** and **perestroika**, while Margaret Thatcher and Ronald Reagan are covered under **New Right**. For reasons of space and accessibility, some seminal thinkers who may not be immediately familiar to readers in the West are included under general entries on intellectual movements, for example Muhammed Iqbal under **Islamic modernism** and Keshab Chandra Sen under **Hindu revivalism**.

ILLUSTRATIONS   Photographs, line drawings, graphs, and maps usually occur on the same page as the entries to which they relate or on a facing page. The picture captions supplement the information given in the text and indicate in bold type the title of the relevant entry. The front endpaper gives a political map of the world, and the back endpaper shows the distribution of the world's chief religions. Other maps, diagrams, and photographs throughout the text amplify or expand the coverage. For example, the entry on **infant mortality** describes the general trends and meaning of such statistics, while the accompanying world map shows the actual rates world-wide in a given period.

STATISTICS, WEIGHTS, AND MEASURES   Both metric measures and their non-metric equivalents are used throughout (thus a measure of distance is given first in kilometres and then in miles). Large measures are generally rounded off, partly for the sake of simplicity and occasionally to reflect differences of opinion as to a precise measurement. One thousand million is taken to equal 1 billion. Dates and sources are given, wherever possible, where statistics occur in the text or illustrations. In most cases statistics have been extracted from publications of the UN and its associate agencies. It is important to emphasize that all statistical information should be treated with caution, no matter how reliable the source. Difficulties in collection or differences in keeping records may lead to substantial discrepancies: for example, the former Eastern bloc traditionally recorded national growth and income differently from the Western model of GNP and GDP, so that figures are not directly comparable. None the less such measures are used for the sake of comparison: the World Bank classifies economies by GNP into low income (GNP per capita of $545 or less in 1988); middle income (GNP per capita of $545–6000 in 1988); and high income (over $6000 in 1988). Such classifications are useful in precisely defining general terms such as developing and developed countries. As a general rule, the term developed countries includes the members of the OECD and the countries of the former Eastern bloc, while the term developing refers to all other countries.

RELATIONSHIP TO OTHER VOLUMES   This survey of peoples and cultures is Volume 7 in a series, the *Oxford Illustrated Encyclopedia*, which comprises eight thematic volumes and an index and ready reference volume.

The volume is self-contained, having no cross-references to any of its companions, and is therefore entirely usable on its own. However, a number of subjects covered here are also examined from different aspects in other volumes: for example, statesmen and women and religious figures in the history volumes, and the technology of communication, transport, and the treatment of major diseases in the volume on inventions and technology. Further information on this volume is given in the Foreword, which offers a fuller explanation of the book's scope and organization.

Abélard, Peter (1079–1142), Christian theologian and philosopher, most widely remembered for his correspondence with Héloïse. He was a creative logician, whose philosophical originality and emphasis on intention and personal conscience in moral theory and practice made him a controversial figure. He advanced a form of *nominalism which brought the debate on *universals to a new level. His *Sic et Non* (*Yes and No*), a collection of opposed texts from scripture, the church fathers, and philosophers, whose resolution was left to the student, was, along with *Sentences* by Peter Lombard (*c*.1100–60), influential in shaping the *scholastic method of disputation.

Aborigines, a term most usually applied to the indigenous people of Australia, such as the *Aranda. Originally these were semi-nomadic *hunter-gatherers, divided into many small bands, with over 200 *Australian Aboriginal languages. Traditionally, the predominant form of social organization was the patrilineal *descent group, based on a system of exogamous marriage (marriage outside an individual's group). This system served to link different kin groups, between which reciprocal exchanges of marriage partners would take place. Males were responsible for *ritual observances, such as *initiation and *circumcision, and often these *rites of passage would also involve food prohibitions, as in the female puberty rite. The Aborigines did not have any written language, but had a considerable oral tradition of mythology. Central to this was the 'dreamtime', when the world was shaped by mythic beings who are thought to be embodied in species of plants, animals, places, or the elements. All Aboriginal art, such as rock painting, was considered to be sacred, and acted to connect the living with the dreamtime. Another aspect of these beliefs is the existence of *totemism, in which clans are seen to relate to certain species of animal or plant. The Aboriginal way of life has been much affected by the colonization of Australia, and few still pursue the traditional way.

abortion, the expulsion of a foetus from the womb before it is able to survive independently. A spontaneous abortion is usually called a miscarriage, the word abortion being reserved for induced terminations. Throughout history women have attempted to end unwanted pregnancies by mechanical or herbal means, but in many countries, the legalization of abortion has been fairly recent. In some it is restricted to cases where the continued pregnancy would endanger the life of the mother, and in others (such as the Republic of Ireland and Iran) it is still illegal. The official Roman Catholic position (not shared by the mainstream Protestant Church) is that the embryo at all stages deserves the full protection which would be afforded to any human being; others who oppose abortion make a similar argument. Those who support abortion argue that women have the right to choose whether to bear a child, and that legal abortion makes the procedure safer, and as available to poor women as to rich. In the USA, in particular, arguments about the legality and morality of abortion have been brought to the political agenda in recent years by Christian fundamentalists and New Right politicians. Improved med-

ical techniques, making a foetus viable from a younger age, undermine the currently accepted 28-week limit for abortion. The World Health Organization has estimated that there are approximately 30 million legal abortions performed in the world every year, but it is thought that about 20 million illegal abortions are also performed. In some countries, abortion is used as a form of birth control since modern contraceptives are either not readily available or accepted; for example, in the former Soviet Union the official abortion rates were six to ten times higher than those in the West, and an estimated one in five women of childbearing age had an abortion every year.

academic freedom, the right to pursue knowledge, to engage in research, or to teach independently of any political control. It is argued that academic freedom is desirable because knowledge is best discovered by the open investigation of facts and opinions. In 1632 Galileo was accused of heresy for stating that the planets circled the sun, not the earth. With the secularization of education, religious interference in academic enquiry has largely given way to political and commercial pressures. The majority of nations exercise some control over their academic and educational systems, but totalitarian regimes exploit this control for the purpose of indoctrination. In the 1930s, for example, thousands of Soviet scientists lost their jobs for teaching orthodox genetics, deemed to clash with Marxist principles. Thousands more (including twenty who were or became Nobel Prize winners) were dismissed by the Nazis because they were Jewish. In recent years, the introduction of 'value for money' criteria for government investment in research, and of 'user pays' sponsorship by businesses, has increasingly affected the direction of academic research. Where academics are civil servants, they are even more susceptible to direct government pressure.

accent, the part of *dialect which refers to pronunciation. Although they are usually difficult to separate, regional accents identify the speaker's place of origin (for example, Scotland, southern USA), and social accents identify the speaker's cultural and educational background. Alternative ways of pronouncing sounds may be good indicators of class-membership. In British English the accent which is not associated with any particular region is RP (received pronunciation), also referred to as BBC, public school, Oxford, or Queen's English. This accent enjoys high prestige for being used by upper classes as well as educated speakers.

acceptance house (accepting house), a merchant *bank (especially in the City of London) whose main function is to 'accept' *bills of exchange. This effectively guarantees a bill of exchange so that it can be traded at a *discount on the money markets.

accounting systems, systems which identify and record the financial transactions of an organization, such as purchases and sales (financial accounting system), or cost information inside the organization (*cost-accounting system). Accrual accounting enters *income and *costs when they are earned or incurred, in contrast to cash accounting, which does so when payment is made. An organization needs to maintain accurate and detailed records of its financial activities to enable management to monitor and control its affairs. There are also legal requirements regarding the provision and publication of financial information relating to some types of organization. Profit-and-loss accounts and

Limestone has traditionally been a favourite medium for sculptors because it is easy to carve. Unfortunately it is also especially vulnerable to the effects of **acid rain**, as seen in this serious erosion at St Paul's Cathedral, London.

balance-sheets provide periodic information on the financial results and status of the organization. (See also *management acccounting.)

acid rain, a chemical *pollution of water supplies, animals, and plants caused by exhaust emissions from the burning of fossil fuels. Rain, snow, and mist become more acid as a result of absorbing waste gases, chiefly oxides of sulphur and nitrogen, emitted from power stations, factories, and motorized transport. Acid rain damages human health by causing bronchial problems, and it corrodes limestone buildings. It increases the acidity of lakes and rivers, causing the death of fish and other animals and plants, as well as the death of forests (see *deforestation). The effect is magnified because acid water releases poisonous metals such as cadmium and mercury that are usually fixed in the soil. Sweden was the first country to notice the impact of acid rain, in the 1960s, but acid rain is probably a major cause of the tree damage found in one-seventh of Europe's forests, mainly in the centre, north, and east, in the north-east of the USA, and in Japan. In 1984 many countries signed a protocol to the Geneva Convention on Long Range Transboundary Air Pollution (1979) agreeing to reduce sulphur emission by 30 per cent by 1993, although four of the heaviest polluters, the UK, USA, Poland, and Spain, did not sign. To reduce sulphur emissions substantially requires the modification or closure of coal-burning power stations. A reduction in nitrogen oxide levels could be achieved by reducing the use and engine speed of cars and lorries, and by fitting catalytic converters, which remove much of this gas (and the hydrocarbons that help produce the acids) from car exhausts;

catalytic converters have been compulsory in Europe since 1992 and have been in widespread use in the USA since the 1970s to control emissions.

act, the name normally given to a *bill once it has been passed by the *legislature of a *state, which then has the force of law within the *jurisdiction of that state. In this sense it is synonymous with *statute law. An Act of Parliament in the UK, for example, is the outcome of a constitutional procedure involving a complex legislative process. Following initial consultations, a *bill is introduced into Parliament, passing through successive stages in both the *House of Commons and *House of Lords, culminating in final approval and the Royal Assent. An act of state refers to the action of one sovereign state towards another state, such as a declaration of war, or an annexation of territory. In the context of international law, a Final Act is the instrument which concludes the proceedings of a conference, such as the Helsinki Final Act of 1975, containing pledges on human rights, which concluded the *Conference on Security and Co-operation in Europe.

actuary, an insurance professional who is concerned with the calculation of risk involved in underwriting *assurance and *insurance policies. Actuarial work relies on past trends and statistics relating to the event to be insured. If a person wishes to take out a term insurance policy, the actuarial calculations will be concerned with an examination of life expectancy to determine the probability of death within the insured period. This probability will be used to calculate the premium to be paid.

acupuncture　*Chinese medicine.

Adi Granth (Punjabi, 'first book'), the most important sacred book of *Sikhism. The original compilation was made under the direction of Guru Arjan (1563–1606), the fifth Sikh *Guru. Written in the Gurmukhi script, the *Adi Granth* consists of the preachings of the first five Gurus, but also includes Muslim and Hindu hymns. It does not contain narrative, but concentrates on religious and social themes, such as the need to achieve oneness with God and the importance of service to others. The work was completed by the tenth Guru, *Gobind Singh, who declared that henceforward there would be no more Gurus: his successor would be the *Adi Granth*, now given the honorific title Guru Granth Sahib ('Holy Book Guru'). For this reason, the *Adi Granth* is treated with great respect: the throne holding the book forms the focus of worship in the *Gurdwara*, or Sikh temple.

adjustment, in economics, a term used to cover policies to adjust the economy to shocks, caused, for example, by sharp changes in *commodity prices, and to promote efficiency and growth. Adjustment policies usually include stabilization policies which are directed at reducing imbalances in a country's economy, particularly *deficits in its *balance of payments, usually by promoting *exports, reducing *imports, increasing government revenue, and cutting public expenditure. Adjustment policies supported by the World Bank also provide for a greater role for the market, with measures such as reduced price controls, *privatization, encouragement of foreign investment, and import liberalization. In the 1980s, world recession, falling commodity prices, and a large debt burden compelled many developing countries, especially in Latin America and Africa, to undertake stabilization and adjustment policies under the auspices of the IMF and the World Bank. Amended versions of such policies are being implemented in the republics of the former Soviet Union and former Eastern bloc in the switch from *planned to *free market economies. Adjustment policies may be slow to take effect, depending in particular on adequate levels of *investment, and are likely to cause hardship as *unemployment rises, *subsidies are cut, and government spending on *social services is reduced. In *Adjustment with a Human Face* (1987), UNICEF called for modified policies to avert such hardship, by maintaining output and investment, creating opportunities for small farmers and the urban poor, reallocating government spending from high-cost areas such as hospitals to low-cost basic services such as clinics, and introducing public-works schemes to generate employment.

Adler *neo-Freudian.

administrative law, that part of *public law which deals with methods of controlling the administrative activities of state bodies. It includes the legal standards which apply to their administrators, the grounds on which administrative acts and decisions are challengeable, and the remedies for administrative misbehaviour. Grounds for *judicial review of administrative action usually include want of power (acting without lawful authority), excess of power (acting outside authority, as where a body misinterprets the scope of its power), and abuse of power (exercising a function in an improper way or for an improper purpose). More generally, administrators are expected to behave in accordance with *natural justice. Administrative law also provides for review by bodies other than traditional courts, such as *ombudsmen, *tribunals, and regulatory bodies.

adoption, the legal transfer of an individual from his or her biological *family to another family. In Western countries, adoption is seen primarily as a way of meeting the needs both of children whose parents cannot care for them and of infertile couples. In Japan, adults as well as children may be adopted in order, for example, to inherit a family business or to ensure care for the adoptive couple in later life. In some parts of the world, adoption is little used, children either being absorbed into the 'extended' family or left to institutional care (*childcare services). Research shows that adoptions of children are generally successful, as strong mutual attachment develops; nevertheless, adoptees often retain a sense of separate identity, and some as adults seek to contact their biological families. In some economically developed countries such as Sweden and The Netherlands, the use of contraception and abortion, and the availability of *social assistance for single parents has so sharply reduced the number of local babies for adoption that the great majority of adoptees are brought in from developing countries, primarily in Latin America and parts of Asia. While inter-country adoption may offer the hope of a better life, there is concern that some children are kidnapped or sold for adoption. Some countries, such as Thailand, accept and seek to regulate adoption by foreigners, since for reasons of custom and religion local adoptions are rare. Other countries, believing that a country ought not to export its children, however impoverished, discourage or ban it.

adult education *continuing education.

Advaita Hinduism (Sanskrit, 'non-duality'), one of the *Vedānta philosophical schools in Hinduism, based on the teaching of Shankara (*c*. AD 700). Shankara systematized the basic principles of the *Upanishads* (part of the *Vedas, the Hindu sacred texts) into a coherent philosophy, according to which there is an essential oneness between ultimate spiritual reality, *Brahman, and the human soul, *ātman. The realization of this identity between Brahman and ātman, which leads to spiritual liberation (*moksha*), cannot be achieved through ritual action, but only through meditation. The diverse and changing world, which prevents us from recognizing the essential truth of non-duality, is nothing but *māyā*, or illusion. Advaita Hinduism is only one of the branches of Vedānta, but it has become well known in Western countries through its modern exponents, in particular the Ramakrishna Mission, founded in Calcutta by Vivekananda in 1897.

Advent (from Latin, *adventus*, coming), the season in the *Christian year preceding *Christmas, first mentioned by the Council of Tours (AD 567). The length of the Advent season varies: in the West it commences on the Sunday nearest to St Andrew's Day (30 November): in the East it lasts forty days. Although lacking the strictness of *Lent, it is traditionally a penitential season of fasting in anticipation both of Christmas and of the expected Second Coming of Christ on Judgement Day. Advent customs include the lighting of candles and, in the West, the liturgical use of purple in Church services.

Adventists, various *Protestant groups, originating in the USA in 1831 as the Evangelical Adventists, who believe in an imminent Second Coming of Christ. There are now about 2 million full members, including two major groups: the 'Second Advent Christians', and the 'Seventh-day Adventists', who strictly observe the sabbath (traditionally a day of abstinence from work and play) on the seventh day (Saturday) and require adult baptism and abstinence from alcohol. (See also *eschatology, *millenarianism.)

adverb *parts of speech.

adversarial procedure, a legal procedure found in countries with *common law systems, in which the two parties to a legal case confront one another in court. According to the procedure, the burden of collating and presenting *evidence falls on each of the parties. (In a criminal trial, these are the *prosecution and the defence.) Evidence is presented in turn by the parties or their representatives, and there is an opportunity for each side to question the other through cross-examination. The role of the *judge is to act as an umpire over the proceedings, to ensure that the trial is conducted according to correct legal procedure, and to evaluate the evidence presented by each side. The adversarial procedure lays emphasis on the argumentative and oratorical skills of the *advocate, in contrast to the *inquisitorial procedure, found in civil law jurisdictions, where the court plays a more active role in eliciting the evidence.

advertising, the use of mass *media to carry paid messages for a commercial purpose or to advance a cause, institution, or political candidate. Advertising has become an integral element in free-market economies; it influences the pricing, packaging, design, display, and sales incentives of a product. Most advertising is channelled through national agencies, which employ copy-writers, art directors, jingle writers, video producers, production specialists, *market researchers, public relations officers, and a media depart-

Evidence for the world-wide spread of **advertising** for consumer brands is found in this wall-painted advertisement in Penang, Malaysia. The familiar slogan 'Coke is it!' proves Samuel Johnson's contention that 'Promise, large promise, is the soul of advertisement'.

ment. Their task is to build over a period of time, and with the use of *agenda-setting, a 'brand image' or 'personality' that dovetails with the psychological profile of a product, person, or cause. In many countries, government is a major advertiser on behalf of state-owned industries and enterprises. In authoritarian regimes, political advertising is co-opted into the *propaganda machine, but it also plays an important role in democratic countries through its involvement in the electoral process. Advertising consultants increasingly influence the planning of election campaigns and the presentation of electoral candidates by manipulating politically sensitive information. Critics point out that advertising influences the cumulative culture of a society by, for example, stimulating people's acquisitive instincts and presenting consumption as the goal of work.

advocate (in law), one whose profession it is to plead for another in court. The title is used in those countries, such as France and Scotland, whose legal systems are based on *Roman law. The Faculty of Advocates is the collective body of Scottish advocates, whose members may appear before any court in Scotland and before the House of Lords. The Lord Advocate is the principal law officer in Scotland. In the USA, the term advocate is sometimes used synonymously with attorney, counsel, or lawyer.

aesthetics, the philosophical study of art and the values, concepts, and kinds of experience associated with art, such as taste, beauty, and the sublime. Aesthetics includes the study of human responses to nature as much as it does the theory of literature and other specific forms of art. In being concerned with conceptual questions, aesthetics is to be distinguished sharply from *psychology; and in seeking to say what is common to all aesthetic experience rather than describe the meaning of particular works of art, it is also distinguished from criticism and interpretation. In classical philosophy, two important discussions are Plato's criticism of art, as in some sense promoting illusion, in *The Republic* (*c*.350 BC) and Aristotle's account of tragedy in his *Poetics* (*c*.340 BC) as a vital function to purge the emotions. Kant's *Critique of Judgement* (1790) is the outstanding modern work of aesthetics, which focuses on the problem of how aesthetic judgements can be subjective and yet lay claim to the agreement of others, and asserts the existence of a special aesthetic attitude marked by disinterestedness.

affirmative action   *positive discrimination.

'affluent society', a term coined by the US economist John Kenneth Galbraith in the title of his book *The Affluent Society* (1958). It refers to the high standard of living of citizens in North America and Western Europe in recent decades, and the economic and social problems arising from such prosperity, which he summed up in the phrase 'private affluence, public squalor'. For instance, aggressive advertising may create artificial needs, high *consumption may over-use scarce resources and create waste and pollution, big businesses may develop *monopoly power, and income and wealth may be unfairly distributed. Galbraith defends a strong government role in the affluent society to maintain economic efficiency and to reduce poverty.

African Charter on Human and People's Rights, a charter adopted by the *Organization of African Unity in 1981 and ratified by thirty-five of its members. The Charter reaffirms the duty of African states to eliminate colonialism, apartheid, and *Zionism, and stresses that civil and political rights cannot be dissociated from economic, social, and cultural rights. The Charter concurs with the *Universal Declaration of Human Rights, and emphasizes the rights of 'peoples'. It establishes the African Commission on Human and People's Rights, based in Dakar, Senegal, a body intended to promote *human rights, as well as to investigate complaints from individuals. However, in many African countries habitual abuse of human rights continues.

African languages *Berber languages, *Chadic languages, *Cushitic languages, *Khoisan languages, *Niger–Congo languages, *Nilo–Saharan languages, *Semitic languages.

African new religions. It is estimated that some 7,000 new religious movements have emerged since the 1930s in sub-Saharan Africa, with some 32 million adherents. Most are a blend of elements of *African traditional religion with elements of an 'introduced' religion, in most cases *Christianity, but also *Islam. On the one hand adoption of elements of the 'introduced religion' may reflect disappointment with contemporary social, political, and economic life leading to adherence to *millenarian expectation of a better future, whereas on the other the inadequacies of mission Christianity in bridging cultural and social barriers, and the weakness of Western medicine in dealing with psychological problems or averting natural disasters are among the reasons for retaining earlier systems of belief and ritual. The new religious movements may be categorized as independent churches; separatist churches; and neo-traditional movements. Examples of independent or indigenous churches would be the Aladura (Yoruba, 'people of prayer') Church in Nigeria; the Harrist Church in the Côte d'Ivoire; the Kimbanguist Church in Zaïre; and the Apostolic Church of John Masowe in Zimbabwe. Such churches tend to be founded by leaders with a strong charismatic appeal and to have a prophetic or millenarian character. They are likely to be associated with a particular ethnic group and may become implicated in political dissidence, as for example the Masowe Church, which was expelled from South Africa on political grounds in 1960. Separatist churches include the Jamaa (Swahili, 'family') movement in Zaïre started by the Belgian Franciscan Placide Tempels; the Legio Maria (Legion of Mary) in Kenya; and the East African Protestant revivalist offshoot known as the Balokole (the sacred ones). Neo-traditional movements such as the Eglise de Dieu de Nos Ancêstres in south-west Zaïre tend to be secret societies or cults which focus on traditional religious practices in a new context and provide a channel for resolving the conflicts between tradition and change which are experienced in most contemporary African societies.

African pastoralists, peoples whose livelihood depends on livestock and *nomadism. Several pastoral peoples have been described as acephalous, meaning that their system of social organization is egalitarian and resistant to political domination by chiefs. In the absence of authoritarian structures, the social organization of such peoples is founded on *kinship and the formation of different *lineages. While seasonal movement of livestock from region to region (transhumance) is essential to secure adequate pasture for their livestock, the nomadism of African pastoralists is limited to a regular return to specific locations. Although some pastoralists, like the *Maasai, were traditionally dependent solely on their livestock, most are not. The *Nuer, for example, also subsist on crops that are grown by the women.

African traditional religions. African traditional religions are closely linked to different ethnic groups, of which there are over 700 south of the Sahara. There is great diversity in both practice and belief, but there are certain common features on the basis of which generalizations may be made. Lacking extensive written scriptures, African traditional religions are based upon *myths and rituals passed down by oral tradition and custom. African traditional religions may be described as systems of beliefs and rituals which make sense of daily experience, rather than metaphysical and moral systems which promise individual salvation in another (spiritual) world. Thus evil and misfortune, for example, are regarded as perverse humanity and a disorder in the right harmony of things which may be set right by healing and propitiation rather than as the work of supernatural powers. In general, a supreme *God or ultimate principle exists in a remote way, and far greater attention is paid to a range of minor deities and spirits. From about the 17th century, as colonization progressed, it seems that the concept of a supreme God became more significant, perhaps in response to the disintegration of political institutions. After contact with Islam and Christianity, many Africans recognized their supreme God to be the same as that in Christianity and Islam, allowing a ready synthesis of certain aspects of the different traditions. In most traditional African belief systems, ancestral spirits are particularly important. The spirits of leaders of the clan or family continue to concern themselves with the well-being of their descendants, and considerable efforts are made to propitiate these spirits through prayers and sacrifices (see *ancestor worship). Other spirit beings may include evil spirits whose power can be harnessed by sorcerers and witches. Charms and amulets to ward off witchcraft are also widespread. In many parts of sub-Saharan Africa, the king or chief was traditionally regarded as semi-divine, and provided both religious and moral leadership. Others concerned with spiritual life include priests; mediums possessed by the spirit of a god or an ancestor; diviners, who foretell the future through magical acts such as throwing the bones; and herbalists. Communal rituals are held for specific purposes such as rain-making or involving a blessing on the harvest. *Rites of passage mark the turning points in an individual's life and maintain the cohesion of the community. Holy places may be a grove or tree or a large temple-like building sacred to the god or spirit whose image may be stored there. (See also entries on the individual peoples of Africa.)

Afro-Asiatic languages *Berber languages, *Chadic languages, *Cushitic languages, *Semitic languages.

afterlife, a term referring to the belief that the human spirit or *soul survives physical death and passes through to a new mode of existence, which is often determined by a person's conduct during life, or by the rituals surrounding death. Conceptions of the afterlife are a common feature of many religions, functioning as a way of putting the actions and experience of this world in a larger perspective. The veneration of ancestral spirits, which implies belief in an afterlife, is common to many religions. In Judaic, Christian, and Islamic thought, the human soul is consigned to *heaven or to *hell, depending on God's judgement. Roman Catholicism teaches furthermore that most souls require purification in purgatory before entry into heaven. Many Roman Catholics also believe in a state called limbo, the abode of unbaptized but otherwise innocent souls (such as infants). According to Hinduism, the soul or *ātman is constantly reborn through a variety of lives until ultimate enlightenment or *moksha occurs, and the cycle of rebirth ceases. Buddhists reject the notion of the individual soul, but they too believe in an endless cycle of *reincarnation until the attainment of *nirvana, the cessation of all desire. (See also *ancestor worship, *funeral customs.)

age (within the social sciences), a principle of social organization often based on different generations, or groups of people of the same age. Age-sets, groups whose membership is determined by the ages of the people involved, are found in many African societies. In some cases age-sets may operate as a form of gerontocracy, or rule by the old, in which the elders play an important part in the *political organization of society. Elders may also be considered as the holders of tradition, and may have control over access to wives and property, as well as wielding power through their knowledge of symbolic and religious systems. Some age-set systems cut across other organizational features such as *kinship and *descent. Young men may be grouped together to undergo ritual *initiation at the same time, as among the *Ndembu or *Maasai, thus helping to form common bonds between them. Age-grades differ from age-sets in that they are not a group as such, but rather a series of stages with a distinctive social status through which all individuals move in the course of their lives.

ageing population, a population in which the proportion of older people is increasing. Populations are ageing worldwide and with unprecedented rapidity: the present average age of individuals and populations, however measured, has no historical parallel. In 1990 there were 488 million people aged 60 or more in the world, constituting 9 per cent of its population. By 2025 the UN forecasts that they will number 1,200 million, 15 per cent of the world's population. In the early 1990s old people formed a far larger proportion of the population of industrialized countries than of developing ones (17 per cent in North America, for instance, compared with 7 per cent in Asia). Yet it is in the developing world that their absolute numbers are expected to increase most dramatically, quadrupling by 2025. The explanation lies in recent sharp rises in *life expectancy (life expectancy at birth was 67 in Brazil in the early 1990s compared with 45 in the 1950s) and lower *birth rates. Almost everywhere in the world, women live longer than men, and the over-80s, who make the greatest demands on health and *social services, are increasing as a porportion of the population. Furthermore, there is an accelerating tendency for old people to live alone. (See also *old age.)

agenda-setting, the process by which public concerns are shaped and the terms of public debate set. Politicians, *interest groups, and *advertising and *public relations agencies are all involved. The term is commonly used to refer to the activities of *television, *radio, and *newspapers in the selection and editing of *news: some issues are highlighted by the length or positioning of items about them, while others are ignored. Furthermore, it is often argued that agenda-setters between them powerfully influence the way in which issues are seen: for example, the emission of greenhouse gases is recognized as a threat to the environment, yet the role of the car is only rarely challenged. Others argue that agenda-setters more commonly respond to the public mood than create it. There is general agreement that agenda-setters are influential in suggesting what the public should be thinking about, even if not controlling what they think.

agent provocateur, a person who joins a group or forms a relationship with an individual in order to encourage the group or the individual to commit illegal acts which may then be punished. *Agents provocateurs* can penetrate trade unions, political parties, revolutionary groups, humanitarian groups, or economic pressure groups, and their activities can take place within or between national societies.

aggression (in international relations), an unprovoked military attack by one state upon another. In 1967 the UN established a special committee to define aggression; in its report in 1974 it discussed such considerations as the direct and indirect use of military force, the first use of force, and the question of proportionality. However, what one state regards as an act of aggression may be regarded by others as a justifiable act. For instance, the Soviet Union and other Warsaw Pact countries justified their invasion of Czechoslovakia in 1968 by the 'Brezhnev doctrine', according to which the intervention was seen as legitimate because it was in the interest of socialist solidarity. The same argument was used to justify the Soviet invasion of Afghanistan in 1979.

At a development project in Bangladesh a bamboo tube-well is used to irrigate half a hectare of farmland. In such countries the insights of **agricultural economics** can be used to improve the techniques of small farmers and reduce hunger and famine.

Agriculture

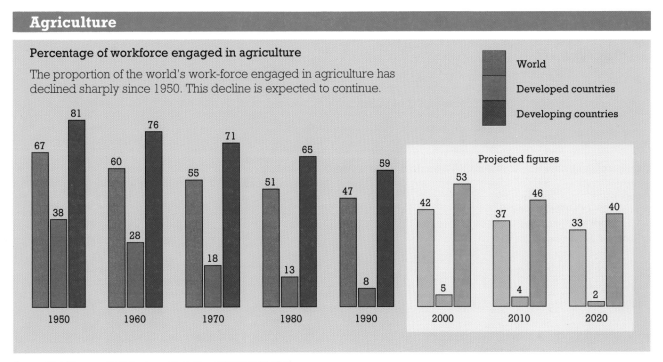

Percentage of workforce engaged in agriculture

The proportion of the world's work-force engaged in agriculture has declined sharply since 1950. This decline is expected to continue.

Legend: World | Developed countries | Developing countries

Projected figures

Source: *World Demographic Estimates and Projections 1950-2025*, U N, 1988

aggression (in psychology), unprovoked and intentional injury of another, or the motivation and feelings behind such action. In a wide sense aggression may include assertiveness and competitiveness at one extreme and predation at the other. A restricted, more common, sense is violence and threat against members of the aggressor's own species. Different parts of the brain control different behaviour patterns. Biological theories of the origin of aggression rely on studies which show that animals can easily be bred for aggression. Doses of the male hormone testosterone increase aggression in adult males of many species. There is some evidence that more assertive women have higher testosterone levels. *Social learning theory provides the other main explanatory hypotheses. An early version, put forward in the 1940s by psychologists from Yale University in the USA such as John Dollard and Neal Miller, held that frustration of goal-directed behaviour causes aggression. Later social learning theorists, especially the Canadian Albert Bandura in the 1970s, showed that frustration is unnecessary, for children imitate adults' aggression without frustration or any other form of distress.

agnosticism (from Greek, *agnostos*, 'unknown'), a term coined in 1869 by T. H. Huxley (1825–95), the British biologist and supporter of *Darwin's theories of evolution, to indicate his position with regard to orthodox religious belief. Influenced by modern scientific thought, the agnostic holds that phenomena which cannot be proved or disproved by material means (such as the existence of God) cannot be the subjects of belief or disbelief. The term is also popularly used to imply scepticism about, or indifference to, religious matters, but it should not be confused with *atheism, which is the denial of the existence of God or any supernatural being.

agricultural economics, a specialized branch of economics, which developed mainly in the first two decades of the 20th century in the USA. Since almost half the world's people earn their income from farming, it is important for economists to analyse agriculture and any associated agribusiness involved in the growing, processing, and distribution of food products. Agricultural economists have practical aims: they study different systems of agriculture, forecast developments such as the impact of climate on harvests, and analyse economic policies towards agriculture. In particular, they have studied the effects of volatile price changes on agricultural producers, and this has contributed to the development of policies of price control and support in virtually all advanced countries (such as the Common Agricultural Policy in the *EC). In the developing world, agricultural economics focuses mainly on the productivity of small, subsistence farmers, and in many parts of the world agrarian reform has led to the development of *collective and *co-operative farms, rather than privately owned farms.

agriculture, the science or practice of cultivating the soil and rearing animals. Types of agriculture vary widely: *hunter-gatherers subsisting without practising agriculture; *pastoralists tending livestock, sometimes with a *nomadic way of life; *shifting cultivation; *plantations specializing in large-scale production of *commodities which rely on cheap labour (formerly on *slavery, and *migrant workers); highly equipped and specialized agribusiness with the latest technology and low concentration of labour; and *collectives or *co-operatives, which in this century have been a cornerstone of *planned economies and of *development strategies in some developing countries. Agriculture may be for subsistence or may specialize heavily in a particular cash crop for export or the domestic market. Patterns of landholding and social structure as well as climate and soil conditions have considerable effect on the type of agriculture practised; these are modified by technology, including irrigation, mechanization, and chemical intervention, and by social changes, including *land reform, and *migration. Population pressure has, over the centuries, been the most important determinant of *land use. The use of high-yield grains, fertilizers, and pesticides in developing countries, especially Asia, from the 1960s onwards brought about massive increases in agricultural output known as the green revolu-

Aid

Aid given

Measures of aid effort differ considerably depending on the figures used. The USA is the largest by volume; it gave $10 billion in aid in 1988. Japan, with $9 billion, was the next largest. The USA is, however, near the bottom among industrialized countries when aid is calculated as a proportion of GNP - 0.2 per cent. The widely accepted international target for industrialized countries is 0.7 per cent of GNP.

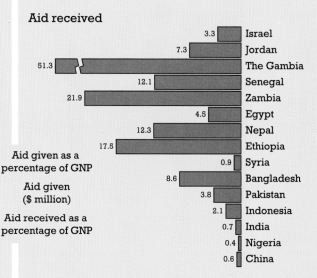

Aid given as a percentage of GNP	Country	Aid given ($ million)
3.04*	Soviet Union	4,212
2.7	Saudi Arabia	2,098
1.1	Norway	985
0.98	The Netherlands	2,231
0.89	Denmark	922
0.87	Sweden	1,529
0.72	France	6,865
0.59	Finland	608
0.51	Libya	129
0.49	Canada	2,342
0.47	Australia	1,101
0.41	Kuwait	108
0.40	Belgium	597
0.40	Germany (FDR)	4,731
n/a	Germany (GDR)	180
0.39	Italy	3,183
0.32	Japan	9,134
0.32	Switzerland	617
0.32	UK	2,645
0.28	New Zealand	105
0.24	Austria	302
0.21	USA	10,141
0.20	Ireland	57

* based on estimated GNP

Aid received

Aid received as a percentage of GNP	Country
3.3	Israel
7.3	Jordan
51.3	The Gambia
12.1	Senegal
21.9	Zambia
4.5	Egypt
12.3	Nepal
17.5	Ethiopia
0.9	Syria
8.6	Bangladesh
3.8	Pakistan
2.1	Indonesia
0.7	India
0.4	Nigeria
0.6	China

The most generous per capita allocations of aid do not necessarily go to the poorest countries. Many government programmes have commercial, political, or strategic purposes. Aid from international agencies such as the UN Children's Fund (UNICEF) and non-governmental organizations such as Oxfam, is more directly concerned with poverty and development.

Source: *World Development Report 1990.* World Bank; *The Economist Book of Vital World Statistics, 1990,* Hutchinson, 1990

tion, with as yet incalculable ecological side-effects. Since 1965 world cereal production (the best indicator of agriculture and nutrition since cereals provide over half the calories in the human diet) has increased by over 70 per cent. Thus India, for example, which formerly suffered regularly from *famine and was forced to spend scarce foreign exchange on food imports is now self-sufficient in food although its population has doubled since independence in 1947. But the green revolution has not yet spread to Africa, to a significant extent, and food shortages and famine persist. Economic thinking emphasizes the importance of agriculture in development: formerly industrialization was seen as the key to economic growth and the agricultural sector was taxed in order to finance investment in industry, but it is now recognized that it is essential to develop agriculture as well in order to alleviate poverty, provide employment, and to meet the basic needs for food of the population, and to boost the domestic market for industrial products. Agriculture is also an important source of export earnings for many developing countries, accounting for many *primary-product exports. Typically, governments may encourage agricultural development by positive pricing and taxation policies, supporting transport, infrastructure, the use of marginal land, research, and education, providing *subsidies, capital, and credit, and, in some cases, by implementing land reform. Agriculture forms a decreasing share of GNP and employment as

development proceeds, and many industrialized countries import food, but most developed countries continue to subsidize agriculture, because it is regarded as a strategic industry, because they wish to preserve the rural environment, and, most importantly, because of the political power of farming *lobbies.

ahimsā (Sanskrit, 'not-desiring-violence'), an important Indian concept which encourages respect for all life. It is most commonly expressed through *vegetarianism. Jain practice prohibits any activity (such as farming) which may cause harm. Buddhist doctrine condemns killing and encourages compassion for all life. Many Buddhists still eat meat, however; meat or fish may be eaten as long as there was no intent on the part of the eater to kill the animal. *Ahimsā* formed the basis of Mahatma Gandhi's policy of non-violent non-co-operation or *satyagraha*.

aid (development aid), the flow of resources as a gift or at below commercial interest rates, typically from richer to poorer countries. With the major exception of military aid, the main purpose of such flows is normally either to alleviate human suffering in the event of a *disaster, or to assist longer-term development (see *development economics). Aid from *non-governmental organizations (NGOs) is in grant form and mostly raised from the general public in donor countries. It is spent on disaster relief and small-scale development projects in developing countries. The motivation for such aid is altruism. Official aid or Overseas Development Assistance (ODA) is that between governments, and is far more significant in volume. It can be split into bilateral and multilateral aid. Bilateral aid is direct government-to-government aid, largely in grant form, and may be strongly motivated by political and, in some cases, commercial considerations. Politically motivated aid may be a means of exerting political influence and maintaining diplomatic, military, and commercial ties. An example is US aid to Egypt and Israel. The commercial benefits of aid are principally that a substantial amount of bilateral aid is tied to purchases from companies from donor countries. These may also lead to further contracts not funded by the donor. Multilateral aid is financed or guaranteed by governments but administered by multilateral development banks (see *World Bank), *UN agencies, the *EC and other international bodies. Aid from multilateral development banks is almost entirely in loans (often concessionary), whereas most of that from the EC is in grant form. The role of aid is controversial, with detractors claiming that aid may distort priorities and create dependency. Aid agencies have been criticized for failure to assess local needs sensitively, both in the case of disasters such as earthquakes or famine, and in the case of development aid such as funding agricultural or health projects.

Aids (*a*cquired *i*mmune *d*eficiency *s*yndrome), a disease complex resulting from infection by HIV (*h*uman *i*mmunodeficiency *v*irus). The virus attacks the body's immune defences, allowing opportunistic infections to thrive, and eventually kill the sufferer. The mean period between first infection and the development of Aids itself is ten years in

In Brazil this clay figure called Ze Cabra-Macho helps to spread the 'safe sex' message through educational slides. He is intended to personalize the message and help raise awareness among construction workers, who, as single young men, are particularly at risk from **Aids**.

North America and Europe, but only three to four years in developing countries, probably because of the different diseases prevalent in different countries and the availability of drugs to treat them. The HIV virus is spread primarily by infected blood and blood products, cervical secretions, occasionally breast milk, and by semen. The syndrome was first recognized in 1981, when a common pattern of symptoms was observed among a small number of homosexual men who had died in the USA. The World Health Organization (WHO) estimates that between 1981 and 1991 about 1.5 million Aids cases occurred. By the year 2000 it is predicted that 40 million people will be infected with the HIV virus and that the number of victims of full-blown Aids will probably approach 10 million, of whom 90 per cent will be from developing countries. In industrialized countries, most cases of Aids in the early years of the epidemic were the result of homosexual contact or the sharing of needles by intravenous drug users; men far outnumbered women with the disease. The transmission of the virus is increasingly through heterosexual contact and the number of HIV-positive women is growing. In developing countries reporting high numbers of cases, *sexually transmitted diseases and poorer general health are thought to be contributing factors to the epidemic spread of Aids among the heterosexual urban population. The countries of central and eastern Africa are hardest hit. In Rwanda, Tanzania, and Uganda 5 to 20 per cent of the sexually active age-group is infected with the HIV virus and in certain risk groups, such as prostitutes, the rate can exceed 80 per cent. The other major transmission route in certain developing countries with a high number of infected women, is via the placenta, from an infected mother to her unborn baby, during childbirth, or during breast-feeding. Of the 40 million people who it is estimated will be infected with HIV by the year 2000, WHO believes 10 million will be children. In areas where Aids is rife, the growing number of infected people showing symptoms of the disease, as well as the growing number of infected babies who may have lost one or both parents to Aids, places enormous burdens on health and social services, which in many developing countries are already at breaking point. Until a cure or a vaccine for Aids can be found, the main strategies for prevention and control are information, counselling, and education, all of which imply major changes in sexual behaviour and drug-injecting practices.

Ainu, a now small ethnic group in northern Japan and the Kuril Islands, who are now mostly assimilated into mainstream culture. Traditionally, the Ainu were hunters and fishers, whose religion centred on local forces of nature, and the sacrifice of a bear at an annual winter ritual. The kinship system was distinct, in that women traced their ancestry through a matrilineal group spanning four generations, and men traced their descent through a patrilineal system, which was also the basis for *ancestor worship, as well as deciding hunting and fishing rights among corporate kin groups.

Akali (Punjabi, 'worshipper of the Timeless One'), a militaristic order of Sikh ascetics. The sect dates from before the formation of the *Khalsa by *Gobind Singh in 1699, but Akalis became its most militant adherents, skilled in fighting and greatly feared. They were at their most prominent under Ranjit Singh (1790–1839), who set up a powerful Sikh kingdom in the Punjab. The name was revived in the 1920s during the struggle to regain control of the *Gurdwaras, or Sikh temples. The *Akali Dal* ('Immortal Army') assisted in the return of *Gurdwara* custodianship to the Sikhs, and since then has played a part in the politics of the Punjab, becoming more sectarian and militant in recent years.

Albanian language, an *Indo-European language spoken by 3 million people in Albania and southern Yugoslavia; there are also small groups of speakers in Greece and southern Italy. It is not closely related to any other language, though it may be connected with the ancient language spoken in Dacia (present-day Romania) before the coming of Latin speakers to the area. The earliest Albanian document dates from the late 15th century, and there is no real literature until the 18th century. An official Roman alphabet has been in use since 1909. There are two distinct dialect groups, *Gheg* in the north and *Tosk* in the south, separated by the River Shkumbin. These are not on the whole mutually intelligible, except for less extreme forms. The official standard language in Albania is based on *Tosk*.

alcohol abuse, the habitual, compulsive, and excessive consumption of alcohol, to the extent where health or social interaction are adversely affected. Figures indicate that alcohol abuse is increasing, especially among women. Excessive alcohol consumption can adversely affect the liver, leading to cirrhosis or liver cancer; it can contribute to *heart disease, high blood pressure, stroke, gastric ulcers, and renal failure; and in pregnancy it can lead to foetal abnormalities. Alcohol is also a major factor in *crime; domestic problems, such as marital breakdown and *child abuse; work problems, such as absenteeism; and accidents, particularly in cars. There is disagreement about treatment: many experts consider that a cure can only be brought about by total abstinence, while others believe that controlled consumption can be achieved. Treatment for alcohol dependence may involve a period of detoxification, followed by individual *counselling or *group therapy. For many people dependent on alcohol, successful treatment is achieved through attending self-help groups, such as Alcoholics Anonymous (AA). Complete prohibition (as in strict Islamic societies, where the penalty is eighty lashes for the drinking of any intoxicant, or the USA in the 1920s) or sudden enforced reductions in availability (as in the Soviet Union in the late 1980s) tend to lead only to illicit production and consumption. Prevention of alcohol abuse is a priority for many governments.

al-Farabī (*c*.873–950), Islamic philosopher. He commented on the logical works of *Aristotle and the political works of *Plato, combining ideas from both in his principal work, *The Ideal City*. This hierarchical society would be headed by a philosopher–prophet, from whom lower ranks would derive their authority. The same structure is evident in his *metaphysics, in which all levels of intelligence and life emanate necessarily from the One, or God, and in his ranking of kinds of knowledge. Philosophical knowledge, acquired through logic, is the highest exercise of reason, but religious knowledge, which dresses itself in symbols accessible to the imagination of lesser thinkers, also has its place.

al-Ghazālī (1058–1111), Islamic theologian and mystic. Born in eastern Iran, al-Ghazālī was one of the leading theological scholars in the Seljuk capital of Baghdad, where he wrote treatises on logic, theology, and jurisprudence. He studied the philosophy of *al-Farabī and *Avicenna, criticizing the latter's work in his *The Inconsistency of the Philosophers*. However, he is best known for his *The Revival of the Religious Sciences*, written after he adopted *Sufism and lived the

monastic life of a mystic. In this, his greatest work, he made a synthesis of orthodox Islam and Sufism.

'Alī (*c*.600–61), a cousin and the son-in-law of *Muḥammad, and the father of Hasan and Husain from whom the progeny of Muḥammad—the Sayyids—descends. The Sunnīs venerate him as the fourth elected caliph, while Shīʿa Muslims claim that he was the rightful nominated successor of Muḥammad. This constitutes the main difference between Shīʿa Islam and Sunnī Islam.

alienation (in sociology), separation or estrangement from fellow human beings, society, or inner self. In his classic formulation in *The Economic and Philosophical Manuscripts of 1844*, *Marx distinguished four principal forms: the worker's distancing from the process of work so that it became a commodity to be sold and lacked intrinsic satisfaction; the worker's lack of control over the product of his labour; detachment from fellow human beings; and estrangement from one's essential human nature. In the 20th century, work in mass production (see *production methods), such as automobile manufacture, has been seen as particularly alienating. The worker must work at the pace dictated by the assembly line, and may have a single repetitive task with no scope for initiative or interaction with others. The recognition of such alienating processes has led to changes in some factories so that workers operate in small groups or produce whole products. The delinquent behaviour of certain groups, for example football hooligans, is sometimes claimed to spring from alienation in a broader sense. The term alienation is also often used to signify feelings of individual powerlessness or disorientation in rapidly changing societies. A related concept is *anomie.

alimony *maintenance after divorce.

alliance (in international relations), an agreement entered into by two or more states for the purpose of mutual co-operation or security. Alliances may be formed for the purpose of waging war, or in order to guarantee security (for example, the treaty establishing *NATO in 1949 states that an attack on one of the members should be regarded as an attack on them all). Alliances may be tacit or embodied in treaty form; they may be secret or open; and they may be limited in time or established on a more permanent basis. In many cases, the co-operation between the different states extends to diplomatic support with regard to foreign policy, as well as joint military exercises, training, and arms procurement.

alphabet, a phonological *writing system with the graphs (letters) representing individual sounds of a *language. In one category of alphabets, called 'consonantal', only the consonants are represented by the letters and the vowels are indicated with diacritics (marks such as dots, accents, and circles above or below the appropriate letters). Hebrew and Arabic are among the languages using scripts based on this principle. In the other category, letters represent both consonants and vowels. Since, however, the correspondence is rarely one-to-one, here too diacritics are often used. Most of the European languages and many others use this kind of alphabet. The wide variety of alphabets world-wide, except possibly for the Indian alphabets, evolved over 4,000 years from the consonantal Semitic script. One of its variants, Phoenician, was the source of the Roman alphabet via Greek. The transition from Phoenician to Greek occurred between *c*.1000 BC and *c*.800 BC; the shapes of the letters altered, and some Semitic consonants, not needed in the Greek phonological system, were now used as vowels. The spread of Christianity from Rome across western Europe was accompanied by the spread of the Roman alphabet. Greek missionaries took Christianity and the Greek alphabet to eastern Europe, which gave rise to the Cyrillic alphabet used for writing Russian. In India, the Devanagari alphabet in which Sanskrit was notated developed independently between the 7th and the 9th centuries. Many modern Indian scripts are based on, and generically termed, Devanagari. *Phonetic alphabets such as the International Phonetic Alphabet (IPA), based on the Roman script, have been developed to represent the sound systems of individual languages universally and more accurately than ordinary alphabetic writing. In China, the Roman alphabet has been introduced since 1958 in a transliteration system called Pinyin to facilitate the pronunciation and comprehension of the Chinese characters, which are logograms.

Altaic, a family of languages, named after the Altai Mountains, which consists of the Turkic, Mongolian, and Manchu–Tungus language-groups. It is not completely clear whether these three form a genetically related group (that is, are descended from one parent language), or whether they owe their undoubted similarities to centuries of contact and mutual influence. An interesting feature which they all share is vowel-harmony, whereby all the vowels in a word must be either all front vowels (produced in the front of the mouth: e, i, ö, ü) or back vowels (a, ı, o, u). Mixtures of the two are not allowed. The thirty Turkic languages are spoken in a band which stretches from Turkey eastwards through Central Asia to north-west China and far into Siberia. They show remarkable similarity considering the distances involved, and neighbouring languages are generally mutually intelligible. The most important language is Turkish, which is spoken by 55 million people. Turkish-speakers reached present-day Turkey in the 11th century, and the first written documents date from the 13th century. The language was written in the Arabic script and heavily influenced by Arabic and Persian, but there was a movement to rid the language of words derived from these languages, following the Language Reform initiated by Kemal Atatürk (the founder of modern Turkey) in 1928, when a script using the Roman alphabet was devised for it. Other important Turkic languages are Azeri, Kazakh, Kirgiz, Turkmen, and Uzbek, written in the Cyrillic *alphabet since the 1940s. There are twelve Mongolian languages, spoken in Mongolia, the Autonomous Region of Mongolia (China), and the autonomous republics of Buryat and Kalmyk in the Russian Federation. The official language of the Mongolian Republic is Mongol, or *Khalkha*. There is a Mongolian literature (mainly Buddhist) which dates back to the 13th century. The sixteen Manchu–Tungus languages have under 100,000 speakers, but are spread over a vast area extending from Siberia to northern China. Manchu, an official language of China under the Qing dynasty (1644–1911) and formerly the main language of communication with the West, is now practically extinct.

alternative medicine   *complementary medicine.

Althusser, Louis (1918–90), French political and social theorist and one of the most influential Marxist thinkers of the 20th century. He advanced his ideas in a series of essay collections, including *For Marx* (1965) and *Reading Capital* (1970). He rejected the 'actually existing socialism' of Eastern Europe and, by offering a new interpretation of *Marx's texts, set out to renew revolutionary theory. Althusser denied that the workings of politics and society could be wholly explained as the outcome of economic class struggle. Culture and ideology were important too. In order to endure, a society depended upon what he termed 'ideological state apparatuses', an elaborate network of cultural and political institutions stretching from the churches and the mass media to school and the family. Althusser's complex writings have aroused diverse responses. Some saw him as a fearless analyst of the deep-rooted assumptions and dilemmas of socialist thought; others as a purveyor of esoteric phrases and explanatory formulae; and others again as an apologist for socialism's failures.

altruism, concern for other people, or unselfish or helpful actions, such as assisting at accidents or emergencies, and giving blood or money. Studies of altruism have covered actions as diverse as giving directions and putting oneself in danger. Most attempts to explain altruism treat it as a form of covert selfishness, for natural selection (see *Darwin) must favour behaviour which increases the individual's own Darwinian fitness. Animals' altruism is therefore usually explained by positing mechanisms which ultimately help the altruist or the survival of its characteristic genes. One mechanism is reciprocal altruism, which promotes co-operative behaviour which involves temporary sacrifices for longer-term pay-offs for the individuals involved. Another mechanism, termed 'kin selection', involves care-giving by parents, which increases the survival chances of the altruist's offspring and thereby of its genes. In humans, cultural norms may modify such innate processes. But most social theorists still see humans as essentially selfish. Research in the 1980s has, however, suggested that *empathy may promote genuine unselfishness. This may be an innate mechanism. Humans in all societies rapidly respond to others' needs. This does not preclude calculation. Willingness to help is affected by how attractive, deserving, and non-threatening the recipient is.

Alzheimer's Disease   *dementia.

Amazonian Indian, an original inhabitant of the Amazonian rain forest in South America, a vast area which shows great linguistic and cultural diversity. The dominant form of social organization is one of semi-nomadic tribes of *hunter-gatherers, who prior to the arrival of Europeans had no domestic animals except dogs. The population is dispersed in small tribal groupings such as the *Yanomano, unlike the confederations that were formed by some *Plains Indians, for example. *Kinship is based on a system of mostly *patrilineal lineage groups, and elaborate *puberty rituals are of central importance, while some tribes are also divided into *totemic clans. The predominant religious beliefs are a form of spirit worship or *animism, in which nature is considered to be inhabited by a variety of spirits, and tribal *shamans are important in mediating between the spirit world and the world of the living. The shamans also function as healers, and frequently use hallucinogenic drugs as a means of entering the spirit world. Other forms of *magical control may include body ornamentation, and some kinds of body painting and tattooing express magical beliefs. The mythology of the Amazonians is diverse, although the French anthropologist *Lévi-Strauss claims to have uncovered significant patterns of similarity among a

Kayapo Indians in traditional dress and paint. Living in the rain forest of central Brazil, the Kayapo are one group of **Amazonian Indians** who are fighting back against exploitation of their land by the Brazilians, and have now accumulated considerable wealth from the mining of gold on their land.

large body of *myth. Contact with Europeans has often produced drastic effects, in particular competing claims from the settlers and the Indians over land use, and the *deforestation of the jungle.

American Convention on Human Rights, a convention drawn up in 1969 by the Inter-American Commission on Human Rights. Only members of the *Organization of American States are entitled to become parties to it: twenty of the thirty-two members have done so. The Convention resembles the *European Convention on Human Rights, setting out the duties of states to respect the civil and political rights of their citizens, without discrimination. Violations of the Convention may be referred to the Inter-American Commission on Human Rights, and, if settlement is not reached, to the Inter-American Court of Human Rights. Although some states with poor human-rights records are non-signatories, the convention is generally believed to be contributing to the promotion of human rights in the region.

Amharic language *Semitic languages.

amnesia *memory disorder.

amnesty, an act erasing from legal liabilities some offence, especially of a political nature. An amnesty may be conditional (for example, on illegal firearms being surrendered or a return to duty by a prescribed date). Amnesty differs from a general pardon in that the former declares the offence abolished, whereas the latter rescinds the punishment.

Amnesty International, a pressure group formed in 1961, whose activities and aims focus on persons imprisoned or maltreated because of their political or religious beliefs ('prisoners of conscience'). With a professional international secretariat in London, Amnesty is based on a network of voluntary local groups and individual members throughout the world, who adopt prisoners of conscience and pursue their cases with the governments concerned or through interna-

tional bodies; methods of investigation include monitoring, fact-finding missions, publicity, and individual correspondence. Amnesty is not associated with any single ideology, government, or political party, and impartiality is central to its Statute. The Statute elaborates the general purposes of the organization, which are: to uphold the *Universal Declaration of Human Rights; to work for the release of those detained, restricted, or otherwise subjected to physical coercion by reason of their beliefs, ethnic origin, gender, colour, or language, provided they have not used or advocated violence; to oppose *detention without trial and to uphold the right to a fair trial; and to oppose use of the death penalty (see *capital punishment) or *torture, whether or not the persons concerned have advocated violence.

amortization, the repayment of the capital value of a *debt, usually by instalments. Amortization is also used to mean *depreciation, the decline in value of a *capital good during its working life.

analytic philosophy, a broad movement in 20th-century philosophy, influential chiefly in Austria, the UK, and the USA, which regards central philosophical problems as primarily demanding clarification or analysis of such notions as meaning, truth, and necessity. Although analytical philosophy is a loosely unified tradition, rather than a specific doctrine, there has been broad agreement on some specific matters. First, philosophy is a distinctive kind of enquiry, which employs methods different from those of the natural or social sciences; additionally, unlike, for instance, biology or economics, it is not addressed to any distinctive realm of facts. Philosophy does not seek to construct theories which build upon or add to our knowledge of the world, but to clarify the knowledge and beliefs we already have. Secondly, this clarification is to be achieved by analysis of the language in which our non-philosophical, common-sense, or scientific knowledge is expressed. This framework leaves ample room for internal divisions. There is, for instance, disagreement between *Russell's view that this kind of clarification will yield answers to the traditional questions of *metaphysics and *epistemology, and *Wittgenstein's contention that such questions are the products of confusions which the careful analysis of language will enable us to avoid. A related dispute concerns whether philosophical analysis can itself be conducted in a systematic way, using the tools and techniques of mathematical *logic, as the *logical positivists held, or whether resolution of philosophical problems demands piecemeal attention to specific areas of ordinary language (see *linguistic philosophy). In general, workers in the tradition are suspicious of system-building, priding themselves on rigour of argument and clarity of expression. Critics of the tradition say it is arid, concerned with minute points of detail, and ignores the major philosophical problems.

anarchism, the view that the state should be abolished and society organized by voluntary means without resort to force or compulsion. According to anarchists, the state is a parasitic body which performs no useful functions, but allows a small privileged class to exploit the remainder of society. Following its abolition, which most anarchists see as requiring a revolutionary struggle, voluntary institutions would emerge to maintain order and co-ordinate production. There is a spectrum of anarchist views on the shape of future society, from the economic individualism of the American anarchist Benjamin Tucker's *Instead of a Book* (1893) to the communism of the émigré Russian Peter

Kropotkin's *The Conquest of Bread* (1906). In the last century, activists such as Mikhail Bakunin (1814–76) played a significant role in radicalizing the European labour movement. Anarchism had its greatest practical success at the outset of the Spanish Civil War (1936–9), when many areas came under anarchist control, but latterly it has been reduced to small individual cells, influential only through their contribution to wider causes such as the *peace movement and *animal rights.

Anatolian languages, a group of *Indo-European languages spoken in Anatolia (modern Turkey) and Syria in the second and first millennia BC. The best attested is Hittite. The other languages, which are rather poorly attested, are Luwian, Lycian, Lydian, and Palaic. Hittite was written in cuneiform on clay tablets discovered in the early 20th century at Boğazköy (ancient Hattusa) in central Turkey. Cuneiform is a script made up of small wedge shapes, in which each character stands for a syllable, and was borrowed from Mesopotamia. The tablets date from the 17th to the 13th centuries BC, which makes Hittite the earliest known Indo-European language. As such it has been extremely valuable for the reconstruction of Indo-European. There are many thousands of tablets, covering religious, historical, political, and legal subject-matter.

ancestor worship, the worship of dead ancestors by the living, based on the belief that the spirits of the dead continue to have a close relation to their kin, and are capable of influencing their affairs. Ancestral spirits can be male or female, and can include all ancestors, those of a few generations, or indeed mythical ancestors. Worship takes many ritual forms, such as propitiatory prayers, offerings, *sacrifice, and festivals of honour. Ancestor worship is found in many *African traditional religions, where the spirits are called on to avert illness, help obtain good crops, or assure fertility. *Chinese religions and *Shinto in Japan stress reverence for ancestors, although in modern China, as the importance of *kinship has declined, so has ancestor worship.

Andean Group (officially, the *Acuerdo de Cartagena* from the Cartagena Agreement which established it), a regional grouping, established in 1969, comprising Bolivia, Colombia, Ecuador, Peru, and Venezuela. Based in Lima, Peru, its two major goals are the reduction of trade barriers and the stimulation of industrial development. It has met with some success, but political problems between and within the member states have hindered progress. In 1987 members signed the Quito Protocol, which included a relaxation of the strict controls on foreign investors in the region (on such matters as share ownership and the repatriation of profits), which had acted as a deterrent to investment.

Anglican Communion, the body of *Protestant Christian Churches around the world which claim descent from the Church in England as reformed in the 16th century. They all recognize the spiritual leadership of the Archbishop of Canterbury, though he does not have any jurisdiction over Anglicans outside England. There are twenty national member Churches, including the Church of England, the largest, with about 16 million full members; the Protestant Episcopal Church of America; the Church of Wales; the Episcopal Church of Scotland; and Anglican and Episcopal Churches in former British colonies or areas of Anglican Missionary activity, for example Japan. There is little formal structure linking the Anglican Churches, but since 1867 their bishops have gathered every ten years at the Lambeth Conference in England, an occasion to affirm the unity of the Anglican Churches and to debate outstanding issues, though the resolutions of the conference have no binding authority. The Anglican Communion is distinguished by considerable diversity in both doctrine and *liturgy, but the Churches unite in acknowledging the three-fold ministry of bishops, priests, and deacons, the authority of the *Bible, and a tradition of liturgical practice or form of worship inherited from the 16th-century Book of Common Prayer. In recent times various issues have strained the unity of the various Churches, and on some, such as the ordination of women, there has been an agreement to differ. There is also great divergence within some of the Anglican Churches. For example, in the Church of England (the established Church in England, recognized by the state, under the titular headship of the UK monarch), the 'high' Church (Anglo-Catholics) stresses the authority of the bishops and priesthood, tradition, and the seven *Sacraments and claims continuity with the pre-Reformation Catholic Church, while the 'low' Church (*evangelicals) sets less store by the sacraments and tradition, and emphasizes the importance of the Bible as the basis of faith. The churches of the Anglican Communion each have individual membership of the *World Council of Churches, and have been active in the ecumenical movement. Anglicans, like *Lutherans, often see themselves as forming a 'bridge' between Roman Catholicism and the more strictly Protestant Churches.

animal rights, an extension to animals of the sensitivity to and respect for life inherent in the concept of *human rights. Those who advocate animal rights claim that because animals possess sentience (the capacity to feel pain, to fear, or to experience enjoyment or happiness), they have a basic right to be treated in ways that respect their independent value. For human beings to exploit animals is a form of 'speciesism'; by analogy to *racism, we allow the interests of our own species to override the interests of other species. The main areas where human beings currently fail to observe animal rights are in intensive farming methods, commercial and sport hunting, and the use of animals for scientific testing and experimentation (vivisection) and in the destruction of their habitats (see *endangered species). Frustrated by the continued abuse of animals, organizations such as the Animal Liberation Front have taken extreme action by fire-bombing shops, raiding laboratories, and threatening scientists.

During the 1970s furs and skins, especially leopard-skin, increased in popularity; today some 20 million furs are traded each year. **Animal rights** groups, such as Lynx, have undermined the appeal of fur clothing by challenging its glamour.

It takes up to 40 dumb animals to make a fur coat.

But only one to wear it.

LYNX

Fighting the fur trade

If you don't want animals gassed, electrocuted, trapped or strangled, don't buy a fur coat. P.O Box 509 Dunmow, Essex Tel: 0371 2016

animism, the attribution of a living soul to all creatures, inanimate objects, and natural phenomena. In anthropology the term denotes the belief that the world is animated by spirits who are capable of harming or helping a person's interests. For example, *Melanesian societies believed in an all-pervasive spirit called *mana*, which was capable of both good and evil. Animistic belief gives rise to all manner of ways in which the spirits may be propitiated or evil avoided, including *taboos and magic charms or amulets. Some 19th-century anthropologists considered animism the most primitive form of *religion, although contemporary scholars prefer not to make such distinctions, and the word is still used in some official classifications of non-Western religions.

annuity, a constant annual payment. The guarantee of the maintenance of such annual payments is also known as an annuity, and can usually be purchased from *insurance companies. A 'certain' annuity is paid over a specified number of years, whereas a 'life' annuity is paid until the death of the named recipient. An annuity may be bought with a lump sum or through a series of contributions. Annuities may be 'immediate' or 'deferred', depending on whether payments to the recipient commence on purchase of the annuity or at a later specified date.

anomie (anomy), the lack or weakness of the usual social or ethical standards in an individual or group. The sociologist *Durkheim, taking the term from the Greek *anomia* (lawlessness), argued that anomie could result from rapid social change. Some US sociologists, in particular Robert K. Merton (1910–), have maintained that anomie can lead to *deviance. Where an individual or group is prevented from achieving widely accepted goals, law-breaking may result. For example, if car ownership is almost universal, poverty may lead to car theft. (See also *alienation.)

anorexia *eating disorder.

anthropology, the study of humanity, divided into two main areas of interest: the physical structure and evolution of mankind, and the social organizations and cultural systems of human groups. In the 19th century, anthropology was concerned with theories of both physical and social evolution, so-called 'primitive' people being regarded as representative of earlier stages of mankind. Both physical and social differences were considered together in theories of *race. In the early 20th century, the study of social and cultural differences became a separate discipline, known as social anthropology in the UK and cultural anthropology in the USA. At the same time, anthropologists started to become more involved in *fieldwork research. Early anthropologists like *Frazer had had little or no experience of the different societies they were writing about, but *Malinowski was one of the first anthropologists to observe a society by living with the people, studying their language as well as their cultural system, and writing about them in an *ethnography, an analysis based on such fieldwork. In the USA, cultural anthropology traces its origins to Franz Boas (1858–1942), who studied various *North-west Indian groups, and whose many notable students included *Mead. Until World War II, most anthropological studies were of 'primitive' people, usually in European colonies, and the dominant theoretical influence in the UK was *functionalism. After World War II, more studies began to be carried out in societies with long traditions of written history in Europe and Asia, and new theoretical approaches, such as

the *structuralism of *Lévi-Strauss, appeared. Modern anthropologists study people in all settings, from industrial cities to remote rain forests. By living within a society and participating in its activities, learning its language, and observing its daily life, the anthropologist builds up a knowledge of that society's *kinship system, *social organization, *culture, *law, *rituals, and *myths. By comparing this cultural system with others, the anthropologist attempts to understand the variety of human social experience as much as possible through the eyes of different people all over the world.

anti-Semitism *Jewish people.

anxiety, a feeling of actual or anticipated unease, similar to fear, but more closely associated with uncertainty. It is associated with bodily changes such as raised heart-rate and perspiration. The relationship between anxiety and uncertainty is shown by the fact that people who are unsure whether they will receive an electric shock have a higher heart-rate and perspire more than those who are sure that a shock is coming. Psychologists distinguish the state of being anxious from the trait of being an anxious person. Levels of trait anxiety appear to be major, and perhaps innate, differences between people. In *psychiatry, anxiety occurs in many psychological disorders, both *neuroses and *psychoses. A notable exception is the *psychopathic personality, where it is precisely the absence of anxiety (failure to worry about the consequences of one's actions) that is the problem. In certain disorders, such as *phobias, in which extreme anxiety is the main feature, the person is incapacitated by fear of, and hence driven to avoid, what in reality are harmless situations. Although drugs (minor tranquillizers) can be used in the treatment of abnormal anxiety, this may lead to dependence and does not relieve the underlying problem, which is better dealt with by *psychotherapy or one of the newer instructional methods (*behaviour therapy), whereby the person is taught self-help techniques of anxiety management. A related term is angst, first used by *Kierkegaard to describe an *existential anxiety or anguish.

ANZUS, an acronym given to a tripartite Pacific security treaty between Australia, New Zealand, and the USA, signed in 1951. Known also as the Pacific Security Treaty, it declares that following an armed attack in the Pacific Area on any of the parties, each would act to meet the common danger, in accordance with its constitutional processes. Following New Zealand's adoption of an anti-nuclear policy, which included the banning of nuclear-armed ships from its ports, the USA suspended its security obligations to New Zealand in 1986. ANZUS continues to govern security relations between Australia and the USA, and between Australia and New Zealand.

Apache, a group of *Plains Indians of the south-western USA. Traditionally, the Apache practised subsistence farming and hunting, and a system of matrilocal (at the home of the wife) residence. They had a reputation as fierce fighters, and resisted domination by the Spanish and Mexicans until the mid-19th century, when their territory was incorporated into the USA. The Apache were not finally subjugated, however, until the end of the 19th century, and many of their chiefs, such as Geronimo, entered into American folklore. They now live in the state of Arizona.

apartheid *segregation.

aphasia, a speech disorder caused by brain damage from strokes, headwounds, or sometimes infectious disease. Two distinct kinds are recognized, named after their discoverers, the French physician Paul Broca (1824–80) and the German physician Carl Wernicke (1848–1905). They are caused by damage to different areas of the brain. Sufferers from Broca's or non-fluent aphasia speak telegraphically, without grammatical features such as prepositions and conjunctions. Sufferers from Wernicke's or fluent aphasia speak fluently and grammatically but have trouble finding the right words. This leads to circumlocution and vague expressions such as 'what's-its-name' and· 'thingumme'. Sometimes speech degenerates into wholly inappropriate word selection or meaningless jargon. Wernicke's aphasics may have difficulty understanding speech even though their perception of other sounds is not affected. Impairment of language does not necessarily imply loss of other faculties such as *intelligence and *memory. Most aphasic people, especially younger ones, spontaneously recover a good deal of speech in time.

appeal, a request made to a higher *court for an alteration of the decision of a lower court. A party who has lost a *civil law case, or a defendant who has been convicted in a criminal case, may appeal to a higher court, either on a question of law (for instance, if there were errors of procedure in the original trial) or, usually in limited circumstances, on questions of fact (which might involve a reconsideration of the evidence and the inferences drawn from it). In order to control the number of appeals, restrictions are often imposed, such as the necessity to obtain leave to appeal from the higher court. A defendant in a criminal case may also appeal for a reduction in his *sentence; and in many countries, the *prosecution can seek a heavier sentence. In some *jurisdictions there is a hierarchy of appellate courts, culminating in a court of ultimate appeal, such as the US Supreme Court, the French *Cour de Cassation*, or the UK House of Lords. Appeals can also be made to the European Court of Human Rights or *European Court of Justice.

a priori, a term from *epistemology meaning knowledge or concepts which can be gained independently of all experience. It is contrasted with *a posteriori* knowledge, in which experience plays an essential role. Statements such as 'all bachelors are unmarried' are known as analytic truths: the concept 'bachelor' and the concept 'unmarried' are interdefinable. Analytic truths, then, provide one form of a priori knowledge. For example, simply because of the meaning of the concept 'bachelor', we know a priori that if John is a bachelor, then John has no wife. On the other hand, knowledge of whether John is a bachelor or not would be *a posteriori* because its discovery requires some form of empirical investigation. The extent of a priori knowledge is much debated. *Rationalists and others, including *Kant, argue that we can have substantial a priori knowledge. *Empiricist philosophies, though, generally limit a priori knowledge to that derivable from analytic truths. (See also *nativism.)

Aquinas, St Thomas (*c*.1224–74), Dominican theologian and philosopher. His *metaphysics revolves around three contrasts, those of potentiality and actuality, form and matter (see *Aristotle), and essence and existence (see *Avicenna). Whether something exists is not settled by an account of what it is. The essence of a thing may involve materiality, but this is not implied by the notion of existence: to be is not to be material. In all material things Aquinas distinguishes their form, or organizing principle, from their matter, which is simply the potential to take on this or another form. Following Aristotle he identified the mind or soul with the form of the body, and sought to reconcile this with the Christian belief in immortality. Thomism, a philosophy rooted in his doctrines, holds a central place in Roman Catholic education to this day.

Arabic language   *Semitic languages.

Arab League (League of Arab States), an organization of Arab states, founded in Egypt in 1945. In 1991 its members were: Algeria, Bahrain, Djibouti, Egypt, Iraq, Jordan, Kuwait, Lebanon, Libya, Mauritania, Morocco, Oman, Palestine, Qatar, Saudi Arabia, Somalia, Sudan, Syria, Tunisia, United Arab Emirates, and Yemen. An annexe to the League's Charter stipulates that Palestine is considered as an independent state and as a full member of the Arab League. The principal aims of the League are to protect the independence and *sovereignty of its members, and to strengthen the ties between them by encouraging co-operation in different fields. Opposition to the state of Israel and the demand for the establishment of a *Palestinian state have been central to the policies of the League. The organization's headquarters were transferred to Tunis during the suspension of Egypt from the League because of President Sadat's peace agreement with Israel's Prime Minister Begin in 1978 (the Camp David Accord). Egypt was readmitted in 1987, and in 1990 Cairo once again became the League's headquarters. In 1989 a mediation committee consisting of three of the members of the Arab League helped to negotiate a ceasefire in Lebanon. In 1990 the League narrowly approved a proposal to dispatch Arab forces to support the US-led coalition against Saddam Hussein's invasion of Kuwait, but the conflict exposed serious divisions among members.

Aranda, a group of central Australian Aborigines. Divided into five sub-tribes, each has a different dialect and different ritual practices. Traditionally, a belief in *reincarnation was fundamental to their religion, which also held that the ancestors were linked to certain natural species in a form of *totemism. Initiation rituals involved physical ordeals, including *circumcision. Witchcraft was thought to be a cause of illness and death, and ritual specialists were used in the process of healing. Despite the cultural contact with settlers that has proved disastrous to some other Aboriginal groups, the Aranda have managed to maintain their distinctive cultural identity.

arbitrage, the simultaneous buying and selling of *goods or *assets in different *markets (which are separated in either space or time) in order to profit from differences in price. Dealers buy at a lower price and sell at the same time at a higher price. As the dealers buy and sell simultaneously, they are not exposed to risk from price movements, in contrast to *speculators, who buy (or sell) in the expectation of a rise (or fall) in the relevant price. Arbitrage most commonly takes place in *commodity markets, the *foreign-exchange market, and the markets for *bills of exchange and *bonds. (See also *futures markets.)

arbitration   *dispute resolution.

archery, the sport of shooting arrows from a bow at a fixed target. Since the 1940s, the traditional English longbow, made of yew, has been replaced by a more accurate composite bow of wood, plastic, and fibreglass. The target stands with its centre 1.3 m (51 inches) above the ground at distances varying from 30 m (98 feet) to 90 m (295 feet). Under international rules, the target has a ten-zone face in five colours. At the centre are two bands of gold (scoring 10, 9 points for each hit), then two bands each of red (8, 7 points), blue (6, 5), black (4, 3), and white (2, 1).

Arctic societies, two distinct cultural groups resident in the region around the North Pole; those of the western hemisphere, now known as the *Inuit, and those of the eastern hemisphere, who include the *Lapps. The societies of the eastern hemisphere are predominantly semi-nomadic *pastoralists, while the Inuit are exclusively hunters. Arctic cultural boundaries are more difficult to define than geographical ones, especially in the eastern hemisphere where the social groupings are more diverse than those in the west. The pastoralists of the east often spend the winter in the coniferous forest, or taiga, of the region, and move their herds during the summer months to the pastures of the Arctic tundra. *Shamanism and spirit worship or *animism were common throughout this region, although such traditional beliefs are now in decline. The Inuit, by contrast, are mostly coastal dwellers, and hunt for fish and small aquatic mammals, such as seal and walrus. The basic unit of social organization is the *family; during the winter, several families congregate in small settlements, and disperse throughout the brief months of summer, although many Inuit now live in permanent settlements.

Arendt, Hannah (1906–75), political philosopher. Born in Germany but migrating to the USA after the rise of Nazism, she developed an original outlook on politics which defies categorization in Left/Right or other conventional terms. In her first book, *The Origins of Totalitarianism* (1951), she identified the *totalitarian regimes of Hitler's Germany and Stalin's Soviet Union as radically new phenomena, whose most prominent characteristic was the use of terror to impose an abstract *ideology on people. Arendt looked for elements in modern European society which could explain the acquiescence of both perpetrators and victims in the horrors of these regimes, in particular the *concentration camps. She pointed especially to the condition of the masses uprooted by social and economic change.

arhat (Sanskrit, 'worthy one'), the ideal person in *Theravāda Buddhism. It is a title given to one who has achieved enlightenment through the teaching of a *Buddha. The *arhat* has freed him- or herself from fear, craving, and the false idea of self; upon death he or she is released from rebirth to enter *nirvana. The Theravāda ideal of the *arhat* contrasts with the *Mahāyāna Buddhist notion of the *bodhisattva, who renounces nirvana in order to lead others to enlightenment.

aristocracy (from Greek, 'the rule of the best'), originally a form of government, but now usually a hereditary social *élite. From *Plato and *Aristotle onwards, it was commonly assumed that political power was best placed in the hands of those who, through education, occupation, or social position, had shown their capacity to exercise it. This assumption was challenged by the democratic sentiments nurtured by the American and French Revolutions (1776 and 1789); the latter provoking, in books such as Edmund Burke's *Reflections on the Revolution in France* (1790) and Louis de Bonald's *Theory of Power* (1796), some of the last explicit

defences of aristocracy. The term now describes a hereditary *social class, normally based on landed property.

Aristotle (384–322 BC), Greek philosopher. A student and critic of *Plato, and the most celebrated philosopher of his own time, Aristotle is also regarded today as a pioneer of many contemporary philosophical questions. His interests were encyclopedic, embracing most of the main branches of philosophy and natural science. His output was massive and a great deal has survived, largely in the form of notes for lectures delivered at the Lyceum, successor to Plato's Academy. Aristotle introduced the systematic study of *logic, developing a system for describing and assessing reasoning that remained the core of the discipline until the 19th century. Contemporary categorial *grammar can be traced to Aristotle's interest in the functioning of words, giving Aristotle a special place in *philosophical logic and in *linguistics. The central questions of Aristotle's *Metaphysics* (What is *substance?) and his *On Coming to be and Passing Away* (How do things come into existence and cease to exist?) are still hotly debated. In *De Anima* (On the Soul) Aristotle discussed the *soul, or psyche; that which makes something alive and capable of the activities characteristic of life. In claiming that the psyche is dependent upon the body, Aristotle anticipated the mind/body debate current in philosophy of *mind. Contemporary *ethics also owes a debt to Aristotle's *Ethics*. His claim that all action aims at *eudaimonia*, or happiness, seemingly has much in common with modern-day *utilitarianism; however, Aristotle's stress on the several virtues is in tension with utilitarianism's promise of a single (if not simple) principle for deciding all moral questions.

armed forces, a term usually referring to the military organization of a country, which is designed to act against the forces of another state, or to defend national interests against attack. For this reason they are distinguished from other armed personnel such as *police forces, armed *militia, or *security services that operate wholly inside the state. The armed forces are traditionally divided into the army, the navy, and the air force. The armed forces of a country may be made up of volunteers or conscripts (see *conscription); *mercenaries usually fight in the armed forces of another country for money, rather than out of national loyalty or ideological reasons. Armed forces usually have a hierarchical structure. At the top, the highest ranking officers are responsible for overall strategy; below them, middle-ranking officers translate that strategy into operational terms; while at the tactical level, the basic soldier carries out the objectives formulated by the officers. The size and capability of an armed force depends on a country's economic resources, the size of its population, and whether it is at peace or at war. In the developed world in particular, advances in technology have given rise to a new kind of armed force, capable of harnessing sophisticated weapons systems and computers.

Armenian Apostolic Church, one of the Monophysite *Christian Churches. It is headed by the Catholicates (supreme ecclesiastical office) of Etchmiadzen, in Armenia, and of Sis (Cilicia) in Turkey (now resident in Lebanon), and the patriarchates of Jerusalem and Istanbul. The Armenian Church is unique in celebrating the birth of Christ as part of the *Epiphany (6 January) and having no separate feast of *Christmas. The Armenian Church has never been in full communion with the Monophysite Churches, and its beliefs are close to those of the *Eastern Orthodox Church, but the church retains the Armenian language, liturgy, and customs.

The British Aerospace Hawk 200, on display at the Farnborough Air Show, UK, in 1984, is designed to be 'low cost' and is meant for countries with small defence budgets. Exports are increasingly important in the **arms trade** as the defence budgets of the major world powers are cut.

There are about 2 million members, principally in Armenia and the USA. There is also an Armenian Catholic rite with its own patriarch in Beirut, which is in communion with the *pope.

Armenian language, an *Indo-European language spoken by nearly 6 million people in Armenia, Turkey, Iran, and (as a result of emigration) in Europe and the USA. The earliest documents go back to the 5th century AD, but the language was certainly established in the south Caucasus area before this date. A thirty-eight-letter alphabet was developed around AD 400 following the introduction of Christianity to the area. Classical Armenian (*Grabar*) is the liturgical language of the Armenian Church. The literary tradition extends from this period to the present day. The language was influenced heavily by Persian and Greek, and also borrowed words from Arabic and Aramaic. Modern Armenian has two standard literary dialects: the Eastern dialect is the official language of Armenia and is based on the dialect of Yerevan; Western Armenian is generally used elsewhere, and is based on the dialect spoken in Istanbul. There are only slight differences between these two varieties; however, there are also many colloquial dialects, some of which are not mutually intelligible.

Armenians, a people whose original homeland was in present-day north-eastern Turkey and Armenia. Subjected at the instigation of the Ottoman and Turkish republican governments to forced mass deportation or massacres in the late 19th and early 20th centuries in which an estimated 1 million

died, the Armenians are a tiny and inconspicuous minority concentrated at present in Istanbul in Turkey; most Armenians are resident in Armenia, Azerbaijan, and Georgia, and in the USA, with minorities in Lebanon and Iran. Speaking Armenian, most Armenians are members of the Armenian Apostolic or the Armenian Catholic Churches. It is estimated that there are over 4 million world-wide. Since the 1970s Armenian terrorists (Armenian Secret Army for the Liberation of Armenia, ASALA) have conducted an efficient campaign, mostly against Turkish officials abroad, in an attempt to gain reparations for Turkey's atrocities against the Armenians, which have never been officially acknowledged by the Turkish government.

arms control, a policy of restraint, exercised by one or more states, in the deployment or use of weapons. The term is particularly used in connection with *nuclear weapons, and should be distinguished from *disarmament, which implies the reduction or elimination of existing forces and weapons. Arms control, on the other hand, is an attempt to manage the *arms race rather than eliminate it. Arms control is intended to introduce some degree of stability and predictability into the relations between adversary states, minimizing the prospects of war, limiting conflict should it occur, and reducing the costs of preparing for war. Arms control agreements and treaties between the USA and the Soviet Union included the Strategic Arms Limitation Talks (SALT) Agreements and Treaties of 1972 and 1979, which limited anti-ballistic missile systems and long-range intercontinental strategic weapons; the Treaty on Intermediate-Range Nuclear Forces (INF) in 1987, limiting forces deployed in Europe; the Treaty on Conventional Forces in Europe (CFE) in 1990; and the strategic arms reduction treaty signed in 1991. A key issue in successful arms control treaties is verification: the checking of the other side's capabilities through such methods as agreed data bases and on-

In **Asante** society women have great economic power. These women run the market at Kumasi, the capital of Ghana, through a system of produce associations, each with an elected leader. Known as the Queen Mother, she can expel traders from the market and controls the quality and quantity of produce sold.

site inspection by observers, as a means of ensuring compliance with the agreement. In recent years, the development of satellite technology has assisted inspection from space.

arms race, a process wherein two or more states, feeling themselves to be insecure or threatened, acquire armaments in succession, each side responding to the acquisition of arms by the other with a further build-up of its own. This action–reaction mechanism may acquire a momentum of its own, fuelling perceptions of insecurity, threat, and the need for more armaments. This is particularly so during times of rapid technological innovation. An important example was the US–Soviet arms race, especially their competition for strategic nuclear weaponry, which started after World War II. Some believe arms races to be a cause of conflict; to others they are a reflection of underlying political distrust, not a cause of it. One theory on arms races is that, if controlled at a key stability point, they may contribute to some kind of strategic stability, akin to a *balance of power.

arms trade, the international trade in weapons, such as guns and explosives as well as complex weapons systems (advanced aircraft and warships, together with their support systems). Much arms-trading in the world is done via an intermediary state, in order to conceal the nation of origin. Supporters of the arms trade argue that it serves as a means

of foreign policy influence, supports allies, and allows research and development costs to be spread over longer production runs, thus lowering costs and preserving national defence industries. Opponents argue that the trade is morally wrong, promotes instability, and fuels regional conflict and diverts money from essential development. They highlight the ironies involved in wars such as the Falklands War (1982) and the Gulf War (1991), where equipment was deployed against those who had sold it in the first place. Concern has also been expressed over the millions of dollars' worth of arms supplied to the developing world, largely by developed countries; such arms sales use up scarce resources and contribute to regional instability. The combined GDP of developing countries is 15 per cent of the developed countries, but they purchase 75 per cent of arms traded every year. In 1989 the largest suppliers of arms to developing countries, principally in the Middle East and Africa, were the former Soviet Union, USA, France, UK, China, Israel, and Brazil. In 1990 the trade in conventional arms was estimated to be worth $40.1 billion.

arrest, the act of seizing and detaining a person with the authority of law. In both common law and civil law jurisdictions, police investigating a crime are empowered to arrest any person whom they suspect has committed it or is implicated in its commission. In many countries, the police require a warrant of arrest, except in the case of serious offences (in English law known as arrestable offences) such as murder or serious theft. After arrest, the rights of a person to leave custody are curtailed, so that further enquiries may be made. In many jurisdictions, the length of time an accused person may be held without charge is limited (see *habeas corpus). The right to liberty is enunciated in many codes of *civil rights and a wrongly arrested or detained person may have redress through the courts.

arson *property crime.

ārtī (from Sanskrit, *ārātrika*), a ceremony of light, which, in *Hinduism, constitutes one of the basic elements of *pūjā, or worship. A tray, upon which are placed items symbolizing the elements, including a lamp with five small candles, is waved before the shrine of a god, and then passed around the worshippers so that they can receive the god's blessing.

Articles of Association, a term unique to UK *company law. It forms the second registrable document necessary for the formation of a *company, the *Memorandum of Association being the first. It regulates the internal affairs of the company and can be altered at will by a majority of the shareholders. The initial articles and any subsequent alterations cannot conflict with the provisions of the Companies' Acts and general principles of company law established by judicial precedent. In civil law systems the material found in the Articles of Association is found in the statutes of the company.

artificial intelligence (AI), 'the science of making machines do things that would require intelligence if done by humans' as defined in 1968 by Marvin Minsky of the Massachusetts Institute of Technology, USA. Sensing, reasoning, and problem-solving are among such tasks. The degree of complexity that constitutes AI tends to be revised upwards with each new generation of computers. The use of computers in mathematics and games such as chess, in which rules are easy to specify, is well established. But most computers act serially, one operation at a time, unlike the human brain. Supercomputers developed in the 1980s use 'parallel processing' to carry out billions of operations per second, but this barely begins to match the capacity of the human brain. Experiments in machine translation in the 1960s revealed the 'frame problem': most human thought processes use vast amounts of background knowledge or 'context' which it is very difficult to duplicate in a computer. 'Pseudo-intelligence' is one term for computer applications being developed in translation systems, semi-automatic offices in which human speech and instructions are turned into a properly laid-out document, in *linguistic and *psycholinguistic studies, and in robotics—replacing human actions by those of a robot, on the production line or in an artificial limb, for example. Robot sensing is used in weapons guidance systems and in product quality control. The impact of such developments is likely to be huge.

Asante (Ashanti), a primarily agricultural people of the tropical forest of Ghana. They farm for subsistence and produce cocoa as an important export crop. Asante society is organized on the principle of matrilineal *descent (from men to men, via their mothers and sisters), but the Asante also recognize spiritual characteristics inherited from the father. The office of *lineage head is symbolized by a lineage stool. The unity of the old Asante kingdom, under the leadership of the Asantehene, used to be represented by the celebrated Golden Stool in the capital city of Kumasi.

Ascension, a major Christian festival celebrated forty days after *Easter Sunday, which commemorates Jesus being taken into heaven. The Ascension constitutes the last of Jesus Christ's resurrection appearances, and signifies his exaltation as Lord of heaven and earth. It is mentioned in the New Testament and Apostles' *Creed and was widely celebrated by the end of the 4th century, with processions to the traditional location of the Ascension, the Mount of Olives.

asceticism (from Greek, *askeo*, 'to exercise' or 'to train'), a system of austere religious practices designed to combat the natural passions and inclinations in order to strengthen spiritual life. The word has its origins in strict regimes of training for athletes, but the idea has formed part of religions and philosophies throughout history. Ascetic practices range from abstinence, fasting, monastic codes, and a life of solitary contemplation and physical austerity as a hermit, to the extremes of flagellation and self-mutilation. Ascetic cults are found in *Christianity, *Hinduism, and *Islam. In many cases, asceticism reflects a low estimation of the human body and physical life. Both Gnosticism and Manichaeism, heretical movements in the early Christian Church, subscribed to dualistic views of the universe, denigrating all that was physical, a belief which led to extreme asceticism among their followers. More orthodox Christians also viewed self-denial and sacrifice as a way of following Christ's example, and by the 4th century, *monasticism, which stipulated celibacy, poverty, and obedience, had become established. Ascetic practices are still especially prominent in Eastern Orthodox communities. In Hinduism, the *sādhu* or holy man increases his spiritual strength through sexual abstinence and fasting, as well as through practices such as self-laceration. Within Islam, some *Sufis stress ascetic practices such as fasting and sleep deprivation. Although *Buddhism, on the other hand, advocates the 'Middle Way', the avoidance of the extremes of both asceticism and *hedonism, Buddhist monasticism includes many ascetic practices and exercises.

Ashkenazi (plural, Ashkenazim), a member of the largest division within Judaism (83 per cent, approximately 10.2 million). The title Ashkenazim refers to Jews from northern, central, and eastern Europe, and, latterly, to their descendants in the USA and Israel. As they moved towards central Europe Ashkenazim adopted *minhagim*, or local customs. These and the language *Yiddish differentiate them from the other major branch within Judaism, the *Sephardim, or Spanish and Portuguese Jews. In addition, the kind of Hebrew used by the Ashkenazim differs from that of the Sephardim.

ashram (from Sanskrit, 'hermitage'), a monastery or retreat centre for spiritual seekers within Hinduism. Visitors are taught *yoga exercises and meditation under the supervision of a *swāmi*, or teacher, and regular worship also takes place. In an environment of peace, prayer, work, and community life, the seeker after truth develops his or her own inner life.

āshrama, the name given by Hindu law books to the four ideal stages of life. The first stage is *brahmachārin*, the student stage, followed by *grihastha*, that of the married householder. Having fulfilled the duties of a householder, the ideal Hindu embarks on *Vāna Prāstha*, retirement as a hermit to seek the truth. The final stage, that of the *sannyāsin* (*sādhu*), or holy person, demands total *asceticism. In practice, few people now achieve either of the last two stages.

'āshūrā', Muslim holy day and voluntary fast day which falls on the tenth of Muharram, the first month of the

Islamic calendar. 'Āshūrā' is a day of mourning, being the anniversary of the martyrdom of Husain and his followers on the battlefield of Karbala (AD 680) commemorated by Shī'as and Sunnīs in their respective traditional ways. The day is marked by pilgrimages to the Shi'a holy places, especially Karbala in present-day Iraq, and mourning rituals which include self-flagellation and passion plays which re-enact Husain's martyrdom.

assassination, the murder of a prominent figure, usually for political or religious reasons. Leaders have been assassinated by lone individuals; as part of a political or religious opposition movement; in the process of a *coup d'état, rebellion, or *revolution; or by covert action conducted by the government of another state. Perhaps the two most notorious assassinations in the 20th century were those of Francis Ferdinand, Archduke of Austria, in 1914, which was an immediate cause of World War I, and US President Kennedy in 1963. There were unsuccessful assassination attempts against US President Reagan and Pope John Paul II in 1981, and against UK Prime Minister Margaret Thatcher in 1984. Other assassinations in the post-1945 world include those of President Sadat of Egypt in 1981, and Prime Ministers Indira and Rajiv Gandhi of India, who were assassinated in 1984 and 1991.

assembly line *production methods.

assessment (in education), the means employed to establish an objective measure of competence in pupils and students. Candidates may be assessed in order to evaluate their achievement, predict their performance, or select them for a further stage. An individual's performance can be compared either with the performance of others ('norm-referenced assessment') or with an established standard of ability ('criterion-referenced assessment'). Most assessment is by examination, which may be written, practical, or oral. In many countries, national agencies independent of schools organize school-leaving examinations such as the *baccalauréat* in France or the *Abitur* in Germany. The justification for these and other externally organized examinations (such as those of professional bodies) is to ensure fairness between candidates. However, preparation for external examinations can dominate the curriculum and put intense pressure on young people. In Japan, competition for the élite schools and universities is so fierce that many candidates attend after-school classes from an early age and spend up to fifteen hours a day studying. Under some assessment schemes (such as the General Certificate of Secondary Education introduced in England and Wales in 1988) examinations have been partially replaced by continuous assessment of the student's work throughout the course.

assets, anything of money value which is owned by an individual or a firm. They appear as positive items on a *balance sheet, as opposed to liabilities, which are negative items. Assets may be classified into fixed assets, current assets, trade assets, and intangibles. Fixed assets include land, buildings, and equipment. Current assets have *liquidity in varying degrees; they include cash, bank deposits, sums owed to the firm in payment of bills, and working *capital. Trade assets are investments in other firms. Intangibles include patents and goodwill. Net (as opposed to gross) assets are those valued after allowing for *depreciation; the distinction between net and gross is important in the case of fixed assets.

Association of South East Asian Nations (ASEAN), an organization of non-communist states in South-east Asia formed in 1967 and based in Jakarta, Indonesia. Its members are Brunei, Indonesia, Malaysia, the Philippines, Singapore, and Thailand. Its objectives are to accelerate economic growth through co-operation and to promote regional stability. Since ASEAN members have historically given more priority to external than intra-ASEAN trade, one of its principal roles has been to negotiate with other countries and with organizations such as the *EC. From its inception ASEAN opposed communist regimes in other Asian countries such as North Vietnam and, subsequently, Laos and Cambodia (Kampuchea). From 1978 it gave political backing to the Khmer Rouge-dominated coalition in Kampuchea, which opposed the Vietnamese-backed regime. In 1992, it agreed to implement an ASEAN free trade area (AFTA) over the following fifteen years.

assurance (in commerce), a (life) assurance policy is an arrangement providing for the payment of a sum of money to a named individual on a specific date (a term or endowment assurance) or at death (a whole-life assurance), in exchange for earlier payments to the insurance fund known as premiums. The sum assured is specified in advance, but, for a higher premium, may also include a proportion of the *profits of the assurance company. These profits are made principally by investing the premiums of policy-holders in marketable *securities.

astrology, the study of the positions and movements of stars regarded as having an influence on human affairs. Astrology was practised by the Babylonians (c.1000–539 BC) and developed by the Greeks and reached Christian Europe via the Arabs. Different systems flourished in China, India, and elsewhere. It was a utilitarian science linked to medicine

Astrology is practised in different forms in many parts of the world. The astrologer, geomancer, and palmist shown here practises in Singapore.

and agriculture, and also an ambitious philosophical system resting on the belief that the stars influenced the entire sublunar world. By studying eclipses, comets, and the movements of the planets in the zodiac, astrologers felt able to predict such effects as wars, plagues, and the weather. They found a key to a person's whole life in his or her horoscope, the disposition of the constellations of the zodiac (first named about 2,000 years ago), and of the planets at his birth. In the 16th century Renaissance popes were enthusiastic patrons and many rulers employed court astrologers for political and medical assistance. In 1586 a papal bull condemned judicial astrology and the Protestant reformers were hostile, leading to disapproval by most Christian Churches. Although astrology is now discredited among most scientists, who say that it is based on calculations invalidated by shifts in the earth's position, it enjoys a lingering popularity, perhaps because it is a source of potent archetypes and symbolism which have been displaced from secular industrialized societies.

atheism (from Greek, *a theos*, 'not god'), the denial of the existence of any *god or supernatural being. It should not be confused with the position of the *agnostic, who holds that as the existence of god cannot be proved or disproved, it should not be subject to belief or disbelief. The atheist maintains, on the other hand, that the very notion of god is meaningless, a view also subscribed to by some Asian religious traditions such as *Theravāda Buddhism. In the 19th century *Marx based his atheism on *materialism, and argued for the abolition of religion, which he saw as upholding an unjust socio-economic order. Communist theory, developed from Marxism, is strictly atheist. *Nietzsche proclaimed the 'death of god' and encouraged man to seek for the meaning of life in himself alone, a position also taken by 20th-century *existentialists such as *Heidegger and *Sartre. The modern philosophical school of *logical positivism is also atheist, arguing that religious speculation is logically ill-founded, since knowledge can only be derived from observation and experience.

athletics, the sports of running, jumping, and throwing, also known as track and field events. Many are modelled on the *Olympic Games of the ancient Greeks, though the development of modern athletics did not begin until about 1850. Athletics meetings are held in summer in a field or stadium, with an oval 400 m (438 yards) running-track laid out in six or more lanes around the perimeter. Within the oval are the various approach runways, pits, and enclosures for the non-track events. In winter, indoor meetings take place on banked tracks with a shorter circuit of, usually, 200 m (219 yards); sprint events are shortened to 50–60 m (55–66 yards), and there are no long-throwing events. At a full outdoor athletics meeting, there may be events for track: sprinting, hurdles, middle- and long-distance running, steeplechase, relays; field: high jump, long jump, triple jump, pole vault, shotput, and throwing events—hammer, discus, javelin; mixed events: decathlon (men) and heptathlon (women); road events: marathon and race walking, which begin and end in the stadium. The women's programme, once fairly restricted, is now almost as broad as the men's, and only the decathlon, hammer, pole vault, and steeplechase are excluded.

ātman (Sanskrit, 'essence'), the Hindu concept which describes the pure, immortal, spiritual essence or *soul of human beings and animals. The *jīvātman* is the inner self or personality of a human being, the essence of all his or her past experiences. It is this *jīvātman* which undergoes *reincarnation, or rebirth, through the processes of *samsara, into a new body after physical death, and which continues to manifest itself in human form according to its conduct in each life. In philosophical discourse, it is represented as the self, the source of awareness and the subject of 'I'-thoughts (*ahampratyaya*), which is distinguished from the objects of awareness. The Hindu schools agreed on the existence of a unified self in every individual, while the Buddhists denied it, claiming that 'I'-thoughts were merely a bundle of sequential states of awareness. Within the Hindu schools, there was much debate on how the *ātman* knows of its own nature (how can I know myself?). In *Advaita, the *jīvātman* is identical with the creator consciousness (*Brahman) which is the ultimate reality and is called the absolute self (*paramātman*). The cycle of births and deaths occurs because of the absence of awareness that the *jīvātman* and *paramātman* are not different (non-dual or *a-dvaita*) from one another. The realization of this absence of duality is equated with liberation (**moksha*) from this cycle.

atomism, the philosophical view that complex items and phenomena are to be understood as composed of some few types of basic, simple constituents, and that the intrinsic features and manner of combination of these simple constituents explain the properties and behaviour of all complexes formed from them. Atomism may be a metaphysical view of all reality, as when it was first proposed by the Greek philosopher Democritus (*c*.460–370 BC), or a stance towards some particular subject area, such as *Hume's psychological atomism of 'impressions' and 'ideas'. Atomism contrasts with holism, according to which the properties of constituents are regarded as abstractions from the complex phenomena in which they figure.

atonement, in Christianity, reconciliation between God and humanity, achieved through the life and death of *Jesus Christ. This concept is rooted in Jewish thought, where atonement was closely linked with animal *sacrifice and later with righteous living and martyrdom (see *Yom Kippur). There is no formal doctrine of the atonement within Christianity, and interpretations have varied throughout Christian history. The idea of Christ's death as a sacrifice, delivering mankind from *sin, is found in the New Testament and has remained a predominant theme in both Roman Catholic and Reformation Churches. Another understanding of the atonement based on scripture stresses the triumph of Christ's life and death over the forces of evil, or, in some contemporary interpretations, the overcoming of *alienation. Other interpretations focus on the exemplary nature of Christ's life and death, or on the powers of God's love revealed in him to transform believers.

attachment (in psychology), the bonding of an infant with his or her caregiver. Investigations of attachment have been one of the major achievements of *child psychology since World War II. The UK child psychiatrist John Bowlby (1907–90) was one of the pioneers, preparing in 1951 an influential study *Material Care and Mental Health* for the World Health Organization, which was alarmed by the plight of the multitude of children orphaned or separated from their families. Research has shown that the infants' successful development and maintenance of a bond with a specific person is necessary for healthy emotional, social, and personality growth. The bond usually develops in the child's second six months and seems to be related to the intensity of the interaction rather than simply to the time spent together. The child often has several attachments, but the most important is usually with the mother, although it may be with the father, siblings, or someone else. What is particularly damaging for a child is if he or she is never able to form attachments (for example, because of placement in an orphanage with transient caregivers) or if attachments are repeatedly broken (for example, because of moves between a series of temporary foster homes). Although the damage can sometimes be repaired if the child is later able to form a strong attachment to an adult, many such children grow up to be lacking in *self-esteem, to be aggressive, delinquent, or subject to *depression and unable themselves to form attachments. Bowlby's main work was the three-volume *Attachment and Loss* (1969–80), in which he explored attachment behaviour and its significance for adults and for children growing up in families as well as for separated children.

attention, the allocation of the brain's processing capacities to allow concentration on mental activity. It is assumed that there is an attentional mechanism that allows the brain to filter out information from the senses that is irrelevant or less important. There is also a need to focus internal brain activity (memories, images, or ideas) and guide the 'train of thought'. Understanding how the mechanism works is probably of central importance to an understanding of the brain. It also has practical implications for the effective use of our limited capacity for attention when monitoring complex systems. Some theorists assume that the brain blocks out irrelevant information quickly, before analysis, to prevent overload. Others assert that the brain processes more information than we realize and that we are only aware of information that is being attended to.

auction, a sale (normally public) in which articles or livestock are sold to the highest bidder. A reserve price may be set by the seller, below which the article will not be sold. Works of art, antiques, houses, commodities, and foreign currencies may be sold by auction.

audit, an examination of the financial records of an organization by an independent body, usually a firm of chartered accountants. Public and private limited companies are required by law to publish annual accounts which have been audited by independent qualified auditors. Increasingly, large companies make use of computerized financial records, which can help to simplify the auditing process. Auditing ensures that the financial records are properly maintained, all financial transactions can be accounted for, and that the accounts of the organization comply with the relevant standards and legislation. It can also, but is not required to, detect fraud (such as stealing by an employee) and prevent the publication of misleading information, particularly to shareholders.

Augustine (of Hippo), St (AD 354–430), Christian bishop, one of the outstanding theologians of the early Christian Church. Born in North Africa of a pagan father and a Christian mother, he was early attracted to Manichaeism, a religious system with both Christian and pagan elements. He taught rhetoric in Rome and then in Milan, where he embraced a Neoplatonic understanding of Christianity. Augustine henceforth lived a monastic life, first in retirement, then as priest and (after 395) as Bishop of Hippo in North Africa. Most of his vast literary output was pastoral or polemical. The *City of God*, a vindication of the Church against paganism, is perhaps his most famous work, apart from his *Confessions*, which contains a striking account of his early life and conversion. His *theology has dominated all later Western theology, with its profound psychological insight and its sense of man's utter dependence on grace, expressed in his doctrine of *predestination, and of the Church and the sacraments.

Australian Aboriginal languages, around 200 languages which were spoken over the whole continent of Australia before colonization. The languages, like their speakers, were disastrously affected by the European invasions which started at the end of the 18th century. Fifty languages are now extinct, and around a hundred more will apparently soon be extinct; many of these are now remembered by just a few old people. This leaves perhaps fifty languages which have a good chance of survival. The number of speakers is estimated to be under 50,000. Languages which have survived best are those in the north and west of the country; those in the eastern third of Australia are either dead or dying. All the Australian languages are related, but they are at least as diverse as the European languages. Although mutual intelligibility between neighbouring languages is quite common, dialect differences between groups of people are important for a sense of self-identity. The languages can be divided into two unequal sub-groups. One small group of diverse languages is spoken in the northernmost part of the Northern Territory and Western Australia. The other group, commonly called Pama-Nyungan, covers the rest of the continent. Within individual languages there are often a number of special speech-styles. For example, initiated men on ceremonial occasions may speak in a specialized variety of the language. There are also avoidance styles of speaking, used to address members of the community that one is not supposed to have contact with, such as one's parents-in-law. All languages have a rich tradition of oral literature. Writing systems based on the Roman alphabet have now been devised for some of the languages.

Austro-Asiatic languages, a group of languages spoken in South-east Asia ('austro-' means 'south') in an area stretching from north-eastern India across to Vietnam and Malaysia. The family consists of three unequal branches; Nicobarese, Munda, and Mon–Khmer. Nicobar is spoken by a very small number of people on the Nicobar Islands in the Bay of Bengal. It is closely related to Mon–Khmer, and some scholars think that it does not deserve a sub-group to itself. Munda is spoken by nearly 7 million people in northeast India. Two languages account for the vast majority of speakers: these are Mundari (1.5 million) and Santali (5 million). Mon–Khmer, the third and largest branch, contains three important languages: Mon, Khmer, and Vietnamese. Mon and Khmer are closely akin to one another, while Vietnamese has developed separately. Mon (*Taliang* in Myanmar (Burma)) is spoken by small groups in Myanmar and Thailand. Khmer is the official language of Cambodia (Kampuchea), where it has around 8 million speakers, and is attested in inscriptions which date back to the 7th century AD. It has borrowed a large number of words from Sanskrit. The scripts of both Mon and Khmer are adapted from a southern Indian original. Vietnamese is by far the largest language in the group, with over 64 million speakers in Vietnam, Laos, and Cambodia. It is a monosyllabic language (that is, most words have only one syllable) with six tones (see *phonology), which it must have developed independently since there is no tone in the other Mon–Khmer languages.

It was written first in Chinese characters, then in a special form of Chinese (*Chu-nom*) adapted to Vietnamese. In the 17th century, Catholic missionaries introduced a script using the Roman alphabet with accents to mark tone, and this is now the official script. Some scholars have made a controversial attempt to link Austro-Asiatic with *Austronesian and *Tai languages to create a super-family called Austric.

Austronesian languages, a large group of languages spread over a huge area in the Indian and Pacific oceans. The central area in which they are spoken is Indonesia, Malaysia, and the Philippines; they extend west to Madagascar, and east to New Zealand and the Pacific islands ('Austronesian' means 'southern islands'). Despite the large distances involved the languages are all remarkably similar to each other, which makes internal sub-grouping difficult. However, it is clear that the Austronesian languages spoken on Taiwan (now almost submerged by Chinese) stand outside the main group. This group, sometimes called Malayo-Polynesian, can be split into a western area and an eastern area by a dividing line which runs through the eastern tip of Papua New Guinea. Although the number of languages on each side of this line is roughly the same (estimated at 300–400 each), almost all the speakers (over 180 million) are found on the western half. The eastern, or Oceanic, languages have around 2 million speakers. They include New Zealand Maori, and languages of Polynesia (such as Samoan, Tahitian, Tongan, and Hawaiian, which is close to extinction), Melanesia, and Micronesia. The largest western language is Javanese, which has over 60 million speakers. It has a long literary tradition, and is first attested in inscriptions of the 8th century AD. However, Malay is the most important language in the area. Forms of Malay are official languages in Indonesia (160 million speakers), Malaysia (15 million), and Singapore (3 million). First written in a script derived from southern India, Malay was later written in the Arabic script, and finally (in the 19th century) in the Roman alphabet. The official language of the Philippines, Filipino, is based on Tagalog, an indigenous language of the Philippines. There are around 10 million native speakers of Tagalog, and Filipino is spoken by most of the population as a second language.

authoritarian state, a state in which political authority is exercised by a person or group who are not responsible to the people they control, and in which there is no legal and orderly method of changing governments. Such systems may be either of the Right or of the Left, and may be either military or civilian in composition. Elections may be held in such states, but are commonly organized on a *one-party basis; *coups of one kind or another, along with *assassinations, are one method of bringing about political change in authoritarian states. The notion is distinct from that of a *totalitarian state, in which all aspects of human life are controlled by the ruling group, but authoritarian rulers are none the less closed off from the demands and needs of the broader population. Examples of authoritarian regimes include those of certain Latin American rulers, such as Alfredo Stroessner of Paraguay (1954–89), and Augusto Pinochet of Chile (1973–90), and the regime of Saddam Hussein in Iraq (1979–   ).

authority, the right to command or rule some group of people. It can be attributed either to individuals ('the authority of the pope') or to institutions ('the authority of Parliament'). Authority, as distinct from *power, exists only when those who comply do so because they recognize the *legitimacy of the body issuing the command. It thus contrasts both with obtaining compliance by force and with rational persuasion. Authority is a pervasive feature of social life, present in families, businesses, schools, and churches as well as in the formal apparatus of the state. *Weber, in a classic analysis in *Economy and Society* (1921), distinguished three basic types of authority: charismatic, the authority of the outstanding individual, seen as carrying out a superhuman mission; traditional, the deference shown to those whose right to rule derives from long-established practice; and rational–legal, the authority of institutions (especially bureaucracies) set up to achieve specific social purposes.

autism, a rare infantile disorder characterized by apparent pensive self-absorption and failure to develop normal relationships, obsessive insistence on sameness which leads to distress if the physical environment or routine is disrupted, and language abnormalities such as monotonous repetition of what others say. There are disagreements about diagnosis, and estimates of incidence vary from four per 10,000 to one per 25,000. About 75 per cent show some mental retardation, but high abilities in arithmetic, memory, music, and sometimes art are quite common. Prognosis is relative to degree of retardation and language ability. The cause is unknown.

automation *production methods.

avatar (from Sanskrit, *avatāra*, 'descent'), Hindu notion of an incarnation or manifestation of the divine on earth. An *avatar* is born independently of the cycle of death and rebirth (*samsara); it ensures that divine will is maintained on earth, either by establishing new religious movements, or by intervening in human affairs. Most common are the ten *avatars* of *Vishnu: Matsya, the fish; Kūrma, the tortoise; Varāha, the boar; Narasimha, the man-lion; Vāmana, the dwarf; Rāma the axe-wielder; Rāma, the prince in the *Rāmāyana epic; Krishna; *Buddha; and Kalki, who is yet to appear.

Averroes (Ibn Rushd) (*c.*1126–98), Islamic philosopher born in Cordoba, Spain. Averroes developed *al-Farabī's view of the relationship between philosophy and religion, which he thought of as distinct ways of apprehending a single truth, and so was able to assert the authority of natural reason in his *Destruction* of al-Ghazālī's *Destruction of the Philosophers*. He considered *Aristotle's works the highest achievement of philosophy; his voluminous commentaries on these were important in introducing Aristotle's thought to Christian scholars. His confidence that philosophical truth, patiently expounded, would harmonize with religious doctrine was not accepted by later philosophers. Thus, his account of the unity of the intellect was held incompatible with personal immortality, and was criticized as such by *Aquinas.

Avesta, Zoroastrian and *Parsi scriptures from *c.*500 BC consisting of hymns, prayers, and rituals, the surviving texts of an ancient body of scripture attributed to Zoroaster, or Zarathustra, the founder of the religion of Zoroastrianism (6th century BC). The core of the *Avesta* is a collection of hymns, or *Gāthās*, which speak of the creator god Ahura Mazdā, and of the judgement awaiting mankind after death.

Avicenna (Ibn Sina) (980–1037), Persian-born Islamic philosopher. In political and religious matters Avicenna largely followed *al-Farabī. His metaphysics made prominent the distinction between *essence* and *existence*: an explanation of why it is that something is must normally appeal to more than an account of what it is. This explanation must finally appeal to something that is simply because of what it is, namely God. This parallels an argument that the actual existence of possible things, which might or might not exist, requires a necessary being, and was influential in medieval discussions of essence and possibility.

āyātollāh (from Arabic, 'sign of God'), title given to Shī'ī, usually Iranian, religious leaders. The title has been in use since the early 20th century in Iran. It may be used for any established *mujtahid*, one who has the right to interpret the law of Islam according to changing conditions. In Sunnī Islam, however, the 'gate of *ijtihād*', or legal interpretation, has been regarded as closed since the end of the 9th century.

Ayer, Sir A(lfred) J(ules) (1910–89), British philosopher. Ayer introduced into British philosophy the doctrines of *logical positivism; his influential book *Language, Truth and Logic* (1936) was written at the age of 25 after discussions with members of the Vienna Circle. The central doctrine of the book was that meaningful propositions could be divided into two kinds: those relating to matters of fact which are essentially testable by observation (see *verificationism), and those pertaining to mathematics and logic, all of which are tautological and should not be regarded as saying anything about the world.

Ayurvedic medicine (from Sanskrit, *āyur*, 'life' and *veda*, 'knowledge'), the traditional medical system of India and Sri Lanka, derived in part from the Hindu sacred texts, the *Vedas, and from later texts of the fifth and second centuries BC. The Ayurvedic system spread to the north, where it influenced Chinese medical thought, and to the west, where it influenced early Greek medicine and was incorporated by Arab scholars into the system known as Unani medicine. Another variant of Ayurveda is Siddha, found in Tamil Nadu and Sri Lanka. The Ayurvedic system aims for a balance of the influence of the five elements (air, water, earth, fire, ether) on the five senses of the body. Treatment involves herbal remedies and touch. In 1970 the Indian Parliament passed legislation drawing up a register of qualified Ayurvedic practitioners.

Azande (Zande), an agricultural people living in southern Sudan, Zaïre, and the Central African Republic. They consist of numerous patrilineal *clans, which are totemic: when a man dies, it is believed that one of his two souls becomes a totemic animal of his clan. The Azande are best known for their belief in witchcraft. In *Witchcraft, Oracles and Magic among the Azande* (1937), the anthropologist *Evans-Pritchard showed how apparently irrational beliefs may be as logical as 'scientific' thinking. The Azande used witchcraft to explain misfortunes; if, for example, a hut were to fall down, injuring a man, he might well recognize that the hut fell because termites had eaten away at the supports, but at the same time he would invoke witchcraft to explain why the hut had fallen at that particular moment. In recent years the Azande have suffered greatly in civil war and natural disasters such as famine in the region.

Aztec language *Mexican and Central American Indian languages.

B

Ba'athism, an Arab political doctrine which combines elements of *socialist thinking with pan-Arabism. This theory of Arab *nationalism conceives of the 'Arab nation' as a single entity stretching from Morocco to Iraq which has been artificially divided by *colonialism and *imperialism. Ba'athism originated in Syria, where the first Ba'ath Party was founded in 1953. Ba'athists have held power in Syria since 1963 and Iraq since 1968, although the two branches of the movement are deeply divided. While the Iraqi leader Saddam Hussein employed the slogans of pan-Arabism to justify his invasion of Kuwait in 1990, the Ba'ath Party in Iraq has been reduced to an instrument of state power.

backgammon, a *board-game in which two players race their pieces or stones around a board divided into four sections or tables. Each section is marked with six long triangular points, and a line called the bar divides the board into inner and outer tables. Moves are dictated by throwing two dice. Each player has fifteen stones (black or white) and 'makes' a point by landing two or more stones on the point. The object is to get all stones into the home or inner table and then move them off the board.

In a street in Izmir, Turkey, a man plays **backgammon**, the most popular board-game of the Middle East. The history of the game can be traced back 5,000 years: a board was found in Tutankhamun's tomb, and it was also popular with the Romans.

badminton, an indoor serve-and-volley racket game played over a net, 1.5 m (5 feet) at the centre. The missile is a shuttle, either cork-based with white goosefeathers fixed to it or made of nylon in one piece. Rackets have whippy handles and small heads 21 cm (8 inches) wide. The court is 13 m (44 feet) long overall, 6 m (20 feet) wide for doubles play and 5 m (17 feet) for singles. Players serve or receive as in *tennis, but only the serving side can score a point. Match-play is usually up to fifteen points in each game, the best of three games deciding the winner.

Baganda, a group of settled farmers in Uganda. The Baganda constituted a kingdom in the 19th century, in which the king was seen as the supreme ruler who exercised his power through a system of district chiefs. The Baganda consist of fifty exogamous (based on marriage outside the group) clans, each distinguished by *totemic symbols. Originally practitioners of a form of *ancestor worship, they are now predominantly Christian.

Bahā'ī, a religion founded in Iran by Bahā'u'llāh (Arabic, 'Glory of God') (1817–92) with about 5 million adherents throughout the world. Following the suppression of the *millenarian Bābī movement in Iran and the execution of its leader, the *Bāb*, or Gate (to the Truth) in 1850, Bahā'u'llah declared himself in 1863 to be the new *prophet heralded by the *Bāb*. Bahā'u'llah acknowledged the revelations of earlier prophets such as Jesus and Muḥammad, but held that the single identity of God must be retaught by new prophecy to each generation. Bahā'īs believe in the spiritual progression of the world to unity and their ideal is an international community with one language. Bahā'ī temples are open to the faithful of all creeds. A Universal House of Justice administers the religion, with its centres in Haifa and Akko (Acre) in Israel. There is no clergy or ritual; spiritual practice includes daily private prayer and an annual period of fasting, which ends with the festival of Nōw Rūz, the Persian New Year at the spring equinox. Bahā'īs stress the equality of women and the importance of monogamous family life. Although Bahā'īs regard the *Koran and Muḥammad with reverence, to Muslims the Bahā'īs are heretics who have displaced the Koran from its position as the final and most important revelation; this has led to persecution in Iran since the religion's inception, with renewed force since the Islamic revolution of 1979. Furthermore, the location of the Bahā'ī world centre in Israel has led to an association of Bahā'īs with that country and made the Bahā'īs a target of anti-Semitic sentiment.

bail, permission for an arrested person's release from custody, often subject to the pledge of money or property as security, until his or her return to court to stand trial. The word may also refer to the money or property so pledged. Accused persons are normally granted bail, unless it is feared that they will abscond, or unless they are accused of a serious crime which they might repeat if released. Bail is a *common law term, but a similar use of surety enabling a suspect to be released from custody before trial exists in *civil law systems.

balance of payments, a record of all transactions occurring in a period of time between the residents of a country and the rest of the world. It consists of a current account, a capital account, and a balancing item (for estimated accounting errors). The current account records the money inflows and outflows arising from *trade in *goods ('visibles') and services ('invisibles'). The invisible items include not only tourism, banking, and other services but also insurance, transfer payments (such as workers sending part of their wage abroad), and flows of property income (rent, interest, profit, and dividends). The capital account records investment and financial asset flows, including inter-government loans and other international transactions by government. The capital and current accounts combined are said to be in surplus if the money inflows exceed the money outflows or in deficit if the reverse applies; surpluses or deficits imply rises or falls respectively in official external reserves. A freely floating *exchange rate will ensure that demand for the domestic currency (or money inflows) equals supply (or money outflows) and an overall balance of payments of zero results. A negative balance of payments may lead to severe depreciation or *devaluation of the home currency, although this will often be avoided by official government financing to support the currency. (See also *balance of trade.)

balance of power (in international relations), a term meaning that international order is preserved by maintaining an equilibrium of power among different states; it can also refer to the deliberate policy of achieving this equilibrium. If one state or group of states seeks a preponderance of power, others may form *alliances in order to counter its attempt at dominance. However, misperceptions of the relative powers of different states might result in war. The idea of the balance of power dominated the foreign policies of the *great powers during the 19th century; it succeeded in maintaining the independence of states, as well as providing some form of international order. After World War I there was a movement towards a system characterized by co-operation (see *collective security) rather than the use of force to maintain equilibrium, but the underlying theory may be considered still to be a key concept in most strategic planning.

balance of trade, the record of money inflows and outflows on the current account of the *balance of payments. The term is used sometimes to refer to *goods ('visibles') only and sometimes to refer to the balance on goods and services ('invisibles') combined. In either case, it signifies the net receipts from abroad resulting from *exports after the value of *imports has been deducted. A trade gap is said to exist when the balance of trade is in deficit, in other words, when payments for imports exceed receipts from exports.

balance sheet, a tabular account of a company's (or other economic agent's) *wealth at a specific moment of time. Commonly it consists of two columns: liabilities on one side and assets on the other. The assets of the company (items owned by or owed to the company) are set against its liabilities. These include not only amounts in money or kind owed to banks and other companies, but also the claims of the company's owners. Thus both columns add up to the same figure. A balance sheet contrasts with a profit-and-loss account, which records a company's expenditure and income during a period of time.

Balinese, an inhabitant of the island of Bali in Indonesia. The island is predominantly agricultural; the staple food is rice, which is cultivated with the aid of complex irrigation and terrace systems, while pigs and cattle are also raised. The religion is a unique form of *Hinduism, although it also incorporates some elements of *animism, and is characterized by elaborate art forms such as wood carving, temple architecture, dance, and music. Stage plays and dances are an integral part of Balinese life, and contain many magical and symbolic motifs. In common with other Hindu societies, the people are organized into a hierarchy of *caste-like groups.

ballooning, the sport and recreation of flying in a basket beneath an inflated balloon. The bag, filled either with hot air from a propane-gas burner or hydrogen gas, rises naturally; descent is controlled by releasing air or gas from the balloon, off-loading sand ballast from the basket, and using a rope drag-line as an anchor. Pilots compete to set records for duration, distance, and altitude. Popular too is the spot-landing event—trying to land as close as possible to a chosen mark.

Baltic languages, a branch of the *Indo-European family quite closely related to *Slavic. The two surviving languages are spoken in the Baltic states of Latvia and Lithuania; in Estonia a form of Finno-Ugric is spoken (see *Uralic languages). A third language, Old Prussian, became extinct around 1700, having been submerged by German. The Baltic languages are extraordinarily archaic, and have preserved many forms useful for the reconstruction of Indo-European. They are written in a modified Latin script. Lithuanian is spoken by 3 million people, and is first attested in written form in 1547. Early written works are, as with Latvian and Old Prussian, translations of religious material. There are two distinct dialects, East and West Lithuanian, each of which has several sub-dialects. A standard written language based on West Lithuanian was adopted at the end of the 19th century. Latvian (Lettish) has 2 million speakers, and is first attested in 1585. There are three main dialects: Central, West, and East. The standard language, which was developed at the end of the 19th century, is based on the Central dialect. The earliest Baltic texts are in Old Prussian.

bank, a financial institution which deals in money, principally by accepting deposits and making loans. Customers' deposits are a bank's liabilities, and loans are its *assets. A bank is distinguished from a non-bank financial institution by the fact that a bank's deposit liabilities are themselves money, that is they are accepted in payments for goods and services and in settlement of debts. Typically, a bank makes a profit by charging a higher rate of *interest for loans than it pays on deposits. The two main types of banks are commercial and *central banks. A central bank is banker to the government, and such banks have become an important instrument of government monetary policy by managing the *money supply and the issue of currency. Commercial banks include clearing banks and merchant banks (see *clearing house). In recent years financial institutions such as *building societies have begun to operate in much the same way as banks. In the UK, discount houses, which borrow and lend in the short-term money market (usually by buying and selling Treasury Bills and *bills of exchange), are also part of the commercial banking system. Commercial banks create money by making loans in excess of their cash reserves; this is possible because customers can spend money without withdrawing cash by paying with cheques, written instructions to the bank to move money from one account to another. Banking systems are based on confidence; if there is a 'run' on a bank, it may be unable to meet its obligations. The ratio between a bank's reserves and its obligations is, however, fixed by law in many countries, and in the USA, for example, most bank deposits must be insured. Merchant banks are banks whose main business is the provision of

long-term credit, and financing for trading enterprises. They perform a variety of services for clients, such as sales of new issues (see *issuing house), the acceptance of bills of exchange, and *portfolio management. A main concern today is to provide advice to firms concerning *mergers and *take-overs, and to supply finance for new businesses. US investment banks purchase new issues of shares or equity which they resell in smaller batches. In *planned economies banks have not been permitted to create money by lending on their own initiative to private producers and consumers. They exist to provide financial services to the government and other customers and charge modest interest rates to cover their expenses, not for profit. In the USA, banks have been confined by law to a single state or locality; consequently many small banks with a limited number of branches operate. By contrast, in the UK, four large banks with many branches dominate the retail banking system. In most countries, a system between these two extremes operates. (See also *debt, *debt crisis.)

Bank of England   *central bank.

bank rate (official discount rate), the rate of *interest at which a *central bank will lend to commercial banks and (sometimes) other financial institutions. Even when no central bank lending is taking place, bank rate will normally be a major influence on short-run interest rates. Changes in bank rate, by affecting market interest rates, may affect the domestic economy by altering *consumption and *investment plans. In addition, a change in short-run interest rates may affect the flow of internationally mobile funds into and out of a country. (See also *balance of payments.)

bankruptcy   *insolvency.

Bantu language   *Niger–Congo languages.

Baptism   *sacrament.

Baptists, a group of closely connected *Protestant Churches, which require baptism of adult believers by total immersion in water. They are one of the largest Protestant groups, with 30 million full members in the USA, and a further 6 million in Africa, Asia, and elsewhere. Congregations have considerable local independence. Baptists are renowned for their defence of religious liberty, their personal commitment, and their *missionary work.

bar mitzvah (Aramaic, 'son of the commandment'). Jewish *rite of passage commemorating male initiation into adulthood and full religious responsibility. *Mitzvah*, commandment, refers to the legally obligatory rituals and rules for living which mark the Jewish way of life, and are adhered to more or less strictly by the different branches of Judaism. The ceremony may be celebrated on the *Shabbat, Monday, or Thursday (the other days on which readings from the Torah are held) following the day after the boy's 13th birthday. It includes reading from the *Torah, and the presentation of a prayer shawl (*tallith*) and prayer book. Orthodox, conservative, and other Jews also present phylacteries, small leather-covered boxes containing verses from the Torah. The day ends with family celebrations at which the child thanks parents and religious instructors. Girls come of age at 12, and this may or may not be marked by a ceremony (*bat mitzvah*), depending on the branch of Judaism. Different rules apply to women, some of them less onerous or pro-

Baseball

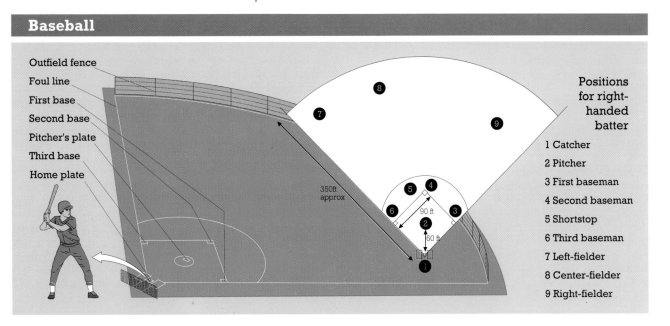

Outfield fence
Foul line
First base
Second base
Pitcher's plate
Third base
Home plate

350ft approx

90 ft

60 ft

Positions for right-handed batter

1 Catcher
2 Pitcher
3 First baseman
4 Second baseman
5 Shortstop
6 Third baseman
7 Left-fielder
8 Center-fielder
9 Right-fielder

hibitive; for example, Orthodox women are prohibited from reading from the Torah and women rabbis are only found in the non-Orthodox branches of Judaism.

barrister, the term used within the legal system of England and Wales, and in countries whose legal systems are modelled on it, for a legal practitioner who is admitted to practise in the superior courts. The primary function of a barrister is to represent a party in court, usually upon the instructions of a *solicitor. In England, all barristers are members of one of the four *Inns of Court. Senior barristers, appointed by the monarch on the recommendation of the Lord Chancellor (the head of the judiciary; see *UK legal system), are known as Queen's (or King's) Counsel (QC). In court they wear silk gowns and are thus known informally as *silks*.

barter, the direct exchange of one (non-monetary) *good or service for another. In a barter economy, to exchange one specified good for another requires that there be someone willing to swap the good being offered for that which is wanted. Otherwise, it is necessary to go through a number of intermediate transactions. Barter is, therefore, not nearly as efficient a system of exchange as using *money, and most barter economies are in due course succeeded by money economies. In situations of hyper-*inflation, where money rapidly loses its value, the use of currency may diminish and people may resort to barter instead.

baseball, a field-game played chiefly in the USA between two teams of nine players, using a bat, ball, and gloves. The focus of play is the diamond, a square with sides of 27 m (90 feet) and a base at each corner. After three outs (an innings), the batting team and the fielding team switch, each team batting in rotation through nine innings. The object is to score more runs than the opposing side. The batter stands at the home-plate facing the pitcher who throws the ball from a mound 18 m (60 feet) away. A fair ball (strike) must pass through the strike-zone, the area above the home-plate between the batter's armpits and knees. If the pitcher throws three strikes, the batter is out. If he throws four 'balls' outside the strike zone, the batter walks to first base. The batter tries to hit the ball away and run to first base or further. If

he hits it over the outfield fence, he automatically scores a home run. When the batter reaches base, a team-mate succeeds him at the home-plate. Fielders guard the bases and the outfield and try to put batters out by catching a hit on the fly or volley, tagging a base-runner, or touching the base, ball-in-hand, before the runner reaches it.

basketball, a game played world-wide between two teams of five on a hard rectangular court 26 m (85 feet) long and

Basketball

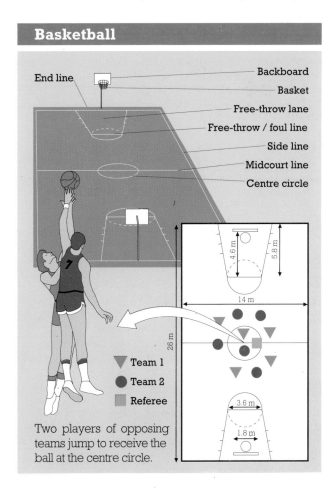

End line
Backboard
Basket
Free-throw lane
Free-throw / foul line
Side line
Midcourt line
Centre circle

4.6 m   5.8 m

14 m

26 m

3.6 m

1.8 m

▼ Team 1
● Team 2
■ Referee

Two players of opposing teams jump to receive the ball at the centre circle.

14 m (46 feet) wide. At each end of the court is a basket, its ring 3 m (10 feet) above the floor and secured to a backboard. The team in possession tries to score a goal by throwing the ball into the basket, and the defending team tries to prevent it and secure possession. Players advance the ball by dribbling (bouncing and tapping it) and passing and may not carry it more than one pace. Only the hands may be used. The team in possession must try a shot at goal within thirty seconds of gaining possession and may shoot from any position on the court. After a goal is scored (two points), the other team puts the ball back in play by passing it in from behind the end-line. Body contact is not allowed, and body-contact fouls are penalized by a free throw from behind the foul-line, drawn 5 m (15 feet) from the backboard. If the player fouled was in the act of shooting and scores, he gets the goal plus one free throw; if his shot misses, he gets two free throws.

Basque, a member of a people living in the Western Pyrenees on both sides of the French–Spanish border. They possess a distinctive culture and language, perhaps the result of their relative isolation from the rest of Europe until comparatively recently. Although the Basque country is divided between France and Spain, they have maintained an identity separate from both states. Basque culture underwent a revival in the late 19th century, which ensured its continuance into the 20th century. In response to what they consider attempts to suppress their culture by the imposition of centralized authority, many Basques in Spain have campaigned for an independent Basque state, some violently in the military wing of the Basque movement ETA (Basque Fatherland and Liberty).

Basque language (Euskara), the language of the *Basque people of the north-west Pyrenees. Four-fifths of the speakers live on the Spanish side of the border; the others live in the French *département* of the Pyrenees Atlantiques. The number of speakers is estimated at slightly under a million, though virtually all are bilingual. The language is also spoken by some people, mostly in the USA, who left Spain after the Civil War (1936–9). Basque consists of a large number of quite diverse dialects, all mutually intelligible. It is related to no known language and is probably a remnant of the pre-*Indo-European languages of Europe. It is first attested after AD 1000 in records of names, then by a few short phrases. The first book appeared in 1545, and this began a written tradition which is still vigorous. There was a Basque cultural renaissance in the late 19th century, but the language suffered under General Franco's regime in Spain (1939–75) and has made only a slight recovery since that time.

BBC (British Broadcasting Corporation), the provider of non-commercial *radio and *television services in the UK and a pioneer in *public service broadcasting. The BBC was founded in 1922 and became an independent public corporation in 1927, operating under a royal charter and financed by licence fees collected by the government and payable initially on all domestic radio receivers, but currently on television sets only. Under John Reith, director-general 1922–37, the BBC became established as a national institution, a broadcasting *monopoly (until a commercial television station was permitted in 1954), and a model for many non-commercial *broadcasting systems world-wide. In the early 1990s, the BBC operated two television channels, five national radio channels, and over forty local and regional radio services within the UK, although government pressure against its monopoly has threatened its position. The renegotiation of its Charter in 1996 may lead to the replacement of the licence fee as its primary source of finance. The BBC World Service, financed by government grant and founded in 1932, broadcasts in English and other languages (37 in 1991) on radio. It started an English language satellite television service in 1991. World Service news reports are widely respected as an independent source of news.

Bedou (plural, Bedouin), Arabic-speaking nomadic *pastoralists living in the deserts of northern Africa and the Middle East. They migrate seasonally with their camels and other animals, following water supplies. The Bedou live off the meat and milk of their camels, as well as the wheat and dates they trade for their livestock. The segmentation of their traditionally patrilineal social groups has led to blood-feuds and raiding between the *lineages, but within each lineage, headed by a sheikh, all men are considered equal. The bedrocks of Bedou society are *Islam, *honour, hospitality, and equality. The settlement policies of the Middle Eastern states through which they pass have restricted the *nomadism of the Bedou, and since the discovery of oil in the Gulf States, many of them have left their tents to pursue wage labour in the modern oil sector.

behaviour genetics, the study of the genetic basis of behaviour and psychological characteristics. Arguments about the importance of hereditary components of behaviour centre around the nature–nurture controversy: whether the characteristic patterns of behaviour shown by an individual are learned or innate. At one extreme it is held that genetic distinctions differentiate humans into types, and at another *behaviourists claim that environment and training shape ability and character. It is, however, likely that both genetic and environmental factors play equally important roles in determining behavioural and psychological characteristics. The methods which have been used to study the genetics of behaviour include, among others, selective breeding of animals and twin studies. In selective-breeding

Ambrosi Junet, a French **Basque**, takes his sheep to summer pastures in the high Pyrenees. The population of his village of Santazi, a small shepherding community in a secluded valley a few miles from the Spanish border, has shrunk from over 1,000 to 390 during the past century.

The mainstay of the diet of the nomadic **Bedouin** is unleavened bread, pulses, olives, and dates. Meat and fat are eaten, but only on special occasions.

experiments, researchers interbreed high- or low-scoring animals. Experiments on rats have shown that it is possible to breed a strain with a particular ability or lack of a particular ability, but if the rats are reared in a poor environment, those from the able strain perform as poorly as those from the less able strain. Twin studies are probably the best-known method of studying the genetic basis of behaviour in humans. Since identical twins share the same genes, differences between them may be ascribed to the effects of environment. Thus human fostering of identical twins who are brought up apart provides an opportunity to study the effects of environment. Studies of both identical and non-identical twins show that the higher the degree of relationship between individuals, the higher the correlation of intelligence-test scores. While this indicates that genetic factors play an important role in determining intelligence, there is also an important environmental component. A study in the USA found that in middle-class families identical twins had more similar intelligence than non-identical twins, whereas in disadvantaged working-class families there was no such difference, implying that heredity plays a far smaller role in an impoverished environment.

behaviourism (in philosophy), a doctrine in the philosophy of *mind that was formulated in response to dissatisfaction with introspection as a means of investigating the mind. Introspective investigation of the mind can be engaged in only by the subject and is notoriously unreliable. Behaviourists believe that the characterization of mental states (such as wanting to get home or being in pain) in terms of patterns of behaviour renders them publicly observable and so scientifically investigable. Being in pain, for a behaviourist, is a matter of behaving in a certain way, as is believing that it is raining. Among philosophical objections to behaviourism is the intuition that to be in pain is more than to behave in a certain way. Objections arise also from within psychology, whose theories need to consider relations between mental states, in addition to relations between mental states and behaviour. Such difficulties led to reformulations of behaviourist theories and to *functionalism.

behaviourism (in psychology), the theory that human behaviour is determined by *conditioning rather than by thoughts and feelings; also the programme of research and the *behaviour therapy based on the theory. The US psychologist *Watson proposed the programme in 1913. It rejected reference to mental processes, consciousness, or the mind, and restricted the subject-matter of *psychology to descriptions of organisms' behaviour and environmental stimuli. Its concept of science was anticipated in the writings of 19th-century positivists such as *Comte. *Pavlov had already laid the foundations for its insistence on controlled experiments, which shifted psychology's preoccupations to the laboratory study of animal *learning. Behaviourism has been particularly influential in the USA, where *Skinner maintained and developed the experimental analysis of behaviour. Even there theorists such as Clark Hull (1884–1952) and Edward Tolman (1886–1959) included unobservable processes such as 'expectation' in their models of learning and behaviour. In the 1950s and 1960s the behaviourist programme was weakened by the demonstrations of the linguist *Chomsky and the Canadian *social learning theorist Albert Bandura (1925–) that human learning could not develop from simple stimulus-response associations. It was further weakened by the rise of *ethology, with its insistence on species-specific innate bases of behaviour and on the need to study animals in their natural habitat. At the same time the growth of *cognitive psychology resurrected the belief that internal processes are the proper subject-matter of psychology. In the late 20th century there are few strict behaviourists in the Skinner mould, but behaviourism, like *psychoanalysis, has played a central role in the development of mainstream psychology.

behaviour therapy (behaviour modification), clinical treatment to change maladaptive patterns of behaviour using techniques which derive from experiments on *learning. It is based on the view that neurotic behaviour is learnt in the same way as normal behaviour and may be eliminated by a manipulation of surroundings which allows the subject to learn new and better responses. It developed in the 1950s from *Watson and *Skinner's ideas about therapeutic applications of *conditioning. The classic text was Joseph Wolpe's *Psychotherapy by Reciprocal Inhibition* (1958). He described how he had made cats fearful and then cured them by inducing them to eat closer and closer to the source of their fear. Behaviour therapy has become popular, in the form of desensitization, for treating *phobias and *obsessions, and has been used with some success for sexual problems and alcohol and drug abuse. It has also been used to try to 'modify' anti-social activities in classrooms. Generally, however, the co-operation of the patient seems necessary. Behaviour therapy does not try to rearrange patients' understanding of themselves or their world. It may therefore appear somewhat mechanistic. More recent approaches, (see *learned helplessness and *locus of control) focus on patients' beliefs about what they are able to do.

Bemba, one of the largest ethnic groups in Zambia. Their Bantu language (see *Niger–Congo languages) has become the *lingua franca of the country. They were traditionally agriculturalists, living off their staple, millet, and shifting their villages every four or five years because of poor soil. The Bemba live in matrilineal *clans, and their traditional religion includes the worship of ancestral spirits. Nowadays many Bemba men spend periods away from their home villages working in Zambia's copper mines, or in South Africa.

Bengali   *Indo-Iranian languages.

Berber, the indigenous peoples of the mountains and deserts of northern Africa. They speak mutually unintelligible dialects of an otherwise grammatically uniform language, although most literate Berber also speak Arabic. The Berber are Sunnī Muslims, and their local tribal groups are often led by a *marabout*, a hereditary religious leader. The Berber peoples include several distinct groups: settled farmers living on terraced, irrigated hillsides in the Atlas mountains; transhumance farmers (who move their livestock seasonally from region to region); and the nomadic *Tuareg of the Sahara.

Berber languages, a group of over twenty languages in North Africa, spoken by about 12 million *Berbers in scattered groups across Morocco, northern Algeria, Libya, and western Egypt, and in a large central-Saharan area in Niger, Mali, and southern Algeria. Berber languages originally covered most of North Africa, but after the 7th century AD were driven back or assimilated by the Arab invasions. As a result of this influence there are many Arabic loan-words in Berber, as well as Phoenician and Latin words which had been borrowed at an earlier date. The earliest attested (but poorly known) language in this family is Numidian (ancient Libyan), which is found written in a unique consonantal script in inscriptions dating from the time of the Roman Empire. A modified version of this script is still in use among the Saharan *Tuareg. The other Berber languages are written in the Arabic script when they are written at all. There is virtually no literature. Scholars have not yet finally decided the internal sub-groupings of the Berber languages. Important groups beside Tuareg include Kabyle (Algeria), Riff (Morocco), and Schluh (Morocco and Mauritania). Berber languages are part of Afro-Asiatic, a larger group which includes *Chadic, *Cushitic, and *Semitic languages.

bereavement, the death of a close friend or relative, followed by the process of grieving. The process has two parts: grief, the personal suffering of loss; and mourning, the social expression of grief. The psychological process of grieving is taken to have four phases: shock and disbelief; yearning for the lost object or person; despair and hopelessness; readjustment and recovery. In Western society many of the rituals of mourning have lost their significance and this, combined with the weakening of family networks, has made bereavement a lonely process, and the bereaved often feels an outcast. By contrast, many other societies have elaborate and prolonged rituals connected with loss (see *funeral customs) and strong support networks. The establishment of bereavement counselling in Western societies is an attempt to provide support for the bereaved.

Berkeley, George (1685–1753), Irish philosopher, Anglican Bishop of Cloyne. One of the British empiricists, he

Japanese offertory dolls, shaped like small Buddhas and beautifully decorated, are placed in most Shinto temples in memory of dead children. Such rituals to commemorate the dead are common to many cultures as part of mourning, the public face of **bereavement**.

rejected the distinction, upheld by *Locke, between primary qualities such as shape, which resemble our sensory ideas of them, and secondary ones such as colour which do not, claiming that the being of perceptible objects is simply to be perceived. He declared the notion of matter self-contradictory, as involving the causal operation of something inert: all that could exist were spirits (minds) and their contents. Since our perceptions are not of our making, they must be induced in us by another mind, which Berkeley took to be that of God. Berkeley also made telling criticisms of the use of infinitesimals in the mathematics of his day. He was one of the most elegant writers of philosophy.

Berne Convention　*copyright.

betting　*gambling.

Bhagavadgītā (Sanskrit, 'Song of the Lord'), a 700-verse section of the *Mahābhārata epic, which describes how the god *Krishna appears to the hero Arjuna on the eve of the final battle, in order to encourage him to fulfil his duty in life by fighting against the forces of evil. The *Bhagavadgītā*, a synthetic text probably written in the 1st or 2nd century AD, reconciles the notion of active duty in society with the opposing ascetic ideal of renunciation and also stresses devotion (*bhakti*) to a personal god as the highest discipline.

Bible, the sacred book of Christianity. All Christian Churches accept two sections of the Bible: the Hebrew scriptures, known as the Old Testament, and specifically Christian writings, known as the New Testament. In addition, some Churches, including the Roman Catholic Church, accept a third section called the Apocrypha, found in the Greek version of the Old Testament (Septuagint). Each section consists of a number of separate books, written at different times by different authors. However, most Christians consider them to be endowed with unique divine authority. The Old Testament is divided by Jews into three: the Law or *Torah, which constitutes the first five books (the Pentateuch), the Prophets, and the Writings. Christians divide it into Histories, Poetic Books, and Prophets. The particular books it contains were agreed in the first three centuries AD. The New Testament consists of the four Gospels, which are concerned with *Jesus Christ's life, death, and resurrection; Acts, an account of the spread of the early Church; letters from prominent members of the early Church; and the visionary Revelation. Most of these books were acknowledged as canonical (accepted as sacred and genuine) by the middle of the 2nd century. The Apocrypha (Greek, 'hidden things') is the name given to a collection of books written between 300 BC and AD 100, not included in the Hebrew Bible. The Roman Catholic Church recognizes almost all of them as canonical.

bicameral assembly, a *legislature with two chambers: a primary chamber elected by universal suffrage, and a second chamber, whose members are either elected or appointed. Under *federalism, as in Australia and the USA, there is a powerful second chamber which often represents the territories in the federal union. In most *unitary states, the second chamber is constitutionally subordinate to the primary chamber, but has some limited capacity to restrain or revise legislation. Various methods including hereditary membership, nomination, functional representation of groups such as farmers or industrialists, and direct and indirect election are used, sometimes in combination, for constituting second chambers in different countries. Several justifications have been given for the retention of a second chamber. It can provide a brake upon hasty or intemperate legislation; it can revise and improve badly drafted legislation. Members sitting for life, or serving longer terms than in the primary chamber, provide continuity and experience. A second chamber may also be less partisan than the primary chamber, or may offer a different perspective, particularly if it is selected on a different basis. These arguments have some substance, though all are difficult to reconcile with the idea that popular sovereignty should find its chief expression through the will of a democratically elected assembly.

bilingualism, a *sociolinguistic phenomenon of linguistic competence in two *languages or more (multilingualism). Bilingualism of whole societies is influenced by migration (as in the case of Turkish guest workers in West Germany), colonialism and imperialism (the expansion of Russian in Lithuania), federation of linguistically diverse groups (Flemish and French speakers in Belgium), and other factors. The use of a particular language is often related to specific domains such as work or school on the one hand and home or church on the other, and it is socially and politically motivated. Sometimes bilingualism is difficult to distinguish from *diglossia.

bill, draft or proposed legislation put before a legislative body. Bills may be introduced by a minister, by an ordinary member of the *legislature, or in some countries by public petition. Passage of a bill normally involves an opportunity for interested opinion to be represented, and for the measure to be discussed, possibly amended, or even rejected in the course of general debate, detailed consideration by committee, and legislative voting. In the UK, bills are often preceded by documents outlining the government's intentions on an issue. Green Papers (so-called because they have green covers) are consultative documents intended to elicit public debate, while White Papers set out the government's proposals, as a preliminary to the drawing up of the bill itself. If approved by the legislature, a bill becomes an *act.

billiards, a family of table-games that are played with various numbers of balls and a cue. English billiards is played with three balls—plain white, spot-white, and red—and six pockets. Players score by pocketing a ball other than their cue-ball, by their cue-ball going in a pocket off another ball, and by cannons, that is, striking the other two balls with the cue-ball.

bill of exchange (known as 'notes' in the USA), a form of *credit used mainly in international *trade. It is a promise to pay a certain sum on a specified future date by the drawer of the bill to the holder of the bill. If a bill is 'accepted' or guaranteed (usually by an *acceptance house), it can be traded in the money markets. If it is accepted by a bank it is known as a bank bill; if by a trader, as a trade bill. Bills of exchange were originally used in domestic trade by merchants who wished to sell goods before paying for them.

bill of lading, a document used in international *trade giving details of the contents of a shipment, the ship carrying the goods, the sender (or consignor), and expected recipient (or consignee). Copies are held by the consignor, by the ship's captain, and by the consignee, who must present the document before being given the goods. A similar document in air transport is an air waybill.

Muslim demonstrators burn an effigy of Salman Rushdie near the Houses of Parliament, London. Parts of his book *The Satanic Verses* were considered to commit **blasphemy** against Muhammed; a death sentence was passed on Rushdie from Iran, and the book was banned in a number of Muslim countries.

bill of rights, a constitutional or legal provision guaranteeing to citizens of a particular state fundamental *civil rights such as free speech, freedom of assembly and worship, and freedom from arbitrary arrest. It is usually part of a constitutional revolution or resettlement. The United States Bill of Rights (1789) consists of the first ten amendments to the US Constitution. The idea of making the bill of rights part of the constitution has been widely followed elsewhere: many Caribbean and African states, Canada, France, Germany, and India, for example, now have constitutional bills of rights under various names. Some of these countries allow *judicial review of legislation for inconsistency with the bill of rights. The UK, Australia, and New Zealand as yet have no constitutional bill of rights.

Binet, Alfred (1857–1911), French psychologist, famous for the invention of the first useful *intelligence tests. Co-founder in 1889 of the first psychology laboratory in France, Binet anticipated much later work in *cognitive psychology. In 1904 the French government asked him to produce a test of children's abilities. He and his colleague Théodore Simon (1873–1961) devised a series of tests of memory, reasoning, and vocabulary of increasing difficulty. Depending on their performance, children could be assigned a 'mental age' which might differ from their actual age. The intelligence quotient (IQ), introduced by William Stern in 1912, denoted the ratio of a child's intelligence to the average for a given age. The tests became the model for all subsequent intelligence tests. Binet and Simon described their work in *The Development of Intelligence in Children* (1908). It was while working on tests for Simon after World War I that *Piaget developed his interest in the stages of children's intellectual growth.

birth rate, the ratio of births to a given population in a specified period. The most common measure, called the 'crude birth rate', is usually calculated as the annual number of births per thousand people. Between 1950 and 1955 and 1985 and 1990 crude birth rates fell from 20 to 13 in Europe, from 43 to 28 in Asia, from 42 to 29 in South America and from 49 to 45 in Africa. The UN expects the falls to continue in all continents and to accelerate in Africa. Despite falls in birth rates and *fertility rates, *population growth is expected to be unavoidable, primarily because the numbers of women of child-bearing age will increase substantially.

Black Churches, a popular name for congregations of Afro-Americans found largely in the USA. They may be of any *Protestant denomination, especially *Baptist, *Methodist, or *Pentecostal. Originating among Black slaves, Black Churches have a strong awareness of political and social injustice, and played an important part in the US Civil Rights Movement of the 1960s and 1970s. Black theology, like *liberation theology, emphasizes the freedom of the oppressed and God's identification with the victims in society. Worship in Black Churches is often informal, with spontaneous singing, shouting, and dancing. Preaching is central, and the Black minister may also be active in community activities and politics.

blackmail, the extraction of unwarranted payment in return for not carrying out a threat (sometimes called demanding money with menaces). Such menaces include the threat of violence or the exposure of past misconduct. In law, it is an essential requirement that the blackmail should concern economic as opposed to any other sort of gain, since the offence is concerned with the invasion of economic interests.

blasphemy, a speech, thought, or action regarded as derogatory to God or to sacred institutions. What is considered blasphemous varies between societies and religions, but it may be regarded as an indicator of what a society and its religious institutions believe must be protected in order to maintain morality and religious integrity. In *Judaism, blasphemy was punishable by death; Jesus was accused of blasphemy because he claimed to be God. In many countries, blasphemy is still regarded as an offence punishable by law. In the UK, the blasphemy laws currently apply only to slanders against Christianity, although there are calls for them to be extended to other religions. Penalties for blasphemy in *Islam are interpreted differently by the four schools of law, but it may be a capital offence.

blindness, partial or complete loss of vision that cannot be corrected by ordinary glasses. A major cause of blindness, particularly in the developing world, is infectious disease, such as trachoma, *sexually transmitted disease, measles, meningitis, and diphtheria. Dietary deficiency also plays a role. The World Health Organization has established national blindness prevention programmes in many developing countries, largely based on *primary health care: training programmes on the early recognition of cataract and trachoma have been set up for community health workers. Facilities to help the blind and partially sighted minimize their *disability, include training in the use of a long white cane or a guide dog to help with mobility; special education and training for jobs; books, textbooks, and other material written in *braille; and braille computer terminals.

Bloom, Benjamin S. (1912–), US educational psychologist and authority on the *curriculum. His work on *cognitive development is widely viewed as a major breakthrough in the improvement of learning and teaching. In his *Taxonomy of Educational Objectives* (1956) he argued that these can be classified hierarchically within three major domains: cognitive (concerned with knowledge); affective (concerned with interests, attitudes, and values); and psychomotor (concerned with physical and manipulative skills). From 1968, and in books such as *Human Characteristics and School Learning* (1976), he elaborated the concept of 'mastery learning'. The acquisition of basic skills involves an identifiable sequence of steps that can be learned by children of widely differing abilities, provided the steps are presented at an appropriate pace, in the correct sequence, and in the student's native language. The process involves testing, instruction, and retesting until the relevant skill is mastered.

blue chip, an *equity (or *share) which carries little risk compared to others. This means that its price on the *stock exchange is less likely to fall or rise rapidly and *dividends are more likely to be paid regularly. Blue-chip firms tend to be large ones with a long record of sound performance.

board-games, competitive games using a baseboard divided into cells or panels. Most are played by two or more people or by two opposing teams. In some, pieces or tokens are arranged in a fixed pattern on the board before play begins; in others, players choose their own arrangements. A chequered pattern is common to many strategic 'war-games' such as *chess, draughts (US, checkers), halma, and go (a Japanese game in which the board is divided into 361 intersections, and players seek to capture their opponents' stones and occupy the larger part of the board). Another family is the route-and-race game, in which players move their counters along a pre-set course arranged in a spiral, serpentine, rectangular, or random pattern, each move determined by throwing a die or dice or spinning a totum. Examples are snakes-and-ladders and ludo (evolved from the Indian game parcheesi).

bodhisattva (Sanskrit, 'a being for enlightenment'), a central ideal within the *Mahāyāna Buddhist tradition, describing both living and transcendent beings who are accorded much respect. Heavenly or transcendent bodhisattvas have achieved enlightenment and freedom from rebirth through the cultivation of various virtues, such as generosity, morality, patience, diligence, meditation, and wisdom, but they renounce *nirvana in order to benefit humanity. Earthly bodhisattvas seek both personal and communal enlightenment through exemplary learning and compassion. This essentially altruistic doctrine distinguishes the bodhisattva from the more individualistic *Theravāda ideal of the *arhat, who seeks nirvana for him- or herself. The term bodhisattva is also used more generally to describe the historical *Buddha before his enlightenment, or other individuals destined to become Buddhas.

body adornment, the transformation of the human body by the use of clothing, jewellery, or decoration. Apart from its purely functional purpose, dress has through the ages been an indicator of *gender, social position, or occupation. In some societies, traditional clothing is worn (the sari in India, for example), while in other societies, fashions are constantly changing, particularly for women, as their role in society is redefined. Other temporary forms of body adornment include face or body painting, for cosmetic or *ritual purposes. Some forms of adornment are more permanent, as in the case of tattooing or cicatrization (a kind of ritual scarring found in some African societies). All body adornment has a symbolic function in that it marks a person's social status, wealth, and, in some cases, *kinship affiliation. In *South Asian societies, differences of *caste may be marked by clothing or facial marks; religious followers or leaders may shave their heads, as in Buddhism and some Christian monasticism, or let their hair grow long, as some Hindus and Rastafarians do. In Western societies, fashion and cosmetics are used as an indicator of social position.

body language   *non-verbal communication.

Boethius (*c*.480–524), philosopher and statesman under the Ostrogoth king Theodoric. His imprisonment for treason led to his writing his best-known work, *The Consolations of Philosophy*, in which he argued that the soul can attain happiness in affliction by meditating on the reality of God. Boethius' chief significance is as a channel by which ancient learning passed into the monastic tradition. His translations of and commentaries on the logical works of *Aristotle provided almost all that was known to Christians of that philosopher until the 12th century, and helped to establish a rich Latin vocabulary of philosophical disputation.

Bolzano, Bernhard (1781–1848), Bohemian philosopher, mathematician, and theologian. In his *Logic and Scientific Methods* (1837) he construed a complete methodology of force, space, and time. As a mathematician he provided proof for the binominal formula and laid the cornerstone for the theory of real numbers, freeing the differential calculus from the concept of infinitesimals. In his insistence that the mathematics of real numbers should be made independent of spatial intuition—the importance of which is illustrated by his proof of the existence of a continuous function nowhere differentiable—Bolzano was an important precursor of *Frege.

bond, a fixed *interest-bearing *security issued by firms or governments which wish to borrow long-term funds. In the USA *debentures are also known as bonds. Most bonds are redeemable: at a date stated on the bond the cash amount specified on the bond will be paid by the issuer to the holder of the bond. Some bonds are irredeemable and the only return on them will be the nominal (or coupon) interest paid. Both redeemable and irredeemable bonds can be traded on the *stock exchange. Bonds may be issued by governments as part of their monetary policy; selling bonds to the public will reduce *liquidity and restrain the growth of the *money supply. A junk bond is a bond that carries a high risk whilst promising a high yield. It is issued by an institution with a low *credit rating, or else is not adequately secured. The use of junk bonds to raise funds, particularly to finance *take-over bids, was prominent in the USA in the 1980s. Junk-bond finance is also known as mezzanine finance because in status it falls halfway between (low-risk) bonds and (full-risk) shares.

bookkeeping, the recording of all financial transactions in an organization, usually recorded as 'debits' or 'credits' depending on whether they represent outflows or inflows of money. Double-entry bookkeeping uses the principle of balance so that, for example, every sale results in an inflow of money and an outflow of product. In this way the accuracy of the records is easily checked. Most bookkeeping is now handled by computer.

Bourse *stock exchange.

Bowlby *attachment.

bowling, a game derived from *skittles. In its most popular form—tenpin bowling—players compete to roll a ball and knock down ten pins set in a triangle 18 m (60 feet) away at the far end of a lane made of polished wood. Balls weigh up to 7 kg (16 pounds) and are fitted with one thumb-hole and two finger-holes. An earlier 19th-century version, called ninepins, was taken by settlers from Europe to North America, where the tenth pin was added, and the game evolved into a popular, highly organized indoor sport. In another game, known as road bowling, played chiefly in Ireland, two players compete in bowling iron balls along a public road; the winner completes the course in fewer throws than his opponent.

bowls, a group of games in which opposing individuals or teams seek to roll their bowls or woods closer to the jack (a small white ball) than their opponents' bowls. The bowl, made of wood, rubber, or composition, weighs up to 1.6 kg (3.5 pounds) and is flattened slightly on one side to impart bias, so that it travels in a curved path. Lawn bowls is played internationally on a level green. In crown-green bowls, played in northern England, the centre of the green is higher than the boundaries.

boxing, also known as the fight game, an international sport in which two opponents attack each other with gloved fists and attempt to win by a knockout (opponent floored for ten seconds) or on points awarded by a referee or judges—according to rules devised by the Marquess of Queensberry in 1865. Modern boxing is highly organized world-wide at professional and amateur levels, and boxers compete in a series of weight divisions from flyweight to heavyweight. A bout takes place in a three-roped boxing ring and is divided into a series of rounds, each of three minutes for professionals and senior amateurs. The sport is opposed by lobbies who claim it is too dangerous; early death and brain damage are the ultimate penalties for some of the young men, many from poor backgrounds, who seek fame and financial security from the sport. Other versions include Chinese, Thai, and French boxing.

boycott, a refusal to have dealings with a person, group, or nation, or to handle its goods (from Captain Boycott, a land-agent in Ireland, so treated in 1880). A boycott of a country whose policies are disapproved of may in its practical effects differ little from the imposition of *sanctions. Some of the best-known examples of boycotts in recent years have been in the sporting field, for example the decision of the USA and other countries not to permit their athletes to compete in the Olympic Games in Moscow in 1980, in protest against the Soviet invasion of Afghanistan the previous year. The displeasure of the international community at the apartheid policies of the South African government also resulted in a much publicized boycott of sporting as well as other links, whereby South African athletes were, until the early 1990s, prohibited from participating in many important international sporting events.

Brahmā, Hindu deity associated with the role of creation. He is often depicted as appearing from a lotus flower that grows in the navel of the sleeping *Vishnu. When he emerges, he creates many worlds, of which this is only one. His consort, Saraswati, is the goddess of art and learning, and, according to tradition, the inventor of the Sanskrit language.

Brahman, a central theological notion within *Hinduism, particularly *Vedānta. It signifies the ultimate holy power, the all-pervading soul or spiritual reality of the universe; eternal, uncreated, and infinite; the source of all things animate and inanimate. The doctrine of Brahman is particularly explored in the *Upanishads, which are the last part of the *Hindu sacred texts, or *Vedas. While Brahman is recognized as the source and purpose of the universe, it is conceptualized impersonally. Within Vedānta, *Advaita takes the reality of Brahman to be language-transcendent, a reality which cannot be captured by the attribution of qualities, and which can only be capable of being experienced (rather than described) as identical with the self; Vishishtādvaita (or qualified non-dualism) holds Brahman to be language-transcendent in terms of logic and possessed of qualities in terms of a devotee's understanding of Brahman as a personal deity, and thinks of Brahman both as consisting of individual souls and being more than their aggregation (as a black cow cannot lack colour but is more than black); Dvaita (dualist Vedānta) holds that Brahman is clearly identifiable as the creator God, a personal deity separate from the souls of individual devotees.

braille, the *writing system for the blind to be read by touch by a fingertip, developed by the French blind teacher, Louis Braille (1809–52). Each sign consists of up to six dots within a rectangle, embossed usually on cardboard. The signs correspond to letters, numbers, punctuation marks, and musical notes.

break-even analysis, a useful way of identifying the profit potential of a business activity. The break-even point occurs in a business calculation where total revenue is equal to total *cost. Normally the break-even point refers to a certain number of items produced: below this number, costs are higher than revenues and a loss ensues: above this number, revenues are higher than costs and a profit ensues. Break-even analysis is the technique for identifying the break-even point by estimating costs and revenues in an actual or potential production process. In the analysis, costs are usually divided into fixed costs and variable costs. Revenue is normally estimated using a fixed selling price giving a straight line relationship with production quantity. The technique is also used to calculate the pay-back period for investment in ongoing activities, which is achieved by plotting expenditure against return.

Brentano, Franz (1838–1917), German philosopher, celebrated for his emphasis on *intentionality as a defining characteristic of mental acts. The idea was introduced in his best-known book, *Psychology from an Empirical Standpoint* (1874). Intentionality is the character of being directed towards an object: you cannot, for example, simply be surprised, but must be surprised *by* something. Brentano never solved the problem that the object of a mental act may not in fact exist, but left it to his followers such as Husserl (see *phenomenonology) and *Meinong to resolve in their different ways. Others of his students at the University of Vienna were *Freud and Tomáš Masaryk, the founder of modern Czechoslovakia.

bridewealth *dowry.

bridge *card-games.

broadcast database, a system of data transmission that broadcasts information in the form of text and graphic displays to viewers at home. Teletext systems, such as the BBC's Ceefax or the IBA's Oracle in the UK, transmit 'pages' of graphic and textual information to television screens as an electronic newspaper or directory. Such systems are one-way; on the other hand, viewdata or videotex systems, such as Prestel in the UK or Minitel in France, have an interactive capacity for users: they give home shoppers and small businesses low-cost on-line access to computerized databanks via a telephone line and a television set with a decoder modem. However, because such systems are two-way, it is possible for the home user's choices to be monitored, thus raising questions about invasion of *privacy.

broadcasting, the transmission of sound and image via radio waves to a mass audience. Today through *radio and *television broadcasts hundreds of millions around the world can listen simultaneously to a pop concert or watch a football match. For every twenty people on earth there are eight radio and three television sets, the overwhelming majority in the industrialized world. Radio and television are key components of what are termed the *mass media. Broadcasting is a major source of *news and other information, entertainment, and education. In the USA it developed primarily as a local service financed by *advertising, with only general supervision and allocation of frequencies by the Federal Communications Commission. Nation-wide *networks provide programmes to affiliated stations and compete for advertising and audience share. There is a similar pattern of services throughout North and South America. In the UK, by contrast, a unified system of national *public service broadcasting, funded by licence fees, was built around the non-commercial *BBC. Independent radio and television services, funded by advertising and closely regulated by a national authority, came later. A similar 'mixed' approach operates in many continental countries. In countries under an authoritarian or communist regime, where the state wishes to exert strong control over public opinion, ownership and control tend to be centralized. The *propaganda potential of radio was demonstrated in World War II and during the cold war, and since television became pre-eminent in the 1950s and 1960s, debates about the ownership, regulation, and underlying philosophy of broadcasting have intensified. Wider access to the airwaves has been demanded by sections of the public in both industrialized and developing countries as demands for a New International Information Order emerged in the 1970s (see *UNESCO). However, in the 1980s, commercial pressure for *deregulation and *privatization of broadcasting services increased everywhere. Concentration of *media ownership continued, yet the number of radio and television stations proliferated. In recent decades broadcasting has been revolutionized by developments in *cable television, *satellite transmission, and *narrowcasting to audience 'segments' and individual subscribers. Radio continues to be a lively medium, for example in community stations. Both radio and television are important elements of *distance education.

broker, a dealer who acts as an intermediary between buyers and sellers in a *market, normally being paid on commission. Examples include *commodity brokers, bill brokers, *insurance brokers, and stockbrokers who deal in *shares. In the UK stock-market prior to the Financial Services Act (1986) jobbers kept their own share book and set prices for shares; thus they acted as 'market makers'. Jobbers did not deal with members of the public. Brokers acted on behalf of members of the public and bought from or sold to jobbers. After the 1986 Act, the distinction between jobbers and brokers disappeared. Any investment firm can now act as a market maker.

Bruner, Jerome (1915–), US psychologist who has made important contributions to *social, *cognitive, and also educational and child psychology. *A Study of Thinking* (1956), with J. Goodnow and G. Austin, focused on the sequence of decisions made in thinking through a problem. It is usually regarded as one of the main contributions to the development of cognitive psychology. In the 1960s Bruner stressed the participation of the pupil in the educational process and argued for an 'integrated science' *curriculum. His work in the 1970s brought out the ways in which children learn non-linguistic communicative skills before they acquire language. Bruner's argument that language development depends on a set of non-linguistic skills contrasts with that of *Chomsky and is described in *Child's Talk: Learning to Use Language* (1983).

Buddha (Sanskrit, 'enlightened one'), a title applied by Buddhists to anyone, earthly or transcendent, who has attained *nirvana. However, the title is most commonly used to refer to Siddhārtha Gautama (*c*.480–400 BC), the historical founder of *Buddhism. According to tradition, he left his life as the son of a prince and became a wandering ascetic, in order to seek the meaning of existence. At the age of 35 he underwent an experience of enlightenment under a Bodhi-tree. He realized that the root of all existence is suffering, but that by following a 'Middle Way' between self-indulgence and extreme *asceticism, man may achieve enlightenment. Buddha travelled around northern India for about 45 years, preaching and gathering together a large number of followers (*sangha*). He attained nirvana at his enlightenment, and at his death, a final nirvana (*parihirvāna*). The focus of Buddhism is on the teaching of the Buddha rather than on Gautama as a unique individual, but he is nevertheless shown great reverence as a supreme teacher and exemplar. *Theravada Buddhism regards Gautama as the pre-eminent Buddha, while *Mahāyāna Buddhism recognizes many revelations of the Buddha ideal.

Buddhism, a major world religion numbering around 300 million followers (exact estimates are impossible since Buddhism does not preclude other religious beliefs). Early Buddhism developed from *Hinduism through the teaching of Siddhārtha Gautama (the *Buddha) and his disciples

Monks collecting alms in Rangoon, Myanmar, where 80 per cent of the people are Buddhist. The Burmese doctrine of 'Social Buddhism' attempts to combine **Buddhism** with Marxism. It suggests that concern for property distracts people from religion, and that greed is an obstacle to meditation.

(*sangha*), around the 5th century BC in northern India. Under leaders such as Ashoka (273–232 BC), who converted to Buddhism and encouraged its spread, the religion provided a stabilizing political structure throughout India. Buddhism gradually spread through central Asia to China, Korea, and Japan, while it declined in popularity in India itself, where Hinduism reasserted its dominance. Owing to its linguistic diversity and geographical extent, Buddhist teaching, scriptures, and observance are complex and varied, but certain main doctrines are characteristic. Buddhism recognizes no creator *God with a monopoly over knowledge and power. Instead it puts forward the doctrine of *dependent origination, or conditioned arising, which states that all phenomena are linked together in an endless chain of dependency. Buddhism teaches that the suffering of the world is caused by desire conditioned by ignorance, but that by following the path of the Buddha, and breaking the link of desire in the chain, release from the cycle of rebirth (*samsara) can be achieved. Three major forms of Buddhism can be distinguished. The most conservative, the *Theravāda school, persists today in South and South-east Asia, particularly in Sri Lanka, Thailand, Myanmar (Burma), and Laos. Theravāda scriptures, the *Tripitaka*, summarize the basic teaching of the Buddha: the *Four Noble Truths and the *Noble Eightfold path. Although this teaching is common throughout Buddhism, the analytical and monastic approach of Theravāda is less widespread than the teaching developed by the *Mahāyāna school, which arose between 150 BC and AD 100. It is now the largest grouping within Buddhism, dominant in China, Japan, Vietnam, and Korea. The final phase of Buddhist expansion, after the 7th century, saw the emergence of *Tantric (Vajrayāna and *Tibetan Buddhism. (See also *Zen Buddhism.)

Buddhist festivals. The Buddhist religious year is based on a lunar calendar, which varies in different Buddhist countries. Festivals generally fall on new or full moons. The three major events of the *Buddha's life, his birth, enlightenment, and entry into *nirvana, are celebrated in all Buddhist countries, but not necessarily at the same time. In *Theravāda countries, all three events are commemorated in the festival of *Wesak (Vesak), which usually takes place in April. Māgha-Pūjā, celebrating the Buddha's teaching of the rules of monastic life, takes place in February. Another important festival, largely confined to Theravāda countries, is the rainy season retreat of Vassa, which brings monks and other followers together for prayer, meditation, and important ordination and initiation ceremonies. It ends with Kathina, a joyous celebration during which monks are presented with robes and other gifts. In *Mahāyāna countries, the three events in Buddha's life are celebrated separately. In China and Japan, there are in addition important festivals commemorating the dead (Ullambana in China, Bon in Japan), which take place in August/September. Mahāyāna countries also celebrate the anniversaries connected with the founders of particular sects. New Year is widely and colourfully celebrated, particularly in Tibet.

Buddhist sacred buildings. A variety of buildings are sacred to Buddhists. They include *stūpas* (or reliquary chambers), monasteries, shrines, and meditation rooms, and vary in size from a simple shrine within the home consisting of a statue or image of the *Buddha, to large temples which may combine several or all of these different buildings. The *stūpa* was originally built to house relics; the form of the original North Indian *stūpas* is the basis of all Buddhist temples' external design, whether Tibetan (*chörten*), Sri Lankan (*dagoba*), or Chinese (pagoda). Worship at a *stūpa* consists of circumambulating the building clockwise in the direction of the sun's path. Monasteries accommodate monks who guide the observance and meditation of Buddhist followers, and often incorporate shrines and meditation rooms. In *Theravāda traditions the shrine contains a statue of the Buddha and copies of *sūtras* (sacred texts). There are sometimes additional statues representing stages in the Buddha's life before which simple offerings may be placed. Followers sit on the floor with bare feet. In the *Mahāyāna traditions there are usually a variety of images in an ornate and colourful style, particularly of the *Bodhisattva Avalokiteshvara. A diverse range of offerings including lights and flowers may be placed before these images, usually to the accompaniment of chanted verses. Meditation rooms are kept calm and uncluttered with a single image and meditative aids such as wall hangings in *Tibetan Buddhism or calligraphy of a sacred text in *Zen Buddhism.

budget, a plan made by a household, a business, or a government of its expected future income and expenditure. The central government budget is normally prepared annually, but may be produced more often in exceptional circumstances. It typically sets out the expected tax receipts (and tax changes) and government expenditure for the following financial year. Since *Keynes, the national budget has been recognized as a major instrument of managing *demand throughout the economy. Aggregate demand tends to increase if a government steps up its own expenditure by more than its income from tax receipts and to decline if government spending rises less than tax receipts. When the government's revenue equals its expenditure, it has a balanced budget. When revenue exceeds (falls short of) expen-

A bull-fight in Mexico, whose capital city has the world's largest bull-ring. **Bull-fighting** is one legacy of Spanish colonialism in South America; many European bull-fighters spend their winters across the Atlantic, where the season runs from December to March.

diture, there is a budget surplus (deficit). A surplus means that the government is on balance repaying debt (to its own citizens or to foreigners); a deficit means that the government is adding to its debts. (See also *deficit financing, *fiscal policy, *national debt.)

building society, a form of savings bank in the UK. It takes in deposits from customers, on which *interest is paid. It then lends these funds to borrowers, mainly in the form of *mortgage loans for the buying of houses. The US equivalents of building societies are savings-and-loan associations. Originally building societies were non-profit-making *co-operatives, but later they entered the mainstream banking system. Since the 1980s they have competed more intensely with *banks, introducing their own banking services such as cheque books and cashpoint cards. Building societies were given the option to turn themselves into banks in 1986.

bull-fighting, a ritual killing of bulls practised chiefly in Spain, parts of Latin America, the South of France, and Portugal. It is considered an integral part of the Spanish heritage, and is known in Spain as the *fiesta nacional* (national celebration). A typical *corrida de toros* (literally, running of the bulls) features six fighting bulls. Three *cuadrillos* (teams), each led by a *matador* (killer), taking two bulls each, put them to death in a traditional sequence of moves using capes, lances, and pairs of barbed sticks. In the final phase, the *matador* plays the bull with his *muleta* (red cloth) and kills it with a climactic sword thrust. In other versions of the sport, the bull may be killed by a mounted bull-fighter (Spanish, *rejoneo*) or grappled with by teams of catchers (Portuguese, *forcado*). In the southern French *course à la cocarde*, the *razeteurs* attempt to remove a rosette attached to the bull's horns; the bull is not harmed, but may inflict considerable damage on his attackers.

bureaucracy, an administrative structure, staffed by a professional body of officials. A bureaucracy theoretically involves a carefully defined division of tasks, following formally defined rules and procedures. The organization is a disciplined hierarchy, in which officials are subject to the authority of their superiors. Authority is impersonal, vested in the rules governing official business. Modern administrative systems like the *civil service, are based on the bureaucratic model. One of the problems of bureaucracy is an inherent tension between uniformity, which is convenient for large-scale administration, and flexibility, which is necessary in dealing with individual cases. In practice, bureaucracies are sometimes deficient, revealing tendencies to excessive rigidity, delay, and unresponsiveness (the popular image of 'red tape'); or else to waste, *corruption, and abuse of power. In some countries, the public may have redress against bureaucratic maladministration through *administrative law and recourse to an *ombudsman.

burglary   *property crime.

burial   *cremation, *funeral customs.

bushido (Japanese, 'way of the warrior'), the strict codes of behaviour, duties, and training of the samurai, the traditional ruling warrior class of Japan. The *bushido* code was influenced by *Shintoism, *Zen Buddhism, and *Confucianism, but its predominant ideals were martial skills, including swordsmanship; duty to the emperor and feudal lords; and a strong emphasis on honour, which dominated everything from speech to ritual suicide or *seppuku* (less correctly termed *hara-kiri). Bushido continues to provide inspirational models for modern Japanese capitalists.

Bushmen   *!Kung San.

cabinet, the body of ministers who confer directly with the head of government. The cabinet may make collective decisions, as it does in the UK and most European democracies, or it may have only an advisory status, as in the case of the President's cabinet in the USA. The size and membership of cabinets vary, but the holders of the major offices of state, such as the ministers responsible for finance, defence, and foreign affairs, are always included. The UK cabinet has normally had around twenty members, chosen by the *prime minister and appointed by the monarch, who are collectively responsible to Parliament for the policy and conduct of the government. It is almost invariably the practice for ministers to be or soon become, a member of one House of Parliament. The convention of collective responsibility means that all members of the cabinet must publicly support its policies or resign. Prime Ministers in Australia and New Zealand have less discretion in cabinet selection. In the USA, the cabinet consists of the heads of executive departments who are chosen by the President with the consent of the *Senate; they themselves are not members of *Congress. In countries which have *coalition governments as a result of an electoral system of *proportional representation, members of different parties may be represented in the cabinet.

cable television, the transmission of *television signals by cable to receiving sets. The original signal may be received direct from a studio by *satellite antenna, microwave ground link, or directly over the air. Cable television was developed in the 1950s to re-transmit broadcasts in regions of the USA with poor 'off-air' reception. A turning point came in 1975 with the Time, Inc. Home Box Office (HBO) transmission of a Muhammad Ali–Joe Frazier heavyweight boxing title fight live from the Philippines; HBO and other cable television companies became television producers in their own right. Cable News Network (CNN) was founded by the US entrepreneur Ted Turner (1938–) in

The **cable television** news network CNN reached its widest audience in 1991 when it broadcast live from Baghdad at the start of the Gulf War.

1980. It carries round-the-clock all-news television which, when reporting a war or other crisis, can rival network viewing figures. Through *satellite broadcasting, CNN is to be found in the world's hotels, government offices, and international businesses. By the mid-1980s half of homes with television in the USA (over half in Canada) had cable television, and there were scores of cable television channels. Elsewhere the figures were much lower; there was little cable television in the UK and none in Italy, although it reached eight out of ten homes in Belgium. The spread of video film rentals and *satellite broadcasting, together with the high cost of cabling, slowed the spread of cable television. The full potential of multi-channel cable systems by which 'one wire' brings telephone, television, *broadcast databases, and other facilities has yet to be realized, but such systems are planned for some areas by the end of the 1990s.

calendar   *Gregorian calendar, *Islamic calendar, *Jewish calendar.

caliph (from Arabic, 'successor' or 'representative'), title given to the heads of the Muslim community following the death of Muḥammad in AD 632, and used in the *Koran, meaning 'successor' or 'viceregent' of God. *Sunnī Muslims accept the authority of the first four 'rightly guided' caliphs: 'Abū Bakr (632–4), immediate successor to Muḥammad; 'Umar (634–44); 'Uthmān (644–56); and *'Alī. Shī'ī Muslims accept authority as passing directly from Muḥammad to 'Alī. The caliphate was abolished with the demise of the Ottoman Empire in 1922, but *Islamic fundamentalists have called for its restitution in recent years.

cancer, diseases caused by the uncontrolled division of cells to form tumours that invade and destroy the tissues in which they arise. The World Health Organization estimates that about 5 million people die of cancer every year. Most common forms of cancer are related in one way or another to ways of life and behaviour: risk factors include *smoking, exposure to substances such as asbestos, or to ultraviolet light or ionizing radiation; a low-fibre diet; and exposure to certain virus infections. However, environmental factors (such as pollution, or natural radiation), as well as genetic predisposition, also play a part. Age is the single most important predictive factor for a majority of cancers, since exposure to risk factors accumulates. With *ageing populations, the absolute number is rising, but the rates for the total population are no higher than in the past. Cancer is a major public health problem in the developing world, since effective diagnosis and treatment are expensive and require highly trained staff. Faced with shrinking health budgets and the imperative to develop *primary health care, some countries are putting greater emphasis on palliative and traditional forms of care.

canoeing, the water sport of controlling and propelling a canoe or kayak. These small lightweight craft, pointed at both ends, are propelled by a double-bladed paddle or a short single-bladed paddle which the paddler operates from a kneeling position. There are three kinds of competition: slalom, wild water or down-river racing, and racing over short- and long-distance courses. Slalom is notably spectacular, the canoeist guiding his craft through rough water and negotiating a sequence of gates hung above the water.

canon law, the rules and laws made by ecclesiastical authority by which a Church and its members are governed. Historically, canon law was the universal law of the western Roman Catholic Church; it has been codified and repromulgated many times in the history of the Church, with the last major revision in 1917. The canon law of the *Anglican Communion has been separate since the 16th-century Reformation. Canon law today is the internal law of a Church governing matters such as the regulation of the clergy, and administration of the sacraments, for example marriage. Especially in countries where Roman Catholicism has been the state religion, canon law has greatly influenced civil law. In the Church of England, because it is an established Church, that is the national church linked to the state, parliamentary approval is required for its decisions to become part of canon law.

cantor (in Judaism), a man, expert in prayer and ritual matters, who leads the congregation of a *synagogue, especially in incantation. The role of the cantor is particularly important within *Orthodox Judaism, which forbids musical instruments as being inappropriate and as involving a form of work not permitted on the Sabbath. After the reading of psalms, the cantor sings of God's deliverance and blessing of the Jews.

capital, an economic term denoting *goods whose part in the production process is to assist in producing other goods and services rather than being available for consumption. The production of capital implies foregone *consumption, that is, saving, because resources have been used to produce capital goods rather than consumer goods. Capital is commonly classified into fixed capital and working capital. Fixed capital, such as buildings and machinery, lasts beyond the production process. Working capital (circulating capital or inventories) comprises *intermediate goods which are used up in the production process. An increase in the stock of capital in any period is termed *investment. Skilled labour is often classified as *human capital. Gross investment less *depreciation leaves net investment. In common usage the word capital may also refer to stocks of personal wealth or money. (See also *factors of production.)

capitalism, an economic system based on *market competition between privately owned enterprises. All human production requires both *labour and *capital. In a capitalist system, capital is supplied either by the single owner of a firm, or by shareholders in the case of a *joint-stock company. Labour is supplied separately by employees who receive a *wage or salary. The residual *profit of the firm after wages and costs have been paid accrues to the owners of capital. Firms compete with one another to sell to customers in what is primarily a *free market, though capitalism can co-exist with substantial state regulation of the economy, as in a *mixed economy. This system gradually replaced the older systems of production by merchant guilds and tied serfs or peasants throughout Western Europe from the 16th century onwards. Since the beginning of the 19th century its main competitor in the industrial societies has been *socialism, which favours the social or public ownership of industry. Defenders of capitalism point to the high rates of *economic growth which this system has achieved, and also to the personal *freedom that private ownership of property bestows. Its critics such as *Marx have claimed that capitalism necessarily involves the exploitation of workers by owners, and that it prevents people from controlling their own working lives. The force of the first charge has been diminished to some extent by state policies of income redistribution and *welfare provision, which are pursued in all contemporary capitalist societies. With the collapse of the leading socialist economies in the 1980s, the main challenge now facing capitalism is to show that the pursuit of private profit can be reconciled with concern for the natural environment and the quality of life. (See also *market socialism.)

capital punishment, the infliction of death by an authorized public authority as *punishment for a *crime. In most jurisdictions where it remains, its use is limited to those who have been convicted of *murder, although in some countries where its use is more frequent it is imposed as a penalty for other offences such as armed robbery (in certain African countries), large-scale embezzlement of state property (the former Soviet Union), *rape and gang-fighting (China), and drug-trafficking (Thailand). A UN survey in 1990 revealed that forty-three countries had abolished the death penalty entirely, seventeen had retained it but only for exceptional crimes such as treason, twenty-four had retained it but not used it for at least ten years, and ninety-seven were still using it. The abolitionist countries were widely scattered, including, for example, the Philippines and Namibia, but were mostly to be found in Europe and Latin America. Although the number of abolitionist states had doubled since the previous survey in 1967, the UN found unwavering official support for capital punishment in many countries in the Middle East, Africa, and Asia. Islamic law (the *sharī'ah) imposes capital punishment for certain offences, and capital punishment is enforced in those countries where the sharī'ah forms the legal code, and in many countries where the sharī'ah is drawn on as the basis for the legal code. Capital punishment has long been the subject of dispute. While proponents argue that it is a necessary deterrent to the most serious crime, more so than the alternative of life *imprisonment, opponents argue either that it is in violation of the human right to life or that inevitable miscarriages of justice will lead to the execution of innocent people. Furthermore, a careful review of the research evidence suggests that capital punishment has no greater deterrent effect than life imprisonment. (See also *extra-judicial execution.)

card-games, games usually played with a pack (or packs) of fifty-two cards derived from the picture cards of the Tarot to which numeral cards were added. The modern pack is divided into four suits—spades, hearts, diamonds, and clubs—each consisting of an ace, king, queen, jack, and nine numeral cards numbered 10 to 2. While the chief function of Tarot cards is fortune-telling, most modern card-games are played either for amusement, albeit competitively, or as a vehicle for gambling. The principal solo games are variations of solitaire or patience, in which the player lays out a number of key cards and tries to build the remaining cards on them in an agreed sequence. In games based on rank, such as whist, players are dealt a hand of cards face down and then lay them out in sequence, trying to defeat other players' cards and collect tricks. Bidding, or declaring in advance how many tricks the player expects to win, produced the modern game of contract bridge. Other games, such as poker, are based on combinations of cards; players bet on their hands and seek to win through a blend of good cards and bluffing.

cargo cults, *millenarian movements originally found in *Melanesian societies. The charismatic leaders of such cults claim that when the new millennium arrives, the ancestors, or a god, will return, bringing the cargo (Western trade goods) that rightfully belongs to the people, having been stolen by white men. The use of the term 'cargo' results from the contact of the Melanesian people with European traders, and the cults can be seen as anti-colonial protest movements. Cult followers often build storehouses, jetties, and airstrips, or adopt European dress and habits in a form of *ritual that anticipates the arrival of cargo. When this fails to materialize, the cult may decline.

Caribbean societies, a diverse range of cultures which include not only the islands of the Caribbean, but also certain coastal regions of South and Central America. Most of the inhabitants are descendants of former *plantation workers, whose culture (known as Creole) is a mix of European and African influences. The characteristic type of *family is known as serial monogamy, in which each person has several partners in succession over a lifetime. Formal *marriage is uncommon, except among the educated élite, as there is little stigma attached to *illegitimacy. The household is often matrifocal, organized around women, with elder women and daughters residing together without any males in permanent residence. Many people are agricultural workers, although *tourism is now an increasingly important element in the economy of the region. Religious cults are popular, sometimes, as in *Rastafarianism, based on African beliefs fused with Christianity. Music is an important element, and like Creole culture in general, is the result of a fusion of different styles and influences.

CARICOM (Caribbean Community and Common Market), an organization of Caribbean countries formed in 1973. Its headquarters are in Georgetown, Guyana. In 1991 its membership comprised the former British Caribbean colonies, now members of the *Commonwealth: Antigua and Barbuda, The Bahamas, Barbados, Dominica, Grenada, Guyana, Jamaica, St Christopher and Nevis, St Lucia, St Vincent and the Grenadines, and Trinidad and Tobago, together with Montserrat (still under British rule) and Belize. In 1990 a proposal to expand membership beyond the English-speaking Commonwealth was rejected. CARICOM has three objectives: economic co-operation through the Caribbean Common Market; the co-ordination of foreign policy; and collaboration in such fields as health, agriculture, and transport. By the early 1990s, trade barriers among members had been substantially reduced.

carnival (derived from the Italian 'farewell to meat'), the festival period before *Lent, celebrated in Roman Catholic countries and communities. Festivities, a succession of parades, masked balls, and theatrical performances in public places, occur between Epiphany (6 January) and Shrove Tuesday, the last day before Lent. Mardi Gras in New Orleans is one of the most famous carnivals. The name, meaning 'Fat Tuesday' in French, refers to the custom of using up all the fats stored over the winter before Lent begins. Other well-known carnivals take place in Rio de Janeiro, Venice, and Trinidad. In North America, carnival also means a travelling fun-fair.

cartel, a group of producers (firms or countries) which attempts to fix the price of its common product or products, usually through restriction of output by cartel members, often by operating a *quota system. The benefit to producers stems from the rise in product price. This is possible because the joint production of the cartel is large enough to exert *monopoly power. The resulting imperfectly competi-

interest until needed. Cash flow is very important. Many organizations have gone bankrupt because, although their long-term financial position was profitable and healthy, they were unable to provide cash in the short term to satisfy their creditors.

caste system, a means of stratification, which groups people according to specific social rank. Variations of caste are found in all Indian religious communities, not only Hindu but Jain, Buddhist, Muslim, and Christian communities as well. All stem from the tripartite social division of the Aryans, who invaded northern India *c*.1500 BC. However, only Hindus developed theological and legal rationales for caste (see *Hindu law). The three divisions or *varnas* consisted of Brahmins (priests and professionals), Kshatriyas (rulers, warriors, and administrators), and Vaishyas (farmers and merchants). Later a fourth *varna* developed, the Shūdras (artisans and labourers). Each *varna* classifies many *jātis* or castes, traditionally determined by occupation, but often linked through geographical locality, marriage, or dietary customs. Religious justification for the *varna-jāti* system stems from the *Rigveda*, the earliest text of the *Vedas, which describes how *Purusha, the original cosmic man, was divided by the gods into specific *varnas*, each of which has its own attributes and role in society. One of the preoccupations of the caste system is the notion of purity and pollution: varying degrees of defilement result from a *jāti*'s occupation, dietary habits, or customs. Those who carried out the most polluting tasks became known as 'untouchables'. Untouchables are outside the *varna* system, although still part of the caste system. Mahatma Gandhi, desiring to improve their status, renamed them *Harijans*, 'Children of God', a title subsequently rejected by them in favour of the name *dalit*, 'depressed'. They remain the most oppressed members of Indian society, despite legislation to reserve government jobs, education places, and parliamentary seats for them. In recent years proposals for similar *positive discrimination for other castes have been a leading issue in Indian politics and caused widespread violence. Critics argue that in a democratic system such policies may amount to little more than electoral bribery and expect that urbanization and modernization will erode the caste system, but others point to the entrenched nature of the caste system and the severe economic and social constraints it places on the lives of those in the lower *jātis*.

casuistry, the attempt to resolve cases of moral conscience, or moral problems such as are created by conflicts of obligations, by subtle reasoning. The term has a derogatory import, carrying the implication that the casuist is responding to the problem in an evasive or quibbling manner.

categorical imperative *ethics.

Caucasian languages, around forty languages spoken by 5 million people in the Caucasus area between the Black Sea and the Caspian Sea. It is unusual to have such a large number of languages concentrated in such a small area, and it is often difficult to draw a clear boundary between what is a language and what is a *dialect. There are two distinct groups, Northern Caucasian and Southern Caucasian, and though they are distantly related, it is doubtful whether they are descended from the same parent language. Southern Caucasian (or Kartvelian) includes Georgian, the most important Caucasian language. Georgian has nearly 3.5 million speakers, and is the official language of Georgia. It is the

In Trinidad the roots of the **carnival** lie in a mixture of the French Catholic tradition and the ecstatic celebrations of newly emancipated slaves. The festivities are accompanied by calypso music played by steel bands.

tive market may be harmful to consumers. Therefore cartels are generally banned within countries. *OPEC is an example of an international cartel.

case law, a system in which the reasoning employed by judges in reaching decisions in cases litigated before them constitutes a source of law by creating a *precedent. Legal systems which operate in this way, such as those in England and Wales and the USA, are sometimes called *common law systems and can be distinguished from code-based or *civil law systems such as are to be found in France and Germany, in which a judge's decision as to the scope of a principle in the code is incapable, on its own, of authoritatively defining or amending the principle for the future. Nevertheless, most systems have elements of both case law and codes. In the UK and the USA, codes are increasingly being provided for specific matters by *statute law, while in French law the *Conseil d'État* (the supreme French administrative body) and the *Cour de Cassation* (the highest court of civil and criminal appeal) have developed a number of general principles through case law. In both systems, statutory codes can sometimes become so overlaid with judicial decisions that the practical effects of the law can be understood only by looking at how cases are decided. Reliance on case law entails the piecemeal development of the law, since it depends on an appropriate case reaching a court of sufficient authority to enunciate a principle or settle a question.

cash crop *shifting cultivation.

cash flow, the cash inflow to, and outflow from, an organization. As many sales and purchases are made on deferred payment terms, it is necessary for an organization to manage its cash to ensure that liabilities can be met when they fall due and that any cash surplus can be invested to earn

only Caucasian language with a long history and an ancient literary tradition. The earliest monuments date from the 5th century AD, and are written in a script derived from Aramaic. The modern Georgian script is a descendant of this. Great works of literature were produced from the 12th century on. The Northern family has two sub-groups, North-West (Abkhazo-Adyghian) and North-East (Nakho-Dagestanian). These two groups are rather different from each other grammatically. The five North-West dialects are notorious for having a large number of consonants (seventy to eighty) and very few vowels; differences between the five dialects are mainly in pronunciation and vocabulary. The North-East group is less closely knit: there are three Nakh dialects, and numerous small languages make up the Dagestanian group. The Caucasian languages were influenced by Arabic and Persian in the past; in recent years, the main source of new vocabulary has been Russian.

causation (in philosophy), the seemingly necessary connection between one event (the cause) and another (the effect). Philosophical discussions of the concept are mainly concerned with analysing what the causal relation actually is, what sort of things are linked by causation (is it objects, events, states, or processes?), and how we can know when one thing causes another (what distinguishes a genuine causal connection from an accidental correlation?). Other questions raised are whether causation is a necessary relation (could a cause operate but its effect fail to occur?), and whether causal relations have a unique temporal direction (can an effect precede its cause? Can a cause be instantaneous with its effect?). Much of the modern debate begins with *Hume, who analysed causation as the 'regular succession' of spatio-temporally proximate objects. He used *sceptical conclusions about the inability of both reason and experience to account for our knowledge of causal relations to support his view that it is based on the psychological phenomenon of custom, or habit. This view enabled Hume to reconcile the view that man is part of the natural causal nexus, with the appearance of *free will. Hume's account awoke *Kant 'from his dogmatic slumbers' to produce his own position in which causal relations are imposed by the mind on to the world. Recent developments in theoretical physics have somewhat diminished the importance of causation, though they seem to support a non-necessary, *probabilistic interpretation. For example, in micro-physics it is not possible to determine with unlimited accuracy, but only in probabilistic terms, both the position and momentum of a particle (according to the uncertainty principle of the physicist Werner Heisenberg, 1901–76).

caving, the study and exploration of natural caves, as opposed to man-made mines and tunnels. Pot-holers specialize in deep caves opening up to the surface. Caves offer an infinite variety of subterranean galleries, chambers, vertical pits, and narrow tunnels, and their unpredictability makes the hobby compelling and dangerous.

Celtic languages, a group of *Indo-European languages which includes Irish and Scots Gaelic, Manx, Welsh, Cornish, and Breton. There are now fewer than 3 million speakers, despite a linguistic and nationalistic revival in the 20th century. Celtic languages were originally spoken throughout Europe, from Spain to Asia Minor (present-day Turkey), but were submerged by other Indo-European languages, notably Romance languages. None of these Continental languages has survived, and only meagre information

about them can be gleaned from place-names and a few inscriptions. The Insular (island) languages fared better. These fall into two groups: Goidelic comprises Irish Gaelic, Scots Gaelic (Erse), and Manx, while Brythonic consists of Welsh, Cornish, and Breton. Irish is first attested, written in runic characters, in inscriptions of the 4th century AD. There was a great literary flowering in the 11th century, but after the 16th century the language began to retreat before English. It was adopted as the official language of the Irish Republic, where it is now spoken by roughly 31 per cent of the population. Scots Gaelic was imported from Ireland in the 5th century AD, and soon developed into a distinct dialect, although Irish remained as the literary language until the 17th century. Scots Gaelic is now spoken by under 100,000 people in the western Highlands and Islands of Scotland. Manx had become extinct as a mother-tongue by the mid-20th century. Welsh is attested from the 8th century, and has a rich medieval poetic tradition. It declined disastrously during the 19th century due to the Industrial Revolution, when thousands of English-speakers were moved to Wales to work in the factories and mines; by the beginning of the 20th century the Welsh-speakers were in a minority. The language has revived, however, since World War II and is now an official language of Wales, with over 750,000 speakers. Breton was introduced to Brittany from the British Isles in the 5th century AD. Its use was not generally encouraged in modern France until the 1950s, and the number of speakers has declined to around 500,000. Cornish became extinct at the beginning of the 19th century.

censorship, restrictions on public and/or private expression, involving the banning or restriction of the publication, utterance, production, or dissemination of written, oral, and visual material of certain types. Censorship can operate as a prior restraint before the fact, as in the case of D-Notices in the UK, restricting the publication of information relating to sensitive security matters; or after the fact, in which case punishment often leads to fear and subsequent self-censorship. Censorship can be employed on political, security, moral, or religious grounds. Most societies use censorship to a greater or lesser degree, whether voluntary or institutional. It can affect artistic freedom, or it can be used in times of war to protect sensitive information that might be of assistance to an enemy. Censorship is used widely by repressive governments to keep their own activities secret and to prevent the dissemination of ideological, philosophical, or political views opposed to their own. (See also *freedom of expression, *freedom of information, *pornography.)

census, an official count of a population or a class of things. Responsibility for population censuses, which supply information essential for planning, is usually taken by governments. Central to the concept of a census are regularity (the UN recommends censuses every ten years) and the complete coverage of all residents, although in some countries only a sample census is taken. Generally, a census yields information on the size and distribution of a population, and its breakdown by age, sex, and, sometimes, race or ethnicity. It may also cover such topics as occupation, housing conditions, and education. The questions to be asked may be disputed. For example, in India, women's organizations have demanded the inclusion of questions about women's unpaid work so that its contribution to the economy can be assessed. Accurate census data are hard to achieve. Even the USA, which has long experience of census-taking and sophisti-

INDEX ON CENSORSHIP

£2.10 $3.60
June 1991
Vol 20 No 6

CHILE
DEATH & THE
MAIDEN
New play by
Ariel Dorfman

AFRICA
SUDAN
Women must go
ZIMBABWE
One-party party
ZAMBIA
A Maja-Pearce
John Mukela
CAMEROON
Pius Njawe

Inside the Soviet
Writers' Union
Sally Laird

A recent cover of *Index on Censorship*, a magazine which
fights **censorship** by printing the work of censored writers
and publishers. Contributions come from wherever work is
censored, and include first-hand testimonials.

cated analytical tools, can estimate its population only
within 2 per cent. In some countries illegal immigrants or
young men avoiding military conscription may evade the
enumerators, or the government may be loath to collect
information about ethnic minorities.

central bank, a *bank at the centre of a country's banking
system. Most central banks, such as the Federal Reserve System in the USA, the Bank of England in the UK, and the
Bundesbank in Germany, control the note issue and, by acting as lender of last resort to other financial institutions,
guarantee the banking system against collapse. In the UK
and some other countries, they license and regulate other
banks within their jurisdiction. They are also responsible for
the execution (and, in some countries, for the formulation)
of monetary policy. There are three principal instruments of
monetary policy. Firstly, the central bank can change the
fraction of deposits which banks must retain as cash. Secondly, the central bank can alter the interest rate known as
*bank rate at which it is prepared to lend to commercial
banks or the money market. Thirdly, the central bank can
engage in open-market operations, buying and selling financial securities. All these methods can be used to influence the
behaviour of banks and hence the amount of money in circulation. Plans to amalgamate national EC currencies into a
single European currency include the unification of national
central banks into a single European System of Central
Banks (ECSB) analogous to the US Federal Reserve System.
It is proposed that the ECSB be given independent legal or
constitutional responsibility for safeguarding price-level

stability in the EC (similar to that of the Bundesbank in Germany), and should not be subordinated on a day-by-day
basis to the financial judgement of the government (as, for
example, in France or the UK).

centralization, the concentration of power in one place
or organization. In territorial terms, centralization normally
implies that most decision-making authority is centred in the
capital city, in which the national government is located.
Centralization can also refer to the aggregation of power in
or by an organization, such as a political party, or by an individual office holder. Excessive centralization can impede
efficient decision-making and administration, and may
aggravate social, regional, or ethnic tensions. This was the
outcome of extremely centralized systems of economic planning used for decades in the former Soviet Union and its
erstwhile satellites in Eastern Europe. (See also *decentralization, *devolution, *federalism, *regionalism.)

Centre (in politics), the position intermediate between
*Left and *Right. Like Left and Right, the meaning of Cen-
tre varies according to time and place, but it suggests moderation and a willingness to compromise between
ideological extremes. Thus in recent political debate, the
Centre has stood for the *mixed economy, as opposed both
to untrammelled *capitalism and dogmatic *socialism.

Chadic languages, a group of over 100 languages with
30 million speakers, situated in central sub-Saharan Africa
to the west, south, and east of Lake Chad. Speakers are
found in southern Niger, northern Nigeria, northern
Cameroon, Chad, and the Central African Republic. Hausa
is by far the most important Chadic language, accounting
for 80 per cent of the total number of speakers (roughly 25
million). It is also used by many as a second language, being
a *lingua franca of Niger and northern Nigeria. (It is an
official language of Nigeria, and is widely used by newspapers and public media in the north of the country.) Hausa
is the only written Chadic language. There are two scripts in
use: an Arabic script called *àjàmí* and a Roman script called
bóokòo. The *àjàmí* script began to be written in the 16th century and is still used; *bóokòo*, however, introduced in the early
20th century, is now the most widespread. Hausa has assimilated a large number of loan-words, mostly from Arabic, but
also from other African languages, and (more recently) from
French and English. Chadic languages are part of Afro-Asiatic, a larger group which includes *Berber, *Cushitic, and
*Semitic.

chain store, one of a group of retail outlets with common
ownership, goods, and prices. The term first appeared in the
USA shortly before World War I, and in the UK in the
inter-war period. Chain stores are usually supplied from the
same warehouses, and most chain stores will usually supply
the same range of goods as the rest of the stores in the chain.
The number of shops necessary to constitute a chain is not
specified, but either regional or national coverage is usually
considered necessary.

chamber of commerce, an association of businesses or
business people located within a specified area who regularly
meet together. Membership may be voluntary or, as in
Germany and The Netherlands, compulsory. The function
of the chamber is to assist its members in their business interests, chiefly through providing information, training, and
representation.

charismatic movement, a movement of spiritual renewal found in Roman Catholicism and Protestantism, but particularly associated with *Pentecostal Churches. Known as 'charismatics', adherents believe that the experiences of the first disciples on receiving the Holy Spirit should be repeated in the present day. Particular emphasis is placed on 'baptism in the Holy Spirit', an experience equivalent to being 'born again' (reconverted to Jesus), often accompanied by 'spiritual gifts'. 'Speaking in tongues'—a highly charged, undeciphered syllabic language said to be directly transmitted by the Holy Spirit—is commonly practised among charismatics. The charismatic movement is strong in Latin America and among Black Churches and is increasingly popular elsewhere.

charity *non-governmental organization, *voluntary organization.

chemical and biological warfare (CBW), the use of synthetic poisonous substances, or organisms such as disease germs, to kill or injure the enemy. They include chlorine and 'mustard' gas (first used in World War I), various nerve gases, defoliant agents, and viruses and bacteria (for example, anthrax). The use of chemical and biological weapons is prohibited by the *Geneva Convention, but their production, possession, or transfer are not. Unlike their World War I counterparts, modern chemical weapons are sophisticated and may be delivered by long-range artillery or missile. The most notorious use of chemical weapons in recent years was Iraq's, against its Kurdish minority in 1988; similar weapons were deployed by Iraq, but not used, in the 1991 Gulf War. Biological weapons were banned under the Biological Weapons Convention of 1972, but research production was permitted for defensive purposes. Agreement regarding the limitation of chemical and biological weapons stands high on the agenda of the *Conference on Disarmament, but many states, particularly in the developing world, are reluctant to give up possession of such weapons because they act as a form of deterrence. Verification of any total ban presents difficulties: declared stocks of chemical and biological weapons can be checked and destroyed, but detection of undeclared production and stockpiling is almost impossible.

Cherokee, a confederation of *Plains Indian settlements, originally in the US states of North Carolina and Tennessee. Traditionally, the Cherokee lived in towns composed of longhouses, and were at first easily assimilated into the expanding USA. They adopted European methods of farming and government, including a bill of rights and a written constitution. The Cherokee also developed a distinct and original written language in the early 19th century, which gave rise to an indigenous literature and, later, a Cherokee-language newspaper. However, they were forcibly removed from their land in the mid-19th century to Oklahoma, and their reservation ceased to exist in the early 20th century.

chess, the best-known of all *board-games and the archetype of war-games played out on a board or table. Two players, white and black, sit at either end of the chessboard, which is divided into sixty-four squares with eight vertical and eight horizontal rows. Each player has sixteen men, which occupy prescribed places at the start of the game. On the first or back row are, from left to right, rook (castle), knight, bishop, queen, king, bishop, knight, rook. On the second row are eight pawns. Each piece has its own fixed type of movement. Players move one piece in turn, and the

Chess has spread around the world from its origins in India or China before the 6th century, as this picture of players in Mexico City testifies. It has also spread socially from its early position as 'the game of kings'.

object of the game is to manœuvre and capture pieces until the opposing king is so cornered that it cannot avoid being captured. This state is called checkmate and ends the game. Among skilled players, the game usually has three phases—the opening, middle game, and end game as the two opponents mobilize the forces available to them, react to loss or gain, and either go for the final kill or try to hold out for a draw. The laws of the game are controlled by the World Chess Federation, which organizes world chess events, including the world championships.

Chicago School (in sociology), a group of sociologists dominant in the USA in the 1920s and 1930s. The most prominent figure in the group, based at the University of Chicago, was Robert E. Park (1864–1944). The Chicago School combined a concern with processes of social change in US cities, a commitment to detailed social research, and theoretical innovation. They held that there was a distinctive urban way of life and recorded the behaviour of diverse social and ethnic groups. They explored patterns of residence, dividing the city into a series of concentric zones from the inner city to the suburbs, and charting the movement of groups between them. Their studies are recognized as landmarks in the analysis of urban structure, ethnic relations, and social problems.

chief, the ruler of a *tribe, *clan, or chiefdom. A chief's claim to position is often traced back to a founding ancestor, and may also incorporate a *creation myth of common origin. A chief exercises certain rights over his subjects, such as the gathering of taxes or tributes, but he also has obligations, which may include *ritual observances, or the distribution of tribute and booty through the society. Other common duties are the maintenance of order through *dispute resolution, and responsibility for defence of the territory against external aggression. Such forms of *political organization are found in many areas of the world, although the power held by chiefs has largely been superseded by other political forms, and a present-day chief may hold only a ceremonial position.

child abuse and neglect, the infliction of physical or emotional harm on children by adults. What behaviour is considered abusive varies between societies and social groups. In some, it is acceptable to beat a child after misbehaviour; in others, it is not. Children may suffer physical injuries; emotional damage through lengthy isolation or rejection; neglect resulting in malnutrition, sickness, or accidental injury. Abuse is most likely to occur in families under stress through poverty or internal conflict. Strategies to deal with the problem range from attempts at prevention by supporting families through *childcare, health, and other *social services to crisis intervention, which often entails removal of the child from the home, permanently or temporarily, as well as attempts to establish acceptable parental behaviour. The term 'collective child abuse' is sometimes used to refer to the damage to children caused by adverse environmental, social, or political conditions. The *UN Convention on the Rights of the Child highlights the responsibility of the state to protect all children and take special measures for child victims of collective abuse. However, the scope for dealing with these problems through international law is limited because the state is often the offender, and while the UN can monitor the activities of governments, there is no system for enforcement.

child benefit, a *social security benefit usually paid, without reference to means, to the mother for the maintenance of a child. First introduced in New Zealand in 1926, child-benefit schemes, which are financed from general taxation, are well established in the industrialized world and frequently found in developing countries. In some places, anxiety about falling birth-rates has been influential in their introduction, although experience indicates that child-benefit schemes have not markedly influenced population trends.

childbirth. Traditionally, women were assisted in childbirth by *midwives and childbirth normally took place at home, but during the 20th century medical intervention increased in the world's rich countries, with most births taking place in hospital. Medical advances, combined with the greatly improved health and nutrition of women, a reduction in the average number of their pregnancies, and their better living conditions, have contributed to a dramatic fall in the perinatal death rates of both mothers and babies. In recent years, there has been a movement towards 'natural' childbirth techniques whereby medical intervention and hospitalization are avoided, and the mother is encouraged to take greater control. In developing countries, however, death rates remain high. The World Health Organization has estimated that more women die of 'maternal causes' in India in one month than die in one year in North America, Europe, Japan, and Australia combined. The majority of maternal deaths and many infant deaths could be avoided by *family planning to help couples space their pregnancies; by screening pregnant women and ensuring that those most at risk are delivered in well-equipped clinics or hospitals; and by training traditional birth attendants.

childcare services, services provided by the state, charities, or commercial organizations to assist parents or to offer substitute parental care. Advice or practical help may be offered, for example through day nurseries or family aides, who assist over-burdened mothers. In Scandinavia, well-developed childcare systems have enabled women to choose to remain in full-time employment, while in the former

planned economies of Eastern Europe and the Soviet Union, state childcare was an important factor in maintaining a fully economically active work-force. Where a full substitute for parental care is necessary, current thinking suggests that institutional care has a negative effect on children to the extent that in Scandinavia placement in residential homes is largely restricted to children coming into care at adolescence. Children in temporary care are usually placed in foster homes and if the child has little prospect of returning home *adoption may be considered.

childhood, a phase in the human life-cycle, stretching roughly from infancy to puberty or to the legal age of majority. Because children can be distinguished from adults by certain biological and cognitive characteristics, childhood is perceived as separate from adulthood, and the transition is normally accompanied by a significant change in social and legal status and marked by *rites of passage and *initiation. The social significance, experience, and duration of childhood are extremely variable, both historically and geographically. For example, before the 20th century, children in Europe generally worked alongside their extended family in factory, field, or mine. In many developing countries, children still work alongside their parents (see *child labour) and young people marry and have children at an age when their

In Karachi, the centre of Pakistan's fishing industry, children earn a pittance shelling prawns. The low cost of employing **child labour** keeps down the price of the processed shellfish, much of which is now exported.

coevals elsewhere are required to remain in school and live under the guardianship of an adult. Despite extreme social and cultural diversity, increasingly it is the Western view of childhood as embodied in the *UN Convention on the Rights of the Child that dominates *social policy and *family policy.

child labour, work performed by children, often under compulsion and in violation of national and international labour standards, for the profit of others and their own sustenance. Most child labourers, some as young as 4 years, are concentrated in developing countries, where they are employed in agriculture, domestic service, or small, unregulated urban enterprises such as weavers' and mechanics' workshops or restaurants. In such societies, the child's contribution to the family's income may be vital to its survival. Child labour prevails where competition is strong, technologies are rudimentary, and production processes simple and routine. Children cannot cope as well as adults with complex work procedures, but they can work faster and are more agile and submissive. Employers use children to reduce labour and capital costs where there are fluctuations in demand and economic uncertainty. Children tend to be paid extremely low wages and some are bonded, working solely to pay off a debt. Many work long hours, frequently with no protection from toxic substances or dangerous machinery, no allowance being made for their physical vulnerability or developmental needs. They are likely to be powerless and unable to organize, and therefore experience severe employment instability. The *UN Convention on the Rights of the Child contains articles requiring signatory states to take measures against child labour, and agencies such as UNICEF are committed to protecting child labourers. The UN estimates that by the end of the 20th century there will be 375 million child labourers world-wide; there are presently an estimated 175 million children working in India alone. (See also *child sexual exploitation.)

child sexual abuse, the exploitation of children by adults in sexual activities to which they are unable to give informed consent, and which violate social taboos. Such activities range from exhibitionism to fondling, *incest, and *rape. The offender is usually a family member or someone closely associated with the child, rather than a stranger. Pre-adolescent girls are the most frequent victims, but children of both sexes and all ages, even infants, are affected. Although the child may be physically harmed, the psychological injury may be even greater and can last a lifetime. Often the victims feel guilty, socially isolated, and humiliated, and because of the fear instilled by the offenders may either not confide in an adult, or if they do, may not be believed. In the case of *incest, the whole family may collude to hide it. Social taboos require the concealment of child sexual abuse, so that the majority goes unreported. Without extensive help (increasingly provided by professional helplines), some victims become abusers themselves in adult life, or are unable to form satisfactory relationships.

child sexual exploitation, the use or trafficking of children in illicit sexual activities for the gratification and financial gain of adults. Those responsible include paedophiles and those who produce *pornography and organize *prostitution and sex tourism. Although some children become involved as a result of their parents' desperation to supplement the family income, child runaways are most at risk, since it is often only by exchanging sexual services for money, food, and shelter that they can survive. The physical and psychological damage suffered by victims is similar to that suffered by victims of *child sexual abuse, but the likelihood of contracting sexually transmitted diseases, and especially of becoming infected with the *Aids virus, or being subjected to violence is far greater. Although many markets in children cross national frontiers, consumers coming from rich countries, for instance, and suppliers from the poor, exploitation takes place in most parts of the world and is apparently increasing. This is partly due to the high value placed on sexual activity with children, and the profits derived from it. It is also due to the bribery and blackmail of officials by the organizers, and the reluctance of nations to admit to the problem and co-operate in confronting it.

Chinese language   *Sino-Tibetan languages.

Chinese medicine, an ancient medical system that goes back for five millennia, and is based on a philosophical speculation that the body, like everything else, is governed by the two principles of *yin and yang. In a healthy person, these complementary polarities are in a state of equilibrium. Diagnosis of disequilibrium is made by examination of the pulses at both wrists; there are twelve different pulses corresponding to the inner organs. Yin and yang energy is conveyed around the body by twelve channels or meridians, and treatment is effected either by moxibustion (the burning of small heaps of dried mugwort) or acupuncture (the insertion of needles) at precise points along these meridians. Herbal decoctions are also used. The first aim of Chinese medicine is to restore the orginal harmony of the body, often by advising on diet or lifestyle, as well as by recognizing conditions which may lead to disease. In the West, acupuncture in particular has become a popular form of *complementary medicine, and new ideas, such as acupuncture of the ear only, have been developed. In China, community health workers in rural areas combine modern scientific methods with traditional herbal remedies and acupuncture.

Chinese philosophy. The essence of Chinese philosophy is humanism: people and their society have captivated the Chinese mind since antiquity. Although there have been comparatively few metaphysical speculations, the Chinese generally see a unity between the individual and the universe. This harmonious relationship between the individual and the natural world characterizes the entire history of Chinese philosophy. During its 4,000 years of recorded history, Chinese philosophy has gone through four major periods. The first of these was the Classical Age, which culminated in the blossoming of the Hundred Schools during the Spring and Autumn (722–481 BC) and the Warring States (403–222 BC) Periods. It was followed by the Middle Period (206 BC–AD 960), when *Confucianism first emerged supreme in the socio-political sphere, only to give way to Neo-*Daoism and *Buddhism. The third period was the Neo-Confucian Stage (960–1850), during which Neo-Confucianism was the unchallenged state ideology. Last came the Modern Era, when *Marxism and *Maoism ousted the indigeneous Chinese schools of thought. Chinese philosophy in the 20th century is still in a formative stage, engaged in a sometimes confusing and chaotic attempt to bring together the whole of the Western philosophical tradition with its own native developments.

Chinese religion. Chinese society is characterized by an unbroken literate tradition from c.1500 BC to the present day and by its persistently centralized government. Despite much regional diversity, linguistic, geographic, and religious, the people of China share one mutually intelligible written language and have traditionally adhered simultaneously to aspects of *Confucianism, *Daoism, and *Buddhism. The official cult of the imperial state was Confucianism, which dominated education. Confucianism and Daoism permeated intellectual life, and the monastic tradition of Buddhism and priesthood of Daoism played a significant role in social life. Co-existing with these three religions were a range of popular beliefs and practices. Primary among these, and indeed the single most important religious practice, is the belief in *ancestor worship, the veneration of ancestors in the father's line of descent. The importance attached to the family unit is underpinned by a belief in the holiness and interdependently sacred nature of all life. In popular religious belief there are many gods and goddesses who may be specific to a locality or have a wider following. They are symbols of order, spirits of the dead, who are part of a bureaucratic heavenly order and are subject to promotion and demotion according to their performance. The inferior counterparts of the gods are demons, who are symbols of disorder and hostile influences. The gods may be approached through food-offerings, special rituals, or charms, which may be offered or performed at popular religious temples, shrines, or holy spots in the landscape. Similarly, offerings are made at the tombs of the family's ancestors, particularly at the time of the annual Spring Festival. The other chief festival is New Year's Day, a festival for all when the powers of life are renewed. In the 20th century, religious practice in mainland China has declined because of government repression following the introduction of communism in 1949. It remains, however, a cogent influence on the Chinese world-view, for example in the importance attached to family life, and flourishes in Taiwan and Hong Kong, despite the influence of westernization.

Chomsky, Noam (1928–), US linguistic philosopher and intellectual, professor at the Massachusetts Institute of Technology. Since the publication of *Syntactic Structures* in 1957, his work has revolutionized *linguistics. He is the founder of generative *grammar, which seeks to provide precise and explicit descriptions of the grammatical systems of *languages, and especially of transformational grammar, a version of generative grammar which derives the superficial structure of a sentence from an abstract underlying structure. He has been a major critic of the behaviourist view that language is just a form of behaviour, and has argued that linguists should focus not on linguistic performance but on the underlying linguistic competence. His main concern has been first *language acquisition. He has argued against empiricist views and for the rationalist position that language acquisition is made possible by the existence of an innate language faculty. Chomsky's other major writings are on US foreign policy and international politics.

Christadelphians, a *millenarian Christian sect which believes that the Christian message principally concerns the Second Coming of Christ to Jerusalem, to establish a *theocracy (government by God), and rejects the doctrine of the *Trinity. The Christadelphian Church was founded by John Thomas in 1848 in the USA, where it is strongest. It probably has about 60,000 full members in all.

Christian Churches. As Christianity spread over the world, a variety of traditions developed within it, which can be seen in the existence of many differing Christian Churches. Divisions between Christians were often occasioned by doctrinal disagreements, though social and political factors also played a part. The major traditions of Christianity are broadly divided along geographical lines. The *Roman Catholic Church is dominant in many countries of southern Europe and their former colonies in Central and South America, and in Poland and Ireland. *Protestant Churches, which broke away from Roman Catholicism in the 16th century, are concentrated in northern Europe and the USA. Emigration and missionary work have established both traditions in Australasia, Africa, and elsewhere. The *Eastern Orthodox Church, which finally separated from the Roman Catholic Church in the 11th century, is primary in parts of Eastern Europe, Belorussia, Georgia, Moldava, the Russian Federation, and parts of the Ukraine, and is scattered throughout the Middle East. The Oriental tradition is one of the most ancient in Christianity, composed of two strands: Nestorian and Monophysite Christianity, which both originated from important differences in doctrine in the 5th century. The Nestorian Church held that Christ united two persons, one divine and one human, while the Monophysites taught that Christ has only one, divine nature. The Monophysites broke with the mainstream Church in the 6th century, eventually forming four important Churches, which accept each other's ministries and sacraments: the *Coptic, *Ethiopian, *Armenian, and *Syrian Churches. These are sometimes known as the Oriental Orthodox Churches, and have held discussions for union with the Eastern Orthodox Church since 1966.

Christian Democracy, the ideology of a number of Centre-Right parties in post-war Europe, attempting to apply Christian principles to the management of industrial society. Arising in reaction both to classical *liberalism and to *Marxism, it sought to create social harmony in place of class divisions, and to use the state as a means of humanizing the capitalist economy. Its religious inspiration was predominantly, though not exclusively, Roman Catholic in character. Much stress was laid on strengthening the family, work associations, and other forms of *community. In economic policy, Christian Democrats have tended to embrace *corporatism; in international relations they have advocated the protection of *human rights, and been strong supporters of European integration. Christian Democratic parties have been powerful in Italy, Germany, and Belgium, often forming the main governing party; weaker, but still of some influence, in France and The Netherlands. Following the accession of President Kennedy in 1960, there was also an upsurge of Christian Democracy in Latin America, with particularly strong parties established in Chile and Venezuela; in the 1980s a similar tendency emerged in most of Central America.

Christianity, the Christian religion, based on the belief that *Jesus Christ is the incarnate Son of God and on his teachings. The world's largest religion, Christianity was originally a sect of *Judaism, and shares the Jewish belief in one omnipotent *God. Jesus, who was a Jew, was believed to be the Messiah and Son of God, the fulfilment in a new way of Jewish *millenarian and *eschatological prophecies of the Saviour. He proclaimed a new *covenant between God and humanity. Central to Christianity is the belief that Jesus is the incarnate Son of God, from which developed the doctrine of the *Trinity, whereby God is three persons, the Father, the Son, and the Holy Spirit, yet one God. Jesus is both God and man, one person in two natures. Jesus' death by crucifixion represents a *sacrifice through which humanity may be redeemed from its sinful condition (see *original sin), and his resurrection from the dead symbolizes the hope of eternal life, as expressed in the doctrine of *atonement. The Christian holy book is the *Bible, the first part of which, the Old Testament, is the same as the Hebrew Scriptures. Christians acknowledge the moral force of the Ten Commandments, but add to these Jesus' teaching of divine love, found in the second part of the Bible, the New Testament, a compilation of writings on Jesus' life and the development of the early Church and Christian doctrines. The doctrine of divine love is considered to be at the heart of God's relationship with humanity, and Christians are called on to display equal love in human relationships. Christianity has from the earliest times been characterized by a strong tradition of communual worship and, in many cases, well-developed ritual, but the *liturgy, or forms of worship, vary strikingly between the different *Christian Churches. Christian Churches also vary in the importance attached to the *sacraments, but the vast majority accept Baptism, in which the believer is initiated into membership of the Church, and the Eucharist, in which bread and wine are blessed and distributed between believers as a memorial or re-enactment of the Last Supper, the *Passover meal celebrated by Jesus and his disciples on the eve of his death. Christians believe in life after death, but the Churches vary in their interpretation of the *afterlife, heaven, and hell. Today Christianity is widespread throughout the world, with rapidly expanding congregations in Africa and South America, where movements such as *liberation theology have attempted to apply the Church's teaching to the problems of poverty and social injustice. Organizations such as the *World Council of Churches promote greater unity within Christianity; *church leaders such as the *pope, head of the *Roman Catholic Church, have historically been based in the West or Near East, but it is expected that developing countries will play a larger part in the leadership of the churches in acknowledgement of their growing congregations.

Christian Science, a religious body concerned with overcoming disease by a faith that denies the existence of matter, suffering, and sickness, based on the teaching of Mary Baker Eddy in *Science and Health* (1875). Centred in Boston, Massachusetts, it is found in all English-speaking countries, with about 600,000 full members. Among its publications is the *Christian Science Monitor*, a daily newspaper.

Christian year, the cyclical calendar of festivals and commemorations observed in Christian Churches, traditionally starting with *Advent. The two main categories are the major festivals celebrating the drama of Jesus' life and work, such as *Christmas and Easter, and the feast-days of various *saints, celebrated on fixed dates each year. In earliest times, the main emphasis was placed on Easter and *Pentecost. *Lent was established as a time of preparation for Easter, and thus the whole Lent–Easter–Pentecost cycle took form. The Christmas–*Epiphany cycle developed somewhat differently as a transformation of the pagan midwinter festival, with Christmas acquiring Advent as its time of preparation. Saints' days were particularly popular and numerous in the Roman Catholic Church, until the Second Vatican Council (1962–5) reduced their number. The different Christian Churches use different methods of calculating the festivals, which are celebrated according to the faith and regional culture of a Church.

Christmas, an annual Christian festival celebrating the birth of *Jesus Christ. The date of Jesus' birth is unknown, but tradition celebrates Christmas Day on 25 December, a date first recorded in AD 336. This almost certainly reflects the birth-date of the Iranian god Mithra, known as the Sun of Righteousness, but it is also close to the Roman Saturnali celebration (17 December), when gifts were given. Thus Christmas celebrations reflect both the pagan winter festival and Christian tradition. The importance of Christmas in the *Christian year varies regionally: in the *Eastern Orthodox Church, *Epiphany is considered to be more important, while most Western Churches exalt *Easter. In the West the festival often begins with midnight mass, celebrating the coming of the light into a darkened world. Christmas is celebrated with the exchange of gifts and feasting.

church, a building for Christian worship. Forms of worship vary greatly among the *Christian Churches and this is reflected in the different structure and layout of church buildings. Many are cross-shaped, and most have a nave, where the congregation stand or sit, and a chancel with seats for a choir and the altar, which is often in a small 'sanctuary' beyond the chancel. Most Western churches face east–west, with the altar at the eastern end. A church which is the seat of a bishop is known as a cathedral; many Protestant churches have rejected bishops and cathedrals although they are retained in the *Anglican Communion. The word 'Church' is also used to refer to the body of Christian believers, perceived as an organic community and symbolized as the mystical body of *Jesus Christ.

Churches of Christ, autonomous conservative *Protestant churches, mainly in the USA, which emerged from the 'Disciples of Christ' movement among early 19th-century *Presbyterians. They consider the *Bible to be all-sufficient and reject all human creeds and writings. There are about 2.5 million members.

church leaders. Systems of leadership and organization differ widely among different *Christian Churches. The *Roman Catholic, *Eastern Orthodox, and *Anglican Churches have an episcopal structure, that is, government by bishops, and claim apostolic succession: that their orders of bishops follow in direct succession from the original apostles. Episcopal Churches are hierarchical. Priests at various levels may celebrate the *sacrament of the Eucharist; the bishop, as higher in rank, may conduct confirmation and ordination, and heads a diocese. An archbishop, also called metropolitan or primate, is usually in charge of a province comprising many dioceses. The title patriarch is used for the heads of the various Eastern Churches. The head of the Roman Catholic Church is the *pope, also described as the Patriarch of Rome. Next in rank to the pope are the cardinals, of whom there are 100, appointed by him. Synod is the name given to church councils, composed at the highest level of bishops, which meet to discuss matters of discipline or doctrine. Synods exist within the Anglican, Roman Catholic, and Russian Orthodox Churches. Some

The central message of **Christianity**, Jesus Christ's life, death, and resurrection from the dead, is commemorated in different ways across the world. Here, at a Good Friday procession in Guatemala, mourners carry statues of the Virgin Mary and other saints. Veneration of the Virgin is particularly widespread in much of Latin America, where it is thought to have been carried forward from pre-Christian cults.

*Protestant churches use the title 'bishop' without claiming apostolic succession, for example the *Methodist Church in the USA and *Lutheran churches in Germany and Scandinavia. Elsewhere the Methodist Church is led by district chairmen and circuit superintendents. The latter title is also used in Lutheran, Presbyterian, and United Reformed churches. Other churches may have ordained ministers or administrative structures, but no formal hierarchy. Women have long played a role in *monasticism as nuns, but only the Lutheran, Methodist, Unitarian, United Reformed, Baptist, Independent, Black-led, and Church of Scotland traditions accept the ordination of women; this is, however, under discussion by the Church of England, but not by the Roman Catholic Church.

Church of England   *Anglican Communion.

CIA   *intelligence services.

cipher, a kind of *code based on transposing letters of the *alphabet used in intelligence, diplomacy, and elsewhere for protecting information from unauthorized people. Messages in cryptograms are encoded following patterns, called algorithms, and are decodable only by someone in possession of the key to a given pattern.

circumcision, the practice of removing the foreskin of the male or the genital labia and/or the clitoris of the female for religious or ritual reasons, usually as a form of *initiation or *rite of passage. It is found in various traditional societies throughout the world, from Africa to Aboriginal Australia. Male circumcision is also an important feature of Judaism and Islam. In Judaism the ceremony, known as *brit* in Hebrew, is performed by a professional *mohel* on the eighth day after birth, usually in the home, and circumcision is seen as a seal of the *covenant between God and the Jewish people. Islamic circumcision, *khitan*, commonly left until early adolescence, follows the tradition or *hadith of Muḥammad, although it is not demanded by the *Koran. Female circumcision, although less common than male, is also found within Arab, African, and other cultures, but some women's groups and those concerned with children's

rights regard the practice as genital mutilation and are campaigning for its abolition in countries which still permit it. It is illegal in the UK.

citizenship, membership of a political society, involving the possession of legal rights, which usually include the rights to vote and stand for political office. For many centuries citizenship was a privileged status extended only to those who fulfilled stipulated conditions such as owning fixed property, but in modern states citizens' rights are usually considered an aspect of *nationality, granted to all those born in a particular country as well as to permanent settlers. Citizens, as opposed to mere subjects, enjoy legal protection against arbitrary decisions by their governments, and they are supposed to play an active role in influencing government policy. The *Left tend to see citizenship as embracing social rights such as those provided by the *welfare state, whereas the *Right advance the idea of an active citizen as someone engaged in charitable work on behalf of the community.

civil defence, activities designed to protect civilians in the event of an enemy attack. In the UK, for example, during World War II, civilians took on many roles, such as firefighters and air-raid wardens, in order to protect the population. After 1945, in the context of potential preparations for nuclear warfare, the term became associated with the development of shelters, warnings, and other means to evacuate and defend the civilian population in the event of an attack. Critics argued that in the event of a nuclear war, no such defence was possible, and that such planning might encourage leaders to assume that a nuclear war was winnable. In some countries there are elaborate provisions for civil defence in the event of a war. Examples are Switzerland and the former Soviet Union, where a comprehensive programme, including compulsory civilian training of a people's *militia, widespread public information, and regular alerts, was developed.

civil disobedience   *direct action.

civil law, a term used to refer to *private law, the law governing the relations between private individuals or bodies, as

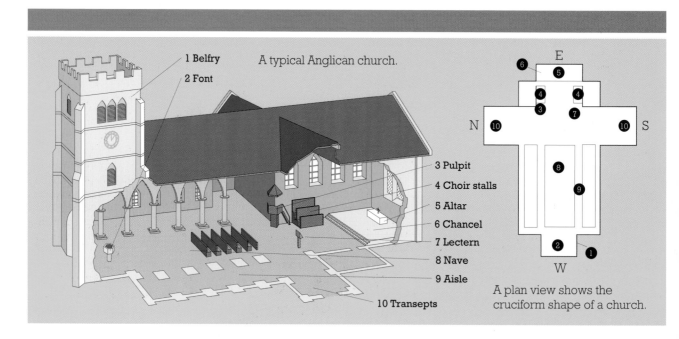

A typical Anglican church.

1 Belfry
2 Font
3 Pulpit
4 Choir stalls
5 Altar
6 Chancel
7 Lectern
8 Nave
9 Aisle
10 Transepts

A plan view shows the cruciform shape of a church.

In a ceremony marking the first stage of initiation into adult life Aborigine boys are prepared for **circumcision** at Milingimbi, Northern Australia. To accompany the ceremony a myth which validates the ritual is sung and played on tapping sticks and didjeridoo.

opposed to *criminal, *administrative, or *constitutional law. Areas covered by civil law include the principles governing commercial transactions, the settlement of disputes in the fields of *tort and *contract, and matters involving family, property, and inheritance. In England, civil and criminal cases are heard in separate *courts of law.

civil law systems, those in which *Roman law has had a decisive influence on legal principles, methods, and terminology in the field of *private law. They are to be found in Continental Europe, Latin America, and parts of Africa and Asia (in modified form). The great 6th-century codification of Roman law, the *Corpus Juris Civilis* ('Body of civil law'), forms the basis of such systems, which are therefore called civil law systems. The development of different nation-states in Europe led to the codification of laws into distinctive systems, most notably the *Code Napoléon*, adopted in France in 1804 (and in other European countries through Napoleonic expansion), and the *Bürgerliches Gesetzbuch*, the German Civil Code, which came into force in 1900. Civil law systems were subsequently exported through the process

of colonial domination (for example, to some African countries and to Latin America) or imported out of respect for an intellectual tradition (for example, in Japan). An important characteristic of civil law codes is the division of private law into conceptual and organizational categories, such as the law of persons, *property, *obligations, and delict (*tort), following the compilations of the Roman jurists. In principle, these codes require no interpretation, only application. In practice, interpretation and judicial development of the law are required. Judicial reasoning is marked by an economy of style, using logical deductions from the principles deemed to underlie the code. Although *case law has acquired an important role as a source of law, there is no system of binding judicial *precedent, as in *common law systems. The civil law has always accorded a higher status to the doctrinal and analytic work of scholars in the universities. Furthermore, court procedures rely less heavily on oral advocacy than is the case in common law systems. Nevertheless, the resolution of legal issues raised by common social, economic, and political problems is often similar, despite the different methodologies and traditions of the two systems.

civil rights, those rights which collectively safeguard political freedom and personal liberty. They are enumerated in the *International Covenant on Civil and Political Rights (1966) and are generally taken to include *freedom of expression, association, movement, conscience, and religion; the right to liberty and to *privacy, the right to vote, and the right to a fair trial. In many countries, civil rights are guaranteed to citizens through a *bill of rights or the *constitution. Civil rights constitute a subset of *human rights. The Civil Rights Movement was the movement in the USA in the 1960s for full legal and civil rights for Blacks.

civil service, a body of officials employed by a *state for the administration of civil affairs. Constitutionally subordinate to the government, the civil service is usually organized into departments with specific functions, such as finance, health care, agriculture, or trade and industry. Under *parliamentary government, an elected minister is the head of each department, and responsible for it to the *legislature. Under presidential government, the *president is administrator-in-chief; subordinate officials are appointed by and answerable to him. Civil servants operate within a hierarchical *bureaucracy, with posts ranging from clerical grades to an administrative élite, which advises elected ministers. In countries which follow the Westminster system, the civil service is traditionally non-partisan and favours anonymity. By contrast, the civil service in France and Germany exhibits considerable *esprit de corps*, regarding itself as the embodiment of the state, above rather than beneath politics. In the USA, top civil servants are often political figures. Like all bureaucracies, the civil services are open to charges of cumbersomeness and abuse of power.

civil society, a term originally applied to any politically organized society, which has come to refer to social institutions and practices that do not form part of the formal apparatus of the *state. According to *social contract theorists such as *Hobbes and *Locke, civil society was formed when individuals, originally in a disorganized state of nature, made a pact of association and agreed to recognize political authority. Modern usage stems chiefly from *Hegel, who in *Philosophy of Right* (1821) applied the term to an economic and social order based on free co-operation between individuals, involving private property, market exchange, corporations, and other voluntary associations. Recently communist regimes have been criticized by their citizens for subjecting all social relationships to political control, thereby obliterating the proper sphere of civil society.

civil war (internal war), a state of sustained, large-scale violent conflict between political, religious, ethnic, or ideological groups within a state. Such conflict can take place in order to overthrow the government, or to secede from the state. An example of the former is the civil war in Russia (1918–20), which followed the 1917 *Revolution; an example of the latter is the American Civil War (1861–5), which resulted from the attempt at *secession on the part of the Confederate States. Groups may resort to war if they feel their interests are not fairly reflected in government, or if they want to impose on the state an alternative ideology or political regime. There is no well-defined characteristic by which a conflict is designated a civil war, but a number of features would generally need to be present. The scale of violence in qualitative and quantitative terms would be an important consideration; factors might include the numbers of people involved, the extent of the geographical area, and the military capability deployed by both sides. A key characteristic is the breakdown of the government's authority: the insurgents would have to exert military and administrative control over a significant proportion of the state's territory and also command the allegiance of a significant

proportion of the state's population. This sort of consideration would determine whether an insurgent force was recognized diplomatically by other states as having 'belligerent status' (that is, recognized as the responsible authority with respect to the territory it controls, and treated on a par with the legitimate government). Many wars since 1945 have been internal or civil wars, brought about by state boundaries fixed in the colonial period which ignore ethnic and religious diversity, resulting in post-colonial struggles for power and influence in the newly created states (see *communal conflict). Such civil wars have often been sustained and even escalated because of intervention by *superpowers, neighbouring states, or other major powers who have acted to protect their own perceived interests or those of client groups within these conflicts. There have been more than thirty civil wars since 1945, including those in Angola, Cambodia, Nicaragua, El Salvador, Lebanon, Nigeria, Mozambique, Ethiopia, Pakistan, Yemen, and Yugoslavia.

clan, a group of people within a wider society who claim descent from a common ancestor and are usually distinguished by a common clan name, as, for example, the Highland clans of Scotland. The term is rather a general one, and can refer to groups organized around different forms of *lineage. In some societies, the ancestor from whom members claim descent may be a mythical figure or, as in forms of *totemism, an animal or other non-human figure. Members of a clan have obligations towards each other, and their *marriages are usually exogamous: that is, members must marry outside the clan.

class   *social class.

class action, litigation pursued by one or more persons for themselves and on behalf of others, either in order to further the interests of a group to which they all belong (as, for example, victims of sex discrimination) or to aggregate their claims in order to strengthen their bargaining power (as, for example, when the victims of a defective drug seek compensation from the manufacturer). Class actions are possible under *civil law in the USA and some other countries, although in practice they are more common and more successful in the USA, where an attorney has a major interest in winning the case, since his or her fee is based on the damages awarded to the whole class of victims, including the client.

classical economics, the system of economic theory expounded in the writings of (mainly British) economists between *Smith (whose *Wealth of Nations* was published in 1776) and *Mill (whose *Principles of Political Economy* appeared in 1848). The principal contributors to classical economic theory were Smith, Jean-Baptiste Say (1767–1832), *Ricardo, Robert Malthus (1766–1834), and Mill. The central idea in classical economics is that of *competition. Although individuals behave solely to benefit themselves, competitive markets (Adam Smith's 'invisible hand') ensure that this is enough to lead to efficient allocation of *resources and *production, and no excess *profits. Government has a desirable economic role (above that of providing law and order) only in the context of market failure, that is, where competition does not exist. The *supply of every *good and every *factor of production will be equal to *demand. The equilibrating element in all markets is price, the price of labour being the wage. This was assumed by the classical economists to tend in the long run to subsistence level, any persistent wage above this level calling forth faster population growth. At the same time, Say's Law, that 'supply creates its own demand', was supposed to rule out persistent or involuntary unemployment of labour. The analysis of *rent was another preoccupation of classical economics because the need was felt to explain and justify the distribution of income among the owners of *labour, *capital, and *land. Ricardo argued that rent was equal to the surplus producible on more fertile land in competition with less fertile land. Classical economics assumes both savings and investment to be predominantly determined by *interest rates, one of the aspects disputed in the 20th century by *Keynes. The classical view of growth theory and economic development was that a stationary state was expected to materialize at some stage in the future. (See also *development economics.) Following the new *marginal analysis pioneered in the second half of the 19th century by the British economist William Stanley Jevons (1835–82), and the Austrian economist Carl Menger (1840–1921), classical economics developed into the neoclassical economics of *Walras, *Pareto, *Marshall, and others. Neo-classical theory remains the scientific core of economic, especially micro-economic, analysis today.

class struggle, the theory of a permanent condition of social conflict between *social classes. Such an idea emerged in the French Revolution (1789), but it was given its theoretical and ideological form by *Marx and Friedrich Engels in the Communist Manifesto (1848), which asserted that 'the history of all society up to now is the history of class struggle'. According to *communist theory, the class struggle is to culminate in the victory of the working class, or proletariat, after which an ideal society based on shared resources would be established. The theory of conflict was underpinnned by *dialectical materialism, according to which the clashes of opposing systems result in positive progress. With the coming to power of the Bolsheviks in Russia (1917) and the Communists in China (1949), a focus on struggle and contradictions came to characterize not only domestic politics but also foreign policy in those countries and others influenced by them. The economic failure of socialism and communism, the collapse of Soviet control over Eastern Europe during the 1980s, and increased opportunities resulting from social change, *industrialization, and enhanced legal rights, such as the right to form *trade unions, have undermined the idea of class struggle. In developing countries, where inequality and poverty may be extreme, notions of class struggle retain some appeal, but are often only loosely linked to those of Marx and Engels.

clearing house, an institution where mutual *debts are settled. For example, the London Bankers' clearing house and the New York clearing house daily calculate the amounts owed by each member *bank to each other bank as a result of that day's cheque transactions by its customers. The debts are then settled by transferring commercial banks' balances at the *central bank. The banks which are members of clearing houses are commercial banks (not merchant banks) and are known as clearing banks.

clientelism, term used to refer to a social or political system based on relations between clients and patrons. It has a long tradition and is found in many contemporary societies, especially in Africa, Asia, and South America. It flourishes where impersonal rules for the allocation of resources are lacking or are ignored. The patron–client relationship, which is often based on *kinship or common geographic origin, is reciprocal with the client performing special duties, giving political support, or contributing to the patron's status, in exchange for the patron's help. The patron may control access to public works contracts, employment or promotion in government service, education and medical treatment, or even protection from the law. In societies where patron–client relations are pervasive, collective action through trade unions or political parties may be difficult to organize. While the system is deeply rooted in some societies, for example the *Mafia in Italy, and provides access to goods, services, and protection for many otherwise powerless people, critics have pointed to the scope for injustice and *corruption, and the tendency of leaders to bolster their position by gathering about them members of their kin or ethnic group, who demand a share of their power and perquisites and exclude others.

climate change   *greenhouse effect, *ozone depletion.

clinical linguistics, the analysis and treatment of *language disorders. These can occur at any level of linguistic organization, *phonetic, *phonological, *grammatical, or *semantic as deviance or delay in learning. A language disability can manifest itself either in spoken or in written language, and either at the production or the comprehension stage. There may be delays in learning language or difficulties in using it. Clinical linguistics uses the theories, methods, and findings of *linguistics to elucidate the nature of pathological conditions in so far as these are manifested in language. (See also *aphasia, *dyslexia.)

clinical psychology, the application of procedures derived from theory and research in *psychology to the assessment and treatment of mental and physical disorders. The term was first used in the 19th century to refer to methods of assessing physical and mental handicap. Assessment of clinical conditions such as brain damage developed during the two World Wars. After World War II clinical psychology also became important for procedures of rehabilitation and especially for the various *psychotherapies. Many of the latter derived initially from *psychoanalysis, but the research on which *learning theories were based gave rise to treatments which did not rely on drugs or make medical assumptions about abnormal behaviour being an 'illness'. These *behaviour therapies have proved fairly successful in the treatment of *phobias and some other disorders. Clinical psychologists are now likely to be eclectic rather than advocates of particular theoretical or therapeutic models. Nevertheless, the view that many abnormalities are at least partly caused by experience ('faulty learning') and can be improved by procedures akin to those of *conditioning remains fundamental to most clinical psychologists.

closed shop (in industrial relations), a workplace in which, by agreement or arrangement, only *trade-union members are employed; it may be a pre-entry or post-entry closed shop, depending on whether a worker must be a union member before being engaged. Pre-entry closed shops give the union control of entry to an occupation. While the closed shop has been part of many *collective-bargaining agreements, particularly in English-speaking industrial countries, it is prohibited or regarded as superfluous, for example, in many European continental countries and in Latin America. The closed shop strengthens the union and may encourage orderly *industrial relations. Opponents of the closed shop argue that it infringes the *civil rights of the individual worker and unduly restricts the freedom of the employer to hire and fire. Some developing countries, such as Mexico and the Philippines, have made legal provision for closed shops; elsewhere governments, as in the UK in the 1980s, have legislated to curb the practice.

coalition government, a government made up of two or more political parties. Coalitions are normally formed in parliamentary systems when no single party has a majority of seats in the *legislature. This is a frequent though not inevitable result of an election held under *proportional representation. In *two-party systems, coalitions are uncommon, because one party normally has a majority in the legislature. Coalitions normally have between two and five parties; many contain the fewest number of parties needed to gain a majority of seats. The distribution of executive posts between the parties is roughly proportional to parliamentary strength. Belgium, France, Germany, The Netherlands, and the Scandinavian countries conform to this overall pattern. 'Grand coalitions' of all major parties are another form of coalition, which tend to be formed in times of national emergency, usually war. Critics of coalition government consider it less stable than government by a single party, because of the need to compromise policies; furthermore, each participating party has the power to bring down the government. This power can give parties with a small number of seats disproportionate influence, as has happened in Israel. However, many coalitions have provided stable government, as, for example, in Germany. Coalition government is also said to encourage a more conciliatory style of politics, in contrast to the adversarial style often practised in two-party systems.

cock-fighting, the sport of setting two game-cocks against each other in a circular cockpit where, in principle, they fight to the death. Banned in the UK and most of North America, it flourishes in some Latin American countries, notably Haiti, Mexico, and Puerto Rico. Along with other brutal animal sports such as dog-fighting, it has recently resurfaced in the UK, indicating that it has continued to exist illegally. The sport attracts gamblers prepared to wager large sums before and during a fight. Game-cocks are trained to fight and in action wear spurs of metal or bone up to 6 cm (2.5 inches) long fixed over their natural spurs. Local rules vary, but a badly injured bird may now be withdrawn

In Bali, Indonesia, fighting cocks are provoked before the fight begins. In Eastern countries where **cock-fighting** is popular, spectators identify strongly with one bird.

instead of being left to die. Fights may have a time limit, and there are provisions for the bird that refuses to fight. His handler sets him breast to breast with the other bird, and if he still refuses, the judge declares that he has quit.

code, a system of rules for matching signs with units of information to facilitate communication, as in the Morse *alphabet in telecommunication, *alphanumeric codes in computer programming, and signals on the railways. Linguists often view *language as a code, a set of rules pairing sounds with meanings.

Code Napoléon (or *Code Civil*), the French civil code, a complete body of written law, adopted in 1804 and largely still in force today. Napoleon himself took an active part in drafting the code, which draws on the philosophical heritage of the 18th-century Enlightenment, as well as the legal heritage of *Roman law. The code enshrines the principles of equality, the separation of civil and ecclesiastical jurisdictions, and the freedom of the individual. With its compressed legislative style (the entire law of *tort is set out in five articles), the *Code* represents perhaps the pinnacle of the codification achievement; versions of it were adopted in various European countries, and later spread through colonization to Latin America and parts of Africa. Today, certain parts of the *Code*, such as family law, have been amended to reflect changing public attitudes, removing, for example, the absolute power of the husband and father in the family.

cognitive development, a child's acquisition, organization, and use of knowledge from infancy to adulthood. The most influential theory was enunciated by *Piaget, who described a universal series of stages in intellectual development. During the sensorimotor period (from birth to 18 months), the infant acquires basic knowledge of objects, causes, space, and time; in the concrete operational period (up to about 11 years) the young child gradually acquires concepts of number, volume, classification, and measurement in specific contexts; in the formal operational stage (11 to adulthood) the adolescent becomes able to reason systematically about hypothetical propositions. Other theorists, notably *Bruner and the Russian psychologist Lev Vygotsky (1896–1934), have laid greater stress on the role of *language development in cognitive growth. It is argued that some specifically human thought processes occur as 'speech for self' and are acquired as language develops over the first five years of life. Social and cultural aspects of language are therefore implicated in the development of thought. Another contemporary approach in *cognitive psychology takes the computer as a model for the changing information-processing capacities of the child. This approach suggests that the basic differences between child and adult may be quantitative rather than qualitative and that development may reflect changes in information-processing capacity.

cognitive dissonance, a state of unpleasant arousal experienced by people who hold inconsistent attitudes or whose behaviour is inconsistent with their beliefs. Dissonance theory suggests that beliefs are determined by psychological needs and that behaviour may cause attitudes rather than vice versa. In *A Theory of Cognitive Dissonance* (1962), Leon Festinger proposed that if people are induced to act inconsistently with their attitudes they will often change their attitudes in an effort to eliminate the feeling of dissonance. Thus a smoker may 'rationalize' his habit by scorning evidence for health damage caused by cigarette smoking.

For some, **collecting** is a way of accumulating objects which will increase in value, while other enthusiasts collect articles which offer a link with the past, as may these remnants of the former East German communist regime, on sale in Berlin.

cognitive psychology, the branch of *psychology dealing with the higher mental faculties: *perception, *memory, *language, and thought. Cognitive psychologists are interested in how humans take in information through the senses (particularly in reading and speech), store it in *memory, and manipulate it during thinking and reasoning. Cognitive psychology has been one of two major developments in psychology since World War II (the other being *social psychology). Its concern with internal mental life and human development contrasts with the weakness of *behaviourism in such areas. Child psychology and *cognitive development are areas of major concern. It includes the study of *attention as an executive controller of mental activity. The computer has provided cognitive psychologists with a metaphor for looking at mental processes, using the language of computer programming and the concepts of information input, storage, retrieval, and processing to describe the brain as an information-processing machine. Cognitive psychology includes research in *artificial intelligence and the brain sciences, in particular neuropsychology. After brain damage, the loss or disruption to cognitive processes, such as an inability to read or speak normally (see *dyslexia and *aphasia), or *memory disorder, can appear in very specific forms, such as loss of memory just for faces or an inability to name familiar objects. Cognitive psychology assumes that the brain is organized in terms of 'faculties', or 'modules' for some functions, with specific areas of the brain sometimes dedicated to specific tasks such as the recognition of faces, putting a name to objects, pronouncing words, or understanding language. Recently the computer metaphor has been abandoned by some scientists, since the brain utilizes fundamentally different principles of computation. They suggest that modelling the electrical activity of large networks of nerve cells in the brain allows a more direct understanding of the brain's possibly unique methods of information-processing.

cohabitation, the situation of two people living together as man and wife. Cohabitation without legal or religious marriage is widespread in poorer communities and is an increasing feature of more affluent societies. A common pattern is for couples to live together before *marriage, and to marry when their first child is expected. In recent years, however, there has been an increasing tendency for unmarried cohabitation to replace marriage altogether, even after the birth of children. This is particularly prevalent in Scandinavian countries. In the UK, the term 'common law marriage' historically referred to a form of marriage once regarded as legally effective in the *common law, despite the absence of formalities. Such relationships are no longer legally recognized, but the expression is still used inaccurately to describe cohabitation. Cohabitees may draw up a formal contract, but the legal effects of such contracts are uncertain. Although a few legal systems treat cohabitation as if it were a marriage, most do not, because this may be seen either to devalue marriage or to deny people the opportunity to avoid control by *family law. Nevertheless, some degree of legal recognition has been inevitable. Thus in some countries legal remedies are available to unmarried cohabiting couples, partly as a response to reasonable expectations they may have held on entering the relationship (such as obtaining a share in property in joint use or in the partner's estate, or to prevent one partner from obtaining unfair advantages over the other), but also out of recognition of their domestic circumstances (for example, protection may be available against *domestic violence).

cohort (in demography and sociology), a group of persons who have experienced the same event in a period. Cohort studies make it possible to compare the experiences of different age-groups in a population or to analyse the experiences of a group over time. In the UK, a notable cohort study (the Medical Research Council National Survey of Health and Development) has followed from birth the progress of 5,000 people born in 1946. It has proved possible to trace the effects of childhood experience, health, and education on subsequent adult life. For example, cohort members who lost a parent through divorce during childhood were earning less and had lower educational attainments at the age of 26 than those whose parents had remained married or who had lost a parent through death.

coin collecting, the hobby of collecting coins (or medals); also known as numismatics. Collecting coins as a hobby dates back at least to the Roman era. Because coins have been struck by many nations since early times and therefore come in an enormous range, most collectors specialize, for example, in particular countries, designs, eras, or denominations. Beginners usually start with coins in circulation and then add to them, collecting through dealers and auctioneers. The highest price paid for a coin was £1 million in a 1980 private sale—for a Greek silver decadrachm c.425 BC. Gold coins, of course, have a substantial intrinsic value and are often treated as a form of investment.

cold war   *East–West relations.

collateral, a marketable *asset which is offered to a lender by a private borrower as a security for the *loan. In the event of the borrower not repaying the loan at the time(s) specified, the lender has some right to take possession and dispose of the collateral, as specified in the loan agreement. In the case of a *mortgage, land or a building is the normal form of collateral. Government borrowers do not normally offer collateral, and this was a central feature of the 1980s international *debt crisis. A notable exception was the loan by the multinational De Beers to the former Soviet Union of $1 billion in 1990, with the collateral in diamond stocks.

collecting, the hobby of collecting objects, usually belonging to a particular group such as paintings, furniture, shells, first editions, comics, cigarette cards, and antique cars. (See also *coin collecting and *stamp collecting.) So wide are some of these fields that many collectors, for financial reasons or for their own satisfaction, prefer to specialize in a particular area. Aesthetic appeal may or may not be a factor, though some collectors keep an eye out for financial gain and the likely resale value at the dealer or auction-house. Few art collectors can afford Old or Modern Masters, but many small areas offer pleasure and reward, and collectors happily specialize in, for example, cartoons and caricatures, profile portraits, marine drawings, decorative tiles, early Victorian picture-trays, or books with painted fore-edges. A recent development has been the rise of sports collecting. In the field of cricketana, there are now specialist collectors in such apparently narrow areas as cricketing aquatints, stat-uettes, autographs, sheet-music covers, bats and miniature bats, scorebooks, caps and blazers, letters, and many others. In this, as in other fields, a specialist literature has arisen to keep collectors informed, and business has swelled at the auction-houses.

collective bargaining (in *industrial relations), negotiations between management and employees' representatives, usually *trade unions, over pay and other conditions of employment. Collective bargaining is the major feature of industrial relations when the employer recognizes a trade union. Negotiations are held when the existing, often annual, pay agreement expires, and can take place nationally, at industry level, or locally in individual workplaces. Talks may also take place over matters such as the number of hours worked, holidays, *productivity, or in the event of a threat to job security or the introduction of new technology. When agreement cannot be reached, an industrial dispute arises, which may lead to conciliation, arbitration, or *industrial action. In some countries the unions co-ordinate their efforts, as in the 'spring offensive' each year in Japan.

collective ownership, ownership of land or of an enterprise in common, by all those who work on or in it (in the case of a *co-operative), or by the state (as a consequence of *nationalization). (The terms public and social ownership are sometimes used in preference to nationalized property.) Collective ownership may date from the creation of a firm, or it may result from the buying out of a company's shareholders, or from their expropriation by the state. The principle of ownership by all is that all should benefit, rather than just the wealthy few. Land and industry are sometimes taken into collective ownership because they are under-employed or inefficiently run, or because the enterprise is bankrupt. Collective ownership, at least in theory, is a cardinal element of *communism, but with the decline of *planned economies there are few countries where wholesale collective ownership is practised. In China, for example, collective farms have to some extent been replaced by farms run by individual households.

collective security, a system of international security co-operation whereby a group of states unites with the agreed purpose of taking joint action to attack an aggressor state if one or more of them is attacked. It is often seen as an alternative to relying on the *balance of power mechanism. Collective-security systems are difficult to put into practice; in the 1930s, the concept of collective security promoted by the League of Nations failed to prevent World War II, because membership of the collective mechanism was not universal. After 1945 the *UN Organization sought to ensure security through collective mechanisms, but because of the persistence of the idea of national *sovereignty and national interest, as well as difficulties in defining *aggression, so far it has been impossible to establish an international collective security force capable of dealing with international conflicts. On the other hand, despite the lack of such a force, the UN was able to demonstrate a collective response in its support of the US-led coalition in the 1991 Gulf War

collectivism, the view that society's affairs, and especially its economic life, should as far as possible be subject to collective control. It is typically opposed to *individualism, private property, and the *free market. Collectivists believe that societies do best when they are consciously directed by some agency, usually but not necessarily the state, to achieve common ends. In the late 19th and early 20th centuries, many socialists described themselves as collectivists; now the term is almost entirely used by individualists to refer to policies and regimes of which they disapprove.

Colombo Plan (Colombo Plan for Co-operative Economic Development in South Asia and the Pacific), a co-operative attempt to strengthen the economies of Asia and the Pacific. The plan was originally formulated by the *Commonwealth, but the largest donor is now the USA. Assistance takes the form of educational aid, training programmes, food aid, loans, equipment, and technical co-operation. The plan has twenty-six members and its headquarters are in Colombo, Sri Lanka.

colony (dependency, protectorate), a country or territory which is settled by and/or subject to the control of another, with supreme legislative and administrative power resting with the controlling country. The terms 'colony' and 'dependency' are often used interchangeably, while a protectorate, although subordinate to a 'protecting' power, may retain some autonomy. Colonies have existed since ancient times, but the modern process of colonialism is mainly associated with the activities of the European powers from the 15th to the 19th centuries. Portugal, Spain, Holland, Britain, and France all acquired control over extensive areas of the Americas, Africa, Asia, and Australasia during this period, but it was the 19th-century process of *imperialism which established the great colonial empires of Britain and France. Most of Europe's colonial possessions were surrendered in the twenty years following World War II in the process known as decolonization, but a few have been retained. The UK, for example, still controls Gibraltar, Hong Kong (due to revert to China in 1997), and the Falkland Islands (Malvinas). Most of Britain's former colonies are members of the *Commonwealth.

COMECON (Council for Mutual Economic Assistance), the English name for an economic organization of Soviet-bloc countries which was dissolved in 1991. Its former members were Bulgaria, Cuba, Czechoslovakia, German Democratic Republic (East Germany), Hungary, Mongolia, Poland, Romania, the Soviet Union, and Vietnam. Set up in 1949, it was the second pillar, with the *Warsaw Pact, of Soviet influence in Europe. Its purpose was to encourage interdependence in trade and production. It achieved little until 1962, when the agreements restricting the satellite countries to limited production and to economic dependency on the Soviet Union were enforced. After the revolutions which overthrew the governments of Eastern Europe in 1989, COMECON was formally disbanded in 1991.

command economy *planned economy.

commercial law, in common law systems, the law of business, covering mercantile law, *company law, *competition law, *insolvency, *intellectual property, and *patents. Commercial law is not a separate branch of law in common law systems, but in civil law systems there is often a distinct body of law codified into a commercial code which contains definitions and applies to specified transactions. In addition to systems of national laws there are also EC laws governing particular areas, for example competition law, and internationally recognized concepts such as the different types of contractual form available for the carriage of goods by sea.

Commodity price fluctuation

Real commodity prices, 1970–87

In 1985 primary commodities, such as sugar and tin, accounted for over half of developing countries' exports (excluding India and China). Shifts in the prices of commodities can seriously affect a country's ability to purchase essential imports. The graph below shows how the price of thirty-three primary commodities fluctuated in the 1970s and fell sharply after 1980. The fluctuations in the price of petroleum are also shown.

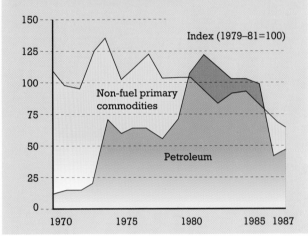

Source: *World Development Report 1988*. World Bank

commodity, a *good; or any raw or semi-processed material which is usually traded internationally. Commodities are classified into agricultural products and minerals. Agricultural products are further classified into foods, which include tree crops, such as coffee, tea, or cocoa, and arable crops, such as wheat, rice, or soybeans, and non-foods, such as timber, natural rubber, or jute. Minerals comprise fossil fuels such as oil, gas, or coal, and metals such as copper, aluminium, or zinc.

commodity market, a *market in a raw or semi-processed material. For many *commodities there is a single world price, or a narrow range of prices, for a particular grade of product (for example, oil); and for many there is a single dominant market where most deals take place. For example, most metal commodities are bought and sold on the London metal exchanges. Commodity stabilization agreements are sometimes made between producing and/or consuming countries to try to stabilize price. These compare with occasional more ambitious attempts to control the long-term level of prices, such as the *OPEC oil *cartel. For a stabilization agreement to work, a central fund is necessary. It is used to buy up quantities of the commodity (thus reducing supply) when the price is below the desired level. These supplies can then be offered for sale when the price is above the desired level. Fluctuations in the world prices of commodities may cause severe hardship, particularly to the economies of developing countries, which tend to be dependent for foreign exchange on the export of a limited range of *primary industry. (See also *futures markets.)

common land, land that is subject to rights of common. These are rights to take the produce from land of which the

A drilling rig at a uranium mine in Kerksdorp, South Africa. A combination of advanced technology and cheap labour have enabled South Africa to exploit its mineral **commodities** successfully, unlike many other African countries.

right-holder is not the owner, for example a right of pasture. They are private rights, and need not be open to all. The right may be restricted, for example, to a portion of the year.

common law systems, the family of legal systems deriving from the law as developed by the King's judges in England and Wales after the Norman conquest in 1066. These include English law and Irish law, and most legal systems in the USA and Commonwealth countries, with modifications where appropriate to local custom (for example, to *Hindu law in India, and to African *customary law in Africa). The common law was not systematically developed from a theoretical basis, as *civil law systems were, but evolved as a pragmatic response to specific disputes. It remained largely in the hands of a small group of professional practitioners, educated through an apprenticeship process; it was from their ranks that judges were appointed. Their professional solidarity meant that common law was largely resistant to *Roman law influence, although this alone was taught in the universities until the famous lectures on English law by Sir William Blackstone (1723–80) at Oxford in the 1750s. As a result of the limited scope of the common law by the 16th century, the Chancellors of England had developed a body of principles and rules, known as *equity, which provided remedies in cases where the common law had failed to do so. Today, these equitable principles and remedies have been

integrated into the mainstream of the common law. In common law systems, *case law is still seen as a central source of law, even if frequently subject to the supreme authority of *statute. Common law procedures tend to maximize the role of *advocates: the judge decides the issues on the basis of material presented in argument, rather than relying on abstract legal principles (see *adversarial procedure). In this way, common law has developed as a response to specific cases, and has been less shaped by the theorizing of legal scholars than has civil law.

common market, a group of countries in which member states have no *tariffs or other restrictions on *trade or movements of resources such as labour or capital between each other, while maintaining common tariffs and restrictions against outside countries. Similar types of institutions are: a free-trade area, where trade between member states is unrestricted but each country may have its own separate trade barriers against outside countries; a customs union, where there is both free trade between members and a common external tariff, but movement of *factors of production such as labour or capital between members is not necessarily unrestricted; and an economic union where, as well as a common market, there exists substantial or complete unification of monetary and *fiscal policy. The *EC is an example of a common market which is endeavouring to move towards economic union.

common security, a concept first introduced by the Swedish Prime Minister Olof Palme, who suggested a 300-km-wide nuclear-free zone straddling the East–West divide (see *East–West relations), in order to provide a security zone, as well as ensuring time and opportunity to cope with the problems of surprise and/or miscalculation. He also called for a strengthening of the role of the *UN in safeguarding security (see *collective security). Subsequent explorations of the idea by theorists and politicians of the different power blocs have stressed the need for a common framework of security, rather than the traditional notion of security as a scarce commodity, which one state achieves at the expense of another. On the broader, international level, common security is concerned with the development of a new type of *world order as formulated by the Stockholm initiative (1991), in which security is considered to be a collective good.

Commonwealth, an association of independent sovereign states, comprising the UK and its former *colonies, which aims to foster common links among members and to promote economic and social development. The successor to the British Empire, the present-day Commonwealth brings together a quarter of the world's population. Although the term 'British Commonwealth of Nations' was used in the interwar period to describe Britain and the Dominions (Canada, New Zealand, Australia, South Africa), the modern-day Commonwealth dates from the granting of independence to the former British colonies of India, Pakistan, and Burma (now Myanmar) in 1947. Since then, most of the UK's former colonies have joined the Commonwealth on achieving independence. The member states of the Commonwealth, which now number forty-nine, are independent in every aspect of domestic and external affairs, but for historical reasons they accept the UK monarch as the symbol of free association of the independent member nations, and as such the Head of the Commonwealth. Apart from this symbolic role of the monarch, the UK is not predominant within the organization. The Commonwealth Secretariat was set up in London in 1965. It operates as an international organization to foster financial and cultural links between all Commonwealth nations. The Commonwealth has no charter but all members subscribe to a set of declarations, among which *North–South relations and the eradication of racial prejudice have been prominent and often controversial themes. The 1979 Lusaka meeting of the Heads of Government paved the way for internationally recognized independence for Zimbabwe, and through the 1980s, the Heads of Government, with the exception of the UK, urged the imposition of economic *sanctions against South Africa as a protest against apartheid.

Commonwealth of Independent States (CIS) (Russian, 'Sodruzhesvto Nezavisimykh Gosudarstv'), a loose association of eleven former Soviet republics. With its headquarters in Minsk, the Commonwealth was established in late 1991 by the Alma Ata agreement, which also recognized the current borders of the member republics: Armenia; Azerbaijan; Belarus; Kazakhstan; Kyrgyzstan; Moldova; Russia; Tadhzikistan; Turkmenistan; Ukraine; and Uzbekistan. Following the dissolution of the former Soviet Union on 26 December 1991 and declarations of independence by all its former republics, the Commonwealth provides a forum for debating and attempting to resolve the immediate problems faced by the Soviet successor states, such as the maintenance or not of a unified military force, co-operation in economic reforms, and representation in international organizations. Policies on potentially unifying issues such as Commonwealth citizenship and a common currency are likely to determine the future role played by the Commonwealth, and its continued existence.

communal conflict, conflict between different groups, often within one state, based upon different *religion, *race, *language, *culture, or history, factors which may all be described as their ethnicity (see *ethnic groups). It may be expressed in a general tension, hostility, and competition for scarce resources, or in forms of oppression or prejudice by one group, often the majority, over another, such as *racism, *segregation, and *discrimination. It may lead to unrest or protests which destabilize a state, *separatist movements, or open armed conflict culminating in *civil war, which undermines the integrity of the state and may lead to *secession. Communal conflict may also be a major source of conflict between states. Conflict may be sparked by a particular issue, such as access to a mutually claimed religious place (the most famous example being Jerusalem, which is holy to Christians, Jews, and Muslims; while in Ayodhya, India, which is one of the seven most sacred Hindu sites, Hindus have attempted to demolish a mosque). Disputes often focus on language and education. Language conflicts in Canada and Belgium, for example, reinforced by religious differences, have been a focus of political tension for decades. In the UK, awareness of being Welsh, Scottish or Irish combines with resentment of English dominance to produce periodic nationalist upsurges. Ethnic conflict is particularly widespread in former colonies, as in Africa, where state borders were drawn with little regard for the cultural or linguistic boundaries of different peoples. It may also be the result of the lifting or loosening of central government authority, as in the former Soviet Union, where the upsurge of ethnic or communal conflicts, for example between Christian *Armenians and Muslim Azeris, may be seen as a result of the weakening of central authority following the policies of

reform introduced by Mikhail Gorbachev in the 1980s. The revival of religion as an increasingly important factor in world politics and the challenge to secularism (see *fundamentalism and *religious politics) is also likely to increase communal conflict in the future. In Sri Lanka, religious and linguistic differences have been the basis of violent conflict between *Tamils and Sinhalese, a conflict with sufficiently destabilizing implications for the entire Indian subcontinent for the Indian army to intervene in an attempt to restore peace. India itself, with some 1,500 languages and dialects, seven religions, and varied ethnic groups and castes, is subject to incessant ethnic strife. In Lebanon, a complex web of ethnic conflict between Christians and Muslims on the one hand, and Sunnī and Shī'a Muslims on the other, caused a long and bloody civil war, exacerbated by external intervention, which led to the virtual disintegration of the state. Northern Ireland has seen a long-running conflict between the Catholic minority and the Protestant majority, also described as sectarianism because it is a conflict between sects of the same religion. Ostensibly political, ideological, or economic conflicts can often be shown to have a tribal, religious, or communal dimension. For example, in post-colonial Angola, the ideological conflict between pro-Soviet and pro-Western groups paralleled the rivalries between different ethnic groups. It is estimated that half the independent states of the world have experienced some form of communal conflict in recent years; the Marxist prediction that distinctions of an ethnic nature would be replaced by a universal working class seems to have been disproved by the strength of ethnic allegiances, which some commentators take to be the strongest form of political awareness.

communicable disease (contagious disease, infectious disease), a disease which can be transferred from one human host to another. The toll of sickness and death from communicable diseases is low in the wealthier countries of the world, but remains high in developing countries, as data from the World Health Organization show (see also *epidemiology). Malaria poses a major threat, with an estimated 100 million acute cases a year. There are 8 million new cases of tuberculosis a year and 3 million die from it, many of them young adults. As a result of the epidemic of *Aids, of which tuberculosis is an early manifestation, its incidence is increasing rapidly, particularly in Africa. Many communicable diseases are chronic, with the result that debilitated sufferers are a constant source of reinfection. Among these are amoebic dysentery, with which WHO believes 400 million are infected, and schistosomiasis (bilharsiasis), with which 200 million are infected. Even where it seems that diseases have disappeared, they may reoccur, as the major cholera epidemic in Peru, which broke out in 1991, the first there for a century, showed.

communication, the mutual exchange of information between individuals, a process central to human experience and social organization. The study of communication involves many disciplines, including *linguistics, *psychology, *sociology, and *anthropology. All forms of communication, from interpersonal to *mass media communications, involve an initiator, who formulates a message and sends it as a signal, by means of a particular channel, to a receiver, who decodes and interprets the *meaning. In interpersonal communication involving face-to-face *conversation, communication is direct, using the code of *language, and reinforced by *non-verbal communication such as body movement, eye contact, gesture, and facial expression.

Information posters and calls for a general strike in Prague in 1989. Such noticeboards formed a crucial method of **communication** in mobilizing popular support for the peaceful revolution of 1989.

Response is also direct. Interpersonal communication can also take place at a distance. Other forms of communication use writing and printing as the means of conveying messages. The invention of the printing press was the first step in the development of mass communication (see *publishing). Books, newspapers, and periodicals are able to convey messages to a wide audience; an even wider audience is reached by *radio and *television, film, and the recording industries. The mass media and the arts impose their own codes and characteristics on to their messages, which can range from relatively straightforward ideological tracts to complex texts carrying multiple layers of possible meaning.

communism, originally a social ideal according to which all goods should be held as common property and distributed according to need, but now mainly used to refer to the economic and political system of countries such as the former Soviet Union, its erstwhile satellites in Eastern Europe, and the People's Republic of China during the period following World War II. The ideal of communism has been embraced by many thinkers, including *Plato, the early Christians and the 16th-century humanist Thomas More (see *utopianism), who saw it as expressing man's social nature to the highest degree. It became the basis of a revolutionary movement through the work of *Marx, who saw communism as the final outcome of the proletarian *revolution that would overthrow capitalism. In Marx's

thought, communism still expressed the ideal of a society in which people would co-operate voluntarily with one another after the state had 'withered away', but in the hands of Vladimir Ilyich Lenin (1870–1924) and his successors in the Soviet Union, this was transformed into a doctrine justifying state control of all aspects of society. The doctrine had two main elements. The first was the leading role of the Communist Party, seen as representing the true interests of the working class. The party was to control the organs of the state, and was itself to be organized according to the principles of 'democratic centralism': the membership of each body in the party hierarchy was formally chosen by the vote of the body below, but policy decisions were to be taken at the top and then imposed rigidly at all lower levels of the hierarchy. The second major element in communist doctrine was the social ownership of *property and central planning of the economy (see *planned economy). In principle, all private ownership of the means of production and all elements of the market economy were to be abolished, and economic life was to be controlled by planning ministries, which would set production targets for factories and *collective farms, fix prices, direct labour, and so forth. Although this principle was never fully implemented, Soviet communism in its heyday stood alone as a society whose every aspect was controlled by a small political élite (during the Stalinist period, 1928–53, by a single individual), and was thus, for many, the leading example of *totalitarianism. Its economic and military achievements nevertheless inspired revolutionary movements in many other countries, and in some developing countries, such as China, Vietnam, North Korea, and Cuba, communist parties came to power and established regimes based more or less closely on the Soviet model. In

Eastern Europe, communist governments were installed under Soviet influence at the end of World War II. But the communist model was increasingly criticized in the West, even by those sympathetic to *Marxism, for its economic inefficiency, its lack of genuine democracy, and its denial of basic human freedoms. In the 1970s most Western communist parties adopted Eurocommunist ideas, which centrally involved the acceptance of democratic institutions and the abandonment of the Leninist theory of 'dictatorship of the proletariat'. During the next decade this questioning of orthodox communism spread to Eastern Europe and the Soviet Union, culminating in a remarkable series of largely peaceful revolutions which removed communist parties from power and opened the way to liberal democracy and the market economy. Communism's historical significance will in future probably be seen as providing a path of transition from agrarian to industrial society, not (as it portrays itself) as the final goal of human history.

community, a body of people living in one place or sharing something which they see as important, such as religion, race, or occupation. As a result of industrialization and technological change, many argue that community in the first sense, based on shared territory, is becoming less important than community in the second sense, based on shared beliefs, characteristics, or interests. For example, a stock-market analyst in Singapore may have more in common with her counterpart in Toronto than with her neighbour, a

The pulling down of the statue of Lenin in Bucharest, Romania, symbolizes the people's rejection of Soviet-style **communism**. The regime of Ceausescu in Romania was one of the more repressive of the totalitarian regimes modelled on the Soviet Union.

retired teacher. The term 'community' is also used to refer to sets of social relationships characterized by close ties and mutual interdependence. In *Community and Association* (1887) the German social theorist Ferdinand Tönnies contrasted *Gemeinschaft* (community) with *Gesellschaft* (association) societies. He held that the former were founded on *kinship, tradition, and strong emotional ties, whereas, increasingly, modern societies were reliant on law, *contract, and the imperatives of trade and business. Many have followed Tönnies in claiming that the transition has had malign effects and that modern industrialized societies are fragmented, often leading to *isolation, *alienation, and *anomie. Against this, others argue that the benefits of closely knit communities can be overstated and point to the greater personal freedom, *privacy, and opportunity which modern societies tend to afford. More generally, the term 'community' is used to distinguish non-institutional from institutional activities and services. Thus a 'community nurse' tends patients at home rather than in hospital.

community care, the policy of caring for people who need assistance because of *mental illness, *mental handicap, physical *disability, or *old age in their own homes or in small residential units rather than in large institutions, such as hospitals. Since the sometimes damaging effects and expense of *institutional care came to public attention in the 1950s, many countries have promoted community care. When working well, such policies enable some people who would otherwise be institutionalized to live in their own homes (specially adapted if necessary) with support from visiting nurses, *social workers, or volunteers. Others may live in sheltered accommodation with resident staff. Experience world-wide shows that most care in the community is provided either by spouses to each other or by women to other family members. While familial affection and a sense of obligation account for this, the burden on carers can become overwhelming. The evidence indicates that people in need of support prefer to live in the community rather than in institutions, but that if they do not have family members on whom to rely or if family relationships are ruptured, loneliness and neglect may be the outcome.

community penalty, a non-custodial *sentence imposed by a *court of law. The range of sentences varies between countries, but may include fines (a common penalty in many countries), *probation, restitution to the victim, and community service. Under some restitution programmes, the court determines a sum which the offender pays from his earnings into an account to reimburse the victim. Under others, the offender and victim are encouraged to reach agreement themselves on the amount. If the offender is not in work, a place on a work scheme may be arranged. Under community service, the offender is required to carry out work of general benefit to the community, such as garden maintenance for elderly people. Restitution and community service are generally organized by the probation service, which supervises the offender. The variety of community penalties and their use has increased in most countries since the 1960s, as a result of a lack of faith in the rehabilitative potential of *imprisonment; they are also far cheaper. Critics who argue that they are inappropriately lenient have been answered in recent years with an increased emphasis on the disciplinary content of such penalties. Offenders may, for example, be forbidden to leave their houses after nightfall and be required to wear electronic tags so that any violation of the curfew can be detected by supervisory staff.

company, a legally defined form of business organization. Although there are a very few unlimited companies, most companies are either private limited companies or public limited companies (PLCs in current UK parlance). In both cases their owners, the shareholders, have the protection of *limited liability for the company's *debts. A public limited company is one whose *shares may be sold to the general public and then traded on the *stock exchange (see *joint-stock company). The sale of shares in private limited companies is restricted. In both cases, companies usually enjoy certain financial and tax advantages over *partnerships and sole proprietorships. The establishment of companies and their operating practices are governed by *company law. The first companies in the UK were set up by Royal Charter, often conferring *monopoly rights in exchange for certain commitments to the monarch.

company law. Both *common law and *civil law systems divide companies into two separate spheres of regulation: public limited companies and private limited companies. The concepts of *limited liability and the company as a separate legal entity, distinct from its members and able to sue and be sued as such are common to both systems. A fundamental difference between private limited companies and public limited companies in both types of jurisdiction is the ability of shares to be transferred to new ownership. Shares in public companies can generally speaking be offered either direct to the public or in the form of bonds (civil law systems), but shares in private companies cannot be offered direct to the public, and frequently the consent of present members must be obtained before outsiders can become shareholders. This distinction in alienability is achieved either by statute law (UK) or stock-market rules (for example, Germany). Harmonization of company law such as accounting and auditing practices within the EC is occurring gradually.

comparative linguistics   *historical and comparative linguistics.

compensation, the making good of a loss, usually through the payment of money. Compensation may be awarded in a number of situations: for example, in the UK an industrial tribunal may award compensation for unfair dismissal or sex discrimination, or money may be paid to victims of violence through criminal injuries compensation schemes. In the case of a breach of *contract or the commission of a *tort (a breach of duty other than a breach of contract, such as *negligence or *defamation), a court may award compensation in the form of *damages. *Common law and *civil law systems recognize the principle of compensation for losses caused by faults for which others are legally responsible. Compensation may be for pecuniary damage, such as lost earnings, or for non-pecuniary damage, such as physical disablement. Determining the appropriate amount of compensation may be complex if, for example, a victim's life expectation is reduced, or he or she has no appreciation of the injury done. Compensation based on fault is generally funded by third-party liability *insurance, which, for some groups like employers or motorists, is usually compulsory. This system of obtaining compensation by determining fault has been criticized as expensive, slow, and unpredictable. A few countries have introduced no-fault compensation schemes, in which victims of accidents automatically receive, from specially constituted funds, compensation based on their needs rather than on proof of fault.

The New Zealand accident compensation scheme, funded by general taxation, led the way in 1972, followed by a similar scheme in Sweden. In parts of Canada, no-fault compensation schemes exist for road accidents alone.

competition (in economics)   *classical economics.

competition law, the law which aims to regulate the abuse of *monopoly power. It tries firstly to prevent firms from making agreements between themselves which have the effect of restricting competition; secondly, to prevent firms which have a dominant position from abusing their position to prevent competition emerging, for example by deliberately underpricing their goods to a level which competitors cannot reach (see *dumping); thirdly, to monitor *mergers between firms which may result in dominance of the market and the decline of competition. In the EC there are two types of legal control; national control and control at the Community level through the Treaty of Rome, in particular Articles 85 and 86. The Treaty of Rome is concerned only with those situations which may affect inter-state trade, but there may be situations where EC law and national law conflict; in such cases it seems that EC law will prevail. Competition law uses its own terminology to classify particular types of agreement. Horizontal restraints on competition arise when two or more firms at the same level in the market-place agree to restrict competition; this is also known as a *cartel, and is regulated by Article 85 of the Treaty of Rome. Vertical restraints can be divided into intra-brand and inter-brand restraints. Intra-brand restraints occur where a producer imposes controls on the way in which his products are distributed; inter-brand restraints are viewed more seriously as they occur when a producer attempts to prevent other products being distributed in competition with his own. Article 86 of the Treaty of Rome concentrates on the abuse of a dominant position within the market-place, particularly through mergers.

complementary medicine (or alternative medicine), a variety of forms of health care that fall outside the official health sector. Such health care provides an alternative to Western or allopathic medicine, which complementary practitioners believe treats symptoms and diseases rather than individuals in their complex physical, emotional, and environmental contexts. Formalized traditional systems of medicine, such as *Ayurvedic and *Chinese medicine, or the practice of traditional healers in Africa, can be termed complementary, as well as newer therapies practised in the Western world, some of which are based on the theories or practices of traditional medicine. Such therapies include acupuncture; homeopathy (which treats symptoms with microscopic doses of substances that cause similar symptoms in the healthy); chiropractice and osteopathy (forms of manipulation); and herbal medicine. In the UK, the practice of these therapies requires training and registration. There are other diagnostic or therapeutic techniques that might be termed fringe medicine. They include iridology (diagnosis from an examination of the eye); reflexology (treatment by massaging the foot in order to cure ailments in other parts of the body); and biofeedback (the use of monitoring equipment to help control involuntary processes, such as heart rate). Many forms of paranormal *healing also come into the category of complementary medicine. In the West there is a growing interest in such alternative therapies, although most conventional medical practitioners do not accept their claims. Some doctors, however, practise holistic medicine, which is the combination of conventional medicine with forms of complementary medicine, self-help skills, and *psychotherapy, in an attempt to treat the whole person and not merely his or her physical symptoms.

comprehensive education, a system of education based on principles of inclusivity rather than selectivity for secondary schools. The model often taken is that of the US high school, which ideally admits all the young people of a neighbourhood and offers both vocational and academic courses. By contrast, in Europe and elsewhere, secondary schooling has historically been restricted to the few and has prepared this group to be the social and intellectual *élite. Since World War II there has been a movement, which has often been accompanied by fierce debate, to transform selective systems into comprehensive systems as the need for a better educated labour-force has become apparent. The chief arguments for comprehensive education are that it promotes equal opportunity, that assessment at 11—the common age for entry to selective schools—is too early in a child's development, and that a comprehensive system encourages flexible and efficient use of resources. Opponents, however, argue that it holds back the development of especially gifted children. In England and Wales, comprehensive schools became general as a result of policy changes introduced by the Labour governments of 1964–70. Previously there was a tripartite state system of grammar, secondary modern, and, often, junior technical schools with entry to grammar schools depending on success in the 'Eleven Plus' examination. However, in comprehensive schools the world over, 'streaming' into different ability groups continues. Furthermore, many countries have a two-stage secondary system that is comprehensive at junior level but has academic and vocational schools at senior level. In developing countries, where school enrolment is not universal, the concept of state comprehensive education is less applicable.

computational linguistics, a term used to refer to two somewhat different kinds of research. On the one hand, it denotes *linguistic research of various kinds that uses computers to process and analyse data, especially the statistical analyses of texts, the making of concordances, and the testing of *grammars. On the other hand, it denotes research that aims to give computers the ability to process human *language in various ways. This includes work on machine translation, speech-recognition systems, and text-to-speech systems.

computer crime, a crime in which a computer is either a tool of crime or is the object of crime. Using a computer as a tool of crime often involves altering, deleting, or adding to data stored on it. Using the 'salami technique', for example, the criminal may illegitimately and regularly transfer funds from many bank accounts but in such small amounts that those defrauded do not notice. Computer crime may also involve illegal access to computer files or networks to obtain confidential information. A computer is the object of crime when it is sabotaged through the planting of computer 'viruses'—for instance, viruses may hold the threat of destroying the databases of large organizations unless money is paid. The increase in the use of computers has resulted in legislation against computer crime in many countries, but detecting and proving offences is difficult and many organizations are unwilling publicly to admit that they are victims.

computer-integrated manufacture (CIM), a production system which covers the whole supply process from design of the product to delivery to the customer. CIM covers the following five categories of techniques: operations strategy, the technique of harmonizing the design, development, manufacturing, and distribution capabilities of an organization with the needs of their market; CAE (computer-aided engineering), including CAD (computer-aided design and draughting), CAM (computer-aided manufacturing), CAT (computer-aided testing), and all the techniques associated with the development of the product and the manufacturing instructions needed to drive the process; methods and facilities planning, including plant *location, level of integration, robotics, quality engineering, and other techniques associated with the manufacturing resources; planning and control systems, including forecasting, warehousing and distribution, production and inventory control, materials management, shop-floor data collection; and organization of people within the design, development, manufacturing, and distribution functions. It is generally accepted that the factory of the future will make use of all these techniques in an integrated and controlled manner, although at present management thinking is a long way from achieving this. A philosophy of implementation is emerging based on the concept of 'islands of automation'. This suggests that computers can be introduced in isolation at different stages of the production process. As long as the introduction is part of an overall strategic plan, and the technology introduced is flexible enough to be combined with other machines introduced later, the process can be successful. If these conditions are not fulfilled businesses will spend large amounts of money improving particular isolated areas of their business without achieving the full potential improvement to overall results.

Comte, Auguste (1798–1857), French philosopher who coined the term 'sociology'. His work is often seen, with that of his compatriot Claude-Henri de Rouvroy, Comte de Saint-Simon (1760–1825), as representing the beginnings of sociological study. Comte maintained that society was like an organism, in which each part had a different role and contributed to the functioning of the whole. These ideas influenced *Durkheim and the development of *functionalism. In his major work *Cours de Philosophie Positive* (1830–42), Comte set out his famous, 'Law of the Three Stages'. He believed that human knowledge and human society evolved through three distinct stages: theological, metaphysical, and positive. In the first, explanation is sought from the action of gods, in the second from more abstract processes such as 'nature', and in the third from the operation of discoverable laws. Comte saw sociology as a 'positive' science founded on the analysis of directly observable phenomena and dubbed his system positivism. His motto, 'Order and Progress', is to this day a feature of the Brazilian flag.

concentration camp, originally a place where non-combatants were accommodated, as instituted by Lord Kitchener during the Second Boer War (1899–1902). The Boers, mainly women and children, were placed there for their own protection from Kitchener's 'scorched earth policy', but mainly to prevent them from aiding the guerrillas. Some 20,000 detainees died, largely as a result of disease. During the *Nazi regime in Germany (1933–45) the term was applied to the place of internment of unwanted persons, specifically *Jews, but also Protestant and Catholic dissidents, communists, gypsies, and the handicapped. The camps (Konzetrazionslager, or KZ) were categorized into *Arbeitslager*, where prisoners were organized into labour battalions, and *Vernichtungslager*, set up for the extermination and incineration of men, women, and children. Among Jews alone, some 4 million perished in the camps. In the Soviet Union, Lenin greatly enlarged (1919) the Tzarist forced labour camps, which were renamed Gulags (Russian acronym for the Main Administration of Corrective Labour Camps) in 1930. An estimated 15 million prisoners were confined to the Gulags during Stalin's *purges, of whom many succumbed to disease, famine, or the firing squad.

conciliation *dispute resolution.

conditioning (in psychology), a change in behaviour due to association between events. It was the basis of *learning theories which dominated academic psychology from World War I to about 1960. Conditioning is usually divided into two kinds: classical or Pavlovian; and operant or instrumental. Both involve the pairing of an event with 'reinforcement', which may be 'positive' (rewards of food, drink, or sex) or 'negative' (punishment such as electric shock). In classical conditioning, which was discovered by *Pavlov, a light or sound is paired with a natural reinforcement. The response which was initially produced by the reinforcement becomes 'conditioned' so that it occurs to the light or sound even when no reinforcement is given. This is therefore a matter of learning an association between two stimuli (the reinforcement and the light or sound) and is referred to as S–S conditioning. Operant conditioning follows the US psychologist Edward Thorndike's (1874–1949) 'law of effect' (1911): that responses become more frequent if followed by satisfying consequences but less frequent if followed by aversive consequences. *Skinner showed that a rat which is rewarded when it 'operates on' its environment by pressing a lever will increase its number of lever-presses. It is therefore associating the stimulus (reinforcement) with its own behaviour (response). This is referred to as S–R conditioning. Psychologists dispute whether these two kinds of conditioning do really differ from each other. Most conditioning experiments have been done with animals. It is very doubtful whether all animal, let alone human, learning is due to conditioning. However, Skinner pointed out that it plays a role, for instance in the unwitting encouragement of misbehaviour when parents reward a child by attending to misbehaviour but ignoring good behaviour. In 1920 *Watson showed that fears can be conditioned and thereby laid the foundations for *behaviour therapy treatments for *phobia.

confederation, a weak form of political union between sovereign states, in order to secure some common purpose. Action by a confederal government requires unanimity among member states; the confederal government generally lacks its own means of taxation, law-making, and enforcement. The federal constitution of the USA was preceded by the Articles of Confederation of 1781 (see *federalism). With the contemporary tendency to *centralization, confederalism is not common: Switzerland is a confederation by name but in practice a federation. Confederal solutions were advocated, but not adopted, to resolve frictions in troubled federations such as Yugoslavia and the former Soviet Union, and some theorists compare the enhanced *EC to a confederation.

Conference on Disarmament, an organization within the framework of the *UN, comprising forty member states,

including the five declared nuclear-weapons states (the USA, the former Soviet Union, France, the UK, and China). Based in Geneva, it has contributed to discussions on the control of *chemical and biological weapons, a nuclear test ban, the arms race in space, and new weapons of mass destruction. So far the Conference has failed to achieve significant positive results because of the reluctance of states to give up arms as deterrents, the problem of achieving significant reductions on both sides, and the difficulty of verification. (See also *arms control, *disarmament.)

Conference on Security and Co-operation in Europe (CSCE), a conference, first set up between 1972 and 1975, which can be considered the major achievement of *détente. The Conference was proposed by the former Soviet Union with the motives of securing agreement to the permanence of post-1945 frontiers, reducing *East–West tension, and furthering co-operation. It was attended by representatives of all the states of Europe (excluding Albania) together with the USA and Canada. Agreement, known as the 'Helsinki Final Act', was reached on security in Europe; co-operation in the fields of economy, science, and technology; and human rights, culture, education, and the free flow of information. Follow-up conferences to oversee progress were held in Belgrade (1977), Madrid (1980), Ottowa (1985), and Paris (1990). At the Paris Summit, thirty-four states (including the united Germany) witnessed the signing of the Treaty on Conventional Forces in Europe (CFE); an agreement that *NATO and the *Warsaw Pact states no longer regard one another as enemies; and the Charter of Paris, comprising a series of principles and institutional developments for greater security in Europe. In early 1992 the former Soviet republics, Croatia, and Slovenia were admitted to the CSCE, bringing the number of members to fifty-one. It has a secretariat based in Prague, and hosts meetings of the heads of states and foreign ministers of member states.

conformity (in psychology), aspects of a person's beliefs, feelings, or behaviour that are due to the influence of other people. Experimental findings about the power of such influence cast doubt on beliefs about the self-determination of individual behaviour. Conformity is distinguished from *obedience by being imitation, often of equals. The person conforming feels he or she is acting voluntarily, whereas obedience is a response to a superior's explicit command and therefore comparatively involuntary. In the 1950s, Solomon Asch (1907–   ) demonstrated that social pressure can induce people to deny the unambiguous evidence of their own senses. He asked people to give oral judgements in small face-to-face groups. When he secretly instructed all but one group member to give several wrong answers on a simple perceptual task, three in four of the lone uninstructed individuals gave the same wrong answer as the group at least once. Most of them lied simply to avoid ridicule: they did not follow the majority when they answered in private. More recently, the French psychologist Serge Moscovici has shown that a minority may influence the majority and actually change the other group members' opinions. This implies that a credible minority produces *persuasion, whereas a majority induces fear of rejection.

Confucianism (Chinese, *rujia* 'teaching of the scholars'), the Chinese religious world-view and code of conduct loosely based on the teachings of *Confucius. The principal texts of Confucianism are the various works which are divided into groups known as the Five, Six, Nine, Twelve, or

Confucian rites in Seoul, South Korea. **Confucianism** was the official ethical system in Korea under the Yi dynasty from the late 14th century to the early 20th century, and remains perhaps the most important set of beliefs there, co-existing with Buddhism, Christianity, and other religious practices.

Thirteen Classics, the last two of which include the *Analects* of Confucius. Most of these are not specifically Confucian; the *Sishu* (a collection of four independent books), was used as a basic Confucian educational text for many years. The philosophical and ethical code worked out by Confucius was adopted and developed into a state cult under the Han dynasty (206 BC–AD 220), with elaborate state ceremonies honouring the emperor and those who had served the empire well. The civil-service examination and educational system were based on the study of the Five Classics, and temples were built in veneration of Confucius throughout the empire. Traditional beliefs such as *yin and yang and the five elements of wood, fire, earth, metal, and water were also incorporated into Confucianism at about this period. Later, the scholar philosopher Zhu Xi (1130–1200) elaborated Confucian doctrines into a coherent spiritual and philosophical world-view known as Neo-Confucianism (*lixue* or *Daoxue*) developed partly as a response to the increased prominence of *Daoism and *Buddhism in Chinese life. As well as developing a metaphysical system based on the twin but complementary concepts of *li*, principle, and *qi*, material force, Zhu Xi wrote authoritative commentaries on the Classics which were the official texts of the Chinese state examinations until 1905. The overwhelming influence of Confucianism on Chinese life has been much restricted in the 20th century since the abolition of the traditional educa-

tional system in 1905 and the establishment of the Republic in 1911. With the adoption of *communism as the state ideology under Mao Zedong (1893–1976), Confucian temples were destroyed and the classics banned, but none the less, Confucian elements prevail in various aspects of Chinese life and its teachings may be discerned in contemporary Chinese socio-political thinking and planning. Confucianism persists in Japan, Korea, Singapore, Taiwan, and Vietnam; today, it is strongest in South Korea and Taiwan, where Confucian shrines and education are maintained on traditional lines.

Confucius (Kong Fuzi, or K'ung Fu-tzu) (*c*.551–479 BC), Chinese philosopher known as the Supreme Sage, whose teaching dominated China for over 2,000 years. A teacher and man of learning, Confucius was principally interested in devising a code of conduct which could be applied both to the administration of the state and to individual morality. He taught respect for the ancestors and recognized the overriding will of heaven, following certain religious practices himself, but he opposed much popular religious practice, and his own teaching focused on the behaviour of man in society. Of cardinal importance was the quality of *ren*, humaneness or love, and *li*, behaviour, the ritual, conduct, or etiquette by which *ren* is brought into daily life or, in the wider sphere, politics. Confucius thought the ideal society would be governed by a select body of superior men or princely persons characterized by their noble behaviour rather than nobility of birth. Throughout his lifetime, Confucius hoped for an opportunity to put his ideas into practice in government, but other than a short-lived period as a minister, this was not to be. His sayings and discourses are contained in the *Analects*, compiled after his death, which is one of the thirteen classic texts of *Confucianism.

conglomerate, a group of firms operating in a disparate range of business activities, but all owned by the same parent or *holding company. A conglomerate is usually established and built up by *take-over or *merger. The holding company may be small relative to the size of the group, but may claim to have the managerial talent to make the acquired firms more efficient.

Congregationalism, *Protestant churches based on local autonomy and the equality of all believers. Baptism and the Lord's Supper are the only *sacraments accepted. As in other reformed churches, there are ministers who carry out pastoral and liturgical duties. Their ordination rests with the congregation they serve; there is no formal hierarchy, though in practice senior ministers exercise oversight in particular areas. The Congregational Church in England and Wales merged with the Presbyterian Church of England in 1972 to form the *United Reformed Church; in the USA the Congregational Christian Churches merged with the Evangelical and Reformed Church in 1957 to form the United Church of Christ.

conscientious objection, the opposition to the bearing of arms or to any type of military training on religious, philosophical, or moral grounds. Many *armed forces are professional, but in cases where there is *conscription it is likely that a minority will object to being called up, either on grounds of *pacifism, or because of objections to a particular war. In most countries conscientious objection is treated as a breach of the law and is penalized. Some countries recognize only specific religious objections; for instance, the

1940 conscription laws in the USA recognized conscientious objectors only if they belonged to a pacifist religious sect; political or personal objections were not recognized. A few countries which still have conscription now recognize religious or philosophical objection, but conscientious objectors are obliged to participate in non-combatant service, or in alternative civilian service in order to fulfil their obligations to the state; in France, this service has a term twice that of military service. In some countries, such as South Africa and the former Soviet Union, political objections to military service have resulted in prison sentences.

conscription, compulsory call-up to take part in a country's *armed forces. Citizens of a state are seen as having an obligation to defend that state by participating in military service. Conscription is generally used to mobilize national forces in times of war, but many countries still retain conscription in peacetime, young men and sometimes women being called up for a term of military service, followed by periodic refresher training. After active training, a conscript may be placed in the reserves. Conscription is retained in countries such as Israel and China (both men and women being called up), and Switzerland. Military service is sometimes regarded as an important component in fostering national unity, especially in countries where divided ethnic loyalties may threaten national cohesion. In the UK conscription, which had continued after World War II in the form of National Service, ended in 1957. In the USA selective service (or the draft) continued after World War II, but in the course of the Vietnam War (1964–75), about 10,000 Americans resisted conscription, many by going abroad, and in 1973 the USA ended the draft and opted for a fully professional army backed up by voluntary reservists.

consent, agreement to the terms of some activity or arrangement. Consent is important in social thought mainly as a criterion of *legitimacy: institutions and practices are held to be legitimate when all those who are subject to them have given their consent. This was developed into a theory of government by *Locke, who in *Two Treatises of Government* (1689) held that governments have rightful authority only when their subjects demonstrate their express or tacit consent. Free *elections are often regarded as the chief means of giving consent to government.

consequentialism, the doctrine in *ethics that the moral rightness or wrongness of an action is decided by its consequences. The kinds of consequences taken to be morally relevant typically include facts about the satisfaction or frustration of people's desires, with the result that there is a very intimate relation between consequentialism and *utilitarianism. Consequentialism is often divided into two forms: act-consequentialism, which assesses actions on an individual basis, and rule-consequentialism, which focuses instead on kinds of action. Consequentialism is strongly opposed to deontology, the view that the moral worth of an action depends upon its according with duty, or its respecting the rights of other individuals. Deontologists characteristically complain that consequentialism leads to a confusion of morality with expediency, since consequentialism seems to allow that the good of one individual may be sacrificed to the good of the many.

conservation, the preservation and care of the natural environment. Conservation embraces all life and the environment that supports it. It may be concerned with the small-

est pond, with sites of scientific interest or scenic beauty, with one of the planet's biomes, such as its rainforests, or with particular species of plants and animals. Conservation may include measures to protect clean air, water supplies, and land, or defend particular habitats against, for example, *deforestation or *desertification, or save *endangered species. International conventions exist concerning the latter, but the preservation of vital habitats is the subject of fewer such agreements; the Convention on Wetlands of International Importance 1971) is one exception. To reach agreement on effective measures to combat *acid rain, the *greenhouse effect, or *ozone depletion requires international collaboration to which the UN through its Environmental Programme is directing increasing attention. *Non-governmental organizations such as Greenpeace and the World Wide Fund For Nature play a role in leading and reflecting public opinion on conservation issues. Conservation is a concern of the *Greens and others who favour *recycling and the use of renewable *energy to conserve resources and reduce *pollution.

conservatism, a political outlook which values and supports established institutions and is critical of proposals for radical social change. Conservatism first took shape as an ideology at the time of the French Revolution, when thinkers such as Edmund Burke (*Reflections on the Revolution in France*, 1790) and Joseph de Maistre (*Considerations on France*, 1796) denounced the revolutionary changes taking place in France as destructive of much that is valuable in society. Since then, conservatism has chiefly been opposed to *liberalism and *socialism. Conservatives have a pessimistic view of human nature. They see people as standing in need of discipline and restraint, and are fearful of the consequences when authority is destroyed and individuals are left to their own devices. They respect tradition as embodying the accumulated wisdom of the ages, and are correspondingly sceptical about untested plans and policies put forward by would-be reformers. Conservatives typically favour: constitutional government as a way of preserving authority without concentrating it in the hands of a despot or dictator; an ordered or ranked society in which people know their proper place and defer to those placed above them in the hierarchy; established religion, in order to integrate people into the fabric of society; and the family, the primary source of moral values and the place where responsible citizens are formed. Conservative economic attitudes have varied with time. Originally conservatives tended to support *protectionist policies in contrast to the *laissez-faire* policies advocated by liberals, but in the 20th century they have increasingly turned to the *free market as the best means of organizing economic activity. This synthesis of conservative and classical liberal beliefs can be seen especially in the thinking of the *New Right. Political parties are rarely wholeheartedly conservative in outlook, but politicians of a conservative disposition can be found in the *Christian Democratic parties of Europe, in the US Republican Party, and in the Conservative (Tory) Party in the UK.

Conservative Judaism, a Jewish movement in the USA occupying a position half-way between *Orthodox Judaism and US *Reform Judaism. Following the ideals of Zachariah Frankel (1801–75), Conservative Jews seek to preserve the essential traditions of *Judaism, while at the same time interpreting and applying the *Torah in ways more suited to the modern world. Like Orthodox Jews, they observe the *Shabbat and follow dietary laws, but with modifications where necessary and in a much less rigorous fashion in most cases. Many Conservative Jews also encourage the study of Hebrew and support *Zionism, but the movement, an influential force in Judaism in the USA, embraces a wide diversity of views.

consociationalism, a form of liberal democracy in societies deeply divided by religious, racial, regional, or linguistic cleavages into two or more distinct segments or communities. Consociational democracy is an alternative to majoritarian rule, and is marked by four main principles: a grand coalition, or executive power-sharing by the political leaders of the communities; a high degree of autonomy for the communities; proportionality of representation and in the allocation of all public resources; and a minority veto when one community perceives its vital interests to be at stake. Clear examples of successful consociational democracy are Austria and The Netherlands after World War II. In Czechoslovakia, a federation of two republics, there are safeguards against domination of one by the other. Elsewhere, for example in Lebanon, consociationalism has not provided a peaceful solution to the divisions of the country. In 1991 the South African government proposed that elements of consociationalism such as executive power-sharing be part of its new constitution.

consortium, a group of firms or nations co-operating for a specific purpose or project, such as a construction contract, in which different members of the consortium carry out different parts of the contract. The Channel tunnel linking France and the UK was constructed by a consortium. A consortium bank is a merchant bank set up by several banks, possibly from several countries, and typically involved in *loan syndication (where the risk of a loan is shared by all the participating banks).

conspiracy, an agreement between two or more persons to do something illegal or reprehensible. A conspiracy to do something illegal is a crime in many countries with *common law systems, but is little known in countries with civil law systems. It is usually concerned with the preparation for the crime, not the crime itself. In the 20th century, the scope of conspiracy law has expanded in some countries in the attempt to reduce *organized crime, *white-collar crime, *fraud, and subversive political activity. Prosecutions often arouse dispute because it is difficult satisfactorily to prove agreement, because those found to be conspirators may be liable for crimes committed by others in furtherance of the conspiracy, and because in joint trials of conspirators, there is a danger of confusion and guilt by association. More generally, charges of conspiracy to commit crimes or *sedition are frequently used by totalitarian governments as a pretext to imprison opponents.

constitution, the rules regulating an association, and particularly the set of basic rules and principles governing the structure, organization, and powers of a *state. A constitution is a fundamental law, specifying the sources, purposes, and uses of public power, and the restraints upon that power. It controls but also legitimizes the government organized under it and operating within it (see *constitutional government). Nearly all constitutions have a wholly documentary basis, the constitution of the UK, which is unwritten (see *UK government), being a rare exception. Most constitutions outline the responsibilities of government and the rights and obligations of citizens. Some are merely statements of national aspirations, rather than rules and doctrines that control the exercise of power. Whether a constitution is stable and effective is likely to depend on how well it incorporates the dominant values of a society, on the respect accorded to it by civilian and military *élites, and on its *legitimacy among the population at large.

constitutional government, a form of government constraining the arbitrary use of public power through a written or unwritten *constitution, in order to make rulers accountable to the people they govern. Under constitutional government, the exercise of power is subject to regular legal and political restraints, reflecting the rights of the governed. To ensure this, public power is generally dispersed to some degree (see *pluralism). Among the best-known structural safeguards are the *separation of powers and the *rule of law. The US constitution (which many more recently constituted democracies have modified and adapted) allocates powers to the *legislature, the *executive, and the *judiciary, but incorporates checks and balances between them to guard against excessive accumulation of power in any branch. There are also frequent elections at federal, state, and local levels. Finally, a constitutionally entrenched *bill of rights (consisting of the first ten amendments to the Constitution) underpins judicial remedies for the redress of grievances. In this way, any democratic constitution creates a balance of rights and responsibilities between citizens and government. In particular, it sustains the belief that government is based upon consent and subject to limits; actions which may be beyond these limits are subject to legal challenge and *judicial review. The main contemporary form of constitutional government, though not the only possible form, is liberal democracy. In this, the constitution provides a stable and legitimate framework within which personal rights are recognized and generally securely established, interests can be effectively represented, political parties may compete peacefully for power, and governments are accountable to the people on the basis of regular, free elections. There are various threats to constitutional government. A pluralistic balance of interests within society may disintegrate; individual liberty may be eroded by steadily encroaching state power; chief executives or other political leaders may usurp authority or evade constitutional obstacles to personal rule; excessive partisanship can destroy the necessary willingness to abide by the rules; poor political or economic performance may undermine faith in the system; and disaffected groups and minorities may turn to violence, and provoke an increasingly authoritarian response. It is not surprising, therefore, that stable and successful constitutional government is a major political accomplishment which has been achieved only in a minority of countries.

consulate *embassy.

consumer, the final purchaser or user of a *good or service. Most goods are used up in the process of *consumption, although this may take some time in the case of durable goods. The consumer of a good is not always the same individual as the purchaser. For instance, a mother (the purchaser) may buy food for her child (the consumer). Because of this, economists may use the household rather than the individual as the basic agent of consumption. Consumer *credit is a *loan made to a consumer to facilitate a purchase. Such credit is often made by (or instigated by) retailers. A common form is hire purchase (instalment credit in the USA). An initial deposit is paid on an item and the balance, plus applicable interest, is paid subsequently in regular instalments. The item being bought by this method does not become the property of the consumer until the final payment is made. Much consumer credit now takes place through the use of *credit cards. Consumer protection is the legislative protection of the consumer from unsafe products and unfair business practices. It is common in the food-retailing sector, but is also designed to protect consumers from inferior quality or unsafe goods, and from unscrupulous methods of selling (including unfair hire-purchase terms).

consumer law. Areas of consumer law include the provision of credit, the regulation of contract terms, and legislation covering specific aspects of consumer goods, for example the regulation of food labelling. All EC member states have different domestic laws covering these issues. In relation to the provision of consumer information each member state makes use of secondary committees; for example, in the UK marketing boards for each product impose and enforce certain standards, while in Germany quality marks are controlled by the owner of that label, who imposes and enforces certain standards. (See also *liability.)

consumption (in economics), using a *good or service to satisfy some material demand of the population. Consumption is measured as the total expenditure in an economy upon goods and services classified as consumption goods, including durable goods such as motor vehicles, refrigerators, or clothing which are used over a number of years. Consumption is the largest component of *national income, and can be divided into consumption by households and consumption by government. That by households is the larger part, and the term is often used to refer to this part alone. The 'consumption function' described by *Keynes is the positive relationship between total household consumption and aggregate personal disposable income. The simple version of this relationship is linear: a household's consumption expenditure rises proportionately as its disposable income increases.

contempt of court (in *common law), disrespect for or disobedience to a *court of law. Civil contempt means disobeying an order of the court, for instance by breaking an *injunction. Criminal contempt is conduct that tends to obstruct, prejudice, or abuse the administration of justice, either in a particular case or generally. Examples of the latter include publishing material prejudicial to a party to legal proceedings, either immediately before or during the proceedings, contempt in the face of the court (which involves the disruption of proceedings) and scandalizing the court (which involves the scurrilous abuse of a judge, or accusations of partiality). The penalty for contempt of court, both civil and criminal, may be a fine or imprisonment.

continental philosophy, a term usually used to distinguish the tradition of modern philosophical thought which developed on the continent of Europe (principally France and Germany) from the *analytic philosophy predominantly practised in the UK and the USA. The point at which the two traditions diverge is often identified with the rise of *phenomenology, founded in Germany by Edmund Husserl (1859–1938) at the turn of this century. The distinctive feature of the phenomenological method has been its endeavour to describe the structures of consciousness, or, more

One of the leading figures of the London-based Campaign for Press and Broadcasting Freedom, the Labour Member of Parliament Tony Benn, supports the **contempt of court** displayed by the publishers of *Spycatcher*, who had defied a court injunction banning publication.

broadly, the part played by the mind in the constitution of reality. The belief that the proper object of philosophical study is an area of being distinct from, and more fundamental than, the reality conceptualized by the natural sciences has been a hallmark of this tradition, which has not fought shy of making large claims about *metaphysics and existence (see *ontology). Phenomenology led to the *existentialism of *Sartre and *Heidegger, and, supplemented by the influence of *structuralist linguistics, to the post-structuralism of *Derrida. By this route contemporary continental philosophy has come to accord a central place to the very issues of language, communication, meaning, and reference which currently dominate analytic philosophy.

contingency fee, payment by a client to a lawyer which is contingent on the outcome of the case. The full fee (normally a percentage of *damages) is paid only if the case is won. In some countries, contingency fees are regarded as unethical, since they are seen to threaten a lawyer's duty not to mislead the court. However, contingency fees are the normal means of financing civil litigation in the USA, where *legal aid in *civil law cases is very restricted.

continuing education, education for adults which replaces or supplements initial education in schools, colleges, and universities. Continuing adult education, often overlooked, has expanded to such an extent in recent years that in some countries more adults than children may be receiving education. It may take many forms, such as evening classes, on-the-job training, and correspondence courses (see *distance education). In developing countries, there is a strong demand for training schemes. Some focus closely on *literacy, numeracy, and work-related skills, while other educators believe collective education of the poor will help them to overcome the problems they face. All over the world, technological developments, changing professional expectations, and the obsolescence of many skills and occupations require adults to train and retrain throughout their lives (see *vocational education). Adults also pursue education for personal satisfaction.

contraception   *family planning.

contracting-out, the transfer of functions previously performed by government employees to voluntary or private agencies. The *New Right has recommended contracting-out as a way of reducing the size and power of the public sector and encouraging competitive pricing, greater efficiency, diversity of supply, and increased consumer choice. Public authorities may contract out practical services such as catering, cleaning, and refuse collection, or professional services such as computing and home nursing. In the USA, private contractors run several prisons. The *regulation of contracted-out services by the public authorities is considered essential to protect public interests.

contract, law of, the rules governing the formation, content, performance, and termination of contracts. A contract is a legally enforceable agreement between two or more persons. In *common law systems, agreements will normally be enforceable only if one party has promised to do (or refrain from doing) specified acts in return for a promise by the other to do likewise. It is this notion of bargain which distinguishes legally binding promises from those which are morally or socially binding only: a contract requires performance by both parties. In *civil law systems, agreements may sometimes be enforceable in favour of a person who has not provided a reciprocal act. In both systems, failure to fulfil a contract without justification will entitle the innocent party to a remedy such as *damages for loss suffered. Contract is central to the organization of modern society: the exchange of goods and services for profit; the sale of labour for reward; and the relationships of companies with each other are all based upon it. Some agreements, however, are unenforceable because they conflict with the public interest or a legal prohibition; typically, these include wagers, child sale, and prostitution. By tradition, the role of the law has been limited to regulating the framework within which people exercise their freedom to contract, but more recently the law in some countries has been used to restrict the terms of certain contracts, in order to protect economically vulnerable groups such as consumers and employees. For businesses, the growth of international trade means more cross-boundary contracts, and increasing pressure for the unification of the contract laws of different countries by means of international agreements.

convention (in politics), a form of international agreement between two or more countries intended to lay down certain obligations which are binding on its signatories. Such agreements may also be known as pacts, protocols, declarations, or *treaties. The use of the term convention was popular in the late 19th and early 20th centuries; for example, it was applied to a series of important international agreements, the *Geneva Conventions, relating to the treatment of prisoners of war and non-combatants. Such agreements form an important part of that body of rules and codes of international conduct known as *international law. The term is often used for agreements reached under the auspices of the UN or other international organization.

conventional warfare, a term referring to warfare between states without resort to *nuclear weapons or *chemical and biological weapons. Recent examples include the Yom Kippur War between Israel and neighbouring Arab states in 1973; the Falklands War between the UK and Argentina in 1982; and the Gulf War between Iraq and the US-led coalition in 1991. Such wars are usually contrasted with nuclear war, which envisages the use of nuclear weapons on some scale, or with unconventional war, which involves tactics such as those employed in guerrilla fighting, or the disregard of established distinctions between combatants and non-combatants. Historically, wars were subject to certain rules and conventions, but the successive influences of science and technology upon warfare have rendered old distinctions less clear. Nuclear weapons and chemical and biological warfare are still regarded as unconventional, but the destructive power and pinpoint accuracy of many conventional weapons serve to blur the distinctions between conventional, unconventional, and nuclear warfare.

conversation, the informal exchange of ideas between individuals by the use of spoken words; the primary form of *communication between people, and the context in which children learn to speak. Conversation is typically interactional, each person taking it in turns to speak and reacting directly to what the previous speaker has said. In recent years, sociologists have analysed conversation, identifying complex rules that govern such matters as the taking of turns, the length of pauses, and the use of conventional opening and closing sequences. Conversation is not only verbal; *non-verbal communication such as body movement, eye contact, gaze direction, and gesture may play just as important a part.

convertible issues   *shares.

conveyancing, the process of transferring ownership of interests in land. The procedure usually involves checking that the vendor is the owner and that the property is not subject to rights of others, and the preparation and execution of the documents of transfer. In some countries transfer is a public act performed before an official.

co-operative, a group of individuals or organizations engaged in economic activity on the basis of common ownership of facilities and profit sharing. Consumer co-operatives are engaged in wholesale and retail trade, and distribute profits (at least in part) to customers who register as members. The retail co-operative movement in the UK originated in the 19th century as a means of reducing the alleged exploitation of consumers in the capitalist system. Distribution and producer co-operatives, in both agriculture and manufacturing, are most common in developing countries and in industrialized countries with centrally planned economies. Co-operatives in industrial market economies include agricultural distribution co-operatives in France, the communal kibbutzim in Israel, and the agricultural and manufacturing co-operatives of Mondragon in the Basque country of northern Spain. In all of these the workers themselves or their representatives have final authority in the running of the enterprise.

Coptic Church (or Egyptian Church), one of the Monophysite *Christian churches, founded in 451. It is led by the patriarch of Alexandria. Members observe five fasts each year: pre-Lent, Lent, pre-Assumption (the feast celebrating the Virgin Mary's ascension into heaven), post-Ascension, and Advent. Coptic was the *Egyptian language used from

Co-operatives are a potent tool of self-help, offering the opportunity for workers to control their economic future. Here in a village near Harare, Zimbabwe, women have formed a co-operative to manufacture peanut butter from locally produced ground nuts.

the 3rd to the 10th century; liturgies in the Coptic Church are still in Coptic, but a parallel Arabic text is provided. Outside Egypt, the church has dioceses in Jerusalem, Sudan, and South Africa; there are about 3.5 million full members. There are also a small number of Catholic Copts.

copyright, the exclusive legal right to reproduce or authorize others to reproduce literary, artistic, or musical material, normally invested in the creator of such material or in his or her employer. This right lasts for the copyright holder's lifetime, and for an additional period of time after his or her death (in the UK, fifty years). Some countries also protect the moral right of authors to be identified with their works, regardless of the ownership of copyright, and to object to any distortion or mutilation of their work which would be prejudicial to their reputation. Reproduction of the copyright work requires permission, and usually involves the payment of royalties for each copy made and sold, as well as protection against plagiarism or piracy (see *performing rights). In the case of films and television programmes, fees are payable to the originators or their distribution companies for each public screening, while broadcasts of recorded music are covered by needle-time agreements that ensure payments to musicians, composers, and publishers. In some countries, authors can also claim lending rights for books borrowed from public libraries. Copyright laws were developed in the 18th century, and in 1886 the Berne Convention gave reciprocal rights to authors in all participating countries. The USA was not a participant in the Berne Convention; in 1952, a less stringent convention, the Universal Copyright Convention, was created in order to establish a minimum level of copyright regulation throughout the world. The USA finally signed the Berne Convention in 1989. Copyright laws have had to change in order to take into account developments in technology; thus in many countries computer programs are now protected on the same basis as literary works. In the case of photocopying, limited photocopying of copyright material for 'fair use' such as research or private study is permitted; in 1990, however, the British Library agreed to introduce a licensed (royalty-paid) document-copying service for profit-making organizations, running parallel to the statutory royalty-free service it provides as part of the 'library privileges' included in the British Copyright, Designs, and Patents Act, 1988. ·(See also *intellectual property.)

corporatism, a political system in which economic and social policy is made through agreements between business associations, trade unions, and government. The term has been used to describe societies which, although formally parliamentary democracies, have given organized interests a large role in the making of policy. In return for this influence, the interest groups involved, primarily employers' associations and trade unions, agree to persuade their members to comply with government directives, for instance by implementing a *prices and incomes policy. One effect of this is to lessen the scope of the *free market, and corporatist arrangements have therefore been criticized by the *New Right for hindering economic growth. All of the advanced capitalist societies display some corporatist features, but the degree of corporatism differs considerably, with countries such as Austria and Sweden near the top of the scale, and countries such as the USA and UK near the bottom.

correlation, a mutual relationship between two or more factors, usually established by the statistical analysis of systematically collected data. For example, many studies have shown that an increase in the consumption of animal fats by a population is correlated with an increase in the incidence of heart attacks. However, a correlation between two factors does not necessarily imply that one has caused the other. They may be linked coincidentally or a third factor may be at work. For instance, the increase in fat consumption may have coincided with an increase in cigarette smoking and it may be this which has affected the incidence of heart attacks. Detecting and explaining correlations are prime tasks for researchers in *social sciences such as *psychology and *economics.

corruption, the abuse of power or misuse of public office for private ends or personal gain. Political corruption

A typical example of the black economy is the sale of goods which break patent or **copyright** laws. In this shop in Abu Dhabi 'pirated' cassettes are on sale; they have been copied without paying the originator the required copyright fee.

Japanese political life has repeatedly been rocked by accusations of bribery and **corruption**. Here Prime Minister Takeshitu resigns in April 1989 amidst allegations of corrupt practice.

encompasses *electoral fraud; the misappropriation of public money and property; and extortion by, and bribery of, politicians and public officials. In all contemporary societies, politicians and officials wield great power: they allocate public funds, levy taxes, grant licences, control access to services, and enforce or circumvent the law. The ideal of disinterested public service which developed in 19th-century Europe is generally accepted as applying not only to officials but also to politicians in most democracies. Corruption is seen as undermining the fair administration of public policies, distorting decision-making, wasting public money, and eroding public trust in the state. Attempts to check flagrant corruption include legal controls, censorious public attitudes, and media vigilance. The ability of the public to scrutinize the activities of public authorities and to hold them accountable is generally thought to be one of the best defences against corruption. Democratic governments in Greece, Japan, and many other countries have in recent years been challenged or brought down by corruption scandals. In the former Eastern bloc, public disgust at the scale of official corruption, on which there were no effective checks, contributed to the collapse of several communist regimes. In developing countries where *one-party government often prevails the model of disinterested public service may not be well entrenched, and older loyalties and traditions may conflict with expectations of impartial decision-making (see *clientelism). This may lead to endemic corruption in day-to-day transactions with government and, in the most serious cases, the diversion by corrupt leaders for their personal use of huge sums raised through taxation and foreign loans and intended for *development. Anger at such abuses has contributed to vigorous campaigns for free expression and multiparty politics in many parts of Africa and Latin America.

cost (in economics), expenditure incurred in the process of production. In the short run, costs can be classified into fixed (or indirect) and variable (or direct) costs. Fixed costs, in some cases also known as overheads, are costs which vary with output. They have to be paid even when there is no output. Examples include *rent, rates, service charges for *capital goods, and *interest payments. Variable costs are those which vary with output, such as wages, raw material,

and costs of intermediate goods. Unit costs are calculated by dividing total production costs by the number of units of output produced, thus arriving at the average cost per unit of output. Opportunity cost is cost measured not in money terms, but in terms of alternative objectives foregone. If suppliers produce refrigerators, the opportunity cost may be that they have sacrificed the opportunity to produce television sets instead. If consumers buy encyclopedias, the opportunity cost may be that they have given up the chance to enjoy an expensive meal in a restaurant. With an ideally functioning *price system, opportunity cost is reflected in money cost. In other words, the price of *resources measures their *value in alternative uses, a key notion in economics.

cost accounting, the provision of cost information for management purposes. Cost information relates to the need to determine costs of production and to determine profitability and efficiency. Cost information is also necessary in planning and controlling budgets within the organization, usually on an annual cycle. Budget and cost control enables efficient cost standards to be maintained and involves a system of reporting to managers.

cost–benefit analysis, a method of appraising *investment projects which takes into account not only the cash outflows and inflows expected to accrue to the investor, but the total economic impact by attempting to measure social consequences in money terms, and by including external (spillover) effects on other parts of the economy. The method is typically used by national and local government authorities in assessing whether major investment projects, public or private, should proceed. The method involves assigning to every relevant cost or benefit a monetary value which represents society's welfare loss or gain. Certain types of cost and benefit may be extremely difficult to quantify, such as the loss of wildlife or a reduced risk of road accidents. Techniques employed to assess these costs include, for instance, assessing how much people are prepared to pay to preserve wildlife, or calculating the money cost of injury or death in road accidents.

Council of Europe, an organization of West European countries, independent of the *EC, which seeks to safeguard the common heritage of its members and to promote economic and social co-operation. Its headquarters is in Strasburg. The organization was set up in 1949, and in 1991 it had twenty-three members: Austria, Belgium, Republic of Cyprus, Denmark, France, Finland, Germany, Greece, Iceland, Republic of Ireland, Italy, Liechtenstein, Luxemburg, Malta, The Netherlands, Norway, Portugal, San Marino, Spain, Sweden, Switzerland, Turkey, and the UK. The Council has limited powers but has made progress in furthering regional co-operation in a variety of fields, notably in working towards the harmonization of national laws within Europe or subjects such as the legal status of *migrant workers and *data protection. The Council is also a forum for discussion of political matters, such as UN activities, international relations, the prevention of *terrorism, and the promotion of *human rights. All members are party to the *European Convention on Human Rights (1950).

counselling (in psychology), guidance offered in the form of discussion rather than any specific type of therapy. Counsellors may have a quantity of specialized knowledge on particular problems, possible solutions, and the potential pitfalls of different solutions, but often they see their role as assisting

People greet troops loyal to President Corazon Aquino after the defeat of an attempted **coup d'état** against her fragile democratic government in the Philippines in December 1989.

those who consult them to find their own solutions. Counselling may be available to help people adapt after physical injury, traumatic shock, when a family has been incapacitated by mental or physical injury, when a marriage is unhappy, when a child has been abused, or when career advice is needed. It may be offered by psychologists, doctors, social workers, or trained lay people. In marriage guidance, the counsellor to some extent acts as an arbitrator, trying to help the couple reach compromises which might meet some of the demands of both parties. In career guidance, counsellors may administer various *psychological tests to assess the clients' capacities and interests. Counselling should be distinguished from *psychotherapy, although there is some overlap. It is less intensive and sometimes more directive, and its clients may have a much wider range of concerns for which they require guidance.

counter-insurgency, the means by which an incumbent government attempts to combat the effectiveness of insurgent groups who are using techniques of *guerrilla warfare or *terrorism in order to defeat or overthrow that government. The broad strategy of counter-insurgency recognizes that revolutionary guerrilla insurgency cannot be defeated solely by using military measures and involves an integration of military, political, social, and economic measures aimed at breaking the crucial link between the insurgents and the civilian population upon which they depend for sustenance and political support. This was referred to by US military planners in Vietnam (1964–72) as 'winning the hearts and minds of the people'. Such principles have perhaps only been applied with success in Malaya, where they were developed by the British in the early 1950s to suppress the communist insurgency.

counter-intelligence services, government organizations dedicated to protecting information and *intelligence services, and to maintaining their secrecy. Such organizations have grown greatly during the 20th century, alongside the growth in espionage, *propaganda, *terrorism, and subversion, reflecting the growth of what has been termed the *national security state. The main purpose of counter-intelligence operations is to prevent the penetration and subversion of the intelligence services, and to maintain control of strategically important information, including technology. This defensive purpose can be allied to that of manipulating the adversary's intelligence services by penetration and subversion, through the use of double-agents or 'disinformation' (the planting of inaccurate or misleading intelligence). Such measures may not only be practised in relation to adversaries: for instance, the Israeli Mossad agency not only safeguards its intelligence against the services of allies such as the US Central Intelligence Agency (CIA), but has also been accused of penetrating and subverting the US intelligence services themselves. Major intelligence services have also developed a capacity for 'covert action', the attempt to exercise influence over the policies and authority of a government from within or outside a country, by using such clandestine means as destabilization, subversion, or the elimination of its prominent members.

counter-revolution, the attempt to overturn or reverse the consequences of *revolution, usually by subversion or military action. Many theories of revolution also contain the notion that the forces of conservatism or reaction, after initial defeat, will regroup and attempt to regain power. In this cause, they may be supported from outside the country by those whose interests are threatened internationally, or by those who have held influence over the country. Radical or revolutionary regimes in Latin America, for example that of the Sandinistas in Nicaragua (1979–90), have also been attacked by counter-revolutionary forces, often with covert or overt support from the USA.

coup d'état, the sudden overthrow of government, especially by military force. The resulting government may assume direct military rule (see *military government) or rule by a faction sponsored by the military (see *junta). In a coup, it is simply the government that undergoes sudden change; a *revolution, on the other hand, involves a radical overturn of a country's entire political, social, and ideological system. Modern *coups d'état* have been most prevalent in Latin America and in the former European colonial territories of the Middle East, Africa, and South-east Asia, but they have also occurred in post-war Europe at times, for example in Portugal (1974), Greece (1967), and the Soviet Union (an attempted coup in 1991).

court-martial, a judicial court consisting of military officers with *jurisdiction to try to punish those charged with military offences. The word also refers to the proceedings of such a court. Most countries have their own military codes of justice, and their own military courts, with the exception of Germany, where military personnel are tried in the civilian courts. In the UK, the court-martial usually consists of a group of serving officers, assisted by a legally qualified judge-advocate, who sums up the evidence and advises on the law. A similar system exists in the USA. In many countries, the findings of a court-martial may be subject to appeal in the civilian courts.

court of law, a place where justice is judicially administered. The function of the court is to decide disputes, award *damages, impose punishments, authorize acts for which application has been made (such as divorce), and exercise other administrative functions. The *jurisdiction and hierarchy of courts vary from country to country. One distinction may be between civil courts and criminal courts; another common distinction exists between courts of general jurisdiction, which deal with a variety of cases, and courts of special jurisdiction, confined to limited issues (such as *courts-martial or *juvenile courts). A further distinction exists between lower and higher courts: lower courts deal with less important matters, and may be presided over by a layman (such as a *magistrate) rather than a *judge; while more difficult or serious cases are heard by superior courts, often presided over by judges of higher status. An appeal against the decision of a lower court may be referred to an appellate court; there may be different levels of such appeal courts, culminating in a court of ultimate authority, such as the House of Lords in the UK, the French *Cour de Cassation* (subject to the *European Court of Justice), or the US Supreme Court. At this level, appeals may be limited to questions of law rather than questions of fact. Courts are presided over by one or more judges or magistrates. In certain cases in Anglo-American systems, the judge is assisted by a *jury of laymen. Court procedure varies in different legal traditions, but parties to a case are generally represented in court by an *advocate or a *barrister.

covenant (in law), a promise made by one person to another in a formal document known as a deed. Such promises are often contained in the *conveyancing deeds by which land is transferred, for example to restrict the purchaser's use of the land to residential purposes. In a commercial context, covenant is an agreement between a borrower and a lender. It specifies conditions of the *loan which are legally binding on the borrower. These may include certain actions to be taken or avoided by the borrower. For instance, a borrower may have to present financial statements to the lender.

covenant (in theology), the central notion of Jewish belief and religious practice, and an important concept in Christian theology of God's commitment to his people. The Jewish covenant was originally offered to Noah by God, who promised to protect Noah's family and later generations from the great flood, and sealed his promise with a rainbow. An unquestioning obedience to God's will earned Abraham a covenant between God and the Jewish peoples: the gift of the land that was to be Israel and the blessing of descendants that were to become the Jewish nation. The practice of *circumcision (Hebrew, *brit*) seven days after birth, connects the individual Jewish male child to a larger covenant. The covenant was codified in the Ten Commandments, recalling God's deliverance of the Jews from Egypt. The ensuing rules govern life in minute detail and form the religious and cultural basis of Judaism. They include diet (see *kosher), dress, morality, and religious ritual. The binding nature of the covenant was reasserted by the *Prophets, who recognized their nation's disobedience towards God and demanded the people's return to righteousness. Some prophets referred to a 'new covenant', a notion later applied in Christianity by Christ to the imminent sacrifice of his life, which seals a renewed covenant between God and the new Israel, the Christian Church.

creation myth, a tale or *myth recounting the origins of the natural world and human society. Myths about the creation of the world, whether they describe the operation of a creator *god, the emergence of the world from primordial parents or a cosmic egg, *sacrifice, or a primordial battle, have great importance within religious beliefs and associated *rituals. Typical features include irreconcilable opposites such as light and dark, or water and earth. Some creation myths refer to the origins of particular *clans or *lineages; these typically tell the story of descent from a single common ancestor or founder. The *Trobriand Islanders of Melanesia, for example, believe that the ancestors of their four clans originally sprang from a particular hole in the ground, and this myth is used to explain differences of rank within the society. Described by the anthropologist *Malinowski as a charter for legitimacy, myths of this kind often act to justify the authority of elders or *chiefs, and may be an important component in the *political organization of society.

creationism *fundamentalism.

creativity, invention, whether in science or the arts. Although creativity is considered a rare personality attribute, found only in gifted individuals, worthwhile innovations are often produced by 'ordinary' people. Creative people may not be a specific personality type but be espe-

Indira Gandhi's son Rajiv lights the funeral pyre at her **cremation** in 1984. Seven years later his own funeral pyre was to be built in the same place, and lit by his son Rahul.

cially well placed to offer novel solutions to problems. A precondition may be particular artistic, scientific, or musical training, coupled with inspiration and hard work. Creativity may reflect the ability to see new relationships among pre-existing elements (see *cognitive psychology). The free play of the imagination may be essential to this process. It is also suggested that bursts of creativity often follow a period of 'incubation', sometimes even of depression, and may result from mental activity beyond the reach of *consciousness.

credit, a *debt incurred through the purchase of *goods and services by delayed payment. A major form of credit is *consumer credit. Bank credit is extended by a *bank (or similar institution) to its customers in the form of overdrafts and *loans. Trade credit is allowed by one trader to another, in the course of business. Credit is vital in facilitating *market transactions, and is liable to have a significant effect on the general level of economic activity. A government wishing to reduce *inflation may wish to limit credit (a credit squeeze) by raising *interest rates (and making credit more expensive since interest represents the price of borrowing) or by instituting more direct credit controls.

credit union, a non-profit-making organization, found mainly in the USA, entitled to provide services to a restricted group of people. Credit unions are typically formed by the employees of a company or other institution. They are normally able to provide cheaper *loans than a

*bank, but are restricted by law as to the amount and conditions of loans.

Cree, an Indian group originally from the Great Lakes area of Canada. The Cree split into two distinct groupings when they were displaced in the mid-19th century. One group became the Woodland Cree, practising sedentary farming, hunting, and gathering, while the other group moved into the Plains area to become the Plains Cree, practising nomadic buffalo hunting. Both groups are culturally and linguistically close to the *Ojibwa.

creed, (from Latin, *credo*, 'I believe'), an authorized, formal statement of Christian belief, the most important being the Nicene Creed and the Apostles' Creed. In early Christianity, brief declarations of belief at baptism varied regionally, but usually made a threefold reference to God the Father, the Son, and the Holy Spirit. The Council of Nicaea (325) issued a formal creed for universal acceptance as a test of orthodoxy. This was later developed into the Nicene Creed, used today in both Western and Eastern Orthodox Eucharistic services. The Apostles' Creed, ascribed in legend to the twelve apostles, first mentioned *c.*390, and found in its present form *c.*700, is used only in the West. The Athanasian Creed is a 5th-century doctrinal statement wrongly attributed to Athanasius, a 4th-century bishop of Alexandria.

cremation, disposal of a corpse by burning it to ashes. The belief in the resurrection of the body meant that cremation was forbidden for Christians, except in cases of emergency, such as the 14th-century Black Death. Cremation became acceptable in the 19th century, largely because of the pressure for space in crowded churchyards. Protestant

Churches, and since 1963 the Roman Catholic Church, allow cremation as an alternative to burial, but it is still forbidden in the Eastern Orthodox Christian Churches, and for Orthodox Jews and Muslims. In the East, cremation has always been the most general method of disposing of the dead, as a way of avoiding pollution from the corpse. In Buddhist, Hindu, and Sikh practice, bodies are usually burned on funeral pyres built close to flowing water, into which the ashes are cast. If possible, devout Hindus return the ashes of the dead to the River Ganges in India. Suttee (from Sanskrit, *sati*, 'virtuous woman'), the custom for a wife to burn herself to death on her dead husband's funeral pyre, was made illegal by the British in India in 1829, but isolated occurrences persist.

Creole *Caribbean societies, *pidgin and creole languages.

cricket, an eleven-a-side summer sport originating in England and now played at Test or top international level in the UK, Australia, New Zealand, the West Indies, India, Pakistan, Sri Lanka, Zimbabwe, and South Africa. The pitch is marked out at or near the centre of the field. It consists principally of two wickets (three stumps, 28 inches (71.12 cm) high, surmounted by two bails, each 4.37 inches (11.11 cm) long, which rest in grooves cut in the top of the stumps) set at a distance of 22 yards (20.12 m) from each other. 'Wicket' also refers to the playing pitch and, as in 'taking a wicket', the dismissal of a batsman. Each side has one or two innings (the time when one side or player is batting) of ten wickets each. Two players from the batting side go in against the fielding side. A bowler begins the first over of six—or (in Australia) eight—balls. Using an overarm action, the ball is delivered (bowled) from one end, and the batsman tries to defend the wicket at the other, if possible hitting the ball away into the field to score runs. As the fielders chase the ball and return it to the stumps, the two batsmen may cross and score one or more runs. If the striking batsman hits the ball across the boundary line, four runs are scored if the ball bounces before crossing and six if it goes out on the full. A batsman may be dismissed in various ways, the most common being bowled (bowler's ball strikes the wicket and dislodges one or both bails), caught (fielder catches ball off bat), leg-before-wicket (batsman struck on leg by a ball which would have hit stumps), and run out (batsman fails to make ground when running). The batting side tries to amass as many runs as possible and then to dismiss the opposing side for less. At professional level, matches may last up to five days.

crime, a punishable act or conduct, prohibited by the *criminal law. It is important to distinguish a criminal act from an immoral one; many crimes are immoral and harmful, but not all immoral or harmful actions are legally prohibited (lying, for example, is not illegal, except in certain circumstances, such as *perjury). By definition, crime is socially determined: what constitutes crime can vary over time and between societies. However, certain categories of crime are recognized almost everywhere: *violent crime, including assault and *homicide; *rape and other *sexual offences; *property crime, including theft and burglary; *white-collar crime, such as fraud and embezzlement; and other crimes against society, such as *drugs offences. Crime is a public, as distinct from a private, wrong; it affects not only the victim but the community, which requires the *punishment of the offender as a way of expressing public condemnation. Within *criminology many theories, based on biology, psychology, and sociology, have been put forward to explain criminal behaviour; criminologists have also sought to measure the extent of crime, and to account for its apparent increase in all modern industrialized societies. Economic growth seems to lead to more opportunities for crime, while liberation from restraints, as occurred in the former Eastern-bloc countries after the overthrow of authoritarian regimes in 1989, may also lead to a rise in crime. Several countries have schemes to compensate victims of crime financially, the first being set up in New Zealand in 1964. In the fight against crime, the police use increasingly complex resources, such as computer records, forensic *evidence, and international co-operation (see *Interpol).

Cricket

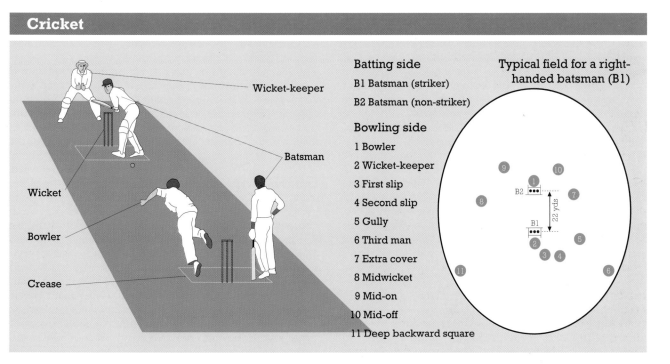

Batting side
B1 Batsman (striker)
B2 Batsman (non-striker)

Bowling side
1 Bowler
2 Wicket-keeper
3 First slip
4 Second slip
5 Gully
6 Third man
7 Extra cover
8 Midwicket
9 Mid-on
10 Mid-off
11 Deep backward square

Wicket-keeper
Batsman
Wicket
Bowler
Crease

Typical field for a right-handed batsman (B1)

criminal law, that branch of the law concerned with wrongdoing against individuals, society, or the state, for which the state has power to seek *punishment through the courts. The major goal of criminal law is deterrence and *punishment, while that of *civil law is individual *compensation. Criminal offences consist of two distinct elements; the physical act (the *actus reus*, 'guilty act') and the requisite mental state with which the act is done (the *mens rea*, 'guilty mind'). For example, in murder the *actus reus* is the unlawful killing of a person, while the *mens rea* is 'malice aforethought' (the intention to kill or cause grievous injury). The criminal law also details the defences that defendants may bring to lessen or negate their liability (*criminal responsibility) and specifies the *punishment which may be inflicted.

criminal responsibility, a concept in *criminal law that defines the degree of knowledge and intention with which an offender commits a crime. Ordinarily, an individual who commits a crime must be fully aware of the harmful nature of what he or she has done, and must have intended or foreseen the consequences or have acted with deliberate recklessness. A person who has not acted voluntarily, or is unaware of what he or she has done, is not normally regarded as criminally responsible, and neither are children under a certain age, an age which varies between societies. All legal systems recognize mental illness as a mitigating factor, though its definition can be problematic. In English law 'insanity' is narrowly defined, requiring proof that the defendant was so severely affected by a specific disorder such as *schizophrenia as not to know what he or she had done or whether it was wrong. Because this test is so narrow, a special defence of diminished responsibility is allowed in the case of murder. It is taken as a partial explanation, reducing the charge to the lesser one of manslaughter (see *homicide).

criminology, the study of criminal behaviour and of the administration of the *criminal law. Salient issues include the measurement, distribution, and causes of *crime, and the operations of law-enforcement agencies. Criminological research has shown that official criminal statistics do not accurately measure crime: when members of the public are surveyed, their reports of their own criminal behaviour and of the crimes of which they have been victims indicate far higher levels. To investigate the distribution of crime and the characteristics of criminals, criminologists examine such factors as their age, sex, ethnic background, social class, and place of residence. Criminologists are also interested in the causes of crime. The Italian physician Cesare Lombroso (1836–1909), who is often identified as the first empirical criminologist, tried to relate criminal behaviour to physical and biological characteristics. Later criminologists have tended to draw on *sociology by considering *social structure and *culture (*anomie, *alienation, or *labelling theory, for example) or on *psychology by considering the effects of childhood experience (*socialization) and personality differences such as *introversion and extroversion. Most would now agree that many explanations have force, but that all are partial. This is probably inevitable given the heterogeneous nature of criminal behaviour. Criminologists also study law enforcement and such subjects as *plea bargaining, *sentencing, and *punishment.

critical path method, a management tool for controlling the progress of any large project where completion on time is important. The method works by breaking down the large project into activities or tasks each with a time allocation. These activities are then logically represented on a network showing their interrelationships in a chronological fashion. For example, if the project was to build a house then the activity 'laying the foundations' must come before 'building the walls', whereas 'interior plumbing' could take place at the same time as 'internal wiring'. As each activity has a time allocation the completed network shows the critical path of activities which must be completed on time if the whole project is not to be delayed. It is also possible to identify the earliest and latest start times for each activity if the overall project is not to be delayed. The technique takes into account both activities (generally represented by a line) and nodes (represented by a circle). A node is a point at which various activities must coincide in either starting or finishing.

critical theory, the radical social theory developed by members of the Institute for Social Research in Frankfurt, Germany (the *Frankfurt School), during the 1930s and later. Following *Marx, they criticized capitalist societies, believing that individuality and freedom were being destroyed, that social injustice was deepening, and that large corporations were eliminating competition and aggrandizing themselves. Through critical theory, they analysed these developments and sought to 'unmask' the discrepancies between the proclaimed goals of, for example, 'democratic' governments and 'free market' economies and the principles by which they in truth operated. Critical theory has influenced scholars in diverse fields. Critical theorists look behind the apparent meaning of, for example, a literary work or the public justification of an institution in order to uncover what they believe to be a hidden, less palatable, reality.

croquet, a tactical lawn game, originating in France during the 17th century, played with four balls, six hoops, and mallets. The court measures approximately 32 by 26 m (35 by 28 yards), and players must hit their balls through the hoops in the correct sequence and finish on a central peg. Tactics include impeding an opponent's progress with devious manœuvres.

cross (in Christianity), a symbol of the wooden gallows on which *Jesus Christ was crucified. The cross is the most universal symbol of Christianity, recalling Christ's suffering and death to redeem mankind, a central doctrine of Christianity. The sign of the cross is used in Christian ceremonial as a benediction, dedication, profession of faith, or prayer. Crucifixes (crosses carrying representations of Christ), became popular within early Christianity and are still used in private prayer, especially in the Roman Catholic Church, as well as images of the Fourteen Stations of the Cross, showing Christ carrying his cross to the place of crucifixion. Representations of the cross include the Greek, with four equal arms; the Latin, with a long base; St Anthony's, in the form of the letter 'T', and St Andrew's, which is diagonal.

cross-country running, the winter sport of racing on foot over a country course containing natural obstacles such as closed gates and water hazards. Championship courses for men are 12–14 km (7.5–9 miles) long in the UK, and shorter in Europe; women's races are usually over 3–5 km (2–3 miles). Races are contested by individuals and teams. The sport has its own specialists and is popular with distance track-runners, who use it to keep fit during their off-season. Some joggers move up to cross-country, but its rigours are not suitable for all.

The behaviour studied as **crowd psychology** can be seen as an inheritance from our tribal past. Here an Italian football crowd gives an atavistic display of territorial ownership through its use of symbolic scarves and its chants.

cross-cultural psychology, the comparison of people from different *cultures to see if they think or feel differently. It is assumed that any differences in behaviour or performance in tests are probably due to *culture, although racial factors or gross differences in physical surroundings might also play a part. Sometimes a researcher hopes to find no difference, thus indicating that a shared characteristic may be innate. *Darwin and many modern psychologists have presented evidence of universality to back their claim that expressions of *emotion are innate. Alternatively, a cross-cultural difference may support a theory that a characteristic is learnt. This kind of work was initiated by anthropologists such as *Malinowski and *Mead, who investigated sex-role acquisition and *psychosexual development among peoples in the Pacific. The original cross-cultural expedition, to the Torres Straits, north of Australia, in 1899, concentrated on comparisons of *perception and *cognitive psychology. Subsequently a belief became established that 'primitive thought' is similar to a child's, as it is 'concrete' and illogical. Modern psychologists do not see such cultural differences as signs of a more primitive stage in the same culture, but rather as signs of development of different appropriate 'tools of thought'.

crowd psychology, the study and theory of the actions and emotions displayed by crowds or other masses of people. A primary controversy concerns the extent to which individuals in crowds cease to behave like themselves and

give way to impulse or the power of the crowd. The French theorist Gustave Le Bon (1841–1931) set the agenda for most discussion in *La psychologie des foules* (1895). He held that important human thoughts and motives operate at an *unconscious level. He suggested that in a crowd people become 'suggestible' and lose conscious control of themselves just as someone under *hypnosis does; the mood of a crowd is 'contagious', and its anonymity and apparent power cause people to yield to dangerous *instincts and disregard personal responsibility. Le Bon's ideas therefore picture persons in a crowd as emotional, irrational, and violent in comparison with individuals alone. This can lead to heroism, but is usually destructive. Evidence from real crowds, let alone riots and lynchings, is comparatively sparse, but studies in smaller groups of role-played panics and analogues of crowd behaviour such as group *conformity, the impact of anonymity, arousal in groups, and social contagion of *emotion, give mixed support for Le Bon's ideas. Studies of real crowds seem to give less support, as individuals' behaviour in football crowds and even race riots seems rule-governed and frequently rational; looting, for instance, tends to be selective and is not often over-audacious.

Crown, the office of a sovereign, and acts performed in the name of the sovereign. The concept refers to the office and not the office-holder, usually an hereditary monarch who is the Crown personified. The whole of government in the UK is carried on in the name of the Crown, which is a legal entity representing the *state and symbolizing its authority and continuity. In those *Commonwealth countries that still acknowledge the UK monarch as *head of state, *Crown prerogatives and immunities remain.

Crown prerogative (royal prerogative), the legal pre-eminence enjoyed by the *Crown, comprising a range of actions which no other agent may lawfully carry out. Crown prerogatives are today almost all delegated to ministers by *statute or exercised by the monarch in accordance with the recommendations of elected ministers and appointed advisers. The most significant prerogative power remaining to the UK monarch would be to invite any one of several party leaders to try to form a *coalition or minority government, if a general election resulted in a 'hung' parliament, in which no party commanded an overall majority.

culture, a general term used in two broad senses: the customs, civilization, and achievements of a particular time or people; and the arts and other manifestations of human intellectual achievement regarded collectively. In the study of society, few words are as difficult to define as culture, and much has been written on its definition alone, including the British–American poet T. S. Eliot's soberly conservative *Notes Towards the Definition of Culture* (1948) and the US literary critic George Steiner's *In Bluebeard's Castle: Notes towards the Redefinition of Culture* (1971). The various meanings of the word may be placed in two main groups: roughly, the anthropological and the artistic. The first defines culture as the whole way of life of a society: its beliefs and its ideas, its institutions and its systems, its laws and its customs. This definition was first elaborated by the Australian archaeologist V. G. Childe in 1929 and was further explored by the British literary critic Raymond Williams in his *Culture and Society* (1958) through the study of British working-class life and history. The second group of meanings defines culture more narrowly, but, in the view of its proponents, more deeply, as the civilized manners of a society, especially as they are expressed in its arts. Here the British poet and critic Matthew Arnold's *Culture and Anarchy* (1869), which defines culture as 'the pursuit of a total perfection, the best that has been thought and said', may still be considered the best introduction. By the first meaning, all humans are cultured because all are members of a culture, whatever its nature. By the same token, an individual tends to approach and judge other cultures from the standpoint of his or her own culture; a crucial idea in *anthropology and other social sciences is cultural *relativism, the view that beliefs are relative rather than absolute. By the second meaning, however, only a minority are likely to be cultured at any one time because culture is a refinement, to be worked for and to be aspired towards.

currency, the current token *money (medium of exchange) used in a country, in the form of notes and coins, usually called cash; or the denomination of a country's money, such as the pound sterling or Swiss franc. (See under individual countries in country section for the names of their currency.) An international ('hard') currency, such as the Deutschmark, is one which is widely acceptable in international *trade, partly because the risk of a fall in its *value is seen as less than for other currencies. The dollar, for example, is used for petroleum transactions. 'Basket currencies', such as the Special Drawing Rights (SDRs) of the *International Monetary Fund and the European Currency Unit (ECU), can also be used to reduce risk in international transactions and to facilitate intergovernmental transactions. The value of such a basket is the combined value of specified amounts of each of the currencies included in it.

curriculum (in education), the subjects which are studied or prescribed for study. The balance between academic and vocational subjects, and the extent of religious or political indoctrination vary, as does the extent of national control over school curricula. Two countries which can trace their systems of detailed national curricula back to the 19th century are Japan (from 1868) and France (from 1875). In both countries this pattern of national education is generally believed to have contributed, as its initiators intended, to national cohesion and to the achievement of high educational standards. The attainments of Japanese children in mathematics and science, for example, are the best in the world. However, in both countries concern that creativity and initiative have been stifled have resulted in calls for reform, calls which in France have led since the early 1980s to greater local decision-making. In the UK, by contrast, where until recently many curricular decisions, especially for primary school children, were devolved to schools and local authorities, the Education Reform Act (1988) gave the government power to introduce a national curriculum for all children in state schools in England and Wales, specifying the subjects to be studied and the time allocated to them, and indicating their content. The term 'hidden curriculum' refers to the unacknowledged ways in which schools transmit values, for example by rewarding individual athletic success but not co-operative enterprise.

Cushitic languages, a group of languages spoken by around 15 million people in Somalia, Ethiopia, and northern Kenya, and in an area further north (spanning the Egypt–Sudan border) between the Nile and the Red Sea. The languages which make up Cushitic are diverse and have been sub-divided into five groups, called for the sake of convenience Northern, Eastern, Southern, Western, and Central Cushitic. However, most scholars now think that the Western languages (spoken by 2 million people in western Ethiopia and northern Kenya) should not be included as part of the Cushitic family, but should form a separate group called Omotic. The other four groups consist of about forty languages. The Eastern group, which includes Galla (Oromo) and Somali, is numerically the most important. Galla is the largest Cushitic language; its dialects (which are all mutually intelligible) are spoken by 10 million people in Ethiopia and Kenya. Somali is spoken by around 5 million people in Somalia (where it is the official language), Ethiopia, and Kenya. Northern Cushitic is represented by Beja, which is spoken in Egypt, the Sudan, and Eritrea. Central Cushitic was originally the major language of Ethiopia before the arrival of speakers of *Semitic languages. Now, however, it is spoken in small linguistic islands which are in danger of being submerged. Most speakers also speak Amharic or Tigrinya. Ethiopia's *Falasha Jews are among the speakers of Central Cushitic. The Southern languages form an isolated group in Tanzania. All Cushitic languages have borrowed words from Arabic, Amharic, and Nilo-Saharan. They are written in the Arabic script, though there is no literary tradition. Cushitic is part of Afro-Asiatic, a larger group which includes Berber, Chadic, and Semitic.

customary law, unwritten rules generally accepted as binding by a community as a result of long use. All legal systems recognize custom as a source of law, although the authority ascribed to it and the extent to which it is recognized in legislative measures and *case law varies. In English law, custom is at the root of much of the *common law, but it is rarely recognized by case law today, while in Japan, where the adoption of codified laws is very recent, courts have given effect to older customs (relating, for example, to marriage), even where they conflict with the civil code. For centuries, sub-Saharan Africa was ruled by customary law, based on traditional beliefs and values, and varying from community to community. It formed the main basis of *dispute resolution, the prime purpose of which was to bring about amicable agreement and restore the cohesion of the group, rather than to pursue abstract ideas of rights and punishment. Colonialism brought Western legal systems to Africa, but customary law continued to be recognized in certain areas (such as family law), with the exception of practices that were considered by the colonialists to be morally repugnant. In independent contemporary African states, such legal pluralism still exists, but there is often tension between the aspirations of some to create modern societies and the preservation of traditional, specifically African, values. For example, legislation to emancipate women may radically disrupt traditional relationships between kin.

customs and excise duties, indirect taxes paid on *goods (see *taxation). Customs duties are *tariffs paid on goods entering (or occasionally leaving) a country. Excise duties are paid on the domestic sale of certain goods and activities, such as alcohol, tobacco, motor fuel, and betting.

customs union   *common market.

cycling, the recreation of riding a bicycle and the various branches of cycle-racing. Several sports can be adapted for playing on bicycles, such as *hockey, *polo, and cycleball (a mounted version of football, using the wheels to propel the ball). Cycle-racing is basically divided into stadium events and road-racing; there is also cyclo-cross, a blend of cycle-racing and *cross-country running held over rough, hilly terrain. Cycle-stadia have steeply banked tracks for sprint events in which skilful manœuvring for position is important. Professional road-racing is established world-wide, but is most popular in Europe, where victory in the Tour de France is the sport's highest prize. The race-circuit, varied from year to year, consists of a gruelling series of stage-races and time-trials, lasting three weeks and covering some 4,828 km (3,000 miles).

Cyrillic alphabet   *alphabet, *Slavic languages.

Dalai Lama (Tibetan, 'Ocean of wisdom and compassion'), title bestowed upon the head of the Yellow Hat monks, the dominant sect in *Tibetan Buddhism, by the Mongol ruler Altan Khan in 1578. The concept of 'lama' (meaning 'none above') is central to the institutions of Tibetan Buddhism. Succession is by incarnation: that is, each monastic leader is regarded as a reincarnation of his predecessor. The Dalai Lama himself is said to be the reincarnation of the important *Bodhisattva Avalokiteshvara. Years are spent seeking out and teaching each new incumbent. The position of Dalai Lama carries full state and religious responsibilities. The present, fourteenth, Dalai Lama, Tenzin Gyatso (1935–   ), was forced into exile in 1959, but his spiritual and political influence remains authoritative for Tibetans.

damages, *compensation in the form of an award of money by a court, constituting the main remedy for loss caused by breach of *contract or the commission of a *tort (that is, a breach of duty other than contractual, such as negligent driving). In *common law systems, contractual damages are intended to give the victim the benefit of the bargain which has not been performed, while tortious damages are intended to put the victim in the position he or she would have been in if the tort had not been committed. Damages may generally be reduced if the plaintiff has contributed in part to the loss.

Dao (Tao) (Chinese, 'way', 'path', 'teaching'), a fundamental concept in *Chinese religion and philosophy, denoting 'the correct way' or moral code. In *Confucianism, *Dao* refers to that which makes correct conduct effective, but in *Daoism, the concept is given an additional spiritual meaning. In the *Daodejing, it is decribed as an Absolute beyond full human understanding or definition. The *Dao* is an ineffable principle which cannot be taught or learnt; Daoists aim to live by a code of inner quietism in accordance with the principles of nature and thus achieve harmony or unity with the *Dao*. To the Moists, who taught universal love, it is the way of ancient sages, sanctioned by the universe or nature (*tien*). This concept prevailed in many traditional Chinese schools of philosophy and took on both metaphysical and ethical meanings in Neo-Confucianism.

Daodejing (Tao-te Ching), '*The Book of the Way and its Power*', a Chinese classic ascribed to Laozi (Lao-tzu; *fl.* 6th century BC), an obscure state official credited as founder of *Daoism. Originally perhaps a handbook for the ruler, the *Daodejing* defines the *Dao* ('way') as absolute reality, the source and end of all being. *De* refers to 'virtue', the latent power acquired through understanding the *Dao*. The *Daodejing* advocates 'unmotivated action': letting things take their natural course according to the spontaneous flow of the *Dao*. It has attracted many in contemporary Western society.

Daoism (Taoism), one of the three main *Chinese religious and philosophical traditions, the others being *Confucianism and *Buddhism. Like Confucianism, Daoism has both a philosophical and a religious, or ritualistic, aspect. However, it is markedly different from the practical teachings of Confucianism in its emphasis on inner contemplation, mystical forms of knowledge, and spontaneous, non-active union with the nature of being. Philosophical Daoism developed from the 5th to the 3rd centuries BC; its tenets are found in the *Daodejing, traditionally attributed to Laozi, and in the text known as the *Zhuangzi after its author. The ultimate reality is the *Dao, in which being and not-being, life and death, are merely aspects of the same reality. Through silence, stillness, and actionless action (*wu wei*) the Daoist aims to achieve unity with the *Dao*. A religious Daoism also developed and was officially recognized in the 3rd century AD; it incorporated certain Buddhist features and developed its own monastic system and cultic practices. Religious Daoism has also tended to be close to certain folk religious practices, and has borrowed elements such as the worship of different local gods. It emphasized the attainment of longevity and physical immortality, which could flow from proximity to the *Dao*, rather than mystical union with the *Dao*, and to this end investigated techniques such as alchemy, magic elixirs, breathing exercises, and meditation. Daoism has been influential in Vietnam, Japan, and Korea, and Daoist religious practice persists in Taiwan. In communist China, Daoist religious practices and monasteries were suppressed, but Daoist thought remains a potent influence in Chinese culture.

darts, the mainly British indoor target-game of throwing small flighted darts at a circular board. The board has twenty sections, numbered 1–20 in a specified order, with an outer ring which scores double the number, an inner treble ring, and a bull's-eye (the centre of the target). Players throw three darts in turn, standing behind a line about 2.5 m (8–9 feet) from the board. The most popular game is 301: players subtract their totals from 301, and to finish must end with a double that brings their score to zero.

Darwin, Charles (1809–82), British naturalist whose ideas and observations have played a decisive role in the life sciences and in the thought of the 20th century. His *On the Origin of Species by Means of Natural Selection* (1859), argues that species are not fixed but evolve through selection. Some individuals have characteristics which better fit them for survival; they are more likely to reproduce and pass their characteristics on to their offspring. Over time distinct species develop. Darwin argued that mankind has evolved in this way. The Austrian Gregor Mendel (1822–84) and later geneticists revealed the mechanisms of variability and the transmission of characteristics. Darwin's work was immediately influential in *psychology when his cousin *Galton, founder of *eugenics, began to study the heritability of *intelligence. Darwin's work gave grounds for belief in the continuity of human and animal *evolution. This belief has seemed to justify much theorizing about humans based on animal experiments. Darwin's *The Expression of the Emotions in Man and Animals* (1872) points out parallels between human and animal body language and *facial expression and remains influential in the study of *emotion and *non-verbal communication.

Dasam Granth (Punjabi, 'tenth book'), a collection of religious poems associated mainly with the tenth Sikh Guru, *Gobind Singh, who was a patron of the arts as well as a warrior. Although the book is not accorded the same authority as the *Adi Granth, verses from the *Dasam Granth* are used by Sikhs in their daily devotions.

data protection, arrangements to ensure that confidential information, and especially computerized information, is available only to people entitled to use it. The twin purposes are to maintain the confidentiality of personal information and business secrets, and to enable the subjects on whom information is stored to ensure its accuracy. Electronic methods for combating unauthorized access to computers are supplemented in many countries by legal requirements. Typically, people who hold information about others are obliged to register with a regulatory agency, to comply with its codes of practice and to permit individuals to check and correct their records. Wrongfully obtaining access to material may be a criminal offence.

deafness, partial or total loss of hearing, which may be congenital (present at birth) or may develop at any age, particularly among the elderly. Some deaf children need special education in separate units, while others may be successfully integrated into normal schools. The deaf are able to communicate by lip-reading or by using a special sign language (see *signing). Total communication usually implies the use of both these methods, as well as speech, finger-spelling, and writing, so that the possibilities of communication are extended and *disability minimized. Those with residual hearing may make use of hearing aids, worn in or behind the ear.

death, causes of. Causes are generally classified into two main types, exogenous (arising from environmental and external causes such as infectious diseases, *famines, natural *disasters, and accidents) and endogenous (arising from a person's genetic make-up). The historical movement from less developed to modern societies has, broadly speaking, been characterized by a shift from exogenous to endogenous causes. This shift has resulted in changes in *mortality rates and *life expectancy. The difference, in contemporary societies, is typified by the difference between countries such as Bangladesh, in which the main causes of death are *communicable diseases, and European countries, in which diseases associated with ageing, such as *cancer and *heart disease, predominate.

death penalty *capital punishment.

death rate *infant mortality rate, *mortality rate.

death squads *extra-judicial execution.

debenture, a fixed *interest-yielding *security (in the USA, a *bond) issued by a firm raising a *loan. Debentures are normally dated for redemption (repayment) by the holder, but may be irredeemable. They may be secured against a particular *asset held by the firm (fixed debentures) or against the whole firm (floating debentures). Debenture holders have higher priority than *shareholders when a *company is liquidated, and can force a company's liquidation if their interest is not paid as due (see *insolvency). Convertible debentures may be changed into ordinary shares at a specified date or dates.

debt, a sum owed by one economic agent to another. A debt is created when *credit or a *loan is supplied. Consumer credit is provided by retailers, finance houses, and others for the purpose of purchasing consumer goods. Trade credit is supplied between companies to facilitate *trade. Bank credit is provided by banks in the form of overdrafts and loans. Debts typically carry *interest charges. The provision of debt is vital to the operation of most economies as it enables people and organizations to spend before income has been received. (See also *national debt.)

debt crisis, the situation arising when people, organizations, or governments cannot pay back the *loans they have been given. They may not even be able to keep up the *interest payments. The mere possibility of a series of non-payments of interest or principal may be enough to cause a financial panic. When depositors fear a *bank failure, they may react by withdrawing their deposits, thus causing the very event they feared. This happened in the USA in the early 1930s and caused a major reduction in the money supply and led to *economic depression. The international debt crisis which started in 1982, when a number of countries had difficulty in servicing and repaying loans to the world's major banks, partly because of very high interest rates, posed a serious threat to the stability of the world banking system. In the event this was forestalled, but not without the banks making substantial losses as they wrote off (cancelled) bad debts. For some debtor countries, external debts to commercial banks, to the *International Monetary Fund, and to other governments remain a continuing constraint on economic advance, and have led to the implementation of *adjustment policies.

decathlon *pentathlon.

decentralization, the transfer of functions from central to regional or local authorities, usually in response to pressure from the regional level, or to the centre's search for efficiency. Federal systems of government are a constitutionally guaranteed form of territorial decentralization (see *federalism). Functional decentralization, by contrast, involves the establishment of local branches of central government departments with no *devolution of the centre's decision-making powers, and is a form of delegation. Most systems of *local government are a hybrid mix of devolution and delegation, allowing limited powers to make local decisions and carry them out within a legally defined framework.

deconstruction, a method of critical analysis of philosophical and literary language, concerned with unravelling the meanings of texts. In *On Grammatology* (1967) the French philosopher Jacques Derrida (1930–) claimed that exposing a text's underlying, but unformulated, ideas revealed meanings which contradicted the apparent meaning or the author's intentions. There was, he argued, no one meaning of a text, but rather a series of often contradictory meanings all elusive and none definitive. Derrida's writings are abstruse, and fierce dispute has erupted over his theory, which some regard as a fearless questioning of the possibility of meaning and others as an adventure playground for intellectual élitism. Deconstruction has been particularly influential in European and Anglo-American literary criticism. Among sociologists and philosophers, deconstruction-

Debt

The map shows the extent to which countries are burdened with debt. The debt service ratio indicates the percentage of a country's foreign currency earnings from exports it has to use to service its debts. A country's debt service ratio, rather than the size of its debt, is generally considered the best indicator of the impact of debt. The higher its ratio the worse its position. Ratios for the world's richest countries are not indicated on the map: their borrowings are usually small in relation to their export earnings, and the World Bank excludes them from its debt tables.

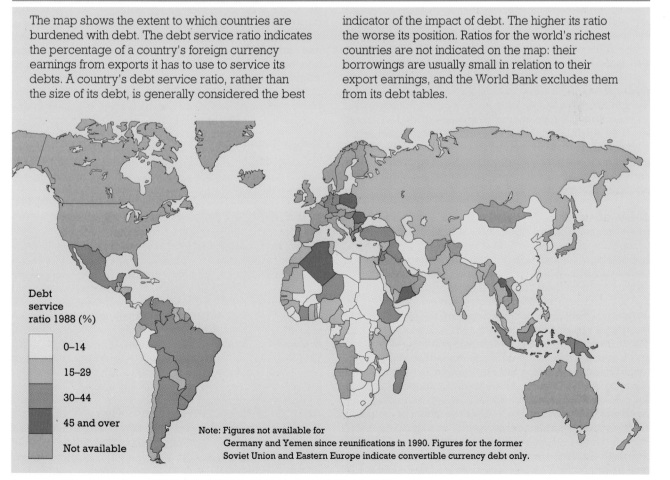

Debt service ratio 1988 (%)

- 0–14
- 15–29
- 30–44
- 45 and over
- Not available

Note: Figures not available for Germany and Yemen since reunifications in 1990. Figures for the former Soviet Union and Eastern Europe indicate convertible currency debt only.

Sources: *World Development Report 1990.* World Bank. 1990. *The Economist Book of Vital Statistics.* 1990.

Derrida's theories of **deconstruction** are summed up in his phrase 'There is nothing outside the text'. His method of close textual analysis to expose the contingency of the views articulated has been widely influential in contemporary literature, linguistics, and psychoanalysis.

ists have questioned the boundaries drawn between categories assumed to be distinct, such as male and female, as well as the meanings of the categories themselves.

deduction, the process or principles by which, in an argument, a conclusion is derived from certain premises. The term is also used, especially in philosophy, with a narrower sense, in which an argument is said to be deductively valid if it is impossible for all its premises to be true and its conclusion false. A simple example might be: 'Some Greeks are philosophers. All Greeks are Europeans. So some Europeans are philosophers.'

defamation, the dissemination of an untrue statement which might damage a person's reputation. False assertions of untrustworthiness or incompetence would be examples. In English law, defamation in a permanent form, such as the written word or film, is known as libel, while defamation in an impermanent form, such as the spoken word, is known as slander. Although an *injunction to prevent publication is sometimes granted by a court, the normal remedy is the award of *damages. Freedom of speech is, however, to some degree protected by defences including truth, fair comment, and public interest. In the USA, the constitutional guarantee of *free speech under the First Amendment has led the Supreme Court to place restrictions on state defamation laws. For instance, a public official alleging defamation may be required to prove that an allegation about a matter of public interest is untrue and motivated by malice.

defence (in international relations), the means taken by a state to defend itself against attack. In an international system devoid of a central authority that can guarantee security

and international order, states have to develop their own means of defence. Many develop their own *armed forces and buy or manufacture their own arms. Some states take up a foreign-policy stance of *neutrality, like Sweden or Switzerland. Others may seek a security guarantee from another state to deter a third (as, for example, in the case of Belize, assisted by the UK in its dispute with Guatemala in 1975 and 1977). Many enter into *alliances to provide a guarantee: Iceland has no armed forces, but it is a member of *NATO and is a strategic air-base for NATO forces. States with few resources, alliance relationships, or strategic positions may find themselves essentially indefensible, especially in the face of a powerful neighbour (for example, Namibia, threatened by the security policies of South Africa in the 1970s and 1980s). Such states may consider a policy of passive defence or non-violent resistance in the face of an external threat, or they may seek defence in the international *rule of law, placing their faith in the power of institutions such as the *UN or the *International Court of Justice.

defence mechanisms (in psychoanalysis), an unconscious process that protects the individual from *anxiety. *Freud argued that anxiety arises from conflict within the individual. It may be due to an ungratified appetite or *instinct or to conflict between an appetite and one's moral beliefs. The mechanisms include repression, keeping memories and wishes in the *unconscious; denial, simply refusing to accept that something is true; sublimation, finding a socially acceptable outlet for a morally unacceptable impulse (such as sexual desire for one's mother); rationalization, giving a rational but specious account of emotionally driven behaviour; regression, retreating to more immature patterns of behaviour; projection, attributing to other people feelings, such as aggression, which one entertains oneself; and reaction-formation, for example acting and feeling affectionately towards someone one hates. Repression is supposedly the main cause of *neurosis. The theory of defence mechanisms was laid out in detail by Anna Freud (1885–1982) in *The Ego and the Mechanisms of Defence* (1937).

Deforestation over thousands of years has left much of the world's land surface barren. Reafforestation, the planting and nurturing of selectively bred types of tree as in this development project in Burkina Faso, West Africa, can help to increase the land's fertility.

deficit financing, expenditure by government in excess of *income. The term is sometimes used to refer to total government spending, including *capital expenditure, and sometimes more narrowly to refer to current expenditure only. Deficit financing was advocated by *Keynes as a temporary means of reflating aggregate *demand in the economy, thus reducing *unemployment. Government borrowing cannot grow faster than *national income indefinitely. This is because the deficit must be financed either by increasing *debt, which will eventually become too large for the government to service out of its revenue (see *debt crisis), or by printing money, which will lead to *inflation. However, most governments regularly run deficits. The reason why this is normal and desirable is that most private (non-government) sectors wish to run surpluses, that is, to accumulate financial claims. This is only possible if another party, usually governments, accumulates the corresponding liabilities. The equilibrium size of government deficits depends on the savings and financial portfolio behaviour of the private sector.

deflation *inflation.

deforestation, the destruction of forest, usually for timber or to clear the land for cultivation or the raising of livestock. Most of western Europe and the Mediterranean lands lost their natural forest centuries ago, and in China wood has been scarce for thousands of years due to deforestation. Today, huge areas of forest, most of it tropical, are being cleared—some 12 million hectares or 2 per cent of the remaining forests each year. In South America, the Amazon rainforest, the world's largest, is particularly under threat and there, as elsewhere, much of the tree-felling is done by multinational companies, which either sell the timber for export or use the cleared land for ranching. As well as decimating the people and the unique wealth of animals and plants in the forests themselves, such destruction threatens the balance of nature on a global scale. The world's trees consume the gas carbon dioxide, which is a major contributor to the *greenhouse effect, and they give out the oxygen animals, including humans, need to breathe. Their roots hold the soil in place, and once they are cut down or burned the soil remains fertile for only a few years, before it is blown or washed away and the land becomes barren. What happened in Lebanon in the eastern Mediterranean, once famous for its cedar trees but now almost bereft of them, has now extended to areas of the Amazon. Reafforestation has been minimal, and usually with a single species of tree (monoculture). Future developments are likely to be in agroforestry, using sophisticated management techniques to cultivate new breeds of trees in combination with grassland and crop plants.

degenerative diseases, a wide range of disorders in which there is progressive impairment of the structure and function of a part of the body. Such diseases impose heavy burdens on sufferers, their families, and health and *social care services, but receive far less attention and expenditure than more dramatic conditions such as *cancer and *heart disease. Until the later stages of illness, *hospital or *institutional care is rarely either wanted by the sufferer or available. Yet the *rehabilitation services required to make life at home tolerable, whether to assist with daily tasks such as washing and eating or to improve life through education and employment, are inadequate in most of the rich countries of the world and almost non-existent elsewhere.

demand (in economics), the willingness and ability of buyers to purchase a *good or service at a given price. If a graph is drawn with price on the vertical axis and quantity demanded on the horizontal axis, a demand curve is the locus of points representing the amount demanded per period of time at each price. For most goods and services, such curves are downward sloping: a rise in price leads to a lower quantity demanded. The 'law of demand' is derived from an analysis of income and substitution effects caused by a change in relative prices. A rise in the price of one good reduces the buying power of a given money income (the income effect) and causes a shift away from the good in question, which is now relatively more expensive, to consumption of other goods (the substitution effect). The extent of this shift relative to a change in price is the price *elasticity of demand. An exception is the *Giffen good. In *macroeconomics, aggregate demand means the total spending in an economy.

dementia, a term used to refer to conditions which result in a progressive decline in the ability to remember, to learn, to think, and to reason. The risk increases with age, being one in five in those over 80. Alzheimer's Disease (first described by Alois Alzheimer, a German neurologist, in 1907) is the commonest form. Its cause is as yet unknown, although research suggests a genetic component, and there is no known cure. At first the individual may lose short-term *memory and have difficulty with everyday tasks. Later disorientation in familiar surroundings and wandering become common, as do personality changes. Finally, the sufferer may become incontinent, immobile, and unable to recognize people and places. The increasing prevalence of the disease as a result of *ageing populations means that services almost everywhere are inadequate.

democracy, a system of government in which sovereignty rests with the whole people, who rule either directly or through representatives. In the contemporary world, democracy is closely associated with the idea of choosing governments by periodic free multiparty elections, but in the past it was understood more literally to mean the people gathering together in an assembly to debate political issues and enact laws. As such, it was compared unfavourably to *monarchy and *aristocracy by most political thinkers, who saw it as unruly and inexpert, and also as impractical in societies bigger than the city-state. The representative system appeared to solve these problems (although it was fiercely criticized by *Rousseau, the greatest theorist of democracy). The chief elements of representative democracy are: freedom of speech and expression; periodic free elections to the *legislature, in which all *citizens are entitled to vote and to stand for office; the right to form competing parties to contest these elections; a government which is responsible to the legislature, and thereby to some degree responsive to public opinion. Where one or more of these elements is absent, as in the 'People's Democracies', the *one-party states of the communist bloc in the period following World War II, the system is unlikely to be genuinely democratic. Within the representative democracies, the major issue has been whether increased popular participation, through *referenda and other such devices, might make these states more democratic in the original sense. There has also been pressure for more democracy at a lower level, particularly in the way that work is organized. The social conditions for stable democratic government have been extensively discussed, with level of economic development apparently the most

A demonstration for **democracy** in Rangoon, Myanmar (Burma). Since the fall of the socialist governments in eastern Europe protest against similar regimes has spread worldwide. In Myanmar, military–socialist rule since 1962 has had disastrous social and economic consequences.

important single factor: the advanced capitalist societies are nearly all representative democracies, whereas many developing societies (India being a striking exception) have *authoritarian governments, despite often laying claim to a democratic structure.

demographic transition, a long-term transformation in which a population changes from high to low rates of *fertility and *mortality. The transition occurred in Europe between the late 18th and mid-20th centuries, coinciding with industrialization. Economic and social factors such as improvements in income, education, and welfare are generally cited as causes. In most but not all countries, the fall in the mortality rate preceded that of the fertility rate, thus stimulating population growth for a time. However, demographers believe that post-transitional rates generally result in near stable populations. Many attempts have been made to extend and revise the theory to cover contemporary populations in developing countries, but these remain controversial owing to the nature and complexity of contributing factors, and the diversity within and between countries.

demography, the systematic study of human populations, addressed primarily to their growth, size, and structure. The main sources of data are the *census and *vital statistics, which developed in the 19th century. In the 20th century, population studies have developed in two main directions. Formal demography is concerned with abstract population mathematics. It shows how rates of *birth, *fertility, *mortality, *marriage, and *migration combine to produce different *population structures, densities, and distributions. Social demography relates this abstract study to the economics and culture of particular societies in different times and places, in order to determine the causes and influence of changing population trends. Sustained declines in fertility and death rates (see *demographic transition) have had major implications for *social policy in modern societies; demographers project population changes to assist in the planning of schooling, transport, health, and other services.

dentistry, the prevention and treatment of diseases of the teeth and gums. Figures collected by the World Health Organization (WHO) indicate a world-wide trend towards a low prevalence of caries (tooth decay) and periodontal disease (disease in the supporting structures) and a marked reduction in edentulousness (the complete loss of teeth). In the industrialized world, where there has been a rapid decline from a high level of disease, this is attributed primarily to the introduction of fluoride toothpaste in the mid-1960s, to improved dental hygiene, and, in some places, reduced sugar consumption. The need for routine professional care for dental disease is likely to fall substantially in these countries. In developing countries, rates of dental disease (which traditionally have been lower than in industrialized countries, probably because of differences in diet) have risen, but are expected to fall gradually. There are few qualified dentists, and basic dental treatment such as the extraction of rotten teeth is often left to traditional practitioners. WHO is supporting the development of basic training, and the distribution of sets of simple, essential low-cost equipment.

deontology *consequentialism, *ethics.

dependency ratio, the ratio of children and older people to adults of working age (usually aged 15–64). Countries with young and rapidly growing populations have the highest dependency ratios. In Africa in the early 1990s, for every 100 adults of working age there were 88 children and 6 older people. In North America, by contrast, there were 32 children and 19 older people. Dependency ratios have important implications for *family policy and the *social services.

dependency theory, an approach to the understanding of underdevelopment in the *Third World, particularly influential in Latin America during the late 1960s and 1970s. Dependency analysis draws on two main lines of economic thought: Marxism and the nationalist, anti-imperialist postulates of Latin American structuralism. It emphasizes the obstacles posed to national development by external conditions. Its basic tenets are the assumption of an asymmetrical relationship between the industrialized countries (centre) and the Third World (periphery), and the subsequent lack of autonomy of the latter. A key text on the subject is F. H. Cardoso and E. Faleto's *Dependency and Development in Latin America* (1979).

dependent origination, otherwise known as 'conditioned arising', the central philosophical teaching of *Buddhism. Buddhists reject the notion of a personal creator *God, who is the origin of all things. Instead, Buddha formulated the idea of dependent origination to explain how all things come into being and how they cease to be. The doctrine states that all aspects of individual existence or modes of being are conditioned by others; in this world of ours there is nothing permanent, independent, or absolute, not even the individual self. It was the understanding of dependent origination, together with *nirvana, which formed the basis of the Buddha's enlightenment and subsequent teaching (*dharma). Dependent origination describes how suffering (the subject of the first of the *Four Noble Truths) comes about, following a series of twelve links or *nidānas*. The chain may begin at any point, but usually starts with ignorance and leads through such states as consciousness, sensation, craving, and clinging, to culminate in birth, ageing, and death. The process of rebirth (*samsara), conditioned by the law of cause and effect (*karma), continues the chain of links indefinitely. This endless series of cycles is graphically depicted in the image of the Wheel of Life. True understanding of dependent origination, however, enables us to break free of this endless wheel. The cessation of spiritual ignorance leads to the cessation of each of the conditioned *nidānas*, in a reverse process, culminating in an escape from karma and samsara, and enlightened entry into nirvana.

depopulation, declining population size in a given area, caused by *migration or *mortality rates in excess of *birth rates. At one time it was believed that the *demographic transition would be followed by the depopulation of Europe, but this belief was disproved by the baby boom after World War II and by better understanding of the causes of *population growth. Today depopulation occurs primarily in rural communities, for example in northern Scotland, southern France, and the Appalachians in the USA. It is caused by migration of young people seeking better opportunities in towns and cities, and it speeds up the process of *urbanization. The immediate impact on population size is compounded by the young age of many of the migrants.

deportation, the removal of an unwanted person from a country. This may be authorized by executive decision in the case of any person who does not have the right of abode under given circumstances. Because deportation can be used without a court order where legal proceedings would be impossible or embarrassing, for example where national security is thought to be threatened, there is a risk of deportation being used to evade the legal controls on *extradition. Deportation may be controversial; for example, where immigration authorities deport persons claiming *political asylum on the grounds that they are in fear for their life, to their country of origin.

depreciation (in economics), the reduction in the value of physical assets due to their wearing out or obsolescence. It normally refers to the deterioration of *capital goods such as buildings and machinery (which represents the difference between gross and net fixed *investment (capital formation) in the national accounts), but may also refer to the depreciation of other assets such as durable household consumption goods. In company accounts depreciation is a *cost to be deducted along with other costs from revenue in order to arrive at a *profit figure. A capital good will be used for a number of years and then be sold or scrapped. The difference between initial cost and scrap value should be spread over the asset life as depreciation in annual accounts. Depre-

The Wheel of Life, shown here in an example from Thiksey Monastery in Ladakh, India, is used in Buddhist teaching as a symbol of the doctrine of **dependent origination**. The pattern of life is cyclical, as in our own cycle of birth, death, and rebirth.

ciation can also be used to mean a fall in the external value of a currency (see also *devaluation, *exchange rates).

depression (in economics), a long period of significant *unemployment or underemployment of labour, capital, and land (the *factors of production). This contrasts with the short-lived unemployment that characterizes a *recession. The causes of depression are debatable, but may include large falls in the *money supply, overproduction, a general lack of *demand, and the use of *tariff barriers to protect national *trade balances. It may be that depression can be avoided or shortened by using *fiscal and monetary measures such as public spending, deficit spending, or tax cuts to reflate aggregate demand. This was true, according to *Keynes, of the global depression in the 1930s.

depression (in psychiatry), an abnormal and persistent state of very low mood, sufficient to interfere with enjoyment of life or ordinary living. Typical accompanying signs are slowness of speech and movement, loss of interest and appetite, disturbed sleep pattern and feelings of guilt, low self-esteem, and pessimism. Depression is common, more so among women. In very severe cases, such as *manic depression, it is a *psychosis which may be accompanied by *hallucinations and feelings of unworthiness and self-blame of delusional intensity. There may be risk of suicide. Contributory factors include genetic predisposition; childhood experience, especially of loss; *stress and feelings of helplessness; and lack of a supportive social network. Spontaneous, possibly cyclical, fluctuations in brain state may also play a significant role. In such cases treatment relies particularly on the use of mood-controlling drugs. *Drug treatments may also be used in milder cases, supplemented by attempts to alleviate the stress causing the depression and to modify the way the person copes with it (see *learned helplessness).

deregulation, the reduction or elimination of specific government *regulation of commercial enterprises and public bodies. In the 1970s the *New Right and others argued that excessive regulation was stifling initiative, preventing the emergence of new suppliers and patterns of service, and denying consumers the benefits of choice and competition. In several Western countries, transport, financial services, and *telecommunications were among the many activities deregulated during the 1980s. By the early 1990s, deregulation was an important concomitant of *privatization in formerly socialist countries, allowing existing enterprises more freedom, and permitting new enterprises to be set up. Experience in the USA of the deregulation of domestic airlines (1978) and of the savings-and-loans banks (1982) suggests that while diversity and choice may be evident at first, insufficient regulation may lead to savage price-wars and to *fraud and, through the resulting collapse of some of the businesses, a 'reconcentration' of the activity in a few hands. In consequence, most governments find it necessary to maintain some degree of regulation of important public services, and of businesses in key sectors of the economy.

Derrida *deconstruction.

dervish (from Persian, 'mendicant'), member of an ascetic or mystical order within *Islam. Emphasizing the emotional, ecstatic, and monastic aspects of religious experience, dervish practices include trance-inducing ecstatic dances (like those of the Mevlevi, or 'whirling dervishes' of Turkey). The dervish fraternities have exerted a powerful influence upon Islamic mysticism. Though signifying a certain detachment from worldliness, most practitioners live a normal life whilst maintaining the special devotional practices of an order.

Descartes, René (1596–1650), French philosopher and mathematician. In mathematics he invented 'Cartesian coordinates', which enabled geometrical properties to be represented numerically. In philosophy he is generally recognized as one of the founders of *rationalism. He pursued certainty about the nature of knowledge by means of his Method of Doubt. This works by suspending judgement on any belief until it can be shown to be systematically derived from more certain beliefs. The aim of the Method is to reach a belief which cannot be doubted, and then to build up knowledge from that basis. In this way *scepticism can be refuted. In his *Discourse on Method* (1637), Descartes claimed that the *a priori belief in his own existence, *Cogito ergo sum* ('I think therefore I am'), was immune to doubt and could, therefore, serve as the basic belief. On this basis Descartes came to hold a *dualist philosophy of *mind; believing the essence of the 'I' to be thinking, and of the physical body to be extension.

descent (in anthropology and genealogy), the tracing of a person's ancestry in a single genealogical line. Many societies emphasize the tracing of unilineal descent, through either male (patrilineal) or female (matrilineal) ancestors only. This has the effect of allocating all members of society to a limited number of bounded groups. The principle of descent as a means of forming social groups like *lineages or *clans can be distinguished from inheritance (the transmission of property), or from succession (the rights to political or ritual positions), and is not necessarily important in the organization of all societies.

desertification, the process by which land becomes desert, usually through a combination of increased drought and the impact of human activity on the land. Desertification came to prominence in the 1970s, when many countries of the semi-arid Sahel zone south of the Sahara in Africa experienced a succession of drought years, soil erosion increased, and sand dunes encroached on formerly productive land, with devastating effects on the people who depend on it. It is estimated that almost a third of the earth's land is at risk or already suffers from desertification and that hundreds of millions of people live on severely affected land. The UN Environment Programme has estimated, for example, that while just 3.5 per cent of southern Africa is natural desert, almost 25 per cent is at high risk of desertification. About 6 million hectares of good land turn to desert each year. Desertification is a natural phenomenon linked to phases in short-term cycles in the climate in which less rain falls in shorter rainy seasons. However, it may be seriously exacerbated or even triggered by *deforestation, over-grazing, and over-cultivation of the land, all of which denude the soil and expose it to erosion by wind and occasional rainfall. The enhanced *greenhouse effect also accelerates desertification. Land bordering deserts is most susceptible and *overpopulation is a major contributing factor.

deskilling, the loss of skills or responsibility resulting from mechanization and automation. The change in printing from typesetting by hand, using heavy metal type, to the use of computer-based equipment linked to automated production of printing plates is one example. H. Braverman in

Labor and Monopoly Capital: The Degradation of Work in the 20th Century (1974) contended that the result was the degradation of human labour, and that deskilling was a deliberate management strategy to reduce the bargaining power of employees. Much research has been done, but there is no agreement. It is unclear, for example, how to weigh the boredom of work on an assembly line against the exhaustion of hard physical work that carries responsibility. Furthermore, some writers and official statistics suggest that technological change has resulted in a greater demand for skills. While some traditional skills disappear, new ones are in demand: automated industries need highly skilled maintenance technicians; the service industry sector (see *tertiary industry), in which individual skills are important, is growing in relation to *heavy industry. Market forces and competitive pricing result in standardized and uniform products. In reaction there is a renewed demand for products requiring skill in their manufacture.

desk-top publishing *publishing.

détente (French, 'relaxation'), the easing of strained relations, especially between states. In recent years, the term has referred to the improvement in *East–West relations (between the USA and the former Soviet Union and their respective allies) which took place during the 1970s, and was marked most significantly by the establishment of the *Conference on Security and Co-operation in Europe (1972–5), by an improvement in relations between the Federal Republic of Germany and the former German Democratic Republic known as 'Ostpolitik', and by the signing of the first Strategic Arms Limitation Treaty (SALT 1) in 1973 (see *arms control). While points of conflict still remained between the two sides, détente was a way of managing *superpower relations at a time when the nuclear capabilities of both sides posed a threat to world peace.

detention without trial, the holding of individuals by the state authorities without due legal process, on the grounds that they are suspected (or could reasonably be suspected) of engaging in activities which undermine the stability or security of the state. Indefinite detention without trial is regarded as a derogation of *human rights, as set out in the *International Covenant on Civil and Political Rights (see also *habeas corpus). The power to detain people without charge or trial is contrary to law in many national legal systems. Detention without trial is an exceptional measure which may be taken by a government in situations where there is a threat to the security or stability of the state or society, for example internal unrest or communal conflict, a terrorist threat (internal or external), or conditions of war. The interpretation of the conditions where detention without trial may be enforced varies; in most democracies, detention without trial is avoided or strictly restricted in duration. For example, the UK Prevention of Terrorism Act (1974) allows detention without charge for up to seven days, after which the individual must be charged or released. In South Africa, on the other hand, a 'state of emergency' declared in 1985 and revoked in 1990 allowed detention without trial for up to ninety days in the first instance and indefinitely in certain circumstances. In many states, particularly those with *authoritarian regimes, detention without trial is routinely used to suppress legitimate political opposition, whether by declaring a 'state of emergency' at will and suspending the law, or by ignoring the law. Human rights organizations have shown that individuals detained without trial are more likely to suffer ill treatment such as *torture during this period, especially if held at secret locations.

determinism *free will.

deterrence *nuclear strategy.

devaluation, a reduction in the price of a domestic *currency in terms of foreign currencies. A devaluation or depreciation in the *exchange rate (the former term is normally used to describe a deliberate change by policy-makers, as against a *market decline of a floating rate) is equivalent to an appreciation or revaluation of foreign currencies with respect to the domestic currency. Home-produced output therefore becomes cheaper in terms of foreign currencies; the resulting increase in competitiveness is usually expected to improve the *balance of trade by boosting exports and slowing down imports, which become more expensive for domestic residents. However, domestic price rises of both imports and exportables may lead to *inflation, which ultimately eliminates the gain in competitiveness. Devaluation, or fear of devaluation, may also lead to the withdrawal of capital held in that currency, causing a shortage of funds for investment.

Devanagari *alphabet, *Indo-European languages.

developing country (less developed country or underdeveloped country), an imprecise term used to describe the poorer countries of the world. One definition offered by the World Bank includes all countries in the low or middle income group, that is with GNP per capita of less than $6,000 in 1988. Like the terms *Third World and *South it is applied to those countries whose economies are not fully modernized (nor centrally planned) and thus includes Latin America, Africa, and most of Asia, as well as a few countries in Europe. Despite diversities, most of these countries had many common economic, political, and social characteristics in the early years after World War II, while also sharing a colonial past. They have generally acted as a bloc in *international politics, especially in the UN, to demand radical changes in the international economic order, in which they are seen to operate at a serious disadvantage. However, in the last forty years there have been considerable differences in development experience, so it is less legitimate to classify these countries into a single group. The growing differences between economies in the developing country category, with some like the prosperous *newly industrializing countries (NICs) becoming richer and others, like Bangladesh or Somalia (sometimes termed the 'least developed countries'), having stagnant or even falling incomes, make it an inadequate term. Yet it remains a useful label to apply to those countries who lag behind the developed world in terms of economic development, technology, and social and political structures, and which, for the most part, face common problems while undergoing structural change and *adjustment in the course of development.

development (in economics), the term used to describe long-term *economic growth in a country and structural change, during the transition from a traditional agrarian-based society to a modern industrialized one; more broadly, a means to eradicate *poverty, raise incomes, and enhance *employment opportunities. The different economic structure of countries permits their broad classification into developed countries, usually those with an advanced *industrialized economy, and *developing countries, those whose economies tend to be based on *primary industries, that is agriculture and minerals. In developing countries as a whole, *GDP grew by 70 per cent between 1965 and 1985, while both *life expectancy and *educational attainment have greatly improved and *infant mortality fell. The factors which contribute to economic growth include an increase in agricultural productivity; investment in education and health; the development of economic infrastructure; the growth of manufacturing industry and eventually of manufacturing exports. An essential precondition is political stability and lack of civil strife. There is considerable controversy about the role of the *market in development; some believe an unfettered market is the most efficient mechanism for promoting economic development, with the role of the government confined to providing social and economic infrastructure. But it is increasingly recognized that an active state can accelerate development, as it has in the highly successful cases of Taiwan and South Korea, so long as it does not stifle incentives or excessively distort prices. Economists have pointed to three major constraints on long-term growth: first, the vicious circle of low real incomes, leading to low savings, investment, and productivity, and back to low incomes. This constraint can be relaxed by foreign *aid. Secondly, inadequate *agricultural growth, in the presence of rapid population growth, leading to poor nutrition, rising food imports, and insufficient cash crop production for exports. In Asia especially, this constraint was relaxed by the green revolution, with technological breakthroughs in developing new highly productive seeds. Thirdly, poor *human capital caused by low investment in health and education. Many countries have made progress in improving human capital over the past half-century, but in Africa and Latin America there was deterioration in most countries in the 1980s. In the 1980s, special problems were caused by external developments—poor and worsening *commodity prices, high interest rates, and the *debt crisis—so that many countries faced acute foreign-exchange problems and had to adopt *adjustment policies, which were often associated with declining per capita incomes and investment. In the world's poorest countries, economic growth has decreased sharply in recent years, and many countries in Africa have had falling per capita incomes.

development economics, the study of economic structure, change, and policy in low- and middle-income countries. The emergence of interest in development economics since World War II is attributed to the gradual replacement of colonial power by independent governments with control over their economic policies and a determination to transform their economies from low-income *primary commodity production to modern industrial states. This was reinforced by the political interests of the major developed countries in promoting *economic development (an interest fuelled by cold war rivalry) and greater public concern for the reduction of world-wide poverty. The field of development economics has certain distinctive characteristics. Firstly, the major differences in economic structure, institutions, and culture among *developing countries as compared with developed countries require that new models be developed or old ones adapted to take these differences into account. Secondly, country-specific research predominates. Countries vary enormously and policy prescriptions must take account of these differences. Thirdly, there is a preoccupation with economic growth and therefore with raising savings and investment rates, and with introducing modern technology. The pessimism about reducing poverty of classical economists such as *Ricardo and Robert Malthus (1766–1834) has been replaced by guarded optimism, brought about by technological development and changes in international trade, for example the green revolution, which raised agricultural productivity, and the emergence of *newly industrializing countries, notably in South-east Asia (Taiwan, South Korea, Hong Kong, and Singapore). A new wave of countries is following their path. There is considerable debate among economists about the appropriate role of government, with a growing school of monetarists and neo-classical economists arguing for minimum government intervention, viewing 'government failures' as more significant than 'market failures'. Others—often described as 'structuralists'—see the need for a strong role for government to help spread technological change in agriculture, promote industry, especially in the early stages of development, and to help ensure adequate provision of the goods and services necessary to meet basic needs.

deviance (in sociology), a form of behaviour which breaks, or is defined as breaking, social rules. What counts as deviance varies between and within societies. For example, in some societies it would be considered deviant for a man to have more than one wife, whereas in others it would be expected. Promiscuous women are often considered deviant, but promiscuity may be taken as a sign of masculinity for men. Which deviant activities are considered to be criminal also varies. For example, in some societies, to be intoxicated in public is a crime. Explanations of deviance are numerous. Human wickedness and unwillingness to conform to rules have been advanced since the earliest times. Academic disciplines such as *psychology, *anthropology, and *sociology have investigated the influence on behaviour of such factors as inheritance, early experience, social class, and poverty. Since deviant behaviour is so variously defined and so widespread, not only explanations but also penalties are diverse.

devolution, the delegation of legislative or decision-making powers to a regional authority. Within this area, decision-making is shared between the devolved authority and the centre, overall constitutional control remaining with the latter. Devolution of power is often proposed as a device for managing the political tensions created by regional cultural, linguistic, or ethnic divisions, which may otherwise be expressed in *separatism. In the UK, a referendum in 1979 for devolution was narrowly won in Scotland but failed to be endorsed by the total electorate, while a similar referendum was overwhelmingly defeated in Wales; and the devolved system of government that existed in Northern Ireland was suspended by direct rule from Westminster in 1972.

Dewey, John (1859–1952), US philosopher and educationalist, associated with the Progressive School Movement in the USA. His pragmatic philosophy (called instrumentalism) held that thought was an instrument, producing theories designed to solve practical problems in many fields such as *logic, *metaphysics, morals, and art (see also *pragmatism). Dewey held that society is in continuous evolution, that democracy is a primary ethical value, and that school is the chief lever of social progress. In works such as *School and Society* (1899), *Democracy and Education* (1916), and *Experience and Education* (1938), Dewey rejected the authoritarian instruction of passive pupils, favouring instead 'child-centred' methods of learning through experiment and discovery, problem-solving, and topic-centred not subject-based lessons. Dewey's ideas have been extremely influential, but some have criticized him for underestimating the importance of systematic learning and the acquisition of skills.

dharma, a central concept within *Hinduism and *Buddhism. The Indo-European root of the word, *dhar*, literally means 'carrying', but has been variously translated as 'law', 'teaching', 'duty', or 'religion'. In Hinduism the term refers to the material and moral order of the world. Each *caste has its own particular *dharma*, or religious and ethical rights and duties. In *Buddhism, where the Pali form *dhamma* is frequently used, the term refers primarily to the universal truth, which was discovered by the *Buddha at the time of his enlightenment and which formed the basis of his teaching. The word also refers to the cosmic laws (karmic rebirth), as well as to morality and righteousness. In philosophy, *dharma* is the characteristic property which determinately or uniquely picks out a thing which is characterized (*dharmin*): for example, light is the *dharma* of a flame. This conception is related to the original idea of appropriateness or 'rightness'. The concept emphasizes the law-like (or 'nomological') way in which the world in its physical, moral, and social senses is ordered. As such it is applied as a regulative idea in all spheres of activity. (See also *Hindu law.)

dialect, a variety of a *language usually associated with a specific region. Regional dialects overlap with other 'lects', for example social dialects (sociolects) and gender dialects (genderlects). Dialects vary in *grammar, vocabulary, and pronunciation or *accent, but they are usually mutually intelligible. While no negative connotations are attached to dialect in *sociolinguistics, they often are in society at large. The dialect with the most prestige in a given speech community becomes the standard. Thus everyone, including the speakers of the standard, uses a dialect. One language may have more than one standard dialect, for example Standard British English and Standard American English. Sometimes two standard dialects of one language coexist within one speech community, leading to *diglossia. Boundaries between regional dialects are not very clear. Dialects form continua and not discrete units. Dialect boundaries coincide with bundles of isoglosses (lines marking the limits of the occurrence of particular linguistic features).

dialectic, a form of argument or reasoning. In the most informal sense of the term, dialectic is simply discussion in which progress towards the truth is made by critical examination. This method is exemplified in *Plato's dialogues. There are, however, several more technical senses of dialectic. One is associated with *Kant, for whom dialectic is the method of showing that any attempt to speculate beyond the limits of possible experience leads to contradictions. Another is associated with *Hegel, for whom dialectic is the interaction of concepts in such a way that one idea (the 'thesis') comes into contradiction with another (the 'antithesis'), out of which a third idea (the *'synthesis') arises, which is more complete and closer to the truth than either of its predecessors. In this latter sense the term was extended to become the *dialectical materialism of *Marxism.

dialectical materialism, the philosophy of *Marxism as developed by Marx's followers, especially in Germany and the former Soviet Union. It unites two central claims: first, human consciousness is a reflex of processes occurring in the natural world; second, these processes display a dialectical pattern in which each developing force generates its opposite or 'negation', leading to a period of revolutionary change in which a higher synthesis of the two opposing forces is achieved.

dice, games determined by throwing a die or several dice. Each die is a cube marked with one to six spots; usually two or three dice are thrown. Dice are used to advance pieces in all manner of *board-games; in gambling games such as craps and crown and anchor, players bet on the outcome of a single throw or series of throws.

dictatorship, a regime in which an individual leader or a small leadership group hold unchallenged power, and in

A feature typical of **dictatorship** is the 'personality cult' of the leader, who is idealized in propaganda and revered by citizens. Here a family bows to a vast statue of Kim Il-sung, who has ruled North Korea since 1948; other visitors have left flowers.

which the leadership is given an exalted status. *Authoritarian regimes can be translated into dictatorships as power is increasingly centralized in the hands of a small group, or as an individual comes to dominate. Frequently, dictatorial leaders dispense with normal legal processes and political institutions, and the regime is sustained by the use of repression and the creation of a *police state. Prominent 20th-century dictatorships were those of Adolf Hitler (1933–45), Benito Mussolini (1922–45), and Joseph Stalin (1924–53).

diglossia, a linguistic phenomenon which occurs when two standard *dialects of one *language coexist within one speech community. One, the high dialect, or variety, is used in formal situations like school and church, and in quality literature. The other, the low variety, is used in informal situations. Classical Arabic and standard German (Hochdeutsch) are examples of high dialects. Colloquial Arabic and the various regional dialects of German (for example, Swiss German) are their low counterparts. Some high and low dialects may be considered distinct languages. The phenomenon then is *bilingualism, not diglossia.

diminishing returns, law of, the principle in economics that increasing the use of only one *factor of production (capital, labour, or land) in the short run leads eventually to the resulting increases in output becoming smaller and smaller. In other words, the marginal productivity (the extra output per unit employed) of the factor eventually declines as more of it is employed. This law assumes that factor inputs are homogeneous, that technology is given, and that all other factors of production remain fixed. It does not specify whether the marginal product (extra output) of the factor eventually falls to zero or becomes negative, which may happen if additional units of a factor eventually reduce the effectiveness of existing factors. The principle applies not only to production but to all areas of economic life—for example, the additional satisfaction obtained by a consumer from additional small amounts of one particular good (quantities of all other goods consumed remaining unchanged) will eventually diminish. The principle typifies the concepts used in *marginal analysis.

diplomacy, the management of international relations, aimed at promoting and ensuring peaceful and routine interactions between states. Diplomacy operates through dialogue and negotiation, rather than the use of force. Permanent representatives have long been sent from one country to another, in order to obtain information, safeguard their own country's interests, and to foster trade and cultural links. Present-day diplomats are guided by a code of protocol laid down by the 1961 Vienna Convention on Diplomatic Relations. They are usually granted special privileges such as *diplomatic immunity by the host state, where their functions include representing their own state and entering into negotiations with the host state; protecting the interests of their own nationals; and promoting economic, scientific, and cultural relations between the two states. Multilateral diplomacy has developed within international organizations such as the UN, where diplomats representing different

A Greenpeace dinghy harries a Japanese whaling vessel in the sort of **direct action** for which it is famous. Despite an international ban, the Japanese continue to hunt for whales, apparently for scientific reasons.

states meet and negotiate. In recent years there has also been an increase in summit diplomacy (face-to-face negotiations between *heads of state), and shuttle diplomacy (the activities of minister or envoys, acting as mediators, who travel between several countries at brief intervals).

diplomatic immunity, an important principle of *international law which involves the granting of reciprocal rights and privileges to a country's official representatives abroad. Diplomatic personnel, their property, and premises are regarded as inviolable, which in practical terms means the exemption of diplomats from the domestic jurisdiction of the country in which they are residing. Violation of diplomatic immunity is regarded as a serious breach of international law. The seizure, by Iranian students, of American hostages at the US *embassy in Tehran (1979–81) met with widespread condemnation by the international community.

direct action, action taken by citizens which bypasses normal constitutional procedures, and aims at direct confrontation with governmental authority. Such action can be taken against a domestic government or against an occupying power, and can be violent or non-violent. Large-scale violence tends to become *guerrilla warfare, *insurrection, or *terrorism, however, while the term direct action is usually associated with non-violent civilian resistance. Such nonviolent resistance is based upon the idea that any government's power to govern rests ultimately upon the *consent and co-operation of its citizens, and that withdrawal of consent and co-operation makes government or occupation very difficult, costly, or eventually impossible. At one end of the spectrum the objective of such action may be simply to persuade a government to change, or to institute a particular policy; at the other it may be the complete downfall of a government or the withdrawal of an occupying military power. Methods of non-violent action include protest and demonstration, protest literature, strikes, sit-ins, boycotts, obstruction, non-co-operation of civil servants, and working to the letter of the law. Non-violent direct action is usually wholly lawful, even if opinions about its legitimacy and efficacy vary greatly. The most prominent case of the use of non-violent direct action was that of Mahatma Gandhi and his followers against the British colonial administration of India from the 1920s to the 1940s. More recently, direct action was used in the Baltic states to demand independence from the former Soviet Union.

disability, a physical or mental incapacity. The World Health Organization (WHO) has estimated that 10 per cent of the world's population is disabled in some way, despite the fact that half of all disabilities are preventable. Causes include traffic accidents, war injuries, infectious diseases, *malnutrition, *psychiatric illness, and *degenerative diseases. WHO has developed a conceptual framework for the assessment of individual and population needs. Impairment is defined as a loss or abnormality of an anatomical, physiological, or psychological function, such as the loss of a leg, vision, or mental functioning. Disability is defined as a partial or complete inability, arising from an impairment, to perform an activity in the manner, or within the range, considered normal for a human being. Examples would be inability to walk or to care for oneself. Handicap is defined as a disadvantage, resulting from impairment or disability, which limits or prevents fulfilment of a role that is normal, depending on age and social factors. Thus impairments and disabilities need not necessarily turn into handicaps. This depends on the individual concerned and, critically, on social responses: inability to walk would not prevent a lawyer from working, if his or her colleagues and clients did not discriminate, and if the office were accessible for a wheelchair. Disability prevention can be related to the WHO classification by reducing the occurrence of impairments, limiting or reversing disability, and preventing a disability from becoming a handicap.

disabled people, services for, services for people with a mental or physical *disability. Where these are well developed, services may include practical assistance at home, day centres offering activities and companionship, *special education, support for employment in sheltered and ordinary work-places, temporary and permanent residential care, and suitable transport, for example through a subsidized taxi service. People with disabilities themselves have in recent years fought to increase both their autonomy (their ability to live according to their own rules) and their independence (their ability to perform key functions such as working, dressing, and eating without assistance from others). In some affluent countries, notably in Scandinavia, Canada, and the USA, measures to increase autonomy and independence have been taken, for instance by adapting housing, and by paying allowances directly to disabled people to spend on services as they wish, rather than leaving decisions to professionals. Discrimination against disabled people is also prohibited by law. In developing countries, where about 80 per cent of the world's disabled people live, but where only 10 per cent of the resources allocated to disability are spent, services are limited, and, as in most of the industrialized world, families bear the main responsibility.

disarmament, a policy aimed at the banning of armaments, or their reduction to the lowest level possible, while maintaining a certain level of security. It is different from *arms control, which seeks to manage the *arms race by maintaining a balance between the capabilities of both sides. Disarmament, on the other hand, envisages a dramatic reduction in arms in order to achieve peace. It may be unilateral, bilateral, or multilateral; and it may apply to certain categories of weapons (as in the 1972 Convention on Biological Weapons) or geographical areas (as in the Antarctic Treaty of 1959, banning the emplacement of nuclear weapons in Antarctica). Proponents of disarmament argue that the manufacture and maintenance of weapons consume vast resources, cause instabilities, and, given the sheer quantity of weaponry, create the risk of accidental war. On the other hand, it is argued that the build-up of weapons is a symptom of conflict and not a cause of it, and that stability is better achieved through a balance of arms. It tends to be in the interest of those who have power and resources to propose disarmament.

disaster, a cataclysmic event, usually of rapid onset, in which one large-scale event causes most of the damage or destruction. The most frequent causes of cataclysmic disasters are earthquakes, tropical cyclones (known as hurricanes in the North Atlantic and South Pacific, cyclones in the Indian Ocean, and typhoons in the North and Western Pacific), floods, and volcanic eruptions. Man-made disasters include environmental catastrophes, for example the nuclear accident at the Chernobyl nuclear reactor in 1986. For geographical reasons, most cataclysmic disasters strike in tropical rather than temperate regions; there is increasing vulnerability as populations grow and people move into more marginal and dangerous areas. Furthermore, an earthquake which strikes in *shanty towns is likely to cause greater hardship and loss of life than one which strikes a well-built town in North America. Similarly, subsistence farmers in developing countries are affected more by, for example, flooding, because they are unlikely to be insured and may be unable to rehabilitate their land. Action to lessen the effects of disasters includes attempts at prevention such as constructing dams, which tend to be expensive and ineffective, or seeking to mitigate the effects, for instance by strengthening buildings or changing crop cycles so that they are harvested before the hurricane season. This can be cost effective, but is not easy to implement. A third approach, preparedness, entailing, for example, evacuation plans and the stockpiling of food, is one which all governments can take at relatively low cost.

disaster, relief of. In all disasters, most needs are met by the victims themselves and their local governments and agencies: international aid can play only a small although useful part by supporting local efforts. Hasty actions, such as the sending of unwanted second-hand clothes, may add to local administrative burdens and be counter-productive. After most disasters, three phases can be identified. In the emergency phase, characterized by activities necessary to save lives, victims usually band together through their families, religious associations, or other groups. Cash to buy food and blankets locally is often needed since outside aid rarely arrives in time. In the 'recovery' phase, which may last six months or more, the victims construct temporary shelters from local materials, make immediate repairs to bridges, roads, and public buildings, and try to return to work. In the reconstruction phase, which may last several years, the victims, having accumulated some cash and hoping that the threat has passed, typically reconstruct buildings and resume economic activity. Most outside relief is directed towards the emergency phase. Yet many aid agencies believe that assistance, in the form of cash, credits, activities that produce jobs, and technical assistance, could more usefully be directed towards the second and third phases and linked to other development *aid.

discount, the amount by which an item is reduced in price from its full or initially declared *value. Firstly, a discount may be a reduction in price offered on any *good or service by a seller. Secondly, the discount on a *security is the amount by which the current price falls short of the issue price; where the current price is above the issue price, it is said to be at a *premium. Thirdly, a discount is the difference between the redemption value of a *bill at maturity and the immediate cash price obtainable for the bill in the *money market. Lastly, the (time-) discount rate is the rate of *interest used for assessing the present value of future *income.

discrimination, unfavourable treatment based on prejudice against certain people or groups. Legislation against discrimination on grounds of *race, nationality, *ethnicity, and *gender, is widespread, usually applying to the supply of goods and services, housing, and employment (see *equal pay). Discrimination on religious grounds is less often covered (for example, it is not unlawful in the UK except in Northern Ireland). Under EC law, member states have to provide remedies for sex discrimination in relation to employment. Whether *positive discrimination is the appropriate legal response to a history of discrimination against particular groups, such as Blacks in the southern states of the USA, is disputed.

dispute resolution, the settlement of conflict between groups or individuals. All societies have to deal with conflicts and disputes, but the methods used vary greatly. Among the more important factors affecting a society's approach to internal disputes are the presence or absence of forms of higher authority like *chiefs or *kingship, and the existence of formal courts, writing, and written law. In many non-industrialized societies, the prime purpose of dispute settlement may be the restoration of normal social relations, rather than the pursuit of abstract ideas of punishment and *justice. This principle can also be seen at work in societies with formal courts and legal procedures. Sometimes social tensions can be expressed and resolved through quite different institutions: the *Azande use ideas about *witchcraft as a means of explaining individual misfortune and blaming it on the action of personal enemies; in this society, disputes can be resolved through *ritual means. The study of dispute settlements can reveal alignments and divisions within a society which might otherwise be concealed, such as between *kinship groups who may be engaged in a *feud. It can also reveal where authority lies within different forms of *political organization: a king, a chief, or a group of elders or other holders of expert knowledge may, in different societies, have the right to settle disputes. In industrialized societies, dispute resolution is more formal and takes various forms. Adjudication connotes the resolution of disputes through a *court of law, that is a body which adopts an impartial stance towards the parties, which has behind it the coercive power of the state, and which is staffed by lawyers. An adjudicating body has authority to intervene in a dispute regardless of the consent of the parties, and produces a binding decision applying the law. Arbitration involves the informal settlement of a dispute according to the rules of law outside the formal processes of courts and legal proceedings by the consent of the parties. International commercial contracts commonly provide for arbitration, thus limiting or in some cases excluding adjudication by the courts. The decision is binding on the parties, subject generally to a right of appeal on points of law to the courts. The advantages of arbitration over adjudication are privacy, cheapness, informality, speed, and flexibility. Mediation (conciliation) is another form of dispute resolution involving the active intervention of a third party in an attempt to resolve a dispute between two other parties outside the processes of law. It differs from arbitration in that any agreement reached is not binding. Examples include the conciliation of industrial disputes, and the use of conciliation on marriage breakdown to enable couples to agree on such matters as the custody of their children.

distance education, a term used for education in which teacher and learner are physically separate. Distance education projects exist in most countries and are directed primarily at adults wishing to obtain qualifications or update occupational skills. They encompass every form of education from basic *literacy to general secondary to agricultural to higher education and teacher training. The Toussaint-Langenscheidt school for teaching foreign languages by correspondence, set up in Berlin in 1856, is generally regarded as the first formally organized correspondence school. Thereafter, correspondence schools multiplied, offering both vocational and academic education. Since the 1960s, many projects, such as the UK's Open University, founded

In the inaccessible Andean areas of rural Colombia literacy levels are low and educational facilities limited. This mixed-age class is learning basic literacy from a radio transmission: an invaluable form of **distance education** in such isolated areas.

in 1969, have successfully linked correspondence with broadcasting and occasional face-to-face tuition. The combination of national television or radio programmes with local study groups can be a particularly effective way of training para-professionals such as health workers. Technological developments such as satellite transmission (which has, for example, made possible the University of the South Pacific) are widening the scope of distance education. Distance education is also used for children, sometimes very successfully. Radio maths lessons developed in Nicaragua were translated into Thai and proved equally effective. However, the experience of the World Bank, which has financed many distance education projects, shows that since creating effective teaching materials is time-consuming and expensive, and since most children need direct contact with teachers to sustain their motivation, distance education cannot, as was once hoped, be seen as a cheap way of supplying mass education to children.

distribution (in economics), the dispersal of *goods and *services by *wholesale and *retail trading to final *consumers; or the location of economic activity or of population throughout a country; or, income distribution, the mechanism by which the rewards of *factors of production (wages and salaries, *profits, *rent) are determined. It also refers to the spread or degree of inequality of incomes among individuals. Such inequalities may be mitigated by government *fiscal policy. (See also *equal pay.)

Dīvālī ('Feast of Lights', from Sanskrit *dīpavalī*, 'little row of lights'), a five-day Hindu festival celebrated towards the end of October, which marks both a new moon and a new year. It takes its name from the lamps (*dīpās*) which are lit at this time. The festival is particularly associated with Lakshmi, the consort of *Vishnu and goddess of prosperity, giving rise to the tradition of financial stock-taking as well as the exchange of gifts. *Dīvālī* is marked by family entertainment and public celebration. Houses are cleaned and decorated,

and spells are cast to ward off financial misfortune. The festival is also celebrated by the Sikhs (see also *Sikh Festivals).

diversification (in economics), an increase in the variety of *goods and services produced by an individual enterprise or *conglomerate, or by an economy. Diversification occurs in many economies as a natural process. In other cases, diversification may be encouraged, either by business owners or by governments, in order to reduce the risk of relying on a narrow range of products; particularly when *demand for those products may be subject to large fluctuations.

dividend, the amount (per *share) of a *company's *profit which is distributed to shareholders. Dividends are normally distributed yearly, but interim dividends may be paid during the year between annual dividends. A maiden dividend is the first dividend paid to shareholders. Dividends are expressed either as an amount of money per share or as a percentage of the nominal *value of the share. The percentage yield of the share is equal to the dividend per share divided by the market price of the share multiplied by 100 over 1.

diving, the pastime and sport of plunging into water. Entering the water from the side of a swimming pool, the object is to enter the water cleanly, the body in a straight line with arms outstretched and fingers pointed. In the sport of diving, competitors take off from a rigid platform 5 m (16 feet) or 10 m (33 feet) above the water or from a flexible springboard. They perform a complicated series of twists and somersaults before striking the water, and judges award marks for each phase of the dive.

division of labour, the specialization of individuals in particular tasks in the production process. Such specialization promotes more efficient production by exploiting differences between individuals and also *economies of scale. The division of labour makes possible mass production of consumer goods such as motor cars and television sets, and becomes pronounced with *industrialization. Individuals, firms, areas, and whole countries now specialize in the production of goods which are then exchanged (traded). For example, the USA exports grain and imports manufactures (from countries such as Germany and Japan), even though it is capable of producing the manufactures itself; the trade pattern reflects the fact that with zero trade the opportunity *cost for the USA of producing additional wheat in terms of manufactures foregone would be far lower than for Germany or Japan, because of the higher land/labour ratio in the USA. This is known as the principle of comparative advantage, and was first formulated by *Ricardo. The result of specialization is greater overall production (and so income) from given resources than would have occurred without division of labour. This says nothing, however, about how that income is distributed. (See also *alienation, *assembly line, and *production methods.)

divorce, the formal ending of a marriage, implying, in monogamous societies, entitlement to re-marry. In some societies, divorce requires an official act, whereas in others it may be effected by the explicit rejection of the wife by the husband in the presence of witnesses followed by finalization in the courts, as under Islamic law, or by the return of the wife to her kin group. Many societies have allowed divorce by consent between the spouses, but where, as in Japan, a woman may have held inferior social status, she may have little choice. This route was closed to Western Europe after the establishment of Christianity, although after the Council of Trent (1563), there was a divergence in the approach to divorce: Roman Catholic countries disallowed divorce entirely, while Protestant countries allowed it on proof of the commission of a matrimonial offence, usually adultery by the woman. Many Catholic countries mitigated the severity of their law by lenient application of the laws of nullity. Since World War II most Western countries have come to allow divorce to be granted without proof of fault when the parties consent or where it can be shown that the marriage has irretrievably broken down (for example, after a period of separation). This has led to high levels of divorce. If the trends of the 1980s are maintained, one in two marriages in the USA and one in three in the UK are likely to end in divorce. Elsewhere in the world where divorce is permitted, rates are rising rapidly. But there is little evidence of a strong movement to return to restrictive divorce. Instead, attention has been concentrated on the extent to which legal processes should supervise the divorce process, control such matters as *maintenance after divorce and the arrangements made for the children, and promote measures, such as conciliation and other alternative means of *dispute resolution, which are designed to save legal costs and reduce the discord, financial hardship, and distress that usually accompany divorce.

Dogon, inhabitants of Mali, who depend mainly on the cultivation of grain crops such as millet for their livelihood. Traditionally they lived in inaccessible villages on steep hillsides, and this isolation encouraged the development of their remarkably intricate cosmology and mythology. To the Dogon, *myths and *symbolism are as real as the material form of things, and every aspect of social life reflects the working of the universe. Dogon villages, for instance, are laid out in such a way as to symbolize the world egg out of which all life is believed to originate. Each district has its own spiritual leader, or *hogon*; nevertheless, the knowledge of myths and symbols is not confined to a priest-caste but is open to anyone who has the patience and intelligence to learn.

domestic violence, violence within the *family, perpetrated by one spouse (or unmarried cohabitee) against another, or else by either parent against the child (see *child abuse and neglect). In the past and in many parts of the world today, the absolute power of a husband over his wife or of parents over their children led to much abuse that was hidden within the family. What appears to be the modern growth of domestic violence may be the result of the oppression of women, and social and economic inequalities leading to stress, frustration, and a cycle of violence, but it may also indicate an increase in the reporting of such matters, and a greater willingness on the part of the authorities in some parts of the world to intervene in family life. The great majority of victims of inter-spousal violence are women. In many countries they have little legal protection and with their responsibility for children and limited earning power find themselves trapped. In a few countries, refuges enable a woman and her children to escape a violent home and legal remedies are available. In the UK, a battered spouse may apply for an *injunction requiring the violent spouse not to molest the complainant, or to leave the home. Some argue that criminal assaults within the family should be treated differently from other violent crime and that, instead of applying the criminal law, therapeutic measures should be

The intermingling of the spiritual and the material influences the way the **Dogon** perceive their houses. Each dwelling is considered symbolically as the body of a man: the hearth is his head, the central workroom his belly, and the grinding-stone his genitalia.

taken to help the family. Others believe that this approach denies equal protection of the law to the victims of domestic violence.

dominoes, a popular table-game played world-wide in many versions. British players use a set of twenty-eight small black rectangular blocks marked on the face with a double set of white spots with values from 6–6 to 0–0. Players draw seven dominoes and lay out one piece in turn, placing it end-on to a piece with a matching number, except in the case of a double-numbered domino which is placed at right angles. The winner is the first to either lay down all his or her pieces or end with the lowest total of spots.

domino theory, a political theory based on an analogy with the way a row of dominoes falls until none remains standing. Popular in the cold war (see *East–West relations), it holds that a political event in one country will lead to its repetition in another, usually neighbouring, country. The term was coined by US President Eisenhower (1890–1969) in 1954 in reference to the communist threat to Indochina, although he also applied it to Central America. His fear was that the collapse of one state to communist forces would lead to the collapse of another, an argument which seemed to be confirmed when the fall of the non-communist government in South Vietnam in 1975 was soon followed by those of Laos and Cambodia.

dowry, the property or money that a woman brings with her into *marriage. The payment is made by the family or kin group of the bride, and generally goes to the new family or household. Dowry is one form of marriage payment, and is not to be confused with bridewealth, where money or property goes in the other direction, from the groom and his kin to the family of the wife. Historically, dowry payments have been most often found in some European, *Middle Eastern, and *South Asian societies, whereas bridewealth is often found in Africa. In modern India, the demand for ever greater dowry payments has led to cases of maltreatment, and even murder, of young brides; this is not, however, a consequence of the dowry system itself, but reflects the impact of change and social mobility on ideas about marriage and standing in India.

Dravidian languages, a group of languages spoken in southern India and northern Sri Lanka, though there are also isolated groups of speakers in north-eastern India and central Pakistan. With over 170 million speakers this group is the fourth largest in the world. It consists of about twenty-five languages which can be divided into four sub-groups: North-West (Brahui), North-East (Kurukh, Malti), Central (Kui, Telugu), and Southern (Tamil, Malayalam, Kannada, Tulu). Brahui is at the greatest distance from the other three, both linguistically and geographically. The four most important languages, which account for 95 per cent of all speakers, have official status in the four states of southern India which were specially created for them after Indian independence: Tamil in Tamil Nadu, Malayalam in Kerala, Kannada in Karnataka, and Telugu in Andhra Pradesh. They have their own scripts and long literary traditions. Tamil (which has about 50 million speakers) is widely spoken outside India, in Malaysia, Indonesia, and throughout Southeast Asia. It has a large literature, and is attested in inscriptions dating from 200 BC. The script is an early adaptation of Brahmi, a north Indian alphabetic script. Tamil *dialects are based both on geography and *caste; there are six regional dialects, and a distinction between Brahmin and non-Brahmin speech. There is also a marked high style (used in literature and formal situations) in contrast to the low style of everyday speech. Malayalam (which has about 25 million speakers) is an old offshoot of the western dialects of Tamil. Telugu has slightly more speakers than Tamil. Like Tamil, the formal and colloquial styles are very different. There are three social dialects, corresponding to the Brahmin, non-Brahmin, and Harijan (untouchable) castes. Kannada (about 25 million speakers) has the same threefold social division and formal/colloquial distinction. The Dravidian languages have taken in a large number of Sanskrit loanwords, and more recently have borrowed from English, Portuguese, and Urdu.

dreaming and sleep research, the study of the brain and other physiological activity of sleepers, and of the effects of sleep deprivation. Sleep is found throughout the animal world, but its occurrence and length vary from species to species. Birds and mammals, including man, have two phases of sleep, quiet (or orthodox) and active (or paradoxical). There are five stages of human sleep, four of them orthodox. Paradoxical sleep is also called Rapid Eye Movement (REM) sleep as the sleeper's eyes move as if they are watching things happen. There is an increase in heart rate, breathing, and blood pressure relative to orthodox sleep, and recordings of the brain's electrical activity show that it increases to resemble that of someone who is awake. Sleepers who are wakened during REM sleep give detailed accounts of dreams, whereas those wakened during the other stages of sleep do not. There are, however, dreamlike experiences at other stages, such as the hypnagogic imagery at sleep onset. Nightmares occur in both paradoxical and orthodox sleep. As a proportion of sleep the REM stage is at its highest in infancy and steadily declines into young adulthood, when it is about 20 to 25 per cent of the total and occurs about five times a night. The proportion of REM sleep increases when sleepers are deprived of it by being wakened. It declines when they are deprived of orthodox sleep. Total sleep deprivation leads to deterioration in concentration and performance on many tasks. After about sixty hours without sleep people begin to experience intermittent visual and auditory *hallucinations. Such findings suggest that sleep and dreams play a protective or restorative role and that dreams may help to integrate novel experiences, but we do not know how these processes work.

dream interpretation (in psychology), attempts to explain or investigate the contents of *dreaming. These have come principally from *psychoanalytic theorists such as *Freud and *Jung. Freud's *The Interpretation of Dreams* (1900) described dreams as the 'royal road to a knowledge of the unconscious activities of the mind'. He distinguished the 'manifest content' which the dreamer recalls from the 'latent content' which the dream symbolically expresses. The latent content consists of anxieties or desires which the dreamer finds unacceptable and has repressed. The 'dream work' transforms these into images which are more acceptable. The psychoanalyst can interpret these images to reveal more about *unconscious contents which may be disrupting the dreamer's everyday life. This theory is largely untestable as dream entities may have multiple symbolic roles. Studies suggest that important wishes and anxieties do manifest themselves in dreams, but this evidence is persuasive exactly when the wish or anxiety does not appear in a disguised form. Jung's theory that dreams contain the archetypal symbols of the 'collective unconscious' and might on occasion prophesy the future, is even harder to test.

drug abuse, the excessive or addictive use of drugs for non-medical purposes, usually in order to affect the user's mental state and perceptions. Most societies accept the use of some mild drugs: for example, alcohol, tannin and caffeine (in tea and coffee), and nicotine (in tobacco). However, the use of certain drugs that are considered particularly addictive or powerful is illegal in most countries. These include narcotics or sedatives (opium and its derivatives, such as morphine and heroin); stimulants (cocaine and amphetamines); and hallucinogens (LSD). Cannabis or marijuana is mainly a sedative, but it can be hallucinogenic. Prescription drugs such as tranquillizers, and ordinary household substances such as glues and solvents may also be abused. The major problem of habitual drug abuse is physical or psychological dependence. In the case of some drugs, such as the opiates, tolerance develops, and more and more of the substance must be taken in order to achieve the desired effect. In the worst cases, everything in the drug user's life is subordinated to the craving for the drug and the steps taken to satisfy that craving. The withdrawal symptoms, when the user ceases taking the drug, may be severe. Other dangers involve the use of non-sterile needles or syringes, which may cause infections or transmit viruses such as hepatitis or *Aids. Drug abuse, especially among the young, has become a major social problem world-wide.

Drug abuse leads to related crimes, such as robbery, *prostitution, and theft to support the habit, or violence while under the influence of drugs (see *drug offences). For many developing countries, drug production and export are important to the economy; the trade is often dominated by *organized crime, as in the case of the drug 'barons' of Colombia. Attempts to prevent and treat drug addiction and to catch and punish drug traffickers consume significant proportions of the time and budgets of health, police, and prison services in many countries.

drug offences, offences connected with the possession, dealing, or smuggling of proscribed drugs, such as heroin, cocaine, and cannabis. The least serious offences relate to the possession of drugs; there are also crimes which may be drug-related, for instance theft, or violence committed under the influence of drugs, or in order to finance a drug habit. Heavy penalties tend to be reserved for drug-pushers (those who sell drugs and thus profit from the addiction of others) and drug-traffickers, who are usually part of the vast international network of *organized crime which controls the cultivation and manufacture of illegal drugs, their importation, and their distribution. In 1990 a UN resolution recognized that drug-trafficking and related criminal activities were a threat to the political stability and security of states as well as to their social and economic fabric. It approved the first international plan to combat illegal drug production and consumption (estimated by the UN to be

A labrador sniffs the luggage of Europe-bound travellers at Karachi Airport to check that it does not contain drugs. Such highly trained dogs are formidable allies of police and customs officials in their struggle against **drug offences**.

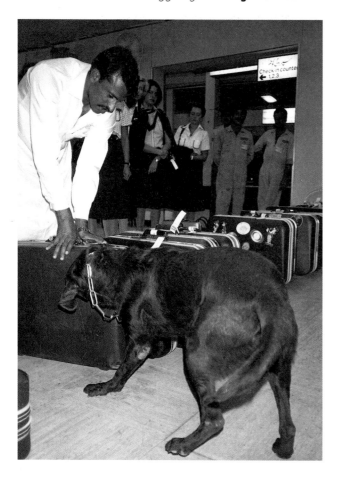

worth $500 billion a year). Building on the UN's 1988 Vienna Convention against the Illicit Traffic in Narcotic Drugs, the plan contains proposals to reduce the growing of coca and poppy plants in the developing world by encouraging alternative legitimate exports and guaranteeing access to international markets. Industrialized countries in which illegal drugs are consumed are to limit the supply of chemicals for their manufacture and the flow of arms to drug cartels. Mechanisms to counteract *money-laundering are also included. Some have argued that the decriminalization of drugs is the only way to check the problem and to deprive the drug cartels of their profits, but others believe this would result in a large increase in addiction.

drug treatments in psychiatry, the use of anxiolytic (anti-anxiety), anti-depressant, and neuroleptic (anti-psychotic) medication to treat the symptoms of the main psychiatric disorders. The increased effectiveness of such drugs produced a psychiatric revolution in the 1950s. The breakthrough came with phenothiazine (chlorpromazine), which was greeted as a possible cure for *schizophrenia. In common with other neuroleptics such as butyrophenones (haloperidol) it alleviates the symptoms of *hallucination and delusion. This control of symptoms has led to a reduction in the need for institutionalization and the possibility of returning psychiatric patients to the community. Later in the 1950s lithium was used as a very successful treatment of mania and bipolar *manic-depression. Drugs to treat anxiety and depression also only alleviate symptoms, but this may help the sufferer to overcome the immediate problem and to recover completely. The anxiolytic benzodiazepines such as diazepam (valium) have a calming effect. Anti-depressant drugs such as imipramine and the monoamine oxidase inhibitors (MAOI) have had some success. All these drugs have side-effects. Lithium is toxic and in high doses can be lethal. Chlorpromazine blocks receptors of the neurotransmitter dopamine. This may lead to loss of motor co-ordination and tremors which are similar to the symptoms of Parkinson's disease. Diazepam may result in dependence and withdrawal symptoms of insomnia and agitation. Anti-depressant MAOI drugs may cause cardiac complications. Overall, the psychiatric revolution produced by drugs has been extremely beneficial, but diazepam, in particular, has often been too casually prescribed. No drug is a sufficient treatment by itself and none provides a cure.

Druze, religious communities living in Lebanon, Syria, and Israel, whose beliefs stem from *Islam or older traditions. Founded by Ismail Darazi (d. 1019), from whom they take their name, the Druze maintain an *Ismaili notion that God manifests himself to mankind in different ages, the last manifestation being the *Shī'īte Fatimid *caliph Hakim, who took the title *imām. He is said not to have died, but to have hidden; he will reappear as a new Muslim messianic leader, or *mahdī* (see *millenarianism). The Druze are led by a hereditary *rais* (chief). They have displayed remarkable cohesion throughout their history, and played a significant role in the civil war in Lebanon (1975–91).

dualism, the general philosophical claim that the world is composed of two ultimate different kinds of *substance, typically mind and matter. *Monism, by contrast, holds that the world is composed of but one kind of substance. *Descartes is usually credited with having provided the most significant articulation of dualism, according to which the world is composed of a single material substance (nature), which is extended and divisible, and a plurality of mental or immaterial substances (God and the minds of individual persons), each of which is unextended and indivisible. Dualism in all of its forms leads to the notorious problem of interaction: namely, of understanding how substances of different kinds can affect one another. Descartes sought to resolve this problem in the case of human beings by claiming that a particular part of the brain (the pineal gland) is responsible for co-ordinating the relations of mind and body. Descartes' solution depends, however, upon the role of God in instituting this arrangement, and a frequent objection to modern, secular dualists is that they have no alternative way of explaining the relation of mind and body. In theology, dualism refers to the perception of the world as motivated by opposing principles of good and evil, as in, for example, *Parsi and some Christian sects' beliefs.

due process in law, the principle expressed in the Fifth and Fourteenth Amendments to the US Constitution that all citizens are entitled to the rights set out in the *Bill of Rights and equal treatment under the law. The due process clauses were intended to impose general objective standards of fairness on public authorities, but have come to enshrine fundamental principles of justice in the USA on which many recent Supreme Court rulings have been based. In international human rights, a comparable principle is that interference with rights be according to the *rule of law; that is, that the same law be applicable to all.

dukkha (Pali, 'suffering'), a central concept within *Buddhism forming the basis of the *Four Noble Truths. Superficially, *dukkha* refers to physical and mental discomfort and pain, particularly that which stems from craving and desire, which can be overcome only through the correct practice of the *Noble Eightfold Path. More profoundly, *dukkha* is one of the *Three Marks of Existence (*trilakshana*). Suffering results from the impermanence and illusory aspect of all things, and thus *dukkha* applies even to those things which are pleasant, since sooner or later they too will pass away.

dumping, the sale of a *good in a foreign *market at a price below that which is economically sustainable in the long run. Sellers will thus normally be making a loss on the dumped items. They are prepared to do this in the short term to dispose of surpluses without driving down prices at home, for instance when they have incorrectly forecast the market and have produced too many goods. It may also be used to establish *monopoly power in the foreign market and prevent competitors from developing or entering ('predatory dumping'). The identification of dumping in practice involves assessing the normal relationship between the export price of a good and its home-market price or *cost of production. This is difficult and liable to be influenced by subjective and political considerations; the sale of surplus US agricultural produce to developing countries is considered by some to be an example of dumping.

Duns Scotus, John (*c*.1266–1308), Franciscan theologian and philosopher, known as the Subtle Doctor. This subtlety is apparent in his conception of *metaphysics as an exploration of being, the most general of concepts, through transcendental notions, that is, notions beyond any of the categories we usually employ in talking about particular things. He held that demonstration of God's existence should not take as given the actual existence of finite things, but should presume only their possibility. God would then be shown to be a necessary being underlying the possibility of all created things.

Durgā-Pūjā (Sanskrit, 'Worship of Durgā'), annual Hindu festival held in honour of Durgā, 'the unfathomable one', an ancient and commonly used name for the Great Goddess, *Shaktī or Devi. The festival, celebrated over nine nights (*Navarātri*) in autumn, is particularly popular in Bengal, and among Bengali Hindus world-wide. In Bengal, a large image of Durgā in her warlike persona (clasping weapons in her ten hands and riding a lion) is carried through the streets and eventually immersed in a river.

Durkheim, Emile (1858–1917), French social theorist, who is recognized as one of the founders of sociology. Durkheim argued that the task of the sociologist was to study the social determinants of behaviour such as the duties, laws, and customs which unite people in society. *The Division of Labour in Society* (1893) traced the movement from what he called 'mechanical' to 'organic' solidarity. He saw the former as characteristic of 'simple' societies, where individuals shared tasks and were subject to common rules. This form of social organization had broken down as society became more differentiated. Modern societies rested on a *division of labour, with the family giving way to the workplace in importance and the expectations governing behaviour becoming specific to the roles people played. Durkheim believed this was a fragile form of society and could give rise to conflict and *anomie. In *Suicide* (1897), Durkheim pioneered the systematic use of statistics in elucidating social problems. He discovered, for example, that suicide rates were higher among soldiers than civilians, and the unmarried than the married, and concluded that explanations peculiar to each individual could not account for these variations. Social factors, such as the degree of integration into society of the different groups, must have contributed. Durkheim also influenced anthropological research, particularly through his later works on *Primitive Classification* (with Marcel Mauss, 1903) and *The Elementary Forms of the Religious Life* (1912).

dynasty, a line of hereditary rulers, in which succession is based on blood relationship. In a dynastic state, there is a ruling family such as the Houses of Bernadotte (Sweden), Windsor (UK), and Bourbon (Spain) rather than a succession of individual rulers. Other contemporary states which have ruling royal dynasties include Belgium, Denmark, Japan, Jordan, Kuwait, Lesotho, Liechtenstein, Luxemburg, Monaco, The Netherlands, Norway, Saudi Arabia, Swaziland, Thailand, and Tonga.

dyslexia, a difficulty in reading that is disproportionate relative to other intellectual abilities. It is considered to be a congenital disability in organizing, which affects short-term *memory, hand skills, and *perception, leading to difficulties with literary skills. It is typified by erratic spelling, often accompanied by letter reversals or word reversals. This indicates that one of the difficulties lies in imposing a consistent spatial orientation on written material. Other possible causes may lie in relating what words look like to how they sound. Recent research suggests that dyslexia is linked to a neurological abnormality that affects vision. There are about 2.5 million dyslexics in the UK, and current research has shown that dyslexia is found among all classes, and is not especially prevalent among the middle classes, as was once thought.

earnings, the rewards to *labour, and sometimes to other *factors of production. The earnings of an individual are the *wages or salaries paid for work. Wage earnings, the total money received, are different from the wage rate, which is the payment for a standard hour or working week without overtime. Business earnings are *company *profits, normally divided between a retained element to be used for future *investment and a *dividend paid out to *shareholders. All earnings can be calculated gross (before tax and other deductions) and net (after all deductions).

Easter, the annual Christian festival celebrating the *resurrection of Jesus after the crucifixion, as recounted in the Gospels. Following ancient custom connected with the dating of the Jewish *Passover, the date of Easter Sunday is calculated in relation to the first full moon after the spring equinox (21 March). Different methods of calculation result in Easter usually being celebrated on different dates in Western and Orthodox churches. The word 'Easter' may derive from the name of the pagan goddess of spring, Eostre. The association of Easter with new life blends Christian and pagan tradition. Easter is the most important Christian festival. Traditionally, catechumens (those undergoing prebaptism instruction) remained awake all Saturday night and were baptized early on Easter Sunday, a practice retained in the *Eastern Orthodox Church and recently resumed by the *Roman Catholic Church. Easter customs include bright illuminations, sunrise services, and the exchange of eggs, symbolizing new life.

Eastern Orthodox Churches, a group of *Christian Churches, historically centred in Eastern Europe, Greece, Ukraine, Russia, Georgia, and the Middle East, which acknowledge the primacy but not the supremacy of the Patriarch of Constantinople. There are about 100 million full members world-wide. The Orthodox Communion is made up of a number of independent autocephalous Churches with their own internal administration which share the same faith and doctrine. These are the four eastern Patriarchates of Constantinople, Alexandria, Antioch (Antakya), and Jerusalem; the Russian, Serbian, Romanian, Bulgarian, and Georgian Patriarchates; and the Orthodox Churches of Cyprus, Greece, Czechoslovakia, Poland, and Albania, with certain other semi-independent Churches. Services have traditionally been held in the vernacular (now

Eastern Orthodox Church

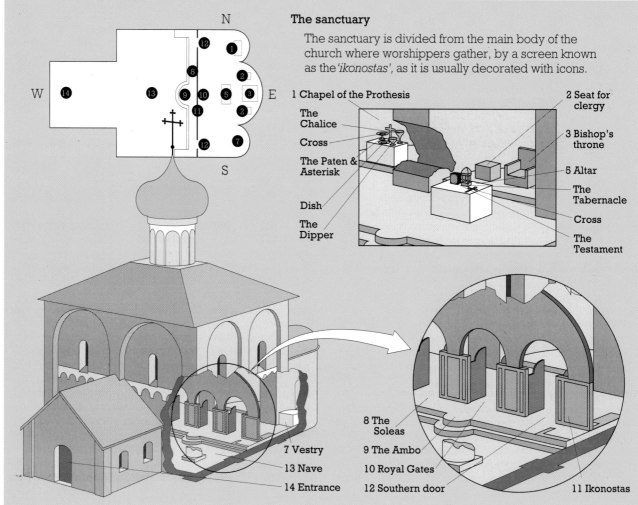

The sanctuary

The sanctuary is divided from the main body of the church where worshippers gather, by a screen known as the 'ikonostas', as it is usually decorated with icons.

1 Chapel of the Prothesis
The Chalice
Cross
The Paten & Asterisk
Dish
The Dipper

2 Seat for clergy
3 Bishop's throne
5 Altar
The Tabernacle
Cross
The Testament

7 Vestry
13 Nave
14 Entrance

8 The Soleas
9 The Ambo
10 Royal Gates
12 Southern door
11 Ikonostas

archaic in some cases, such as Old Slavonic), leading sometimes to an association with nationalism. The Orthodox Churches attach great importance to the role of Councils, in contrast to Roman Catholic emphasis on the pope's authority, and their central beliefs are based on the seven Church Councils held up to AD 787. Doctrinally, the principal difference from Roman Catholicism is the role of the Holy Spirit in the *Trinity. The Orthodox acknowledge seven *sacraments, with some flexibility since, for example, burial or a monastic commitment may also be regarded as a sacrament. Communion is taken only four or five times a year, and parish priests are permitted to marry, although the higher clergy, who are usually from the monasteries, are not. Divorce is permitted under certain circumstances. Monasticism is important, but there are no centralized orders, each monastery being a self-governing unit. The veneration of icons, which are believed to have a mediatory role, is central in Orthodox worship. The Orthodox celebrate many of the principal festivals of the *Christian year according to a different calendar from the Western Church. Subject to much persecution during the era of communist ascendancy in Eastern Europe and the former Soviet Union, the Orthodox Churches have recently been permitted to operate freely again.

East–West relations, the relationship existing from the end of World War II between the USA and its allies on one side (the West) and the former Soviet Union and its allies on the other (the East). After the war the USA and the Soviet Union emerged as *superpowers based on opposing ideologies, with global interests. The USA had a stake in the security of Western Europe, while the Soviet Union extended its influence over the countries of the Eastern bloc, despite Eastern European discontent, leading to the Yugoslav break with Stalin in 1948 and Soviet repression of dissidents in Poland, Czechoslovakia, and elsewhere. Both sides possessed increasing nuclear capabilities. The bipolar split in world politics became evident in the *alliance systems of *NATO and the *Warsaw Pact. The period of mutual distrust and rivalry that ensued, characterized by ideological differences, the dissemination of *propaganda, the build-up of arms, military threat, and occasional misunderstandings and crises, became known as the cold war. Each side built up its nuclear arsenals (see *arms race) and attempted to extend its sphere of influence in the developing world. However, the rigid polarization of the first period of the cold war was broken down in the early 1960s by an ideological split between the communist regimes of China and the Soviet Union, and the formation of the *Non-Aligned Movement, an attempt to remain independent from both East and West. During the 1970s there was a period of *détente when relations improved, only to deteriorate because of the Soviet invasion of Afghanistan (1979), which triggered what many called the second cold war. However, the 1980s saw the rise of *glasnost and perestroika in the Soviet Union, progress made in arms agreements (see *arms control), the withdrawal of the Soviet army from Afghanistan in 1988, the demise of communism in the Eastern bloc, the reunification of Germany in 1990, and the disbanding of the Warsaw Pact in the same year. With the demilitarization of East–West relations and prospects of greater co-operation between the two sides, the East–West balance of power may cease to be an overriding factor in shaping international relations.

eating disorder, an abnormal preoccupation with eating. The most common eating disorder is obesity. Another form is pica, the habitual eating of non-edible substances. Two overlapping forms, which are most common among adolescent girls, are *anorexia nervosa, a potentially life-threatening pattern of self-starvation driven by a delusion that the body is overweight, and bulimia nervosa, characterized by alternating gross overeating and vomiting. Explanations, none entirely satisfactory but all probably true to some extent, include social pressure on girls to be slim; stress effects on the functioning of brain centres controlling eating; expression of underlying personality disorder; and reaction to a conflict-ridden family situation. Treatment may include *counselling, psychotherapy, and drugs.

EC (European Community), an association of West European countries whose origins lie in efforts by European governments to promote regional co-operation after World War II. In 1991 its membership, identical to that of the *EEC, comprised Belgium, Denmark, France, Germany, Greece, Ireland, Italy, Luxemburg, The Netherlands, Portugal, Spain, and the UK. Malta (1990), Austria, Sweden, Switzerland (1991) and Finland (1992) have applied for EC membership; and Norway and the countries of Eastern Europe are expected to apply by the end of the 1990s. The principal EC bodies are located in Brussels, Luxemburg, and Strasburg. The EC consists of three distinct Communities: the European Coal and Steel Community (ECSC), established by the Paris Treaty of 1952, as well as the EEC and European Atomic Energy Community (EURATOM), both established by the Treaties of Rome in March 1957. Under a 'merger' treaty which became effective in 1967, they now share a single institutional framework comprising the *European Commission, the *European Council of Ministers, the *European Court of Justice, and the *European Parliament; these are assisted by the advisory Economic and Social Committee, and by the Court of Auditors. This framework is increasingly referred to simply as the European Community or Communities. Political union is the ultimate goal of the three communities, and the merger treaty was seen as a step to the setting up of a single European community to be governed by one treaty. Such political integration is far from complete, and members disagree as to its extent, and the speed at which it should proceed. Some political co-operation already exists through the system known as European Political Co-operation (EPC), set up in 1969 and formalized under the Single European Act (1987). The Maastricht Treaty (1992) moved towards greater political union on the three 'pillars' of monetary policy, including the establishment of a European *central bank and implementation of a single currency; foreign and security policy, designating the *Western European Union as the EC's defence wing; and co-operation on *immigration, *political asylum, and policing. The UK, which has opposed any suggestion of *federalism, opted out of a common policy on social issues to be adopted by other members.

ecology (Greek, *oikos*, 'house' or 'living place', and *logos*, 'study'), the study of the relations of organisms to one another and to their surroundings. Much of ecology is concerned with the ecosystem, a complex web linking all living organisms of the planet. In a narrower and more popular sense, ecology is about man's effect on the *environment. Environmentalists, *Greens, and others believe that the widely held view of the earth as a treasure-house to be plundered, and irresponsible use of industrial processes have had a disastrous effect on the ecosystem. *Acid rain, *deforestation, *desertification, *endangered species, *global warm-

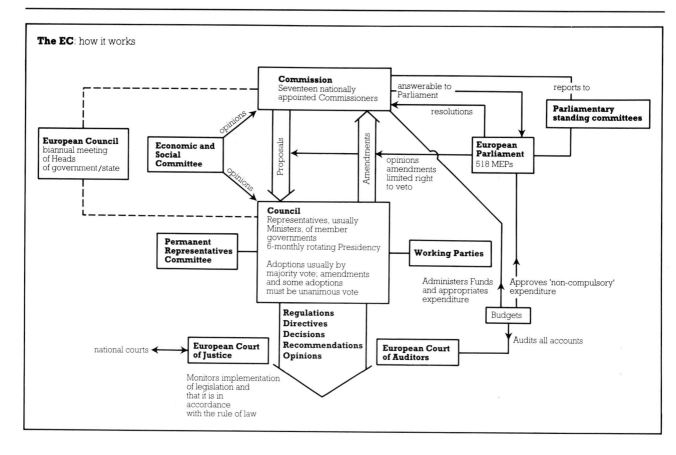

The EC: how it works

ing, *pollution, and *ozone depletion are all aspects of this negative impact. *Conservation measures and the use of renewable *energy sources are part of the positive action that is required to counter it.

econometrics, the application of statistical techniques to the quantitative estimation of economic relationships. It falls into two parts: theoretical and applied. As many standard statistical assumptions do not hold when considering economic phenomena, there is a need for a specialized branch of statistical theory, theoretical econometrics. Applied econometrics, on the other hand, uses statistical techniques (including those specifically developed by theoretical econometricians) to test economic theories and to quantify economic models.

economic forecasting, making predictions about economic variables, either *macro-economic (for a country or a group of countries) or *micro-economic (for an individual product or *market). Economic forecasting employs a range of methods, from market research to complex mathematical models relying on a number of key behavioural assumptions. (See also *risk analysis.)

economic growth, the increase in the productive capacity of an economy. The growth rate is measured as the percentage increase per year in *GNP or *national income. Economic growth, in the sense of income per head, is normally assumed to lead to a higher *standard of living. Governments therefore have an interest in promoting it. Key determinants include technological advance and the rate of *investment out of income. Population increase may promote overall economic growth, but not necessarily growth of incomes per head. The distribution of gains from economic growth also needs to be considered; economic growth may

not make all groups better off. There may also be negative *externalities arising from economic growth, such as congestion and pollution. These should, if possible, be taken into account when judgements are made about people's standard of living. (See also *cost–benefit analysis.)

economics, schools of. From the mid-16th century to the final quarter of the 20th century, economic thought can be split into five main historical schools: *mercantilism; the economics of the French physiocrats; *classical (and neoclassical) economics; *Keynesianism; and *monetarism. The schools overlap, and they represent broad categories of thought which do not necessarily encompass the views of all economists. The mercantilists, between the mid-16th and mid-18th centuries, argued that the *wealth of nations depended on their *balance of trade. With the simple monetary system that existed, proponents of the theory were concerned to maximize the amount of precious metals in the country. *Protectionism was encouraged. Classical critics of mercantilism, beginning with the philosopher *Hume, demonstrated that attempts to accumulate bullion were likely to prove self-defeating, because inflows of gold would raise domestic price levels to the point of making domestic producers uncompetitive, therefore causing gold to flow out again as more *imports were bought. The French physiocrats of the 18th century, led by François Quesnay (1694–1774), accorded pre-eminence to the agricultural sector, which they saw as the only source of wealth, and also the source of tax revenue. They believed in the role of government being limited to preserving the natural order. They also believed in free trade. Thus their approach was *laissez-faire. The physiocrats' ideas of laissez-faire and free trade were adopted by the classical economists. Much of modern *micro-economics stems from the theories of classical economics, centring on *Smith's Wealth of Nations (1776). The *marginal analysis of the 19th century led to the development of neo-classical economics as a refinement and progression from classical economics. It clarified the mode of interaction of supply and demand through the price mechanism, and resolved a number of problems that had troubled classical economic theory, for example the apparent paradox that diamonds (an inessential luxury) are usually more 'valuable' than water (a necessity of life). The principal contributors to classical and then neo-classical economics include, in chronological order: Smith, Robert Malthus (1766–1834), *Ricardo, *Mill, William Stanley Jevons (1835–82), *Marshall, Arthur Cecil Pigou (1877–1959), *Walras, *Pareto, and Francis Ysidro Edgeworth (1845–1926). The central tenet in classical economics is that of competition. The law of *supply and demand ensures that the price of a good balances supply and demand. Competitive markets ensure that the self-seeking behaviour of individuals results in efficient, socially optimal allocation of *resources and *production. This is Adam Smith's 'invisible hand'. The role of government is limited to intervention in cases where a *market does not exist or works imperfectly. In the early part of the 20th century, economists argued over the role of government in controlling *unemployment caused by fluctuations in *demand. Those in the classical tradition argued that government should maintain a balanced budget; others argued for government expenditure financed by budget deficits. The issue was resolved by *Keynes in 1936 in *The General Theory of Employment, Interest and Money*. This work laid the foundation of what is now called *macro-economics. Keynesianism favours demand management by government through the use of both *fiscal and monetary policy. *Monetarism, prominent in the 1970s and 1980s, represented a resurgence and updating of pre-Keynesian thought on macro-economic issues. It stressed the importance of the *money supply as the means of controlling aggregate money demand and *inflation but rejected the notion that either monetary or fiscal policy could exercise any lasting influence on the level of output and *employment: the money supply, it was argued, determined only the price level, not the volume of output and employment. (See also *Marxism, *positive economics.)

economies of scale (increasing returns to scale), in economics, the situation in which an equal proportional increase in all inputs leads to a more than proportional increase in output. This implies that (with given input prices) average *costs fall with increased output. Economies of scale may be internal to a firm or external. Internal economies of scale result from, for example, the *division of labour or indivisibilities (minimum efficient size) of fixed or working capital. They commonly arise only over a certain range of output. Since it is large firms which tend to profit from economies of scale, this causes the emergence of *oligopoly or *monopoly, where a few firms or a single firm dominate the market. External economies of scale are of two kinds. Firstly, technological economies exist when an industry benefits from the shared experiences or facilities of its member firms. Secondly, financial advantages occur when there are industry-wide savings in the expenditure needed to create demand, carry out market research, or otherwise maintain profitability. Diseconomies of scale (output increasing less than proportionately with inputs) may arise if an organization becomes too unwieldy or bureaucratic.

education, the transmission of knowledge and understanding, and the development of the individual personality, by *teaching or example. Political theorists as diverse as *Plato and *Marx have argued that education gives people power to change their lives. It also enables whole societies to develop. The value of education can be illustrated by its impact in poorer countries. The World Bank has found that where adults have had even a few years of education, their families are often smaller and their children healthier and that their labour may be more productive (see *human capital, and *education and development). For the individual, education means access to better-paid, more varied jobs and higher status. School systems are usually divided chronologically into *pre-school, *primary, *secondary, and *higher education. The expansion of universal state provisions in industrialized countries, including *comprehensive education, has been built on the older traditions of *independent education. Of increasing importance in recent years have been *adult and *vocational education and *literacy campaigns. The organization of education often reflects the outcome of struggles between the competing interests of, for example, governments, employers, teaching unions, religious bodies, parents, and children. Governments usually wish to hold down the potentially limitless costs of education while ensuring the production of a skilled and law-abiding citizenry, whereas others may have concerns about *curriculum, assessment, discipline, and access. In consequence, battles may be fought, but are rarely conclusively won.

education, access to, the opportunity or right to obtain formal education. Economic power—of entire nations or individual parents—is the chief determinant of access to education. In some industrialized countries, spending per capita on education is fifty times that in some parts of sub-Saharan Africa. The benefits are clear. Enrolment rates are significantly higher in industrialized countries and drop-out rates much lower. In very poor countries drop-out rates from primary school average around 50 per cent, and fewer than a quarter of children may attend secondary school. In poorer families, children may be inadequately nourished, leading to impaired development and loss of energy and concentration; encouragement to study may be lacking, especially if the family needs the child's labour or earning power or believes the education available to be so poor as to confer no advantage. School fees, charged in many countries for secondary education, are another deterrent. In countries without universal education, enrolment in urban areas may be more than double that in rural areas. Furthermore, boys usually outnumber girls. The gap is widest in Africa and parts of the Indian sub-continent, where there are almost twice as many boys as girls in secondary school, though the gap is narrowing.

education and development, the relationship between formal education and economic and social development. Research indicates that investment in *education is necessary to effect changes in social and economic life. Labour *productivity can be increased by education (see *human capital), but several years of *primary education are required before effective *literacy is achieved, and in the poorest countries, half the children drop out before this. Some economists have suggested that literacy rates of 30–40 per cent may be necessary before sustained economic growth can occur. Improved levels of education are also associated with falls in *fertility rates. In the developing countries as a whole, adult literacy has risen sharply, and enrolment rates both in primary and secondary schools in many parts of

Education

These charts show the increase from 1975 to 1985 in the number of pupils enrolled in primary, secondary, or further education as a percentage of the relevant age group. This increase in every region, at every level, for both boys and girls, is a considerable achievement given the very large increases in the eligible population in the developing countries. Another notable advance is the narrowing of the gap between boys' and girls' enrolment, though boys still significantly outnumber girls at all levels except in the developed countries.

Percentage of a given age enrolled in primary, secondary or further education

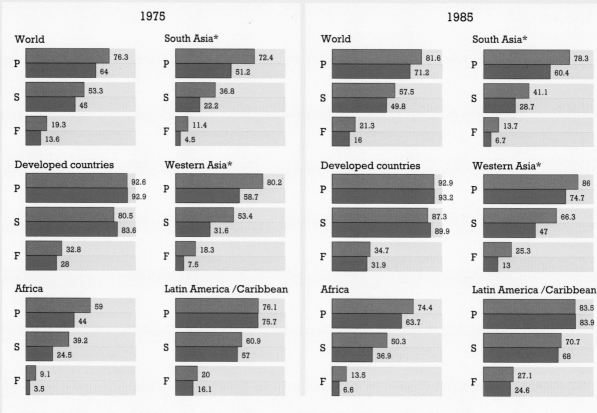

1975

World
P 76.3 / 64
S 53.3 / 45
F 19.3 / 13.6

South Asia*
P 72.4 / 51.2
S 36.8 / 22.2
F 11.4 / 4.5

Developed countries
P 92.6 / 92.9
S 80.5 / 83.6
F 32.8 / 28

Western Asia*
P 80.2 / 58.7
S 53.4 / 31.6
F 18.3 / 7.5

Africa
P 59 / 44
S 39.2 / 24.5
F 9.1 / 3.5

Latin America /Caribbean
P 76.1 / 75.7
S 60.9 / 57
F 20 / 16.1

1985

World
P 81.6 / 71.2
S 57.5 / 49.8
F 21.3 / 16

South Asia*
P 78.3 / 60.4
S 41.1 / 28.7
F 13.7 / 6.7

Developed countries
P 92.9 / 93.2
S 87.3 / 89.9
F 34.7 / 31.9

Western Asia*
P 86 / 74.7
S 66.3 / 47
F 25.3 / 13

Africa
P 74.4 / 63.7
S 50.3 / 36.9
F 13.5 / 6.6

Latin America /Caribbean
P 83.5 / 83.9
S 70.7 / 68
F 27.1 / 24.6

* Western Asia: Cyprus, Iraq, Israel, Jordan, Kuwait, Lebanon, Oman, Qatar, Saudia Arabia, Syria, Turkey, United Arab Emirates, Yemen.

* South Asia: Afghanistan, Bangladesh, Bhutan, Cambodia, India, Indonesia, Iran, Laos, Malaysia, Myanmar, Nepal, Pakistan, Philippines, Singapore, Sri Lanka, Thailand, Vietnam.

| P Primary school (6–11yrs) | S Secondary school (12–17yrs) | F Further education (18–23 yrs) | Boys | Girls |

- The USA spends $1,257 per child per year on education compared with just $15 in a typical sub-Saharan African country.

- The economic crisis of the 1980s forced 37 developing countries to cut education spending by a quarter in order to keep up the interest payments on foreign debts.

- Approximately one-quarter of the world's adults are illiterate; two-thirds of these are women.

Sources: *Tendances et projections des effectifs scolaires par degre d'enseignement et par age*, 1960-2000, UNESCO, Paris, 1984. *The Economist Book of Vital World Statistics*, Hutchinson, 1990; *The State of the World's Children* 1989, UNICEF, Oxford University Press, 1989; United Nations Statistical Office.

Latin America and Asia have increased. On the other hand, as a result of economic decline, education budgets have been sharply cut over the last decade in most of the poorest countries in the world. The education systems in some of these countries have been described by the UN Children's Fund (UNICEF) as on the brink of collapse. Nevertheless, some argue that attempting to model the education systems of the poorest nations on those of the richest has led to a disastrous mismatch of resources, with under-investment in primary and *vocational education, and over-investment in *higher education. According to the World Bank the average dollar invested in primary education returns twice as much as one invested in higher education in terms of the productivity, health, and well-being of a country's citizens.

education, financing of. Most *primary, *secondary, and *higher education is financed by general taxation. A few countries have imposed fees for primary education, but such fees are generally modest and rarely cover more than 10–15 per cent of recurrent costs. Fees meet a larger proportion at the secondary level (20 per cent in Sierra Leone and 44 per cent in Lesotho). Fees for higher education are often met by scholarships, and university students in many countries receive a stipend. After World War II, public spending on education rose steadily in most countries both in real terms and as a percentage of GNP. By the mid-1970s the largest share of many national budgets was going to education; where education was not first it was usually exceeded only by *military expenditure. Since then growth in education spending in many industrialized countries has slowed and in many parts of the developing world spending has fallen. The level of expenditure per student in industrialized countries is vastly more than that of developing countries. The ratio can be 50:1. Bolivia spends the equivalent of $0.80 per primary school pupil for classroom materials, whereas Italy spends $75 and Sweden more than $300.

EEC (European Economic Community), an economic organization of West European states, set up by the Treaties of Rome in March 1957. The EEC, which is based in Brussels, is the best known of the three communities that together form the *EC. It was set up following discussions at Messina in 1955 between the foreign ministers of the six member countries of the European Coal and Steel Community (ECSC) (Belgium, France, Federal Republic of Germany, Italy, Luxemburg, and The Netherlands), who wished to promote further economic integration in Europe. The Treaties of Rome laid out the rules for an establishment of a European Common Market. They included provisions for the free movement of labour and capital between member countries, the abolition of customs barriers and cartels, and the fostering of common agricultural and trading policies. The expansion of the EEC dates from 1973, when the UK, the Republic of Ireland, and Denmark were admitted. (The UK's earlier efforts to enter were blocked by France.) Greece joined in 1981, and Spain and Portugal in 1986. In 1991, the organization had a membership of twelve: Belgium, Denmark, France, Germany, Greece, Republic of Ireland, Italy, Luxemburg, The Netherlands, Portugal, Spain, and the UK. Co-operation in the EEC is most organized in the area of *agriculture, and the Common Agricultural Policy (CAP) has been the largest item in the EC budget. In 1979 EC members set up the *European Monetary System (EMS) to stabilize exchange rates. In the 1980s, new initiatives, including the Single European Act (1987) and the Maastricht Treaty (1992) were taken to speed the progress of economic integration. The Single European Market, effective from the end of 1992, was agreed, and proposals were put forward for eventual Economic and Monetary Union (EMU). With regard to trade beyond the Community, the EEC has established special trading relationships with a number of countries or groups of countries, notably with African, Caribbean, and Pacific (ACP) countries under the Lomé Conventions, and more recently with Eastern Europe. With the *European Free Trade Association (EFTA), the EEC has established a frontier-free zone known as the European Economic Area (EEA).

egalitarianism, the belief that society should pursue policies that make people more equal in certain respects. Forms of egalitarianism feature in many religious, social, and political movements, but it has developed particularly in the West since the French Revolution (1789) and with the spread of *communism. Most liberal democracies are committed to equality before the law (everyone should have the same legal rights and access to the courts), political equality (everyone

should be able to vote and stand for office), and equality of opportunity (everyone should be free to compete on an equal footing for jobs, offices, and educational places). More controversial are proposals to bring about greater material equality, for instance by *land reform or by redistributing income through the tax system. Critics of egalitarianism claim that such proposals would infringe personal freedom and diminish economic productivity. Its defenders point to the human costs of *poverty and argue that large inequalities in living standards are unacceptable. (See also *equal pay, *human rights.)

egoism, self-interest as the moral basis of behaviour. Egoism thus stands opposed to claims that there are moral demands on individuals which are binding and may require them to abandon their own interests. The egoist (usually in contrast to the amoralist) is thought of as seeking to demonstrate the rationality of his position; most arguments against egoism attempt to show that some inconsistency is involved in the egoist's claim that his self-interest, but not that of other people, provides him with a source of justification. The first detailed arguments for egoism are presented by Glaucon in *Plato's *Republic* (*c*.350 BC): Glaucon argues that, granted a 'ring of invisibility', by means of which sanctions could be evaded, a person would have no reason to be just. The 19th-century German philosopher Max Stirner attempted, in *The Ego and His Own* (1845), to defend a comprehensive theory of egoism. (See also *altruism.)

Egyptian language, the language spoken in Egypt in antiquity. Its daughter language, Coptic, died out in the 17th century AD. It thus has one of the longest histories of any language. There is a vast literature, both secular (historical and legal texts) and religious (myths, hymns, and rituals). From 650 BC the classicizing tendencies of the scribes gave way to Demotic ('of the people') Egyptian, and Demotic inscriptions are found until the mid-5th century AD. Coptic became dominant in the 4th century AD, but started to decline after the introduction of Arabic in the 7th century (see *Semitic languages). Egyptian inscriptions were written in hieroglyphs (highly stylized pictorial symbols). There were also two cursive scripts based on the hieroglyphs: Hieratic, used for religious documents; and Demotic, for ordinary documents. Coptic was written in the Greek alphabet, with seven extra letters taken from Demotic. Egyptian is part of Afro-Asiatic, a larger group which includes *Berber, *Chadic, *Cushitic, and Semitic languages.

elasticity (in economics), a measure of the degree to which one variable responds to a change in another. Elasticity is a ratio: the proportionate change in the dependent variable divided by the proportionate change in the independent variable. (A proportionate change is the change in a variable divided by the total variable.) For instance, price elasticity of demand measures the proportionate change in the quantity demanded that arises from a proportionate change in price. Here price is the independent variable, since a change in price causes a change in demand, which is therefore the dependent variable. Similarly, income elasticity of demand measures the proportionate change in demand arising from a change in consumers' incomes. The concept helps economists to analyse the effects of policy and other changes. For example, a reduction in motor vehicle prices may boost sales, particularly if buyers believe that the cut is only temporary. If, say, a 10 per cent cut in prices is followed by a 20 per cent rise in the number of cars sold, then one could conclude that the short-run price elasticity of demand for cars is −2 (minus, because the quantities have opposite signs). Price elasticity may help them to predict how a change in the *exchange rate will affect *exports and *imports. Income elasticity may be useful in analysing the effect of a change in tax rates on consumer spending.

elections, the means by which people make political choices by voting for leaders and office-holders. In competitive elections, there are alternatives to choose from; in political elections on a national scale, the main purpose of competitive elections is to determine the composition of the government. However, real choice exists in perhaps only one-third of the world's states. In many developing countries, and in those communist states that remain, elections are non-competitive: there is no choice of candidates or political parties, and the electoral process exists purely as a *legitimizing device, in order to demonstrate an apparent show of support for the government on the part of the population. When elections are free and fair, and do provide an effective choice, they also perform additional functions. They generate respect for the political system by reinforcing its *authority and stability; they confer dignity on the individual *citizen through his or her right to vote (see *franchise); and they provide a line of communication between politicians and people, ensuring that the government is sensitive to popular demands and can be held accountable for its actions. The frequency with which elections are held, the selection of candidates and of those eligible to vote, the rules governing polling procedures, and the methods by which voters' preferences are translated into seats vary widely (see *electoral systems).

electoral fraud, the manipulation of the electoral process to produce a result that does not reflect the free choice of the electorate. Abuses range from false campaign propaganda that discredits rival candidates; bribery and intimidation of voters (see *corruption); multiple voting on the part of individuals, gerrymandering (manipulating the boundaries of a constituency to give undue influence to some party or class); and dishonest counting of the votes. Safeguards include up-to-date registers of eligible voters, legal limitations on campaign spending, secret ballots, and the presence of impartial observers at vote-counting.

electoral systems, sets of rules for conducting *elections. These specify who can vote and how, which offices are subject to election and how frequently, the regulations governing campaigns, and how votes are to be translated into seats in a *legislature. In some countries, such as Australia and Belgium, electoral participation is considered a duty as well as a right, and is therefore compulsory. In such countries, and in countries where registration is automatic, the turnout at elections is high. By contrast, in the USA, where voter registration is left to the initiative of individuals or political parties, turnout is exceptionally low (30–50 per cent). There are rules governing the frequency of elections, whether local or national, as well as the terms for which certain office-holders may be elected. Electoral systems also specify certain campaign practices, such as limits on expenditure, access to the *mass media, and polling procedures. The most important function of electoral systems, however, is to determine the composition of the government by converting votes to seats. Systems are either *majoritarian (in which case a candidate wins either by a first-past-the-post plurality of the votes, or by a 50 per cent or other specified majority), or *proportional (in which case the distribution of seats is proportional to the number of votes cast for the competing parties). Ideally, an electoral system should help to create effective government, which is none the less acceptable in the eyes of the people (see *legitimacy). It should act as a safety-valve, allowing unpopular governments to be removed, and at the same time it should draw people into politics rather than shutting them out. In practice, however, electoral systems can only meet some of these requirements at the expense of others. For example, a majoritarian system may produce a stable government at the expense of minority parties who feel that they are not being represented, while a proportional system, which is more representative of the population as a whole, may result in unstable *coalitions.

elementary education   *primary education.

élite, a select group or class. The Italian theorists *Pareto and Gaetano Mosca (1858–1941) maintained in a series of influential writings that social groups and societies were inevitably headed by élites: the classless societies advocated by *Marxists were impossible. The German sociologist Robert Michels (1876–1936) argued that even political parties with democratic aims would come to be dominated by élites through the 'iron law of oligarchy'. The existence of élites in the USA has been much discussed, as they are sometimes held to undermine its democratic basis. Charles Wright Mills in *The Power Elite* (1956) pointed to the domination of the USA by an élite from business, political, and military life which he termed the *military–industrial complex. Élites may be forced to change their character. In newly independent countries the revolutionary élites which have fought for change may, after a struggle, be displaced by the next more pragmatic generation. Elites which do not renew themselves by recruiting new members and remaining open to talent risk, as Mosca held, 'exhaustion that is wont to bring on great social cataclysms'. Arguably the rigid exclusivity of the governing élites of the communist regimes in Eastern Europe and the former Soviet Union contributed to their downfall in 1989 and 1991.

Jozsef Antall casts his vote on the April 1990 **elections** in Hungary, which his Democratic Forum Party was to win. Despite the initial enthusiasm for democracy, in an important by-election in Budapest just one year later the 21 per cent turnout invalidated the poll.

embargo *sanctions.

embassy, the headquarters of a *diplomatic mission in a foreign country; the site where diplomatic business is conducted; and often the residence of the ambassador, who is a country's highest-ranking overseas representative. Permanent diplomatic missions date from the 15th century, and their activities are conducted on the basis of established rules and conventions, some of which, like the principle of *diplomatic immunity, have the status of *international law. While embassies are concerned with diplomatic or intergovernmental relations, the function of a consulate is to protect the citizens and interests (often commercial) of the country they represent. Consulates are set up under reciprocal bilateral treaties and are to be found in major ports and towns; embassies are exclusively located in capital cities.

emergency powers, powers assumed by governments when circumstances appear to demand a suspension of normal political or legal processes. Justifications for such moves can include natural disasters, insurrection or riot, and either civil or international war. Typically, the taking of emergency powers involves the suspension of parliamentary procedures; the establishment of special legal procedures, including special courts, and *detention without trial; and the suspension of *civil rights, such as freedom of movement, information, and speech. Sometimes, emergency powers can lead to the imposition of *martial law through the military authorities. The government of South Africa, faced with widespread violence in opposition to *apartheid during the 1980s, imposed a state of emergency in certain areas between 1985 and 1990, which led to severe restrictions on the right to political activity and the reporting of events. Emergency powers can be an important mechanism for the maintenance of *authoritarian states or *dictatorships, and even in democracies, such powers may continue after the need for them has passed.

emigration, the movement of people permanently or semi-permanently from one country to another. The term out-migration refers to internal movement from one part of a country to another. The main motivation for both these types of *migration is economic improvement; adolescents and young adults are most likely to move. Wars, and racial, religious, and political persecution have resulted in the forced emigration of *refugees. Europe's net emigration from 1800 to 1914 was of the order of 50 million persons, over half of whom settled permanently in the USA (total emigration was greater, since some 30 per cent returned to Europe). About half a million people still emigrate to the USA each year. Sustained emigration in the 20th century also includes movements from Europe to the Americas, Australia, and New Zealand, from South Asia to the UK, from parts of south-eastern to northern Europe, and from North Africa to France. The economic consequences of emigration are complex. The advantages for the country of origin from remittances sent by emigrants, for example, may be counterbalanced by brain drain, that is the loss of skilled workers.

emotion (in psychology), a state taken to involve feelings, physiological changes, and expressive reactions. Arguments about emotion concern the degree to which it is a biological remnant of the evolutionary past, and the degree and manner to which emotions are differentiated from each other. Those who follow *Darwin, who set out his views in *The Expression of the Emotions in Man and Animals* (1872), regard at least basic emotions as innate, and assume that emotions are differentiated by distinct innate expressive and instrumental behaviour. By contrast, those who see emotions as social constructs assume they are differentiated by the way they fit into the social world. The number of basic emotions is disputed, but many would concur with *Watson in accepting fear, rage, and love. The work of *James on emotion in his 1884 article 'What is an emotion?' in *Mind* has had lasting impact. James argued that 'our feeling of the [bodily] changes as they occur IS the emotion', that is, that emotion is a physiological response to an environmental stimulus. A modified version of this theory, known as the James–Lange theory from the contribution to it of the Danish physician C. G. Lange (1834–1900), is found in the leading contemporary theory of emotion developed by the US psychologist Stanley Schachter in *Emotion, Obesity, and Crime* (1971), which links physiological arousal to cognitive evaluation.

emotivism, the philosophical view that the meaning of a moral statement consists in its expressing an emotional attitude. For example, an emotivist would understand 'You ought not to have done that' as expressing the speaker's feelings of disapprobation towards a person's action. Emotivism is formulated in the first place as a theory about the meaning of moral language, but it follows that, for an emotivist, there are no objective moral facts, and that no truth is uncovered by moral argument. Emotivism was first advanced by *Ayer in close association with *logical positivism.

empiricism, a doctrine in the theory of knowledge (see *epistemology) which stresses the primacy of sense-experience over reason in the acquisition and justification of knowledge. It thus stands opposed to *rationalism, and limits *a priori knowledge. Although explicit empiricist notions can be found in medieval philosophy, and perhaps even earlier, its main impetus was gained during the 17th-century revolution in physics, when adherence to empiricist controls was advocated as an antidote to scientifically unproductive metaphysical speculation. The demand for philosophy to be responsive to the needs of science is a theme that has been invariant through the empiricist tradition from *Locke and *Hume to *Russell and the *logical positivists, and is present also in *pragmatism. (See also *verificationism.)

employment, the utilization of *labour, or the situation of a person who is in the paid employ of another person or an organization. The term refers, in economics, to the use of *factors of production, which include *land and *capital, as well as labour. Statistics of labour employment tend to omit home-makers and care-givers, nearly all women, who do unpaid work. Most workers are in paid employment—almost all workers in socialist countries, over three-quarters in other industrialized countries, and between one-quarter and three-quarters in developing countries. Self-employed workers make up between a quarter and half of the paid labour-force in developing countries, particularly in *agriculture and in the *informal sector, where day, seasonal, and other temporary labour is common. Part-time work and outwork are common forms of employment, and *migrant labour is important in many economies. Current trends in developing countries show rural employment declining and service and industrial employment increasing (see *primary, *secondary, and *tertiary industry). Industrialized countries have seen a fall in industrial employment and an increase in service-sector working. There is a trend world-wide towards a greater proportion of women among paid workers.

Employment

These graphs compare the activities of the workforce in Pakistan, a developing country, and Canada, an industrialized one. A fall in the agricultural sector and a rise in the service sector typically occur as countries become more prosperous. Most of the world's economies fall between those of Pakistan and Canada.

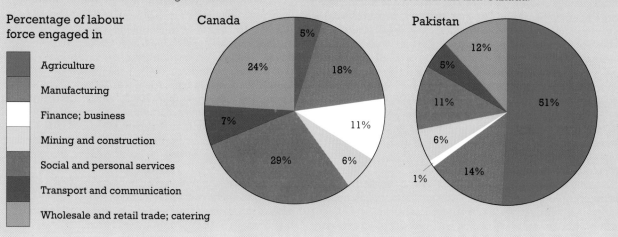

Percentage of labour force engaged in

- Agriculture
- Manufacturing
- Finance; business
- Mining and construction
- Social and personal services
- Transport and communication
- Wholesale and retail trade; catering

Discrimination in access to employment and to *equal pay affects women, young workers, and members of ethnic minorities in particular. They tend to have the least well-paid employment and to be the first to lose their job in times of *recession. *Trade unions and bodies such as the *International Labour Organization seek to influence levels and conditions of employment world-wide, as do the *monetary, *fiscal, and *education policies of governments.

endangered species, animals or plants which are threatened with extinction, usually because of man's impact on the ecosystem (see *ecology). At present there are probably some 10 million species on the planet, mostly plants and invertebrates, but scientists predict that by the end of the century at least 1 million of these will be extinct. Although animals and plants have always become extinct, the process has been greatly accelerated by *pollution, *hunting, and the destruction of habitats through *deforestation, for example of the Amazon and other rainforests. Ecologists suggest four arguments for conserving species: we should respect our fellow species (see *animal rights); many species, such as oxygen-producing plankton in the ocean, play a vital role in the ecosystem, not yet fully understood; many species provide, or could provide, food, drugs, and other useful chemicals; for many developing countries 'wildlife tourism' is or could be an important source of revenue. About 500 species and subspecies of mammal (there are 4,000 in all) are listed in the Convention on International Trade in Endangered Species of Wild Flora and Fauna (CITES), including all the whales and their relatives, all big cats, and all primates except man. Most countries have ratified CITES, but it is widely flouted. Another agency for species *conservation, the International Union for the Conservation of Nature and Natural Resources (IUCN), lists species at risk in its *Red Data Books*. Large mammals such as the African elephant, hunted for its ivory tusks, and the Asian tiger, hunted for its skin, may be protected by government programmes, but the fate of many other plants and animals is sealed.

energy, renewable, energy derived from a source which is unlimited (such as wind or sun) as opposed to those which are finite (particularly fossil fuels). The generation of this energy can use various sources of power: the sun (producing solar power); wind and waves; tides, their energy being harnessed through river barrages; running water, as in hydroelectric power; and power from water heated by volcanic rocks (geothermal power). Biomass (material from living things such as wood and dung) is another such source, provided that any felled trees are replaced by planting. Interest in renewable energy was stimulated in the 1960s by the *ecology movement, and in the 1970s by oil price rises, which focused attention on the finite nature of oil, gas, and coal reserves. Renewable energy is already widely used, especially in developing countries: hydroelectric installations provide a quarter of the world's electricity supplies and three-quarters for developing countries. There are many other examples of the successful use of renewable energy: in Brazil sugar cane is converted into ethanol fuel for cars; in Sweden refuse incinerators provide 8 per cent of district heating; China has 4.5 million domestic 'biogas' appliances, which treat human, animal, and agricultural waste, and produce cooking gas for 20 million people; in France there are more than 40 geothermal schemes for domestic heating. The use of renewable energy has environmental advantages; it is also usually cheaper. Most forms contribute little or nothing to the *greenhouse effect or other forms of *pollution, and they avoid the risks of nuclear power (which, although theoretically an unlimited source, is usually not considered a form of renewable energy). Other major contributions to solving the world's energy crisis will be the conservation of energy through improved insulation of houses, the development of more energy-efficient machines, *recycling, and changing lifestyles so as to use less energy.

Engels *Marxism, *matriarchy.

English language, the language spoken by an estimated 300 million people as a first language in the UK, Ireland, the USA, Canada, Australia, and New Zealand. It has official status in over fifty countries, notably in sub-Saharan Africa and southern Asia, and is the most widely used second language in the world. Germanic speakers began settling in

England from northern Germany and southern Denmark from about AD 450, and Viking invasions in the 9th century added a Scandinavian element to the language. The Old English period runs from the appearance of the first texts in the late 7th century to the mid-11th century, when the Norman invasion radically changed the nature of English. Over 50 per cent of the vocabulary was replaced by words taken from French and Latin during the subsequent Middle English period (1100–1500). The Modern English period saw the language taken beyond Britain and the establishment of new regional varieties, such as American English. English spelling does not accurately reflect the spoken language, as it goes back to a period before the introduction of printing in 1476. Samuel Johnson's *Dictionary* of 1755 began the process of standardizing modern spelling. English grammar is relatively simple; the language has a remarkable capacity for absorbing foreign words, which has resulted in a large and international vocabulary.

entrepôt *free port.

entrepreneur, the organizer (and sometimes the owner) of a business, who employs *factors of production to create *goods and services for sale. The entrepreneur bears part or all of the risk of the enterprise and, if successful, is rewarded by making a *profit. In large *companies the entrepreneurial functions of ownership and control are normally split. *Shareholders own the company and bear some of the risk, as do creditors, while day-to-day control is in the hands of salaried managers.

environment (in *ecology), the physical surroundings of an organism or organisms, including biological, physical, and chemical factors. Planning, caring for, and *conservation of the human environment, both built and natural, became of increasing concern in the years following World War II, as reflected in the UK by the creation of the Department of the Environment in 1970 to deal with town *planning and conservation as well as housing. Since then the environmental movement has broadened public concern so that the term now encompasses wildlife and *endangered species and habitats, and the threat to planetary systems posed by *pollution, *deforestation, and other effects of human activity. In philosophy, environmentalism stresses the influence of the physical environment on man's development and activities. (See human *geography and, by contrast, *Gaia hypothesis.)

epidemiology, the study of the incidence and distribution of diseases, and of their control and prevention. Epidemiologists deal with information on thousands or millions of people (see *vital statistics) and discern disease, associations, and trends. For example, studies comparing rates of *cancer and *heart disease in communities with different diets and ways of life have established the role of *smoking and the consumption of saturated fat in the development of both. Epidemiology is thus fundamental to *preventive medicine and *public health. To reduce the spread of *communicable disease the World Health Organization recommends the provision of safe water supplies and sanitation and improved housing and nutrition. *Immunization against specific childhood diseases is markedly successful, but the control of parasites is less so. Some parasites, notably the anopheles mosquito, which causes malaria, are increasingly resistant to pesticides. To ensure prevention of disease, treatment, often by drugs, is directed towards sufferers for their own benefit and to prevent them from acting as carriers. Rising *life expectancy demonstrates the progress in the control of communicable disease.

Epiphany, an annual Christian festival on 6 January, originally commemorating the manifestation of Jesus' divinity at his baptism. First mentioned by Clement of Alexandria (AD 217), by the 4th century it was widely celebrated. In the West, Epiphany came to commemorate the revelation of Jesus to the Gentiles, in the visit of the Magi or Wise Men.

epistemology, the philosophical theory of knowledge. It is generally assumed that the difference between a belief which makes a genuine claim to knowledge, and one which is a mere statement of opinion, is that the former can somehow be justified. Epistemology can be regarded as the investigation of what constitutes that justification, and how, or whether, it can be attained. *Scepticism is the position which holds that justification, and hence knowledge, is not possible. Traditionally conflicting theories about knowledge have been *rationalism, which claims that ultimate justification for our beliefs is to be found in reason (see *a priori), and *empiricism, which argues that it is to be found in our sense-experiences. The traditional debate, then, has concerned the nature of the foundation of knowledge. More recently, however, attention has been focused on the structure of knowledge, that is, how our true beliefs are related to one another. The assumption that knowledge has to have a starting-point in any sort of foundation has been questioned by the Coherence Theory of Knowledge, which suggests, instead, that a belief is justified to the extent to which it fits in, or coheres with, all our other beliefs.

equal pay, equality of treatment in payment for *labour, either for the same work or work of equal value. The right to equal pay in paid employment is recognized by the *UN and by the *International Labour Organization. The concept most often refers to the comparison between women's and men's pay in the same enterprise, industry, or country, but it applies also to workers of different ethnicity or in different countries. Much of the work done by women is in the home or the community and receives no remuneration. In European market economies the gap between male and female earnings in manufacturing in 1985 ranged from 10 to 20 per cent in Scandinavian countries (Sweden, Denmark, and Norway) to 30 to 35 per cent in the UK, Ireland, and Switzerland. Equal pay for women doing the same work as men is now widespread, even general in most countries, but occupational segregation continues to result in lower pay in predominantly female sectors of employment such as shops, catering, and domestic work. The 1970s and 1980s saw the introduction of equal pay laws in many countries, for example the 1970 Equal Pay Act in the UK. In developing countries *minimum wage laws provide some protection to lower-paid workers in certain regions and trades. Apart from legislation, *collective bargaining and better access to *education and training are strategies for improving prospects of equal pay. (See also *egalitarianism.)

equilibrium, an economic concept which describes a situation in which there are no forces at work to bring about a change. For instance, an equilibrium price in a *market is one where there is no excess *demand to drive price up and no excess *supply to drive price down; at equilibrium, demand will equal supply. *National income will be in equilibrium when aggregate demand is equal to aggregate supply (that is, when the amount that people want to spend on a nation's goods and services exactly coincides with the nation's planned output). Economists distinguish between general and partial equilibrium analysis. General equilibrium occurs when there is a state of equilibrium in all product markets and in all markets for *factors of production (see *Walras). Partial equilibrium (see *Marshall) focuses on the behaviour of a single market assumed to be small in relation to the economic system as a whole.

equity (in law), a body of principles developed historically in England by the Court of Chancery to overcome unfairness resulting from the inflexibility and limitations of the law applied in the *common law courts. These principles, based on conscience, were usually given effect through the creation of new remedies, which could require a litigant who had successfully established legal rights before a common law court to use those rights for the benefit of a person (a 'beneficiary') who had a better claim in equity. In time, such beneficiaries were considered to possess equitable rights. These did not destroy legal rights, but took precedence over them. The *trust, in which a legal owner holds property for the benefit of beneficiaries, is a notable creation of this system; specific performance (by which a party to a contract may be ordered to carry out his part of the bargain rather than pay *damages) and the *injunction were also equitable remedies. Today, most common law systems have integrated equitable principles and remedies into the mainstream of their law, but they are still regarded as distinct in conceptual analysis. In economics, equity refers to an ordinary *share or the ordinary share capital of a *company. An equity market is where shares are traded and usually forms the greater part of a *stock exchange.

ergonomics, a field of study directed specifically towards the problems of the individual at work which impinge on work performance. It examines the effect on work performance of both internal and external factors. Internal factors are such things as the anatomical, physiological, and psychological factors affecting the work. External factors include such things as machine design, layout of equipment, speed of work, and lighting and heating conditions. These concerns have led ergonomics to be divided into two main fields. Firstly, how machines should be designed to ensure that no unnecessary effort is required for people operating them. Controls should be easily reached and operated, and instrument panels clearly visible and capable of being read quickly and accurately. The second main field of ergonomics is the design and control of optimum working conditions. The level and intensity of lighting, noise levels in the working environment, and temperature levels are typical concerns. Colour is also important: ergonomic study of workers using visual display units led to many screens having green printing, identified as the most restful colour and least likely to cause eye-strain and headaches. Ergonomics has grown in importance as it has been recognized that the performance of a machine is inextricably linked to the performance of the person who operates it.

eschatology, a term used primarily in Christian and Jewish theology to refer to the 'last things', including the ultimate fate of the world and the individual soul. However, almost all religions of the world have eschatological features, which may be divided into those based on mythological explanations of the origins and end of the world (see *creation myths) and those based on historical explanations. The biblical accounts of the history of the Jewish people and the teaching and parables of Jesus are examples of historical eschatology, leading to *millenarian expectations of the coming of the Messiah among Jews, and of the Second Coming among Christians. Contrasting with such views is the expectation of the apocalyptic or cataclysmic intervention of God in history. In both Hinduism and Buddhism, eschatological beliefs focus on the longing for release from the cycle of birth and rebirth (see *dependent origination, *reincarnation, *samsara).

Eskimo *Inuit.

Eskimo–Aleut languages, a group of about ten languages spoken by 90,000 people in Greenland, northern Canada, Alaska, the Aleutian islands, and the Chukchi peninsula of Siberia. Most of the speakers are *Inuit (Eskimo); Aleut accounts for just 700 people on the Aleutian islands off Alaska. The two languages are not mutually intelligible. Eskimo has two branches: Yupik, spoken in Alaska and Siberia, and Inuit (or Inupiaq), which is spoken in Canada and Greenland. There are numerous dialects of Eskimo, and in general only neighbouring ones are mutually intelligible. Greenlandic Eskimo, which has the most speakers, is an official language of Greenland, and is used in schools and on the radio. The first book in Eskimo was published in Greenland in 1742, using an adapted Roman script. Since then the Eskimo languages have been written in various adapted Roman scripts; Siberian Eskimo (which has less than 800 speakers) is written in the Cyrillic *alphabet.

Esperanto, an artificial language invented in 1887 by a Pole, Ludwig Lazarus Zamenhof (1859–1917). He published *Fundamento de Esperanto*, the definitive guide to the structure of the language, in 1905, the year of the first Universal Congress of Esperanto. The word-roots of Esperanto are taken from the European languages, and especially from Romance. All words are spelled exactly as they are pronounced. The *grammar is simple, and perfectly regular. For example, all nouns end in -o and add -j in the plural; there is an object case (accusative) which adds -n (making singular -on, plural -ojn); adjectives end in -a and agree with the noun they refer to in number and case; verbs end in -s in all persons. There are present, past, and future tenses, which are distinguished by different vowels before the final ending: -a in the present, -i in the past, and -o in the future. Thus 'I am' is *mi estas* (= est + a + s). A large amount of world literature has been translated into Esperanto, and there are also original compositions and journals in the language. There are over sixty countries with national Esperanto associations, but probably far more people are able to understand it than speak it fluently. A move to have Esperanto accepted as an official language of the UN failed in 1966.

ethics, the philosophical study of the nature and grounds of moral thought and action. Ethical theories in this pure sense are sharply distinguished from moral systems, which are directed towards drawing up particular sets of rules by which to live (such as Christian morality), and from practical or applied ethics, the analysis of arguments advanced for particular moral conclusions (such as the rightness or wrongness of abortion). The most fundamental question in ethics is usually taken to be the justification of morality, that is whether or not it can be demonstrated that moral action is rational. Schools of ethics can be divided, very roughly, into three sorts. The first, which derives from *Aristotle's *Ethics*, gives pride of place to the virtues, such as justice, charity, and generosity, which are thought of as dispositions to act in ways that both tend to the fulfilment of the person who has them and to benefit the society of which he or she is a member. Aristotle's ethics are also often described as *naturalistic, in that he seeks to exhibit a harmony between morality and human nature. The second, which is defended in most depth by *Kant, is the school which makes the concept of duty central to morality (called 'deontology'). Kant argued that the only thing which is good in itself (as opposed to merely good as a means) is a 'good will', one which is freely in accordance with duty. Knowledge of one's duty, for Kant, follows from a realization that one is a rational being, and thus bound to obey what he called the 'categorical imperative', the requirement to respect all rational beings as autonomous 'ends in themselves'. Kant's views of morality are intimately connected with his view of *free will. The third school of ethics is *utilitarianism whose goal is the 'greatest happiness of the greatest number'. Ethical theories may also be divided in another way, according to whether or not they allow that there is such a thing as objective moral truth; *Hume, as a subjectivist, held that morality is profoundly rooted in our 'sentiments'. Ethics in this century has been largely preoccupied with analysing the meaning of moral language, as in *Ayer's theory of *emotivism, whereby the meaning of a moral statement consists in its expressing an emotional attitude.

Ethiopian Orthodox Church, or Abyssinian Church, a Monophysite *Christian church. It was closely associated with the *Coptic Church, before becoming virtually independent, with its own patriarch, in the 1950s. It observes some Jewish practices, such as circumcision and keeping the sabbath. Its scriptures include books not usually considered *canonical, such as the First Book of Enoch. Distinctions are made between two kinds of clergy: those who administer the sacraments, who may not be educated, and those who teach, who are trained, often at the seminary in Addis Ababa. There are about 7 million full members. The literary language Ge'ez, a *Semitic language of the Southern Peripheral group, is the liturgical and biblical language.

ethnic conflict *communal conflict.

ethnic groups, groups of people who think of themselves as sharing some common element of cultural or racial identity. These ideas about cultural distinctiveness are expressed through the concept of ethnicity. Ideas about ethnicity involve the criteria of both insiders, or members of the group, and outsiders, or non-members, so that ethnicity is as often defined by what or who it excludes as by what or who it includes. This reveals an important principle: ethnicity and membership of an ethnic group are based on relations between different groups of people. People are aware of 'belonging' to a particular group or *culture by virtue of their differences from some other group or culture (see *social identity theory). It seems likely that ideas about ethnic identity were less clear-cut and more fluid in non-industrial societies. The existence of different ethnic groups poses a problem for modern *nation-states, which base their *legitimacy on ideas of one state for one group of people (the nation) with a common culture. Some modern states try to ensure the existence of a common culture for all their people through control over education and communication media like newspapers, radio, and television. Disputes with ethnic minorities often focus on problems of education and

language, as in the case of the *Basques of Spain or the *Tamils of Sri Lanka. In both cases, the groups feel their identity and community is threatened by a central state controlled by people who do not share their culture and language. In this sort of dispute ethnic groups assert their own claims to form a separate nation, and the issue becomes an aspect of *nationalism. In other cases, as with many immigrant groups in the USA, people remain attached to particular signs of their ethnic identity, even though they accommodate themselves to the culture and politics of their new state. In the modern world, ethnic problems are especially common in former colonies, such as those in Africa, whose boundaries were drawn with little regard for the cultural or linguistic boundaries of different peoples. But the upsurge of minority conflict like those in the republics of the former Soviet Union and in Eastern Europe, shows that the problem of ethnicity is by no means confined to developing countries. (See also *race.)

ethnography, the study of the social organization and culture of a particular group of people. The term refers to two distinct but interrelated ideas: the practice of conducting *fieldwork in a particular place based on participant observation by the ethnographer, and the putting together of a written description and analysis based on these fieldwork experiences. Ethnography provides the raw material for all modern *anthropology.

ethnolinguistics, the study of the relations between linguistic and cultural behaviour. It combines the study of cognitive structures (patterns of thinking) from *ethnography and social *anthropology, and of *semantics from *linguistics. Ways of categorizing meaning and experience in different cultures are studied in relation to the forms and vocabulary of *languages. Areas of study include *kinship terms, types of insults, plant categorization, and types of talk. Ethnolinguistics overlaps with *sociolinguistics, forming a discipline known as ethnography of communication.

ethnomethodology, the study of the methods used by people to construct and maintain everyday life. It was devised by the US sociologist Harold Garfinkel (1917–), who conducted experiments disrupting everyday expectations in order to show how social life is conventionally ordered. For example, he asked students to return home and act like lodgers; the reactions of relatives would demonstrate the fragile intricacy of the social world. Ethnomethodology is much concerned with the analysis of *conversation.

ethology, the study of animal behaviour, usually in its natural environment, and the application of insights and methods derived from such work to observational study of humans. Its theoretical orientation was based on *Darwin's dictum that patterns of behaviour as well as bodily structure are subject to the selective processes of evolution. Its classical formulation is in the works of the Austrian Konrad Lorenz (1903–89) and the Dutchman Nikolaas Tinbergen (1907–88), particularly the latter's *The Study of Instinct* (1951). Tinbergen showed that complex patterns of behaviour might appear with little influence of *learning when innately programmed 'sign stimuli' release them. An example is the food-begging of herring gull chicks, which is 'released' by the orange spot on the adult bird's yellow beak. Lorenz demonstrated how experience might direct a fixed action pattern when he discovered *imprinting. Goslings adopted him as their 'mother' because he was the first mobile object

The new-born baby's reflex to suck is a clear example of the instinctive behaviour shared by humans with other mammals, which forms the basis of **ethology**.

they encountered when newly hatched. Lorenz and Tinbergen generally played down the role of learning, but in the 1950s and 1960s it became clear that animals' natural behaviour is more flexible, particularly in higher species such as primates. Modern studies of animal behaviour nevertheless accept Tinbergen's view that any behaviour must be explained in four ways: its immediate cause; its appearance and progress in the development of the individual; its adaptive function—how it improves the species' chance of survival; its evolutionary history—how the species developed such behaviour as part of its repertoire. Ethology spread into systematic observation of human, particularly children's, behaviour, and arguments about innateness of *facial expression and other non-verbal *communication. Bowlby's theory of *attachment is another application of ethological ideas.

etymology, a branch of *historical linguistics studying the ancestry of the form and meaning of words. It draws on the theory of regular sound change in the development of one *language or across languages. For example, 'king' is related to Old English *cyning*, and the Welsh *pedwar* (meaning 'four') is related to the Latin *quattuor*.

eugenics, the study and doctrine of improving a population by controlled breeding for desirable inherited characteristics. The concept was widely discussed in Britain, the USA, and Europe in the late 19th and early 20th centuries, the term having been coined by the British psychologist *Galton in 1883. Advocates of eugenics seek either to encourage the procreation of supposedly superior human beings or to prevent the procreation of supposedly inferior ones. Any complete eugenic policy would involve decisions about which characteristics were desirable and which undesirable, assumptions that these characteristics were inherited rather than socially determined, and a degree of compulsion. Because eugenic ideas flourished under *Nazism, they became discredited and are not often voiced. However, implicitly eugenic practices continue in many parts of the world: for example, the denial to handicapped people of the right to have children, selective sterilization, and amniocentesis followed by the offer of *abortion if chromosomal abnormality emerges.

Eurocommunism *communism.

Eurodollar, a US dollar deposit held by an individual or an institution in a bank outside the USA (most frequently in Europe). Eurodollars constitute a stock of internationally mobile funds, which act as a source of easily transferable *credit and which facilitate *trade. Banks benefit by borrowing and lending dollars at different *interest rates. The Eurodollar market originated in the late 1950s. Subsequently the market also began to function in other *currencies too; thus the term Euro-currency developed.

European Commission (Commission of the European Communities), one of the principal institutions of the *EC, and the one responsible for planning Community policies. Its loyalties are to the Community as a whole, rather than to the individual member states. The present-day European Commission dates from 1967, when a treaty merging the three executive bodies of the three different Communities (the *EEC, the European Coal and Steel Community, and the European Atomic Energy Community) came into effect. The Commission heads a large Secretariat in Brussels, which submits proposals for consideration by the *Council of Ministers. The Commission is also charged with the implementation of decisions, once they have been made by the Council. It also acts as a mediator between the different Community members. There are seventeen commissioners, appointed by the governments of the member states: two from the UK, Germany, France, Italy, and Spain, and one from other EC member states. Each commissioner has responsibility for a different policy area. The President of the Commission is normally appointed for a four-year term.

European Convention on Human Rights (European Convention for the Protection of Human Rights and Fundamental Freedoms), a convention drawn up in 1950 by the *Council of Europe, as an attempt to enforce certain of the rights stated in the *Universal Declaration of Human Rights. All members of the Council are parties to it. The European Convention emphasizes *civil rights such as the right to life and liberty, the right to a fair trial, and freedom of conscience and association. Any breach of the Convention by a state may be referred (by an individual, a group, or another state) to the European Commission on Human Rights. The Commission will deal with the matter only if all domestic remedies have been tried. If the Commission fails to obtain a settlement of the case, it is referred to the European Court of Human Rights sitting in Strasburg, France, which consists of judges, chosen by member states of the Council of Europe, who are independent of the governments of their countries. To bring a case to the Court takes several years and the direct protection conferred on citizens within member states is limited. None the less, the Convention has influenced decisions of national courts and legislatures on such subjects as detention pending trial and corporal punishment. States which are parties to the Convention are obliged to ensure that their law accords with the Court's rulings, but the Court recognizes that states must have some discretion in giving effect to its requirements.

European Council of Ministers (Council of the European Communities), one of the principal institutions of the *EC, and its pivotal decision-making body. The Council, which meets in Brussels, consists of ministers from the governments of each of the twelve member states, and is therefore the institution representing the particular interests of each of these states. Although referred to as the Council, there are in practice a number of different councils, each dealing with different policy areas. Because ministers are only able to be in Brussels for short periods, a Committee of Permanent Representatives (COREPER), consisting of the ambassadors of the member states, aided by a committee of civil servants, prepares the issues awaiting ministerial decision. The office of President of the Council is held for six-month periods by each member state in rotation. The Council acts on proposals submitted to it by the *Commission, after consultation with the *European Parliament and sometimes the Economic and Social Committee. The Council is also responsible for co-ordinating the general economic policies of its members, and for ensuring that the provisions of the EC treaties are implemented. Since December 1974, the heads of government of Community countries have met twice yearly in the capital of the country holding the Council presidency. These meetings or summits are known as the European Council. This Council discusses matters relating to the Community, as well as matters handled by the European Political Co-operation system (EPC), under which Community foreign ministers meet four times yearly to co-ordinate aspects of their foreign policies.

European Court of Justice, one of the principal institutions of the *EC, and its main judicial body. The Court, which is based in Luxemburg, was established in 1957 under the Treaties of Rome. It hears cases involving alleged breaches of Community law. It is responsible for interpreting and applying Community treaties, and ensuring that they are fairly observed. It is the final arbiter of Community law, and there is no further appeal. The Court derives its authority from the fact that Community law prevails over national law in cases of conflict. The Court comprises thirteen judges, including at least one from each member state, who are appointed by EC member governments and serve for six-year periods. Because of an increase in the number of cases that have come before the Court, a lower court, or Court of First Instance, has been set up to deal with minor cases.

European Free Trade Association (EFTA), an organization of western and northern European countries which aims to create an industrial free-trade area among its members. The Association was set up in 1960 by eight countries who wished to reduce trade barriers and thereby create a larger market for their manufactured goods, but who were not ready to accept the broader political and economic obligations implied by membership of the *EEC. EFTA is based in Geneva. Its membership of six (following the departure of the UK and Denmark in 1973, when they joined the

EEC) comprises: Austria, Finland, Iceland, Norway, Sweden, and Switzerland. A series of agreements link *EC and EFTA members, and the trend is towards growing collaboration. In 1984, an EFTA–EC tariff-free zone was established, and in the Luxemburg Declaration of the same year, guidelines were laid down for developing the EC–EFTA relationship and for the creation of a European Economic Area, comprising all EC–EFTA countries. Austria, Sweden, Switzerland, and Finland have applied for EC membership, casting some doubt on the survival of EFTA.

European languages *Baltic languages, *Germanic languages, *Indo-European languages, *Romance languages, *Slavic languages, *Uralic languages.

European Monetary System (EMS), a system devised by *EC members which aims to promote monetary stability by limiting exchange-rate fluctuations. The system was set up in 1979 by the then nine members of the EC. The EMS comprises three principal elements: the European Currency Unit (ECU), which is the monetary unit used in EC transactions; the Exchange Rate Mechanism (ERM), whereby those member states taking part agree to maintain currency fluctuations within certain agreed limits; and the European Monetary Co-operation Fund, which issues the ECU and oversees the ERM. The 1992 Maastricht Treaty provided for steps towards Economic and Monetary Union (EMU) (proposed in 1989 by the then President of the *European Commission, Jacques Delors), including a European Monetary Institute which will become a European *central bank, and the introduction of a single European currency.

European Parliament, one of the principal institutions of the *EC. Set up in 1952 under the terms of the treaty which established the European Steel and Coal Community (ECSC), the Parliament was replaced and extended in 1958 to serve two new communities, the *EEC and the European Atomic Energy Community (EURATOM). Meeting in Strasburg and Luxemburg, it has 518 seats, distributed among Community members by the size of their populations; members are directly elected by the citizens of the member states. Elections to the European Parliament first took place in 1979 and are held at five-year intervals. The Parliament is consulted on all major EC issues, including the annual budget, and it advises on legislation. Although it has the theoretical power to dismiss the *European Commission by a vote of censure, its actual powers are restricted, and its role has been advisory rather than legislative. However, under the European Co-operation Procedure formalized under the Single European Act (1987), the Parliament was given a greater say over the proposals for the completion of a single European market in 1992, and under the Maastricht Treaty (1992) the powers of the Parliament were enhanced to include the right of veto on some bills, further budgetary control, and a say in the membership of the Commission.

euthanasia (Greek, 'good death'), a term used to describe the practice of ending a human life to relieve a person from physical suffering or prolonged coma, usually due to terminal or degenerative illness. In most *jurisdictions, it is illegal, but calls have been made for the legalization of voluntary euthanasia, that is euthanasia with the active consent of the patient, a situation that is accepted in practice in The Netherlands. Arguments against voluntary euthanasia are that the patient may not be in a fit state to consent or otherwise; that he or she may feel pressured by relatives into consenting; and that the acceptance of voluntary euthanasia might lead to involuntary euthanasia (the decision by an individual or by society to end the life of someone who cannot give consent), or even to compulsory euthanasia (the elimination of those considered unfit). In 1990 the US Supreme Court endorsed the view that the Fourteenth Amendment to the Constitution guaranteed the right to avoid unwanted medical treatment, but only in cases where patients had made their wishes known earlier. The withholding of treatment such as respirators and intravenous feeding for the terminally ill (sometimes termed 'passive euthanasia') is, however, regarded by some not as euthanasia but as allowing nature to run its course.

evangelicalism, a term applied to various Protestant groups which emphasize the authority of the Bible, *missionary work, and personal commitment to Christ after being revitalized or 'born again' in him. The word has been used to distinguish *Lutherans from *Reformed Calvinists, and for the Christian revival of the 18th century. In the present day, there are numerous Lutheran and United Protestant churches which include 'evangelical' in their name, such as the Norwegian Evangelical Lutheran Church. However, the term is also used in a more general sense in many Protestant churches. 'Conservative evangelicals' are closely associated with what is known as *'fundamentalism', a belief in the verbal inspiration and literal truth of the *Bible, thus upholding, for example, the biblical accounts of creation and rejecting biblical criticism. 'Liberal evangelicals', however, accept liberal theological ideas and a critical approach to the Bible, while still emphasizing the importance of the relationship of the believer to God.

Evans-Pritchard, Sir Edward (Evan) (1902–73), British social anthropologist. His *fieldwork in the Sudan in the 1920s and 1930s resulted in two of the best-known *ethnographies of sub-Saharan Africa, *Witchcraft, Oracles and Magic among the Azande* (1937), and *The Nuer* (1940), which made a substantial contribution to the study of *kinship, *magic, *religion, *political organization, and *dispute resolution. Although his early work was often described as belonging to the school known as *functionalism, and although Evans-Pritchard himself was strongly influenced by French sociologists like *Durkheim, he also argued that anthropology was essentially an art like history, rather than a science like biology, and that it should concentrate on the description and translation of particular cultures, rather than attempt to create generalized theories.

evidence (in law), material items, documents, or verbal testimony submitted to a *court of law to prove or disprove a case. In *common law systems, the use of a *jury before whom evidence is presented has led to the development of an extensive body of rules, known as the law of evidence, regulating the ways in which evidence is presented and witnesses are cross-examined. For example, advocates are usually prohibited from asking witnesses leading questions (that is, questions asked in a manner which suggests the answer sought by the questioner), and it is usual that only witnesses' first-hand knowledge of facts is admissible, and not opinions or second-hand information (hearsay). Rules also govern the admissibility of tape recordings or video films of interviews as evidence. The term 'forensic evidence' refers to material items which have been analysed by forensic scientists: included are *fingerprints; bloodstains, other body fluids, fibres, and hairs; and the chemical and microscopic analysis

of glass, paper, and paint. Technical advances in forensic techniques include genetic fingerprinting, and electrostatic document analysis.

evil eye, a belief, found in many *peasant societies, that certain people have the power to inflict harm on other people, animals, or crops simply by looking at them. The evil eye is often attributed to old women, strangers, or deformed individuals, who are thought to be motivated by jealousy, which can work unconsciously. Charms, amulets, or protective gestures may be used to ward off the evil.

evolution, social, the belief that a culture or a society can be explained as the product of a single process of systematic change leading from simple to complex forms. In the 19th century, social evolution was already well established even before *Darwin published his theories of biological evolution. Human societies were also thought to undergo a process of natural development from simple to complex, not only in their social organization, but also in their beliefs. According to this idea, all existing societies could be placed on a single scale of evolution, leading invariably to Western industrial society as the pinnacle of achievement. Anthropologists like *Frazer, for example, viewed certain *rituals and *magic as primitive forms of science, while other theories were advanced to explain the origin and development of social institutions such as *marriage and the *family. Societies and cultures that were less developed in technological terms were seen as more primitive, and hence representative of earlier stages of social evolution. In practice, social evolutionism became less an account of change than a way of cataloguing societies and cultural traits in terms of an imagined historical scheme. Later anthropologists such as *Malinowski and *Evans-Pritchard attacked the unproven assumptions about history and change on which such classifications were based, and social evolutionism now has few adherents among modern social anthropologists, although its assumptions persist in ideas about economic development, as well as in popular understandings of primitive societies as 'earlier' versions of Western societies.

exchange rate, the price of one *currency in terms of another (or in terms of other international units of account such as *International Monetary Fund Special Drawing Rights). Currencies are bought and sold in the foreign-exchange markets, and an exchange rate is said to be freely floating if it is determined by the *supply and demand for the currency without any government or *central bank intervention in the market for the specific purpose of influencing the rate. By contrast, a fixed rate is one declared and maintained (usually within some narrow range of fluctuation) by the authorities through market intervention as necessary from day to day. If, for instance, the rate needs to be raised, the central bank will enter the foreign-exchange market as a buyer of the currency in order to increase demand and, therefore, price. There are various exchange-rate regimes between the two extremes of freely floating and fixed. In some circumstances, a government may institute exchange controls to limit the purchase and sale of foreign currency. In the 1970s and 1980s, many countries, including the UK, used a 'managed-float' system; however, central-bank management has not been sufficient to prevent great swings in the value of currencies, caused in part by the fact that much foreign-exchange trading is now made for the sake of short-term speculative profit. Changes in the exchange rate such as *devaluation or depreciation may be used to improve an unsatisfactory *balance of payments or macro-economic situation by making exports cheaper, but the extreme instability of currencies in recent years is considered detrimental to real economic productivity and stability. Systems such as the EC's Exchange Rate Mechanism, which is part of the *European Monetary System, exist to create monetary stability by pegging member currencies to rates against which limited fluctuations are permitted. (See also *franc zone, *gold bullion, *gold standard.)

executive (in politics), the leading decision-making office or offices within a system of government. Traditionally, the executive branch was distinct from both the *legislature and the *judiciary (see *separation of powers); it was that part of government concerned with implementing decisions and putting laws into effect. The modern executive is better understood as the centre-piece of the machinery of government decision-making, both initiating policies and overseeing their implementation. It provides national leadership, there being few areas of society beyond its potential concern. Executives, however, vary considerably in structure, composition, and power. A fundamental distinction can be made between collegial and hierarchical types. A *cabinet is a collegial form of executive, based upon decision-making by members of equal standing. An executive *president, by contrast, stands at the apex of a hierarchical executive. Cabinet government in the UK and presidential government in the USA respectively illustrate these types. The boundary of the executive, however, is not always distinct: in addition to junior ministers, it may in practice embrace personal advisers, senior civil servants, and military leaders. Both in function and in membership, the executive may also overlap with the legislature: this is an inherent feature of *parliamentary systems of government.

existence *ontology.

existentialism, a movement in mid-20th-century *continental philosophy. In the post-war years it gripped the imagination of many thinkers, writers, and artists. Its appeal lay partly in its ability to reflect the *alienation and experience of atrocity in 20th-century Europe. Existentialist philosophers speculated about the nature of reality, but subordinated traditional *metaphysical and *epistemological questions to an anthropocentric perspective, in which there takes place a dramatic, often tragic, confrontation between man and the world. Existentialist thought tends to disparage scientific knowledge, particularly *psychology, in so far as it claims to be a science, and to insist on the absence of objective values, stressing instead the reality and significance of human freedom. Influenced by *Kierkegaard, existentialism gave rise to a tradition of Christian existentialism, but the best-known exponents of existentialism in its atheistic form are *Heidegger and *Sartre. Existentialism cannot be easily identified with any single set of philosophical ideas. It took contemporary inspiration from Husserl's *phenomenology, but derived also from various sources in 19th-century philosophy, including *Nietzsche and Kierkegaard, whose conception of the 'individual' may be regarded as a prototype for the existentialist view of the human being as solitary, contingent, and self-creating.

exorcism *spirit possession.

expectation (in psychology), a belief about the future course of events. Prominent in the theories of the US psy-

chologist Edward Tolman (1886–1959) and the German Kurt Lewin (1890–1947), it is now regarded as a major factor in *learning and *motivation. It was clear by the 1950s that the essential feature of animal learning was expectation, although *behaviourists tried to produce alternative non-mental explanations. For example, an animal eventually stops turning towards a repeated stimulus, such as a click, but turns again when the click does not occur at the usual (expected) interval. Expectation that one cannot succeed in a task generally results in a loss of motivation. The Austrian psychologist Fritz Heider (1896–1988) claimed that people's theories of success and failure involve both ability and effort. Children who attribute their school failures to lack of effort rather than lack of ability are more likely to succeed in future. Other people's expectations also influence motivation. Schoolchildren are affected by both their parents' and their teachers' expectations. Employees who are set clear goals frequently improve their performance and job satisfaction. In all cases high but realistic expectations seem most effective. (See also *learned helplessness, *social learning theory, *social understanding.)

exports, *goods (visible exports) and services (invisible exports) which are sold by one country to another. *Trade occurs because countries possess resources such as commodities, or are relatively more efficient in the production of some goods and services than of others (see *Ricardo). By specializing in the production of these goods and trading some of them, countries can obtain more goods and services than if no trade had occurred. Restrictions on exports include export taxes (imposed by the producing country), and *tariffs, *quotas, variable levies, health and safety regulations, and technical regulations (imposed by the importing country). Exports may also be limited by transport costs. Export subsidies are a means of assisting exports. Many economists believe development of exports plays a key role in the growth of an entire economy. Policies of promoting exports of manufactured goods rather than *import-substitution, have been largely responsible for the outstanding economic growth of *newly industrializing countries such as Taiwan and South Korea, where exports account for about half of GNP, while a strategy of promoting agricultural exports has been remarkably successful in the Côte d'Ivoire.

externality (in economics), an activity or part of an activity which is not given a market price, but which nevertheless has either a negative or a positive effect on the welfare of others. Negative externalities may be generated by, or have an impact upon, consumers (somebody playing loud music which annoys a neighbour), or producers (a factory polluting a river which causes problems for a fish farm downstream), or a combination of both (aircraft noise keeping local residents awake). An example of a positive externality is when one firm sets up a training programme which increases the supply of qualified workers to another firm. There is an incentive for such a firm to internalize the positive externality by, for example, encouraging other firms to contribute to the cost of the training programme. In general, correction of externalities as a form of *market failure may require taxes and subsidies to restrict negative and promote positive externalities respectively. Alternatively, legislation could be used against negative externalities like pollution.

extradition, the removal of a person from one country to face criminal charges in another. In *international law, extradition is available only between states which have con-

F

Dominic McGlinchey is extradited from Northern Ireland to face charges in the Republic in 1985. The usual protection from **extradition** for political offences was waived because, in the words of the judge, 'brutal offences are so serious that their criminality exceeds their political aspects'.

cluded an extradition treaty with each other. Such treaties require a court to sanction the extradition, and do not normally permit extradition for political offences.

extra-judicial execution, the killing by state authorities of individuals, groups, and even whole sections of society outside the proper judicial process. It can be in the form of murder by so-called 'death-squads' (covert groups of usually secret political or military intelligence officers), or in the form of summary execution by an official agency of the state after a perfunctory secret trial. Extra-judicial execution is a widespread phenomenon used particularly by repressive political regimes to eliminate political opponents or even minority ethnic groups (see *genocide). Victims are often tortured before being murdered and disposed of in mass graves. In 1983 it was estimated that during the previous fifteen years over 2 million people had been eliminated in this way by military or extremist regimes, and such extra-judicial execution has shown no sign of abating.

extroversion/introversion, terms first used by *Jung to distinguish between those who are sociable and outgoing and those who are not. Many personality theorists regard it as a fundamental difference between people. In *Psychological Types* (1921), Jung suggested that introverts are mistrustful and focus on the subjective and private aspects of experience, whereas extroverts direct their energies to the outside world and their relationships with other people. The British psychologist Hans Eysenck (1916–) developed this idea in a series of books starting with *Dimensions of Personality* (1947). He argued that extroversion–introversion is a continuum, and many people lie in the middle rather than at one extreme. Eysenck held that it is a biological difference: introverts' nervous systems are more aroused than those of extroverts. As too much or too little arousal is unpleasant, introverts avoid stimulation, while extroverts seek it.

facial expression, an important form of *non-verbal communication between individual humans. *Darwin argued that facial and other expressive actions are innate. He cited evidence of the universality of human expressions and of similarities between them and the expressions of other mammals, especially other primates. In contrast, 20th-century anthropologists have described the enormous variation in the expressive behaviour of different cultures. Recent work supports a modified Darwinian view. The basic facial expressions of happiness and sadness seem to be universal and the expressions of disgust, anger, fear, and surprise almost so. These six expressions appear very early in blind or brain-damaged as well as normal infants, and are therefore unlikely to be learnt. But different cultures have different rules about the appropriateness of displaying particular *emotions. Facial muscles are controlled by two different nerve pathways, one is from the cortex, the brain's highly developed outer layer, which is responsible for our learning ability, and the other from lower brain centres, which control emotion. This explains how facial expressions can be innate and associated with particular emotions, but also come under subsequent control through *social learning.

factors of production (in economics), the inputs or *resources needed for a productive activity. They are normally categorized into *capital, *labour, and *land. Other categories may be used in a particular analysis, for example *human capital generated by education. Some, including *Marx, have claimed labour to be the only true factor of production; it is the application of labour which is said to give value to capital and land (see *labour theory of value). Other economists believe that the *entrepreneur, who organizes production, represents a fourth factor of production.

Falasha, a people found in Ethiopia (where they are called *Esra'el*), who probably converted to *Judaism through contact with Egyptian and Arab Jews. They worship in mosques, and, uniquely within modern Judaism, perform *sacrifices. They maintain monasteries, observe *circumcision rites and most major Jewish festivals, but instead of Hebrew they employ an Ethiopian liturgical language, Ge'ez (a *Semitic language), in which their scriptures are written; in daily usage they speak Central *Cushitic. They have no knowledge of the *Talmud; for them only the Pentateuch is relevant. They were recognized as Jewish by Israel's chief rabbinate in 1973. In the 1980s and early 1990s, many Falashas were provided with sanctuary in Israel. Falashas number approximately 65,000.

falsificationism   *Popper.

family, the basic *kinship group in all societies. Families have several functions: they usually provide vital support for their members, in the form of security, shelter, clothing, and food; they fulfil the sexual and reproductive needs of the parent members; they are important in caring for, educating, and socializing children; and they care for older family members. From the earliest years, patterns of behaviour and beliefs are learned from the family. Family relationships are central to the psychological development of children, while at the same time family conflicts may result in severe psychological problems. *Domestic violence, including *child abuse and neglect and *child sexual abuse, are manifestations of the darker side of family life. Families vary enormously in structure and size from society to society, as do the roles played by the various degrees of kin. For instance, the nuclear family usually consists of two adults and their children, biological or adopted. The extended family may include three or four generations, as well as uncles, aunts, and cousins. These may live and work together in common *households, or exist simply as an extended kin network, linked by social relationships. The relatives belonging to the extended family are of varying relevance to the individual, according to the society in which he or she lives. In recent years, Western societies have seen an increase in the number of one-parent families, which may consist of an unmarried mother and her child or children, or else of a father or mother, left without a partner through death or *divorce, and his or her children. This is often an intermediate stage before the formation of another two-adult family, which establishes a series of step-relationships, in which the absent parent may or may not play a part. Because of the family's importance to society as the basic provider of care, protection, and support for the future generation, states normally regulate its functions by means of *family law and *family policy.

family court, a special *court of law dealing with legal problems arising out of family relationships and, sometimes, with offences committed by children (see *juvenile delinquency). A family court may operate in the same way as any other court, but is often associated with a special mode of *dispute resolution. This may entail incorporating into the court itself a panel of lay counsellors, who endeavour to produce a settlement informally, as in Japan. Elsewhere, the family court may retain a more traditional method of decision-making by a judge or *magistrate, but may link extensive *counselling and welfare services to the court administration, as in Australia. Both these arrangements can result in difficulties because of conflict between the counselling services and the ultimately coercive authority of the court. (See also *juvenile court.)

family law, the branch of law concerned with relations between family members, as well as the role of the state in supervising these relationships. Historically, and, in traditional societies, currently, family law has mainly concerned relationships between families, controlling the terms on which women from one family become integrated into another through devices such as *dowry and bridewealth, the attribution of legal rights over the children, and the devolution of property. In such systems, legal rights of individuals, particularly of women and children, are subordinated to the interests of the family group. In the West the influence of Christianity and the social changes of industrialization enhanced the position of the marrying couple at the expense of family groups, but left legal power concentrated in the hands of the husband, and subjected both parties to restrictive *divorce laws. Since World War II, Western family law has been marked by progressive liberalization of divorce law and a quest for equality between husband and wife. This has led to greater emphasis on securing the quality of the conjugal relationship and regulating the consequences of its breakdown, through measures such as

*maintenance after divorce. More recent concerns have been over the extent to which children have rights and how best to safeguard them against *child abuse and neglect, and, in view of the increase in unmarried *cohabitation, how to respond to domestic relationships between unmarried people, whether of the same or the opposite sex. Technological advances have also required solutions to problems raised by artificial methods of fertilization, surrogate parenthood, and post-operative transsexualism.

family planning, a term used to refer to measures to limit or space the children born to a couple or to a woman. These measures include the use of contraception and sterilization of men and women (the most common method in developing countries). *Abortion is promoted as a means of birth control in some government programmes, but most family-planning policy-makers are concerned with preventing conception and regard abortion as a back-up for failed contraception. Concern about spiralling *population growth has led to extensive family-planning programmes in many nations, although artificial means of contraception are forbidden by the *Roman Catholic Church. In most of the world, *fertility rates and *birth rates have dropped sharply since the introduction of the contraceptive pill in the early 1960s. Better education and work opportunities for women, and reduced *infant mortality (which gives parents confidence that the children they do bear are likely to survive) have also contributed. The World Health Organization estimates that about 70 per cent of married women of reproductive age in the industrialized world use contraceptive measures or devices, and about 45 per cent of women in

Family Planning

In just two decades the percentage of people in developing countries using modern family planning has more than quadrupled. Today over half of women who want no more children - temporarily or permanently - are able to fulfil their wish.

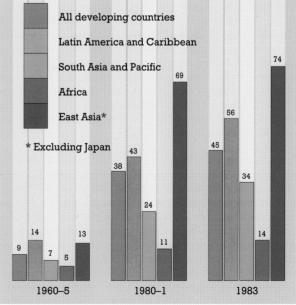

Source: *The State of World Population 1989*. UN. Fund for Population Activities, New York, 1989

A small-scale local **family-planning** talk in Lesotho. Such gatherings are a valuable aid in generating understanding of population problems in rural areas.

developing countries. Thailand, with one of the most effective programmes, stresses the immediate practical and economic benefits for families of lowered fertility. Nevertheless, there are still more than thirty countries (the majority in Africa and the Middle East) where most people have virtually no access to modern services. Here, as elsewhere, breast-feeding helps by reducing the fertility of the mother. In order to reduce its birth rate, in the late 1970s China enforced a policy that allowed only one child per couple. The result was dramatic: whereas 126 million babies were born from 1970 to 1975, only 98 million were born from 1975 to 1980.

family policy, the use of *social policies to achieve political objectives concerning the formation and maintenance of families, as well as child-rearing and the care of dependants within families. In advanced industrialized societies, family policy typically takes two forms: the design of cash benefits (such as *child benefits) so as to encourage certain kinds of behaviour, and the use of *social services to provide child care. In many countries, there is an ambivalence within family policy: on the one hand, the objective is to maintain the traditional pattern of the family, consisting of a father-provider, a mother-carer, and children below working age (see *patriarchy); on the other hand, another objective is the support of one-parent families and of mothers who re-enter the work-force. A growing problem is the care of the adult disabled and the frail elderly within the family, which tends to fall on female carers (see *old age). In many developing countries, family policy concentrates on the question of population control (see *family planning). This policy is difficult to enforce, however, particularly in rural areas. States have sometimes attempted to change the whole pattern of family life through their policies, a notorious example being Ceausescu's Romania (1967–89), where enforced child-bearing was decreed in order to boost the number of workers. The Israeli kibbutz or agricultural collective is another example of an attempt to break away from the stereotypes of the family: members of the kibbutz live communally and bring their children up collectively, but even here, parent–child relationships are encouraged.

family therapy, a counselling or psychiatric treatment involving some or all members of a family as a group. It uses a wide range of therapeutic techniques and diagnostic models, including self-assessment videos and role-playing. It began in the USA in the 1940s and 1950s, when it fitted the consensus shared by the then dominant orthodoxies of *psychoanalysis and reinforcement theories of *learning. Both conceived a child's psychological growth as determined by how its parents relate to it. The British anthropologist Gregory Bateson (1904–80) attributed thought disorder in *schizophrenia and emotional blunting to confusion caused by ambiguous communication within the family (*Steps to an Ecology of Mind*, 1972). His compatriot, the psychiatrist R(onald) D(avid) Laing (1927–89), took this further with the idea that the families of schizophrenics are themselves sick and require treatment because they prevent the child from achieving 'authentic' psychological development (*Sanity, Madness and the Family*, 1964). Therapies have been developed, particularly in the USA and Italy, to try to alter the way in which family members relate and to alert them to 'scapegoating' the family member who seems mentally ill. Attempts have been made to use family therapy for all kinds of problems, such as anorexia, child-abuse, or bed-wetting, as well as schizophrenia. There is also marital therapy of a similar kind.

famine, widespread acute starvation in a population associated with a sharp increase in mortality. The victims die not only from starvation but also from diseases that are fatal to the debilitated, and which spread rapidly as a result of massive population movements in search of food. Famine should be distinguished from chronic *malnutrition. In India, the last major famine occurred in 1943 (more recent threatened famines having been averted mainly by public intervention), but chronic malnutrition is quite widespread. China, by contrast, has tackled chronic malnutrition more successfully, but fell victim to a famine in 1958–61 in which it is estimated over 20 million people died. Famine is more geographically confined than malnutrition; most famines in recent decades have occurred in sub-Saharan Africa, with a few exceptions, as in Bangladesh in 1974 and Cambodia (Kampuchea) in 1979–80. Although a natural *disaster such as flood, drought, or crop failure may be the prime initiator of a famine, its impact depends on the organization and prosperity of the society. The most catastrophic recent famines have been exacerbated by war, political rivalries, and the destruction of distribution systems. More generally, while a fall in the availability of food may be one factor in famines, many commentators, including the economist Amartya Sen in his influential book *Poverty and Famines* (1981), have argued that an equally important factor is the loss of ability of large numbers of people to secure adequate food, for example as a result of loss of employment and therefore income, or food price-rises. This analysis has important implications for *famine relief and prevention.

famine relief, prevention or relief of widespread acute starvation. While the direct supply of *food aid to the starving through international relief efforts may be necessary in *disasters, better approaches to averting incipient famines may include government interventions in local markets to ensure adequate supplies and prevent escalating prices, and measures to increase people's capacity to purchase food themselves, for example by guaranteeing employment during crises. Cash transfers are often more effective than food rations: cash is faster to move and easier to administer, and

Famine

Causes of Famine

Famine is caused not only by natural disasters such as drought and flooding, but by other man-made catastrophes such as war or economic crisis, which cause people to flee their homes and abandon their livelihoods, or deprive them of the means to purchase food

Food production may be disrupted by crop failure:

- Weather (drought, flooding, prolonged cold weather)
- Pests and plant disease
- War (displacing farmers, destroying crops)

Food distribution may be disrupted by:

- Lack of transport or fuel
- Delay, sabotage, and inefficiency
- War (blockading roads, airlifts, and rail links, destroying vehicles, looting and pillage

Food purchase may be disrupted by poverty:

- Unemployment
- Inflation and price rises
- Black marketeering and hoarding

In the past 20 years, famine and disease resulting from malnutrition claimed lives all over the world.

- In 1973 an estimated 100,000 died in West Africa
- In 1973–4 and 1984–5 between 250–750,000 died in Ethiopia
- In 1974 24–100,000 died in Bangladesh

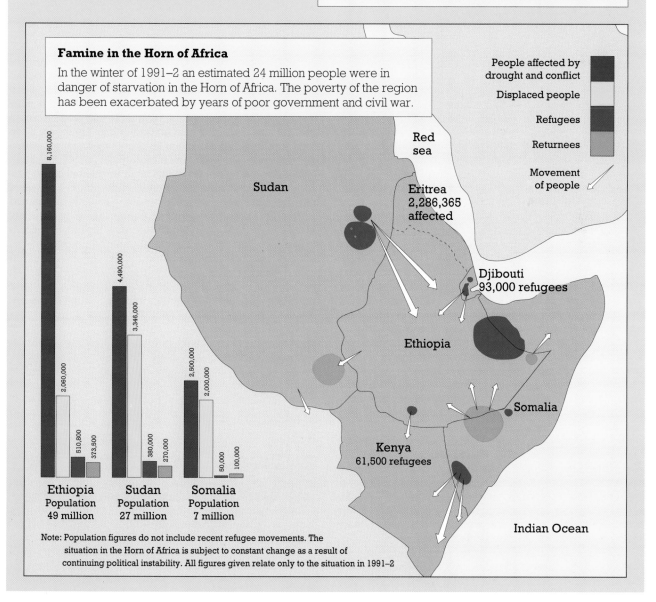

Famine in the Horn of Africa

In the winter of 1991–2 an estimated 24 million people were in danger of starvation in the Horn of Africa. The poverty of the region has been exacerbated by years of poor government and civil war.

People affected by drought and conflict

Displaced people

Refugees

Returnees

Movement of people

Red sea

Sudan

Eritrea 2,286,365 affected

Djibouti 93,000 refugees

Ethiopia

Somalia

Kenya 61,500 refugees

Indian Ocean

Ethiopia
Population 49 million

8,160,000
2,060,000
510,800
373,500

Sudan
Population 27 million

4,490,000
3,346,000
380,000
270,000

Somalia
Population 7 million

2,500,000
2,000,000
50,000
100,000

Note: Population figures do not include recent refugee movements. The situation in the Horn of Africa is subject to constant change as a result of continuing political instability. All figures given relate only to the situation in 1991–2

Source: *Situation Report, Special Emergency Programme for the Horn of Africa, No.1, October 1991. Poverty and Famine*, Amartya Sen, Oxford 1981

This woman is one of the hundreds of thousands who starved in the Ethiopian **famine** of 1984–5. Partly the result of the failure of rains and poor harvests, the famine was exacerbated by Ethiopia's political instability and economic underdevelopment, which makes its citizens particularly vulnerable.

it does not harm the market for local produce and thus farmers' incentives. If food is available within the affected country, and trade and markets work reasonably well, this approach can achieve notable success, as a programme in Maharashtra state in India in 1970–3, which has been used as a model by others, has demonstrated. In this programme, famine was averted by the employment of nearly 5 million labourers on public works, and a scheme of relief for those without able-bodied relatives and unable to work. In Africa, the governments of Botswana, Cape Verde, Kenya, and Zimbabwe, among many others, took decisive action during the 1980s to ensure that adequate food was available by purchasing food on the international market; by food distribution within the country using both public distribution systems (for example, health clinics) and private traders; and the creation of public employment schemes. However, famine persists in societies subject to civil war, where often famine relief efforts have not been successful, apart from temporary relief through *food aid.

fantasy, a daydream arising from conscious or unconscious wishes or attitudes. Theorizing about fantasy and imagination goes back at least to Aristotle, but proper psychological interest in it has been a recent phenomenon,

partly due to *behaviourism's denial of the possibility of studying mental content and partly perhaps because it was not taken seriously. Recent work suggests that fantasy and visualization are valuable human capacities. Children who engage in fantasy concentrate better, have more positive emotions, and often cope better with relationships. Fantasy visualization has been used in various *psychotherapies. Patients fantasize to induce mild anxiety with which relaxation techniques help them to deal, or they use attractive fantasies as part of a relaxation procedure. Sports psychologists encourage their charges to visualize themselves succeeding so as to build up their confidence. Visualizing one's plans as they might appear to others may give a more realistic estimate of what one might do.

Farsi   *Indo-Iranian languages.

fascism, a political ideology of the first half of the 20th century, whose central belief was that the individual should be subjugated to the needs of the state, which in turn should be directed by a strong leader embodying the will of the nation. Fascism originally flourished in Italy in the 1920s with the rise of Benito Mussolini (1883–1945), but fascist regimes were also established in Germany (see *Nazism) and Spain, and there were strong fascist movements in the 1930s and 1940s in many other countries. The appeal of fascism lay in its image of order and discipline in contrast to the licentiousness and economic turmoil of the liberal democracies. Fascist movements adopted a paramilitary structure and when in power attempted to impose a military discipline on the whole of society at the expense of individual freedom (though, despite the socialist elements in fascist ideology, there was little interference with private ownership). Democratic institutions were replaced by the cult of the single leader, whose pronouncements were unchallengeable. Fascism was thus a form of *totalitarianism, but it attracted mass support in the countries where it came to power and was finally defeated only by military means in the course of World War II. Some political scientists have detected ele-

The South African AWB (Afrikaner Resistance Movement), a far-right White organization, owes much to **fascism** in its belief in the superiority of the White race and its dependence on a strong leader—Eugene Terreblanche. The movement's flag clearly evokes the swastika of the German Third Reich.

Fertility Rate

The chart below shows a marked and accelerating decrease in total fertility rate in all regions except Africa. Fewer children may mean more time for women to devote to activites outside the home. Combined with improved education and job opportunities, reduced fertility can lead to greater autonomy and economic independence for women.

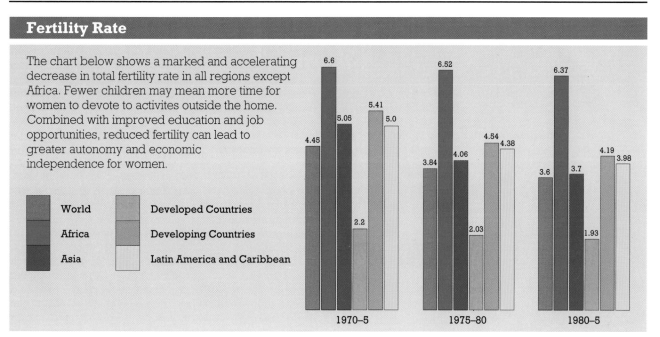

Source: *World Population Trends and Policies 1989. Monitoring Report*, UN, 1989.

ments of fascism in subsequent authoritarian regimes, especially military dictatorships in developing countries, but in no instance have these regimes explicitly adopted a fascist ideology.

fatwā   *sharī'ah.

federalism, a form of government involving a constitutionally guaranteed territorial dispersion of power. Federalism contrasts with the *unitary system of government, in that *sovereignty is shared within a national or possibly supra-national framework. A federal constitution allocates powers to different levels of government, some to the central government, and others to the governments of the territories making up the federation. Powers may be allocated either exclusively to one level, or concurrently to both. Unlike a *confederation, where the confederal government usually lacks its own institutions, each level of government in a federal system maintains institutions, imposes its own laws and taxes, and acts directly on the population. Federalism is often seen as an appropriate constitutional solution for a political system based on an originally limited degree of unity, a diverse or dispersed population, or a large area, as in Australia, Czechoslovakia, India, Pakistan, Switzerland, the former Soviet Union, and the USA. Among the disadvantages of federalism are duplication and complexity. The USA, for instance, has fifty-one complete systems of elections, government, administration, and justice. Relations between levels of government and between the territories in a federation are usually rivalrous and sometimes hostile.

Federal Reserve   *central bank.

feminism   *women's movement.

fencing, the world-wide sport of duelling with one of three weapons: foil, épée, and sabre. Women compete in foil only. A fencer scores by hitting his or her opponent's target area. To avoid injury, fencers wear a face mask, padded jacket, and glove. The first to score five hits—or lead the scoring when the time (six minutes) expires—wins the bout.

fertility rate, a calculation essential to the prediction of population changes and, in particular, of *population growth. The most commonly used rate is the 'total fertility rate' (TFR). The TFR for a country represents the number of children projected to be born, on average, to each woman upon completion of her child-bearing years. Between 1950 and 1955, and 1985 and 1990, TFRs fell in Europe from 2.6 to 1.7 (well below the replacement level of 2.1), from 5.9 to 3.6 in South America, from 6.0 to 3.5 in Asia, and from 6.6 to 6.2 in Africa. Many factors affect fertility rates, not least beliefs, traditions, familial affections, religious sentiments, and the value of the labour children can perform, but improving health and education may provide the surest way to achieve sustained declines. Evidence shows that, in general, it is only when couples believe that their children have a reasonable chance of survival to adulthood that they are willing sharply to reduce family size. In many parts of sub-Saharan Africa, where more than 20 per cent of children die before their fifth birthdays, parents can have no such confidence. Evidence also shows that where women are better educated and have easy access to *family planning they marry later and have fewer children.

fetish (from Portuguese, *feitiço*, 'charm'), an inanimate object which is worshipped in the belief that it possesses some supernatural power. The word was used by early Portuguese travellers to describe the magical objects such as shells, sticks, stones, or wooden carvings which they encountered in West Africa. In the 19th century, fetishism was thought to be a primitive form of religion. The word is now most often used metaphorically to describe a person's abnormal obsession with any sort of object.

feud, an organized state of mutual hostility between groups. Hostility may exist between *families, or between *kinship or territorial groupings like *clans and *lineages, and the feud may persist over a number of years, or even generations. Anthropologists have shown that feuds are not anarchic outbreaks of violence, but often involve the recognition of rules about the appropriate use of and response to violence by both sides of the dispute, perhaps in defence of

Scientists comparing genetic **fingerprints** to see if they match; each 'fingerprint' is a bar-code printed on x-ray film. The technique was invented at Leicester University, UK, in 1983 and provides a different pattern for each genetically unique individual.

*honour. Feuds are most commonly found in societies with either weak or remote central authorities; in these societies the feud can function as a form of *dispute resolution.

fieldwork, the basic research method of modern social and cultural anthropology; the term refers to the gathering of data concerning social or cultural groups by means of personal observation. *Ethnographic fieldwork was most notably pioneered by *Malinowski, who argued that only close and prolonged contact with the society to be studied could reveal its true character. This process is now often referred to as participant observation. The fieldworker resides with a social group for a year or two, learns the local language, and participates in the daily life of the group, at the same time recording and analysing such features as *kinship groups, *rituals, seasonal activities, and the like.

Filipino   *Austronesian languages.

finance company, a term covering various types of financial intermediaries, in particular finance houses. These specialize in providing *consumer credit through hire purchase. They also collect commercial *debts for other companies, an activity known as factoring, and sometimes supply short-term bridging *loans.

financial regulation, government rules and regulations to supervise financial activities. In the UK, the Financial Services Act (1986) established the Securities and Investment Board (SIB), and required all investment businesses to be authorized by the SIB or by a self-regulating body. It also provided for the *regulation of *take-overs and *insider trading. In the USA, the Securities and Exchange Commission (SEC) was created in 1934 to supervise *stock-exchange trading and investigate alleged abuses such as market-rigging and insider trading.

financial sector   *tertiary industry.

fingerprint, an impression left by the finger tips. Since no two people share the same fingerprints, it is a widespread means of identification, used in particular by the police (since 1901 in the UK) to identify criminals. In most countries a central fingerprint record is kept of those convicted of serious offences so that matches may be made when the police investigate new crimes. Genetic fingerprinting is a new technique based on the fact that no two persons possess the same patterns of DNA, which make up the individual genetic code. These patterns may be obtained from any part of the body, for example hair, white blood cells, or from semen, and computerized DNA profiles have therefore been used as a means of identification of criminals. There have been calls for legislation to permit the genetic fingerprinting of convicted criminals, as an aid to crime detection.

Finno-Ugric languages   *Uralic languages.

firm, theory of the, a body of *micro-economic analysis ideas which models the behaviour of firms with regard to price, output, and employment. The traditional theory of the firm assumes that firms maximize *profits under *perfect competition with perfect information and certainty about future events. This simple theoretical framework is very powerful at explaining decisions by firms. It is also important in building theories of *markets and of resource allocation. The modern theory of the firm includes adaptions to the traditional theory designed to make it more realistic. Firstly, imperfect competition is analysed. Secondly, allowance is made for managers not seeking to maximize profits; for example, they may instead wish to maximize sales. Thirdly, information is recognized to be neither ubiquitous nor costless. Uncertainty and risk will alter the behaviour of firms.

fiscal policy, that part of government policy concerned with *taxation and public-sector expenditure, usually set out in an annual *budget. The difference between tax revenue and public expenditure is the *public-sector deficit. In accordance with *Keynes' economic thinking, fiscal policy may be used to help regulate aggregate demand in the economy; this is known as demand management. By increasing expenditure or reducing tax rates (an easing of fiscal policy), the government can increase aggregate demand. Alternatively, a tightening of fiscal policy will reduce aggregate demand. The exponents of *monetarism, however, disagree; they believe the level of output and employment should be self-regulating provided the price level is kept stable by means of appropriate control over the money supply.

Fisher, Irving (1867–1947), US economist, famous principally for his work on *interest rates and *investment, and on the *quantity theory of money equation. The rate of interest is determined by two things: the strength of individuals' preferences for income now rather than later (which Fisher called time preferences); and the ability of technology to convert current income into future income. His work on investment attempts to predict how much a given firm will choose to invest. According to Fisher's equation firms will stop investing when any further investment will not increase the sum of discounted future profits. This sum of discounted future profits is (or should be) equal to the present value of the firm.

fishing, the pastime of catching fish, usually with a rod and line, when it is also known as angling. Most fishermen specialize in the fish they try to catch—game (salmon, trout), coarse (other freshwater species), or seafish—and this determines the type and weight of rod they choose, and whether they use edible bait (bait-fishing), natural or artificial flies (fly-fishing), or a fish or metal lure made up to resemble a fish (bait-casting or spinning, and trolling). In colder climates, ice-fishing through a hole bored in the ice is a popular winter pastime.

Five Pillars of Islam, the basic duties and religious observances of *Islam. The first pillar, īmān (faith), prescribes regular recitation of the shahādah, a summarized confession of belief, itself often referred to as the first pillar, which affirms the unity of God and the sole authority of the Prophet *Muḥammad: 'There is no god but Allah; and Muḥammad is the Messenger of Allah'. The second pillar is daily worship, salāh (salāt), to which believers are called by the *muezzin, performed five times: at dawn, noon, in the afternoon, after sunset, and at night. Three pre-conditions must be observed before worship: a clear conscience, a clean body, and a clean environment. Wuḍū, the observance of ritual cleansing, always precedes worship. A prayer mat or carpet ensures a clean environment, and is placed pointing towards *Mecca. Ritual worship is compulsory and follows a fixed pattern of standing, bowing, prostration, and kneeling, and recitation from the *Koran. The third pillar, ṣawm, lays down abstinence from food, drink, and sexual relations during the daylight hours of *Ramadan; the rule does not generally apply to children below the age of 12, the infirm, or nursing mothers. Ẓakāt (purification of wealth), an obligation upon those who have enough wealth, demands the donation of 2.5 per cent of yearly income to support the Muslim community, in one of eight prescribed ways. It is administered in some Muslim countries by official collectors. This differs from charity (ṣadaqa), which can be given by any Muslim. The final duty is that all those who are physically and financially able should perform the *pilgrimage (ḥajj) to Mecca at least once in a lifetime. The pilgrimage takes place in the twelfth month, Dhu al-Ḥijja, and entails a number of ritual and ceremonial acts, including the adoption of plain white clothing, symbolizing spiritual equality. It culminates, after ten days, in the Festival of Sacrifice, *'īd ul-Aḍḥā. *Jihād (striving) is sometimes referred to as a sixth Pillar of Islam, but it has no such official status.

fives, a group of handball games played with a small hard ball and gloves in an indoor or outdoor walled court. Related to the Irish–American game of handball (which employs a rubber ball and in which the players wear softer gloves), fives developed at three English public schools which produced the three games of Winchester fives, Eton fives, and Rugby fives.

flexible response, a central theme in the development of *nuclear strategy, concerned with response to *aggression at an appropriate level, leaving the option open for an escala-

tion to a higher level if necessary. Until the late 1950s, the US policy was one of massive retaliation, but, with the election of President Kennedy in 1960, the policy changed to one of flexible response, which was adopted by *NATO in 1967. The aim of flexible response was to be ready for any Soviet escalation of armed conflict, a strategy that demanded vast resources devoted to defence (larger *armed forces; small-, medium-, and long-range nuclear weapons; and long-range air- and sea-lift capacity). A few years later, the Soviet Union adopted the same policy, and in principle each of the *superpowers possessed a vast array of weapons and an overall strategic plan allowing prompt and appropriate response to actions by the other. However, this policy of matching force with force contributed to a major increase in the volume of weaponry and *military expenditure in both the USA and the former Soviet Union and their allies, as well as to strategic instability. (See also *arms race.)

flotation (in economics), the offer for sale of new *shares in a *company as a means of raising *capital. The term is normally used of share sales by companies not previously quoted on the *stock exchange, but may also refer to capital raising by established companies for major *investments.

folklore, the traditional beliefs, knowledge, customs, and orally transmitted culture of a group of people. Many studies of folklore are concerned with oral traditions such as folktales and legends, rhymes and proverbs, or folk-music. Folklore is generally seen as co-existing with a dominant, literate culture in the place where it is studied. It is often associated with marginalized minority or *ethnic groups, and folklore study is often an important part of nationalist movements.

food aid, food supplied by richer to poorer countries as a form of *aid. Food aid constitutes about a fifth of the USA's assistance to other countries, and is a significant proportion of the aid donated by all countries through UN agencies and the EC. Most food aid is known as 'programme food aid' and is given for *balance of payments support. The recipient country saves foreign exchange by not having to buy food abroad and, by selling the food aid in its own country, can raise funds for other purposes. 'Project food aid', by contrast, is supplied for *disasters, and such specific purposes as food-for-work or supplementary child-feeding projects to combat *malnutrition. An argument for food aid is that much of it represents Western production surpluses which would otherwise benefit no one. Direct distribution may also be essential in severe *famines as in Ethiopia, Somalia, and Sudan in the 1980s and 1990s. Increasingly, however, problems with food aid have been recognized: food transport from continent to continent can be slow and expensive; within the affected countries, storage, transport, and distribution problems may be immense; supply from feeding centres may cause harmful population migrations; and sudden large imports may adversely affect local farmers and traders, thus depressing future local production. If the central objective is to ensure food security for the poor, other methods are necessary as supplements and alternatives (see *famine relief).

food customs, the social or religious regulations surrounding the preparation, serving, and eating of food and drink. Eating together (commensality) is a basic human act, which denotes the friendliness and common purpose of a

Football

Association Football

Penalty kick mark
Centre circle
Touch-line
Halfway line
Penalty area
Goal area
Goal-line
Corner-kick area
Goal net

90-120 m
16.5 m
5.5 m
40.32 m
18.32 m
45-90 m
9.15 m

Sweeper formation

1 Goalkeeper
2 Sweeper
3, 4, and 5 Defenders
6, 7, 8, and 9 Midfield players
10 and 11 Forwards

Rugby Union

Dead ball line
Touch-in goal-line
In goal
Goal-line
Halfway line
Touch-line

Scrum formation

1 and 3 Props
2 Hooker
4 and 5 Locks
6 and 7 Flankers
8 Number 8
9 Scrum half-back
10 Stand-off
11 and 14 Wing three-quarter-backs
12 and 13 Centre three-quarter backs
15 Full-back

100 m
10 m
69 m
15 m
22 m
5 m
5.6 m
22 m

Australian Football

Goal behind
Boundary line

6.4 m
45.7 m
45.7 m
135-185 m
110-155 m

1 Full-forward
2 Full-back
3 Half-back
4 Half-forward
5 Centre
6 Followers
7 Rovers

American Football

Offense
1 Center
2 Guard x 2
3 Tackle x 2
4 Tight end
5 Wide receiver
6 Quarter-back
7 Running back x 2
8 Split end

18ft.6 in (5.64 m)
160 ft (48.8 m)
30 ft (9.14 m)
300 ft (91.4 m)

Goal post
Goal line
2-yard line
Inbounds line
Side line
Side zone
End zone
End line

Defense ▼ 1 Nose tackle 2 Defensive end x 2 3 Linebacker x 4 4 Safety x 2 5 Cornerback x 2

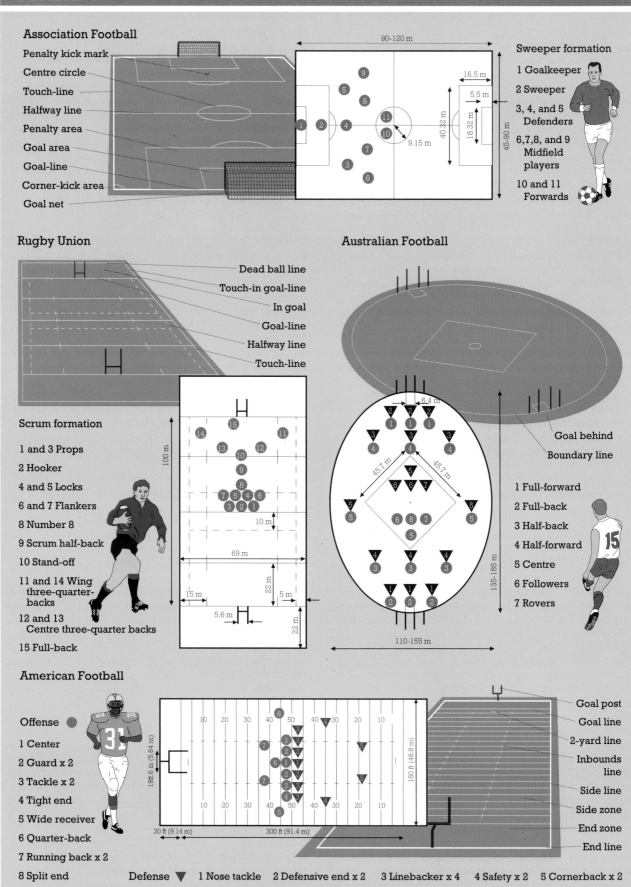

group. Feasts are often used to mark *rites of passage, such as marriages, or religious festivals, such as Christmas, and symbolic meals (for example, the Christian Eucharist) play an important part in some religions (see also *sacrifice). Fasting, the avoidance of food, may also be regarded as a religious act, as in various *ascetic cults, or as in temporary periods of fasting like *Ramadan. All societies select certain foods as especially valuable and mark off others as wholly inedible or *taboo. Many ritual observances include some measures of this sort, while some religions forbid certain sorts of food under any circumstances. For example, *totemism often includes a prohibition on eating the animal or plant that is the group totem; dietary laws within Judaism forbid the eating of any foods not regarded as *kosher or legitimate; and alcohol, among other things, is strictly prohibited for Muslims. Other food prohibitions can be calendrical: that is, certain forms of food may not be eaten on certain days or at particular times of the year. Certain types of food may also be seen as the privilege of certain persons, or groups of people, and in this way may serve as an indicator of social status and *rank. Among Hindus in *South Asian societies, eating meat (especially beef) may be a sign of belonging to a low *caste, while higher caste people will usually not eat cooked food of any sort if it has been prepared by people of low caste.

football, the world's most popular group of team-games in which two sides compete to carry an oval football across the other team's goal-line or kick an oval or round ball between a pair of goal-posts. All forms of football began with the crude version played in medieval Wales and England: in a typical game, two villages fought over an air-filled pig's bladder, trying to propel it to an agreed victory mark; rules were minimal and bloodshed frequent. In the 19th century, members of various public schools set about defining rules for their favoured version of football, and a basic distinction was established between games which involved handling an oval ball and those in which players kicked a round ball. In 1863 supporters of the second group formed the Football Association, and this became the first parent organization for the great world game of Association football or soccer, the eleven-a-side game in which the object is to kick or head the ball into the opponents' goal. In 1871 English supporters of the handling game formed the Rugby Football Union. In Rugby Union, a fifteen-a-side game, the chief object is to run the oval ball across the opponents' goal-line and ground it to score a try. In 1895 a breakaway group formed the Northern Football Union, ancestor of Rugby League, a thirteen-a-side game similar in many ways to Rugby Union, but in which players may receive payment. American football, the gridiron game, evolved during the 1880s, is derived from Rugby Union; the chief differences are the line of scrimmage, the introduction of the quarter-back (the chief play-maker), forward passing, blocking players not in possession of the ball, and the division of each team's players into offensive and defensive squads. In Gaelic football, a hybrid game played in Ireland, players score a goal by kicking or punching the ball between the posts and under the crossbar. In Australian Rules football, played on an oval pitch, a goal is scored by kicking the ball between the two central goal-posts.

forgery, the offence of creating a false instrument (a document of a formal or informal character) with a view to having it accepted as genuine. Forgery is therefore usually a preparatory step to some other crime involving deception.

Such instruments may be any device on which information is stored: typically, share certificates, stamps, credit cards, passports, or birth certificates. The forging of coins or banknotes is known as counterfeiting.

Foucault, Michel (1926–84), French historian and social philosopher. Foucault sought to reveal the origins and thereby the arbitrary character of the ideas and practices which make up everyday life in the modern world. He wanted to free people from the mistaken belief that such ideas and practices had a rational foundation. He was concerned especially with the 'sciences' of man contained in disciplines such as medicine, psychology, and social administration. In *Madness and Civilization* (1961), for instance, he examined the way in which the concepts of sanity and madness had emerged to define mental illness. In *Discipline and Punish* (1975) he analysed the disciplinary methods employed in prisons as exemplifying the way in which the human sciences could impose standards of 'normal' behaviour on people. In this work there emerged the idea that forms of thought are also relations of *power which constrain human beings. It was possible to struggle against the domination of existing patterns of thought and behaviour, but never to escape entirely from power relations.

Four Noble Truths, the basic teaching of the *Buddha in his first sermon in the deer park at Varanasi (Benares), when he explained the cause and nature of suffering, and the goal of enlightenment. The Four Noble Truths follow the structure of a medical diagnosis. The first truth recognizes that there is a disease: suffering (*dukkha*), which is the basis of all existence. The second truth determines the cause of the disease: desire (*tanha*). The third truth acknowledges that there is a cure for the disease, and the fourth truth states what that cure is: the following of the *Noble Eightfold Path.

franchise (in economics), a right to use a trade mark, name, or production technique in exchange for payment. Companies such as the fast-food outlets Wimpy and Kentucky Fried Chicken use franchising to market their products through a network of independent franchisees. A franchise will be granted only if the franchisee meets the quality standards set by the franchising company. The main arguments in favour of a franchise system are that it provides incentives for the franchisee, and that it keeps down the distribution costs of the franchisor.

franchise (suffrage), the right to vote in an election. In most modern *democracies, the franchise is an inalienable right which applies to all adult *citizens over a certain minimum age, which ranges from 18 to 25. This has not always been the case. Originally, where voting rights existed at all, they were the privilege of limited groups, who had to fulfil certain qualifications of age, sex, race, income, property, or education. During the 19th and 20th centuries, the franchise was gradually extended, this extension occurring at different times in different countries. First of all, working-class males were integrated into politics; where universal manhood suffrage occurred early and peaceably, as in the USA, it encouraged subsequent political stability. Women were the next group to be given the vote; this occurred first in New Zealand (1893), but women still do not have the vote in certain countries, particularly in the Middle East. The most recent general extension of the franchise has been in countries where the minimum voting age was lowered from 21 to 18. The extension of votes to ethnic minorities has been more complex. For example, even after the abolition of slavery in the southern states of the USA, Blacks were still denied the vote through the imposition of unaffordable poll taxes to discourage registration, and through unfair literacy tests, but the *Civil Rights Movement in the 1960s led to the prohibition of discrimination in voting, as well as in education and the use of public facilities. Under colonial rule in many countries in Africa and Asia, voting restrictions, such as literacy or property qualifications, were imposed on ethnic populations, and universal suffrage was only achieved after independence from the colonial power. Despite the fact that universal adult suffrage applies in most modern states, a right to vote in theory does not automatically imply a right to vote in practice; difficulties in registration often effectively disenfranchise certain groups, especially the poor and uneducated. Categories of individuals not allowed to vote include convicted prisoners in penal institutions, the mentally ill, aliens, and those convicted of corrupt or illegal electoral practices; in some countries, an educational qualification of basic literacy may be required, but in others special allowance is made for illiteracy in voting procedures. In the UK, members of the House of Lords may not vote.

Franc Zone, a monetary union covering all countries and groups of countries whose currencies are linked to the French franc at a fixed rate of exchange and who agree to hold their reserves mainly in the form of French francs and to exchange them on the Paris market. Each has its own central issuing bank and its currency is freely convertible into French francs. The Franc Zone is based on agreements between France and each country or group of countries. The members in 1990 were Benin, Burkina Faso, Cameroon, the Central African Republic, Chad, the Comoros, Côte d'Ivoire, Equatorial Guinea, France, its Overseas Departments and Territories, Gabon, Mali, Niger, Senegal, and Togo.

Frankfurt School, an influential group of thinkers based at the Institute for Social Research founded in 1923 at the University of Frankfurt, Germany. During the Nazi ascendancy, many members fled to the USA and the Institute was affiliated to the University of Columbia, New York, between 1934 and 1949. One of its most brilliant scholars was Theodor Adorno (1903–69), best known for *The Authoritarian Personality* (1950), a study of *fascism and the type of personality drawn to it. Others were Max Horkheimer, the director from 1930 to 1958, and *Marcuse. From the 1960s *Habermas took forward some of its ideas. The School was notable for its attempts to integrate disciplines such as philosophy, psychology, and economics and, by building on the work of *Marx, to construct new critiques of *capitalism. Developing what it called *critical theory, it analysed the role of multinational companies, technology, and mass communication. Its members feared the increased control of capitalism over all aspects of life and favoured *socialism. The School emphasized the importance of theory building and of theorists' attempts to transform society. In this it was opposed to positivist social scientists, who favoured investigative research and a detached rather than a partisan approach.

fraud, criminal deception to obtain unjust advantage or to injure the rights or interests of others. Although fraud is not new, it has been described as the archetypal modern crime, opportunities for fraud having multiplied with, for example, the increased use of credit-cards, computers, and the auto-

mated transmission of money across the world. Fraud involves crimes by individuals such as tax evasion, by businesses such as the submission of insurance claims for ships which have been deliberately scuttled (see *white-collar crime), and by criminal organizations such as the fraudulent diversion of hundreds of millions of pounds in subsidies from the *EC's Common Agricultural Policy (see *organized crime). Fraud has caused heavy losses not only in capitalist but also in communist countries. Because fraud is often complex, international, and committed by people of high status, law-enforcement agencies typically have difficulty in uncovering it, securing convictions, and obtaining sentences commensurate with the damage caused. Mounting public concern has led in some countries to the setting up of specialist investigative agencies (in the UK, the Serious Fraud Office was established in 1986), closer *regulation of businesses and of professionals such as lawyers and accountants whose expertise is crucial for many sophisticated frauds. Attempts to increase international collaboration by tackling *money-laundering, improving *extradition procedures, and enabling investigative agencies to use evidence obtained in one country in a trial in another, are as yet limited.

Frazer, Sir James George (1854–1941), British anthropologist. His most famous work was the multi-volume study *The Golden Bough* (1907–15), in which he sought to prove that human beliefs followed an evolutionary progression from *magic and *religion to modern science. Frazer's research methods were those of the 'armchair anthropologist', who relied on library and documentary sources rather than *fieldwork and first-hand experience of different societies. Although he is now rarely read by anthropologists, Frazer's ideas had widespread influence outside anthropology on figures such as T. S. Eliot, D. H. Lawrence, and *Freud.

freedom, the condition in which people, individually or collectively, can control their own lives without interference either by other people or by some outside political authority. In the modern world, the demand for political freedom takes two main forms: the demand of nations that they should throw off foreign rule, and govern themselves through their own political institutions; and the demand of individuals that the state should not interfere in areas of life that are deemed to be private. This last demand includes specific freedoms such as *freedom of expression and worship, freedom of association, and (more controversially) economic freedom in the sense of the freedom to buy, sell, and contract with any willing party. Political philosophers such as Isaiah Berlin ('Two Concepts of Liberty', 1958) have drawn a distinction between negative and positive senses of freedom, where being negatively free means simply not being prevented or deterred by other people from achieving one's goals, whereas being positively free means having the capacity (the resources, the mental determination, and so on) to achieve those goals. Freedom, although an important political value, must be limited for its own sake and for the sake of other ends. The best-known principle for deciding this is enunciated in *Mill's essay *On Liberty* (1859): people should be free to act as they like except when their actions cause harm to other people. (See also *freedom of expression, *freedom of information, *free will, *human rights.)

freedom of expression (free speech), the right of every individual to free expression of his or her opinions, including the right to receive or impart information through any *medium. It is one of the basic *human rights, included in the *Universal Declaration on Human Rights and the *European Convention on Human Rights, and enshrined in the First Amendment to the US Constitution. Freedom of expression is regarded as a fundamental part of the democratic process, assisting the emergence of the truth, as well as providing a means of self-fulfilment for the individual. The term implies freedom of conscience and religion, the *freedom of the press, and free participation in political activity, none of which are tolerated in totalitarian societies. However, even in democratic societies, freedom of expression is not an absolute right. It can be curtailed by considerations of national security, or subject to laws relating to *privacy, *defamation, *pornography, incitement to racial hatred, *contempt of court, protection of confidences, and *copyright.

freedom of information, the principle that information held by state authorities should be available to the public. In most Western democratic countries other than the UK there is legislation which requires state agencies, and sometimes private bodies, to make files available to people with a legitimate interest in seeing them, subject to restrictions necessary to protect competing interests, such as national security, and the *privacy and commercial rights of others (see *data protection). Freedom of information encourages democratic accountability by making possible informed debate by citizens and legislatures of public policy and government performance, and by allowing people the right to check the accuracy of records held about them. Under totalitarian regimes, information is rigidly controlled. Citizens have no right to investigate or challenge government activities. Even demographic information (on population movements, or patterns of disease, for example) may be suppressed. Information and speculation about individuals gathered through informers, the *secret services, and, often, *technological surveillance, is never open to public scrutiny.

freedom of the press, the freedom to print information and opinions without previous licence or prior restraint (see *censorship), subject to the laws regarding such matters as *defamation or *pornography. John Milton attacked the pre-publication licensing laws of his day, and his arguments expressed in the *Areopagitica* (1644) can be seen as one of the great defences of press freedom. Today, advocates of press freedom within democratic societies argue for a wider *freedom of expression than that normally granted to the individual. Specific press freedoms include the right to found a newspaper free from licensing restraints; editorial freedom; the right of access to public institutions; and the confidentiality of the journalist's sources. In democratic countries, press freedom may come into conflict with other rights, such as the individual's right to *privacy, or the right of reply to adverse comments made by the press. In totalitarian states, press freedom is non-existent, the media being controlled by the state, and free expression driven underground, as was the case in the *samizdat publications of the former Soviet Union and erstwhile Eastern bloc countries.

free market, an economy in which buying, selling, and other transactions can be conducted on whatever terms the parties choose without *intervention by the state. This means, for example, that prices are not fixed, and there is no *regulation or subsidization of production or employment. Prices are therefore determined solely by the forces of *supply and demand. The ideal of a perfectly free market is central to *libertarianism and the *New Right ideology, on grounds both of freedom of choice and of economic efficiency—see, for instance, *Friedman's *Capitalism and Freedom* (1962). These claims, however, depend on conditions of widespread competition and full information (see *perfect competition), which are often not fulfilled in reality, and so even governments sympathetic to free-market ideas are obliged to regulate markets to protect consumers and to prevent the emergence of monopolies and cartels. Producer groups, too, may prefer the stability of a regulated market to the hazards of open competition, as the US economist John Kenneth Galbraith argued in *The New Industrial State* (1967). None the less relatively free markets appear to be indispensable to economic growth, and are being introduced in many countries that are pursuing policies of *liberalization in the wake of failures of government planning (see *planned economy). Although it is possible (in theory) to envisage a form of *market socialism in which optimum prices are set by the government, the free exchange of goods, services, and labour is likely in practice to lead to a *capitalist form of economic organization.

free port, a port which accepts entry and exit of goods and services without the imposition of tariffs or taxes. The purpose of free ports is to encourage entrepôt trade, where incoming goods can await re-export without going through customs, and to give a competitive advantage to a particular port or compensate for a competitive disadvantage.

free speech   *freedom of expression.

free trade   *trade.

free-trade area   *common market.

free will, the philosophical problem of understanding how it is possible for people to be held morally responsible for their actions, given that there is reason for thinking that what they do is determined by causes. The problem of free will originates in the context of *theology: if *God is omniscient and omnipotent, it appears to follow that everything people do is foreknown by God, and determined by God's will. The same problem, in a secular context, is often seen in terms of a clash between morality and science: whereas moral practices (such as punishment) require our actions to be free, science tells us that everything we do is governed by the inexorable laws of nature; the deterministic view is of the world, including people, as just a vast machine, all of whose movements could in principle, given enough information, be predicted by physical science. Two important views of the nature of free will are those of the libertarian and the compatibilist. Libertarians, such as *Kant, hold that free will consists in the ability to do otherwise than one in fact does, that is, power of choice, and that this involves a suspension of the laws of nature. Libertarians have difficulty in explaining how this is possible, and Kant thought that for there to be free will, people had to be thought of as being in some sense outside the bounds of nature. Compatibilists such as *Hume, by contrast, deny that this much is needed for free will. They hold instead that a person acts freely so long as he is not constrained by external forces, such as the will of another person. For a compatibilist it is enough for a person to have acted freely that he knew what he was doing and that his action expressed his desires or character. Compatibilists face in turn the problem of explaining why the factors which determine a person's desires or character, such as their genetic make-up or upbringing, over which they

The **free port** of Singapore is the world's fourth largest port and a leading example of the benefits of encouraging entrepôt trade. More than half of imports are re-exported, particularly rubber, petroleum, textiles, timber, and tin.

have no control, should not be regarded as depriving them of free will.

Frege, Gottlob (1848–1925), German mathematician, logician, and philosopher. Frege's central works, *The Foundations of Arithmetic* (1884) and *The Basic Laws of Arithmetic* (1893, 1903), aimed to show that arithmetic and numerical analysis may be derived from principles of pure *logic. To this end he produced a rigorous systematization of logic which formed the basis of subsequent developments in mathematical logic, and a philosophical account of meaning which has had a similar influence in *semantics and *linguistics. His works were closely studied by *Russell and *Wittgenstein. Through them his concerns have come to be distinctive of much 20th-century British and US philosophy.

Freud, Sigmund (1856–1939), Austrian psychologist and psychotherapist who pioneered *psychoanalysis. Following a medical training, in which he specialized in neurology, he turned to the study of *hysteria. *Studies on Hysteria* (1895), written with Josef Breuer (1842–1925), established the framework of psychoanalytic theories about *neurosis: that the symptoms result from (and have a symbolic relation to) an emotional trauma which the patient has 'forgotten'. The memory, however, acts in the *unconscious to disrupt the patient's thoughts and feelings. To gain access to unconscious material the therapist uses *hypnosis, *dream analysis, or free association. Freud published *The Interpretation of Dreams* in 1900. He noticed the importance of sexual themes

in this material and argued that sexual 'memories' were really childhood fantasies which represented infantile sexual desires. This thesis of childhood sexuality, laid out in *Three Essays on the Theory of Sexuality* (1905), became central to Freud's thinking about normal and abnormal *psychosexual development. His theories came from clinical observations about which he wrote case histories; some of which, however, were subsequently shown to have been self-censored. There are many sources of distortion in such data and Freud's preoccupation with sexual explanations sometimes led him to ignore more obvious possibilities. Freudian theory enjoyed great popularity in the 1940s and 1950s, when academics such as the *social learning theorists at Yale University in the USA attempted to test his ideas by experiment, but they were rarely confirmed. Freud and his followers developed such key concepts as displacement, identification, projection, regression, repression, and sublimation (see *defence mechanisms). His ideas remain controversial and influential not only in the treatment of psychiatric illness, but in the arts and social sciences. Later psychoanalytic theorists who follow Freud are known as *neo-Freudian.

Friedman, Milton (1912–), US economist. A pioneer of contemporary *monetarism, Friedman is famous principally for his defence of the self-regulating *free-market economy and his unshakeable hostility to *Keynes' theory of discretionary management by government policy of aggregate demand. He reformulated the *quantity theory of money as a post-Keynesian theory of money demand. In *A Theory of the Consumption Function* (1957), Friedman developed a hypothesis of 'permanent income' in which he argued that expectations of future income were as important as current income in determining consumers' expenditure, a refinement of the Keynesian *'consumption/function' which, however, implied rejection of Keynesian notions about the economy's proneness to instability. Winner of the Nobel Prize for Economics in 1976, Friedman has had enormous influence on economic practice, especially that of conservative governments in the 1970s and 1980s.

friendly society, a UK institution originally set up in the 19th century as a self-help or *co-operative organization, and now a tax-efficient way of saving. Friendly societies are monitored by the Registrar of Friendly Societies and have specified limitations on their activities. The most common form of friendly society is the *building society; others are similar to life *assurance companies.

fringe benefits, payments in cash or kind made to employees in addition to wages and salaries. They include such items as free or subsidized meals, *pension or *loan arrangements, *discounts, and company cars. Statutory requirements such as sick leave and holiday pay are sometimes included in the definition.

Froebel, Friedrich (1782–1852), German educator whose theories did much to transform Western education. Profoundly convinced of humanity's spiritual dimension, Froebel argued for a system that attended to mind, body, and spirit. Influenced by both *Rousseau and *Kant, he also categorized three stages of teaching. This led him, firstly, to emphasize the child's internal characteristics through *play; then to meet the growing child's need to comprehend his or

Sigmund **Freud** and his daughter Anna walking in the Dolomites in 1913. Freud analysed Anna over several years, breaking his own professional rules; she manifested her devotion to him by becoming a psychoanalyst herself, remaining unmarried, and nursing him through his final illness.

her external environment; and finally to bring this to synthesis in the adolescent. Such theorizing caused him to set up, at Blankenburg in 1837, the first *kindergarten* (children's garden), or school for young children. Here the emphasis was on play, and the child's discovery of his or her own capacity. It is this aspect of his work which has endured, and continues to influence education today.

Fulani language   *Niger–Congo languages.

functionalism (in philosophy), a doctrine in the philosophy of *mind formulated as a response to the failure of *behaviourism to give an intuitively satisfying account of the mind. Functionalism claims that we can give a full account of a mental state only if we appeal to all its causes and all its effects, rather than just its behavioural effects. So functionalism, unlike behaviourism, can see mental states as causally interacting with other mental states and so can solve many of the difficulties inherent in the behaviourist approach.

functionalism (in social science), the theory that social institutions and cultural values can be explained in terms of the functions they perform in the cultural or social system as a whole. The existence of customs, institutions, and beliefs within a given society is explained as serving some individual or collective purpose or function. In anthropology, the idea of functionalism is often associated with *Malinowski, who sought to explain cultural phenomena as responses to a limited set of individual biological needs. Other social anthropologists stressed instead the idea of the social system as an integrated, functioning whole. A synthesis of the ideas of functionalism was attempted by the US sociologist *Parsons, and functionalism was especially influential in US sociology in the mid-20th century. Originally conceived as a criticism of the theory of social *evolution, functionalism has itself been criticized for ignoring the importance of historical development, and for viewing societies as existing in a state of equilibrium, with little possibility of change.

fundamentalism (in *Christianity), a religious movement which developed in the early 20th century among Protestants in the USA. A conservative response to *Darwin's theory of evolution, atheistic ideologies such as *Marxism, and new techniques of biblical criticism, fundamentalism aims to maintain the traditional doctrines of the Church and the infallible authority of the *Bible. Fundamentalism is associated with *evangelicalism, and has re-emerged in recent years as an influential movement, particularly in the USA, where fundamentalist views reach a wide audience through religious broadcasting. Fundamentalists often have a clearly defined social agenda which they see as traditionalist. They oppose abortion, support anti-pornographic legislation, and promote the teaching of creationism in schools, that is, the biblical account of the creation, rather than evolutionary theories. *Millenarian ideas rooted in biblical prophecies of the Second Coming have led to fundamentalist support for the state of Israel; anti-communism is expressed in support for a strongly armed USA. US fundamentalists have been active missionaries, and derivative or parallel movements are now found world-wide. The term fundamentalist is loosely used of those in any religion who seek a return to fundamental doctrines. (See also *Hindu revivalism, *Islamic fundamentalism.)

funeral customs, rituals and beliefs concerning the death of an individual and the disposal of the corpse, usually

At a Daoist funeral in Ganshu, China, close relatives (dressed in shrouds) chant prayers to assist the journey of the soul and burn paper money to ensure that it is adequately provided for. The great reverence paid to ancestors in Chinese culture enhances the significance of **funerals**.

involving religious observance. Many religions believe that there is a distinction between physical and spiritual life, and that something of the individual survives death, either to be reborn through *reincarnation or to fulfil its spiritual destiny in the *afterlife. In most religions and cultures it is important that the correct funerary procedures are followed, in order to assist the passage of the dead person from this world to the next. All societies, religious or not, have to deal with the problem of the death of their members and the *bereavement of the living. Like other transitions in an individual's life, death is usually marked by a *rite of passage in which central values are restated and important social bonds re-emphasized. Funerals provide an opportunity for relatives of the deceased to mourn death publicly; they are also a means of coping with the social disruption that occurs with death. Precise customs vary in different religions and traditions, but common features include the washing and laying out of the corpse (which may be embalmed); the wake, or watching over the dead body, usually the night before the funeral, which provides the opportunity for a gathering of relatives and friends; the disposal of the corpse by burial, *cremation, or other means such as exposure to the elements often accompanied by religious rituals; and the period of mourning following the funeral.

further education *higher education.

futures markets (forward markets), markets in which contracts to buy and sell at future dates are traded. Futures markets exist for foreign *currencies, some goods (chiefly *commodities), and *securities. Dealers contract to buy or sell a specified amount for a specified price on a specified future date. In some cases the contract itself may be subsequently traded. Futures markets exist to diminish risk by removing price uncertainty from particular transactions. With agricultural commodities crops may be sold before harvest (the amount specified in the deal being whatever a certain acreage yields), thus insuring the farmer against harvest failure. (See also *arbitrage, *hedging.)

Gaia hypothesis, the theory, put forward by the British scientist James E. Lovelock in the early 1970s, that the earth is a single organism. Gaia was the ancient Greeks' earth goddess, and in *Gaia: A New Look at Life on Earth* (1979), Lovelock suggests that the earth is self-regulating, like the human body. For example, the more or less constant composition of the earth's atmosphere over geological time has been maintained by a delicate balance between living organisms, oceans, and atmosphere. Focusing on biological feedback processes, the theory has the possible implication that if mankind disturbs the earth's natural ecological balance, the planet itself will compensate by undermining man's domination. In distinction to the traditional view that organisms merely adapt to their environments, the Gaia theory holds that they also modify that environment to make it more hospitable to themselves.

Galbraith *affluent society.

Galla language *Cushitic languages.

Galton, Francis (1822–1911), British psychologist, explorer, meteorologist, founder of *eugenics and pioneer of the study of *intelligence and other differences between people. Inspired by his cousin *Darwin's *Origin of Species* (1859), Galton published *Hereditary Genius* (1869), in which he relied on biographical data to show that particular talents often run in families. He carried out the first study of twins (1876). As identical twins have identical genes, variants of twin-studies have remained the fundamental method to separate effects of heredity from those of experience or the environment ('nature versus nurture'; see *behaviour genetics). He also investigated individual differences in mental imagery and verbal associations, topics which are still of central concern to cognitive psychology. His development of viable methods for *psychology were as important as his ideas. His principal methodological contribution was to show the applicability of statistics to psychological data, inventing various techniques, notably correlation.

gambling, the pastime of betting on the outcome of a sporting contest or chance event. The stake is usually either money or money exchanged for chips or tokens, and the degree of skill required varies widely. In a sophisticated card-game such as poker, no player can expect to win consistently by relying on chance alone, whereas in casino games such as roulette and various forms of *dice, players depend on a random factor such as the turn of a wheel to bring them a win. What such players can control is the scale of their winnings or losses, both by the amount of stake money they venture and by their skill in offsetting long-odds losses with short-odds gains—in roulette, by betting on red or black, for example, where the odds are even—while at the same time placing more risky bets on single numbers or combinations. In some forms of gambling such as horse-racing or football pools, the players do not take part in the event but may use their knowledge of the current form of the horses or football teams to predict the outcome of a race or series of matches.

game-shooting, the sport of shooting birds and mammals. To protect the game, seasonal limits and codes of conduct are usually imposed: in the UK, 12 August to 10 December for grouse shooting, 1 October to 1 February for pheasant shooting, and 1 September to 1 February for partridge shooting. Shooting may be of big game, such as deer, antelope, bear, and wild boar, or of small game, such as grouse, partridge, pheasant, duck, geese, and rabbit.

game theory *rational choice theory.

GATT (General Agreement on Tariffs and Trade), an international trade agreement. Established under the auspices of the *UN in 1948 and with a secretariat in Geneva, it aims to promote international trade by reducing *tariffs and other trade restrictions through multilateral negotiations and a code of conduct covering the commercial relations of member countries. Ninety-six countries are party to it and a further twenty-eight apply GATT *de facto*. Between them they account for 90 per cent of world trade. GATT promoted the post-war expansion of world trade through the reduction of trade barriers, but the poorer countries felt its terms favoured the developed countries, a criticism that led to the founding of *UNCTAD and to an agreement in 1965 that developing countries should not be expected to offer reciprocity when negotiating with developed countries. GATT has been less influential in relation to non-tariff barriers, some types of which increased in the 1970s and 1980s. These include *quotas and requirements that products meet certain health and environmental standards. In the eighth round of talks by GATT members on trade liberalization (called 'the Uruguay Round' because the talks commenced in 1986 in Uruguay), the issue of farm *subsidies has been a source of major disagreement.

GDP (gross domestic product), a measure of the total flow of *goods and services produced by an economy in a specified time period (normally a year). GDP is calculated by summing the output of all firms and the government. A firm's output is its *value added, which is the total sales revenue minus the cost of any intermediate goods purchased from other producers. Government output is measured by summing the wages and salaries of public servants. GDP is initially measured 'at market prices'. Then the indirect taxes, which raise prices above production cost, are subtracted and *subsidies are added. The result is GDP 'at factor cost', which measures the *costs of producing the goods and services. Net domestic product is GDP minus *depreciation of fixed *capital goods. (See also *GNP.)

gender (in social science), the distinction of people on the basis of a person's biological sex. Patterns of work, individual behaviour, and status are ascribed to people according to gender; throughout the world such perceived distinctions often become the basis for male domination. From birth, children are treated differently and are taught or mimic the social roles characteristic of their gender, whether male or female. The extent to which gender-specific biological factors, such as hormones, affect a person's behaviour is unclear, and there is considerable debate among psychologists over whether biology, *socialization, or other factors dictate gender-related behaviour. The range of behaviour within each sex, as well as the number of people who choose sexual partners and life-styles contrary to their expected gender roles, indicate that these roles are not simply dictated and fixed by nature. Moreover, in different societies, roles are rigid to a varying degree. The extent of variation shows that definitions of maleness and femaleness are, to a large extent, socially specific. In hunter-gatherer societies, for instance, where there is a high level of equality between the sexes, roles are less rigid than in settled peasant societies. The concept of gender has been important in feminist arguments against male domination. (See also *patriarchy, *sex differences.)

Geneva Conventions, a series of international agreements on the treatment of victims of war, ratified in whole or partially by the majority of states and certain non-state organizations such as the PLO (the Palestine Liberation Organization) and SWAPO (the South West Africa People's Organization). The first Geneva Convention was established by the Swiss founder of the Red Cross, Henri Dunant, in 1864, and concerned the treatment of the wounded in war. Subsequent Conventions in 1907, 1929, 1949, and 1977 covered the treatment of prisoners of war and the protection of civilians, forbidding such acts as *deportation, *torture, *hostage-taking, collective punishment or reprisals, and the use of chemical and biological weapons. The 1977 Convention dealt with more extensive non-combatant protection, and covered problems arising from internal wars.

genocide, the systematic policy of destruction of a group or nation on grounds of race or ethnic origin. Following the

In March 1988 Iraq made a chemical attack on the Kurdish town of Halabja in northern Iraq. An estimated 4,000 died, lending some credence to claims of **genocide** against the Kurds.

Nazi policy of genocide of the Jews and of ethnic groups such as gypsies, the Convention on the Prevention and Punishment of the Crime of Genocide was adopted by the UN in 1948. The Convention establishes that genocide is not to be regarded as a matter of domestic jurisdiction within a state, but rather is to be seen as a matter of fundamental concern to the international community. It also establishes the principle of individual accountability on the part of those carrying out the killings. Since the signing of the Convention, many conflicts in the world have split groups along ethnic or tribal lines (see *communal conflict), and claims of genocide have been made. Examples include the Nigeria–Biafra conflict in 1969; Uganda in the 1970s; the Pol Pot regime in Kampuchea (Cambodia) (1976–9); and Iraq's treatment of the Kurds (1986–   ). The international community has failed in most cases to respond effectively to claims of genocide: firm evidence is hard to obtain; there are problems in determining the appropriate tribunal; perhaps most importantly, states are reluctant to intervene in the domestic affairs of another state on the grounds that this is a violation of national *sovereignty.

geography, human, the study and body of knowledge concerning the relationship between the earth's surface and the people who live on it. Karl Ritter (1779–1859), the founder of modern human geography, emphasized the influence of the natural environment on human activity and development. Subsequently human geographers tended to concern themselves primarily with the uniqueness of particular peoples and regions. Since the 1950s more effort has gone into discovering the universal laws that may govern human behaviour and organization over the surface of

the planet. There has been a fragmentation of study into fields such as industrial, urban, agricultural, transport, and political geography, *demography, and *ecology. For some, human geography has become a spatial science, involving locational analysis of the proximity and distribution of centres of human activity. Mathematical modelling often plays an important part in such work. Another trend, often seen as conflicting, has been to study the distribution of wealth, resources, and the provision of education and health services. There is an increasing understanding that present human geography cannot be understood without reference to the past, through the field of historical geography. Mental maps are now compiled to record individuals' experience of spatial patterns, as opposed to the actual distribution of human activity. *Ethnic group, *social class, and *gender are all factors that are increasingly taken into account.

geopolitics, an approach to understanding international politics which seeks to explain the political behaviour of states in terms of geographical variables such as size or location. The term is particularly associated with the work of the Swede R. J. Kjellen (1864–1922) and the German Karl Haushofer (1869–1946). Haushofer's perception of geopolitics as involving the struggle between states to occupy the world was taken up by the Nazi Party in Germany to justify its expansionist goals, a connection which helped to bring the subject into disrepute. However, the use of the term in the sense of stressing the interplay of geographical and political factors in international relations has remained. It is considered particularly helpful in understanding the problems facing strategically sensitive areas of the world.

Germanic languages, a group of *Indo-European languages which originated in northern Europe. They fall into three main branches: East, North, and West Germanic. The East Germanic languages, which included Gothic, are now extinct. Gothic provides the earliest written Germanic in the form of Ulfilas's Gothic Bible of AD 350. North Germanic includes Swedish (9 million speakers), Danish (5 million), Norwegian (4.5 million), and Icelandic (250,000). Swedish, Danish, and Norwegian are on the whole mutually intelligible, though their standard literary languages are quite distinct. The earliest evidence of Scandinavian consists of runic inscriptions (formed by shaping Roman or Greek characters to suit carving) from the period AD 200–600. Written documents date from 750. Swedish was standardized in 1526, Danish in 1550. Norwegian, however, has much of its vocabulary in common with Danish, but has preserved a pronunciation similar to Swedish. Standardized 'Dano-Norwegian' (*Bokmål*) was adopted in 1863, and a reconstructed New Norwegian (*Nynorsk*), based on spoken dialects, was adopted in 1907. *Nynorsk* is taught in schools as a literary language, but is not widely spoken as a mother-tongue. Icelandic is an extraordinarily archaic Scandinavian language. West Germanic includes *English, Frisian, German, Dutch, *Yiddish, and Afrikaans. Frisian, the closest cousin of English, is spoken by 400,000 in northern Holland and Germany. German has 94 million speakers in Germany, Austria, and Switzerland. There are three broad dialect bands: Low, (spoken in the North), Central, and High (spoken in southern Germany and Austria). The standard language spoken by Germans is based on east Central German. The first written texts date from the 8th century. Dutch, which includes a large number of diverse dialects, is spoken by 20 million people in The Netherlands and Belgium (where it is sometimes called Flemish). Afrikaans is a derivative of Dutch

spoken in South Africa. *Yiddish, the traditional language of Central and East European Jews, is written in the Hebrew script and contains many Hebrew and Slavic elements.

gerrymandering   *electoral fraud.

Gestalt psychology (German, *Gestalt*, 'form'), an approach, particularly to *perception and cognitive problems, developed from 1912 onwards by Max Wertheimer (1880–1943), Kurt Koffka (1886–1941), and Wolfgang Köhler (1887–1967), all of whom emigrated from Europe to the USA. Their principal claim was that the structural laws of wholes determine what occurs in their parts rather than vice versa. They used examples, such as squares or melodies, in which we can perceive the same form (*Gestalt*) even when its constituent parts such as size or key are different. Their empirical work, which centred on problem-solving and *visual illusions, showed that the mind imposes on its surroundings interpretations that it is constantly trying to simplify—an idea at odds with those of *reductionism and *behaviourism. The Gestalt psychologists anticipated modern *cognitive psychology and were a dominant influence on the development of *social psychology after World War II.

Gestalt therapy, a psychotherapy which emphasizes awareness, immediate experience, and personal responsibility. It is not an offshoot of *Gestalt psychology, but was developed largely under the influence of the German-born psychoanalyst Fritz Perls (1893–1970), drawing on ideas from many sources. Popular in the USA since the late 1960s, Gestalt therapy adopts a holistic approach, giving equal weight to mind and body. Conflicts within the individual's personality are explored, sometimes by acting them out, and in a group session, with the object of removing obstacles to personal growth.

gesture   *non-verbal communication.

ghetto, a historical term for the Jewish quarter in a city, now used for residential areas in which minority ethnic or cultural groups predominate. Exclusiveness reflects, on the one hand, the desire of such peoples to protect and preserve their religious, group, and family values; on the other, it often reflects prejudice, *discrimination, and economic structures in the wider society and may even be the result of forced *segregation policies.

ghost dance, a *millennial movement which spread among the North American *Plains Indians during the second half of the 19th century. The ghost dance, which involved dancing for days on end, was said to presage the end of the world, when the white settlers would leave and the Indians would have their lands restored.

Giffen goods (in economics), goods which do not obey the 'law of demand', in that the amount demanded of a Giffen good becomes greater if the price increases, rather than less. The name is that of Sir Robert Giffen (1837–1910), who observed that when the price of bread rose, the demand for it by the poor also rose. This is because the income effect of the price change was both negative and larger than the substitution effect. A negative income effect occurs when the amount of bread demanded falls as real income rises, because when people are better off they prefer higher-grade food. A good displaying a negative income effect is known as an inferior good. Inferiority is a necessary but not sufficient condition for a good to be a Giffen good. Also necessary is the condition that this income effect be greater than the substitution effect, the tendency to substitute cheaper for more expensive products following a relative price change. The fact that expenditure on bread accounted for a large part of total income in the case cited contributed to the (negative) income effect being larger than the substitution effect, because a rise in the price of bread made the poor significantly poorer and therefore unable to afford meat and other non-bread foodstuffs. As a result they bought more bread.

gift, an object transferred from one person or group of people to another without immediate direct repayment. The importance of the gift as a basic medium for creating and maintaining social ties has been recognized in *sociology and *anthropology. Gifts can create relationships of obligation between individuals and groups. This obligation can take many forms, but is usually marked by principles of reciprocity, in that the person who gives the gift also expects, at some time in the future, to be the recipient of a gift in return. The act of giving is sometimes seen as more important than the value of the gift itself, and thus gifts have a symbolic value, as in the exchange of Christmas cards in Western societies, which is accompanied by powerful feelings of obligation out of proportion to the low practical value of the cards. Gift-giving is also important in *rituals such as *marriage, or may be connected with religious beliefs, as in the giving of gifts to members of religious orders or to deities. Other forms of gift-giving may be related to calendrical events or to *rites of passage that mark a change in social status. Gifts may also serve to maintain social links over distances, as in the traditional *kula exchange system of the Trobriand Islanders, described by *Malinowski. Gifts may also express complex issues concerning social status and prestige, as in the case of the *potlatch of the North-west Indians, or the ritual pig-feasts of many *New Guinea Highland societies. The importance of the gift as a basic medium for creating and maintaining social ties was first pointed out by the French sociologist Marcel Mauss in his *Essai sur le don* (1925). Mauss's theme of reciprocity was subsequently developed by Lévi-Strauss to account for forms of marriage alliance in which patterns of *kinship are systems in which women are exchanged as gifts between groups of men.

gilt-edged securities (gilts), UK government *bonds (marketable *securities with an original maturity of not less than twelve months). The term gilt-edged means that there is no significant danger of the government failing to pay interest or redeem the bonds.

glasnost and perestroika, the concepts of 'openness' and 'restructuring' whose effects led to major changes in Soviet society as well as profoundly influencing the world *balance of power and *East–West relations. Introduced into Soviet domestic politics by Mikhail Gorbachev 1931–), who became Soviet leader in 1985, the concepts are described in his book *Perestroika* (1987). The twin processes aimed to reduce inefficiency and corruption in the former Soviet Union, and to encourage political liberalization. Internally the results of the 'Gorbachev doctrine' were mixed and contributed to growing unrest, provoked by nationalist demands, *commual conflict, and economic discontent, which in 1991 brought about the disintegration of the structure of the Soviet Union, the secession of the Baltic republics, the displacement of the Communist Party from its formerly dominant position, and the formation of a new

This variation on the theme of the traditional Russian doll for sale in the streets of Moscow depicts Soviet leaders with the word 'perestroika' painted on Gorbachev's image. Such entrepreneurship was an early sign of the break with orthodoxy created by **glasnost**.

*Commonwealth of Independent States. Externally *glasnost* and *perestroika* contributed to the abandonment of Soviet control over the Eastern bloc, the withdrawal of Soviet troops and support from Afghanistan, and a growing reluctance to become involved in conflicts in developing countries as well as a growing rapprochement with the West, which brought the cold war to a close.

gliding, the sport of flying in unpowered heavier-than-air craft which use upward currents of air to gain altitude after being towed aloft by a powered plane. In hang-gliding, wings are fitted to a lightweight frame. The flier launches himself on foot over a steep incline and tries to glide like a bird.

global warming   *greenhouse effect.

GNP (gross national product), the most widely used measure of national prosperity. It is based on *GDP, to which is added property income (interest, profits, and dividends arising from the ownership of assets) accruing to domestic residents from abroad minus similar income paid from the domestic economy to foreigners. The GDP is the gross product produced within the geographical boundary of a country, whereas the GNP is the gross product accruing to the residents of the country. Net national product is GNP minus *depreciation.

Gobind Singh (1666–1708), the tenth and last of the Sikh *Gurus. He became Guru at the age of nine, following the execution of his father, the ninth Guru, at the hands of the Mogul emperor Aurangzeb. Gobind Singh encouraged the militarization of the Sikhs against the Mogul empire. During *Baisakhi* (the new year festival) in 1699, he called upon five Sikhs to give up their lives, but instead of killing the volunteers he rewarded their courage and loyalty by initiating them into the *Khalsa*, a newly formed army of soldier-saints. At the time of his death, Gobind Singh declared that there would be no living Guru after him, but that authority would be invested in the *Adi Granth*, the sacred book of the Sikhs.

god, a conception of transcendence as a personal being or deity. Conceptions of transcendence, which are always found in *religion, vary in the degree to which they are personal or impersonal, mythical or abstract. God as One, All-Powerful, and All-Merciful in *Islam may be said to be relatively impersonal when compared to Christian conceptions of God as a father, but both are quite personalized and related to myth when set beside the Hindu notion of *Brahman, or the Buddhist concept of *dependent origination. Mythic conceptions of god typically make use of human imagery and terms; a god may be portrayed with emotions, with gender, or with a body. It is important to remember that a god is not perceived as a conception, but as transcendence itself. A god is thus generally beyond human concepts and human understanding, and contrastive language is often used to describe god; god can be both manifest and hidden, male and female, just and merciful, good and evil, creator and destroyer, one and many. Various forms of worship, from *sacrifice to public acts of honour, to private prayer, are typically linked with concepts of god. Emotions such as awe, fear, and gratitude are often experienced in such religious activities with god as their object. Religions vary in the number of gods acknowledged. Some are polytheistic, with complex pantheons as, for example, in ancient Greece and some forms of *Hinduism. Others, like *Judaism and *Islam, insist on a strict monotheism. It is also possible to combine polytheistic and monotheistic conceptions of god in a metaphysical or epistemological hierarchy. In many *African religions, a supreme being is worshipped over and above lesser deities. In some branches of Hinduism, *Vishnu and *Shiva are each conceived as a monotheistic god who manifests himself in other gods. *Advaita Hindus affirm that personal gods are necessary for those of lesser spiritual capabilities, but ultimate reality is best understood as Brahman. Scholars have disagreed about whether or not there is any pattern to the diversity of conceptions of transcendence. Earlier in this century, scholars assumed that there was such a pattern, and some argued for an evolution from polytheism to monotheism to impersonal abstraction, while others saw a devolution from original monotheism to polytheism and pantheism. Contemporary scholars, however, are generally less sanguine about the existence of such patterns.

Goffman, Erving (1922–82), US sociologist, particularly concerned with the analysis of daily life. Drawing on *symbolic interactionism, he maintained that social life could be understood using a dramatic analogy, where life is a stage, human beings are players, and expectations of front stage and back stage behaviour diverge. In a restaurant, the diners may sit in elegant comfort, while 'behind the green baize door' staff labour in pandemonium. Such divergencies are to be found in most organizations and social groups. Goffman's delight in the scrutiny of social encounters led to influential books on *stigma and on *'total institutions' such as prisons, but since many of his observations arose from his own participation in the activities he dissected, they have proved difficult to replicate and confirm.

gold bullion, bulk quantities of gold in the form of ingots and bars as opposed to coins. Gold bullion forms part of the international reserves held by *central banks. It is not as important in the international monetary system now as

Gross National Product

Gross National Product (GNP) per capita is the main criterion used to distinguish countries at different stages of economic development by the World Bank and the UN. Low- and middle-income countries (except those in Eastern Europe) are often termed 'developing countries'. High-income countries (with the exception of the Middle Eastern oil exporters) are generally termed 'industrialized' or 'developed'.

Groups
of economies

0–$545
Low-income
economies

$546–5,999
Middle-income
economies

Over $6,000
High-income
economies

Not available

Note: Figures not available for Germany and Yemen following reunifications in 1990 or for the former Soviet Union and Yugoslavia following disintegration in 1991/2.

Sources: *World Development Report, 1990* World Bank, Oxford University Press, 1989

under the *gold standard or the Bretton Woods international monetary system of fixed exchange rates which ended in 1971, but it still plays a residual role.

gold standard, a monetary system under which a country's monetary authority maintains convertibility of its *currency into gold at a fixed price by standing ready to exchange its currency for gold on demand at the price declared (plus or minus a small margin which reflects the cost of shipping gold). *Exchange rates between the currencies of member countries are then necessarily fixed. Each monetary authority has to maintain a certain reserve of gold to honour its obligation; the size of the reserve in relation to the domestic *money supply or to changes in it may or may not be established by law. Under a 'full' gold standard (or gold specie standard), such as existed before 1914, convertibility applied to all citizens and gold coins circulated as money. Under the 'gold exchange' standard, such as existed in the later 1920s, convertibility applies only among monetary authorities, and there is no circulation of gold coin. The gold standard is not currently in effect anywhere in the world.

golf, a popular target game played world-wide by amateurs and professionals, using a selection of wood- and metal-faced clubs to hit a small white ball across uneven terrain and hole it in a circular cup with the least number of strokes. A full-length golf course, usually 4,600–6,400 m (5,000–7,000 yards) in length, consists of eighteen holes of varied character, laid out with a long, narrow fairway of mown grass terminating in a roughly circular green where a flag marks the hole. Along the way are numerous hazards: long grass, bushes, and trees next to the fairway, perhaps a stream or lake, and almost always a series of sand bunkers. Golf has proved a compelling sport for both players and spectators, and the money prizes at the top level are among the highest in sport. A handicap system allows for even competition among players of differing abilities.

Good Friday, the annual Christian commemoration of the crucifixion of *Jesus Christ, directly preceding *Easter Sunday. It is a time of fasting and penance, often with a three-hour service from noon until 3 pm in which the Passion or suffering of Jesus on the cross is narrated. Good Friday is known as 'Great Friday' in the Orthodox Church.

goods (in economics), physical commodities which either directly or indirectly provide for the satisfaction of human wants. Consumer goods (or final-demand goods) are those used for *consumption purposes. They can be classified into non-durable goods (such as food) and durable goods (such as refrigerators). Producer goods are those used to produce other goods and services. These comprise intermediate goods (raw materials and semi-finished items) and fixed *capital goods (buildings and equipment). Services are normally distinguished from goods by their intangible nature. They are normally consumed at the instant of their production, as in the case of a haircut. 'Bads' also exist; they have a negative value and an adverse effect on human satisfaction (for example, pollution). Public goods are those which, when consumed by one individual, are not depleted (for example, street lighting and national defence).

government, a term referring both to the act of rule and the institutions through which it is conducted. The act of government is the exercise of influence and control through law and coercion over any group of people, but particularly those formed into a *state. The institutions of government comprise the leading offices of state, and the systems of representation and administration; they can be divided into the *executive, the *legislature, and the *judiciary. The term may also refer to the broad relationship, involving both *consent and constraint, between this set of institutions and the population living within its jurisdiction. Throughout history, governments have extracted resources from society in return for providing order and security. Increasingly, modern governments have come to regulate economic life and provide extensive social *welfare. Most are also large employers. Even in capitalist liberal *democracies, the contemporary role of government is therefore substantial. The balance between law and coercion varies between governments. Broadly, however, absolutist non-constitutional regimes relying heavily on the threat or use of coercion such as *authoritarian or totalitarian governments may be contrasted with *constitutional governments, in which public power is subject to effective restraints. There are numerous variations in the structure of governments such as presidential government (see *president), *parliamentary government, *federalism, *unitary state, and *one-party state.

government housing, housing which is built, allocated, and managed by central or local government. It is usually intended for low-income groups, but sometimes for others such as members of the armed services or civil servants. Government involvement in housing began in the late 19th century in some industrializing nations as *urbanization caused overcrowding, which threatened *public health and order. Within communist states, most new construction has typically been by the government or by co-operatives. Across the world, government housing has greatly increased the amount of accommodation for urban populations, and raised standards by supplying *water, *sanitation, electricity, and separate units for each household. Demand from those in inferior, usually privately rented, accommodation and from the *homeless outstrips supply. None the less, some government housing has been criticized for its monotonous design and inferior construction, its inadequate maintenance, and sometimes authoritarian management. As a result of its connection with the poor it may be stigmatized. In developing countries, government housing has often proved unsuitable for the poor because of its distance from workplaces, the size of payments required, and the limited and inflexible space provided. In many *shanty towns, by contrast, residents combine home and workplace, and informal social networks sustain them within a low-income economy. In consequence, many governments have given up building low-income housing, concentrating instead on rehabilitating *slums and *shanty towns.

grammar, the study of the formal properties of words and sentences. Traditionally, it includes morphology, which describes the ways in which words are formed from smaller units or other words, and syntax, which describes how words combine into sentences. It sometimes also includes *phonology and *semantics. Grammar is descriptive, that is, concerned to describe the facts, and not prescriptive, that is, concerned to recommend or prohibit particular forms. A central branch of modern *linguistics is generative grammar, which seeks to provide precise formal descriptions of the grammatical systems of languages and to develop a theory of universal grammar: a set of general statements about the structure of human languages. Transformational grammar is a form of generative grammar which makes use of operations known as 'transformations', which systematically indicate the links between various types of sentence and derive one type from the other.

Gramsci, Antonio (1891–1937), Italian social theorist. As a young man, Gramsci was a revolutionary socialist, active in promoting factory councils as the basis of a socialist society. He helped to found the Italian Communist Party in 1921, but was arrested in 1926 and remained in prison until his death. In *Prison Notebooks* (1947), he expounded a form of *Marxism that played down the determining role of economics in social change. According to Gramsci, human consciousness was by no means a simple reflection of the material world, but played an active and independent role in shaping that world. Thus the key to the struggle between capitalist and working classes was the battle of ideas in which the latter sought to overthrow the *hegemony of the former and to become the dominant intellectual force. This meant that Marxists should pay less attention to economics and more to winning control of the cultural institutions through which ideas were disseminated. Gramsci's ideas were later influential among the *New Left.

great power, a state seen as playing a major role in international politics. A great power possesses economic, diplomatic, and military strength and influence, and its interests extend beyond its own borders. It is the great powers that make the key moves in international affairs, are involved in the major conflicts, and make the peace when it has to be made. The term is usually associated with the emergence of Austria, Russia, Prussia, France, and Great Britain as great powers in Europe after the Congress of Vienna in 1815; they worked together under a loose agreement known as the Concert of Europe. After World War I, the USA grew in importance, while after World War II, the USA and the former Soviet Union, through their industrial strength, global influence, and nuclear capabilities, attained the status of *superpowers, and world events became dominated by bipolarity. The UK and France have declined from their former great power status, although they are still recognized by the *UN, together with the USA, Russia, and China, as permanent members of the *Security Council with power of *veto. The number of great powers at any time (whether the system is bipolar or multipolar) is considered a key feature of the international system, important in determining the level and nature of *war.

Greek language, the *Indo-European language for which we have the longest record, dating from 1400 BC. Mycenean Greek, the earliest phase, is known from clay tablets written in a syllabary (a writing system where each sign stands for a syllable) called Linear B. They date from *c*.1400 BC to the collapse of Mycenean civilization in about 1150 BC. The ensuing dark ages of Greece ended with the introduction of the Greek alphabet (adapted from Phoenician) in the early 8th century BC. The great period of classical Greek literature began in the late 6th century and spanned the next two centuries. But there was no standard ancient Greek language; each city-state had its own dialect. By the end of the 5th century Athens had established herself as the leading cultural centre in Greece, and by 300 BC a *koiné* (common language) based on the Athenian dialect of Attic–Ionic had emerged, which became a *lingua franca throughout the eastern Mediterranean. During the Byzantine era (AD 330–1453) and the period of Turkish rule

(1453–1822) the *koiné* continued to be used as an archaizing literary language, while the colloquial language evolved separately. After Greek independence an archaic or 'puristic' language (*katharévousa*) was resurrected as the official language. In the 20th century this was gradually replaced by the colloquial (demotic) language, though the *katharévousa* was reinstated during the regime of the military junta (1967–76). Modern Greek is spoken by around 10 million people, and a flourishing demotic literary tradition has evolved.

Green (in politics), an advocate of a system of life which is sustainable and which respects the laws of *ecology. The Green movement is made up of numerous pressure groups, national and international, as well as Green political parties in many countries. Pressure groups include Friends of the Earth, Greenpeace (famed for direct actions to defend species, such as whales, and environments), and the World Wide Fund for Nature. Greens share a philosophy based on most of the following strands: respect for and *conservation of the earth and its wealth; the rejection of materialism and the need to build a sustainable alternative to the present system of industrial *capitalism, away from the quantitative growth measured by *GNP towards qualitative *development, hence the need for *recycling and renewable *energy; a commitment to lasting security through non-nuclear defence and a commitment to open, participatory democracy at every level; the importance of building a new kind of society based on self-reliant decentralized communities, and of acknowledging the importance of satisfying work and human-scale technology; a willingness to share the earth's wealth among all its peoples; and a recognition of the rights of future generations. Green parties have enjoyed limited political success since their emergence in the early 1970s. The world's first was the Values Party founded in New Zealand in 1972, closely followed by the British Ecology Party in 1973. In the former Eastern bloc countries political changes have led to a mushrooming of ecological pressure groups and there are growing ecological movements in India, Africa, Latin America, and elsewhere.

Green Paper   *bill.

greenhouse effect, the insulation of the earth by certain gases present in the atmosphere and, in common parlance, the raising of the earth's temperature caused by the increase in such gases due to the burning of fossil fuels, forests, and grasslands. The greenhouse gases—chiefly carbon dioxide but also methane, nitrous oxide, and chlorofluorocarbons (CFCs)—hold the sun's heat like the glass of a greenhouse, allowing energy from the sun to penetrate the atmosphere but preventing radiation from the warmed earth from escaping. Without greenhouse gases there would be no life. However, although most greenhouse gases occur naturally (methane, for example, is produced by rotting animal and vegetable matter), rapid *industrialization and *pollution have accelerated their production and affected the ecological balance. The increased human population itself produces more gases, as do the animals raised for food, and the rotting of the waste they produce. *Deforestation exacerbates the process of global warming, since trees absorb carbon dioxide. It is difficult to predict the extent and effects of global warming, but in 1990 scientists of the International Panel on Climate Change suggested that world temperatures may have risen by 0.5 °C in the past century and be set to rise a further 1 °C by 2030 and 3–4 °C by 2090, unless drastic action is taken. The rises forecast disastrous consequences for mankind—especially for the poor and those in low-lying regions—including *famine, death, and mass migration. Expansion of ocean waters and melting of polar icecaps would raise sea levels by up to 1 m (2–3 feet) within a century, flooding such highly populated deltas as the Ganges in Bangladesh. Many low-lying islands might disappear. Climate zones could shift latitude by hundreds of miles, bringing further *desertification and affecting grain-producing areas such as the Great Plains of the USA. There is already evidence of the freak weather predicted by scientists, such as unpredictable rainfall, storms, and droughts, as in Ethiopia and the US grain-belt. Scientists propose various solutions. Some suggest a limit to growth in industrial production, consumption, and population, while others favour technical solutions such as transporting excess water to inland basins, removing greenhouse gases from exhausts before they reach the atmosphere, or planting more trees. Increased use of renewable *energy and better energy conservation will also play a role. Governments are considering the introduction of 'green taxes' and tighter limits on all types of exhaust emission.

Gresham's Law (in economics), a law named after Sir Thomas Gresham (1519–79) who declared that 'bad money drives out good'. If there are two coins in circulation with different ratios of face value to intrinsic value (in terms of the precious metal content of the coins), then the coin with the relatively higher intrinsic value will tend to be taken out of circulation for hoarding or melting down.

greyhound racing, an international sport that is primarily a vehicle for betting. Up to eight (usually six) trained greyhounds, noted for swiftness, race each other round an oval circuit approximately 370–490 m (400–550 yards) long in pursuit of a mechanical hare. At the beginning of the race, the dogs wait in traps lined across the course. The hare moves past the traps on an electric rail, triggering the trap doors when it is some 11 m (12 yards) ahead of the dogs. The winner is the first greyhound whose nose crosses the winning line.

Group of 7 (G7), a grouping of the world's seven richest industrial democracies. The G7 was set up in 1975 with the aim of co-ordinating efforts to promote growth and stability in the world economy, and to bring the world's key *exchange rates into line. The original five members (France, Japan, the UK, the USA, and West Germany) were joined in 1976 by Canada and Italy, with the EC acquiring observer status in 1977. The G7 has no permanent headquarters, but holds regular meetings between the finance ministers and central-bank governors of member countries. The annual meeting of the G7 heads of state is of growing importance, and now includes discussion of key foreign policy issues. The 1991 summit was marked by the invitation to the then Soviet President Mikhail Gorbachev to attend post-summit discussions on the Soviet economy's transition to a *free market. Attempts to agree on the reduction of agricultural subsidies in order to facilitate the *GATT talks have been another crucial debate in recent summits.

group therapy, the psychotherapeutic treatment of several persons at once. Groups, usually composed of six to twelve, meet regularly with one or two therapists. The object is that the shared experience and interaction of group members may prove mutually beneficial by allowing individuals to recognize patterns of behaviour and feeling in themselves

and in each other. Group therapy may be used in therapeutic communities, for example for victims of *child sexual abuse, for depressives, and for the rehabilitation of alcoholics and drug abusers. Membership of such a group may increase the individual's sense of confidence and support for others. With the help of skilled therapists group members gain insight into those neurotic mechanisms in themselves and others which block their development. They learn to come to terms with negative experiences, thus freeing them to re-establish contact between themselves, others, and their environment. Extensions of group activities include psychodrama, in which members act out roles relevant to the problems of each of them in turn, one object of which is to make the individual aware of the differences between the image he has of himself and how he or she is perceived by others.

guardian, one who looks after the interests of a child (the ward), and is entitled to exercise parental rights and duties over him or her. A guardian may be appointed by a *will or by a *court, either after the death of a child's parents or if the parents are unable or unwilling to fulfil their parental role. Guardianship is a legal status that gives the guardian broadly the same rights and duties as those of a natural parent: for example, financial maintenance, care and custody, and responsibility for education.

guerrilla warfare, an 'indirect' military strategy, the essence of which is to avoid full-scale military confrontation while keeping the enemy under pressure with many small-scale skirmishes. The technique is suited to harsh terrain, particularly jungle and mountainous areas, and has been used effectively by materially weak forces against militarily strong opponents, where there are few opportunities for conventional military forces to use superior firepower in well-defined military 'fronts'. It can be used as part of a much larger conventional land war, or as a means of initiating revolutionary war or wars of national liberation. The opponents of guerrillas often deny them legitimacy by referring to them as *terrorists, as was the case in Zimbabwe in the 1970s. Guerrilla warfare is usually an 'intermediate' stage in a conflict used to gain administrative control of territory and political support from the populace; ultimate military success usually depends on transforming it into conventional warfare. The most spectacular success of such a strategy was the Chinese revolution, culminating in 1949. Other notable successes have been the Cuban revolution of 1959 and the wars in Indo-China of the 1950s and 1960s, in which neither the French nor the Americans were ultimately able to prevail despite apparently superior military power and technology. These wars produced three of the most prominent exponents of revolutionary guerrilla warfare: Mao Zedong, Che Guevara, and Vo Nguyen Giap respectively. On the other hand, many other guerrilla wars, particularly in South America, have been unsuccessful.

Gulf Co-operation Council (Co-operation Council for the Arab States of the Gulf; GCC), an organization of Arab Gulf states, established in 1981 to promote regional co-operation. The GCC has six members: Abu Dhabi, Bahrain, Kuwait, Oman, Qatar, and Saudi Arabia. Its headquarters are in Saudi Arabia. Initially seeking to encourage collaboration in economic, social, and cultural affairs, the GCC later extended its scope to cover common security problems, and in 1984 set up a joint defence force. It supported Iraq in the Iran–Iraq War (1980–8). The organization's failure to offer any decisive response to the Iraqi invasion of Kuwait in 1990 led to suggestions that it be strengthened and expanded. After the Gulf War ceasefire in February 1991, the GCC countries joined with Egypt and Syria in agreeing to set up an Arab peace force as part of a broader plan to strengthen regional security.

Gurdwara (Punjabi, 'door of the guru'), the Sikh place of worship. The term can refer to any place where the sacred book of the Sikhs, the *Adi Granth*, is kept, as well as to a temple. The centre-piece of the temple is a throne or dais holding the *Adi Granth*. The book, usually covered by a canopy, is brought out to be read early in the morning and returned to its resting place in the evening. It is fanned with a sceptre set with peacock feathers or animal hairs as a sign of its authority. There are no priests in *Sikhism; any Sikh, man or woman, may conduct a service. Worshippers cover their heads and remove their shoes when entering the temple. Men and women sit separately on the floor facing the sacred book. Portions of the text are read and hymns are sung to the accompaniment of music. *Karah parshad*, a mixture of semolina, clarified butter, sugar, and water, which has been stirred with a *kirpan* or dagger, is distributed at the end of the service. The Sikh temple is a community centre, visited by many people throughout the day, as well as a place of worship; it also contains a *langar*, or communal kitchen, where food is distributed. The holiest Sikh temple is the *Harimandir*, or Golden Temple, built in 1604 at Amritsar in the Punjab, India. The temple, which stands on a lake, has four doors, indicating that it is open to all *castes.

guru (Hindi, 'teacher', from Sanskrit, 'heavy'), in *Hinduism, a spiritual teacher who assists people in their search for God, leading them from darkness to enlightenment. Hindus are encouraged to seek a guru to help them attain *moksha*, or spiritual liberation. In *Sikhism, the term applies to any of the first ten leaders of the Sikh religion. Sikhism was founded in the 15th century by Guru *Nanak, whose authority and personality were transferred to nine further Gurus in succession. They include the third, Amar Das (1479–1574), who introduced the *langar*, or communal kitchen; the fifth, Arjan Dev (1563–1606), who founded the *Harimandir* or Golden Temple at Amritsar, compiled the *Adi Granth*, the Sikh holy book, and was martyred by the Mogul emperor Jahangir; and the tenth, *Gobind Singh, who founded the *Khalsa*, or army of soldier-saints. Before his death, he declared that the religious authority of the Guru was considered to be vested in the *Adi Granth* from that time on. The ten Sikh Gurus are seen as perfect men who have achieved spiritual union with God and have escaped from the cycle of *reincarnation.

gymnastics, a competitive sport demanding strength, agility, and artistic execution, practised at the highest level at the *Olympic Games. In national and international events, men compete in six set exercises: floor exercises, vault, pommel horse, parallel bars, horizontal bars, and rings. Women compete in four: floor exercises, vault, beam, and asymmetrical bars. Competitors are required to perform two routines on each apparatus, one a compulsory set and the other of the athlete's own devising. Marks are awarded by judges out of ten. At a more everyday level, the term gymnastics also covers a broader range of fitness exercises, using apparatus such as that mentioned above and carried out in a gymnasium, which, in English-speaking countries, means a room or hall set aside for physical activities.

Central European **gypsies**, or Tziganes, in their traditional hooped wagon, a reminder of the brightly painted caravans once associated with the gypsy people.

gypsies (from 'Egypt', supposed to be their place of origin), also known as Romany (from Romany, *Rom*, man), a nomadic people originating in northern India and today found mostly in Europe and parts of North Africa, and also in North and South America. It is estimated that there are some 6 million gypsies world-wide, speaking a distinct *Indo-Iranian language, Romany. Traditionally, gypsies were *nomads who travelled in groups of households of varying sizes, under the authority of a chief, who is elected for life. They worked as horse-traders, metal- or basket-workers, wood-carvers, and fortune-tellers. Gypsy music, performed in public exclusively by men, remains highly popular and lucrative in Central Europe. The gypsy code demands that women be subservient to men and that married women always wear a headscarf. Gypsies have often been persecuted, most notably under the Nazis when some 500,000 perished between 1933 and 1945. Post-war communist regimes throughout Eastern Europe forced gypsies to settle in high-rise housing blocks in industrial towns, breaking up extended families and forcing them to work in factories. Post-communist governments have allowed gypsies to form political parties and to campaign for recognition as an ethnic minority. Associations and pressure groups such as the Hungarian 'Phralipe' (Romany, 'brotherhood') have been formed to campaign for special schools and for books in the Romany language. However, the majority still face racial discrimination, are poorly housed, often unemployed, and have a lower life expectancy than their compatriots.

habeas corpus (Latin, 'you must have the body'), an ancient *common-law right which, in the form developed in England since the 15th century, requires an official to provide legal justification before the courts for the imprisonment of a detained person. A habeas corpus writ is a means of testing whether a person has been accorded full legal rights (see *due process in law); it does not establish his or her guilt or innocence. It is regarded as a crucial safeguard of the rights of the individual, providing practical and symbolic protection against arbitrary imprisonment in England and Wales, and other countries whose legal systems have developed from the English, such as the USA, Canada, Australia, and New Zealand. Habeas corpus is generally not found in *civil law systems, although in some cases comparable legislation exists. The *International Covenant on Civil and Political Rights stipulates comparable legal justification in court for arrest or detention. (See also *detention without trial.)

Habermas, Jürgen (1929–   ), German philosopher and social theorist. Habermas is the leading contemporary representative of the *Frankfurt School of *critical theory. His central concern is with the problem of knowledge, and in particular with finding a rational vantage-point from which the practices and belief systems of *capitalism can be criticized. In his first major book, *Knowledge and Human Interests* (1968), he argued that there were three basic forms of knowledge, corresponding to three central human interests: technical control over nature, understanding and communicating with others, and liberating ourselves from domination. Under capitalism the first interest and its corresponding form of knowledge, empirical science, has become dominant. Later, Habermas attempted to identify an alternative form of rationality by looking at what people must assume about one another if they are going to communicate (for instance, that each sincerely believes what he asserts). These presuppositions of rational *communication are invoked to define an 'ideal speech situation', in which only argumentative means may be used to convince others of the truth of propositions. Habermas believed that the legitimacy of social *norms can be assessed by asking whether they would be accepted in such an ideal speech situation.

hadīth (Arabic, 'traditions'), the teachings and acts of *Muhammad and his followers, constituting the *sunna*, or 'rules of life', the basis of the *sharī'ah. Although disputed, the *hadīth* are highly revered sources of historical, moral, religious, and ritual authority, second only to the authority of the *Koran. Six *hadīth* collections, chiefly the one compiled by Bukhari (AD 810–70), are accepted as authoritative by orthodox *Sunnīs, whilst five, based upon the authority of the Caliph 'Alī and the other *imāms*, are accepted by *Shī'īs.

hajj   *pilgrimage.

hallucination, a sensation or perception experienced as real but without any external stimulus. An hallucination can occur in any of the five senses. Drugs, exhaustion, and sensory deprivation can produce hallucinations in normal people. Different kinds of hallucination are associated with different pathological conditions. For example, 'organic' *psychoses (caused by degenerative changes in the brain) may produce fragmentary visual hallucinations, while hallucinations in the form of voices which speak about the patient are a primary symptom of *schizophrenia, one of the 'functional' psychoses.

Hanukkah (Feast of Lights or Dedication), Jewish festival which lasts eight days during November or December. The festival commemorates the cleansing of the Temple in Jerusalem by Judas Maccabeus in 165 BC, after it had been given over to idolatry by Antiochus Epiphanes, who denied the Jews access. An eight-branched receptacle for oil or candles (*menorah*) is lit, signifying, among other things, the seven days of creation. On each day of Hanukkah, one more candle is lit, and the ceremony culminates in games and the exchange of presents.

hara-kiri (Japanese, 'belly-cutting'), the Western term for ritual suicide, more properly termed *seppuku*, practised by Japanese samurai warriors. In *Zen Buddhism the belly is the spiritual centre of the body, thus hara-kiri may be understood as a spiritual act. The samurai preferred death to dishonour, and *seppuku*, a legal and ceremonial process, was performed to avoid disgrace, to atone for a failure of duty, or to demonstrate loyalty and resolve. (See also *bushido*.)

Hare Krishna (International Society for Krishna Consciousness), a modern Hindu sect brought to the West in the 1960s by A. C. Bhaktivedanta Swami, and based on the teachings of Guru Chaitanya (1486–1534). Members attend temple services or dedicate themselves fully to an austere, monastic life of service and devotion to Krishna. The way of Krishna Consciousness forbids alcohol and demands a vegetarian diet. Followers stress the spiritual benefits of music, ecstatic trance, and chanting, particularly the *mantra 'Hare Krishna, Hare Rama', as a way of concentrating the mind in devotion on Krishna's various manifestations in the *avatars of *Vishnu. Full members often assume Hindu dress and customs, and are encouraged to chant and proselytize in the streets.

Hasidim (from Hebrew, 'pious'), a mystical movement within *Judaism, which first found expression in 12th-century Germany. Modern Hasidim evolved in 18th-century Poland, where its leader, Ba'al Shem Tov (1700–60), taught a return to faith and piety. The movement was influenced by the *Kabbalah, and advocated repeated prayer, song, chanting, and dance as joyous ways of perceiving God in all aspects of daily life. After rapid growth amongst the repressed Jewish communities of eastern Europe, the movement was curtailed by the rise of modernism. Today the largest groups of Hasidim are to be found in the USA and Israel, where their leaders, *zaddikim* ('saints'), are in the forefront of the movement for religious legislation, and are determined defenders of *Orthodox Judaism. Followers are distinguished by their black dress, reminiscent of clothes worn in Poland in the 17th–18th centuries, and curled sidelocks, as well as by their acceptance of the Orthodox Jewish prohibition against cutting the beard, which probably originated in a wish to be distinguished from unbelievers.

Hausa, the most numerous of the peoples of north-western Nigeria and southern Niger. Their traditional trading activities contributed to the spread of the Hausa language as a *lingua franca throughout most of West Africa (see *Chadic languages). Many Hausa were converted to Islam in the 13th century. Their society is hierarchical, consisting of several hereditary classes. In the wet season, the land is cultivated collectively by members of a patrilineage; millet, sorghum, and maize are grown for subsistence, while cotton, tobacco, and groundnuts are important cash crops. In the dry season, the Hausa take time off to travel or to trade.

havan (from Sanskrit, 'homa', 'fire offering'), one of the elements of Hindu worship, or *pūjā. It originates from the sacrificial fire of the Vedic rites. The priest lights a sacred fire on a portable altar and throws melted butter (ghee) on it. In wedding ceremonies, the bride and groom take seven steps around the sacrificial fire.

Hayek, Friedrich August von (1899–1992), Austrian-born economist and political scientist. A prolific writer, Hayek was a *libertarian, famous for his strong defence of *laissez-faire liberalism and *free-market economics. His tract, *The Road to Serfdom* (1944), condemned social democracy and the *welfare state as harbingers of *totalitarianism. In economic theory he emphasized the importance of market prices as disseminators of information to market participants, both about each others' behaviour and about technological possibilities. He also made contributions to capital theory and *trade-cycle theory.

head of state, the office which personifies the *state in law and international relations. This may be a ceremonial position: in countries like the UK, Belgium, Norway, Sweden, The Netherlands, Spain, and Thailand, the head of state is a constitutional *monarch who reigns but does not rule. In other countries, such as Germany, India, Switzerland, and Greece, the head of state is a symbolic *president who car-

Following the traditions of **Hasidim** these Jews in Stamford Hill, London are wearing orthodox costume for prayers: each wears a skull-cap (*yarmelka*) to cover his head, a prayer shawl (*tallit*), and phylacteries (*tephillin*)—boxes containing portions of the Torah—tied to his forehead and left upper arm.

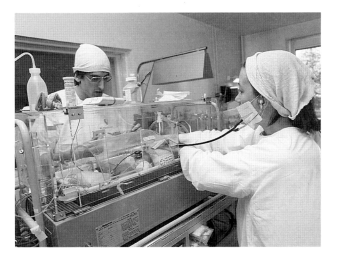

The expansion of sophisticated medical techniques since World War II has led to an ever-growing bill for **health care**. In the consequent struggle for resources care for premature babies, who need expensive equipment and intensive nursing, may suffer.

ries out mainly ceremonial duties. The head of state can, however, hold executive power and responsibilities, as in the US, or in France, where the president wields important political power, including the appointment of the *prime minister.

healing, the curing of a sickness or disorder, a key activity in every society. Since ancient civilization, both simple and complex methods of healing have existed, many of which are still common today. Different healing systems around the world include Western medicine, homoeopathy, and *Ayurvedic medicine. All healing depends upon a particular theory of the human body and the nature of sickness. Much of Western medicine, for instance, is based around the notion of germs and viruses which attack the body. Other systems are based upon belief in non-physical causes and cures for sickness. In many parts of the world, ideas of *spirit possession and *witchcraft are common explanations for illness. In India, for example, sickness is often ascribed to evil spirits which have entered the body. The banishing or exorcism of this spirit, through charms, spells, and sometimes physical means, cures the patient. Belief plays a vital role, as it does in all healing. Here, religious belief, and emotional and bodily well-being are linked; sickness is seen as spiritual and not just physical. Different systems are often used together, depending upon local beliefs. Healers are usually specialists, but small-scale healing methods may also be practised by non-experts. Herbal medicine and first aid are both examples. In most systems, however, there are ailments where only specialists can effect a cure. Their power to do this usually depends upon their knowledge. This may be passed in secret from practitioner to practitioner. Ideas of the spiritual power of the healer may also be of importance. The practice of Western medicine depends largely on knowledge, for instance, whilst exorcists of spirits are usually believed to possess special religious powers.

health-care finance, the financing of a country's health-care system, either through insurance schemes or by government *taxation. In some countries, such as the USA, health insurance is voluntary and health care is financed through a combination of private insurance and government schemes, such as Medicare for the elderly and Medicaid for the poor. In most European countries health insurance is compulsory. Funding through taxation can be by central government, as in the UK, or by local government, as in Sweden. In developing countries, it is common for basic health services to be funded by the government, with the wealthy paying directly for more sophisticated facilities. The rising costs of health care, caused primarily by the cost of high technology medicine and by *ageing populations, are a universal problem. A rich country typically spends 8 per cent of GNP on health, while a poor country may spend less than 1 per cent of a much lower GNP. Yet the amount a country spends does not correlate exactly with the level of health. A study by UNICEF of countries with a low per capita GNP found huge disparities: at one extreme, exemplified by Afghanistan, one child in three may be expected to die before reaching the age of 5 compared with one in twenty in China and Sri Lanka. The high level of achievement in China and Sri Lanka did not require heavy health spending, but rather a coherent approach backed by political leadership and popular support using *public health, *preventive medicine, *primary health care, and, in the case of China, the integration of traditional and modern medicine. Targeting resources on the most vulnerable, as in a special programme for mothers and children in Chile,

A power station in Bitterfeld, Germany, belches pollution into the air. The lack of environmental controls on **heavy industry** in former Soviet-bloc countries has left a legacy of serious health hazards, with high levels of respiratory diseases in industrial areas.

which achieved a 40 per cent reduction in infant mortality at a time of economic instability, is also beneficial. The World Health Organization recommends such approaches to the cost-effective use of health finance.

health screening, a way of detecting disease by examining people before they show symptoms. In developed countries, pregnant women are often screened for diseases which may affect the health of the foetus, such as syphilis or diabetes, and the foetus may be screened for a range of abnormalities such as spina bifida or Down's Syndrome. Infants and children are routinely screened for defects in hearing or vision, and adults may be screened for cervical *cancer, *heart disease, or *Aids. Screening programmes have had some notable successes in detecting and thereby reducing certain diseases (tuberculosis and glaucoma are examples), but there are drawbacks. Some tests, such as chorionic villus sampling for foetal abnormality, may not be completely safe. Other tests may not be very accurate, while screening many people in order to detect a few cases of disease can be expensive. Also, there may be little point in detecting a disease early if little can be done to treat it, or if early treatment has no advantage over later treatment. These difficulties have slowed the development of breast-cancer screening programmes, and make it likely that mass screening will remain confined to a few diseases.

heart disease (cardio-vascular disease), a congenital or acquired abnormality in the structure or function of the heart. It is estimated that about half the deaths in the developed world are caused by cardio-vascular disease. Some aspects of the modern Western way of life have been identified as risk factors for the disease, particularly *smoking, excessive consumption of animal fats, *stress, and lack of exercise. There is evidence to suggest that heart attacks can be prevented (or at least postponed) if people change their behaviour. However, there are other factors such as family predisposition, sex (men are more prone to the disease than women, who are conferred a degree of protection by female hormones), and high blood-pressure. In developing countries, cardio-vascular disease accounts for an increasing proportion of deaths, following changes in the way people live, particularly in urban areas. In Brazil, for instance, it is already the most common cause of death. This imposes further burdens on over-stretched health-care systems.

heaven, a place believed to be the dwelling place of God, and of the righteous after death. In Judaeo-Christian belief, heaven is a state in which, after judgement, the saved *soul sees God face to face in the beatific vision. In traditional Christian belief, the human body, in a glorified form, will be reunited with the soul in heaven after the Last Judgement. In Islamic belief, heaven is depicted as a blissful paradise of material delights, a description which is generally supposed to be more allegorical than literal. In Eastern religions, concepts of heaven vary. *Pure Land Buddhist sects believe that followers can be born into a paradisical state through devotion to the *Buddha Amitābha, but the true goal of *Hinduism and *Buddhism is *nirvana, a state of enlightenment and union with the divine. Until that state is reached, the cycle of *reincarnation can include rebirth in temporary heavens and *hells.

heavy industry, a broad grouping of large-scale industries, usually operating with heavy machinery or plant, which require extensive capital investment. Heavy industry includes metal-processing such as steel and iron manufacturing, petroleum-refining, hydroelectric plants, motor-vehicle production, and so on. Heavy industry has declined in relative importance in the second half of the 20th century, and has been held responsible for much environmental damage and *pollution.

Hebrew language   *Semitic languages.

hedging, action taken to avoid the risks of possible future changes in prices. To hedge against *inflation, *assets can be bought which rise in nominal *value at or above the rate of inflation. Such assets may include *land, *securities, or index-linked assets (see *indexation). To hedge against changes in the prices of specific goods over a specific period of time, *futures markets (where they exist) can be used. Producers may reduce or eliminate the risk of making a loss as a result of falling output prices by selling their output in advance on a futures market. More commonly, exporters who incur production *costs in terms of their domestic *currency but who invoice in terms of a foreign currency may wish to sell their anticipated sales receipts on the forward exchange market.

hedonism, both an ethical view and a psychological theory. As an ethical view, hedonism states that the only things that have value in themselves are states of pleasure or happiness. As a psychological theory, hedonism states that all action is determined and explained by the desire for pleasure or happiness. Hedonism in this second sense seems to conflict with the view that people are, at least sometimes, motivated by moral requirements and that they may prefer to sacrifice their own prospects for the sake of others, making hedonism akin to *egoism. *Mill defended hedonism in both senses as part of his argument for *utilitarianism.

Hegel, George Wilhelm Friedrich (1770–1831), German philosopher, strongly influenced by Romanticism, and *idealist successor to *Kant. Hegel began by modifying Kant's metaphysical system in two fundamental respects: he argued that Kant's division of reality into knowable and unknowable realms was incoherent, and he introduced the dimension of history. The system that resulted (elaborated in *The Phenomenology of Mind*, 1807) viewed the world as the evolution of *Geist*, or Spirit, in a direction of increasing rationality, as *Geist* attained ever higher levels of self-consciousness. This process was for Hegel to be described by means of the *dialectic, a form of logic quite different from *deduction, in which each stage of history is composed of a thesis, contradicted by an antithesis, out of whose conflict there emerges a new and higher thesis, which is contradicted by a new antithesis, and so on. Hegel's *monistic vision, in which history is governed by necessary laws, and the world forms an organic whole, proclaimed that 'the rational is the real'.

hegemony (from Greek, 'leader'), leadership, especially by a state which exercises dominance within an international system, other states having to define their positions in relation to this dominant state. Within the study of *international relations, the term is exclusively applied to the industrialized nations of the developed world. According to the hegemonic stability theory developed by US theorists in the 1970s, stability within international economic relationships is dependent on the dominance of one power, which establishes a framework of rules and expectations, and encourages compliance with them. Recent discussion has concerned the decline of US hegemony in the political and economic world order. In *War and Change in World Politics* (1984), the US political theorist Robert Gilpin used the term hegemonic war to denote major wars which occur when the leading power in the international system changes. In another sense, hegemony is the dominance of a class within the state over the remaining classes. The latter sense is due chiefly to the Italian Marxist *Gramsci. According to Gramsci, the ruling class exercised hegemony by manipulating the institutions of civil society (such as the media, the schools, the churches) so that its own beliefs and values were foisted upon the rest of society.

Heidegger, Martin (1889–1976), German philosopher, a student of Husserl (see *phenomenology) and important contributor to *existentialism. In his central work, *Being and Time* (1927), Heidegger attempted to return philosophy to contemplation of what he took to be the outstandingly important question, 'What is being?' Though he never claimed to be able to answer this question, Heidegger evolved a new philosophical vocabulary in which traditional *metaphysics and *epistemology gave way to an analysis of the distinctive features of human existence (referred to by Heidegger as *Dasein*, 'being there'). Heidegger's philosophical achievement is sometimes argued to be tainted by his involvement with *Nazism.

hell, the abode of evil spirits, and the place where the wicked are believed to be condemned to eternal punishment after death. In *Judaism, the notion of *Sheol*, the shadowy underworld of departed souls, gave way to that of *Gehenna*, a place for punishing the wicked. Christian theologians today define hell as the eternal deprivation of God's presence, the logical outcome of the soul's adherence to its own will and rejection of the will of God. It is traditionally described as a fiery subterranean abyss, populated by demons and ruled over by Satan or Lucifer, a fallen angel who rebelled against God and was cast out of *heaven. *Islam also depicts hell (*Jahannam*, a name derived from *Gehenna*) as full of fire and torment, but punishment there is not necessarily eternal. In Hindu and Buddhist belief there are multiple hells (as there are multiple heavens) through which beings may pass as part of the cycle of *reincarnation.

heredity   *behaviour genetics.

higher education, formal education after completion of a full *secondary education. It takes place in a university or place of similar status, such as some teachers' colleges and polytechnics, is usually full-time, and leads to the award of a degree. Like 'tertiary education' the term higher education sometimes embraces any formal education after secondary school, including shorter courses that are of below degree level. In industrialized countries and much of Latin America, about one in four young adults, men and women, is now able to attend a university or training college. However, in both Africa and the Indian sub-continent, tertiary education is available to fewer than 10 per cent of young men and fewer than 5 per cent of young women. The relatively high cost of higher education—it is some twenty-five times more expensive per student year than primary education—is a major factor in development and education policies. Most first-degree courses last three or four years (longer for professions such as medicine), and a minority of graduates go on to an advanced master's or doctor's degree course. Research is an important activity in most higher education institutions. Current trends include a greater emphasis on *vocational education, an increasing proportion of women students and number of mature students, and the introduction of new methods of study such as *distance learning and use of the television, as in the UK's Open University. (See also *continuing education.)

hi-jacking, the takeover of an aircraft, ship, train, bus, or other vehicle, usually in passage, in order to achieve some criminal or political objective. During the 1960s the term was applied to the takeover of planes in an attempt to seek political asylum or as a terrorist act carried out by or on behalf of groups seeking political objectives. The 1970s saw many hi-jackings, a number of which were carried out by groups with an interest in the Arab–Israeli conflict. The Convention for the Suppression of Unlawful Seizure of Aircraft (The Hague, 1970), and the Convention for the Suppression of Unlawful Acts against the Safety of Civil Aircraft (Montreal, 1971), as well as increased airport security, have proved effective in reducing the incidence of hi-jacking.

hijrah (Arabic, emigration), the departure of *Muḥammad and following him of about one hundred followers separately from Mecca, where they faced opposition and persecution, to Medina in AD 622, from where Muḥammad's teaching spread. The significance of this event was realized during the reign of the *Caliph 'Umar, who made 622 the first year of the *Islamic calendar, in recognition that the community phase of Islam dates from then.

Hindi language *Indo-Iranian languages.

Hindu festivals. The Hindu religious year is based on a lunar calendar. Each lunar month is divided into two, the 'light' half, the fortnight approaching the new moon, and the 'dark' half, the fortnight following its wane. There is no characteristic Hindu year, since Hindus celebrate hundreds of different festivals, which vary from place to place. The following are some of the main ones: *Dīvālī ('Festival of Lights') in October or November celebrates the new year. *Holi is a joyful spring festival in February or March. The birth of Rāma is celebrated in April or May with the nine-day festival of Rāma-navami, during which stories from the *Rāmāyana are narrated. Rāksha Bandan (July or August), celebrated mainly in northern and western India, marks the middle of the monsoon. During this festival, women tie threads symbolizing mutual protection around their brothers' wrists. In August or September, Janmashtami commemorates the birth of Krishna, while September or October sees the major festival of Navarātri (another nine-day festival), connected with the autumnal equinox. During this time *Durgā-pūjā, commemorating the Great Goddess Durgā, is celebrated, and the nine-day festival ends with Dussehra, commemorating the death of Rāvana, as recounted in the Rāmāyana.

Hinduism, the religion of the majority of the people of India. Because of its evolution over more than 4,000 years, Hinduism embraces a vast diversity of religious beliefs and practices, and is neither dogmatic nor evangelical. Despite the lack of a binding theological creed, several features unify Hindu consciousness. One is respect for the *Vedas, the earliest Hindu sacred texts. Fundamental to many schools of Hindu philosophical thought (in particular Vedānta) is the belief in an eternal and all-pervading principle of ultimate reality, *Brahman. Brahman itself is without individual per-

A mandala shrine to Durgā, the great goddess who reflects the matriarchal tendency of the early influences of **Hinduism**. She is portrayed as a powerful creative–destructive energy, sometimes ferocious, sometimes serene, and is the object of intense devotion amongst followers.

sonality, but for most Hindus, religious worship on a practical level is directed towards numerous personal gods and goddesses, the most important being *Vishnu, *Shiva, and the Great Goddess (*Shakti, Durgā, or *Kālī). Each of these is the object of monotheistic devotion, and their individual cults (Vaishnavism, Shaivism, and Shāktism) constitute in practice the three major forms of Hinduism. Most Hindus regard the sacredness of the land of India and the *caste system as central to their religion. Other common teachings concern the moral law of cause and effect (*karma), the nature of the soul (*ātman), reincarnation (*samsara), and, for many Hindu traditions, the possibility of union with Brahman through *moksha, or spiritual liberation. Running through Hinduism is a constant tension between the importance of one's duty in society (dharma) and the ideal of world renunciation, a conflict which is illustrated in the *Bhagavadgītā ('Song of the Lord'), part of the epic poem the *Mahābhārata. Hindu worship (*pūjā) is based at home, at a local shrine, or within the mandir (*Hindu temple), and it includes essential daily rituals, popular public celebrations of festivals, familial rites of passage, and non-essential but highly regarded acts such as pilgrimage to one of India's many sites of religious significance, most notably the River Ganges and the town of Varanasi (Benares). Hinduism is followed by approximately 600 million Indians, and, through migration, has spread to East Africa, South Africa, Southeast Asia, the Caribbean, Canada, the USA, and the UK.

Hindu law, the attempt to systematize and order the personal conduct and religious duties of Hindus around the world. Traditionally, a body of guidelines and principles of conduct for Hindus was found in the *shāstra* (treatises). Of these the *Dharmashastra*, composed mostly in verse from the 6th century BC to the 18th century AD, which are treatises on the *dharma, or spiritual obligations in keeping with the material and moral order of the universe, are the closest to law in the Western sense. Hinduism has few universal norms of conduct, but rather diversity in behaviour is expected according to differences in age, gender, and social background. Nor was there any central legal or ecclesiastical authority capable of standardizing the norms of behaviour appropriate to such groups. Thus the *Dharmashastra* explicitly allow for variants of local custom. Through the concept of *dharma*, Hindu law has influenced the Buddhist societies of South-east Asia such as Myanmar (Burma), Thailand, and Cambodia (Kampuchea). In India, the British attempted in 1771 to codify the *Dharmashastra* according to the principles of English common law, and produced a hybrid Anglo-Hindu law. Since Indian independence in 1947, much Hindu law has been codified; it applies only to Hindus and co-exists with a secular legal system and with other systems of religious law, such as the *sharī'ah. Although all laws founded on the *caste system have been formally repealed, many Hindus still conduct themselves in accordance with these laws, for example, in avoiding mixed marriages.

Hindu revivalism, a term usually given to the many trends associated with Hindu responses in the 19th and early 20th centuries to the encounter with the West. It is also called a 'reformation', a 'renaissance', or 'neo-Hinduism'. It is characterized by the Hinduization of Western concepts or an interpretation of indigenous concepts in the light of Western categories. There are many thinkers and ideas associated with this process. Raja Ram Mohun Roy (1772–1833) was the forerunner of new Hinduism; he learned English, first located Hindu ideas in the context of Western ones in order to promote Hindu self-understanding and founded the reform movement the Brahmo Samaj (Society of God). Debendranath Tagore (1817–1905) was his successor as leader of the Society; he explicitly questioned the infallibility

of the *Vedas* and called for an experimental spirituality based on the aphorisms of the *Upanishads*. Keshab Chandra Sen (1838–84) sought inspirational sources within Hinduism which could demonstrate the universal harmony between experience in different religions, especially *Christianity and *Vedānta Hinduism. The most famous figure was Vivekananda (1863–1902) who claimed that Vedānta was the Hindu exemplification of that oneness to which all religions aspired and that the idea and practice of tolerance and universality were India's gift to the world; he admired Western self-confidence and scientific success, and formed a model of mutual influence in which the West taught its material skills to India which reciprocated with its spiritual teachings. Bankim Chandra Chatterji (1838–94) derived a claim for national self-assertion by attempting to give a secular and humanistic reading to the Hindu religious tradition. Dayanand Saraswati (1824–83), founder of the Arya Samaj (Society of Aryans) tried to emphasize the global significance of Vedic teachings by discerning scientific and technological ideas in them. Bal Gangadhar Tilak (1856–1920) harnessed Hindu cultural practices to the expression of nationalist sentiments; Madan Mohan Malaviya, founder of Benares Hindu University, aimed at combining Western methodology and traditional subjects of study; Bipin Chandra Pal (1858–1932) used his own tradition to articulate a political ideology for the first time in modern India; and Isvara Chandra Vidyasagar (1820–91) wrote books on Sanskrit grammar and Bengali history which drew on European rational methods. New Hindu thinking made certain characteristic assertions: Hinduism, as a religious doctrine, especially *Advaita Vedānta, has traditionally maintained open-minded acceptance of different traditions, and in a sense all other religions ultimately tend toward the same spiritual goals which Hinduism posits; Hindu universalism is a vehicle for the expression of Hindu self-assertion, for universalism is India's unique contribution to the world; the oneness of all beings affirmed in Advaita is the foundation of an ethic of social responsibility and reformative action, such that a viable Hindu moral philosophy is directly derivable from Hindu metaphysics; Hindu spirituality is necessary for the West, just as the dynamism of Western rationality and science will help modern India. The term

Hindu Temple

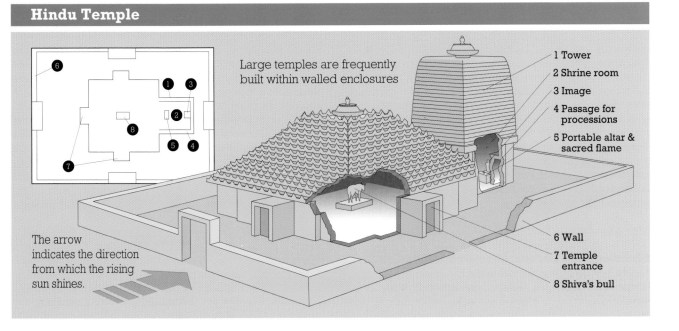

Large temples are frequently built within walled enclosures

1 Tower
2 Shrine room
3 Image
4 Passage for processions
5 Portable altar & sacred flame
6 Wall
7 Temple entrance
8 Shiva's bull

The arrow indicates the direction from which the rising sun shines.

Hindu revivalism is also used to describe the ideology of *nationalism based on allegedly Hindu values which is professed by some groups in contemporary Indian politics.

Hindu sacred texts, the writings, primarily in Sanskrit, originally part of an oral tradition, which constitute the scriptures of *Hinduism. They are divided into two main categories: *shruti* ('that which is heard') and *smriti* ('that which is remembered'). The *shruti* texts, regarded as divine revelation, consist of the *Vedas*, which were fixed in Sanskrit between 1500 and 500 BC. There are four original collections of texts, the oldest and most important being the *Rigveda*, hymns of praise. The four *Vedas* were later supplemented by further explanatory texts; the most significant of these are the *Upanishads*, which form the basis of the philosophical school of *Vedānta. The *smriti* texts are not considered to be divine revelation, but they too stem from a long oral tradition. They include the two great epic poems, the *Rāmāyana* and the *Mahābhārata. The latter contains the famous section known as the *Bhagavadgītā*, a philosophical work exploring the notion of duty. A supplement, the *Harivamsha* (*c.* AD 300–400), contains many stories about the boy *Krishna. Another *smriti* text is the *Laws of Manu* (*c.* AD 200–100 BC), which deals with religious ritual, law, and custom. Later texts include the *Yoga-Sūtras*, attributed to Patañjali (*c.* AD 200–300), and the *Purānas* (*c.* AD 400–1200), a popular collection of stories about the creation of the world and the lives of the gods. They have become the scriptures of the common people. Other texts in Hindi and Tamil are also considered to be sacred by some Hindus. There is, however, no single canon of authoritative literature whose contents are acceptable to all Hindus.

Hindu temple (*mandir*), the place of public worship for Hindus. Its basic shape is square, in order to signify the perfect ordering of space. The primary function of a temple is to provide a pure sanctuary for the deity, away from the pollution of the external world. Thus the most important part of the building is the shrine room, containing the image (*murti*) of the particular deity to whom the temple is dedicated. A tower (*sikhara*) rises above the shrine room, and around it runs a sheltered passageway (*pradakshinā*) for circumambulating the deity as part of worship. Near the shrine is a portable altar holding the sacred flame. The other parts of the temple are the entrance gateway and porch, which face east, and a pillared hall which leads to the shrine room by way of some steps. Worshippers sit on the floor of the hall, facing the shrine, and they join in the chanting and singing while the image is dressed in robes and welcomed as an honoured guest. Other statues and shrines are found throughout the temple. Some larger temples may be built within a walled enclosure and are approached through pyramid gateways (*gopura*). Such enclosures may also contain a stone statue, the vehicle (*vāhana*, 'mount'), and the traditional riding animal associated with the deity. While the temple is used for public worship or *pūjā, many Hindus also worship before their own private shrines at home. (See diagram on previous page.)

hire purchase *consumer.

historical and comparative linguistics, a type of *linguistics which studies the ways in which specific *languages have developed and the ways in which languages in general can change, and which seeks by comparing languages with a common ancestor to learn something about the nature of the ancestor. This type of linguistics was particularly important in the 19th century, when the details of the *Indo-European family of languages were mapped out. It was commonly known at that time as comparative philology. Recent work in historical linguistics has drawn on the insights of theoretical linguistics and *sociolinguistics.

historicism, the view that concepts and writings should not be regarded as if they were timeless, and that they should instead be understood in terms of the historical context in which they developed. To describe an approach as historicist is to say that it attempts to make sense of a text, idea, or theory by locating it with reference to its predecessors and seeing what historical forces influenced its production. It is a moot point whether or not historicism, when it is carried through consistently, implies *relativism: that is, that there is no truth outside particular historical outlooks. Historicism was first philosophically articulated in the 18th century by the Italian philosopher Giovanni Battista Vico (1668–1744), and later elaborated by *Hegel, for whom philosophical knowledge involved retracing the entire history of human thought.

Hobbes, Thomas (1588–1679), English political philosopher. He is famous chiefly for his defence of absolute government, mounted in the debate surrounding the English Civil War (1642–9), and best presented in his masterpiece *Leviathan* (1651). His political thinking was grounded in a materialist metaphysics and a pessimistic view of human beings as driven by innate passions, especially the fear of violent death. In the absence of government, these passions would lead men into interminable conflict with one another for the means of survival; human life would be 'solitary, poor, nasty, brutish and short'. Understanding this, rational men would agree to surrender all their rights to a sovereign capable of enforcing peace. The sovereign must have unlimited authority, and must permit no internal divisions of power, since, according to Hobbes, any such limitation or division would be a source of renewed conflict. Hobbes's bleak but remorselessly consistent philosophy won him few friends, but his case for unconditional submission to any government capable of preserving order remains a challenge to more liberal *social contract theories.

hockey, field, an amateur game most keenly pursued in the UK and Commonwealth countries and in Europe. Eleven players on each side use a hooked stick to hit or push a hard ball into their opponents' goal. The pitch, some 90 m (100 yards) long by 55 m (60 yards) wide, is similar in dimensions to various types of *football pitch but the goal is smaller, the posts being 3.6 m (4 yards) apart and the crossbar 2.1 m (7 feet) high. Scoring shots must be struck inside the 'circle', a semi-circular line of 15 m (16 yards) radius drawn around the goal. Increasingly goalkeepers wear thick body-padding to protect themselves, together with leg-guards, gloves, and a barred helmet. Hockey is a difficult game to keep flowing, especially on bumpy pitches, and clubs are turning increasingly to plastic, all-weather surfaces.

hockey, ice, a six-a-side skating version of field hockey played on ice with a puck or rubber disc. Originating in Canada in the 1870s, it is the fastest team game in the world. The rink should be some 60 m (200 feet) long and 26 m (85 feet) wide, surrounded by barrier boards up to 1.2 m (4 feet) high. All players wear specialized protective padding, the goalminders most of all. A team consists of some twenty

Field hockey

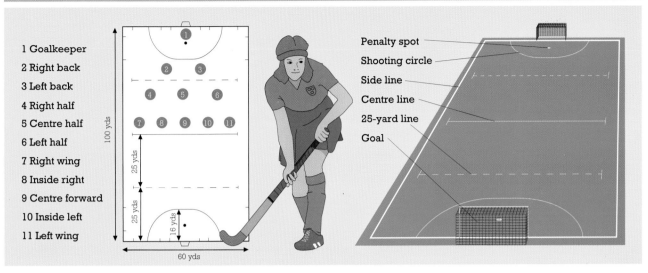

1 Goalkeeper
2 Right back
3 Left back
4 Right half
5 Centre half
6 Left half
7 Right wing
8 Inside right
9 Centre forward
10 Inside left
11 Left wing

Penalty spot
Shooting circle
Side line
Centre line
25-yard line
Goal

players who (usually with the exception of the goalminder) periodically replace each other on the ice. There are three periods of 20 minutes each. The world's top professionals play in the National Hockey League of North America. At the *Olympic Games the most prominent nations have been the USA, the former Soviet Union, Canada, Czechoslovakia, Sweden, and Finland.

holding company, a *company which owns enough of another to have control of it. The latter may be wholly owned or part-owned (commonly, but not necessarily, more than 50 per cent of the *shares). A holding company may have control of one or more companies, any of which may have far more *capital than the holding company itself (see *conglomerate). The advantages of a holding company are that it may be able to provide centralized management, financial, and marketing expertise, while preserving some of the relative efficiencies of small businesses.

Holi, major Hindu spring festival celebrated in northern India, occurring over the full moon in February or March, and originating from an ancient fertility festival. According to mythical tradition, the young prince Prahlāda, a worshipper of *Vishnu, survived an ordeal by fire despite the evil demoness Holikā. Bonfires are lit to symbolize the triumph of good over evil. The festival is also associated with the merry pranks of the young *Krishna, and it is celebrated in boisterous and sometimes licentious ways. The usual restrictions of *caste and gender are disregarded, and participants enjoy throwing coloured water and powdered dyes at each other.

holism *atomism.

homelessness, the problem of those lacking a home. In all countries, those most at risk of homelessness have low, unstable or negligible incomes, have been forced to move by *war or *communal conflict (see *refugee) or the need to find work (see *migration) or are disadvantaged by racial *discrimination, or by mental or physical *disability. Homelessness is defined in international reports in two ways. According to the narrower definition, the homeless are those who lack any shelter, such as people living in public places such as railway stations and parks. Immediate ways of

reducing their numbers include increasing the supply of cheap rented accommodation, ensuring that those who are disabled receive appropriate care, and providing emergency shelters. According to the broader definition, the homeless include not only those sleeping outside, but also people who do not have adequate shelter with defined legal rights as owners or tenants. They may be forced to rely on temporary hostels in towns or communal shacks in the countryside, or to live in dangerous and insanitary *shanty towns or *squatter camps. The UN estimates that their numbers exceed 1

Ice hockey

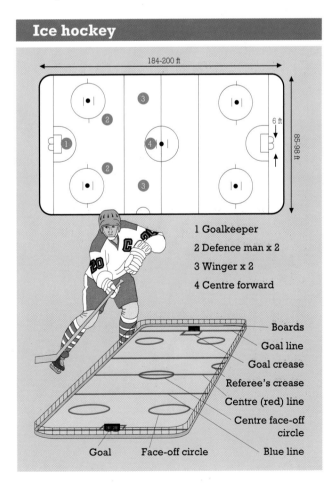

1 Goalkeeper
2 Defence man x 2
3 Winger x 2
4 Centre forward

Boards
Goal line
Goal crease
Referee's crease
Centre (red) line
Centre face-off circle
Blue line

Goal   Face-off circle

billion world-wide. Among the policies advocated to tackle this broader problem are government action to increase the supply and reduce the cost of housing to people on low incomes (for example, by ensuring easier access to credit to permit the purchase of housing, or of land and materials so that people can build themselves); the enhancement of the earning capacity of the poor through training schemes so that they can afford better accommodation; and the provision of low cost *government housing and of subsidized housing managed by non-profit organizations such as churches, co-operatives, and housing associations.

homicide, the killing of a human being by another. Some homicide may be considered lawful, as when a convicted offender is executed by the state, or excusable, as in self-defence. Unlawful homicide is treated by almost all legal systems as a crime of extreme gravity. Homicide is often categorized into different types, which attract different punishments. Within the UK legal system and many which are related to it (see *common law systems), two major categories are recognized: murder and manslaughter. In both murder and manslaughter, the *actus reus* ('guilty act') is identical: the unlawful killing of the victim, but the categorization of the act depends on the offender's *criminal responsibility. Murder requires the offender to have killed the victim with 'malice aforethought' (that is intending to kill or to cause grievous injury), while manslaughter does not. In *civil law systems, all unlawful killings are usually classified as homicide, but there may be different penalties, according to the circumstances of the crime. In many jurisdictions, the punishment for deliberate murder is the *death penalty. In English law, the mandatory death penalty was replaced in

Shakespearian actor Ian McKellan and the Member of Parliament Peter Tatchell join a demonstration in 1988 against Section 28 of the British Local Government Act. This section prohibits local authorities from 'intentionally promoting **homosexuality**' and has been considered to undermine equal opportunities for all citizens.

1965 by a mandatory life sentence. In practice, life is an indeterminate sentence, which may be longer or shorter than a fixed term of imprisonment. The offender may, after a number of years, be released on licence, which means remaining under the surveillance of the police and *probation service for the duration of his or her life, and submitting to restrictions such as limitations on travel.

homosexuality, a sexual preference for members of one's own sex, distinguished from heterosexuality (preference for members of the opposite sex) and bisexuality (attraction towards either sex). Homosexual women are usually known as lesbians (from the Greek island of Lesbos, home of the 7th-century BC homosexual poet Sappho). At different times and in different cultures, homosexual behaviour has been approved of, tolerated, or banned. Christian doctrine, for example, following St Paul and upheld by the Roman Catholic and some Anglican Churches, has traditionally frowned upon homosexuality. Estimates of the occurrence of homosexuality vary, as do theories of its cause. There is a conflict between theories of nature and those of nurture (see *behaviour genetics). Early psychologists, such as Richard von Krafft-Ebing (1840–1902) and Havelock Ellis (1859–1939), regarded homosexuality as a congenital condition which was a deviation from the norm. There is some evidence, from the study of identical and non-identical twins (see *behaviour genetics), that genetic factors may enter into homosexuality, but other theorists suggest that it is determined by critical childhood experiences, or by *social learning. Lack of available contact with the opposite sex (as in prisons, military camps, or boarding schools) may be a cause of homosexual behaviour in individuals who generally think of themselves as heterosexual, and this factor, as well as the wide variation in the extent and acceptability of homosexual behaviour in different societies, also suggests that it is in part socially determined. For many years in Western societies homosexuality was subject to social disapproval and legal punishment. Nowadays, however, it is more commonly argued that homosexuality should be regarded as a variant

of sexual behaviour, and not as a pathological condition. Homosexual behaviour between adults in private is generally legal in most states of the USA and in Europe; in the UK, it was made legal in 1967, although it is still illegal to commit homosexual acts with a young person under 21, or to commit homosexual acts in public places. In recent years, following the civil rights movements of the 1960s, many homosexuals have publicly acknowledged their sexual preferences (a process known as 'coming out'), and have chosen to describe themselves as 'gay'. They have demanded equal rights in such matters as housing or employment practices, and the right for their partnerships to be treated on an equal footing with heterosexual marriages. However, the spread of *Aids among male homosexuals has led, in some instances, to a resurgence of *discrimination.

honour, adherence to what is right or an accepted standard of conduct; a reputation for this. It is a concept closely related to that of shame, the sense of having acted improperly. Anthropologists distinguish 'shame cultures' from 'guilt cultures'. A shame culture is held to conform to external pressures, while a guilt culture is held to rely on 'internalized conviction of sin'. Shame is often associated with closely controlled sexual behaviour and careful covering of the body, particularly in the case of women. The concepts of honour and shame are particularly prevalent in Mediterranean and Middle Eastern societies. Here, family pride and honour are seen as crucial, and members often defend it at great cost. Because of this, vendettas or *feuds may be taken out against individuals who have harmed the group, in order to restore its members' honour. The reputation of women is central to family honour: if daughters have illicit sexual relations, or act improperly in other ways, the honour of all family members is damaged. In 20th-century Japan, for example, the code of honour is extended to the place of work, reflecting the diminution of importance of *kinship groups in industrialized societies.

Hopi, a group of pueblo (village)-dwelling Indians in northeastern Arizona in the USA. The Hopi are sedentary farmers, growing maize, beans, and cotton, with some sheep farming. Each village is divided into clans, which are ruled by a chief, who is also the religious leader. Although a very small group, their religious and ritual life has captured the imagination of European artists and writers.

horse-racing, the sport in which specially bred and trained horses race against each other before spectators, many of whom bet enthusiastically on the outcome of each race (see *gambling). In the UK, the chief categories are flat-racing—a summer sport organized by the Jockey Club—and jump-racing, a winter sport subdivided into hurdle-racing and steeplechasing and organized according to National Hunt rules. Most jockeys taking part in these programmes are professional; for amateur riders, there are point-to-point races held over cross-country courses and organized by local hunts. Top horses and jockeys now travel the world to race. Other major horse-racing countries are Ireland, France, Italy, and the USA. Also popular in North America is trotting, or harness-racing, in which the driver sits behind the horse in a cart or sulky.

horse-riding, the international pastime of owning or hiring a horse or pony and taking it out for rides either alone or in an organized expedition. The term also covers a group of competitive activities that are distinct from *horse-racing

and are known as equestrian events. Dressage involves a series of tests to reveal how a horse moves and to measure its development and state of training. Show-jumping is more spectacular and tests both horse and rider over a series of fences; in competitions, time is as much a decisive factor as the horse's ability to jump a clear round. Three-day eventing is an all-round test with separate competitions each day for dressage, speed, and jumping ability over a cross-country course, and with show-jumping on the final day.

horseshoe-pitching, a game played by two or more contestants in which the objective is to throw a horseshoe so that it encircles a 35.5 cm (14 inch) vertical iron peg. The standard pitching distance is 14.57 m (40 feet) for men and 10.93 m (30 feet) for women. It is popular in the USA where annual world competitions are held. Quoits is similar to horseshoe-pitching except that metal (or rope) rings are pitched on to pegs that are 2.5 cm (1 inch) high—from 9.1 m (30 feet) for men and 6.0 m (20 feet) for women. Quoits is a common pastime on board ship.

hospital, an institution providing medical or surgical treatment, as well as nursing care for the ill or injured. A typical general hospital in a modern health system investigates and treats a wide range of patients requiring medical care or surgery. The majority of people in rich countries are born in a hospital and die in one. Hospitals with special functions include hospitals, often long-stay, for those with psychiatric illnesses or the elderly. Another kind of hospital, the hospice, aims to bring peace and comfort to the dying by offering expert care and a tranquil atmosphere. In recent years, the central role of the hospital within the *health-care system has been questioned. In the world's rich countries, control of the escalating costs is sought by restricting drugs and equipment, reducing the length of patients' stay so as to use beds and operating theatres more intensively, placing greater responsibilities on *paramedical workers, *primary health care, *social care services, and families, and increasing doctors' accountability. Developing countries can seldom afford an adequate number of well-equipped hospitals, and access is often restricted to the rich or those in big cities. Despite this, it is quite common for hospitals to account for two-thirds of total government expenditure on health and for one-half of this to be the cost of one or two major national hospitals. In response, many governments are trying to increase the cost-effectiveness of their hospitals, and to divert expenditure to *preventive medicine. Thus, for example, in Pakistan, a nation-wide *immunization effort was financed by postponing for five years the building of a single urban hospital.

hostage-taking, the capture and holding of persons as bargaining counters. Criminal hostage-taking usually has the purpose of extorting money from individuals, companies, or governments, or is used as a means of escaping capture during or after a criminal act. Political terrorist organizations may use hostage-taking to extort money in order to finance their organizations, but they also use such actions as a means of achieving political objectives. For example, often hostages are taken to bargain for the release of convicted terrorists held in prison. Hostage-taking has become a particular feature of the complex international politics of the Middle East, where hostage-taking has been used covertly by governments in order to exert political pressure on neighbouring states or on the governments of European countries and the USA. During the 1980s Iran and

Syria in particular are thought to have sponsored groups in Lebanon who have held Western hostages for long periods of time, in part in an attempt to secure the release of prisoners held by Israel. In 1979, when the Islamic Republic was declared in Iran, the occupants of the US embassy in Tehran were taken hostage on the grounds of US complicity in plots to restore the Shah, and were not released until January 1981. In 1990, after its invasion of Kuwait, Iraq took hostage foreign (mainly Western) citizens resident in Iraq and Kuwait, whom it threatened to use as a 'human shield' in areas of strategic importance.

household, a group of people sharing a common residence and enjoying common resources, such as food. Simply living together does not necessarily make a household; anthropologists sometimes define a household as a domestic arrangement in which all food is purchased from a common fund and prepared at a common hearth. Household arrangements are often complicated, and there is great variation in the forms they take all over the world. They may consist of a simple nuclear *family, consisting of parents and children, or an extended family, consisting of several generations. In India, for example, households often include parents, all their children and all their children's spouses and children, and sometimes the parents' own brothers and sisters. In many household types, all property is shared, and members work as well as live together. This is common in many *peasant societies, where brothers, living together with their elderly parents and unmarried siblings, as well as their own wives and children, own and work land together.

House of Commons, the primary chamber of the UK *legislature (the Houses of Parliament), and the elected part of the government. Members of Parliament are elected from 650 single-member constituencies by universal adult suffrage in plurality (first-past-the-post) *elections held at least every five years. The presiding officer of the Commons is the Speaker, who functions in a strictly non-partisan way. The House of Commons is organized along adversarial lines, its proceedings normally controlled by a disciplined party majority. The exercise by the House of Commons of its powers in matters of legislation, finance, scrutiny, and enquiry are thus in practice largely party-dominated, subject to the rights conventionally accorded to the opposition. On the other hand, an increasing role is played by all-party committees, such as standing committees, which consider and amend *bills, or select committees, which monitor the workings of government departments, taking evidence, questioning witnesses, and issuing reports. Following a general election, or a change of leadership, the leader of the party commanding an overall majority in the House of Commons is invited by the monarch to become *prime minister and form a *cabinet. (See also *UK government.)

House of Lords, the non-elected second chamber of the UK Houses of Parliament, comprising the Lords Spiritual (twenty-six archbishops and bishops in order of seniority), the Lords Temporal (approximately 1,000 hereditary and life peers), and the Lords of Appeal in Ordinary (Law Lords), the most senior members of the *judiciary. Non-hereditary peers have been created since the Life Peerages Act of 1958; they tend to be more active members of the Lords than many hereditary peers. A former equal of the *House of Commons, but constitutionally subordinate to it since the Parliament Acts of 1911 and 1949, the House of Lords retains a suspensive veto on legislation of one year,

except for financial legislation. It still performs several useful parliamentary roles. These include the revision of *bills from the Commons, the initiation of non-controversial legislation, scrutiny of the *executive, and enquiry by select committee. Debate in the Lords is less raucously partisan and sometimes better informed than in the Commons. The House of Lords is the highest court of appeal in the *UK legal system, but only the Law Lords take part when it acts in this capacity.

House of Representatives, one of the two chambers of the US Congress, the other being the *Senate. The House of Representatives comprises 435 members, the number for each state being determined by population, though every state is entitled to at least one Representative. Members are elected for a two-year term, all terms running concurrently. A Representative (popularly called Congressman) must be at least 25 years of age, a US citizen for at least seven years, and an inhabitant of the state represented. The right to originate finance bills is given to the House by the Constitution. The House also has the power to begin *impeachment proceedings, through which the *President, a judge, or other official can be removed from office for misbehaviour, if the resolution of the House to impeach is adopted by the Senate. The House of Representatives is organized along party lines, by majority and minority party leaderships. The majority party in the House does not necessarily coincide with the majority party in the Senate, or the party of the *President. A noted feature of both the House of Representatives and the Senate is the system of specialized standing committees and numerous sub-committees, through which most of the legislature's work is accomplished; these committees, which often display striking autonomy in their decisions, conduct most congressional business, dealing with different classes of bills, as well as scrutinizing government departments.

housing, buildings for human habitation. Housing choices may be measured on three dimensions: quality (concern with standards of accommodation), security (concern with occupancy rights), and opportunity (concern with the relationship of housing to other goods such as *employment and *education). Households make different trade-offs between the three. A poor family may be compelled to give a higher priority to proximity to unskilled jobs (opportunity) than to quality or security. In general, as households become richer their choices expand, but are always influenced by the physical availability of housing, by controls on access (*government housing may be reserved for civil servants, and ethnic minorities may be debarred from purchasing in certain areas; see *segregation), and by costs, which in turn are influenced by *subsidies and *tax concessions, and by the effects of land speculation and government planning policies. In the richer countries of the world, ensuring a supply of adequate housing is seen as an important responsibility of governments and many have built rental housing and encouraged owner occupation through subsidies. None the less, certain groups such as migrants and one-parent families remain at risk of *homelessness. In the developing world, explosive *population growth, shortage of government resources, and the inability of many citizens to pay more than a tiny sum towards housing costs has led governments to limit their commitment to government housing and to recognize that they cannot assume responsibility for housing their populations. Instead they are concentrating on upgrading *shanty towns and *slums, on supplying *water, *sanitation, and other services, and on community development and self-help initiatives.

human capital, a term used in economics to indicate that education, training, and improvements in health are investments which raise output, and can therefore be described as creating 'human capital'. Traditionally, economic analysis concentrated on investment in physical *capital such as machinery, but especially since 1964, when the US economist Gary Becker published *Human Capital*, the concept has powerfully influenced debates about education and the labour market. There are difficulties in measuring the returns in human capital of different kinds of education and health care. Private returns consist of the extra earnings and improved employment opportunities that education confers on the individual. Numerous investigations have found rates of return on education of well over 10 per cent in developing countries; usually the returns for primary education are higher than for other levels of education, and the highest returns are found in the poorest countries. However, these estimates may exaggerate returns to society because education does not simply improve productivity by imparting knowledge and skills, but also serves as a 'screening device' to enable employers to pick individuals with higher innate ability or with personal characteristics which make them more productive. But there are other benefits from education which are not included in the estimates of extra earnings, which raise social returns. Female education, especially, raises the health and nutrition of children, and is usually associated with smaller size of families.

humanism, an outlook of a kind which in some sense places man at the centre of the universe. There is no systematic theory of humanism, but any world-view which claims that the only source of value in the world is man, or more loosely that man supplies the true measure of value, may be described as humanist. The relations between humanism and religious thought are complex, but humanism is in some respects opposed to religious belief, by virtue of the humanist's belief in human perfectibility, contradicting the doctrine of *original sin. In this way humanism also has connections with *individualism, the notion that the goal for man includes the fulfilment of each person by the cultivation of his or her own individual nature, and with a belief in the possibility of social progress. Historically, humanism was fully articulated for the first time (as, for example, in the writings of the Dutch humanist Erasmus, 1466–1536) in the 15th-century Renaissance, where it was manifested in a resurgence of interest in the culture of ancient Greece and Rome, and in artistic achievement, conceived as contributing directly to the glory of man rather than God. *Marx may be correctly described as a humanist, and in this century humanism has been given expression, in both secular and religious forms, in *existentialism.

humanistic psychology, an approach to psychological study and therapy which reacts against mainstream *psychology's apparent willingness to treat humans as objects of investigation and manipulation. Humanistic psychology emphasizes co-operation, *empathy, and mutual respect between psychologist and patient ('client'). Its philosophical ancestry is traceable through *existentialism to *Rousseau. Key concepts for most humanistic psychologists are the 'real self' and 'self-actualization', as expounded by the Scottish psychiatrist R(onald) D(avid) Laing (1927–90) and the US psychotherapist *Rogers. Humanistic psychologists encourage self-expression, self-discovery, and 'personal growth' through insight and emotional experience. There is no clear set of doctrines or single therapeutic approach. Techniques

The Mothers of the Plaza de Mayo, Argentina, began their silent vigils in the main square of Buenos Aires, carrying photographs of their relatives who had been killed by the military regime (1976–83). They caught the public imagination and became the centre of protests against **human rights** violations, which culminated in the trial of the military leaders responsible.

are drawn from many traditions, and include forms of exercise to foster bodily awareness and reduce tensions, and also self-disclosure or role-playing, as in psychodrama and *group therapy. Humanistic psychology offers an appropriate attitude for *psychotherapy, but may have limited use in challenging the experimental approach of academic psychology because the two are based on different premises.

human rights, the rights to which all humans are held to be entitled. The human rights guaranteed by international codes fall into three broad classes: first, individual civil and political liberties (freedom from arbitrary *arrest, *detention without trial, and *torture or other maltreatment; *freedom of movement, association, and expression; religious, conscientious, and philosophical liberty); secondly, social and economic rights and freedoms (rights to *education, health care, work, fair conditions of *employment, and maintenance of at least a minimum standard of living); thirdly, the 'third-generation' collective rights (the rights of peoples), designed to advance the position of minorities and bolster *self-determination and equality (see *egalitarianism), as well as to control the capacity of richer nations to use their resources to exploit poor ones. The international codes which set out these rights include the *Universal Declaration of Human Rights (1948); the *European Convention on Human Rights (1950); the *International Covenant on Civil and Political Rights (1966); the *International Convention on Economic, Social, and Cultural Rights (1969); the *African Charter on Human and People's Rights (1981); and the *International Convention on the Rights of the Child (1989). These treaties bind states which are parties to them in *international law, but do not automatically form part of the municipal law of any state. However, they require states to ensure that *citizens have adequate legal redress for breaches of the guaranteed rights. (See also *bill of rights, *civil rights.)

Hume, David (1711–76), Scottish philosopher and historian, probably the most influential writer of the *empiricist school. His guiding thought that the sole origin of knowledge is in experience led him to criticize the common views of *causation and *induction. He argued that as we cannot literally perceive the connection between a cause and its effect, our knowledge of causal phenomena is merely that the appearance of certain objects regularly follows certain others, and that an inductive inference is not truly a process of reasoning, but one of custom or habit. His philosophy limited the role of reason in our knowledge of the world, and emphasized that many human responses are in line with animal habit. These conclusions stirred *Kant into producing a philosophical system which re-emphasized the role of reason.

hunger-strike, the attempt to demonstrate commitment to a political or other cause by refusing food and/or drink. Hunger-strikes may be carried out by those imprisoned for political or other reasons, to achieve changes in conditions, or to force a review of their cases. An example of such use is that of members of the IRA, who during the 1970s and 1980s staged hunger-strikes in an effort to obtain the status of political, rather than criminal, prisoners at prisons in Northern Ireland. Hunger-strikes may also be used as public demonstrations of protest or commitment, as for example by Mahatma Gandhi and his followers during the struggle for Indian independence from the 1920s.

hunter-gatherers, people who subsist from the natural environment, without involvement in agriculture or animal husbandry. They survive by gathering wild fruit and vegetables, and by hunting. Theirs is the earliest and simplest form of human organization, and has been found all over the world: Australian *Aborigines, the Arctic *Inuit, and the *!Kung-San in southern Africa are all examples of hunter-gatherers. They have a *nomadic way of life, following seasonal food supplies. They are organized in bands consisting of close kin, but these bands fluctuate in size as members move in and out, according to food availability. *Marriage is a very loose institution, and *lineage is not considered of great importance. Hunter-gatherer society is egalitarian: leadership is usually based on individual ability and is not hereditary. Relations between men and women are also more egalitarian than in many sedentary societies, though

The high aristocracy of fox **hunting** is to be found in the meets of the 'Shire' counties of England. Famous Shire packs include the Belvoir, the Cottesmore, the Pytchleys, and the Quorn hounds, seen below.

there is a basic division of labour, the men hunting game while the women do most of the gathering. Today, many hunter-gatherers are threatened by economic development, which is destroying the natural environment upon which their survival depends.

hunting, the pursuit of game or other wild animals for profit or for sport. In the UK, the most popular legitimate form of hunting is the cross-country pursuit of foxes by their scent by mounted members of a hunt and hounds, the latter being controlled by the notes blown on the huntsman's horn. In beagling, hares are the quarry, and the hunters run with or behind their dogs. Some proponents of *animal rights who oppose hunting say it is cruel and not a true sport; supporters maintain it is necessary (for purposes of culling or controlling overpopulation) as well as enjoyable.

Huron, a confederation of four Indian tribes from what is now Ontario, Canada. The Huron were culturally similar to the *Iroquois, and also lived in fortified villages, relying on farming for much of their food. They were driven out of their original territory by the Iroquois expansion of the 17th century, and by the mid-19th century were living in Kansas. They were later resettled in north-east Oklahoma.

Husserl   *phenomenology.

hypnosis, a trance-like condition involving apparent alteration in *consciousness and *memory, during which the hypnotized subject becomes susceptible to the hypnotist's suggestions. These may produce anaesthesia (absence of sensation), analgesia (insensitivity to pain), paralysis, or apparent regression to childhood functioning. Post-hypnotic suggestions made during hypnosis influence the subject after the trance has ended and may induce the subject to forget what has occurred during hypnosis (post-hypnotic amnesia). Hypnosis is a contentious issue. Some believe it is simply a form of role-playing in which subjects voluntarily act in a way they believe typical of those 'hypnotized'. They point to evidence that there is no physiological sign, for example in brainwave patterns, of any change in consciousness. Others believe that hypnosis is a special state of consciousness, pointing out that similar trance-like states, often resulting from repetitive stimuli such as drumming, have been reported since ancient times and in all cultures. Hypnotic suggestibility differs from person to person. A tendency to vivid daydreams and willingness to be hypnotized characterize those who are susceptible. Hypnosis has been used in *dentistry, obstetrics, and *psychotherapy. In all cases the patient's belief in its efficacy seems crucial. It was the study of hypnosis which led *Freud to explore the unconscious mind and develop his theory of *psychoanalysis.

hysteria, a *neurosis often featuring emotional outbursts, sensory abnormalities, such as eyesight failure, paralysis, or defects of motor co-ordination, for example lameness. There is no evidence of an organic cause. It was while treating hysteria that *Freud formulated his basic *psychoanalytic ideas. He suggested that the symptoms were a 'conversion' of repressed sexual conflicts. It is possible that he developed this theory, one of the most influential in psychology, on the basis of over-generalization from an atypical illness which occurred in a particular cultural milieu. More recent writers have considered the role of *anxiety, *stress, and *depression in the genesis of hysterical symptoms. The condition causes much distress to sufferers, but is difficult to treat.

I

Ibo, one of the largest groups of people in south-eastern Nigeria, speaking the Ibo or Igbo language (see *Niger-Congo languages). Despite their number, the Ibo historically had no chief and lacked a strong ethnic identity. Nevertheless they united in opposition to British colonial rule, and played a large part in the struggle for independence. In 1967–70 an Ibo attempt at secession led to the Biafran war (Biafra being the name they gave their secessionist state), in which they were defeated. Their political organization is egalitarian: both men and women belong to *age-sets, the older age-sets being responsible for the regulation of the social and economic life of the village, as well as *dispute resolution. Land is inherited by the men, but there is some variance between patrilineal and double descent. Traditionally the men cultivate yams and the women are responsible for other crops, such as maize; recently the cultivation of rice as a cash crop has been introduced.

ice hockey   *hockey, ice.

ice-sailing   *sailing.

An **Ibo** mask representing a maiden spirit. Ibo religion is based on a complex mythology involving a creator god, an earth goddess, and numerous deities and spirits, as well as the worship of ancestors. Revelation of the will of the gods is sought by divination and oracles.

This sign, placed on the fence surrounding a site where there is a danger of electric shock, has a clear message. The triangular shape is an **ideogram**, since it is conventionally used to mean 'warning'; the more representational picture inside is a pictogram.

ice-skating, a popular pastime carried out on outdoor rinks, frozen ponds, lakes, and rivers as well as in purpose-built indoor rinks equipped with an artificial surface. Beginners progress through basic movements to learn elementary turns and spins; they may then go on to ice-dancing and figure-skating, both of which are competitive sports practised to *Olympic level. Another activity is long-distance or speed-skating, especially popular in countries with large expanses of outdoor ice, such as the USA, Canada, The Netherlands, Scandinavian countries, Russia, and elsewhere in north-eastern Europe.

idealism (in philosophy), a set of views according to which the physical world is dependent upon the mind; we somehow create the world. These doctrines are not as counterintuitive as they seem because idealists are not saying that our experience of the world is other than it is, but that the explanation of our experience is other than we take it to be. So an idealist will not deny that tables and chairs are physical objects but he or she will give an account of what it is to be a physical object that makes the physical dependent upon the mental. So, for example, *Berkeley would say that an object is simply a collection of 'ideas' (instances of *universals) that are coherent: for there to be a table in the room is for any perceiver present to experience those consistent and connected perceptions which the realist about material objects would claim to be caused by the table's mind-independent existence. *Kant and *Hegel are among the greater exponents of other forms of idealism.

ideogram, an abstract or conventional graphic *sign representing a thing or notion. Ideograms constitute a component of the Egyptian hieroglyphic and the Chinese logographic *writing systems. A contemporary example of an ideogram is the diagonal line across road signs expressing prohibition. Ideograms are to be distinguished from the less abstract *pictograms.

ideology, a political belief-system which both explains the world as it currently is and suggests how it should be changed. The term was given currency by *Marx, who used it to describe the belief-systems of *social classes, and espe-

The relaxation of Soviet emigration policies has led to massive **immigration** by Soviet Jews to Israel. From 13,000 arrivals in 1989 the numbers rose to 185,000 in 1990.

cially that of the capitalist class or bourgeoisie. Bourgeois ideology involved *false consciousness, and in that respect was contrasted with the 'scientific' outlook that represented the true consciousness of the working class. This ideology/science contrast has since generally been dropped in favour of the view that all political outlooks rest on assumptions that cannot be proved, and are to that degree ideological. Some have sought to reserve the term for political outlooks that are seen as rigid and extreme in contrast to those that are more pragmatic and moderate. In this sense, social scientists in the 1950s and 1960s, such as Edward Shils and Daniel Bell, claimed that Western societies were witnessing 'the end of ideology', pointing especially to the demise of *Marxism as an all-embracing vision of society. It seems better, however, to recognize the pervasiveness of ideology as the means by which people order their perceptions of the social world, whether or not they consciously subscribe to a political creed.

'Īd ul-Ādḥā (Arabic, 'festival of sacrifice'), one of the two major annual Muslim festivals, which occurs on the tenth day of the twelfth month (*Dhu al-Hijja*). It marks the completion of the *pilgrimage (*ḥajj*) to Mecca, and commemorates Abraham's willingness to sacrifice his son Ishmael. The substitution of a ram for Ishmael is symbolized by the *sacrifice of animals, performed by both pilgrims and believers throughout the world, and is followed by prayer and celebration. The flesh of the animal is cooked and shared by the donors or given to the poor. The second major festival, *'Īd ul-Fitr*, marks the end of the month of *Ramadan.

illegitimacy, the status of a child born outside marriage. Historically, and in many countries today the illegitimate child has suffered social stigma and has been subject to legal discrimination, particularly in matters of succession; in some countries, the illegitimate child has been denied *civil rights as well. The child's father similarly has no rights or claims over the child. Such discrimination runs counter to the egalitarian ideals of many modern societies, however; both the European Convention on the Status of Children Born out of Wedlock (1975) and decisions of the US Supreme Court (1977) demanded equality between children born within and outside marriage. In the UK, children are now treated alike, whatever their status, apart from the cases of succession to titles and to *citizenship. The abolition of discrimination against illegitimate children does not necessarily confer rights on their fathers, however, and there are variations in the circumstances in which Western legal systems allow fathers to acquire rights over their illegitimate children.

image, a term with more than one application, referring primarily to visual reproductions of reality (such as photographs) which have *meanings at both a representational or 'denotative' level ('what is shown') and an interpretative or 'connotative' level ('what is meant'). By extension, image can also refer to any imaginative conception or evaluation drawn from a *text or collection of texts; for example, representations of women or black people in certain *newspapers, novels, or film genres. Images are often coded with meanings, on the assumption that audiences will decode the *signs in a spontaneous and unconscious manner. *Advertising works in this way, associating products with appealing images, in order to trigger psychological responses. In a similar way, attention to style and fashion help to project a particular self-image to other people.

imām (Arabic, 'leader'), among Sunnī Muslims a title conferred upon the person chosen by the community to lead congregational prayer in a *mosque. Although the *imām* is usually a person who possesses a theological education, no special qualification is necessary, and any respectable Muslim may fulfil the duty of leading the prayer. The term is also applied by Sunnī Muslims to the orthodox caliphs, and to any important teacher or religious leader. In Shī'ī belief, the title has a complex range of meaning. It indicates the highest rank of authority, spiritual and legitimately temporal, bestowed by the Prophet on a direct descendant of Muḥammad and 'Alī; or the *imām* of the time under Divine guidance. The larger sect of the Shī'as, the Ithna 'Asharīs, believe in twelve *imāms* the last being associated with the *millenarian notion of a disappeared leader, or *mahdī*, who will return to instigate a retun to pure Islamic ideals, and whose function and authority is maintained by a *mujtahid* or *āyātollāh. The *imāms* are held to be semi-divine, the repository of secret mystical knowledge and a source of spiritual renewal without whose existence, manifest or hidden, the world would not continue. Shī'a Muslims have commonly endowed worldly rulers with *legitimacy by associating them with the concept of the imamate in some way.

immigration, the movement of people as permanent settlers into a country not their own. The principal motives for immigration are usually the search for better wages and for secure employment, but some immigrants are *refugees fleeing political or natural disasters. In recent years, the main flows of immigrants have been from less developed to more developed economies, Germany, the USA, the UK, Canada, Australia, and Italy being the principal destinations (see *emigration). Immigration policies differ, but most countries restrict by law the number of immigrants they will accept, and impose educational, financial, or other requirements on applicants for temporary or permanent residence, or *citizenship. Discrimination (for or against) immigrants from particular countries is not uncommon. Illegal immigrants may be expelled, and *migrant workers may be offered financial and technical assistance as an incentive to return to their country of origin.

immunization, the production of immunity to a disease by artificial means. In the richer countries of the world, mass immunization of children against major childhood diseases has been successful in reducing *morbidity and *mortality rates. In 1974 when the World Health Organization launched the Expanded Programme on Immunization, fewer than 5 per cent of children in developing countries were immunized. By 1991 four-fifths of the world's children were protected by immunization against diphtheria, whooping cough, tetanus, measles, polio, and tuberculosis, and WHO estimated that 2 million lives were being saved each year. None the less, there is still a heavy toll in preventable disease, with more than a million cases of measles, which is often fatal to malnourished children, for example. New goals for the 1990s are to eradicate neonatal tetanus and polio and to reduce measles by 90 per cent. WHO's global eradication of smallpox in 1977 through systematic immunization, and through tracking down the last carriers for treatment, has set a dramatic and encouraging precedent.

impeachment, a judicial procedure by which a public official may be tried by the *legislature for treason or other serious crime. In the UK, the impeachment procedure has passed into disuse since the 18th century, but has never been abolished. In the USA, the House of Representatives institutes the impeachment proceedings and the Senate acts as judge. In 1974 the House of Representatives was preparing articles of impeachment against President Richard Nixon (1913–) on the grounds of obstruction of justice and misuse of power after he refused to co-operate with inquiries into the illegal electronic *surveillance of his political opponents at the Watergate Hotel in Washington, DC. He pre-empted proceedings by resigning.

imperfect competition   *perfect competition.

imperialism, the policy of extending a country's influence over less powerful states. Historically imperialism has existed in all periods: Greece, Rome, Ottoman Turkey, Spain, and Britain have all extended their respective domains over societies at different times, giving way to forms of imperial rule. What has been labelled 'classical imperialism' usually refers to the period of expansion of the modern industrial powers from the 1880s until World War I. The term 'neo-imperialism' is sometimes used to describe certain (usually economic) policies of the developed world, notably the USA and the former Soviet Union, towards the *developing countries in the post-World War II era. Explanations for the causes of imperialism, be they political, military, economic, or religious, have stimulated a long intellectual debate in which John Atkinson Hobson's *Imperialism, A Study* (1902) and Vladimir Ilyich Lenin's *Imperialism, the Highest Stage of Capitalism* (1917) are regarded as historical landmarks, both setting the bases for economic theories of imperialism. In 1953 in a famous essay published in *The Economic History Review* entitled 'The imperialism of free trade', John Gallager and Ronald Robinson popularized the term 'informal imperialism', which includes forms of indirect control over subordinate societies through economic means. The term 'informal imperialism', which is subject to a lively debate to this day, has been criticized for its vagueness by scholars who prefer to restrict the definition of imperialism to political and territorial domination.

imports, an economic term denoting flows of *goods (visible imports) and services (invisible imports) into a country from abroad, the opposite of *exports, which are flows of goods and services out of the country. When imports flow into a country, the payment for them flows out and is recorded as a debit item on the *balance of trade. Exports mean a money inflow and are credit items. In the 1950s and 1960s policies of import substitution, that is protection (by *quotas and *tariffs) and domestic production of goods which would otherwise be imported, were favoured in many less developed countries as a means of reducing external dependence, encouraging *industrialization, and improving the balance of trade. However, such policies tended to be self-defeating because many countries lacked the capital and expertise to produce a range of goods cheaply, especially when protectionism encouraged an artificially high *exchange rate and so handicapped exports. Most economists today agree that policies of export promotion are a more satisfactory means of economic development.

imprinting, a process of early learning by which the newborn forms *attachment to the object it sees first after birth.

It was made famous by the Austrian pioneer in *ethology, Konrad Lorenz (1903–89), who described it in *Studies on Animal and Human Behaviour* (1935). Recently hatched swimming and walking birds, such as ducklings, follow almost any noticeable moving object, normally their mother, thereby improving their chances of survival. Such 'filial imprinting' is attachment to an individual care-giver. 'Sexual imprinting' is preference for the species of that same individual in later mate selection. Imprinting is a form of learning which requires no reward. Indeed, the more effort the young has to exert to follow, the stronger the imprinting is. It shows how *instinct interacts with circumstance in the development of behaviour and how important early experience may be.

imprisonment, the confinement of an offender in a penal institution, usually for a fixed length of time. In those jurisdictions where the *death penalty is not available, imprisonment is generally considered to be the most severe punishment which can be inflicted. The length of a custodial sentence is determined in part by the seriousness of the offence, but *sentencing practice varies widely throughout the world. In countries that emphasize the punitive and

In many countries the physical conditions of **imprisonment** are themselves part of the punishment, as the sordid state of this room at Bedford Prison, UK, makes clear. In others, such as The Netherlands a more liberal approach stresses improved conditions and the importance of rehabilitation and education.

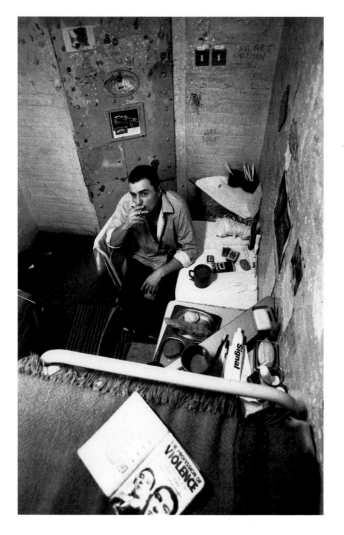

deterrent objectives of *punishment, sentences are usually longer. In many jurisdictions, a prisoner is automatically released after serving a certain proportion of the sentence, subject to good behaviour; this is known as remission. A prisoner may also apply for *parole. The custodial establishment in which prisoners serve their sentence will be determined by the security risk which they represent. Some prisons, for particularly dangerous offenders, are maximum security, while in open prisons, prisoners have greater access to their families and in some jurisdictions may be allowed conjugal visits. In some countries, there is provision for weekend imprisonment so that offenders may continue working during the term of their sentence. On the other hand, many prisons all over the world are notorious for overcrowding, violence, intimidation, and insanitary conditions, the resultant grievances sometimes leading to riots. Prison reformers have argued that incarceration (especially if conditions are harsh and degrading) leads to a hardening of criminal attitudes and to an increase in recidivism (reoffending once the prisoner is released). In consequence, *community penalties are widely used in preference to imprisonment.

incest, sexual relations between certain categories of close kin. These categories vary between societies, but some measure of prohibition of incest is generally found in all societies. Prohibited categories can range from specified individuals, such as, for example, parents, brothers, sisters, or cousins, to much larger groups of kin who may be only distantly related. Although it is often thought that incest prohibitions are designed to avert the incidence of genetic in-breeding, there is little evidence for this; the variety of prohibitions that exist in different societies suggests that this explanation cannot account for them all. The incest *taboo, as it is often termed, is sometimes seen as maintaining certain forms of *marriage by encouraging people to look outside their own social group for partners. *Lévi-Strauss, for example, has argued that this gave rise to the principle of reciprocal exchange of wives between kin groups, and that incest prohibitions are the basis for all human social organization. In modern societies, incest (particularly between a father and a daughter) is seen as a form of *child sexual abuse.

income, a flow of receipts (usually money) to an economic unit (an individual, household, firm, government, or nation) over a specified time period. It is paid chiefly to the owners of employed *factors of production: wages and salaries for labour; *rent for *land; *interest and *profit for *capital. Income may also include transfer payments. These are payments made by private individuals (such as gifts) or government (such as *old-age benefits) for which no productive service is exchanged. Disposable income is the income left for spending or saving when all transfer payments have been added and all deductions (such as direct tax and national insurance contributions) have been subtracted. (See also *GDP, *GNP, national income.)

incomes policy *prices and incomes policy.

independence *self-determination, *sovereignty.

independent education, education offered in schools and other educational institutions for which the state is not responsible. The proportion of primary school children in independent education ranges from, for example, none in the People's Republic of China (where it is banned) to more than a quarter in some sub-Saharan African countries, Belgium, Spain, and Hong Kong. In most countries religious bodies are the principal providers. Some independent schools charge fees, while others are free. Independent schools complement state schools, either by offering programmes parents and children find preferable or, as in many developing countries (where their numbers are increasing rapidly), by offering facilities which governments cannot afford. They are sometimes supported by state subsidy and in the UK are awarded charitable status, which exempts them from income tax. In many countries the state exercises some control, at least over the *curriculum. The system in The Netherlands represents a compromise: two out of three children attend independently run schools, which are financed and regulated by the state but guaranteed ideological freedom. Although the arguments for state and for *comprehensive education are strong, it is notable that the schools of many educational pioneers from *Montessori to *Steiner have been independent. Independent schools offer scope for experiment and, many believe, are an important safeguard against state ideological control over children.

indexation, the formal linking of (typically) wage rates, salaries, or *bond prices to the movement of an index number. This latter records the percentage change in average prices, volumes, or money values from a base period (when the index number is set at 100). The most common index used for this purpose is an index of general *inflation such as a *retail price index (RPI). Wages and salaries in high-inflation countries have from time to time been indexed to the rate of inflation to maintain the purchasing power of people's incomes. Indexed bonds are those with interest and capital repayments that change in line with an index; for example, in the UK there are some gilt-edged securities which are linked to the RPI.

index, financial, a series of numbers starting from a base period (where the index is set at 100) and representing the average percentage change in prices since the base period. A financial index is typically of *share prices, but may also be of other types of financial assets. It is a useful device for seeing how prices in a market stand and how they have changed over time. Most share indices are updated continuously during trading hours. Indices are either unweighted or weighted averages of a number of prices. In the latter case, a weight is assigned to each company according to its total asset value, so that changes in the share price of bigger companies have more impact on the overall index. Often only a small number of share prices are used in the calculation of the index, but movements in these shares are seen as representative of general trends. Examples of financial indexes are the Financial Times Indices (London) (of which the most commonly quoted is the Financial Times Stock Exchange index of the leading 100 companies), the Dow Jones Index (New York), and the Nikkei-Dow Jones Average (Tokyo), the CAC-40 (Paris), the Dax Index (a Frankfurt index of *blue-chip shares), the All Ordinaries (Sydney), and the Hang Seng Index, the oldest of three Hong Kong indices which have now been amalgamated to form the Hong Kong index.

Indian philosophy, the pre- and non-Islamic systems of thought usually described by the Sanskrit terms *darshana* ('way of seeing') and *ānvīkshikī* ('investigation'). Indian thinkers were usually attached to one or another tradition or school with a specifically religious character, and Indian philosophy is characterized by an intimate relationship between argumentative analysis of various ideas regarding knowledge, language, logic, the natural world, and so on, and the defence of particular interpretations of scriptural doctrines of spiritual release. Some sections of the *Vedas* have elaborate arguments about the relationship between human action and cosmic order which provided later thinkers with material for discussion on ethics and on the role of language. The *Upanishads* provide early metaphysical speculation on the nature of the self (*ātman*), on god and supernatural powers, and on the nature of the cosmos. Classical Hindu philosophy is broadly divided into the Six Schools of Thought (*shaddarshana*): Pūrva Mīmāmsa; Uttara Mīmāmsa or Vedānta; Yoga; Sāmkhya; Nyāya; and Vaisheshika. They originated roughly between the 4th century BC and the 4th century AD. Over the next thousand years, the Pūrva Mīmāmsa branched into two sub-schools, and the Vedānta into three; while Yoga and Sāmkhya merged, as did Nyāya and Vaisheshika. Two other schools were the Lokāyata (or Chārvaka) and the Grammarians (who often owed nominal allegiance to one of the traditional schools). The Buddhist schools, which arose as competing interpretations of the Buddha's teachings, were the Hīnāyana (the Sautāntrika and the Vaibhāshika) and the Mahāyana (the Mādhhyamika or Shūnyavada (see *Nāgārjuna) and the Yogāchāra or Vijñānavāda). The separate religious schools of the Jains, however, practised broadly the same philosophy. Some of the Six Schools of Thought were primarily associated with one particular view. Thus the Pūrva Mimāmsa argued for a real and independent world, without a creator god, marked by cosmic laws which humans had to be in consonance with through following rules of language provided by the *Vedas*. The Vedānta Advaitins argued for a world which could not be established as either independent of, or dependent on, subjective grasp for its existence; such a world would be transcended when subjects realized that their consciousness was identical with the creator consciousness (*Brahman). The Sāmkhya–Yoga school attempted to define the elements of the natural and spiritual worlds, while Nyāya–Vaisheshika, which argued for a god-created world independent of any mental of subjective power of construction, became the school of *logic, developing sophisticated tools for the analysis of the content of cognition, knowledge-claims, relations, and so on, which others, especially the Advaitins, made use of. The Buddhists too developed their own tools of logic and presented radical views challenging common assumptions about reality: the 'idealist' Yogāchāra said that the world was a mental construct; and the Mādhyamika evolved a *dialectic against philosophical claims that a coherent view of reality is possible, which Advaita in turn used for its own ends. There was a debate between the Grammarians and the Pūrva Mimāmsa about the nature of language and its relationship with the world. The Jains attempted to create a system of categorizing the truth and falsity of philosophical claims which showed the superiority of their own method of pursuing salvation. Other arguments included the role of scriptural authority in the regulation of society, the consequences of action, moral law, and the methods of attaining special spiritual states. The nature of the self or soul was also a subject of debate. Indian philosophy thus pursued the same fields of investigation as Western *philosophy; however, rather than the purely theoretical examination found in modern Western philosophy, it has traditionally concerned itself with establishing philosophical positions as the foundation for the spiritual claims of each school.

Indo-European languages

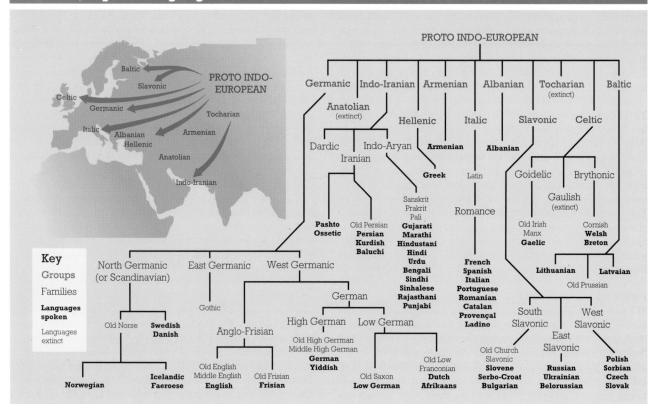

Indian thought, contemporary. Modern Indian thought takes three interrelated forms depending on the style and concerns of its proponents. First, traditionalists, usually called *pundits*, trained in Sanskrit, attempt to preserve the classical tradition through commentaries and discussions chiefly in social and religious contexts, and are generally not much concerned with contemporary philosophical developments in the West and elsewhere. They are not interested in interacting with other social groups and tend not to be known outside the circle of interested Sanskrit scholars. They preserve most clearly the linguistic tradition of classical Sanskrit learning. Secondly, ideological thinkers who, especially in the 19th and early 20th centuries, responded to Western denigration of Indian moral and intellectual values by appealing to the greatness of significant past Indian thinkers and texts. Their primary aim was to develop an understanding of India's past which allowed them to claim that it had an intellectual tradition, but they themselves did not construct philosophical systems. They were often social activists and reformers (see *Hindu revivalism). Others, such as Mahatma Gandhi (1869–1948) and Jawaharlal Nehru (1889–1964), are often considered to be thinkers in this sense because of their ideological views about the achievements and potential of Indian culture. The third and final category includes academic thinkers who follow largely Western models in addressing tightly focused issues with the apparatus of technical terminology. Though they accept that there is an unavoidable use of Western modes of discussion, especially because of the predominant use of English and German, they argue that their reconstructed understanding of the tradition is merely a contemporary method of preserving the classical tradition, and as such, quintessentially Indian. The authoritative translation and interpretation of classical Sanskrit texts is an important element of this modern study

and several Western scholars have contributed to this field. Examples of such Indian philosophers are A. K. Coomaraswamy (1877–1947), who sought to develop a perennial philosophy whose metaphysical and aesthetic bases would nourish the continuity of different traditional cultures; S. Radhakrishnan, best-known of modern thinkers, who wrote on both his own interpretation of *Advaita *Vedānta, and on comparative analyses of Indian and Western ideas, especially the supposed parallel between Advaita and *idealism; Sri Aurobindo Ghosh (1872–1950), whose later philosophy combined with his saintly character to produce a vision of the spiritual and moral anticipation of all humanity; K. C. Bhattacharya, an authentically modern thinker whose primary aim was to develop an entire system of thought which used both Western elements like the philosophy of *Kant and *Hegel, and Indian elements like Advaita Vedānta (which is the dominant paradigm of modern reconstruction); and B. K. Motilal (1936–91), who employed Western analytic methods in reconstructing classical Indian *epistemology, theory of language, and *metaphysics, in order to contribute to contemporary debate in these areas in the West.

individualism, the belief that societies are nothing more than collections of individuals. It may embrace three more specific theses: that we can understand how societies function by looking at the behaviour of the individuals who compose them; that only individuals and their characteristics are of moral significance; and that individuals ought to be granted as much freedom as possible to pursue their own ends. These are separate beliefs, although often held together. Individualism in the third sense is a political doctrine whose antithesis is *collectivism. It claims that the role of the state should be reduced as far as possible so as to provide maximum scope for individuals to act on their own initiative. It is closely associated with a commitment to the *free market as the economic system that allows people to co-operate with one another with the minimum of compulsion. Prominent advocates of individualism include the British social philosopher Herbert Spencer (1820–1903), the US sociologist William Graham Sumner (1840–1910), and the Austrian economist *Hayek.

Indo-European languages, a family of languages spoken originally throughout Europe, Asia Minor (present-day Asian Turkey), Iran, northern and central India, and as far east as Chinese Turkestan. Following the period of European colonial expansion, which began in the late 15th century, modern Indo-European languages (notably *English, and the *Romance languages of Spanish, Portuguese, and French) spread to much of the rest of the world, including the Americas, Australasia, and the continent of Africa. Virtually all the modern languages of Europe belong to this group, the only exceptions being Basque, Finnish, Hungarian, and Turkish. There are ten main branches to the family, which are listed in order of antiquity; *Anatolian (now extinct), *Indo-Iranian, *Greek (a single language), *Italic, *Germanic, *Armenian (a single language), Tocharian (now extinct, once spoken in what is now northern Chinese Turkestan), *Celtic, Balto-Slavic (see *Baltic; *Slavic), and *Albanian (a single language). These languages share family characteristics such as basic vocabulary and grammatical inflections. The parent language can be reconstructed by comparing the daughter languages, especially the ancient ones. This language was spoken some time before 3000 BC, and split up during the subsequent millennia.

Indo-Iranian languages, the largest sub-group within *Indo-European languages. Modern Indo-Iranian languages have official status in Afghanistan, Bangladesh, India, Iran, Nepal, Pakistan, and Tadzhikistan, and are also spoken elsewhere. Speakers number approximately 700 million. The group falls into two distinct branches: Indic (or Indo-Aryan) and Iranian, both of which have very long histories. They split from each other in prehistoric times, and might well be classed as two separate groups within Indo-European. The earliest stage of Indic is called Sanskrit (meaning 'polished'). The most archaic form, Vedic Sanskrit, dates from around 1500 BC, and continued in use for over 1,000 years. This is the language in which the *Rigveda* and other sacred texts were composed. The period of classical Sanskrit, the great language of Hindu culture, runs from the 6th century BC to about AD 1000. Sanskrit continued in use as a literary language after it was no longer spoken as a mother tongue, and is still current as a *lingua franca among Hindu scholars. The middle stage of Indic is represented by a number of languages called the Prakrits ('vernaculars'), which overlapped to a large extent with Sanskrit. The main literary languages of the middle stage were Maharastri and Shauraseni; Pali, the language of the Buddhist writings, may also be included. The modern Indic vernaculars had begun to emerge by the 10th century AD. Of these the most important are Hindi (India) and Urdu (Pakistan). These are practically the same language, but Hindi is written in the traditional Indian Devanagari script (used for Sanskrit), while Urdu is written in the Arabic alphabet. Hindi is associated with Hinduism, while Urdu, which was spoken by Persian and Turkish invaders, is associated with Islam and has assimilated many Arabic and Persian words. Bengali, the national language of Bangladesh, is spoken by

some 60 million in India; Assamese, Gujarati, and Marathi in India, Punjabi and Sindhi in Pakistan, and Romany, the *gypsy language, are other Indic languages. Iranian too has three main stages. The two oldest forms date from the 6th century BC. Avestan (north-east Iran) is the language of Zoroastrian sacred poetry (see *Parsi), while Old Persian (south-west Iran) is the language of the cuneiform inscriptions of the Achaemenid emperors (6th–4th centuries BC). Middle Iranian is represented by Middle Persian (southern Iran), Parthian (northern Iran), and an Eastern group spoken mainly in Central Asia. Of modern Iranian languages the largest is Farsi (modern Persian), the official language of Iran. Others are Pashto (Afghanistan), Tadzhik (Tadzikistan), and Kurdish (see *Kurds).

induction (in logic), a process in which previously observed regularities are taken as the ground for predicting future regularities. For example, from the basis that all swans observed up to the present have been white, we could infer that all future swans will be white. As this example shows, however, inductive inferences are fallible: they can lead from true premises to false conclusions (there are black swans in Australia). This has led to doubts whether inductive inferences can be the basis of scientific reasoning (see *Popper) and even whether they are processes of reasoning at all (see *Hume). (See also *probability.)

industrial action, a term used to refer to action taken to apply pressure to the other party involved in *industrial relations between employers and employees. It usually follows a breakdown in *collective bargaining, although in Japan it may precede negotiations. Industrial action by employees directly involved in a dispute may be supported by secondary action from other *trade-union members (also known as sympathetic or solidarity action). Industrial action by employees is intended to disrupt production and may include overtime bans (refusal to work beyond normal

A sit-in at a car plant in South Korea conveys a vivid impression of the power of a mass of workers when expressed through **industrial action**. South Korea has restricted the right to form independent trade unions.

hours); the go-slow or work-to-rule (strict adherence to employment contracts); and strikes and *picketing. Sit-ins (US, sit-downs), occupations, and boycotts or 'blacking' also occur. In a strike the employees withdraw their *labour. Official action, as opposed to unofficial action, is industrial action supported or organized by a trade union. Official strikers may be paid by their union in compensation for lost wages. The general strike of all workers in a country or location usually has wider political aims. Industrial action may also be taken by employers in the form of lock-outs (refusal to admit employees to their workplaces), punitive dismissals, or the operation of blacklists of potential employees. The right to strike is recognized in most countries, but subject to restrictions which may include a ban on strikes in essential services or the public sector, obligatory cooling-off periods or ballots before strike action, compulsory conciliation or arbitration, and limits to picketing, all of which have been incorporated at times in *industrial law.

industrial democracy, participation by employees in industrial management and decision-taking. Traditionally, *trade unions in industrialized market economies such as the USA and UK have not wished to participate in management. However, in recent decades participation has effectively increased through *collective bargaining in many countries. Tripartite consultation between government, employers, and unions concerning economic and social policy has become common in many countries. Participation through works councils of employees' and, often, management representatives has become more common in Europe since the 1970s, and also in developing countries. In some countries, for example Germany, there is legal provision for workers' representatives on some boards of directors. Profit-sharing among employees and the introduction of quality circles in the workplace have also been adduced as evidence of increasing participation. Most *co-operatives involve some workers' management, or participation. The Yugoslav system of self-management, with its degree of workers' control, has influenced practice in some developing countries. Finally, in centrally planned economies trade unions have participated up to national level in decision-making on a wide range of economic and social issues.

industrialization, the growth to significant relative size of *secondary (manufacturing) industry in an economy which was previously dominated by *primary production, such as *agriculture, fisheries, and the extraction of minerals. When industrialization takes place, primary *employment falls, either absolutely or as a proportion of total employment, as *resources of *labour and *capital are shifted into manufacturing industry. A number of countries, such as the USA, the UK, and Germany, went through this process (known in the UK as the Industrial Revolution) in the 19th and early 20th centuries. In many less developed countries, industrialization is equated with *development, that is modernization, progress, and *economic growth, a viewpoint often, though not always, justified by the circumstances of the individual countries. In recent decades there has been rapid industrialization in many developing countries, in particular those known as the *newly industrializing countries; economic growth in these countries has generally exceeded that in those benefiting from ample natural resources, excepting certain oil-rich countries. Development plans favouring industrialization via *import substitution have been superseded in many countries by policies of *export promotion. Industrialization has been welcomed as

providing *employment for growing populations whom the land could no longer support; but since much industry is located in cities, there have been associated problems of massive *urbanization and, often, *pollution of the environment. The relationship between industrialization and development continues, therefore, to be debated. In the latter decades of the 20th century, the phenomenon of deindustrialization has been witnessed in industrialized countries. This means that in these countries manufacturing employment accounts for a shrinking proportion of total employment, as a result of the growth both of manufacturing *productivity and of *tertiary employment.

industrial relations, the relationship between managers (often referred to as 'the employers') and workers (usually represented by *trade unions) in the workplace. It is accepted that the objectives of managers may differ from those of their subordinates, leading to industrial conflict. Differing objectives are most commonly expressed in terms of disagreements over *wage or pay rates, but also occur in the areas of working practices (hours of work, working conditions, and conditions of employment). Industrial disagreements sometimes have a political dimension and have led to much emotive debate and intervention by government ministers. The miners' strikes of 1989 and 1990 in the former Soviet Union provide examples of the political dimensions of *industrial action. Although it is common for most attention to be focused on industrial disputes there are many less well-publicized aspects of industrial relations in which managers and other employees work effectively as a team, resulting in high levels of *productivity. In order for the two sides of the industrial relationship to work harmoniously together a number of procedures exist to facilitate the resolution of any disputes that may arise. Joint consultation is the system by which discussion of matters of common interest to managers and workers can occur. Often this takes place in a committee, or a workers' council, of employers' and employees' representatives which meets regularly. The main role is often advisory. Pay and conditions of employment are usually not covered by joint consultation but left to *collective bargaining in separate negotiations between union and employer. Procedure agreements exist in many industries as a means of avoiding strikes, lockouts, or other forms of organized coercive action. They provide an agreed step-by-step process to resolve disputes with the aim of avoiding industrial action. (See *dispute resolution.) Arbitration and conciliation are methods of settling an industrial conflict or dispute by using an independent third party. Conciliation is a process whereby an independent third party assists the two parties to a dispute to reach agreement. Conciliation differs from arbitration in that it assists in a general way and does not involve the reaching of a binding decision. In the UK the major independent third party used in industrial disputes is ACAS (the Advisory Conciliation and Arbitration Service). An ACAS conciliation officer assists the two disputing parties (usually management and trade union) to reach an agreement, offering guidance to both sides separately and then, at a later stage together. The results of arbitration are not legally binding in the UK (unlike the USA), but normally are accepted as the basis for settlement.

industrial relations law, the law governing *industrial relations, particularly *collective bargaining, and the conduct and role of *trade unions. In many countries employment laws make provision against unfair dismissal or *discrimination, and for holiday and sick leave, *equal pay,

Infant mortality

The infant mortality rate (IMR), defined as the number of children per 1,000 who die before their first birthdays, ranges from 5 in Iceland and Japan to 172 in Afghanistan. It is falling in most countries. A country's wealth is usually a prime determinant of its IMR, yet some countries such as China, Sri Lanka, Cuba, Costa Rica, Chile, and Jamaica, have achieved a much lower IMR than their incomes would suggest through investment in primary health care.

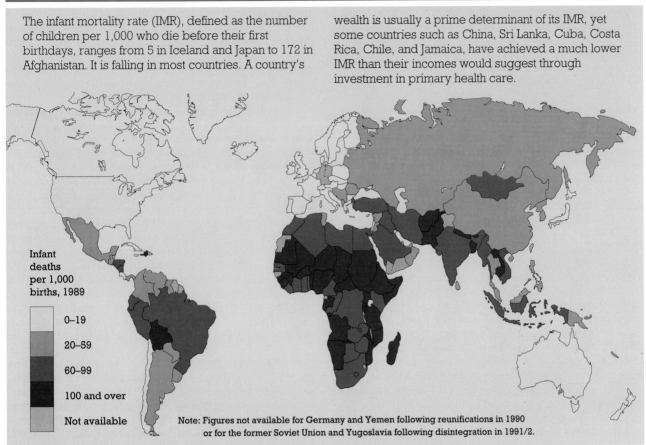

Infant deaths per 1,000 births, 1989

- 0–19
- 20–59
- 60–99
- 100 and over
- Not available

Note: Figures not available for Germany and Yemen following reunifications in 1990 or for the former Soviet Union and Yugoslavia following disintegration in 1991/2.

Sources: *World Development Report 1991* UNDP, New York; *World Resources 1990-91* World Resources Institute, New York

and employers' social security contributions. Legislation that sets pay levels such as the *minimum wage, also affects industrial relations. Legislation or case law in many countries restricts the lock-out of workers by their employer. However, the term industrial (or labour) law also refers to the law as it affects the role and conduct of trade unions. In socialist countries (centrally planned economies), trade unions have been integrated by law into management planning. In some industrial market economies (for example, the USA), the law lays down rights and procedures for union recognition. Legislation may provide for a measure of *industrial democracy or participation, as in Germany since 1952 and now increasingly elsewhere in Europe. In developing countries the law tends to intervene more often in the resolution of disputes. However, in all countries recourse to the law is usually a last resort. Industrial relations law may also be introduced to curb *industrial action. This was the case in the UK in the 1980s, when restrictions were placed on forms of action including sympathy and political strikes, some immunities against legal action were removed, ballots became obligatory before strike action, and the use of *injunctions and sequestration against unions was facilitated. The law may require conciliation and/or arbitration in the event of disputes, as in Australia and New Zealand, where labour courts can impose a settlement. In most countries the law bans or restricts strikes by public employees, especially those in essential services.

industry *primary industry, *secondary industry, *tertiary industry.

infant mortality rate, a calculation in *demography indicating the level of infant deaths. The infant mortality rate of a population over a year is calculated as the number of deaths of infants before their first birthday for every thousand live births. Between 1950 and 1955 and 1985 and 1990, rates fell in every part of the globe from 62 to 13 in Europe, from 126 to 58 in South America, from 181 to 73 in Asia, and from 187 to 106 in Africa. Improved nutrition, sanitation, living conditions, and health services, as well as reduced *fertility rates (which lessen the ill-health of mothers), have all contributed to improvements in infant mortality rates. The rate is often considered to be the best single indicator of the general health and social conditions of a population.

infertility, the inability to conceive a child. In much of the world an estimated 6 per cent of couples are involuntarily childless, excepting Africa, where the proportion is about 10 per cent, and the Middle East and Latin America, where the proportion is about 3 per cent. Investigating and treating infertility is complex and costly and is largely confined to wealthy industrialized countries. Childless couples may decide on *adoption, but some couples decide on artificial insemination by a donor to enable the woman to bear a child although her partner is infertile. Women may be treated for infertility by drugs or surgery. Where this is unsuccessful in vitro fertilization (IVF), by which eggs are fertilized outside the body by sperm and then replaced in the womb, may be tried. IVF has opened the way to the use of sperm on eggs donated (or illegally sold) to the couple by strangers or relatives. Embryos created by IVF may also be frozen for later implantation. In surrogate motherhood, another woman may volunteer or be paid to bear a child fertilized by the husband of the childless couple's sperm. Such medical advances raise ethical and legal questions of great complexity, and in many countries fertility treatments are supervised by a regulatory body with the backing of the law. In the UK the Human Fertility and Embryology Authority was established in 1991.

inflation, a persistent upward movement of the general price level (or, in other words, a decline in the value or purchasing power of *money), usually measured as a percentage rate per annum (see *retail price index). Keeping inflation low is a major economic objective for most governments since, although there is no conclusive proof that inflation adversely affects economic growth, it tends to generate a number of unwelcome effects. First, it penalizes holders of cash and those on fixed incomes. Secondly, it may distort the allocation of resources by altering relative prices, including 'real' *interest rates (the 'real' rates being nominal rates minus the (expected) inflation rate) and *exchange rates. This may also be associated with a redistribution of income and wealth between creditors and debtors since the interest repaid after inflation will be lower than previously expected in real terms. Levels at which taxation is paid may also be distorted. Thirdly, price confusion may arise: consumers may not know the market price for a rarely bought commodity. Fourthly, inflation magnifies uncertainty about the future, which discourages investment. Lastly, inflation may make exports and import-competing goods more expensive and thus adversely affect the *balance of trade unless the exchange rate is devalued. Economic theories about the causes of inflation include the *monetarist *quantity theory of money according to which inflation is caused by a faster growth in the money supply than in aggregate output. Monetarists prescribe tight control of the money supply, with the possible consequence of high and prolonged unemployment, in order to reduce inflation. A second theory is based directly on *Keynes' theory of income determination. This 'demand pull' theory postulates that inflation arises when aggregate demand for goods and services exceeds supply, usually as a result of incorrect monetary or *fiscal policies. A further model to explain inflation, also derived from Keynes' analysis, is the 'cost-push' theory, whereby costs are increased by a rise in import prices or in one of the components of domestic income (most commonly wages),leading to a price-wage spiral. *Prices-and-incomes policies have been used on this approach to control inflation, but are widely discredited today on the grounds that they tend to disrupt market mechanisms and cause shortages. In some developing countries, notably in Latin America, extremely high rates of inflation have been attributed to structural imbalances caused by rapid development, and also, or alternatively, to an exorbitantly high rate of imports, which cannot be paid for by an equally high rate of exports, and so leads to continued falls in the exchange rate and hence ever-higher prices of imports.

informal sector, a term used broadly to describe that part of a country's economic system which operates in some way outside the legal and statistical framework. The economic activity may itself be illegal, for example the production and trade of prohibited *drugs or smuggling; or it may be unreported to the government in order to avoid the payment of taxes or compliance with relevant legislation, for example labour laws which specify conditions of work and *minimum wages. In many developing countries, the informal sector has expanded as people migrate to cities and find insufficient employment opportunities. These migrant labourers often become *slum dwellers or *squatters who engage in whatever form of self-employment they can find. Economists and government planners, who had formerly disparaged as marginal or attempted to control such informal-sector activity, are now tending to recognize at least the vigour and size of such informal sectors. Characterized by ease of entry, reliance on indigenous resources, family ownership of enterprises, small scale of operation, labour-intensive and adapted technology, skills acquired outside the formal school system, and unregulated and competitive markets, the informal sector is estimated to account for between 30 and 70 per cent of the economically active population in most developing countries. One result of the existence of the informal sector is the failure of national accounts to measure fully the size of a national economy. Although informal-sector economic activity may be vigorous, levels of productivity are likely to be low and policies now focus on strategies to provide further investment for the informal sector or to develop links between the informal sector and organized sector, which is characterized by difficult entry, frequent reliance on overseas resources, corporate ownership, capital-intensive technology which is often imported, formally acquired skills, and government-protected markets.

information technology, the application of a combination of computing, telecommunications, and microelectronics to the collection, processing, storage, and transmission of information. Information-processing of one kind or another is a key activity in all advanced industrial economies, permeating areas such as banking, finance, design, manufacturing, and transport planning, as well as fields such as journalism, publishing, and broadcasting. Information technology has transformed libraries by introducing new forms of data storage; it has cut costs and speeded production times for newspapers, and has made possible instantaneous global television links; and it has greatly facilitated business communication through word-processing, desk-top publishing, the exchange of electronic mail from one computer to another, and the transmission of documents by fax machines (see *telecommunications). Information technology raises problems of *privacy and *freedom of information, as data is gathered about citizens who may not have access to records held about them (see *data protection, *surveillance).

infrastructure, a term referring most commonly to a country's stock of fixed *capital in basic services, notably roads and other communications networks, and public utilities such as energy, *water, and *sanitation. Infrastructure may also be interpreted as including health services and *education, since these contribute to society's *human capital by improving the work-force's quality and productivity.

initiation, a process of admission into a section of society or a particular role, through the use of *ritual. Initiation is usually marked by a *rite of passage, as the individual passes from one status to another. Initiation may be a religious rite, denoting full admission into a particular religion, as in ceremonies such as Baptism, Confirmation, or *bar mitzvah; or it may mark a change in social role: for example, admission to the status of warrior in *Maasai society, or admission to the status of graduate in the graduation ceremony of a university. Initiation ceremonies are also used when an individual is admitted to a common-interest society, such as the *Masonic Order, US college fraternities, or German student brotherhoods (*Brüderschaften*).

injunction, a court order aimed at either restraining a person from performing a particular action, or compelling him or her to do something. In *common law systems it is granted at the court's discretion, especially where *damages would be inadequate or inappropriate; for example, an injunction may restrain a person from playing loud music in a residential area at night or prevent the publication of defamatory material. Failure to comply with an injunction constitutes *contempt of court, which may result in imprisonment. In the USA injunctions are often used to protect constitutional rights. The injunction is a remedy little used in *civil law systems, with the exception of Germany, where it is used to protect against interference with property, and to supplement the slander laws.

Inns of Court, four sets of buildings in London (Inner Temple, Middle Temple, Lincoln's Inn, and Gray's Inn) belonging to the legal societies of England and Wales with the exclusive right of 'calling persons to the bar' (the partition, real or imaginary, across a law court, separating the judge, jury, and certain lawyers from the public), and thereby enabling them to practise as *barristers. Each Inn is governed by officers called benchers (Masters of the Bench), who mainly comprise judges and Queen's Counsels (QCs).

inquest, a legal or judicial inquiry to determine matters of fact. In *common law systems, the term is used to denote a coroner's inquest, a legal inquiry which has to take place in the event of a sudden, violent, or suspicious death, in order to determine the cause. Coroners' inquests are sometimes held before a *jury, but are not criminal proceedings. If unlawful *homicide is suspected and criminal proceedings are likely, the coroner will usually adjourn the inquest. If the inquest jury find that a particular person caused the death in circumstances amounting to homicide, that person may stand trial. Other verdicts may be death from natural causes, accidental death, and *suicide. The coroner may make recommendations (for example, about a dangerous product) to prevent similar deaths in future. Coroners also hold inquests on treasure trove (money, gold, or silver which is found and the ownership of which is unknown).

inquisitorial procedure, a legal procedure found in countries with *civil law systems in which the judge takes an active role in the conduct of a case by leading the investigations, examining the evidence, and interrogating witnesses. Under the *adversarial procedure, used in *common law countries, these responsibilities lie with the legal representatives of both parties. Three distinct stages are apparent in the inquisitorial system: the filing of pleadings and the appointment of a hearing judge; the collation and presentation of evidence; and the consideration by a bench of judges, including the hearing judge, of the report on the case and written submissions on the law by lawyers acting for the parties. Oral argument is only heard about selected issues. There are several fundamental distinctions between the inquisitorial and adversarial systems: in the former, heavy emphasis is placed on the written, as opposed to the spoken, word; the hearing judge may pursue enquiries not suggested by the parties' lawyers; and instead of a rigid turn-taking in the presentation of evidence by opposing sides, there is a more continuous flow of evidence.

insider trading, the buying or selling of financial *assets (typically *shares) by individuals or organizations who have access to privileged information affecting the likely future movement of the asset's market price. Such trading is commonly illegal.

insolvency, the condition of being unable to pay one's *debts or to discharge one's liabilities. Either a firm or an individual may become insolvent: a firm is insolvent if its *liabilities exceed its *assets (excluding its equity capital). Insolvency is not synonymous with bankruptcy; if an insolvent individual, trader, or firm is not successful in raising funds to discharge liabilities, the insolvent trader or person, or his or her creditors, may petition to the Bankruptcy Court to be declared bankrupt. Debtors who are not insolvent may also in certain cases petition for bankruptcy. A receiver is appointed to examine the financial position of the debtor or insolvent. During this time the receiver controls and administers the debtor or insolvent's finances. If bankruptcy is then declared, the receiver or another is made trustee of the bankrupt's property, which is distributed for the benefit of all his or her creditors, some of whom, such as secured creditors or preference-shareholders, may take priority over others. In the case of a company, bankruptcy is often synonymous with the liquidation, or winding up, of the company, but it may sometimes provide an opportunity for the company to be restructured and to be maintained as a going concern or for a *management buy-out. In the case of an individual bankrupt, he or she is discharged from bankruptcy after meeting his or her obligations and after a period set by the court. The effect of bankruptcy proceedings is thus to eliminate indebtedness, and their purpose to provide creditors with an equitable settlement of debt.

instinct, a set of behaviour patterns which develops, without learning, in all members of a species and serves functional ends, such as eating, drinking, and reproduction. The claim that such patterns are innate does not imply that they cannot be modified by learning or environmental pressure. Complex organisms like humans have less fixed behaviour than simpler ones.

institutional care, a form of care in which children or adults who are homeless, mentally ill, mentally or physically handicapped, debilitated by age, or thought to require containment are accommodated in residential institutions. Psychiatric hospitals, orphanages, and other institutions multiplied in Europe and elsewhere in the 19th century in response to the pressures of industrialization, urbanization, and an increasing population. While for short periods (for instance, during an acute episode of *mental illness) residential placement may be a useful option, it is argued that long-term institutional care tends to be harmful and takes on the characteristics of a *total institution. Furthermore, residential institutions are costly to run and difficult to staff. Many countries have sought both to improve institutional care by better staff-training and management, and improved physical conditions. In many industrialized countries, the policy known as 'deinstitutionalization' has resulted in a dramatic emptying of mental hospitals without the parallel development of *community care services. Supporters of the policy argue that the lives of former patients have become fuller, freer, and more productive, but others describe it as inhumane, citing the rise in young, chronically ill patients, the difficulty in finding treatment, and the cutting of funds to mental health services.

insurance, a guarantee against risk provided by an insurance company in the form of an insurance policy, a contract paid for by one or more premiums (regular payments) in exchange for a guarantee of financial compensation in some specified circumstance. Insurance is commonly classified into general insurance and life *assurance. General insurance covers policy holders against risks such as fire and theft. Life assurance guarantees a payment in the event of the policy holder's death or after the passage of a certain number of years. *Social insurance is a generic term for *social security schemes based on the insurance principle and organized by governments. (See also *endowment policy.)

integration (in economics), the merging into common ownership or organization of businesses operating in the same market (horizontal integration), in successive production stages of a particular good or group of goods (vertical integration), or in totally different sectors of the economy (conglomerate integration). Horizontal integration, in particular, is the merging of companies that are competitors. The reasons for firms to seek integration may include the existence of *economies of scale, and the pursuit of *monopoly power (which is also why governments may wish to limit or prevent *mergers). For a group of economic regions or nation-states such as the *EC, integration refers to the process of increasing mutual trade and factor mobility and seeking to harmonize or co-ordinate economic policy and performance among the members.

intellectual property, an internationally recognized term for legal protection of products of the intellect. Such protection has developed by analogy with that given to conventional *property. The term intellectual property covers protection of aesthetic works by *copyright, inventions by *patents, ideas and information by the legal obligation of confidentiality, and certain business interests by way of *trademarks. Most countries have intellectual property laws, and international agreements exist. The World Intellectual Property Organization (WIPO), an agency of the UN, is responsible for promoting the protection of intellectual property throughout the world and attempting to harmonize different intellectual property laws. In some parts of the world, particularly in South-east Asia, the piracy of Western books, records, videos, computer programs, and brand-name products has been a growing problem, despite the fact that certain Asian countries have begun to introduce their own intellectual property laws and have made efforts to join the international copyright community.

intelligence, the ability to acquire, organize, and use knowledge, differing between individuals and basic to all processes of reasoning. Capacity to learn and to adapt to the environment is also said to be an attribute of intelligence. As measured by *intelligence tests, there is some correlation between intelligence, educational achievement, and occupational status. However, there are many forms of intelligence. Mentally handicapped 'idiots savants' occasionally show prodigious memory or exceptional drawing skills. Child psychologists emphasize qualitatively distinct stages in intelligence, as *cognitive development progresses from infancy to adulthood. Intelligence in technological societies may also be defined in relation to verbal and spatial skills, which make for success in school. Heredity, the environment, and the interplay between the two probably all play a role in the development of intelligence, but their relative importance is disputed. (See *behaviour genetics.)

intelligence services, government organizations dedicated to the collection and evaluation of information, primarily about the intentions of other countries that are seen as adversaries. Such information can be economic, political, or military, and can relate either to general trends or to specific groups such as *terrorists, individuals, and institutions. Much intelligence is gathered from public sources, but intelligence services have also developed extensive covert activities, designed to protect and enhance national security. They have also acquired functions in *counter-intelligence, in order to safeguard their own operations and to manipulate those of adversaries. Among the most significant intelligence services are those of the USA (primarily the Central Intelligence Agency, or CIA), the UK (the Security Service (SS) and the Secret Intelligence Service (SIS), popularly known as MI5 and MI6, which deal respectively with internal security and intelligence-gathering abroad), France (Direction Générale de la Sécurité Extérieure, or DGSE), Israel (Mossad), China (Social Affairs Department), and, formerly, the Soviet KGB. In most cases, intelligence services distinguish between civilian and military operations: thus, the CIA operates alongside such bodies as the Defense Intelligence Agency (DIA) and the National Security Agency (NSA). Many national intelligence services also regard it as their job to monitor events, groups, and personalities in their own societies, reflecting the growth of the *national security state during the cold war period, and arousing political and legal objections in several Western countries. In *authoritarian states, intelligence services are often closely allied to the political, police, and propaganda organizations. In industrial espionage, businesses seek to acquire trade secrets of design, manufacturing processes, research, and future plans from their competitors.

intelligence test, a measure of individual differences in *intelligence, the first being devised by *Binet in 1908. The most widely known is the Wechsler test, which measures verbal and non-verbal abilities such as vocabulary, reasoning by analogy, memory, and spatial abilities to yield an Intelligence Quotient (IQ). For any population the average IQ score is 100. An IQ test score higher than 130 is obtained by no more than 5 per cent of the population and this may define intellectual giftedness. In the UK a score below 70 legally defines mental handicap. In recent years, other measures have been developed, such as reaction-time tasks, in which speed and accuracy of response are taken as a measure of *intelligence. Any intelligence test is a partial and inadequate measure of an individual's mind. In particular, what is tested may not be what will be most useful in everyday life; and so-called 'culture-fair' tests, where such factors as socio-cultural bias in test materials, variations among test subjects in language skill, motivation, test-taking attitudes, and rapport with the tester have been taken into account, have failed to live up to their name.

intentionality, a doctrine in the philosophy of the *mind (which has, however, nothing to do with intention in the sense of 'meaning to do something'). *Brentano proposed that mental phenomena should be distinguished from physical phenomena by virtue of their being 'directed towards objects'. By this he meant that a mental state such as Jane's thought about John must be understood in terms of its special relation of 'aboutness' to John: John so to speak 'exists intentionally' in Jane's mind. Brentano's doctrine is widely accepted as showing something crucial about the mental, but the underlying nature of intentionality remains puzzling.

interdependence, in politics and economics, a state of mutual dependence, characterized by the sensitivity of states to the actions of others. The concept was particularly fashionable in analysing international relations in the 1970s when it was perceived that the growing ties or transnational relations between states rendered inappropriate the old 'realist' or state-centric view of international relations and called for a new approach. Yet while interdependence has become an increasingly important aspect of the world scene, with its consequences being evident in the great diversity of activity among *international or transnational organizations, it has so far failed to undermine the system of nation-states.

interest (in economics), payments made by a borrower to a lender during specified time periods in return for the use of a capital sum. To the borrower these payments represent the cost of borrowing. To the lender they are a reward for postponing *consumption (by saving rather than spending) and for the risk of making the loan. The rate of interest for a specified time period is the percentage ratio of the interest paid to the capital sum borrowed. If £100 is borrowed for one year and £8 interest is repaid in addition to the £100, the rate of interest is $8/100 \times 100/1 = 0.08$ or 8 per cent per annum. The proximate determinants of interest rates are the supply of and demand for funds. The real rate of interest is the nominal or money rate minus the economy's (expected) rate of price inflation. The *central bank influences the money rate of interest as part of its conduct of monetary policy.

interest group, a voluntary association, aiming to influence government or public opinion in order to protect its interests or promote its objectives. A distinction is commonly made between sectional groups, such as *trade unions or employers' organizations, who defend social and economic interests, and promotional or pressure groups, who espouse a particular cause or belief such as voluntary relief agencies, or environmental groups. Interest and pressure groups mostly rely upon persuasion, through contacts with ministers and civil servants, through *lobbying the *legislature and *political parties, or through efforts to influence public opinion. In many cases, interest groups aid and assist in the preparation of legislation by appearing before legislative committee hearings as in the USA. Pressure-group tactics may go beyond this, however, and include the threat or use of *sanctions, such as strikes or *boycotts, or the attempt to bribe public officials (see *corruption). Despite cynicism, at times well justified, about their motives and methods, interest groups are indispensable intermediaries in the process of communication between citizens and government in *pluralist liberal democracies.

Influencing public opinion through publicized stunts is an important tactic of the **interest group**. In June 1990 the French farming lobby artificially transplanted a wheatfield to the Champs Elysées to draw attention to its members' financial difficulties.

International Atomic Energy Agency (IAEA), an international organization based in Vienna, Austria, which was established in 1957, under the auspices of the *UN. The Agency, of which 113 states are members, encourages the peaceful uses of atomic power in such fields as agriculture,

medicine, industry, and energy supply. It offers technical assistance and guidance on safety standards. It seeks to ensure that nuclear materials and equipment intended for peaceful use are not diverted to military purposes. In accordance with the *Nuclear Non-Proliferation Treaty (1968), it inspects nuclear installations in those states that have acceded to it. The IAEA played an important role in dealing with the consequences of the accident at the Chernobyl nuclear power plant in Ukraine in 1986. After the 1991 Gulf War, IAEA inspectors established the existence of Iraq's secret nuclear weapons programme, leading to calls for stronger measures, including more special inspections, to prevent proliferation.

International Court of Justice, one of the six principal organs of the *UN, and its main judicial body. The Court sits at The Hague in The Netherlands. It has fifteen judges elected for renewable nine-year terms by the General Assembly and the Security Council. Only states, not individuals, can be parties to cases before the Court. Its jurisdiction is not binding and depends on the consent of the states concerned. While it has not been prominent in preventing or ending wars, it has given judgments in some important disputes and contributed to the development of *international law. Among the cases brought to the court have been those by Australia and New Zealand against France over nuclear testing in the Pacific in 1973, and Nicaragua's case against the USA over the placing of mines in its harbours in 1984.

International Covenant on Civil and Political Rights, a covenant adopted by the *UN in 1966. Eighty-eight countries are signatories. The covenant promulgates the civil and political rights enumerated in the *Universal Declaration of Human Rights of 1948. Whereas the Declaration is not legally binding, the covenant has the legal force of a treaty for the parties to it. The rights safeguarded include *freedom of expression, conscience, and movement; the right to liberty and *privacy, the right to vote, and the right to a fair trial. These rights are to apply without discrimination, and legal remedies are to be available within each state against breaches of the covenant. Signatories undertake to respect its provisions and to submit reports to a human rights committee within the UN. This committee is also responsible for a procedure through which states, and, in certain circumstances, individuals, may complain of non-compliance. By comparison with the *International Covenant on Economic, Social and Cultural Rights adopted in the same year, this covenant is more specific in its delineation of rights, stronger in affirming states' obligations, and better provided with means of review and supervision.

International Covenant on Economic, Social and Cultural Rights, a covenant adopted by the *UN in 1966. Ninety-two countries are signatories. The covenant promotes, but has no mechanism to enforce, the economic, social, and cultural rights enumerated in the *Universal Declaration of Human Rights of 1948. Whereas the Declaration is not legally binding, the Covenant has the legal force of a treaty for the parties to it. The rights safeguarded include such rights as the right to work, to education, and to participation in cultural life.

International Labour Organization (ILO), an agency founded in 1919 to improve labour and living standards throughout the world. At first affiliated to the League of Nations, in 1946 the ILO became the first specialized agency of the *UN. The ILO sets international guidelines for improving working conditions, *trade-union rights, the rights of women and children, *minimum wage levels, hours, and health and safety at work. It provides technical assistance to developing countries, promotes *employment, and researches and reports on trends in employment and *industrial-relations practice and law. The ILO received the Nobel Peace Prize in 1967.

international law, sometimes called the law of nations, the body of rules and principles which states consider legally binding on them in their *international relations. The three major sources of international law according to Article 38 of the Statute of the *International Court of Justice are: international *conventions or *treaties; international customs; and the general principles of law as recognized by civilized nations. Modern international law has evolved over the last 400 years. It grew, in part, out of the usages and practices of modern European states in their relations with each other. It is particularly associated with the Dutch jurist and philosopher Hugo Grotius (1583–1645), author of *The Law of Peace and War* (1625). The 19th century saw a great expansion in international law when the rise of powerful new states, the expansion of European colonialism, new industrial innovations, and the increased destructiveness of war, made it urgent that states should devise a system of rules to regulate the conduct of their international affairs. The 20th century has also seen major advances. The Permanent Court of Arbitration was established by the Hague Conferences of 1899 and 1907, and the Permanent Court of International Justice was set up in 1921 and succeeded in 1946 by the *International Court of Justice. Since World War II *international organizations such as the *UN and its related bodies have also contributed to the expansion and increased scope of international law to include not only political and strategic affairs, with which international law in earlier periods had been primarily concerned, but also economic, social, communications, and environmental matters. Because international law, unlike domestic or municipal law, has no dependable machinery behind it, and therefore no effective means of securing its enforcement, it is often said that states show little respect for international law or even that strictly speaking it should not be called law at all. Yet states clearly do accept that international law is law and, contrary to popular belief, they usually obey it, partly through custom and respect for public opinion, and partly because it is in their mutual interests that they should do so. Far from being ineffective, international law has over the past few centuries played a vital role in shaping today's international society as witnessed by the development of an elaborate system of rules which touches on virtually every aspect of inter-state relations: relating to land, sea, air, outer space, *diplomacy, *neutrality, *warfare, *human rights, and the environment. While there is a tendency to focus on the failures of international law in the realm of peace and war, these are the exception rather than the rule. By the early 1990s international law had not only shown its durability and its flexibility by expanding to cover new areas of international relations, but also its efficacy when, through the machinery of the UN, Iraq's aggression against Kuwait in 1990 was effectively repudiated.

International Monetary Fund (IMF), an international economic institution, and specialized agency of the *UN. The IMF was established in 1945 and is based in Washington, DC. In 1991 it had 151 members. Unlike the *World Bank, to which it is closely allied, the IMF is not a development agency. Its principal aims are to encourage international monetary co-operation and the expansion of international trade, to stabilize *exchange rates, and to eliminate foreign-exchange restrictions. Member states subscribe funds in accordance with their wealth. The Fund has supplemented its resources by borrowing from countries with ample reserves and by creating a new reserve asset, the Special Drawing Right (see *currency). The Fund offers its members an orderly system for settling financial transactions among themselves. It also makes loans to countries with *balance-of-payments difficulties. In recent years most have been developing countries. Such loans are normally conditional on changes in their economic policies (see *adjustment) designed to improve economic performance. Since these changes often entail cuts in public expenditure, welfare services, and subsidies, and increases in the cost of living, the IMF's conditions have at times been a source of controversy between the IMF and recipient nations. Furthermore, implementation of an IMF-approved programme has typically been necessary for them to secure renewal of their large-scale loans from commercial banks. In 1986 the Fund established a 'structural adjustment facility' to provide assistance to low-income developing countries.

international organizations, a body set up by a multilateral agreement between two or more countries, aimed at promoting the common interests of its members. Such organizations are 'formal, continuous' structures; that is, they hold regular meetings and have a permanent secretariat or headquarters. International organizations have proliferated since the mid-19th century with the growing awareness of the problems of co-existence among states, and the need to regulate relations between them. The term is now often applied to both inter-governmental organizations (IGOs), comprising states or government representatives of member countries, and *transnational, or *non-governmental organizations (NGOs), whose members are non-state actors, such as charities or religious groups. International organizations may be universal in scope, such as the *UN and its different agencies, or restricted to a particular geographical region, such as the *EC, the *Organization of American States or the *Arab League, in which case they may also be referred to as *regional organizations.

international relations *balance of power, *East–West relations, *international law, *North–South relations, *regionalism, *transnational relations.

international society, a concept of the solidarity of states going back to the idea of a 'great society of states' first put forward by the Dutch jurist and humanist Hugo Grotius (1583–1645). For neo-Grotian theorists, the existence of *international law, *diplomacy, and *international organizations suggests a world community beyond the nation-state, characterized by co-operation and communal values. Those who wish to see an international society, as opposed to a mere international system of interacting and often conflicting states, envisage a *world order in which the only legitimate use of force is restricted to international society itself, in defence of international law (see *collective security).

Interpol (International Criminal Police Organization), an international organization of police forces, aimed at promoting exchange of information and more effective law enforcement. Interpol was established in 1923, in Vienna, and since the end of World War II its headquarters has been in Paris. Its operations are based on co-operation between its members, the national police forces of 138 countries, and on a central clearing-house for information which maintains records on international criminals. The growing internationalization of crime has created an increasing need for Interpol's services, particularly in dealing with arms smuggling, drugs networks, *money-laundering, and those who take refuge in other countries after committing offences. Although Interpol can provide information and assist in locating offenders, it cannot arrest or imprison them, and national governments have the power to block *deportation and *extradition which can limit international co-operation. Although the extensive membership of Interpol is useful, it can also pose problems, as in cases where certain countries decline to work seriously with others, for political reasons.

intervention (in economics), any action by government designed to alter or limit the *market forces of *supply and *demand. Examples are the *regulation of industry by price control or quantity restrictions, trade *protectionism, and official financing to support the *balance of payments or the *exchange rate. In practice, nearly all governments today are in some measure interventionist, but there is much debate among both economists and politicians over the degree of intervention that is desirable.

Inuit, an *Arctic society more commonly known as the Eskimo. They are mostly coastal dwellers, and fishing is their principal source of food, together with the hunting of aquatic mammals such as seals and walrus, which not only provide food but also skins for clothing. Like many other semi-nomadic societies, such as the *Lapps, the basis of their social organization is the *family and household. During the winter months families gather to form larger groups, which disperse in the summer months, and live in temporary shelters. The igloo, or ice shelter, was not as common traditionally as huts made from turf or even driftwood. The Inuit way of life has changed considerably with the introduction of modern technology, and many now live in permanent settlements.

inventory, a listing of the assets of an organization, but usually relating specifically to stock. Organizations need to keep records of stocks of raw materials, semi-finished, and finished but unsold goods to help determine profitability and efficiency levels. Annual financial records need to take account of inventory costs. In times of *inflation a particular problem is how to value inventory when the value of some assets rises above the cost paid for them. In financial accounts stock values are reported at the lower of cost and market value. A re-evaluation of assets may be necessary each year so that any appreciation in market value can be taken into account.

investment, a term referring to expenditure on the formation or maintenance of physical *capital, whether fixed (buildings and machinery) or producers' inventories. Investment is a crucial factor in economic growth. In common usage, the word has a wider meaning, being used also to refer to acquisition of financial *assets, particularly the purchase of *shares.

investment trust, a company which uses all its capital to buy a portfolio of shares in other companies for investment purposes, rather than to gain control of them. Shareholders of investment trusts (closed-end mutual funds in the USA) and unit holders in unit trusts (open-end mutual funds in the USA) both gain the advantages of a widespread portfolio. In the latter case a unit-trust holding is not a share holding in the unit-trust company, but a certificate representing the underlying bundle of shares held by that institution.

Iroquois, Indians of the north-eastern woodlands of the USA and Canada. Unlike the *Plains Indians, the Iroquois traditionally lived in permanent fortified villages. The men were *hunter-gatherers, while the women grew crops of maize, squash, and beans. Descent was *matrilineal, and women had a high status. The Iroquois were not a distinct *tribe, but a confederation or league, consisting of five tribes. This was highly organized, with decisions being taken by voting among the tribal members, and then in council by each tribal representative. The Iroquois were also skilled warriors, and expanded the confederation by conquest, until the height of their powers in the mid-17th century. Like other Indian groups, the power of the Iroquois was eventually eclipsed by the European colonists.

Islam, the religion of Muslims, revealed through *Muhammad, the Prophet of Allah. The name comes from Arabic, meaning 'submission' to God. The cardinal principle of Islam is *tawhīd* (making one), the absolute unity of God, Allah, the universal creator whose omnipotence is supreme. This is expressed in the *shahādah:* 'There is no god but Allah and Muhammad is his Messenger'. Human authority lies with a succession of prophets, of whom the most important are Noah, Abraham (regarded by Muslims as 'the father of Islam'), Moses, and Jesus, with Muhammad as the final 'Seal of the Prophets'. Islam has two major sects: *Sunnī and *Shī'a Islam. Shī'īs revere *'Alī, the son-in-law of Muhammad, as the first successor of Muhammad. Divine origin and authority is attributed to the *Koran, the 'recitation' of the word and will of God, as revealed by the Angel Gabriel to Muhammad, superseding and fulfilling all other religious scriptures. Religious practice is based upon observance of the *Five Pillars of Islam. Public worship occurs in a *mosque, where prayer is led by an *imām. Attendance at the mosque, which is not required of women, is compulsory for men on Fridays and special festivals and meritorious on all days. Moral and religious law is disseminated through the *sharī'ah*, based on the Koran and the *hadīth*, a canon of belief and social regulation. There are four schools of law in Sunnī Islam; disputes have traditionally been resolved by *'ijma'*, or consensus. Islam does not recognize a clergy which intermediates between the individual and God; however, religious and legal officials exist to give leadership on matters of faith and doctrine, particularly within the Shī'a branch of Islam. Parallel to the formal practice of Islam is the *Sufi or mystical movement through which an individual may experience direct intuitive awareness of God. Sufi fraternities such as *dervishes form an important element in Muslim spiritual life and society. Islam is the official religion of forty-five states world-wide, with some 800 million followers concentrated within the Middle East, North Africa, and parts of central, south, and east Asia.

Islamic calendar, a calendar based upon lunar months. Unlike the Gregorian solar calendar, it avoids the use of leap years, and therefore each Muslim year begins eleven to twelve days earlier than the previous one. The Muslim era begins with the *hijrah, the year in which Muhammad left Mecca for Medina, AD 622. Although it is impossible to match the Muslim months exactly with the Gregorian months, a formula exists for calculating corresponding Gregorian years with Muslim years: AH (After Hijrah) = $33/32$ (AD-622), or AD = $32/33$ (AH$+622$). *Muharram* is the first month of the new year. The Prophet's birthday falls in the third month, *Rabī 'ul-Awwal*, regarded by many Muslims as the most important date in human history, since it was through Muhammad that Allah's will was revealed. The ninth month, *Ramadan, is a month of fasting, and ends with the festival of *'īd-ul-fitr* The 'Night of Power', on which Muhammad received the first of many revelations from the Angel Gabriel, is commemorated on the night of the 26th/27th of this month.

Islamic fundamentalism, the belief that the revitalization of Islamic society can only come about through a return to the fundamental principles and practices of early Islam. Fundamentalist movements have often been a response to political and economic decline, which is ascribed to spiritual and moral decay. For example, in the 18th and 19th centuries, the disintegration of Muslim political and economic power and the ascendancy of the West were instrumental in the emergence of a number of differing revivalist movements. Despite major differences, these movements shared the belief that religion is integral to both state and society, in contrast to the Western secular view that religion and politics should be separated, and advocated a return to a life patterned on the 7th-century political community of the faithful established by Muhammad at Medina, governed by the *sharī'ah (Islamic law), and supported if need be by *jihād (holy war). In the 20th century, activist organizations such as the Muslim Brotherhood, which was founded in Egypt in 1928 and has or had national independent organizations in Jordan, Kuwait, Palestine, Sudan, and Syria, and is influential in Afghanistan, India, and Pakistan, and other more radical groups such as Hizbullah (Party of God) have become prominent. Such groups are characterized by emphasis on the literal interpretation of the Koran and *sharī'ah*. By contrast with *Islamic modernists, fundamentalists tend to stress the penal code and restrictions on women contained in the *sharī'ah*, at least in part because such provisions have become symbols of cultural identity and antagonism to *westernization. The Muslim Brotherhood advocates presidential rule with an elected consultative council replicating the *shūra* of Muhammad's day. Many fundamentalists regard multiparty politics as divisive of the Muslim community. Some may be Islamic socialists, who are careful to denounce the materialism and atheism of *Marxism, but deplore the inequities of *capitalism, especially its reliance on usury, which is forbidden in the Koran. Some Western observers have regarded the recent resurgence in Islamic religious practice and the Iranian Revolution of 1979 as further examples of fundamentalism, but it is not accurate to regard all Muslim religious practice, however strict, as fundamentalist, while scholarly examination of the constitutional structure of the Islamic Republic of Iran reveals radical innovations which are not fundamentalist. There is, however, no doubt that the Iranian revolution has been an inspiring example to many Muslims of all persuasions throughout the world.

The fifth basic religious observance of **Islam** is the *hajj* pilgrimage to the Ka'aba in Mecca, culminating in the circling of the sacred shrine seven times. Every Muslim aims to complete the pilgrimage, and the numbers are usually huge.

Supporters of the Algerian Islamic Salvation Front (FIS) on strike outside the Central Bank. In early 1992 the FIS was suppressed by the authorities who feared its electoral success would result in an **Islamic fundamentalist** state.

Islamic law *shari'ah.

Islamic modernism, a movement in Islamic thought which seeks to reinterpret Islam to meet the changing circumstances of contemporary life. By contrast with *Islamic fundamentalism, Islamic modernism is a response to Western imperialism and economic dominance which attempts to reform legal, educational, and social structures. From the 19th century leading Muslim thinkers such as Jamal al-Din al-Afghani (1838–1897) and his followers in Egypt, Muhammad Abduh (1849–1905) and Rashid Rida (1865–1935), were concerned at the stagnation they perceived in Muslim intellectual, political, and social life. They advocated the reform of the *shari'ah by reopening the door of *ijtihad*, or reinterpretation, which orthodox Sunnī Muslims have regarded as closed since the 9th century. Western scientific advances should not be rejected as incompatible with Islam, but should be integrated into the structure of a religion which is essentially scientific. Abduh distinguished between an inner unchanging core of Islamic belief and practice, and outer layers of regulations which could be varied in accordance with contemporary social practice. His reinterpretation of the law on these lines was continued by Rida, who drew on a traditional legal principle of public interest to formulate new laws. The Egyptian modernists' concern with the establishment of a modern Muslim state was echoed in India,

most influentially by the poet-philosopher, lawyer, and politician Muhammad Iqbal (1875–1938). Influenced by his study of Western philosophers such as *Hegel, *Fichte, and *Nietzsche, Iqbal developed his own synthesis and interpretation of Islam. His view of the community as a religio-political state based on the supremacy of the *shari'ah was influential in the establishment of Pakistan in 1947. Like the Egyptian modernists Iqbal distinguished between the immutable core of the *shari'ah*, and the regulations which were the product of human interpretation, and called for the renewal of *ijtihad* by the *legislature rather than by the *'ulama'. Like many Islamic modernists, Iqbal favoured pan-Islamism and the ideal of a transnational Muslim community which transcended nationalism, which he thought could be embodied in a Muslim League of Nations. Islamic modernism has had widespread influence in most Muslim countries, but despite its emphasis on the reform of the *shari'ah*, no systematic reform has ever been undertaken.

Ismā'īlīs, members of *Shī'ī sects (Musta'lians in India and Yemen, and Nizāris in Afghanistan, East Africa, India, Iran, and Syria,), who split from Shī'ī orthodoxy in the 8th century over the identity of the seventh *imām*, upholding the claims of Ismā'īl, from whom the sect takes its name. The family of the Aga Khan claims descent from Ismā'īl.

issuing house, an institution (in the US or UK usually a merchant *bank) which manages on behalf of a client company the raising of *capital through the selling of newly issued *securities. The confidence of investors may be influenced by the reputation of the issuing houses, which are selective in the issues they will organize. The issuing house may *underwrite (promise to buy) some or all of the securities issued if they remain unsold.

Italic languages, the early *Indo-European languages of Italy, of which Latin was by far the most important. They fall into two main groups: Oscan–Umbrian, which is named after its two major languages, but includes minor dialects of central Italy; and Latin–Faliscan. Oscan and Umbrian share broadly the same patterns of grammar and inflection as Latin, but diverge widely in *phonology and vocabulary. Faliscan is attested in a small number of inscriptions from Falerii, north of Rome. Latin was the language of Rome which spread with Roman political power; first in Italy, and later throughout the whole of Europe and the Mediterranean world. Earliest inscriptions date from the 6th century BC, but the great period of Latin literature began in the late 3rd century BC and continued for some 400 years. By the 9th century colloquial (or vulgar) Latin and the literary language were quite separate, and vulgar Latin evolved into the various *Romance dialects. Latin has had a unique influence on Western culture, for two main reasons: the political and cultural influence of the Romans; and the fact that Latin became the official language of the Christian Church in the West. Scientific, medical, and legal terms are still by convention taken from Latin.

J

Jainism, Indian religion and philosophy numbering some 3 million adherents. It is based on the teaching of twenty-four *tirthankaras* or *jinas* ('conquerors'), the last and greatest being the founder Mahavira (*fl. c.*500 BC). Jains do not believe in a creator God, but all followers attempt to live according to the rules of right knowledge, faith, and conduct. This will ensure the conquest of the bondage of physical existence and freedom from rebirth without supernatural aid. Central to Jain practice is the notion of **ahimsa*, respect for all life. *Ahimsa* demands strict vegetarianism and prohibits any action which directly or otherwise causes suffering to any living creature. Life is not only the property of animals and plants but also of entities such as stones, running water, and other natural objects. This theory has imbued the Jains with a kind of respect for nature not found in any other classical religious tradition. There are lay Jains, but release from the cycle of birth and death, **samsara*, calls for vows of celibacy and a severe regime of contemplation and self-denial, which may culminate in self-inflicted death by starvation. Jainism is tolerant towards other religions, and is not evangelical. In India its followers are mainly found in Gujarat and Maharashtra states. Although their relative size has been small throughout history, the influence of the Jains on Indian culture and the continuity of their history have been such that they are regarded as one of India's major religious traditions. Mahatma Gandhi's non-violent movements were significantly influenced by the Jains.

James, William (1842–1910), US philosopher and pioneer psychologist, who taught the world's first psychology course at the laboratory he set up at Harvard University in 1875 and whose *Principles of Psychology* (1890) is one of the subject's few classic texts. Three of its important ideas concerned **emotion*, **consciousness*, and the self. James claimed that bodily changes which are themselves **instinctive* responses to events cause emotion, rather than being its effects or concomitants. He held that consciousness is a constantly changing process or flow which has no states. His theory of the 'stream of consciousness' had a major conceptual impact (and an effect on literary theory and practice). James divided the 'self as known' into three, frequently conflicting, parts: the 'material me', the 'social me', and the 'spiritual me'. His ideas influenced the **symbolic inter-actionists* and underlie modern approaches to **self-esteem*, the **self concept*, and **self presentation*. *The Varieties of Religious Experience* (1902) was one of the earliest books on the psychology of **religion*. James's philosophy of **pragmatism* was an attempt to define knowledge and truth in terms of the success for the individual of efforts to control the environment, rather than of **perception*.

Japanese language, the language spoken by 123 million people in Japan. It is unclear what other languages Japanese is related to, and there has been considerable argument over this question. It seems to be distantly related to Korean, and many scholars now connect it with the **Altaic* group. There are many regional dialects, some of which are mutually unintelligible; however, virtually all Japanese people also speak the Common Standard Language, based on the dialect of Tokyo, which is used for official and educational purposes. The earliest attested Japanese, written in Chinese characters, dates from the 8th century AD. Modern Japanese is written in a mixture of Kanji, which consists of around 2,000 characters borrowed from Chinese, and Kana, which are phonetic characters based on Chinese. There are two varieties of Kana, Hiragana and Katakana; the former is used for writing Japanese, the latter for transliterating foreign words (representing them in native, rather than foreign, letters). The influence of Chinese on Japanese has been enormous; about 60 per cent of Japanese vocabulary is made up of borrowings from Chinese. In the 20th century there have also been borrowings from European languages, notably English. Important stylistic distinctions are observed in Japanese; speech will vary according to whether the setting is formal or informal, whether the speaker is male or female, and whether he or she is addressing a social superior.

Japanese society. Japan is marked by the homogeneity of its population. Its geographical remoteness naturally led to separate development, a trend accentuated by the government's policy of closing the country to the outside world from the 17th to the late 19th century. There is to this day a strong sense of insider and outsider. Within Japan, outsiders such as the Korean minority or the *burakumin* (communities practicing low-class trades), though legally emancipated, suffer social disabilities, whilst foreigners are known generally as 'outside persons' (*gaijin*). Linguistic separateness makes international contact uneasy, even though economic success has given the country a dominant world-wide role. Loyalty to the group and especially to its leader is the ruling ethical concept. The emperor may no longer be a god, but he remains the symbol of the nation, with continuing ritual duties associated with the **Shinto* religion. At every level there is a focus of loyalty and duty: for wife and children, towards the paterfamilias; for students, towards their professors; for employees, towards their company chairman; and for politicians, towards the leader of the personal grouping or faction within a larger political party. The strength of these ties emphasizes the indifference to outsiders or those of another grouping. Although Japan appears to have assumed the trappings of a modern Western state, most of its citizens prefer the traditional diet, traditional housing, and traditional styles of relaxation. A family may baptize its children by Christian rites, but marry them in a Shinto ceremony and expect its elders' obsequies to be carried out in a Buddhist temple. Hedonism often coexists with austerity. The insecurity of life in Japan, subject as it is to earthquakes and typhoons, has led to a sense of the transience of life, not yet obliterated by the comforts of late 20th-century living. Most Japanese prefer to look for security within the group with which they are at home, and to seek agreement by consensus rather than the confrontation of opposing views, both within the group and when they have to deal with outsiders.

Japji (Punjabi, 'you recite and understand'), a hymn composed by the first Sikh **Guru*, **Nanak*, and found in the opening section of the **Adi Granth*, the Sikh sacred book. The devout Sikh is expected to rise early, wash, and then recite the thirty-eight verses of the *Japji* from memory. The hymn sums up Guru Nanak's teaching: the belief in the absolute unity of God (*Ik Omkar*, 'One Creator'), who is omnipotent and omnipresent, beyond time and without form.

jargon, a variety of **language* featuring a high level of technical vocabulary. It serves professionals (in medicine,

linguistics, and elsewhere) to convey specialized subject-matter. Its unintelligibility to outsiders often provokes public irritation, so it has a derogatory sense. The use of jargon such as criminal argot often marks group membership. Jargon partly overlaps with *slang.

Javanese   *Austronesian languages.

Jehovah's Witness, a member of a Christian sect believing in the imminent end of time and the elevation of 144,000 'elect of Jehovah' to be with God in a Messianic kingdom. They deny most of the fundamental Christian doctrines and refuse to acknowledge the claims of the state when these conflict with the sect's principles. It was founded by Charles Russell in 1878 in Pittsburgh, USA, together with his magazine *The Watchtower*, which is still published and acts as the sect's focal point. There are about 2 million members, mainly in English-speaking countries.

Jesuits, formally known as the Society of Jesus, a religious order of the Roman Catholic Church, founded in 1534 by St Ignatius Loyola and approved by Pope Paul III in 1540. Despite periods of suppression, the Jesuits remain a powerful intellectual body. Governed by a General Congregation, they elect a Superior General with life tenure. A special vow of obedience to the pope is taken. Jesuits have traditionally engaged in international missionary and educational work. Since the Second Vatican Council (1962–5), they have played a leading role in Roman Catholic reforms.

Jesus Christ (*c*.6 BC–AD 30), the central figure of *Christianity, believed by his followers to be the Son of God. In Christian belief Jesus Christ is fully divine, of one essence with God the Father and God the Holy Spirit in the doctrine of the *Trinity. He was born a Jew in the Roman province of Palestine. The principal sources for his life and teaching are the Gospels of the *Bible. Through his *miracles and preaching with the use of parables and proverbs, he proclaimed the Kingdom of God and taught the ethical and religious qualities demanded of those who were to enter it. His crucifixion and death were followed, according to Christian belief, by his resurrection from the dead. The compassion he displayed in life to the poor and lowly is held up as an example of Christian conduct, and his sacrifice of his life is the core of the doctrine of *atonement, by which God redeems humanity from *sin. The *Christian calendar of festivals revolves around the life of Jesus Christ, and the drama of his life, suffering, death, and resurrection lies at the heart of Christian ritual and belief.

Jewish calendar, a lunar calendar, normally consisting of twelve months, which alternate between 29 and 30 days, as each lunar month is actually 29.5 days. Tradition calculates the day of creation as occurring in 3760 BC; the present Jewish year is therefore calculated by adding 3,760 to the present Gregorian year.

Jewish law   *Talmud.

Jewish people, a people of Hebrew descent or those whose religion or cultural and political orientation is

Orthodox Jews reading from the Torah, or scrolls of the law, at the Wailing Wall in Jerusalem. There are deep divisions of religion, culture, and politics among the **Jewish people**, but many would defend Israel's claim to Jerusalem as its capital.

*Judaism. Jewish identity today is based more on a sense of shared history than ethnic or linguistic attributes. A common religious faith is no longer a unifying factor, with secularism (particularly in the West) on the rise and a decrease in religious observance on the one hand, and increased sectarian division on the other. *Orthodox Jews, for example, do not recognize many of the other branches of Jews, some of whom they regard as idol-worshippers, and they deplore the secularism of *Zionism. It is estimated there are 15 million Jews world-wide, with about 40 per cent in the *USA, 20 per cent in *Israel, 12 per cent in the *Soviet Union, and significant numbers in Argentina, Brazil, Canada, France, South Africa, and the UK. The *Falasha, a people of Ethiopia, are also recognized as Jewish. Mainly city-dwellers in their recent history, many Jews today are immigrants following massive population movements as a result of anti-Semitism, which found its most violent expression in the Nazi Holocaust of World War II, when an estimated 6 million Jews were murdered. More recently, large numbers of Soviet Jews have emigrated to Israel, following the relaxation of Soviet emigration laws. However, in most societies Jews are now more assimilated than ever before, although retaining self-identity as Jews; they retain prominence far beyond their numerical significance in world political, cultural, and economic affairs.

Jewish year, the annual cycle of festivals in Judaism. It starts with *Rosh Hashanah in the month of Tishri (September–October), a time of judgement by God, during which the fate of the coming year is determined. Rosh Hashanah is also a time of repentance, and, during *Yom Kippur, fasting. Sukkot (Feast of *Tabernacles), commemorating the Jews' desert wanderings after the Exodus from Egypt, occurs five days later. Cheshvan is followed by Kislev, and the celebration of *Hanukkah, which extends into Tevet (December–January). After Shevat (January–February), the fifteenth day of Adar marks the festival of *Purim. Nisan (March–April) brings *Passover, commemorating both spring and the Exodus. The period between Passover and *Pentecost (the rest of Nisan, Ityar (April–May), and part of Sivan (May–June)) is a time of semi-mourning during which no marriages may occur. The months of Tammuz (June–July) and Av (July–August) are associated with deep mourning for the destruction of the Temple and the exile of the Jews. The final month, Elul (August–September), begins preparation for the new year.

jihād, usually translated from Arabic as 'holy war', literally struggle or striving. One of the basic duties of a Muslim, prescribed as a religious duty by the *Koran and *ḥadīth, is to struggle against external threats to the vigour of the Islamic community and also against personal resistance to the rules of divine law within oneself. *Jihād* in theory is controlled by the strict laws of war in Islam, which prescribe conditions under which war may be declared, usually against an enemy who inhibits observance of the faith. Those who die fighting in a *jihād* are accorded a *martyr's place in heaven. In recent years, the concept of *jihād* has played a significant role in some *Islamic fundamentalist and revivalist movements, justifying political violence or *terrorism.

job evaluation, a technique used to arrange in order of relative value (as expressed in pay rates) the tasks within an organization. Job evaluation is a system for grading based on an analysis of the characteristics of different jobs and how closely they are related. Thus the concern is not with how well an individual is carrying out a job but with the job itself. Emphasis is placed on determining the qualifications and experience necessary to perform the job, and on the responsibilities of the particular post in the organization. There are a number of different methods for evaluating jobs. For example, a points system may be used with points awarded to a particular post according to a range of factors such as the level of education and training needed, physical skills and effort levels, responsibility for supervision of others, external contacts, level of internal contacts. The points for each job are compared and put into grade bands which are then used to determine salary levels. Annual increments are often used to reflect the growing experience achieved by an employee. In a large organization a more general classification system may be necessary and job evaluation may be based on: a brief description of the work, education and training requirements for the job, examples of typical work to be carried out and of typical jobs in the grade. A number of detailed job evaluation systems have been developed which cover all types of jobs. The overall aim is to achieve an equitable balance between the job undertaken and the remuneration provided so that harmonious *industrial relations are achieved. Job evaluation is used to establish pay differentials that have been distorted by inflation, to assist implementing *equal pay policies, and to adopt pay scales to changes resulting from new technology.

job satisfaction, the extent to which employees are content with their workplace experience. Job satisfaction in employees is extremely difficult to measure as no standard criteria for doing so exist. Tasks that bore some people interest others and some people will work hard even though dissatisfied with their work (for example, to earn more money). If employees are dissatisfied in their work they will tend to take as much time off as possible or leave. Levels of punctuality, rates of absenteeism, and the rate of labour turnover are perhaps the best indicators to measure job satisfaction. One method of improving job satisfaction is job enrichment. Job enrichment involves employees being given more responsibility and further training in their work. However, not all employees are likely to want more responsibility. It is important to research employees' feelings before taking action. The use of questionnaires asking employees what they like most and least about their jobs is one way of investigating levels of job satisfaction. (See also *alienation.)

joint-stock company, a company whose *capital ownership is split into small equal parts known as *shares (or common stock in the USA). Numerous investors can own different proportions of the company, all protected by *limited liability for the company's *debts. Thus any company with shares is a joint-stock company, including all public limited companies (PLCs).

journalism, the collection and dissemination of news and other information for *newspapers, periodicals, *broadcasting, and *television. Print journalism falls broadly into three divisions: news, features, and comment. News and features are usually submitted by staff reporters, correspondents, freelances (or stringers), and news agencies. News concentrates on factual reporting of current events, while features examine a subject in detail, and also cater for general interest topics such as the arts. A newspaper's editorial stance is most evident in its current or 'leader' column, where views on one or more of the main news stories are given. Broadsheet newspaper journalism often allows reporters the space

for an in-depth news account. Broadcast journalism's strength is its immediacy. For example, at the beginning of the 1991 Gulf War Cable News Network (CNN) journalists broadcast live from Baghdad as the US-led coalition bombed the city (see *cable television). The National Union of Journalists in the UK and Ireland, enjoins journalists to respect objectivity, accuracy, individual *privacy, and the confidentiality of sources. In tabloid journalism, particularly, these requirements may be ignored in the quest to attract advertisers and project the views of the newspaper's proprietor. In the UK, broadcast journalism is more strictly controlled than newspaper journalism, and television and radio journalists are usually required to give as objective an account of events as possible. Journalists around the world are constantly under pressure to relinquish their independent status. Concern that the presence of journalists and camera crews may influence events being covered (as in Beijing in 1989 when pro-democracy demonstrators were encouraged by world-wide interest) can lead totalitarian governments to control or ban them, and democratic ones to request limited coverage. (See also *agenda-setting.)

Judaism, the religion of the *Jewish people. The central belief of Judaism is faith in one God, summarized in the Shema, recited in all public and private devotions, the first verse of which is translated, 'Hear, O Israel: the Lord our God, the Lord is one'. Jews believe that God created both heaven and earth and ordained the Jewish people as the inheritors of a unique relationship with God, through the *Covenant he made with Abraham. There is also a *millenarian belief in the prophesied appearance of a Messiah, an 'anointed' figure who will initiate a time when all Jews will be gathered back to the land of Israel. Jewish religious practice is based on obedience to the *Torah, which governs every aspect of spiritual, religious, and moral life and is summarized in the Ten Commandments. In rabbinic tradition, the total number of biblical commandments (*mitzvot*) is given as 613. Further commentaries and oral traditions are codified within the *Mishnah and *Talmud. Public worship occurs in the local *synagogue and religious authority is vested in the *Rabbi, but many distinctive features of religious observance, particularly those surrounding diet (see *kosher) and *Shabbat worship, are centred in the home. Contemporary Judaism divides into several branches. *Orthodox Jews maintain the sole authority of the Torah as the indisputable revealed word of God. This is repudiated by *Liberal and *Reform Judaism, which express, to varying degrees, radical departures from traditional biblical observance. In the USA, *Conservative Judaism represents a compromise between the Orthodox and Reform movements. A further development, *Zionism, expresses a combination of nationalistic and religious demands which resulted in the foundation of the state of Israel in 1948.

judge, a public officer appointed to hear and try cases in a *court of law. A judge may sit alone, or with lay assessors, with a *jury, or, as is common in appeal courts, with other judges. Where a judge sits with a jury, it is usually the jurors who decide questions of fact, such as guilt or innocence, while the judge decides on questions of law (such as whether *evidence is admissible), and passes sentence. In *common law systems, it is an accepted part of the judge's task not only to apply the law, but also to interpret it. In certain circumstances, decisions by judges can set *precedents which may, or even must, be followed. In *civil law systems, there is traditionally little scope for judges to make law by setting precedents, but as new problems arise that are not covered by existing legal provisions, judges are increasingly having to play a part in the interpretation and development of the law. Judges attain their positions in a variety of ways. In England, judges are appointed by or on the advice of the Lord Chancellor (the highest judicial officer of the Crown) from practising lawyers of many years' standing. On the other hand, judges in France, Italy, Germany, and most civil law systems are career judges: young people, having qualified by examination, enter the judicial service direct, and are promoted to higher courts on the basis of age, ability, and experience. In the USA, judges of the Supreme Court, known as Justices, are appointed for life by the President, subject to confirmation by the Senate. In some states in the USA, judges, especially in the lower courts, are popularly elected. In totalitarian regimes, judges are appointed by or with the agreement of the ruling power and are often subservient to it. The independence of judges from political interference is generally considered essential for the protection of civil liberties. (See also *judiciary.)

judicial review, a legal procedure in which the judiciary reviews the legality or constitutionality of the behaviour or decisions of another public body. There are broadly two types of judicial review: judicial review of administrative action (see *administrative law), and judicial review of *legislation. The latter allows judges to strike down legislation held to be inconsistent with the constitution and is most common in jurisdictions with an entrenched *constitution, such as the USA, Australia, Canada, France, and Germany, and particularly in those countries with a *bill of rights.

judiciary, the body of *judges within a legal system making up the third branch of *government, the other two being the *legislature and the *executive. An independent judiciary is a bulwark of *constitutional government and essential for the *rule of law, but the relationship between politics and the judiciary is complex. Political influences are often present in the appointment of judges. In the USA, for instance, the *President nominates and the *Senate must confirm appointments to the federal judiciary. It is often argued that judicial independence is a fiction: the judiciary is not immune from class loyalty, ideological bias, or professional self-interest. However, despite these influences, judges operate within a set of institutional values generated by law and professional practice. Constitutional interpretation by the judiciary can be of great importance. This is especially so where *judicial review has taken root, as in the USA: legislative acts or executive decisions may be invalidated by the judiciary as incompatible with the constitution. The need to adjudicate between different levels of government means that judicial interpretation is more important under federal rather than unitary constitutions. Judicial review in the UK has traditionally been limited by the doctrine of parliamentary sovereignty and the absence of a written constitution, but administrative decisions are now increasingly subject to legal challenge. This is of growing importance at the supranational level, in such bodies as the *European Court of Justice, through the application of EC law to member countries, and in the *International Court of Justice.

judo *martial arts.

Jung, Carl Gustav (1875–1961), Swiss psychiatrist, the founder of 'analytical psychology'. He worked with *Freud in the early development of *psychoanalysis, but became

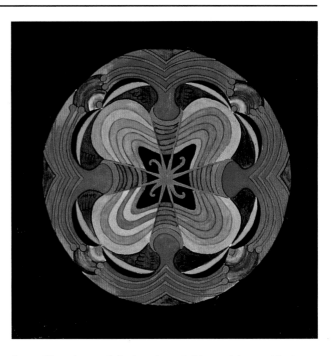

One of **Jung**'s mandala drawings. In his autobiographical book, *Memories, Dreams, Reflections* (1961) Jung claimed that symmetrical patterns moving within a circle reflect the state of the self, and that the round rose windows of Europe's medieval cathedrals are supreme examples of its expression.

dissatisfied with Freud's preoccupation with *instinctive sexual and self-preservative motivation. Jung posited both a personal and a collective *unconscious. The collective unconscious and the archetypes which are its manifestation underlie the personal. Jung observed that many patients described dreams that exhibited parallels with myths and symbols from different traditions. He regarded the mandala, an instrument of contemplation in Tantric yoga, as an archetypal symbol of the self, and was attracted to the idea that the archetypes afford evidence of communion with a divine mind, and that, by extension, the division in man is an expression of divine conflict. In personality development, Jung described a process of 'individuation' leading to greater *extroversion or introversion, and also to the dominance of one of the four functions of thinking, feeling, intuition, and sensation. Disturbance in the process causes *neurosis. Although Jung's belief in the occult and precognition in dreams has prejudiced some against him, his theories of *symbolism and work on personality types have been of enormous influence.

junk bond *bond.

junta (Spanish, 'council', 'meeting'), a term applied to a group of political or military leaders forming an administrative council or committee, particularly in the aftermath of a *coup d'état or *revolution when there is no legal government. The term has been widely used in Latin America to describe military regimes such as that of General Galtieri in Argentina during the 1980s. If a single dominant leader or small group emerges from a junta, it can be transformed into a *dictatorship.

jurisdiction, the authority of nations, or of states within nations, to legislate and to enforce their *legislation through judicial and administrative action. The term is also used to refer to the territory over which their authority extends. Within the USA and other *federal systems, the federal government has jurisdiction over some matters and the state governments over others.

jurisprudence, the philosophy or science of law. It entails philosophical and practical enquiry into law and legal systems and encompasses at least four broad types of study. First, there are studies of legal systems to identify their constituent elements such as rules, rights, and duties, and the bonds between them. There are different theories about the relationship between legal rules and morality (see *justice). Legal positivists have regarded legal systems as distinct from systems of morality, while exponents of *natural law have disagreed. Secondly, there are studies of the growth and social impact of law in such fields as medicine, business, and the environment. Thirdly, there are studies of the behaviour and beliefs of legal officers and institutions (*police, *legislatures, and *juries, for example). This field was pioneered by US 'legal realists', who argued that legal rules were often not the decisive factor in the outcome of cases. Other factors such as inter-organizational rivalry or public attitudes to a particular crime might outweigh them. Finally, there are studies which look at all the social mechanisms which we associate with the law, in particular those maintaining order and resolving disputes. Studies by anthropologists of *dispute resolution processes are increasingly influencing the use (notably in *family law) of conciliation procedures alongside or instead of judicial decision-making. The term jurisprudence, derived from French usage, can also refer more narrowly to the *case law built up by courts and especially by international law courts.

jury, a group of lay persons (usually twelve) summoned to a *court of law or an *inquest in order to decide the facts of a case and give a verdict. The jury system is found almost exclusively in the UK and in countries influenced by the English legal system. In the UK, juries are mainly used in criminal trials, or in a few civil cases such as libel. In the USA there are two types of jury: the grand jury, which investigates possible criminal wrongdoing, hears the state's *evidence, and if satisfied that a trial should take place, hands down a formal accusation or indictment; and the petit or trial jury, which is used in both criminal and civil trials. The members of a jury are randomly selected, but the defendant has the right to challenge the composition of the jury and to object to jurors on the grounds of prejudice or unsuitability. Jurors may also be challenged with no reason being given. The role of the jury is to decide on questions of fact and to issue a verdict, while the *judge directs them on matters of law and sums up the evidence for them. The verdict of the jury is traditionally expected to be unanimous, but where this is impossible, a majority verdict may be sufficient. The use of a jury is intended to ensure that the defendant is given a fair trial by ordinary people chosen at random, who bring to the proceedings impartiality and common sense. On the other hand, it is sometimes argued, particularly in complex cases involving fraud, for instance, that juries of lay people may be incapable of understanding the issues or the evidence put before them.

justice, an action or state of affairs held to be morally right and fair. Theories of justice have been elaborated by philosophers, political scientists, legal theorists, economists, and others. Both *Plato and *Aristotle regarded justice as the essential virtue which enables humans to live together in harmony. In this wider sense justice is closely linked with morality and *ethics. In recent times, many theorists have been concerned with theories of social justice which examine the question of *poverty and the distribution of resources in a society. A further question is the relation between legal systems and justice, which is examined by *jurisprudence. Ideas of equality pervade most theories of justice and it is usually accepted that departures from equality are unjust and must be justified. However, the nature of equality and the grounds for justifying inequality are highly controversial. (See also *egalitarianism.) Despite the popular expectation that the law exists to achieve just results and will operate in procedurally just ways, there is ample potential for conflict between legal systems, *natural law, and morality, which gives rise to difficult questions about the nature and application of justice.

juvenile court, a special *court of law dealing with legal problems connected with children and young people. These may be either criminal matters such as offences committed by children (see *juvenile delinquency), or civil matters such as the problems of abandoned or neglected children. Juvenile courts originated in the USA in 1889. It was believed that children who offended should be treated differently from adult offenders, and that they were in need more of reform than of punishment. Juvenile courts are now found in Europe, Latin America, Japan, and elsewhere. Sometimes matters normally dealt with in a juvenile court come before a *family court. There are wide variations in procedure and structure in juvenile courts, but in general they tend to be less formal and intimidating than ordinary courts. It is now widely accepted, however, that the special treatment given to young offenders in juvenile courts carries the risk of depriving them of the procedural rights enjoyed by adult offenders. These include the right to legal representation, as well as requirements that the offender should be proved beyond reasonable doubt to have committed a specific offence, and that the measures taken by the court should relate to the offence proven, rather than to the offender's social background.

juvenile delinquency, criminal or anti-social activities by children and young people. Statistics tend to show that a high proportion of crime is committed by young people. (In England and Wales almost half known offenders are under 20.) Commonly committed crimes include theft (often shoplifting), vandalism, and car-stealing. The term juvenile delinquency is also used to refer to behaviour which, though not prohibited to adults, is in many societies illegal for children and young people, such as drinking alcohol, running away from home, and sexual activities. Numerous causal theories have been advanced (see *crime). Juvenile delinquents are treated differently from adult offenders, in many countries are being dealt with in *juvenile courts. The emphasis is often on rehabilitation rather than *punishment, with the young person being placed on *probation or working for the benefit of the community (see *community penalties). Since young people who commit serious offences and who are placed in custody, either in special young offenders institutions or adult prisons, are highly likely to reoffend on release and to be reincarcerated, attempts are made in many countries to keep them out of custody by the use of intensive supervision.

Ka'aba, the sacred shrine in Mecca, Saudi Arabia, to which Muslims turn daily in prayer, and the focal point for Muslim pilgrimage. It is a cube-shaped building covered with a black cloth, embroidered in gold with Koranic quotations. In a wall of the Ka'aba is embedded a sacred black stone. A tradition says that the black stone was given to Abraham by the Angel Gabriel, and it is believed to symbolize God's covenant with the worshipper. The authentic Muslim tradition goes that the Ka'aba was originally built by Abraham. (See also *Five Pillars of Islam.)

Kabbalah (Hebrew, 'tradition'), the main tradition of Jewish *mysticism. Kabbalistic belief maintains the possibility of a direct 'vision' of divine attributes, based upon *astrology and the study of occult interpretations of the Old Testament and other texts, which define the spiritual and symbolic value of numbers and letters. The main Kabbalistic work, the *Zohar* ('Splendour'), a 13th-century mystical interpretation of the *Torah, was influential in modern *Hasidic teaching. It taught ten ways of understanding God, whilst maintaining that God himself is beyond comprehension.

Kachin, a group of people found in the remote north-east of Myanmar (Burma). Traditionally practising *shifting cultivation, there are two main groupings: those who live in the hills and those who inhabit the valley floors. The former practise *ancestor and spirit worship, while the latter are Buddhists. In his analysis of their political organization, *The Political Systems of Highland Burma* (1954), the anthropologist Edmund Leach (1910–89) showed how political authority among the different groups can shift between hierarchical and egalitarian forms. According to Leach neither form is stable and different Kachin communities can be understood as going through a process of change between one political form and another. The kinship system is based on patrilineal descent and a system of marriage exchange. The Kachin have always maintained their separate cultural identity, and resisted all forms of outside domination. The Kachin state is presently a semi-autonomous region of Myanmar.

Kālī (Hindi, 'the Black One'), another name for the Great Goddess *Shakti or Dēvi, the consort of *Shiva, who is worshipped independently of him. Kālī represents destructive, primal energy, and is associated with disease and death. She is often depicted as a fearsome and bloody figure bearing weapons. Despite this terrifying aspect, she has many devoted followers, particularly among the lower *castes in India.

Kanak, an *ethnic group from the French colony of New Caledonia, in *Melanesia. Originally a pejorative term, the word Kanak now covers all the groups of indigenous people on the island, who had for many years been confined to reserves, working mainly on the French-owned plantations, and in the nickel mines. An influx of European settlers has resulted in the Kanaks becoming a minority, now approximately 44 per cent of the population. Having gained the vote in the 1950s, they are now pressing for autonomy or independence from France.

Kant, Immanuel (1724–1804), German philosopher, responsible for the doctrine of transcendental *idealism. Kant's *metaphysical system is presented in the *Critique of Pure Reason* (1781), his most important work. Kant sought to transcend the opposition between *rationalism and *empiricism by showing how knowledge of the external world necessarily involves both experience and the application of metaphysical concepts which do not themselves derive from experience. Kant's proofs of the necessity of presupposing such concepts as *substance and *causality in all judgements about the external world take the form of *transcendental arguments. Kant took it to be a consequence of his arguments that we cannot legitimately claim to have knowledge of (although we can form thoughts about) the world as it really is. The world thus divides for Kant into a realm of objects partly constituted by the human mind (appearances or 'phenomena'), and a realm of unknown independent objects (things-in-themselves or 'noumena'). Speculation about the latter, according to Kant, inevitably ends in contradictions. Kant thought that *scepticism could in this way be defeated and idealism of *Berkeley's kind avoided. In further works, Kant elaborated the consequences of his metaphysics for *ethics and *aesthetics.

karate   *martial arts.

Karen, an *ethnic group found in southern Myanmar (Burma). The Karen are split into two main groupings, the 'white', consisting of two sub-groups, and the 'red', consisting of four sub-groups. Although they are one of the largest ethnic minorities in Myanmar, they are also widely dispersed. They have managed to resist cultural and political integration into the state, despite repeated attempts to impose integration on them by force.

karma (Sanskrit, 'deed'), central moral concept within Indian religion, denoting the underlying moral law of cause and effect which generates the process of birth, death, and rebirth (*samsara) until liberation. In *Hinduism, karma binds the *soul to rebirth; it refers to single thoughts or deeds, their consequences, and the sum of all consequences, which determine one's condition and disposition in a future life. Karmic release is achieved by surrender to the will of God, acting righteously, and thus building up good karma. *Buddhism rejects the continuity of the 'soul' through various lives, but it admits a causal connection between them. The intention behind a deed, whether good or bad, is the factor which determines individual spiritual destiny. Release from rebirth depends on knowledge of the Real. This knowledge, in turn, permits action that is without hate, desire, or delusion, and which is therefore karmically neutral. The notion of karma is neither fatalistic nor deterministic, since, although it dictates the situation into which one is born, it does not definitively affect the manner in which one may choose to act.

Keynes, John Maynard (1883–1946), British economist. The founder of modern *macro-economics, through his seminal work *The General Theory of Employment, Interest and Money* (1936) Keynes argued that, contrary to the presuppositions of *classical and neo-classical economics, a market economy will not invariably maintain or move towards full employment of resources, but may, on the contrary, become stuck in a situation of underemployment. This is because the movement of prices and interest rates may not in themselves provide the necessary incentives for producers to employ

This portrait of **Keynes** with his wife Lydia Lopokova was painted in 1952. Keynes's theory that state intervention coupled with government borrowing stimulated a nation's economic growth, was to have profound influence on Western policies for the best part of the 20th century.

idle resources. In particular, Keynes rejected the idea that wage cuts would be a reliable cure for unemployment as resting on an erroneous view of the labour market, which assumed that the price of labour could be altered without significantly affecting *demand (or supply) conditions in the rest of the economy at large. In correcting this error, Keynes argued first that cuts in money-wages did not directly bring cuts in real wages but resulted rather in lower prices and thus in an increased purchasing power of the economy's *money supply. This in turn would raise aggregate demand and therefore employment only in so far as it led to lower interest rates and thence to higher investment expenditure. Such expenditure would also increase *consumption demand through the *multiplier effect on household incomes. If the private sector's will to invest could not be adequately stimulated, the government would have to step in with outlays on public works or other (relatively) direct boosts to aggregate demand. Keynes played a major role in the Bretton Woods conference (1944), which led to the establishment of the *International Monetary Fund and the *World Bank. After World War II his views were raised almost to the level of orthodoxy and underpinned the foundation of the British *welfare state. In recent years, however, the validity of 'Keynesian economics' has been questioned and in part abandoned.

Keynesianism, a school of or group of schools of economic thought stemming from *Keynes's *General Theory of Employment, Interest and Money* (1936). In the theoretical domain, it favours models of the economy in which money-wages are inflexible and employment levels variable. In the policy domain, it favours the active control of aggregate *demand by government through the use of monetary and *fiscal measures. In both respects Keynesianism is opposed by various versions of *monetarism, including neo-*classical economics.

KGB *intelligence services.

Khalsa (Punjabi, 'pure ones'), a group within *Sikhism consisting of those who have accepted full initiation into the faith. The *Khalsa* was instituted by the tenth Sikh *Guru, *Gobind Singh, in 1699, when he formed an army of soldier-saints, prepared to fight for their faith. Nowadays, both men and women can be initiated into the *Khalsa* by drinking *amrit* ('nectar'; a mixture of sugar and water) in the presence of five Sikhs, and promising to wear the 'five Ks': uncut hair (*kesh*); a comb (*kangha*); a bracelet (*kara*); shorts (*kaccha*); and a sword or dagger (*kirpan*). To these male members added the turban, giving the Sikhs a distinctive appearance. In addition, smoking, alcohol, and sexual incontinence are forbidden. Members of the *Khalsa* must accept the teachings of the *Gurus, and be prepared to sacrifice all for the faith. Men who are initiated are given the additional name of *Singh* ('lion'), while women adopt the additional name of *Kaur* ('princess').

Khoisan languages, the smallest language group in Africa, spoken around the Kalahari Desert in Angola, Namibia, Botswana, and South Africa. The group as a whole has less than 130,000 speakers, and few of the languages have more than 1,000 speakers each. Khoisan is spoken by two main groups of people; the Khoikoi, a cattle-herding people, and the *!Kung-San, a hunter-gatherer people of the Kalahari. Khoisan languages are most well known for their 'clicks'; a click is a suction noise made either by the tongue (written 'tut' or 'tsk' in English as a noise of disapproval), or by the lips (in which case a noise rather like a kiss is produced). These noises are ordinary language-sounds (or phonemes, see *phonology) in Khoisan. A few of the languages have been recorded, but some have already become extinct, and others are in danger of extinction.

Kierkegaard, Søren Aabye (1813–55), Danish philosopher. Kierkegaard trained as a theologian and his writings, which border on *ethics and *theology and are often polemical, describe the human predicament in a way which is fiercely Protestant, highlighting themes of faith, choice, dread, and anguish, giving prority to man's relation to God. *Hegel's optimistic and rational vision of the world figured as a target in many of Kierkegaard's works. Foremost among Kierkegaard's concepts are his idea of the 'existing individual', and his notion of 'subjective truth'. In *Either-Or* (1843) Kierkegaard described the radical choice to be made between the 'aesthetic' and the 'ethical' forms of human existence. He developed an 'existential *dialectic', according to which the different stages of existence are aesthetic, ethical, and religious. Kierkegaard's writings were an important influence on *existentialism.

Kikuyu, a Bantu-speaking people of Kenya, living in the Highlands. In their traditional society they are grouped into patrilineages known as *mbari*, and their economy depends on the cultivation of crops such as millet. Many Kikuyu were dispossessed of land by White farmers, and this in part encouraged their struggle against colonial rule. In the 1950s some Kikuyu were responsible for the Mau Mau uprising against British rule, and later on it was the Kikuyu who led the independence movement resulting in Kenyan independence in 1963. They still dominate political life. Many Kikuyu are still landless, however, and now work in Nairobi's factories, living in suburban slums.

kingship, a form of *political organization in which individual power is held by a *monarch or king. Political systems of this kind have been found all over the world. Kings were often treated as gods, and within this system of divine kingship, the well-being of the king was often believed to embody the well-being of the people as a whole. A sick or weak king might mean a sick or weak society, and he could be killed in order to maintain the health of the body politic. The *symbolism of kingship, as seen in *rituals of royal power, often served to mark out kings as different in kind from their subjects. Although kingship still survives in parts of the world, kings are now rarely believed to have supernatural powers, and ideas of divine kingship have given way to other kinds of political theory, such as *democracy.

kinship, a system of relationships between people either through biological links, such as parentage and *descent, or through social links such as *marriage. Kinship is important in all societies, although kinship systems vary from society to society. The organization of economic life, access to political power, the conduct of religious ritual: all of these areas of life may be organized and explained in terms of kinship. Kinship systems may involve rules concerning descent, inheritance, succession, *incest and *marriage, as well as structuring the more intimate world of friendship and *fam-

A class of children in Indonesia learning the **Koran**. Knowledge of the 7th-century Arabic text is a fundamental part of religious observance: many Muslims memorize the Koran in its entirety, thus earning themselves the title of *Hafiz*.

ily. The comparative study of kinship has been one of the central concerns of social *anthropology. Anthropologists have divided in analysing kinship either in terms of alliances such as marriage, following *Levi-Strauss, or in terms of descent. Recently emphasis has been placed on the relationship between kinship and economic life.

kites, building and flying kites of paper, plastic, or cloth on the end of a hand-line, originally an Asian invention, now adopted world-wide. An early function of the kite, named after a type of hawk, was to ward off evil spirits when flown above a house at night. Today's kite-fliers aim more for sustained flight and a graceful shape. The most common designs are hexagonal, diamond, and box-shaped, with or without a tail to maintain balance. Fliers depend on a moderate wind speed of 13–32 km/h (8–20 m.p.h.) to launch their kites and keep them aloft.

Klein *neo-Freudian.

Kōan (Japanese, 'public notice'), meditative aid of the Rinzai sect of Japanese *Zen Buddhism. Kōans are essentially paradoxical and seemingly nonsensical statements (for example, 'What is the sound of one hand clapping?'); as such they are a practical means of forcing us to realize that truth lies not only beyond ordinary conceptual distinctions but beyond all concepts.

Koran (Qu'rān), the sacred book of *Islam. Written in classical Arabic, the Koran is held to contain the word and will of God as revealed to *Muḥammad by the Angel Gabriel (*c*. AD 610–32). The first revelation on *Lailat al-Qadr*, the Night of Power, is commemorated during *Ramadan. The text was established (651–2) under Caliph 'Uthmān; it comprises 114 chapters or *sūras*, written in rhyming prose with lines of differing length. The book itself is held to represent the very word of God, being an accurate copy of the eternal and heavenly Koran. The divine origin and authority of the Koran evokes extreme reverence among Muslims, for whom it is God's chosen means of communication with mankind. For this reason, for many years translations of the Koran were not permitted, and although today translations of the Koran exist, Muslims are taught to memorize and chant the original Arabic text. Calligraphic renditions of the text are a distinctive aid to worship in Islam.

Korean language, the language spoken in North and South Korea by 64 million people. It is not closely related to any other language, but has been connected with *Altaic by many scholars, and may be distantly related to *Japanese. The official standard language has been based on the dialect of Seoul since the 14th century, when Seoul became the political centre of the country. The partition of Korea following World War II has resulted in two standard languages, based on the dialects of Pyongyang (North) and Seoul (South), but the differences are small. Korean was written in Chinese characters until the 15th century, when an alphabetic script was invented. But the alphabet was not generally accepted by Korean scholars, and Chinese characters remained in use until the beginning of the 20th century. The Korean alphabet was adopted officially in North Korea after the Korean War (1950–3) and is now used exclusively. Policy has wavered in South Korea, however, and a mixture of Chinese characters and the alphabetic script is taught in schools. It is estimated that 50 per cent of Korean words are borrowings from Chinese.

kosher (Hebrew, 'proper'), a term most commonly used to describe food and wine which are suitable for Jews, based upon prohibitions found in the *Torah. Animals that have divided hooves and do not chew the cud (pigs), as well as shellfish, certain birds, and most insects, are forbidden, as is any mixing of meat and milk, or any meat which still contains its 'life' blood. These rules also apply to utensils used in the preparation of food to the extent of having separate dishes or refrigerators. Strict kosher observance is maintained within *Orthodox communities, but not as rigorously in *Reform and other traditions of Judaism.

Kripke, Saul (1940–   ), US philosopher. Kripke claims that many philosophical claims have been based on a failure to distinguish between the metaphysical notion of necessity, the epistemological notion of *a priori reasoning, and the linguistic notion of analyticity. In *Naming and Necessity* (1972), Kripke asserts that there is no reason to believe that something is necessarily true (that is, it could not have been otherwise) if it is only knowable a priori (independently of experience). Kripke's work has prompted philosophers to reconsider traditional views of, for instance, the necessity of *essence*, those features of something, perhaps having to do with its scientifically discoverable make-up, that make it what it is.

Krishna (Sanskrit, 'black'), one of the most popular of the Hindu deities, and hero of many myths, most notably in the *Mahābhārata* epic. The eighth *avatar of *Vishnu, he is commonly worshipped as a god in his own right. He both inspires and gives love and devotion, and is the focus of many *bhakti* (devotional) cults. In many representations, Krishna is depicted playing the flute, with which he charmed his lover Rādhā.

kula, an elaborate system of ceremonial *gift exchange which links a number of islands off the north-east coast of New Guinea. Among them are the *Trobriand Islands, where the kula was first described by *Malinowski. The kula involves the circulation of shell necklaces and bracelets along trade routes; the necklaces are exchanged in one direction, and the bracelets in the other. People travel long distances between islands to take part in kula exchanges, and the possession of particular necklaces and valuables is a source of great prestige and status.

!Kung-San (Kalahari bushmen), a dwindling group of nomadic *hunter-gatherers, living in the southern African Kalahari desert and speaking one of the *Khoisan languages. Their traditional social unit is the camp, consisting of a group of siblings and cousins, who move around in territory surrounding water holes, often sheltering in caves. Many rock surfaces still bear witness to the !Kung-San's rich mythology and skill in drawing. The groups do not regard their territories as property in the strict sense, nor are there any organized political structures: a camp leader may be a man or a woman whose skills and judgement are respected, but decisions are made by consensus. The !Kung-San depend for their livelihood on fruits, berries, and nuts gathered by the women and on animals hunted by the men. This traditional way of life is rapidly disappearing, however; recent settlement by migrating farmers has introduced property relations and wage labour to !Kung society.

Kurds, a people who live mostly in eastern Turkey, western Iran, and northern Iraq, speaking two main dialects of Kurdish, an Indo-European language. Estimates put their numbers at about 12 million in Turkey, 5 million in Syria, and 4 million in Iraq. There are about 500,000 in Syria and 100,000 in Armenia. Formerly nomadic pastoralists, the Kurds are now mainly settled agriculturalists, increasing numbers of whom have moved as *migrant labourers to towns for work. Traditional social organization remains an important factor, with local religious and political leaders (*sheikhs* and *ağas* respectively) influential. Most Kurds are Sunnī Muslims, but some are Shī'ī and there are small Christian, Yezedi, Jewish, and Zoroastrian minorities. The Kurds have resisted domination by central governments for centuries; following World War I the Treaty of Sèvres provided for the establishment of an independent state of Kurdistan, but this was never implemented. In Turkey, where the government has only recently acknowledged the very existence of the Kurdish minority, the Kurds have been systematically oppressed and subjected to forcible resettlement, resulting in a separatist guerrilla war fought by the Marxist PKK (Kurdish Workers' Party). In Iran, a brief attempt at autonomy immediately after the 1979 Revolution was suppressed. In Iraq, the Kurds have historically suffered less cultural repression and even came close to establishing an autonomous province in 1970–4, but since 1988 the Iraqi government has carried out a systematic campaign of repression, including the use of poison gas and chemical weapons on civilians, destruction of Kurdish villages, and forced deportation. An uprising by the guerrilla fighters or *peshmerga* (those who face death) in 1991 after Iraq's defeat in the Gulf War met with limited success, but hundreds of thousands have fled intermittently since then to Turkey and Iran for short-term refuge.

Kwa languages   *Niger–Congo languages.

Kwakiutl, a *North-west Indian tribe from British Columbia. Like other people from the same area, the Kwakiutl were traditionally sedentary *hunter-gatherers. Each small village was considered as a separate social unit, and was further subdivided into small groups. Rank and hierarchy were based on a system which included all tribes, villages, subdivisions, and individuals. Status was signified by the adoption of a particular title to which prestige was attached and this was determined by birth. The number of ranks or names was, however, limited within the groups. Individuals might occupy several ranks, but the status and prestige that the names conferred had to be maintained by displays of wealth, distributed within a system of reciprocal *gift exchange, known as *potlatch, a form of conspicuous consumption common to all the North-west coastal tribes. Mythology was represented through *ritual dances, involving the use of elaborately carved and painted wooden masks.

labelling theory, a sociological theory concerned with the processes by which individuals and groups are defined as not conforming with social rules. It is particularly associated with the US sociologist Howard Becker, author of *Outsiders* (1963). Labelling theory concentrates on the social responses to, and social definitions of, *deviance, rather than on the reasons for committing acts seen as deviant. Thus Becker and his followers are concerned with why *homosexuality is labelled as deviant in some societies but not in others, rather than with the motivations of homosexual men and women. They maintain that dominant groups label as deviant other groups who threaten them, thereby denying the legitimacy of their actions. Their ideas have been criticized for failing to explain the reasons for the behaviour which is labelled. None the less, the proposition that an act is deviant because it is so labelled rather than because it is inherently so, has entered public debate on issues such as *illegitimacy and *drug-taking in many parts of the world.

labour (in economics), the *factor of production which helps to produce *goods and services through the application of human physical and intellectual effort. The other main factors are *capital and *land. (In a wider sense, all work, unpaid as well as paid, is labour.) Labour finds many different types of *employment, both manual and non-manual, with different levels of skill, *productivity, and *cost, in the various sectors of *industry. *Division of labour underlies the creation of the modern economy, especially the process of *industrialization. The cost of labour includes the *wage rate or salary, plus the cost of providing *fringe benefits and statutory benefits, such as paid leave and *pensions. Mobility of labour refers to the movement of workers from one area or occupation to another (geographical and occupational mobility respectively). Flexibility of labour in the workplace may be counterposed in management terms to *restrictive practices. As a social group, labour has traditionally comprised manual workers, organized in *trade unions, and has found a political voice in Labour parties in, for example, the UK and Australia. Apart from *collective bargaining, *industrial relations between labour and capital are also modified by *industrial law.

labour theory of value (in economics), the theory that the *value of any goods or service stems from the labour input required to produce it. *Smith first introduced the idea, which was more specifically developed by *Ricardo and by *Marx. Ricardo argued that the amount of labour used in production was a rough guide to value and relative prices. Marx, however, argued that all value stems from labour. Other *factors of production have value only because labour has been applied to them in the past. Moreover, labour has a use value (total value) and an exchange value (the cost of hiring labour). The difference is *surplus value, which is extracted from the workers by the capitalist. Alternatives to the labour theory include general-use theories, the value of a *commodity being based on the use to which it can be put, and marginal *utility theory, which states that the price of any commodity is equal to the utility obtained from the last unit purchased. Non-Marxists now generally equate value with market prices, and view these as being determined by *supply-side and *demand-side factors jointly.

lacrosse, a ball-and-goal game for teams of ten a side, popular in Australia, Canada, the UK, and the USA, and deriving from an ancient game played by North American Indians. Players carry a stick with a triangular net at one end in which they catch the hard rubber ball, pass it, and shoot at goal. The pitch is a rectangle some 100 m (110 yards) long by 64 m (70 yards) wide.

Laing *humanistic psychology.

laissez-faire (French, 'let do'), a term originally employed by the French physiocrats in the 18th century. They maintained that society should be governed according to an inherent natural order, and that the soil is the only source of wealth and proper object of taxation. Subsequently taken up by *classical economists like *Smith, it signifies minimum government *intervention in the economic system, and maximum scope for *market forces. In time the expression came to be associated with the absence of any general government schemes for the relief of poverty. (See also theories of *economics.)

land (in economics), a *factor of production. Broadly defined, it comprises all resources occurring naturally, including not just the surface of the continents and the sea but also the fertility of the soil, minerals, fish, and any other facet of the physical environment used in production.

land reform, the changing of systems of land tenure, usually at government initiative. Systems of land tenure vary considerably, and have great importance for the social and political structure of a society. Land may be held corporately by *lineages, in small individual plots, or by a tiny number of wealthy landowners. Land reform has varied purposes and takes different forms: it may aim to create a more equal society by abolishing feudalism, winning the support of peasants, and giving them a greater stake in society; it may also aim to increase economic efficiency by creating a pattern of landholding which maximizes investment and productivity; or it may seek to impose a socialist pattern of ownership, where individual land ownership is not in general permitted. Reforms have varied from the redistribution of land, to the imposition of land ceilings (so that no single owner controls more than a certain area), and from the complete abolition of private ownership, to attempts to alter the terms under which tenants work private owners' land, such as the terms of *sharecropping agreements. In modern times, the first land redistribution was that in France following the Revolution (1789), which established the pattern of small family farms which continues today. In Britain there was no government-initiated reform, but the Enclosures movement (16th to 19th centuries) pushed many peasants off the land into the towns, and led to the development of industry and of large-scale farming. In Russia, limited land reform giving the land to the peasants accompanied the emancipation of the serfs in 1861, but the land was again taken away with the abolition of private ownership of land from 1918, and extensive *collectivization. A similar process occurred in much of Eastern Europe, but the individual right to own land has been reintroduced in the early 1990s. In developing countries that espouse *communism, such as China, Cuba, and Vietnam, there has also been extensive collectivization, while in Mozambique and Ethiopia all land title was declared the nation's and the rights of the tillers of the land and their descendants guaranteed. Some land reforms in Asia have been very effective in increasing land ownership among peasants, including those in Taiwan, South Korea, and Malaysia, where a system of *co-operative land settlement resembling the Israeli use of kibbutzim, has been employed. In Latin America, attempts at reform have often been impeded by factors such as the high level of foreign ownership, prevalence of very large *plantations, and opposition from politically powerful landowners. In the Middle East, a successful reform in Egypt in 1952 has been the model for reforms elsewhere, with varying degrees of success. State compensation to landowners whose land is expropriated is often in the form of state bonds; a noteworthy exception being in Taiwan, where shares in public industry were given in compensation, emphasizing the need for *industrialization to provide employment in countries where rapid population growth means that the land, however equitably distributed, cannot provide a living for all. The redistribution of land from large estates into small peasant farms has nearly always had the effect of raising productivity and reducing *poverty, leading to renewed interest in land reform since World War II. However, powerful vested interests often prevent effective reform. (See also *agriculture.)

land use, the way *land is used, analysed according to a system of classification that usually reflects differences in rural areas. The UN's Food and Agriculture Organization categorizes land into cropland (over one-tenth of total world land surface area); permanent pasture (a quarter); forest and woodland (under a third); and other, including land not used for cultivation or pasture, built-on areas, and wetlands (one-third). Such land-use categories may give an incomplete picture, unless different crop combinations and types of farming are taken into account. The slow growth in cropland area is tailing off, and *deforestation accounts for a decline in forest and woodland.

language, the method of human communication, either spoken or written, consisting of the use of words in an agreed way. Scholars of *linguistics conceive of language in various ways. For example, *Saussure viewed language as an arbitrary and conventional system of *signs used for communication, while for *Chomsky it is a set of rules and principles in the mind of a speaker. Language is central to the transmission of culture. For example, the study of verbal *taboo—that which is so sacred or important that it cannot be talked about unless using ritual speech or euphemisms—reveals society's values and beliefs. The use of language also has important political implications. It may be an indicator of identity for ethnic minorities whose identity or existence is threatened, and it expresses group or class membership, as in the use of *dialect or *jargon. Distinguishing between languages is often more a matter of social, historical, and administrative than of linguistic criteria. If the languages have no standard forms, or if the local dialects are not affected by the standard forms, it may be impossible to find a boundary between them. For example, the dialects of Spain, France, and Italy form a continuum and it used to be hard to say where the linguistic borders were. Standard languages themselves do not always differ more than dialects; for instance, Danish, Swedish, and Norwegian are easily mutually intelligible. The ability of humans to acquire and use language is the primary feature distinguishing them

For minority groups **language** represents a vital part of their culture, and its defence can arouse strong passions. Here Welsh parents in the UK, demonstrating in favour of a directive from their county council that primary-school teachers must speak Welsh to their pupils, outnumber a rival group who oppose it.

from animals, although animals are capable of using signalling systems. Bees' communication by dancing is an example. Such systems, however, are inborn rather than acquired and lack the complexity of human language.

language development, the acquisition by children of their native language. Speech is complex, yet it is readily mastered by most babies. The infant must learn to produce the sounds of the language (*phonology), the rules that govern their sequencing into words and sentences (*grammar and *syntax), the meanings of words (*semantics), and how people use language in conversation. The behavioural view, associated with *Skinner, suggests that speech is acquired by rewarding the production of appropriate language. This theory has difficulty in explaining why the child persists in producing ungrammatical utterances even when reward is absent. The nativist view, associated with *Chomsky, is that humans are equipped at birth with species-specific neurological systems to acquire language. There is good evidence for 'lateralization' of speech functions in the left hemisphere of the brain. The *cognitive approach stresses the contribution of general intellectual abilities. For example, the child's early language reflects knowledge of the agents and objects of actions, rather than the specific grammatical categories of verbs and nouns. Each of these theories accounts for part of language development, but none is sufficient to explain the whole process.

languages, classification of, a major task in *linguistics. Linguists commonly distinguish between natural languages, those which human beings speak, and artificial languages, such as computer languages and logical systems.

They classify natural languages in two different ways: genetic and formal. Genetic classifications group together languages which have a common ancestor. For example, most of the languages of Europe and northern India, including English, French, German, Hindi, Italian, Russian, and Welsh, are classified as *Indo-European languages because it can be shown that they are descended from a common source. Likewise, Arabic, Hebrew, and Maltese are classified as *Semitic languages. Formal classifications group together languages which have *grammatical properties in common, whether or not they are related. It was once common to classify languages on the basis of the nature and extent of their word-formation processes. More recently, it has been common to classify languages on the basis of the order of the main constituents of a sentence: subject, verb and object. English has the order subject–verb–object. In the sentence *John loves Mary*, *John* is the subject, *loves* the verb, and *Mary* the object. Other languages, for example Turkish, have the order subject–object–verb (*Murat Yasemin'i seviyor*, 'Murat loves Yasemin') and others, for example Welsh, have the order verb–subject–object. It is also common to classify languages on the basis of how fixed or free word order is in a sentence.

language universals, propositions true of all languages. Some are fairly simple and concrete, such as the proposition that all languages have vowels and consonants. Many are of the form that if a language has property A, it also has property B. Most, however, are quite complex and abstract.

Laozi *Daoism.

Lapp, an *Arctic society of semi-nomadic *pastoralists, sometimes known as the Sameh, found also in Norway, Sweden, Finland, and the Russian Federation. Their seasonal migration with the reindeer herds begins in the spring, when small groups of between ten and a hundred people move from their winter encampments to pastures for the calving season. In early summer, there is a second move to highland pasture, followed by a move back to the lowland pasture in the autumn, before the final move to winter quarters. In common with other pastoralists, the basic unit of social organization is the family, and there is no overall form of authority. Kinship and trading links provide the basis for creating bonds that extend beyond the immediate family group. Although *shamanism was the traditional form of religious belief, many Lapps are now Christians, and have settled in permanent villages.

Latin *Italic languages.

Latvian *Baltic languages.

law, that collection of precepts creating obligations within the community to which they apply. Secular legal systems may be differentiated from moral and religious laws by the derivation of their constituent elements from identifiable political sources. Although often associated with the infliction of *punishment in case of violation, it is clear that laws perform many functions other than penal, such as conferring powers on individuals to enter *contracts, form companies, transfer *property, and make wills (typical subjects of *private law), as well as defining social and power relationships (see *administrative law, *jurisprudence, *public law). Law may have originated from expectations about how disputes between individuals should be resolved (see

*dispute resolution), generating custom and eventually *case law. The Roman legal theorists reduced these practices into systematic expositions which acquired their own authority. The 6th-century codification of *Roman law, *Corpus Juris Civilis* ('Body of Civil Law'), forms the basis of the systems of most continental European countries, which are therefore called *civil law systems. Many of these countries codified their laws during or after the Napoleonic era (1799–1815), but these codes retained many of the concepts of the civil law. The law in England developed relatively independently from civil law influence, and it formed the basis of the *common law systems which evolved in countries colonized by Britain. In many countries, the precepts of religious communities or of tribal custom govern various aspects of the lives of their members (particularly in *family law), alongside the law of the state, resulting in legal pluralism (see *Hindu law, *sharī'ah (Islamic law), *Talmud (Jewish law), *customary law). Besides the national law identified with particular states, a body of principles has developed over the years governing relationships between states. This includes the laws governing diplomatic relations and the observance of treaties. This customary *international law has been supplemented in the 20th century by institutional mechanisms such as the *International Court of Justice and the *UN. International law binds states, but still lacks effective means of collective enforcement. In recent years, a new body of supra-national law, which can bind states as well as individuals within states, has arisen within the *EC under the Treaty of Rome and subsequent agreements.

lawyer, a person versed in the law, or professionally qualified to practise law in some capacity. In the widest sense, the term embraces every branch of the profession, including *advocates, *barristers, *solicitors, sheriffs (see *Scots law), and *judges (except lay judges) as well as law teachers, *notaries, and legal draftsmen.

learned helplessness, a theory of *depression formulated by the US psychologist Martin Seligman in his book *Helplessness* (1975) and later developed into an attributional theory (see *social understanding). Learned helplessness occurs in response to prolonged or repeated inescapable punishment of some sort, the key sympton being a passive, listless, or defeatist response to simple problems. Bad events are believed to be caused by factors—such as stupidity, or weakness of will—which are 'internal' (an aspect of oneself), 'stable' (will remain), and 'global' (affect other areas of one's life). Good events in contrast are believed to have external, transient, and specific causes, such as momentary good luck. The concept is therefore related to other *locus of control theories. *Psychotherapy may provide effective treatment.

Left (in politics), a term applied to ideas, movements, and parties of a radical or progressive character, usually associated with *socialism. Following the example of the representatives of the Third Estate at the time of the French Revolution (1789), members of legislative assemblies holding liberal, democratic, or egalitarian views have tended to sit on the left of their chambers. What counts as 'Left' varies with time and place: classical liberal views, for instance, would count as 'Right' nowadays, but were 'Left' when first espoused in the late 18th century.

legal aid, professional legal advice and assistance, including representation in *courts of law and *tribunals, given either free or for a reduced sum to people on low incomes.

For many people, one of the basic *civil rights, the right of access to the courts, is meaningless because they cannot afford the cost of litigation. In criminal cases, too, a person accused of a crime may not be able to afford an effective defence. In the USA, the Supreme Court has ruled that the Constitution guarantees the right of representation for persons accused of serious crimes, and assistance is provided by salaried lawyers, usually called public defenders, whose fees are paid from tax revenues. In other systems, developed in the UK, France, and Germany, the state pays the fees of lawyers in private practice to enable them to undertake legal aid work in both criminal and civil cases. Many countries also provide legal services through publicly funded law centres. Restrictions on public expenditure render these schemes vulnerable to underfinancing, and payments to participating lawyers may be lower than the normal fees, making it difficult to attract competent practitioners. More recent developments have therefore sought to make the legal process itself cheaper and more accessible by promoting alternative methods of *dispute resolution.

legislation, the form of law made through enactment by a person or body authorized by law to do so, known as the *legislature. Legislation can be divided into primary legislation, or *statute law, and delegated legislation, which takes the form of regulations made by subordinate bodies. Reformers use legislation to achieve social and economic change by enacting programmes which can, in democratic states, be submitted for electoral approval. Legislation differs from judge-made *common law, which is heavily dependent on individual cases and does not so readily allow for democratic accountability. Legislation reduces the power of *judges to make law, but they everywhere retain scope for creativity when interpreting it. (See also *judicial review.)

legislature, a national assembly with the principal or sole function of making or changing *law. Legislatures are often, but need not be, elected bodies, and go by different names such as Chamber of Deputies, Congress, Diet, Legislative Assembly, Parliament, or Supreme Soviet. They may be *bicameral, as in the USA or UK, or unicameral, as in New Zealand or Israel. A freely elected assembly is regarded as an important component of *democracy; the elected or otherwise representative status of members confers *legitimacy and authority on a legislature. Legislatures exist in the majority of countries, but their election or appointment need not necessarily follow a democratic procedure. In addition to legislating, legislatures may have other functions such as appointing, controlling, or dismissing *governments; scrutinizing government operations; considering and approving (or amending) financial provisions; and providing a forum for political debate. Members of legislatures are formally equal and make decisions collectively according to established procedures. There are many different types of legislature, but they may be categorized according to the relative effectiveness and independence of the legislature in relation to the *executive. Two main types emerge: firstly, presidential government, where the legislature is separate from the executive, although in the USA, for example, the *president (the chief executive) has the right to veto legislation as well as to propose it; secondly, *parliamentary government, as in the UK, where members of the executive are drawn from the legislature. Mixed or transitional relationships between the legislature and the executive are also common, as in France, Czechoslovakia, and Egypt. In the USA

congressional committees must first pass any bill before it is debated in Congress. In the UK the role of Parliament is largely to ratify the will of a party-dominated government which may count on the support of its majority in the *House of Commons, although all-party parliamentary committees which deliberate proposed legislation go some way to redressing the balance of power between Parliament and the executive. In most communist countries, the constitution has provided formally for a strong legislature, but the real power has traditionally been with the Communist Party and the executive; recent democratic changes in many such countries have relatively easily tipped the balance to implementing the law fully. The strength and independence of the legislature may be measured by its capacity to initiate legislation (particularly financial), to modify or throw out draft legislation, and to influence or alter budgets. Some political theorists argue that party-dominated or *one-party legislatures lack independence and impartiality. However, in practice, most legislation is drafted by *civil servants, and rule-making powers are often delegated to the executive; thus the legislative function may be dispersed across various organs of government and is not the exclusive preserve of a national assembly. (See also *separation of powers.)

legitimacy, as attributed to a regime or social institution, the quality of being rightful or lawful. A government is legitimate when its subjects recognize that it has the right to wield *authority. Such recognition may have a number of sources. In some cases it derives from historical tradition, as when the son of the previous king is acknowledged to be the legitimate heir. In other cases it may derive from popular *consent, as when the legitimacy of a democratically elected government is recognized. Social institutions such as a market economy also require supporting beliefs that establish their legitimacy if they are to survive without resort to force.

Leibniz, Gottfried Wilhelm, Baron von (1647–1716), German philosopher and mathematician. Leibniz believed in an infinity of *substances created by God and kept in existence by God at all times, which he called monads. He conceived monads to be simple entities, without parts, which could neither act upon or be acted upon by other substances. Despite this lack of interaction, talk of causes and effects is not senseless because there is a pre-established harmony between the states of all substances such that it is possible to infer from the state of one substance, the state of another. The world, which is constituted of these substances and works according to this pre-established harmony, was created by God because, although it is not perfect, it is the best possible world (a view lampooned by the French philosopher Voltaire in *Candide* (1759). Leibniz believed that every monad has a 'complete concept', which embraces everything that can truly be said about that substance, a concept such that only an omniscient being such as God could have. Thus, each substance is independent of each other, it is possible to infer from any one state of a substance every other, and each substance can be uniquely identified by its complete concept. The final consequence is the socalled 'identity of indiscernibles', or Leibniz's law: the claim that if the descriptions of objects *a* and *b* are exactly alike then *a* is *b*.

leisure, free time, hence all sporting, artistic, and recreational activities carried out in non-working hours. Traditional leisure activities date from the days when free time was brief and had to be enjoyed near or in the home. They include many forms of *sports, gardening, *fishing, *collecting hobbies, *board and card games, eating out, *gambling, and drinking. Since the 1960s a great increase in time available for leisure in the industrialized nations has come about through a combination of factors, among them the shorter working week and longer holidays, the liberating effects of automation in the workplace, and greater life expectancy. Better diet and health care, greater mobility through car ownership, the growth of cheap air travel, and, in wealthy countries, the availability of land no longer required for agriculture, have encouraged *tourism and outdoor leisure pursuits. The changing times have produced a greater appetite for *continuing education. Such leisure activities are largely confined to the industrialized world; in most developing countries concepts such as leisure, personal fitness, and holidays are regarded as scarce luxuries.

Leninism   *communism.

Lent, a forty-day period in the *Christian year, of fasting and penance in preparation for *Easter, traditionally commemorating *Jesus' temptations and crucifixion. Fixed by the date of Easter, Lent is measured differently in East and West, as the East excludes weekends from its forty-day fast while the West excludes only Sunday. Beginning in the West on what is known as Ash Wednesday, Lent includes Holy Week (the week preceding Easter) and concludes at dawn on Easter Sunday. The traditional rules of abstinence in Lent have been largely abandoned in the West. However, the custom of voluntary abstinence from some food or pleasure is still widely observed by Christians, and extra commitment to Christian study or attendance at worship is encouraged.

letter of credit, an order from a domestic bank to a foreign bank instructing the latter to make a specified payment to a named individual, firm, or institution. Letters of credit are often used as guarantees to exporters that they will receive payment for goods sent abroad.

Lévi-Strauss, Claude (1908–), French anthropologist, regarded as the first person to apply the theoretical approach known as *structuralism to *anthropology. His early *fieldwork was carried out in Brazil in the 1930s, and his first major theoretical work, *Les Structures élémentaires de la parenté* (1949) focused on systems of *kinship and *marriage, which he analysed as structures of exchange. His later works contained a more detailed consideration of structuralism and its relationship to linguistic theory, through the analysis of *myth and systems of classification. Lévi-Strauss also criticized previous approaches to *totemism, which he treated as part of a more general human propensity to classify and order the world. In all this work, Lévi-Strauss argued that people's thought processes exhibited the same structural properties the world over. Lévi-Strauss's many writings are characterized by a difficult but dazzling literary style and by his use of fragments of *ethnography from many different societies; his work is in the tradition of earlier literary anthropologists like *Frazer, and is quite different from the *fieldwork-based approaches which have dominated British and US anthropology since *Malinowski.

li (Chinese, 'proprietousness', 'rites'), the term used in *Chinese philosophy to denote the way in which external conduct harmonizes with internal cultivation, by actualizing goodwill and concern towards others, *ren, in everyday behaviour and action. It is the most central of the five leading concepts of morality in classical *Confucianism. In antiquity, the term originally applied to ceremonies and rituals, especially those concerned with honouring ancestors. Gradually *li* became equated with etiquette and inextricably linked with state ritual. In Confucian thought, however, it refers to a learned skill possessed by a superior individual, which matches correct action with a natural concern for another person. *Li* is the form in which true humanity is realized, a manifestation of both inner self-cultivation and harmony with the universe.

libel   *defamation.

liberal democracy   *constitutional government.

liberalism, a political outlook attaching supreme importance to safeguarding the freedom of the *individual within society. Liberal ideas first took shape in the struggle for religious *toleration in the 16th and 17th centuries. The liberal view was that religion was a private matter; it was not the business of the *state to enforce a particular creed (see *religion and politics). This later developed into a more general doctrine of the limited and constitutional state, whose boundaries were set by the natural rights of the individual (for instance in the political thought of *Locke). Around 1800 liberalism became associated with the doctrines of the *free market and *laissez-faire, and reducing the role of the state in the economic sphere. This tendency was reversed later in the 19th century with the arrival of 'New Liberalism', committed to social reform and welfare legislation. In contemporary debate both schools of thought are represented, some liberals harking back to the *classical economic ideas of the late 18th century (for instance, *Hayek), others embracing the *mixed economy and the *welfare state (for instance, *Rawls). Despite their economic disagreements, liberals unite in upholding the importance of personal liberty in the face of encroachment by the state, leading to demands for *constitutional government, *civil rights, and the protection of *privacy.

liberalization (in economics), a term used to refer to policies which aim to create a *free market by minimizing government *intervention. Such policies include lifting restrictions such as *protectionism on international trade, the *deregulation and internationalization of the financial sector, *privatization, de-unionization, and the reduction or phasing-out of other regulatory arrangements such as *prices and incomes policies. Liberalization is often associated with the *New Right and *libertarian dislike of government intervention; such policies have featured in most *adjustment strategies in recent years. Proponents consider liberalization essential to unlock entrepreneurial abilities and increase the *investment necessary for *economic growth, but sceptics argue that some government intervention is necessary. For example, some protectionist measures and *subsidies may be necessary to promote *industrialization, *economies of scale, and learning, especially in the early stages of *development; and there may be considerable hardship and even civil unrest if the burden of economic adjustment is not eased by measures to counteract *unemployment and higher prices. Recent evidence shows that some high-growth economies have combined extensive government interventions with a market orientation.

Liberal Judaism, a Jewish movement which began in about 1780 in Germany, in response to the need to redefine

The politicized role of Father Jean-Bertrand Aristide, elected President of Haiti in 1990 and deposed in 1991, is a good example of some of the underlying principles of **liberation theology**, which holds that the Church should play an active part in redressing injustice.

the meaning and practical observance of the *Torah in a changing society. Liberals saw the Torah's revelations as progressive rather than static, expressing God's teaching rather than God's law. This allowed for evolution in religious law and practice and resulted in dramatic changes in both diet and custom, including the use of the vernacular in services and the relaxation of *Shabbat laws. In Europe the movement is also known as Progressive, and is roughly equivalent to US *Reform Judaism.

liberation theology (in Christianity), a theological movement developed in the 1960s principally by Latin American *Roman Catholics. Liberation theology is a response to the widespread poverty and social injustice found in much of Latin America. Drawing on *Marxism and the ideas of *dependency theory, which viewed the inequalities of the Third World as springing from dependence on the exploitative capitalism of the developed world, liberation theology attempts to address the problems of political and social inequality in addition to the spiritual matters often regarded as the only legitimate concern of the Church as societies became more secular in the 19th century. Works such as Gustavo Gutierrez's *A Theology of Liberation* (1971) argue that freedom must encompass both political and religious spheres, changing not only individuals but also the structure of society. Liberation theology differs from the ideas of other Christian theologians such as Reinhold Niebuhr, who in *Moral Man and Immoral Society* (1932) acknowledged the injustice of human society but emphasized the importance of inner spiritual life given the impossibility of achieving real justice in a flawed world. Liberation theology raises controversial questions about the Church's relationship with non-Christian ideologies, about the connection between *religion and politics, and the Christian response to social inequality and poverty, which have led to its rejection by some Roman Catholic authorities.

libertarianism, a radical form of *liberalism, which holds that the role of the state should be reduced to an absolute minimum and looks to private *property and *market exchange as the basis of the good society. According to libertarians, the role of the state should be confined to police pro-

tection, the enforcement of contracts, and national defence. Some would go further still, and claim that personal protection could be provided by private associations on a market basis; here libertarianism becomes a form of *anarchism. As an ideology it has been influential chiefly in the USA, where the Libertarian Party has polled nearly 1 million votes in recent elections. *Nozick has offered a recent defence of the minimal state position.

library, a repository of recorded knowledge. Libraries have existed since ancient times, but became accessible to the general public in the 19th century with the growth of *literacy and the development of free public book-lending libraries, strengthened by the support of philanthropists such as Andrew Carnegie (1835–1919). Libraries today are a public service and an important source of knowledge and education, with specialist libraries for scholars, and school and children's libraries to encourage reading skills. The Dewey decimal classification introduced in the USA in 1874 and subsequently adopted internationally, has been supplemented in recent years through the application of *information technology. Most countries operate a system of copyright libraries which by law house all books published in that country: the UK copyright libraries are the British Library, Bodleian Library, Oxford, National Library of Scotland, National Library of Wales, Trinity College Library, Dublin, and University Library, Cambridge. In the USA, the Library of Congress, Washington, DC, is the national library where all copyright material must be deposited and catalogued.

life expectancy, the average number of further years that a person of a specified age in a given population may expect to live. The most common calculation is life expectancy at birth, often used as an indicator of the *public health and social development of a country. Between 1950 and 1955 and 1985 and 1990, life expectancy at birth rose from 65 to 74 years in Europe, from 51 to 65 years in South America, from 41 to 61 years in Asia, and from 38 to 52 years in Africa. The UN predicts that this convergence will continue. One consequence of increased life expectancy is an *ageing population (especially of women, whose life expectancy is longer than that of men). (See also *mortality rate.)

light industry, a group of small-scale *secondary (manufacturing) industries operating without the use of heavy capital equipment and plant. For some types of light industry, such as textile and clothing production or food-processing, a skilled work-force is not essential, whereas for others, such as electronics and the manufacture of computer hardware, a highly skilled work-force is needed. Light industry is often found in developing countries or the *informal sector because it can be established without large capital *investment.

limited liability, a limitation on the financial liability of the *shareholders in a *company for the *debts of that company; they can lose only the nominal *value of their shareholdings. A limited company may be a private limited company or a public limited company; the latter is one whose shares are traded on the *stock exchange. Owners of businesses with unlimited liability may have to use their personal property to pay the debts of the business.

lineage, a group of people who can trace *descent from a common progenitor. Lineages are always based on unilineal descent, either through males (patrilineages) or females (matrilineages). This is because unilineal descent allocates people to different, distinct groups. Lineages form important political bodies in African societies such as the *Nuer, where particular lineages are associated with particular territories, and where lineage structure is the key to *political organization. Sometimes different lineages combine to form larger groupings like *clans or *tribes, while lineages themselves may be subdivided into smaller descent groups; anthropologists call these systems of nesting units segmentary lineage systems. Lineage systems are a good example of the political importance of *kinship organization in some societies.

lingua franca, a *language used among people with no common native language. English and French are the most widespread lingua francas today. Other examples include Swahili in East Africa and Latin in medieval Europe. Originally the term meant 'French language' and referred to a variety of Provençal used during the Crusades (11th–14th centuries) by Crusaders of different native languages, later expanded by the inclusion of elements from other languages.

linguistic philosophy, a method of doing *philosophy which emphasizes the analysis of concepts as they are used in everyday natural (as opposed to artificial) languages such as English. Suggested by the work of *Wittgenstein, it is part of the tradition of *analytic philosophy and prominent in British philosophy in the 1950s and 1960s, when its leading figures were Gilbert Ryle (1900–76) and J(ohn) L(angshaw) Austin (1911–60). Philosophers who embrace this methodology are convinced that many philosophical problems arise because of the lack of clarity that results from the way in which we use language; in particular, from our lack of attention to the differences between words and phrases that are used in superficially similar ways. For example, Austin approached the problem of *free will by contrasting the use of 'if' in 'he could have done so if he had chosen' with the uses of 'if' in straightforward indicative conditionals such as 'if it is raining you will get wet'.

linguistic relativity   Sapir–Whorf hypothesis.

linguistics, the science of *language. As a science, it is concerned to develop theories and evaluate them on the basis of objective data. Measurement and experiment are also features of some branches of linguistics. Central to modern linguistics is the study of languages as formal systems through *grammar, *phonology, and *semantics. Also important is the study in *psycholinguistics of the way language is used by speakers, and the study in *sociolinguistics of the way language functions in society. Modern linguistics is mainly synchronic (concerned with languages at a single point in time), but some work is diachronic (concerned with language change over time). A further important distinction is between theoretical or descriptive linguistics, which is concerned to increase our understanding of language, and applied linguistics, which seeks to use this understanding in various ways, especially in connection with language teaching. Historical and comparative linguistics studies the development of particular languages and their relationship to each other.

lip-reading, a way of understanding spoken *language by watching the position of the lips of the speaker, used by the deaf as an alternative to *signing. Because the position of the lips is the same for several sounds, for example, 'm', 'b', and 'p', a special signing system distinguishing between the sounds often accompanies the speaker's performance.

liquidity (in economics), the ease with which an *asset can be exchanged for *money promptly and at little or no loss. For example, most deposits in banks and building societies are highly liquid, since they can be easily turned into cash. Shares and bonds may also be fairly liquid, if there is a well-organized and accessible market in these assets. Fixed *capital, including housing, is typically an illiquid asset; even if a buyer can be found, selling takes time and transaction costs are significant. Liquidity preference, a term taken from *Keynes, is the desire to hold money as opposed to other assets. If investors and treasury managers favour liquid assets, this may be a sign of lack of confidence and businesses may suffer from low *investment.

liquidation   *insolvency.

literacy, the ability to read and write. According to *UNESCO, a person is literate 'who can with understanding both read and write a short simple statement on his everyday life', while a functionally literate person can 'engage in all those activities in which literacy is required for the effective functioning of his group and community'. Even taking the first more restricted definition, it is estimated that only three in four of the world's adults are literate. Levels of illiteracy are highest among women because, historically, women have had less access to *education than men. In 1985 two-thirds of the world's illiterates were women. The size of this gender gap is accounted for chiefly by the extremely large numbers of illiterate women in countries in South Asia such as Bangladesh and Pakistan. Although illiteracy worldwide has been significantly reduced since World War II, recent figures suggest a slackening of pace. The task is complex. For example, a literacy student can achieve fluency more rapidly in his or her mother tongue than in a second language. But the multiplicity of languages and dialects within many developing nations, for example *Niger–Congo languages in Africa, and the fact that some are spoken but not written can present formidable obstacles to literacy teaching in the mother-tongue. In China, a nation with almost a fifth of the world's population, a command of at least 2,000 characters is necessary. Although Japanese experience shows that ideographic writing is not a bar to universal literacy, in China it imposes a heavy educational burden. None the less, much can be achieved by energetic national action as a UNESCO study of successful campaigns in countries as diverse as Brazil, Cuba, Myanmar, Somalia, and Tanzania discovered. The need has also been recognized for follow-up courses for literacy campaign graduates and for governmental action such as the support of printing and publishing to consolidate the gains of literacy campaigns.

Lithuanian   *Baltic languages.

liturgy (in Christianity), an act of worship, specifically the ordered services of the Church. *Christian churches have different liturgies with varying emphases. The principal form of liturgy is called the 'Mass' in the *Roman Catholic Church, but in *Eastern Orthodox churches 'the Divine Liturgy', and sometimes (in all churches) 'the Eucharist'. The Eucharist is one of the two principal *sacraments, the other being Baptism. The Roman Catholic Mass has been held in the vernacular or spoken language of a country since

1970 following the Second Vatican Council (1962–5). In *Protestant churches the liturgy is usually less formal, with the emphasis on the sermon and readings from the *Bible, and the Eucharist is celebrated less often. In most churches there has been increased emphasis on lay participation in recent years, though in the Catholic, Orthodox, and Anglican Churches a priest is needed for the consecration and celebration of the Eucharist.

live broadcasting, the transmission by radio wave of sound and image simultaneously with their registration by microphone and camera. The term covers live broadcasts direct from the studio, but usually refers to outside, on-location coverage of unrehearsed newsworthy events, or of sporting and entertainment occasions. It has been facilitated by 'electronic news gathering' based on portable videotape cameras, and *satellite transmission and is used more extensively by Cable News Network for news coverage than by any other company. Unedited 'real-time' sound and image, including the spontaneous reactions of the commentator, can have enormous impact.

Lloyd's of London (Corporation of Lloyds), an institution which acts as an international *market for those wanting to buy and sell *insurance (particularly marine insurance). There are some 20,000 members (the *underwriters), who pay out if a successful claim is made. They commonly form syndicates to deal with insurance *brokers, who act as intermediaries between underwriters and clients seeking insurance cover against risks. The Lloyd's Register of Shipping is the world's largest ship-classification society.

loan, a sum borrowed by one individual or organization from another. A loan may be secured; that is, the lender may be entitled to *collateral (some *asset belonging to the borrower, ownership of which is forfeited to the lender if the loan agreement is broken). Borrowers usually pay *interest in addition to repaying the capital sum borrowed.

lobbying, the activities of individuals or *interest groups seeking to win support from elected politicians, ministers and administrators, or public opinion, either by direct contact or through the mass media. The term originates from the attempts of interest groups in the USA to influence politicians by meeting them in the lobbies of Congress or state *legislatures. Lobbying activities are largely unregulated yet are firmly established in all liberal democracies. Lobbyists seek to influence public policy by reasoned argument, *public-relations campaigns, mass letter writing, or sometimes the offer of favours (see *corruption). In some countries, attempts have been made to regulate the activities of lobbyists by requiring them to report contributions and expenditure.

local government, administration by local or regional authorities. In *unitary states, local government is the conferment of limited legislative and executive powers by central government upon local authorities. These generally consist of councils of locally elected representatives, who appoint paid officials to provide a range of services or to act as agents of the central government in a specified locality. Under *federalism, local government is responsible to and under the legal control of the territories making up the federal union, rather than the federal government. The concerns of local government may include *education, local highways, municipal services, some areas of social welfare,

and recreation. The degree to which local government is locally representative varies in different countries.

location of firms, the geographical spread of firms throughout a country. Location theory was developed by *Weber, amongst others, to explain the location decisions of firms individually and collectively. Transport costs are important in many cases. Location may be at the site of raw materials (if their bulk makes transport expensive), or at the site of the sale of output (if transport of the finished good is more expensive than the transport of raw materials), or at some intermediate transhipment point. Variations in the costs of land and other inputs also influence decisions, as do the availability and cost of *labour. *Demand for the firm's output may determine its location. For some firms, often referred to as 'footloose', transport costs are insignificant; environmental factors such as climate may prove dominant in deciding location for these firms, for example those in the US 'sunbelt'. Large companies, particularly *multinationals, may locate their plant in a variety of different locations.

Locke, John (1632–1704), English philosopher and liberal political theorist. In *An Essay Concerning Human Understanding* (1690) he presented an *empiricist framework intended to clarify the grounds and limits of human knowledge. Locke regarded himself as an 'underlabourer' for the new 17th-century sciences and was influenced by Robert Boyle's (1627–91) atomic theory of chemistry. He attacked *Descartes's claim that we possess innate ideas, and tried to

The new **Lloyd's of London** building combines the traditional and the modern to convey an impression of stability and strength. Yet tax changes in the UK and a series of vast international catastrophes threaten its position as the world's leading insurance market.

show how all knowledge arose from, and was limited by, experience. Like Boyle, he distinguished between primary and secondary qualities, and argued that although our ideas of the former are actually possessed by material objects, the latter depended on the existence of a perceiver (see *Berkeley). He also distinguished between the real and nominal essence of a *substance, arguing that the nominal essence was a compound of the ideas we can have of an object, but that real essence was unknowable, even by science.

locus of control, a theory about the place (locus) people believe is the seat of control over their lives: 'internals' believe control is in their own hands, 'externals' believe in luck or other people's power over them. The US psychologist Julian Rotter (1899–) proposed a *social learning theory model of *personality development, in which control beliefs underlie many differences of personality and *motivation between people. His questionnaire to tap people's control beliefs, published in 1966, has been used world-wide. Research has borne out many of Rotter's claims, showing that internality is associated with political activism and general eagerness to control one's surroundings, while externality is associated with *depression and inability to cope with *stress. However, doubts have been expressed about whether people have general beliefs about their control and also about the universality of the range of topics in Rotter's questionnaire. (See also *learned helplessness.)

logical positivism, a set of doctrines espoused most famously by a group of philosophers calling themselves the Vienna Circle, who met in Vienna during the 1920s and 1930s. In the tradition of *analytic philosophy and influenced strongly by *empiricism and especially by *Hume, logical positivism was an attempt to develop empiricist views with the help of *logic and mathematics, in particular, in the work of *Russell and the young *Wittgenstein. According to logical positivists, sense experience is all we can appeal to in justifying our beliefs or in explaining the meaning of our words. These views give rise to the *Verificationist Principle on which the meaning of a sentence is the procedure by which it can be verified. The logical positivists believed that adoption of their ideas would dissolve all the problems of philosophy because any question to which the answer could not be provided by some experience would be meaningless. Logical positivism was spread in the UK by *Ayer's work and in the USA by the forced emigration of *Carnap.

logic, formal, the study of reasoning and, in particular, argumentation; the putting forward of reasons for a conclusion. Logic is not concerned with the subject of an argument but with its form schematically represented. For example, the arguments; *all men are mortal, Socrates is a man, Socrates is mortal*, and *all lying is wicked, that is a lie, that is wicked*, share a form despite the difference in their subject, and that form can be represented by the schema; All As are B, C is an A, C is a B. Logic describes and explains the *validity of arguments by describing and explaining the validity of argument schema; a particular argument is valid only if it is an instance of a valid argument schema. No universal logic characterizes all valid arguments because there are so many different types. Instead different logical systems have been developed and classified by appeal to their logical constants, the words around whose meanings the validity of the arguments revolve. For example, propositional logic deals with arguments whose validity revolves around the meaning of the words (or phrases) *if*, *and*, *or*, *not*, and *if-and-only-if*, whilst the constants of predicate logic (whose precursor was the *syllogistic logic of *Aristotle) are these plus the words *all* and *some*. There are formal logics under construction that characterize arguments of many kinds, including those involving time (tense logic), morality (deontic logic), belief (epistemic logic), and possibility (*modal logic). The question of which words can play the role of logical constants is important in *philosophical logic. The study of formal logic is a prerequisite for any work with computers, including *artificial intelligence. (See also *deduction, *induction.)

logicism, a school of research into the foundations of mathematics. It aimed to reduce the concepts and principles of mathematics to the concepts and principles of *logic. The philosophers who pioneered this approach were *Frege and *Russell. Generally considered a failure, logicism nevertheless yielded new insights and forms the basis of the modern perception of the relation between mathematics and logic.

long run, an economic concept, first put forward by *Marshall, denoting the period of time sufficient to enable producers to change the amounts employed of *all* *factors of production, including buildings and machinery. It is thus not a fixed period of time, but varies from industry to industry, normally depending on technological factors. Marshall distinguished the long run from the short run, which refers to the period during which only some factors, such as labour, can be changed. The difference between long and short run may be illustrated by the case of a firm whose products suddenly face increased demand. The firm wishes to raise output, but in the short run can do so only by increasing the labour input, leading to an increased labour/capital ratio, which may reduce efficiency and increase unit costs. In the long run the firm can install additional capital equipment and so reduce the labour/capital ratio again. (See also *cost.)

loss, the deficit made by a firm whose *costs are greater than its revenues from sales. A firm may incur short-term losses in the hope of future profits, and some companies in a group may do so for the purpose of maximizing the group's profits. A loss for the whole group is known as a consolidated loss. (See also *profit.)

Lotus Sūtra (Sanskrit, *Saddharma Pundarīka Sūtra*, 'Lotus of the True Law'), a collection of Buddhist teachings dating from around the 1st century AD. It is recognized by *Mahāyāna Buddhists as containing the essential teachings of the *Buddha, and thus the most complete discourse of their doctrine. It contains a speech given by the transcendent, rather than earthly, Buddha to all sentient creatures. In it he explains the many ways to enlightenment: the role of the Buddha; the benefits of appealing to Bodhisattvas, particularly Avalokiteshvara (see *Dalai Lama); the meaning of Buddha-nature; and the importance of faith.

Lutheran Church, a *Protestant Church widespread in Germany, Scandinavia, and the USA, and also found in Canada and Australasia, with about 25 million full members. Traditional Lutheran teaching, based on that of Martin Luther (*c.*1483–1546), emphasizes that faith alone is necessary for salvation. Many Lutheran Churches are established, with the head of state as the head of the Church. Lutheran services lay more stress on the sermon and less on the celebration of the Eucharist than do Roman Catholic or Eastern Orthodox services.

M

Maasai (Masai), *pastoralists living in Kenya and Tanzania. In the past they dominated the grasslands of the Rift Valley, raiding their neighbours for cattle. Traditionally, the Maasai live off the blood and milk of their cattle, although they also keep sheep and goats. Maasai men belong to *age-sets; following *circumcision, a group of young men become *moran* (warriors), and for ten years are responsible for herding the cattle and killing predators. Once the *moran* become junior elders they are allowed to marry. The Maasai are under pressure to give up *pastoralism and settle in villages.

Mach, Ernst (1838–1916), Austrian physicist and philosopher of science. His belief that all knowledge of the world comes from sensations, and that science should be solely concerned with observables, inspired the *logical positivist philosophers of the Vienna Circle in the 1920s, and also scientists such as Albert Einstein (1879–1955) in the formulation of his theory of relativity, and the 'Copenhagen school' of

Amongst the **Maasai** a girl's initiation into womanhood corresponds to the boy's initiation as warrior. She relinquishes her childhood name, her head is shaved, and her face decorated. Soon afterwards she will marry and must leave her own family and village to live with her husband.

quantum mechanics. In commemoration of his work on aerodynamics, his name has been preserved in the Mach number.

Machiavelli, Niccolò (1469–1527), Italian statesman and political theorist. He is best known for *The Prince* (1513), a book of advice to monarchs on the best means to acquire and retain power. In apparent disregard of traditional morality, Machiavelli argued that princes should use cruelty, deception, and other such devices to strengthen themselves in the eyes of their people. His underlying belief, however, was that a strong *state was necessary to achieve all other human ends. This lay behind his *Discourses on the First Ten Books of Titus Livy* (c.1513–17), in which the achievements of the Roman republic were analysed in order to understand what successful republican government required. Machiavelli stressed the need to preserve the public spirit or *virtu* of the citizens from corruption. He wrote as a political realist, conveying lessons learnt by observing the world as it is. By interpreting this realism as a cynical contempt for moral restraints, 'Machiavellian' has come to mean 'scheming and deceitful'.

macro-economics, the areas of economics which view the economy as a single unit, rather than as a large collection of individual economic agents and markets. It is thus concerned with the behaviour of broad economic aggregates, notably aggregate *demand (and its components *consumption, *investment, and government spending), *national income, the *balance of payments, the level of *employment, and the price level. A central focus of macro-economics is the role of government, especially the impact of monetary and *fiscal policy on economic performance. Different schools of economic thought develop different models of macro-economic behaviour. *Keynesians assume inflexible money-wages and make national output dependent on government *intervention in the economy. *Classical economics and *monetarism are more likely to assume flexible wages and prices and make national output essentially independent of government policy.

Mafia, an international secret society originating in its modern form in Sicily in the early 19th century, and now active world-wide. It is a self-governing society which requires its members to live by a code of silence and eschew all co-operation with legitimate authorities: the right to avenge wrongs lies with the victim and his family. The Mafia is involved in drug-trafficking (*drug offences), organized *prostitution, *fraud, *theft, and *kidnapping. It imposes on businesses protection 'tax' (that is, immunity from molestation obtained by payment under threat of violence) estimated to amount to many millions. Those within the Church or law enforcement agencies who have taken action against the Mafia have often been murdered or threatened. In the USA, the Mafia is notable also for its infiltration of legitimate businesses; for example, in transport, construction, gambling, and fast-food, and its use of these businesses for *money-laundering. Numerous attempts by the authorities both in the USA and in Italy to undermine Mafia activities have as yet been unsuccessful.

magic, a belief that specific ends can be achieved through *ritual actions, often involving spells and incantations, which invoke supernatural forces. Studies of magic have often been linked to studies of *religion. Early anthropologists like *Frazer saw magic as a stage in social *evolution, and regarded it as a kind of primitive science, but this was challenged by *Malinowski, whose own interpretation of magic, in keeping with his *functionalism, treated it as a means to allow emotional expression. Contrary to the predictions of sociologists like *Weber, magic has not disappeared, despite the advances of scientific rationalism.

magistrate, in a broad sense, any person exercising judicial authority. In England and Wales, a magistrate is usually a lay person who has shown an interest in public affairs, but who is not legally qualified. Such magistrates are advised in court on matters of law by a *solicitor known as a clerk of the justices. A stipendiary magistrate is a full-time salaried magistrate who must be a *barrister or a *solicitor. Magistrates' courts are mainly concerned with criminal law. It is their job to decide whether those charged with a serious offence should be tried before a *judge and *jury, while they themselves both try and sentence those charged with less serious offences. They also adjudicate on certain claims under *civil law.

Mahābhārata, classical Sanskrit epic (*c.*400 BC–AD 200), regarded as one of the *Hindu sacred texts. It describes the tragic war between two branches of the Bharata dynasty: the Pāndavas, the forces of good, and the Kauravas, the forces of evil. The hero of the epic is Arjuna, whose long dialogue with Krishna at the climax of the poem is known as the *Bhagavadgītā*.

Mahāyāna, a major grouping within *Buddhism, distinct from *Theravāda Buddhism. It arose during the 1st century AD and spread mainly throughout north-eastern Asia. It is sometimes called Northern Buddhism. Whilst nominally accepting the Theravāda canon, essential Mahāyāna beliefs are based upon supplementary texts, written in *Sanskrit, rather than *Pali, particularly the *Lotus Sūtra. Mahāyāna belief emphasizes universal enlightenment; its followers belong to all sections of society and need not be monks, hence its name, which means 'Great Vehicle'. Followers seek personal enlightenment for the sake of all, rather than the individual. This distinctive notion is best displayed in the *Bodhisattva ideal of Avalokiteshvara (see *Dalai Lama), whose pre-eminent wisdom and outstanding compassion served to benefit all followers, as well as providing the perfect example of the Mahāyāna religious ideal. There are two main philosophical schools within Mahāyāna Buddhism: the Mādhyamika school, which emphasizes the illusory and essentially empty (*shūnyata) nature of all things, as well as the importance of *prajñā* (wisdom); and the Yogāchāra school, which lays stress on meditative concentration (*samādhi*). (See also *Indian philosophy.)

mahdī *millenarianism.

mahjong, a game for four played with tiles, originally from China and the Far East and brought to the West after World War I. In its modified English-language version, a complete set of tiles (once made of ivory, wood, or bone, now of plastic) consists of a suit of thirty-six bamboo tiles (four sets, numbered 1–9), thirty-six circles, and thirty-six characters similarly subdivided, twelve dragons (red, green, and white) and sixteen winds (East, North, West, and South), with the optional addition of sixteen flowers and seasons. Players draw thirteen tiles by a complicated process from four 'walls' (the Great Wall of China) and play anti-clockwise in turn, discarding one tile and picking up another. The winner is

After two years of marriage to the actress Joan Collins, her fourth husband Peter Holm (seen here) was awarded a sizeable **maintenance after divorce** through the US courts.

the first to collect four 'pungs' (three like tiles of the same suit and rank) and a pair, or another scoring set, such as combinations of a quong (a pung plus the first matching tile) and a chow (a run of three tiles of the same suit). There are also other special winning combinations such as seven pairs (seven sisters).

Maimonides (1134–1204), Jewish philosopher, physician, and authority on the Law, born at Cordoba in southern Spain. His *The Torah Reviewed* is a code of Jewish law (see *Torah) which systematized all Jewish law and doctrine. Like *al-Farabī Maimonides sought to reconcile religious doctrine with philosophical and scientific beliefs by allegorical reinterpretation. His *Guide of the Perplexed* is addressed to those whose early philosophical education faces them with the apparent need to choose between religious and natural knowledge. He holds that each can be pursued within its proper sphere, but that this harmony can be appreciated only by those of strong intellect. This élitist doctrine, together with its devout aims, results in the deliberate obscurity of the *Guide*, designed to deter and to hide from weaker minds a view by which they could be only confused.

maintenance after divorce (USA, alimony), a financial provision made by the economically stronger spouse to the other spouse after *divorce. Maintenance may consist of a sum payable for the benefit of the parent and a further sum for the benefit of the children. The presumption in many countries has been that a man should financially support both his wife and any children after divorce. However, in the UK, in many parts of the USA, and elsewhere, each spouse is entitled to a share in the family property on divorce, but further maintenance is normally payable only to a spouse who is caring for children. Many dispute whether this adequately compensates a spouse who has spent years caring for children or who has subordinated a career to a partner's. It is common for the liable spouse, usually the father, not to fulfil his obligations, sometimes because he is supporting a new family. This may result in his former spouse and children becoming dependent on *social security benefits. Many governments, alarmed by increasing costs to the taxpayer and following initiatives in the USA and in Australia, have devised formulae to simplify calculations of parental liability and to improve collection.

Maitreya (Sanskrit, 'friendly one'), the future *Buddha, now residing in heaven, awaiting his rebirth on earth. His appearance is keenly anticipated by all Buddhists. In eastern Asia he is often depicted as a fat, laughing figure, holding a bag of good fortune and a rosary, representing good deeds, ready to restore truth on earth.

majoritarian representation, a system of electoral representation based on single-member constituencies, in which the winner of the seat must either receive the highest number of votes among several alternatives, or else receive more than 50 per cent, or some other stipulated proportion of the vote, such as two-thirds. A notable example of majoritarian representation is the first-past-the-post, plurality system found in the UK. Here, the leading candidate in each constituency is elected from one ballot, regardless of the narrowness of the margin of victory. In majority systems, found in such countries as Australia, Canada, and France, the party or candidate receiving over 50 per cent of the vote wins the seat. In cases where no candidate secures 50 per cent of the total vote, a second ballot is often used, as in France. Only the two candidates with the highest number of votes on the first ballot stand in the second ballot. Australia uses the system of the alternative vote, in which voters rank candidates in order of preference. If no candidate wins a majority of first preferences, the bottom candidate is eliminated and these votes are redistributed according to second preferences. This process continues until one candidate does have a majority. Majoritarian systems, particularly the plurality formula, tend to favour large *political parties, which are able to gain a majority of seats in the *legislature. This reduces the need for *coalitions, which are more characteristic of systems of *proportional representation.

Malay language   *Austronesian languages.

Malinowski, Bronislaw (Kaspar) (1884–1942), Polish anthropologist, who pioneered the use of intensive *fieldwork in British anthropology. Malinowski was a noted critic of earlier theories of social *evolution, and is generally regarded as a founder of *functionalism, but his theoretical contributions have been mostly forgotten, while his vivid *ethnography (the study of a particular society) still captures the imagination of new readers. Between 1914 and 1918, Malinowski spent more than two years living as a 'participant-observer' on the *Trobriand Islands in the south Pacific, researching the life of the people. The first major product of this work was his account of the *kula system, *Argonauts of the Western Pacific* (1922). Like his later studies of Trobriand life, it provided an unprecedented richness of detail in its descriptions.

malnutrition, a chronic condition brought about by insufficient intake or absorption of food. For children under 5, World Health Organization standardized measures of weight for age are used, with moderate malnutrition meaning less than 75 per cent of these standards, and severe malnutrition less than 60 per cent. Two other commonly used terms are stunting, in which a child's height for age falls below international measures, usually indicating past nutritional deficiencies, and wasting, in which a child's weight for height is below international measures, usually indicating current deficiencies. The World Bank estimates that about one-sixth of people in the developing world may not have a sufficient calorie intake to prevent stunted growth and serious health risks, and that another third may not have

Although an overall insufficiency of food is the major cause of **malnutrition**, the protein deficiency disease kwashiorkor results from weaning babies on to an exclusively starch-based diet. Education programmes, such as this one in Togo, can convince mothers of the need to include locally available protein in their children's diets.

enough for an active working life. Malnutrition is associated with increased vulnerability to disease, poor school performance among children, and lower productivity among adults. Malnutrition among babies is a major factor in high *infant mortality rates. Many countries give priority to mothers and children, some having programmes to distribute subsidized or free food through health centres. Evidence from Chile and elsewhere shows that the fastest reductions in child malnutrition are obtained when health and *immunization programmes are combined with nutrition programmes and targeted on the most needy. Other programmes are designed to enable families to buy more of their own food, for example by providing work for the unemployed with payment in cash or food, or by giving stamps to the poor to exchange for food, or by subsidizing staple foods.

management accounting, the provision of financial information to assist in management control and decision-making. Originally, management accounting was concerned with the need to establish the costs of manufacturing products and providing services. Subsequently, it was extended to include cost control through budgeting and forward business planning. For example, financial planning involves setting a budget for each department as a guide for the department's manager. Management accounting also enables managers to determine product profitability and to investigate inefficiencies. Management accounts are often more detailed than the financial accounts prescribed by law and which all companies must keep. They analyse information in a different way which is more relevant to the needs of, for example, manufacturing management. Where this is the case it is vital that a procedure exists to reconcile the two forms of accounts so that, although they may be different in presentation, their overall meaning is the same.

management buy-out, the purchase by managers of (a self-contained or specialist part of) the organization employing them, for example a firm or division of a conglomerate or part of an *insolvent organization. Similarly, government employees may bid for a company being *privatized, or to provide a service which is being *contracted out from the public sector. The attraction to managers of owning the company they operate is to increase their responsibility and control, and to share more fully in the fruits of their efforts and the risks of the business than if they remain salaried employees. Managers are commonly assisted in buy-outs by tax-relief incentives and the provision of bank loans.

management science, the application of quantitative techniques (those involving making measurements) to business decision-making. Management science covers the whole range of decision-making by management, for example, *operations research, *production management, *marketing, *personnel management, and cost accounting. Management science operates by forming a quantitative representation of a business problem, that is by putting a numerical value on the factors involved. This modelling process enables the major elements of the decision to be identified and considered in relation to the whole problem. Alternative solutions can then be put forward and evaluated and an optimum solution found. There is always a need to balance the quantitative approach with behaviourial considerations, keeping in mind that business decisions involve people. Whilst past experience can be used to suggest how people might react in the future, conditions change and consequently people's future reactions are not always predictable. Thus management science techniques should be used as an aid to business decision-making not as a substitute for it.

mandate, the authority to act for another; specifically, a term used to describe the system of government applied to the colonies lost by Germany and Turkey at the end of World War I. Such mandated territories included Turkey's imperial possessions in the Middle East, and Germany's colonies in Central and South-West Africa. Mandates were not, strictly speaking, *colonies, nor fully independent countries, but were entrusted, under the supervision of the League of Nations, to the care and guidance of certain countries, notably Britain and France, until such a time as they were deemed ready for full independence. In practice the mandate system was fraught with difficulties and provoked considerable resentment. Most mandated territories, with the important exceptions of Palestine and Namibia, had achieved independence by World War II.

manic depression, a cyclical mood disorder in which periods of hyperactivity, elation, self-importance, and (often unwarranted) optimism alternate with the despair of *depression. Although in extreme form it has the disorganizing quality of *psychosis, lesser degrees of manic-depressive behaviour can be seen in some moody people who, in the 'up' phase, can often manage feats of great creativity or achievement: the British World War II leader Winston Churchill was a notable example. Manic depression, the tendency to which is inherited, is due to spontaneous fluctuations in the levels of chemicals in the *brain that control mood. Accordingly, the most successful treatment is with mood-stabilizing *drug treatment that acts to redress this imbalance of brain chemistry.

manpower planning, the forecasting of requirements of employees of all kinds and levels in an organization and matching these demands with the likely supply (availability) of such employees. The demand for manpower within the organization will depend on how successful the organization is and whether it is involved in expansion or take-over activity. Manpower planning in an organization is made more difficult because many of the factors affecting the supply of and demand for manpower are outside the control of the organization. Supply can be affected by political and economic changes, for example, the *EC requires greater labour mobility between member countries. The advent of the free market within the Community in 1992 has made manpower planning even more important as skilled workers are able to move freely to the country where they are offered the best conditions. A buoyant economy increases competition for manpower and shortages can occur, thereby forcing up wage-rates.

manslaughter *homicide.

mantra (from Sanskrit, 'spell' or 'charm'), a mystic formula or verse, used in Hinduism and Buddhism, which by repeated chanting forms an aid to *meditation. Mantras are believed to have magical qualities, such as the ability to protect the user from evil powers. Hindu mantras are based either on Sanskrit verses taken from the *Vedas, or on sacred syllables, such as Om (Aum), which represents supreme reality. (See also *Tantra.)

manufacturing industry *secondary industry.

Maoism, the communist doctrines of Mao Zedong (1893–1976). Mao devoted considerable time to the theoretical basis of the communist state in China, and his ideas reflect the influence both of traditional Chinese thought and of the structure of Chinese society. Maoism's principal difference from Marxist–Leninism is the importance it attaches to the peasantry as the powerhouse of the revolution and communist state, rather than to the urban proletariat, which was at the time not well developed in China. A central idea is that of permanent revolution, which led to the radical reform movements known as the Great Leap Forward (1958) and the Cultural Revolution (1966). By contrast with the former Soviet Union, where large-scale *industrialization was favoured and a ruling communist *élite emerged, Maoism emphasized the continuing importance of the peasantry, small-scale industry, and agricultural *collectivization. In order to avoid the emergence of a bourgeois élite, city workers and intellectuals were sent to the countryside to perform compulsory 'educational' agricultural labour. Such policies proved economically and socially disastrous and have been largely reversed in present-day China. However,

Maoist revolutionary theory and strategies for guerrilla warfare are still influential in some developing countries.

Maori, the original inhabitants of New Zealand. Although originally *Polynesian, the Maoris have their own distinct culture.Their language is one of the *Austronesian languages. Tribal structure was traditionally based on common ancestry, and sub-tribes were the landholding groups. The family was the basis for agricultural production, and also for *ritual events. Vigorous Maori opposition to colonization led to a series of wars which finally ended in 1872. Maori culture went through a period of revival in the early 20th century, which led to parliamentary representation, and the introduction of the Maori language into schools. In more recent years, another phase of cultural revival has maintained the distinctiveness of the Maori.

marathon, a long-distance running-race, standardized in 1908 at 42,195 m (26 miles 385 yards). It commemorates the heroic run in 490 BC by a Greek soldier from Marathon to Athens to bring news of the Greek victory against the Persians. The race was introduced in 1896 at the first modern *Olympic Games (held in Athens) and is now recognized as the ultimate test for distance-runners of either sex. Winners cover the course in little more than two hours. Public enthusiasm for amateur long-distance running has made the marathon a regular annual event in some communities, and big marathons such as the London or Boston attract huge fields, usually fronted by 200 serious or reasonable club-runners. The full distance is too severe for many, and the half-marathon has become a widely accepted substitute.

Marcuse, Herbert (1898–1979), German-born philosopher who fled Nazism and settled in the USA after 1934. A member of the *Frankfurt School, he advocated radical social change and in the 1960s was a cult figure for student revolutionaries and the *New Left. *Eros and Civilization* (1955) was a bold attempt to synthesize the ideas of *Freud and *Marx. 'He was', according to the British philosopher Anthony Quinton, 'as committed to the erotic liberation of the unconscious from repression by the conscious mind as he was to the revolutionary liberation of the masses from political and economic domination by the capitalist ruling class.' Marcuse was especially known for his analysis of the repressive nature of modern society, whether capitalist (*One-Dimensional Man*, 1964), or communist (*Soviet Marxism*, 1958).

marginal analysis (in economics), an analysis which uses the concept of marginal or small incremental qualities. The marginal change in variable A with respect to variable B is the change in A associated with a small change in B. For instance, the marginal propensity to consume measures the change in *consumption arising from a change in income. This notion underlies the Keynesian *macro-economic model of the *multiplier. In *micro-economics marginal analysis is particularly useful. For example, the amount of a food purchased by a consumer can be seen as determined at the point where the additional satisfaction ('utility') obtained from the last ('marginal') unit purchased at a given moment first matches the price of the food in question. This assumes that the price is given and that (at least beyond a certain point) marginal utility diminishes with each increase in the quantity of the food purchased (see also *diminishing returns). Somewhat ambiguously, on the production side, a profit-maximizing firm will increase output as long as its marginal revenue (the addition to total revenue from sup-

plying an extra unit of output) is greater than its marginal cost (the addition to total costs from that same unit of output), because the marginal unit of output is then clearly adding to profit. The firm will reach its optimum output where marginal revenue is equal to marginal cost. The same analysis can be applied to the employment of *factors of production.

market (in economics), the arrangements to permit or facilitate exchange between buyers and sellers. Some markets have a specific location (for example, livestock markets or *stock exchanges), but this need not be the case (for example, housing markets or the *foreign-exchange markets). In any market, buyers demand goods or services, and sellers supply them. In a well-functioning *free market, price will respond to market forces to equilibrate *demand and *supply. If would-be purchases exceed would-be sales, price will rise, thus reducing demand and drawing forth more supply. The reverse will happen if planned sales exceed planned purchases. Markets are, therefore, of crucial importance to the allocation of resources. If markets do not exist or have undesirable features, such as *monopoly power, government *intervention may be appropriate. In a *planned (or 'command') economy, direct allocation by government order is the norm as opposed to a market economy, where decisions are decentralized and co-ordinated through markets.

marketing, the creation or enlargement of *demand for a good or service by a company. It may involve the use of *market research, mass media *advertising, and other forms of promotion, including sponsorship, special offers, and free gifts; packaging at point of sale (see *merchandizing); pricing; product policy, including the creation of brands and new product development; personal selling; and distribution. Successful marketing involves defining and satisfying customers' needs. Although marketing was developed in relation to consumer goods, the principles of marketing are being applied increasingly to industrial goods, to services, and for non-profit-making activities such as charities and local and national government activities. An international dimension to marketing is becoming more common as business activity grows.

market research, the study of consumers' needs and preferences, and of the acceptability of goods and services offered for sale; in economics, the study of the requirements of *markets. Generally the aim is to obtain information that will help design a product or service and its presentation (packaging and *marketing) so that sales and profits can be maximized. Techniques may be relatively simple: testing the expectations of sales staff, for example, or looking at previous sales of the same or a similar product, or at competing products. More sophisticated surveys of consumer attitudes may be conducted, by mail, telephone, or personal interview, with a population sample selected with due attention to age, sex, socio-economic grouping, or geographical location (see *social classification). A new product may be test-launched in a limited area. Market research achieved recognition as an occupation in the 1920s and 1930s; after World War II, US and Japanese companies took the lead in its use and development.

market socialism, a form of *socialism combining social ownership of the means of production with extensive use of market mechanisms in the economy. The theorists who set forth this doctrine in the 1930s and 1940s were Oskar Lange and Abba P. Lerner (hence 'Lange–Lerner socialism'). It aims to reap the efficiency advantages of the market while distributing resources more equally than under *capitalism, for instance by converting enterprises into workers' *co-operatives. Such proposals have frequently been put forward by reformers in Eastern Europe, and on occasion (especially in Yugoslavia and Hungary) partially implemented. In China too, in recent years, responsibility for *agriculture, for example, has been switched from *collective farms to households. In most states, if some sort of market mechanism is not officially permitted, an *informal or black economy is likely to develop.

Maronite, member of an Eastern Christian community in communion with the *Roman Catholic Church. Numbering about 1 million, Maronites are found principally in *Lebanon, but have migrated also to Cyprus, Egypt, Palestine, Egypt, and the USA. The Maronite liturgy is in Syriac (see *Syrian Orthodox Church), and their ecclesiastical head, under the pope, is the patriarch of Antioch (Antakya in present-day Turkey), who resides in Lebanon. Since the establishment of the state of Lebanon in 1944, the Maronites have been prominent in politics, with the office of President traditionally held by a Maronite. In the Lebanese civil war (1975–91) the Maronites were split into two factions: the Phalangists and Chamounists.

The priest (seated) guides the bride, who has been decorated and adorned by members of her family, and groom through one of the many elaborate rituals that make up a Hindu **marriage** ceremony. The pair sits within a rope which symbolizes the joining of man and woman.

marriage, a socially recognized relationship between a man and a woman, which accords status to their offspring. All cultures organize and structure the relationships between men and women through which society as a whole reproduces itself, but there is great variation in the rights and duties associated with marriage in different societies. In many cultures, marriage is theoretically regarded as a permanent bond, dissoluble only through *divorce, but marriage may also be a temporary arrangement. In Iran and other Muslim countries, for example, the early Islamic practice of temporary marriage still co-exists with permanent marriage. Most Western legal systems have since World War II attempted to provide equal rights in law for both parties to a marriage, but in other systems, such as, for instance, Islamic law (the *shari'ah) men and women are not accorded the same rights. Marriage is central to *kinship organization, and the whole pattern of a society can be affected by its pattern of marriage. A person may have only one partner (monogamy) or many partners (polygamy: in polygyny, a man has more than one wife, and in polyandry, a woman has more than one husband). Most societies have rules prohibiting marriage amongst certain categories of kin (see *incest), and people may indeed be forced to marry outside their own group (exogamy). On the other hand, people also often marry within a circumscribed category (endogamy), as in the *caste systems of Indian society, or they may be expected to marry partners from a particular category of kin, like certain sorts of cousin. In some societies, a widow is expected to marry her husband's brother. Although Western societies place great emphasis on romantic attraction and individual choice of marriage partner, marriage always involves a much wider group of people than the husband and wife; most other societies recognize this, and the wider kin group plays an important part in the choice of marriage partner, and in the exchange of *gifts and payments such as *dowry and bridewealth. Marriage can be seen as an important *rite of passage; it involves particular *rituals, often religious in character, which emphasize the importance of marriage to society as a whole. However, unmarried *cohabitation is an increasing phenomenon world-wide.

Marshall, Alfred (1842–1924), British *classical economist. Marshall was largely responsible for the development of partial (as opposed to general) equilibrium *micro-economics, the theoretical analysis of resource allocation by examining the mechanism of *supply and *demand in a representative individual market, assuming this market to be negligibly small in relation to the economic system as a whole. In the process Marshall invented the tool of demand and supply curves; the term *elasticity to denote a relation between two proportionate changes; and the concept of consumer's surplus to denote the difference between the maximum amount of money that consumers would be prepared to pay for a specified quantity of a good and the amount that they actually have to pay at the given market price. Marshall also greatly extended the theory of rent inherited from *Ricardo (see *profit).

martial arts, a group of fighting techniques developed in Oriental countries and now practised world-wide. They demand a high degree of physical fitness and muscular control in which timing is all-important. They offer a valued means of self-defence and are also practised as competitive sports. Jujitsu is a Japanese method of self-defence involving throws, arm- and wrist-locks, kicks, chopping movements, and punches. It gave birth to the modern combat sport of

Tai kwan do (Korean, 'kick-fist-art') is one of the many traditional **martial arts** which has developed into a dynamic combat sport. It was introduced as a demonstration sport at the 1988 Olympic Games, held in Seoul, Korea, the sport's country of origin.

judo, a form of wrestling from a standing position. Karate students learn deep mental control as a prelude to unleashing latent forces which enable them to deliver lethal blows with the hands and feet. Kung-fu is the Chinese form of kick-fighting; variations are practised also in Taiwan and Thailand. Aikido is a Japanese form of wrestling that uses circular moves, wrist-locks, and throws. Kendo, also from Japan, is Samurai fencing, carried out with long staffs; contestants wear padded gloves, a breastplate, and face-mask. Another version, tai kwan do, originated in Korea.

martial law, government by military authorities in times of emergency, such as *war or civil unrest. Martial law may also be imposed over long periods to stifle opposition to a particular regime. It imposes a more restrictive regime than is normal, and often *civil rights such as free speech are suspended. The term is sometimes applied to the body of laws which govern members of the armed forces, but this is more accurately called military law.

martyr (Greek, 'witness'), one who suffers persecution and death for persistence in religious faith, or for any great cause. In Christianity, martyrs, ranked before all other *saints, were venerated for their courage and faith, and were considered powerful intercessors between man and God. Until 1969 it was Roman Catholic practice to preserve relics of the martyrs in every consecrated altar. The term originally applied to early Christians such as St Stephen, the first martyr, who were put to death for their faith, and, more recently, has been applied to El Salvador's Archbishop Oscar Romero, who was assassinated in 1980, and to those in the former communist bloc persecuted for their faith. In Islam, the shahīd ('witness') is a similar concept: those who die in a *jihād or holy war are considered martyrs, and are guaranteed a place in heaven. Shī'īte Muslims regard the martyrdom of Husain (in AD 680), commemorated at *'āshūrā' as the turning-point in their history. Sikhs commemorate the martyrdoms of two of their *gurus, Arjan and Tegh Bahadur. In Judaism, the six million Jews killed during World War II are remembered as martyrs.

Marx, Karl (1818–83), German social scientist and revolutionary. Originally a disciple of *Hegel, Marx's involvement with radical groups in Germany and France during the 1840s led him to espouse *communism and to formulate a far-reaching critique of *capitalism, a system which he condemned as the major source of human *alienation. Convinced of the centrality of economics to human life, he reversed Hegel's formulation that mind or spirit determines the course of human history, to develop the *materialist interpretation of history which came to form the core of *Marxism. Later, Marx devoted most of his attention to the economics of capitalism, with the aim of demonstrating its increasingly exploitative and crisis-ridden character. These researches culminated in *Das Kapital* (1867; edited by Friedrich Engels 1885–94). In his more journalistic writings Marx analysed the political events of the day from a class perspective. He was also spasmodically active in labour and socialist movements, helping to found the First International in 1864. Since his death, his extensive body of writings has exercised an immense influence on socialist movements and *political parties throughout the world.

Marxism, the system of economic and political ideas first developed by *Marx and Friedrich Engels (1820–95) and later developed by their followers together with *dialectical materialism to form the basis for the theory and practice of *communism. At the heart of Marxism lies the materialist conception of history, according to which the development of all human societies is ultimately determined by the methods of production that people adopt to meet their needs. A particular technique of production determines first of all a set of property relations to organize production (for instance slavery, feudalism, *capitalism), and secondly the politics, religion, philosophy, and so on of a given society. The conflict between the particular social classes which emerged led to the next stage of social *evolution. Feudalism had been followed by capitalism, which was destined to make way for *socialism/communism. In this way Marx and Engels sought to establish the centrality of classes and the *class struggle. Their attention was focused on capitalist societies, which they viewed as increasingly polarized between an exploiting capitalist class and an impoverished working class. Crucial to Marx's economic analysis of capitalism was his normative elaboration of the *labour theory of value held by the classical economists *Smith and *Ricardo. Marx saw capitalists as expropriating the *surplus value created by workers, and accumulating ever-further capital, as the workers (the proletariat) grew ever poorer. The development of industry would render capitalism obsolete, at which point the working class would be ready to overthrow the system by revolutionary means and establish a socialist society. Marx and Engels said little about the economics and politics of socialism; after their death, Lenin and his followers in the former Soviet Union and elsewhere used Marxist ideas to underpin *communism, the ideology later being dubbed 'Marxism–Leninism', while other Marxists were critical of communist methods and regarded the Russian revolution (1917) as premature. Since then Marxists have had to grapple with the failure of the socialist societies to live up to the humanistic beliefs of Marx himself, and also with political developments, such as the rise of fascism, that appeared to contradict historical materialism. Such shortcomings when put into practice mean that to embrace Marxism wholesale now requires a considerable leap of faith. However, Marx's injunction that to understand a society we should first investigate its mode of production continues to influence many social scientists and historians who would not accept the complete theory.

Masonic Order, a widespread secret fraternal society, whose members are known as freemasons. The society, inspired by the medieval guilds of stonemasons, was formed in London in 1717 to encourage mutual brotherliness and self-help. Members of the different 'Lodges' of the Order, open to men only, are drawn particularly from professional classes. Masonic practice is noted for its rites of *initiation, involving oaths of allegiance, and for its use of *symbolism: for example, moral law, brotherhood, and rectitude are symbolized by the sacred book, the compasses, and the square. Freemasons recognize each other through a series of secret signs, passwords, and handshakes. Freemasonry is not a religion, although members generally believe in a Supreme Being, and follow the precepts of morality, charity, and obedience to the law. In parts of Europe, particularly Italy and France, freemasonry has traditionally attracted anti-clericals and free-thinkers, and has thus encountered opposition from the Roman Catholic Church, which regards the principles, oaths, and secrecy of freemasonry as incompatible with its doctrines. Today the Masonic Order remains most popular in the UK and other English-speaking countries.

mass media, the means of producing and disseminating news, information, and entertainment to a universal audience. The term commonly refers to print and *broadcasting news *media—*newspapers, magazines, *radio, and *television—but may encompass cinema, the sound-recording industry, and even paperback *publishing and photography. Benefiting from *economies of scale, spreading risks by *diversification, and operating with an extensive *division of labour, the mass media are industrial operations of considerable size and influence in political, economic, and cultural life. Key factors in the nature of the messages carried, the way they are conveyed by the mass media, and their impact for the individual and society are *news selection, *agenda-setting, and *censorship; the quality of *journalism; and the effects of modern *telecommunications technology, such as in electronic news gathering. The mass media have been credited with helping to fashion a mass society characterized by greater consensus, public participation, and awareness of the 'global village' in which we live, but also, more negatively, by increasing conformity, passivity, and *alienation. Mergers and acquisitions, as well as the integration of production, distribution, and equipment supply, have produced media empires operating on a multinational or indeed world-wide basis. In non-industrialized countries and those with *authoritarian or *totalitarian governments, government ownership or control more directly affect the mass media. The degree of control exercised by the mass media, their power to influence public opinion, their allegiance to political *ideologies, and what is seen as a tendency to pander to the lowest common denominator of public taste, have been hotly debated. At the same time, accusations of 'cultural imperialism' have been made: during the 1970s and 1980s, many developing countries felt that because of the economic power of the Western mass media, Western programmes and Western values had been allowed to overwhelm local programmes and local values. On the other hand, calls by the Non-Aligned countries and by *UNESCO for a New World Information Order as a means of controlling the mass media and redressing the balance came up against the principle of the *freedom of the press, and the proposal was dropped. Advances in *satellite broadcasting in the 1980s further strengthened the position of exporters of information and entertainment.

mass production *production methods.

materialism, the philosophical view that reality is material or physical. Materialism is therefore a form of *monism. Materialism is rarely argued for directly, and is usually taken to be borne out by the success of the physical sciences. *Hobbes may be cited as a modern proponent of materialism. For materialism to be true, minds or mental states must in some sense be identical with physical phenomena (presumably states of the brain or nervous system), a proposition which raises complex philosophical questions. A different sense of materialism is associated with *Marx. Here materialism is not so much an ontological claim, as a theory about how best to explain human history, society, and thought. Marx's materialism asserts that a society is determined by its state of material development (its powers of economic production and so forth), in opposition to the *idealist claim that it is thought alone which autonomously determines the course of human development.

maternity leave *parental leave.

matriarchy, the authority of women over men, the converse of *patriarchy. Some 19th-century thinkers, including the German social theorist Friedrich Engels (1820–95), believed that matriarchy was the characteristic form of the earliest human societies. In *The Origin of the Family, Private Property and the State* (1884) he argued that evidence could be found in myths, in the early history of religions, and in the tendency for agricultural societies to worship the fertility principle in the form of a goddess. Matrilineality, whereby power (often that of men) is inherited through the female line of *descent, found in certain peoples in non-industrial societies, was interpreted as a vestige of bygone matriarchy. The evidence for these conclusions is not fully accepted, but the possible existence of matriarchal societies is an important strand in feminist arguments against male domination.

matrilineality *descent, *lineage.

Mawlid an-Nabi (Arabic, 'time of the prophet'), a festival celebrating the birthday of the Prophet *Muḥammad, believed to be 20 August 570. Celebrations are spread throughout the month of *Rabi' ul-Awwal* (culminating on the twelfth day), and include the re-telling of stories about Muḥammad's life, to expound his personality and spiritual greatness. The day is significant because it commemorates the birth of the 'messenger of God', who passed on the divine revelation of the *Koran to mankind. The celebration of the birthdays of founding fathers began within the *Sufi tradition, but spread throughout Islam, despite opposition from ultra-orthodox groups such as the *Wahhābī.

māyā (Sanskrit, 'wizardry', 'illusion'), a term used in Hinduism to denote the illusory nature of reality. In the *Upanishads it is linked with the notions of magic and deceit. This world is like the show of a magician in that we believe that what we see in the phenomenal world is real, but we are deluded by the skill of the magician. In Advaita, *māyā* indicates that, as in a magic show, sensory certainty is insufficient for knowledge. Nothing in the nature of our cognition (*jñāna*) of the world actually rules out the possibility that reality is not what is experienced ordinarily. Knowledge in fact consists, as can be seen from the teachings of the *Upanishads, in the realization that the natural world is ever-changing, multi-formed, and not ultimately real, despite our experience that it is so, and that reality is *Brahman, itself idenitifiable with the realized self (*ātman). Only through *vidyā* or knowledge do we come to a true understanding of the eternal and unchanging nature of Brahman, and achieve ultimate escape from *māyā*.

McLuhan, (Herbert) Marshall (1911–80), Canadian literary and *communications theorist, known for his theories on the *mass media, developed in his book *Understanding Media* (1964). McLuhan regarded the printed word as a less immediate and more detached medium than aural communication, such as television and believed that the print media would eventually give way before electronic media, such as *television and computers. In his view, the message transmitted by any form of communication was fundamentally influenced by the medium in which it was sent, hence his aphorism 'the medium is the message'. His term 'the global village' conveys the idea that the *mass media have 'shrunk' the world through their pervasive cultural influence.

Mead, Margaret (1901–78), US anthropologist. Mead's fluent writing style and committed discussion of topical issues made her the most famous anthropologist of her generation. In her best-known work, *Coming of Age in Samoa* (1928), Mead argued that US teenage problems were the product of cultural influences, not natural forces; Samoan adolescents lived in a culture with a more relaxed attitude to pre-marital sex and appeared to suffer none of the traumas that affected US teenagers and their families. Many Samoans resented this picture of their culture, and Mead's findings, which were based on relatively limited *fieldwork, have provoked bitter controversy since her death.

meaning, the interpretation of any *communication, message, or *sign by the recipient. The 'meaning of meaning' has vexed philosophers, linguists, psychologists, anthropologists, and sociologists for years; it is the central object of study of *semantics. Compilers of dictionaries convey the 'meaning' of words by observing how they are used, but their definitions, themselves expressed in other words, are only approximations. Since a message may have different connotations for different readers, and may in addition be shaped by the particular discourse or language of the *medium used, understanding will depend on knowledge of the *codes employed. Meaning is a product of *culture or *ideology; when it is presented as fixed or finite, it becomes a type of *myth supporting a dominant value-system. This is the overt purpose of *propaganda, but is equally powerful in more subtle forms of bias that impose a preferred meaning on apparently neutral information.

mediation   *dispute resolution.

medical ethics, a term used to refer to moral issues arising within health care. Attention has focused, for example, on the proper limits of confidentiality, how far doctors are morally obliged to involve patients in decisions about treatment, on *euthanasia, the allocation of scarce medical resources, the moral status of the human embryo and foetus (see *abortion), genetic engineering, medical participation in *torture, and the principles that should govern clinical trials on human subjects. Philosophers, lawyers, and theologians, as well as health-care professionals, are to be found working on medical ethics, often within hospital-based ethical committees. Legislation on these issues rarely keeps pace with scientific developments and is invariably contentious.

medical profession, the range of medical practitioners, qualified to practise medicine. In developed countries, the patient's first point of contact has traditionally been the general practitioner, who can make a first diagnosis and refer the patient if necessary to a specialist. This is still the pattern in countries such as Australia, Denmark, The Netherlands, and the UK, but in the USA and elsewhere, general practice has declined and patients often go directly to a specialist. In developing countries, doctors trained in the Western style tend to be scarce and are often concentrated in hospitals and in the big cities. Because of the expense of training doctors, many countries are using *paramedical workers to an increasing degree.

meditation, a means of developing spiritual awareness or devotion to God through various techniques of concentration and contemplation. Meditation may be verbal, a form of prayer, or recitation; or it may be physical, a technique which calms the mind and promotes relaxation. In Christianity, meditation consists of devout reflection on themes from the *Bible or from the lives of *saints, an intellectual means of deepening spiritual insight. In Eastern religions, meditation is a method of achieving enlightenment or liberation, as the individual spirit is integrated into a greater spiritual or cosmic reality. *Yoga, for example, employs discipline over physical and mental processes in order to attain purification. In many religions, meditation is assisted through the repetition of sacred syllables, names, or texts, such as Hindu and Buddhist *mantras or Islamic *dhikr*, or through focusing on images and symbols, known as mandalas. Other practices include the use of rhythmic movement and dance, or devices such as prayer beads, rosaries, or prayer wheels. Eastern methods of meditation have been popularized in the West in recent years by organizations such as the Transcendental Meditation movement.

medium (plural, media), any means of *communication used to convey information. The medium may be voice or body language (see *non-verbal communication); it may be writing, print, pictures; or it may be some mechanical means such as *radio, *television, sound recording, or film.

A village woman in Jisham county, China, receives a physical check-up from a member of the **medical profession**. In China, as in most of the developing world, health care in rural areas is based on out-patient consultations in health clinics, as distinct from the more expensive hospital-based system typical in the West.

*McLuhan observed that 'the medium is the message', indicating that the type of medium chosen has a strong influence on the *meaning of what is communicated. 'The media' is a term often used to refer to what are more properly known as *mass media: the press, radio, and television.

megacity, a term used for a very large city. Cities with more than 4 million people were unknown until London reached that figure in the 1880s. By 1980 there were thirty-five such cities. In its *Global Report on Human Settlement* (1987), the UN agency Habitat forecast that by the year 2000 there would be sixty-six, fifty of them in the developing world. Among these large cities is a sub-group of 'megacities' or, as the UN describes them, 'agglomerations'. In 1980 there were seven agglomerations with populations of more than 10 million. By the turn of the century, if present trends continue, there could be twenty-two, all but five in the developing countries. São Paulo could have around 25 million inhabitants and Tokyo/Yokohama 20 million, and Mexico City, Bombay, and New York/NE New Jersey might have passed 15 million, while Bangkok, Beijing, Buenos Aires, Cairo, Calcutta, Delhi, Dhaka, Jakarta, Karachi, Los Angeles, Manila, Moscow, Osaka/Kobe, Rio de Janeiro, Shanghai, Seoul, and Tehran could be housing more than 10 million. Many large cities are already facing severe difficulties in meeting the needs of their populations for *water, energy, food, and *employment. (See also *urbanization.)

Meinong, Alexius (1852–1920), Austrian philosopher. His main contribution was his 'theory of objects', a classification of the varieties of objects of mental acts; these included 'objectives', the objects of belief and other 'propositional attitudes', in the terminology now widespread among analytic philosophers. Like *Frege, he distinguished sharply between merely entertaining an objective and judging it to be true. *Russell studied and wrote about his work. He is principally remembered among *analytic philosophers for holding that non-existent objects can be the object of mental acts, and referents of (what most would consider to be) empty terms: what Meinong dismissed as a 'prejudice in favour of the actual', Russell is widely held to have vindicated by means of his theory of descriptions.

melā (Sanskrit, 'assembly'), a Hindu religious gathering. It is particularly associated with the pilgrimage festival of Kumbh Mela, a riverside fair held in turn at four sacred sites on the banks of the Ganges, Godāvari, and Sipra rivers, where people come in their millions to bathe. Smaller fairs or *jatras*, at which local deities are venerated, form an important part of the Indian religious calendar.

Melanesian societies, those of the central Pacific between the Equator and the Tropic of Capricorn. This region, which includes *New Guinea and the *Trobriand Islands, contains a diversity of cultures, as well as many distinct languages, which are part of the *Austronesian languages group. The usual form of settlement is small villages, with the inhabitants practising *shifting cultivation as well as rearing pigs and chickens, while *hunting and gathering, as well as fishing, add to the basic crop cultivation. Property, in the form of land, belongs to *kinship groups, which can be either patrilineal or matrilineal, and although the patterns of kinship vary throughout the region, some common features do exist. All the Melanesian societies are divided into *clans, mostly exogamous (based on marriage outside an individual's group), which claim descent from a common ancestor.

Some of these may be *totemic, and governed by *taboos and certain *food prohibitions. Although some of these societies have hereditary chiefs, and rely on tribal elders for *dispute settlement, power and status can be achieved through the acquisition of wealth, or oratorical skills, which are of great importance in the *ceremonies and *rituals of the region. *Gifts are important in creating and maintaining bonds between individuals and *kin groups; ritual exchange can spread over wide areas as in the *kula system of the Trobriands. *Ancestor worship is a common feature of the region; the spirits of the dead are thought to be potentially injurious, and must be controlled through ritual means. The region as a whole has been greatly affected by contact with Europeans; one result has been the growth of *millenarian movements such as *cargo cults.

Memorandum of Association (in UK company law), the document which sets out the name of the company, the *share capital of the company, and the registered office of the company. It is one of two documents which must be registered in order to set up a company, the other being the *Articles of Association. The Memorandum must be signed by each subscriber for shares, of which there must be at least two. Until the Memorandum is registered by the Registrar of Companies, the company cannot legally exist. In civil law systems, the Memorandum is replaced by the Company's Statutes, which contain similar material and must be attested to and registered in a similar way.

memory, the retention across time of learned knowledge, skills, or behaviour, the items retained, and the ability to recall them. The study of memory falls into two subject areas, biology and psychology. Psychologists have distinguished between two main types of memory. Short-term, or primary, memory is used for the temporary holding of information that is of current concern. It has been associated with *attention and the contents of *consciousness, although now it is described as a 'working memory', by contrast with the long-term, or permanent, memory that contains inactive stored information which can be retrieved and placed into short-term holding if required for current thought processes. Psychologists also distinguish different parts of memory in the long-term store, those for visual images, personal life-events, knowledge of word meanings, and skilled physical behaviour, for example. It is thought certain that some long-term change in the brain's physiology must act as a mechanism for memory, possibly through changes in the connections between nerve fibres. The mechanism of short-term memory is thought possibly to be electrical in nature, involving the temporary activation of information being currently processed or 'thought about' by the brain. The study of *memory disorders may throw light on some of these questions. A quite different, social, phenomenon, which may be called 'collective memory', is connected with the formation of *myth and *stereotype.

memory disorder, an inability either to recall previously learned knowledge or life-events, or to retain new knowledge after brain damage. 'Retrograde amnesia' results in not being able to recall events prior to the onset of the amnesia, though how far back in time this period extends varies, typically shrinking with time. 'Anterograde amnesia' involves the inability to form new *memory traces after the onset of amnesia. Certain types of memories and intellectual abilities may survive the onset of amnesia, such as previously learned skills (like playing the piano), or previously learned knowledge of certain topics, despite the inability to recall specific life events. A common cause of brain damage resulting in amnesia is head injury in road traffic accidents. *Aphasia, the loss of learned speech skills, may result from such a blow. Deficiency of thiamine (vitamin B¹), which can result from excessive alcohol drinking, can cause amnesia, which is also associated with *dementia. There is as yet no overall agreement about how normal memory functions, and no accepted treatment for memory loss; eventual spontaneous recovery is common in amnesia from head injury.

Mencius *ren.

Mennonites, a Protestant group founded in The Netherlands by Menno Simons (1496–1561). In accordance with their emphasis on the autonomy of the local Church, Mennonite beliefs are varied, but they unite in upholding adult Baptism and *pacifism, and rejecting worldly concerns in favour of withdrawal from society. There are about 500,000 full members, mainly in North America. The Amish Church of the USA, whose members are known for the strict anti-modernism of their way of life, is a conservative branch of the Mennonites.

mental handicap, imperfect mental development, characterized by limited intelligence and a restricted capacity to learn the social and intellectual skills for independent living. Mental handicap, which is usually present at birth and is a permanent *disability, should be distinguished from *mental illness which usually affects adults and is often successfully treated. Among its many causes are genetic and chromosomal abnormalities; damage to the foetus through the mother's heavy drinking or drug use, or through an infection such as rubella; and injury at birth. Levels of mental handicap, which are measured by *intelligence tests, range from mild (indicating slow development), to profound (indicating the need for constant care). The most severely affected often have multiple disabilities of sight, hearing, speech, and movement. In industrialized countries, about 2 per cent of the population are mentally handicapped, of whom one-fifth are severely affected. Reliable estimates for developing countries are not available. All over the world, families bear most of the responsibility for their care. People with mental handicaps have the same capacity to feel joy and pain as other human beings and often the same desire to love and to be loved. Yet they are vulnerable to neglect, exploitation, and ill treatment. In the 19th century large residential institutions were set up for them. More recently *special education, sheltered workshops and accomodation have been developed in some countries, but in others services barely exist. From the 1960s, the 'normalization movement' in Scandinavia and the USA has advocated that patterns of life as close as possible to the regular ways of society be made available to all people with mental handicaps. While *eugenic policies to sterilize people with mental handicaps persist in some societies, in others their rights to marry and to found a family are recognized.

mental illness, a disorder of the mind. Mental illnesses include *psychoses (that is severe conditions such as *schizophrenia and *manic depression), *neuroses (less severe but none the less distressing conditions such as *phobias and *obsessions), *depression, *dementia and *personality disorders. Mental illness is widespread, those at special risk including victims of *disaster, *communal conflict and *war; *refugees and migrants; older people and ethnic minorities. *Bereavement, marriage breakdown, and *unemployment also place people at risk. The World Health Organization estimates that at any time at least 350 million people are affected by it world-wide. In the UK, where it ranks alongside heart and circulatory disorders as a major cause of ill health, research suggests that one in ten people suffer mental illness each year. Of these about 10 per cent are afflicted by psychotic illness, about 30 per cent by acute *stress and *personality disorders, and 60 per cent by neurotic conditions and depression. Many forms of treatment are available (see *psychiatry), and in the UK, as elsewhere, the vast majority of people are treated through the *primary health care services or as out-patients. Of the small minority requiring hospital admission most enter voluntarily, only a few being subject to compulsion. Across the world it is common for those who are severely mentally ill to be stigmatized, feared, abused, and neglected either in *institutional care or as a result of a policy of too rapid deinstitutionalization. Increasingly, users of mental health services, their families, and professionals are uniting to demand comprehensive services encompassing not only medical treatment and hospital admission when necessary, but sheltered accommodation and employment for the severely disabled, day-care and home-visiting services, and support to families. Yet according to the World Federation for Mental Health, in every country per capita expenditure for the mentally ill is far less than for the physically ill and most of what is spent goes on hospital rather than *community care.

mercantile law, the law covering *bills of exchange and contracts for the carriage of goods by sea and marine insurance. In a common law system, mercantile law must first have belonged to a body of custom known as law merchant, that is the general custom of merchants; once such custom has been recognized by judicial decision it becomes part of mercantile law. Law merchant is supposed to be a flexible body of law constantly expanding and changing to take account of commercial practices. In a civil law system the term mercantile law is synonomous with the code covering *commercial law.

mercantilism, a scheme of thought in economics widely accepted from the mid-16th to the mid-18th century which views a nation's *wealth as dependent chiefly on its *balance of trade. Proponents argued for government *intervention to maximize trade surpluses and the accumulation of reserves of precious metals. *Hume contradicted the mercantilist view in a celebrated essay in 1752, arguing that a country's bullion reserves were essentially determined by the size of its economy and its consequential need for *money as a circulating medium, and would not be permanently influenced either way by government interference with trade.

mercenary, a soldier who joins an army (usually a foreign army) for payment, rather than from political obligation or affiliation. Most mercenaries serve in the ranks, not as officers. Before the rise of nationalism in Europe, many armies were composed of mercenaries; poor conditions or disaffection often caused them to desert to seek a better living in another army. In the modern era, mercenaries from Europe have frequently been engaged to fight in other countries, particularly in Africa. They often take part in *civil wars, being hired either by government forces or by rebel forces.

merchandizing, the promotion of *goods and *services for sale to *consumers, particularly through *advertising,

A youngster targeted by the **merchandizing** campaign of an American cartoon series which, on the back of its TV programmes, was able to flood homes with consumer goods netting millions of dollars for the manufacturer.

packaging, and display. Merchandizing at the point of sale in *retail trading outlets can take the form of packaging, window displays, labelling, devising a special layout, offering discounts or free samples and gifts, and promotion of sales by staff. In the USA merchandizing includes the wider functions of *marketing.

merger, the joining of two or more *companies of similar status by mutual agreement. A merger may be contrasted with a *take-over, where either mutual agreement or similarity of status is lacking. The merging of competitors at the same stage of production is a form of horizontal *integration, and the merging of a supplier with a customer is a form of *vertical integration. Both these forms of merger may create *monopoly power, and so may be disallowed by government. Governmental mechanisms to allow or disallow large mergers are a significant part of anti-monopoly policy in many countries and in the EC.

Merina, the dominant ethnic group of Madagascar. The Merina are now mainly agriculturalists living in villages based on *rice cultivation. From the late 18th century their kingdom expanded rapidly to become the major political power on the island before French colonization. Inheritance is bilateral, that is, through both the male and female line. Their traditional religion is based on *ancestor worship and they are famous for their elaborate tombs and *funeral customs. The Merina also possess a distinct language and script as well as an extensive written literature.

meritocracy, a society in which all positions, such as jobs or offices, are awarded entirely on the basis of individual merit. A meritocracy would result if equality of opportunity were fully realized, so that access to privileged positions depended entirely on each person's abilities and efforts. In *The Rise of the Meritocracy* (1958), Michael Young satirized such a society for its heartless treatment of the less able.

Merleau-Ponty, Maurice (1908–61), French philosopher who followed Husserl's call for a *phenomenological investigation of consciousness, but developed this programme in distinctive ways that have many of the features of *existentialism. Merleau-Ponty attempted in his main work, *Phénoménologie de la perception* (1945), to describe the unique relationship to the world enjoyed by the human subject in perception, which he presented as the key to solving *metaphysical problems. By emphasizing the philosophical significance of the human body, and the limits to human autonomy, Merleau-Ponty stood in sharp opposition to his contemporary, *Sartre.

metaphysics (from Greek, 'the things after the physics', from the ordering of *Aristotle's works), that branch of philosophy which studies the most general categories and concepts which are presupposed in descriptions of ourselves and the world. Examples are *causality, *substance, *ontology, *time, and reality. Metaphysical questions have a very broad scope. Whereas the physical scientist might ask 'How does x cause y?', the metaphysician asks 'What does it mean for anything to cause anything else?' Whereas the chemist might investigate particular substances, the metaphysician asks what it means to be a *substance, and whether there is one basic substance, or many. Metaphysical questions can become the subject of more specialized philosophical inquiry. We can ask whether our actions are subject to causality, which gives rise to the problem of *free will. And the question of whether our mental experiences involve a separate substance from body is a major issue in the philosophy of *mind. Although metaphysics dates back to the ancient Greeks, there have been occasions on which its status as a legitimate inquiry have been questioned. The rise of science in the 17th century led to attempts by philosophers such as *Hume and *Locke to limit the claims of metaphysics, and earlier this century scientifically minded philosophers such as the *logical positivists claimed that metaphysical assertions were meaningless.

Methodist Church, a *Protestant Church that originated during the Christian revival under the English minister and preacher John Wesley (1703–91) and eventually separated from the *Anglican Church of England. It has spread especially in English-speaking countries and has over 15 million full members, including about 10 million in the USA. Methodism has a strong tradition of missionary work and concern with social welfare, and emphasizes the believer's personal relationship with God, and his inspiration, without an insistence on theological detail.

Mexican and Central American Indian languages, languages spoken by the indigenous peoples of Central America before the Spanish invasion of 1519. Most are still spoken, in spite of a dramatic fall in the number of speakers, but linguistic boundaries do not correspond with modern political borders. The region is a meeting-place for the language groups of North and South America (it is generally believed that the indigenous peoples of South America travelled there from the North via this narrow area), which is an argument in favour of the theory that most American Indian languages are related, however distantly. Central American languages may be classified into three groups: Northern Amerind, Central Amerind, and a southern group called Chibchan-Paezan. Mexico has speakers of languages belonging to all three groups. Hokan and Penutian are Northern Amerind languages; Hokan is spoken in the north-east of the country and in the south Californian peninsula, while Penutian is spoken in eastern and southern Mexico, and includes the important Mayan languages Yucatec, Quiché, Cakchiquel, Kekchi, and Mam. Two families belonging to Central Amerind are spoken throughout Mexico: Uto-Aztecan and Oto-Manguean. Uto-Aztecan, which includes the Comanche, Hopi, and Aztec languages, stretches from Mexico up into the western USA; Aztec, the most important Mexican language, has about a million speakers. Oto-Manguean is spoken by over 1.5 million people in southern Mexico; there are seventeen languages, of which the most important are Otomi, Mixtec, and Zapotec. The Chibchan-Paezan languages are spoken in a small area in south-west Mexico, and throughout Central America from Guatemala to Panama. The Pre-Columbian civilizations of the region had an oral rather than written literature, although Mayan had a writing system which has not yet been properly deciphered. Spanish-based scripts have been devised for some languages.

mezzanine finance   *bond.

micro-economics, those parts of economics concerned with the behaviour of individual decision-making units (economic agents), as opposed to *macro-economics, which studies broad aggregates such as national income and the price level. Economic agents comprise households (consumers) and firms. Agents interact in markets, buying and selling goods and services. Consumer *demand theory studies the quantities purchased by consumers, as derived from consumer preferences, income, and output prices. The production function of a firm describes alternative combinations of inputs (*factors of production) needed to produce varying quantities of output. Together with data on input prices, the production function enables average and marginal production costs to be derived; and this, together with information on firms' objectives and on market structure, determines *supply conditions in the product market and the demand by firms for resources. Market price equilibrates supply and demand. Economists have focused on the sense in which the market mechanism may bring about an optimum allocation of resources; on the various forms of market structure which prevent this; and on the scope for government *intervention to cure or mitigate market failure. (See also *marginal analysis, *Marshall, *Pareto, *Walras.)

Midrash (Hebrew, 'exposition'), in Judaism, the interpretation of the Hebrew scriptures using the oral traditions codified in the *Mishnah. The Halakhic *Midrashim* (from *halakhah*, 'law') are legal collections of interpretations based on Exodus, Leviticus, Numbers, and Deuteronomy. The Haggadic *Midrashim* (from *haggadah*, 'narrative') are the non-legal collections, which examine biblical lore; some of these are homilies on the special readings for festivals, for example the *Haggadah* read at *Passover.

midwifery, the practice and profession of a person, usually a woman, who attends a mother during pregnancy, *childbirth, and in the first days of a child's life. In developed countries, midwives usually undergo a nursing training followed by specialist courses in obstetrics and gynaecology. In the industrialized world midwives work as part of a broad team of health professionals and most births take place in hospital. In developing countries, half of all births are attended by untrained traditional midwives, but an increasing number of countries have established training courses in essential obstetric care and safe motherhood.

migrant labourers, people who move over large distances or cross national borders in order to obtain work. This separation of work and home may be temporary or seasonal, or it may last for several years. Much migrant labour

Migrant labourers empty dustbins in the early hours in Munich, Germany. The position of the country's several million *Gastarbeiter* or 'guest workers', who only have annual work permits, is seriously threatened by the high level of unemployment in the east of the country.

is unskilled and some is illegal (when migrant workers do not have work permits). Migrant workers sometimes perform tasks considered menial or undesirable and may be paid very low wages, especially if they are illegal immigrants who are not protected by law and are thereby prevented from joining *trade unions. Migrant labourers may also be vulnerable to expulsion, loss of livelihood, or *discrimination if relations between the host country and their country of origin deteriorate. In many parts of the world, agricultural workers move seasonally, following the harvest as the crops ripen. Thousands of workers come into the USA every year from Mexico, for example, in order to help with the harvest. In Africa men often move from their villages to urban areas, in order to work in mines or factories; they may stay for several years in the same job, but most do not lose contact with their families, sending back part of their wages. Other examples include Turks who work in northern European countries, Thais who go to Japan, or Pakistanis, Filipinos, and others who migrate to the oil-rich states of the Middle East in search of work. Migrant labourers are often younger men and women who leave their families at home and send back their wages as foreign-exchange remittances which may make a sizeable difference in the home country's *balance of payments. (See also *immigration.)

migration, the permanent or semi-permanent change of residence by an individual or group. Together with rates of births, *mortality, and *fertility, migration is a principal component of population change. Migration is distinct from mobility, which includes temporary movements such as *transhumance, commuting, and *tourism. Migration may be international (see *emigration, *immigration) or internal within a country (see *depopulation, *urbanization). The latter is the most common. Return migration usually refers to individuals who live or work for one or more extended periods in a city or country away from their place of birth, later returning home; circulation may refer to repeated back-and-forth movements of this kind, or to other regular patterns of migration between two or more places; chain migration builds up networks of friends and relations from the same home town or village, to facilitate further such movements. *Migrant labourers may be from any of these categories. The main motives for migration are economic: the search for secure employment and better wages. Political and cultural differences, notably in the case of *refugees, are also important.

military expenditure, that part of a state budget devoted to the research, development, and acquisition of military equipment, as well as the payment of the *armed forces. The *arms race of recent years, as well as the growing technological sophistication of much modern equipment, led to a vast increase in military expenditure; for example, US military expenditure in 1989 amounted to nearly $300 billion. There have been debates about the extent of military expenditure, which may divert funds from social expenditure and cause severe economic problems, as in the former Soviet Union in the 1980s and 1990s. Following the end of the cold war and the collapse of *communism in the Eastern bloc countries, a start has been made by the military superpowers in reducing defence expenditure. However cogent the arguments for reduction, there are

usually well-entrenched interest groups such as the *military–industrial complex, which oppose it. In many developing countries, on the other hand, the trend continues towards a rise in military expenditure. Many poor countries spend two or three times as much on military expenditure as on education or health. The UN Development Programme has estimated developing countries' military expenditure at $173 billion (1987) and has urged aid donors and international organizations like the World Bank and IMF to press for reductions in military spending and the *arms trade.

military government, a form of rule in which the major institutions of government are controlled, either directly or indirectly, by the military. Military government usually arises as a result of a military *coup d'état. Military leadership may be by a small group (often called a *junta) or by an individual 'strong man'. In the contemporary world, military governments are common in states where political institutions and democratic traditions are weak. This has been particularly the case in Latin America and in the former colonial territories of Africa and the Middle East, but they have also been found in countries such as Greece, Portugal, Spain, and Turkey. Very often, military governments come to power as a means of preventing political anarchy in cases where political parties are not strong enough or cannot secure sufficient support to provide stable government. In these circumstances the military leadership often sees itself as the arbiter of political conflict. In practice, far from being politically neutral, the military often intervenes on behalf of a particular political faction or political ideology. Military governments can be from the Left or the Right of the political spectrum. Whatever their orientation, most military governments appeal to patriotism and claim to be an agent

Following a pattern common in the developing world, the **military government** in Mozambique came to power after a successful struggle for independence from a colonial power. Frelimo (the Mozambique Liberation Front) was the sole political party from 1974 until the initiation of democratization in late 1990.

of modernization, especially in non-industrial or traditional societies. Many military governments are repressive by nature, and ignore the *civil and *human rights of their citizens, justifying such action by the imposition of *martial law to maintain stability.

military–industrial complex, the interdependence within a state of the military and the industrial sectors. *Armed forces need equipment, and manufacturers want to make it. The scale of *military expenditure, particularly at a time of arms build-up (see *arms race), means that many sectors of the economy are highly dependent upon lucrative defence contracts. US President Eisenhower warned in 1961 of the potential unwarranted influence of the conjoined military and industrial forces on foreign policy formation, defence budgeting, and the wider allocation of national resources. The military–industrial complex dominated the economy of the former Soviet Union after World War II, where it was estimated to employ some 9 million in 1,500 factories and 900 research institutes, and is a feature in other countries with developed arms industries.

militia, a military organization composed of permanently armed citizens and available for territorial or local defence, which can be called up for combat in times of emergency. These non-professional soldiers normally undertake limited training, for example by joining their units for a certain period each year, and are also generally restricted to infantry or light-armoured roles on land. In certain cases (for example, the National Guard in the USA), the militia can play a role in air and coastal defence. Such countries as Israel, Switzerland, Yugoslavia, and Sweden have based much of their defence planning on the use of militia units, and people's militias also had a pervasive influence in communist states such as East Germany and Czechoslovakia. Militia forces can also play an important role in internal conflicts, where they may be raised and controlled by factions; in such cases, the dividing line between militia and *guerrilla forces can be blurred.

Mill, J(ohn) S(tuart) (1806–73), British philosopher and economist. Mill was strictly educated by his father in the *utilitarian school of moral and political philosophy. His own contribution was to broaden the basis of that philosophy with insights from continental thought, especially the need for a historical understanding of contemporary institutions. The upshot was a sophisticated statement of *liberalism. In *On Liberty* (1859), he argued that a protected sphere of personal freedom was essential to individual self-development, and defended the principle that society might only interfere with an individual's thought or behaviour in order to prevent harm to others. In *Considerations on Representative Government* (1861), he outlined a political system that would combine widespread popular participation with the protection of minorities and a proper role for the intellectual élite. He was a leading exponent of *classical economics, and wrote widely on economic issues, tempering a liberal belief in *laissez-faire* with enthusiasm for a more equal distribution of social resources.

millenarianism (or millennialism), the belief in the imminent end of the present world order and the establishment of a new and radically different one. Millenarian movements, which are found all over the world in many different societies, usually occur at times of change and upheaval. The millenarian idea that divine or supernatural intervention will bring about a reversal of worldly expectations resulting in an earthly paradise, tends to appeal to those who are dispossessed both culturally and economically. Millenarianism may often be interpreted as a form of political or social protest; the world is perceived as dominated by enemies who will be overthrown by the forces of good. The awaited new order may be a return to a traditional way of life, as in the *ghost dance movement of the Plains Indians, or a fusion of both old and new, as in the *cargo cults of Melanesia. Much millenarianism has its roots in the Jewish expectation of the coming of the Messiah. It takes its name from the early Christians' anticipation of Christ's Second Coming, to be followed by a millennium, or thousand-year reign of peace and tranquillity. In Christianity, the early expectation of Christ's imminent return to this world was replaced by the theologian St *Augustine's allegorical model of an other-worldly City of God. Millenarian Christian beliefs thereafter became associated with dissident sects, and are expressed today in the beliefs of sects such as the *Jehovah's Witnesses, Seventh Day *Adventists, *Christadelphians, and *Mormons. The idea of establishing Christ's kingdom on earth in the New World was an idea with millenarian overtones found amongst 17th- and 18th-century settlers, and is echoed in an inchoate conviction in the USA that the country's role in the world has God's backing. In Islam, *Shī'ī Muslims and sects such as the *Druze await the return of the hidden *imām or mahdī; in the Islamic Republic of Iran, the spiritual leader, the *Walī Faqīh*, is stated to be the leader in the absence of the *mahdī*. The *Bahā'ī religion originates from a millenarian proclamation in 1844, the 1,000th anniversary of the hidden *imām*'s disappearance. For many Jews, the establishment of the state of Israel was the fulfilment of millenarian beliefs (see *Zionism), and the Afro-Caribbean *Rastafarian cult envisages the black people's repatriation to Africa. Millenarian beliefs are less prominent in Buddhism, but in Hinduism, Kalki, the last *avatar of *Vishnu, is expected to destroy the degeneration of this age and instigate a new cosmic era. The philosopher Bertrand Russell pointed out that even a strictly secular ideology such as *Marxism is patterned on millenarian beliefs in its expectation of an ideal society in the future.

Minangkabau, the inhabitants of west central Sumatra, in the Indonesian archipelago. The Minangkabau are *rice cultivators, followers of *Islam, and are a particularly famous example of a *matrilineal society. Traditionally, they lived in wooden longhouses, and each person, either female or male, remained a member of their maternal longhouse. Whereas the children stayed with their mother at all times, the husbands often spent time living in their maternal longhouse, as well as in that of their wife. In their own longhouse, the men could inherit property and have some influence over their sisters' children. In the wife's longhouse, however, the husband had no property rights.

mind, philosophy of, the examination of a family of problems revolving around the concept of the mind. The mental may be distinguished from the physical in various ways: *intentionality and consciousness provide two important features of mental states. One extreme position in the philosophy of mind is represented by Descartes' *dualism, where it is claimed that minds are utterly distinct *substances. An important part of Descartes' argument for this position is the claim that mental states are known in a special way: they are directly given, transparent to their owner, and known infallibly. This position has been sharply attacked by *Wittgenstein, who argued (in his *private language argument) that Descartes' view makes knowledge of other people's minds impossible, and that our understanding of the mind is bound up with behaviour. Philosophers of a *monist and *materialist bent, who believe that reality is physical and explained by natural science, have sought in various ways to understand the mind in material terms. Behaviourism, now unfashionable, advocated that psychology should concern itself exclusively with observation of behaviour, disregarding introspection altogether. Others have proposed bluntly that mental states are the same as states of the brain. Dissatisfaction with these overly simple attempts to incorporate the mental into the physical realm led to the development of *functionalism. This view grew out of attention to the analogy between minds and computers, and has itself been subject to criticism arising out of development in the theory of *artificial intelligence.

minimum wage, a state-sanctioned and legally enforceable minimum rate of pay. The practice of minimum wage regulation, first developed in New Zealand and Australia around 1900, is widespread in both developing and industrialized countries. In some countries, regulations affect workers in only a few low-paid occupations, whereas in most countries in Africa, Latin America, and the Middle East, employees in almost all occupations are covered although those working in the *informal sector may not benefit. Although minimum wage rates tend to be low, infrequently updated, and difficult to enforce, they have, according to the *International Labour Organization, contributed to an improvement in wage levels in many places, especially where collective bargaining through trade unions is weak or non-existent. Economists disagree about whether the enforcement of minimum wage levels results in increased *unemployment.

miracle (from Latin, *mirari*, 'to wonder at'), an event which seems to transcend the normal natural order and is therefore attributed to a supernatural agency. Belief in miracles is common to practically all religions, particularly in their popular forms. The biographies of great religious leaders, such as Buddha, Jesus, or Muḥammad, commonly include stories of miraculous happenings. Muḥammad, however, denied that he possessed miraculous powers, choosing to regard the *Koran as the great miracle. In Christianity the issue of the literal truth of a miracle is of greater importance than in other religions because of the function of miracles within Jesus' mission: the virgin birth, the miracles of healing, and the resurrection are all believed to attest Jesus' divinity. However, there has been a questioning of the necessity for belief in miracles and their veracity in all religious traditions since the advances in scientific knowledge of the 19th and 20th centuries. Conversely, the presence of miracles in religious narratives is often taken by non-believers or sceptics as a sign of their spuriousness.

Mishnah (Hebrew, 'teaching by repetition'), the earliest and most authoritative collection of Jewish oral laws or traditions, the final compilation of which was under the direction of Rabbi Judah (AD 135–217). The Mishnah is composed of six major sections: religious laws concerning agriculture; ritual and religious observance; women, marriage, and family life; civil and criminal law; the Temple and rules pertaining to sacrifice; and laws on ritual purity. The Gemara (Aramaic, 'completion') are the commentaries on the Mishnah which together constitute the *Talmud.

missionary, one who propagates a religious faith. Missionary activity has been a feature of *Christianity more than any other religion since its earliest days. Most Roman Catholic missionary activity is administered by the Rome-based Congregation for the Propagation of the Faith, known as the Propaganda. Foreign missions are run by the various religious orders and lay missionary societies who report to the Propaganda. Protestant missionary activity expanded with the development of trading companies and *colonization from the 17th century. Missions of all denominations often promote *education and medical services in order to contribute to the practical needs of potential converts before introducing spiritual concerns. Following World War II, many states restricted proselytizing missionary activity, sometimes, as in China, for ideological reasons, and sometimes, as in the newly independent states of Africa, because it was felt to be a form of cultural imperialism through its association with the process of colonialism. The Second Vatican Council (1962–5) acknowledged such sensibilities in stressing the need for adapting the *liturgy and for understanding different peoples and cultures, whilst continuing to emphasize the importance of mission activity. The social aspects of mission work, however, such as medicine and education have increasingly become the preserve of governments and international aid agencies, which include among their number *non-governmental organizations with a Christian complexion such as Christian Aid. The centrality of recruiting new converts in Christianity is not found in other religions; in Islam conversion is deemed desirable, but it is not a religious duty, while in Orthodox Judaism the process of conversion is deliberately arduous.

mixed economy, an economy which has both a predominant *private sector and a sizeable *public sector, so that resources are allocated both by the *market and by the *state. In the private sector, the market or *price system will determine what quantities of goods and services are produced, and to whom they are distributed. In the public sector, such decisions will be made by government. The economies of all modern states except the communist *planned economies are mixed. The relative importance of the two sectors varies, however, and in the 1980s many countries favoured *privatization and *deregulation of public-sector enterprises. In a mixed economy, there may also be some government *intervention in private-sector economic activity.

modal logic, that branch of *logic which deals with arguments involving the notions of necessity and *possibility. Some of the most basic agreed principles of modal reasoning are, for instance, that whatever is necessarily the case is in fact the case, and whatever is in fact the case is possibly the case; similarly, whatever follows necessarily from something necessary is itself necessary. Beyond a basic level of agreement, however, there is much room for debate over which principles of inference properly reflect our intuitive understanding of the notions of possibility and necessity, so that a number of different systems of modal reasoning have been developed.

moksha (Sanskrit, 'release' or 'liberation'), the release of the *soul (*ātman) from the bonds of *samsara, the cycle of birth, death, and rebirth. It is the highest spiritual goal within most schools of *Hinduism. In *Advaita Hinduism, *moksha* implies the realization of the soul's identity with *Brahman. In more general germs, *moksha* may be achieved

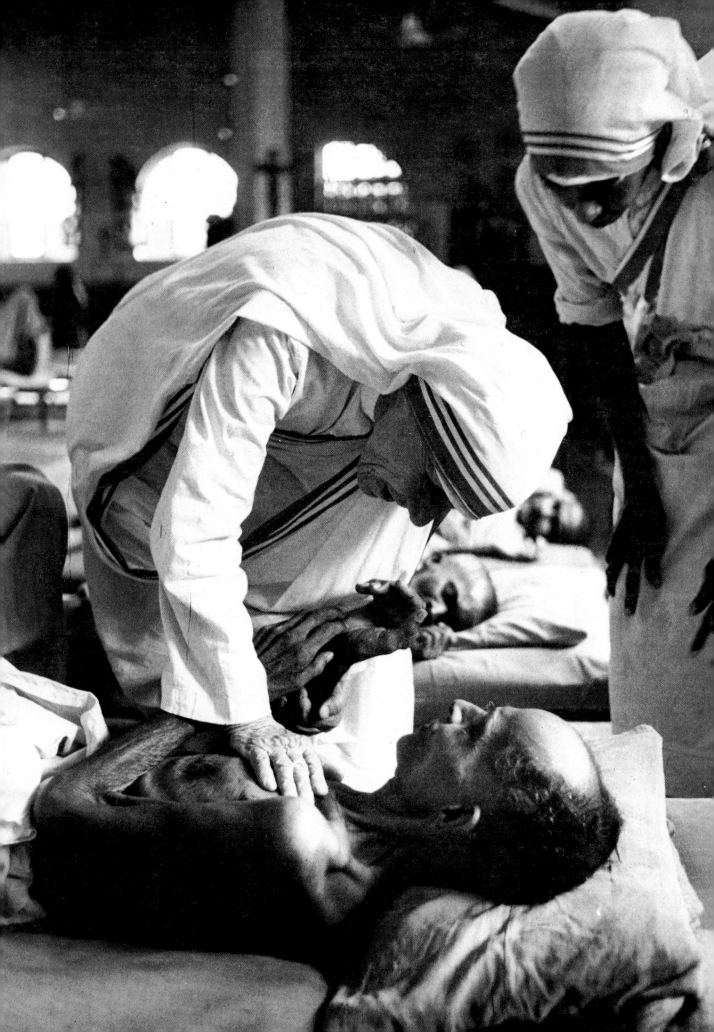

through following one of four 'paths'. The hardest is through knowledge, *jñāna*, requiring detailed scriptural study to gain an intellectual understanding of Brahman and *ātman*. *Yoga requires the help of a teacher; meditation and controlled breathing release hidden spiritual energy, which lengthens life and hastens the *ātman* towards liberation. The third path is that of selfless activity or *karma (the cycle of cause and effect); by serving God and society in accordance with the duties or *dharma pertaining to one's rank in life, the spirit is gradually released from the bonds of bad karma, which tie it to the cycle of samsara. The easiest route to liberation is through *bhakti*, or devotion to a chosen deity. Meditation upon the image and name of the deity, regular worship, and the presentation of offerings, inculcate an emotional awareness of the nature of God.

monarchy, rule, commonly hereditary, by or in the name of a single individual. Absolute monarchs wielding unlimited authority were once the norm throughout Europe, but are now rare. Most contemporary monarchs are constitutional rulers, with severely limited or even purely ceremonial powers. Succession to the position of monarch is usually hereditary (see *dynasty), though other methods, including election, have been known. The association of monarchy with *aristocracy and privilege can be politically divisive, but constitutional monarchs are often effective symbols of national unity above party politics.

monasticism, religious communities or institutions which are meant to further the communal and individual practice of *asceticism. Monasticism has been important in *Christianity since its early days, evolving from the asceticism practised in the 3rd century by men fleeing from Roman persecution in Mediterranean countries to the Egyptian desert, where they sought union with God. In the *Eastern Orthodox Churches monasteries are still based on the Rule of St Basil the Great (*c*.329–79), the first known Christian monastic rule, which prescribes physical and mental labour as well as prayer and contemplation. Orthodox monasteries, of which the most famous are at Mount Athos in Greece, are self-governing units which are not part of an order. In *Roman Catholicism, however, there are numerous orders whose members are often bound by vows of poverty, prayer, and *meditation. Communities have both spiritual and practical functions, such as *education and *social work. Among these, the Benedictine order, based on the Rule of Benedict of Nursia (*c*.480–*c*.550), emphasizes a balance of prayer, Bible reading, rest, and physical work. The Cistercian Order follows the reformed Benedictine Rule, and Cistercians of the Strict Observance (Trappist) form the largest contemplative order. The Dominican Order, founded by St Dominic in 1220, and the Franciscan Order, founded by St Francis of Assisi in 1209, were originally mendicant orders of friars, living from charity, although now most of their members are based in community houses. The Dominicans are particularly devoted to theological study and preaching. (See also *Jesuits.) Monasticism in the *Anglican Churches has become more prominent since the 19th-century Anglo-Catholic movement, with the re-foundation of some ancient orders and the establishment of new orders such as the

The important contribution made by women to **monasticism** is continued in the 20th century by Mother Theresa and her order of the Missionaries of Charity. The order runs a home in Calcutta for the dying and destitute, and has expanded to fourteen other countries.

Community of the Resurrection, founded in 1892. The ecumenical Taizé community in France, founded in 1940, is the best-known Protestant order. Although Christian monasticism is declining in Europe, it is expanding in the developing world and plays an important role there in providing educational and other welfare services. In *Buddhism, especially Theravāda Buddhism, monastic order, or *sangha, is an important element, with well over 250,000 members despite the hostility of communist governments in China and elsewhere. In return for food and support from ordinary people, monks and, uncommonly, nuns offer pastoral advice, education, and religious example. In *Islam, the closest equivalent to monasticism is *Sufism and the Sufi orders. In *Hinduism monasticism takes the form of *ashrams, or retreats, where the influence of a guru or holy man and practices such as *yoga are important. In the Hindu concept of the four ideal stages of life, *ashrama, the last two stages, following parenthood, are devoted to contemplation and asceticism. The strictness of *Jainist monastic life, which may include self-mortification to the point of starvation, is perhaps unparalleled in the contemporary world. There are also *Taoist and *Zen Buddhist monastic orders in which meditation is of prime importance.

monetarism, a school of economics which emerged mainly in the 1960s and 1970s, with *Friedman as its leading exponent. It is a revival of the *classical (pre-*Keynesian) approach to *macro-economics. Monetarist models assume that money, prices, and wages are flexible but that aggregate output and *employment will automatically tend towards an optimal equilibrium. Therefore government policy should concentrate on achieving and maintaining the stability of the price level, which monetarists believe depends on proper management of the *money supply mainly through monetary rather than *fiscal policy. Hence 'monetarism'. Moreover, there is a strong preference for automatic, rule-based rather than discretionary conduct of policy. (See also theories of *economics, *quantity theory of money.)

money, the general medium of exchange allowing goods and services to be valued in money terms and exchanged for money, rather than traded directly as would occur in a *barter economy. This primary function of money entails three others: money is a unit of account, a store of value, and a unit of deferred payment (a unit of account over time). Historically, *commodity money, then token money, and then *debt money have developed. Commodity money is money in the form of an ordinary good with intrinsic use value (such as precious metals). Token money (such as banknotes) has an intrinsic value less than its face value. Debt money is a medium of exchange based on a debt. In particular, a cheque draws on the debt of a *bank to the holder of a bank deposit. Money markets deal in short-term lending and borrowing of money. (See also *currency, *exchange rate.)

money-laundering, a term used to describe the attempt to recycle illegitimate profits from crime in a legitimate form. It is often undertaken by those involved in *organized crime in order to protect the proceeds of illicit activities, such as *drug trafficking, from the threat of confiscation by the authorities. Money-laundering procedures are also sometimes used by governments in an attempt to conceal the origins of money obtained in a way they do not wish to be made public, such as through arms deals. Methods of money-laundering include investment in legitimate shares or property, or the setting up of a network of front companies, or bank accounts in false names, as a way of handling the proceeds of crime. In many jurisdictions, banks or financial institutions which knowingly launder such proceeds are subject to heavy penalties. In 1990 twelve members of the Council of Europe signed the Convention on the Laundering, Search, Seizure and Confiscation of the Proceeds of Crime. Under the Convention, money-laundering is recognized as a crime and the signatories agreed to legislate for the court confiscation of convicted drug dealers' assets and for the surveillance of the telephones and computer systems of suspected drug criminals.

money supply (in economics), the amount of *money circulating in an economy at a moment in time. The definition of what comprises money varies because various different assets can be used as a medium of exchange. One major definition includes notes and coins in circulation (that is, not in bank vaults) and bank sight (or current) accounts on which cheques can be drawn. However, the type of accounts with chequing facilities may change. In the 1980s they came to include interest-bearing accounts in many cases; and in the UK, for example, cheques may also be drawn on some building society accounts. Even without chequing facilities, if deposits can quickly be moved from one account to another, it may be advisable to include non-sight bank accounts in the money-supply measure. More generally, near-money comprises financial assets which are *liquid (quickly transferable into money); elements of near-money (for example, money-market deposits) may also be included in money-supply measures. (See also *monetarism.)

Mongolian language *Altaic languages.

monism, the philosophical belief that the world consists entirely of a single *substance or kind of substance. Opposed to the *dualism of mind and body, the most obvious forms of monism claim either that the world is entirely material (*materialism) or that it is entirely mental (*idealism). Monist doctrines will frequently explain the *apparent* differences between kinds of things as subjective, resulting from our different ways of understanding a single thing. The most extreme monism, held, for example, by *Spinoza, claims that the world is a single thing, and that all seeming diversity is a product of partial understanding.

Mon–Khmer languages *Austro-Asiatic languages.

monopoly (in economics), a situation in which there is a single supplier (a monopolist) in the *market for a good or service. Monopoly power is the ability of a single producing firm to affect price so as to make profits above those necessary to cover costs, including a normal return on capital. Such profits are known as super-normal or monopoly profits. Monopoly power may also accrue to oligopolistic firms (see *oligopoly). Monopoly in a particular variety or brand of a product does not necessarily lead to monopoly profits. When there are many firms with monopolies in slightly different products which are substitutable, the situation is known as monopolistic competition. Governments may try to restrict the emergence of monopolies since a monopoly's power to influence prices and supplies of a good is commonly considered detrimental. (See also *competition law, *economy of scale.)

monopsony (in economics), a situation in which there is a single buyer (a monopsonist) in the market for a particular

At the age of 80 Dr **Montessori** sees her ideas about early education enacted in a school in Smithfield, London. Her system overturned contemporary teaching methods based on Victorian disciplines in which 'children, like butterflies mounted on pins, are fastened each to his place'.

good or service. This may be compared with *monopoly, where there is a single seller. Monopsony power is the ability to affect price through buying power. An example of a monopsonistic market is that of defence equipment, where most sales are to one buyer, the national government.

Montesquieu *separation of powers.

Montessori, Maria (1870–1952), Italian educational pioneer. The first woman to graduate in medicine in Italy, she became infant schools organizer in Rome, founded a series of schools, and initiated a world-famous movement based on principles set out in *The Montessori Method* (1912) and *The Secret of Childhood* (1936). The Montessori system is based on belief in the child's creativity, drive to learn, and wish to be treated as an individual. Everything in the 'House of Childhood'—scaled-down furniture, climbing frames, wooden shapes inserted into puzzle frames—is geared to the child, whose physical activity and sensory experience are preparations for intellectual discovery. The teacher organizes the environment in which the child works, but remains in the background: the emphasis is on self-education and initiative. Montessori's ideas have had a profound influence on *pre-school and *primary education.

Montreal Protocol *ozone depletion.

Moonies *Unification Church.

moral philosophy *ethics.

moral right *copyright.

Moravian Church, a small *Protestant Church, founded in 1722, which has its origins in the Hussite Bohemian Brethren in Central Europe and is closely linked to the *Lutherans. Worship is kept simple; Moravian hymns are famous, and reflect the Church's emphasis on direct spiritual experience and good conduct rather than elaborate doctrines. Though it has only about 200,000 full members it has been a powerful influence on Protestant thinkers, such as John Wesley, the founder of *Methodism, and is effective in missionary, educational, and ecumenical activity.

morbidity rate, a measure used to indicate the incidence or prevalence of a disease in a population. By the incidence of a disease is meant the number of new cases occurring within a defined population (say 100,000) over a given period (say a year). By the prevalence of a disease is meant the total number of cases, old and new, existing at any one time in a defined population. In order to collect accurate information about morbidity, most countries require doctors to notify a central register of the occurrence of certain diseases. Data about morbidity rates and *mortality rates are essential to *preventive medicine and *public health.

Mormon, a member of the Church of Jesus Christ of Latter-Day Saints, a *millenarian religious movement founded in the USA by Joseph Smith in 1830. With headquarters in Salt Lake City, Utah, the Mormons base their creed on the Bible and the *Book of Mormon* and other volumes revealed to Joseph Smith. Mormonism is characterized by an elaborately hierarchical organization and ritual, and there is strict control over the lives of members, numbering over 5 million. Mormon beliefs diverge sharply from orthodox Christianity, which is held to be a corrupt faith. Doctrines include the expectation of the Second Coming of Christ, baptism of adults, and belief in *prophecy.

morphology *grammar.

mortality rate, the ratio of deaths to a given population over a specified period. The most common measure, called 'the crude death rate', is usually calculated as the annual number of deaths per thousand population. Between 1950 and 1955 and 1985 and 1990, the crude death rate in Europe remained unchanged at 11, but in South America it fell from 15 to 8, in Asia from 24 to 9, and in Africa from 27 to 15. These rapid falls, which were not at first accompanied by parallel falls in *birth rates, contributed to major *population growth. The analysis of the mortality rates of populations as a whole and of sub-groups according to their age, sex, occupation, and residence have played a critical role in establishing the patterns and causes of *disease (see *epidemiology) and paving the way for preventive measures (see *public health).

mortgage, a legal contract between a borrower (mortgagor) and a lender (mortgagee) secured by *assets (commonly land or buildings) owned by the borrower. The ownership of the assets is transferred to the lender only if certain conditions of the *loan agreement are broken. A mortgage is unlike a hire-purchase agreement (see *consumer) in that the mortgaged property belongs to the borrower. Mortgages of various kinds are typically extended by *building societies, *banks, and *insurance companies to businesses and individual house-buyers. In the USA most housing loans are made by savings-and-loan associations. The security for the loan is the house, and the mortgage lapses when the loan is fully repaid along with all the *interest due. The mortgagee has the technical right to occupy the property until the loan is repaid, but in practice the mortgage permits the borrower to occupy. In case of default, a mortgagee has a number of remedies, but normally seeks possession and sells the property.

mosque (from Arabic, *masjid*, 'place of prostration'), a holy building used as a meeting place, for public prayer and worship, and for study within *Islam. The term occurs in the *Koran, particularly in connection with the *Ka'aba in Mecca, and the building of a mosque was one of the first actions performed by *Muḥammad upon arrival at Medina. Traditionally built of brick or stone, mosques are square or rectangular in shape, surrounding a courtyard which usually contains washing facilities. Minarets, towers from which the *muezzin calls followers to prayer, mark the corners or front. Shoes are removed on entry, and women must cover their heads. The *qibla* wall marks the direction of Mecca with a niche (*miḥrāb*), to the right of which stands a pulpit (*minbar*), from which the Friday sermon is preached. There is usually a partitioned area for female worshippers, whose attendance at mosque prayer is not compulsory. All images of human or animal forms are forbidden, but mosques are often decorated with calligraphic extracts from the Koran, and geometric designs derived from calligraphy representing eternity. (See illustration overleaf.)

motivation, the processes which lead people to act in a certain manner in particular circumstances. Psychologists have assumed that human and animal activity originates from innate biological drives, such as sex, hunger, and thirst. Early discussions, like that of the British psychologist William McDougall (1871–1938) concentrated on *instinct. But approaches as different as Freudian *psychoanalysis and *learning theory have concentrated on the modification and shaping of such drives through experience. *Behaviouristic learning theory posited that animals and humans develop patterns of behaviour through reinforcement by rewards and punishments. *Freud emphasized how human instincts are controlled by moral norms which are learned and respected through fear of punishment. Both appear to be wrong. *Social learning theorists have shown that human children learn without reward or punishment and the American H. F. Harlow (1905–81) showed that other primates may do so too. Parental warmth and use of incentives, not punishment, help children to acquire clear standards of conduct. Since Edward Tolman published *Purposive Behavior in Animals and Men* in 1932, psychologists have shown increasing interest in the way behaviour is organized around the pursuit of goals and in the plans adopted to reach them. This has led to greater interest in the *cognitive features of motivation. *Expectation also plays a role in motivation.

motorbike-racing, the international sport of racing motorbikes, either on a special track or on public roads. Races are usually graded by engine size, and the most common classes are 500, 350, 250 and 125 cc, with additional races for motorbikes with side-cars. Grass-track racing also has its following, and in moto-cross or scrambling the bikes race over rough hilly terrain. (See also *speedway-racing.)

motor-racing, the various forms of racing in specially built or adapted cars. Long-distance road-racing is known as rallying; the Monte Carlo Rally, first held in 1911, is the most famous and the Paris–Dakar is currently the most dangerous. Track-racing is divided into categories such as Formula Three, Formula Two, and Formula One. The last named is the most prestigious, and Grand Prix cars are built by such famous designers as Ferrari, McLaren, and Williams, whose drivers battle for the world championship over a nine-month season at celebrated venues all over the world, such as Silverstone in England and Monza in Italy. In the USA, motor-racing is particularly varied, with categories for club-racing (sports cars), off-road racing (four-wheel-drive vehicles), stock-cars, drag-racers, which compete in ferocious sprints over a short straight course, and races such as the Indianapolis 500 for high-powered racing cars.

motor skills, development of, the growth of children's co-ordination and ability to master complex movements and manipulate their surroundings. Many human motor *skills develop as 'milestones' in maturation without explicit training or even encouragement. For instance, children normally sit and reach for things by 6 months, crawl by 9, and walk by 18 months. Other skills, some of which we take for granted, require external guidance and stimulation, although *imitation plays a large part in children's acquisition of normal practical and *social skills. *Social learning theory has produced studies on the role of demonstration and imitation in motor skill learning, but we still do not know how children and adults reproduce movements they observe. To acquire a skill a child must develop (a) knowledge about the typical behaviour of its environment, for example the way a ball or shuttlecock flies, (b) control of its own muscular movements, and (c) the capacity to co-ordinate the two. Fine control of movement is not possible before the age of about 4, when brain cells are sufficiently mature.

mountaineering, the sport of climbing mountains. It was first taken up as a sport in the mid-19th century, when groups of English climbers began tackling the European Alps, helped by Swiss, Italian, and French guides. Edward Whymper was one of the first great mountaineers, present at the first ascent, in 1865, of the Matterhorn (4,478 m/16,690 feet). After the Alps, interest moved to other great ranges, such as the Andes, the Rockies, the high peaks of Africa, and the Himalayas. Mount Everest, at 8,848 m (29,028 feet), became the ultimate goal, conquered in 1953 by Edmund Hillary and Tenzing Norgay. Mountaineering calls for courage, technical skill, and sound judgement if the climber is to survive the rigours of rock climbing, bivouacking on narrow icy ledges, and coping with crevasses and ice falls.

muezzin (Arabic, 'caller of the call to prayer'), a man who calls the faithful to prayer, usually, in Muslim countries, from a minaret, a tower attached to a *mosque. The muezzin's voice is taped or amplified by loudspeakers in many countries today, but his role retains its importance, since the call to prayer is determined by the sun, and changes daily. Muezzins also chant the *Koran at special services such as funerals and the Friday prayer.

muftī   *sharī'ah.

Muhammad (c.570–632), the founding Prophet of *Islam. He was born in Mecca, but was orphaned early. In about

Mosque

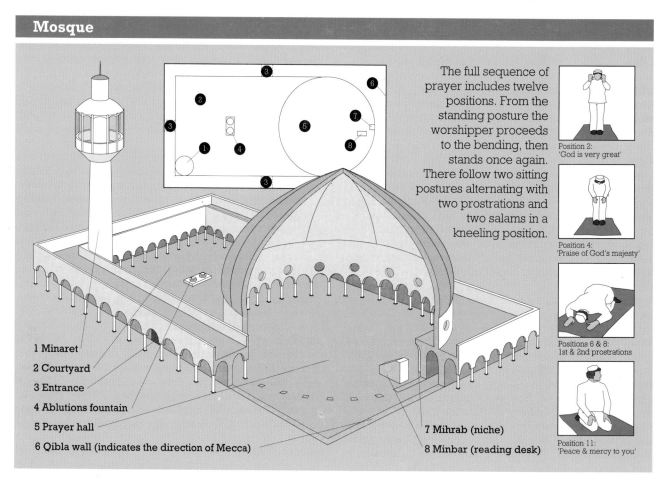

The full sequence of prayer includes twelve positions. From the standing posture the worshipper proceeds to the bending, then stands once again. There follow two sitting postures alternating with two prostrations and two salams in a kneeling position.

Position 2: 'God is very great'

Position 4: 'Praise of God's majesty'

Positions 6 & 8: 1st & 2nd prostrations

Position 11: 'Peace & mercy to you'

1 Minaret
2 Courtyard
3 Entrance
4 Ablutions fountain
5 Prayer hall
6 Qibla wall (indicates the direction of Mecca)
7 Mihrab (niche)
8 Minbar (reading desk)

AD 610 on the 'Night of Power', during one of his regular meditative retreats to desert caves, Muḥammad received the first of many visions in which the Angel Gabriel appeared and recited the word of God to him, initiating his prophetic mission. Gabriel's words were later transcribed as the *Koran, which revealed the oneness of God, Allah. Muḥammad's demands for the ending of idolatry and for a more just society resulted in persecution. His departure (*hijrah) for Medina in c.622 is the turning point in the history of Islam. Subsequently he and his followers were able to capture Mecca, where he re-dedicated the *Ka'aba to the worship of Allah. Muḥammad is honoured by Muslims, as the last and most important of the *prophets, and his life is venerated as an example of holiness, but he is not worshipped in his own right nor does he intermediate between the believer and God. Muslims believe that Muḥammad's life is the culmination of the prophetic era, and that Islam is the fulfilment of the earlier revelations of the prophets of Christianity and Judaism.

multinational corporation, a firm which produces and sells goods and services in more than one country. Such firms, also called transnationals, locate themselves in a number of countries in order to achieve lower *costs (including lower tax payments) and larger *profits. They often employ tens of thousands of workers and earn large profits for their shareholders. Many of the largest multinationals, such as IBM (USA), Shell (UK/Netherlands), and Toyota (Japan), earn more income in a year than the *national income of small developing nations. Of the world's hundred biggest economic units, it has been estimated that half are nations and the other half are multinational corporations. However, there are also some comparatively small businesses which become multinational in order to gain certain advantages. For instance, they may be helped to circumvent *tariff barriers and produce within a *common market. Many firms have moved into Western European countries in order to operate within the *EC. Some analysts welcome the arrival of multinationals because they create jobs, *investment, and *income within the host economy. Others accuse multinationals of stifling local competition, of profiting from low wages, of using up scarce resources, and of seeking to exercise undue influence on the political system of the countries where they operate.

multiparty system, a political system in which political parties are freely permitted to exist and regularly have a decisive influence on the formation of *government by participating in *elections. A fully multiparty system is a crucial indicator of democratic conditions; many states which profess *democracy severely curtail their citizens' rights to form *political parties, either banning parties of a certain persuasion which is perceived as extremist or threatening, such as *communism or *Islamic fundamentalism, or restricting the formation of parties which may attract more electoral support than the ruling party or parties. More technically, in the study of politics, multiparty systems of three or more parties are normally contrasted with *one-party and *two-party systems. In this technical sense, multiparty systems are often found in countries with multiple social, ethnic, religious, or regional divisions, some of which may themselves be represented by political parties. Multiparty systems are also associated with *proportional representation: several parties may achieve representation in a *national assembly, none of which has a majority of seats, resulting in government by *coalition. Such multiparty systems, more common than the two-party systems characteristic of the UK and the USA, are found in Belgium, Canada, Italy, Israel, The Netherlands, and most of the Scandinavian countries.

multiplier, an economic concept first propounded by the British economist Richard Kahn in 1931 and incorporated in a modified form by *Keynes into his *General Theory* in 1936; the multiplier measures the total change in 'real' *national income resulting from an initial change in some component of aggregate *demand, assuming that there are unemployed resources and approximately stable prices. For example, an increase in government expenditure of £100 million on road building initially raises national income by that amount. Employees and shareholders of the road-building companies receive this increase in income. If there is a marginal propensity to consume (see *marginal analysis) of, say, three-quarters, then they will spend three-quarters × £100 million on *consumption. This then increases the income of other suppliers and retailers by £75 million. They, in turn, spend three-quarters × three-quarters × £100 million (= £56.25 million), and so on. Thus the total impact of the initial expenditure is magnified. In this case, national income will rise by £100 million × (1 ÷ (1 − three-quarters)) = £400 million. In this sample example, therefore, the multiplier is equal to 1 ÷ (1 − marginal propensity to consume).

murder *homicide.

museum, a building or site used for the exhibition and storage of works of art, antiquities, and objects of scientific and historical interest. The origins of museums go back to classical times with the *museion* (Greek, 'temple of the muses') at Alexandria, celebrated for its collection of artefacts and its *library. Although there were many private princely collections in, for example, 15th-century Italy, the first modern museum dates back to the foundation of the Ashmolean Museum in Oxford (1683), which was the first public collection in the world. The 18th and 19th centuries saw national and civic museums such as London's South Kensington Museums, founded after the Great Exhibition in 1851, established throughout Europe and North America. The 20th century has seen a vast expansion in museums. For many countries in the post-colonial era, national museums displaying a country's history establish and determine cultural identity. In Europe and North America changes in science and technology and the consequent demise of many important industries and the erosion of traditional ways of life have provided impetus for museums of industrial archaeology and folk life, often on open-air sites where buildings and machinery are preserved and actors dressed in costume re-create the past, for example the Norwegian Folk Museum outside Oslo, founded in 1896 (see illustration overleaf). Though education remains the primary aim of museums, the use of sophisticated display techniques and specially designed interiors means that they play a key part in providing entertainment and are a major part of the tourism industry, attracting millions of visitors yearly.

mutiny, an open revolt against authority; for example of prisoners against a prison governor, or sailors on a commercial vessel against the captain. It is also one of the gravest offences against military law, committed by any member of the forces who combines with one or more others (who may be civilians) to resist or usurp the lawful military authority, avoid operations against an enemy, or go over to the enemy. Military personnel accused of mutiny are proceeded against

Traditional houses with grass growing on the roof for insulation in the open-air Folk Museum in Oslo, Norway. The **museum** was a pioneer in presenting real-life buildings as part of its display.

in *courts martial, while civilians are dealt with under ordinary *criminal law.

mutual fund *investment trust.

Myrdal, Gunnar (1898–1987), Swedish economist and sociologist. He is known for *The American Dilemma* (1944), a study of the disadvantaged position of Blacks in the USA, his work on the economic implications of social democracy, and on *development-economics issues, especially in the Asian context. In *Rich Lands and Poor* (1957), he argued that international market forces tend, unless corrected, to operate to the disadvantage of developing countries. For example, their economies tend to concentrate on the export of *primary products, which are subject to fluctuating demand and prices. He also contributed to *interest theory and population studies.

mysticism, the concepts, activities, and experiences of unity between a person and ultimate reality. It is found typically in a *religion which conceives of transcendence as an unseen but essential unity of all that exists. Thus, mystical ideas, practices, and experiences are central to *Buddhism, *Hinduism (see *Advaita) and *Daoism. Mysticism may also be found in religions which conceive of transcendence as radically other than the world, but in such cases it is often less important or even the subject of dispute, as in *Islam (see *Sufism), Judaism (see *Kabbalah), and *Christianity. These disputes are the result of mystics in these communities valuing individual experiences even when they do not confirm authoritative beliefs. A wide variety of practices is associated with mystical experiences: most important is *meditation, but other techniques of concentration including contemplative prayer are also recommended. Auxiliary practices include breath control, *asceticism, and rhythmic movement or exercise. Subject to more dispute is the mystical use of hallucinatory drugs, alcohol, and sexual activity. Mystics commonly place a high cognitive value on their experiences, but also consider these experiences as ineffable. They sometimes try to communicate the nature of their otherwise indescribable experiences with metaphors: mystics in Christianity and Islam frequently use bridal imagery or the imagery of a lover re-united with his beloved. This universal theme of the ineffability of mystical experience has led some scholars to argue that all mystical experiences are fundamentally the same, while other scholars have emphasized the fact that the imagery employed by mystics is almost always linked to the mainstream concepts of their religious tradition.

myth, a traditional story about the past, often including religious or fantastic elements. Myths of some sort can be found in all societies, although they may function in different ways. They may be attempts to explain the origins of the universe and of mankind (see *creation myth), the development of political institutions, or the reasons for *ritual practices; on the other hand, they may simply be told for the love of a good story. Myths often describe the deeds of gods or supernatural beings, or of heroes, like the *trickster, who have supernatural powers that enable them to change from human to animal form, or to perform extraordinary deeds. Anthropologists have spent a great deal of time trying to differentiate myth from history, but it is clear that history can serve the same functions as myth, and the two types of tale about the past blur into one another. Theorists like *Frazer regarded myths as a form of early religious or scientific thought. This approach was later criticized by *Malinowski, who saw myth as providing a justification for the social order. The Romanian–US historian of religion Mircea Eliade (1907–86) regarded myth as a religious phenomenon, man's attempt to return to the original act of creation. *Lévi-Strauss has argued that it is not the content but the structure of myth which is important, since it reveals universal mental processes. In *psychology, myths are regarded as an important basis for human behaviour. Both *Freud and *Jung made extensive use of myths in their work. Whatever the theories regarding the origin and functions of myths, they remain fundamental to the human consciousness.

N

Nāgārjuna (c. AD 150–250), the first important Buddhist philosopher and founder of the Mādhyamika sect, a branch of *Mahāyāna Buddhism. Nāgārjuna was a south Indian monk and mystic. Several works are attributed to him, including the *Memorial Verses on the Middle Teaching* (*Mādhyamika-kārikā*). His teaching was based upon the reduction of his opponent's arguments to nonsense, indicating that all things are relative and without true substance; 'empty' (*shūnyatā*). His major achievement was the philosophical justification of a middle way which directly concurred with the teachings of the *Buddha.

Nagas, a group of tribes in the densely forested state of Nagaland, in north-eastern India. The Nagas, who consist of different cultural and linguistic groupings, live in small hillside villages, and practise *shifting cultivation, as well as some hunting and gathering. Political organization varies from tribe to tribe as among the *Kachin of the same region. Many of the Nagas are now Christians, having converted from their traditional beliefs of spirit worship.

Nanak (1469–1539), the founder of *Sikhism and the first Sikh *Guru. He was born into a Hindu family at Talwandi in the Punjab (now known as Nankana Sahib, in present-day Pakistan). Legends about his life are contained in the four *janam sakhis* ('evidences of his life'). As a child, Nanak learned about *Islam as well as *Hinduism, and he used to compose hymns together with a Muslim musician. He was a householder for the first part of his life, but at the age of 30 he underwent a religious experience. He had a vision of God, who called him to go out into the world to repeat the divine name. After this experience, Nanak proclaimed that he was neither a Hindu nor a Muslim; he gave away all his possessions and became a wandering preacher, hoping to bring Muslims and Hindus together by expounding his message of the oneness of God and the equality of men. He returned to the Punjab after years of travelling and set up a community of disciples, who became known as Sikhs (from Sanskrit, *shishya*, 'pupil'). His teachings in the form of short devotional hymns are contained in the *Adi Granth.

narrowcasting, the transmission of *television and *radio programmes, information, or *advertising direct to an identified target audience, as opposed to more traditional *broadcasting to a general, undifferentiated audience. In the 1980s, advertisers on television and elsewhere became concerned to reach specific 'segments' of the audience, in order to tap the collective wealth of, for example, Black people or other groups hitherto unheeded, such as children, and the elderly. Geographical location, language and professional or leisure interests may also help to identify target groups. In Singapore, for instance, with a population of less than 3 million, more than a dozen radio stations are targeted towards the speakers of Malay, Mandarin, English, and to different age-groups. Narrowcasting has developed particularly in *cable television, where religious, sports, youth, and leisure-interest programmes operate alongside twenty-four-hour news and film channels. Magazines too have become increasingly specialized as audiences have moved away from broad publications such as Time-Warner's *Life*. Making an electronic *database accessible to subscribers is another form of narrowcasting.

national assembly   *legislature.

national debt (public debt), the *debt of a country's government, created through borrowing by the public sector. Some of the debt is typically in marketable form (government securities) and some non-marketable (national savings deposits and certificates). It may be held by residents or non-residents of the country in question. Interest on the debt is paid principally from tax revenues. The *public sector borrowing requirement (approximately equal to the *budget deficit) represents the yearly addition to the national debt. (See also *deficit financing, *fiscal policy.)

national income (net national product at factor cost), a measure of the money value of all goods and services produced in an economy in a given period (normally a year) and accruing to the country's residents. It is equal to *GDP (gross domestic product) plus or minus net property income from abroad and minus depreciation of fixed *capital. (See also *GNP (gross national product).)

nationalism, the demand by members of a nation for political self-government, which normally entails the found-

A heap of several thousand Soviet military passports abandoned by Lithuanian conscripts symbolizes a rejection of control by the former Soviet Union. Members of the movement for **nationalism** in Lithuania declared the country's independence in March 1990, and this was finally recognized by Moscow in September 1991.

ing of an independent state. Nations are very hard to define, but roughly speaking they are bodies of people who identify with one another and acknowledge a common loyalty by virtue of *descent, *language, *culture, or *religion. Such national identities have proved remarkably resilient in the modern world, and they have been a potent source of political change. Early nationalist movements, such as those in Germany and Italy in the 19th century, were typically concerned to build large and powerful *states out of existing small principalities. In the present century nationalists have more often sought either to throw off imperial or colonial rule (many developing countries have witnessed nationalist movements aiming at the formation of independent states) or else to break away from an established state. Recent European movements, such as those of the Scots, the Basques, and the many minorities or nationalities within the erstwhile Soviet Union, show nationalism taking this *secessionist form. Liberals and socialists have often been inclined to dismiss nationalism as an irrational phenomenon arising from the most primitive elements in human nature, but few would now deny the mobilizing power of national sentiments and allegiances. (See also *communal conflict, *ethnic groups, *self-determination.)

nationality, an aspect of a person's status in relation to a state. Each state lays down its own conditions for nationality; these may typically include place of birth and parenthood. An individual may have no nationality (if the state in which he or she is born does not automatically grant nationality) or several. It is possible to acquire a new nationality by *naturalization. International law imposes obligations on states as to the treatment of non-nationals (aliens). Under the *Geneva Convention, in time of war, nationals of enemy states ('enemy' as distinct from 'friendly' aliens) may be interned but must not be used as *hostages.

nationalization, the policy of taking land, firms, or whole industries into public ownership and running them under government-appointed management. Since the early years of the 20th century, nationalization was a declared aim of labour and socialist parties in developed countries such as the UK and France, while *statist policies in developing countries also favoured nationalization as a means of *development and political independence. While land, industry, and other enterprises were first taken wholesale into state ownership in the former Soviet Union after the 1917 Revolution, nationalization has also been carried out by many capitalist governments. The typical nationalized industry is a public utility (such as electricity, gas, water, post, and telecommunications), partly because these may be natural *monopolies and partly because these industries tend to be viewed as part of a country's basic *infrastructure and therefore most appropriately retained in the *public sector. Numerous examples can also be found, however, of other types of nationalized enterprise, notably in *banking and manufacturing. The top management of nationalized industries is appointed by the government, which also monitors the industry and sets performance targets for it (for example, a target rate of return on *capital employed). It may also fix the industry's pricing policy. Nationalization has been seen as a means of increasing efficiency and breaking up concentrations of private wealth, but many critics now claim that nationalized industries suffer from inefficiency and poor performance because of a lack of competition and a poor incentive structure for employees. As a result, they recommend the *privatization of such industries. In the UK, most public utilities were privatized in the 1980s. In the USA, many have never been in public ownership.

national park, a land area which a national government decides to preserve from everyday farming or industrial development so that its natural resources may be enjoyed by the general public. Now a world-wide movement, it received considerable impetus in the USA when the National Parks Service was founded in 1916. Yellowstone National Park, the country's oldest, was established in Wyoming in 1872; its protected wildlife includes antelope, bear, bison, deer, elk, moose, and many species of bird. The aims of national parks vary from one nation to another, the emphasis being placed on land or wildlife or both and on preserving cultural sites. In countries such as Peru, the government seeks to protect local peoples in their original territory, guarding their hunting and gathering grounds from intrusive visitors. Other examples of countries with extensive national parks are Australia, Kenya, Germany, and the UK. The chief problem facing the authorities concerns the damage inflicted by the tourists for whom these areas were created. Solutions include keeping the main tourist facilities, such as hotels and restaurants, outside the parks, and limiting public access within them, thus protecting vulnerable wildlife.

national security state, a phrase used to describe and account for the growth of the national security apparatus within society, particularly during the cold war era (1946–90). The combination of the external threat from ideological and political adversaries, and the internal threat of subversion, as well as the importance of protecting nuclear weapons programmes, have been seen by many as leading to the growth of military organization and its counterparts in the *intelligence and *counter-intelligence communities. One particular expression of the process is the *military–industrial complex, which is said to grow up around the common interests of the military, the intelligence services, and the defence-related industries. Both the USA and the former Soviet Union may be seen as examples of this, and countries such as the UK and France have developed smaller-scale national security communities. It is often argued that the militarization of government leads to bias and distortion because of the priority given to military security and secrecy, leading in some cases to the infringement of *civil rights.

nation-state, a territorial and social entity formed when *state and nation coincide; that is, when a people, united by a common sense of *culture, history, *race, *religion, or *language, feels itself to be a 'nation', coincident with the territorial boundaries of the state (see *self-determination). The resultant nation-state thus forms a single and sovereign political community, whose institutions are regarded as *legitimate by an overwhelming majority of the population. States almost everywhere use *symbols, *rituals, monuments, the *educational system, *mass media, or *military service to foster a sense of national identity, not always successfully. Nation-states are regarded as the *international norm, based on mutual recognition and membership of international organizations such as the UN. However, for historical reasons in the period following decolonization in the 20th century, the boundaries of many states were drawn on artificial lines which do not reflect ethnic or religious boundaries, giving rise to inbuilt divisions, majorities, or minorities. In such states, conflict is likely to arise between the disparate elements. (See also *communal conflict.)

nativism, a school of philosophical thought according to which at least some of our concepts are innate, such that they are prior to and (sometimes) independent of our sense experience. Famous nativists were *Plato, *Descartes, and *Kant. Nativism was eschewed by the British *empiricists *Locke, *Berkeley, and *Hume, who believed that all our concepts are acquired through experience and that at birth our minds are *tabulae rasae* ('clean slates'). The dilemma facing nativists is similar to that of the nature–nurture debate (see *behaviour genetics), because even if some concepts are innate they may need to be triggered by experience, and it is very difficult to disentangle the contribution of experience from whatever was innate. Contemporary nativists include *Chomsky. (See also *a priori.)

NATO (North Atlantic Treaty Organization), an *alliance founded in 1949 with the intention of safeguarding Europe and the North Atlantic area. According to the Treaty, the members (the USA, Belgium, Canada, Denmark, France, Germany, Greece, Iceland, Italy, Luxemburg, The Netherlands, Norway, Portugal, Spain, Turkey, and the UK) agree that an attack on one of them shall be considered an attack against them all. The Treaty also encourages political, economic, and social co-operation. NATO headquarters are in Brussels, and its highest organ is the North Atlantic Council, which meets at the level of heads of governments, ministers, or permanent representatives. Under the North Atlantic Council is the Military Committee, whose executive agency, composed of representatives of chiefs of staff, is based in Washington, DC. NATO committed the USA to the defence of Europe during the period of poor *East–West relations (the cold war); the former Soviet Union and its allies formed the *Warsaw Pact in 1955 as a counter-measure. The rapid changes in the former Eastern bloc countries after 1989 and the dissolution of the Warsaw Pact (1991) led to a reassessment of the role of NATO, and the extent to which NATO members should alter the scope of the alliance. In early 1992 the former Soviet republics were admitted to a new co-operation council whose members are the 16 existing members of NATO and the former members of the Warsaw Pact.

naturalism (in philosophy), an outlook which stresses the role of facts about human nature in explaining human thought, and, more generally, sees human beings firmly as parts of the natural order. Naturalism is broadly opposed to religious and metaphysical outlooks. Thus naturalism is frequently (although not necessarily) associated with *materialism and a high estimation of the physical sciences. Naturalist theories have both an explanatory and a justificatory aspect. They seek in the first instance to show that it is possible to explain why we think the way we do in terms of facts about our natural constitution; and they then seek to show that by appealing to those facts it is possible to provide as much of a justification for our ways of thinking as can reasonably be demanded. There are important strains of naturalism in the philosophies of *Hume and *Wittgenstein. *Ethical naturalism regards moral judgements as grounded in, and perhaps even as deducible from, facts about human nature.

naturalization, the process of satisfying the legal conditions for acquiring a new *nationality. The conditions, which vary widely between states, lay down eligibility criteria such as period of residence, linguistic proficiency, and knowledge of the *constitution. In some countries, new nationals are permitted to retain their original nationality and thus hold dual nationality.

natural justice, a doctrine of *administrative law which requires administrators to comply with minimal standards of fairness based on *natural law. The main requirements are that the decision-maker be free of bias or personal interest, and that the persons affected should have an opportunity to put their case. Natural justice applies only to the procedures followed in reaching a decision, and not to the decision itself. An example would be the conduct of immigration officials in interviewing aliens. Breaches of natural justice may lead to the resulting decision being quashed.

natural law (in philosophy), unchanging moral principles common to all people by virtue of their nature as human beings. The existence and nature of natural law has been much discussed by theorists throughout the ages. *Aristotle believed that there were universal and immutable laws laid down by nature, while the medieval theologian and philosopher St Thomas *Aquinas regarded natural law as that part of divine law which was discoverable through human reason. According to such theories, human laws derive their validity from natural law, and if a law conflicts with moral values, it is not fit to be regarded as a law. Later theorists developed the idea of natural rights, based on natural law. During the 18th century, the belief that man possessed an inalienable right to 'life, liberty, and the pursuit of happiness' was used to justify the overthrow of oppressive systems, such as British colonial rule in America in 1783, or the *ancien régime* in France before the Revolution in 1789, and underpinned the *constitutions of the succeeding republics. The belief that there are universal and immutable principles of natural law has been challenged by legal positivists (see *jurisprudence), who deny any element of moral value in the definition of law, and who define it in purely descriptive terms as the observable *legislation of a generally recognized authority. Since World War II, however, there has been renewed interest in natural law ideas, and some contemporary theorists have stressed the essential relationship between legal and moral values. Most people today would regard the *human rights elucidated in the *Universal Declaration of Human Rights as natural rights.

nature–nurture debate   *behaviour genetics.

Navajo, an Indian group of over fifty *clans, who were originally nomadic *hunter-gatherers from north-east Arizona. Often engaged in sporadic warfare with the pueblo (village)-dwelling Indians such as the *Hopi, the Navajo were resettled in the mid-19th century, becoming, by and large, sheep farmers. They are now the largest single tribe in the USA. Their *kinship organization is based on extended matrilineal groups, in which women have a high status. Recent discoveries of oil and mineral reserves on their reservation have become an extra source of material wealth.

Nazism, the ideology of the National Socialist German Workers' Party, which ruled Germany under Adolf Hitler from 1933 to 1945. It combined two essential doctrines: the *fascist belief in national unity, secured by a *one-party state with one supreme leader embodying the national will; and the *racist belief in the superiority of the Aryan peoples, implying that Slavs, Jews, and other races might be subjugated and if necessary exterminated. The defeat of Hitler and world-wide revulsion at his *genocidal policies have ensured the virtual disappearance of Nazism from mainstream politics. However, it retains an influence on certain far Right groups on the fringe of politics.

Ndebele, a *Bantu-speaking people, living in southern Zimbabwe. Traditionally they live in kraals, groups of family homesteads. The women grow maize, the staple crop, and the men herd the cattle. Cattle are regarded as a sign of prestige and are used in marriage payments (*lobola*) (see *dowry). Under colonial rule many Ndebele lost their lands and became industrial or domestic workers. They joined with the more dominant *Shona in the independence struggle, but ethnic differences are still a source of tension between the two groups.

negligence (in *common law), the breach of a duty of care owed by one person to another. Many duties of care are well established: motorist to other road-users; employer to employee; manufacturer to consumer; doctor to patient. However, the concept is flexible and allows the courts to hold that a duty of care exists between parties who stand in a sufficiently proximate relationship to one another, such as a building society surveyor and the purchaser of a house. The duty of care is breached when the defendant's failure to take reasonable care causes foreseeable damage to the plaintiff. The growth of liability *insurance has led to courts being increasingly ready to find breaches of reasonable care, and actions for negligence have become the major means by which accident victims receive *compensation. The extent to which the possibility of an accusation of fault constitutes a deterrent against careless conduct is widely debated, and some legal systems have replaced *damages for negligence with no-fault compensation schemes.

neo-classical economics *classical economics, *theories of economics.

Neo-Confucianism *Confucianism.

neo-Freudian, a term for influential *psychoanalytic writers inspired by, but differing from, *Freud. Loosely, it includes *Jung, Melanie Klein (1882–1960), and Wilhelm Reich (1895–1957). Frequently, however, it is restricted to those who rejected Freud's model of human development as the manifestation of instinctual drives and their often unsatisfactory suppression through fear of retribution. In contrast, they emphasized that individuals develop through a process of integration into a social and cultural world which may be benign rather than hostile. They also denied that early infant–parent relationships exclusively caused the healthy or unhealthy development of personality, and they did not accept Freud's doctrine of the *unconscious mind. The Austrian Alfred Adler (1870–1937) viewed people's behaviour as explicable in terms of the goals they adopt and their general attempt to develop their capacities and overcome a sense of their own imperfection and inferiority. The American Harry Stack Sullivan (1892–1949) saw personality as a matter of how people relate to others throughout their lives, with adolescence a particularly important time in development. His compatriot Erik Erikson (1902–79) shared a very similar psychoanalytic orientation. He also discussed developmental 'tasks' and crises that occur throughout life.

Nestorian Church (East Syrian, Chaldean, or Assyrian Church), an Oriental *Christian Church. It has about 170,000 members, who are found mostly in Iraq, Iran, Syria, and the USA, where the Patriarch resides. The liturgical language is Syriac (see *Syrian Orthodox Church).

netball, a seven-a-side ball game related to *basketball, usually played outdoors and almost exclusively by girls and women, mainly in the UK and Commonwealth countries. The court is 30 m (100 feet) long by 15 m (50 feet) wide and divided into three equal areas. The goal, an open net, is mounted on a 3 m (10 feet) high post at each end, surrounded by a semicircular shooting circle 5 m (16 feet) in radius. The game is played between two teams, each consisting of seven players. Each player has a designated position and may only enter limited areas of the court. Only the goal-shooter (GS) and goal-attack (GA) may shoot at goal.

neurosis, a type of *mental illness in which a person persistently over-reacts emotionally and behaves in an inappropriate way, while knowing that it is irrational to do so. By contrast, in *psychosis, this insight is lost. A common example is a *phobia, in which there is a crippling fear of, say, social situations or public places. In more complicated cases there may be periodic *depression, *obsession, impulsiveness, and self-damaging behaviour, including *suicidal gestures. In a few cases the neurosis can be traced to a single cause, such as an experience in war or of civilian disaster. However, most neuroses reflect long-standing personality difficulties, and originate in an interaction between early environmental influences (for example, parental deprivation, loss, or abuse) and inherited temperamental factors, such as a strong tendency to *anxiety that makes the individual more vulnerable to *stress.

neutrality, the status of countries that are not parties to an international conflict. Certain rights and obligations apply; for example, ships of a neutral state are usually allowed to leave a blockaded port, and escaped *political prisoners may seek *political asylum in the territory of a neutral. More generally, states may acquire a reputation, role, or status as a neutral in international politics (for instance, Austria, Ireland, Sweden, and Switzerland). Japan and Germany are not neutral in status, but since World War II their constitutions have forbidden involvement in international conflicts.

New Age movement, a cultural movement covering a broad range of beliefs and activities and characterized by a rejection of Western values and culture and the promotion of an integrated or 'holistic' approach in areas such as religion, medicine, philosophy, *astrology, and the environment. Although the movement originated in, and is strongly associated with, California and the West Coast of the USA, its influence spread throughout the USA and northern Europe, and became established in communities such as Findhorn in Scotland from about the beginning of the 1970s. Many of its components, including a wide range of alternative and complementary therapies, the practice of Eastern religions, and a fascination with the occult and *parapsychology, seem to follow directly from aspects of the 'hippie' movement of the 1960s. However, it has attracted not only an older age group but also middle-class people with money and status within society.

New Guinea highlands, the highland areas of *Papua New Guinea, which contain a large number of different tribal and linguistic groupings. Partly due to the mountainous and heavily forested terrain, little was known about these people until comparatively recently. The tribes permanently occupy land in small villages, and practise subsistence agriculture, hunting, and the raising of pigs. Gender is important in social organization and the sexual division of labour is strict: men prepare the land while women plant and harvest the crops as well as tending the pigs. After *marriage, residence tends to be virilocal (at the husband's home), but the men and older boys live in communal houses. Young boys often undergo *initiation rituals which involve their seclusion from women, and certain *food prohibitions. The *clan system is organized on the principles of exogamous (marriage outside the group) patrilineal *descent groups, and marriage between them often involves a public exchange of wealth between the two groups. *Ritual and ceremony such as *gift-giving play an important role in Papuan societies, not least in determining rank and hierarchy. Leadership can be achieved through the acquisition of wealth and prestige, such people becoming known as 'big men'. Status and power are not transferable or hereditary, and so in principle each male has the opportunity to attain high status.

New International Economic Order (NIEO), a set of demands formulated by a group of *Third World countries at a special session of the *UN General Assembly in 1974 which envisage a restructuring of the present international economic system to improve the position of the developing countries (the South) with respect to the advanced industrialized countries (the North). These demands include increased control by developing countries over their own resources, the promotion of *industrialization, an increase in *development assistance, and alleviation of *debt problems. While the demand for an NIEO was in part a reflection of frustration at the inability to break out of the cycle of underdevelopment, it also drew inspiration from the experience of *OPEC in successfully raising world energy prices. By the 1990s the NIEO had not materialized, having met the joint obstacles of Western resistance, and lack of commitment and support from the developing countries themselves.

New Left, a movement of radical intellectuals in the 1960s, spanning the leading Western societies. The New *Left was socialist in inspiration, but it was critical of orthodox *communism as practised in Eastern Europe at the time (as well as of existing socialist and communist parties in the West). Its members focused their attention on cultural factors such as the *mass media and the growth of consumption which stemmed revolutionary opposition to *capitalism. Seminal books were Raymond Williams's *Culture and Society* (1958) and *Marcuse's *One-Dimensional Man* (1964). New Left ideas were influential mainly in movements such as that against the Vietnam War (1964–75), and played a large role in the student uprising in Paris in May 1968, which led to educational and administrative reforms.

newly industrializing country (NIC), a term used to describe a country traditionally placed in the *Third World or *developing country category which has experienced rapid economic growth since the 1970s. East Asian countries including Hong Kong, Singapore, South Korea, and Taiwan, are regarded as the leading NICs, while some putative NICs such as Brazil, Malaysia, Mexico, and Thailand have also been identified. While it is debatable that the NICs are joining the ranks of the advanced industrialized countries, they stand out among developing states for their achievement of self-sustained, *export-led economic growth, while the East Asian NICs have also avoided the *debt problems

commonly associated with many developing countries, particularly in Latin America.

New Right, an intellectual movement of the 1970s and 1980s which sought to reformulate the basis of *Right-wing opposition to *social democracy and *socialism. New Right thinkers, whose influence was greatest in the USA and the UK, drew in varying proportions upon the ideas of *libertarianism and *conservatism. (*Nozick's *Anarchy, State and Utopia* (1974) and Roger Scruton's *The Meaning of Conservatism* (1980) represent the two ends of this spectrum; *Hayek's *Law, Legislation and Liberty* (1973–9) falls somewhere in between.) The libertarian strain could be seen in their defence of the *free market, and their belief that the role of government had been over-extended and now needed to be reduced. This meant, for example, the *privatization of firms and industries owned by the state, *monetarist policies, and a shift away from the *welfare state towards private insurance as a way of coping with ill health and old age. The conservative strain appeared in their strong commitment to law and order, and in their belief that the family unit needed to be strengthened. Some New Right thinkers embraced *public choice theory, holding that the actions of governments were to be explained in terms of the self-interest of the politicians and bureaucrats who staffed them. New Right ideas were for the most part not novel in themselves, but they marked a radical break with the post-war consensus about the role of the state in society. Their influence could be seen in the crusading style adopted by the governments led by Margaret Thatcher and Ronald Reagan in the 1980s.

news, regularly updated reports of recent or continuing world, national, and local events, presented through *newspapers and *broadcasting. The nature and variety of news reports available in a country depends in part on the respect accorded to *freedom of the press; the selection, presentation, and topicality of the news depends on those engaged in *journalism, and the technology used in gathering it (see *live broadcasting and *satellite broadcasting) and transmitting it (see *television, *radio, and *newspaper). News is collected under the constraints of time and distance, cost, competition with other news providers, and bias due to the influence of government, *advertising, and cultural viewpoint. *News agencies, press conferences, and press releases provide much of the raw material. The news may be 'managed' by politicians or *public relations firms, who seek favourable exposure by leaking confidential information, setting up 'photo-opportunities', or building speeches around brief, dramatic 'sound-bites' aimed at news bulletins. The editor's task of selecting, shortening, and re-presenting the work of his or her reporters is an integral part of creating a newspaper or newscast. News values (what makes a story newsworthy or worth including) often stress what is biggest or has most obvious impact. The news tends to be defined by editors as a blend of what they believe their audience want and need to know. Happenings may be reported in isolation rather than as parts of diffuse and complicated social or natural processes. Despite journalism's claims and aims of objectivity, news is a manufactured and perishable commodity, sometimes conveyed through simple but easily grasped *stereotypes, and carrying and reinforcing ideological messages. (See also *agenda-setting.)

news agency (US, wire service), a local, national, or international organization that collects reports and photographs from staff correspondents and supplies them by telegraph,

The Times, one of the oldest and most influential of British **newspapers**, has changed hands many times since its foundation in 1785. Seen here is the Australian businessman Rupert Murdoch who became its proprietor in 1981.

telephone link, or *satellite to subscribing *newspapers or *broadcasting companies. News agencies play a key role in the production line that turns events into *news. A small local paper can carry first-hand foreign reports, while major newspapers and broadcasting stations use agency wire services to supplement reports from their own correspondents. The big four international news agencies are Associated Press and United Press International based in the USA, Agence France-Presse in France, and Reuters in the UK. TASS, once the chief news agency of the former Soviet Union, is under challenge from the independent Interfax. Two companies specializing in television news film are Visnews and World Television News. Agency news values and stories reflect the needs of their mainly US and European subscribers. Subscribers elsewhere provide less revenue and their interests are less consistently covered.

newspaper, a daily or weekly publication containing *news, comment, information, and other features. Most newspapers are paid for, but *advertising is an important source of revenue, and provides most of it in US newspapers. 'Free newspapers' are financed entirely by advertising and carry no cover price. Although the pre-eminence of newspapers as a news medium has been challenged, first by *radio, then by *television, and although a trend towards fewer newspapers targeted at a narrower audience is often apparent, they remain popular and influential. Large-circulation newspapers spread in Europe and the USA in the 18th century as printing techniques improved. Government *censorship was a frequent curb on *freedom of the press, although a radical underground press often gave voice to anti-establishment views, then as now. 'Press barons' exercised considerable power through newspaper empires built up in the late 19th and the 20th centuries. By the 1970s newspapers in the UK divided between the 'quality' broadsheet press carrying news and analysis, and the popular tabloid (half-sheet) papers largely devoted to gossip and entertainment. Although they can lead to high-quality, enterprising *journalism, the circulation wars that break out between newspapers can have a damaging effect on the journalism offered: what are seen as over-simplification,

*stereotyping, and invasion of *privacy have led to many complaints. The perceived political bias of many newspapers and increasing concentration of ownership of the *mass media have also caused concern. Only in the late 20th century has it become possible, with electronic and satellite transmission, to publish the same newspaper simultaneously over large territories. The technique was pioneered in 1983 by the *Wall Street Journal* which publishes both a US and a European edition. In the 1970s and 1980s, changes in production technology were introduced, such as direct input of copy and working on video screens by journalists. The Australian-born businessman Rupert Murdoch's News Corporation, the world's largest publisher of English-language newspapers and the first global multi-media corporation, introduced new production technology to its London newspaper titles in 1986. This resulted in all British newspapers adopting the new 'cold type' technology. Many newspaper print workers lost their jobs in consequence. Among the world's famous 'quality' papers are: the *New York Times*, *Washington Post*, and *Wall Street Journal* (USA), *Izvestia*, *Pravda* (Russia), *People's Daily* (China), *The Times of India*, *La Prensa* (Argentina), *Asahi Shimbun* (Japan), *Frankfurter Allgemeine* (Germany), *Financial Times*, *The Guardian*, *The Independent*, *The Observer*, *The Telegraph*, *The Times* (UK), *Figaro*, *Le Monde* (France), and *La Repubblica* (Italy).

new town, a planned urban centre created in a rural area, often with government sponsorship. Industrialists seeking to provide housing and amenities for their workers made some of the first full-scale experiments in creating socially and economically integrated communities. Within the UK, G. Cadbury built Bournville (1895) near Birmingham, and William Hesketh Lever built Port Sunlight (1887) near Liverpool. The British town planner and social reformer Ebenezer Howard recommended in *Garden Cities of Tomorrow* (1902) the foundation of 'garden cities', where the population would be limited to about 30,000, land use controlled for public benefit, and a surrounding 'green belt' of agricultural land would prevent urban sprawl. Between 1945 and 1980 twenty-eight new towns were built in the UK, the last to be started being Milton Keynes in 1967. In the USA, over 100 new towns have been built, including private as well as government projects. New towns and cities have been created in many other countries, a notable example being the designs by the French architect Le Corbusier for Chandigarh, capital of Punjab and Haryana states in India, which was built in the 1950s. New towns are sometimes built to promote development in areas of rural *depopulation or, as in the case of Brasilia, the capital of Brazil since 1960, to open up previously unexploited territory.

Nietzsche, Friedrich (1844–1900), German philosopher. Nietzsche, who trained as a philologist, is in the first instance distinguished by the extraordinary literary quality of his writings, which he regarded as inseparable from their philosophical content. Originally under the influence of *Schopenhauer, Nietzsche's first book, *The Birth of Tragedy* (1872), identified in Greek tragedy, with whose spirit he associated Wagner's operas, an artistic mode of salvation. In subsequent works, such as *Beyond Good and Evil* (1886), Nietzsche pursued a devastating critique of religious and ethical (particularly Christian) conceptions of life, arguing for a 'revaluation of all values'. The concept of the 'will to power' played an important part in Nietzsche's view that *metaphysical systems are to be evaluated not in terms of their truth or falsity, but in terms of the kind of will to which they give expression, and their role in promoting or suppressing the value of life.

Niger–Congo languages, the main language-group of the southern two-thirds of Africa, stretching as far north as Senegal on the west coast and southern Kenya on the east coast. It is a vast and very diverse family, with over 1,000 languages and numerous dialects. Scholars have divided it into six main groups which represent divisions that occurred over 5,000 years ago: Adamawa–Eastern; Benue–Congo; Kwa; Mande; Voltaic (also called Gur); and West Atlantic. Although resemblances can be found between neighbouring languages, there is no single characteristic common to all of them. Benue–Congo is by far the largest group; its sub-group Bantu dominates most of the southern half of Africa. Bantu has around 550 languages and over 150 million speakers. The most important Bantu language is Swahili, which is used as a *lingua franca by up to 50 million speakers on the north-east coast of Africa, and is an official language of Kenya and Tanzania. It is the only Niger–Congo language with international status, and has borrowed a large number of words from Arabic, and, more recently, from French and English. It is almost unique in the Niger–Congo family in no longer making use of tone (see *phonology). Other prominent Bantu languages are Kongo in the west (7 million speakers), and *Zulu and *Xhosa (each with 5 million speakers) in the south. Closely related is the Kwa group, whose major languages are *Yoruba (18 million speakers, mostly in south-west Nigeria), and *Ibo (13 million speakers in south-east Nigeria). An important West Atlantic language is Fulani, which stretches from northern Senegal through to Burkina Faso and northern Nigeria. The languages which make up Adamawa–Eastern, Mande, and Voltaic are on the whole spoken by relatively small groups of people.

Nilo-Saharan languages, a group of languages spoken in east-central Africa around the southern Nile, Chari, and Niger rivers. The group is a small one, and speakers are often found in 'islands' surrounded by other languages. The six main groups are Chari-Nile, a very large group; Fur, a single language spoken in western Sudan; Koma, a group of two languages on the Ethiopia–Sudan border; Maban, a small group in Chad; Saharan, a group which extends from north-east Nigeria into central and northern Chad; and Songhai, a single language spoken along the River Niger in Mali and Niger. Chari-Nile is an important and diverse group in its own right, with four distinct branches. The largest of these is Eastern Sudanic, which includes the group of languages known as Nilotic. Nilotic languages are spoken in southern Sudan, Uganda, western Kenya, and northern Tanzania. Nubian is also an Eastern Sudanic language, spoken along the Nile south of Aswan. It is interesting in having an early written tradition; between the 8th and 11th centuries, after the arrival of Christianity, Nubian was written in Coptic (an alphabet derived from Greek). It was later written in Arabic, following the adoption of Islam.

nirvana (Sanskrit, 'extinguished' or 'blown out'), a term describing the state of bliss entered into by enlightened or liberated beings, before or after death. In *Hinduism, nirvana is the release from endless rebirths (*samsara) into the highest form of consciousness where the *soul finds union with *Brahman. In *Buddhism it is the perfect suspension of volition and cognition, and the removal of all traces of personal emotion. While some Buddhist schools take this to be a movement into a transcendent mode of existence, others question such positive linguistic description, and only point out negatively that it is what is not given by worldly pursuit, desire, and consequent sorrow (*dukkha) of successive lives (samsara).

Noble Eightfold Path, a central Buddhist teaching, which outlines the practical paths towards the extinction of desire and suffering, thus attaining *nirvana or release from endless rebirth (*samsara). It is the last of the *Four Noble Truths, as defined by the *Buddha. It is also known as the Middle Way. The Path leads out of the vicious circle of existence and up the creative spiral of enlightenment. The eight stages divide into three: right (or perfect) viewpoint and right resolve, which concern the understanding of the Four Noble Truths and the acceptance of the Path as the way forward; right speech, action, and livelihood, which concern correct behaviour; and finally right effort, mindfulness, and concentration, which develop the higher realms of spiritual understanding, by overcoming 'unskilful' states of mind, and encouraging inner collectedness through *meditation. This meditation itself deepens understanding and wisdom, so that the sequence of virtue, meditation, and wisdom grows ever more refined, until 'stream-entry' is achieved, the first glimpse of nirvana. Once this transitional stage is reached, a higher form of the Eightfold Path is followed, leading to the state of the *arhat.

no-go areas, areas which are taken to be outside the control of legitimate governmental authorities, owing to the prevalence of anti-government forces. In urban areas, the term can be applied to parts of cities beyond the control of the police, such as those in Latin America controlled by drugs cartels; large rural areas have also been 'off-limits' to security forces in countries such as Colombia. The UK government has been faced with the problem of no-go areas in the border regions between Northern Ireland and the Irish Republic. (See also *civil war, *guerrilla.)

nomadism, the diverse traditional ways of life practised by peoples who move regularly from place to place to ensure a source of food and livelihood. Nomads are constantly on the move, unlike *migrant workers, who leave their homes and find work in one place on an irregular or permanent basis. There are three broad categories. Firstly, some *hunter-gatherers move at varying intervals in search of plants and game. Secondly, transhumance is practised by pastoralists (tenders of flocks or herds) such as the *Kurds, *Basques, or *Nuer, who move their livestock back and forth on a seasonal or periodic basis from relatively fixed points, commonly between mountain pastures in the summer and valley pastures in the winter, or wet- and dry-season pastures. Thirdly, tinker or trader nomads, such as *gypsies or *Tuareg move on a regular basis to trade or practise small crafts. Nomads are likely to have permanent homes in one or more centres, but they may also travel in movable dwellings such as tents and caravans. Traditionally, many nomadic peoples have elaborate *lineage-based systems of *kinship. Nomadism has declined sharply in the 20th century, for economic reasons such as *industrialization or changes in *agriculture, and for political reasons which include the emergence of *nation-states which discourage the free movement of peoples across frontiers; different patterns of land tenure; and the dislike of increasingly centralized governments for a way of life regarded as aberrant and insusceptible to government control. (See also *African pastoralists.)

nomenklatura, a practice of the former Soviet political system by which the Communist Party exercised control over important appointments. It comprised a list of responsible posts, such as ministerial positions, newspaper editors, factory managers, heads of schools, and other institutions, together with a list of individuals approved by the Party to hold such positions. This created an *élite within Soviet society with special rights and privileges, such as access to special shops, hospitals, or schools. It was one of the targets of Mikhail Gorbachev's programme of *glasnost and perestroika.

nominalism, a philosophical view which denies the existence of abstract objects and *universals, holding that these are not required to explain the significance of words apparently referring to them. Nominalism holds that all that really exists are particular, usually physical, objects, and that properties, numbers, and sets (for instance) are not further things in the world, but merely features of our way of thinking or speaking about those things that do exist. In making claims about what there really is, nominalism is a thesis about existence (see *ontology); but it also involves views about meaning related to *reductionism.

Non-Aligned Movement (NAM), a group of developing countries united by their desire to remain independent from both the Western powers and the Soviet bloc and thus to keep out of *East–West conflicts. In 1990, the movement had 102 members. Non-alignment started as an Asian movement with Prime Minister Nehru of India (1889–1964) as its leading figure, soon to be joined by President Tito of Yugoslavia (1892–1980), and President Nasser of Egypt (1918–70). Inspired by the Bandung Conference of 1955, in which Asian and African states met to discuss world peace and co-operation, the first Non-Aligned Summit was held in Belgrade in 1961, followed by further summits held in different non-aligned capitals, usually at three-year intervals. Gradually the movement was joined by most newly independent nations, and the scope of its interests widened. Members still maintained an anti-cold war stand, but increasingly became concerned with other issues of particular concern to the developing world, notably economic *development. The movement grew in importance during the 1960s and 1970s, becoming the most influential *Third World grouping, with considerable impact on world politics, particularly in the UN. The Co-ordinating Bureau of Non-Aligned Countries was set up in September 1973 in Algiers with the aim of working towards the establishment of a *New International Economic Order. A novel development at the NAM summit in 1989, which followed the revolutions in Eastern Europe, was the guest appearance of former *Warsaw Pact member countries.

non-governmental organization (NGO), an *international organization consisting of non-governmental representatives of states, a characteristic which distinguishes it from the international governmental organization (IGO), such as the *UN, which consists primarily or wholly of government representatives. Non-governmental organizations bring together groups, associations, organizations, and individuals from within different countries. They include religious, professional, and sporting bodies, *trade-union groups, *political parties, charities, and other *voluntary organizations. These are 'non-state actors' on the world stage and their interactions give rise to *transnational relations. NGOs have played an increasingly important role in international politics in the 20th century. Some well-known

A project in Bangladesh funded by Islamic Relief, a UK-based **non-governmental organization** with charitable status. The smaller NGOs are often the most efficient and cost-effective in alleviating need.

examples are the International Red Cross, *Amnesty International, the Salvation Army, and Oxfam.

non-verbal communication, the ways in which information is conveyed between individuals face to face in addition to or instead of speech. *Conversation between individuals is invariably (and often involuntarily) accompanied by non-verbal communication: posture and position, eye contact, gaze direction, *facial expressions, and gesticulations. 'Body language' of this kind may reinforce the message conveyed by speech, or it may subtly contradict it (as when eye contact is avoided, for instance). Much body movement is involuntary, but we also make use of voluntary gestures, recognized actions performed in order to express a meaning, such as shrugging the shoulders, giving a thumbs-up sign, or pointing. There are world-wide similarities in facial expression of emotion. However, in the case of certain gestures there may be significant differences in meaning from one culture or community to another. For example, joining the thumb and index fingers to form a circle may signify approval, disapproval, or an overt sexual invitation. Where such gestures are widely recognized they often replace speech entirely, as is also the case in systems such as sign language for the deaf (see *signing).

norm (Latin, *norma*, 'carpenter's square'), a standard common to members of a social group. The norms of a society guide the actions of its members, who are expected to conform with them. Failure to fit in with the norms of a group (see *deviance) can result in social or legal penalties. Members of a society learn its norms through the process of *socialization.

North American Indian languages, languages spoken by the indigenous peoples of Canada and North America before the arrival of Europeans, who had a disastrous effect on them. Fewer than half of the 300 languages which were originally spoken in North America have survived, and many are remembered now by just a few old people; there are only fifty which have more than 1,000 speakers. In this respect northern languages have suffered more than those in Central and South America. The classification of the American languages into families is complicated and controversial. The northern languages can be classed into two groups: a clear-cut family called Na–Dené, and a large group called Northern Amerind, which in turn consists of four important sub-groups. Na–Dené is spoken in Alaska and western Canada, and in a substantial island stretching over California, Arizona, and New Mexico. There are thirty-four languages, including Navaho and Apache, and 200,000 speakers. Navaho, the largest language, is spoken by 120,000 people, a figure which has increased over recent years. The four groups which make up Northern Amerind are called Almosan, Keres–Siouan, Penutian, and Hokan. The most important member of Almosan is Algonkian, which is spoken by over 90,000 people across central and eastern Canada, and the centre and eastern coast of the USA. Its speakers include members of well-known groups such as Ojibwa, Cree, Blackfoot, and Cheyenne. Keres–Siouan has around 45,000 speakers in the central and eastern USA (including Sioux and Crow in the centre, and Cherokee and

Mohawk in the east). Penutian is a huge group which has bands of speakers stretching from western Canada and the western USA across to the south-east USA and southern Mexico. It has 3.2 million speakers altogether, and includes Chinook and Muskogee. The Mayan languages of Central America are also included (see *Mexican and Central American Indian languages). Hokan is a group of twenty-eight languages (50,000 speakers) of the south-western USA and eastern Mexico. The northern languages have no indigenous scripts, but modern scripts have been devised and some oral literature has been transcribed.

North–South relations, a term used to describe the relationship existing between the advanced industrialized countries (the North) and the *Third World, or *developing countries (the South). North–South relations became an issue in *international politics following the process of decolonization, which brought a large number of new *states into an international system in which they found themselves to be at a serious disadvantage, particularly in economic terms. The developing countries of the South tried through various means to reduce their *dependence on the North. They were particularly active in the UN, notably in the *United Nations Conference on Trade and Development (UNCTAD) in 1964, where the framework was established for a set of demands for a new deal on world trade. The position of the South looked stronger by the late 1970s: *OPEC (the Organization of Petroleum Exporting Countries) had set an example to all developing countries by successfully raising world energy prices, the demand for a *New International Economic Order had been presented to a UN General Assembly session in 1974, and the issue of North–South relations had been made the subject of an international commission which met from 1977 to 1979 under the chairmanship of Willy Brandt (1913–   ). In its now famous report *North–South: A Programme for Survival* (1980), the commission urgently recommended reforms to reduce the existing inequalities in North–South economic relations. It has been estimated, for example, that inequalities in income between Europe and the Indian subcontinent have increased from 2:1 to 70:1 in the past 100 years. Few such reforms materialized. The developing countries have also proved unable to introduce major changes to the prevailing international economic order, partly due to lack of solidarity among themselves.

Two internationally understood **non-verbal communications** had their specific origins in the Allied victory sign of World War II and the half-raised fist of the 1960s Black Power movement. Both are seen here at a pro-democracy rally in Mongolia.

North-west Indians, the inhabitants of the Pacific seaboard of Canada and Alaska, including the *Kwakiutl, *Tlingit, and *Tsimshian. Traditionally, they lived from fishing and some hunting. These societies were highly stratified, with a rigid set of statuses, from chief to commoner to slave. Rank and hierarchy were determined by *descent, which was generally matrilineal. The village was the basic social unit, and consisted of permanent log dwellings. Their mythology linked each member of a particular village to one common ancestor. The North-west Indians developed a distinctive and highly sophisticated style of painted woodcarving, some of which became known as 'totem poles', and acted as signs of status, prestige, and wealth. In general terms, status was a combination of privileges, inherited through descent, and would include, for example, the use of a particular fishing ground, or the right to take berries from a particular tree. Status was not a permanent condition, but had to be earned, and one of the most spectacular ways to do this was the *potlatch, a feast at which valuable goods and items would be distributed or even destroyed.

notary (from Latin, *notarius*, one who takes notes of judicial proceedings), an official who is authorized to perform certain legal formalities. A notary's functions encompass drawing up and certifying documents and contracts, administering oaths, and taking sworn statements for use in court proceedings. In some countries, notaries belong to an independent profession, while in others they are civil servants.

Nozick, Robert (1938-), US political philosopher. Nozick is a radical *libertarian who argues that liberty and equality are incompatible and that liberty (particularly the liberty that comes from ownership) must take priority. In *Anarchy, State and Utopia* (1974), Nozick developed his Entitlement Theory of Justice, according to which things are not like 'manna from heaven' but come into existence already owned. According to Nozick all taxation is forced labour except that required to maintain the so-called 'night-watchman' state, a minimal state whose task is to protect property.

nuclear proliferation, the spread of nuclear weapons. Vertical proliferation is concerned with the development of more and different types of weapons by the existing nuclear weapons states, often in response to evolutions in *nuclear strategy. Such proliferation may be checked by *arms control agreements. Horizontal proliferation, on the other hand, refers to the spread of these weapons to currently non-nuclear states. The five declared nuclear weapons states are the USA, the former Soviet Union (nuclear weapons being located in Belarus, Kazakhstan, Russia, and Ukraine), the UK, France, and China. It is widely believed that Israel has nuclear weapons, and India detonated what it called a peaceful nuclear device in 1974. In 1981, knowing that Iraq was developing a nuclear weapons capability, the Israelis bombed their reactor. Others thought to be capable of producing weapons include Pakistan, Argentina, Brazil, and South Africa. The horizontal proliferation of nuclear weapons is controlled by international constraints, including the 1963 Partial Test Ban Treaty; the 1968 Non-Proliferation Treaty (which, however, has not been signed by some countries, such as Israel, India, Pakistan, and South Africa, which have the potential for developing nuclear weapons, and was only signed by the declared nuclear powers of China and France in 1992); and the Safeguards Regime of the *International Atomic Energy Agency, designed to prevent the transfer of nuclear energy materials into weapons production. However, the weak nature of such constraints was indicated by the confirmation after the 1991 Gulf War of Iraq's development of nuclear weapons despite its membership of the Non-Proliferation Treaty. Following the demise of the Soviet Union, concern was voiced that Soviet nuclear scientists might contribute to nuclear proliferation by making their expertise available to third-party countries, and international diplomacy concentrated on reaching agreement on disarming the nuclear capacity of the Soviet successor states.

nuclear strategy, the political and strategic functions of *nuclear weapons, including the problems of nuclear deterrence. Once the former Soviet Union acquired nuclear weapons in 1949, the key problem was how, in the context of the cold war (see *East–West relations) the opposing sides could seek to make political gains, threaten each other with unacceptable damage in case of serious provocation, and yet limit the risk of nuclear war. Deterrence aims at discouraging hostile action through fear of retaliation, proportionate to the damage threatened. For deterrence to work, the threat of retaliation must be credible. The concept of extended deterrence involves retaliation in defence of one's allies, as in the case of the USA's commitment to the defence of Europe, and much depends on the credibility of one state's risking its own homeland in defence of its allies. Deterrence involves not only making clear the intention to use nuclear weapons if need be, but also the retention of a capability to do so, hence the escalation of nuclear arms on both sides (see *arms race). Another strategic device is the 'strategic triad', the development of nuclear systems on land, at sea, or in the air, to ensure that if the opponent strikes first (in a pre-emptive strike), sufficient forces would survive to inflict unacceptable damage in retaliation (an assured second strike capability). Developments in missile accuracy and the ability to locate fixed missile sites by the use of satellites prompted searches for alternative, mobile missiles. Nuclear strategy has also been concerned with *arms control and the preservation of a balance of nuclear arms on both sides.

nuclear weapons, explosive devices that owe their destructive power to the energy released by nuclear fission or nuclear fusion. A typical nuclear explosion releases about half its energy as shock or blast, a third as heat, and the rest as radiation. At first, nuclear bombs were carried on long-range aircraft, but in the 1950s, long-range ballistic missiles were developed, capable of travelling thousands of kilometres. Intermediate-range ballistic missiles and tactical or battlefield weapons were also developed. The Cruise missile is propelled by a small jet engine in flight and can reach its target with great accuracy thanks to a computerized system. Because nuclear devices are weapons of mass destruction, and global nuclear war would have incalculable effects on the environment and life on earth, restraints have been placed on the proliferation of such weapons through *arms control and non-proliferation treaties (see *nuclear proliferation); *nuclear strategy itself has been based on deterrence and a maintenance of a *balance of power, rather than on a planned use of nuclear weapons.

Nuer, a people living in southern Sudan, between the River Nile and Ethiopia. The anthropologist *Evans-Pritchard, who published a study of the Nuer in 1940, saw them as archetypal African *pastoralists. Apart from meat and milk, the Nuer depend for their livelihood on crops such as millet, grown by the women. Nuer men are characterized by an aggressive egalitarianism, and their social life is dominated by their love for cattle, which are used as bridewealth. The social and political organization of the Nuer is 'segmentary' and based on *kinship; that is, there is no central authority, leadership belonging to the heads of various *lineages. This segmentation has led to much antagonism between patrilineages at a local level, and *feuds are often settled by payments of cattle. The Nuer way of life has been disrupted by civil war and *famine, and many are *refugees.

nuisance (in *common law), a continuing act or state of affairs which unreasonably interferes with people's use or enjoyment of land, or with public health and safety. Thus a factory which emits noise and fumes on to another's land may create a nuisance. Those affected may seek an *injunction to restrain the nuisance, or may make a claim for *damages. Public nuisance, such as obstructing the highway, is a criminal offence.

nursery education *pre-school education.

obedience, acting in accordance with a superior's instructions. The most famous studies of obedience, performed by the US psychologist Stanley Milgram, are described in his *Obedience to Authority* (1973). Milgram set up an experiment supposedly to test the effects of electric shocks on people's learning ability. The 'learner' was a confederate of the experimenter and received no shocks, but acted as if he did. Twenty-six out of forty males in the original study obeyed the experimenter's instructions and administered massive, potentially lethal, shocks to the victim when he gave wrong answers. Milgram argued that under orders people abandon personal responsibility. He compared this to the behaviour of ordinary soldiers who massacre prisoners or civilians and defend their actions as 'obeying orders'. Those who took part generally believed the shocks were genuine and many were acutely distressed by what they had done. The studies caused an outcry and a change in the American Psychological Association's rules about experimental procedure.

obligation, political, the duty of ordinary citizens to abide by the laws of the state. Modern political theory has tried to demonstrate the grounds and limits of such an obligation. One popular answer has been *utilitarian: we should obey the law because, and to the extent that, it is in the public interest to do so. A second approach is provided by theories of *social contract, such as *Locke's *Two Treatises of Government* (1689). Here it is argued that we have consented to government, and in so doing agreed to abide by duly enacted laws. On this approach, political obligations are owed only to certain governments (for example, those where *legitimacy derives from democratic *elections) and within certain limits (for example, obligation ceases if the government should infringe *human rights). A more radical view is that political obligation is a myth, and people should keep or break the law as their conscience dictates—see, for instance, Robert Paul Wolff, *In Defence of Anarchism* (1970). Such a view often lies behind advocacy of *civil disobedience.

obligations, law of, a collective term covering the laws of *tort, *contract, and restitution. A legal obligation is a concept known primarily but not exclusively in *civil law rather than *common law systems; it connotes the idea of something owed by one person to another. Obligations may be created by the will of the parties, as, for example, under a contract, or they may be imposed by law. Thus in some countries adults are legally obliged to maintain their children and close kin.

obsession, a morbid preoccupation which in *psychiatry is seen in several types of mental disorder, including *psychosis, where it may take on a delusional quality. However, it most commonly forms part of obsessive–compulsive *neurosis in which the person knows the obsession is irrational, but is unable to control an endlessly recurrent, intrusive thought, such as doubt ('Am I *really* sure I locked the door?') or fear of harming others. Obsessional states are usually grouped, as anxiety-based disorders, alongside *phobias and, although much more resistant to change, they are often treated with similar methods of *behaviour therapy.

Ockham, William of (*c.*1285–1349), theologian, philosopher, and a leading figure in the growth of the 'modern' or 'terminist' logic. This made central the questions of how and to what the subject and predicate terms in a sentence refer. Ockham's answers to these questions embodied his *nominalist response to the problem of *universals: words expressing our general thoughts refer only to particular, individual things. In accord with this he held that intuitive knowledge of individuals, acquired in experience, is fundamental to all knowledge. His views are thus generally sympathetic to *empiricism.

Ockham's razor   *ontology.

OECD (Organization for Economic Co-operation and Development), an organization of industrialized countries, established in 1961, and based in Paris, which seeks to promote co-ordination of economic and social policies among members, to make resources of capital and training available to developing countries, to contribute to the expansion of world trade, and to foster co-operation in fields such as education, energy, and transport. In 1991 its members were Australia, Austria, Belgium, Canada, Denmark, Finland, France, Germany, Greece, Iceland, Ireland, Italy, Japan, Luxemburg, The Netherlands, New Zealand, Norway, Portugal, Spain, Sweden, Switzerland, Turkey, the UK, and the USA. Yugoslavia participates with special associate status. The OECD prepares an influential annual report on the economy of each member country.

Ojibwa, the Indians who formerly inhabited the territory around Lake Superior in North America. The Ojibwa were hunters and fishers as well as subsistence farmers, and were constantly feuding with the *Sioux. They also developed a unique form of picture-writing. During the 17th century they expanded their territory as far as North Dakota, and became one of the biggest tribes in North America. Since the early 19th century they have been living on reservations in North Dakota, Michigan, Minnesota, and Wisconsin.

old age, the final stage of life, variously defined across the world, but often taken to coincide with the period during which a person is no longer expected, or no longer able, to carry the workload or responsibilities normal for their society. For the purpose of international comparisons, the UN takes old age to begin at 60 for both men and women. Yet those aged over 60 are typically in good physical and mental health; a survey in Fiji, the Philippines, and Malaysia found 80 to 90 per cent could live independently without difficulty. Many observers have suggested that because of increased *life expectancy and improved health, a distinction should be drawn between the 'young-old' and the 'old-old'. The former, whom the French describe as in their 'Third Age', often live active healthy lives. The latter, in their 'Fourth Age', tend to suffer from increasing mental and physical frailty. Attitudes to, and experiences of, ageing vary. Studies have found that in some pre-industrial societies older people, if considered burdensome, were neglected or abandoned, but in many others, they occupied powerful positions controlling land tenure and family relationships, and were respected for their knowledge and experience in agriculture, health, religion, and other spheres. Increasingly, professionals such as doctors and teachers, and the *mass media are responsible for transmitting information and shaping attitudes so that the knowledge of older people tends to be seen as obsolete. In developing countries, where most must work to survive, lack of education and incapacity for strenuous activity can result in unemployment and destitution. Those in the richest countries, by contrast, are tending to retire younger (some by choice or compulsion by 55) and most can draw on *old-age benefits, *social services, and medical care. In all parts of the world, however, there is discrimination against older people both in the workplace and the wider society.

old age, family support in. In most societies, family support for older people is enjoined by custom and law. Within Islam, for example, the Koran prescribes dignity, respect, and assistance for older family members, obligations which are reflected in legislation requiring children to support their parents in states such as Algeria, Syria, and Tunisia. However, rapid social change is everywhere affecting family relationships. The mass *migration of young workers from country to town and between countries, has left many older people isolated. While some are supported by remittances from relatives, a study in India found that only half of *migrants remitted any money and that remittances more frequently passed from husbands to wives and from parents to children than from children to parents. Even when families are not geographically separated, expectations are changing, and in many countries the extended family centred on the grandfather or father has almost disappeared. All over the world, where they have a choice, young people are choosing to live in a nuclear family with their own children, while work and leisure pursuits are increasingly segregated by age. None the less, many older people, particularly older women, have an important role in caring for grandchildren and in housing daughters with children after marriage or relationship breakdown. A survey of black South African pensioners found that as a result of low income, acute housing shortage and the sense of familial obligation, all those renting homes of their own shared them with younger family members, the average household size being seven. In this society, as elsewhere, relations between older people and their children are often reciprocal. Furthermore, numerous studies from all over the world have shown that despite changing family patterns, the practical assistance given by families to their older members, even in the richest countries, far exceeds that given by the social care services. Looking after those who are severely disabled and especially *dementia sufferers can be a drain on both material and emotional resources, and attempts are being made in some countries to support relatives.

old age, services for, services designed to supply practical, financial, or social support to older people. Those who are mentally or physically infirm are particularly likely to be at risk of neglect or abuse in their own homes or in institutional care. There are great disparities in the quality and availability of services and, with an *ageing population across the world, universal concern about rising costs. The Netherlands is considered to have one of the best national programmes with co-ordinated health and *social care services, extensive assistance to enable people to remain in their own homes (with home nursing, domestic help, and physical adaptations available) and substantial *social security benefits. Even here the costs cause alarm: on average, the annual cost of health care for someone over 80 is nine times the cost for someone under 20. In many developing countries, eligibility for *old-age benefits is restricted and social services are few. A West African study found that elderly women were dependent on relatives or those nearby, and

while most received assistance, some did not. Help Age International (an umbrella organization for national 'age-care' agencies) argues that the programmes for older people established in richer countries rely too heavily on inflexible public services and the residential segregation of old people, and are too costly for developing countries. It recommends self-financing projects with low capital costs which stimulate a community response from young and old, and give benefits according to need. Successful existing projects around the world provide basic services and necessities such as food and clothing, and teach skills so that older people without a family or pension can earn a basic income.

old-age benefit, a *social-security benefit paid to those above retirement age. Some form of old-age benefit is to be found in about 130 of the world's countries, but in many, especially developing countries, only a small minority (often government employees) are covered. Some old-age benefits are paid on the basis of contributions (*social insurance) and others on the basis of right, or of need (*social assistance). In countries where such benefits are widely available, they have contributed to a substantial improvement in the well-being of older people, an increase in their independence from other family members, and a reduction in poverty. Traditionally, the sum paid has been linked either to the subsistence cost of living in the country, or to the previous income (and contributions) of the recipient. The recent tendency is to combine the two, by paying a flat-rate benefit to everyone, and an earnings-related supplement. The revision of benefits is usually designed to maintain either their purchasing power or their relationship to the income of the working population. Those who can afford to do so often supplement their state benefits with occupational pensions (to which they and their employers have contributed) and pensions derived from private *insurance. The rapid increase in the numbers of old people across the world (see *ageing population) and the proportionate decrease in the working population (see *dependency ratio) have raised concerns about the future financing of old-age benefits. Many schemes are financed in such a way that current workers and employers directly provide the funds from which pensioners are paid, in the expectation that future generations will do the same. If a shrinking work-force is unable or unwilling to provide funds, a cut in benefit levels or eligibility, or a rise in the retirement age, however unpopular, may become unavoidable.

oligopoly (in economics), a market structure comprising a small number of firms. It is a form of imperfect competition (see *perfect competition). Oligopolists may have *monopoly power, and the ability to affect price and to make super-normal *profits. The main characteristic of oligopoly is that when firms make decisions on price and output levels, they take into account the expected decisions or reactions of competing firms. Thus they frequently avoid competing on price, preferring instead to compete in other ways (for example *advertising), and occasionally to form *cartels.

Olympic Games, a world festival of sport inspired by the ancient Greek games held at Olympia until AD 393. The modern version owes its existence to Baron de Coubertin, a French aristocrat, and was conceived as a championship for amateur sportsmen to be staged every four years. For the first Games in 1896, athletes from twelve nations travelled to Athens to compete in *gymnastics, *athletics, *cycling, *fencing, lawn *tennis, *shooting, *swimming, *weight-lifting, and *wrestling. Apart from intervals for the two World Wars, and despite various politically motivated boycotts, the Games have continued ever since, at venues including, in recent years, Mexico City, Munich, Montreal, Moscow, Los Angeles, and Seoul; the Barcelona Games of 1992 was the twenty-fifth in the modern series. A separate Winter Olympics began in 1924, held in the winter months preceding the summer Games. Chief focus of every summer Olympics is the main stadium, where track- and field-athletics are held; women's athletic events were introduced in 1928. The programme now includes a great diversity of sports, but has become increasingly dominated by nationalism and commercialism. In 1988 professional tennis players were allowed to take part, final evidence that the principle of amateurism had been abandoned.

ombudsman (Swedish, 'agent' or 'representative'), a person responsible for investigating complaints against government officials. The office originated in Sweden in 1809. The late 20th century has seen an explosion in the number of countries with ombudsmen, perhaps stimulated by the increasing activities of public bureaucracy and by the readiness of members of the public to complain: ombudsmen are now established in Australia, Canada, Denmark, Finland, New Zealand, Sweden, the UK, some states of the USA, and elsewhere. Ombudsmen are impartial and independent of the government of the day; their powers vary widely. Some are permitted to make legally binding awards of compensation, while others merely make recommendations. Some can investigate allegations of illegality, and even institute legal proceedings, while others are restricted to matters of maladministration. Recently there has been a tendency to extend the term to officials who monitor and handle complaints in the private sector.

one-party state, a political system in which one *political party monopolizes state authority and does not permit effective electoral challenge from other parties. Ruling parties in a one-party state justify their position by reference to a 'higher' authority than the rule of the people. This may be ideological, such as the dictatorship of the proletariat in *communist states, or the glory of the nation in *fascist states. In many developing countries, *authoritarian regimes maintain one-party states in the name of national unity and economic development. One-party systems vary considerably. For example, even among the unreformed communist states, there was a significant difference between the former Soviet Union, where communist rule was dominant, and some East European states such as Poland, where some measure of *pluralism was permitted. In some developing countries, the single ruling party is based on the support of a particular ethnic grouping or on personal attachment to a leader, and becomes a device through which political *patronage is distributed to regional or ethnic supporters. In such one-party states, the party may exert less rigidly structured control than in ideologically based one-party states where the doctrines of the party, such as communism, are held to imply particular methods of managing economic and social institutions. In many countries, however, *ideology and ethnic politics coincide to produce a party such as the Syrian Ba'athist party, which is controlled by an Alevi minority and the ideology of *Ba'athism, or Arab socialism.

ontological argument, an argument first presented by St Anselm (1033–1109), claiming to establish the existence of God *a priori, that is, in a way that depends only on the con-

cept of God, and draws on no factual premiss. The ontological argument is thus contrasted with various cosmological arguments, which seek to demonstrate the existence of God as creator from the existence or order of the natural world. Anselm's argument held that God is the most perfect conceivable being; that a God who exists in reality is of greater perfection than one who exists only as a conception in man's mind; and that therefore God, as maximally perfect, must exist in reality. The argument was repeated by *Descartes, and criticized by *Kant, who questioned whether we may, as the argument presupposes, think of existence as a feature something might have or lack. The worth of the argument remains a live philosophical question.

ontology, the philosophical study of the nature of being. Although this can be taken to be the study of what it is for anything to exist at all, as in *Heidegger's work, ontological questions are also concerned with what, in particular, exists. Thus our common-sense ontology would include the material objects with which we interact (such as trees, tables, and mountains), but should it also contain abstract mathematical entities (sets and numbers) or the sub-atomic entities of the theoretical sciences (such as protons and muons)? Closely linked is the question of *reductionism. For example, can minds be reduced to bodies, or mathematics to *logic? A major question is how we are to decide ontological issues. Ockham's razor, the principle, formulated by William of *Ockham in about 1340, that we should not multiply entities beyond necessity, is generally thought of as a principle in the theory of knowledge or *epistemology, and was used as such by *Russell. But in recent philosophy this has also often been linked to questions of meaning, as in *logical positivism.

OPEC (Organization of Petroleum Exporting Countries), an organization of major oil-producing countries, established in 1960, with its headquarters in Vienna. In 1991, OPEC's members were Algeria, Ecuador, Gabon, Indonesia, Iran, Iraq, Kuwait, Libya, Nigeria, Qatar, the United Arab Emirates, Saudi Arabia, and Venezuela. Its activities encompass all aspects of oil negotiations, such as establishing crude oil prices and production *quotas. The organization rose to prominence in the mid-1970s after it virtually quadrupled the price of oil over a three-month

Arab oil ministers meeting in an extraordinary session of **OPEC** in 1973 when the cartel succeeded in raising the price of oil by 200 per cent over three months.

period at the end of 1973, and imposed an embargo on Western consumers who had supported Israel in the Arab–Israel (Yom Kippur) War. OPEC's successful use of the 'oil weapon' had important repercussions for *North–South relations, inspiring greater assertiveness among developing countries, and giving weight to their demands for a *New International Economic Order. During the 1980s, however, the influence of OPEC on world oil prices declined as Western industrialized countries began to exploit their own oil resources, found alternative forms of fuel, or initiated programmes to cut the use of energy. The Organization of Arab Petroleum Exporting Countries (OAPEC), based in Kuwait, was established in 1968, to co-ordinate the different aspects of the Arab petroleum industry, and safeguard its members' interests.

operations research, the application of scientific techniques to the processes and methods of business. Operations research is a set of techniques which can be applied to business problems using some form of quantitative representation as an aid to (but not as a substitute for) decision-making. The aim of operations research is to find optimal courses of action using available resources, using methods such as project management (see *critical path analysis) and simulation techniques. One example of operations research is queuing theory, which can be applied to service situations such as banks (or supermarkets) and used to determine how many service tills (or checkouts) are needed to provide a given level of service speed or cost. Another concerns the routing of delivery schedules in a distribution operation. Scientifically devised routing can increase the number of 'drops' undertaken by one van and decrease the total number of vans and drivers needed.

opinion poll, a sample survey of public opinion on a topic of current concern. The sample of the population questioned can either be random, or one which is designed to reflect the social, educational, or vocational proportions of the population as a whole (quota sample). The study of statistics in *elections (psephology) is used to calculate the margins of error and to assess the accuracy of the inferences made from the sample to the population as a whole. Opinion polls provide a snapshot of public opinion at a particular moment, but they rarely track opinion over time, as do some fuller surveys conducted by academics. However, provided that the sample is properly drawn, and the questions are phrased so as to avoid bias, opinion polls provide a measure of what ordinary people feel about an issue, or how they might vote in an election, both of which may be of significance to political strategists. On the other hand, opinion polls have been criticized for failing to provide a true picture of public opinion, for invading people's *privacy, or even for influencing public opinion itself, by creating a 'bandwagon' effect.

Opus Dei (Latin, 'work of God'), a Roman Catholic organization founded in 1928 by the Spanish priest Josemaria Escrivá de Balaguer. Members, of whom there are 76,000 world-wide, may be either priests or lay people, in which case they are encouraged to retain their social position and pursue their profession. Particularly active in General Franco's Spain (1939–75), the organization has exercised considerable, but controversial, conservative influence on public affairs. It maintains a number of educational establishments, including the Universities of Pamplona and Navarre. There is a separate branch for women, segregation of the sexes being an important principle. Opus Dei emphasizes the austere and conservative aspect of Catholicism; members follow a range of ascetic and spiritual practices, which include daily 'mortification' in the form of brief self-flagellation, and celibacy is encouraged. Active recruitment has resulted in a growing membership world-wide.

organic farming, farming without the use of artificial fertilizers or pesticides. Many farmers in wealthier countries 'go organic' because of the increased demand for food without artificial chemicals, partly as a result of research showing the damaging effect of pesticides and fertilizers on human health and the environment. Excessive use of chemicals may also damage the soil. Organic methods include use of natural fertilizers such as manure, kelp, and compost, and planting clover and other legumes to fix nitrogen in the soil. To combat pests and disease, crops may be mixed, and natural predators introduced (biological control). Antibiotics are not used as prophylactics (as in much conventional farming), but only in case of sickness in the animal. Standards of organic farming are set by independent national organizations such as the Soil Association in the UK, and by the International Federation of Organic Agricultural Movements (IFOAM). IFOAM encourages organic farmers to minimize *pollution, use fewer non-renewable raw materials, and limit mechanization.

organic growth (in economics), the growth of a firm through expansion of its own output rather than by the acquisition of other firms. Organic growth contrasts with growth by *take-over or *merger, and is typically achieved through the re-investment of *profits in productive activity. In some countries (mainly the UK and the USA) the threat of take-over bids has become so common since World War II that it may have reduced organic growth. This is because firms undertaking *investment for future growth may be more vulnerable to take-over in the short term, and because too much management time is spent concentrating on accomplishing or avoiding take-overs and mergers.

organizational theory, the theory of the operation of organizations and how individuals in organizations behave. Individuals in organizations take up roles: formal roles as managers, supervisors, and employees, and informal roles which may help or hinder the organization. When individuals go to work they take with them their personality, attitudes, preferences, and other behaviourial characteristics. These behaviour patterns impinge on the organization, and it is important that they are taken into account when formal organizational structures are planned. Many theories of organizations have been put forward. In the classical model heavy emphasis was placed on formal structures and on responsibility, authority, and lines of command. Human relations theories of organizations stressed the importance of good human relations in order to achieve good performance by individuals. The systems theory views organizations as systems which input resources (raw material, employees, ideas) and convert them into outputs (finished goods and services).

Organization of African Unity (OAU), an association of African states. It was founded in 1963 to promote unity and solidarity among African states and the elimination of colonialism. All African states except South Africa have at one time belonged. The leaders of thirty-two African countries signed its charter at a conference in Addis Ababa in

In the Golden Triangle of Myanmar, Thailand, and Laos, Khun Sa, seen here with some of the members of his 20,000-strong private army, dominates a powerful network of **organized crime**. He controls 60 per cent of the local production of opium, refines it into heroin, and exports it to the West.

1963. There is an annual assembly of heads of state and government, a council of ministers, a general secretariat, and a commission for mediation, conciliation, and arbitration. The OAU has attempted to bring about reconciliation in regional conflicts, and has supported sanctions against South Africa to bring about the end of apartheid.

Organization of American States (OAS), a regional international organization. Originally founded in 1890 on US initiative for mainly commercial purposes, the OAS adopted its present name and charter in 1948. The major objective of the thirty-two American states which comprise the OAS is to work with the *UN to ensure the peaceful resolution of disputes among its members, to promote justice, to foster economic development, and to defend the sovereignty and territorial integrity of the signatory nations. In general, the OAS has taken an anti-communist stance, and Cuba's membership is currently suspended from OAS activities.

organized crime, the activities of an organization of individuals who profit on a continuing basis from *crime. Organized crime may refer to street gangs; to permanent teams of skilled thieves or confidence tricksters, operating on a small scale; or, more commonly, to criminals responsible for large-scale, often sophisticated international projects, such as art theft and drugs smuggling (see *drug offences). Criminal organizations are often based on shared ethnic or geographical origin (examples would be the Chinese Tongs and the Italian *Mafia). They penetrate many areas of business life, as well as committing offences such as cargo-theft, *fraud, *kidnapping, extracting protection payments, and supplying illegal goods and services. In Japan, a criminal organization known as the Yamaguchi has existed for over 300 years and in modern times more than 100,000 gangsters (*yakusa*) are estimated to be organized in gangs. In the republics of the former Soviet Union, the *vorovkoi mir* ('thieves world'), controls a large-scale black market in consumer goods, especially food. Organized crime poses special problems for enforcement agencies since it is often hidden behind legitimate enterprises, is able to translate the proceeds of crime into businesses, cash, or property (see *money-laundering), and is sometimes able to buy protection from legal action by bribing officials (see *corruption).

organ transplant, the transfer of an organ from a donor to a recipient. Though a kidney, for example, may be given by a live donor, patients dying in hospital are the major source of organs for transplant. How best to provide such organs has been keenly debated. Different strategies include encouraging would-be donors to carry donor cards; allowing organs to be used unless the deceased patient has stipulated otherwise (opting out); and requiring doctors to approach relatives of deceased patients (required request). Cost is another focus of controversy: heart transplants, in particular, have come to symbolize the kind of high-technology medicine, of uncertain benefit, that many think is given too high a priority relative to more basic health care. Another concern is that a desire to use organs for transplant may occasionally result in premature withdrawal of life support; this has prompted calls for stricter segregation of the medical teams responsible for donor and recipient. Finally, it is debatable whether people should be allowed to sell their own organs (usually one of their kidneys) for transplant—a practice now illegal in many jurisdictions.

Orientalism, the study of or interest in the culture of Asia and the Arab parts of Africa. European contacts with the Arab and Ottoman worlds from the 12th to the 18th centuries and the intellectual revolution of the 18th-century Enlightenment led to the systematic study of Asian languages and thereby their culture and history. The 19th-century growth of colonialism and imperialism resulted in the development of views justifying the imposition and continuation of colonial rule: that 'Asiatic' peoples preferred despotic and undemocratic governments; that such peoples were deceitful and lacking in objectivity; and that Eastern societies were irrational and childlike. In recent years scholars, most notably the Palestinian literary critic Edward Said in *Orientalism* (1978) have argued that Western culture uses the term 'orient' to define, subject, interpret, and control the peoples and societies of Asia and the Arab world. Others, however, argue that the term is a useful academic description of the study of particular regions.

original sin, in *Christianity, the doctrine that the *sin of Adam, the first man, has been inherited by all humanity, and confers a tendency to do wrong. The concept of original sin is not explicitly set out in the *Bible, but was firmly established in the writings of St *Augustine. Although certain early theologians maintained that the human will is capable of good without the help of divine grace, this was branded as a heresy and the doctrine of original sin widely accepted. It has served Christianity as an explanation for what is seen as the imperfection of the human condition. Christians believe in redemption from sin through *Jesus Christ's death on the cross, and the *sacrament of Baptism symbolizes the washing away of this sin, through acceptance into the Church. Jesus Christ and, according to Roman Catholics, the Virgin Mary, are believed to be free of original sin.

Orthodox Church   *Eastern Orthodox Churches.

Orthodox Judaism, a major branch within *Judaism which teaches that the *Torah contains all the divine reve-

A pro-birth-control poster in Chengdu, China, where family planning is officially an obligation for every citizen. By the 1960s China was experiencing serious **overpopulation** which led the government to recommend that 50 per cent of rural and 80 per cent of urban couples have only one child.

lation that Jews require. Religious practice demands the strict observance of 613 rules (*mitzvot*), which govern moral behaviour, dress, religious customs, diet, work, observance of the *Shabbat, and personal hygiene. When interpretation of the Torah is required, reference is made to the *Talmud, whose religious authority is second only to the Torah. Unlike modern movements (*Liberal, *Reform, and *Conservative Judaism), whom they do not recognize, Orthodox Jews maintain the separation of sexes in synagogue worship. There is only an Orthodox rabbinate in Israel, with the result that all official religion in that country is Orthodox controlled. While many Orthodox Jews support *Zionism, they deplore the secular origins of the movement and the fact that *Israel is not a fully religious state. For example, the Orthodox recognize a person as Jewish only if he or she has a Jewish mother or undergoes an arduous process of conversion; whereas the Law of Return governing emigration to Israel accepts all those with a Jewish grandmother as potential Israeli citizens.

overpopulation, an excess of people in relation to the resources available to sustain them. The UN's forecast of *population growth suggests that between 1990 and 2025 the world's population will increase from 5.3 billion to 8.5 billion. Almost all of this increase will occur in the developing countries of Asia, Africa, and Latin America. By the late 1980s, 67 nations with 85 per cent of the developing world's population officially considered their growth rates too high. The UN Population Fund now argues that environmental degradation is the gravest immediate threat posed by overpopulation, rather than shortages of food, fuel, and minerals as previously thought. Overpopulation (together with excessive consumption by the developed world) is already contributing to *desertification, loss of agricultural productivity through overuse of land, the destruction of forests and, through the increased burning of fossil fuels, the *greenhouse effect. Already many poor countries, especially in sub-Saharan Africa, are losing their ability to feed, shelter, and educate even their present populations, yet these are the very countries where population growth is expected to be highest. The UN Population Fund believes that only *development can stabilize the world's population and calls for *sanitation, *education, health care, and *family planning in order to reduce *fertility rates. However, the youthful age structure of the world's population means that the effects will only slowly be felt. In consequence, many believe that overpopulation is one of the severest challenges facing the planet.

ozone depletion, the thinning or puncturing of the protective ozone layer in the earth's atmosphere caused by waste products from industrial production. The ozone layer, high in the stratosphere, filters out many of the sun's harmful rays, including ultraviolet (UV). An increase in UV radiation would decrease crop yields and photosynthesis by ocean plankton, affect climate, cause more human sunburn and skin *cancer, and affect the body's ability to fight disease. During the 1980s the scientific community accepted that it was man-made chlorofluorocarbons (CFCs), mainly used in aerosols, in refrigeration, and in foam manufacture, that were responsible for the destruction of the ozone layer, first observed as a 'hole' over the Antarctic in 1982. Over fifty governments signed the Montreal Protocol in 1987, committing themselves to halving output of CFCs by the end of the century. In 1990 agreement was reached to phase out CFC production by the year 2000, but environmental groups argue that nothing short of an immediate total ban will stop the damage in time.

P

pacifism, the belief that *war is never justifiable, no matter how good the cause or how great the threat to one's country. Pacifism springs either from religious faith, as in the case of *Quakers, or else from a humanist belief in the sanctity of life; the religious underpinning can be seen in works such as Tolstoy's *Christianity and Pacifism* (1883). In its purest form it prohibits all use of violence, even in self-defence. Pacifists advocate non-violent means of resisting oppression, drawing especially on the experience of Gandhi's campaign against the British in India (1920–47). Some pacifists, however, while refusing personally to take part in war, would support the use of force by international bodies such as the UN. In this century many states have respected the beliefs of pacifists by recognizing *conscientious objection as a ground for refusing *conscription. (See also *peace movement.)

Palaeosiberian languages, a group of four very small languages which are not genetically related, but which are grouped together because of the similarities arising from extended contact and mutual influence. They once occupied large parts of Siberia and eastern Asia, but were pushed to the periphery by other languages (notably *Altaic and Russian), hence the name Palaeosiberian, which means 'old Siberian'. The largest of the four is a group of five languages called Luorawetlan (or Chukchi–Kamchatkan), spoken in north-eastern Siberia on the Chukchi and Kamchatka peninsulas. The group as a whole has fewer than 25,000 speakers; the largest language within it, Chukchi, has perhaps 12,000 speakers. The second largest is a language-isolate called Gilyuk, which has around 3,000 speakers on Sakhalin island, Siberia, and the nearby mainland. The third is a group of languages called Yeniseian, which was spoken along the River Yenisey in the Russian Federation. Only one language, Ket, survives, and has around 1,000 speakers. Finally, Yukaghir is spoken in small 'islands' in north-eastern Siberia, and has some mere 500 speakers. It has been suggested that Yugakhir is related to *Uralic, but this remains very uncertain. None of the Palaeosiberian languages was written until the 1930s, though *pictograms (on birch-bark) were quite widely used. A script based on the Roman alphabet was initially devised, but was subsequently replaced by one based on the Cyrillic *alphabet.

Palestinians, an Arabic-speaking people who formed the indigenous population of Palestine (a historical region of the Middle East along the Mediterranean now divided between Israel and Jordan), before the establishment of the state of Israel. It is estimated there are 5.25 million Palestinians world-wide, of whom over 1 million live in the territory known as the West Bank (of the River Jordan), which was annexed by Jordan in 1950 and has been under Israeli occupation since 1967. A further half a million live in the territory known as the Gaza Strip, which was administered by Egypt until it too was occupied by Israel in 1967. There are Palestinian refugee camps in Israel, Jordan, Lebanon, and Syria: there are an estimated 929,000 Palestinian refugees in Jordan (where, in all, Palestinians account for about half the population); there are 302,000 refugees in Lebanon, and 280,000 in Syria; and Palestinians are scattered as migrant workers in both professional and menial jobs throughout the world, but particularly in the Gulf States. Deprived of their historic homeland, the Palestinians now claim the right to *self-determination in a Palestinian state. They recognize as their sole legitimate representative the Palestine Liberation Organization (PLO) which was founded in 1964 and is now based in Tunisia. It is an umbrella organization of Palestinian groups of which the most important is al-Fatah. Its leader, Yasir Arafat, is also chairman of the PLO. Democratic elections are held to the Palestine National Council which acts as a Palestinian parliament despite the scattered nature of the electorate. The PLO was recognized by the *Arab League and the UN in 1974 following the UN debate in 1967 which recognized the right to self-determination of every state (resolution 242). Much criticized for its alleged involvement in terrorism, the PLO has attempted in recent years to distance itself from, and reduce, acts of violence and terrorism, but twenty-four years of occupation and repression have led to the ongoing Palestinian *intifaḍa* (uprising) in the Israeli-occupied territories and ensure that violent resistance continues. The PLO recognized Israel's right to exist in 1989 and called for a two-state solution in Palestine; talks between Israel and others continue to founder on Israel's refusal to recognize the Palestinian right to self-determination and reluctance to cede the West Bank, and the reluctance of Israel's principal ally, the USA, to enforce UN resolutions calling for Israeli withdrawal. Palestinian support for Saddam Hussein in the 1991 Gulf War discredited the PLO politically and had disastrous consequences for individual Palestinians resident in Kuwait and other Gulf States; none the less the war again brought the realization that without a settlement of the Arab–Israeli conflict there will never be lasting peace in the Middle East, and an international peace conference was convened in late 1991 under the aegis of the USA, which warned Israel that future US aid would be conditional on Israeli willingness to negotiate.

Pacifism is widespread in Japan, and the Japanese peace movement keeps alive the memory of the suffering caused by war. At a ceremony in Pace Memorial Park, Hiroshima to mark the anniversary of the dropping of the atomic bomb, survivors burn offerings in honour of the victims.

Pali *Indo-Iranian languages.

Papuan languages, languages spoken on Papua New Guinea and surrounding small islands by an estimated 3 million people. The 750 languages which make up Papuan, although highly diverse, are now known to be members of one family. Approximately one-sixth of the world's languages are spoken in this small area (as well as several thousand dialects), which means that it has the highest language concentration in the world, and has resulted in heavy mutual influence. There has also been some influence from *Austronesian languages, which are spoken by people living in the coastal area of Papua New Guinea. Around four-fifths of the country is occupied by a single group of over 500 languages called the trans-New Guinea phylum, while a second group contains about 100 more, and the others fall into smaller groups. The number of speakers of the Papuan languages ranges from a few hundred in some cases to tens of thousands in others. Enga, which is spoken by 165,000 people in the West Highlands of New Guinea, has most speakers. It has been suggested that the extinct languages of Tasmania were also Papuan, but there is no conclusive evidence that they were not part of the Australian family.

paradox (in *logic), the situation that arises when from a set of premisses, all of which would generally be accepted as true, a conclusion is reached by a valid deductive argument that is self-contradictory or that conflicts with other generally accepted beliefs. When a paradox appears we are forced to reject some generally accepted belief or find some way of dissolving the paradox, perhaps by re-interpreting the premisses or the conclusion. The best-known paradox is that of the Liar, where Epimenedes, the Cretan, claims 'all Cretans are liars': if this is true then it is a lie (false), but if it is false then it is true.

paramedical worker, a partially qualified person who plays a part in the health care system. Some paramedical workers have substantial training and play a leading role in *primary health care: nurses in some parts of the world carry out basic medical techniques previously performed by doctors. Another group (often known as 'barefoot doctors') are normally recruited from the population they are to serve and are briefly trained for specific functions such as checking children for *immunization or administering malaria medicines. The country most closely associated with the barefoot doctor is China, where millions of peasants were recruited as the basis of a decentralized post-revolutionary health system. Despite the difficulties of creating and maintaining successful schemes, they are widely accepted as necessary for effective *family planning, health, and nutrition services. In general, experience suggests that tasks should be few and well defined, necessary supplies must be available, and supervision and encouragement must be given by trained workers. In some places, workers have become involved in broader attempts to challenge poverty and patterns of land ownership which they see as contributing to ill health. In the health care system of a developed country, the paramedical worker might be a laboratory analyst, radiographer (who operates X-ray machines for diagnosis and treatment), physiotherapist (expert in physical rehabilitation), speech therapist or pharmacist. New paramedical occupations are constantly evolving: for example, some ambulance staff have become highly skilled in using portable life-saving equipment and do some work once done only by doctors in casualty departments. Their growth has been rapid in recent years, encouraged partly by concerns over the rising cost of medical care.

paranoia, an exaggerated degree of mistrust in others, in extreme cases a feeling of being persecuted, usually accompanied by a feeling of self-importance. Paranoid ideas may form part of the more general disintegration of thinking found in *schizophrenia or they may be found in people who are not regarded as mentally ill, but who are touchy, opinionated, and arrogant. More common among men, paranoid delusions bear a disconcerting resemblance to the beliefs propagated by some religious or political leaders. In the 20th century both Hitler and Stalin expressed paranoid ideas, and murdered those they perceived as persecutors.

parapsychology, the study of human experience and behaviour which suggests that people may gain knowledge or control of their environment in ways which cannot be explained by known mechanisms. An example is the experience of shock which turns out to coincide with the death of a relative many miles away. Surveys since World War II show that most people believe they have experienced such paranormal events. Landmark experiments were described in Joseph B. Rhine's *Extrasensory Perception* (1934). Participants tried to name the shape printed on a card when neither they nor anyone else was looking at the target card (clairvoyance), when someone else was looking at it (telepathy), or before the cards were shuffled and one shown (precognition). Researchers reported many successful demonstrations of these abilities, which do not, however, seem reliable. Proponents of telepathy argue that it is unreliable because telepathic signals are easily drowned by other sensory input, a view supported by demonstrations that depriving people of immediate sensory input or relaxing them through *hypnosis or meditation seems to increase telepathic receptivity. Rhine also reported that some people could will dice to fall one way rather than another (psychokinesis). Recent studies demonstrate people's (limited) influence over computer-randomized events. These results do not persuade sceptics, who allege that parapsychologists suppress non-supportive findings. More serious is the lack of any clear theory, and the chasm between the implied non-physical mechanisms and those recognized by the scientific community.

parental leave, leave of absence from work granted to one or other of the parents to care for a child. Most European countries have provision for maternity leave before and after the birth of a child, with a guaranteed return to work afterwards, although there is no such federal scheme in the USA. In the UK, a woman who has been with the same employer for two years is entitled to eleven weeks' leave before the birth of a child and up to twenty-nine weeks after. A number of employers allow fathers a short period of paid leave after the child's birth. Sweden has the most extensive system of parental leave; parents can choose which of them should take advantage of it. Leave taken within a year of the child's birth is granted on generous terms; furthermore, either parent may work reduced hours on lower pay until the child is 8, and they also have extensive rights to parental leave to look after sick children. The provision of parental leave is important in helping women, in particular, to achieve their full economic potential while raising a family.

Pareto, Vilfredo (1848–1923), Italian economist and sociologist. Pareto's work as a sociologist emphasized the role of *élites; more important is his path-breaking contribution in economics, where he achieved a fusion of welfare economics (see *positive economics) with the general equilibrium analysis pioneered by *Walras. In *Course of Political*

Economy (1906), he was concerned to demonstrate in what precise sense a system of ideally functioning *markets generates maximum social welfare, on the assumption that *utility, or satisfaction, is not a measurable and inter-personally comparable substance, but merely a shorthand way of referring to individuals' subjective preference scales ('ordinal' as opposed to 'cardinal' utility). In other words, any individual is assumed able to choose between any two alternative *consumption bundles, and in so doing maximizes utility. Pareto showed that in certain specified conditions the market system generates a situation, now called a Pareto optimum, in which no single consumer can be made subjectively better off without making at least one other worse off.

parliament *House of Commons, *House of Lords, *legislature.

parliamentary government, a system of representative *government in which the *executive and the popularly elected branch of the *legislature are closely interdependent. The executive, headed by a *prime minister and *cabinet, is drawn from this assembly, and holds office so long as it retains its confidence. This connection gives parliamentary government *legitimacy based on popular support, and provides a direct channel of accountability from the government to the electorate. There are two main variants of parliamentary government, depending on the nature of the legislative party system: cabinet-dominated and assembly-dominated. The former is where the cabinet enjoys disciplined majority support in the assembly from either a single *political party, as typically in the UK, or by a durable *coalition of parties, as in several continental European countries such as Belgium and The Netherlands. This gives the executive considerable strength and stability. In the assembly-dominated variant of parliamentary government, the executive depends upon shifting coalitions within the assembly, as, for example, in Italy or Israel, where the life-span of cabinets has tended to be short. Most Commonwealth countries coming to independence after World War II adopted the parliamentary system of government, but the majority, particularly in Africa, have subsequently amended their constitutions and introduced a *presidential executive system. (See also *prime ministerial government.)

parole (release on licence), the release of a prisoner before expiry of the sentence, on the promise of good behaviour. Depending upon the jurisdiction, a prisoner may apply for parole after serving either a minimum amount of time in custody or a certain proportion of his or her *sentence. It differs from remission (the automatic and unconditional release of a prisoner after serving a certain proportion of the sentence, subject to good behaviour) in that it is discretionary, and the parolee must keep to the conditions of release, which will include supervision by a *probation officer, or face recall to prison to serve the unexpired portion of his or her sentence.

Parsi (Parsee), the name given to the Indian followers of the ancient Persian religion of Zoroastrianism. The Parsis emigrated to India from Iran in about the 8th–10th centuries, to avoid persecution by Muslims. Their belief and worship are based on the *Avesta, the scripture attributed to Zoroaster (628–*c*.551 BC; also known as Zarathrustra). Parsis are monotheists, believers in one God, but they subscribe to the dualist belief that the earth is a battleground for the forces of good (*Ahura Mazdā*) and evil (*Angra Mainyu*). Religious prac-

tice includes the fire temple, where a sacred flame is kept alight, and the tower of silence, upon which the dead are left exposed. Parsis in India live chiefly in Bombay and surrounding areas. They form a wealthy, well-educated, and influential group, noted for the equal role they allow to women. In Iran, a sect called the Gabars, numbering about 25,000, maintains the traditions of Zoroastrianism. There are also significant Parsi communities outside India, for example in London.

Parsons, Talcott (1902–79), US sociologist who synthesized the ideas of *functionalism and attempted to establish a system of analysis which could encompass all aspects of human behaviour, both individual and group. Parsons's interests and writings ranged widely from the specially protected role normally accorded to sick people, to the analysis of business and the professions, and to the effects on the USA of becoming a world power after World War II. Much concerned with how order and cohesion are maintained in societies, Parsons emphasized the shared values which make it possible for people to live together. He further argued that the different parts of a society, such as its educational and political systems, play distinctive roles in maintaining its equilibrium. Parsons is recognized as one of the most influential sociologists of the 20th century, but critics argue that he paid too little attention to conflict and change. Among his major writings are *The Structure of Social Action* (1937) and *The Social System* (1951).

partnership (in business), a form of organization in which by legal agreement two or more people join together for business purposes. Partnerships are common in professions such as accountancy, law, and architecture, where little capital is needed. A partnership contrasts with sole proprietorships on the one hand, and *companies on the other. An advantage is that partners with different specializations can join together to provide a more comprehensive service. Disadvantages are the possibility of disagreements between partners and the risk caused by the lack of limited liability.

parts of speech, a set of categories to classify words in a *grammar. In modern *linguistics, the term 'lexical categories' is often preferred. The most important parts of speech are probably noun, verb, and adjective, but others, such as preposition, adverb, article, and conjunction, are also noteworthy. All these parts of speech are used in the sentence, 'The old man often talked to the boys and girls'. *Man*, *boys*, and *girls* are nouns, *talked* is a verb, and *old* is an adjective. *To* is a preposition, *often* is an adverb, *the* is an article and *and* is a conjunction. Traditionally, the parts of speech are defined in terms of meaning. Thus, nouns are said to refer to persons or things, verbs to actions, and adjectives to qualities. In modern linguistics, however, they are defined in formal terms. Nouns in English, for example, normally have plural forms and can be preceded by an article, verbs normally have a number of different tense forms, and adjectives normally have a comparative form formed with the ending -*er* or the word *more*.

Passover (Hebrew, *Pesach*, 'Feast of Unleavened Bread'), a major Jewish festival celebrated in spring (March–April) and lasting eight days. It marks God's angel 'passing over' the houses of the enslaved Jews in Egypt which had been marked with the blood of a lamb, thus saving their first-born from death and allowing them to escape to the desert. Houses are thoroughly cleaned to remove all leaven (raising

The annual migration to the mountains of Qashqai
pastoralists near Shiraz in southern Iran. The arid plains
where the Qashgai winter their flocks of sheep and goats do
not provide sufficient pasturage in the hot dry summers.

agent for bread, such as yeast), because traditionally the Jews
ate unleavened bread before their Exodus, having had no
time to let it rise. The Seder ('order') meal occurs on the first
and second nights. In commemorating the Exodus from
slavery, Passover recalls and renews the unique historical
identity of the Jewish people to be saved by God, a destiny
emphasized by a series of questions about the meaning of
the festival which must be asked by the youngest present.
The answers are found in the *Haggadah*, or narrative, on the
Passover story, which is read.

pastoralist, a herder such as the *Lapps in Europe or the
*Maasai in Africa. Ecological factors, such as seasonal vari-
ation in available pasture land or the existence of semi-
desert and tundra which will only support shifting grazing
are very important in determining the pattern of pastoralists'
lives. Many pastoralists practise forms of *nomadism. Transhumance, or seasonal movement back and forth (for
example, the Lapps' move from lowland pasture in the winter to highland pasture in the summer), is a form of pastoralism, and tends to be practised by sheep, reindeer, and
goat herders; it is also found among the yak herders of Tibet.
Although the collaboration of a large number of people is
needed for successful husbandry and movement of stock, the
family or household tends to be the basic unit of social
organization, due to the seasonal requirements for the larger
groups to disperse. Livestock is not only important as a
source of food but also for wealth and status, as the use of
livestock as *dowry, for example, establishes relationships
and social position, and status may often depend on the successful use of such relationships to accumulate wealth. *Age-

sets are often an important part of pastoral social organization, acting to create and sustain relationships over large distances and long periods of time.

patent, the exclusive right to make, use, or sell a specified
invention for a limited time. Patents thus form part of general *intellectual property legislation, like *copyright, or the
registration of *trade marks. The term patent derives from
the medieval letters patent conferred by a sovereign granting monopolistic control of specific goods to an individual.
Today, such a right is conferred in almost all countries on an
inventor (or his or her employer) of a new invention, capable
of industrial adaptation. The exclusive monopoly is not conferred automatically, as in the case of copyright; patentees
must define and disclose the invention to their national
Patent Office, which investigates as far as possible whether
the invention is new and non-obvious, and then publishes
the application. Protection only has effect in the country in
which application has been made, but patents can also be
applied for through the Patent Co-operation Treaty, an
international system for the multiple filing of patent applications, or the European Patent Convention, which grants
protection to an invention in all countries that are parties to
the convention. The World Intellectual Property Organization (WIPO) is working towards a treaty setting the norms
for patent protection, and basic standards of intellectual
property protection have also been discussed in *GATT
talks.

paternalism, the management of an economic enterprise,
or a country, in an authoritarian manner that also attends to
the needs of the inferior party, supposedly in a way that reflects relations between a father and his child. The classic
examples given of paternalism are the *plantations of the
Old and New Worlds, and factories in the early years of
*industrialization in Europe and the USA. However, pater-

nalism, or the effort to make an appearance of it, is still present in many agricultural, industrial, and business organizations today. The 'company unions' initiated by employers in the USA in the 1920s and 1930s were employee representation plans to motivate and integrate workers into the company, along with welfare measures such as company housing and leisure facilities. Similar steps were taken at that time in Japanese companies. In both cases part of the motivation was to absorb labour militancy and exclude *trade unions.

Pathan, the dominant *ethnic group of south-east Afghanistan and north-west Pakistan, speaking Pashto, an Iranian language. They consist of sixty *tribes and over 5 million people. Each tribe traces its origins to one ancestor, and is divided into *clans and sub-clans. The family is patriarchal, and *feuds, which sometimes span generations, can be inherited. Although some Pathans are *pastoralists, the majority are farmers, and the rights to land are determined through a complex system of genealogy, while status and rank are also largely inherited. The Pathans are devout Muslims, who have resisted domination by other groups and have a reputation as fierce warriors.

patriarchy, the authority and control of men over women, the converse of *matriarchy. The concept of patriarchy, according to which men control the social institutions and the dominant ideology, has been seen as the general, perhaps the universal, condition of society. For some apologists, patriarchy is justified by the different reproductive functions of men and women. The concept has been attacked by feminist writers, such as Kate Millett in *Sexual Politics* (1969), who saw male political power in the relationship between the sexes, expressed in the sexual act, as the basis of patriarchy. *Gender, the *family, and the processes of *socialization can all be viewed in terms of patriarchy: the traditional view of the family as consisting of father-provider and mother-carer, each fulfilling their allotted tasks, is thought to be influential in reinforcing gender stereotypes in children. Feminists consider *pornography, *rape, and other violence against women, and the subordinate position of women in the workplace and in the home to be associated with patriarchy.

patrilineality *descent, *lineage.

patronage, political, a system of rewards conferred by a political superior (the patron) on a subordinate in exchange for political support. Political patronage is a universal phenomenon, but assumes its greatest importance in states where patrons control access to public goods and services, such as government employment, education, and housing (see *clientelism, *nomenklatura). Political patronage is often associated with *corruption and in many countries there are legal prohibitions against obtaining political office through the promise or supply of rewards to supporters.

Pavlov, Ivan Petrovich (1849–1936), Russian experimental physiologist. He received a Nobel Prize in 1904 for work on the digestive system, but is best known for his discoveries about *conditioning, which were described in *Conditioned Reflexes* (1926) and became the basis of *behaviourism and *learning theory. Pavlov noticed that dogs salivated and secreted other digestive juices when they anticipated food. Anticipation could be aroused by the sight and smell of food, but also by other associated stimuli such as sounds of their keeper's approach. Pavlov inferred that learning is based on association. 'Unconditional' reflexes, such as salivating, which are innate responses to unconditional stimuli, such as food, can be produced by other stimuli which do not naturally produce them, so long as the latter are appropriately paired with the unconditional stimuli. The new 'conditional' stimuli then produce the response in the absence of the original unconditional stimulus. Pavlov demonstrated the circumstances in which such conditioning will occur and persevere or disappear. He saw that these phenomena might explain aspects of human behaviour. For instance, he used conditioning to produce and cure experimental *neurosis in laboratory animals. Pavlov has been a major influence on psychology in the 20th century.

peacekeeping, a process whereby external forces may be used to intervene in a conflict once it has broken out, with a view to effecting a ceasefire, ensuring that it is observed, keeping the conflicting parties apart, and perhaps preparing the way for mediation. A peacekeeping force should have the sanction of a supranational organization such as the *UN; its members should be drawn from those member states of the organization who are not nationally identified with the conflict; and it should operate within strict guidelines (for instance, members may not fire unless fired upon). The peacekeeping mechanism of the UN is now relatively well developed; peacekeeping forces have been sent to the Congo (1960), Cyprus (1964), and the Golan Heights (1974). The UN also sends unarmed observer missions to countries where there is conflict; for instance, the UN Iran–Iraq

Austrian soldiers from the UN **peace-keeping** force in Cyprus (UNFICYP) patrol the deserted village of Athra. The UNFICYP was introduced in 1964, and with intercommunal antagonism still rife and a settlement proving elusive, the Security Council has extended its mandate.

Military Observer Group (UNIIMOG), established in 1988, or the UN Angola Verification Mission (UNAVEM), established in 1989.

peace movement, in the broadest sense, that section of society which opposes, in some degree, *war and preparations for war on moral, religious, philosophical, or political grounds. This group includes those who take an absolutist, *pacifist stand, such as *Quakers, and some *conscientious objectors, as well as many types of international reformers who seek to enhance the *rule of law in international politics, but who perhaps recognize the concept of a just war. In the narrower sense, the term peace movement has been applied to groups who have articulated views on peace in particular times, places, and circumstances, such as the protesters against the Vietnam War, the opponents of cruise missiles (see *nuclear weapons) in Europe in the 1980s, or members of Arab–Israeli peace centres in Israel such as Neve Shalom, where Jews and Arabs work together in communities and schools.

peasants, people who live off the products of their own small-scale farming, but who may also sell some of their crops or give over a share for tax or as a *sharecropping arrangement with a landlord. Contrary to the predictions of writers such as *Marx, the revolutions of the 20th century did not take place in industrial societies, but rather in countries such as the former Soviet Union, China, Cuba, and Vietnam, where most of the population were peasants. This has made peasants a focus of study for social scientists looking at social change and economic *development. Peasants feature prominently in studies of rural Mediterranean societies, but they are found in almost all parts of the world, especially Latin America, Asia, and Africa. Peasant *agricultural production is usually organized through *family and household, with *gender and *age often the main lines of division in the work-force. The extent of economic inequality within peasant societies varies greatly, and there has been much argument about whether peasant societies are internally divided by *social class. As well as economic organization, peasant beliefs such as the *evil eye have been studied, together with the relationship between local peasant *culture and the culture of the wider society to which they belong. (See also *land reform.)

pelota, a group of handball games derived from the French *jeu de paume* and especially popular in Latin America. In *rebot*, a five-a-side game played in the Basque provinces, players catch the ball in a wicker basket attached to the wrist and hurl it back against the end wall of the court. The speed of the ball makes it one of the fastest of all ball games.

PEN (Poets, Playwrights, Editors, Essayists, Novelists), an international association of writers, founded in London in 1921. Membership of the association is open to all writers who subscribe to its principles. PEN promotes friendship between writers from all countries; it fights for *freedom of expression and against *censorship throughout the world, supporting those who have been imprisoned or harassed for speaking out against their governments, or for publishing unpopular views; it raises money for refugee writers; and it promotes the translation of works by its members.

pension   *old-age benefit, *social insurance.

Pentateuch   *Torah.

pentathlon, an athletic contest derived from the ancient *Olympic Games, now reserved for women. Contestants earn points from their performance over one or two days in five events: 100 m hurdles; shot; high jump; long jump; and 200 m. The men's event equivalent to the pentathlon is the decathlon, involving the following ten events: 100 m; long jump; shot put; high jump; and 400 m (first day); and 110 m hurdles; discus; pole vault; javelin; and 1,500 m (second day). Modern pentathlon is different: a multisport contest which includes fencing, swimming, horse-riding, shooting, and running.

Pentecost, Jewish and Christian festivals occurring fifty days after *Passover and *Easter respectively. The Jewish festival celebrates the giving of the Ten Commandments and is the continuation of an ancient Hebrew harvest festival. The Christian festival, also called Whit Sunday, commemorates the descent of the Holy Spirit on to the disciples. It marks the end of Eastertide.

Pentecostal Movement, a part of the *charismatic movement among *Protestants, which started at the beginning of the 20th century. Pentecostalists believe the modern Church should display the same spiritual gifts as the early Church, and advocate what is called 'Baptism in the Holy Spirit', the power of healing, prophesying, and 'speaking in tongues' (the uttering in a heightened spiritual state, of incomprehensible syllables). Usually they hold conservative *evangelical beliefs. Pentecostal Churches have over 35 million full members, and are particularly strong in Latin America. In the UK there are two main groups: the Assemblies of God and the Elim Church.

perception (in philosophy), the sensory process by means of which we get knowledge of the external world. The philosophical problem of perception is *epistemological: how are we to justify perceptual claims to knowledge? This question is not answered by psychology, which already assumes the existence of an external world. The main difficulty consists in showing why we should trust our perceptual experiences, given that we have apparently identical kinds of experience which are illusory, such as dream and hallucination. Philosophical theories of perception include representational realism, which says that external objects are hypothesized in order to explain and match our experiences, and phenomenalism, according to which external objects are in fact nothing but bundles of experiences.

perception (in psychology), the processes intervening between sensation and the mental organization of the experience (cognition). Common sense urges us to trust our senses, but scientists are familiar with *visual illusions and other errors in perception. The initial sensation involves changes in the nerve cells close to the source of the stimulus, and also selection between stimuli. In vision, for example, different distributions of radiant energy give rise to the experience of hue (red, yellow, violet), brightness, and saturation. At the other extreme, our ability to recognize, remember, and describe objects depends on how we name them. A drawing will be remembered and described as having different characteristics depending on how it is named. Furthermore, perception may be influenced or determined by language (see *Sapir–Whorf hypothesis). Attempts to understand the early stages of perception are often linked to characteristics of neurological processes. Thus the fact that any coloured patch can be matched by combinations of only three different lights probably results from the three classes of photoreceptor that mediate colour vision in the eye's retina. There have been attempts to pursue this approach further, either to find out how different neural transformations affect our experience or to find the neurophysiological states corresponding to specific perceived objects (for example, Grandma). Other attempts to describe perceptual processes in psychological terms are usually too vague to produce testable predictions. Some approaches suggest that 'unconscious inference' links our experience, for example of the distance of an object to both the size of its image on the retina and our knowledge of the object's actual size.

perestroika   *glasnost.

perfect competition, a *market structure in which all agents take the market price as given; they cannot alter it because they lack the market power to do so. This implies that there are a large number of firms producing an identical product; perfect entry to and exit from the industry (new firms are able to set up easily); perfect information; and no transport costs. The consequence of these assumptions is that firms will make no excess *profit in the *long run, since any excess profit in the short run will attract new firms into the market, and the increased *supply will drive down the market price, thus eroding the excess profits. Imperfect competition comprises a set of market structures where some or all of these assumptions do not hold; the principal categories arise from *monopoly and *oligopoly.

performing rights, the right to perform, play, or show a *copyright work in public, or to broadcast a work on radio or television; one of the rights protected by copyright. Thus a drama society must obtain permission from the author before it can put on his or her play, or a shopkeeper must obtain the consent of the copyright owner before playing a piece of music in the shop. Because of difficulties in enforcing such rights, they are frequently assigned to 'collecting societies', such as the UK Performing Right Society, who act on behalf of the copyright owners in licensing and enforcing the rights. Performing rights must be differentiated from rights in performances; that is, the rights of performers not to have their performances recorded and reproduced without permission.

perjury (in *common law), the making of a false statement while under oath in a *court of law, before a tribunal, or in front of someone having power at law to hear *evidence. The statement must be materially important, and made wilfully rather than through inadvertence. Perjury is an offence not because lying is immoral, but because it obstructs the efficient administration of justice.

Persian language   *Indo-Iranian languages.

personal identity, that which makes a person the same over time. Philosophical theories of personal identity try to identify what makes a person one and the same at the beginning and at the end of his or her life. The problem of personal identity was first explored in detail by *Locke. He was dissatisfied with Descartes's *dualist view that persons are immaterial *substances (or *souls), since he thought it perfectly possible that a person should be connected to a different substance every minute of their lives, everything else about them remaining unchanged. He also thought that a person could not just be a physical organism, a view which

does indeed seem wrong when we consider that a person's brain, with all their memories and personality, could in principle be transferred to a different body. On Locke's view, the key to personal identity lies in *memory: a person at one point in time will be the same as a person at an earlier point in time, if he can remember performing the actions of the earlier person. There are many difficulties with this view, intuitively appealing as it may seem: what are we to say, for example, of a person whose memory fails completely? Some philosophers, despairing of finding a solution to the problem, deny that there is such a thing as true personal identity, and hold instead that persons are just streams of experiences that might, in principle, merge into one another.

personality, the stable differences between people in social, emotional, and motivational characteristics. The most common approaches to personality in psychology are trait theories, which attempt to show that people do have a limited number of stable characteristics, which exist in a different degree in everyone. Most models of personality development are fairly deterministic, differing only about the relative importance of experience and heredity. The most thoroughly worked out model is *Freud's description of *psychosexual development, which stresses experience. By contrast, research in *behaviour genetics has shown that animals may easily be bred with stable characteristics which seem analogous to human personality traits, such as *aggression and emotionality. They have also shown how these traits are modified by experience and circumstances. In humans twin studies have also suggested that certain characteristics such as *extroversion and neuroticism may be innate. *Learning theorists have attacked the evidence of heritability and stability. Their view has traditionally been equally deterministic, as typified by *Watson's argument that *conditioning would account for adult personality. Recently however theorists like Albert Bandura have offered a *social learning approach to personality. Another important social learning model is *locus of control. This is one of a number of approaches which claim that differences in the way people think affect behaviour, *emotion, and *motivation, and are therefore major personality differences. The most thoroughly worked out of these is the US psychologist George Kelly's *The Psychology of Personal Constructs* (1955).

personality disorder, a term in *psychiatry denoting the state of individuals who do not suffer from a clearly identifiable mental illness but who nevertheless show a profound defect of character and temperament that noticeably interferes with their social relations. There is no agreement about their causes. Some categorizations of personality disorder are purely descriptive, recognizing, for instance, aggressive or dependent types. Others imply parallels between personality types and psychiatric disorders which they resemble. For example, schizoid personality is supposed to share some lesser features of *schizophrenia, such as social withdrawal and difficulty in expressing feelings. Other recognized types are *obsessional, *hysterical, *paranoid, and an antisocial set of traits often referred to as sociopathic or *psychopathic. Personality disorders are often detectable by the time sufferers reach their teens, but may become less noticeable as they get older. Since personality disorders are difficult to change, treatment consists largely of helping sufferers through *counselling and giving practical support so that they can cope better and cause less distress to others. *Drug treatment for specific symptoms such as *depression and *anxiety may also be tried.

personnel management, the work of those, usually specialists, within an organization concerned with *manpower planning, with recruitment and selection of staff, with their training, and with performance review. Dismissal procedures, conditions of *employment, *job evaluation, *wage structures, and *collective bargaining with *trade unions are other significant parts of the personnel management role.

person perception (in psychology), the way people form impressions of others. People have to make sense of others rapidly and on the basis of limited information. They therefore form predominantly evaluative impressions of others, and interpret later information about them in that light. This leads to the 'halo' effect, giving those we like the benefit of the doubt, but refusing to acknowledge good in those we dislike. This effect also appears when people observe others, who have already been described as either 'warm' or 'cold'. People also rely on implicit personality theories, assumptions about which characteristics occur together in the same person, for example happy, talkative, and extrovert. Such beliefs and processes incline to over-simplification and perhaps inaccurate judgements. However, some psychologists dispute such a pessimistic conclusion.

persuasion, the act of attempting to make people change their beliefs or behaviour. The rise of the *mass media led in the mid-20th century to increased interest in the art of persuasion, especially in the fields of *politics and *advertising, *marketing, and *public relations. The art became big business, and sometimes the responsibility of new government departments. It was understood early on that a communicator's credibility depended on apparent expertise and disinterestedness, but less rational considerations, such as the communicator's demeanour, attractiveness, or familiarity may also play a major role. Sequence of information, amount of detail, and explicitness of conclusions also affect persuasion. Reference to negative effects of not acting as advocated can result in fear or resistance, and thereby reduce persuasion. Low self-confidence and good mood seem to make an audience more susceptible to persuasion. New ideas spread by *conformity with persons whose views or status others respect. It is possible to 'inoculate' people against *propaganda by giving them weak versions of an opponent's arguments and revealing their flaws.

pétanque, a ball-and-target game similar to lawn bowls, also known as boule. The wooden jack is thrown by a player in the chosen starting circle to a point between 6 and 10 m (19.5 and 33 feet) distant. The players then toss metal balls (weighing between 620 g and 800 g/22 and 28 ounces) in an attempt to place them as close as possible to the jack. Play resumes with the winner throwing the jack from its position in the previous game. Unlike lawn bowls, pétanque may be played along village streets or in back yards.

phenomenology, a philosophical method developed by the German philosopher Edmund Husserl (1859–1938) and widely employed in *continental philosophy. The key tenet of phenomenology, defined in *Cartesian Meditations* (1931), is that philosophical truth is to be obtained by examining the nature and content of consciousness. Phenomenological investigation emphasizes that consciousness is *intentional, and employs the 'phenomenological reduction', an operation whereby we suspend belief in, or 'bracket', the existence of the things we have consciousness of, such as the external world. This is not undertaken with a view to promoting *scepticism about the external world, but in order to focus on what survives such a reduction: namely, pure consciousness. Husserl thought that we could in this way uncover a special realm of 'essences', and find out how reality is constituted by consciousness. Husserl insisted that phenomenology had nothing to do with introspection in the ordinary sense, and that it was not a form of psychology. Husserl's phenomenology was never brought to completion, but it led directly to *existentialism.

philology   *historical and comparative linguistics.

philosophical logic, the philosophical study of *logic, and the concepts introduced in constructing logical systems. For example, the notion of *validity upon which logical systems depend is defined in terms of negation, *truth, and *possibility, the explication of which is the province of philosophical logic. Similarly any logical system will stipulate an interpretation of the logical constants (words such as 'and', 'or', 'if') and it is the task of the philosopher of logic to examine and if possible to justify such interpretations.

philosophy (Greek, 'love of wisdom'), the use of reason and argument in the search for truth and the nature of reality, especially of the causes and nature of things and of the principles governing existence, *perception, human behaviour, and the material universe. Philosophical activities can also be directed at understanding and clarifying the concepts, methods, and doctrines of other disciplines, or at reasoning itself (see *philosophical logic) and the concepts, methods, and doctrines of such general notions as *truth, *possibility, knowledge (*epistemology), *necessity, existence (*ontology and *metaphysics), and proof. Philosophy has many different areas, classified according to the subject-matter of the problems being addressed; thus, philosophy of *mind is concerned with questions such as 'how does the mental interact with the physical?'; philosophy of mathematics with questions such as 'what constitutes a proof?'; of *religion ('does *God exist?'); of *science ('what constitutes good evidence for a hypothesis?'); of *ethics; of *politics; and indeed of any other discipline. The first philosophers were also the first scientists, people who asked questions about the physical world and who attempted to answer them by observation (see *empiricism) and reasoning (see *rationalism) rather than by appealing to magic or to a God of some kind. These people, known as the pre-Socratics, were the precursors of *Socrates, *Plato, and *Aristotle, the three great philosophers who set the agenda for many of the philosophical questions debated today. Philosophy regularly gives birth to new disciplines as one group of the questions it is trying to answer become amenable to study by the physical sciences. *Psychology, for example, is a discipline that is still in the process of separating itself from philosophy. Great advances in scientific thinking have usually been accompanied by great advances in philosophical thinking. For example, Galileo's work on the mechanics of planetary motion in the late 16th century was a motivating force in *Descartes's work on knowledge and justification, while the physicist Albert Einstein (1879–1955) paid tribute to *Hume as one of the philosophers whose work inspired his theory of relativity. In the 20th century, the principal schools of philosophy are *continental philosophy and logico-*analytic philosophy. Within these principal schools, however, there are major divisions according to sides taken in the various great disputes of philosophy. For example, until fairly recently it was a matter of great concern whether someone was a *dualist or a *monist—whether they believed that there are two different sorts of *substance (the physical and the mental), or only one sort—either the physical (*materialism) or the mental. There are also major disputes about whether or not there are such things as 'innate ideas', concepts that are inborn rather than acquired through experience, and whether we can make sense of a world that is independent of us and our minds (*realism) or whether the mind is in fact more fundamental than some extra-mental reality (*idealism). Rather than being empirical scientists, philosophers try to discern the logical form of the problems in which they are interested and to discover hidden fallacies or habits of mind which might be obscuring understanding. The only experiments indulged in by philosophers are *thought experiments. The interpretation of various doctrines in modern physics is currently of great interest to philosophers: at least one interpretation of the laws of quantum physics would invalidate some of the rules of classical logic. Moreover, advances in engineering, computing and psychology have brought us close to the production of an *artificial intelligence, a fact of interest not only to philosophers of mind, but one that introduces ethical questions of great importance. Major areas in which philosophy can be applied to the problems of everyday life are moral and political philosophy, especially in *medical ethics such as the prevention of conception and the enhancement of fertility. In such cases very deep moral problems arise, the solutions to which require sustained and critical examination of what is right and what is wrong. These investigations are usually carried out by interdisciplinary committees in which philosophers play a major part.

phobia, a type of *anxiety disorder in which there is an unfounded or disproportionate fear of, and consequent urge to avoid, some object or situation. Specific phobias, for example of snakes or spiders, are common and not necessarily disabling in everyday life. Of more concern in *psychiatry is agoraphobia, a fear of public places, which may limit the person's freedom of movement. In treatment by *behaviour therapy, patients confront a series of increasingly potent examples of what they fear. When they can cope with the less terrifying encounters they move on to those they find worse. The patients are often also taught relaxation techniques or other strategies to overcome the build-up of anxiety.

phoneme   *phonology.

phonetics, the analysis of speech sounds as physical entities from the point of view of their production (articulatory phonetics), transmission (acoustic phonetics), and perception (auditory phonetics). Sounds (or phones) are broadly classified as vowels and consonants. Vowels are further described in articulatory terms with respect to the degree of mouth opening, and the positions of the tongue and the lips. Consonants are described with reference to the manner in which the air passes through the vocal tract and the participating speech organs. Among the disciplines drawing on phonetic studies are foreign-language teaching, *clinical linguistics, *phonology, and *sociolinguistics. Many of the applications of phonetics depend on accurate written records (transcriptions) of spoken texts. These use phonetic *alphabets, which have been developed to represent the sound systems of individual languages universally, and more accurately than ordinary alphabets. The International Phonetic Alphabet (IPA), a British invention of 1889, is a widely used example.

phonology, a branch of *linguistics investigating the organization of sounds in *languages. Its major insight is that different sounds may count as a single sound within a language. For example, the p sound in *pill* differs from the p sound in *spill*: only the former is aspirated, followed by a short puff of air. This difference never distinguishes one word from another in English and speakers are unaware of it. A number of sounds that count as a single sound in this way are known as a phoneme. Speech can largely be analysed as a sequence of phoneme segments, but speech also has features extending beyond one segment, notably intonation and tone. Intonation refers to the patterns of pitch or melody performing various grammatical and semantic functions. Tone is a similar feature of individual words, distinguishing one word from another, in so-called tone languages such as Chinese and the Niger–Congo languages.

Piaget, Jean (1896–1980), Swiss polymath biologist, philosopher, and developmental psychologist, responsible for the most comprehensive theory of intellectual development (*cognitive development). Trained as a biologist with an interest in the evolution of organisms, he moved into *child psychology when he realized that intellectual abilities slowly evolve in the child. While working in *Binet's Paris laboratory he became fascinated by the errors children make in *intelligence tests, and proceeded to study the development of logical thinking. He began with the pre-school child's knowledge of the physical environment, especially through the 'conservation' tasks, which test understanding of properties such as number, volume, or mass. The pre-school child fails to understand that such properties remain constant despite surface transformations in appearance. Piaget proposed a universal series of stages of intellectual development from a sensorimotor stage in infants, in which knowledge is expressed through action, through to a formal operational stage characterizing adulthood when reasoning becomes possible with respect to hypothetical situations. Piaget's ideas about the stage-like development of a child's intellect and discovery-based learning have been influential in *education and the design of *curricula.

picketing, a form of *industrial action where people stand outside a workplace in order to discourage other employees from going into work. Pickets may try to prevent deliveries to or from the workplace from crossing the picket line. Secondary picketing is picketing by workers at a workplace other than that of those directly involved in a dispute. Flying pickets move rapidly from one site to another, while the strength of mass pickets is in their numbers.

pictogram, a graphic sign showing an entity or an idea in a direct, representational way. The pictographic system is the oldest form of *writing. Contemporary examples of pictograms can be seen in road signs and other public places. Pictograms are to be distingushed from the more abstract *ideograms.

pidgin and creole languages (from a Chinese corruption of English 'business' and Spanish *criollo*, 'native'), two related types of *language. A pidgin is a *grammatically, lexically, and functionally simplified form of the dominant language in a language contact situation such as colonialism. Pidgins are not 'corrupt' or 'debased' versions of the source language but highly structured varieties with most attributes of a 'normal' language. Well-known pidgins have been derived from English, French, and Portuguese. Creoles are

Yunaited Sios bisop lusim hailans bihain long 16 yia

ISSAC SOKA i raitim

LAPUN bisop bilong Yunaited Sios long Hailans rijon, Bennie Collins i lusim Enga long 22 Novemba na go bek long Yunaitet Kingdom. Bishop Collins wantaim meri bilong em Gwen i bin stap long Enga inap 16-yai olgeta wantaim tupela pikinini meri na wanpela boi.

Taim Bisop Bennie wantaim meri bilong em Gwen i bin pinisim skul bilong tupela long Oksfot Yunivesti, ol i kam stret na mekim wok misin long Hailans. Long dispela taim tupela i lainim planti samting long ol asples na pipel bihain pasin na sindaun bilong ol asples pipel.

Gwen i olsem ol meri hailans stret bikos em i save givim susu long pikinini bilong em na karim em long hailans bilum raun wantaim ol arapela meri hailans. I kam inap nau, taim bilong tupela i pinis nau na tupela i mas go bek long kantri wantaim ol pikinini.

Mista na Misis Collins i kamap long ples balus na ol manmeri i krai nogut tru long lusim tupela i go. Bisop Collins i mekim las toktok bilong em long ol manmeri long ol i mas putim ol yet long han bilong bikpela God tasol na mekim ol samting em i laikim.

Mista na Misis Collins i lusim ol manmeri bilong Enga na long dispela nupela Bisop i redi long kisim wok bilong Collins. Nupela Bisop em Reveren Seru Beraki bilong Fiji husat bai lukautim nau Hailans rijon.

Gorbachev bungim Pop

• Pop John Paul II i toktok wantaim Presiden bilong Rasia, Gorbachev long Novemba 18. Rasia lida i kamap long Rom long toktok wantaim gavman lida na bungim Pop.

The article shown above is from the newspaper *Wantok*, meaning 'friend', published weekly in Papua New Guinea. It is entirely in Tok Pisin, a **pidgin** language spoken by 1 million people in the country and based on English.

pidgins which have acquired native speakers. When this happens there is rapid development in vocabulary, grammar, and style. The status of creoles is the same as that of other natural languages, only their history is different. Being creative adaptations of their source languages, pidgins and creoles are of great interest to *sociolinguistics in the study of socially motivated language change.

pigeon-racing, the sport of breeding and training pigeons to race from a common release-point back to their loft. On arrival, the owner removes a coded race-ring from the bird's leg and places it in a timing clock to record its performance. Pigeon-racing is especially popular in northern England, Belgium, and Germany, where individual owners, known as fanciers, join a local club. To give the birds an equal chance and minimize the effects of changing wind-forces during a race, each club has a small fixed radius of membership.

pilgrimage, travel to sacred places undertaken in order to gain spiritual merit or healing, or as an act of penance or thanksgiving. Most religions have pilgrimage sites, such as sacred rivers, shrines, or buildings, which have traditional religious significance. Every devout Muslim tries to make the *hajj* or pilgrimage to the *Ka'aba in Mecca at least once in a lifetime; Karbala and Najaf in Iraq are sacred to *Shī'ī Muslims. The Ganges at Varanasi (Benares) and the Golden Temple at Amritsar are pilgrimage sites for Hindus and Sikhs respectively. Sites of Christian pilgrimage include Jerusalem (also visited by Jews and Muslims), Rome, and Lourdes in southern France. Whatever the religion and wherever the site of pilgrimage, there are similarities in the structure of all pilgrimages, which may be seen as the equivalent of a *rite of passage with a similar three stages: the start of the journey; the journey itself, and the stay at the shrine or site where the sacred is encountered; the return home. Pilgrimages often involve techniques to encourage and enhance religious experience, and changes in religious status.

pinyin   *alphabet, *Sino-Tibetan languages.

Plains Indians, the original inhabitants of the Plains region of North America. Traditionally, there were two main types, sedentary farmers and nomadic hunters. The introduction of the horse in the early 18th century had a profound effect, with many tribes such as the *Sioux and the *Cree moving into the Plains area. These equestrian *nomads became adept buffalo hunters. During the winter months, the tribes split into small groups. Sporadic warfare was endemic, and status for men was often measured by success through warfare and other dangerous exploits. Although *marriage was mostly monogamous, there were cases of polygyny, especially among those of high status. Patrilineal exogamous clans (based on marriage outside the group) were common, and many of the tribes contained secret societies, or warrior societies, organized as *age-sets, and often involving some form of *totemism. In many tribes, like the *Iroquois, women had a high status. Among men rank was not inherited but had to be achieved through warfare, as well as through generosity towards widows and orphans; *adoption was also a common practice. The title of *chief was largely a matter of prestige, as authority was exercised by the consensus of those of high status, who would act as arbiters in *dispute resolution. In some cases the warrior societies would act to keep the peace. Belief in *magic and elemental spirits was also common.

plaintiff, the person who brings an action on his or her own behalf in a civil suit against a defendant. A plaintiff should be contrasted with the *prosecution in criminal cases, which brings an action on behalf of the state. Commonly, the plaintiff will be suing for *damages for loss suffered as the result of the defendant's actions, or seeking an *injunction to prevent the defendant from engaging in certain behaviour.

planned economy (command economy), one in which (most) resources are allocated centrally by government, rather than by *markets through the operation of the *price system. All *land and *capital in such an economy is owned by the state, and factories are given resources to reach specified targets. The distribution of *income is likewise determined centrally. Eastern Europe, the Soviet Union, and China in the period 1945–90 were closest to this definition of a planned economy, although in some sectors markets and private enterprise continued to exist (in particular in *agriculture and the black economy or *informal sector). The main problems associated with central planning are chronic inefficiency and rigidity in resource allocation, the costs of a large bureaucracy, and lack of incentives for workers and managers. State power over the economy is also associated with authoritarian government and lack of individual freedom (although authoritarian governments are also found in association with capitalist market economies). However, a centrally planned economy may be better able to meet specific priorities, such as fast economic growth or high military expenditure. (See also *free market, *market economy, *market socialism *mixed economy.)

plantation workers, people who work on large estates which produce *commodities such as coffee, tea, sugar, or fruit, usually on a large scale, and for export. Most plantations were founded by foreign colonialists in tropical countries, and can still be found in many parts of the less developed world: in Latin America, where commodity production and regional specialization have increased over the years, and in the Caribbean, South Asia, and parts of Africa. Plantations rely on cheap labour, which is unskilled and very highly supervised. In the Caribbean and the southern states of the USA, African *slaves were used in plantations until the 19th century. Plantation workers even now are often almost entirely dependent upon the plantation, which functions as an enclosed world. Housing, and sometimes health and education facilities, are provided, and family groups have often lived on a plantation for many generations without leaving it.

Plato (c.428–348 BC), Greek philosopher, disciple of *Socrates and teacher of *Aristotle. His work, in dialogue form, is still highly influential. The early dialogues, for example, *Gorgias* and *Protagoras*, are concerned mainly with *ethics, and are negative in character, showing only that we do not understand, for example, what virtue in itself is. Plato is not interested in the various examples of virtue that we see around us, but in virtue itself, what it is and how we can know about it, very much the questions of contemporary ethics. Plato's extraordinarily influential and robust positive doctrines include the Theory of Forms (see *universals), introduced in the *Phaedo*. For Plato, the Forms are changeless and eternal objects of thought appealed to in the explanation of the acquisition of concepts, the possibility of knowledge, and the meaning of words. Thus, particular acts *are* virtuous, are called 'virtuous' and can be known to be virtuous because they are related to the Form of Virtue. The question of just what there is a Form of was examined in the *Parmenides*; their existence was disputed by Aristotle, and is still argued about today. Plato is also noted for his theory of *anamnesis* (recollection) (developed in the *Meno*), according to which much of our knowledge is not acquired through experience, but is known at birth, experience serving merely to jog memory. This theory is a form of *nativism, still a subject of great philosophical interest. The subject-matter of the Platonic dialogues (whose chronology is still a matter of scholarly dispute) spans all areas of philosophy, although the work for which Plato is best known is probably *The Republic*, a treatise on political theory in which he displays both democratic and totalitarian tendencies.

play, an activity carried out for amusement, often based in *fantasy and typical of, but not restricted to, the young. Play is intentional, it tends to be repetitive, and often involves imaginative use of objects. Play is often social, when humour may have a role, but it may be solitary. In either case, reality may be subordinated to the imagination of the child. It may serve to use up surplus energy; to enable the child to develop and comprehend social relationships, or to practise complex motor skills (including speech); or to develop symbolic processes and rehearse intellectual skills, as in *language development. Ritualized forms of play form the basis of games of skill, or of chance. Games may also involve social processes such as competition and rivalry, again sometimes under conditions in which the real world is subordinated to the imaginary world.

plea bargaining (in law), a negotiation which may affect the outcome of a criminal case. It can take several forms. A judge may let it be known that if the accused pleads guilty, he will receive a lower sentence. In other cases, the *prosecution and defence reach an agreement by which the accused pleads guilty in return for an offer from the prosecution (for example, the dropping of other charges, which may be more serious, or the prosecution's influence in requesting a lighter sentence). Plea bargaining is common in the USA; it has the advantage of securing admissions in cases that might be difficult to prove, but can result in the prosecution habitually abandoning more serious charges, which may undermine the administration of justice.

plebiscite *referendum.

Plotinus (AD 205–70), Platonist philosopher. After study in Alexandria he established a Platonic school in Rome. His only writings (*The Enneads*), edited by his follower Porphyry (232–303), were written, without revisions, to record the results of his deeply felt and closely argued exposition of a metaphysical, ascetic Platonism. Although he insisted that everything he taught was to be found in *Plato's writings, his philosophy was both original and profoundly influential. The central idea was of the Three Hypostases: the One, Intellect, and Soul. He was known for his kindliness, and for his opposition to Gnostics, occultists, and Christians. Porphyry commented that he 'seemed ashamed to be in a body', but he denied that the physical universe was wholly corrupt. Later Platonists, because of him, have been much more receptive to the claims of art than Plato was.

pluralism (in politics), a condition in which *power is diffused throughout society with no single group controlling all decisions. A pluralist state is one in which decision-making is divided among many independent groups: for example, government ministers, *civil servants, *interest groups, and local officials. Like exponents of élitism, who believe that power is concentrated in the hands of an *élite, advocates of pluralism acknowledge that, even in a *democracy, decisions are made by a small minority, but they maintain that no single group should dominate all decisions. They also believe that individuals should have an opportunity to become involved in making decisions, even if they often choose not to do so. The intellectual origins of pluralism are in the USA, where the *separation of powers built into the Constitution was a deliberate, and largely successful, attempt to create political pluralism.

Plymouth Brethren, a strict Protestant group, so called because of their early establishment in Plymouth, England, by John Nelson Darby (1800–82) in 1831. The Brethren underwent a major division in 1849, becoming what are known as the 'Exclusive Brethren' and the 'Open Brethren', the latter being the less rigorous. They advocate adult Baptism and reject clergy.

police, a body of civilian officers with particular responsibility for upholding the law and maintaining public order through *crime prevention and crime investigation. National police forces developed in Western Europe and

North America during the 18th and 19th centuries, and have since been adopted by almost all *nation-states. In some countries, the national police force is supplemented or paralleled by regional or local bodies, or by groups set up for particular purposes such as riot control, serious crime detection (for example, the US Federal Bureau of Investigation, or FBI), and other tasks such as traffic control. In addition, national organizations such as railway or airport systems frequently develop their own police forces, with powers of arrest and detention within their areas of operation. Military police forces are given the same powers in respect of service personnel. Most police services make a distinction between uniformed and plain-clothes operations; the former patrol the streets and act as a first line of defence against crime, while the latter are detectives who investigate crime, and who often have close links with *intelligence and *counter-intelligence bodies. Since the late 19th century, there has been a notable development of secret or political police forces, charged with the control of social life and the monitoring of dissident or subversive elements (see *police state).

police state, a state in which a national police organization, often secret, is under the direct control of an *authoritarian government, whose political purposes it serves, sometimes to the extent of becoming a state within a state. The inhabitants of a police state experience restrictions on their mobility, and on their freedom to express or communicate political or other views, which are subject to police monitoring or enforcement. In some cases, the exercise of police control is supported by systems such as internal passports or internal exile, or by punishment camps; likewise, there is often a strict system of *censorship and extensive secrecy. The operation of the KGB (Komitet Gosudarstvennoy Bezopasnosti) in the former Soviet Union, of the so-called *Stasi* (Staatssicherheitsdienst) in East Germany before its reunification with the West, and of the *Securitate* in Romania illustrate the ways in which political, military, and police functions can overlap in authoritarian or *totalitarian societies. Some interpretations of the *national security state suggest that it tends to degenerate into a form of police state, since the need to ensure national security can act as the rationale for ever-increasing control of the citizenry.

political asylum, the protection given by a state to a political *refugee from another country. The 1951 UN Convention Relating to the Status of Refugees defines as a refugee a person who, 'owing to well-founded fear of being persecuted for reasons of race, religion, nationality, membership of a particular social group or political opinion, is outside the country of his nationality and is unable or, owing to such fear, is unwilling to avail himself of the protection of that country...or...to return to it'. The Convention does not guarantee a right to asylum; strictly speaking, in *international law, the right of asylum is not the individual's but the state's to grant protection in its sovereign territory. However, the Convention does declare that a refugee should be expelled only on grounds of national security and should not be returned to a territory where his or her life or freedom is threatened. For humanitarian reasons, most countries acknowledge the right to asylum; however, the asylum-seeker may encounter difficulty in establishing his or her legal status as a refugee.

political organization, the distinctive way in which any *society organizes the working of power and authority. All societies have some form of political organization, which may be concerned with the maintenance of order, and the protection of common territory and resources from external threat, or may be closely tied to religious ideas and the control of important *rituals. Some societies have forms of political organization without any institution we could call a *state; these are sometimes referred to as headless or acephalous societies, as there is no obvious single focus of power. Examples include egalitarian *hunter-gatherers like the *!Kung San, and societies in which political organization is closely tied to *kinship organization, like the *Nuer. In some societies the political order is viewed as a copy of the heavenly order, and the rulers are treated like gods, as in forms of divine *kingship. In these cases, political organization is bound up with ritual organization, although political rituals are as important in modern *democracies as in ancient kingdoms. Political organization is not only found at the highest levels, it is also found locally, where *dispute resolution and *feuds may reveal the workings of *power and authority. In many societies access to power depends on *kinship, especially *descent, but this is often accompanied by considerable competition for political office; even the most 'traditional' society usually shows a great deal of flexibility in deciding who should become a *chief or king. There are few societies today, however, in which the role of the *nation or state does not play a crucial part in political organization, and many figures of traditional authority, like chiefs or kings, now occupy a mainly ceremonial role. Most modern states recognize that ultimate authority lies in the people, and in these circumstances the presence of different *ethnic groups within a single state often leads to conflicts.

political party, a permanent organization which aims to occupy decisive positions of authority within the state, usually but not always through *electoral means. In contrast to an *interest group, a party seeks to form the *government and not just to influence it. Parties are a response to the emergence of the mass electorate. Originally, parties were little more than loose coalitions of notables, but with the extension of the *franchise, parties had to develop a modern organization and a coherent set of policies in order to cultivate electoral support. Parties exist in almost all countries, except where they are banned or suppressed. They may be based on ethnic, religious, or regional identifications or on differing *ideologies. They combine specific interests into an overall political programme, they provide a link between the people and the government, and, if they succeed in achieving power, they reward their supporters and activists with government positions and, sometimes, with benefits such as government contracts (see *patronage). Political parties, whether they operate under *one-party, *two-party, or *multiparty systems, are necessary for the creation of a viable government, and have become an indispensable feature of politics in the modern world.

political prisoner, a person detained or imprisoned because of his or her political beliefs or activities, under laws designed to restrict dissent or opposition. Given the nature of the 'offence' concerned, such detention or imprisonment often takes place under *emergency powers, without trial or appeal; likewise, release of political prisoners is often less a reflection of legal processes than of political change. Perhaps the world's best-known political prisoner of recent times is Nelson Mandela, who was held in South Africa from 1963 to 1990, having originally been convicted of involvement in subversive activities carried out by the African National Congress. Political prisoners who have not espoused vio-

Narguesse Chayessteh, an Iranian teacher, displays evidence of the cigarette burning which she endured during her 17 months as a **political prisoner**. Many political dissidents were subject to torture and imprisonment in the aftermath of the Iranian revolution of 1979.

lence are also sometimes referred to as prisoners of conscience, and form part of the concern of pressure groups such as *Amnesty International. In some countries, classification of prisoners as political may be a matter of serious dispute, as, for example, in Northern Ireland, since it may convey certain privileges not available to criminal offenders. Insurgent or dissident groups often claim political status, since this confers legitimacy on their cause, and enables them to justify the use of violence for political means (see *political violence).

political protest, the use of acts or demonstrations to draw attention to situations, or to particular policies pursued by governments, in which political oppression or injustice is perceived to be present. In many cases, political protest is used by groups or individuals who have little hope of achieving change through processes such as *elections, either because elections have been denied, or because their views are representative of a minority or outsider interest. Individual political protests can take the form, for example, of *hunger-strikes, of self-immolation, or self-imprisonment. Larger-scale political protests can take the form of marches, demonstrations, and strikes. Some of the largest mass political protests have been those against racial *discrimination in the USA during the 1960s, against nuclear weapons in Western Europe during the early 1960s and 1980s, against the communist regimes of Eastern Europe during 1989 and 1990, and against centralized control in the former Soviet Union in the early 1990s. In some cases, the line between peaceful protests (whether individual or mass) and political violence can be very narrow; thus, in 1989–90, the protests against the Ceausescu regime in Romania led to outbreaks of near-*civil war, and the peaceful protest of Chinese stu-

dents in Tiananmen Square, Beijing (1989), led to the use of extreme violence by military authorities.

political trial (show trial), a legal or quasi-legal process in which those on trial are accused of offences against the existing political system or state. It may be used as a means of providing 'legal' respectability for measures taken on political grounds. Those on trial may face trumped-up charges and be denied proper legal representation. Equally, trials conducted under some national security legislation can be attacked as 'political trials' by those who are accused. There is frequently a link between the taking of *emergency powers, the establishment of special courts, and the holding of political trials. In the former Soviet Union, for example, the trials and public confessions of large numbers of citizens in the 1930s, 1940s, and 1950s were used as a basis for *purges of unreliable elements in military or political life. Likewise, in China, the student protests of the late 1980s in Tiananmen Square, Beijing, were followed by political trials, which led to the execution of several student leaders. Those convicted by political trials can become *political prisoners or face *capital punishment.

political violence, the use of violence in order to achieve political objectives. This can range from random violence that breaks out during legitimate political demonstrations, to systematic and organized murder and destruction used to achieve political objectives. The justification for political violence is a problematic issue for both political theorists and those concerned with bringing about political change. It has been argued that the legitimacy of political violence depends on whether or not there exist peaceful, constitutional, and democratic means for bringing about political change or satisfying legitimate interests. Thus, for some theorists, political violence may be justified in repressive political systems but not in democratic political systems. In the contemporary world, political violence has been 'internationalized' by the existence of non-state national groups; for example, the Palestine Liberation Organization, who have used violence in an attempt to pressure the international community to help them achieve their political objectives, in this case a national territory. (See also *terrorism.)

politics, the study and practice of government and the exercise of authority. Efforts are made to influence, gain, or wield *power at various levels of *government, both internally and internationally, rather than in private settings and associations. Modes of political activity are highly diverse, varying from *dispute resolution and formal *elections to the threat or use of outright coercion or force. The degree to which people can engage in political activity also varies in different countries: in open societies, individuals have more freedom to participate in the exercise of political power than in closed societies, where such power is restricted to small groups.

poll tax *taxation.

pollution, the introduction into the environment of substances which are detrimental to human health, to other animals, and to plants. It is estimated that the minority resident in industrialized countries is responsible for 80 to 90 per cent of world pollution. The process of *industrialization has led to the growth of industrial diseases in the workplace and has produced gases such as sulphur dioxide and carbon dioxide, which form blankets of 'smog' over industrial cities. Despite

'Smoking mountain' rubbish dumps in Manila, the Philippines, illustrate the negative side of industrialization. The growth in the country's textile, leatherware, food-processing, and tourist industries has been bought at the expense of such **pollution**.

legislation to control emissions, air pollution continues to be a problem, particularly because of the increased volume of vehicle exhaust gases. *Acid rain, the enhanced *greenhouse effect, and *ozone depletion are all forms of atmospheric pollution. The explosion of artificial chemicals on to the market as drugs, fertilizers, and additives in manufacturing and foods has broadened the scope of pollutants so that there are literally hundreds. Among the most dangerous and widespread (some still widely used, particularly in developing countries) are: industrial waste which have entered water supplies; DDT, a pesticide; asbestos, used to fire-proof buildings; and nuclear radiation from the normal operation of power plants, weapons manufacture, and nuclear-power accidents. Other forms of pollution are: untreated sewage and toxic waste dumped at sea; electromagnetic radiation from electronic equipment and power cables in offices and the home; and noise and light pollution. Industrialists often produce scientific evidence to show that pollution falls within acceptable levels, but levels are regularly revised downwards as new research is carried out. For governments, the control of pollution involves competing priorities of health, industry, and commerce. Where industrial development is at a premium, as in developing countries or the former Eastern bloc, relatively high levels of pollution, especially in urban areas, have been officially sanctioned.

polo, a ball-and-goal game of Central Asian origin played on horseback by teams of four. Players attempt to hit a wooden ball with the side of a mallet through a pair of goal posts on a grass field 182.88 m by 274.32 m (200 yards by 300 yards). The game, which is divided into four to eight chukkas of seven minutes each, is as much a test of horsemanship as of ball-playing skills.

Polynesian societies, those of the eastern central Pacific, including Hawaiians and Samoans, and the people of Tikopia. As well as these relatively small islands of volcanic origin, this culture contains the larger land mass of New Zealand with its *Maori culture. Polynesian languages are members of the *Austronesian group. Polynesians were accomplished sailors and navigators, and established trade routes throughout the region. As well as fishing, they also cultivated small plots of land, whose ownership was vested in corporate kin groups. Their societies were highly stratified, with systems of rank and hierarchy supported by a *creation myth and a complex *kinship system. This had two basic forms, the first with patrilineal *descent from a common ancestor. This depended on both mythology and tradition to validate status. The second form also traced a common ancestor, but ranked people in terms of the whole society and the kin group to which they belonged. Family structures varied between different areas. Religion focused on spirit worship, with a strong emphasis on the idea of *mana*, or power, which was thought to belong to objects as well as people. A system of *taboos and *food prohibitions protected the chief from contact with those who, it was thought, would dilute his *mana*.

pope (in Western Christianity), the bishop of Rome (residing at the *Vatican), and the supreme head of the *Roman Catholic Church. In the *Eastern Orthodox Church, the patriarch of Alexandria is sometimes called the pope, and the title may be used of any priest. Within the Roman Catholic Church, the pope is believed to be the spiritual descendant of St Peter, leader of Jesus' disciples, and his title 'Vicar of Christ' expresses a claim to universal jurisdiction over all Christians. The official doctrine of papal infallibility was promulgated at the First Vatican Council in 1870, to the effect that under certain conditions, when speaking *ex cathedra* (Latin, 'from the throne') on matters of doctrine, faith, or morality, the pope cannot be in error. Since the Second Vatican Council (1962–5) the Roman Catholic Church has emphasized the importance of the bishops working together with the pope on these matters. The pope uses encyclicals (written mandates), circular letters, and, on more important matters, bulls, or apostolic letters, to communicate his views. In recent years, the pope has become an increasingly visible figure, travelling throughout the world on missions to strengthen the Roman Catholic faith and assert the relevance of the Christian message.

Popper, Karl (1902–), Austrian-born philosopher. He published political works hostile to *Marxism, and *psychoanalysis, which he dubbed intellectual superstitions, but is best known for his contribution to the philosophy of *science concerning the correct characterization of the scientific method. Because of the fallibility of *induction, Popper claimed that science could not progress by this method. He suggested, instead, that it used the hypothetico-deductive method. This works by making bold theoretical conjectures, which the scientist then tries to refute by experiment. Science progresses, then, not by verifying its theories by experiment, but by falsification, the active weeding out of those theories that fail experimental testing.

Polo

200 yd
8 yd
40 yd
30 yd
60 yd
300 yd

Goal line
Touch line
Goal
Safety area

1 and 2 Forwards
3 and 4 Backs

population, age structure of, the composition of a population according to the numbers of people in each age-group. The age structure of a population is the cumulative result of past *fertility, *mortality, and *migration and an important determinant of *population growth. The typically very different age structures of developing and advanced industrialized countries may be seen by constructing 'population pyramids' to show the numbers in each age-group. Developing countries characteristically have triangular profiles. In advanced industrialized countries, the age groups are more similar in size.

population, sex ratio in, the ratio of males to females in a given population. The most common calculation normally shows a male predominance at birth of 105 males to 100 females. This gradually declines with age, reflecting superior female *life expectancy. Large deviations from the normal sex ratio (as in India, where the 1991 census found 110 males for every 100 females) indicate practices for ensuring the survival of some (usually male) offspring at the expense of others. *Migration can affect sex ratios, as in South Africa, where for many years a substantial Black male population has worked far from the 'homelands' in which their families were compelled to live.

population density, the number of people relative to the territory in which they live. Over the world's land surface it surpassed 400 persons per 1,000 ha in the early 1990s. The Asian city-states of Hong Kong, Macau, and Singapore, with rates of over 44,000 per 1,000 ha, have the highest densities in the world. High densities as a result of *urbanization are also to be found in many of the rapidly growing cities of Asia, Africa, and the Americas, such as Bombay, Nairobi, and São Paulo. Bangladesh is one of the most densely populated countries in the world, with the result that many of the its inhabitants are compelled to live in low-lying frequently flooded areas. Where people are directly dependent on the land and the food it produces, there is a clear link between their numbers, the productivity of the land, the wealth produced, and living standards. Densely settled farming areas where people live from what they produce may be prosperous, but are often poor because the land cannot support such high numbers of people. In cities, high population density is not necessarily associated with *poverty. Some of the wealthiest people live in high-density urban areas (though rarely with the same numbers of people per room as in the poorest areas) and millions of families of modest means live reasonable lives in them. In cities, the question is whether people, through their resources, skill, acquired wealth, or control over others, can earn a sufficient income, and whether the city has the infrastructure to supply adequate services. For example, The Netherlands and Singapore have high population densities and high living standards, the wider world being the source of their wealth, not just the land they occupy.

population growth, the rate of increase of the world's population, currently at some 90 million people a year. Between 1950 and 1990, the world's population grew from 2.5 billion to 5.3 billion. The UN forecasts that by the year 2025 it will reach 8.5 billion. It is predicted that 3 billion of these additional people will live in the developing regions of Africa, Asia, and Latin America, and only 200 million in the developed regions. By that date 84 per cent of the world's population will be living in the developing regions, compared with 67 per cent in 1950. While population predictions are not infallible, particularly for individual countries, global population forecasts have proved reasonably reliable. In the past, population growth was low because in most societies both *birth rates and *mortality rates were high and roughly balanced each other. With the introduction in many developing countries after World War II of improved health, housing, sanitation, and education, mortality rates fell rapidly, but birth rates and *fertility rates remained high, in accordance with traditional values, leading to unprecedented population growth. By the early 1990s, mortality rates were close to their anticipated minimum, and birth rates had declined or were starting to decline in most countries. If these trends continue, population growth will eventually return to low rates, with births and deaths stabilized at low rather than at high levels (see *demographic transition). However, the youthful age structure of the population in the developing world, where a large proportion of young people have yet to reach their reproductive years, means that the absolute number of births, and the total population, will continue to rise rapidly for twenty to thirty years, if present trends continue, thereby contributing to increasing *overpopulation.

populism, a style of politics that claims to represent the true feelings and aspirations of the people in contrast to the prevailing political establishment. Populist leaders often stand outside existing *political parties and attempt to mobilize the people directly by articulating grievances against the ruling *élite or against foreigners. Examples of populist movements include the Russian Narodniks and the American People's Party in the late 19th century, and in the 1950s the Poujadists in France and the Perónists in Argentina. Often these movements have a specifically agrarian basis. They promise salvation to the poor and exploited by offering a vision of national regeneration, but usually little by way of concrete policies to achieve this.

pornography, the exhibition or description of sexual activity in the printed word, films, or the visual arts, which is intended to stimulate erotic rather than aesthetic feelings.

Population growth

While the population in most of Europe is falling or rising only slowly, population growth in many parts of the world is explosive. Although the average annual growth rate for the world's population, which reached a peak of 2.1 per cent in 1965–70, had fallen to 1.7 per cent in 1980–9, the youthful age structure of the population in many countries and high fertility rates in some, resulted in their experiencing annual average growth rates of more than 3 per cent.

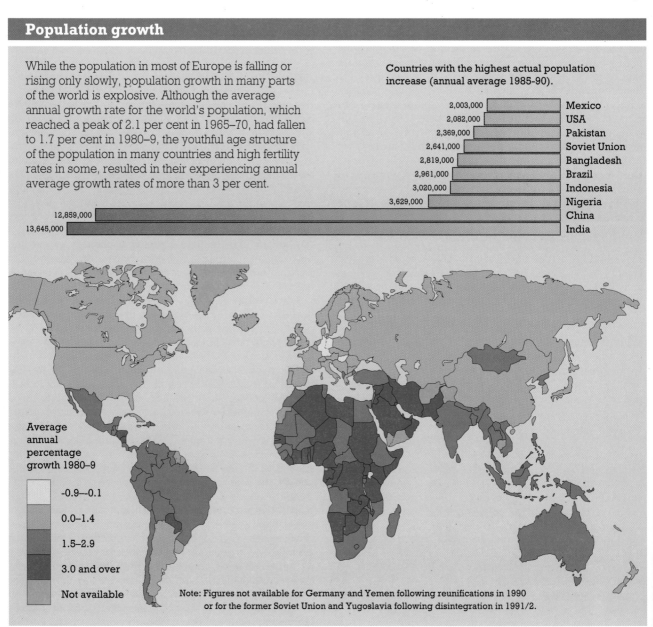

Countries with the highest actual population increase (annual average 1985-90).

2,003,000	Mexico
2,082,000	USA
2,369,000	Pakistan
2,641,000	Soviet Union
2,819,000	Bangladesh
2,961,000	Brazil
3,020,000	Indonesia
3,629,000	Nigeria
12,859,000	China
13,645,000	India

Average annual percentage growth 1980–9

- -0.9–-0.1
- 0.0–1.4
- 1.5–2.9
- 3.0 and over
- Not available

Note: Figures not available for Germany and Yemen following reunifications in 1990 or for the former Soviet Union and Yugoslavia following disintegration in 1991/2.

Source: *World Bank Atlas. 1990.*

Some pornography can be classified as obscene material, a term usually defined as 'tending to deprave or corrupt', although it is notoriously difficult to determine the extent to which obscene material has this effect. Standards change over time, so that writings once held to be pornography may now be held to be literature (for example, D. H. Lawrence's *Lady Chatterley's Lover*, 1928). Different countries have varying standards and different ways of controlling the publication and sale of pornography. Pornographic material itself may range from 'soft' pornography, which produces low levels of arousal, to 'hard-core' pornography, which may involve sadistic violence against women, bestiality (sexual intercourse between a person and an animal), and paedophilia (sexual desire directed towards children). The liberal argument against the banning or censoring of pornography is based on the notion of *freedom of expression, and the belief that the attempt to define what is or is not pornographic may lead to more widespread *censorship. Moral and religious arguments against pornography focus on its perceived tendency to deprave the individual, to undermine conjugal relationships, and to bring about a deterioration in the moral climate of society. In their belief that pornography has a social effect, often leading to an increase in violent and sexual crimes, moral objectors are joined by feminist critics of pornography, who see soft pornography as degrading women through distorted depictions of them as sex objects (see *sexism), and hard-core pornography as encouraging violence against women by depicting them as willing victims of pain and humiliation. The causal connection between pornography and violent and sexual crimes has been hotly debated, but so far the evidence has proved inconclusive.

positive discrimination (US, affirmative action), a term describing policies which aim to counteract the inferior position of groups which have been subjected to *discrimination, especially in terms of *employment, *education, and access to *housing. Supporters of positive discrimination maintain that past negative discrimination against certain groups means that to achieve equality of opportunity they must be given preferential treatment. This may entail, for example, giving a job or university place to a Black candidate who is less well qualified than a White candidate. Such policies have been pursued in the USA in the belief that legislation against racial discrimination may not bring equality, and in the former Soviet Union, in the hope of creating support for the central doctrine of communism among new élites. In India, attempts to reserve jobs and university places for the 'scheduled *castes' (untouchables) are another form of positive discrimination. Opponents of positive discrimination argue that it is unjust and leads to resentment in the majority population, thereby increasing antagonism.

positive economics, that aspect of economics which seeks to discover and explain how actual economies function. It is concerned with what is, not what ought to be, the case. This compares with normative economics, which concerns itself with what ought to be, the derivation of prescriptive statements based on value judgements. Examples of general statements in positive economics are 'as national income rises, so does consumption'; or 'as the price of a good increases, so the quantity demanded falls'. Neither of these statements need be true in all cases. We have to make certain assumptions, including the assumption that other changes do not occur simultaneously to counter the impact of the particular change being considered. In contrast, normative economic statements cannot be empirically proved

or disproved. An example is 'unemployment benefit should be abolished'. A related positive statement would be 'if unemployment benefit is abolished, inequality will increase'. Welfare economics is a generalization of normative economics, examining how economic activity ought to be organized in order to increase economic efficiency and improve human welfare.

positivism *Comte, *social sciences.

post-industrial society, a society whose economy is based on the production of services (see *tertiary industry) rather than manufactured goods (see *secondary industry). The modern concept was elaborated by US sociologist Daniel Bell in his *The Coming of Post-Industrial Society* (1973). According to Bell, a post-industrial society (the USA is taken to be a model) places a high value on 'knowledge' and most of its citizens are well educated. The reduction in industrial production entails the shrinking and eventual abolition of the traditional working class, most citizens being employed in clerical or professional jobs. According to some theorists, in such a society work would become less important, leaving more time for *leisure and for less intensive work. Critics of the idea point out that supposedly post-industrial societies are still dependent on industrial production, but that the factories are now in the *developing countries. They also suggest that the expansion in education and research has largely been concerned with improving industrial production processes rather than with pure knowledge.

post-modernism, a contemporary movement in reaction against that designated 'modern', which has been influential in many spheres: it has influenced art, literature, philosophy and the analysis of contemporary society, *deconstructionism being one of the approaches associated with it. The term came to be widely used in the 1970s to describe the rejection by some architects of the Modern Movement in architecture and the austere functionalism of its buildings. Post-modern architects introduced ornament, colour, and sculpture, often mixing styles in a 'jokey' manner. Post-modernists attack all systems of thought and meaning from traditional *religion to scientific reason, *Freudian analysis to *Marxism—anything with claims to truth. Many hold that Western societies have entered a post-modern phase in which the succession of images projected through the *mass media (and especially *television, videos, and *advertising) defines reality. Post-modernist writings (such as Salman Rushdie's *Satanic Verses* (1988) and Umbert Eco's *Foucault's Pendulum* (1988)) are characterized by their emphasis on the meaninglessness of all 'higher truths', a constant merging of fact and fiction, reality and image. Post-modernism's critics express scepticism about what they see as its pretentious jargon and its cynical and superficial approach to understanding the world.

potlatch, a ritual based on *gift exchange found among *North-West Indians. Potlatches were ritual feasts in which competitors for positions of status sought to outdo each other by giving ever more lavish gifts. The arrival of Europeans in the area during the 19th century, and the changes this brought to the local economy, caused a huge escalation in the scale of potlatches. Large quantities of European trade goods like blankets were not only given away but were also publicly destroyed ito force a rival to equal the gesture.

poverty, the inability to attain a minimal standard of living. Absolute poverty occurs where people have inadequate incomes to attain subsistence standards of nutrition and lack access to basic health care and education. Relative poverty occurs where people fall significantly below average standards of the society in which they live. Absolute poverty is usually calculated by estimating whether households have sufficient income (including own production) to acquire enough food for a healthy life. But the precise 'poverty line' in unavoidably arbitrary because people differ in how much food they need and the distribution of food within the household can also vary. Moreover, an income-based measure of poverty does not capture some essential dimensions of human welfare; households with no access to health or education services are also poor, even if their food needs are met. Therefore, consumption-based measures are often supplemented with others such as *life expectancy and school enrolment rates. In many societies, the poverty line also has a relative element, including income sufficient for people to participate fully in society. For example, in some societies indoor plumbing is a luxury, but in industrialized countries it is regarded as a necessity. The 'head count' measures of poverty—simply counting all people who fall below the poverty line—has been criticized for failing to indicate how far incomes fall below the poverty line. Other, more complex, measures of poverty have therefore been proposed. Many countries construct poverty lines in order to set levels of *social security benefits or 'target' *social services to the most needy. The perception of poverty has evolved historically and varies tremendously between cultures. In general, as countries become wealthier, their perception of the acceptable minimum level of consumption (the poverty line) changes.

poverty, distribution of, the distribution of those unable to attain a minimal standard of living. The World Bank has devised a global poverty line (see *poverty) based on the poverty lines estimated for several countries with low average incomes. In its *World Development Report 1990: Poverty* it reported that about 1.1 billion people in developing countries lived in poverty (defined as living on less than $370 a year) in the mid-1980s. Nearly half of them were to be found in South Asia in countries such as Bangladesh, India, and Pakistan, and another third in sub-Saharan Africa. In these regions, too, about half the population is poor. The Middle East and North Africa have the next highest proportion in poverty, at about a third, followed by Latin America and the Caribbean, East Asia and China at about a fifth. In rich countries, too, there are poor people, but their poverty is mainly relative to the affluence of other members of their society, not entailing inadequate subsistence as elsewhere. The poor are to be found disproportionately in rural areas with high *population densities, in resource-poor areas such as the High Andes in South America, in overcrowded cities where population has outrun productive employment opportunities or, in industrialized countries, especially during *recessions, where the decline of industry has caused high *unemployment. Maldistribution of assets, including *land, *capital, and *education is an important component in poverty. Without assets, such as land, the poor must hire out their labour and without education (see *human capital); they are confined to unskilled work. When their capacity to work is restricted or obliterated by malnutrition, ill health, or old age, their position is even more precarious. Almost everywhere, households headed by women are poorer than those headed by men. The World Bank's experience suggests that the most rapid and politically sustainable progress in eradicating poverty has been made in those countries, such as Indonesia and Malaysia, which have implemented a two-part strategy. They have promoted the productive use of the poor's most abundant asset, labour, and by investing in *primary health care, nutrition, *family planning, and *primary education have enabled the poor to take full advantage of new opportunities. It is also necessary to have a safety-net *social assistance programme of benefits in cash or kind for those who are either temporarily or permanently unable to work. *Land reform has also been an essential aspect of poverty reduction in many societies.

power (in political theory), the capacity to achieve desired ends in the face of resistance. The study of human societies focuses on the power of an individual person, a group, or an institution such as a state *vis-à-vis* others; for example, the power of the US President over Congress, or the power of business over government. Power in this sense means the capacity to induce others to do things they would not otherwise have done; there is a range of ways of exercising power, from *authority to force. There are two main views about the distribution of power in contemporary societies. On one view, élitism, power is concentrated in the hands of a relatively cohesive *élite made up of the leading politicians, industrialists, financiers, military chiefs, and so on (see C. Wright Mills, *The Power Elite*, 1956). On the other view, *pluralism, power is more widely dispersed among a variety of interest and pressure groups, each of which is able to wield influence in its own particular sphere of decision-making (see Robert Dahl, *Who Governs*, 1961). The fact that both views have some plausibility illustrates how difficult it is to find an objective way of measuring power.

power politics, sometimes called realism, a view of world politics which holds that since the world is divided into sovereign states, each state must seek to enhance its national interests by developing and maximizing its own means to power (economic, political, or military) and necessarily competing with others. The idea that the prime motivations in international politics are self-interest and expediency goes back to *Machiavelli's *The Prince* (1513) and *Hobbes's *Leviathan* (1651). For the realist, military capability is the most important means of furthering the interests of the state; stability and order are achieved through the *balance of power, rather than through the co-operation of states within the framework of *international law and *international organizations.

pragmatism, a US philosophical tradition, originally developed by Charles Peirce (1839–1914) and then extended by, amongst others, *James and *Dewey. Its main claims, easily caricatured, are that statements only have meaning to the extent that they can affect our actions, and that *truth is, ultimately, what works for a scientifically sophisticated community. It thus has strong affinities with, but is more subtle than, positivism. Although pilloried by *Russell, it has had a powerful influence on many modern philosophers, especially those drawn towards coherence theories of truth and *epistemology.

prasād (Sanskrit, *prasāda*, 'edible grace'), the food and water offered to a deity as part of Hindu worship or *pūjā. The deity is believed to accept and return the offering and thus consecrates it. The food is then distributed among the worshippers, who thereby receive the god's favour. All food may become *prasāda* if silently offered to the deity before consumption.

precedent, a judicial decision containing a statement of a legal principle which is authoritative not only in that case but also in future cases. The power of courts to make law through precedents operates only in *case law systems. Generally, decisions of higher courts are said to bind lower courts. Only those parts of the reasoning which justify the decision (Latin, *ratio decidendi*) are binding; other remarks (Latin, *obiter dicta*) are only persuasive. Even the *ratio decidendi* of a case does not bind if, in the view of later judges, it was reached without regard to an important consideration or if it has been superseded by *statute or (in some *jurisdictions) changed circumstances. Precedent operates more rigidly in the UK than in the USA, where *judicial review of legislation for inconsistency with an entrenched *constitution gives courts the freedom to re-interpret the constitution without being strictly bound by precedent.

predestination, the belief that all aspects of life and *afterlife are foreordained by God. In Christian *theology, this belief is not incompatible with the notion of *free will: God predestines to salvation those whose future faith and merits he foreknows. The doctrine of predestination is closely linked to that of God's grace: only through divine grace, God's free favour, can man be saved. The French Protestant theologian John Calvin (1509–64) advanced the extreme notion that not only are some souls predestined to salvation, others are predestined to damnation, regardless of their merit or guilt. This idea challenges the idea of free will and implies fatalism. Islamic belief in the predetermined will of Allah (*qadar*) is similarly fatalistic, but in practice the devout Muslim attempts to bring his behaviour into line with the will of Allah, in order to retain responsibility for his actions. The Hindu notion of *karma differs from that of predestination, in that appropriate behaviour in this life determines the quality of future *reincarnations.

prejudice, a bias for, or more usually against, an individual, *gender, or a particular social group without just grounds. Theories of *motivation influenced by the work of *Freud have treated prejudiced behaviour as *aggression which has been displaced from its proper target to low-status social groups as a safe outlet. Best known of these theories is *The Authoritarian Personality* (1950) by the German social theorist Theodor Adorno. It looked for an explanation of *Nazi anti-Semitism in a rigid and repressive family upbringing which led children to admire power but also to develop displaced hostility. The view that *stereotypes typify the oversimplification common to all human thinking about categories (see, for example, *person perception) has led to modern *cognitive theories of prejudice, particularly *social identity theory. It has been assumed that contact between members of different racial groups will reduce prejudice and *racism; this assumption underlay desegregation in the USA (see *segregation). Contact does produce more positive attitudes, but the improvement may not extend beyond the context where contact occurs (school or workplace), and contact in settings which confirm stereotypes or increase hostility may increase prejudice.

Presbyterian Church, a *Reformed *Protestant Church which is governed by elders or presbyters, rather than bishops, in an attempt to follow the biblical pattern. Presbyterian churches oppose state intervention in religious affairs; they advocate the primacy of the Bible as a rule of faith. Worship is usually in simple chapels. The official Church of Scotland, with 1.25 million members, is one of the largest; Presbyteri-

The inauguration of Mary Robinson, Ireland's first woman **president**, at Dublin Castle on 3 December 1990. Robinson, a civil rights lawyer, attributed her victory to votes from the women of Ireland, who 'instead of rocking the cradle rocked the system'.

ans are also widespread in the USA. The Presbyterian and *Congregational Churches in England joined as the *United Reformed Church in 1972.

pre-school education, the education of children before they enter compulsory *primary school. Since children's early experiences significantly affect their subsequent progress, the chief aim in most nursery schools and playgroups is to stimulate their social and intellectual development and to prepare them for school. Some schemes, such as Project Headstart initiated in the USA in 1965, are designed to give under-privileged children a better chance at school and to improve their health and nutrition as well as their education. Another function of some pre-school establishments, such as day nurseries, is to care for the children of working parents. Pre-school education in developing countries is rare, but in industrialized countries it is increasing. In France it is available for 2-year-olds and more or less universal for 4- and 5-year-olds; nine out of ten 5-year-olds attend kindergarten in the USA. In the former Soviet Union, China, Israel, and some European countries, state-provided education is an accepted part of early childhood, but in many others it is limited. Most pre-school education focuses on the child's all-round development rather than on the acquisition of specific skills; group activity such as play, games, making things, painting, singing, making music, exercise, and listening to stories is encouraged. Oral development is stressed before *literacy. The ideas of *Piaget, and *Bruner about *cognitive development have become, with the work of *Montessori and *Froebel, major influences on early childhood education.

president, a non-monarchical *head of state, a post which may also be combined with *executive power and responsibilities. In constitutional states, presidents are chosen in various ways; the most common methods are election by the *legislature, by an electoral college, or by direct popular election (see *electoral systems). The main distinction is between presidential and parliamentary types of executive. In parliamentary systems, a presidential head of state has a mainly ceremonial role, receiving ambassadors, formally appointing ministers, conferring honours, and so forth. Such a president sometimes exercises significant choice among party leaders in the formation of a new government, as in Germany, for instance. Under presidential systems, by contrast, the president is usually elected separately from the legislature for a fixed term of office. He is chief executive and commander-in-chief of the armed forces, as well as head of state. The *US government is headed by such a president. The French Fifth Republic is a constitutional hybrid in which the president is a directly elected head of state, sharing executive authority with a *prime minister appointed by him but who is also accountable to the *national assembly. In many undemocratic regimes, on the other hand, the president is in reality an autocrat, usually backed by the armed forces, and sustained by a combination of force, *corruption, and *electoral fraud.

pressure group *interest group, *lobbying.

preventive medicine, measures taken by the community as a whole, or by individuals, to prevent disease and promote health. According to the World Heath Organization, most of the world's major health problems could be reduced through changes in behaviour. On the level of *public health, better *sanitation, the provision of safe *water, reduced atmospheric *pollution, improved nutrition, *immunization, and *health screening programmes have been effective in preventing disease. Action can also be taken to regulate behaviour, either directly, for example by requiring the wearing of seat belts to reduce injuries in traffic accidents, or indirectly, for example by raising taxes on alcohol to reduce drinking. Health education alerts the population to the risks of certain forms of behaviour (such as *smoking, over-consumption of fatty foods, or promiscuous and unprotected sex, in order to reduce the risks of *cancer, *heart disease, or *Aids. Despite health educationalists' attempts to promote a healthy way of life rather than simply to denounce hazardous behaviour, change comes slowly, if at all. Furthermore, effective preventive measures against most *degenerative diseases have yet to be discovered.

prices and incomes policy, a policy which attempts by regulation or persuasion to influence changes in money prices and incomes, in order to curb or prevent *inflation. By contrast, *fiscal and monetary policies influence pay settlements and prices only indirectly. Incomes policy, which may also be used to redistribute income, typically involves government agreements with *trade unions and industry to restrain increases in pay and prices. This approach, besides being of questionable long-term effectiveness, carries potential dangers of misallocation of resources by interfering with the *price system. An alternative form of incomes policy is to tax companies who grant wage increases above some stipulated rate. Incomes policies were once much favoured as a means of combating inflation, but are largely discredited in favour of *free-market approaches.

price system (price mechanism) (in economics), the mechanism of allocating resources by equating *supply and *demand in *markets through the movement of prices. Where demand is greater than supply, suppliers can raise the price and still sell all their goods. Such a price increase normally has the effect of reducing demand and enlarging supply. Price will increase until demand equals supply. Where demand is less than supply, then similarly the price will tend to fall as suppliers try to undercut each other. This fall in price leads to greater demand and reduced supply. The price system allocates resources by way of decentralized decision-taking. This tends to be quicker and more efficient than central planning, because of the costs to the planning authority of acquiring and processing information. Elements of centrally determined resource allocation may none the less be appropriate where markets for particular goods and services are missing or are highly imperfect. (See also *externalities, law of *supply and demand.)

primary education, the initial stage of education for children between the ages of, typically, 6 and 11 and concentrating on skills such as *literacy and numeracy. Primary, or elementary, education differs from *pre-school education in its greater emphasis on formal study, and from *secondary education in the less specialized nature of the instruction offered. There is considerable variation between national *school systems. In the UK most children start the first of 6 years of primary school at the age of 5, while in the former Soviet Union children entered their eight-year school at the age of 8. In a typical primary school class in the industrialized world, one teacher takes all the lessons with the twenty to thirty children. Over half the school time is spent on reading, writing, arithmetic, and speaking aloud. Elements of history, geography, nature study, science, and social studies may be integrated into this approach, and there may be periods of physical education, music, art, drama, and religious instruction. Two theoretical approaches to primary education have been influential. One is founded on the ideas of 'progressive' educationalists such as *Montessori and *Dewey, who have favoured a focus on developing the individual child rather than learning by rote. The other builds on the research of such developmental psychologists as *Piaget and *Bruner. Primary education is compulsory in the industrialized world and almost all school-age children are enrolled and attend classes. In recent decades there has been a huge increase in enrolment in developing countries, where four out of five children of primary school age are now enrolled. Investment in primary education is the stated educational priority in many developing countries and the UN has called for a shift of resources away from *secondary and *higher to primary education. (See also *education and development, access to *education.)

primary election, a preliminary *election in which voters can decide who will be the party candidate at the next local or national election. Primaries were pioneered in the USA as a reaction to *corruption, *patronage, and manipulation by *political party leaders in the selection of candidates. Closed primaries are restricted to registered party voters, and open primaries occur when all voters can participate in a cross-party exercise. The Australian Labor Party runs a similar 'pre-selection' ballot for the selection of candidates. The advantage of primaries is that they further political choice and participation.

primary health care, the level of health care with which patients first come into contact. It is seen by the World Health Organization as the linchpin of health services. In affluent countries, it is normally provided by a general medical practitioner or district nurse. In the developing world, it is delivered through *paramedical workers with varying amounts of training. Most medical problems can be dealt with at the primary health care level, including the diagnosis and treatment of common ailments, advice, and preventive measures such as *immunization. Based on the rational use of scarce health resources as well as on social equity, the principles of primary health care are now widely accepted, although hospital-based care still consumes a larger proportion of health budgets in all countries. Attracting and retaining trained staff is a significant problem, particularly in rural areas. In some countries, incentives, such as housing, are given to compensate for the lost advantages of working in modern, urban facilities.

primary industry; any economic activity which involves exploitation of natural *resources. *Agriculture, fishing, and mining are major examples of primary industry. It is the dominant form of economic activity in traditional less developed economies. In terms of world *trade, primary industry tends to be economically unstable as a result of changing *commodity prices and unpredictable factors such as climate. Furthermore, the prices fetched by many primary products on international markets have tended to fall in relation to those of manufactured goods. Many countries whose economies are based on primary industries have therefore tried to *diversify into *secondary or *tertiary industries. (See also *exports, *imports.)

prime minister (premier or chief minister), the member of a *government charged with speaking for it in the principal chamber of the *legislature. Where the *head of state is a constitutional *monarch without significant *executive powers, the prime minister is effectively the head of the executive branch, initiating policies and making decisions, even though in constitutional theory he or she merely 'advises' the monarch. Where the head of state is a ceremonial *president, the chief executive is again normally the prime minister. In some countries, however, such as France, executive power is shared between president and prime minister. The relationship between the two offices is then more variable, and potentially conflictual. Where, as is the case in the UK, the prime minister is indisputably head of the executive, the office derives its strength from the prime minister's twin roles as chairman of the *cabinet and leader of the majority *political party in the *House of Commons. (See also *prime ministerial government.)

prime ministerial government, a form of *parliamentary government in which collective decision-making by the *cabinet gives way to domination by the prime minister in a near-presidential manner. The power of the prime minister is compounded from several sources, including his or her authority as party leader and control over the executive, as well as the use of cabinet committees, 'partial executives', and independent advisers, in order to bypass the full cabinet. Increasing personalization of politics and *elections, has also tended to elevate prime ministers above their ministerial colleagues, and to link the success of a *political party to the popularity of its leader. In the UK, given the strength of party discipline in the *House of Commons and the prime minister's wide powers of *patronage and appointment, the tendency towards prime ministerial government under a forceful incumbent can be very strong. In its extreme form, prime ministerial government results in a system dominated

by its chief executive but without the checks and balances that characterize the constitutional presidential executive. Prime ministerial government is less likely to develop where the prime minister leads a *coalition.

privacy, right of, the right, particularly developed in US law, to freedom from interference or *surveillance. In the individualistic societies of the West, privacy is considered a component of individual liberty, but in other societies ideas of personal space may be very different, to the extent that privacy is not regarded as a right or a need. In the USA and Canada, the constitution makes provision for the right to privacy and personal autonomy, although for public figures these rights may be limited (see *defamation). Technological advances in obtaining and storing information may jeopardize the individual's right to privacy, with the result that many countries have introduced *data protection laws.

private education   *independent education.

private language (in philosophy), the notion of a language that can, of necessity, be understood by only one speaker because its words refer to the speaker's own sensations and experiences to which no one else has access. *Wittgenstein argued in the *Philosophical Investigations* (1953) that no such language could exist because it would not be possible for the speaker to make a principled distinction between his using a word correctly and his merely seeming to use it correctly: If 'red' refers to a private experience then only I can determine whether 'red' is being used correctly, but how do I *know* I am using it correctly rather than mistakenly applying it to something quite different on each occasion? Memory is not much help because I can also be mistaken about what I remember. A private language should be distinguished from a coded language used by someone to write a private diary because this is a language that could, in principle, be understood by someone else.

private law, that part of the law which governs relations between private individuals or bodies. It typically deals with obligations relating to the *family, *property, private *companies, and *contracts, and with *torts. However, the range of matters which are regarded as intrinsically private or public varies between societies. In some (such as France), relationships with public bodies are governed by different rules and administered by different courts from relationships between private people or bodies. In the UK, the distinction between *public law and private law is much less well developed.

private sector, those parts of the economy neither owned by the state nor under the direct control of government. Thus it includes households, all privately owned businesses, and non-profit-making organizations such as charities and private research institutes. (See also *public sector.)

privatization, the total or partial transfer of ownership or management of resources from the *public sector to the *private sector. Typically it involves some combination of the sale of *shares, withdrawal of government control, and the contracting out of government-purchased services to private producers. The motives for privatization may be budgetary, economic (to remove inefficiency), or political (to diminish the economic role of the state and to widen share ownership). Advocates of privatization argue that it enhances efficiency, consumer choice, and quality of service,

Public telephones in Argentina, where the **privatization** of the national telephone company, ENTEL, was a central plank of Peronist President Menem's policy for reducing the 20 per cent of the country's work-force employed in the public sector at his election in 1989.

reduces political interference, and raises *capital. With the growth in popularity of *free-market ideas, privatization has become widespread, replacing earlier 'statist' policies whereby it was thought the state should control many industries for reasons of public interest. Governments in Western Europe committed themselves to it in the early 1980s because of a loss of faith in state-run *nationalized industries. By the 1990s it had become an equally central part of economic *liberalization in the formerly socialist states of the Eastern bloc. Notable government initiatives were also pursued in many parts of the developing world, but in some countries a lack of capital and management experience, and opposition from public employees, have presented formidable obstacles. Recent studies indicate that privatization does not necessarily increase competition (a private monopoly may be created), that neither the private nor the public sector is intrinsically more efficient (profitability depending primarily on informed investment, worker motivation, and management control), and that both sectors are interdependent for economic growth. Furthermore, whenever important public services such as water or electricity have been privatized, new systems of *regulation to ensure accountability and consumer protection and to prevent profiteering have proved necessary.

probate, the formal confirmation of a *will granted by the appropriate authority to the person (the executor) who is entrusted with distribution of the assets of the person making the will (the testator). This is normally granted on application by the executor. Where a will is disputed, proof must take place in a formal probate action. In some jurisdictions there is a specific Court of Probate, but in England the High Court is responsible.

probation, a *sentence imposed by a *court of law by which an offender is supervised by a probation officer for a fixed period as an alternative to other *community penalties or to *imprisonment. The court may impose additional requirements such as residence at a hostel or treatment for a mental disorder. The aim of probation is both to assist the offender and to control his or her criminal behaviour. Although this mixture of *counselling and surveillance is inherently fraught with conflict, many offenders complete

their orders successfully. Probation is frequently used in the treatment of young offenders (see *juvenile delinquency). If the offender fails to comply with the order, he or she may be returned to court and given another sentence.

production (in economics), the process of transforming *resources (inputs of *factors of production) into outputs of *goods and services. In economic theory, the production function represents the technological relationship between the maximum amount of output that can be produced from various combinations of inputs. Given input prices along with a production function, a firm's *cost curves (showing production costs per unit of output) can be derived; and thence, once the firm's objective (for example, *profit maximization) and the *demand conditions facing the firm are known, its level of output is also determined.

production management, the planning, co-ordination, and control of the processes involved in the manufacture of products in an organization. It plans how raw materials are to be transformed into products and services efficiently and effectively by the work-force. The choice of *production method enables an organization to produce the right amounts of each of its products to fixed deadlines.

production method, the process by which an organization transforms inputs such as raw materials, by using capital equipment and labour, into added value output in the form of *goods and/or services. There are several major types. Mass production refers to large-scale processes which produce a narrow range of standardized products. A major advantage is that mass production usually provides *economies of scale, enabling the organization to compete on price terms. However, in the 1980s there was a move away from standardization in products to variety and more customization. This trend did not negate the advantages of mass production but required the refinement of production methods, for example using automation and more flexible means of manufacture. Automation involves the use of capital-intensive production control systems which require little or no labour input to operate. Technological advances have made automatic control systems possible in many business processes. Good examples are automatic bar code scanners at supermarket checkouts, which enable constant updating of stock, and robots in car manufacturing processes used to carry out routine tasks on assembly lines. Automation should increase efficiency, speed, and accuracy in the performance of repetitive processes and reduce the need for labour input. Batch production is used where a defined quantity of a product is required at one time. In the same factory many different types of product are being made simultaneously, moving from one machining centre to the next. Sometimes the batches will move into a store to wait until they are needed for subsequent manufacture or assembly. The task of scheduling this form of production efficiently is extremely difficult. This is a very traditional form of production in engineering. Batch manufacture is now being superseded by more modern methods using automation and giving greater flexibility. Process manufacture is a term frequently applied to a product which is made by a small number of simple and related operations, for example, cosmetics and pharmaceuticals. The product is generally amorphous, perhaps a liquid or powder, unlike the products of batch production which are usually engineered metal parts. Process manufacture is usually very capital intensive because it uses large, expensive plant. Flow production involves the use of an assembly line whereby a complicated product such as a motor-car can have many operations performed in sequence. Each operative performs one function as the product is moved along an assembly line, which is usually automated. Automation, including the use of robotics, is common in this type of production, and increases accuracy and quality. (See also *computer integrated manufacture.)

productivity, the amount of output produced per unit of input of a *factor of production. Where total output is measured, productivity measures the rate of output (for example, output per worker-hour). Average productivity is the ratio of total output to total input of the factor in question. Marginal productivity measures the additional output from an additional unit of factor input (*see marginal analysis). Increases in productivity, which are an important source of *economic growth, may come about as a result of technological advance in *capital or as a result of altered working practices.

profession, an occupation, especially one which involves advanced learning or science. Law and medicine are generally taken as the prime examples, but there are many others. Professions in the USA and the UK, where they have been intensively studied, have often been held to share such characteristics as high status, service to the community, the possession of a distinct body of knowledge, adherence to a code of conduct, and self-regulation through a professional association, which may control entry through examinations, and the disciplining of members. Whether occupations such as teaching and the Church, which exhibit some, but not all, of these characteristics, should be deemed vocations rather than professions has often been disputed. Critics see professions as exclusive organizations protecting their own interests, power, and rewards. The demands of the professions for wide discretion in their work and in the disciplining of their members may conflict with the public interest in the maintaining of professional standards and in the equitable distribution of the resources (such as medical treatments) which they control. Such conflict may result in curbs on professional autonomy.

profit (in economics), the difference between sales revenue and production *costs. Economists classify profit into normal profit and excess or super-normal profit. Normal profit is the level of profit which makes it just worthwhile for an entrepreneur to stay in business in the *long run; it is equivalent to the *opportunity cost of *capital and of the entrepreneur's time. While an accountant includes normal profit in the definition of profit, an economist tends to include it in costs of production. Therefore, economic profits represent excess or super-normal profits, which act as a market signal, attracting new firms into an industry so long as there is *perfect competition. In *Marshall's terminology, excess profits are identical to economic *rent. In capitalist systems, some of the profits of an enterprise are usually reinvested in it to ensure that it remains competitive, while the rest accrue to the owner or shareholders. Critics of capitalism such as Marx argued that it is the *surplus value created by workers which is being expropriated. They believed that in a *planned economy profits would be shared equitably among the workers. In practice, however, the lack of incentive to make profits in a planned economy (the surplus being retained by the state) is an important factor in their failure.

proletariat   *Marxism.

propaganda, the attempt to shape or manipulate people's beliefs or actions through the use of information, arguments, or symbols. Propaganda may be printed, broadcast, or visual, but common to all these forms is the attempt to manage and control communication and thereby to affect people's views of the world. All governments engage more or less in propaganda activities, describing them in many cases as public information programmes, and these can be used to influence opinions and actions both at home and abroad. The extent to which propaganda succeeds depends on the freedom of access to alternative views. One common form of propaganda is the dissemination of information designed to create a favourable image of a government or society; another is the use of 'black propaganda' to create suspicions of either the intentions or the actions of another state. Thus, during the cold war (1946–90), Radio Moscow, Radio Free Europe, and the Voice of America were active in promoting the images of their own societies and attacking their opponents. With the growth of international communications systems, propaganda has become an ever more potent political tool, as evidenced, for example, by the attempt by both sides to influence world public opinion through television during the 1991 Gulf War.

property   *property law.

An Iranian **propaganda** poster from the Iran–Iraq war (1980–9) attacks the alliance at that time between the USA and Iraq. The USA feared that an Iranian victory in the war would lead to Iranian dominance in the region and the spread of anti-American sentiment.

property crime, a term used to describe *crimes which involve property, as contrasted with crimes against the person (see *violent crime). In most societies, owning property is seen as a right that must be protected from illegitimate interference, which may take the form either of appropriation, or of damage and destruction. In law, distinctions are usually made according to the means employed, the nature and value of the property, and the 'criminal intent' or its absence. In English law, for example, theft is the dishonest appropriation of property belonging to another with the intention of permanently depriving that other of it. Burglary, a more serious offence, means entering a building or any part of it as a trespasser, with the intention of stealing or damaging property, or raping or inflicting grievous bodily harm on occupants. Arson falls within the second category of property crime, and involves the malicious burning of a house or other building. One could also include vandalism in this category. Crimes against property appear to be particularly prevalent in economically advanced societies which emphasize personal success and material possessions and in which traditional forms of *social control such as close surveillance of young people by adults have diminished.

property law, the law governing the right to control and dispose of property. Property law concerns the allocation not only of material objects such as land or goods, but also of intangibles such as *intellectual property. In private property systems, such as are found in capitalist countries, allocation is based on the concept of individual ownership, which typically confers on the owner of a given resource the exclusive rights to use, occupy, derive income from, and transfer it. Many defences of private property have been offered: it is essential to the operation of *capitalism; it respects the individual need for *privacy; it provides a bulwark against encroachment by the *state. By contrast, in collective property systems such as are found in communist countries, allocation of resources is determined by the public authorities. Where the system is fully implemented, private ownership is not permitted and accordingly businesses and properties cannot be bought and sold, nor can they be passed on by inheritance (see *collective ownership, *cooperative, *land reform). In the countries of central Europe which have abandoned *communism, and in the former Soviet Union, the passage of new property laws has been seen as an essential prerequisite for the growth of indigenous business activities and the attraction of foreign investment. Such laws are necessary both to determine if those dispossessed when the communists came to power are entitled to physical restitution or financial compensation, and to establish the basis on which future business relations are to be conducted. Many countries recognize a 'right of private property' in their constitutions or as signatories to international agreements. In some, such as the Universal Declaration on Human Rights, the institution of private property is guaranteed. In others, such as the Fifth Amendment of the Constitution of the USA, the guarantee is simply that property will not be expropriated without *due process of law or *compensation.

prophet, a person regarded as speaking from divine inspiration in order to reveal the will of God, criticize the present order, or predict future events, such as the end of the world, or the coming of Judgement Day (see *millenarianism). The prophets of the Old Testament of the *Bible strove to instil a moral vision into Jewish belief and practice, and later provided Christianity with a prophetic ideal, fulfilled by *Jesus Christ. The 'gift of prophecy' continues to be a feature of *charismatic Christian movements, and 'inspired utterances' are also characteristic of *Quakerism. In Islam, the term Prophet refers to *Muḥammad, who, through the angel Gabriel, received and revealed the *Koran, the divine word of Allah. Muḥammad is regarded as the last of a long line of prophets, who include Jesus Christ. *Bahā'īs believe that the religion's founder Bahā'u'llah is a further successor to this line of prophets.

proportional representation, an *electoral system which seeks to give parties a share of seats proportional to the number of votes cast for them. Apart from the UK, Canada, and the USA, most *liberal democracies use some form of proportional representation (or PR) rather than *majoritarian representation. In a PR system, the size of a constituency is critical. Each constituency has several seats, and the more seats it has, the more proportional the outcome is likely to be. A common form of PR is the list system. In this, the elector casts a vote for a *political party's entire list of candidates; the number of seats eventually awarded to a party is determined by the number of votes its list receives. If a party is allocated, say, ten seats, then under a strict list system, the top ten candidates on the party's list would be elected. However, in practice, most list systems also allow voters some choice between the candidates of the party they vote for. Belgium, Finland, Italy, Norway, and Switzerland are examples of countries using the list system. The other main form of PR is the single transferable vote, as used in Ireland and Malta. Here, voters rank candidates in order of preference, and complex computations are necessary in order to achieve a result. The main characteristic of this system is that it emphasizes candidates, rather than parties. Whichever form of PR is adopted, however, the normal result is that no party wins a majority of seats in the legislature, often resulting in *coalition governments.

prosecution, the institution and pursuit of a criminal charge in court. The function of the prosecutor is to act on behalf of the state in the best interests of justice. In France, prosecution is conducted by officers of a branch of the *civil service, while in the USA, states have their own prosecutors (district attorneys), who are usually elected to office. In England and Wales the Crown Prosecution Service (CPS) was set up in 1985 to ensure the separation of investigation and prosecution, for both of which the police had formerly been responsible. Once a person has been charged with an offence by the police, the CPS decides whether there is sufficient *evidence for a prosecution, and whether it would be in the public interest.

prostitution, the sale and purchase of sexual relations. Most prostitutes are women, although there are male and homosexual prostitutes; the system of prostitution, however, is almost exclusively organized by men. The attitude of the law to prostitution varies in different jurisdictions. In some it is illegal; in others, it is not in itself unlawful, but certain activities associated with it, such as soliciting, kerb-crawling, brothel-keeping, and 'living off immoral earnings', are illegal; in others it is lawful and subject only to medical controls. Prostitution is usually motivated by poverty; in some places, for example in cities like Bangkok and Calcutta, poverty has generated vast numbers of prostitutes involved in the growing trade of 'sex tourism' and *child sexual exploitation. Across the world, the activities of the prostitutes and their clients are contributing to the rapid spread of

Some of Bangkok's 200,000 prostitutes in a go-go bar in the tourist area of the city. For many Thai women **prostitution** is the only escape route from poverty: they can earn ten times the wage of a waitress or building worker.

the *Aids virus. Feminists tend to view prostitution not as an individual crime but as a system which exploits women; on the other hand, some prostitutes claim that they provide a public service and have campaigned for legalization.

protectionism, the use by government of any measure designed to restrict international *trade or to give artificial competitive assistance to domestic producers. It most commonly involves attempts to reduce *imports by *tariffs, *quotas, and other barriers. Non-tariff barriers also include health and safety regulations, bias in government purchasing, and 'voluntary export restraint' (VER) agreements, among others. Export taxes similarly restrict trade, while export and producer *subsidies give a cost advantage to domestic firms. Although protection may be beneficial (particularly in the short run) to the domestic country as a whole, for example by helping a new industry to develop, it more commonly gives advantages to producers, who may have political interests or lobbies at the expense of consumers who face narrowed choice and higher prices. The *GATT (General Agreement on Tariffs and Trade) is an international agreement intended to reduce trade restrictions world-wide.

Protestant Churches, Western Churches that broke away from the authority of the Church of Rome during the 16th-century Reformation, or divided off from these later. All hold their services in the vernacular (the language spoken in the country), and most emphasize the Bible as the sole source of revelation needed for salvation. A few are 'established' as part of a state–church system, including some *Lutheran Churches, the Scottish *Presbyterian Church, and the Church of England; this last is one of the *Anglican Churches, which include some Roman Catholic traditions that distinguish them from most other Protestants. Others,

including *Baptists, *Congregationalists, *Methodists, *Moravians, and *Pentecostalists, are 'nonconformist' or 'Free', having no connection with the state. Some groups which started within Protestant communities, such as *Adventists, *Jehovah's Witnesses, *Mormons, and *Unitarians, have moved further from the generally agreed Christian doctrines and are not usually accepted by others as Christian Churches.

Protestant ethic, a term developed by the sociologist *Weber to describe qualities of hard work, abstention from luxury, reason, and the steady accumulation of wealth which he associated with northern European Protestantism. In *The Protestant Ethic and the Spirit of Capitalism* (1905) Weber held that these qualities had been particularly conducive to the development of *capitalism in Europe. For Protestants, individual salvation could be gained by hard work and service, in contrast to the Roman Catholic belief that individual grace was not dependent on merit. There has been much debate about Weber's proposition, and about whether he stereotyped capitalism and Protestantism. However, a link between the Protestant ethic and the development of capitalism is still widely accepted.

psephology   *opinion poll.

psychiatry, a branch of medicine concerned with the study and treatment of *mental illness. The conditions coming within its scope are mainly those in which there is no established damage to, or disease of, the brain (these are the province of neurology) and include *psychoses such as *schizophrenia; *neuroses such as *phobias; *depression; *dementia; and *personality disorders. Psychiatrists, who generally work with other professionals such as psychiatric nurses, *clinical psychologists and *social workers, offer varied treatments. These include *drug treatment, electro-convulsive therapy (ECT) (for some forms of depression), *behaviour therapy, *family therapy, *group therapy, *psychotherapy, and individual *counselling and support. The practice of psychiatry is fraught with difficulties. The ethical permissibility of many treatments has been challenged on the grounds that they may have damaging side effects, be of questionable efficacy, and may pose a threat to patients unable, because of illness, to give informed consent. Another problem is that although only a small proportion of mentally ill people are a threat to themselves and an even smaller proportion a threat to others, dangerousness cannot accurately be predicted. The claim by the Hungarian-American psychiatrist Thomas Szasz in *The Myth of Mental Illness* (1961) that psychiatrists were modern-day inquisitors labelling behaviour in order to control people's conduct, was one of the catalysts of a movement which has resulted in the USA and elsewhere in deinstitutionalization and in restrictions by law on the powers of psychiatrists to detain and treat the mentally ill. In response, psychiatrists argue that mental illness, far from being a myth, is to be found in every society, is shown by research to be the result of the interaction of biological (probably inherited) predispositions and environmental factors, and is the cause of immense distress to sufferers and their families for which treatment, even if imperfect, is sought. In 1977 the psychiatrists' international body, the World Psychiatric Association, promulgated the Declaration of Hawaii, a set of ethical guidelines to promote high standards and prevent the misuse of psychiatry, not least in countries where political dissenters are diagnosed as mentally ill and incarcerated.

psychoanalysis, a theory of and therapy for the mental disorders known as *neuroses, and a general theory of *personality and emotional development constructed almost entirely by *Freud. The therapy is one-to-one, over an extended period, and investigates the interaction between the conscious and, by free association of ideas, the unconscious mind, bringing to light repressed fears and conflicts. The theory has been of enormous influence in 20th-century thinking and culture. It gives a central role to the drives of *instinct and the way that *socialization may pervert such drives through too much indulgence or control (see *psychosexual development). Psychoanalysis stresses that instincts and emotions may remain, unacknowledged, in the *unconscious and profoundly affect thought and behaviour. Freud believed that instincts from childhood onwards revolve round physical gratification and are broadly sexual. Subsequently, however, he suggested that we have destructive as well as sexual instincts. The Austrian-British psychoanalyst Melanie Klein (1882–1960) took this idea of *thanatos* (death) and *eros* (love) much further; her work with children is probably the most important contribution to psychoanalysis after Freud. At this period the anthropologist *Malinowski demonstrated that the importance of sexual instincts in personality may not be a universal feature of human development. In *The Ego and the Id* (1923), Freud proposed a tripartite division of the personality into ego ('I'), id ('it'), and super-ego. The id is unconscious and contains primitive emotions and drives. The super-ego contains ideals and moral values. The ego steers between the two, trying to reconcile their demands and the constraints of the real world. It is the seat of *consciousness, but its *defence mechanisms are not conscious processes. Later *neo-Freudian theorists placed more stress on development of the ego and less on the unconscious and sexual motivation (*Jung rejected the centrality of the latter). The theory of psychoanalysis, which is arguably the most inclusive in *psychology has fundamental conceptual weaknesses. Many of its claims are impossible to test by experiment, or, where tested, have not been confirmed. Psychoanalytical therapy seems less effective than some more economic forms of *psychotherapy, *behavioural therapy, and other treatments offered by *psychiatry.

psycholinguistics, a branch of *linguistics concerned with the ways in which human beings process *language and especially with how they plan and produce utterances and perceive and interpret the utterances of others. It looks at such matters as speech errors and the comprehension difficulties that arise with certain types of sentences, and is often concerned with linguists' proposals about the nature of human linguistic knowledge. Psycholinguistics is sometimes seen as including the study of *language development and *clinical linguistics, but these may also be viewed as separate branches of enquiry.

psychological test, a test designed to estimate individuals' capacities or to characterize them on some other basis. There are many standard tests of achievement, ability, and personality, as well as more controversial ones of *cognitive styles based on the finding that people do not all rely on the same perceptual cues or process incoming information in the same way. A test must be reliable and valid. It is reliable if it is free from random error, for example if a person who is unchanged in relevant respects obtains the same result on different occasions or on different versions of the same test. A test is valid if it 'measures' what it is meant to.

An *intelligence test is valid if it correlates with an everyday criterion of intelligence such as academic achievement. A personality test of extroversion is valid if it distinguishes the criterion group of people who exhibit extrovert social behaviour.

psychology, 'the science of mental life', in the words of *James, one of its great figures. Psychology concerns both the normal and abnormal workings of the mind, whereas *psychiatry only deals with the latter. The earliest scientific psychology was the study in the 19th century of sensory *perception. This and other major psychological problems were defined earlier by the philosophers *Locke and *Hume, who theorized about *emotion, *motivation, sensation, *memory, and understanding. The first psychology courses were established in the 1870s by *Wundt at Leipzig and James at Harvard. Experimental method and the development of statistical tests have been crucial to psychology's advance. But major discoveries have been made through more informal work, such as the conversational studies of children's reasoning by *Piaget. In Austria, *Freud created *psychoanalysis in the course of treating *neurosis, but turned it into a general theory of *personality, motivation, child development, and *mental illness. A recurrent question in *behaviour genetics is the relative impact of heredity and experience, particularly very early experience. *Galton introduced modern methods for investigating this, still a dominant issue in studies of *sex differences and of *intelligence and personality. Progress in mid-20th-century psychology centred on *learning theories, especially those of *behaviourism, associated with *Watson, and *Skinner. These derived general laws of learning from animal experiments on the control of behaviour through *conditioning. This work has had important applications in *clinical psychology and the treatment of *psychiatric illness. However, in the 1950s behaviourism's oversimplified conceptual base and sacrifice of realism to experimental rigour came to seem increasingly inadequate. This was one reason for the rise of *humanistic psychology. Technological advances are helping to overcome these problems: it is now possible to record the activities of the brain in various ways; knowledge of genetics has increased dramatically; and computers assist in statistical analysis. Computers have also provided a reference point for *cognitive psychology, which since World War II has become the dominant area of research. It grew out of work on memory and problem-solving, and from the analogy with computers (see *artificial intelligence). It concerns itself with just those kinds of questions for which behaviourism appeared manifestly inadequate: *language development, and the nature and development of human thought and knowledge. Cognitive psychology shares its ancestry in German *Gestalt psychology with modern *social psychology, the other major development since World War II. Social psychology addresses such topics as *prejudice, *relationships, and misunderstandings of ourselves and others. It has also been influenced by *ethology. Psychology finds application in industry, *advertising, *education, child-rearing, and, through *clinical psychology, in the diagnosis and treatment of *psychiatric illness.

psychopathic personality, a term used in *psychiatry to describe a persistently anti-social individual whose abnormally aggressive or irresponsible behaviour cannot be ascribed to low intelligence but stems from a *personality disorder which is largely insusceptible to treatment. There is no agreement on its causes. Characteristic of the disorder are a failure to make loving relationships, impulsive actions, a lack of guilt, and a failure to learn from adverse experiences. Although many people with a psychopathic personality are superficially charming, they show a striking indifference to the feelings of others, being self-centred and heartless. At the extreme, they may callously inflict pain and degradation. Their work record is often unstable and offences are repeated. Many are sent to prison. Although numerous approaches have been tried, the evidence suggests that there is little effective treatment.

psychosexual development, the theory of the role of early experience in determining adult *personality, constructed by *Freud, founder of *psychoanalysis. Freud claimed that the child passes through oral, anal, and phallic stages, a latency period, and the genital stage of puberty. In the oral stage the child's primary pleasure comes from the mouth and its activities, including feeding and exploration. The anal stage is associated with toilet-training: the child must learn to control its impulses. In the phallic stage, at about four, the child's interest shifts to its genitals. It also develops a sexual interest in the parent of the opposite sex and hostility and fear ('castration anxiety') to the parent of the same sex. These feelings are called the Oedipus complex in boys and the Electra complex in girls after characters in Greek myths who sexually loved and murdered the parent of the opposite sex. The hostility and its *anxieties are resolved by identification with the same-sex parent. Those who become 'fixated' at any stage, due to over- or undergratification, may develop problems in adulthood, or characteristics of a so-called oral or anal personality. The former is talkative, generous, and interested in food and drink; the latter is orderly, mean, and obstinate. Empirical evidence supports the occurrence together of these anal characteristics and, more weakly, of the oral characteristics, but they have not been demonstrated to derive in the way Freud argued. His claims about the phallic stage and its sex differences are not well supported, particularly in the application of 'penis envy' to women. However, there is some evidence that over-involvement with the mother may be related to sexual difficulties in males. Later theorists have used evidence from *anthropology and *ethology to build on Freud's ideas and to show that the course of sexual development is influenced by the surrounding culture. In *Childhood and Society* (1950), the US psychologist Erik Erikson (1902–79) expanded Freud's model to eight stages, which cover the entire lifespan. *Bowlby's theory of *attachment and maternal deprivation also derives from the Freudian model.

psychosis (in *psychiatry), the term used to refer to serious forms of *mental illness in which thinking and feeling become so aberrant that the individual loses a grip on reality, may suffer *hallucinations and delusions (as in *paranoia), yet fails to appreciate that anything is wrong. The symptoms can be a sign of brain damage, due for example to longstanding *alcoholism, or the result of taking drugs like LSD (lysergic acid diethylamide). Otherwise the symptoms are most likely to indicate that the person is suffering from *schizophrenia or *manic depression, the two most common forms of psychosis. Psychosis can be contrasted with *neurosis, in which the individual is fully aware of his or her irrational behaviour or emotional reactions.

psychosomatic disorders, bodily diseases caused at least in part by emotional stress. Examples are some forms of ulcer, *heart disease, asthma, and skin complaints. Contentiously, some would argue that all illness is partly psychosomatic, including *cancer. This belief accounts for the popularity of certain forms of 'alternative medicine' that employ psychological techniques such as relaxation.

psychotherapy, the treatment of emotional or behavioural problems by psychological means, often in one-to-one interviews or small groups. *Freud devised the first systematic approach, initially discussing patients' problems with them, but later allowing them to do most of the talking in a procedure called free association of ideas. This has been the model for subsequent psychotherapies. Modern *psychoanalysis and cognitive therapies associated with theories such as *learned helplessness concentrate on the patient's beliefs. Other therapies, such as those within *humanistic psychology, attend to the patient's emotional state or sensitivity. The distinction, however, is not clear-cut, as all these therapies involve intense exploration of the patient's conflicts, and most rely on the emotion generated in therapy as a force in the patient's recovery. In contrast, *behaviour therapies derive from the view that neurosis is a matter of maladaptive *conditioning and concentrate on modifying patients' behaviour. There are arguments about the effectiveness of psychotherapies, but it is generally agreed that success depends on a secure, confiding relationship between the therapist and patient, and on a shared confidence in the capacity of the therapist and his or her theory to explain and eliminate the problem.

puberty rites, *rituals which mark the transition from childhood to adulthood. Many societies mark the approach of physical maturity by a ritual of some sort; for girls this usually occurs at the time of first menstruation, but for boys the timing varies from society to society. In some cultures, *initiation into adult society involves *circumcision, or submission to certain ordeals as a trial of endurance. Where societies mark this particular transition with a ritual, it tends to show the same structure as other *rites of passage: the young people are first separated from their former roles, forced to spend time away from the normal world of everyday life, and then invited to re-enter society in their new role. Puberty rites often provide important expressions of a particular society's ideas about *gender and what it means to be an adult.

public choice theory, a branch of *rational choice theory which analyses political processes and decisions by reference to the personal goals of politicians, bureaucrats, and other participants. Politicians are seen as motivated not by *ideology but by the desire to win office and increase their power; civil servants by the desire to expand their administrative empires and increase their salaries; voters by the desire to maximize the benefits they receive from government policy. Public choice theory, whose classic statements include James Buchanan and Gordon Tullock's *The Calculus of Consent* (1962) and Anthony Downs's *An Economic Theory of Democracy* (1957), examines how the political system will work given these assumptions. For instance, what will parties do to maximize their chance of winning elections? How will governments allocate their budgets between different groups of claimants? It is particularly concerned with cases in which the pursuit of private interests produces outcomes that no one wants. Public choice theorists such as Buchanan believe that the growth of public expenditure in this century is such a case, and have argued for legal restraints obliging the government to balance its budget, an argument that has recently been influential with the *New Right. This approach leads naturally to advocacy of *constitutional government, where the constitution serves to limit the damaging pursuit of private interests in politics.

public finance, government income and expenditure. Public-finance economics analyses *fiscal policy and studies the effects of *taxation and government expenditure on individuals, firms, and national economic aggregates. A special area of public-finance economics is social *cost–benefit analysis, which is used to assess the full economic consequences of government expenditure.

public health, a speciality within *medicine that aims to identify and prevent the environmental and social causes of ill health. It is based on *epidemiology, the study of disease within a population. The traditional concerns of public health include *sanitation and *water supply, air and noise *pollution, food hygiene, nutrition, *housing conditions, and the health and safety of people at work. More recently, public health doctors have also examined the health consequences of social problems such as *unemployment and *poverty. Where other branches of medicine concentrate on the individual, public health focuses on groups and society as a whole. In affluent countries, problems are often tackled by *preventive medicine, and by government regulations, which set standards in everything from food-processing to machinery noise. Sophisticated public health laboratories are also used to identify health hazards, to monitor outbreaks of infectious diseases such as *Aids or influenza, or to trace the source in episodes of food poisoning. It is generally agreed that most of the major advances in *life expectancy in developed countries over the last century have been due mainly to improvements in public health, rather than to the efforts of curative medicine. Likewise, most of the current health problems in developing countries can be attributed to poor public health.

public law, that part of the law which deals with the functions, duties, and powers of state bodies, the relationships between state bodies, and the relationships of state bodies with private individuals and organizations. The term is usually employed in contradistinction to *private law. Public law includes rules of the *constitution and *administrative law, together with much of the law of civil liberties. It is recognized in many societies that the special functions of state bodies necessitate treatment which is different from, and sometimes less indulgent than, that which citizens normally receive.

public ownership *nationalization.

public relations (PR), the management of the public's perception of a business or other organization. PR emerged in the early 20th century as a distinct occupation serving big business corporations in the USA; it was pioneered by Edward L. Bernays, author of *The Engineering of Consent*. Much PR activity is directed at journalists; it therefore operates indirectly, as opposed to *advertising or *marketing direct. PR techniques include the press conference, where journalists are invited to listen to a statement, ask questions, then report; and the written press release. 'Issue management' involves the advance identification of possible problem areas. Other PR functions are speech-writing, and preparation of booklets and reports for customers, shareholders, or other key groups. PR services are widely used by

governments, political parties, and charities, as well as by business.

public sector, the part of the economy under direct national or local government control as contrasted with the *private sector. On the production side, it comprises public services, such as *nationalized industries, and public (state-owned) corporations. On the spending side, government expenditure includes government outlays on goods and services together with transfer payments, such as *pensions and *social security payments. Some of the outlays are on what economic theory calls public or collective goods, that is goods whose consumption by one individual does not preclude consumption by others, such as street lighting and national defence. It may also supply merit goods, such as education, if it considers that private-sector provision would be inadequate to the needs of society.

public sector borrowing requirement (PSBR) (US, government sector deficit, combined budget deficit), the amount which the government needs to borrow to finance its *budget deficit in any given time period, typically a year. The PSBR is equal to the public sector financial deficit (government expenditure minus taxation) plus government lending to other sectors. A negative PSBR is known as a public sector debt repayment (PSDR). (See also *national debt.)

public service broadcasting, a philosophy of non-commercial *radio and *television production. It was devised largely by one man, John Reith (1889–1971), first director-general of the *BBC. Reith claimed that the duty of *broadcasting in a democracy was to 'inform, educate, and entertain' the public, not to meet the requirements of commercial *advertising or government. The concept assumes wide-ranging programmes of high quality, catering for all interests, tastes, and social minorities, available to the whole population, and measured in relation to 'cultural value', not simply size of audience. In 1954 the first not-for-profit educational television station went on air in the USA, hitherto the preserve of the commercial *networks. The new 'ETV' stations in the USA combined into a national, non-commercial Public Broadcasting System in 1969.

publishing, the commissioning, editing, production, and marketing of printed materials such as books, periodicals, journals, specialized magazines, and works of music. The publisher co-ordinates the activities of the author, editor, printer, and bookseller. An essential ingredient in publishing is the contract between publisher and author or composer, which sets out the rights and obligations of both parties. These include *copyright, royalties (the sum paid to an author/composer for each copy of the book sold or public performance of a work), and translation and subsidiary sales rights such as broadcasting and television (sometimes with the help of his or her agent). Modern publishing houses have developed different departments specializing in editing, manufacturing, designing, accounting and marketing, and distribution, while the printing and binding is often done in a country with lower costs. The great innovation of the paperback book (known as pocket book on the Continent), pioneered by Penguin, increased the market for a wide variety of literature, as has the marketing revolution of the 1960s when books were increasingly displayed and sold in public service areas such as airports and food shops. A development that now challenges traditional publishing is the growth in new technologies for the storage, transmission, and distribution of data. Microcomputers with specialized programs and laser printers facilitate desk-top publishing (DTP), which cuts out expensive typesetting and makes even very short runs of highly specialized work economic to produce. DTP is now a growing area in the field of *information technology.

pūjā (Sanskrit, 'worship'), religious observance within *Hinduism, usually involving worship offered to a god or goddess. Personal acts may include lighting incense, giving offerings to the deity, prayer, and the recitation of *mantras. Communal acts of worship, conducted by priests or *pūjāris*, consist of three elements: **havan*, the offering of fire, **ārti*, worship using lights, and the distribution of **prasād* ('edible grace'), the left-over food that has been offered to the god. *Pūjā* in a *Hindu temple may also include a circumambulation of the image of the deity.

punishment (in law), a penalty inflicted for a *crime. World-wide, punishments range from fines to hard labour, *imprisonment, solitary confinement, corporal punishment (including flogging and amputation) and *capital punishment. Since inflicting harm on people is normally prohibited by law and considered morally abhorrent, punishment requires justification. Over the centuries, philosophers, legal theorists, and social reformers have advanced justifications for punishment. The dominant approaches are retributive and utilitarian. A retributivist claims that punishment is justified because people deserve it; a utilitarian points to the useful results of punishment. The idea of retribution—that someone who has wronged others should be penalized and that punishment restores the moral order—is strongly upheld in many societies. *Kant illustrated the idea by arguing that an island society about to disband should still execute its last murderer. For the utilitarian, punishment may have a number of purposes. It may incapacitate the offender temporarily (by imprisonment) or permanently (execution).

This man was sentenced by the Islamic court to receive 100 lashes with a whip in a public square, after having been convicted of making love with a married woman. The sentence was to be carried out in two parts; shown below is the first **punishment**.

It may deter him or others from future wrongdoing. It may demonstrate a society's revulsion at a particular crime or type of crime. It is usually argued that punishment should be proportionate to the crime, but what is judged to be a proportionate *sentence varies widely. In a study by the International Bar Association, involving twenty-three countries and federal states, three judges in each country were asked how they would sentence certain crimes based on identical facts and offenders' criminal histories. For a hypothetical rape case the sentences ranged from 18 months' imprisonment in the Irish Republic to 50 years in Texas. The penalties for a drug offender ranged from a fine in Denmark to a life sentence in Hong Kong, and for tax fraud from a large fine in Australia to 10 years' jail in Germany.

Punjabi *Indo-Iranian languages.

puppet state (puppet regime), a country or government which is ostensibly independent, but is in reality under the control of another stronger power. Following the Japanese invasion of the Chinese province of Manchuria in September 1931, a puppet state called Manchukuo was set up. Similarly the invasion of Afghanistan by the then Soviet Union in 1979 and the invasion of Cambodia (Kampuchea) by Vietnam in 1978 led to the establishment of two puppet regimes backed by invaders.

purdah (from Persian, 'curtain'), the seclusion of women in Islamic society. In the early Muslim period the Persian and Byzantine practice of secluding women was adopted. The *Koran does not stipulate seclusion, although it prescribes modesty for both men and women. In contemporary Muslim society the seclusion and rights of *women are important issues, which are debated in the context of a return to the **sharī'ah* and the rights and wrongs of *westernization.

Pure Land Buddhism, popular Chinese and Japanese schools of thought within *Mahāyāna Buddhism. It is believed that heavenly *Buddhas preside over 'Pure Lands', mystical universes in which a believer may be reborn through faith and through devout prayers to the particular Buddha. In the Buddha's presence, *nirvana may more easily be achieved. The Buddha Amitābha (Amida) is the most important Buddha of these schools of thought and is often associated with the very notion of Pure Land Buddhism.

purge (in politics), the process by which unreliable or dissident elements within a *political party or *government are eliminated, by political, legal, or other means. This 'elimination' may range from dismissal and exile to imprisonment or execution. A purge aims to cleanse the party or government of members who are seen as surplus to requirements or a potential source of opposition to the leadership. Although *authoritarian regimes or those with a strong ideological tinge are the most frequent practitioners of the purge, it can also be used within democratic systems, to bring political changes without *elections. Purges have taken place in the USA and in other Western democracies, notably by Senator Joseph McCarthy and his Senate Committee, when many people accused of communist sympathies in the USA between 1950 and 1954 lost their livelihoods. On a much vaster scale, the 'Stalin purges' of the late 1930s and 1940s in the former Soviet Union led to deaths of an estimated 15 million, while the Great Proletarian Cultural Revolution in China (1966–76) also led to the punishment, political disgrace, or death, of millions.

Purim ('Feast of Esther'), a Jewish festival celebrating the legendary foiling by Esther, the beautiful Jewish wife of the Persian king, of his countrymen's plot to slaughter the Persian Jews. *Pur* means 'lot', and recalls the casting of lots by the vizier Haman to set the date for their annihilation. Thanks to Esther the plot was uncovered and the fateful date was chosen by the Jews to trigger the slaughter of the Persians. Readings from the *Book of Esther* commemorate the salvation of the Persian Jews.

Purusha (Sanskrit, 'man', 'person'), the mythical primal man in Hindu mythology, who was sacrificed by the gods, and from whose dead body sprang the three early *Vedas*, the four major divisions of Hindu society (*castes), and the gods of nature. In the *Vedānta, teaching based upon the Vedas, *Purusha* is identified with the notion of *ātman, and thus with *Brahman. The dualistic philosophy of Sānkhya equates it with pure consciousness, or spirit, as opposed to matter (*prakriti*).

puzzles, the pastime of devising and solving problems using words, numbers, symbols, or the manipulation of objects. The most popular word-game is the crossword puzzle, a feature of many daily newspapers, which requires the solver to fill in the blank squares of a grid by answering numbered clues 'across' and 'down'. Clues can be very sophisticated, based on cryptic references to literature, history, or puns. In a shorter puzzle such as the logogram, the problem is to make shorter words out of a long word; in an anagram, to unscramble letters to form a word. Oral word-games include charades, in which a word, title, or phrase is broken down into syllables or elements and mimed, and Twenty Questions, in which players try to identify a word or object by asking questions about it that must be answered 'yes' or 'no'. Visual puzzles include noughts-and-crosses and tangrams—arranging geometric shapes to form recognizable objects. Many other puzzles have a mathematical base, such as cryptarithms and magic squares.

pygmy, a term used to describe widely scattered peoples characterized by their shortness of stature. The most notable of these are the Mbuti, who live in the Ituri Forest of Zaire. They are *hunter-gatherers, but they also have social and economic ties with agricultural peoples living at the edge of the forest. The Mbuti are subservient in their relations with these neighbours, but when they live among themselves in the forest, their society is remarkably egalitarian. They are organized into patrilineal groups; decisions are made jointly, women playing a full part in all discussions, and childcare is shared among all adults.

Pythagoreans, followers of the mathematician and philosopher Pythagoras (*c*.570–*c*.495 BC), forming a mystical sect centred in southern Italy. Pythagoras' anti-*empiricist philosophy lent itself to religious embodiment. His doctrine that 'all things are numbers' rejected the surface appearance of things as illusory: genuine knowledge of the natures of things, and so appreciation of the underlying order of the world, could be had only by understanding them in arithmetical terms. Pythagoras' view was inspired by his development of the arithmetical theory of harmony in music, and was a major influence on *Plato.

Quakers (correctly termed 'The Society of Friends'), a Christian body which rejects the formal structures of *creed and *sacraments and usually of clergy and *liturgy, emphasizing instead the individual's search for 'inner light'. Founded by George Fox in the 17th century, Quakers spread throughout Europe and created the American state of Pennsylvania. Quakers are known for their social reform, pacifism, and support for philanthropic ventures. They played an important role in the abolition of *slavery, and were instrumental in the foundation of the British-based charity Oxfam, amongst others.

quality control, a system for ensuring that predetermined standards are met in a process. A number of stages can be involved: a check that materials received for the production process are of sufficient quality and consistency; a check that quality standards are being maintained during the production process; finally, a check that the finished product meets quality standards, carried out by inspecting a sample of each production batch. Modern techniques have concentrated on two areas to improve quality: the human and the mechanistic. Following Japanese methods, staff may be formed into 'quality circles' representing all grades of workers and concentrating together on the improvement of quality in specific areas. Computers are also widely used to monitor the output of production machines, stopping the process when the statistically monitored quality level appears to be consistently deteriorating. Quality control is a vital activity. If defective products are not detected before delivery, not only are costs incurred, but the organization's reputation may suffer, causing a reduction in customer confidence and satisfaction levels.

quango (quasi-autonomous non-governmental organization), a special agency or body, often of a regulatory nature, ostensibly of independent standing, and typically straddling the public–private boundary in the economy. Quangos usually receive financial support from the government, which makes senior appointments. Examples include broadcasting authorities, supervisory bodies in the gas, electricity, and water industries, data-protection organizations, and sports and arts councils. The proliferation of quangos reflects recognition, even by *New Right opponents of state intervention and *nationalization, of the need for private interests to be regulated for the public good in certain situations.

quantity theory of money (in economics), a theory of the price level or alternatively of the demand for money, most frequently summarized in the equation developed by the economist *Fisher: $MV = PT$, where M is the *money supply, V is velocity (the speed at which money circulates round the economy), P is the general price level, and T represents the total volume of goods and services transacted. The equation in itself is an identity (it is always true by definition), since the left-hand side represents the total value of money transactions in a given time period and the right-hand side represents the total *value of goods and services sold in that same time period. The quantity theory, however, assumes T and V to be (approximately) constant, so that P is proportional to, and determined by, M. *Monetarists interpret the equation as indicating that *inflation (a rise in P) is caused by the money supply (M) growing faster over time than the economy's capacity to produce goods and services (T). The theory has been criticized on a number of grounds: for instance, that neither V nor T are constant, and that M cannot be adequately monitored or controlled by the authorities.

Québécois, a Canadian of French descent from Quebec province. The Québécois maintain their separate identity through the use of both written and spoken French, in a country which is predominantly English-speaking. Both languages are now recognized by the government as official, and many of the Québécois are bilingual. There have been separatist demands for Quebec to become an independent state, and the province now has a measure of autonomy from the central government. Québécois culture is based on the traditions and folklore of the rural population, including distinct forms of singing, dancing, and music.

Quechua language *South American and Caribbean Indian languages.

quotas (in economics), a limit on physical quantity, most commonly set upon output or *imports. A *cartel, such as *OPEC, may allocate a quota to each producer in order to restrict supplies and keep the product price up to an agreed or target level. The success of such a strategy depends upon the willingness of individual producers to remain within their agreed quota. In international trade, a country or common market may set a maximum level of imports of a specified good in a given time, as a method of *protection. Quotas may be preferred to *tariffs if a country wants the absolute volume of imports to be kept below a certain level.

rabbi (Hebrew, 'master'), the title given to Jewish religious teachers, and, after the Temple's destruction in AD 70, used of any ordained exponent of Jewish Law (see *Talmud). Rabbi Judah (AD 135–217), compiler of the authoritative *Mishnah, is considered the rabbinic exemplar. The rabbi is not a priest and there is usually not a rabbi at every synagogue; he may conduct services and be invited to preach sermons, but he is not essential in, for example, Orthodox marriages. Rabbis are responsible for the religious instruction of the young, and are expected to marry and have children as an example to the community. *Liberal, *Reform, and *Conservative Judaism now permit the ordination of women rabbis, but Orthodox Judaism does not.

race, an imprecise term referring to the division of humanity into different groups according to real or imagined common *descent. Such divisions are usually based on physical characteristics such as skin and hair colour, and shape of eyes and nose, which are related to the geographical origins of a particular group. In the 19th century, it was believed that human beings could be unambiguously classed as members of particular races, and that social and cultural differences could be explained on racial grounds. The notion of race as a rigid classification or genetic system has largely been abandoned, and it is generally acknowledged that human races are relative sub-divisions of one species, which have migrated and interbred over time. There is, however, a small minority of exponents of much-disputed theories that race and attributes such as intelligence are connected. (See also *ethnic group.)

racism, the belief that human abilities are determined by *race or *ethnic group, often expressed as an assertion of superiority by one race or group over another, and *prejudice against or even hatred of particular groups. Often race is confused with '*culture', so that dislike of certain cultural practices is used to condemn a racial group as a whole. Racism is often an underlying issue in the political and economic factors that lead to world wars and strife. It is explicit in some political ideologies, such as *fascism. An extreme example of the consequences of racism is that of the German *Nazis, whose belief that fair-haired Nordic or Germanic peoples were far superior to Jews and other 'non-Aryans' led to the *genocide of millions of Jews, Slavs, and gypsies in Europe during Nazi rule (1933–45). Racism has also been responsible for political systems such as apartheid in South Africa, which keep different races apart, ensuring that they use separate facilities and do not meet socially. Even where it is not institutionalized, racism may still have a great influence, affecting the access to education or employment that is given to ethnic groups.

radio, sound *broadcasting. In the first quarter of the 20th century, 'wireless telegraphy' of messages in dot-and-dash Morse code (used largely at sea) progressed to 'radio telephony' of speech and music. By 1925 there were some 600 radio stations broadcasting world-wide and radio soon became ubiquitous, offering entertainment and instruction, *news and *advertising; innovations included soap operas and quiz shows. Because radio frequencies are widely used in communications by aircraft, ships, police, and for all the messages carried by *satellite transmission, as well as by broadcasting services, access to them is regulated by national agencies, such as the Federal Communications Commission in the USA, and by the International Telecommunications Union, a specialized agency of the UN. In the USA, commercial radio is financed by *advertising, and control is minimal apart from allocation of wavelengths to stations. Most other governments exercise greater control, and some encourage *public service broadcasting. Shortwave radio broadcasting spread during World War II for news and armed forces networks. After television supplanted radio as the chief broadcasting *medium, some stations began to target more local or specialist interest audiences (see *narrowcasting). Chat shows, phone-ins, and disc-jockeys came to greater prominence. Radio sets became portable with the development of the transistor in 1948, and the number of stations and receiving sets multiplied: in the late 1980s there was one set per six persons in developing countries compared with over one set per person in the industrialized world. Community stations have been set up in response to demands for citizens' access, notably in Europe. In Japan local mini-stations broadcast up to a distance of half a mile. The future of radio lies largely in its potential for developing countries and in new technologies such as microwave *satellite communication: both possibilities raise the same questions of access and control voiced by earlier generations of amateur radio 'hams' and by enthusiasts for citizen's band (CB) radio, which was deregulated in the USA in 1983 and subsequently in other countries.

Ramadan, the ninth month of the Islamic calendar, commemorating the revelation of the *Koran; Ramadan is prescribed as a time of fasting for all healthy Muslims. Fasting, which fulfils *sawm*, one of the *Five Pillars of Islam, occurs throughout the daylight hours and includes abstinence from tobacco and sexual intercourse as well as food and drink. Only the young, pregnant or nursing mothers, or the sick are exempt. The month is a time for introspection and spiritual renewal. The celebratory festival of *'id-ul-fitr*, 'Feast of breaking the fast', occurs at the end of the month. It is marked by a ritual bath, and the wearing of new clothes, as well as by almsgiving and prayer. Friends are visited and received with mutual blessings, and specially prepared sweets and perfumes are enjoyed. The festival is a time for cementing family and community relationships.

Rāmāyana, classical Sanskrit epic poem (composed *c.*400–100 BC), regarded as one of the *Hindu sacred texts. It deals with the adventures of Rāma (one of the *avatars or incarnations of *Vishnu), whose wife Sītā is abducted by the demon Rāvana, the King of Lanka. She is recovered by Rāma, with the help of the monkey god Hanuman. In the figures of Rāma and Sītā, ideals of courage, faithfulness, duty, and obedience are portrayed.

rape, the crime of having sexual intercourse with a person (usually female but also male) who has not freely given consent. Rape is considered a violent *crime as well as a *sexual offence. Evidence suggests that in as many as half of all rapes, the attacker is already known to the victim, and, furthermore, that most rapes are planned and systematic. Police studies uncover few false allegations by victims. However, it is thought that many rapes go unreported, in part because victims often experience problems in reporting rape

since police procedures may be felt to be as humiliating as the assault itself. Rape is difficult to prove in law, since it is usually one person's word against another's: conviction hinges on proving that the victim has not consented and that the attacker realized this, with the result that the characters of both parties and the victim's sexual history may be described in court in trying to prove or disprove consent. The acquittal rate is high, and those convicted are often given lenient sentences; in English law, the maximum penalty is life *imprisonment, but this is rarely imposed. Recent writers have argued that, contrary to popular beliefs that women enjoy or provoke rape, that men commit rape because of uncontrollable sexual urges, or that women make false accusations of rape, it is an expression of male domination and exploitation of women. They have stressed that rape is a degrading assault which is both physically and psychologically traumatic.

Rastafarianism, an expanding religious and political movement, originating from a Jamaican cult which worships Haile Selassie I (Ras Tafari, 1892–1975), the former Emperor of Ethiopia, as divine. The movement was influenced by the Black activists of the 1930s, particularly Marcus Garvey (1887–1940), who attempted to 'repossess' Africa for the Black race. Rastafarianism combines elements of *African religion, Black supremacy, and biblical narrative, particularly exodus and *millenarian liberation themes, with Afro-Caribbean culture. Its adherents believe the Blacks to be the lost tribes of Israel, who will eventually be redeemed by repatriation to Africa. The movement lacks both clergy and church, and ritual practice is largely spontaneous. Rastafarians express their sense of brotherhood through certain symbols: their hairstyle, known as 'dreadlocks'; the use of the Ethiopian national colours red, black, green, and gold; their dietary habits (avoidance of pork); and the occasional use of cannabis as an aid to *meditation. Reggae music, particularly that of Bob Marley (1945–81), provides an important medium for the popular dissemination of Rastafarian ideas.

A **Rastafarian** at Notting Hill Carnival celebrates the Jamaican activist Marcus Garvey's centenary. Garvey argued for the return of Blacks to Africa and drew a parallel between their exile through slavery and that of the Jews in Babylon.

rational choice theory, an approach to the explanation of social behaviour which treats it as the outcome of the rational pursuit of personal goals by individuals. It assumes that individuals have definite preferences over possible states of the world, that these preferences are held consistently, and that individuals will always try to act so as to obtain their preferred outcome. These assumptions have long been standard in the field of economics, but the rational choice approach has in recent years been increasingly influential in other areas of social scientific research. For instance, sociologists have sought to explain phenomena such as criminal behaviour or the choice of marriage partners in terms of the costs and benefits of the alternative courses of action open to rational individuals. *Public choice theorists have applied the rational choice approach to politics. In these fields it competes especially with explanations in terms of cultural *socialization and adherence to social *norms. An important branch of rational choice theory is game theory, which examines what happens when each of a number of people has to decide how to act without knowing how the others will act, where the outcome depends on what the others will in fact do. Of especial significance are cases where individually rational choices produce a result that is bad for everybody. For instance, it may be rational for each person to use a polluting form of transport such as the motor car, even though it is in everyone's overall interest that pollution be reduced. Game theory explores possible ways of escaping from such dilemmas.

rationalism, a broad philosophical position characterized by the claim that *reason is, in some way, a source of knowledge. This claim can mean either that reason provides us with *a priori concepts (or innate ideas) which can give the content of knowledge, or, more simply, that sense-experience gives the content which then has to be corrected, and justified, by reason. Rationalist is the common label for 17th-century continental philosophers such as *Descartes, *Leibniz, and *Spinoza. In the works of these authors, much emphasis is put on systematic justification, and mathematics, especially geometry, is often taken to be the template of an ideal rationalist *epistemology. Traditionally, rationalism stands opposed to *empiricism, in which experience provides us with all of our concepts, and is the ultimate source of justification of knowledge claims. Philosophers such as *Kant attempted to synthesize the insights of the two.

Rawls, John (1921–), US political philosopher. In *A Theory of Justice* (1971), Rawls revived the idea of a *social contract as a way of re-laying the foundations of *liberalism. He asked his readers to imagine a group of people debating the future shape of their society without knowing anything specific about their personal abilities or tastes, or the place they would occupy in that society. He argued that agreement would emerge on two basic principles of *social justice, the first specifying that each person should have the greatest possible liberty compatible with an equal liberty for others, the second specifying that income and other rewards should be distributed in whatever way produced the highest level of benefit for the worst-off group in society, provided there was equality of opportunity to compete for the more favoured positions. After two decades of sustained criticism, Rawls no longer claims universal validity for his theory, saying rather that it reflects the traditions of modern liberal *democracy.

reading, the comprehension and pronunciation of the written language. The complex psychological processes involved vary, depending on how the particular symbol system represents units of the spoken language. In an *alphabetic system, such as English, word spelling specifies pronunciation to a greater or lesser degree. In picture scripts, such as Chinese or Egyptian hieroglyphics, the symbols represent whole words. According to one major theory, reading is done 'by ear', through 'phonic mediation', a process of the successive association of the graphemes with their vocal counterparts (phonemes), which are combined into words with associated meanings. Recent research suggests that rhyming games may assist in drawing the child's attention to the phonetic structure of language. According to another theory, reading is done 'by eye': complete graphic words are perceived by the eye and their meanings are retrieved from the mental lexicon or guessed on the basis of the context. It is likely that readers use different combinations of both strategies depending on the kind of reading activity: reading aloud, critical reading, proof reading, reading for learning, or skimming. Most research has been carried out on reading alphabetic writing, but apparently, whatever the *writing system, reading strategies are basically the same. There are diverse competing techniques for teaching children *literacy, but no single favoured approach exists. Learning to read is a basic object of education, and its importance for the individual and society is recognized in literacy campaigns. A common reading difficulty for individuals is *dyslexia.

realism (in philosophy), a view of any subject area or range of judgements which holds that what is true or false in that area is determinately fixed by how things stand in the world, independently of our opinions on the matter, or the evidence we can have for those opinions. Realism about one subject-matter does not imply realism about another; for example, few would imagine that whether a story is really funny is a wholly objective question, not tied to whether people find it so. There are different sorts of realism about the same subject-matter; for example, one can be a realist with respect to moral values because one believes that the world actually contains moral values that exist independently of us, or because one believes that talk of moral values can be reduced to talk of social custom or the greatest happiness of the greatest number (see *utilitarianism). Various philosophical doctrines have opposed realism in particular areas: *emotivism is a form of anti-realism about morality; instrumentalism (see *science, philosophy of) is an anti-realist attitude to scientific theories. A principal motivation for anti-realist views has been the difficulty of explaining how we can come to know the realist's completely independent facts.

reason (rationality), the faculty of making judgements and inferences. Reason may be divided into theoretical and practical reason. Theoretical reason aims at true belief; practical reason aims at right action. The operations of reason can also be divided into *deductive and *inductive forms, and can to some extent be formally described by *logic. Reason is distinguished from other faculties, such as *perception, *emotion, and imagination. The relative power of reason and desire is a central philosophical question; *Hume famously claimed that practical reason can only ever be the 'slave of the passions'. Possession of reason is often said to provide the essential difference between man and other members of the animal kingdom. *Descartes described human reason as 'universal', meaning that a being that has reason is not limited to a fixed stock of responses, and connected the faculty of reason with the ability to use *language. The existence of reason provides a major challenge for a *naturalistic view of persons.

recession (in economics), a period of underemployment of *resources in an economy, due to a temporary reduction in aggregate *demand. It is now technically defined as two consecutive quarters of falling output. It is normally viewed as a phase of the *trade cycle—the typical cyclical fluctuation of aggregate demand relative to supply potential. A slump is a severe recession. Economic *depression is the term used to denote a more sustained period of *unemployment.

recycling, the re-use of items, or materials in discarded manufactured goods instead of taking further raw materials from the earth. It saves resources, though it may not necessarily be cheaper than using new materials, and is of growing relevance for reducing environmental *pollution. Recycling of paper has become important in view of accelerating *deforestation. French, German, Japanese, and Norwegian authorities have taken steps to set up stable markets for recycled paper. Metals, plastics, and glass can also be recycled, and removing these materials from domestic refuse helps reduce the growing problem of waste disposal. Such 'external recycling' contrasts with 'internal recycling' during an industrial process, for example the resmelting and recasting of metal turnings and offcuts. The technology, legislation, and application of recycling domestic waste is advanced in Japan and Germany. The USA has taken an increasing interest: in some states those who fail to recycle their waste can be prosecuted, and in an increasing number of states domestic waste must be sorted by the householder before collection in order to assist recycling. Green parties have suggested encouraging recycling by charging a natural resources tax on newly manufactured items: the surcharge on a new car would be returnable when the wreck of the car is delivered for the metal to be recycled. Governments could also charge manufacturers a tax to pay for the disposal of non-renewable packaging.

reductionism, the claim that philosophically problematic notions can be adequately explained by appeal to more basic ones. The claim that a notion is problematic is, of course, relative to a philosophical position. Hence *empiricist philosophers have sometimes tried to reduce notions of which we can have no sense-experience to those that we do (see *logical positivism and *positivism.) On a larger scale, physicalism is the claim that, ultimately, all scientific explanations can be given in terms of theoretical physics.

referendum, an electoral device through which voters are allowed to express their opinion directly on an issue. A referendum may or may not be legally binding, depending on its constitutional status. A government may call a referendum in order to test public opinion, or to decide questions which cut across party lines, such as issues involving morality (for example, *divorce) or *constitution (for example, membership of the *EC). Referendums may be optional, as in the case of ordinary legislation, or mandatory, as in the case of constitutional amendments in the states of the USA. The initiative, a less common device, is a referendum held at the request of a number of electors who wish to vote on a particular issue. Referendums were first held in 16th-century Switzerland; other countries making substantial use of referendums include Australia, Denmark, France, and New Zealand.

reflation (in economics), the stimulation of aggregate demand after a period of slow *economic growth or rising *unemployment. Reflation may be instigated by government through *fiscal and/or monetary expansion, for example higher government spending, lower tax rates, and easier or cheaper credit. Such policies may, however, lead to *inflation. The opposite (tight) policies are often referred to as disinflation or restraint. Governments and *central banks may also mix, say, high interest rates and expansionary budgets in order to achieve particular combinations of impacts on different variables (for example, output and the *balance of payments, or output and *price measures).

Reformed Churches, a term which refers to all *Protestant Churches, but is usually kept for those in the tradition of the French Protestant theologian John Calvin (1509–64). They emphasize that the Bible contains all that is necessary for salvation, and traditionally hold that God in his absolute power through *predestination wills who is to be saved or damned, though many Reformed Churches have modified this strict doctrine. Many countries have their own Reformed Churches; there are about 20 million full members in all. The Dutch Reformed Church in South Africa has provoked controversy in the past by its support of apartheid. (See also *predestination.)

Reform Judaism, a term which, in the UK, refers to a movement, founded in Germany by Zachariah Frankel (1801–75), in reaction to the perceived laxity of *Liberal Judaism. Frankel questioned the wholly divine inspiration of the *Torah, whilst retaining observance of some Jewish laws and traditions. In the UK, Reform Jews might be regarded as being on the 'right' of the *Liberal or Progressive movement. In the USA the term Reform Judaism refers to the whole of the Liberal tradition, brought across by German immigrants in the 19th century. American Reform Jews are roughly equivalent to British *Liberal Jews.

refugee, a person who, for political, racial, or ideological reasons, or as a result of crises such as *famine or *disaster, has been forced to flee his or her home country. The 20th century has seen massive and unprecedented numbers of

Through drawing, a Ugandan boy is able to express his experience of the sacking of his village. In 1979 Ugandan **refugees**, fleeing the civil war in their own country, began arriving in southern Sudan, putting enormous strain on that country's economy.

Refugees

Principal countries from which the world's refugees have fled (1990)

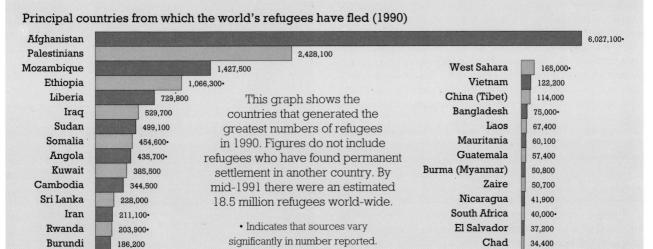

Afghanistan	6,027,100•
Palestinians	2,428,100
Mozambique	1,427,500
Ethiopia	1,066,300•
Liberia	729,800
Iraq	529,700
Sudan	499,100
Somalia	454,600•
Angola	435,700•
Kuwait	385,500
Cambodia	344,500
Sri Lanka	228,000
Iran	211,100•
Rwanda	203,900•
Burundi	186,200

West Sahara	165,000•
Vietnam	122,200
China (Tibet)	114,000
Bangladesh	75,000•
Laos	67,400
Mauritania	60,100
Guatemala	57,400
Burma (Myanmar)	50,800
Zaire	50,700
Nicaragua	41,900
South Africa	40,000•
El Salvador	37,200
Chad	34,400

This graph shows the countries that generated the greatest numbers of refugees in 1990. Figures do not include refugees who have found permanent settlement in another country. By mid-1991 there were an estimated 18.5 million refugees world-wide.

• Indicates that sources vary significantly in number reported.

Countries which are host to the largest numbers of refugees (1990)

This map shows the concentrations of refugees and asylum-seekers who are unable or unwilling to repatriate due to fear of persecution or violence in their homelands. It includes those, primarily in Europe and North America, who applied for asylum in the previous years (but not those who applied in earlier years); The map does not show refugees who have settled permanently in a country not their own. Of an estimated 16.69 million refugees in 1990, 5.44 million were in Africa and 9.8 million in the Middle East or South Asia.

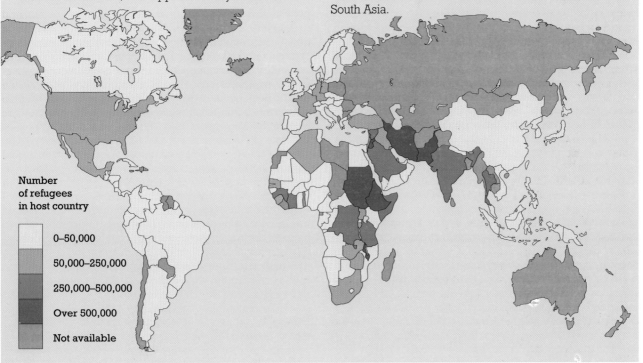

Number of refugees in host country

- 0–50,000
- 50,000–250,000
- 250,000–500,000
- Over 500,000
- Not available

Source: *World Refugee Survey*, 1991

refugees; it was estimated in 1990 that there are 15 million world-wide, with the overwhelming majority in developing countries. The root causes of refugee movements are complex and varied, but the two main contributory factors are armed conflicts or serious internal disturbances, and *human rights violations, all of which are exacerbated by *nationalism, *communal conflict, foreign intervention, *population growth, and the increasing availability of arms. However, governments are often reluctant to grant *political asylum to refugees because they fear damaging relations with the country of origin, encouraging a mass influx, offering protection to ideologically unsound groups, and incurring an economic burden. Despite the explicit terms to the contrary of the 1951 UN Convention relating to the Status of Refugees, governments may close their borders to refugees, treat refugees as illegal immigrants, expel new arrivals, or subject them to incarceration or harassment. Government responses may be motivated by ideological reasons. Thus refugees from the former Eastern bloc from the 1950s to the 1970s were likely to be regarded as defectors possessing valuable intelligence, whereas the response in Europe and North America to growing numbers of refugees from developing countries was to apply increasingly restrictive admissions policies (important exceptions being Chileans and other Latin Americans in the 1970s, and the Indo-Chinese in the early 1980s, both of which groups were able to secure popular sympathy). In Pakistan, for example, some 2.8 million Afghan refugees have received massive relief, whereas Iranian refugees receive virtually no government assistance. Even if refugees are successful in obtaining legal status, the problems in rebuilding a satisfactory social and economic life are huge. The office of the *UN High Commissioner for Refugees and other agencies attempt to mitigate immediate problems such as lack of food and housing. In the long term, however, the future of many refugees is bleak: they may be unable to return home (repatriation is the wish of most refugees) because the circumstances which they fled remain unchanged; prospects for resettlement in a third country may be slim, and, even where they exist, the facilities to help refugees adapt to a new environment such as teaching a new language or skills may be lacking; many face a future in ill-equipped long-term refugee camps.

regionalism (international), the promotion of unity, *integration, and co-operation between states in a particular geographical region, the most important expression of which has been the formation of associations or groupings among proximate states known as regional organizations. Some examples are the *Arab League (1945), the *EEC (1957), and the *Organization of African Unity (1963). Regionalism was once frowned on by the advocates of universal *international organizations such as the League of Nations or the UN, but it became popular in the 1960s with the proliferation of a large number of regional organizations in different parts of the world. While the achievements of many of these organizations have been limited, the success of the *EC has acted as an inspiration, particularly to regional groupings in the developing world. The European experience, in particular the EC's creation of a single market together with the impact produced by the easing of the cold war and the consequent loosening of the bipolar nature of the international system, led to a revived interest in regionalism at the beginning of the 1990s. This resulted in the appearance of new regional groupings, while older organizations looked for ways to enrich their existing agendas.

regionalization, the encouragement of intermediate forms of government between central and local levels. The aim is sometimes to develop local cultures and institutions, and often to promote more uniform economic growth between different regions of a state. Regionalization involves the delegation of some powers from the centre, but should be distinguished from *federalism, since full sovereignty is not conferred. Delegation can be democratic, normally by widening the decision-making powers of locally elected bodies; or it can be functional, in which responsibilities of the centre are transferred to non-elected regional structures. An example would be the French system of regional planning, which involves functions traditionally associated with central rather than local government. Spain and Belgium have adopted even stronger forms of regionalization closer to federalism, which involve the *devolution of sovereign powers to regionally elected bodies.

regional policy, central government programmes aimed at adjusting economic and social disparities between

The micro-computer playing a vital role in the **rehabilitation** of physically disabled youngsters. A simple extension keyboard allows them to use a maths program teaching the use of sets, while increasing their confidence with modern technological machinery.

regions. Such policies may be positive or negative. Positive policies aim to foster regional development by encouraging investment through such means as tax incentives, grant aid, and liberalization of planning controls for the private sector in designated areas. Negative policies are intended to discourage development in more affluent areas, for example by stricter planning controls. Public-sector regional policies usually include infrastructural development, for example roads and communications, but may involve larger projects, such as the movement of a capital city into a region (for example, Brasilia in Brazil). In countries such as Sweden, Canada, and Ireland, regional policy has a social dimension: inducements are offered by the government to settlers in developing regions.

regulation, the use of government authority to constrain the activities of commercial enterprises, public bodies, and members of the professions, in the public interest. Regulation is generally held to be necessary when the operation of the market will not afford sufficient protection: to prevent enterprises transferring social costs to others (for instance, by discharging untreated chemical effluent); to protect consumers against dominant or monopolistic suppliers; to redress the balance where there is an 'information asymmetry' between the amateur consumer (of health or financial services, for instance) and the professional provider. Governments have also used regulation to maintain an orderly market in such spheres as air travel and banking. 'Structural regulation' determines which firms or individuals (or categories of them) are allowed to engage in certain activities by such measures as enforcing entry restrictions or requiring professional qualifications. 'Conduct regulation' seeks to control behaviour, for example by enforcing rules against monopolistic activities. Concern about excessive regulation, notably in transport and *telecommunications, has led to attempts at *deregulation. Some commentators have observed that these should more properly be seen—as in *financial regulation in the UK—as a shift in emphasis from structural to conduct regulation. Regulation may be the responsibility of external bodies (such as the Securities and Exchange Commission in the USA) or of self-regulatory bodies established by trades or *professions to monitor and discipline their own members.

rehabilitation (in medicine), the attempt to restore partially or completely lost abilities or functions. It includes all measures aimed at reducing the impact of *disability. It is becoming more important with the increasing incidence of chronic *degenerative diseases, as well as of accidents, which in developing countries have reached epidemic levels. The rehabilitation of disabled people requires the co-operation of doctors, occupational therapists, physiotherapists, *social workers, and psychologists. Rehabilitation procedures range from the simple (such as the supply of glasses) to complex and multi-disciplinary interventions, such as those following a stroke, which may leave the victim partially paralysed, incontinent, and unable to speak. Rehabilitation involves persistent and intensive work with patients on an individual basis. Rewards are limited, and the outcome uncertain; and therefore this area of health care is often undervalued and underfunded, despite its benefits to the patient.

reincarnation, a term denoting the rebirth of the human *soul in another form after death. It is most commonly associated with Indian thought, but is also found amoung Australian *Aborigine peoples, and in *African traditional religions. In *Hinduism, a single soul or *ātman is subject to an endless cycle of births, deaths, and rebirths, through the process of *samsara. What one does in this life determines one's condition in the next, according to *karma, the law of cause and effect. The soul achieves liberation from this cycle through *moksha. *Jains also believe in the absolute soul, which after death awaits rebirth in a new body. In *Buddhism, however, the concept of 'non-self' (anatta), one of the *Three Marks of Existence, is a central belief. There is no personal or transcendent soul, and therefore no continuing spiritual entity. Rebirth is explained through the process of *dependent origination, in which each embodied existence, conditioned by karma, is linked to the next.

relationships (in psychology), genetic, elective (chosen), or institutional bonds between people. Relationships—at work, in the *community, in the *family, or between partners—are the substance of *society. For the individual, breakdown or lack of satisfactory close personal relationships may have a devastating effect on mental and physical health. *Social psychologists have studied relationships such as those of status, power, co-operation, and competition, trying, for instance, to show how a manager's relations with workers may affect job satisfaction and productivity. However, more attention has been given to close elective or familial relationships. Clinical and child psychologists have assumed that relationships between parents and children are potentially crucial to the children's emotional and intellectual development (see *attachment, *family therapy, *Freud, *psychosexual development). Theories in this area have possibly overemphasized the role of the mother and undervalued the role of the child's relationships outside the family. Social psychologists have studied friendship as well as romantic or marital relationships and *sexual behaviour. Factors found to affect the choices made in forming a close sexual relationship include mutual physical attraction and similarity of *attitudes and *personality. There is no evidence that 'complementary' characteristics or needs play any role. Belief that another relationship is readily available

is a major factor in the break-up of relationships and in *divorce. It has been suggested that a preoccupation with exchange of resources (some of which are intangible) underlies all relationships, but such theories are weak. In the late 1980s some psychologists tried to explain mate choice by reference to *sociobiology or the attachments formed by the partners in childhood. Recent attempts at the long-term study of relationships have had mixed success as volunteers may not offer a typical sample and the constant intervention of an observer may affect the course of the relationship.

relativism, the idea that truth, knowledge, or moral judgements are relative to situations, and only valid for the particular society in which they are found. Ethical relativism holds that there are no universal or absolute ethical standards, since each society develops its own. Similarly, cultural relativism posits the theory that a culture can only be understood from the point of view of its own values or customs. The idea that beliefs are relative rather than absolute is an important tool in *anthropology; for example, *Azande ideas about witchcraft can only be understood if we accept the assumptions that the Azande make about the world, which are coherent and logical in their own terms. Really consistent relativism, however, would deny the possibility of understanding any other society at all, and few anthropologists or philosophers would go this far, just as few would apply strict moral relativism to their own decisions.

religion, those areas of human life which presuppose the existence and importance of a transcendent unseen. In an important sense, religion is an extension of an ordinary human propensity to assume that there is 'more to life than meets the eye'. Thus a religious worldview is one that sees the world in depth, as being both what it appears to be, and, in an essential way, something more. We may call religious those areas where humans give a primacy to this 'more' as ultimate reality and order their lives around it. There has been no society which has not sought to give order and meaning to life through some form of religion. Religion, as an orientation to transcendence, always links concepts, activities, and experiences. Usually religion is associated with social institutions which have professional attendants, such as a temple or church with its priests, who are seen as guardians and preservers; such institutions give religion a public character, even though they may co-exist with individual beliefs. Transcendence has been conceived in a wide variety of very particular ways, but this diversity may be grouped into two basic types: transcendence is either radically *other* than the world or it provides an essential unity to all that exists. For example, Christian thought sees *God as a creator distinct from his creation, whereas the *Advaita form of *Hinduism defines transcendence as the absolute ground of Being, *Brahman, which is identical with the eternal Self (*ātman) of a person. Both types of conceptions of transcendence may co-exist in a single religious tradition, however, as in Islamic mysticism and Buddhist devotionalism. Knowledge about transcendence, the world, and human life is communicated in *myths, but it may also come through *symbols, images, doctrines, *philosophy, and the behaviour of charismatic individuals. Transcendence has been conceived both personally, as gods and goddesses, and, impersonally, as natural forces or an abstract order. Religious activities are seen as an approach to transcendence and thus they vary according to the conception with which they are associated. When transcendence is understood as Other, then characteristically, some form of worship will be

the dominant religious activity. When transcendence is conceived more immanently, then *meditation or self-reflection will be the typical religious activity. Moreover, religious concepts are often learned in activities. Religious experiences often occur in the context of religious activities; the act of worship, for example, is conducive to a sense of awe. They always reflect the concepts of the experiencer: Christians experience *Jesus, not the *Buddha. Religious experiences are often highly valued in a community, as long as they do not contradict authoritative beliefs.

religion and politics, the relationship between spiritual and secular authority, and the effects of religious principles or beliefs on political life. This has always been fraught with potential conflict. Religion is acknowledged to be a crucial source of *legitimacy and political mobilization in all societies, ranging from those which are avowedly secularist, such as communist regimes, to those which are *theocracies, such as Iran, or Tibet before Chinese rule was imposed in 1951, or those where conformity to a state religion plays an important part in national life, as in Saudi Arabia. A complex example is Israel, a state founded on *Zionism, a secular movement which claims the territory of Israel on historical and religious grounds. Many states have tried to weaken the power of the religious body by creating a state religious body, as in England, Scotland, and most of northern Europe following the 16th-century Reformation, where national churches were legally established in an attempt at control. Likewise, many great Islamic dynasties tried to assimilate the *'ulamā'; more recently, the secular government of Turkey has attempted to reduce the authority of Islam by creating a State Directorate of Religious Affairs. In the former Soviet Union, religious activity was circumscribed or even banned until 1991 when freedom of belief was reinstated. The authorities had tried to control the remaining religious institutions by bringing them under state supervision. In the USA, by contrast, the separation of church and state is formally enshrined in the First Amendment to the Constitution (1791), exemplifying the principle of secularism, the view that religion should be separate from public life, which first came to prominence among philosophers of the 18th-century Enlightenment. Secularization and the decline of religious belief and observance were regarded by many as hallmarks of modernization and Western liberal democracy until recent years, but since the Iranian Islamic Revolution (1979) and the spread of *Islamic fundamentalism, the resurgence of the *New Right and *fundamentalist values in US political life in the 1980s, and the virtual collapse of most secular communist regimes by the end of that decade, religion has been very widely acknowledged as a powerful element in both individual and public life.

religious education, education offered in schools and other educational institutions for which religious bodies are responsible, or instruction in the tenets of a *religion. Many schools and universities began as religious foundations educating their adherents or providing for underprivileged children. The tradition continues in, for example, the Koran

An historic demonstration in Red Square, Moscow on 1 May 1990 pinpoints resistance to the attempt to control **religion and politics** in the communist Soviet Union for seventy-three years. As the Communist Party's centralized hold on power declined, churches were reopened to thronging congregations.

schools of Islam, in Buddhist schools, and in the schools established by Roman Catholic religious orders. Religious schools were banned in the Soviet Union after the revolution of 1917 and certain other countries such as China, Cuba, and Albania when they fell under communist rule. These restrictions are gradually being lifted. Elsewhere religious schools are generally permitted and sometimes financially supported by the state, though most are subject to careful oversight. In many countries religious bodies are the main providers of *independent education. The question of religious education within state schools has long been contentious. In some nations, such as Turkey, a secular state by constitutional provision, it is limited, but in parts of the world where one religion is dominant (as Roman Catholicism is in Central America or Islam in the Middle East) it is often compulsory.

ren (*jen*) (Chinese, 'humaneness'), the term used in *Confucianism to denote the demonstration of love, concern, and respect for all humanity. The Chinese character for *ren* is composed of the signs for 'two' and 'human being', indicating that true humanity lies in human relationships. Generally, *ren* is the essence of all virtues; more specifically it is akin to loyalty and a fundamental necessity in the conduct of the 'Five Relationships', between ruler and minister, husband and wife, father and son, elder and younger brother, friend and friend, whose harmonious working *Confucius regarded as the basis of the ideal society presided over by 'princely persons'. Filial piety is stressed as the heart of family relationships and a model for the community and political conduct. It is the function of the inferior of the relationship to obey, and of the superior to exercise righteousness and benevolence. Confucius regarded *ren* as a virtue which must be instilled or learnt, but later Chinese philosophers, notably Mencius (Meng-tzu, *c.*371–289 BC), thought *ren* was innate, and human nature naturally good, a subject much discussed in later Chinese philosophy.

rent, the price paid per period of time for the services provided by a *factor of production or a *good. Typically rent is paid for the use of *land or buildings, but it may also apply to the hire of *capital goods and durable consumer goods. Economic rent, a concept developed in the work of *Ricardo and *Marshall, is the excess payment to a factor of production over its opportunity *cost, that is over and above the payment it would receive in its best alternative use (see *profit). Rent control is the control by government of the rent that may be charged for accommodation; a ceiling may be imposed to provide cheap *housing for the poor. However, the reduced rents are liable to lead to a reduction in the supply of rented accommodation.

representative government *democracy, *pluralism.

republic, a state in which supreme power is held by the people, their elected representatives, or by an elected or nominated president rather than a monarch. The *head of state in a republic is normally a *president, either directly or indirectly elected. A republican head of state may also be chief executive, but the office may be simply a ceremonial position. Republican forms of government have a long history, dating from ancient Greece and Rome. Though the powers of government nominally derive from the people, a republic is not necessarily democratic. Historically, most have been oligarchies dominated by the wealthy and well born. The republican form of government received a pow-

Gum Department store in Moscow. In the last years of the Soviet Union, its magnificent arcades were bare of merchandise, demonstrating the failure of the **retail-trading** system under communism.

erful impetus from the American and French revolutions (1776 and 1789), becoming associated in the 19th century with the spread of liberal, nationalist, and democratic ideas.

resale price maintenance (RPM), a *restrictive practice whereby a manufacturer enforces a minimum price for its product at the point of sale to the final *consumer. RPM used to be common in the UK, but it was made illegal in 1964 unless the manufacturer could make a case to the Restrictive Practices Court that RPM was in the public interest for its product. As a result RPM in the UK continues only in the case of books, where it is known as the 'net book agreement', and for certain drugs and medicines.

research and development (R & D), the invention of new products and *production techniques, together with the improvement of existing products and techniques. R & D may be either publicly or privately funded, and is an important source of improved *productivity and *economic growth.

resources (in economics), those scarce elements used for producing *goods and services. They can be categorized

into three: *land, *labour, and *capital. Land is normally defined to include all naturally occurring resources as well as the use of land surface area. Labour includes the efforts of workers, managers, and *entrepreneurs. Capital comprises goods which are themselves used in the production process. Skilled or qualified labour is often described as incorporating *human capital. (See also *factors of production.)

restrictive practice, an agreement to limit competition or output in industry. Restrictive *trade agreements between firms may be formal or informal. Examples are *cartels and price agreements, which set prices higher than would otherwise occur, in order to extract *monopoly profits. Members of *trade unions and certain professions may benefit from procedures which restrict competition between those doing the same kind of work and which limit entry into the *labour-market. Employers may seek to end alleged overstaffing or inflexible work practices because they restrict *productivity, as may governments through *deregulation. Some restrictive practices are banned, but some, such as certain state monopolies or *closed shops, may be allowed if they are considered to be in the public interest.

resurrection, rising from the dead; in Christianity, the word used to signify *Jesus' return from the dead as recounted in the New Testament and traditionally celebrated on *Easter Sunday. Theologians differ over whether Jesus' resurrection was a physical or spiritual event, but the resurrection is a crucial doctrine of Christanity because it is believed that, through Jesus' triumph over death, all Christians have the opportunity to share in the *afterlife. The idea of resurrection is found in ancient Near Eastern religions, and both the Greeks and Romans believed in the immortality of the *soul. The Christian doctrine of resurrection is based on Jewish prophecies of resurrection found in the Old Testament; both Muslims and Zoroastrians hold similar beliefs in the resurrection of the dead before the Day of Judgement. The idea of resurrection is, however, more central to Christian belief and doctrine than to that of any other religion.

retail price index (RPI, or cost-of-living index), a measure of changes in the average price level of *consumption goods and services. Movements of such an index are commonly used as the starting point for pay claims. The RPI is typically a base-weighted index, that is, it measures changes in the money cost of the bundle of consumption goods which households bought in the base year. Each item in the sample is given a share or 'weight' in the overall index, according to its importance in the average base-year household budget. The selection of goods and weights used for the index will eventually need revision as tastes and average incomes change. Family expenditure surveys are carried out at intervals, to monitor changes in spending patterns and thus facilitate updating of the items in the RPI sample of goods.

retail trading, the sale of *goods in relatively small quantities to ultimate consumers for personal or household use, not resale (unlike *wholesale trading). The goods may be fast-selling foodstuffs, toiletries, or clothing, or consumer durables such as electric appliances. (Retail trading may also be taken to include services such as water, gas, or electricity supplies, telephone, entertainment, transport, and the services of doctors, lawyers, accountants, and bankers.) Most retailing is via shops or stores. In the USA, *chain stores account for a third of retail sales, and self-service *super-markets for three-quarters of food-store sales. Such outlets offer goods at lower prices permitted by *economies of scale. The ancient institution of the bazaar or market has re-emerged recently in the form of shopping malls. These group shops, offices, and services such as banks, restaurants, and cinemas under one roof and around heated or air-conditioned pedestrian areas with plants and fountains. In the USA, these malls realize over half of retail sales. Like super-markets, many are accessible only by motor transport. Current trends in retailing include a continuing reduction in the number of 'middlemen' between wholesaler and final pur-chaser; and the increasing prominence of *advertising, *marketing, and point-of-sale *merchandizing. Non-shop forms of retailing are: direct marketing through mail-order or catalogue houses, and broadcast advertisements with pay-ment by credit card; personal door-to-door or telephone sales; and vending machines.

revisionism, a term used primarily within the socialist tradition to describe the views of those who depart from the prevailing orthodoxy, usually in the direction of greater moderation. The first 'revisionist' was Edward Bernstein (1850–1932), a German socialist who challenged some cen-tral tenets of *Marxism and argued for a gradual, non-revolutionary transition to *socialism. Latterly the term has been applied particularly to those who believe that their basic aims can be achieved without extensive public owner-ship of industry.

revolution (in politics), the transformation of a political system or regime through a relatively rapid and concen-trated process, often but not always accompanied by *polit-ical violence. It should be distinguished from a *_coup d'état_, which refers to the sudden overthrow of a government, and not of the political system as a whole. The American and French Revolutions of 1776 and 1789 established the assumption that a radical break with previous governmental patterns was central to revolution; the Bolshevik Revolution of 1917 in Russia further established that such transforma-tion should extend to the social, economic, and cultural aspects of the state concerned. A related idea central to *Marxism and *Maoism is that of 'permanent revolution', in which it is argued that post-revolutionary society should be subject to continual radical change or *purges so that no reactionary groups can achieve power or conduct a *counter-revolution. For example, in China, the leadership of Mao Zedong instigated the Cultural Revolution of 1965–8 as a means of reinvigorating revolutionary thought and action. Revolutionary groups may operate within the estab-lished order, or outside it, in which case they are often orga-nized into 'cells' or 'cadres', the irreducible unit of political action. Specific revolutionary actions aimed at destabilizing the established system can include subversion, demonstra-tions, or political violence. It is often argued that revolutions undergo distinct phases of development, with the pre-revolutionary stage demonstrating specific tensions and conflicts, and the post-revolutionary stage often leading to the emergence of an *authoritarian state, but much of the Marxist-dominated revolutionary theory of the 20th century has been undermined by the different pattern of revolutions in recent years, from the Iranian Islamic revolution (1979) to those, largely peaceful, of the former Eastern bloc in the late 1980s.

The signal that heralded nation-wide support for the Czech **revolution** of 1989 was the ringing of handbells and keyrings by crowds gathered on the Letna Plain above Prague (seen here). The peal of the cathedral bells in the city below was taken up by outlying churches and relayed across the breadth of the country.

Ricardo, David (1772–1823), British political economist, together with *Smith the founder of British *classical eco-nomics and of economics as an independent discipline. Probably the most celebrated aspect of his work was his three-*factor model of income distribution (with *wages, *profit, and *rent) in the context of a corn-producing eco-nomy. He argued that real wages tend to remain steady at subsistence level and that unit production *costs will tend to equality on all agricultural land. In addition, profits are uni-form, the owners of capital offering higher amounts to landowners for the use of more fertile land. The resulting surplus of income on such land is rent. As more and more marginal land is cultivated (due to rising population), rent increases and profits are squeezed. In a multi-good econ-omy, the so-called Ricardo effect arises when labour becomes relatively more expensive than *capital, the price of labour-intensive relative to capital-intensive goods goes up, and demand and resources are shifted to capital-intensive goods. Among other contributions, Ricardo is also famous for his pioneering formulation of the law of compar-ative advantage in international *trade. This states that if, in the absence of trade, the price (or marginal opportunity cost) of good A in terms of good B is higher in country 1 than in country 2, then (ignoring transport costs) trade is economi-cally beneficial to both countries, even if the absolute production costs of both A and B are lower in one of the two countries than in the other.

rice cultivation, the major form of food production in southern and South-east Asia. Rice is the staple food of this region, and the growing cycle requires that the young shoots are kept submerged in shallow water, usually in irrigated fields known as paddy fields; this in turn requires the use of extensive irrigation systems, and the terracing of hillsides. As rice is a high-yield crop, several harvests can be gathered each year. Most of the production is carried out by *peasant farmers and *sharecroppers; in some cases control over the water supply, and the resources to build extensive irrigation systems become a political issue.

Right (in politics), term applied to ideas, movements, and parties of a conservative or reactionary character. Following the example of the nobility at the time of the French Revolution (1789), members of legislative assemblies holding authoritarian, anti-democratic, or anti-socialist views have tended to sit on the right of their chambers. As with *'Left', the meaning of 'Right' varies with context, denoting at different times conservative, liberal, or even *fascist outlooks. (For recent trends, see *New Right.)

rights issue *shares.

risk analysis, the analysis of possible outcomes of management decisions, especially those involving capital *investment. Risk analysis assesses the likely good and harmful results for a company of prospective decisions, often using statistical probability techniques. In the case of investment, the expected returns will be calculated to compare them with the current cost of the capital. A recent extension to risk analysis used by *multinational corporations is scenario planning, which looks at broad company strategy in the context of different possible developments within the world economy.

rites of passage, a term first used by the Belgian anthropologist Arnold van Gennep (1873–1957) for *rituals in which a person passes from one status or role to another. Such rituals constitute forms of *initiation, and commonly have three distinct stages. The first involves the separation of the individual from his or her current role. The second stage is a period of transition, and the third is a process of re-incorporation, when the individuals concerned assume their new social role. This structure can be seen in many different rituals, especially those known as life-crisis rituals such as *marriage, *funerals, or *puberty rites. In marriage, for example, the bride and groom have to pass from the status of bachelor and spinster to that of married person; in puberty rites the individual moves from child to adult. Rites of passage are also seen in rituals which mark the passing of time, or the changing of seasons. As well as a strong ritual structure, rites of passage usually involve the use of *symbolism, often designed to reaffirm the importance of certain central values. In the transition phase, though, the symbolism is often turned upside down. Amongst the *Ndembu, the male initiates are stripped of their clothes and sent out into the bush for a time. In many contexts in Western society, similar reversals may occur, as, for instance, in the initiation of new apprentices at a factory, or new students into a college fraternity, which often involves some kind of ordeal. The reversal of symbolism also occurs in rituals which mark the passing of time, like the annual *carnival before the aus-

The Oxford University degree ceremony shown here can be considered to form part of the participants' **rites of passage**. They leave the Sheldonian Theatre as students, change their gowns and put on symbolic hoods, and re-enter to be accepted as graduates.

terities of *Lent, when everyday values would be briefly turned upside down. Thus the final phase of the rite of passage reaffirms the values of society, and a new state of equilibrium is achieved.

ritual, a term used for various sorts of stylized behaviour, often, but not always, religious. In attempting to define ritual, different anthropologists stress different things: the formal nature of ritual, or the religious context, or the fact that it fulfils collective expectations and often involves collective action. Ritual is thus closely linked to areas like *magic, *myth, and *religion, and includes activities such as *circumcision, *marriage, and *funerals. In addition it is an important feature of *political organization in most societies. One important group of rituals are those *rites of passage which involve a transition from one status or position in society to another. The collective action in rituals can create a powerful response both in the participants and in those watching, whether they be mourners at a funeral, cheering crowds at a royal wedding, or spectators at a football match. The French sociologist *Durkheim thought that ritual made people aware of the collective power of society over the individual, and that rituals were a necessary source of social integration.

Rogers, Carl Ranson (1902–87), US psychotherapist and theorist about the self, a founder of *humanistic psychology. Rogers argued that *psychotherapy would be successful only if the therapist felt care, *empathy, and 'unconditional positive regard' for the patient. Evidence supports this claim. His *Client-centered Therapy* (1951) held that therapists should be 'non-directive', listening to their patients (or 'clients') without offering explicit guidance. Rogers thought that the basis of psychological maladjustment is a discrepancy between people's beliefs about what they are (*self-concept) and what they ought to be (ideal self), and that in therapy the clients' self-disclosures change these beliefs. His ideas are supported by evidence that such discrepancy does increase the risk of both mental and physical illness. Rogers also claimed that everyone should aim for 'self-actualization', 'growing' to become his or her 'real self'. After 1968 he dissociated himself from academic psychology's 'methods of studying people as objects'.

role (in sociology), the forms of behaviour and expectations associated with a social position. An individual may fulfil many roles: doctor, mother, daughter, and snooker-player. For each, the expected mode of behaviour is different. A study of roles shows how individual behaviour is shaped socially. For sociologists, roles are the building blocks of social institutions and of societies.

roller-skating, the international sport and pastime of skating on wheels clamped to the shoes or a pair of all-in-one boots fitted with wheels. In recent years roller-skating has found a fresh appeal among children and the under-twenties, linked in part to the craze for skateboarding and supported by new rink facilities at local leisure centres. In crowded cities such as New York, people skate to work for exercise and to cut their journey time. Roller-skating can be adapted to games such as hockey, and has its own competitions for speed-skating, figure-skating, and dancing.

Roman Catholic Church, the *Christian Church under the spiritual authority of the *pope, with over 400 million full members. Until the 16th-century Reformation the Roman Catholic Church was the sole church of Western Christendom. The Church has an elaborately organized centralized hierarchy of bishops and priests, who must be celibate, under the pope, whose authority is based on the doctrine of the Petrine Succession, that is, that the popes are the spiritual heirs to the power vested in St Peter by Jesus. The Roman Catholic Church is characterized by the paramount authority of the pope, as expressed in the doctrine of papal infallibility promulgated in 1870, and even rulings which are not technically infallible enjoy great authority. This has led to controversial rulings such as that in 1967 forbidding the use of contraception and reiterating the condemnation of *abortion. The Roman Catholic Church differs from Protestantism in the importance it attaches to tradition, in addition to the authority of the *Bible. The importance of the seven *sacraments and the celebration of the *liturgy have developed as part of the traditions of the church. The majority of worshippers follow the Roman rite, but there are five Eastern-rite groups which accept the authority of the pope. They are the Byzantine, Antiochene, Alexandrian, Chaldean, and Armenian rites, which encompass a number of different churches. Veneration of the Virgin Mary and the saints is a further aspect of Roman Catholic traditionalism. The centralized authority of the Church has led to a high degree of elucidation of doctrine and belief, such as the different categories of *sin and the qualities of purgatory, heaven, and hell. The Church maintains its opposition to *divorce, but has recognized the need for reform and renewal; the liturgy, once universally held in Latin, is now held in the vernacular or language spoken by the people. *Monasticism remains important, but the importance of lay movements such as the South American 'base communities' is increasingly recognized. The Church participates in the ecumenical movement by sending observers to the *World Council of Churches. In recent years the Church has taken a more active role in world events, by its sustained opposition to atheist political and economic systems such as *communism in Eastern Europe and through the development of movements in South America such as *liberation theology, which address the problems of endemic poverty and oppression.

Romance languages, the daughter languages of *Latin, spoken by some 500 million people in Europe, the Americas, and elsewhere in the world. Opinions on the number of languages vary, since what constitutes a language is often a question with a political as well as linguistic dimension. There are five national languages: Spanish, Portuguese, French, Italian, and Romanian; three with official regional status: Rhetic (eastern Switzerland), Catalan, and Galician (Spain); while two more, Sardinian and Occitan of southern France, deserve the title on purely linguistic grounds. There are many dialects of Romance languages (for example, Sicilian) which differ more from the 'national standard' than, for example, Spanish and Portuguese differ from each other. Dalmatian, a language spoken in northern Yugoslavia, became extinct in about 1900. There is no straightforward way of sub-grouping the languages. In different ways they have all been influenced by each other and by changing political boundaries in Europe. Geographical proximity is generally the largest factor in linguistic similarity. Spanish is the most widely spoken, with 280 million speakers and national status in nineteen countries (the three largest being Spain, Mexico, and Argentina). Catalan (6 million speakers), which is not a dialect of Spanish but a language closely related to Occitan, has official status in Andorra, and is also spoken in the Roussillon region of France. Portuguese is the national language of Portugal (10 million speakers) and Brazil (147 million), and is an official language in former colonies such as Angola and Mozambique. A related language, Galician (*Gallego*) is spoken in north-west Spain. French is spoken by 66 million people in France, Belgium, Switzerland, and Canada, and is an official language in former colonies in North Africa and elsewhere. It is an important international language. The Occitan dialects of the south (which include Provençal) still have over 10 million speakers, though most are bilingual. There have always been many regional dialects in Italy. Since unification in 1861 the standard language has been based on the dialect of Florence, but 50 per cent of the population still claim a non-standard dialect as their mother-tongue. Romanian is spoken by 27 million people in Romania and Moldava. It is written in the Roman *alphabet in Romania and the Cyrillic alphabet in Moldava and other parts of the former Soviet Union where it is spoken. It is rather different from the western Romance languages, and has borrowed words from Slavic and Turkish. Related dialects (Arumanian and Megleno) are spoken in northern Greece.

Roman law, the body of law developed in Rome between about 150 BC and AD 250 and codified by the Emperor Justinian I (482–565) in his *Corpus Juris Civilis* ('Body of civil law'). Roman law re-emerged in the 11th century as a popular subject of study in the Italian universities; later it evolved into the common core of the *civil (or Romano-Germanic) law family of legal systems, which established itself in the lands of the Holy Roman Empire. The ideas of Roman law were dominant in the French *Code Napoléon, adopted in 1804, and in later civil codes adopted in Germany, Switzerland, and Austria. The codification movement appealed to the perceived higher rationality of Roman law as providing a logically consistent set of principles and rules for solving disputes.

Rosh Hashanah (Hebrew, 'beginning of the year'), a two-day Jewish festival accepted as marking the religious new year in the seventh month Tishri (usually falling in September or October). A ram's horn, or shofar, is blown a hundred times as a call to repentance and spiritual self-examination. The festival is also known as a Day of Judgement, a time for each Jew to review his or her standing with God. It is also traditionally the anniversary of the creation, and of the birthdays of Abraham, Isaac, and Jacob. The following day is a fast day and is the first of Ten Penitential Days of repentance and forgiveness, which culminate in *Yom Kippur.

rounders, a bat-and-ball game played mainly in Britain and said to be a forerunner of *baseball. Two teams of nine take turns to bat and field, and a match consists of two innings each. The batter uses a rounded stick and faces up to the bowler, who delivers the hard leather ball with an underarm action from a square 7.5 m (25 feet) away. The batter tries to hit the ball forward of his or her square and runs to first post or further, continuing if possible to fourth post and scoring a rounder. Fielders can dismiss batters by catching a hit on the full or touching the ball to a post before the batter can reach it.

Rousseau, Jean-Jacques (1712–78), Swiss-French social and political philosopher. The central question of Rousseau's thought was how individuals, with their complex psychological make-up, could be reconciled to the demands of *society. In his *Discours sur l'origine de l'inégalité des hommes* (1755), he traced the corrupting effects of society on human beings who, he believed, were by nature good and had originally lived in a condition of innocent isolation. Private property and the division of labour had created an artificial social inequality and a false morality. In *Du Contrat social* (1762), Rousseau argued that the people's only means of salvation was to surrender all their rights to a sovereign state, in which they themselves would compose the *legislature. He envisaged a city-state whose citizens assembled to deliberate on matters of common concern and expressed a 'general will' which, Rousseau claimed, must necessarily be just. These views had a powerful influence on later ideas of *democracy, and, in particular, on the radical wing of the French Revolution. (See also *social contract.)

rowing, the world-wide sport of propelling an oared boat faster than its rivals. In sculling, the rower pulls two oars, and in ordinary rowing one oar. Racing boats are long and slender, and fitted with sliding seats and outriggers to hold the oars. Main competitions, or regattas, feature races for single and double sculls, coxed and coxless pairs (with and without a separate steersman), coxless fours, quadruple sculls (coxed and coxless), and eights. The world's most famous boat race is the annual Putney to Mortlake contest on the River Thames between the eights of Oxford and Cambridge Universities.

royalty, a fee or tax paid to the owner of an *asset in return for the right to produce and sell. Such assets may consist of intellectual property (patents for inventors, *copyright for writers, composers, and musicians) or of mineral *resources (oil, gas, metal ores). A *franchise is a form of royalty.

rugby *football.

rule of law, the principle that the actions of government and private citizens alike should comply with legal rules and be evaluated according to law. It implies that a legal system should minimize the use of retrospective *legislation; that laws should be reasonably clear and well publicized, and

avoid arbitrary *discrimination between subjects; that *judges should be independent and unbiased; and legal processes should be accessible to all. These procedural requirements are applicable to many different systems of government. In recent years it has also been suggested that the rule of law requires enforcement of what are claimed as natural *human rights, such as racial equality or freedom from hunger, an idea that links the rule of law closely to *natural law.

Russell, Bertrand (Arthur William) (1872–1970), the most influential British philosopher of the 20th century. Along with G(eorge) E(dward) Moore (1873–1958), Russell reacted against the *idealism dominant around 1900, and re-established the *empiricist tradition of such philosophers as *Hume. Russell introduced to English-speaking philosophers the enormous advances made in *logic by *Frege, and held that the new tools provided by mathematical logic enabled empiricist philosophy to be conducted in a systematic, scientific way. His method of logical constructions aimed to detail the complex relationships which abstract or theoretical objects have to sense experience, so validating experience as an adequate basis for all knowledge. Although his philosophical output was massive, Russell was never a narrowly academic figure. He was imprisoned for pacifist activities during World War I, and later ostracized for his views on sexual morality (see *Marriage and Morals*, 1929). After World War II he became a leading spokesman of opposition to nuclear weapons.

Russian language *Slavic languages.

S

sacrament, a religious ceremony or act regarded as an outward sign of spiritual grace. In *Christianity, the term applies to the seven rites of Baptism, Confirmation, the Eucharist, Penance, Ordination, Extreme Unction, and Matrimony. Both the *Roman Catholic and *Eastern Orthodox Churches accept all these as sacraments, while most *Protestant churches give this name to only two of them, the Eucharist and Baptism, which were, they believe, actually ordained by Jesus Christ himself; the *Quakers and *Salvation Army accept no form of 'outward observance' of the sacraments. *Anglican churches accept all seven, but give priority to the Eucharist and Baptism. Baptism is the Christian *initiation rite, purifying the individual through sprinkling of or immersion in water, or anointing with oil. Confirmation, usually a laying-on of hands and anointing, confirms the baptized believer in membership of the Church. The Eucharist, or practice of sharing bread and wine, re-enacts the Last Supper, at which Jesus and his disciples shared bread and wine, and recalls mankind's

In Pakistan the head of a family sacrifices a cow at the joyful festival of 'Īd-ul-Fitr, which follows the fasting month of Ramadan. In Islam **sacrifice** is also carried out at the end of the ḥajj pilgrimage to Mecca.

redemption by Jesus' *sacrifice on the cross. Christian Churches interpret the Eucharist differently: for the Roman Catholic and Orthodox Churches the bread and wine become Jesus' body and blood, a change known as 'transubstantiation' by Roman Catholics; most Protestant churches regard the Eucharist as a symbol of Jesus' sacrifice and the unity of the community of believers. In Penance, the believer confesses *sins, receives absolution from a priest, and is allocated a penance. Extreme Unction is the anointing of the gravely ill with oil.

sacrifice, a ritual offering to a deity or suprahuman being in which an object is renounced and sometimes destroyed. Forms of sacrifice have been found in most known religions, with diverse materials and rites, and varying motives and intentions. The object offered is usually alive or symbolizes life in some way, but may also be an item of value. Sacrifice may involve killing, burning, destroying, or burying the creature or object which is offered, or substituting for such action a representation of it. The intentions of most sacrifices may be generally categorized as praise, thanksgiving, supplication, or expiation (including purification and propitiation). Scholars have held differing theories as to the origins of sacrifice, with each theory explaining well particular examples of sacrifices, but not the whole phenomenon. Some have seen sacrifice as a form of gift, either in homage or as a bribe to the deity, which, like human *gift-giving, carries an implied obligation. Others have noted that sacrifice may take the form of a communal meal, in which the ritual of slaying and bond of eating together strengthen the community. It is also thought that sacrifice is used as a means to

Twelve-metre yachts from New Zealand **sailing** during the America's Cup competition. The race is named after the 'America', the yacht from New York which won the first race (then called the 100 Guinea Cup) around the Isle of Wight in 1851.

establish a link between the sacred and profane worlds by establishing a relationship with the divine. Yet another theory suggests that performing sacrifice is a means of triggering divine or magical forces rather than a way of addressing a particular divine recipient. Examples of sacrificial rites in practice today include the Christian *sacrament of the Eucharist, which renders present Jesus' death on the cross in *atonement, or expiation, of mankind's sins. Christianity inherited the idea of expiatory sacrifice from ancient Judaism, but since the Babylonian exile (586–538 BC), sacrifice has not been practised by Jews and has been replaced by prayer as the central rite of Judaism. In Christianity, the reforming Churches see the Eucharist as a sacrament of commemoration with no sacrificial power; from its earliest days, Christianity has also stressed the need for self-sacrifice or inner renunciation, leading to an emphasis on *asceticism. Islam allows no place for sacrifice in formal worship, but it is widespread in Muslim societies during the *ḥajj*, or pilgrimage, and at the *ʿīd ul-aḍḥā, as a remembrance of Abraham's sacrifice and as an act of charity (*zakāt*, one of the *Five Pillars of Islam), since the flesh of the animal sacrificed is distributed to the poor. In Hinduism, food offerings (*prasād*) are a common part of *pūjā, or worship. In accordance with the doctrine of *ahimsa, Buddhism forbids blood sacrifice, but ancient practices survive in new guises, as in Tibet, for example, where the ancient custom of human sacrifice has been replaced by dough offerings at shrines.

sailing, the sport and pastime of taking out a sailing boat either for pleasure, to take part in a race, or as a solo feat of skill and endurance. The size of boat ranges from a small 3 m (10 feet) long dinghy to ocean cruisers of 23 m (75 feet) or more, capable of sailing round the world. Among the more famous yachting trophies is the Admiral's Cup, contested every year by teams of three offshore racing yachts, which sail four races. The America's Cup is an international challenge trophy, dominated by the USA, which brings enormous prestige to the winning captain and crew but demands a forbiddingly large financial investment to produce a winning design.

saint (from Latin, *sanctus*, 'holy'), a person of remarkable holiness or powerful religious example. In the early Christian Church, all members were referred to as saints; later on the term came to mean those who were assumed, because of their holiness during life or the manner of their death, to have merited *heaven. The *martyrs were considered to be first in rank among the saints. It was believed that the relics of saints had the power to work *miracles. In the Roman Catholic Church, the processes of beatification and canonization are lengthy: to be admitted as a saint a person must have been an outstanding exemplar during life, and must have performed authenticated *miracles before and after death. In 1969 the Church dropped several saints from the liturgical calendar because of doubts that they ever existed; among them was the popular St Christopher. Most religions recognize the status of holy men and women, from Hindu sadhus to Theravāda Buddhist *arahats and Mahāyāna Buddhist *bodhisattvas. *Islam, however, specifically rejects the notion of sainthood, although there are popular local cults of saints, *wali*, particularly in Sufi and Shīʿī practice.

salvage (in maritime law), the right to reward of those who have voluntarily saved ships and goods from dangers at sea. Such rules of public policy are recognized by all modern maritime states, and have been extended to cover salvage of aircraft and salvage of lives as well as property. A salvor may retain the goods until payment of salvage, which should cover all expenses properly incurred. No such general right exists where a person saves property on land from loss or danger, although some legal systems, notably civil law systems, do grant such rights.

Salvation Army, an international Protestant body, organized in military fashion, concerned with *mission and *social work. Founded by William Booth in London in 1865, the Salvation Army today is a *non-governmental organization operating in eighty countries world-wide with its headquarters in the UK. Officers, who may be men or women, are required to practise obedience and abstinence from alcohol. The Salvation Army is renowned for its work with the poor and homeless, and for its uniformed brass bands.

samādhi (Sanskrit, 'making firm', 'putting together'), a term used in *Hinduism to describe the highest goal of *yoga, wherein it represents a total absorption or concentration upon the object of *meditation. If this is God, then liberation (*moksha*) is attained. The death of a person who has reached this goal is also considered a *samādhi*, and by extension the term can also refer to the site of such a saint's cremation. In *Buddhism, *samādhi* is a stage of meditation, and the last stage of the *Noble Eightfold Path.

samizdat (Russian, 'self publishing'), unofficial writings circulated in the former Soviet Union and Eastern bloc, expressing the views of dissident groups and individuals in defiance of official *censorship and controls. The samizdat movement took shape in the 1950s in the Soviet Union, and was intensified following the death of Stalin and the 'thaw' of the mid-1950s. It experienced rapid growth after the Helsinki Agreement, at the *Conference on Security and Co-operation in Europe (1975), reporting, for example, on the violation of *human rights and on *pollution.

Samoan, an inhabitant of the *Polynesian islands of Western and American Samoa. Traditionally subsistence farmers and fishers, the Samoans are perhaps best known from *Mead's controversial portrait of a sexually permissive society. In fact Samoan society is highly stratified and many Samoans have complained about Mead's description of their culture. *Kinship is based on the *descent line, that is, a group of people who can trace their patrilineal descent to a common mythical ancestor. Titles, rather than property, are inherited, and each of these is linked to rank. Every kin group holds a number of such titles, and these enable it to participate in village councils. As several descent groups are present in each village, seniority of title, and hence position of village chief, is determined by reference to mythology.

sample (in social research), a representative portion of a larger population. Sampling is used by investigators where it would be impractical to study a whole population. Thus *opinion polls are based on a sample of the electorate. The simplest type is the random, in which each member of a population has an equal chance of being selected. This may be done by selecting, for example, every fifteenth member. However, if an investigator wishes to ensure a particular group is sufficiently represented (for example, people over 85), stratified random sampling may be used. The population is divided into sub-groups (in this case by age) and a sample drawn from each.

samsara (Sanskrit, 'journeying through'), a central notion within *Hinduism and *Buddhism which denotes the way in which successive lives are determined by the laws of *karma. In Hinduism, the *soul continues to be reborn in a variety of forms, according to its actions in past lives, until release (*moksha) is achieved. Buddhism rejects the existence of the soul but clearly recognizes a spiritual link between successive lives (see *dependent origination). The cycle of samsara involves many different forms of life, and Buddhists believe in five realms of rebirth: the realm of gods, that of human beings, that of animals, that of ghosts, and a hellish realm. Because all creatures are subject to samsara, Buddhists respect all forms of life, but only humans, who are capable of recognizing both desire and ignorance, may find enlightenment and release from samsara through *nirvana.

samskāra (Sanskrit, 'making perfect'), a term that most commonly refers to personal *rites of passage and purification within *Hinduism. There are sixteen *samskāras*, beginning with rituals connected with conception, pregnancy, and birth; they continue by marking each stage of life, until the final set of ceremonies after death. Few modern Hindus go through all the *samskāras* recommended in the Hindu lawbooks, but for men from the three highest *castes, the most important is the adoption of the Sacred Thread, a celebration of religious maturity. The wearers of the Sacred Thread are called *dvija*, or twice-born. For women, the most important *samskāra* is marriage.

sanctions, coercive or punitive measures taken by one or more countries (or an *international organization) against another to force a change in policy or to secure fulfilment of international obligations. Such measures may involve *boycott and the complete or partial interruption of economic and cultural links, communications, and diplomatic relations. The *UN *Security Council is empowered to order mandatory sanctions against an offending country; for example, sanctions were applied against Rhodesia (1966–79)

following Ian Smith's unilateral declaration of independence in November 1965, and against Iraq in 1990 following its invasion of Kuwait. However, their efficacy has often been called into question.

sangha (Pali, 'crowd', 'host', or 'assembly'), a term originally used in *Buddhism to describe the followers of the Buddha. *Theravāda Buddhism limits the expression to monastic orders, which consist of monks (*bhikshu*), nuns (*bhikshunī*), and novices (*shrāmanera*), who exert a strong social and religious influence. In *Mahāyāna traditions the term is extended to include the entire Buddhist community, especially in areas where the monastic tradition has been weakened, particularly in China and Tibet, by political repression. In *Hinduism, *sangha* denotes any group of people who follow a guru or teacher in order to gain spiritual understanding.

sanitation, the disposal of sewage and waste. Deficiencies in sanitation services and *water supply are principal reasons for the high incidence of communicable diseases in developing countries. By 1990 the World Health Organization estimated that facilities for the sanitary disposal of wastes were available, even on a generous estimate, to two-thirds of urban residents in developing countries, and one-fifth of rural residents, and that improvements in services were not keeping pace with *population growth. The World Bank argued in *Investing in Development* (1985) that a wide variety of simple sanitation systems can reach hygienic standards at reasonable costs. Water-based sewerage systems can rarely be justified since their high costs severely restrict the numbers served. However, the disposal of excreta is associated with ritualized practices and taboos in most societies, and this has had a bearing on the acceptability of lower-cost technologies which are less convenient than in-house plumbing and water-borne sewage. Convincing potential users of the benefits of improved waste disposal may be difficult when the solution advocated is confined, considered unclean, or is shared with others, and potential health benefits are long-term. Experience shows that users, and particularly women as providers of health care and carriers of water, must be involved in the planning, implementation, and operation of sanitation and water projects.

Sanskrit *Indo-Iranian languages.

Sapir–Whorf hypothesis, a psycholinguistic theory that a *culture's language embodies the way in which it understands the world and dictates how those who use that language think about the world. This may be due to structural factors, such as the way time is expressed in verb tenses, as well as to more superficially obvious features such as vocabulary. The theory is named after the US anthropologist and linguist Edward Sapir (1884–1939) and his pupil Benjamin Lee Whorf (1897–1941), who developed an extreme version of it in his essays about American Indian languages published in *Language, Thought and Reality* (1956). Much of the research has concentrated on the vocabulary of colour terms, since languages differ in their number of colour words and the distinctions they make along the spectrum. There is limited evidence that this may affect colour matching, but no evidence for the gross differences that limited colour vocabularies might be expected to produce. The idea that language may affect thought has been hotly disputed in educational and child psychology, with Lev Vygotsky (1896–1934) in favour and *Piaget against. A weak version of the theory appears in the claim that dialects or lower-class speech may diminish speakers' ability to think or communicate adequately. Another influential version appears in *Wittgenstein's philosophy.

Sartre, Jean-Paul (1905–80), French philosopher and writer, chief proponent of *existentialism in the post-war years. His central philosophical work, *L'Etre et le néant* (1943), attempted to characterize the fundamental structures of human existence by describing the clash between consciousness and the objective world, in such a way as to give prominence to what Sartre considered the defining feature of human beings: their freedom. His literary works (notably *La Nausée*, 1938, *Chemins de la liberté*, 1945–9, and numerous plays) paralleled and illustrated his philosophical project. Sartre's later writings concentrated on political questions, notably *Marxism, and include a multi-volume study of Flaubert.

sat-cit-ānanda (sathchidananda), a combination of three Sanskrit terms in Hinduism: *sat*, a state of being, unconditioned by change of form or name; *cit*, consciousness not limited by personal awareness; *ānanda*, joy without the restrictions of particular emotions. These terms relate to the three qualities of existence, cognition, and volition which characterize all sentient beings. The absolute or ultimate principle of God or the impersonal *Brahman is minimally conceived of as being without any of the conditions, limitations, or restrictions which qualify individual sentient creatures. Realization (*moksha) of Brahman consists in the freedom from these qualifications and/or the attainment of

Sartre at a demonstration in memory of victims of Nazism at Père Lachaise Cemetery, in the recently liberated Paris of 1944. World War II confirmed Sartre's belief that man's defining characteristic, freedom, must be expressed through political activity.

that absolute state. Within *Vedānta there is a debate as to whether Brahman can be positively described in our limited language without logical incoherence, as 'absolute being-consciousness-bliss'; or only negatively, as not being circumscribed by impermanent existence, individualized awareness, and transient joy in the way ordinary souls are.

satellite broadcasting, the re-transmission via satellite of *television and *radio broadcasts, transmitted from the earth back to distant points on the earth's surface. Satellite broadcasts reach the individual television receiver via microwave frequencies or cable from ground stations, or from a direct broadcasting satellite (DBS), via small 'backyard antenna' dishes. Satellites can make news, sporting, and other images available to world-wide audiences of over a billion people. Easily transported 'earth terminals' 2–3 m (7–10 feet) in diameter can transmit direct to satellites which have spurred the growth of *cable television and *narrowcasting. In the USA, Home Box Office began transmission to cable stations in 1975 by satellite. US *networks have used satellites to distribute their programmes since the 1980s. Many local stations, especially in radio, alternate satellite-transmitted programmes—often news, sports, and other more specialized channels—with local *advertising. Satellite *broadcasting can be cheaper, more reliable, and more flexible than traditional links. Future developments may be in direct broadcasts to rural areas (of potential benefit in developing countries), and delivery of high-definition images (HDTV). However, many multichannel DBS systems rely on cheap programming from the USA, which may elicit complaints of cultural imperialism.

satellite transmission, the use of a satellite in the communication of any signal (telephone, telegraph, *radio, video, or *television) enabling messages to be exchanged across great distances, and providing remote communities with access to global *telecommunications. There are thousands of artificial satellites, many engaged in *satellite broadcasting. Over a dozen countries have their own satellite systems, and the services of the world-wide Intelsat consortium are used by over 110 countries. Satellite links are also used for up-to-the-minute stockmarket reports and teleconferencing, in weather forecasting, mapping, land-use management, navigation, and for military purposes. Such broadcasts may be 'scrambled' or encoded for security and require a decoder. Two-way satellite communications systems suitable for business use (V-sat) are in use in the USA, but they are not yet widespread elsewhere. The international regulation of satellite transmission is the concern of the UN Committee on the Peaceful Uses of Outer Space; issues raised include the regulation of spy satellites, which make use of information gathered by one country about another, as well as direct satellite broadcasting from one country to another.

Saussure, Ferdinand de (1857–1913), Swiss linguist, pioneer of *semiotics. His major contribution was to the theoretical foundations of *language studies. He distinguished between two aspects of language: *langue*, a system shared by a community of speakers, and *parole*, the actual linguistic behaviour of individual speakers. He made it explicit that the study of *langue* can be 'diachronic' or 'historical', focusing on linguistic change in history, or 'synchronic', treating languages as temporarily self-contained systems. He also argued that synchronic linguistics must view *langue* as structured systems of interrelated elements. He broke language down into linguistic units such as *phonemes and words, which, he argued, could only be defined in relation to other such units in terms of syntagmatic (co-occurrence) relationships and paradigmatic (substitution) relationships. The idea that every element in a system both defines and is defined by all other elements underlies *structuralist linguistics and has been extended to other fields of enquiry, giving rise to semiotics. Saussure's theories were published posthumously in *Cours de linguistique générale* (1916), which is based on his own and his students' lecture notes.

savings-and-loan association   *building society.

Say's Law   *classical economics.

Scandinavian languages   *Germanic languages.

scarcity, a situation where there is less of a certain good than people would like to consume if its cost were zero. Similarly, a *resource is scarce if firms and individuals would like to use more of it at zero price than exists. Thus air is not scarce, but labour and cars are. If any resource required in the production of a good is scarce, then the good itself will be scarce; conversely, goods scarcity implies at least some resource scarcity. In the presence of scarcity some method of resource allocation is needed for economic efficiency. Economics itself has been defined (by the UK economist Lionel Robbins in 1930) as 'a science which studies human behaviour as a relation between ends and scarce means which have alternative uses'. (See also opportunity *cost.)

scepticism, any philosophical position which maintains that our beliefs about a certain subject-matter cannot be justified. *Epistemology, the philosophical theory of knowledge, has often been regarded as the search for an effective answer to scepticism. Scepticism can be either global or local. Global scepticism is concerned with all our beliefs about the external world, and claims that we can have no knowledge of the way that the world really is. Local scepticism is more specific, and only claims that beliefs in a certain area, such as *ethics, cannot be justified. Local scepticism can be used as a way of showing that commonly accepted beliefs about a subject cannot be maintained because they lead to a sceptical conclusion. *Hume, for example, used scepticism in this way in his discussion of *induction.

schizophrenia, a *mental illness characterized by disturbances in thoughts, feelings, and actions and the relationships between them. In an acute episode, the symptoms may include delusions, hallucinations such as imaginary voices, and bizarre behaviour. Many who experience an acute episode recover well, but if the disease becomes chronic, the mental torment drives some sufferers to become apathetic and withdrawn, while others become unpredictable, demanding, and sometimes aggressive. The risk of *suicide is high. World Health Organization studies have found that about one person in a hundred world-wide will suffer an episode during their lifetime. The causes of schizophrenia are unknown, but research suggests that it arises from a disturbance in the biochemical balance in the brain triggered by stress, hormonal changes, or other factors in predisposed individuals. The predisposition is sometimes inherited. There is no evidence for the theory (once widely disseminated) that faulty upbringing can cause schizophrenia. *Drug treatment can control symptoms but not cure the illness, and can have severe side effects. WHO has found that

Children in a physics lesson in a Russian secondary school. The **school system** in the former Soviet Union focused on creating productive future employees by enhancing the status of work and involving children in practical projects from the earliest opportunity.

a higher proportion of sufferers recover in developing than in industrialized countries, possibly because they can sometimes be contained in larger, more supportive family networks. If the disease becomes severely disabling, sufferers need long-term treatment and support. However, hospital care and community services are likely to be inadequate because of the lack of finance in developing countries and the trend towards de-institutionalization in industrialized countries.

scholasticism, the philosophy practised in the 'Schools' or medieval universities. Medieval philosophical writing often has a very formal style, derived from the dominant pattern of teaching in the universities. First a question is raised; the views of several previous philosophers or Church authorities on the question are then expounded and criticized in turn; finally the author's own answer to the question is presented and defended, often in a way which draws attention to minute points of agreement and disagreement with his predecessors. In the best hands, this method of presentation can convey the impression of a powerful, original mind exploiting the resources of an active intellectual tradition. Lesser writers seem merely to adopt the formulas of argument, contributing little but dry and pointless distinctions. The pejorative use of the term derives from this latter group.

school system, the institutions and principles that make up the formal *education of a country. In the 20th century, many schools throughout the world have been set up according to the system developed in the industrialized countries of the West. The state system provides nine out of ten school places in many countries, but often a parallel system of *independent education remains in place. Most schools are co-educational, but traditional single-sex schools survive and are becoming more numerous in Islamic countries. Sometimes control of the system is highly centralized, as in Japan and, formerly, the Soviet Union. In the USA and Australia, responsibility devolves to states. In Switzerland there are said to be as many school systems (twenty-six) as there are cantons. Some systems, as in the UK and the USA, are *comprehensive. That is, children can expect to continue from the beginning of *primary education to the end of compulsory schooling without hindrance. Elsewhere secondary school places are limited (as in much of the developing world) or schools are academically selective and entrance is by examination. In some countries, only a half day of schooling can be offered. In industrialized countries, children typically learn basic *literacy and numeracy in primary school. In *secondary school, from about 11, children gradually specialize—often after some three years—in arts or science subjects, and *vocational studies may begin. Examination success at the end of secondary school, at around 16 to 18 years of age, gains entry to some form of *higher education. At every stage, some children drop out from pressure to earn or lack of money, lack of motivation, or simply because there are not enough schools.

Schopenhauer, Arthur (1788–1860), German philosopher. In his main work, *The World as Will and Representation* (1818), Schopenhauer took *Kant's *idealist metaphysics as his starting-point. He accepted Kant's thesis that the external world is constituted by our minds, and in this sense is a 'representation'. But he denied that the world as it is in itself is unknowable and identified it instead with 'will'. Will in Schopenhauer's sense is a blind, surging force, without purpose or direction. This, he argued, vindicates a profoundly pessimistic view of human life, to which art and aesthetic contemplation provide a partial antidote.

Schumpeter, Joseph (1883–1950), Austrian economist and social philosopher. A prominent member of the Austrian School of economics, he was interested less in technical questions of economics than in long-term patterns of economic change. In *Capitalism, Socialism and Democracy* (1942), he predicted that *capitalism's very success would lead to its demise. The size of economic enterprises would grow, competition would give way to *oligopoly and *monopoly, and there would be less and less scope for the individual entrepreneur. The inevitable (though unwelcome) outcome would be a form of *socialism where economic decisions were made centrally by bureaucratic means. He also put forward a view of *democracy as a political method whereby individuals acquire the power to make decisions by means of a competitive struggle for the people's vote. He contrasted this with the more traditional view that democratic decisions reflect the general will of the people, which, he said, made wildly unrealistic demands on the political capacities of the ordinary person.

science, philosophy of, the investigation of the concepts and methods of the natural and social sciences. There are two major themes. Historically the most important is the realism debate which dates back to the time of the pioneer astronomer scientists Galileo (1564–1642) and Copernicus (1473–1543) and is concerned with the interpretation of scientific theories. The question is whether these theories should be regarded as true descriptions of the world (scientific realism) or whether they are rather instruments which are not literally true, but simply useful in that they enable us to make successful predictions about immediately observable phenomena (instrumentalism). A more recent debate concerning the nature of scientific progress is the rationality

debate, which asks how we can characterize the 'scientific method', or even whether such a single, universal method can be identified (see *Popper). Both debates have strong links with *epistemology, the theory of knowledge. On the question of scientific rationality we can ask what sort of justification there can be for the choice of one scientific theory over another. And in the realism issue, we can ask whether we have adequate justification for regarding scientific statements as literally true. A further question is the relationship between the natural sciences (such as physics and chemistry) and the *social sciences (such as *economics and *sociology). Should they be regarded as close enough to share the same methods (as in *Comte's positivism)? Or are the methods of the natural sciences inappropriate for the subject-matter of the social sciences? Do the natural and social sciences even have the same aim? It has been argued that the aim of natural science is prediction and control of natural processes, whereas the aim of the social sciences is to understand human behaviour. The question of *reductionism plays a role here: can sociology be reduced to *psychology, and psychology in turn to a more physically grounded neuroscience? Or are social and psychological processes irreducible?

Scientology, a religious system based on the teachings of the US science-fiction writer, L. Ron Hubbard (1911–86). The Church of Scientology, which evolved from a type of psychotherapy called 'Dianetics', was established in 1955. Its teachings combine 'psychotherapy' with aspects of *Christianity, *Hinduism, and *Buddhism. The basic belief is that humans are immortal beings called Thetans, who progress towards enlightenment through a process of *reincarnation. In order to rediscover the Thetan within, members undergo 'auditing', a rigorous interview process, including lie-detector tests, to increase self-awareness. Controversially, the results are stored for future reference and guidance; the financial demands that Scientology makes on its members have also aroused controversy.

Scots law, the law applicable in Scotland, which remains resistant to the dominant influence of English law within the *UK legal system. Scots law came under early Anglo-Saxon–Norman influence in the feudal period (11th to 13th centuries), but Scotland's later political and cultural alliance with France led to the importation during the 14th to 16th centuries of *Roman law doctrines by Scottish law students returning from continental universities. The separate Scottish legal system, court structure, and procedures have been preserved until today, despite the union of the two kingdoms in 1603 and of the two parliaments in 1707. Scots law is more highly systematized, relying, like other *civil law systems, more on general principles (such as the law of *obligations) than on *case law and *precedent. The chief inferior *courts in Scotland are sheriff courts, with both a civil and a criminal jurisdiction. The sheriff is the title of the *judge, and the public prosecutor is known as the procurator fiscal. The Lord Advocate is the chief law officer in Scotland, with ultimate responsibility for Crown prosecutions. The superior Scottish civil court is the Court of Session, and the superior criminal court is the High Court of Justiciary. The supreme Scottish civil court is the House of Lords, sitting in London, and consisting usually of three English judges and two Scottish judges. This fact, together with the increased volume of legislation from the English-dominated Westminster Parliament, means that there is a considerable English influence over Scots law, a trend resisted by many Scottish lawyers.

secession, the declaration, or attempted declaration, of independence by parts of a state. The right of secession may be included in the constitution of a state, for example in federal systems, but in many cases the attempt to secede centres on a power struggle and can lead to violent conflict or *civil war, in which outside states sometimes become involved. The most notable secessions of the 20th century were perhaps those of the republics of the former Soviet Union (1991). The growth of federal systems in newly independent states after the collapse of the British and other empires, partly in acknowledgement that *nation-states include disparate ethnic groups and territories, has led to several attempted secessions, including that of Biafra from Nigeria (1969–71), and the actual secession of Bangladesh (formerly East Pakistan) from Pakistan (1971). (See also *separatism.)

secondary education, the instruction of children from the age of about 11, on leaving *primary school, to the time when they enter employment or continue into *higher or *vocational education. Changes in secondary education in the 20th century have been influenced by the expansion of enrolments resulting from *population growth and the desire to equalize educational opportunities between *social classes and ethnic and racial groupings. There has been a great increase, noticeably in the developed world, of occupations requiring extensive formal education. Nations are constantly required to revise their curriculum, adjust their facilities, and retrain their teachers. In most industrialized countries, nearly all children receive their secondary education free, at least to the lower grades (in many developing countries, schooling for the majority does not continue beyond the age of 12). In the 1940s the USA and Sweden pioneered comprehensive secondary schools, later adopted by many other countries, in which all pupils were offered both academic and vocational curricula under one roof. The methods used in secondary education in Asia, Latin America, and Africa remain greatly influenced by the earlier teaching methods of Europe and North America, in which pupils were taught to learn by rote and recitation and all activities were dominated by the teacher. While this method is also used in the ideologically driven educational systems of China and Cuba, most of the secondary school population in these countries attends part-time, vocationally oriented middle schools where all pupils are expected to involve themselves in approved work projects. Current teaching in Europe and North America attempts broadly to develop the intellect, with the teacher again dominating the learning process through lecturing, demonstrations, questioning, and debate. More recently, a third method which attempts to anticipate employment needs has been gaining ground. In this, education is process led, that is, in conjunction with a firm foundation in the humanities, social sciences, and the natural sciences, pupils are encouraged to develop skills and attitudes which mirror social needs and *employment opportunities. Pupils are given a relevant and realistic context to the knowledge acquired and are asked to locate, define, and analyse a problem holistically. For example, the needs of the community are presented, and pupils are asked to plan solutions, make models, and evaluate their work. The aim is to create an awareness of the process of social and economic *development in a complex world.

secondary industry (manufacturing industry), any economic activity which takes raw materials and transforms them through the *production process into *goods. Secondary industry includes construction, fuel-processing, and other power generation; it may be divided into *heavy and *light industry. Secondary industry is traditionally seen as the principal means of *development and *economic growth for developing economies, where *primary industry predominates; but in the advanced industrialized economies, such as the USA or UK, *tertiary industry has tended to supersede manufactured heavy industry. This partly reflects changes in (global) technology and demand pattern, and, partly, a shift in comparative advantage, with heavy industry moving to *newly industrializing countries such as Taiwan and South Korea.

sectarianism *communal conflict.

secularism *religion and politics.

security, a document issued by firms, institutions, and governments which gives the owner of the security certain property rights and/or the right to receive *interest or *dividends. Securities are commonly traded on *stock exchanges. If the current price of a security is higher than its issue price or nominal *value, the security is said to be at a premium (see also *discount). Types of securities include fixed-interest-bearing securities, normally representing debts such as *debentures, preference *shares, and *bonds (including all government securities such as *gilts); and variable income securities, essentially shares. Preference shares are an intermediate category; they normally carry a fixed dividend having priority over the dividend on other shares but not amounting to a legal entitlement like the interest on bonds. An investor's collection of securities is known as a portfolio.

Security Council, one of the six principal organs of the *UN, based at UN headquarters in New York, whose prime responsibility is to maintain world peace and security. The Security Council, which first met in January 1946, consists of five permanent members (the USA, Russia, China, France, and the UK), and ten non-permanent members elected by the *UN General Assembly for two-year terms on a rotating basis. With the changes in the economic and political *balance of power since the end of the cold war, a change in the permanent membership to admit Germany, Japan, the EC, or other regional powers, is likely to come under discussion. The Security Council can investigate any international dispute, and recommend ways of achieving a settlement, including 'enforcement measures', such as *sanctions, or the use of force by UN members. It is also responsible for peace-keeping forces such as UNIFIL (United Nations Interim Force in Lebanon), which was established in 1978 to confirm the withdrawal of Israeli forces from southern Lebanon, or UNIIMOG (United Nations Iran–Iraq Military Observer Group), established in 1988 to monitor the ceasefire after the Iran–Iraq War. Decisions taken by the Security Council require a majority of nine, including all five permanent members. This rule of *great power unanimity, usually referred to as the right of veto, has been the cause of controversy, as during the cold war, when the activities of the Security Council were frequently paralysed by the failure of the five permanent members to adopt a common position in international crises. However, the improvement in *East–West relations by the early 1990s meant that the Security Council had a chance of functioning effectively.

security services, governmental organizations with responsibility for protecting national security and for countering non-military threats to it. The term 'security services' covers organizations such as *intelligence services, *counter-intelligence services, and branches of the *police concerned with public order or official secrets. Even in liberal-*democratic regimes, the security services are likely to be insulated from public or parliamentary scrutiny, on the grounds that open debate about their operations would be detrimental to the national interest. Thus, in the USA, the National Security Act (1948) and in the UK the Official Secrets Acts (1911, 1939, 1989) are the essential foundations of the security services, and in each case the influence of the *legislature over their activities is severely limited. In *authoritarian states, or those with *military governments, the security services may act as important mechanisms of state control over the lives of citizens (see *police state). One of the most characteristic activities of security services is that of spying, also known as espionage, either within or outside their home state. A central feature of the post-1945 period in industrial countries has been the growth of private security services, aimed at protecting property or commercial activities, and the accompanying growth of activities such as industrial espionage.

sedition, any activity aimed at undermining an established government, usually by speech or writing rather than the use of violence. Sedition is generally taken to be a less serious offence than *treason, but has been a frequent concern of governments, particularly in wartime or times of international tension. The McCarthyite 'witch hunts' of the 1950s in the USA saw many Americans, including prominent public figures, accused of seditious activity, primarily as the result of alleged association with the Communist Party. Likewise, dissident groups in the former Eastern bloc and the erstwhile Soviet Union were accused of sedition or 'anti-state activities' when mounting protests or circulating *samizdat publications.

segregation, the enforced separation of groups by *race or *gender. Segregation affects the provision of schooling, transport, and other public facilities, land, and accommodation. The best-known example is probably that of apartheid ('separate development') in South Africa, designed to separate not only Whites from Blacks, but also non-White groups from each other. The legislation forming the cornerstones of apartheid was repealed in 1991. In the southern states of the USA, segregation laws forced Blacks to attend separate schools until the Supreme Court declared (1954) the so-called 'separate but equal' principle unconstitutional. Segregation on grounds of gender or *caste may be enforced for religio-social reasons, as in Saudi Arabia, where women have separate educational and transport facilities, or in India, where place of residence may be dictated by caste.

self-concept, a set of beliefs that people hold about themselves. There is a tradition of self-reflection in the works of philosophers such as St *Augustine, *Descartes, *Hume, and *James, whose discussion in *The Principles of Psychology* (1890) provides the immediate source for many approaches to the self and self-concept today. The *Chicago School of *symbolic interactionism, particularly in the work of the social psychologist G. H. Mead (1863–1931), gave the 'self' a central role in its theories of child development and *socialization. For Mead, an individual's self and *personality develop through and reflect consciousness of others' *attitudes to him or her. More recently *social, clinical, and *cognitive psychologists have investigated ways in which beliefs about oneself may affect one's behaviour, *emotions, and thought

processes. People's beliefs about their own abilities and about the nature of ability affect their determination, and thereby the development of their skills. If there is a discrepancy between what one thinks one is and what one thinks one ought to be, or wishes to be, this may occasion *anxiety or *depression.

self-determination, the right of a people to choose its political future and, by extension, the right to choose independence and statehood. Largely a phenomenon of the 20th century, it is enshrined in the UN Charter. Factors such as *ethnicity, *nationality, *language, or *religion, define a people's self-identity, but such definitions are likely to be controversial. Claims of self-determination often have a territorial basis, giving rise to *separatism or *secession.

self-presentation, tactics people employ to control the impression they make on others. The ways in which people define and project themselves in interaction with others have been a central concern of the American *symbolic interactionists including *Goffman. He held in *The Presentation of Self in Everyday Life* (1959) that the self is co-extensive with the social roles the individual acts out in public. Goffman produced detailed anecdotal descriptions of the 'protective' and 'corrective' actions people routinely take to 'save face' for themselves and others.

semantics, a branch of *linguistics studying meaning. For some linguists it is concerned with all aspects of meaning, but for others it is concerned just with those aspects that are independent of context, context-dependent aspects of meaning such as politeness or conversational interaction being the province of pragmatics. On either view, it deals with such matters as ambiguity, where an expression (word, phrase, or sentence) has more than one meaning; synonymy, where two expressions mean the same; and entailment, where one sentence follows from another. It draws on work in *logic and *philosophy.

semiotics, the study of natural and artificial *signs and sign systems. It postulates that *communication is a *code. For example, in *language, signs like sounds and words are arranged in a particular manner, following rules of *grammar, into a speech system. Other communication systems include gesturing (see *non-verbal communication), the structure of *myths, symbolic rites, styles in clothing, and *food customs. The semiotic approach to *language was advocated by *Saussure, but other linguists have rejected it as descriptively inadequate. They claim that language understanding and interpretation involve not only the decoding of a linguistic sign but also processes of inference.

Semitic languages, an important group of languages presently spoken throughout North Africa, the Arabian peninsula, and the Middle East. They fall into two major halves, the Eastern branch and the Western branch. All modern Semitic languages are descendants of the Western branch. The Eastern group was extremely important in antiquity, however; Akkadian (which later developed into Babylonian and Assyrian) was the great language of ancient Mesopotamia during the second and first millennia BC. The cuneiform (a script of wedge-shaped syllabic characters) tablets bearing these languages were rediscovered and deciphered in the 19th century. Western Semitic falls into two branches, South and Central. South Semitic is the Ethiopian branch, of which the two main languages are Tigrinya (spoken in Tigre and Eritrea) and Amharic, the official language of Ethiopia (13 million speakers). Central Semitic is much larger, and includes Arabic, Hebrew, Phoenician, and Aramaic. By far the largest Semitic language is Arabic, which has over 150 million native speakers, and is used by many more as a second language. There are two varieties: classical Arabic, the language of Islam, has remained virtually unchanged since the 7th century AD, and is used both as a literary language and as a *lingua franca throughout the Arab world. Colloquial Arabic is not a single language, but consists of the numerous modern dialects spoken in everyday life, which differ from region to region. These are not necessarily mutually intelligible. Maltese is also an Arabic language, although it is written in the Roman *alphabet. Hebrew has a long and interesting history: the Jewish scriptures were written in biblical Hebrew between about 1200 and 200 BC, but the language began to decline as a spoken language by the end of the 6th century BC and was almost supplanted by Aramaic by the time of Jesus Christ. However, the language was maintained by Jews down the centuries as a religious and literary language, and was resurrected (with modifications) as a living language at the beginning of the 20th century. It is now the official language of Israel, where it has 4 million speakers. Aramaic, which replaced Hebrew as the spoken language in Palestine, has a descendant called Syriac, which has only 300,000 speakers in scattered groups across the Middle East. Phoenician is now extinct, but was important in the first millennium BC, being the language of an active trading and colonizing people. Semitic is part of Afro-Asiatic, a larger group which includes ancient Egyptian, Berber, Chadic, and Cushitic.

Senate, US, the second chamber of the US Congress, representing the fifty states of the union. Each state has two senators, regardless of population, directly elected since 1913. One-third of the Senate is re-elected every two years. The US Senate is unusual among second chambers in that it is broadly co-equal in power with the *House of Representatives, the other chamber of the *bicameral US *legislature. Fewer in number and with the security of a six-year term, senators are more prominent political figures than most Representatives. The Senate, with its committees and subcommittees, constitutes a formidable counterweight to the *President. Presidential appointments of high federal officials are subject to the advice and consent of the Senate, which also has the power to ratify foreign treaties and to impeach the president, both by a two-thirds majority.

sense data, a technical term used by philosophers to refer to the basic simple units of *perception. Sense data are usually explained by considering ordinary cases of perceptual illusion, such as the appearance which a stick partly submerged in water gives of being bent; or the elliptical appearance of a round coin seen from an angle. These cases are said to show that what we are directly aware of are never physical objects but only complex sensory appearances, which can be analysed into patches of colour and sensations; it is these which are called sense data. How we go from knowledge of these elements to knowledge of a physical world is the problem of perception.

sentence (in law), the decision of a *court of law, especially the *punishment allotted to a person convicted in a criminal trial. Sometimes courts are constrained by mandatory penalties: *capital punishment for *homicide, for instance. A maximum penalty for each category of offence is normally

set. Fixed penalties, or penalties fixed within a narrow range, are known as tariff sentences; they are intended to ensure retribution according to the severity of the crime and equity between offenders. Their disadvantage is that they pay little or no regard to differences between offenders. Therefore, in most legal systems *judges exercise some discretion, taking into account such factors as the offender's age and previous convictions, and the circumstances of the *crime. Such sentences give less weight to retribution and to the deterrence of others, and more to the needs and deserts of the individual. Their disadvantage is that different penalties may be inflicted for similar offences, arousing justified claims of unfairness. Furthermore, the disparities may sometimes arise from conscious or unconscious bias, for example against a particular ethnic group. In an attempt to reduce unwarranted differences, specially established sentencing commissions in some US states (notably Minnesota and Pennsylvania) have devised guidelines which indicate the range of permissible variations in sentences for each offence.

separation of powers, a classic doctrine of liberal government, usually associated with the French philosopher Montesquieu (1689–1755), although the tripartite division was earlier suggested by *Aristotle and *Locke. In *The Spirit of the Laws* (1748), Montesquieu set out that the three branches of government—the *legislature, the *executive, and the *judiciary—should be constitutionally separate from each other, both in function and in persons. This produces institutions that are relatively independent from one another and supports a system of checks and balances, preventing any one branch of government from dominating the others. The doctrine is enshrined in the US Constitution, which provides a formal separation of Congress, President, and Supreme Court. The separation, however, is not total and some collaboration, especially between President and Congress, is necessary if the system is to work at all (see *US government). In countries with *parliamentary government, the executive and legislature are fused and have overlapping functions. In the UK, the executive, formed from the majority in Parliament, dominates the legislature. The judiciary, however, does stand to one side and is largely independent of legislative and executive processes, although the head of the judiciary, the Lord Chancellor, is a member of the *cabinet (executive) as well as the presiding officer of the *House of Lords (legislature). (See also *pluralism.)

separatism, the aim of establishing an independent political unit to represent a particular ethnic, religious, or other grouping, sometimes associated with the aim of *secession or *self-determination. A driving force behind separatism is the perception of a distinct geographical, ethnic, religious, or cultural identity, which becomes associated with a political movement. The desire for control over the destiny of the group in political, economic, and cultural terms may lead to demands for independence which may express themselves in peaceful protest as well as *political violence or forms of *nationalism. Separatism may lead to internal conflict, *civil war, and intervention. There are a number of different separatist forces in the Punjab in *India, for instance; other separatist movements are those in Eritrea and the *Basques in Spain and France. In some cases, calls for separatism may be satisfied by *devolution, that is, enhanced local self-government, or semi-autonomy.

Sephardi (plural, Sephardim, from Hebrew, 'sefarad', Spain), a member of the southern branch of the *Jewish peo-

A house search in Kashmir, India is one sign of increasing tension in the area. As in the neighbouring state of Punjab there are calls for **separatism** by the Kashmir Liberation Front, but the situation is complicated by calls from rival Muslim terrorist groups for the state to join Pakistan.

ple. They number 17 per cent of the world's Jewish population, and many are resident in Israel, where they formed over half the population until the influx of Soviet Jews in the 1990s. The term refers to those Jews who were resident in Portugal and Spain until their expulsion in 1492, when they settled elsewhere in Europe, North Africa, and the lands of the Ottoman Empire. Sephardic Jews speak Ladino, a form of medieval Spanish with Hebrew, Arabic, and Turkish elements, and they preserve the Babylonian Jewish traditions rather than the Palestinian traditions of the *Ashkenazim. Today the term Sephardim is commonly applied to all 'oriental' Jews, that is, those of the Middle East and North Africa, whatever their origin.

Serbo-Croat language   *Slavic languages.

service industry   *tertiary industry.

settlement (in law), the resolution of a dispute outside the courtroom, either directly, by negotiations between the parties or their representatives or insurers, or indirectly, through a third party. The use of a third party is characteristic of mediation and arbitration, two forms of *dispute resolution. In *civil cases, there are considerable pressures on the person bringing the case to settle, although this may involve the partial compromising of the claim. Pressure to reach a settlement is caused by difficulties in obtaining evidence, legal costs, and uncertainty about the outcome of the case.

Seventh-day Adventist   *Adventist, *millenarianism.

sex differences (in psychology), differences in males and females. Statistics showing sex differences are often unreliable, since there may be differential reporting of abilities and disabilities between the sexes. However, it has been repeatedly shown that females have greater verbal skills and males greater visual–spatial and mathematical skills. The origin of these differences in genetic or environmental factors continues to be hotly disputed. Temperamental differences, especially in the display of aggression, are often linked to hormones and to the primary and secondary sexual characteristics important for reproduction. There are well-documented sex differences in the age of reaching puberty, in total body growth, in longevity, and in susceptibility to *neuroses and *depression. No fully satisfactory theory exists to explain how such biological differences interact with social processes to give rise to tertiary level characteristics, such as the lesser representation of females among mathematicians or in the sciences. Differential growth rates may result in a variance in the patterns of brain differentiation for verbal and spatial skills. The distribution of such abilities between the sexes, although overlapping, would then show a different range. Sex roles within the social system (see *gender) may further exaggerate such inherent sex differences as children learn through *socialization to take their place in the social world.

sexism, *discrimination against an individual or a group on the grounds of biological sex (see *gender). While the term can apply to any such discrimination, it is usually employed to describe the attitudes of those who regard women as inferior, or as objects to be used for sexual pleasure. Some feminists argue that the male domination of women characteristic of *patriarchy is not a feature of an individual relationship but rather an inevitable result of *social structure, influencing all areas of life: work opportunities, family roles, sexual relationships, and the social and legal systems. The *women's movement aims to end sexism, allowing women to take control over their own lives, as well as liberating men from the role of oppressor.

sexual behaviour, any activity aimed at procreation or erotic gratification. Accepted sexual practice varies across cultures and historical epochs, a point emphasized by anthropologists such as *Mead, who argued that there is no single pattern of relations between the sexes, and no particular sexual orientation (or position) which is natural and proper. Some societies are monogamous, others polygamous; some encourage premarital sex, others condemn it; in some *homosexuality is accepted, in others it is a criminal offence. Studies of the intimate aspects of human sex are comparatively recent, and most have contented themselves with people's reports of what they do. The Kinsey Reports (*Sexual Behaviour in the Human Male* (1948) and *Sexual Behaviour in the Human Female* (1953)) were the first famous studies of this kind, and questionnaire surveys became popular in the 1970s, although there is some doubt about the honesty of people's answers to such surveys. Virginia Masters and William Johnson, however, went much further. Their *Human Sexual Response* (1966) reported their conclusions from laboratory observations of people's sex acts. More conventional studies have related people's reports on their sexual activities and preferences to factors such as *personality, attitudes, and *gender, usually with unsurprising findings. *Extroverts claim to have had sex earlier, more often, and with more partners. Women have less interest in premarital and in impersonal sex than men. In the 1970s there was evidence that Western women's attitudes were 'catching up', but in the 1980s there was a resurgence of more conservative attitudes, especially among women. Examples of the practical application of psychologists' work on sex include studies of the use (or lack of use) of contraceptives, as well as sex therapy for psychosexual problems.

sexual harassment, unwanted attention or intimidation, usually directed by men against women, which may range from leering and suggestive remarks to unwanted pressure for sexual favours, unwanted touching, sexual assault, and even *rape. It is a particular problem in the workplace, although it may occur elsewhere. Harassment may take forms that are not purely sexual, such as victimization; it is often seen as an issue of power rather than one of sex, particularly if the man is in a position of authority over the woman. Taking action against harassment may be difficult, since sexual harassment is not a criminal offence unless it goes as far as sexual assault or *rape. Many trade unions and women's groups have campaigned for codes of practice within workplaces and institutions, and sex *discrimination legislation may be used to obtain redress against some forms of harassment.

sexually-transmitted disease (STD; venereal disease), a *communicable disease usually or primarily spread by sexual contact. Besides gonorrhoea and syphilis, there are many extremely prevalent but less serious infections such as

During the preliminary stages, **sexual behaviour** is limited to subtle body gestures. In this scene from *Gentlemen Prefer Blondes* (1953) Marilyn Monroe protects herself by tucking in her leg and closing her hands over her knee, while her co-star displays his interest by the angle of his shoulder and foot.

genital herpes and chlamydia. Such diseases are difficult to contain: their stigma may prevent people seeking treatment; both partners must be treated in concert; and, in their early stages, the diseases may be virtually symptom-free, especially in women, so that one carrier may unwittingly infect several partners before seeking treatment. With the use of antibiotic and sulphonamide drugs, few people die of these diseases today (*Aids being an important exception), but untreated gonorrhoea or chlamydial infections are a significant cause of *infertility in both women and men, as well as causing miscarriages, stillbirths, and birth defects. Genital ulcers have been identified as a risk factor in the transmission of HIV, the virus that causes Aids. Sexually-transmitted diseases are increasing in almost every country in the world, largely as a result of the social and moral changes that tend to accompany migration and urbanization.

sexual offences, crimes of a sexual nature, many of which are also crimes of violence. Crimes involving non-consensual sexual aggression include *rape and indecent assault: violations of privacy and personal security that in most societies are considered particularly serious. Feminists argue that many sexual offences against women are not the result of uncontrolled sexual desires, but are rather the expression of a need to humiliate or exercise domination over the victim. Under authoritarian regimes women and children may frequently be the victims of sexual assaults by members of the *security forces. A second category of sexual offences focuses on the protection of those thought vulnerable, such as people who are mentally handicapped or children (see *child sexual abuse). More controversial are sexual offences in a third category, those which are intended to maintain standards of morality; thus *homosexual acts and *prostitution are illegal in some societies.

Shabbat (Sabbath, from Hebrew, 'rest'), the Jewish weekly holy day, beginning on Friday evening and ending at sunset on Saturday, during which time no work is permitted (except in liberal traditions), in obedience to the Fourth Commandment. Among Orthodox Jews the prohibition of work is taken to ban any creative or causal activity, such as writing, travelling, or switching on an electric light. Ritual is based primarily in the home, although *synagogue attendance is usual on both days. The Sabbath begins on Friday evening, when the mother lights and blesses the Shabbat candles in preparation for the Shabbat meal, at which the father will bless two loaves of bread called *challah*. The *Kiddush* ('Sanctification') prayer is said over a cup of wine, and the bread is broken, sprinkled with salt, and eaten. At the end of the meal, a concluding prayer, the *havdalah* ('differentiation'), is said, which marks God's distinction between the sacred and profane, and indicates the Shabbat's difference from other days.

Shakti (Sanskrit, 'power', 'energy'), a name of the Great Goddess or Devī, one of the most important of the monotheistic deities worshipped by Hindus. As the earth mother she is the object of widespread popular devotion in India. She is also the consort of *Shiva, but is worshipped independently of him. In her benevolent aspect she is known as Umā, Pārvatī, or Ambikā (little mother), while in her fearful and destructive aspect she appears as Kālī or *Durgā. She is also identified with Lakshmi, goddess of wealth and good fortune, the consort of *Vishnu. Shāktism, the cult of Shakti, is, with Vaishnavism and Shaivism, one of the three major forms of *Hinduism.

shamanism, a kind of religious practice focused on specific individuals, known as shamans, who are able to act as mediums between the human and the supernatural. Although shaman is originally a Siberian word, the term is applied in a wide variety of contexts in Africa, Asia, and the Americas. Typically male, shamans combine both religious and *healing functions, and their authority derives from personal religious experience, such as *spirit possession, rather than from an institutional role. Shamanic experiences can involve the use of hallucinogenic drugs, or sensory deprivation or stimulation, all of which may help the shaman establish contact with the spirit world. Shamans are often regarded as possessing superior wisdom and knowledge. In certain circumstances they are thought capable of inflicting illness as well as curing it.

shame *honour.

shanty town, a popular term for settlements in which most of the structures are constructed by residents and where, initially at least, *water, *sanitation, and other services are lacking. The UN agency Habitat in its *Global Report on Human Settlements* (1987) uses the term 'informal settlement'. The land on which an informal settlement is built has usually either been seized illegally by *squatters, or purchased, but without permission from the municipal authorities for construction on it. In fourteen cities in developing countries studied by the UN, one-third to four-fifths of the inhabitants lived in informal settlements and the proportion was rising rapidly: Nouakchott, Mauritania, for example, had 5,000 inhabitants in 1965 and 270,000 in 1985, with most of the extra inhabitants in illegal shanty or tent encampments. Although informal settlements are frequently on unsuitable sites, such as steep hillsides, are overcrowded, lack services, and are constructed from recycled materials, many have held that they offer the best hope of housing the poor. In an influential work, *Housing by People* (1976), the UK architect F. J. C. Turner contended that they afford cheap and flexible workspace and accommodation, and can, over time, in favourable circumstances, be improved. Residents are often willing to upgrade their own homes and communal facilities if they are given some security of tenure. Most municipal authorities now believe it more satisfactory to accommodate informal housing than to build *government housing. With the encouragement of the World Bank and other international organizations, authorities have sometimes devised 'sites-and-services' projects which supply basic infrastructure on new sites and let the owners build the rest at their own pace. Such ventures cannot, however, be afforded by the very poor. Narrowly targeting improvements in water and sanitation in existing settlements tends to reach them more effectively. Both schemes have proved administratively complex and many argue that only more radical policies to tackle such issues as land speculation and income distribution within and between countries can ameliorate *housing problems in the developing world.

share, a *security issued by a *company to raise long-term *capital. The ordinary shareholders of a *joint-stock company are its owners. In proportion to the shares they own, they are entitled to voting rights (to elect the directors of the company), to *dividends, and to the proceeds which remain from the liquidation of the company after all other creditors have been repaid in the event of bankruptcy. Preference shareholders take priority over ordinary shareholders in this event. They also receive their fixed dividend before any divi-

dend can be paid to ordinary shareholders. To raise capital, a company may offer new shares through an *issuing house. Alternatively, it may avoid the high cost of such an issue by seeking new capital from existing shareholders; this is known as a rights issue. A scrip issue (or share split) raises no new capital but merely alters the denomination of the company's shares, facilitating transactions in the shares in smaller lots. A convertible issue is a way of raising *loan capital which gives the option of conversion to shares.

sharecropping, a form of land tenancy in which a landlord allows land to be used in return for a share of the tenant's crops or labour. Sharecropping is found all over the world, especially among *peasant societies in developing countries; for example, it is widespread in many parts of Asia, especially in areas where rural population densities are high. It is associated with hierarchical social relations. There is substantial variation in the form of sharecropping agreements. Sometimes the landlord may share production costs (of seeds or labour, for instance) and sometimes not at all. Tenants may face a variety of restrictions, such as in the type of crops produced.

sharī'ah (from Arabic, 'path'), the law of Islam. The *sharī'ah* is the way of life prescribed for Muslims, based on the *Koran and the *ḥadīth. The *sharī'ah*, the path of religion, contains, and is sometimes identified with *fiqh*, jurisprudence, or the science of the *sharī'ah* worked out by the four orthodox schools in Sunnī Islam and by Imām Ja'far Sādiq (*c*.700–65) and other *imāms in Shī'ī Islam. Although the *sharī'ah* has no codification as in some Western law systems, the *fiqh* books may be considered the equivalent of law books. Legal opinions based on *fiqh* known as *fatwās* are given by scholars known as *muftīs*. A religious law, believed to be divinely revealed, the *sharī'ah* may be divided into two major categories: duties to God, which are summarized in the *Five Pillars of Islam; and duties to fellow men, including penal, commercial, and family law. In religious terms, all human actions may be classified into the following five categories: obligatory (in this category omission is punished); meritorious; indifferent; reprehensible; and forbidden (a category divided into different types of *sin). Each of the schools of law divides actions into somewhat different categories for legal purposes. From the earliest times Islamic rulers have supplemented the *sharī'ah* with secular law based on customary law and edicts issued to meet the political conditions of the day. Beginning in the 19th century, *westernization and colonization led to the introduction of Western civil, commercial, and penal codes in many Islamic countries; for example, in the Ottoman empire (the Turkish empire which ruled much of the Middle East and south-eastern Europe from the 16th to the early 20th centuries) a commercial code based on the French commercial code was adopted in 1850 and a new system of courts set up to implement it. By the middle years of the 20th century, in the majority of countries with a predominantly or partially Muslim population, the *sharī'ah* was applied only to family law; and in a number of countries the *sharī'ah* courts were abolished and a unified system of courts established. However, Turkey, Albania, and the former Soviet republics with a pre-

A **shanty town** or *favela* in Rio de Janeiro, Brazil's second-largest city. Even if a shanty town manages to obtain water supplies, facilities for the disposal of waste are likely to lag behind. It is estimated, for example, that less than 2 per cent of urban sewage in Latin America is treated.

dominantly Muslim population are the only Muslim countries to have adopted fully secular legal systems and to have abolished the *sharī'ah* entirely. Most other Muslim countries have adopted a mixed system. For example, in Egypt a civil code based on a compromise between Islamic and Western law was drawn up in 1949 and later adopted by Syria and Libya. In Iran and Saudi Arabia, the *sharī'ah* is the basis of the legal system, with special religio-legal bodies to ensure its correct application in all areas of government. The question of the reintroduction of all or part of the *sharī'ah* as happened in Iran and Sudan, is an issue for many Muslim countries, causing heated debate in some cases between *Islamic fundamentalists and *Islamic modernists. Pakistan announced plans to make the *sharī'ah* the supreme law of the land in 1991 whereas in Algeria the authorities closed down the pro-*sharī'ah* Islamic Salvation Front in early 1992.

shifting cultivation, a form of agriculture now usually practised in tropical conditions. Also known as slash-and-burn or swidden, it involves the use of a patch of newly cleared forest land for one or occasionally two seasons, before moving cultivation on to a new piece of land. The forest is generally cleared, then burned, before seeds are sown; the crops use the nutrients from the burnt forest. Although regarded with hostility by governments, shifting cultivation can provide a stable living at low population densities. However, it does require a high ratio of land to people as it takes a period of at least ten years for the forest to regenerate to support a further crop after cultivation. Shifting cultivation has been the basic mode of subsistence for many people in all parts of the world for thousands of years, but recent population increases in some areas, and the use of shifting cultivation for growing cash crops, that is, crops produced for sale or barter rather than subsistence, have led to a drastic shortening of the fallow cycle, and a rapid degeneration of the soil.

Shī'ī (Shi'ite) (from Arabic, 'sectarian'), a member of the minority Shī'ah division within *Islam, which consists of about one-fifth of all Muslims. Shī'īs are in the majority in Iran (where Shī'ī Islam is the state religion), southern Iraq, and parts of Yemen, and are also found in Syria, Lebanon, East Africa, northern India, and Pakistan. Originating as the partisans of *'Alī, Shī'īs now differ from *Sunnī Muslims primarily in the importance they attach to the continuing authority of the *imāms, who are the authentic interpreters of the *sunna* (customs), the code of conduct based on the *Koran and *ḥadīth. The suffering of the House of the Prophet, chiefly of Ḥusain and his martyrdom in Karbala, and the *millenarian expectation of a future *imām* or *mahdī* who is in occultation, permeate much Shī'ī thinking, providing a set of beliefs in which oppression and injustice figure largely. There are hundreds of different Shī'ī sects: the main ones are the Zaydis, *Isma'īlīs, and Ithna Ashariya (or Twelvers, who await the return of the hidden twelfth *imām*).

Shingon Buddhism (Japanese, 'School of the True Word'), one of the largest and most esoteric of Japanese Buddhist schools, founded by Kūkai (AD 774–835). Like many other *Mahāyāna schools, Shingon understands that enlightenment is already a universal property of humanity. That is, we are *Buddhas without knowing it. The teaching of a Buddha, however, is comprehensible only to initiates, and is passed from master to disciple. Since it cannot be expounded through words, it is transmitted by means of mandalas, or visual aids, by bodily postures, particularly

All **Shinto** shrines have a *torii* or gateway dividing the sacred and secular domains. This straw rope is a symbolic representation of the *torii* at one of Japan's oldest and most important Shinto sites, the Ise shrine in Southern Honshu.

hand gestures (*mudrās*), by *meditation, and by rituals from which many immediate spiritual and, unusually, material benefits may accrue.

Shinto (Chinese/Japanese, 'the Way of the Gods'), a Japanese religion dating from prehistoric times, based on the worship of *kami*, sacred powers associated with natural features such as mountains or rivers. Shinto is not a highly conceptualized religion; it is tolerant and adaptable, laying emphasis on high standards of behaviour and on daily rituals, rather than on doctrine. There is no official Shinto scripture, although the *Kojiki* (Records of Ancient Matters) and *Nihon-gi* (Chronicles of Japan), 8th-century compilations based on oral tradition, contain myths and stories about creation and the gods. During the 5th century AD, the spread of *Confucianism introduced *ancestor worship to Shinto, and in the 6th century *Buddhist beliefs became incorporated into the ancient religion, some *kami* being regarded as incarnations of *Buddhas or *bodhisattvas. During the 19th century the rise of the unified Japanese state saw the development of state Shinto: the emperor came to be worshipped as a descendant of the sun goddess Amaterasu. State Shinto became the dominant form of the religion, which informed all public life and encouraged extreme nationalism, until it was rescinded by the emperor (under US pressure) in 1945. It was replaced by the older form, shrine Shinto, the worship of *kami* in shrines or sanctuaries, tended by priests. In the home, the *kami* are housed within a *kami-dana*, or 'godshelf'. Personal worship involves purification rites and daily prayers to the *kami*. Shinto is regarded as the religion of life, while Buddhism is seen as that of death; marriages are therefore celebrated according to Shinto tradition, while people generally choose Buddhist rites for funerals. Pilgrimages to temples and shrines, particularly those on mountains, are widespread during the new year, spring, and autumn festivals. Festival worship includes the chanting of prayers, the playing of ceremonial music, and the offering of food. A set of different practices is associated with sect Shinto, new religious movements with a Shinto foundation.

Shiva (Sanskrit, 'the kind or auspicious one'), one of the most important of the monotheistic deities found in the Hindu tradition. Shiva is worshipped in several apparently contradictory aspects, whose combination gives emphasis to his incomprehensible transcendence. He is seen as a giver of blessings, and is also a symbol of sensuality, represented by the lingam or phallus. On the other hand, he is sometimes depicted as an ascetic, seated in meditation in the Himalayas. Shiva is also the god of destruction and dissolution. In his manifestation as Shiva Nataraja, the four-armed Lord of the Dance, he tramples on the forces of ignorance and chaos, and keeps creation in balance. His female consort appears variously as Pārvatī, *Durgā, or Kālī, and he is sometimes also paired with the Great Goddess, *Shakti. Shaivism, the cult of Shiva, is, with Vaishnavism and Shaktism, one of the three main forms of *Hinduism.

Shona, the largest group of Bantu-speaking people living in north and east Zimbabwe. Traditionally, they are farmers of maize, the primary staple, and other crops; cattle are valued for their milk but also for *lobola*, or marriage payments (see *dowry). Following White settlement in the late 19th century, many Shona were forced off their tribal lands and on to the labour-market. The Shona joined forces with the *Ndebele in the fight against colonialism, but it is the more numerous Shona who now dominate independent Zimbabwe. The traditional enmity between the two groups has resulted in continuing inter-ethnic strife.

shopping   *retail trading, *supermarket.

shorthand (stenography), speedy *writing abbreviating the letters or the sounds of words, and replacing frequent words and expressions by single *signs. It serves to record speech in business, *journalism, and elsewhere. Shorthand originated in ancient Greece. Modern systems, developed since the 17th century, draw on the Roman or the phonetic *alphabets, or abstract symbols.

shūnyāta (Sanskrit, 'emptiness', 'void'), a central concept within the Vajrayana and *Mahāyāna schools of *Buddhism. Early Buddhism acknowledged that all things are essentially impermanent, lacking in substance, and conditioned by suffering. *Mahāyāna schools developed this notion as the fundamental truth (*dharma*) upon which all others are based. It defines the world in that all things are devoid of content including the very concept of emptiness itself (as it would have to be if everything is empty). 'Emptiness' is the logical state of all reality, for any one particular thing can be shown, according to them, to not be what it is taken to be. Mahāyāna schools differentiate their philosophy from that of Theravāda with the following illustration: in Theravāda all reality is like an empty vessel, whereas within Mahāyāna the vessel itself is rejected. The Mahāyāna notion is further developed within the philosophical Madhyamika tradition. It is argued that all claims of knowledge are unjustifiable, all statements are reducible to contradiction, all action unable to attain the goal. These claims, of course, undercut themselves. But this paradoxical and self-refuting sceptical pursuit leads to an understanding of the futility of using language and concepts and a realization that volition and cognition are not ultimately real, that they are *shūnya* (empty) of meaning and significance. Such a realization results in the attainment of *nirvana (liberation).

sign, a key term in semiology or *semiotics (the study of symbols or signs), which denotes the link between the physical object (the signifier) and the mental concept (the signified). The Swiss linguist *Saussure described language as a *code combining signs (words) which have meaning only in a particular cultural context. Signs can be direct or abstract, according to the relationship between signifier and signified. The US logician Charles Peirce (1839–1914) proposed three categories: the iconic sign is a resemblance or representation of the signifier (drawings, maps, photographs); the indexical sign has a physical connection (smoke = fire, a uniform = police officer); and the symbolic sign is wholly conceptual and relies on social convention for its meaning (the Christian cross, the warning triangle traffic sign). These categories often overlap. Photographs, for example, may carry meaning both at the level of realistic depiction and at a secondary conceptual or symbolic level. Thus a photograph of a baby is a realistic image of a particular child, but may at the same time signify the vulnerability of childhood or the importance of family life.

signing, an independent linguistic system used by the deaf. It is a system of hand shapes and movements in relation to the upper part of the signer's body. The complexity of its *grammar (the rules of sign and sentence formation) and expressiveness equals that of spoken languages. Sign languages have their own *dialects, undergo linguistic change, and for some are acquired as their native tongue. Among the many different, mutually unintelligible sign languages, the American Sign Language (ASL) is the most widespread. Finger spelling and cued speech which aids *lip-reading are alternative forms of signing, which are 'parasitically' dependent on spoken language.

Sikh festivals. The *Gurpurbs* are Sikh festivals which celebrate the birth and death anniversaries of the ten *Gurus. The most important are the birthdays of Guru *Nanak and Guru *Gobind Singh, the first and the last Gurus, and the martyrdoms of Guru Arjan Dev (who founded the Golden Temple at Amritsar in 1577) and Guru Tegh Bahadur (the father of Gobind Singh). *Gurpurbs* are marked by the *Akhand Path*, the continuous reading of the *Adi Granth, the Sikh holy book, which takes place in the forty-eight hours before the festival. Another important Sikh festival is *Baisakhi*, on 13 April, a new year festival begun by Guru Amar Das, the third Guru. It also commemorates Gobind Singh's foundation of the *Khalsa, which took place during the 1699 *Baisakhi*. In addition to the *Gurpurbs*, Sikhs have adopted certain Hindu festivals. *Hola Mohalla*, the equivalent of *Holi, was set up by Gobind Singh as a counter to some of the excesses of *Holi, and in order to encourage a separate Sikh identity. The Sikh celebration of *Dīvālī commemorates the release from prison of Guru Hargobind, the sixth Guru. Resistance against injustice and the triumph of good over evil are central themes of the Sikh *Dīvālī*.

Sikhism (from Sanskrit, *shishya*, 'pupil'), a monotheistic religion founded in the Punjab in the late 15th century by Guru *Nanak. Sikhism, which derives from both *Islam and *Hinduism, combines belief in one eternal and omnipotent God with acceptance of the Hindu concepts of *karma and *reincarnation. Sikhism preaches the equality of mankind and rejects the *caste system. The aim of the believer is to root out selfishness and achieve oneness with God through the repetition of his many names. Through union with God, the Sikh achieves *mukti* (the same concept as Hindu *moksha, liberation from the cycle of birth, death, and rebirth). Nanak was the first of a line of ten *Gurus, ending with *Gobind Singh, who proclaimed that his successor as perpetual Guru was to be the *Adi Granth, the Sikhs' holy book. Gobind

Singh also established the **Khalsa*, a brotherhood of soldier-saints. Nowadays the *Khalsa* consists of both men and women who have undergone full initiation into the faith. Sikhism has no priests; any Sikh, of either sex, can conduct a service. Worship may consist of private devotions (for instance, the reciting of the **Japji*) or public services in the **gurdwara*, or Sikh temple. The focus of *gurdwara* worship is the reading of the *Adi Granth*, which, as the Guru Granth Sahib ('Holy Book Guru'), is venerated as the successor to the ten historical Gurus. Apart from the *Harimandir*, or Golden Temple, at Amritsar, India, other important places for Sikhs are Patna (the birthplace of Gobind Singh), Anandpur (where the *Khalsa* was established), and Nander (where Gobind Singh died). Important decisons affecting the Sikh community are taken by a committee of leaders from these holy places. While the majority of Sikhs live in the Punjab in India, where Sikh separatism has become a militant political movement, many others have emigrated to the UK, the USA, Canada, East Africa, and South Africa. They number about 14 million in all.

sin, a notion within Judaism, Christianity, and Islam implying deliberate disobedience against the known will of God.

The Golden Temple at Amritsar, India, symbolizes many aspects of **Sikhism**. Positioned in the centre of a pool, it represents the beauty of religious devotion growing from the murky water of life, while its outer courtyard has four entrances, suggesting that the Sikh religion is open to all.

In a wider sense it can indicate any moral evil or failure to live up to some moral law, but more specifically it applies to those religions that worship a personal deity. Judaism, Christianity, and Islam explain mankind's fallen state and the presence of evil by referring to the idea of *original sin: Adam, the first man, misused his *free will in choosing to eat the forbidden fruit of the tree of knowledge, and as a result mankind became predisposed to sin. Roman Catholic theology distinguishes between this original sin and what it calls actual sin: evil acts performed in thought, word, or deed. There are further distinctions between venial and mortal sins: venial sin does not wholly deprive the *soul of God's grace, while mortal sin involves deliberate disobedience against the known will of God with full knowledge and consent; it must furthermore concern a grave matter. Unless such a sin is confessed to a priest and fully repented, the sinner will be condemned to *hell. Traditionally the seven deadly sins are pride, covetousness, lust, anger, gluttony, envy, and sloth. Practices to remove sins or repent from them include Baptism, Confession, and periods of abstinence and repentance such as *Yom Kippur and *Lent.

singing-games, games played by children all over the world, and featuring a song which the players dramatize with actions. In 'Oranges and Lemons', a popular party-game spiced with a dash of danger, the players sing the nursery rhyme and dance in turn under the fateful 'chopper', which falls and symbolically beheads the player passing beneath it during the final words of the song. Another favourite is 'London Bridge is falling down'. Others, such as 'Nuts in May', may have links with the old festivals that celebrated May Day, while 'Farmer's in his Den' is one of a number of ring-games. Children's singing-games are updated and revivified by each succeeding generation and often illuminate the preoccupations and fashions of an era, as seen from the playground.

Sino-Tibetan languages, the second largest group of languages in the world, with well over 1 billion speakers. It has two branches: Sinitic, which comprises the Chinese languages spoken in China, Singapore, Hong Kong, Taiwan, and elsewhere, and Tibeto-Burman, a group of languages spoken in Tibet, Burma, Nepal, and parts of northern India and Bangladesh. All employ a system of tones (pitch and contour) which distinguish otherwise similar words. Chinese is spoken by 95 per cent of the population of China; 75 per cent of the population of Singapore; and almost the entire populations of Taiwan and Hong Kong, which makes it the language with the largest number of speakers in the world. In fact, Chinese is not just one language, but consists of at least five languages, which for political and cultural reasons are referred to as dialects. Nevertheless, they are not mutually intelligible; they are about as divergent as the Romance languages of Europe. Seventy per cent of China's population now speak Mandarin, or Modern Standard Chinese (*Putonghua*), a uniform spoken language created in the early 20th century which is based on the dialect of Beijing. The other language-groups are Hakka, Min, Wu, and Yue, the latter including Cantonese, the dialect of Guangzhou and Hong Kong. Written Chinese is understood by all speakers, however, since Chinese characters can be read in any dialect. The script is logographic (one character for each word), and is first attested in the 18th century BC. In modern Chinese about 2,000 characters are required for basic *literacy. In the 1950s a system of transliteration into the Roman *alphabet called Pinyin ('phonetic spelling') was officially adopted. It is designed to aid the learning of the characters and the *Putonghua*, and replaces the earlier systems, such as Wade-Giles, which is still used in Hong Kong. Thus Peking becomes Běijīng, and Mao Tse-tung becomes Mao Zédōng. The two most important languages of Tibeto-Burman are Tibetan (4 million speakers) and Burmese (around 35 million speakers). Both have long traditions of Buddhist literature, written in scripts derived from an Indian original. Burmese has taken a considerable amount of vocabulary from Pali, an Indian language which exerted a huge cultural influence on it. There are also loan-words from Mon (an *Austro-Asiatic language) and more recently from English.

Sioux, a confederation of seven Indian tribes, who were displaced in the mid-18th century by the *Ojibwa, and settled in Minnesota in the USA. In common with other *Plains Indians, the Sioux were nomadic buffalo hunters, who gathered in tribes during the summer months, and dispersed into family groups during the winter. The Sioux were again displaced from the Black Hills of Dakota, although they vigorously resisted domination. Today they are to be found in the states of Minnesota, Nebraska, Dakota, and Montana.

skandha (Sanskrit, 'group', 'heap'), a term used within *Buddhism to describe the five central factors which combine to make up a 'person'. Each factor is a group or aggregate of related states. The first factor is physical appearance, shape or form, while the remaining four concern mental states: sense *perception and feeling; mental perception; intentions which initiate action; and finally discriminative consciousness. The *skandhas* are sometimes described as 'the aggregates of attachment', a term that applies to the craving and desire that are a basic cause of suffering (*dukkha*). The *skandhas* are revealed through the processes of birth, old age, death, lifespan, and change: they are without essence, impermanent, empty, and laden with suffering. Each particular association of *skandhas* ends at death, and any link between lives is maintained through the process of *karma.

skiing, the winter sport of gliding over snow on long shaped runners known as skis, aided by poles in either hand. Skiing developed some 5,000 years ago as a mode of transport and is still used as such in rural areas of northern and central Europe. Ski technology has advanced rapidly since the 1950s, and modern skis are made of metal and fibreglass with sharp bottom edges to give control at speed and add bite when turning. Skiing events may be divided into Nordic and Alpine. The former incorporates cross-country and jumping skills, while Alpine skiing includes downhill racing and slalom down a zigzag course with artificial obstacles.

Skinner, Burrhus Frederic (1904–1990), US psychologist who developed operant *conditioning. The most effective disciple of *Watson's *behaviourism, Skinner held that all behaviour is under the control of 'reinforcement' (reward and punishment), but unlike Watson he never denied a role to heredity. His discoveries form the basis for *behaviour therapy and 'behaviour modification', which is used, for instance, to eliminate unwanted or encourage new behaviour in retarded or disruptive children. He developed the Skinner box in which a rat's or pigeon's learning could be studied efficiently. In the box a simple response such as a peck or bar-press is rewarded with food or drink. The 'schedule of reinforcement' can be varied, for example, a reward for every ten presses (fixed ratio reinforcement). Different schedules produce different speeds of learning and

of extinction, that is, gradual cessation of responding when reward is no longer given. Occasional reinforcement on a random schedule keeps an unrewarded animal responding longest. Skinner compared this to the behaviour of human slot-machine players. *The Behaviour of Organisms* (1938) gives Skinner's account of such conditioning experiments. After World War II Skinner investigated how conditioning could build up complex behavioural responses. His main interest was to show how basic learning principles explain and govern all forms of human behaviour, with practical applications in *socialization, *education, and behaviour therapy.

skittles, a popular European game related to *bowling. Teams and individuals compete to knock down nine pins set in a diamond at the far end of an alley, each player usually having three balls. In France the game of boule, a version of skittles, is played on rough ground, usually with metal balls.

slander   *defamation.

slang, a colloquial variety of *language without the technicalities of *jargon, used within peer or professional groups such as adolescents, employees, or ethnic groups. Slang marks group identity and is often used for secrecy and protection, elimination of outsiders, and verbal play, for example in Cockney rhyming slang where 'godfors', short for 'God forbids', stands for kids. In slang, commonly used words acquire unconventional meanings, for example 'corn' may mean 'money' among teenagers in the UK. Original slang terms often enter general use, as in the case of the medieval Latin *testa* meaning 'hard shell', which as *tête* came to replace the formal French word *chef* for 'head'.

slavery, the ownership of one person by another, who controls the slave's life and labour. Slaves are viewed by their dominators as property, and are bought and sold accordingly. They are usually used for their labour, but sexual rights over them may also be an important element. Slaves are usually not native to the areas where they are held; they are uprooted from their homes, and may be deliberately prevented from developing *kinship ties. Slavery is closely associated with racial *prejudice, the belief that one *race is superior to another. Slave-owning societies can be found throughout history; one of the most significant examples was the use of African slave labour in the *plantations of the Caribbean and the southern states of the USA during the 18th and early 19th centuries. The word slave is now applied by the UN to anyone who cannot voluntarily withdraw his or her labour; the UN estimates that some 200 million such slaves exist, principally in Asia, Africa, and South America, where bonded labourers (persons who bind themselves and their labour over for a fixed period in order to pay off a debt, earn a fixed sum, or other compensation such as transport or housing) and child slavery are widespread. (See also *child labour, *child sexual exploitation.)

Slavic languages, a group of *Indo-European languages spoken in central and eastern Europe. They fall into three groups (South, West, and East Slavic), but they have remained close to each other in grammar, phonology, and basic vocabulary, and the spoken languages are not as sharply distinguished as the literary languages. Within each of the three groups there is a degree of mutual intelligibility. The earliest written Slavic is Old Church Slavonic, the language of the Slavic Orthodox Church, dating from the 9th century AD. The modern South Slavic group includes Serbo-Croat (17 million speakers), Slovene (2 million), Macedonian (1 million), and Bulgarian (8 million). Serbo-Croat, which is spoken in Yugoslavia and its former republics, has three distinct dialects and is written in both the Cyrillic and Roman alphabets. The Cyrillic alphabet, which is based on the Greek alphabet, was developed in the 9th century for the Slavs by the Orthodox missionaries St Cyril and St Methodius. Slovene is spoken in Slovenia. The Macedonian dialects are intermediate (both linguistically and geographically) between Serbo-Croat and Bulgarian. Bulgarian has a western and an eastern dialect. The eastern dialect is the basis of the literary language that developed in the 18th century and uses the Cyrillic alphabet. West Slavic includes Czech, Slovak, and Polish, all of which use modified Latin alphabets. Czech (9.5 million speakers) and Slovak (4.5 million) are mutually intelligible. Czech was influenced by German, Slovak by Hungarian. Polish (37 million speakers) is first attested in texts from the 14th century. East Slavic comprises Russian, Belorussian, and Ukrainian, all of which are written in the Cyrillic alphabet. Russian is spoken by 150 million as a mother-tongue, and throughout the former Soviet Union by virtue of having been its official language. It has been heavily influenced by South Slavic due to the cultural prestige of Old Church Slavonic. Ukrainian has 40 million speakers in Ukraine, Belorussian has 10 million in Belarus; both have borrowed quite heavily from Polish.

sleep *dreaming.

Slovene language *Slavic languages.

slum, a dilapidated urban area, often encompassing residential, manufacturing, commercial, and retail uses. By contrast with *shanty towns, slums are usually located in inner cities. The housing tends either to be built specially for the poor (the shop-house tenements of South-east Asia are examples) or converted from other uses: for example, the *khans* (warehouses or hostels) of the Middle East or the *mohallas* (old mansions) in Delhi. Cheap rooming houses are also abundant. In many of the old cities of Asia, Latin America, and the Middle East, inner-city slums are the main province of the urban poor, housing more of them than shanty towns. The buildings tend to be overcrowded, badly maintained by landlords, inadequately served by *water and *sanitation and at risk from fire. Yet despite their physical disadvantages, inner-city slums have always played an important role in providing for migrants, immigrants, and the poor. Rents may be low, and the frequent proximity of residence and workplace and the easy access to city-centre jobs and amenities can be advantageous. Policies to deal with rapacious landlords by rent control, and with poor physical conditions by *urban renewal and the supply of *government housing to those displaced have often proved disappointing, sometimes leading to the creation of new areas of deteriorating housing and social problems, usually on urban peripheries. In Austria, Italy, and elsewhere in Europe, slum clearance has been replaced by a policy of rehabilitating buildings. Unless such a policy is accompanied by controls on access, and rent or mortgage subsidies, the poor tend to be displaced by more prosperous inhabitants in a process known popularly as gentrification.

Smith, Adam (1723–90), Scottish philosopher and economist, the founder of *classical economics. In his revolutionary work, *An Inquiry into the Nature and Causes of the*

A Liverpool **slum** offers stark evidence of aimless existence. Shifts in manufacturing and trading patterns have brought about urban decay in cities around the world which, a few generations before, had carried civic pride among their people.

Wealth of Nations (1776), he focused on the creation of *wealth, and noted the importance of manufacturing industry as well as *agriculture. He argued that to increase wealth, *division of labour and a high proportion of productive to non-productive activity is needed. The larger the market, the greater the scope for specialization and division of labour. Smith ascribed the *value of a *good to its labour input, but its price to the interaction of *supply and demand. Central to his analysis is the role of competition. He argued that, in the presence of competition, individuals pursuing selfish economic ends would be led, 'as if by an invisible hand', to maximize the well-being of society as a whole. From this analysis, he prescribed a minimum of government *intervention in the economic system. (See also *laissez-faire.)

smoking, inhaling the smoke of tobacco leaves. Tobacco contains the drug nicotine, which is a stimulant and can be addictive. Smoking has been proved to cause lung *cancer and cancers of the mouth, larynx, and oesophagus; chest diseases such as bronchitis and emphysema; and to contribute to *heart disease. Men have traditionally smoked more than women, but there has been an increase in smoking among women, leading to additional health problems. Women smokers have a higher risk of diseases of the circulatory system, particularly if smoking is combined with the contraceptive pill; smoking during pregnancy may put the unborn baby at risk, or lead to lighter birth weight; and smoking can have an adverse effect on fertility. The children of smokers are more likely than those of non-smokers to suffer from asthma and other respiratory diseases. Studies have shown that passive smoking (the inhalation of other people's smoke) can also have harmful effects, particularly on those already suffering from heart or lung disease. Many governments have taken action to discourage smoking, for instance by putting health warnings on packets of cigarettes, banning smoking in public places, restricting advertising, and increasing duties on tobacco, but such measures are limited by the *lobbying and influence of the international tobacco industry. In industrialized countries, smoking is declining, but a recent trend has been an increase in smoking in developing countries, to which the tobacco companies are directing their main marketing efforts. This is expected by the World Health Organization to lead to an epidemic of smoking-related diseases. Many developing countries are major tobacco growers and exporters; the crop uses land that many argue might be put to more beneficial uses.

snooker, a development of *billiards played mainly in the UK. The table is set with fifteen red balls and six colours. Players use a white cue ball to pot, in sequence, first a red then a colour, continuing in a prescribed manner until the table is cleared. Professional snooker commands large television audiences. Pool (or pocket billiards) is a variant of snooker that is popular in the USA. There are fifteen numbered balls that must be potted in sequence by the cue ball.

soccer *football.

social assistance, a generic term for *social security schemes in which payments are based on need, rather than entitlement through *social insurance. In countries with social insurance schemes, social assistance may be available as a safety net for those who fall outside their scope. This is the case in the UK, where it is known as 'income support'. Elsewhere, limited social assistance may be available to certain groups, such as infirm elderly people without family support. The principal features of social assistance are that the whole cost is met by taxation, that the benefit is designed to bring the applicant's total income up to a community-determined minimum, allowing for such factors as family size, and that the benefit is paid only if the applicant's total resources leave him or her below that minimum. Payments under social assistance schemes are usually inadequate and the application procedures (which may be designed to deter) are often felt to be humiliating. A recent trend has been to link payments to the acceptance of training or employment at minimal rates of pay. Several US states have 'workfare' schemes and the UK and France have remodelled their schemes to encourage re-entry into the labour-market and to penalize those who reject it.

social care services, services offering assistance with personal and social problems. They encompass *childcare services and services for those who are old, mentally or physically handicapped, or mentally ill. In some countries, assistance is given to people with drug and alcohol problems and to *migrants. Some social care staff may be trained social workers (see *social work) and others para-professionals. Their objectives are to support individuals and families who are in difficulties; to alter and control people's behaviour for their own and others' benefit; and to protect the interests of vulnerable individuals. Since World War II, social care services established by law and supplied by government, *voluntary organizations, and private agencies have grown rapidly in most industrialized countries. In some, the state-run services are the responsibility of local government departments concerned solely with social care (in England and Wales these are known as social services departments). In others, social care services are administered by health or *social security agencies. Social care services may be provided in a person's own home, in a day-care centre, or in residential care. Services are financed by taxation and, to a lesser extent, user charges.

social class, a division or order of society. Many observers have distinguished between the systems of *social stratification found in pre-industrial societies, in which distinctions are primarily of rank and rest on long-established rights and duties, and the systems found in industrialized societies which are based on social class. In *The Communist Manifesto* (1848) *Marx identified classes in relation to the means of production. In capitalist societies, the dominant class, 'the bourgeoisie', owned the means of production, while 'the proletariat' laboured, their surplus production belonging not to themselves but to the bourgeoisie (see *surplus value). For Marx, the criterion of class was economic. *Weber, who, with Marx, has strongly influenced 20th-century debate, defined the term more broadly to refer to an individual's ability to command resources: class position might be determined by skills as well as property. Weber also regarded *status as a factor in social stratification. Mid-20th-century sociologists took up the idea of status to the point where some, especially in the USA, denied the existence of clear economic class divisions in their country, while in communist states, classless societies were predicted. However, evidence from across the world suggests that social class divisions based on occupation and economic standing are to be found in every society. Class position is linked not only to command of private goods such as cars or household appliances, but also to access to resources such as health care, *education, and *housing.

social classification, the classification of individuals according to social, economic, demographic, or other criteria. Population censuses and surveys publish statistics which break the main groupings down into *professional; intermediate; skilled non-manual; skilled manual; partly skilled; and unskilled. In the 1970s the retailing and marketing industry in the West began to classify potential customers in social grades A to E: A, higher managerial, administrative, or professional; B, intermediate managerial, administrative, or professional; C1, supervisory or clerical, and junior managerial, administrative, or professional; C2, skilled manual workers; D, semi-skilled and unskilled manual workers; and E, state pensioners, casual, or lowest-grade workers. In recent years the revolution in information technology has led to huge advances in collecting and storing personal data, allowing the classification of consumers into over sixty profile types. The gathering of geo-demographic information on which this is based has become increasingly sophisticated, with marketeers employing, for example, the electronic point of sale at the supermarket to record transactions made with cash cards to access information about the customer.

social contract, an agreement among the members of a society to acknowledge the authority of a set of rules or a political regime. Social contract theories became popular in the 16th and 17th centuries as a means of explaining the rightful origin of government and hence the *political obligations of subjects. Postulating an original state of nature without political authority, contract theorists such as *Hobbes (*Leviathan*, 1651) and *Locke (*Two Treatises of Government*, 1689), argued that it would be in each person's interest to agree to the establishment of government. The terms of the agreement fixed the proper form and scope of government, absolute in Hobbes' case, constitutionally limited in Locke's. If the government overstepped the mark, the contract was broken and subjects had the right to rebel. Such theories were later criticized for their unhistorical character. Recently the social contract tradition has been revived, especially by *Rawls (*A Theory of Justice*, 1971), to address problems of distributive justice, and by *public choice theorists to establish the limits of state activity. In contemporary politics the idea of a social contract is sometimes used to describe *corporatist arrangements, whereby the major interest groups in society agree to collaborate with government.

social control, the term used by sociologists for the process by which order is maintained in *society and its institutions. All societies and institutions are controlled, but in a variety of ways. Some rely on force and terror, while in others the consent of the governed plays an important part. The law, with the backing of *police, *courts, and prisons, is always a key component. But social control can also be achieved by more subtle means—the inculcation of beliefs in children, the propagation of national myths, the systematic reward of some behaviour by high pay and status, and the threat of loss of livelihood to those who challenge the established order. Much of the social control of individuals and small groups is achieved by mutual surveillance: the person who steps out of line may be ostracized or stigmatized (see *deviance). Social control is essential to the functioning of any society, but the debate about the proper balance between social control and individual liberty is of perennial interest to philosophers as diverse as *Nozick, *Mill, *Hobbes, *Aristotle, and *Plato.

social democracy, a form of society in which democratic political methods are used to create greater social equality through the redistribution of resources. At the beginning of the 20th century, social democracy was virtually synonymous with *socialism. After the break with *communist parties in the 1920s, however, social democratic parties were distinguished by their commitment to parliamentary *democracy and their moderate, gradualist programmes of social change. Over time, they abandoned their commitment to public ownership of industry (see *nationalization), seeking instead to make capitalist economies work in a fairer way by implementing equality of opportunity (see *egalitarianism) and by using progressive taxation to provide *social security and *welfare programmes for the poorer members of society. Most Western societies since World War II have adopted social democratic policies to some degree, with the Scandinavian countries going furthest in this direction. In recent years, such policies have been attacked by the *New Right, who claim that they inflate the *public sector and slow down economic growth. (See also *market socialism.)

social identity theory, a recent theory of *prejudice developed by the British psychologist Henri Tajfel (1919–82). Tajfel argued that belonging to a group is sufficient to make one prejudiced against other groups (out-

groups). He suggested that human thought naturally categorizes objects in both the social and the non-social world. People's *self-concept includes assumptions about their membership of social categories or groups such as *race and *gender. These constitute their social identity. To maintain self-esteem people tend to regard categories or groups to which they belong as better than those to which they do not belong. Many empirical findings supported the theory, but experiments have resulted in contradictory predictions about its effects. Although, the theory predicts that those whose identification with a group is strongest should show most bias, this is not the case in practice.

social insurance, a generic term for *social security schemes based on the insurance principle. By paying contributions into government-run insurance funds, individuals become eligible to claim benefits. Benefits which may be financed this way include *unemployment benefit, *old-age benefit, maternity benefit, survivor's benefit (for widows, widowers, and orphans), sickness benefit, and medical benefit. Today industrialized countries operate schemes encompassing all or most of these benefits. The revenue base is broad, with contributions from workers, employers, and, sometimes, general *taxation. Since participation is compulsory for most adults, risks are widely shared and coverage is extensive. The claimant's right to benefit depends largely on his or her contribution record. In some countries, attempts have been made to minimize such typical shortcomings as the failure to provide for those not in remunerative employment, and the limits set on the level and duration of benefits. Social insurance schemes have given unprecedented financial security to people living in industrialized countries and sharply reduced *poverty. In developing countries, however, *insurance benefits for *unemployment and *old age rarely cover more than a small minority. In Latin American countries, which have had the longest experience with social insurance, coverage has generally been limited to people employed in the formal sector in urban areas. In countries in which a high proportion of the population, especially in rural areas, is self-employed or intermittently employed at subsistence level, contributions cannot be levied either from employers or from employees. Nor is the complex administration required for social insurance at present feasible.

socialism, a political outlook which favours the conscious direction of social life, involving in particular limits on the private ownership of industry. It covers a wide range of positions from *communism at one extreme to *social democracy at the other, and is therefore difficult to define with precision. It is less easy to say what socialists are for than what they are against, namely untrammelled *capitalism, which in socialist eyes enriches the owners of capital at the expense of their employees, provides no security for the poor, and sacrifices the welfare of society to private gain. Most socialists have responded by arguing for social ownership of the means of production, either in the form of state ownership (see *nationalization and *statism), or else in the form of ownership by the workers themselves (see *syndicalism). They have also often advocated replacing the market economy by some kind of *planned economy. The aim of these measures is to make industry socially responsible, and to bring about a much greater degree of equality in living standards. In addition, socialists have argued for special provision for those in need, in the form, for instance, of a *welfare state. A major source of division within the socialist tradition has been how to get from capitalism to socialism;

whether by means of a revolutionary upheaval, or by gradual, parliamentary methods; the first position is represented by *Marx and Engels in *The Communist Manifesto* (1848), the second by Bernstein (see *revisionism) in *Evolutionary Socialism* (1898). These debates have been somewhat overshadowed in recent years by the question of whether socialism is viable at all as an alternative to capitalism. Many Western socialists now opt for *social democracy, others for *market socialism. It is only in certain developing countries that traditional socialist aims still attract widespread support among political leaders.

socialization, the process by which individuals are fitted into *society. It is a complex process which continues through life and is conveniently divided into three main stages. The first takes place mainly in the *family, where most children are still reared. While the nature of the family may vary from society to society, it still has a formative role. Psychologists have pointed to the patterned ways in which children move through different stages of development and how these relate to human society. *Social learning theory and the theory of *psychosexual development are two influential approaches. Stress on the importance of the mother, in particular by John Bowlby (see *attachment), who maintained that maternal deprivation could adversely affect the social development of the infant, is now much disputed; the emphasis has shifted to the role of love in general. In early years the child may become attuned to certain *gender roles in the family and these may be reinforced at the secondary stage of socialization, which takes place mainly in the school. Socialization takes place through contact between children and adults other than parents, as well as with parents, and this becomes increasingly so as the individual develops. Children also learn from the example offered by authority figures in school, such as teachers, and there may be conflict between these and the patterns offered by parents. The third stage of socialization is even more diverse, the individual being affected by contact with other adults and, increasingly, by the *mass media.

social justice, justice in the distribution of resources throughout a society. Ideas of social *justice are applied not to transactions between individuals, but to the major institutions of a society, such as its *property and *welfare systems. The aim is to shape these institutions so that as far as possible everyone receives the resources that they deserve or that they need (to cite two of the most prominent criteria). Such ideas are popular with *liberals and *social democrats, but they are strongly opposed by *libertarians such as *Hayek and *Nozick, who claim that the demand for social justice is an error, since there is no agency responsible for distributing resources throughout society. *Rawls is prominent among recent theorists of social justice, in particular for his principle that income and other goods should be distributed in whatever way brings the greatest benefit to the least advantaged members of society.

social learning theory, an adaptation of principles of *learning to explain aspects of personality and behaviour. In *Social Learning and Imitation* (1941) and other works, the US psychologists John Dollard and Neal Miller explained phenomena described by *Freud as the products of mechanisms outlined by their *behaviourist colleague Clark Hull (1884–1952). They held that complex repertoires of behaviour are developed through reward and punishment ('reinforcement'). They applied their ideas to *neurosis and

its cure, but are now best known for their theory that *aggression results from the frustration of goal-directed behaviour. Later, in a series of books such as *Aggression* (1973) and *Social Foundations of Thought and Language* (1985), the Canadian psychologist Albert Bandura paid particular attention to children's capacity for imitation and ability to learn by abstracting rules from their observation of others' performances, showing that such learning occurs without reinforcement. Modern social learning theory emphasizes *cognitive rather than *motivational factors, and the roles of curiosity and the individual's belief in his or her ability to act effectively (see *locus of control).

social mobility, the movement of individuals up or down a social hierarchy. Most commonly, the term refers to occupational change. Intra-generational social mobility involves the movement of an individual over his or her lifetime. Inter-generational social mobility involves a change in the individual's occupational position compared with that of his or her parents. In industrial and *post-industrial societies, the number of non-manual higher-status jobs is growing, thus increasing the scope for upward social mobility. The recognition that these jobs require *secondary or *higher education has helped to fuel a world-wide boom in the demand for education (see *education, access to). Social mobility may enhance the stability and efficiency of a society (as well as being seen as desirable on grounds of *social justice) by admitting ambitious or able people to the *élite. However, individuals 'left behind' by the mobility of others may become an *underclass, and have often been regarded as potential recruits for extremist political organizations.

social ownership   *nationalization.

social policy, a term used to refer to public policy which bears upon the welfare of the individual. Through social policies, governments seek to modify social arrangements and influence individual behaviour. Policies are typically implemented by setting up *social services like *education and health, and employing professionals in them, transferring money to individuals through *social security, and manipulating the *taxation system (for instance, by exempting philanthropic donations from tax). Just as important is the use of legislation to compel some activities such as school attendance, or debar others such as *abortion. Social policies are influenced by *ideology and tend to be dominated by economic policies. In some prosperous countries, especially in northern Europe, the state accepts responsibility for all its citizens (see *welfare state), whereas elsewhere greater emphasis may be placed on individual responsibility, and the development of social policies may be subordinated to the country's economic growth or survival. Recent thinking on social policy has emphasized its importance to political stabilization in advanced economies; the way that social welfare may be channelled through the taxation system or work-related benefits; and the scope for the *privatization or *contracting-out of matters like health or pensions.

social psychology, the study of how people understand, influence, and relate to one another. It covers topics of great political and social importance, including *aggression, *altruism, *attitude, *conformity, *communication, *person perception, *persuasion, *relationships, *sexual behaviour, and *social understanding. During the 1970s and 1980s the last two (*cognitive) topics have probably been the ones most researched. Social psychology emerged as a distinct area of

In Caribbean countries such as Barbados, shown here, the share of government spending on **social services** such as education has tended to be appreciably higher than in other countries with comparable incomes.

research after World War II, primarily in the USA. Among the major figures were Theodor Adorno (1903–69), on *prejudice, and Fritz Heider (1896–1988) and Solomon Asch on person perception and conformity. The ideas of George Herbert Mead (1863–1931) about the self and *self-concept have resurfaced in psychology through the influence of *Goffman's work on *self-presentation. In general, US social psychology has been individualistic, stressing environmental rather than innate determinants of behaviour. By contrast, European contributions have often focused on genetic factors, as in *ethology and *sociobiology. Modern European social psychologists have attempted to develop theories of collective rather than individual phenomena. In France, for instance, Serge Moscovici has modified *Durkheim's claim that central ideas affecting individuals' thought and behaviour derive from their *culture, by producing evidence that these collective ideas are susceptible to change through novel discoveries and inventions made by individuals.

social sciences, branches of the study of human society and social relationships. The disciplines usually encompassed, at least in some of their aspects, are: *anthropology, *demography, *economics, *geography, *political science, *psychology, and *sociology. The codification of the social sciences began in the 18th century, when the success of the natural sciences inspired the belief that humanity could be investigated similarly. Early approaches often sought to adapt to social enquiry the methods used to investigate the natural world. Laws were postulated and evidence for them sought. This approach has been called *naturalism or positivism. Such methods and views persist to the present day, and some social scientists share objectives with natural scientists. They seek to test hypotheses and to explain and predict phenomena. They use experiments and statistical techniques to establish *correlations. Economists and psychologists are frequently to be found in this group. However, from the late 19th century many writers, among them, most notably, the German sociologist *Weber, maintained that the social sciences could still be rigorous without copying the methods of natural science. Rather than looking for law-like statements or working numerically, the social scientist could be more interpretive and intuitive. Social scientists following this approach tend to lay greater stress on the observation and interpretation of complex phenomena as they occur in the world rather than in experiments, and on eliciting the views of those being studied. Anthropologists and sociologists are frequently to be found in this group. While the quantitative and qualitative approaches have different antecedents and are used for different purposes, the understanding of a phenomenon or problem often requires a combination. For example, attempts to understand, ameliorate, and prevent *famines in Africa require the skills not only of economists, who analyse the effects of fluctuations in commodity prices on the ability of nations to import foodstuffs, but also of anthropologists, who investigate the ways in which farmers themselves husband their resources in a drought, thus helping aid agencies to formulate appropriate strategies. Social scientists are found in almost every society in the world, as their work is used by governments and public and private bodies in the attempt not only to understand the world, but to master it. It is increasingly recognized that the great challenges of *over-population, environmental degradation, economic revival in the former Eastern bloc and Africa, and the spread of *Aids cannot be met by technical or technological solutions alone. It is necessary to understand why people act as they do and to analyse the interaction of a multiplicity of forces. However, disagreements among social scientists in their analyses of issues and in their proposals for action, and their increasing specialization, mean that the policy-maker wishing to use social science research findings is faced with a formidable task.

social security, a system of financial maintenance organized by government to protect individuals against the loss of earnings resulting from sickness, unemployment (*unemployment benefit), old age (*old-age benefit), and other misfortunes; to meet medical costs; and to give support to families with children (*child benefit). The term covers *social insurance schemes and *social assistance schemes. Schemes have developed in industrialized countries since the late 19th century in response to the emergence of a large class of factory workers dependent on the regular payment of wages, and to the dislocation caused by two World Wars and the economic depression of the 1920s and 1930s. By the 1970s almost the entire population of industrialized countries was protected, but rising costs were causing alarm. With social security receipts accounting for a quarter of *GDP in some countries, governments have raised insurance contributions and reduced benefits while boosting the importance of occupational and personal insurance. Most developing countries have neither the money nor the administrative infrastructure for social security systems, although some countries, such as Chile and Costa Rica, have insurance schemes and others, such as Thailand, are introducing them. Consequently, their citizens are vulnerable to the financial consequences not only of *disasters such as *famine and flood, but also of misfortunes such as sickness and *unemployment, and of *old age. In these countries, it may be more practical to follow policies designed to raise incomes and to make better services available free.

social services, state welfare services delivered in kind rather than cash. These can include health, *education, *social care, and, in some countries, *housing, food supplements, and *employment services. Nations with highly developed social services are often termed *welfare states. In many parts of the world, the state is closely involved in planning and monitoring its social services, but permits a multiplicity of public, private, and voluntary organizations to supply them. In industrialized countries, if services are designed for universal use, like the UK's national health service and the French education system, public pressure for high standards is likely and national solidarity may be reinforced, but costs are high. If services are selective, resources may be concentrated on those in most need, but determining eligibility can be administratively complex, and there is a danger of creating inferior, stigmatized services, as has happened with welfare housing in the USA. In the developing world, the UN believes governments can improve basic social services even in times of financial stringency by reallocating government expenditure away from *military expenditure and costly services benefiting the élite towards low-cost interventions such as *primary health care, basic *education, and self-build *housing, and by targeting services to the poorest. In Tamil Nadu in India, for example, targeted food supplements combined with other nutrition and health measures cut severe *malnutrition by half within two years. Such targeting is, however, administratively complex and may jeopardize the broad-based support essential for the social services if they are to grow.

social skills, the ability to control one's interaction with others in ways which produce satisfactory results. *Self-presentation is one interpretation. Social skills training is a form of *behaviour therapy which has developed to help people overcome crippling social anxieties. For instance, assertiveness training may help overcome shyness about complaining or speaking to other people. The therapist generally 'models' the behaviour and gets the patient to imitate it. Therapists have also tried to change the behaviour of mentally handicapped, institutionalized, or mentally ill people, in the hope that by gaining social approval and self-respect they would further improve their social skills. However, willingness and ability to learn seem crucial, with the result that such training works better in improving, say, salespeople's techniques than in helping the retarded or socially inept.

social stratification, a term used by social scientists to refer to the hierarchical differentiation of groups within a society. Virtually all societies are stratified, but the bases differ. Indian society is stratified by *caste, whereas in most industrialized societies it is *social class (normally defined by occupation) which is central. Adherents of *functionalism often maintain that stratification is important for the continued existence of society, whereas others point to its role in social conflict.

social structure, a term used by sociologists to refer to the discernible pattern of interrelationships in a society which endure over time. The social structure of a society is often held either to influence (see *Parsons) or to determine (see *Marx) the experience of its members. Thus, in a racially segregated society, the poverty of one race and the wealth of another may be explained not by the inherent characteristics of the two groups, but by the social structure. In such a society, the operation and interrelationship of, for example, legal, political, and educational institutions can be shown to favour one group at the expense of the other.

social understanding (in psychology), the way in which people explain or, more generally, understand their own and others' behaviour. The seminal work is *The Psychology of Interpersonal Relations* (1958) by the Austrian-born Fritz Heider (1896–1988). He held that people make sense of the transient and ambiguous data of experience by relating them to beliefs about relatively stable and unobservable causal factors such as people's dispositions and abilities. (*Self-concept enters in here.) Heider also pointed out biases in people's understanding of others' behaviour. We tend to assume, for instance, that others think as we do. We exaggerate the role of factors such as ability, character, or intent, and underestimate the role of environmental factors such as social pressure or the difficulty of the task in which a person is engaged. There is still disagreement about the reasons for these biases. Recent studies have indicated that people have ideas (often called 'scripts') about typical sequences of behaviour. They do not need a special process of causal reasoning because the scripts give ready-made predictions and ready-made explanations of people's actions. Psychologists have used Heider's ideas to try to understand how people's beliefs about success and failure affect their *motivation and may predispose them to *depression. (See also *person perception, *social identity theory.)

social work, an occupation directed towards the alleviation of personal and social problems. Beginning as an unpaid activity associated with *voluntary organizations and churches in the 19th century, it has emerged in the 20th century as a professionally trained occupation in the USA and in many *welfare states. Social workers play a major role in *social care services, by assisting children and families, old people, and those incapacitated by illness or handicap, and by counselling people with personal problems such as alcohol addiction or marriage breakdown. In many countries, social workers are being asked to play a bigger role in controlling deviant, delinquent, and criminal behaviour, but are required not to intrude on family privacy or abrogate the civil rights of those with whom they work. In some countries, notably in the developing world where their numbers are small, they are often involved in assessments for financial assistance, in relief work, and community development.

society, an organized and interdependent community of people. The term generally refers to a relatively large group, such as the citizens of a *nation-state. It is often used in contrast to the term 'individual', to refer to the collectivity of which an individual is part, but which goes beyond those, such as family members and fellow workers, with whom he is in immediate contact. The relationship of the individual to society has been the subject of perennial debate. Philosophers such as *Plato have speculated on the obligations of the *citizen. Psychologists such as *Piaget have examined how children learn to live with others. Political theorists such as *Hobbes have debated the way in which order is maintained, whether by force or consent. Sociologists such as *Durkheim and social anthropologists such as *Malinowski have investigated how behaviour comes to be categorized as acceptable or unacceptable. To be human is to influence and to be influenced by others, to shape and be shaped by society.

sociobiology, the study of the biological bases of social behaviour in humans and animals. In the 1940s and 1950s *ethology set out to explain behaviour in terms of its evolutionary history and adaptive function. Sociobiology grew up round discussions of various apparent anomalies of *Darwin's evolutionary theory such as *altruism, described as sociobiology's 'central theoretical problem' in Edward Wilson's *Sociobiology, the New Synthesis* (1975). An example is the honey bee, which perishes by stinging in defence of the hive. This instinctive behaviour, which seems useless for the individual, although it may be valuable for the hive, is explicable by the UK zoologist W. D. Hamilton's theory of kin selection (1964): the bee-sting increases the survival chances of the genes which determine it, as its bearer cannot reproduce but the relatives which it is protecting can. For humans, an example sometimes suggested is male *aggression. Sociobiological assumptions about adaptiveness and biological selfishness in human behaviour, however, are fraught with difficulties because human culture may act as a buffer against evolutionary mechanisms and moral or legal prescriptions determine some of our actions. Human behaviour may also be maladaptive in the man-made social and physical environment in which we live even if it was highly adaptive in other environments with different demands.

Nevertheless sociobiology attempts to explain aspects of human sexuality and parental behaviour as well as altruism.

sociolinguistics, the study of the relationshp between *language and *society. Sociolinguistic work on urban and social *dialects correlates the use of language varieties (such as standard and non-standard) with speakers' age, *social class, *gender, *education, and so on. It studies the significance and the role of stylistic and functional varieties of a language in society. Speakers' social status, beliefs, and value systems are revealed by studying such topics as forms of address, speech acts (requests, apologies, compliments, and the like), linguistic routines (greetings and leave-takings) attitudes to language varieties, humour, taboo, *bilingualism, and *pidgin and creole languages.

sociology, the systematic study of the development, structure, and functioning of society. The late 19th-century writings of *Marx, *Weber, and *Durkheim laid the foundations of sociology. All three analysed many facets of their own societies, in the more general context of observing the causes and consequences of the transition from traditional pre-industrial life to modern societies. The fundamental postulate of sociology is that human beings act not by their own free decisions taken rationally, but under the influence of history and culture, and the expectations and demands of others: human beings are both the products and the makers of their societies. Sociologists are less concerned with the characteristics of individuals than with patterns of behaviour (between doctors and patients, for instance, or priests and parishioners), which recur irrespective of the individuals involved. During the 20th century, sociologists have been particularly interested in the influence of *role, *status, *class, and *power on experience and behaviour, in the *family and in the *community; in the factors which contribute to cohesion and conflict; in *social structure and *social stratification; and in social problems such as *crime, *drug addiction, and *domestic violence. There are many approaches to sociology, from the *functionalism of *Parsons to the *Marxism of the *Frankfurt School. While some sociologists are primarily theorists, many analyse data gathered through interviews, observation, and surveys. Sociological findings are used increasingly by governments and businesses such as *advertising and *public relations.

Socrates (*c*.470–399 BC), Greek philosopher and teacher of *Plato. Socrates practised philosophy by the method of dialectic, posing questions on such matters as the nature of justice, virtue, or friendship, and subjecting the answers offered to careful analysis and counter-argument. He did not claim to have answers to these questions, but only that he recognized his own ignorance, and that this recognition is a pre-requisite of wisdom. Although his investigations are inconclusive, they develop a view of what wisdom would be: a complete and discursive grasp of centrally important concepts.

softball, a version of *baseball. It is played with a smaller diamond, a shorter bat, and a ball which is not soft but larger and heavier than a baseball, with a circumference of 30 cm (12 inches). The effect of the smaller playing area is to speed up the action, and the larger ball, delivered at speed with an underarm action from 14 m (46 feet) for men and 12 m (40 feet) for women, gives the pitcher a greater advantage over the batter. In high-class games, scores therefore tend to be low. Each team of nine plays seven innings, and the principles of play are similar to those in baseball. Softball began in the USA and since the 1960s has spread to many countries, including Canada, Japan, the Philippines, Australia, and much of Latin America.

solicitor (in English law), a lawyer engaged directly by a client to carry out legal administrative work (such as the conveyancing of property or the drafting of wills), or to give advice on the *law. A solicitor has a right of audience in inferior *courts, but in higher courts, he or she instructs a *barrister, specializing in the legal area in question, to represent the client. Under reforms enacted in 1990, however, solicitors will, if they fulfil certain conditions, themselves be granted rights of audience in the higher courts, thus removing the monopoly hitherto enjoyed by barristers.

solipsism, the view that the only thing that exists is oneself, or at least that the only thing of which there can be any knowledge is oneself. A solipsist therefore denies both that there is an external physical world and that there are any other minds. Solipsism is typically based on the claims that all that we can perceive are our immediate experiences or states of mind, and that these do not supply an adequate basis for knowledge of anything further.

Somali language *Cushitic languages.

sophists, a group of travelling professional lecturers centred in Sicily and southern Italy in the 5th century BC, who offered to teach the rhetorical and argumentative skills necessary in public life. Their readiness to argue either cause in a dispute brought them condemnation from *Plato as self-interested imitators of wisdom lacking any concern for the truth, a view reflected in the modern meaning of 'sophistical'. However, the most renowned sophists, such as Protagoras and Gorgias, drew relativist or *sceptical conclusions from the defensibility of opposed claims, indicating a seriousness of purpose which Plato failed to acknowledge.

soul, the spiritual or immaterial element believed to exist within mankind (and sometimes within all living things). The term is often used to denote that which confers individuality on a person, sustains the emotions, intellect, and spiritual aspirations, and is believed to survive the body after death. However, in some religions an individual may have multiple souls. There are different theories about the nature of the soul. In Hinduism, the *ātman or soul is reborn again and again within different bodies through *reincarnation; Advaita Hindus identify this soul with *Brahman, the universal spirit or ultimate reality into which it is totally subsumed, once its unity with the cosmos is fully perceived. Buddhists, while also believing in reincarnation, reject the idea of the individual soul or self (see *Three Marks of Existence). Christianity, on the other hand, regards each soul as immortal and as a new, separate creation of God. The body is regarded as the temple of the soul, and becomes sacred through association. Veneration of dead souls, such as *ancestor worship, is found in many African religions and forms a significant part of Chinese and Japanese practice (see *Shinto).

South American and Caribbean Indian languages, languages spoken by the indigenous peoples of this region before the arrival of European (mainly Spanish and Portuguese) invaders. Nowadays they are spoken by an estimated 12 million people; many are poorly known, and many

became extinct before they could be recorded. The task of classifying them into groups is difficult and controversial. The languages can be divided into four main groups, which may (at a very distant level) be related to each other and to the Amerind families of North and Central America (see *Mexican and Central American Indian languages; *North American Indian languages). The four groups are Chibchan–Paezan, Andean, Equatorial–Tucanoan, and Ge–Pano–Carib. Chibchan–Paezan, which is also spoken in Central America and Florida, stretches down the west coast of South America, though islands of speakers are found in the northern central region. It has around 200,000 speakers. Andean is a huge language-group which extends down the west coast from Ecuador to the southern tip of the continent. It has only twenty languages, but they are spoken by 9 million people. Six million of these speak Quechua, which was the official language of the Inca empire, and was later adopted by the Spanish in their dealings with the Indians, acquiring the status of a literary language in the 17th and 18th centuries. It is now an important *lingua franca. Equatorial is spoken by 3 million people on the Caribbean islands and all over northern and central South America. Two language families, Arawak and Tupi, account for most of the speakers. The fifty Tucanoan languages have just 35,000 speakers scattered throughout Brazil. Ge–Pano–Carib is spread over a vast area of South America east of the Andes, but has relatively few speakers. Carib is spoken in the north, Ge in the east (Brazil), and Panoan in a band which stretches from Peru down to Uruguay. None of the languages were written until the 16th century, when Roman Catholic missionaries prepared grammars and dictionaries and translated Christian texts.

South Asian societies, peoples of the region which includes the modern states of *India, *Pakistan, *Bangladesh, *Sri Lanka, and *Nepal. Society in this region, despite a number of large cities and growing industry in some areas, remains overwhelmingly rural and agricultural. The area shows great ethnic diversity, containing many different groups, including the *Sherpa, *Nagas, and *Pathans. There is a broad division between north and south based on language (the many northern languages belong to the *Indo-European family, which is related to modern European languages, the southern languages belong to the *Dravidian family) and agriculture (*rice cultivators in the south, wheat farmers in the north). The dominant religion is *Hinduism, and local communities are divided by *caste, which is expressed in ideas about *purity and pollution and restric-

This 'soul catcher' made of polished bone and inlaid with shell is from the Tlingit culture of the north-west coast of America. Such a tool was a vital piece of equipment for the shaman who used it to recapture the wandering **soul** of a sick person.

tions on *marriage. Control of land throughout South Asia is of great economic and political importance, and many low castes are also landless labourers. *Islam predominates in Pakistan and Bangladesh, although Muslims are found throughout the region. Other religions which started in this area, such as *Buddhism, *Jainism, and *Sikhism, are now mostly confined to limited parts of the region. Social organization, in which the village and extended families and households are important components, has been affected by a long history of foreign rule, first by Muslim invaders then by British colonialists. Since the colonial withdrawal in the 1940s political stability has been occasionally threatened by regional, linguistic, and religious differences, which have sometimes surfaced in violent confrontation as in the Punjab and Sri Lanka.

South-east Asian societies, geographically defined as peoples within an area bounded by Myanmar (Burma) in the west, the Philippines in the east, and Indonesia in the south. This region includes a wide variety of ethnic groups and a diversity of social organization, including, for example, the *Kachin, *Minangkabau, and *Balinese. This area is dominated by *rice cultivators, often employing complex irrigation systems, and various forms of *shifting cultivation. Most of the population are *peasant farmers, but cash crops such as rubber, cotton, and sugar are important. There are also many urban areas, such as Singapore, which have become increasingly important as world trading centres. Social organization is often based on the nuclear *family and the house. Three main religions, *Buddhism, *Hinduism, and *Islam, have had a major cultural impact on these societies.

Southern African Development Co-ordination Conference (SADCC), an organization of southern African countries whose principal goals are to reduce its members' economic dependence on South Africa, and to promote regional integration. The SADCC was formally established in April 1980 with the signature of the Lusaka Declaration, which bore the title: 'Southern Africa: Towards Economic Liberation'. In 1990 its members were Angola, Botswana, Lesotho, Malawi, Mozambique, Namibia, Swaziland, Tanzania, Zambia, and Zimbabwe. The organization is based in Botswana. Members aim to reduce their dependence on South Africa for rail and air links and port facilities, imports of raw materials and manufactured goods, and electricity supply. The organization has attracted substantial foreign aid to fund its projects, and during the 1980s SADCC was regarded as one of the most successful of Africa's regional groupings. However, with recent political change in South Africa, the continuing role of the SADCC is under question as members open trading and diplomatic links with South Africa.

South Pacific Forum, a gathering of heads of government of the independent states of the South Pacific. It met first in 1971. In 1990 its members were Australia, the Cook Islands, Fiji, Kiribati, the Marshall Islands, the Federated States of Micronesia, Nauru, New Zealand, Niue, Papua New Guinea, Solomon Islands, Tonga, Tuvalu, Vanuatu, and Western Samoa. Informal discussions on common problems are held annually or when urgently required. The Forum has no written constitution and decisions are reached by agreement. In 1985 it adopted a treaty declaring a nuclear-free zone in the South Pacific. It has discussed threats to the region posed by the predicted rise in sea levels

due to *global warming and by overfishing. In 1989 it demanded an end to the use of driftnets, which, by sweeping 48 km (30 miles) of ocean at a time, threaten the survival of marine species. Under this and other pressure, the main nations responsible, Japan and Taiwan, have acceded. Its secretariat is provided by the South Pacific Bureau for Economic Co-operation based in Suva, Fiji, which also promotes trade, transport, and tourism in the region.

sovereignty, supreme and independent authority over a given territory. Sovereignty is usually vested in the people of the territory, who delegate it to the *government administering the *state on their behalf. Internally, sovereignty implies a *legitimate source of rule within society, above which there is no higher authority. This can in practice diverge from and conflict with the actual power of a ruling *élite. A stable and legitimate system of government requires both the right to control a society and the means for doing so. Externally, the claim to sovereign control of a given territory is normally recognized by other sovereign states either *de facto* (because it exists in fact) or *de jure* (by right). In practice, *international law imposes restrictions upon the sovereign power of states, which are not allowed to act simply as they please within their territory.

space (in philosophy). Questions about the nature of space and its relations to objects are, along with questions about the nature of *time and its relation to events, amongst the oldest and most pervasive questions in philosophy. One such question is whether space is real and whether it could exist even in the absence of any objects; whether there could be empty space. The 'absolutist' view of space sees space as a container within which objects exist and enter into relations with each other. A difficulty with this view is that we want to ask the questions: what is outside the container? what are its 'walls' made of? what size is the container and what shape? An alternative view, the 'relativist' view of space, sees space as dependent for its existence upon the objects in it—so that any proposition about space can be understood as a proposition about objects and their relations to each other and there can be no sense in the idea of empty space. A difficulty with this view is that relations between objects are themselves spatial, so we have not fully analysed the idea of space by saying that it consists in relations between objects. In recent times, mathematicians have represented space not as a container in the Euclidean manner, but as a finite sphere, our conceptions of which depend upon our having chosen one geometry in which to interpret our observation. These views culminated in the work of the physicist Albert Einstein (1879–1955), who showed that space and time are not separate dimensions but one space–time dimension, the geometry of which is seen as real and such that it can be appealed to in explanation of various phenomena.

Spanish language *Romance languages.

special armed services, élite sections of the *armed services designed for action in particularly sensitive or dangerous circumstances. Almost all organized armed forces have special units whose duties include the protection of the government itself or the carrying out of particularly dangerous operations. In *authoritarian states, such forces are often under the personal control of the ruler, and charged with his or her protection. One characteristic of such forces is high mobility, combined with lethal firepower and the combination of tactics and weapons from army, naval, and air forces.

The British Special Air Service (SAS) and Special Boat Service (SBS) are two of the most widely known special forces, along with the Soviet Spetznaz; others include Republican Guards in Iraq, and the Israeli Sayarot. In wartime, the functions of these forces include operations behind enemy lines; in peacetime, they have been used for hostage rescue operations by a variety of states. Special armed services tend to follow their own codes of conduct and discipline, which sometimes leads regular soldiers or civilians to regard them as being beyond the law.

special education, a term used for educational programmes and services for people with learning difficulties. It is estimated that one child in ten world-wide has learning difficulties. Some have a specific learning *disability such as *dyslexia. Others fall behind as a result of social or emotional difficulties. Still others are *deaf or *blind or physically or *mentally handicapped. In poor countries inadequate pre-natal and post-natal care, infectious diseases, and malnutrition cause many of these disabilities. Yet UNESCO has estimated that 85 per cent of the world's disabled population reside in nations where few or no special education facilities exist. Where developing countries do provide special education it is usually only for children with severe impairments. In many countries special education is segregated. Internationally there is a trend towards 'normalization' or 'mainstreaming' of special education in state schools. This is prompted by a belief that it will enhance the dignity and motivation of students with learning difficulties as well as improve their education. Cost–benefit analyses by UNESCO and others have shown that, overall, 80–90 per cent of handicapped people are employable if appropriate education and training programmes are completed.

speculator (in economics), someone who trades in *markets with the specific objective of profiting from changes in prices. Speculators may operate in markets for *goods (chiefly *commodities), *currencies, and *securities. They buy when they believe the price is going to rise, and sell when they think it is going to fall. A large amount of speculative activity in a market may itself affect prices. For example, speculative purchases made in the expectation of a price rise may increase *demand and thus push the price up. Detractors of a market economy cite speculation as a negative side-effect and possible cause of market disruption or collapse if taken too far.

speech   *communication, *conversation, *language.

speedway racing, a sport in which four riders race adapted lightweight motorbikes with no brakes round an oval track some 275 m (300 yards) to 410 m (450 yards) in length, sliding dramatically through bends and accelerating on the straights. A professional sport in Britain, it is also popular in Australia, where it began in the 1920s, New Zealand, Czechoslovakia, Poland, and Sweden.

Spinoza, Baruch de (1632–77), philosopher of Jewish extraction who lived and worked in Holland. Spinoza is regarded as one of the three great *rationalist thinkers: he was strongly influenced by *Descartes, and developed Cartesian ideas in directions which contrasted with those of *Leibniz. Spinoza's greatest work, his *Ethics* (1677), is strictly organized in terms of axioms and deductions, manifesting his aspiration to construct a philosophical system on the analogy with mathematical science. Spinoza's outlook is

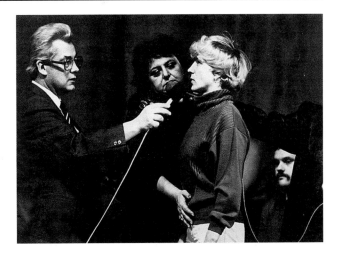

One of the few means of exploring the supernatural to be officially sanctioned by atheistic communist regimes, was **spiritualism**. A medium is seen here conducting a seance on Soviet TV.

profoundly *monistic: the world is conceived as a single infinite substance, with which God is also identical. What we ordinarily take to be distinct things, such as physical objects and persons, are for Spinoza only modes of that substance. Spinoza also articulated the view that the mental and the physical are but different attributes of the same thing (a view now referred to as psycho-physical parallelism). One of the most fascinating parts of Spinoza's philosophy is his account of 'human bondage'—enslavement by passion—and of the liberating role of the intellect, as involving a recognition that all human action is strictly determined.

spirit possession, the belief that a person can be possessed by a spirit or supernatural being, which can act and speak through his or her body. The spirits may be those of dead ancestors, demons, saints, or gods, and possession may be thought a blessing marking a person out as favoured by the gods (as in *shamanism), or an affliction requiring exorcism (driving out by invocation to a superior spirit being) and healing. Possession is usually accompanied by symptoms of trance. Sometimes it occurs spontaneously, but it may also be induced in the context of *rituals involving dance and music. In many parts of the world, spirit possession disproportionately affects groups of people, such as women or the poor, excluded from power and public life, and it may be seen as a form of safety valve for the outlet of their feelings of frustration, anger, and protest.

spiritualism, the name given to a movement with the belief that the spirits of the dead can communicate with the living by means of a medium, a person regarded as sensitive to the spirit world. It is an ancient belief, common to many religions; spirit mediums are active in *African religions, for instance. The spiritualist movement originated in occult happenings experienced by the Fox family in New York State in 1848. The Fox sisters became mediums, and the practice of seances, attempts to seek messages from the spirit world, became widespread on both sides of the Atlantic. Many followers of spiritualism are anxious to obtain evidence of life after death, or to make contact with the spirits of loved ones who have died. Psychic phenomena common at seances include clairvoyance, telepathy, and trance states, while physical manifestations include table turning, auto-

Squash

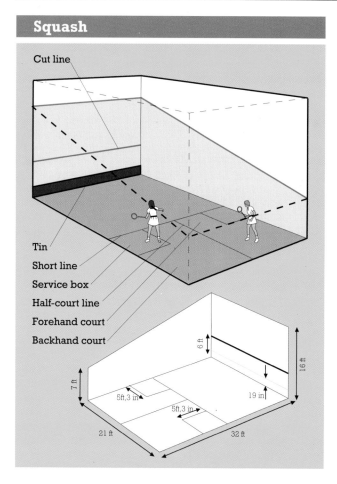

Cut line
Tin
Short line
Service box
Half-court line
Forehand court
Backhand court

6 ft
16 ft
7 ft
5ft, 3 in
5ft, 3 in
19 in
21 ft
32 ft

matic writing, levitation, and the appearance of ectoplasm, a viscous substance supposed to emanate from the body of the medium during a trance. Spiritualist beliefs and practices have been attacked both by established churches, which regard spiritualism as dabbling in the occult, and by those who believe that spiritualist manifestations are based on trickery and sleight of hand. The Society of Psychical Research was set up in London in 1882 in order to make a scientific study of such phenomena. (See also *parapsychology.)

squash, a fast-paced racket-and-ball game played in an enclosed rectangular court measuring 10 m (32 feet) by 6 m (21 feet). From a small square on one side of the court, the server hits the small rubber ball against the front wall so that it rebounds into the back half of the other side of the court. The receiver returns the ball, and the rally continues until one player either fails to reach the ball before it has bounced twice or hits it out of bounds. First to score nine points wins the game, and only the server may score; if the server loses a point, service passes to the other player. In the American (as opposed to the International) game, the court is almost a metre narrower, the ball is harder, the game is up to 15 points, and points count irrespective of service. Squash probably originated in the 19th century from the older and faster game of rackets, in which the court is almost twice the size, the rackets are heavier and with larger handles, and the ball is smaller and much harder. Of the few rackets courts in existence, most are in the UK. A variant of squash that is becoming extremely popular in the US is racketball. This is a racket-and-ball game played in a completely enclosed indoor court, roughly the size of a squash court. The rackets

are like tennis rackets but with much shorter handles, and the rubber ball (which is larger than a squash ball) is very bouncy. Unlike squash, the ball can bounce off the ceiling, but otherwise scoring and mode of play are quite similar.

squatter, a person who takes unauthorized possession of unoccupied premises or land, usually to live there. Squatting generally results from *housing shortages, but whereas in rich countries squatters tend surreptitiously to take single buildings, in poorer ones the illegal occupation of land has been on so great a scale as to persuade the authorities often to condone it, and sometimes to grant squatters legal title. Large-scale land seizures are sometimes carried out rapidly at night after careful planning: this is reflected in some designations for squatter settlements: in Mexico, *barrios paracaidistas* ('parachute settlements') and in Turkey, *gecekondu* ('built overnight'). The land chosen tends to be in public, not private, ownership and to be unwanted by others because, for example, it is on a waste-dump or subject to flooding. Squatters may also squeeze into small patches of land, near motorways for instance. Once the land is occupied, the residents begin to build shelters leading to the creation of *shanty towns. When the growth of such settlements initially accelerated (in Latin America in the 1940s and in sub-Saharan Africa in the 1960s), government reaction was often eviction of residents to distant camps and demolition of the structures. When it became apparent that this did not stem *migration to cities and destroyed not only housing stock but *informal-sector jobs, most governments became more tolerant of squatter settlements. In recent years, rapid *urbanization has reduced the supply of accessible public land and increased competition for it.

stabilization policies, policies which attempt to lessen short-run fluctuations in aggregate *demand and *national income. The chief methods of stabilization policy are monetary policy (control of the *money supply and interest rates) and *fiscal policy (government *taxation and expenditure). So-called automatic stabilizers include unemployment benefit (which leads to additional government expenditure when there is *unemployment) and income tax (since total income tax revenue rises with money national income). An important problem with stabilization is that of time lags, which arise in diagnosing a problem, in deciding upon and implementing action, and in that action taking effect. Another is the possibility that the effectiveness of systematic stabilization measures may be undermined by anticipatory actions on the part of producers and consumers.

stamp collecting (philately), the hobby of collecting postage stamps (or related material). Collecting followed soon after the issue of the first adhesive stamp (the UK penny black in 1840) and has now become a world-wide hobby enjoyed by young and old alike. Because of the proliferation of stamp issues, requiring catalogues to be revised annually, most collectors tend to specialize in particular countries' pictorial themes or such features as watermarks and cancellations. Stamps may be swapped among collectors, who often form local societies, or purchased through dealers or auctioneers. The most famous individual stamp is the 1 cent British Guiana black on magenta issued in 1856, only one copy of which is known to exist, and prices paid for rarities of this kind can approach £1 million. Stamp collecting is a hobby to which many postal systems now cater, from which many countries generate revenue, and in which many speculators invest.

standard of living, a term used to describe the material well-being of individuals. It is measured by the purchasing power of *income in terms of currently produced goods and services. For international comparisons and comparisons across time, real *national income (or *GNP) per capita is often used as a crude measure. When private consumption rather than GNP per capita is employed as the measure, separate allowance has to be made for the social wage (public services such as education and health care provided free at the point of use). It may also be appropriate to allow for other elements such as the quality of the environment.

state, the organization with legal supremacy, ultimately backed up by coercion, over a specific territory and population. Where states exercise *de facto* control over their territory (whether by right or not), they are usually given diplomatic recognition by other states and supra-national organizations such as the *UN. However, *de facto* recognition by the international community does not, in itself, bestow *legitimacy within the state. The structure and organization of the state are usually defined, nominally at least, by a *constitution. The boundaries of the state are not always clear-cut, but the core consists of the *executive, the *civil service, the *judiciary, the *police, and the *armed forces, which give the state its capacity to make and enforce decisions. Most states also include *legislatures. *Political parties, however, would not normally be considered to form part of the state in liberal *democracies. A state is a *nation-state if the bond of *nationalism coincides with the boundaries of the state.

state terrorism, repressive measures employed by a government against its own population; or *terrorism instigated or sponsored by a government against other states or individuals. In the first case, terrorist measures are employed by the state in order to coerce, intimidate, repress, and ultimately eliminate opponents. The most prominent practitioners of state terrorism in the 20th century were the Nazi regime in Germany (1933–45) and the Stalinist regime in the former Soviet Union (1924–53); but some contemporary *authoritarian states employ terrorist methods against their own populations, including threats, arbitrary arrest, *detention without trial, *torture, abduction, and *extra-judicial execution. The second form of state terrorism is often pursued by governments as a means of confronting or subverting other powers, which they do not have the military strength or will to attack directly. For example, the Libyan government is alleged to have financed and armed external terrorist groups such as the Irish Republican Army; Iran is believed to have been instrumental in instigating or supporting acts of terror by Islamic fundamentalist organizations; while the USA, as emerged in the Iran–Contra scandal of 1986, secretly sold arms to Iran in order, it was alleged, to fund the Contra rebels in Nicaragua.

statism, state control of social life, especially political control of the economy. It is less a coherent doctrine in its own right than a corollary of other doctrines, for instance, *socialist or other advocacy of the *nationalization of industry, or the *fascist belief in the supremacy of the state. In its extreme version, statism becomes *totalitarianism.

status, the position held by an individual or group or the esteem accorded to that individual or group. Status is sometimes used as a measure of *social stratification alternative or additional to that of *social class, in particular in the writing of *Weber.

statute law, law contained in enactments of the supreme legislative body in a jurisdiction. Proposed legislation is usually introduced in draft, and if approved (with or without amendment) in the manner provided for under the constitution, becomes law. Statute law usually overrides all other sources of law such as *case law and *customary law. Exceptions are any entrenched constitutional provisions or, in member states of the European Communities, provisions of Community law which have direct effect in member states.

Steiner, Rudolph (1861–1925), Austrian visionary whose ideas have influenced practical endeavours in agriculture, medicine, and education. The founder of anthroposophy, a mystical religious system evolved from *theosophy, Steiner urged harmony between the spiritual, creative, intellectual, and economic aspects of life and stressed man's relationship with the natural world. His pioneering interest in *ecology led to the 'biodynamic movement' based on *organic farming principles. Anthroposophical medical practitioners (who are also fully qualified doctors and in Germany run five sizeable hospitals) encourage physical and spiritual wholeness through art and movement, rhythmic massage, and specially devised medicines. There are 400 Steiner (or Waldorf) schools world-wide which seek to support the child's natural development. Steiner's principles also underlie the Camphill Movement, a network of schools, workshops, and residential communities for the benefit of *mentally handicapped children and adults. The capacity of all to contribute, to participate, and to enjoy life is recognized. In the residential villages for adults, residents and co-workers share a communal life and often seek economic self-sufficiency through running farms, bakeries, and craft workshops.

stereotype, an over-simplified definition of a social group, organization, or nation which provides a convenient but invariable *image. Stereotypes encourage simplistic judgements. They are often used in the *mass media because they provide instantly recognized cues, but their constant repetition may be highly prejudicial to identified groups (such as Black or homosexual people, Jews, American tourists, trade unionists, and so on). *Propaganda makes use of stereotypes in order to reinforce *prejudice against targeted groups.

stigma (in sociology), a mark or sign of disgrace or discredit. Individuals or groups may be stigmatized in a process akin to *labelling, leading them to become social outcasts. Defining and maintaining the boundaries between the 'normal' and the 'deviant' is an important function in all societies. In *Stigma* (1963), the US sociologist *Goffman maintained that typical stigmatized conditions include supposed blemishes of character (such as *homosexuality and *alcohol dependence), bodily defects (such as *deafness and *infertility), and the 'tribal' attributes of *race and *religion.

stock, a *security: in the USA 'common stock' means ordinary *shares, and in the UK 'government stock' means government *bonds or *gilt-edged stock. In a different sense, an *inventory: a quantity of raw materials, work in progress, or finished products held by a firm as part of a that firm's working *capital.

stock exchange, a *market in which *securities are bought and sold. Most capital cities have stock exchanges, as do some provincial cities. The world's largest stock exchanges are to be found in New York (Wall Street), Paris (the Bourse), Frankfurt, Tokyo, and London. All stock

Dealers on the Tokyo foreign-exchange market panic as the dollar hits a record low in April 1987. The Tokyo **stock exchange** is important but unpredictable: because of time differences it conducts its day's business before Western markets open, and its large fluctuations can have serious consequences.

exchanges make it possible for firms to raise long-term *capital by issuing securities to investors, who can then use the stock exchange to sell their securities when they wish. Investors normally buy and sell through *brokers, and in most stock exchanges deals are now conducted using computers. A 'bull market' is a term used to describe a market situation in which potential investors are optimistic, so that potential buyers outnumber sellers and security prices are on an upward trend. The opposite is a 'bear market', in which sellers predominate and prices are on a falling trend.

stoicism, a movement in philosophy founded by Zeno of Citium around 300 BC, the name deriving from the colonnade, or *stoa*, in Athens where Zeno lectured. Zeno's followers propounded various *metaphysical systems, united chiefly by their *ethical implications. All were variants on the pantheistic theme that the world constitutes a single, organically unified and benevolent whole, in which apparent evil results only from our limited view. Thus the requirement of wisdom and a good life is to accept inwardly one's place in an all-inclusive harmony, and to meet misfortune with self-control and calm fortitude.

Strategic Defense Initiative (SDI), the research, development, and deployment of space- and land-based defensive systems using directed-energy weapons and kinetic-energy weapons, and sophisticated surveillance systems to intercept and shoot down enemy missiles. The programme, known in popular parlance as 'Star Wars', was announced by US President Ronald Reagan in 1983. It was seen as a means of ending the insecurities and weapons proliferation associated with nuclear deterrence. The former Soviet Union, which already had an active research programme concentrating on particle beam and laser weapons, regarded SDI as a potential threat to its land-based missile systems. Hugely expensive (with an estimated $21 billion spent on SDI research between 1983 and 1991) and technically very difficult to achieve, the US programme was later scaled down; it was reorientated in 1991 as Global Protection Against Limited Strike (GPALS). Following the end of the cold war, the Russian President Boris Yeltsin proposed a joint global defence system incorporating the Star Wars technology to shield the world from nuclear attack.

street-games, a variety of race, chase, and ball-games played in the street by children world-wide. Many street-games are variations of much older games, some going back to *rituals. Most games belong to any time of the year. The games may be adaptations of conventional sports such as tag or be chanting and *singing-games. Other games include marbles, spinning tops, rolling a hoop with a stick, skipping, hop-scotch, wiggling with a hula hoop, catching a boomerang or frisbee, and skateboarding. An essential is that equipment be minimal or easily improvised. Some are played as an accompaniment to singing-games.

stress, the term used for a demand on physical or mental strength, or distress caused by this. Stress is a major health issue of modern society. It was defined by Hans Selye in *Stress* (1950) as a physiological response to noxious or aversive stimuli. Most people now working on stress would regard this definition as too restrictive. Although the physical effects of stress such as *heart disease, hypertension, lowered immunity, and gastric ulcers are dramatic and important, lower levels of stress—measurable in changed activity of the heart, brain, and hormonal system—also impair people's health, satisfaction, and efficiency. Early investigations concentrated on physical stressors such as extreme temperature, noise, illness, and injuries. More recent studies have emphasized the impact of factors such as work-load, crowding, *bereavement, and poor *relationships. These psychological factors are less well defined than Selye's physical ones, but they appear to cause both mental and physical illness. Research shows the importance of per-

Boys playing Chinese chequers in a *hutung* or alleyway in Beijing. These alleys which surround the courtyard houses typical of the Chinese capital are too narrow for cars and are quiet enough to allow children to play a variety of **street-games**.

ceptions of control over the source of stress. For example, noise affects concentration, but one experiment showed that people worked more efficiently through noise if they were told that they could switch it off whenever they wanted to. Such research is increasingly being used, particularly in the workplace, both in the organization of work and in the application of new technology.

strict liability, legal liability for a crime, breach of contract, or wrongful act, which does not require the victim to prove intention or *negligence on the part of the defendant. For example, in many countries the owner of a dangerous animal is strictly liable for any injury it causes, regardless of the precautions he or she claims to have taken, and a manufacturer is strictly liable if the product he or she makes proves defective and causes damage.

strike *industrial action.

structuralism, a method of study in which the phenomenon to be analysed is seen as comprising a system of structures, which are regarded as more important than the isolated elements that make them up. Structuralism derives from the linguistic theories of *Saussure in the early 20th century. Saussure regarded language as a vast network of structures; he broke it down into its minimal components (linguistic units such as phonemes and words), which could be defined only in relation to other such units. Saussure's linguistic theories were applied by the anthropologist *Lévi-Strauss in his study of *myth, *kinship, and *totemism, which he analysed as though they were language systems. He believed that the structures he identified corresponded to structures inherent in the human mind. Structuralism came to be applied to other areas, such as *sociology and literary criticism. From the 1960s literary structuralism flourished, particularly in France. Although it was never a unified critical school, certain ideas were predominant. The elements making up a literary work were held to have no intrinsic significance; their importance came from the relationships between them, such as parallelism, opposition, and so on. Literary structuralism was analytical rather than evaluative, regarding 'the content' of a narrative as less important than its structure.

subsidy, a payment made by government to producers or distributors in order to bring the market price of a product below its *factor cost. It is thus a negative indirect tax. The purpose may be to sustain producers in an otherwise nonviable activity, or to benefit consumers by reducing the price of a necessity, such as basic foodstuffs.

subsistence crop *shifting cultivation.

substance, a philosophical term meaning roughly a thing, or independently existing thing. Philosophical questions about substance are questions about what things, or kinds of things, fundamentally exist. *Aristotle characterized a substance grammatically as 'what is neither said of nor in a subject'. So, for instance, in 'Sam is running', *running* is said of, or said to be a feature of, *Sam*, but *Sam* cannot in this sense be said of anything else. Things can in turn be said of *running*, as in 'running is healthy', but here it seems clear that what are ultimately being spoken of are people, individual things, or substances, who run: people who run tend to be healthy. Again, *Sam* is something independent in a way that *running* is not: *Sam* can exist without *running*, but *running* can-

not exist unless someone runs. As well as this primary sense of substance, Aristotle recognized a secondary sense in which it answers the question *what* something is: 'Sam is running' tells us what *Sam* happens to be doing, but 'Sam is a man' tells us what kind of thing *Sam* fundamentally is. Primary substances are thus the individual things the world fundamentally contains, and secondary substances the basic kinds into which these things fall. In its long history the notion of substance has been modified and applied in various areas of philosophy. The *rationalist *Descartes made the notion central to his *epistemology: true knowledge of the world must rest on insight into the essential natures of the basic kinds of things it contains, in Descartes's *dualist philosophy, minds and material things. From *Locke onwards *empiricists, doubting our ability to achieve this insight, have been wary of the notion of substance. Even so, Locke's philosophy reluctantly casts substance in various roles: whatever it is that has the various properties we speak of in describing the world, or what lies behind and causes our diverse perceptions of it. That nothing can fill all the roles ascribed to substance perhaps explains why the notion has frequently fallen into philosophical disrepute. (See also *Leibniz.)

suffrage *franchise, *women's suffrage.

Sufism, the mystical and devotional aspect of Islam. Sufism arose in the early Islamic period as a reaction against the strict formality of orthodox teaching, and was organized into orders from the 12th century. Today, it is common to find an individual combining membership of a Sufi order with participation in everyday working and family life. The central aim of Sufism is to know God directly, and to this end the varied brotherhoods and groups of Sufism have adopted differing practices and beliefs. *Asceticism and *meditational practices such as *dhikr* (recitation) and *sama'* (dance) are amongst the most common Sufi practices. Veneration of Muḥammad, Sufi saints, and leaders who are held to be intermediaries with God is widespread, contrary to orthodox Muslim practice. Influenced by the beliefs of other faiths, amongst them neo-Platonism and *Buddhism, but deeply rooted in Islamic spiritualism, Sufism has played an important role in conversion and, sometimes, as an outlet for popular social and political discontent, although it has found a following amongst rulers as well as the ruled. (See also *mysticism.)

suicide, the intentional killing of oneself. In some societies, suicide used to be regarded as praiseworthy, or obligatory in certain circumstances, as for instance the Japanese *seppuku* or hara-kiri, ritual disembowelling in order to escape humiliation or demonstrate loyalty, or the Hindu practice of suttee, the voluntary burning of a widow after her husband's death. On the other hand, suicide is forbidden in Islam, Judaism, and Christianity. For centuries in Christian countries, suicide was considered a crime, and those who committed it were refused burial in consecrated ground. Criminal penalties for attempting suicide were only abolished in 1961 in England and Wales, and it is still a crime to help someone to commit suicide. The Voluntary Euthanasia Society has campaigned for the right to assist a suicide, particularly in cases where terminal illness is involved (see *euthanasia). The cause of suicide has been the subject of much debate, from the theories of *Durkheim, who regarded it as the result of social maladaptation, to psychological theories stressing the inverted aggressive impulses underlying it. It is generally held nowadays that many different social and psychological factors play a part. It is also recognized that suicide threats should be taken seriously, contrary to the received opinion that those who threaten to kill themselves do not actually do it. Unsuccessful suicide attempts may be deliberately unsuccessful, a 'cry for help', or they may well lead to a future, fatal attempt. Organizations such as the Samaritans, who operate telephone helplines, have had some success. Suicide is not only a tragedy for the victim: it has a profoundly damaging effect on the families and friends who survive the victim, often leaving them with feelings of grief, guilt, and anger.

sumo   *wrestling.

Sunnī (from Arabic, *sunna*, 'tradition'), the belief and practice of mainstream, as opposed to *Shī'ī, *Islam. Sunnī Muslims, constituting over 80 per cent of all believers, follow the *sunna*, or rules of life based on the *ḥadīth* collected in the *Sihah Satta*, six authentic books of Tradition. Sunnīs recognize the order of succession of the first four *caliphs, whereas Shī'īs believe authority begins with 'Alī, the fourth caliph. Sunnīs follow one of the four schools of law: the Hanafī, prevalent in the Middle East and Pakistan; the Malikite, found in western and northern Africa; the Shafite, found in Egypt, East Africa, Malaysia, and Indonesia; and the Hanbalite in Saudi Arabia.

supermarket, a large self-service store selling a range of goods, often but not always specializing in a single sector such as food. Supermarkets were a major development in *retail trading in many countries in the second half of the 20th century. Self-service reduced waiting time and staff costs. *Economics of scale permitted goods to be offered at lower prices than in traditional shops. Shortages of shop labour, and the attractions of out-of-town shopping (facilitated by wider car ownership), have assisted the growth of chains of supermarkets, many of which are sited outside town centres to take advantage of cheaper land. Hypermarket is the name given in the UK to large self-service stores with car-parking facilities: a group of shops under the same roof, often out of the town centre, is known in the USA as a mall and is an increasingly widespread form of retail trading.

superpower, a nation or state that has a dominant position in world politics, with power to act decisively in matters of global interest. The classic definition is that by the US political scientist William Fox, who said that a superpower is a *great power plus great mobility of power. The term was used to describe the dominant powers in the international system since World War II: the USA and the former Soviet Union. What made them superpowers was not only their resources and potential, the extent of their interests beyond their borders, and their economic and diplomatic power and influence, but also their military capabilities and their *nuclear weapons, which took power beyond that associated with the term great power.

superstition, a rather broad term, loosely used to describe false or irrational beliefs concerning supernatural forces or spirits. Use of the term is relative and subjective, and it has been applied at times to any form of religion or belief other than that which the person using the term happens to believe in. That being said, many people in many societies subscribe, either seriously or half-seriously, to beliefs concerning good and bad luck, the warding off of evil, the pre-

The painting of eyes on the prow of a boat is a widespread **superstition**. The eyes, painted here by a Singapore fisherman, may be to enable the boat to find its way or to outstare the 'evil eye'.

diction of the future, or the healing of sickness, whether these beliefs are common to a particular society as a whole (as in the case of the *evil eye), or whether they are beliefs held simply by a family or an individual.

supply (in economics), the amount of a *good or service that a firm or industry wishes to sell at a given price. For a competitive industry a supply curve can be drawn relating quantity supplied (on the horizontal axis) to price (on the vertical axis). The supply curve in such a case is normally positively sloped; an increase in price brings forth an increase in supply. In the case of *monopoly no separate supply curve exists. The firm will set supply (output) at the point where monopoly *profits are maximized. This is the output where marginal revenue equals marginal cost, that is the revenue from an additional unit of output just covers the additional cost of production. This depends on the slope of the *demand curve for the product. (See also *marginal analysis.)

supply and demand, law of, the economic principle that in a competitive market the amount supplied of a good in any period will tend to equal the amount demanded. The mechanism which facilitates this result is that of price. Typically, as the price of a good increases, the quantity demanded decreases, and the quantity supplied increases, so there will normally be one price at which supply equals demand, known as the equilibrium price. There are exceptions to this. Over a certain range the demand for a good may increase as price increases (goods with snob value; and *Giffen goods), and it is also possible for supply to decrease when price increases (for example, peasant farmers reducing production and enjoying more leisure). In such cases there may be more than one equilibrium price, and some equilibria may be unstable. These exceptions aside, if demand is greater than supply, then some consumers will be willing to pay more for the good, and firms will be able to charge higher prices whilst still being able to sell all their output. This leads to a rise in the price of the good, which in turn stimulates supply and reduces the quantity demanded (thus reducing the excess demand). The process continues until supply and demand are equal. Conversely, if supply is greater than demand, suppliers will tend to undercut each other and price will fall, raising demand and reducing supply until, again, supply equals demand.

surfing, the world-wide sport of riding ocean breakers on a long narrow board, a shorter belly board, a lightweight canoe, or by keeping the body rigid with arms above the head. Originally developed in Polynesia where people were required to manoeuvre through surf to land, it was popularized in the 1920s in Hawaii, where riders can surf for distances of 0.8 km (0.5 mile) or more. Surfing is practised wherever wave conditions permit and is especially popular in Australia, the USA, New Zealand, South Africa, and Latin America.

surplus value, a term employed by *Marx to denote the difference between the use value of labour (the value of the productive output of labour) and its exchange value (*wage) in his *labour theory of value. Surplus value arises only in the case of labour, not other *factors of production, and is seen as being appropriated by the capitalist in the form of *profit.

surveillance (technological), the monitoring of behaviour from a distance by means of electronic equipment or other technological means. A major feature of *security service activities during the 20th century has been the use of technological means to gather information on the opinions or activities of citizens with or without their consent. Such means include telephone tapping, powerful directional microphones, and various forms of loudspeaker devices or 'bugs'. Because surreptitious surveillance threatens *privacy, in most countries it is subject to legal controls, and can be employed only under a warrant issued by a specified authority, such as a judge in the USA and Australia, or a special tribunal in Germany. Electronic tagging is a form of non-surreptitious surveillance consisting of a device attached to convicted offenders or defendants on *bail, allowing their whereabouts to be monitored, and thus providing an alternative to imprisonment. Another common means of surveillance is the use of closed-circuit television systems in public places as a means of detecting and deterring crime. (See also *data protection.)

Suttee   *cremation.

Swahili   *Niger–Congo languages.

swimming, the art of moving the body through water. Swimming is one of the best forms of physical exercise and a popular sport. Strokes used in competitive swimming include backstroke, breaststroke, front crawl, and butterfly. The ability to swim is essential to other sports such as *diving, water-polo, water-skiing, *surfing, and skin-diving. As a leisure activity, swimming in the sea has been provided with an added dimension through snorkelling (using a breathing-tube for supplying air to an underwater swimmer).

syllogism, a type of argument consisting of two premises followed by a conclusion, in each of which two terms are related. A simple example would be: all Athenians are Greeks; all Greeks are Europeans; so all Athenians are Europeans. The various patterns of *valid syllogism were first studied by *Aristotle.

symbolic interactionism, a form of sociology which stresses the place of *symbols in social interaction. Closely associated with the *Chicago School US philosopher George H. Mead (1863–1931), and the sociologist *Goffman, it pays particular attention to the creation of the human personality in social interaction, by considering how people develop a sense of themselves. They learn through a process of interaction with others and with society, but do not always react directly. The symbolic nature of the interaction is paramount. They may never see their president or monarch, but are still subjects, relating to their power. Considered by some as an alternative to *functionalism, symbolic interactionism has helped to elaborate ideas about *deviance, *role, and *socialization.

symbolism, any system of meaning and representation that might act as a form of *communication. A symbol is anything that can be used to stand for, or represent, something else. A word (written or spoken) is a symbol, but so is a traffic sign, or a gesture, or a work of art (or part of a work of art). Some symbols, such as *ideograms and *pictograms, have simple, paired meanings, like 'red' meaning 'stop' on a traffic light, or a flag denoting a particular country. Others evoke much more complex responses (see *symbolic interactionism). In many works of art, symbols are deliberately used for allegorical or representational effect, while in others, communication is more suggestive and subjective: a poem or a piece of music, for example, may 'mean' different things to different people. All human beings use symbols and meanings, but every culture tends to have certain central symbols which are considered especially important. *Jung took this idea a stage further by elaborating a theory of archetypal symbols which exist in the 'collective unconscious' and are common to all cultures. Anthropologists like *Lévi-Strauss also claim that an analysis of the structure of symbolism can reveal universal principles of thought. All *rituals contain symbolic elements, and can themselves be interpreted as symbolic statements about society and social relations which reflect the human need to classify the world. Symbols not only act as signs which denote certain values and meanings, they also carry with them connotations of other meanings. In this way, all symbolism involves ambiguity and potential argument over meaning. The very ambiguity of a symbol can help to make it effective as a means of uniting people politically, despite serious differences; symbols of *kingship or *nationalism are good examples of productively ambiguous symbolism.

synagogue (from Greek, 'bringing together'), the Jewish place of worship, originally called the *beth ha knesset*, 'house of assembly'. Synagogues also provide religious instruction and are centres of legal authority. Synagogues arose after the Babylonian Exile (586 BC) and after the destruction of the Temple (AD 70) they spread rapidly, forming and remaining a focal point for Jewish life. Synagogues may be of any shape, but all share several features. Internally the central focus is the Ark (*Aron ha-kodesh*). This is a cupboard in the wall facing Jerusalem, which contains the scrolls of the Law (see *Torah), and which is screened by a curtain (*parochet*).

Synagogue

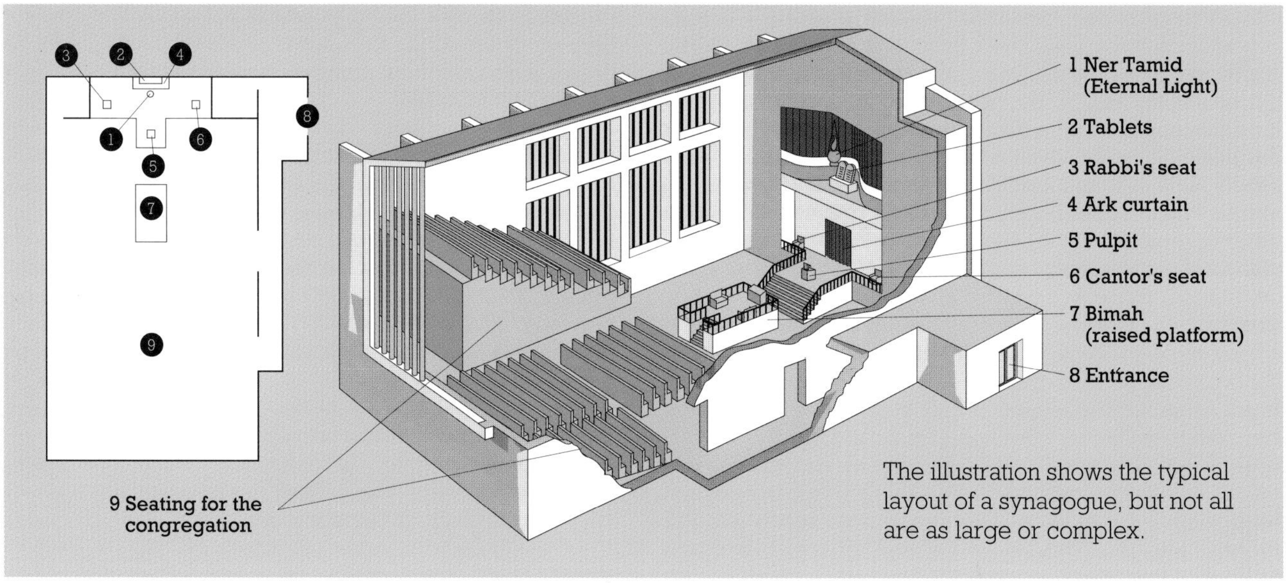

1 Ner Tamid (Eternal Light)
2 Tablets
3 Rabbi's seat
4 Ark curtain
5 Pulpit
6 Cantor's seat
7 Bimah (raised platform)
8 Entrance
9 Seating for the congregation

The illustration shows the typical layout of a synagogue, but not all are as large or complex.

Above the Ark are two tablets with the first two words of each of the Ten Commandments inscribed upon them. A light, the *ner tamid* ('lamp of perpetual light'), is suspended in front of it and represents both God's presence and the continuity of Judaism. During a service a scroll is removed from the Ark and transferred to a reading desk (*bimah*), from where it is read aloud. Some older synagogues contain a *mikvah*, or ritual bath. Synagogues allow no human or divine images, although the Magen David, a six-pointed star, representing aspects of the divine, and representations of the two Lions of Judah, may be present. In *Orthodox Judaism the sexes are separated, singing is unaccompanied, led by the *cantor, and services are in Hebrew. All Orthodox Jews wear a *tallit* or prayer shawl. *Reform Judaism (*Conservative Judaism in the USA) may allow family seating and musical accompaniment, and part of the service may be in a language other than Hebrew. *Liberal Judaism (Reform, in the USA) permits mixed-sex seating, and musical accompaniment; *tallits* are rarely worn, and worship, usually held on Friday evening, is in the vernacular.

syndicalism, a form of militant *trade unionism, aiming ultimately at the overthrow of *capitalism and its replacement by a form of *socialism. Syndicalist movements appeared in several Western societies, especially France, Italy, and Spain, in the late 19th and early 20th centuries. For radical workers, they served as an alternative to parliamentary socialist parties. Syndicalism shares with *anarchism an abhorrence of the state. The syndicalist aim was a society in which workers themselves, through their trade unions, would own the means of production. The path of change lay through industrial agitation, and especially the general strike, which would usher in a *revolution.

synod *church leaders.

syntax *grammar.

synthesis, a method for arriving at knowledge, opposed to analysis. The origin of this contrast lies in contrasting methods in geometry. Whereas analysis proceeds by breaking ideas down into their constituents and tracing them back to

their foundations, synthesis goes in the other direction: it shows how elements can be put together so as to compose new wholes. Synthesis has a similar but more technical sense in the context of Hegel's *dialectic. For *Kant, synthesis is the spontaneous activity of the mind in combining and unifying the isolated data of sensation.

Syrian Orthodox Church, or Jacobite Church, one of the Monophysite *Christian Churches, and sharing the doctrines of the *Armenian, *Coptic, and *Ethiopian Churches. It has about 800,000 full members, who are found on the Malabar coast in India as well as in the Middle East. Its centre is at Antioch (now Antakya in Turkey), the seat of its Patriarch. There are also some 80,000 Syrian Catholics in the Middle East, with a patriarch in Beirut. Syriac, a branch of Aramaic (the language of Palestine in the time of Jesus Christ), is the language of the rite of the Syrian Churches (see *Semitic languages).

T

Tabernacles, Feast of (Hebrew, *sukkot*, 'booth'), Jewish autumn festival lasting eight days. It recalls the offerings made by Jews at the end of the harvest and God's care for the Jews during the period in the wilderness after the Exodus (*c.*1300 BC) living in tabernacles, that is portable dwellings. New *sukkot*, in which all meals are eaten, are constructed of branches. Citrus fruit, myrtle, palm, and willow are borne in joyful procession around the synagogue. Called the *arba minim*, they represent four parts of the body and symbolize respectively: affection (heart), faithfulness (eyes), uprightness (spine), and humility (lips), indicating that God is worshipped with all faculties.

table tennis, a miniature indoor version of *tennis, played with small bats and a hollow plastic ball on a tabletop with a central net. A full-sized table measures 2.7 m (9 feet) by 1.5 m (5 feet). Games are up to twenty-one points, and players serve in sequences of five points then change over. Skilled players use cut and spin to swerve the ball through the air and make it deviate or accelerate on bouncing. In recent years China has been the dominant nation, with other champions emerging from Korea, Japan, and Eastern Europe.

taboo, a system of *ritual prohibitions forbidding contact with certain things or people. Taboo is originally a Polynesian word, but has been extended in general usage to refer to anything which is forbidden. In *Polynesian societies, taboo was part of a complex system of ritual observances, closely tied to ideas of rank. More generally, taboo is used to describe such things as food prohibitions, which can also be related to ideas of rank and hierarchy. In 19th-century *anthropology, the idea of taboo was usually associated with the food prohibitions of *totemism, and the marriage prohibitions of *incest.

Taiji (T'ai-chi) (Chinese, 'Great Ultimate', literally, 'ridge beam'), in Chinese philosophy, an expression of supreme or ultimate reality; the fundamental force from which spring *yin and yang and all creation. The notion was first mentioned in the *Yijing and was borrowed by Zhu Xi (Chu Hsi), a founder of neo-*Confucianism, who used it to define the unity of matter and the structure of the universe.

Taiji Quan (Chinese, 'Grand Ultimate Fist'), Chinese boxing. In this self-defence method, slow, regular movements are used to harmonize the forces of *yin and yang within the body, in order to improve health, remove tension, and increase energy.

Tai languages, a group of around sixty closely related languages spoken in Thailand and Laos, as well as in northern Burma and Assam to the west, and northern Vietnam and southern China to the east. They are spoken by over 60 million people. The languages fall into three sub-groups: North, Central, and South-West. South-West Tai has by far the largest number of speakers, since it includes Thai and Lao, the two biggest languages in the group. The Tai languages differ in pronunciation and spelling, but do not differ very much in grammar; the degree of divergence has been compared to that of the *Romance languages of Europe. Most words have only one syllable, and tone (see *phonology) is important. Squashed as they are between the giant cultures of India and China, the Tai languages have assimilated much from their larger neighbours. The eastern languages have tended to borrow especially from Chinese, the western languages from Sanskrit and Pali (see *Indo-Iranian languages). Thai, the official language of Thailand, is the largest language in the group; estimates as to the number of speakers vary, but it is probably in the region of 35 million. It has taken in a large number of Sanskrit and Pali words for cultural and technical vocabulary. The script was borrowed from Khmer, and is derived ultimately from the Indian Devanagari script, which was adapted for Thai in the 13th century. There is no very ancient Thai literature, since Pali was regarded as the literary language by Thai scholars. Lao, the official language of Laos, has over 15 million speakers, and Zhuang, a Northern-group language spoken in southern China, has over 10 million. The Tai languages have been linked with *Austronesian languages to form a superfamily called Austro-Tai, but this remains controversial.

take-over, the purchase of one firm or group of firms by another. Most take-overs occur by one of two methods. First, a *company may be taken over by the purchase of its *shares on a *stock exchange. This may happen over a period of time or (more usually) in response to an offer to buy shares at above the existing market price (a take-over bid). Secondly, a heavily indebted firm may be taken over by its creditors; in effect, the firm's *debts are converted into shares. A take-over is usually different from a *merger in that it is often (but not invariably) opposed by the firm being acquired. (See also *organic growth.)

Talmud (Hebrew, 'study'), the compilation of scholarly interpretations and commentaries on Jewish oral law codified in the *Mishnah. These interpretations and commentaries are also known as the *Gemara*. There are two major versions: the Palestinian or Jerusalem Talmud (completed *c.* AD 400) and the Babylonian Talmud (completed *c.* AD 500). Both are based on the same Mishnah, but the Babylonian Talmud is more extensive and considered more authoritative. The Talmud is primarily a legal compilation, but it also includes non-legal sections known as *Haggadah* (narratives). The standard version of the Talmud prints part of the Mishnah and the relevant Talmud on each page. The Talmud is the basis of later codifications of Jewish law (*Halakhah*), the most influential of which is the *Shulhan Arukh* ('Laid Table') (1565). Until the 18th century, Jewish communities in Europe had judicial autonomy and were subject to their own rabbinic courts. With the various reform movements thereafter the different branches of Judaism have viewed the Talmud and *Halakhah* differently. *Orthodox Jews regard the oral law and the written law of the Pentateuch (see *Torah) as equally divine and immutable sources of law which must be strictly observed. Reform Judaism, however, negates the divinity of the oral law and places emphasis on the authority of the Pentateuch. Conservative Jews take a position between these two, regarding the law as evolutionary. Thus Jewish law on aspects of religious practice such as diet and keeping the *Shabbat applies in differing degrees to Jewish communities throughout the world, with the exception of Israel, where the state acknowledges Jewish law as a source for secular law and recognizes rabbinical courts, which adjudicate exclusively in matters of marriage and divorce concerning Jews, and have concurrent jurisdiction with civil courts in all matters of personal status, if all the parties concerned consent. Questions of constitutional, criminal, and private law are, however, the domain of secular Israeli law, contrary to the declared aim of Orthodox Judaism that Israel become a fully Talmudic state.

Tamil, a member of an *ethnic group from southern *India, who also form a sizeable minority in parts of *Sri Lanka. The Tamils consist of a variety of groups and *castes, but are united through their common language which is a member of the *Dravidian language group and literature. The great majority are Hindus, but there are also Tamil-speaking Muslims and Christians. While Tamils in the south of India have their own federal state, Tamil Nadu, those in Sri Lanka believe themselves the victims of prejudice from the majority Sinhalese population, who control the government; since the 1950s the Tamil campaign for an independent state or regional autonomy has led to conflict, which has been at the level of civil war since the 1980s.

tantra (Sanskrit, 'loom'), an esoteric tradition in both *Hinduism and *Buddhism, which, through magical texts (*mantras), *meditation, and rituals, leads the practitioner to spiritual liberation and supernatural powers. In Hinduism, tantric practice, which may involve indulgence in normally forbidden taboos, is designed to awaken the energy of *Shakti. Tantric Buddhism or Vajrayāna ('Diamond Vehicle') is an important element in *Tibetan Buddhism. Meditation is based upon medical, occult, and astrological texts, as well as on mantras, *mudrās* (symbolic hand gestures), and mandalas (visual aids such as sacred diagrams).

Taoism *Daoism.

Tarahumara, an Indian group who are indigenous subsistence farmers of northern Mexico. They originally practised a form of dispersed cultivation, with frequent seasonal mobility, but now they tend to be settled. Although nominally Roman Catholic, the Tarahumara have several saint cults, which mix non-Christian religious practices, such as the use of the hallucinogenic drug mescalin (found in the peyote cactus) with more recently adopted beliefs.

tariff, a tax imposed on *imports, in the form of either an *ad valorem* tariff (a percentage of value) or a specified amount per unit quantity. The purpose of a tariff may be to protect a domestic industry, to reduce the level of imports for *balance of payments purposes, to retaliate against foreign *protectionism or unfair trade practices, or to raise revenue. Tariffs may be non-discriminatory, applying to all exporting countries equally, or preferential to some countries and discriminatory against others.

Tarski, Alfred (1902–), Polish mathematical logician and philosopher. Although it constitutes only a small part of his achievement in mathematics, Tarski is renowned amongst philosophers for work in essays of the 1930s on the notions of truth and logical consequence (republished in *Logic, Semantics and Metamathematics*, 1972). Tarski showed how to give these philosophically problematic notions mathematically precise definitions, at least in so far as they apply to formal languages in which (for instance) arithmetic and set theory can be expressed. The first reaction of philosophers was to count themselves freed at a stroke from the traditional problems of truth. More recently, and more soberly, philosophers have debated its relevance to the coherence and correspondence theories of *truth.

taxation, the compulsory transfer of money (taxes) to the central or local government from individuals, firms, and other groups, normally on an annual basis. The tax rate is either an absolute sum per unit of a product or else is the percentage of the *value of the taxable item which is payable. Taxation has several roles. First, it provides income for the government. In general, the higher the rate of tax, the higher the revenue raised from it. However, this is not necessarily the case. For example, high rates of income tax may lead to more tax avoidance and evasion (legal and illegal non-payment respectively), and also to emigration of some high earners and reduction of effort by others. These events may be sufficient to reduce income tax revenue when the tax rate is increased. Secondly, taxation may be used, together with government expenditure, to alter the distribution of *income and *wealth. To analyse the effect of taxation in reducing inequality, and also to analyse the effect of possible future changes in the tax rates, taxes can be measured by their progressiveness. A progressive tax is one which reduces inequality (taking an increasing proportion of income as income rises), and a regressive tax is one which increases inequality (taking a decreasing proportion of income as income rises). Thirdly, taxation can be used to change relative prices of *goods and services and so affect *demand patterns. Many governments tax alcohol and cigarettes at high rates partly to reduce *consumption of these items. Taxes on *imports (*tariffs) may also be used with this objective in mind. Fourthly, changes in tax can be used to influence aggregate demand (see *fiscal policy). Taxes can be classified into direct and indirect taxes. Direct taxes are those levied on individuals and companies, and include capital gains tax, corporation tax, income tax, inheritance tax, poll tax, property tax, and wealth tax. Indirect taxes are those levied on expenditure, and include *customs and excise duties, sales tax, and value added tax. A disadvantage of direct taxation is that it can reduce incentives to work and to save. However, much indirect taxation has the property (normally considered a source of injustice) of being regressive. Capital gains tax is a tax on realized increases on certain capital *assets (an asset is realized when it is sold). Individuals and companies are liable. Corporation tax is a tax on net company *profits. It may be structured in conjunction with income tax on company dividends and with capital gains tax to encourage either (larger) retention of earnings by companies or (larger) dividend payouts. Income tax is a tax on income, and is normally set at several percentage rates, each payable in a different income band. Rates normally increase with income (they are progressive). Taxes at higher rates are payable on additional income above the specified income thresholds. Typically, the first tax rate is zero per cent, so individuals on low incomes pay no tax. Inheritance tax or death duty is a tax paid on inherited *wealth. Poll tax (the short-lived 'community charge' in the UK) is a tax levied equally on all (or all adult) members of a community. Property taxes or rates are taxes (usually progressive with the value of property) levied on holders of property. Wealth tax is a tax on (all) forms of immovable and movable wealth. Sales tax is a tax on goods and services at point of sale. Value added tax (VAT) is a tax on the value added by a firm on a produced good or service. In other words, it is a tax levied on the difference between the sales price of the item and the costs of the bought-in inputs (intermediate goods) needed to produce the item.

tax haven, a place where rates of direct *taxation are low and exchange controls non-existent or minimal, so that individuals and firms move *capital funds there from abroad to avoid taxation. Tax havens are typically small countries such as Luxemburg or the Bahamas. Wealthy individuals may find it advantageous to live in tax havens as 'tax exiles'.

teaching, the profession of teachers and the work of education they carry out. Research commissioned by the World Bank shows that a teacher's qualifications, experience, education level, and knowledge have significant consequences for what children achieve. The trend world-wide is for all teachers to receive *higher education and specialist teacher training, but in most developing countries the percentage of unqualified or insufficiently qualified teachers is high. Although teachers are rarely well paid, their salaries tend to account for a very high proportion of the costs of education—often between 70 and 90 per cent. The majority of teachers are appointed by a centralized government agency or department which controls curricula and finances education. Decentralized teaching is strongest in the USA and India, where considerable responsibility for education is delegated to each state and community. Other countries, among them the UK, share the control and administration of teaching between national and local authorities. Most teaching owes something to each of two contrasting traditions—the traditional one that emphasizes formal instruction, often by rote, to impart a body of knowledge, the other focusing on the development of the individual student. *Froebel, *Montessori, *Dewey, *Bloom, *Bruner, and *Piaget are among the educationalists and psychologists who have particularly influenced teaching methods in the latter tradition. Current trends point to a holistic approach whereby teachers are required to develop interdisciplinary curricula whose aim is to enable pupils to find solutions to a specific need by, for example, mastering elements of business studies, home economics, physics, crafts, and communication skills.

technocracy, rule by an *élite of technically or scientifically qualified persons. Since the early 19th century, many social thinkers have looked forward to a time when both industry and government would be directed by those with the technical expertise to provide correct answers to economic and social problems. Prominent among them was the French aristocrat Henri de Saint-Simon (1760–1825), whose many writings, including *Du système industriel* (1821–2), advocated a society administered by scientists and industrialists. For some, technocracy is the only rational way of organizing society; for others it represents the destruction of human values in the name of material progress.

telecommunications, the long-distance transmission of voice or data by means of wire, *radio, computer, or *satellite. Telephone and telegraph systems, invented in the 19th century, converted speech or letter symbols into electric impulses for transmission; while the original systems needed wires to carry signals individually, modern systems are capable of handling thousands of messages at once to link distant points. Modern telecommunications systems also include teleprinter facilities, such as telex, in which a typed message is relayed and printed out; fax (facsimile transmission), in which documents and other graphic matter are transmitted as a signal by means of a telephone and printed by a small scanner-printer; and the exchange of computer data through telephone links (electronic mail). Traditionally, telecommunications systems were delivered by a monopoly supplier, usually a branch of government concerned with the postal, telephone, and telegraphic services (in Europe, the PTTs). In the USA the American Telephone and Telegraph was privately owned, but was still subject to government regulations. As the traditional forms of telecommunications were challenged by computer-based forms of *communication, there were calls for the breakup and *deregulation of the old telecommunications monopolies. In 1984 American Telephone and Telegraph, once the largest company in the world, providing four-fifths of the USA's telephones, and nearly all its home and international long-distance services, had its monopoly broken by the government. It was split into twenty-two local telephone companies grouped into seven regional companies. In Japan the huge Nippon Telegraph and Telephone Company faces similar governmental pressure to break up its monopoly. Markets are also being opened up in Australia and New Zealand, but in most of Europe the retention of a minimum provision of telephone services has been preferred to a policy of greater competition and technological innovation. The use of sophisticated telecommunications systems is transforming all aspects of business, political, and social life, bringing different societies closer together, and enabling speedy decisions to be taken.

teleology, explanation by reference to ends, purposes, or function, as in, 'Why do you have such big teeth, Grandmama?'—'All the better to eat you with, my dear!' *Aristotle considered teleological explanations to be a particularly illuminating kind of causal explanation, and contrasted them with explanations citing efficient causes, the prior state of affairs that brings something about. In Aristotle the value of teleological explanations rests on his *metaphysical doctrine of forms (see *universals), the fundamental kinds into which all things fall, and which define their proper ends. Without some such metaphysical underpinning, the use of such explanations is hard to justify; in particular, the mechanistic world-view characteristic of much of modern science emphasizes efficient causation and seems to leave little room for purposefulness. The great achievement of *Darwin's theory of evolution was to show how some teleological explanations in biology could be rested on a mechanistic foundation. How far this kind of reconciliation is possible is a live issue in the philosophy of *science. Perhaps the most famous teleological argument is that for the existence of *God, which takes our observations of the regularity and coherence of the world around us and our experience of the conjunction of regularity and design, to conclude that there must be a designer.

television, the most important of the entertainment *mass media, in which images and sounds are transmitted via radio-frequency electromagnetic waves or electrical cable. Television was first demonstrated by the Scot John Logie Baird in 1926. Regular black-and-white television broadcasts began in Germany in 1935, the *BBC followed suit in 1936, and the USA's National Broadcasting Company *network in 1939. In the 1950s television began to supplant cinema and radio in commercial importance and in the size of its audience. Colour television developed in the 1950s and early 1960s. In the Americas, commercial television, financed by *advertising, has always been dominant, but elsewhere state television is a significant component of services. From hesitant beginnings in 1962, transatlantic and then world-wide transmission of live pictures via *satellite

The Mursi of south-western Ethiopia watch a film made about them by a visiting TV crew. For such people **television** is a mixed blessing: while helping them to understand their place in the modern world it can also undermine faith in their traditional way of life.

has made television as flexible as *radio for *newscasts. Satellite services, like *cable television, are paid for per view or by subscription. The 'global village' predicted by the Canadian communications theorist *McLuhan in the 1960s is now a possibility. A single programme, such as the Live Aid pop concert for Ethiopian famine relief in 1985, can now reach hundreds of millions of people simultaneously in virtually every country of the world. The video recorder and use of the television receiver for *broadcast database information have further extended television's uses. There were 477 sets per 1,000 people in industrial countries in 1986, but only 40 sets per 1,000 in the developing countries, some of which, such as India, had fewer than 10 sets per 1,000. This, however, understates the access people all over the world have to television. The ubiquity of television's images of the world about us have renewed debate about the cultural and political roles of *broadcasting. The growing concentration of media ownership in the hands of a few companies has at times been at the expense of *public service broadcasting. The concern of developing countries that television is an instrument of cultural imperialism has led to demands for a New World Information Order with re-apportionment of the radio spectrum, dominated as it is by the industrial countries. Domestic critics see television as responsible for declin-

ing social values, particularly by portraying violence in entertainment programmes. The influence of *advertising on programme content is another area of controversy.

tennis, lawn, a racket-and-ball game. It is generally played outdoors, but indoor courts are becoming increasingly popular. The court measures 24 m (78 feet) by 8 m (27 feet) for singles with a pair of 'tramlines' at the side for doubles. The server stands on the baseline and serves the ball, usually with an overarm action, across the net into the receiver's right-hand court. The players rally until the ball hits the net and remains on the hitter's side, bounces twice, or goes out of play without bouncing in the court. The server then serves into the receiver's left-hand court. Players need four points to win a game, scored as fifteen, thirty, forty, and game. If they level at forty, deuce is called, and one player must win two clear points (advantage and game) to take the game. Players need six games and a lead of two games to win a set. Nowadays, if the set continues to 6–6, a tie-break is called. Women's matches are played over three sets and men's championships usually over five. The most prestigious championships take place in Paris (French Open), London (Wimbledon), New York (US Open), and Melbourne (Australian Open). Lawn tennis derives from the ancient game of real (or royal) tennis or (in France) *jeu de paume*. This is a racket-and-ball game played in an indoor court.

terrorism, the practice of using violent and intimidating acts, especially for political ends. *State terrorism implies either the use of terror by state authorities in order to suppress opposition, or state sponsorship of terrorist activities. Terrorism is also used by political groups in order to bring pressure to bear on state authorities to accede to political demands. Terrorism has been used most commonly by revolutionary groups whose objective is the overthrow of a particular state authority, and by nationalist groups seeking national *self-determination. Techniques of terrorism involve bombing and shooting attacks against property and individuals, the *assassination of significant persons associated with the established government or security forces, *hostage-taking, and *hi-jacking of aircraft, trains, ships, and buses. Terrorist acts are rarely indiscriminate (though the immediate effects on victims may be) or random, though it may be intended to appear so if that produces the desired effect of a generalized state of public fear. The major objectives of terrorism are: to keep a particular cause in the forefront of public consciousness; to pressure the political authorities to concede the terrorists' demands by inducing a state of public fear; and to induce a government to betray its own commitment to freedom and democracy by imposing illiberal security measures in order to contain such violence. The overthrow of governments or the achievement of national independence have rarely been achieved by terrorist techniques; on the other hand, by keeping a cause in the forefront of domestic and international political agendas, terrorism may be seen in retrospect to have played a role if those objectives are ultimately achieved, and to have imposed heavy costs on governments, even if they are not. Among the most prominent groups that have used terrorist techniques are: the Palestine Liberation Organization (PLO) and its offshoots; the Provisional Irish Republican Army (IRA); the Basque nationalist movement (ETA); the Red Brigades (Italy); and the Baader-Meinhof group, which became the Red Army Faction (Germany). International collaboration against terrorism has not proved easy since it involves the close co-operation of legal and police authorities from many different states (see *Interpol), which have different domestic laws as well as different international and foreign policy interests. The European Convention on the Suppression of Terrorism (1977), the 'Trevi system' of co-operation among EC members (1976), which has now spread to Council of Europe states, the Tokyo summit declaration on terrorism in 1986, and the participation of the former Soviet Union in anti-terrorist collaboration have all helped to establish a climate of international co-operation. However, it is less easy to set up specific mechanisms to counter the terrorist threat. For example, it has often been difficult to get common provisions on airport security; and laws on *extradition, which are the subject of specific bilateral treaties between states, often produce complex legal problems, the result of which may be that alleged terrorists are not brought to trial.

The bombing of the Grand Hotel, Brighton by the IRA during the Conservative Party Conference of October 1984 was one of the most effective examples of **terrorism** in the UK. Five people, including a Member of Parliament, were killed by the blast and many members of the government were injured.

tertiary industry (service industry), any economic activity which involves the production of services rather than *goods. Services are characterized by being intangible and consumed at the moment of production. Examples include *tourism, *banking, *insurance, wholesale and *retail distribution, *telecommunications, transport, catering and cleaning, and *journalism *Social services such as health and *education, which are commonly at least partly under central government control, are also tertiary industries. Industrialized nations such as the USA, Japan, Germany, and other western European countries, where the tertiary industries are the fastest-growing sectors, are considered to be in a *post-industrial phase. Such growth has been stimulated by the development of *information technology. A number of small countries, notably Hong Kong, Singapore, Bahrain, and Panama, have specifically developed as centres of tertiary industry, often by specializing in financial services and shipping. (See also *primary industry, *secondary industry.)

theocracy, a society governed by priests, or one whose government is heavily influenced by religious leaders. Originally it meant a system where divine law was the basis of all humanly enacted law, and in which religious and political hierarchies were merged as in Tibet until Chinese occupation in 1951. There are no theocracies in this strict sense in the modern world, but the term is applied where governments are forced to comply with the edicts of religious authorities, especially over moral issues. The clearest example of a theocracy in this broader sense is Iran since the fall of the Shah in 1979. (See also *religion and politics.)

theology (from Greek, 'the study of God'), the study of beliefs to do with God and his relationship to the world, including the study of scripture, *philosophy, comparative religion, and church history. Theology is usually undertaken from the standpoint of faith. It may be practised in the context of all religions, but has flourished most in the contexts of the monotheistic religions, *Judaism, *Islam, and, in particular, *Christianity. In both Judaism and Islam, the codification of religious law (see *Talmud and *shari'ah) has been considered a separate discipline and has often taken precedence over theology. Both religions lay stress on the indivisible unity of God and his unknowability by humans, and their theologians were not therefore as exercised with the problem of God's nature as were Christian theologians. In Christianity, however, the interaction between ideas of essentially Jewish provenance and the Greco–Roman world, and the systematic attempts to define *Jesus' relationship to God the Father and the Holy Spirit (see *Trinity), the relationship of divine and human nature in the person of Jesus, and the significance of his birth, crucifixion, and resurrection, have led to a long history of theological argument. The basic formulations of Christian belief were promulgated at the three great councils of Nicaea (325), Constantinople (381), and Chalcedon (451), which are recognized by both the Eastern Orthodox and Western *Christian Churches. After the great schism between the Churches in the 11th century, different traditions developed. The Eastern Church is, in essentials, faithful to the early delineation of Christianity; in the West there ensued a period of theological and philosophical development known as *scholasticism. Increased contact between Judaism, Islam, and Christianity and the translation of Greek philosophy into Latin and Arabic led to an intellectual flowering in all three religions, exemplified in the work of Christian theologians such as Anselm (1033–1109) and St Thomas *Aquinas, the Muslim philoso-

Reverential respect was shown to the Ayatollah Khomeini in the modern-day **theocracy** of Iran. He was the leader of a politicized Shi'a clergy who successfully reversed the westernization and secularization of their country.

pher *Avicenna, and the Jewish philosopher *Maimonides. However, in later years scholasticism lost much of its vitality. The *humanism of the 15th-century Renaissance challenged theologians, and Martin Luther (1483–1546) initiated the Reformation, the division of the Western Church into Protestant and Roman Catholic Churches, with a theology centred upon the conviction that salvation ('justification') was by faith alone. He expressed this in biblical rather than philosophical terms, and took less interest in philosophical discussion of the nature of God. For John Calvin (1509–64), the leading figure in Protestantism after Luther's death, the doctrine of justification by faith was extended to an emphasis on salvation by God's grace, in which the doctrine of *predestination was central. By the 18th and 19th centuries Christian theology faced profound challenges from philosophers such as *Locke, *Hume, *Descartes, *Kant, and *Hegel, and from the rise of science, from the critical study of historical documents and the scriptures, and from key developments in modern thought such as *Darwin's theory of evolution, *Freud's theory of psychoanalysis, and *Marxism, all of which have contributed to more widespread secularism Theologians have responded in two ways: by retreating into defensive positions as in *fundamentalism; or by trying to integrate new insights into Christian belief, as in the 19th-century 'liberal' theology; or in contemporary movements such as feminist and *liberation theology.

theosophy (Greek, 'divine wisdom'), a religious philosophy claiming insight into the nature of God and the universe through direct experience, making use of such means as *mysticism, *meditation, occult practices, and hidden meanings in sacred texts. Theosophists include Neoplatonists and Gnostics, but nowadays they are more generally identified with members of the Theosophical Society, founded in New York by Helena Blavatsky (1831–91). The ideas of the society were heavily influenced by *Hindu thought, and its base moved to India, where its leading exponents was Annie Besant (1847–1933). The Theosophical Society, with branches throughout the world, aims for the universal brotherhood of man, and the spiritual exploration of unexplained laws of nature. Theosophy has attracted many intellectuals, including the educationalist *Steiner.

Theravāda (Pali, 'teaching of the elders'), one of the most important groupings within *Buddhism, predominant in Sri Lanka and South-East Asia. It is also known as Southern Buddhism. The Theravāda school takes as its canon of scripture the *Tripitaka, written in Pali, which contains the original teachings of the *Buddha: the *Four Noble Truths, the *Noble Eightfold Path, and the doctrine of *dependent origination. Theravāda differs from the other great school, the *Mahāyāna, in its emphasis on individual, rather than universal enlightenment. Theravāda Buddhism also stresses the pre-eminence of Gautama *Buddha, who is saintly rather than transcendent. Personal liberation is attained through the observance of a strict moral code, rather than through grace. Theravāda emphasizes meditation and wisdom, as well as compassion. Initiation into a monastic order (*sangha), traditionally thought essential for enlightenment, is giving way to an increasing lay community, especially in Sri Lanka, but the Theravāda ideal of the saintly monk or *arhat remains important.

Third World, a collective term of French origin (le Tiers monde) originally employed in a UN classification system to distinguish between the developed capitalist countries, (First World), the developed communist countries (Second World), and the remaining under developed countries (Third World). The Third World thus includes most of Africa (excluding South Africa), Asia (except Japan), and Latin America. It emerged as a distinct entity in international politics following the process known as decolonization, which brought independence to a large group of African and Asian countries in the 1950s and 1960s. Their shared historical experience (*colonialism) and common problems (*poverty and under-*development), together with those of Latin America, led them to act as a bloc in international forums, particularly the *UN. The Third World advocated *non-alignment in East–West relations and formulated a set of demands to reform the existing international economic system known as the *New International Economic Order (NIEO). Like the term *developing country or simply the South, with which it is used interchangeably, the Third World is in many ways an imprecise and unsatisfactory definition, largely because it encompasses an enormous variety of countries with very different economic, social, and political conditions. It also has a pejorative connotation. Yet despite efforts to redefine the term and introduce new categories such as less developed, middle income, and *newly industrializing country (NIC), its use is still widespread.

The 17th-century Potola (palace) in Lhasa, Tibet, the traditional centre of **Tibetan Buddhism**. From here the Dalai Lama or 'lama great as the ocean' exercised temporal power while the Panchen Lama or 'jewel of the scholars' held spiritual sway. The current Dalai Lama lives in exile in Dharmsala, northern India.

thought experiment, a philosophical method used for the analysis of concepts (most notably the concept of *personal identity). It works by testing our intuitions in an imagined situation. For example, if a person were to split as amoeba do, which of the resulting two people would be identical with the person prior to the split? Thought experiments are also used in the natural sciences: Isaac Newton (1642–1727) used them when considering the nature of light, and Albert Einstein (1879–1955) relied on them for the development of his theories of relativity.

Threefold Refuge (Three Jewels), a verbal sign of commitment, much like a confession of faith, recited by all Buddhists. The *Buddha, his teaching (*dharma), and the monastic order (*sangha) are regarded as three jewels of inestimable worth, and the phrase 'I go to the Buddha for refuge, I go to the *dharma* for refuge, I go to the *sangha* for refuge' expresses commitment to the precepts of *Buddhism.

Three Marks of Existence, the three fundamental factors that characterize all phenomena, according to *Buddhism. The first mark of existence is *dukkha*, or suffering, which reflects the human experience of pain, disease, ageing, and death. The reason for this suffering is *anicca*, or impermanence, the second mark of existence. Everything is transitory, subject to change, decay, and death. Belief in a permanent state of existence is a deception by our senses. Finally, the reason for this impermanence is explained by the third mark of existence, *anatta*, or 'non-self'. All things lack an essence, or in the case of a person, a self or soul. This doctrine is an important difference between Buddhism and *Hinduism, which postulates the continuity of an ultimate self, or *ātman. To a Buddhist, the realization of the truth of

the Three Marks of Existence is a necessary component of enlightenment.

Tibetan Buddhism, a distinctive form of *Mahāyāna Buddhism found in Tibet. The predominant sect, the Yellow Hats, is headed by the *Dalai Lama, who is both a religious and political leader. Tibetan Buddhists revere the *Bodhisattva of Compassion, Avalokiteshvara, and they believe that each Dalai Lama is his *reincarnation. Much of the ritual of Tibetan Buddhism is based on the esoteric tradition of *tantra, as well as the ancient *shamanism of the earlier Bon religion of Tibet. Worship includes the recitation of *mantras and prayers, and the singing of hymns to the accompaniment of horns and drums. The Tibetan canon of scripture includes the *Kangur* (see *Tripitaka) and the *Tenjur* (further commentaries). The *Tibetan Book of the Dead* (*Bardo Thödröl*) describes consciousness between death and rebirth.

Tibeto-Burman languages   *Sino-Tibetan languages.

Tikopia, a small Polynesian island, whose inhabitants practise subsistence agriculture and fishing. Land is divided according to *clan interest, *lineage interest, and the rights of the *chief. In common with other *Polynesian societies, the village is the basic social unit, although villages do not have a formal leader. *Marriage is virilocal (resident at the husband's family's home), and *kinship is organized on the basis of *patrilineal *descent groups. Traditional authority was exercised through the clan chiefs, and the use of *ritual was an important part of this process. However, since the majority of the islanders converted to Christianity in the mid-1950s, these rituals have fallen into disuse.

time. Despite its seeming familiarity and the large extent to which temporal notions occur in our everyday thoughts, the nature of time has been a longstanding philosophical issue. Many kinds of questions, both general and specific, have been raised. For instance, is time a process which is independent of the events which occur in it, as the absolutist position maintains, so that there can be time without change? Or is time not really an entity which can exist without events at all, as on the relational view, in which talk of the 'flow of time' is merely a way of speaking of sequences of events? And is time real in the sense that it exists independently of all perceivers? Or is it, as *Kant maintained, an *a priori element of our conceptual apparatus, something we impose on to reality in order to make the world comprehensible? More specific questions are: Does time have a beginning and an end? Could time be circular? does time, of necessity, only ever flow in one direction? Can we make sense of the possibility of travelling backwards in time? And more recently, what is the relation between time and *causation? Science has always played a much larger part in the discussion of these issues than in many philosophical disputes, because of the role of time in scientific theories. In the 17th century, for instance, Isaac Newton argued that time was both real and absolute, a view which brought him into conflict with *Leibniz. Recent theoretical developments in physics have brought about a revolution in our way of thinking about time. Most notably, whereas it had always been assumed that *space and time were separate dimensions, modern science now combines them into a single four-dimensional space–time manifold.

time-and-motion study, the analysis of a task so as to arrive at the correct time needed to do the task or to suggest

ways in which the task can be speeded up. Where small jobs are repeated many times, by breaking down the task into its basic component parts, it may be possible to suggest changes which, cumulatively, make major savings in time and/or effort. The technique has been criticized for failing to take the human element into account. People have different abilities under various conditions and their work performance will vary at different times of the day or week. However, the need to identify standard units of work is important in *production management in order to plan output levels, to identify unit costs, and to maximize efficiency.

Tlingit, a group of fourteen tribes of *North-west Indians, found in south-eastern Alaska and British Columbia. The Tlingit have a complex *clan organization, organized around three phatries (groups of clans), which are *matrilineal with exogamous (outside the group) *marriage. The phatries, however, have no political unity, and no chiefs, and their main function is to determine the choice of marriage partners. The local clans control territorial rights for hunting and fishing, and also act to enforce *dispute resolution. Rank and hierarchy were partly determined by inheritance, but also partly through the display of wealth in the *potlatch system

toleration, a willingness to accept or permit speech or behaviour contrary to one's own beliefs. As a political ideal it is central to *liberalism, and like the latter can be traced back to the religious struggles in Europe during the 16th and 17th centuries, which culminated in the recognition of the rights of dissenting Churches and sects to worship in their own way (see *religion and politics). Toleration has been more recently discussed in relation to co-existence between different *ethnic and cultural groups within society. In this context, toleration implies not simply refraining from harming groups different from one's own, but enabling them to develop as minorities with their own distinct identities. Other writers have discussed the more controversial issue of the limits of toleration, for example the right to indulge in speech or behaviour found morally repugnant by others, such as *blasphemy, or incitement to racial hatred. Most countries limit their *freedom of expression in this domain for the sake of social harmony and peace.

tone languages   *phonology.

Torah (from Hebrew, 'teaching'), in the broadest sense, the essential doctrines, law, and narratives of *Judaism, held to be God's fullest truth for mankind. In a narrow sense, the Torah refers to the Pentateuch, the first five books of the *Bible, which are believed to have been revealed to Moses on Mount Sinai. In order, they are: Genesis, Exodus, Leviticus, Numbers, and Deuteronomy. The Pentateuch is kept in all Jewish *synagogues and readings from it are an important part of the Jewish liturgy. The term Torah may also include the oral law compilations and commentaries of the *Talmud and the *Mishnah and is sometimes extended also to refer to the *Midrash* and other commentaries on the law.

tort (from medieval Latin *tortum*, 'wrong'), a breach of duty, other than a breach of contract, leading to liability for *damages or in certain circumstances an injunction. The aim of the law of tort is to secure *compensation for personal injury or damage to property, as well as to protect other interests, such as reputation (see *defamation) or *privacy. *Common law systems tend towards a proliferation of individual torts, whereas *civil law systems, in which a tort is usually called a delict, have recourse to a general principle of responsibility, which operates in the majority of cases. In addition to compensating the victim, the law of tort also encourages those whose activities carry risks for society (such as drivers of cars, or manufacturers of potentially dangerous products) to undertake them with care. Those whose activities carry special risks are in some legal systems subject to *strict liability. Even in the codified systems of the civil law, but particularly in common law systems, tort law is largely judge-made law, and liability is subject to judicial perceptions of the correct limits of personal responsibility.

torture, the systematic inflicting of pain, bodily damage, or extreme psychological stress on captives in order to punish, to extract information or confessions to crime, or to intimidate. Methods of torture range from beatings, sexual assaults, solitary confinement, threats to relatives, to the use of mind-changing drugs and electric-shock devices. Torture is most often used by repressive political regimes in order to eliminate internal dissent or departures from official orthodoxy, which might undermine their authority. The *Universal Declaration on Human Rights (1948) forbids the use of torture by governments, but the view of the *human rights monitoring group, *Amnesty International, which maintains systematic records on the use of torture, is that torture is still a widespread phenomenon, which is regularly

A political prisoner freed by the Tigré People's Liberation Front in Ethiopia in 1986 demonstrates the method of **torture** used against him. An estimated 2 million people died in purges during the fourteen years of the Marxist Mengistu regime which collapsed in 1991.

and systematically used by more than 100 regimes in the early 1990s.

total institution, an institution which completely absorbs the lives of those within it and separates them from the rest of society. The concept was formulated by the US sociologist *Goffman, following research in a psychiatric hospital. He cited prisons, hospitals, and, at the extreme, *concentration camps as examples. In *Asylums* (1961), Goffman described the methods by which control is exercised and the dehumanizing effect on both the inmates and staff. A total institution strips identity from inmates—their clothes are communal, personal possessions are removed, *privacy is denied, and a rigid routine imposed. Some inmates actively collaborate with the staff, others become passive and dejected, while others again find subtle ways of defying and subverting the regime. The Romanian asylums for mentally handicapped adults and orphaned children, revealed to the world after the fall of the dictator Nicolae Ceausescu in 1989, displayed in gross form the characteristics of total institutions.

totalitarianism, a political system in which all individual activities and social relationships are subject to surveillance and control by the state. The idea originated in the 1930s and 1940s, when observers noted points of similarity between *Nazism under Hitler and *communism under Stalin: one-party government headed by a single powerful individual; promotion of an official *ideology through all media of communication; government control of the economy; and extensive use of terror tactics by the secret police. Together these features pointed to a society in which power was highly centralized and in which no individual could escape from the attentions of the state. A totalitarian regime is a specifically modern form of *authoritarian state, requiring as it does an advanced technology of *social control. Some observers (most notably *Arendt) have explained the emergence of such regimes with reference to the growth of mass society: where the bonds of *community break down, atomized individuals can be mobilized by the propaganda of political leaders. The classic case of totalitarianism is the former Soviet Union under Stalin; features of totalitarianism are also to be found in a number of developing countries governed by authoritarian regimes.

totem, an animal or species which is regarded as the original ancestor of a particular *clan. Totemism is often associated with *ritual observances and prohibitions on eating the flesh of the animal concerned. The symbol of the totemic animal may be tattooed on the skin as a body adornment, represented in masks, or carved on poles (as among the Indians of the Pacific North-West). At one time, totemism, which is found in Australia, Melanesia, North America, and other parts of the world, was believed to be the original, primitive form of all *religion. Writers such as *Freud, *Frazer, and *Durkheim all incorporated it into their schemes of religious and social *evolution. As evolutionism gave way to *functionalism in *anthropology, *Malinowski analysed totemism as an attempt to control, through *ritual practices, the fertility of the species to which the totem belonged. The most recent theory of totemism is that of *Lévi-Strauss, who argues that totemism is just one aspect of the general human desire to classify and order the world.

tourism, travelling for leisure either in a different region of one's own country, or in another country, originating in the 'grand tours' of Europe in the 18th and 19th centuries by wealthy families. Tourism has become a major industry, accounting for over 5 per cent of world trade and generating foreign currency and widespread employment, both direct and indirect, for many nations, as well as business in the packaging and promotion of tours and the chartering of cheap flights. Before 1939 an estimated 1 million travelled abroad each year, but by 1990 there were more than 400 million international travellers. Many developing countries possess the potential to be ideal tourist locations, such as the Caribbean islands, and derive a major part of their revenue from tourism. However, the benefits of tourism, such as increased foreign-exchange revenues, higher employment, and even enhanced international understanding, may be outweighed by the damage done to local communities and the environment, and the repatriation of profits by foreign investors.

trade, the exchange of goods and services for money (domestic *currency or *foreign exchange), for other goods and services (*barter or counter-trade), or in payment of *debt/extension of credit. Wholesale trade is trade in large volumes. It occurs between firms, and the seller's profit margin is normally less than it would be with smaller volumes. *Retail trade is trade at the point of sale to the final consumer. This trade typically occurs in shops, but may occur in other ways (for example, mail-order selling). When using the term trade, economists are often referring to international trade. This consists of *imports and *exports. Trade in goods is known as visible trade, trade in services as invisible trade. Free trade is said to exist when there is no government intervention which either encourages or discourages international trade. The view of classical and neoclassical economists is that free trade encourages each country to specialize in the production and export of those goods and services in which it has a comparative advantage, leading to gains for all trading countries; *Ricardo said trade would increase 'the sum of commodities and mass of enjoyments'. In practice *protectionism is common. This may take the form of *tariffs; *quotas; variable levies (tariffs used, in particular, by the EC Common Agricultural Policy, which change weekly); health, safety, and other regulations; restrictions imposed to stop dumping (the selling of underpriced goods possibly but not necessarily in order to stifle competition); and 'voluntary export restraint' (VER) agreements (as used by the USA and EC). A VER agreement is a bilateral agreement made between an importer and an exporter in which the exporter agrees not to export more than a certain amount of a good in exchange for some (possibly non-trade-related) concession by the importing country. The demand for such diverse methods of protectionism in part stems from a (usually unjustified) desire to restrict trade by means which are not disallowed by the *GATT. (See also *balance of trade, *exchange rate.)

trade cycle (business cycles), more or less regular cyclical fluctuations in the level of aggregate *demand, and hence of *national income. The amplitude of such cycles can sometimes be lessened by means of *stabilization policies. The causes of trade cycles vary. Many theoretical models focus on fluctuations in the level of *investment by firms as the cause of the cycles. However, changes in investment may themselves stem from several different causes, including demand 'shocks' (such as the jump in world oil prices in 1973–4, which affected other components of demand besides investment) and sudden changes in monetary policy and*interest rates.

Faked goods bearing the **trademark** of famous manufacturers are produced in countries such as Taiwan and retail at a fraction of the original. Seen here are counterfeit watches being crushed by Cartier of Switzerland.

trade mark, an identification symbol (name and/or logo) legally registered or established by use in order to distinguish the goods of a particular manufacturer. Such a device may be one of the manufacturer's most effective marketing tools, and as such it is protected by *intellectual property laws. A trade mark need not be registered if it has become well established, but registration gives an immediate right to prevent someone else making use of the same trade-mark, without the need to prove that the manufacturer has established a reputation in the use of the device. A service mark is the same sort of device as a trade-mark, but it applies to services rather than manufactured goods.

trade union (US, labor union), an organization representing employees in negotiations with employers. Trade unions are funded by membership subscriptions and are usually run by an elected executive and full-time officials, and elected workplace representatives (shop stewards in Britain). Their main economic objectives are to attain good *wages, good working conditions, and secure *employment for their members. Types of trade union include enterprise or company unions restricted to a single company (common in Japan); craft unions for workers with similar skills in different industries (traditional, and common, for example, in the UK); industrial unions representing all the workers in a specific industry (common in Germany); and general unions, which represent broad groups of workers in different industries and occupations. White-collar (non-manual) and women workers are increasing in total and as a proportion of all trade unionists. Trade unions aim to achieve their workplace *industrial relations objectives through *collective bargaining, supported when necessary by *industrial action. Most unions also have wider political objectives and seek to influence government economic and social policies through national representative organizations such as the Trades Union Congress (TUC) in the UK or the American Federation of Labor and Congress of Industrial Organizations (AFL–CIO) in the USA, and through local trades councils. Trade unions often have links with political parties respectively, for example the Labour Party in the UK. In some European countries, such as France, there are two trade union centres, affiliated to the socialist and communist parties respectively. In the former Soviet Union and other centrally planned economies, where union membership has exceeded 90 per cent, trade unions were integrated in government decision-making. Elsewhere, union membership fluctuates with political and economic vicissitudes, especially in developing countries, where it ranges from under 10 per cent (India) to over 40 per cent (Algeria). The last figure is typical for many industrialized market economies, where membership ranges from 15 per cent (France, Portugal, Spain, USA) to 90 per cent (Finland, Sweden). A significant development since World War II has been the increasing participation of trade unions in government and tripartite bodies at national or industry level (see *corporatism). This is reflected at workplace level, in forms of participation and limited *industrial democracy. The two main world organizations of trade unions are the World Federation of Trade Unions (WFTU), with its centre in Paris, and the International Confederation of Free Trade Unions (ICFTU), which has its office in Brussels.

transcendental argument, a special form of philosophical argument invented by *Kant, intended to defeat *scepticism. Transcendental arguments seek to derive metaphysical conclusions about how the world must be by considering what is necessary for a certain kind of thought or experience. The following is an important example from Kant: if a thinker is to be able to consider himself as a separate entity, and use the pronoun 'I', then the thinker must presuppose the existence of an external world; without such a presupposition, there can be no consciousness of oneself as a thinker. If successful, the argument shows that scepticism about the existence of an external world is self-defeating.

transhumance *nomadism, *pastoralism.

transnational relations, a term used to describe the wide variety of relationships and activities between groups and individuals in different states that are not controlled by governments (non-state actors). Transnational interactions take place *across* national boundaries, they do not include intergovernmental relations conducted at a state-to-state level or through international governmental organizations (IGOs). The most important sources of such activities are *non-governmental organizations (NGOs), including religious groups, charities, and other social, economic, or political organizations which operate in two or more countries, and transnational or *multinational corporations (MNCs), firms that manage economic units in two or more countries. The great increase in transnational activities since World War II led some political scientists to suggest that the old state-centric view of the world should be replaced by one based on the concept of *interdependence. While transnational relations are undoubtedly important, the *nation-state has proved to be highly resilient to their challenge.

treason, betrayal of a *state, either during wartime or during peacetime, through acts aimed at undermining its security and giving 'aid and comfort to the enemy'. The punishment for acts of treason is usually either *capital punishment or prolonged imprisonment, in keeping with the view that it is one of the most heinous of crimes. Varieties of treasonable activity can include plotting to overthrow the state, insulting a monarch or ruler (*lèse-majesté*), spying, and acting on behalf of enemy states in wartime. One danger inherent in the accusation of treason is that it can be used by a govenment against its political opponents, who can be accused of betraying the country.

treaty, a written agreement between two or more states, intended to create certain rights and obligations between them which are considered binding in *international law. Treaties are one of the most important sources of international law. They are usually worked out by government representatives and are later subject to ratification before their formal signature. Treaties are generally regarded as the highest and most formal of the many kinds of agreements between *states, such as pacts, protocols, declarations, or *conventions. Examples of treaties signed in the 20th century include the Versailles Treaty, of June 1919, which was part of the peace settlement which formally ended World War I; the North Atlantic Treaty, signed in April 1949, which established the North Atlantic Treaty Organization (NATO); and the Treaty of Rome of March 1957, which marked the foundation of the European Economic Community (*EEC). Despite their binding nature, treaties may lapse through war or renunciation by one or more of their signatories, as was the case after the Iranian Revolution of 1979, when the new Islamic Republican government renounced both the pro-Western Central Treaty Organization (CENTO), of which it was a member, as well as a long-standing Treaty of Friendship with the former Soviet Union, signed in 1921.

Treaty of Rome *EC.

tribe, a word used to describe any group of people sharing common *descent or a common *language or *culture. The word itself was first used in English for the divisions of the ancient Hebrews in the Old Testament of the Bible. In the 19th century, the term came to be used more and more for groups of people, who might now be called *ethnic groups, in particular parts of the colonized world, like Africa. In *South Asian societies, the word 'tribal' is used to designate certain groups of people, usually living in remote hill areas, but there is now considerable argument about whether these people really are different from their Hindu neighbours. In *anthropology, the word tribe has been used to describe a society which is more technologically complex than *hunter-gatherer societies, but whose *political organization is based on *kinship rather than a centralized state. This definition, though, is based on ideas of social *evolution, which many anthropologists would now reject, and the very idea of what constitutes a tribe is now controversial.

tribunal, a body, other than an ordinary *court of law, appointed to adjudicate on disputed matters, for example between a *citizen and a *government department, or between individuals. Examples in the UK are social security tribunals and industrial tribunals, which hear disputes between employers and employees. There are also tribunals set up to enforce discipline within professional groups, such as doctors. In the UK tribunals are usually presided over by a legally qualified chairman, but they are largely composed of laymen, and are conducted less formally than courts of law. The tribunal's decisions, while based on rules of law, often concern broad discretionary issues and require members to bring their own experience to bear in reaching their conclusions and are subject to judicial control, according to the principle of *ultra vires*: it is important that tribunals observe the rules of *natural justice and act within the limits of their jurisdiction and prescribed procedure.

trickster, a mythological figure, both animal and human, endowed with magical qualities, with the aid of which he plays tricks on society. He is both clever and foolish (and trickster tales usually involve some measure of each), but is also capable of superhuman feats and miraculous metamorphoses. The trickster is an example of a mythical character who appears in folk traditions all over the world, from Reynard the Fox to the trickster god Eshu in *Yoruba tales.

Trikāya (Sanskrit, 'three bodies'), a *Mahāyāna Buddhist doctrine referring to the three aspects of a *Buddha. The *nirmānakāya* ('transformation body') refers to the transient body of a Buddha as he appears on earth. The *sambhogakāya* ('enjoyment body') is the beautiful form in which a buddha appears to *bodhisattvas for their enjoyment and enlightenment. Finally, the term *dharmakāya* ('body of the law') identifies the Buddha with absolute reality itself.

Trinity, a central doctrine of Christianity: that *God is one substance, but three persons, Father, Son, and Holy Spirit. This doctrine is not found explicitly in the New Testament, although some threefold formulas are used. Early Christian creeds used Trinitarian language, but this raised theological problems. Recognition of *Jesus Christ's divinity seemed to threaten Christian monotheism, while denial of his divinity put salvation in doubt. Hence the doctrine of the Trinity represents the radical reformulation of the doctrine of God to meet the demands of Christian faith. It was formulated in a series of great Church councils in the 3rd and 4th centuries, at which first the Son was declared to be of one essence with the Father, and later the equal dignity of the Holy Spirit was affirmed.

Tripitaka, Tipitaka (Pali, 'three baskets'), the sacred scriptures of *Theravāda Buddhism, written in Pali. They consist of three *pitakas* or 'baskets', which collect together the sayings and teachings of the *Buddha. The *Vinaya-pitaka* ('discipline basket') presents the origins of, and behaviour codes for, Buddhist monks and nuns (*sangha). The *Sūtra-pitaka* ('teaching basket') records the words of the Buddha and his immediate disciples. The last section, the *Abhidharma-pitaka* ('higher teaching basket') contains analytical comments on the teachings expounded in the *Sūtra-pitaka*.

Trobriand Islanders, the inhabitants of a group of islands off the coast of New Guinea in Melanesia. The islanders are in the main subsistence farmers, practising *shifting cultivation and pig breeding. They are organized in matrilineal *clans, whose members trace their origins to one ancestor in a kind of *totemism. Like other *Melanesian societies, the Trobrianders traded throughout the surrounding islands, and are perhaps best known through the work of *Malinowski, who drew attention to their system of *gift exchange known as the *kula. The accumulation of prestige through such exchange is a central concern of social life. Since colonial rule they have added a unique form of cricket to their ritual system.

trust (in law), an arrangement whereby funds or assets are managed by one person (known as a *trustee) for the benefit of another (a beneficiary). In England, the trust developed in the *common law system in the court of *Equity, and there is no direct equivalent in *civil law systems. The duties of the trustee are determined both by the general law and by the express instructions of the person who established the trust. The trustee is ostensible owner of the trust property but must keep the trust property separate from his own assets, must invest and preserve it, and distribute income from it in accordance with the terms of the trust. The trust is a flexible device, used in different circumstances and for different purposes. Historically, it facilitated the holding of family property over several generations. Today it is used, for example, as a device for arranging financial affairs to minimize taxation, as a way in which ownership of land can be shared, and as a means by which funds are held for a charitable purpose. In the UK, a trust also refers to a financial institution such as an *investment trust, which facilitates *stock exchange trading by small-scale investors. In the USA, a trust is a *conglomerate or a group of *companies who form a *cartel to fix prices or restrict competition. Hence US legislation to maintain competition and break up cartels is known as 'anti-trust'.

trusteeship (in politics), a system devised after World War II by the *UN for administering certain non-self-governing territories, notably former Japanese and Italian colonies. UN trusteeship is modelled on the *mandates system established by the League of Nations after World War I. Reports on trust territories are submitted to the UN Trusteeship Council, whose role is to superintend their transition to self-government. As a result of the decolonization process virtually all such territories have achieved independence, with the exception of certain small US-administered Pacific islands.

truth. All sciences, in the broadest sense, aim at uncovering truths, but in doing so what are they aiming at? The question, 'What is truth?', or 'What makes anything true?' belongs not to any particular science but to *philosophy. Philosophers themselves are fundamentally divided over the meaning and importance of the question: some regard it as philosophy's distinctive question, towards answering which all their more specific enquiries are in essence directed; others count the issue as confused, or as so general that nothing useful can be said. Asking 'What makes it true that cyanide is poisonous?' will call forth one answer; 'What makes it true that Mozart is a greater composer than Mendelssohn?' demands another. It hardly seems likely that there will be anything common to both answers that reflects a common concern with truth, in addition to their diverse concerns with medicine and music. Philosophers thus persuaded that there is no real question of truth can make little of the continuing opposition between the two major traditional answers to that question: the correspondence and coherence theories of truth. The correspondence theory holds that the truth of a statement or belief lies in a relation of congruence or conformity to the fact or state of affairs it describes. The coherence theory denies that the truth of any of our beliefs can be a matter of matching up to completely independent facts, emphasizing instead the interdependence and organization of our total system of beliefs.

Tsimshian, a *North-West Indian society, found in the north of British Columbia. Like the *Tlingit, they are organized into *matrilineal kin groups (see *kinship), with four major phatries (groups of clans). These groups controlled the land and the rights for hunting and fishing. Also known as house groups, members of these lineages inherit certain

The romantic image of the **Tuareg**, with their blue robes and nomadic lifestyle, contrasts sharply with the reality of their daily life—a struggle to exist in a harsh environment of scorching days and freezing nights.

names or titles, as well as crests, which confer prestige. Status could also be gained through displays of wealth, as among the *Tlingit.

Tuareg, a group of *Berbers, relatively few in number, who roam over a vast territory in North Africa. In the past they criss-crossed the Sahara in their caravans, trading between the Mediterranean and the Sahel, and subsisting on dates and millet, which they traded for their livestock. Traditional Tuareg society is hierarchical and feudal, the different castes being mutually interdependent. Traditionally it is Tuareg men who go veiled, not the women. In recent years the *nomadism of the Tuareg has been threatened both by trading restrictions and by Sahelian droughts.

Turkic languages   *Altaic languages.

turnover, the gross sales revenue of a firm in a given period. In a different but related sense, the rate of *stock turnover measures the number of times the average stock of a business is sold in a given time period, usually one year.

two-party system, a pattern of party competition in which two leading *political parties dominate national politics and alternate in forming the government. Such a pattern, usually associated with *majoritarian government, is found in the UK and the USA. In the USA, national and state *elections are contested by the Democrats and the Republicans, with occasional interventions from independent candidates. The parties themselves, however, lack a rigid structure, contain a wide range of opinion, and are less polarized than the two major parties in the UK, Labour and Conservative. Two-party politics in the UK has traditionally been associated with an adversarial political style, sharp oscillations in public policy, and clear accountability of the government to the electorate. Minor parties may attract a fair amount of support, but because of the first-past-the-post system of majoritarian representation, the best they can hope for is to hold the balance of power in a *coalition government.

UK government, a liberal *democracy, based on a system of representative *parliamentary government. The *head of state is a constitutional, hereditary *monarch, in whose name *government is carried on (see *Crown, *Crown prerogative), but who wields no effective political power. There is no written *constitution: constitutional law derives largely from *legislation on specific subjects (such as frequency of *elections), legal decisions, and 'conventions', which are unwritten rules based on past practice. The *legislature, based at Westminster, is a *bicameral Parliament with a primary chamber (the *House of Commons) elected by universal suffrage, and a non-elected second chamber (the *House of Lords). British government has been based on *political parties for well over a century, and most of this time has been characterized by a *two-party system. Minor parties become important only when they hold the balance of power. Parliament operates along disciplined adversarial lines. The leader of the majority in the House of Commons becomes the *prime minister, who forms the government from members of his or her party. The second largest coherent grouping forms the constitutionally recognized official opposition. Institutionally, all major functions of government are controlled from centralized departments, each headed by a minister and run by appointed civil servants. A limited amount of funtional decentralization has taken many labour-intensive government departments out of the capital city. Scotland, Wales, and Northern Ireland have at present a limited degree of administrative *devolution, but the UK remains a *unitary state, with a traditional emphasis on the legislative supremacy of Parliament. There are two tiers of *local government, county and district, each having its own elected council which appoints officers to administer services and possesses the authority to issue subordinate legislation in the form of by-laws.

UK legal system, a term covering the plurality of legal systems that exist in England and Wales, Scotland, and Northern Ireland. (The Channel Islands and the Isle of Man are not part of the UK, but are subject to certain UK legislation.) The dominant legal tradition is that of the *common law, although there are significant *Roman law influences in *Scots law, and the influence of Norman custom in the Channel Islands and Norse custom in the Isle of Man. Parliament in Westminster has authority to legislate throughout the realm, but not infrequently legislation is limited territor-

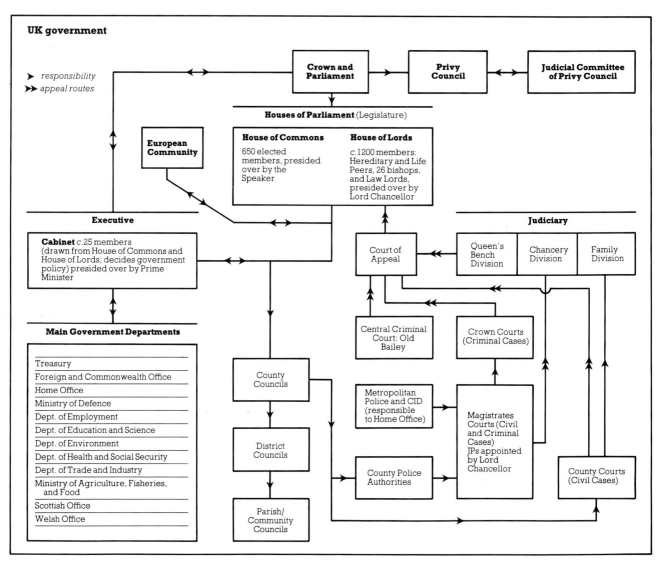

ially; for example, the Abortion Act (1967) does not apply in Northern Ireland. However, in practical terms, there is a single UK law in areas such as company law, taxation, welfare law, and labour law, where there is a high level of *legislation and regulation. Each legal system has its own separately organized legal profession. It also has its own hierarchy of courts, superior and inferior; its own structure of binding judicial precedent; and its own traditions and customs. However, the *House of Lords is the highest court of appeal, except in cases from the Channel Islands and the Isle of Man, which go to the Privy Council, and criminal cases in Scotland, which go to the Scottish High Court of Justiciary. The Lord Chancellor is responsible for the administration of justice in England and Wales. He is a member of the Cabinet, presides over the House of Lords when it exercises its legislative function, and may take part in its judicial role. The Attorney-General, also a member of the government, is the Crown's principal legal adviser. The Director of Public Prosecutions heads the Crown Prosecution Service, which conducts the majority of criminal *prosecutions. Until 1972 there was a separate Attorney-General for Northern Ireland; in Scotland, the equivalent position is held by the Lord Advocate. As a member state of the EC, the whole of the UK is subject to EC law; certain cases which raise community law questions (in matters of customs, taxation, agriculture, or immigration, for instance) must be referred to the *European Court of Justice.

'ulamā' (Arabic, 'scholars'), collective title for teachers of Islamic law and theology. Traditionally, the *'ulamā'* expressed the consensus of the Muslim community on matters of jurisprudence, government, and religion, and played a clerical role similar to that of the Christian priesthood, although Islam acknowledges no intermediary between the believer and God and there is no administrative institution or hierarchy among them. However, in many Muslim countries the role of the *'ulamā'* has been eroded by the secularization of education, law, and society. In many Muslim countries, the *madrasah* (theological seminary) for the teaching of Islamic sciences is separate from secular education. The authority of the *'ulamā'* and the **sharī'ah* (Islamic law) are central issues in Islamic society today.

ultra vires (Latin, 'beyond [one's] powers'), the principle that when a person or body behaves in a manner which falls outside the ambit of its powers, the behaviour is unlawful and cannot usually affect the legal rights or duties of other people. The principle of *ultra vires* is particularly important in *company law and *administrative law.

unconscious mind (subconscious), in *psychoanalysis, the site of memories and wishes which, according to *Freud, cannot be recalled to consciousness but which continue to influence thought and behaviour. They have not merely been forgotten, but repressed by *defence mechanisms because recall is painful. The unconscious contents manifest themselves in *dreams and in errors of speech ('Freudian slips') of the tongue or forgetting appointments. Psychoanalytic therapy is based on the belief that the contents of the unconscious cause neurotic symptoms precisely because they are 'dammed up' by repression of traumas experienced earlier on in life. The psychoanalyst aims to help the patient to release unconscious material into consciousness, and, by releasing suppressed feeling of, for example, anger, fear, or aggression, to shed them. A more recent concept in *cognitive psychology is that the brain can accept and analyse

information unconsciously, rather like the *artificial intelligence of a computer. This unconscious processing of information is basic to human behaviour.

UN Convention on the Rights of the Child, an international treaty, adopted in 1989. The rights apply to all persons under 18 except in countries where the age of majority is lower. The Convention declares the *family to be the natural environment for children, and states that in all actions concerning children account should be taken of their best interests. It promulgates the child's right to a name and *nationality, to *privacy, freedom of association, thought, conscience, and religion. The obligations of others, especially parents and the state, are documented. The state, for example, must provide *childcare for those with working parents, *education, *health care, and protection from *child sexual exploitation, *child abuse and neglect, drug abuse, and *child labour. The treaty indicates the special protections required by vulnerable children such as the victims of armed conflict, handicapped and *refugee children, and the children of minorities. It is binding on states which ratify it, but there is no mechanism for enforcement.

UNCTAD (United Nations Conference on Trade and Development), a permanent agency of the *UN, with its heaquarters in Geneva. Established in 1964, the conference meets at four-year intervals. Its goal is to promote international trade, particularly between countries at different stages of development, and to encourage economic growth in developing countries. UNCTAD has played an important role in devising economic measures to favour less developed countries, for example in securing advantageous prices for primary *commodities, on which many developing countries depend for their export earnings, and in ensuring that their manufactured goods receive preferential *tariff treatment. At UNCTAD's first meeting in 1964, a group of developing countries formed themselves into a bloc, known as the 'Group of 77', to establish a strong negotiating position on trade and development issues. In 1990 the membership of UNCTAD included all UN countries, plus the Holy See, the two Koreas, Liechtenstein, Monaco, Namibia, San Marino, Switzerland, and Tonga.

underclass, a subordinate *social class, usually the lowest. *Immigrant workers, and sometimes women workers, have been seen as an underclass, often highly exploited, and forced to accept low-paid, low-status occupations removed from legal protection. In the USA and some other countries the term is used of people who are unemployed (long-term) and possibly involved in crime or dependent on drugs. They may have little or no access to social services such as education and health, which other citizens take for granted. There is a fear that underclass membership is perpetuated from one generation to the next. The underclass may pose a threat to the rest of society, taking part in violence and *crime because its members feel they have little to lose.

underwriting, the action of guaranteeing against possible *loss in exchange for a *commission or *premium(s). The term is mainly used in two contexts. In the London insurance market, underwriters are members of *Lloyd's, whose capital is on offer to provide insurance cover. In the new issues market underwriters such as *issuing houses or other financial institutions guarantee to buy or retain any *securities left unsold at a particular flotation, in the event that they are not bought by the investing public.

The problems of homelessness and **unemployment** are as widespread in the developed as the developing world. Here, homeless men in the USA receive free food in a Chicago soup kitchen.

unemployment, a measure of the proportion of the available work-force without a job. Inefficiency, waste, and individual suffering are all aspects of unemployment, which tends to affect disproportionately women, young people, seasonal and migrant workers, and unskilled workers. Official statistics are based on various concepts of 'availability for work', but probably underestimate levels of unemployment and underemployment (people who are not, but want to be, fully employed); both these affect developing countries particularly. In the 1970s and 1980s unemployment levels rose in many countries for reasons that are disputed and unclear. At the same time state unemployment benefits tended to fall. In developing countries, in Latin America for example, population expansion, out-of-date forms of land tenure and the mechanization of agriculture have driven many people off the land to join growing numbers of urban unemployed. In some industrialized countries (UK, Ireland, and Spain), unemployment was at historically high levels, with the proportion of long-term unemployed rising; such unemployment is in part structural, arising from the decline of *secondary industries such as coal and steel. In centrally planned or statist economies, government policy was to maintain low or zero levels of unemployment; however, that such statistics are misleading or cushioned by permitting redundant posts to continue to be filled is evidenced by soaring unemployment in eastern Germany, where unemployment figures reached 50 per cent within a year of German reunification in 1990.

unemployment benefit, a *social security benefit paid to the involuntarily unemployed. Statutory unemployment benefit schemes are to be found in only forty, mainly industrialized, countries, a third of the number in which *old-age benefit schemes exist. The difference reflects concern about its effects on work incentives, and the difficulties of establishing eligibility for unemployment benefit, especially in countries where most of the population are self-employed and earn erratically. Most schemes are based on *social insurance. Those who have left work voluntarily, or as a

result of a labour dispute or their own misconduct, or who cannot show that they are capable of work and willing to take it, may have their claims disallowed. The benefit is commonly about 60 per cent of previous earnings within a minimum and maximum band, for a prescribed time. The International Labour Organization suggests at least thirteen weeks' benefit be payable in any year. In some countries, *social assistance is available for those who are ineligible or whose eligibility has expired.

Unification Church, a religious movement founded by Sun Myung Moon (1920–   ) in South Korea in 1954. Members are popularly known as the 'Moonies'. Its theology, found in the *Divine Principle*, claims that a sinless man (often thought to be Moon himself) could save the world and form the kingdom of God on earth. There are said to be 3 million members. The movement has attracted controversy through its business practices and accusations that it brainwashes new recruits.

Unitarians, *Protestants who affirm the unity of God and reject the divinity of Christ and the doctrine of the *Trinity. The first Unitarian Church was founded in London by Theophilus Lindsey in 1773, based on ideas reaching back to the 16th-century Reformation. There are about 300,000 full members of Unitarian Churches, including those in the USA, who have merged with the Universalist Church.

unitary state, a political system, found in the majority of the world's *nation-states, where the central government has sovereign authority over *local government, and can alter or abolish it by the ordinary legal process. The powers and functions of government may be decentralized into various levels, branches, or departments, but all are ultimately under central control. The UK is often cited as an example of a unitary state, with a system of local government repeatedly refashioned by central government. The concentration of *sovereignty in a unitary state contrasts sharply with the constitutionally guaranteed dispersal of political authority which characterizes *federalism.

UNESCO (United Nations Educational, Scientific and Cultural Organization), a specialized agency of the *UN, founded in 1946 and based in Paris, which promotes international collaboration in *education, science, *culture, and *communication. In education, it supports the spread of *literacy, *continuing education, and universal *primary education; and in science, assists developing countries, and international interchange between scientists. It encourages the preservation of monuments and sites, and of other aspects of culture such as oral traditions, music, and dance. By 1989 UNESCO's 'World Heritage List', designed to protect landmarks of 'outstanding universal value', comprised 315 sites in sixty-seven countries. In the field of communication, UNESCO is committed to the free flow of information. In 1980 its supreme governing body approved a New World Information and Communication Order despite opposition from those who believed it threatened press freedom (see *mass media). In 1984 the USA (which had been due to supply about a quarter of UNESCO's budget) and in 1985 the UK and Singapore withdrew, alleging financial mismanagement and political bias against Western countries.

United Nations General Assembly (UNGA), the main deliberative organ of the *UN, where representatives of every member country sit and have a vote. The Assembly, based at UN headquarters in New York, can discuss and make recommendations on all questions which fall within the scope of the UN Charter; it is also responsible for the UN budget. It first met in January 1946 and meets for three months annually in regular session, although both special and emergency sessions can also be convened. Such sessions have been held to discuss issues of particular importance, such as the Palestinian problem, disarmament, or the sanctioning of the US-led war against Iraq in 1991; or in cases where the Security Council has failed to agree on a course of action in an international dispute, such as occurred in Afghanistan (1980), Namibia (1981), and the Israeli-occupied Arab territories (1982). Decisions on important questions require a two-thirds majority, otherwise a simple majority is sufficient. In the UN's early years, the USA could normally command a majority in the General Assembly. But with the dramatic increase in new members following decolonization, the balance shifted to favour the developing countries, who were often unwilling to endorse the policies of either superpower, preferring to adopt a *non-aligned stance.

United Nations High Commission for Refugees, Office of (UNHCR),

a UN body established in 1951 to replace the International Refugee Organization. The headquarters are in Geneva, and there are five Regional Bureaux. The UNHCR has two primary functions: to extend international protection to *refugees under the terms of the 1951 UN Convention relating to the Status of Refugees, and, specifically, to ensure refugees obtain *political asylum and are not forcibly returned to a territory where they fear persecution; and to provide emergency relief such as food, shelter, and medical assistance, and, in the long term, to assist in voluntary repatriation, or resettlement and integration into a new community.

United Nations Organization (UN),

an international organization established in 1945 as successor to the League of Nations, with the goal of working for peace, security, and co-operation among the nations of the world. Its permanent headquarters are in New York. The term 'United Nations' was first used in a Declaration of the United Nations in January 1942, when representatives of twenty-six Allied nations

A **UNESCO**-sponsored project to teach literacy to the Urn Indians of the Lake Titicaca region in Peru.

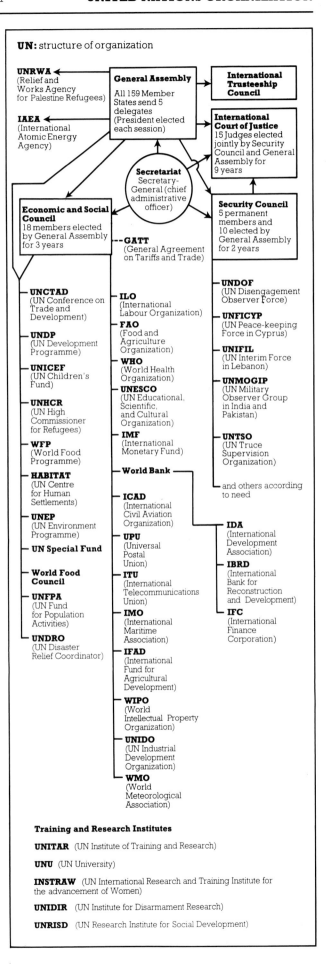

UN: structure of organization

UNRWA (Relief and Works Agency for Palestine Refugees)

IAEA (International Atomic Energy Agency)

General Assembly All 159 Member States send 5 delegates (President elected each session)

International Trusteeship Council

International Court of Justice 15 Judges elected jointly by Security Council and General Assembly for 9 years

Secretariat Secretary-General (chief administrative officer)

Economic and Social Council 18 members elected by General Assembly for 3 years

GATT (General Agreement on Tariffs and Trade)

Security Council 5 permanent members and 10 elected by General Assembly for 2 years

UNCTAD (UN Conference on Trade and Development)

UNDP (UN Development Programme)

UNICEF (UN Children's Fund)

UNHCR (UN High Commissioner for Refugees)

WFP (World Food Programme)

HABITAT (UN Centre for Human Settlements)

UNEP (UN Environment Programme)

UN Special Fund

World Food Council

UNFPA (UN Fund for Population Activities)

UNDRO (UN Disaster Relief Coordinator)

ILO (International Labour Organization)

FAO (Food and Agriculture Organization)

WHO (World Health Organization)

UNESCO (UN Educational, Scientific, and Cultural Organization)

IMF (International Monetary Fund)

World Bank

ICAD (International Civil Aviation Organization)

UPU (Universal Postal Union)

ITU (International Telecommunications Union)

IMO (International Maritime Association)

IFAD (International Fund for Agricultural Development)

WIPO (World Intellectual Property Organization)

UNIDO (UN Industrial Development Organization)

WMO (World Meteorological Association)

UNDOF (UN Disengagement Observer Force)

UNFICYP (UN Peace-keeping Force in Cyprus)

UNIFIL (UN Interim Force in Lebanon)

UNMOGIP (UN Military Observer Group in India and Pakistan)

UNTSO (UN Truce Supervision Organization)

and others according to need

IDA (International Development Association)

IBRD (International Bank for Reconstruction and Development)

IFC (International Finance Corporation)

Training and Research Institutes

UNITAR (UN Institute of Training and Research)

UNU (UN University)

INSTRAW (UN International Research and Training Institute for the advancement of Women)

UNIDIR (UN Institute for Disarmament Research)

UNRISD (UN Research Institute for Social Development)

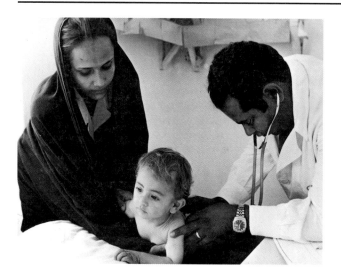

Among the subsidiary organs of the **UN** is the UN Relief and Works Agency, which runs community health programmes such as this one at the Palestinian refugee camp of Jabalia, in the Gaza strip.

pledged their governments to continue fighting together against the Axis powers, but it was only after further conferences held at Dumbarton Oaks, Washington, in 1944, and San Francisco in 1945 that representatives of fifty Allied countries signed the document, known as the Charter, setting up the new organization. The UN grew rapidly as newly independent nations, created as a result of decolonization, applied for membership. In 1991 the organization had 159 members, important exceptions being Switzerland and the two Koreas. In order to carry out its many functions, the UN is served by a wide range of organs and institutions. The six principal organs of the UN are the General Assembly (UNGA), the *Security Council, the *International Court of Justice, the Economic and Social Council (which deals with international economic, social, cultural, educational, health and related matters), the Trusteeship Council (which administers those territories held in trust by the UN), and the Secretariat, which is responsible for the general administration of the UN. The Secretariat is headed by the Secretary General, appointed for a five-year renewable term by the General Assembly. There have been seven Secretary Generals since the UN was founded: Trygve Lie (Norway), 1946–53; Dag Hammarskjöld (Sweden), 1953–61; U-Thant (Burma), 1961–71; Kurt Waldheim (Austria), 1971–81; Javier Pérez de Cuéllar (Peru), 1981–91; and Boutros Boutros Galli (Egypt) 1991–). The UN is also served by nineteen intergovernmental agencies known as the specialized agencies, dealing with economic and social questions. They include the *International Atomic Energy Agency (IAEA), the *International Monetary Fund (IMF), the UN Educational, Scientific, and Cultural Organization (*UNESCO), and the *World Health Organization (WHO). Other organs which are part of the UN system include the UN Conference on Trade and Development (*UNCTAD), and the UN High Commission for Refugees (*UNHCR).

United Reformed Church, a Protestant body formed in 1972 by the union of the *Congregational Church of England and Wales and the *Presbyterian Church of England. This was the first union of different Protestant denominations in the UK. Traditionally, the Presbyterians were governed by local and national assemblies, while Congrega-

tionalism affirmed the independence of local congregations, a principle modified but not abandoned in the United Church. It currently has twelve provinces in the UK, with about 1,100 ministers and 200,000 members.

unit trust   *investment trust.

Universal Declaration of Human Rights, an international declaration, adopted in 1948 by the General Assembly of the UN (with the six members of the former Soviet bloc, Saudi Arabia, and South Africa abstaining). It declares that all human beings are born free and equal in dignity and rights, and are entitled to the rights and freedoms set out in the Declaration without discrimination on the grounds of race, colour, sex, language, political opinion, or religion. The rights enumerated include *civil rights such as freedom of expression, conscience, movement, peaceful assembly, and association; and economic and social rights such as those to work, to an adequate standard of living, to education, and to participation in cultural life. The exercise of an individual's rights and freedoms is limited only by respect for the rights and freedoms of others. The Declaration is not legally binding but it has underpinned the activities of the UN, affected both national and *international law, and widely influenced debates on *human rights. In 1966 the General Assembly adopted two Covenants, the *International Covenant on Civil and Political Rights and the International Covenant on Economic, Social, and Cultural Rights which embody the rights in the Declaration, and have legal force.

universals. These are appealed to in philosophy in explanation of how we are able to think or speak in quite general terms, to say such things as 'squirrels are red', rather than just 'that thing is that colour'. They are also appealed to in explanation of our ability to form concepts (which are ideas of types of things), and to know, of some particular thing, whether or not it is an instance of a concept. So, the word 'squirrel' expresses the concept *squirrel*, and one who possesses the concept *squirrel* knows of the various things in the world whether they are squirrels or not. When we form a concept we come to know a universal, or type. The first and most famous theory of universals was *Plato's theory of Forms. Philosophers still discuss the question of whether universals exist independently of the objects that are instances of them or exist only by virtue of being exemplified by particular things (see *nominalism).

Upanishads, *Hindu sacred texts, the final part of the *Vedas. They are also known as Vedānta, 'the end of the Vedas'. They consist of discussions between gurus (teachers) and their disciples concerning the nature of ultimate spiritual reality (*Brahman), the soul (*ātman), and the cycle of death and rebirth (*samsara). They form the basis for the later philosophical school of *Vedānta.

Uralic languages, a family of languages spoken over a large area of northern Europe and Asia. They stretch from north Scandinavia and the Baltic region across the Ural mountains into northern Asia and Siberia. Uralic has two unequal branches: Finno-Ugric, made up of Finnic and Ugric which have 22 million speakers, and Samoyedic, which has just 30,000. The two major Finnic languages are Finnish (Suomi), with 5 million speakers, and Estonian, with nearly 1.5 million speakers, which are closely related to each other. The first written texts date from the 16th century.

Two smaller Finnic languages are Karelian (140,000 speakers), which is spoken in the territory bordering the Russian Federation and Finland; and Lapp (30,000 speakers), which consists of three mutually unintelligible dialects spoken in northern Scandinavia and the Kola peninsula of the northern Russian Federation. There are three Ugric languages: Hungarian (Magyar) is the largest, spoken by 11 million people in Hungary and 3 million in neighbouring countries. It is the only major non-*Indo-European language in central Europe, and has taken in an unusually high number of loanwords, from Slavonic, Turkish, German, and Latin. The first Hungarian text dates from around AD 1200. The other two Ugric languages, Mansi and Khanti, are spoken along the River Ob in the Russian Federation. The Samoyedic languages are spoken by 30,000 people scattered over a vast area of northern Russia and Siberia. There are four surviving languages: the largest, Nenets, accounts for 25,000 of the Samoyedic speakers. The main Uralic languages employ a variety of vowel harmony (see *Altaic); those within the former Soviet Union are written in the Cyrillic *alphabet, while the others are written in the Roman alphabet.

urbanization, the increase in the proportion of a population living in urban areas; also the process by which an area loses its rural character and way of life. In the former sense, urbanization is a consequence mainly of rural–urban *migration. Urbanization in the 20th century has proceeded at an unprecedented rate. In 1900 the UK became the first country to be predominantly urban. In 1920 only about 14 per cent of the world's population lived in urban areas, but by 1950 the proportion had reached one-quarter, and by 1990, 43 per cent. If present trends continue, nearly half the world's population will live in towns and cities at the turn of the century, and the figure could reach 60 per cent by 2025. Industrialized countries are the most urbanized: in the early 1990s, about three-quarters of their people lived in urban areas, compared with one-third in developing countries. Yet patterns of *population growth mean that urban settlements in developing countries are growing three times faster than in industrialized countries and that by the year 2000 urban residents will outnumber rural residents in most developing countries. The natural increase of the existing population is the main component of population growth in some of the fastest-growing cities and *megacities. Elsewhere, for example in Seoul in South Korea and Lagos in Nigeria, migration in search of work accounts for most of urban growth. In industrialized countries, urban growth has become more gradual; the populations of many big old cities have started to shrink, as disadvantages of city life, such as overcrowding, *pollution, and *crime, have become more pronounced, and as manufacturing industry has relocated in search of lower costs either in the same country or, often, in developing countries. Attempts to reverse the trend to urbanization, for instance by migration controls, have failed. For governments to ensure *housing, *water, *sanitation, and work for the equivalent of 30,000 extra urban dwellers each day in industrialized countries and 140,000 in developing countries is a task of enormous magnitude.

urban renewal, the redevelopment of run-down urban areas. Some schemes include a mixture of new and rehabilitated buildings, while others entail wholly new developments, often on a massive scale. In inner cities, small dilapidated buildings and semi-derelict areas whose typical uses (rental housing, small shops, and workshops) offer low yields, are commonly replaced by large commercial properties with offices and retail space, offering high yields. Land freed by deindustrialization such as redundant dockyards and steelworks may also be used. Comprehensive renewal programmes entailing major investment by government and private companies, and concerned not only with buildings but also with *housing, *employment, and income-generation, have revitalized the centres of numerous cities, among them Glasgow in Scotland, and Baltimore and Cleveland in the USA. Yet in almost all urban renewal programmes, the fate of displaced persons and functions requires consideration. Relocation to more spacious but distant facilities may be welcome to some residents and traders and disastrous to others. In developing countries, demolishing *slums without replacement intensifies overcrowding, increases *homelessness and shelter costs, and often causes loss of income by destroying jobs in the *informal economy.

Urdu *Indo-Iranian languages.

US government, a federal republic and liberal *democracy, established under the Constitution adopted in 1789. This vests legislative power in a *bicameral Congress, consisting of the *House of Representatives and the *Senate. *Executive power is conferred on the *President, separately elected for a fixed term of four years. *Judicial power is vested in the Supreme Court, which has a crucial role in constitutional interpretation. The branches of the federal government are in this way separate, but the exercise of their powers is subject to checks, brakes, and balances between the branches (see *separation of powers). The President, for example, may veto *legislation passed by the Congress, which may in turn override a presidential veto by a two-thirds majority. The US Constitution thus systematically disperses power within the federal government. Power is also divided between the federal government and the fifty states, each with its own *constitution, elected *government and legal system (see *federalism). This dispersal of constitutional authority is matched by decentralized *political parties. Political offices are contested nationwide by the Republican and Democratic parties, but these are loose coalitions, providing only limited co-ordination between different branches and levels of government. US democracy is highly *pluralistic. Because of extensive power dispersal, government mainly operates through coalition-building and a tendency to compromise. (See diagram overleaf.)

US legal system, the legal systems of the different states of the USA, as well as the federal *jurisdiction. The dominant legal tradition is that of the *common law (except in the state of Louisiana, which is influenced by *civil law), but the common law has had to adapt to the particular needs of a federal state with a written *constitution. For instance, the doctrine of judicial *precedent has always been much more loosely applied than in English law because of the plethora of parallel jurisdictions. The federal *legislature is Congress, consisting of the House of Representatives and the Senate; the executive consists of the president and his *cabinet; while the federal *judiciary consists of the Federal Supreme Court, District Courts, and Courts of Appeal. However, each state has its own *constitution and its own legislature, executive, and judiciary. State law regulates the criminal law and matters of personal status (family law), as well as *tort and *contract. Each state also regulates its own legal profession. However, the federal jurisdiction is empowered to rule on constitutional matters; to regulate foreign trade and trade between states; and to protect civil liberties. The Attorney-

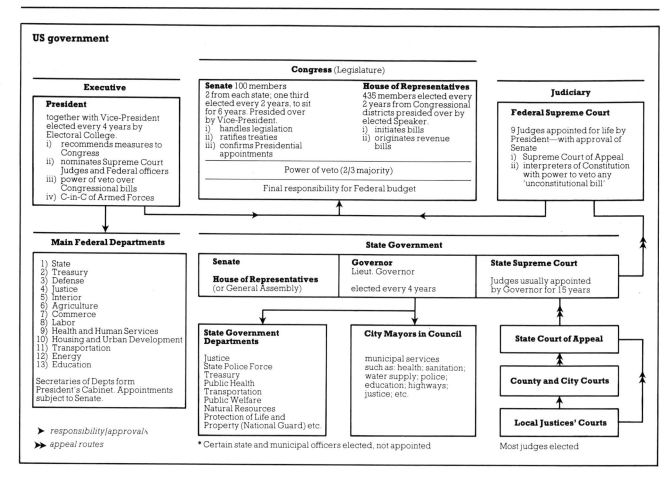

US government

Executive

President

together with Vice-President elected every 4 years by Electoral College.
i) recommends measures to Congress
ii) nominates Supreme Court Judges and Federal officers
iii) power of veto over Congressional bills
iv) C-in-C of Armed Forces

Congress (Legislature)

Senate 100 members 2 from each state; one third elected every 2 years, to sit for 6 years. Presided over by Vice-President.
i) handles legislation
ii) ratifies treaties
iii) confirms Presidential appointments

House of Representatives 435 members elected every 2 years from Congressional districts presided over by elected Speaker.
i) initiates bills
ii) originates revenue bills

Power of veto (2/3 majority)

Final responsibility for Federal budget

Judiciary

Federal Supreme Court

9 Judges appointed for life by President—with approval of Senate
i) Supreme Court of Appeal
ii) interpreters of Constitution with power to veto any 'unconstitutional bill'

Main Federal Departments

1) State
2) Treasury
3) Defense
4) Justice
5) Interior
6) Agriculture
7) Commerce
8) Labor
9) Health and Human Services
10) Housing and Urban Development
11) Transportation
12) Energy
13) Education

Secretaries of Depts form President's Cabinet. Appointments subject to Senate.

State Government

Senate

House of Representatives
(or General Assembly)

Governor
Lieut. Governor

elected every 4 years

State Supreme Court

Judges usually appointed by Governor for 15 years

State Government Departments

Justice
State Police Force
Treasury
Public Health
Transportation
Public Welfare
Natural Resources
Protection of Life and Property (National Guard) etc.

City Mayors in Council

municipal services such as: health; sanitation; water supply; police; education; highways; justice; etc.

State Court of Appeal

County and City Courts

Local Justices' Courts

➤ *responsibility/approval*
➤➤ *appeal routes*

* Certain state and municipal officers elected, not appointed

Most judges elected

General is the chief law officer of the federal government and head of the Department of Justice, with responsibility for the enforcement of federal laws concerning *civil rights, environmental protection, and corruption within government. The Federal Supreme Court is the highest court of appeal, above state Supreme Courts; it also has the power to veto any unconstitutional *bill. Judges at all levels are elected or appointed by executive or legislative authority. Despite the proliferation of different laws in different states, at law school, US law students study the law on a US-wide basis, comparing the solutions reached in different states. Another unifying feature is the publication of *Restatements*, privately published non-legislative textbooks which restate the law in force in the fifty states in a systematic form.

utilitarianism, an ethical theory advanced by Jeremy Bentham (1748–1832) and refined by *Mill. Utilitarianism identifies the goal of morality as 'the greatest happiness of the greatest number', and, in *consequentialist fashion, it says that an action is right in so far as it tends to promote that goal. Although the problems of utilitarianism are many, and include the fundamental difficulty of comparing quantitatively the happiness of one person with that of another, it has proved a remarkably persistent doctrine which continues to attract adherents. Part of its appeal lies in its apparent clarity and simplicity: the concept of happiness seems much less obscure than rival moral concepts such as that of a natural right, and the rule, 'Maximize happiness', seems to offer a decisive and factual procedure for deciding what to do. Utilitarianism is particularly attractive as a method for public decision-making. Utilitarianism finds it hard, however, to explain why we value things other than happiness, such as equality and *justice.

utility, in economics, the satisfaction gained from the *consumption of *goods and services. *Classical economists developed a theory of *demand in terms of diminishing marginal utility. This suggested that the utility gained from the consumption of extra units of a product would decline as more of the product was consumed. Hence the price that consumers would be prepared to pay would fall as more of a product was demanded. However, this theory depended on the notion that utility could be measured in units ('cardinal utility'). Later theories of demand accepted instead that utility cannot be measured in absolute terms, but assumed that consumers can rank products or combinations of products in order of preference ('ordinal utility').

Utopianism, a form of speculative thinking in which ideal societies are depicted in order to highlight the defects of those we inhabit. The original *Utopia*, published in 1516 by Sir Thomas More, depicted a society whose members lived communally and abstemiously, sharing property, and working under the direction of spiritual leaders. Some of More's ideas have reappeared in later Utopian writings: for instance, the idea of a harmonious society in which everyone works together according to a rational plan. Many 19th-century Utopias were *socialist in inspiration, but the genre is not tied to any particular political creed. It is not always easy to say, moreover, whether the aim of Utopian writing is to describe an ideal society which the author would like to see brought into existence, or simply to satirize present society by imagining a very different set of arrangements. In the 20th century, so-called 'dystopias' extrapolate present trends to present a nightmarish vision of the future (Huxley's *Brave New World* (1932) and Orwell's *1984* (1949) are literary examples) in the hope that such developments can be forestalled.

validity, that feature of arguments or chains of reasoning studied by the science of *logic. The notion of validity may be defined in two ways. The first uses the notion of truth: an argument is valid if the truth of its conclusion is guaranteed by the truth of its premises (see *deduction). The second appeals to basic accepted patterns of reasoning or principles of inference, for example that given 'A' and 'If A then B' one may infer 'B': a conclusion validly follows from certain premisses if it can be derived from them in accordance with basic principles. A central question in modern work in logic is whether a complete set of principles of reasoning can be specified, so that any argument valid in the first sense is also valid in the second.

value (in economics), the capacity of a *good or service to provide satisfaction (*utility) to its purchaser; or, the *resources employed in its *production and hence its opportunity *cost in terms of alternative outputs foregone. *Microeconomic theory shows that in a well-functioning market system, the price of an item reflects the value of the last (marginal) unit sold and bought. Value added by a firm is that part of the gross value of its output (the firm's revenue) that has been created by the firm in question. In other words, it represents revenue minus the input costs of raw materials, bought-in services, and semi-finished items. More generally, economists have debated how value is created (see *labour theory of value).

value judgement, a judgement which accords value of a certain kind, especially moral value, to an object. The contrast is with a factual judgement. An example of a value judgement would be 'Torture is evil'; of a factual judgement, 'Torture is widespread'. Value judgements have immediate implications for what ought to be done. That there is a gap between judgements of fact and value was argued by *Hume, who made the point that no value judgement can be *deduced from any number or kind of factual judgements. Those who accept Hume's claim often go on to say that the meaning of value judgement is not descriptive but prescriptive or emotive.

Vatican Council   *pope.

Vedānta (Sanskrit, 'the end of the Veda'), a term applied both to the teaching of the *Upanishads (commentaries attached to the *Vedas) and to the most influential of the orthodox schools of Hindu philosophy, based on Upanishad doctrine. Important exponents of Vedānta include Shankara (c. AD 788–820), who stressed non-dualism (*Advaita Hinduism); Rāmānuja (c.1017–1137), who advocated *bhakti*, or devotion to a personal God, identified with *Vishnu; and Madhva (c.1199–1278), who rejected the monism of Shankara and asserted the separate identity of the world, God, and souls. He too believed that ignorance could be overcome through *bhakti*. Despite these differences of emphasis, the Vedānta schools share a belief in the supremacy of *Brahman, the transmigration of souls (*samsara), the desirability of release from the cycle of reincarnation (*moksha), and the ability of the soul or *ātman to direct

its own actions and thus determine its status in the next incarnation. Inspired by the idea of the ultimate equality of individual souls, exponents of Vedānta in the 20th century stress the need for social justice and a casteless society. (See also *Indian philosophy.)

Vedas, the most authoritative of the *Hindu sacred texts, regarded as *shruti*, the product of divine revelation. They are the earliest Sanskrit scriptures of the Indo-Aryans. The basic four collections of *Vedas* consist of the *Rigveda*, hymns of praise to the nature gods, particularly Agni, the fire god, and Indra, the warrior god; the *Yajurveda*, a collection of sacrificial rites; the *Sāmaveda*, containing the melodies and chants required for special sacrifices; and the *Atharvaveda* (included later in the canon), which consists of occult formulas and spells. Later on, commentaries were added, stemming from different schools. The *Brāhmanas* are detailed explanations of the sacrifices, for the use of priests. The *āranyakas* are works suitable for the hermit, while the *Upanishads* are mystical and philosophical works. They are also known as *Vedānta, or 'end of the *Vedas*', and form the basis of the philosophical school of the same name.

vegetarian, a person whose diet does not contain meat, nor in most cases fish. Vegans exclude all animal products from their diet, including eggs and dairy foods, and may avoid all use of animal products, such as wool and leather. There are two interconnected arguments for vegetarianism, political and moral. The moral argument, based on the moral status of animals (see *animal rights), denies man the right to kill them; the Buddhist doctrine of *ahimsa follows a similar argument. The political argument measures the high cost in resources of meat production against the background of *famine and *malnutrition in many countries. Recent medical research suggesting that excessive protein and fat consumption is the cause of many diseases has also encouraged vegetarianism among those who can afford meat in their diet.

verification   *arms control.

verificationism (in philosophy), the view that the meaning of a proposition is its method of verification, the procedure by which its truth or falsity can be determined by observation or experience. Verificationism was adopted by the *logical positivists and was strongly influenced by the *empiricist tradition. The verificationist claim resulted in many, if not all, of the propositions of *metaphysics being rendered meaningless: as they cannot be verified, they cannot have meaning. It also resulted in the propositions of mathematics and of logic (which are of course consistent with all observations) being seen as meaningful only in the sense of being tautologies; they tell us nothing and merely show us how things are. As any non-tautological proposition that cannot be verified by observation is deemed meaningless, this renders all the propositions of ethics and of aesthetics meaningless too, and useful only as expressions of emotion or exclamations. A major problem for verificationism is that it puts the meaning of all scientific generalizations in jeopardy because these cannot be conclusively verified by observation.

vertical integration, an industrial structure involving unified ownership or control of two or more stages of production. Complete vertical integration means that a company controls a production process from start to finish: from the extraction of raw materials to the final retail sale. Vertical integration may be achieved through *organic growth, or through *merger or *take-over. There may be significant *economies of scale from vertical integration, but it may also lead to *monopoly power. Well-known historical examples of vertically integrated firms were the major *multinational oil companies such as BP, Exxon, and Shell, before the 'OPEC' revolution of 1973–4 deprived them of control over major sources of crude oil.

veto (Latin, 'I forbid'), the refusal by a country or an individual to approve a course of action proposed by another country, group of countries, or organization. If majority voting is not permitted, and decisions must be carried by a unanimous vote, the individual, group, or country which does not agree with the majority has in effect the power of veto, as happens in the *European Council of Ministers where decisions in certain policy areas must be unanimous. The US Constitution gives the *President the right to veto any bill passed by Congress. In the context of the UN *Security Council, the right of veto refers to the power of each of the five permanent members (USA, Russia, China, the UK, and France) to oppose any resolution with which it does not agree. During the cold war, which found the USA and the former Soviet Union in disagreement on a wide range of international issues (see *East–West relations), the right of veto often paralysed the workings of the Security Council. The easing of the conflict at the end of the 1980s, however, saw new restraint exercised with regard to the veto, as demonstrated by the resolutions passed against the Iraqi invasion of Kuwait in 1990.

vicarious liability, the legal liability imposed on one person for the crimes or wrongful actions of another. Thus in many countries, an employer is vicariously liable for certain actions of employees in the course of employment, for example *libel or breach of *contract. Vicarious liability also ensures that the employer, who benefits from profits generated by the employee, bears responsibility for any losses.

Vietnamese language   *Austro-Asiatic languages.

violent crime, a term used to describe crimes against the person, as contrasted with *property crime. Violent crime includes the *common law offences of assault (the threat of personal violence) and battery (actual personal violence), although the term assault is generally used to cover both. Other violent crimes are robbery (the use of force in the commission of a theft, as in the case of mugging); *domestic violence, and *homicide. Many *sexual offences, such as indecent assault and *rape, involve violence. Violent crimes are of particular concern to the public; they are often associated with drunkenness, drug dependency, the availability of weapons, frustration, and hopelessness. Some propose stiffer sentencing as a deterrent, while others advocate prevention (for example, education programmes) or protective measures (such as personal alarms, or protective screens for counter staff). In some countries there are support and compensation schemes for the victims of violent crime, who often suffer shock and lasting psychological distress in addition to their physical injuries.

Vishnu (Sanskrit, 'all-pervader', 'worker'), one of the most important of the monotheistic deities worshipped by Hindus. He is regarded as the preserver of the cosmos and the restorer of moral order, and he is said to have appeared in several earthly incarnations (*avatars), in particular Rāma and Krishna. Vishnu's consort is the goddess of wealth and beauty, Lakshmi. Vaishnavism, the worship of Vishnu, is one of the major forms of modern Hinduism, alongside Shaivism and Shāktism. It is characterized by *bhakti*, or devotion to the god as a means of escape from the cycle of birth, death, and rebirth (*samsara).

vital statistics, statistics relating to births, marriages, and deaths. Registration of these events (compulsory in parts of Scandinavia since the 17th century and widespread in Europe and North America from the 19th century) is mandatory in many parts of the world. Where the information is comprehensive, it may be used not only in population forecasting and government planning, but also in *epidemiology, to uncover the links between the circumstances in which people live and the diseases from which they die. An unexpectedly high incidence of deaths from cancer near a toxic waste dump might suggest a connection if all other factors could be ruled out.

vocational education, education for a particular occupation. Industrialized countries have seen a fall in demand for unskilled workers, and an increase in jobs in the professional, technical, commercial, and administrative sector. Vocational education is traditionally associated with trades and crafts: young people were apprenticed to employers for a number of years and learned on the job. Today the focus has shifted from the workplace to *secondary and *higher education institutions, and from employers' to government provision and finance. Trainees in most occupations combine workplace training with study at a technical or academic institution. In the former Soviet Union, school and work were always strongly linked from *primary school. Germany provides nine out of ten young people not entering higher education with vocational training, and training is planned from national down to local level through tripartite committees of government representatives, employers, and trade unions. In some countries, skills are being grouped and 'job families' created so that individuals can move between jobs with similar technical requirements. In others 'competency-based education' is advocated to equip individuals with 'transferable' as well as specific skills. In developing countries, where it is traditional for children to work from an early age, only a tiny proportion of students follow a formal vocational programme, while the long specialist training of professionals such as doctors, lawyers, and engineers is a costly burden. Training places for technicians, nurses, teachers, and other essential workers are often limited. World-wide, there is a slow but steady increase in the numbers of women training for occupations of influence in science, technology, law, and business. It is also becoming clear that one course of vocational education is not enough for a lifetime. Retraining through *continuing education is essential.

volleyball, a handball game played world-wide by two teams of six separated by a net 2.4 m (8 feet) high for men and 2.2 m (7 feet) for women. The court measures 18 m (59 feet) by 9 m (30 feet), and the object is to ground the ball in the opponents' half of the court. The server stands behind the baseline and hits the ball into the opponents' court. A receiver tries to prevent the ball from hitting the ground and passes it to a team-mate, who may then hit it back across the net or set it up for a better-positioned team-mate to hit a winning shot. Opponents meanwhile jump and try to block

Devotees 'fire walking' at a **voodoo** ceremony in Haiti, the world centre of the religion. At such cult services followers are possessed by *loa*—spirits of African gods, Roman Catholic saints, or deified ancestors—who empower them to give supernatural counsel and to perform extraordinary physical feats.

the return. Only the serving team may score, and the first to fifteen points (with a lead of two points) wins the set. Matches are decided by the best of three or five sets.

voluntary organization, a non-profit organization operating for the public good. Voluntary organizations range from small local support groups (for instance, for blind people) with no paid staff, to large international agencies with paid professionals (sometimes known as *non-governmental organizations) such as Save the Children Fund and the World Wide Fund for Nature. Their activities encompass directly supplying services such as shelters for the *homeless, pioneering new services such as hospices for *Aids victims, and campaigning for policy change, such as an end to commercial whaling. Until the 20th century, *social services were provided almost entirely by voluntary groups and organizations, often run by *missionaries or religious bodies. In the 20th century their responsibilities have tended to diminish, as the state's have expanded, but the pattern is variable. Scandinavian countries with well-developed *welfare states have few voluntary organizations, as, for different reasons, do most African and Asian countries, although those that do exist may play a major part in *social care services. In communist countries, voluntary organizations were outlawed on the grounds that the state could meet all needs. The recent trend away from government inter-

vention has led to their growth on the grounds that they can supply services more cheaply than state agencies, give scope for diverse approaches to social problems, harness the sense of social responsibility of unpaid volunteers, and offer choice to service users. New patterns of service are emerging where state social care agencies contract out services to voluntary organizations, but retain responsibility for their finance and *regulation.

voodoo, a religious practice based in the southern states of the USA, the Caribbean, and Brazil; it is the chief religion of the majority of the people of Haiti. Voodoo was brought to the Caribbean by West African slaves; the name derives from *vodu*, 'god', or 'spirit' in the language of the Fon people of Benin. Voodoo combines *ancestor worship and belief in African deities with *Roman Catholic elements, dating from the time of colonization. The *loa*, identified as ancestors, saints, or gods, communicate with the individual by *spirit possession, during collective worship, presided over by priests or priestesses, which involves song, drumming, ecstatic dance, and ritual sacrifice. Voodoo has become associated in the popular imagination with its use of *obeah*, 'sympathetic' magic practices in which objects or images (such as dolls) are used as substitutes for reality, and beliefs such as that a sorcerer can raise the corpse of a dead person (*zombi*) to be used as a slave. Such practices are not, however, typical of ordinary voodoo ritualizing. In Haiti the Roman Catholic Church, which for many years denounced voodoo, has come to coexist with it.

voting   *election, *electoral system, *franchise.

voting behaviour, patterns of electoral choice conditioned by political, social, and psychological forces. Exactly what combination of these factors determines the voting patterns of groups and individuals can not be known with certainty, but a number of models have sought to isolate particular influences. The sociological model emphasizes people's social characteristics, such as their *social class, housing tenure, and education. By contrast, the party identification model stresses the emotional attachments acquired early in life through the family, which create a lifetime bond to a particular party. Finally, the *rational choice model stresses that voters choose between parties instrumentally, just as they would between different products, selecting the one of most use to them. The value of models varies between countries and over time. For example, social changes during recent decades have led to a decline in popular identification with the parties, a trend known as dealignment. Voting is now more influenced by popular judgements of the policies and by the performance of the parties (the party 'image'), particularly in office. These judgements are particularly important in explaining why some voters (though still a minority in most countries) change their vote from one *election to the next. Such 'floating voters', who vote in response to topical issues rather than out of loyalty to one party or another, may play an important role in determining the outcome of an election.

wage, an agreed regular payment for *labour services, and the chief component of the cost of labour. The term wage is commonly reserved for weekly payment, and salary for monthly payment (both types are covered by the term pay). Wages can be paid either at an hourly rate (in which case there may be additional payments such as overtime pay) or for work accomplished (piece rate). Wages and salaries are set by *market forces modified by the *collective bargaining of *trade unions. While wages have maintained their real value over the economic ups and downs in many industrialized countries, wage earners in Latin America and in Africa south of the Sahara suffered a drop of up to 30 or 40 per cent in real income in the first half of the 1980s. Given the patterns of self-employment and casual work in many developing countries, wages may be a less important part of household income than in industrialized countries. *Minimum wage legislation supposedly provides some protection for the low paid in both developing and some industrialized countries.

Wahhābī, a revivalist Muslim movement founded by 'Abd al-Wahhāb (1703–92). The Wahhābi movement was the formative influence in the establishment of the state of Saudi Arabia, and dominates Saudi religious and political life, including the administration of the holy towns of Mecca and Medina. The Wahhābīs are austerely orthodox *Sunnī Muslims who oppose popular religious practices such as the *Sufi veneration of saints and tombs, on the grounds that these are an idolatrous departure from monotheism.

Wall Street   *stock exchange.

Walras, Marie-Esprit Léon (1834–1910), French economist and pioneer of the mathematical model of general economic *equilibrium in which he demonstrated the mutual interdependence of all prices and quantities in the economic system. In *Elements of Pure Economics* (1874–7), Walras grappled with the problem of how equilibrium market prices could be arrived at; in his theoretical analysis he imagined an economy-wide auctioneer to act as a means of communication and to ensure that equilibrium prices are established with the help of hypothetical bids from economic agents before any actual transactions take place.

war, a state of strife or conflict between two or more states, involving their *armed forces. The most influential theoretician of war until the advent of the nuclear age in the 1950s was the Prussian general Carl von Clausewitz. His major work on strategy, *On War* (1833), which maintained that 'war is nothing but a continuation of political intercourse with the admixture of different means', has been studied closely in every country that has since engaged in war, including Germany, Japan, the former Soviet Union, and the USA. His basic ideas on the importance of psychological and accidental factors, and the targeting of enemy forces, resources, and will to fight, remain valid. War may be classified into different categories, according to scale (general or world wars, regional wars, or wars limited to a particular objective); or means (*conventional, nuclear, or *guerrilla wars). In *inter-national law, there are rules and principles regulating armed conflict between states, with the aim of minimizing destruction, ensuring just treatment of prisoners and non-combatants, and establishing means, such as safe conducts and flags of truce, to permit communications between the belligerents. The Hague Conventions of 1899 and 1907 codify rules with regard to the conduct of war, while the *Geneva Conventions of 1864, 1907, 1929, 1949, and 1977 are mainly concerned with the rights of prisoners of war and non-combatants.

war crimes, certain activities in *war that violate the rules governing the established rules of warfare, as set out in the Hague and *Geneva Conventions. In most societies, activities such as the killing of prisoners, their *torture or enslavement, *hostage-taking and the deportation and killing of civilians, are deemed to be war crimes. Present-day attitudes to war crimes have been influenced by the trials at Nuremberg and Tokyo in 1945–6 of German and Japanese wartime leaders. In the course of these proceedings, it was made clear that an individual was to be held responsible for his or her actions even if carrying out the orders of a higher authority. During the Vietnam War (1964–75), US soldiers were indicted on charges of killing civilians; and Iraq's hostage-taking and maltreatment of prisoners during its occupation of Kuwait (1990–1) also led to calls for those responsible to be tried for war crimes.

Warsaw Pact (the Warsaw Treaty Organization), an agreement signed in 1955 by the former Soviet Union, Albania, Bulgaria, Czechoslovakia, the former German Democratic Republic, Hungary, Poland, and Romania, following the admission of the Federal Republic of Germany to *NATO. Yugoslavia refused to join, and Albania left in 1968. The treaty pledged immediate mutual assistance in case of armed *aggression, and established a system of joint military command. In practice, the Pact was dominated by the former Soviet Union, militarily and politically. Originally having a duration of twenty years, the Pact was extended in 1975 and 1985. With the fundamental changes that overtook the Eastern bloc countries in 1989 and 1990, the Soviet system of security in that part of the world ended, and so did the Pact. The German Democratic Republic left in September 1990, just prior to German reunification. After the Eastern bloc members of the Pact ordered Soviet troops out of their territory, the Pact was wound up as a formal military alliance in February 1991.

water supply, the provision and storage of water for an area. In addition to meeting requirements for drinking, cooking, and washing, clean water is essential for manufacturing and commercial activities, which may account for 30 per cent of water consumption in Europe. Deficiencies in water supply and *sanitation services are the principal reasons for the high incidence of *communicable diseases in developing countries. Inadequate water supplies also force people to spend excessive time collecting water; more than six hours a day per family in rural East Africa. By the 1990s the World Health Organization estimated that while three-quarters of urban residents in developing countries had access to safe water (often from standpipes), only a half of rural residents did, and that although numbers served were rising, *population growth was outstripping increased provi-

US troops occupy Iraq in 1991 after the **war** in which the US-led coalition drove the Iraqis out of Kuwait.

sion. The global use of water doubled between 1940 and 1980 and is likely to do so again before the year 2000. Where the priority is to supply as many people as possible, the World Bank argues in *Investing in Development* (1985) that resources should first be spent on standpipes and courtyard connections; these can contribute to improved health. Connections to individual houses are more convenient, but cost ten times more. Waste water collection must be planned in conjunction with water supply, or excess waste water can become a hazard, negating the benefits of clean water supply. Rural needs can generally be met at lower per capita costs than urban needs, corresponding to lower standards of service, but low incomes, the absence of commercial users, and the attachment of villagers to their traditional, free sources of supply lessen the prospects for recovering capital costs. This, together with the fact that rural residents often have less political influence than urban dwellers, accounts for the slow progress in rural water supply: substantial capital contributions from central government are required, and often contributions from the local population in labour, land, and materials.

Watson, John Broadus (1878–1958), US psychologist, founder of *behaviourism. He argued that a psychological science must restrict itself to the 'prediction and control' of observable behaviour. Influenced by *Pavlov, he argued in *Psychology from the Standpoint of a Behaviourist* (1919), that human *language, *personality and psychiatric disorders could all be explained by *conditioning. His most important work sprang from the theory of conditioned *emotion put forward in this book. In an experiment on an 11-month-old child Watson produced conditioned fear reactions to a white rat by frightening the boy with a loud noise when the rat was present. Watson took this as evidence against *Freud's ideas about *neurosis. Many psychologists considered it confirmed the conditioned nature of *phobias, although there is now considerable doubt whether conditioning can make any object at all elicit fear. Although Watson did not devise a cure for the child's acquired fear, this experiment stands behind the theory and practice of all modern *behaviour therapy.

wealth (in economics), the stock of *assets accumulated by individuals, households, businesses, or nations. These assets can be physical possessions (such as consumer durables and buildings), financial assets (such as bank accounts and *shares), *'human capital' (such as people's skills and talents), or natural *resources (such as mineral deposits). The term 'marketable wealth' is applied to those assets which are relatively *liquid; they can be easily turned into *money. Wealth may be accumulated by saving out of current *income or it may be inherited. Wealth, in turn, can create income. For instance, owners of bank deposits are paid *interest and shareholders receive *dividends. A nation will be described as wealthy if it has a high *national income per head, a high *standard of living, a well-qualified labour-force and plentiful natural resources. However, environmental factors ought also to be considered. An industrialized nation may produce a high *GNP, but may suffer from numerous negative *externalities (such as pollution and excessive *urbanization) which detract from the quality of life of its inhabitants. Moreover, even in a wealthy nation, many may live in *poverty.

Weber, Max (1864–1920), German sociologist, one of the founders of *sociology. His ideas, which spanned subjects from economic history to the sociology of music, continue to be extremely influential. Weber argued that there was a link between the emergence of Protestantism (in the 16th century) and what he termed the *Protestant ethic, and the rise of capitalism. He was one of the first to see the importance of *bureaucracy, which he analysed as a form of social organization which consisted of a hierarchy of paid, clearly defined offices, filled by individuals selected on merit who were free and able to progress up the hierarchy, which itself was controlled from the top. Weber refined the analysis of *social stratification, arguing, for example, that an individual's class could depend on the possession of skills as well as on property ownership and occupation, and he stressed the role of *status in social inequality. According to Weber, sociology should concern itself with the interpretation and explanation of social behaviour, not simply with its observation and description, thus distancing himself from approaches influenced by *Comte's positivism. Weber was concerned with the responsibilities of the social scientist and argued for the pursuit of 'value-freedom' in academic life: personal beliefs must not interfere with investigation and analysis. Weber's major work, published posthumously, is *Economy and Society* (1922).

welfare economics   *positive economics.

welfare state, a political system in which *social policy becomes a primary activity of government and the state accepts responsibility for the welfare of all its citizens. There is no one definition of what transforms an advanced industrialized state into a welfare state; it requires both a comprehensive range of state-supported *social services and a political consensus that welfare objectives (such as health, *education, and income maintenance) should be secured for all citizens on the basis of need rather than means. On these criteria, the USA, with its incomplete coverage of the population for social benefits and overriding commitment to a *free-market economy, would not be a welfare state, but Canada, Australia, and New Zealand would be. Sweden is usually taken as the purest example because of its interventionist labour market policy and integrated health care system, but Belgium and The Netherlands have more generous *social security systems. In a welfare state, the proportion of *GNP allocated to social expenditure can rise as high as 40 per cent, but usually around half of this is the transfer of money through taxes and cash benefits like pensions rather than expenditure on services. More significant in entrenching a welfare state is high public employment in health, education, and social services. The concept has always been attacked by conservatives concerned about disincentives to work, and to familial and personal responsibility. In recent years the principal challenge to the welfare state has been that politically acceptable tax levels are too low to sustain good-quality services, resulting in cuts in benefits, *deregulation, and *contracting-out of services.

Wesak (Vesak), the most important of the *Theravāda Buddhist festivals, commemorating the birth, enlightenment, and death (and thus *nirvana) of the *Buddha. It is celebrated on the full moon in the lunar month of Wesak (April/May), and it is a time of temple worship, the presentation of alms, and the renewal of vows.

Western European Union (WEU), a European regional security alliance. In 1991 its members were Belgium, France, Italy, Luxemburg, Germany, The Netherlands, the UK,

Portugal, and Spain. The WEU was founded in 1955; it replaced the Brussels Treaty Organization formed in 1948. Its Secretariat is in Paris. For many years the WEU played a minor role in European affairs. The organization was revived in 1984, and in 1989 resolutions were adopted to strengthen its role in dealing with West European defence concerns. The WEU helped to co-ordinate Europe's contribution to the anti-Iraq coalition in the Gulf War in 1991. In the *EC discussions on developing a common defence and security policy, the WEU played an important role, as a bridge between the EC and *NATO, and in the Maastricht Treaty (1992), it was formally designated as the basis for an EC defence identity.

westernization, the process by which a country or society adopts the customs and institutions that are said to characterize the Western world. For some governments and élites in *developing countries, westernization has been seen as synonymous with modernization and development and therefore as a desirable goal. Another more recent tendency, however, part of what Hedley Bull and others have termed 'the revolt against the west' in *The Expansion of International Society* (1984), is to regard westernization as a pernicious process equated with the negative aspects of *capitalism, which undermines local customs and values, and which should therefore be strongly opposed. The Iranian Revolution of 1979 was, at least in part, a reaction to the westernizing policies of the Shah Muhammad Reza Pahlavi (1919–80), which neglected the traditional, particularly religious, values in Iranian society, and the anti-Western theme has, to a greater or lesser degree, been taken up by *Islamic fundamentalist movements throughout the Muslim world.

white-collar crime, a term coined by the US sociologist Edwin Sutherland in *White Collar Crime* (1949) and defined there as 'crime committed by a person of respectability and high social status in the course of his occupation'. Those typically involved include businessmen, politicians, administrative officials, doctors, and stockbrokers. It is often perpetrated by whole organizations, or groups within those organizations, rather than individuals. For example, members of a corporation might conspire with members of another to contravene the USA's anti-trust legislation, which seeks to ensure healthy competition in the marketplace for the benefit of consumers; a politician might attempt to bribe the director of a newspaper to ensure favourable coverage; a doctor might make out false prescriptions to non-existent patients and claim the cost back for himself; or a company director might use inside information in order to gain personal profits on the stock market. Research has shown that these people rarely see themselves as criminal, and are often not seen as such by the public, partly because white-collar crime is usually not violent and often harms no specific victim, and partly because white-collar criminals are often not detected or taken to court. Serious consequences include losses to shareholders, failure of companies, and adverse effects on the safety of workers or consumers and on the environment.

White Paper   *bill.

wholesale trading, the buying of *stock in bulk from manufacturers in order to sell at a profit to retailers. Some wholesalers sell directly to the public at (or just above) wholesale prices. Large retailers may do their own wholesaling to reduce their combined costs of operation.

will (in law), a transfer of *property which is intended to take effect on death. The term is also used to denote the document setting out the intentions of the person making the will (the testator). In England, this must be signed by the testator and the making of the signature verified by two witnesses. In other countries, it is possible to create a will by other methods, including oral declaration before several witnesses, declaration before a public official, and signed writing by the testator alone. A will is revocable at any time before death, and in some cases is automatically revoked by the divorce or marriage of the testator. A will does not take effect until death, and does not affect the ability of the testator to deal with his or her property. On the testator's death, an executor is appointed who, after obtaining *probate, distributes the property in accordance with the will.

windsurfing, the sport of offshore sailing on a surfboard. As opposed to *surfing, which requires specific wave conditions, windsurfing needs a relatively calm sea and light winds. The mast is usually clipped into the board, and the sailor uses a horizontal crossbar to manœuvre the sail and catch the wind.

witchcraft, the power to harm others by supernatural means. In his study of the *Azande, *Evans-Pritchard made a distinction between witchcraft and sorcery, on the basis that witchcraft is an inherited power which may be used unconsciously, whereas sorcery is learnt and involves the conscious, malevolent use of *magic. When an Azande suffered misfortune, witchcraft was a common explanation, and divination could reveal who the witch was. Once revealed, the witch, male or female, usually a personal enemy, would be required to make some sort of reparation. For the Azande, then, belief in witchcraft serves as a perfectly logical explanation of misfortune, and is part of a process of expressing social tension and *dispute resolution. Studies by both historians and anthropologists have pointed out the important function that belief in witchcraft has had in different societies, while raising serious doubts about whether there ever really were any witches. In the 20th century, in Europe and the USA, a new kind of witchcraft has manifested itself, which claims to be a revival of pre-Christian pagan religion. It is practised by a small number of adherents in covens or assemblies and has at times been associated with animal *sacrifice and *child sexual abuse.

Wittgenstein, Ludwig (Josef Johann) (1889–1951), Austrian-born philosopher. Perhaps the most influential philosopher of this century, Wittgenstein came to philosophy through an interest in the foundations of mathematics, which he studied under *Russell at Cambridge. He rapidly concluded that problems in *Frege's and Russell's attempts to base arithmetic on logical principles stemmed from a misunderstanding of the nature of logical principles themselves. He held that to have a right view of logic we must first solve all problems connected with the meaningfulness of simple, contingent statements. He addressed these in his *Tractatus Logico-Philosophicus* (1922), which, he said, 'shows how little has been done when these problems are solved'. Philosophical problems are no more than confusions, brought about by the misleading ways in which we express ourselves in language. Philosophy aims to get rid of these confusions, not to construct any theories of its own. He always retained this view, but later thought that he had been wrong to imagine that we could hope for a single, comprehensive remedy for all philosophical confusions. His later

The blockade of the US military base at Greenham Common in the UK in the 1980s by women opposing the cruise missiles located at the base was an example of the solidarity of the **women's movement**.

work, exemplified in the posthumous *Philosophical Investigations* (1953), is therefore less abstract, and involves detailed examination of areas of language, such as those concerned with experience, intentions, and knowledge, which give rise to a lack of clarity in our thought.

women's movement (developing world), a movement, less well-defined than its counterpart in the Western world, which aims at equality between men and women. In developing countries, women generally suffer from a greater degree of inequality than their counterparts in Western countries. Their participation in the paid labour force and their *literacy rates tend to be lower, and their *fertility rates and maternal mortality rates tend to be higher. High fertility rates, low educational attainment, and, sometimes, religious or social traditions are responsible for women's limited role in economic, public, and political life. Those who are in paid *employment tend to be relegated to low-paid and unskilled occupations, while in general women's workload, including caring for extended *families, agricultural work, gathering fuel and fetching water, is greater than that of men. In many countries women have tried to improve their status, for example by opposing bridewealth (see *dowry) in traditional African societies, or dress restrictions and seclusion codes in Islamic societies (see *purdah). Women have achieved most in those countries where they have participated in liberation struggles: in Vietnam, Nicaragua, Mozambique, and Angola, for instance, national revolutionary groups have made women's equality part of their political platform. Elsewhere, women's groups have tended to be largely middle class, as is, for instance, the thriving women's movement in India, which opposes certain social practices such as arranged *marriages.

women's movement, (Western world), a broad-based movement aimed at achieving equality between men and women. Ideas associated with feminism originated in antiquity, but the real struggle for equality dates back to the 18th-century Enlightenment, and to Mary Wollstonecraft's book *A Vindication of the Rights of Women* (1792), which called

for equal opportunities for women. In the 19th and early 20th centuries, the movement concentrated on the achievement of *women's suffrage. The contemporary women's movement has its roots in works such as Simone de Beauvoir's *Le Deuxième Sexe* (1949); *The Feminine Mystique* (1963) by the US feminist and founder of the National Organization for Women, Betty Friedan; *Sexual Politics* (1969) by the US writer Kate Millett; and *The Female Eunuch* (1970) by the Australian-born feminist Germaine Greer. The women's movement challenges the patriarchal nature of modern society (see *patriarchy), and argues that male domination is implicit in all personal and professional relationships. Feminists believe that male superiority is not the inevitable result of physical or intellectual differences, and they are concerned with changing those sexual stereotypes that confine women to subservient or domestic roles. There are three discernible strands in the women's movement: solidarity and consciousness-raising, through which small groups of women reassess their roles and position in society; public campaigns on issues such as *abortion, *equal pay and work opportunities, *childcare provision, *pornography, and *domestic violence against women; and the academic discipline of women's studies, which provides the theoretical underpinning of the movement. Although the women's movement is agreed on broad aims, since the 1970s it has been divided on the best way of achieving them. Mainstream feminists continue to work through education and support networks in order to improve the position of women in society as it is, while radical feminists who advocate separatism argue that any interaction with men is bound to result in exploitation, and that women should aim at total independence of men to the extent of foregoing motherhood if need be. In reaction to this uncompromising stand, some post-feminist writers have acknowledged the central and fulfilling role of children and *family in women's lives and have expressed disillusionment with women's apparent sexual liberation and wish to mimic male roles. A number of women have achieved equality in the workplace, but in the absence of adequate support structures, they still experience problems in reconciling their careers with family life. (See also *gender, *sexism.)

women's suffrage, the right of adult women to vote in local and national *elections (see *franchise). Women's suffrage was first advocated by Mary Wollstonecraft in *A Vindication of the Rights of Women* (1792), and throughout the 19th century, in Britain and the USA, calls were made for voting rights for women. In 1893 New Zealand granted women the right to vote, and Australia followed in 1902. In Britain, during the early years of the 20th century, the Women's Social and Political Union, led by Emmeline Pankhurst and her daughter Christabel, campaigned for the right to vote in national elections, often adopting militant methods. In 1918 women over 30 were granted the vote, the age being lowered to 21 in 1928. During the years following World War I, women were granted the vote in many countries, including the former Soviet Union (1917), Germany, Poland, Austria, and Sweden (1919), and the USA (1920). During and after World War II, further countries, such as France (1944), Italy (1945), China (1947), and India (1949), granted women the vote, as did most developing countries gaining independence after decolonization. In Switzerland, women were denied the vote until 1971, and suffrage was restricted in some cantons until more recently. Women still do not have the vote in countries such as Saudi Arabia (where all suffrage is restricted), Kuwait, and Jordan.

World Bank, an international economic organization and specialized agency of the *UN, based in Washington, DC. It comprises two legally and financially distinct organizations which are, however, administered by the same staff: the International Bank for Reconstruction and Development (IBRD), established in 1945, and the International Development Association (IDA), established in 1960. The World Bank receives its funds from member countries (the USA being the largest contributor) and from borrowing on world money markets. Its purpose is to provide funds and technical assistance to help the economies of developing countries and it works closely with the *International Monetary Fund. The IBRD (which was owned by the governments of 152 countries in 1991) lends to those at a more advanced stage of economic growth at just below commercial interest rates. Some of the projects supported by the IBRD, particularly those which have entailed large-scale industrial developments and construction projects such as dams and roads, have been criticized for overburdening states with *debt and harming indigenous *development and the environment. In recent years, it has shifted its emphasis to investments in *agriculture, small-scale enterprises, *education, *family planning, health, and nutrition in an attempt directly to improve the well-being of the vast numbers of poor people in developing countries. The IDA, which had 137 member states in 1991, gives assistance to the poorest countries on more favourable terms than IBRD. IDA credits, which are made only to governments, can be repaid over forty to fifty years with a grace period of ten years and without interest.

World Council of Churches (WCC), an interdenominational organization of *Christian Churches, created in 1948. With the exception of the Roman Catholic Church, which sends accredited observers, most of the world's Churches are members. The World Council of Churches is the most important of a number of ecumenical movements advocating greater unity amongst the Christian Churches. The Council is also active in disaster relief.

World Health Organization (WHO), an intergovernmental organization, part of the *UN system, of which 166 states are members. WHO was established in 1948. Its head office is in Geneva, Switzerland. Member states provide WHO's finance and decide its policy at the annual World Health Assembly. WHO's two main functions are to act as a directing and co-ordinating authority on international health work and to encourage technological co-operation between member states. To this end, the organization promotes *public health; provides information, advice, and assistance; and sponsors research. In 1981 the World Health Assembly adopted a global strategy, *Health for All by the Year 2000*. This recognized health as a fundamental right, and affirmed WHO's commitment to *primary health care as a means of ensuring equitable access to services and the most efficient use of resources. It advocated concentration on *public health measures to provide safe drinking *water and adequate *sanitation, the *immunization of all children against major *communicable diseases, and the reduction of *malnutrition. In addition, an intensified effort should be made to prevent and combat endemic diseases such as malaria and tuberculosis, and to give access to essential *drugs and to *family planning services.

world order, a state of peace and stability within international relations, regarded as the traditional goal of international politics. The proponents of *power politics or realism seek to achieve order through the use of power, specifically military power, while others believe that despite conflicts between states there exists an *international society supported by *international law and *diplomacy. This concept of world order as the absence of *war has been criticized by developing countries, who envisage a *New International Economic Order, claiming that reform is necessary so that poorer states may participate in international affairs on something approaching equal terms. Some theorists examining the concept of world order have focused on global problems such as the nuclear threat, environmental damage, and the gap between the developed and developing worlds, and have envisaged a world consisting of interdependent societies and communities rather than conflicting and competing states (see *interdependence).

wrestling, the ancient sport of hand-to-hand grappling, practised world-wide according to a variety of disciplines. Two styles, Greco–Roman and all-in or freestyle, are contested at the *Olympic Games. There are ten classes, ranging from 48 kg (106 pounds) to 130 kg (286 pounds). Contestants wear leotards and light boots, and bouts last for three three-minute rounds unless previously decided by a fall or disqualification. In Greco–Roman wrestling, no holds are allowed below the waist, and the legs may not be used to grip an opponent. Freestyle is faster and permits any fair hold, throw, or trip. Bouts are won on points or by a fall, pinning the opponent's shoulders to the mat for one second. Sumo wrestling, which requires both bulk and speed, is practised at the highest level only in Japan. Victory goes to the wrestler who forces his opponent to the mat or across the rope in a circular ring.

writing, a system of inscribed *signs replacing or recording spoken *language. Various writing systems world-wide have developed independently. The earliest forms of writing are non-*phonological; that is, they do not represent the sounds

A **World Health Organization** team in India spraying against the larvae of the *Anopheles* mosquito, which passes the malarial blood parasite to man. WHO embarked on a world-wide spraying campaign in 1948, but lack of money and the mosquitoes' development of resistance to the sprays have hampered their efforts.

Sumo, a specialized form of **wrestling**, has been a popular sport in Japan since at least the 8th century. The sport began as part of a ceremony to ensure a good harvest, and still includes ritualistic elements, such as the sprinkling of salt in the fighting circle.

Xhosa, the second largest ethnic group in South Africa after the *Zulu, with their own language, Xhosa, which is a member of the *Niger–Congo language group. Traditionally the Xhosa are agriculturalists, growing maize and sorghum, but they also keep cattle, which play an important part in social and religious customs, such as *lobola*, or marriage payments. Many Xhosa live in the semi-autonomous 'homelands' of Transkei and Ciskei, nominally independent states created as part of South Africa's apartheid policy of 'separate development', but others, largely men, have been drawn into South Africa's labour-market as *migrant farm labourers and industrial workers. The necessity for men to live away from their families, in urban slums or single-sex dormitories, has disrupted the traditional family and community life of the Xhosa, who have also suffered greatly in recent years from poverty, discrimination, and endemic political violence, including repeated clashes with members of the rival Zulu clan.

Xun Zi *Chinese philosophy.

of a language. The *pictograms of pictographic writing (direct representations of simple objects and notions) date back to 3000 BC. Pictographic writing evolved into ideographic. *Ideograms depict more abstract concepts, ideas, and expressions. Egyptian hieroglyphs are an example of ideographic writing, which typically is a mixture of pictograms, ideograms, and representations of certain sounds of the language (phonograms). In logographic writing systems like Chinese, logograms represent words or their parts (morphemes) and usually include *semantic and *phonetic components. There are two purely *phonological writing systems: syllabaries, where the symbols correspond to the syllables of words; and *alphabetic systems, where the symbols directly correspond to individual sounds (phonemes).

Wundt, Wilhelm Max (1832–1920), German philosopher and physiologist; a founder of experimental and academic *psychology. His most important book is *Principles of Physiological Psychology* (1873–4), which presented psychology as an independent scientific discipline and proposed the principle that experimental psychology would find its future in close alliance with the anatomy and physiology of the central nervous system. In 1879 he established the first laboratory dedicated to experimental psychology, which became the prototype for other psychology departments.

Yanomano, a large forest tribe of *Amazonian Indians, living on the Brazilian and Venezuelan border. The Yanomano practise *shifting cultivation, growing crops such as sweet potatoes and cassava, and live in villages of up to twenty families. Their religion is a mixture of *shamanism and spirit worship, with a common belief that spirits of plants cause illness. Villages constantly *feud with one another, and a great deal of social life goes into the creation of alliances, many of which are formed through *kinship ties between exogamous (marriage outside the group) patrilineal groups. In common with many other Indians of the Amazonian region, the Yanomano are under increasing threat from *deforestation and other activities such as gold-mining.

Yiddish (German, *Jüdisch*, 'Jewish'), a language spoken by *Ashkenazi Jews in central and eastern Europe. It developed in the 9th century from German, but soon acquired a distinctive character of its own. It is now written in the Hebrew alphabet. Many words have been borrowed from Slavic, as well as from Hebrew–Aramaic (see *Semitic languages). Western Yiddish (dialects of Germany and Holland) was the medium of spoken communication between European Jews until the 18th century, when it was replaced by a new literary language based on Eastern Yiddish from the Baltic and Slavic lands. There is a continuous literary tradition (both religious and secular) from the 12th century to the present day. Modern Standard Yiddish is based on the East European dialect. Before World War II there were 11 million speakers in Europe; now the number of speakers world-wide is estimated at under 5 million, mainly Jews living in North America, Latin America, Israel, and the republics of the former Soviet Union.

Yijing (I Ching; Chinese, 'Classic of Changes'), an ancient Chinese text, forming part of the five classic texts of *Confucianism. Originally it was a book of divination, but during the Han Dynasty (206–20 AD) the original meaning of the book was expanded and a comprehensive system of cosmology was developed in a series of appendices or 'wings'. It stresses constant change and transformation, occasioned by the interaction of *yin and yang. The book contains eight trigrams (characters formed of three strokes) which subdivide to produce sixty-four hexagrams. The first two trigrams are Heaven and Earth, which are equated with yang and yin respectively. They are the father and mother of all other trigrams, and, in turn, of all creation. Themselves springing from the great ultimate, they produce by their interaction all the phenomena of the universe. The eight trigrams and the sixty-four hexagrams therefore symbolize all possible situations or mutations of creation. By studying these hexagrams and their interpretations the scholar may come to know the activities of the universe. Thus universal patterns of change can be related to immediate worldly concerns, and the likely outcome of particular events can be deduced. The *Yijing* is still used as a practical means of solving everyday problems, both in China and in the West.

yin and yang (or in Japanese, *in-yō*), two opposing forces whose complementary interaction forms and sustains the universe according to Eastern thought. Originally 'yin' described the cold, northern side of a mountain, and 'yang' the hot, southern slope. By the 3rd century BC, yin, the passive force, was taken in China to represent the earth, darkness, and all that is feminine and receptive, while yang, the active force, represents light, the sky, and all that is masculine and penetrating. The common symbol of yin and yang resembles the light and dark halves of a circle, curving one into the other. Each holds a small particle of the other in it. This balance between yin and yang applies to all human affairs as well as to all physical processes.

yoga (Sanskrit, 'yoking', 'union'), any form of religious activity, particularly within *Hinduism, which is designed to link or harness the practitioner to the desire or knowledge of the divine. In particular, yoga is one of the six orthodox systems of Hindu philosophy, based on the yoga Sūtras (doctrinal works) of Patañjali. The highest yogic form, Rāja yoga, aims at the spiritual purification of the practitioner through a series of eight stages, requiring expert teaching and guidance. The first four teach restraint and religious observance, followed by physical preparations involving postures (*āsanas*, such as the Lotus position) and breathing exercises (*prānāyāma*). The next stages involve the withdrawal of the senses, concentration of the mind, and meditation, until the final stage, *samādhi*, or union with the divine, is achieved. In Western countries, the first four stages (the basis of Hatha Yoga) have become popular as a form of exercise and relaxation, and the control of breathing and the use of postures in particular have been adapted to numerous fitness courses. In a wider sense, yoga refers to the different paths leading to a spiritual liberation (*moksha*); as well as Rāja yoga, these include karma yoga (selfless action), *bhakti*-yoga, devotion to a personal deity, and *jñāna*-yoga, the way of intellectual knowledge. Yoga is not limited to Hindu practice and may be found within other religions, such as *Tibetan Buddhism.

Yom Kippur (Hebrew, 'Day of Atonement'), the holiest day in the Jewish year, a time for *meditation and for the expiation of sins, marked by abstention from food, drink, and sexual relations. It is celebrated from the evening of the ninth day of the lunar month of Tishri. Referred to as the *Shabbat Shabbaton, or Sabbath of Sabbaths, in the Bible, Yom Kippur is the day of the year when cessation from work is most strictly kept. Jews attend the *synagogue for a day of prayers, confessing collective and personal guilt, and asking for absolution from God. Prayers are said for God's forgiveness for those who have died in the past year; friends ask and grant forgiveness of each other for the offences of the past year. The Book of Jonah is read. Uniquely in Jewish worship, the congregation kneels at the mention of God's name.

Yoruba, a people of southern Nigeria with their own language, a member of the *Niger–Congo language group. They are traditionally town dwellers, living around a central market. Each town used to be ruled by an *oba*, a king said to have divine powers. The men are traditionally farmers; palm oil and cocoa are now major cash crops. It is the women who are the traders, controlling much of the market system. Many Yoruba are now Christians or Muslims, living in the cities of Ibadan and Lagos, but they have not lost their ethnic identity; they group together with other Yoruba to form mutual aid and credit societies.

Z

Zaibatsu, large privately owned Japanese conglomerates. The five major *Zaibatsu* (Mitsubishi, Mitsui, Okura, Sumitomo, Yasuda) controlled much of Japanese industry and trade up to World War II. In 1948 a decree limited the influence of the traditional *Zaibatsu* families, and prevented members of these families from continuing to hold official positions in *Zaibatsu* companies. The influence of the *Zaibatsu* therefore declined.

Zen Buddhism (Chinese, *ch'an*, from Sanskrit, *dhyāna*, 'meditation'), a school of *Buddhism which originated in China in the 7th century. It was introduced to Japan in the 12th century. It teaches that everyone has the potential to achieve enlightenment by overcoming ignorance. This is not achieved through scriptural texts or ritual worship, but through *satori*, a sudden enlightenment experience, which is usually achieved under the guidance of a teacher. Different branches of Zen teach different methods of achieving enlightenment, such as *meditation on paradoxical statements (*kōans*), and seating posture (*zazen*).

zero population growth, a goal advocated to avert *overpopulation whereby *birth rates and *mortality rates in a country (together with *immigration and *emigration) are permanently balanced. It has more or less been achieved in some of the countries of Europe (see *demographic transition). However, it is not usually possible in countries where the number of young adults is growing rapidly, as it is in most developing countries. Even in China, which instituted a coercive policy of limiting each couple to one child in the late 1970s and achieved a dramatic fall in its birth rate, the population is still increasing as the many women born in earlier population booms reach child-bearing age. Zero population growth remains a controversial aim as *population growth has historically been an important component of social and economic development, and some have seen exhortations by the rich world to the poor to have fewer children as racist.

Zhuangzi (Chuang-tzu), a classic text of *Daoism written by Zhuangzi (*c.*369–286 BC). Although Zhuangzi's philosophy differs from that found in the *Daodejing, his concept of *Dao* was a further naturalization of Laozi's concept. To him all things change at all moments and though they are different and conflicting, *Dao* transforms and unites them into a harmonious whole. The ideal person does not interfere with the Way of Nature but is at one with it. Thus the mystical and metaphysical features of Daoist thought are ultimately vehicles for addressing human problems. In life the individual must return to the simplicity and purity of the *Dao* in order to achieve true freedom.

Zhu Xi *Confucianism.

Zionism, a movement founded in 1897 by the Hungarian Jewish writer Theodore Herzl (1860–1904) for the establishment of a Jewish homeland in Palestine. It resulted in the formation of the state of Israel in 1948. Originally a secular movement, Zionism has its foundation in the *millenarian belief that the Jews, the chosen people of God, will be reunited from diaspora (dispersion or exile) in their rightful homeland. It was further strengthened by the persecution and annihilation of the *Jewish people in World War II. Today, Zionism remains an important issue in Israeli domestic politics and in the politics of the Middle East, since the question of the existence of the state of Israel and its claim to all the biblical territory of Israel has not been satisfactorily reconciled with the rights of the *Palestinians. The continuing right of all Jews world-wide, whatever their nationality, to emigrate to Israel and to take Israeli citizenship, is a fundamental principle of Zionism, and the World Zionist Congress, an independent body, exists to support Jewish emigration to Israel.

zoos (zoological gardens), places where wild and domesticated animals are exhibited in enclosures. Many of the more eminent zoos are run by scientific societies whose primary aims are to initiate research, help with the conservation of rare species (see *endangered species), and provide an educational centre for the study of animals. Modern zoos date from the mid-18th century, some developing from private menageries and some from other scientific collections. The Paris Zoo, for example, began in 1626 as a physic garden growing medicinal herbs, to which the botanist Comte de Buffon added the *Ménagerie*. The larger zoos maintain a balanced collection of mammals, birds, and sea creatures housed in a separate aquarium building. World-wide, there are more than 1,000 animal collections open to the public, and among the best-known are those in Berlin, the Bronx (New York Zoological Park), London, Washington DC, Paris, Beijing, San Diego, Toronto, and Vienna.

Zoroastrian *Parsi.

Zulu, the largest ethnic group in South Africa, descended from the Nguni peoples of Natal with their own language, Zulu, which is part of the *Niger–Congo Group. They formed a powerful military empire in the 19th century, before their defeat by the Whites. Traditional Zulu society is based on the *clan system, the clan consisting of several patrilineal households, under the leadership of a chief. Some Zulu still live in the traditional way in the 'homeland' (or nominally independent state, in practice dependent on South Africa) of KwaZulu, but many men are employed as poorly paid industrial workers in South Africa, living in suburban 'townships', dormitory towns for Black workers, established in accordance with the apartheid principle of separate development. In recent years the Zulu Inkatha movement has clashed violently with other Black groups in South Africa, particularly the *Xhosa.

Countries of the World

In the closing decade of the 20th century, the political picture of the world has altered dramatically with the birth of new nations and demise of others following the disappearance of the majority of the world's communist regimes. Many longstanding conflicts are within sight of resolution, and many dictatorial regimes are giving way to freely elected democratic governments. Yet abuses of human rights, conflict, civil war, poverty, and famine persist, and, in many regions, worsen.

This section provides a summary of the political and economic structure of the majority of the world's independent nation-states. In some cases, colonies such as Hong Kong or nations occupied by another have been included because their importance has been judged to be too great to omit them. In other cases, such as the Federated States of Micronesia or Guam, a number of very small states which share similar features have been grouped under one heading.

A small map shows the location of each country or group of countries. In the case of very small countries such as islands, the map should be regarded as an indicator which is not accurately drawn to scale. Tables provide vital statistical and other information, including a breakdown of the religious and ethnic divisions of a country and its principal languages.

Every effort has been made to ensure that the information given is up to date and correct. It is, however, important to note that in all cases, particularly in potentially controversial areas such as ethnicity and religion, figures are unlikely to be fully reliable, due to the difficulty of collecting information, or, sometimes, reluctance to do so for political reasons. Moreover, in the case of ethnicity, there may be limited consistency between the ethnic groups listed in different countries. This is because such classification depends on the criteria used by the country concerned in collecting information, reflecting the fact that the definition of what is or is not an ethnic group varies according to the society in question.

Another difficult area is that of nuclear capacity. Sometimes, a country may possess the wherewithal to produce nuclear weapons, or have actually produced them, although its declared capacity is only 'research'. We have followed the neutral categories given in the World Resources Institute's *World Resources 1990–91*.

In order to save space, international organizations are given in their abbreviated form. Entries describing each organization and giving its full title are to be found in the main alphabetic section of the Encyclopedia.

Cross-references (indicated by an asterisk) only refer to entries within this section.

Afghanistan

Da Afghānestān Jamhawrīyat

CAPITAL Kabul
AREA 652,225 km² (251,825 sq. mi.)
POPULATION 14.825 million (1989)
POPULATION GROWTH 1.4% p.a.
GDP PER CAPITA $143 (1988)
CURRENCY 1 afghani = 100 puls
LIFE EXPECTANCY 41 (male) 42 (female)
POPULATION UNDER 15 YEARS 42%
LITERACY RATE 23.7% (1985)
RELIGION Sunnī Muslim 93.0%; Shī'ī Muslim 7.0%
ETHNIC GROUPS Pathan (Pashto) 52.3%; Tajik 20.3%; Uzbek 8.7%; Hazara 8.7%; Chahar Aimak 2.9%; Turkmen 2.0%; Baluchi 1.0%
LANGUAGE Pashto, Dari (Persian) (both official); minority languages
NUCLEAR CAPACITY No
LABOUR FORCE IN AGRICULTURE 56% (1988)
MAIN INTERNATIONAL ORGANIZATIONS UN; Colombo Plan; Non-Aligned Movement

Afghanistan is a republic governed by an Islamic Council. The Soviet-backed government was ousted by the Mujahidin (Islamic guerrillas) in 1992. Afghanistan was invaded by the Soviet army in 1979 and remained under Soviet military occupation until their withdrawal in 1989. Soviet and US arms supplies to the government and Mujahidin respectively ceased in 1991, and the UN attempted unsuccessfully to instal an interim government. The prolonged and bitter civil war between Soviet forces and the puppet government, and the splintered Mujahidin guerrillas has given way to fighting and shifting allegiances between the seven rival Mujahidin factions which control different regions of the country and claim allegiance from the different ethnic groups. Agriculture, mainly sheep-raising and subsistence farming, is the mainstay of the economy, which has been devastated by the civil war; there are widespread food shortages, giving rise to fears of famine, and illegal opium production is prevalent An estimated 6 million Afghan refugees fled the civil war, mainly to Pakistan and Iran. Afghanistan is divided on religious and ethnic grounds: in the north Sunnī Tajik, Turkmen, and Uzbek peoples predominate, while the economically disadvantaged Shī'ī Hazara people are found in central Afghanistan. Sunnī Pathans, who form the largest ethnic group, have traditionally held power in Kabul.

Albania

Republika e Shqipërisë

CAPITAL Tirana
AREA 28,748 km² (11,100 sq. mi.)
POPULATION 3.197 million (1989)
POPULATION GROWTH 2.0% p.a.
GDP PER CAPITA $1,102 (1988)
CURRENCY 1 lek = 100 qindars
LIFE EXPECTANCY 69 (male) 74 (female)
POPULATION UNDER 15 YEARS 32.6%
LITERACY RATE Virtually 100% (1989)
RELIGION Non-religious 55.4%; Muslim 20.5%; atheist 18.7%; Eastern Orthodox 5.4%
ETHNIC GROUPS Albanian, with Greek and gypsy minorities
LANGUAGE Albanian (official); Greek; Macedonian; Romany
NUCLEAR CAPACITY No
LABOUR FORCE IN AGRICULTURE 49.8% (1988)
MAIN INTERNATIONAL ORGANIZATIONS UN; CSCE; North Atlantic Co-operation Council

Albania is a multiparty republic, which was a one-party state controlled by the communist Albanian Labour Party until 1991. The communists held power in the first free elections in 1991, but were displaced in elections in 1992. Albania has modified its isolationist foreign policy, and is re-establishing diplomatic links abroad. Economic reforms, which include the privatization of farmland, state enterprises, and housing, the abolition of price subsidies, and the liberalization of trade are being implemented. Shortages of food and consumer goods, high inflation, a wage freeze, and the end of price-fixing have led to social unrest and high rates of crime and exacerbated existing conditions of extreme deprivation and poverty. The economy is primarily agricultural, but crude oil is exported, and petrol-refining is an important industry. The main crops are wheat, maize, potatoes, sugar-beet, citrus fruits, grapes, olives, and tobacco. Chromite (chromium ore), copper, nickel, and coal are mined. Up to 80 per cent of Albania's power is hydroelectric, although the drought of recent years has affected both power supplies and agriculture. Industry, which is limited, is in great need of modernization and has suffered from a ban on foreign investment. The main exports are minerals and foodstuffs. Albania was officially an atheist country until freedom of conscience was restored in 1990.

Algeria

al-Jumhūrīyah al-Jazā'irīyah ad-
Dīmuqrāṭīyah ash-Shaʿbīyah

CAPITAL Algiers
AREA 2,381,741 km² (919,595 sq. mi.)
POPULATION 24.579 million (1989)
POPULATION GROWTH 3.0% p.a.
GDP PER CAPITA $2,269 (1988)
CURRENCY 1 Algerian dinar =
100 centimes
LIFE EXPECTANCY 61 (male) 64 (female)
POPULATION UNDER 15 YEARS 44.4%
LITERACY RATE 44.7% (1982)
RELIGION Sunnī Muslim 99.1%; Roman Catholic 0.5%
ETHNIC GROUPS Arab 82.6%; Berber 17.0%; French 0.1%
LANGUAGE Arabic (official); Berber; French
NUCLEAR CAPACITY 1 research reactor
LABOUR FORCE IN AGRICULTURE 25.7% (1988)
MAIN INTERNATIONAL ORGANIZATIONS UN; Arab League; OAPEC;
OPEC; Maghreb Union; Non-Aligned Movement; OAU

Algeria is a republic ruled by a military-backed High State Council. It became independent from France in 1962. It was a one-party state governed by the socialist Front de Libération Nationale (FLN) until 1989, when other political parties were legalized. The success of the fundamentalist Front Islamique du Salut (FIS) at local elections and its expected success in national elections led in early 1992 to the government's fall, the cancellation of elections, and the banning of the FIS. Industry, mainly state-owned, is based on oil-refining, but cement and steel are also produced. The country's main exports are crude oil, petroleum products, and natural gas. Agriculture is limited: the northern mountainous region is suited only to grazing and timber, and the south of the country is the Sahara Desert. Algeria imports much of its food, the EC being the major trading partner. High-quality roads link a country which has developed health and education services. High levels of debt and unemployment, and shortages of foreign exchange have caused growing economic and social problems.

American Samoa *Polynesia.

Andorra

Principat d'Andorra

CAPITAL Andorra la Vella
AREA 468 km² (181 sq. mi.)
POPULATION 50,000 (1989)
POPULATION GROWTH 3.8% p.a.
GNP PER CAPITA $9,000 (1983) (GDP n.a.)
CURRENCY French francs, Spanish pesetas
LIFE EXPECTANCY 70 (male) 70 (female)
POPULATION UNDER 15 YEARS 19.0%
LITERACY RATE Virtually 100% (1987)
RELIGION Roman Catholic 94.2%; Jewish 0.4%; Jehovah's Witnesses
0.3%; Protestant 0.2%
ETHNIC GROUPS Spanish 55.1%; Andorran 27.5%; French 7.4%;
Portuguese 4.1%; British 1.5%
LANGUAGE Catalan (official); French; Spanish
NUCLEAR CAPACITY No
LABOUR FORCE IN AGRICULTURE 0.6% (1986)

Andorra is a co-principality, with sovereignty shared between the French President and the Bishop of Urgell in Spain. A General Council of the Valleys submits proposals to the permanent delegations of each co-prince. Tourism is the main industry, employing 37 per cent of the labour-force, with commerce, forestry, and the construction industry also of importance.

Angola

República Popular de Angola

CAPITAL Luanda
AREA 1,246,700 km² (481,354 sq. mi.)

POPULATION 9.739 million (1989)
POPULATION GROWTH 2.7% p.a.
GDP PER CAPITA $569 (1988)
CURRENCY 1 kwanza = 100 lwei
LIFE EXPECTANCY 43 (male) 46 (female)
POPULATION UNDER 15 YEARS 44.9%
LITERACY RATE 28% (1980)
RELIGION Roman Catholic 68.7%;
Protestant 19.8%; traditional beliefs
9.5%
ETHNIC GROUPS Ovimbundu 37.2%;
Mbundu 21.6%; Kongo 13.2%; Portuguese and Mestizo
LANGUAGE Portuguese (official); Umbundu; African Bantu languages
NUCLEAR CAPACITY No
LABOUR FORCE IN AGRICULTURE 70.6% (1988)
MAIN INTERNATIONAL ORGANIZATIONS UN; OAU; Non-Aligned
Movement; SADCC

Angola is a one-party socialist republic ruled by the Popular Movement for the Liberation of Angola (MPLA), which received substantial backing from the former Soviet Union and Cuba. It became independent from Portugal in 1975. Large parts of the country are controlled by the South African- and US-backed guerrilla force, the National Union for the Total Independence of Angola (UNITA), which is made up mainly of Ovimbundu people. The prospects of a withdrawal of foreign backing and military stalemate indicate a settlement may be close, and a peace agreement was signed in 1991. The oil-producing province of Cabinda is an enclave in Zaire, which does not accept Angola's sovereignty over it. Potentially Africa's richest country, Angola has a wealth of mineral deposits, including the oil produced in Cabinda, on which the economy is heavily dependent, diamonds, and iron ore. Exports include crude oil, petroleum products, coffee, diamonds, and mahogany hardwoods. Agricultural crops include sugar-cane, bananas, palm oil, and tobacco. Industry is limited to food-processing and metal-refining. Electricity is generated mainly from hydroelectric dams. The economy has suffered major disruption from the civil war, which has caused widespread migration, famine, and destitution; it is badly in need of investment in infrastructure. An estimated 800,000 internally displaced people and some 300,000 refugees in Zaire and Zambia are beginning to return home.

Antarctica

Antarctica is the fifth largest and the southernmost continent, with an estimated area of 14,200 sq. km. A primitive native population of animal and plant species exists in the cold climate. There is no permanent human population, though a number of scientific and meteorological stations operate there. Territorial claims have been made on various sectors of Antarctica, defined by longitude, by Norway, Australia, France, New Zealand, Argentina, Chile, and the UK, with overlapping claims by the last three. All claims were suspended by the Antarctic Treaty of 1959, signed additionally by the USA, former Soviet Union, Belgium, Japan, and South Africa. The Treaty has since been ratified by other countries. The Treaty provides for a free and demilitarized continent, and encourages co-operative scientific research and exploration between countries. A variety of international programmes has since been undertaken. Antarctica is a nuclear-free zone, with weapons-testing and waste disposal expressly forbidden. The Treaty also established the continent as a conservation area for flora and fauna. A 50-year ban on all minerals exploration was agreed in 1991. Among recent scientific discoveries have been the remains of a large number of meteorites, and the first observation of the thinning of the ozone layer was made there in the mid-1980s.

Antigua and Barbuda

Antigua and Barbuda

CAPITAL Saint John's
AREA 441.6 km² (170.5 sq. mi.)

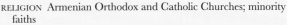

POPULATION 78,400 (1989)
POPULATION GROWTH 1.2% p.a.
GDP PER CAPITA $170 (1985)
CURRENCY 1 East Caribbean dollar =
 100 cents
LIFE EXPECTANCY 70 (male) 74 (female)
POPULATION UNDER 15 YEARS 37.2%
LITERACY RATE 90.0%
RELIGION Anglican 44.5%; other
 Protestant (mainly Moravian, Methodist,
 and Seventh-day Adventist) 41.6%;
 Roman Catholic 10.2%; Rastafarian 0.7%
ETHNIC GROUPS Black 94.4%; Mixed 3.5%; White 1.3%
LANGUAGE English (official); English creole
NUCLEAR CAPACITY No
LABOUR FORCE IN AGRICULTURE 9.0%
MAIN INTERNATIONAL ORGANIZATIONS UN; Commonwealth;
 CARICOM

Antigua and Barbuda is a three-island parliamentary monarchy whose head of state is the UK monarch. It became independent from the UK in 1981. Political life has been dominated since 1956 by the Antigua Labour Party. The mainstay of the economy is up-market tourism. Manufacturing industry includes clothing and the assembly of electrical components for re-export. Agriculture has been neglected, resulting in dependence on food imports, which exacerbates the high foreign debt.

Argentina

República Argentina
CAPITAL Buenos Aires
AREA 2,780,092 km² (1,073,399 sq. mi.)
POPULATION 32.425 million (1989)
POPULATION GROWTH 1.5% p.a.
GDP PER CAPITA $2,759 (1988)
CURRENCY 1 dollar = 1,000 austral
LIFE EXPECTANCY 67 (male) 74 (female)
POPULATION UNDER 15 YEARS 29.9%
LITERACY RATE 95.5% (1985)

RELIGION Roman Catholic 92.0%; Protestant 3.0%; Jewish 2.0%
ETHNIC GROUPS White, mainly Spanish and Italian extraction
 85.0%; Mestizo, Amerindian and other 15.0%
LANGUAGE Spanish (official); Italian; Amerindian languages
NUCLEAR CAPACITY Civil and research (7 reactors)
LABOUR FORCE IN AGRICULTURE 10.9% (1988)
MAIN INTERNATIONAL ORGANIZATIONS UN; OAS; Non-Aligned
 Movement

Argentina is a multiparty republic which emerged from a period of repressive military rule in 1983. Both president and vice-president must be Roman Catholic. There is a territorial dispute with the UK over the Falkland Islands (Malvinas), and a portion of the Antarctic continent, and with Chile over the Argentine territory of Tierra del Fuego. Argentina's coastal areas are densely populated with almost one-third of the population concentrated in Buenos Aires. The principal exports are agricultural products such as cereals, soya beans, and meat, but there is also a broad range of manufacturing industry, of which petroleum products and chemicals are significant exports. A high percentage of agricultural land is taken up by large cattle-raising estates. Argentina has some oil and natural gas deposits whose exploitation is important to the development of industry. There is also a long-standing programme to develop nuclear technology. In recent years government policies, including extensive privatization, have successfully reduced very high rates of inflation.

Armenia

Haikakan Hanrapetoutioun
CAPITAL Yerevan
AREA 29,766 km² (11,490 sq. mi.)
POPULATION 3.5 million
CURRENCY rouble

RELIGION Armenian Orthodox and Catholic Churches; minority
 faiths
ETHNIC GROUPS Armenian 93.0%; Azeri 2.0%; Russian and Kurdish
 minorities
LANGUAGE Armenian (official); Russian; minority languages
MAIN INTERNATIONAL ORGANIZATIONS UN; Commonwealth of
 Independent States; CSCE; North Atlantic Co-operation Council

Armenia is a republic. Formerly a Soviet republic, it became fully independent on the dissolution of the Soviet Union in late 1991. However, it remains economically interdependent with the other former Soviet republics. Armenia is forming its own army, in part as a result of conflict in neighbouring Azerbaijan between Armenians and Azeris in the autonomous region of Nagorno Karabagh, which has a predominantly Armenian population. The region of Nakhichevan is an enclave within Armenia which is controlled by Azerbaijan. Mineral resources include copper, lead, and zinc, and there has been rapid industrial expansion, particularly in mechanical engineering, chemicals production, and mining. Agriculture, which includes cotton, rice, tobacco, fruit, and viticulture, remains important. There is considerable hydroelectric potential, but Armenia is dependent on imports for its other energy requirements.

Aruba

Aruba
CAPITAL Oranjestad
AREA 193 km² (75 sq. mi.)
POPULATION 61,300 (1989)
POPULATION GROWTH −0.7% p.a.
 (negative)
GDP PER CAPITA $8,480 (1987)
CURRENCY 1 Aruban florin = 100 cents
LIFE EXPECTANCY 72 (male) 77 (female)
POPULATION UNDER 15 YEARS 25.9%

LITERACY RATE 95.0% (1985)
RELIGION Roman Catholic 88.5%; Protestant 7.4%; other Christian
 1.1%
ETHNIC GROUPS Mostly Netherlands Antillean
 (Dutch/Spanish/Black/Amerindian) Creole
LANGUAGE Dutch (official); Papiamento (a creole language)
NUCLEAR CAPACITY No
LABOUR FORCE IN AGRICULTURE 0.2% (1981)

Aruba is an autonomous territory of The Netherlands. It has full control of internal affairs and is due to become independent in 1996. Tourism is the dominant sector of the economy; Aruba's oil refinery closed in 1985, leaving the economy dependent on Dutch aid. There is some light industry.

Atlantic Islands

Saint Helena is a UK colony which includes the dependencies of Ascension, Tristan da Cunha, Inaccessible, and Nightingale Islands. Economic activity is limited since there are no industries or minerals, and agriculture is restricted. The labour-force is employed mainly by a US air and missile base, and at telecommunications and weather stations. English is spoken, and the Anglican faith predominates. South Georgia and the South Sandwich Islands have been UK territories since 1985, with executive power vested in the Falkland Islands Commissioner. There is no permanent population. A small UK military garrison is stationed on South Georgia, and there is a biological research station on Bird Island.

Australia

Commonwealth of Australia

CAPITAL Canberra
AREA 7,682,300 km² (2,966,200 sq. mi.)
POPULATION 16.804 million (1989)
POPULATION GROWTH 1.4% p.a.
GDP PER CAPITA $14,083 (1988)
CURRENCY 1 Australian dollar = 100 cents
LIFE EXPECTANCY 73 (male) 80 (female)
POPULATION UNDER 15 YEARS 22.2%
LITERACY RATE 99.5% (1980)
RELIGION Anglican 26.1%; Roman Catholic 26.0%; other Protestant
    20.8%; Eastern Orthodox, Muslim, Jewish, and Buddhist
    minorities
ETHNIC GROUPS native-born 78.2% (of which 1.5% Aboriginal);
    country of origin of foreign-born: UK 7.2%; Asia and Middle East
    3.9%; New Zealand 1.9%; Italy 1.6%; Africa and Americas 1.5%;
    Yugoslavia 1.0%; Greece 1.0%
LANGUAGE English (official); minority and Aboriginal languages
NUCLEAR CAPACITY 2 research reactors; uranium producer
LABOUR FORCE IN AGRICULTURE 5.3% (1988)
MAIN INTERNATIONAL ORGANIZATIONS UN; OECD; Colombo Plan;
    ANZUS Pact; South Pacific Commission; Commonwealth

Australia is a multiparty parliamentary monarchy whose head of
state is the UK monarch. There is a federal constitution and a government for each of its eight states and territories. The federal government
has responsibility for finance, external affairs, immigration, and communications, and the state governments have responsibility for health,
education, law and order, and public utilities. Over 80 per cent of Aus-
tralians are city-dwellers, mainly along the south-east coast. Australia
has the world's highest rate of home ownership and a high rate of personal savings. The economy is based on mining, agriculture, and industry. Agricultural land, which is periodically devastated by drought,
accounts for 64 per cent of Australia's territory, almost all of this
devoted to cattle and sheep. Australia is the world's leading wool producer and largest beef exporter, as well as being an important wheat
producer. Paramount in mineral production, Australia is the world's
leading exporter of iron ore and aluminium, and highly important in
producing coal, nickel, zinc, and other metals. Domestic crude oil
meets 70 per cent of domestic needs and is also exported. Manufacturing industry is aimed principally at domestic markets, and is comparatively undeveloped and vulnerable to competition from Asian
neighbours. Japan and the USA are Australia's main trading partners,
to which raw materials are supplied. Although Australia's trading relationship with countries of the Pacific Rim and Asia is well established,
the formation of European and American trading blocs is viewed with
concern; there is also recurrent concern over the servicing of a sizeable
foreign debt.

Australian External Territories are South Pacific territories
placed under Australian authority, most of them in 1933. The Cocos
(or Keeling) Islands is a group of some twenty-seven coral islands. West
Island has a European majority, while Home Island has a predominantly Malay population. A small amount of copra is exported. Christmas Island is an electoral district of the Northern Territory, and has
had an island assembly since 1985. The economy is based on the
extraction of phosphates, which are verging on exhaustion. Norfolk
Island has a large degree of self-government, public revenues being
derived largely from tourism and the sale of postage stamps. Forestry is
being developed. Other External Territories include the Heard and
McDonald Islands, the Territory of Ashmore and Cartier Islands, and
the Territory of local Sea Islands. By the Antarctic Treaty of 1959 (see
*Antarctica) Australia agreed to use the Australian Antarctic Territory
to participate in peaceful international scientific investigation. There
are three research stations: Mawson, Wilkes, and Davis.

Austria

Republik Österreich

CAPITAL Vienna
AREA 83,857 km² (32,377 sq. mi.)
POPULATION 7.603 million (1989)
POPULATION GROWTH 0.1% p.a.

Much of the population of **Australia** is concentrated in the coastal
regions. Sophisticated systems such as the flying doctor shown here
provide services for isolated outback communities.

GDP PER CAPITA $16,675 (1988)
CURRENCY 1 Schilling = 100 Groschen
LIFE EXPECTANCY 71 (male) 78 (female)
POPULATION UNDER 15 YEARS 17.6%
LITERACY RATE Virtually 100% (1986)
RELIGION Roman Catholic 84.3%; non-
    religious and atheist 6.0%; Evangelical
    5.6%; Muslim, Jewish, and other
    minorities
ETHNIC GROUPS Austrian 96.1%; Yugoslav
    1.7%; Turkish 0.8%; German 0.5%
LANGUAGE German (official) and minority languages
NUCLEAR CAPACITY 3 research reactors
LABOUR FORCE IN AGRICULTURE 6.3% (1988)
MAIN INTERNATIONAL ORGANIZATIONS UN; OECD; EFTA; Council
    of Europe; CSCE

Austria is a neutral multiparty federal republic of nine states (*Länder*),
each with its own provincial assembly. Forty-one per cent of Austria's
land is under forest, and timber and paper products account for 10 per
cent of exports. The economy is primarily industrial, with agriculture
contributing a mere 3 per cent of GDP. Foreign trade is the mainstay
of the economy, with machinery accounting for over a quarter of
exports. Austria is the world's largest source of high-grade graphite,
and has other mineral deposits, including crude oil, natural gas, and
uranium. Tourism is also important. Austria applied to join the EC in
1989, and trade is largely with Western Europe, especially Germany.
A large portion of the Austrian economy has been in public hands since
World War II, but a privatization programme now aims to enhance
productivity and reduce the large public debt.

Azerbaijan

Azarbaijchan Respublikasy

CAPITAL Baku
AREA 88,606 km² (33,430 sq. mi.)
POPULATION 7.1 million
CURRENCY rouble
RELIGION Shi'i Muslim; minority religions
ETHNIC GROUPS Azeri 83.0%; Armenian
    6.0%; Russian 6.0%
LANGUAGE Azeri Turkish (official);
    Armenian, Russian, and other minority
    languages
MAIN INTERNATIONAL ORGANIZATIONS UN; Commonwealth of
    Independent States; CSCE; North Atlantic Co-operation Council

Azerbaijan is a republic which achieved full independence from the
former Soviet Union following its dissolution in late 1991. It retains a
degree of economic interdependence with the other former Soviet
republics. Azerbaijan has a border dispute with Iran, and a violent dispute with its neighbour Armenia over the status of the predominantly

Armenian autonomous region of Nagorno Karabagh within Azerbaijan. Azerbaijan has sovereignty over the region of Nakhichevan within Armenia. Azerbaijan was the world's leader in petroleum production at the beginning of the 20th century, and has rich mineral resources, including petroleum, gas, and metal ores. Industry concentrates on power, manufacturing, and chemicals production. Cotton and tobacco are the main crops; viticulture is also important.

The Bahamas

The Commonwealth of The Bahamas

CAPITAL Nassau
AREA 13,939 km² (5,382 sq. mi.)
POPULATION 249,000 (1989)
POPULATION GROWTH 1.8% p.a.
GDP PER CAPITA $10,833 (1988)
CURRENCY 1 Bahamian dollar = 100 cents
LIFE EXPECTANCY 67 (male) 74 (female)
POPULATION UNDER 15 YEARS 38.0%
LITERACY RATE 89.0% (1984)
RELIGION Non-Anglican Protestant 55.2%; Anglican 20.1%; Roman Catholic 18.8%
ETHNIC GROUPS Black 72.3%; Mixed 14.2%; White 12.9%
LANGUAGE English (official); English creole; French (Haitian) creole
NUCLEAR CAPACITY No
LABOUR FORCE IN AGRICULTURE 6.7% (1988)
MAIN INTERNATIONAL ORGANIZATIONS UN; OAS; Commonwealth; CARICOM

The Bahamas is a parliamentary monarchy whose head of state is the UK monarch. It became independent from the UK in 1973. Tourism makes a large contribution to the economy, while exports are dominated by petroleum products, refined from imported crude oil. A favourable system of taxation has led to The Bahamas becoming an important financial centre. There is some industry, and shipping has expanded since free-flag status was established in 1976.

Bahrain

Dawlat al-Baḥrayn

CAPITAL Manama
AREA 691 km² (267 sq. mi.)
POPULATION 489,000 (1989)
POPULATION GROWTH 3.7% p.a.
GDP PER CAPITA $7,583 (1988)
CURRENCY 1 Bahrain dinar = 1,000 fils
LIFE EXPECTANCY 69 (male) 73 (female)
POPULATION UNDER 15 YEARS 32.7%
LITERACY RATE 75.1% (1986)
RELIGION Shīʿī Muslim 60.0%; Sunnī Muslim 40.0%; Christian minority
ETHNIC GROUPS Bahraini Arab 68.0%; Iranian, Indian, and Pakistani 24.7%; other Arab 4.1%; European 2.5%
LANGUAGE Arabic (official) and minority languages
NUCLEAR CAPACITY No
LABOUR FORCE IN AGRICULTURE 1.9% (1988)
MAIN INTERNATIONAL ORGANIZATIONS UN; Arab League; OAPEC; OPEC; GCC

Bahrain is an absolute emirate. Although the ruling family is Sunnī, about 60 per cent of Bahrainis are Shīʿī. The country's exports are dominated by crude oil and petroleum products from a large oil refinery on Bahrain Island. An aluminium smelter constitutes the largest non-oil industry in the Gulf; there is also a growing banking and communications sector. Shipbuilding and repair in dry docks are also significant. Islam is the state religion. There is an array of social services: medical care is free, as is schooling to technical college level.

Bangladesh

Gana Prajātantrī Bangladesh

CAPITAL Dhaka
AREA 143,998 km² (55,598 sq. mi.)
POPULATION 110.29 million (1989)
POPULATION GROWTH 2.0% p.a.
GDP PER CAPITA $179 (1988)
CURRENCY 1 Bangladesh taka = 100 paisa
LIFE EXPECTANCY 51 (male) 50 (female)
POPULATION UNDER 15 YEARS 43.9%
LITERACY RATE 33.1% (1985)
RELIGION Muslim 86.6%; Hindu 12.1%; Buddhist 0.6%; Christian 0.3%
ETHNIC GROUPS Bengali 97.7%; Bihārī 1.3%; minority tribes 1.0%;
LANGUAGE Bengali (official) 99.0%; Urdu; Bihārī; Hindi
NUCLEAR CAPACITY No
LABOUR FORCE IN AGRICULTURE 69.9% (1988)
MAIN INTERNATIONAL ORGANIZATIONS UN; Commonwealth; Colombo Plan

Bangladesh is a multiparty republic subject to military interventions and political instability. The forced resignation and subsequent arrest of the president in 1990 paved the way for the first fully free elections since 1982. The country grows 70 per cent of the world's supply of jute, and jute products are an important export, despite falling world demand. Other exports include clothing, shrimp, and leather goods. Industry is limited; the economy is primarily agrarian, with rice the most important food crop. There are substantial undeveloped reserves of oil, coal, and natural gas. The country is one of the world's poorest and most densely populated, being subject to frequent devastation by cyclones and flooding, and it relies heavily on foreign aid.

Barbados

Barbados

CAPITAL Bridgetown
AREA 430 km² (166 sq. mi.)
POPULATION 255,000 (1989)
POPULATION GROWTH 0.3% p.a.
GDP PER CAPITA $5,840 (1988)
CURRENCY 1 Barbados dollar = 100 cents
LIFE EXPECTANCY 71 (male) 77 (female)
POPULATION UNDER 15 YEARS 25.3%
LITERACY RATE 98.0%
RELIGION Anglican 39.7%; non-religious 17.5%; Pentecostal 7.6%; Methodist 7.1%; Roman Catholic 4.4%
ETHNIC GROUPS Black 80.0%; Mixed 16.0%; White 4.0%
LANGUAGE English (official)
NUCLEAR CAPACITY No
LABOUR FORCE IN AGRICULTURE 7.2% (1988)
MAIN INTERNATIONAL ORGANIZATIONS UN; OAS; CARICOM; Commonwealth

Barbados is an island parliamentary monarchy whose head of state is the UK monarch. It became independent from the UK in 1966. The principal economic activity is tourism, but agriculture, with sugar-cane the main crop, remains important, and limited manufacturing industry includes food-processing, clothing, and assembly work. Offshore petroleum and natural gas reserves make an important contribution to the economy, and there is a developing services sector.

Belarus (Belorussia)

Respublika Belarus

CAPITAL Minsk
AREA 207,600 km² (80,134 sq. mi.)
POPULATION 10.3 million
CURRENCY rouble/Belorussian coupons
RELIGION Eastern Orthodox Church
ETHNIC GROUPS Belorussian 78.0%; Russian 13.0%; Ukrainian, Polish, and Jewish minorities
LANGUAGE Belorussian (official); Russian and minority languages
NUCLEAR CAPACITY Defence and civil
MAIN INTERNATIONAL ORGANIZATIONS UN; Commonwealth of Independent States; CSCE; North Atlantic Co-operation Council

Belarus is a republic which bcame fully independent following the dissolution of the former Soviet Union in late 1991. Petroleum reserves in the south of the country are exploited, but other mineral resources are meagre. Industry is well developed: Belarus was the major Soviet supplier of heavy engineering equipment, transport and agricultural equipment, electronic and consumer goods, chemicals, timber, and textiles. Much industry was dependent on processing raw materials from other parts of the former Soviet Union, and Belarus is seeking new sources of supply and new markets for its finished goods. Peat is used to generate electricity, but much of Belarus's energy requirements are.met by imports. Agriculture concentrates on livestock- and dairy-farming, potatoes, sugar-beet, and flax.

Belgium

Koninkrijk België/Royaume de Belgique

CAPITAL Brussels
AREA 30,518 km² (11,783 sq. mi.)
POPULATION 9.878 million (1989)
POPULATION GROWTH 0.0% p.a.
GDP PER CAPITA $15,394 (1988)
CURRENCY 1 Belgian franc = 100 centimes
LIFE EXPECTANCY 72 (male) 78 (female)
POPULATION UNDER 15 YEARS 18.1%
LITERACY RATE Virtually 100% (1988)
RELIGION Roman Catholic 90.0%; Muslim 1.1%; Protestant 0.4%
ETHNIC GROUPS Belgian 91.1%; Italian 2.8%; Moroccan 1.1%; French 1.1%; Dutch, Turkish, and other minorities
LANGUAGE Flemish, French, German (all official); Italian
NUCLEAR CAPACITY Civil and research (12 reactors)
LABOUR FORCE IN AGRICULTURE 2.4% (1987)
MAIN INTERNATIONAL ORGANIZATIONS UN; EC; NATO; OECD; Council of Europe; CSCE

Belgium is a parliamentary monarchy. Three linguistically based regional assemblies provide a measure of autonomy for the nine provinces. Belgium is divided linguistically between the Dutch- (or Flemish-) speaking north, the French-speaking (Walloon) south, and the small German enclave on the eastern frontier. Brussels is officially bilingual. The constitution requires equal numbers of French- and Flemish-speakers in the government. Manufacturing industries such as steel, textiles, engineering, and chemicals dominate the economy, but service industries are of increasing importance due to the location of the EC's headquarters in Brussels. Other than coal, Belgium has no natural resources, and processes imported raw materials. Major exports include steel, chemicals, motor vehicles, and foodstuffs. Agriculture is limited to production for the domestic market.

Belize

Belize

CAPITAL Belmopan
AREA 22,965 km² (8,867 sq. mi.)
POPULATION 185,000 (1989)
POPULATION GROWTH 2.6% p.a. (1987)
GNP PER CAPITA $1,250 (1987) (GDP n.a.)
CURRENCY 1 Belize dollar = 100 cents
LIFE EXPECTANCY 66 (male) 71 (female)
POPULATION UNDER 15 YEARS 44.5%
LITERACY RATE 93.0% (1985)
RELIGION Roman Catholic 62.0%; Anglican 12.0%; Methodist 6.0%
ETHNIC GROUPS Creole (predominantly Black) 40.0%; Mestizo (Maya-Spanish) 33.0%; Garifuna 8.0%; Maya 7.0%; European 4.0%; Ketchi 3.0%; East Indian 2.0%
LANGUAGE English (official); English creole; Spanish; Mayan; Garifuna
NUCLEAR CAPACITY No
LABOUR FORCE IN AGRICULTURE 27.6% (1983–4)
MAIN INTERNATIONAL ORGANIZATIONS UN; Commonwealth; CARICOM

Belize is a parliamentary monarchy whose head of state is the UK monarch. Belize's neighbour Guatemala has not yet recognized its independence (1981), and a long-standing claim to Belize's entire ter-ritory is in abeyance. Belize has a predominantly agricultural economy. Industry is limited mainly to food-processing, and the chief exports are processed sugar, clothing, and citrus products. Tourism is another important source of revenue.

Benin

République Populaire de Bénin

CAPITAL Porto Novo
AREA 112,600 km² (43,450 sq. mi.)
POPULATION 4.592 million (1989)
POPULATION GROWTH 3.2% p.a.
GDP PER CAPITA $389 (1988)
CURRENCY 1 CFA franc = 100 centimes
LIFE EXPECTANCY 45 (male) 48 (female)
POPULATION UNDER 15 YEARS 47.5%
LITERACY RATE 28.0% (1980)
RELIGION Traditional beliefs 61.4%; Roman Catholic 18.5%; Muslim 15.2%; Protestant 2.8%
ETHNIC GROUPS Fon-Ewe 55.5%; Bargu 22.5%; Yoruba 13.6%
LANGUAGE French (official); Fon-Ewe; Bargu; Yoruba
NUCLEAR CAPACITY No
LABOUR FORCE IN AGRICULTURE 63.3% (1988)
MAIN INTERNATIONAL ORGANIZATIONS UN; OAU; Non-Aligned Movement; ECOWAS; Franc Zone

Benin is a multiparty republic which held its first free elections in 1991. It became independent from France in 1960. A Marxist–Leninist one-party state from 1974 to 1990, Benin is making the transition to a free market economy, with World Bank and IMF support. Benin has an agricultural economy, with exports of cocoa, cotton, and palm products. There is some light industry, especially food-processing, brewing, and palm-oil processing. There are mineral deposits of off-shore oil, chromium, and phosphates; oil production began in 1982, but has disappointed expectations.

Bermuda

Bermuda

CAPITAL Hamilton
AREA 54 km² (21 sq. mi.)
POPULATION 58,800 (1989)
POPULATION GROWTH 0.9% p.a. (1988)
GNP PER CAPITA $23,100 (1986–7) (GDP n.a.)
CURRENCY 1 Bermuda dollar = 100 cents
LIFE EXPECTANCY 69 (male) 77 (female) (1987)
POPULATION UNDER 15 YEARS 21.3%
LITERACY RATE 96.9% (1980)
RELIGION Anglican 37.3%; Methodist 16.3%; Roman Catholic 13.8%; non-religious 7.8%
ETHNIC GROUPS Black 61.3%; White 37.3%
LANGUAGE English (official)
NUCLEAR CAPACITY No
LABOUR FORCE IN AGRICULTURE 1.4% (1988)
MAIN INTERNATIONAL ORGANIZATIONS Commonwealth

Bermuda is a UK colony with self-government, except in security matters and external affairs. Tourism is the most important industry, while medical products account for over half of total exports. International finance and insurance flourish due to low levels of taxation and well-developed communications systems. Over 10 per cent of Bermuda's land is occupied by US military and naval bases.

Bhutan

Druk-Yul

CAPITAL Thimphu
AREA 47,000 km² (18,150 sq. mi.)
POPULATION 1.408 million (1989)
POPULATION GROWTH 2.1% p.a.

Tin miners at Cerro Rico mine, Potusi, **Bolivia**. For a period in the 1980s, the nationalized mining industry was managed by the unions, but after 1985 a series of measures of economic liberalization included privatization, closure, or rental of many mines, leading to the loss of thousands of jobs.

GDP PER CAPITA $197 (1988)
CURRENCY 1 ngultrum = 100 chetrum
  (Indian rupee also legal tender)
LIFE EXPECTANCY 45 (male) 47 (female)
POPULATION UNDER 15 YEARS 39.7%
LITERACY RATE 18.0% (1977)
RELIGION Buddhist 69.6%; Hindu 24.6%;
  Muslim 5.0%
ETHNIC GROUPS Bhutia 62.5%; Gerung
  15.5%; Assamese 13.2%
LANGUAGE Dzongkha (a Tibetan dialect) (official); Gurung; Assamese
NUCLEAR CAPACITY No
LABOUR FORCE IN AGRICULTURE 91.1% (1988)
MAIN INTERNATIONAL ORGANIZATIONS UN; Colombo Plan; Non-
  Aligned Movement

Bhutan is a parliamentary monarchy. India, the major export destination, guides foreign policy and provides an annual subsidy. Tourism is significant in a largely agricultural economy with some light industry. Only about 9 per cent of Bhutan's mountainous territory is cultivated; the chief crops are rice, maize, and fruit. Principal exports are electricity and wood products.

Bolivia

República de Bolivia

CAPITAL La Paz (administrative); Sucre
  (judicial)
AREA 1,098,581 km² (424,164 sq. mi.)
POPULATION 7.193 million (1989)
POPULATION GROWTH 2.8% p.a.
GDP PER CAPITA $858 (1988)
CURRENCY 1 boliviano = 100 centavos
LIFE EXPECTANCY 51 (male) 55 (female)
POPULATION UNDER 15 YEARS 43.9%
LITERACY RATE 65.8% (1987)

RELIGION Roman Catholic 92.5%; Bahā'ī 2.6%
ETHNIC GROUPS Mestizo 31.0%; Quechua 25.0%; Aymara 17.0%;
  White (mainly Spanish extraction) 15.0%
LANGUAGE Spanish, Aymara, Quechua (all official)
NUCLEAR CAPACITY No
LABOUR FORCE IN AGRICULTURE 42.5% (1988)
MAIN INTERNATIONAL ORGANIZATIONS UN; OAS; Andean Group

Bolivia is a multiparty republic which has suffered protracted political instability and periods of military rule. Landlocked, it claims a strip of land on the Chilean coast, which would give direct access to the Pacific. Mining is the principal industry, and Bolivia is developing its capacity to smelt mineral ore. Other industry includes chemicals, textiles, and food-processing. Natural gas accounts for 60 per cent of exports, while tin, of which Bolivia is one of the world's largest producers, provides another 30 per cent. Bolivia produces enough petroleum for internal consumption. Agriculture is the mainstay of the economy despite periodic droughts and floods. Principal crops are sugar-cane, potatoes, and maize. The coca plant, from the leaves of which the drug cocaine is produced, grows freely; it is smuggled to Colombia for processing. Bolivia's economy has suffered from fluctuating commodity prices, especially for tin, a large external debt, high inflation, and lack of investment.

Bosnia-Herzegovina

Republika Bosna i Hercegovina

CAPITAL Sarajevo
AREA 51,129 km² (19,741 sq. mi.)
POPULATION 4.3 million
CURRENCY dinar
RELIGION Muslim 44.0%; Eastern Ortho-
  dox 31.0%; Roman Catholic 17.0%
ETHNIC GROUPS Muslim Slav 44.0%; Serb
  31.0%; Croat 17.0%
LANGUAGE Serbo-Croat (official)

Bosnia-Herzegovina is a republic which gained independence from Yugoslavia in early 1992. There is civil war between the Eastern Orthodox Serbian population, which opposed independence and has set up its own Serbian autonomous provinces, and the Muslim and Roman Catholic Croat populations which voted for independence in a referendum in early 1992. Talks under EC auspices seek a confederal solution, devolving power to Muslim, Serb, and Croat cantons. However, the Croat population of western Herzegovina favours union with Croatia, as do some of the Serb population with Serbia. The poorest of the former Yugoslav republics, Bosnia-Herzegovina has a variety of mineral resources, including coal, iron, copper, chrome, manganese, cinnabar, zinc, and mercury. Much of the land is mountainous and under forest. Livestock and sheep are raised, and the principal crops are cereals, fruits, citrus, and tobacco. Industry comprises mining, steelworks, and oil refineries. Many Bosnians are migrant workers in Western Europe.

Botswana

Botswana (Tswana)/Republic of Botswana

CAPITAL Gaborone
AREA 581,730 km² (224,607 sq. mi.)
POPULATION 1.25 million (1989)
POPULATION GROWTH 3.7% p.a.
GDP PER CAPITA $1,488 (1988)
CURRENCY 1 pula = 100 thebe
LIFE EXPECTANCY 56 (male) 62 (female)
POPULATION UNDER 15 YEARS 48.5%
LITERACY RATE 71.0% (1985)
RELIGION Traditional beliefs 49.2%; Protestant 29.0%; African
  Christian 11.8%; Roman Catholic 9.4%
ETHNIC GROUPS Tswana 97.0%; Shona, !Kung San (Bushmen),
  Khoikhoin (Hottentot), and Ndebele minorities
LANGUAGE Tswana, English (both official); Shona and local
  languages
NUCLEAR CAPACITY No
LABOUR FORCE IN AGRICULTURE 43.2% (1985)
MAIN INTERNATIONAL ORGANIZATIONS UN; OAU; SADCC; Non-
  Aligned Movement; Commonwealth

Botswana is a multiparty republic with a national assembly complemented by an advisory house of chiefs. It became independent from the UK in 1966. Diamonds are the chief export, producing revenues which have supported a high growth rate, making Botswana the world's fastest growing economy in the post-war period. It is thought that further mineral wealth awaits discovery; other exports are copper-nickel matte and beef. Agriculture is mainly pastoral, but recent droughts have decimated cattle herds. A large proportion of the work-force is employed in South African mines. Landlocked, Botswana depends on South Africa for much of its trade and imports. It is part of the Southern African Customs Union.

Brazil

República Federativa do Brasil

CAPITAL Brasília
AREA 8,511,965 km² (3,286,488 sq. mi.)
POPULATION 147.404 million (1989)
POPULATION GROWTH 2.2% p.a.
GDP PER CAPITA $2,451 (1988)
CURRENCY 1 cruzeiro = 100 centavos
LIFE EXPECTANCY 62 (male) 68 (female)
POPULATION UNDER 15 YEARS 35.2%
LITERACY RATE 79.3% (1986)
RELIGION Roman Catholic 87.8%; Protestant 6.1%
ETHNIC GROUPS Mulatto 22.0%; Portuguese 15.0%; Mestizo 12.0%;
  Italian 11.0%; Black 11.0%; Spanish 10.0%; German 3.0%;
  Japanese 0.8%; Amerindian 0.1%
LANGUAGE Portuguese (official); German; Japanese; Italian;
  Amerindian languages
NUCLEAR CAPACITY Civil and research (5 reactors); uranium
  producer
LABOUR FORCE IN AGRICULTURE 25.6% (1988)
MAIN INTERNATIONAL ORGANIZATIONS UN; OAS

Brazil is a multiparty federal republic consisting of twenty-three states, three federal territories, and one federal district. Each state has a governor and its own assembly. The 1988 constitution enhanced the powers of the Congress and transferred substantial financial control to the states, while the military retained significant influence. A huge,

newly industrialized country, Brazil has the eighth largest economy in the world. Industry is concentrated in the centre and south, while the drought-prone north and north-east remain undeveloped. The destruction of up to 12 per cent of the vast Amazon rain forests causes world-wide concern. Agriculture has been neglected in favour of industry and food imports have increased, but crops such as sugar and cocoa and agricultural exports such as coffee, soya beans, and orange concentrates remain important. Tin, iron ore, machinery, and other industrial products now account for more than half of all exports. Brazil also has one of the world's largest capacities for hydroelectric power production and valuable mineral deposits: it is the largest Western producer of chrome ore and the world's only commercially viable source of high-grade crystal quartz. There is a programme to develop nuclear technology which goes back to the late 1960s. High inflation, a massive foreign debt, and extreme inequalities in wealth distribution have restricted economic growth and led to severe social problems including an estimated 3 million street children.

Brunei

Negara Brunei Darussalam

CAPITAL Bandar Seri Begawan
AREA 5,765 km² (2,226 sq. mi.)
POPULATION 251,000 (1989)
POPULATION GROWTH 2.8% p.a. (1988)
GNP PER CAPITA $15,400 (1986) (GDP n.a.)
CURRENCY 1 Brunei dollar = 100 cents
LIFE EXPECTANCY 70 (male) 73 (female)
  (1986)
POPULATION UNDER 15 YEARS 36.7%
LITERACY RATE 80.3% (1984)
RELIGION Muslim 63.4%; Buddhist 14.0%; Christian 9.7%
ETHNIC GROUPS Malay 68.8%; Chinese 18.3%; Indian and other
  7.9%; other indigenous 5.0%;
LANGUAGE Malay, English (both official); Chinese; minority language
NUCLEAR CAPACITY No
LABOUR FORCE IN AGRICULTURE 3.5% (1986)
MAIN INTERNATIONAL ORGANIZATIONS UN; Commonwealth;
  ASEAN

Brunei is an absolute monarchy. Political parties, but not elections, are permitted; the Sultan effectively has supreme political and executive powers. The state religion is Islam, and there are plans to bring the legal system into line with Islamic teaching. The economy is almost entirely dependent on oil and natural gas, with one of the world's largest gas liquefaction plants.

Bulgaria

Republika Bŭlgaria

CAPITAL Sofia
AREA 110,994 km² (42,855 sq. mi.)
POPULATION 8.987 million (1989)
POPULATION GROWTH 0.1% p.a.
GDP PER CAPITA $2,217 (1988)
CURRENCY 1 lev = 100 stotinki
LIFE EXPECTANCY 69 (male) 75 (female)
POPULATION UNDER 15 YEARS 20.0%
LITERACY RATE 95.5% (1980)
RELIGION atheist 64.5%; Eastern Orthodox 26.7%; Muslim 7.5%;
  Protestant 0.7%; Roman Catholic 0.5%
ETHNIC GROUPS Bulgarian 85.3%; Turkish 8.5%; gypsy 2.6%;
  Macedonian 2.5%; Armenian 0.3%; Russian 0.2%
LANGUAGE Bulgarian (official); Turkish; Romany; Macedonian;
  minority languages
NUCLEAR CAPACITY Civil and research (6 reactors)
LABOUR FORCE IN AGRICULTURE 20.1% (1987)
MAIN INTERNATIONAL ORGANIZATIONS UN; CSCE; North Atlantic
  Co-operation Council

Bulgaria is a multiparty republic, which was formerly a communist republic closely allied to the Soviet Union. The first free elections were held in 1990, following a wave of mass popular demonstrations. An economic reform programme with IMF support started in 1991, permitting private ownership of land, the return of collectivized land to former owners, and the privatization of small businesses. The reforms have caused increased hardship for the Bulgarian population, already subject to food shortages; the removal of subsidies has led to higher prices for basic commodities, despite compensatory wage increases. Bulgaria's mineral resources include coal, iron ore, copper, lead, zinc, and petroleum from the Black Sea. Agricultural products include wheat, maize, barley, sugar-beet, grapes, and tobacco, which are exported along with wine and spirits. Manufacturing industry specializes in electrical and transport equipment, steel, and chemicals; plans to introduce high-technology production units have so far been unsuccessful. Tourism is a significant source of revenue. Attempts to impose the Bulgarian language and culture on the Turkish minority resulted in the emigration to Turkey of some 300,000 in 1989, leading to labour shortages; about one-sixth have since returned.

Burkina Faso

Burkina Faso

CAPITAL Ouagadougou
AREA 274,200 km² (105,869 sq. mi.)
POPULATION 8.714 million (1989)
POPULATION GROWTH 2.8% p.a.
GDP PER CAPITA $204 (1988)
CURRENCY 1 CFA franc = 100 centimes
LIFE EXPECTANCY 46 (male) 49 (female)
POPULATION UNDER 15 YEARS 43.8%
LITERACY RATE 13.2% (1985)
RELIGION Traditional beliefs 65.0%; Muslim 25.0%; Roman Catholic 9.8%; Protestant 2.4%
ETHNIC GROUPS Mossi 47.9%; Mande 8.8%; Fulani 8.3%; Lobi 6.9%; Bobo 6.8%; Senufo 6.0%; Grunshi 5.0%; Bunasi 5.0%; Gurma 4.5%
LANGUAGE French (official); Mossi; Dyula; Fulani; Lobi; local languages
NUCLEAR CAPACITY No
LABOUR FORCE IN AGRICULTURE 84.9% (1988)
MAIN INTERNATIONAL ORGANIZATIONS UN; OAU; Non-Aligned Movement; Franc Zone; ECOWAS

Burkina Faso is a landlocked republic which held multiparty elections in late 1991, which were boycotted by the opposition. It became independent from France in 1960. It is one of the poorest countries in the world, heavily dependent on western aid. The economy is mainly agricultural and vulnerable to drought, with most of the population engaged in subsistence agriculture. The major exports are cotton and gold. There is some industry, mostly state-owned, with largely unexploited mineral deposits of gold, manganese, and zinc. Many Burkinabé seek employment abroad.

Burundi

Republika y'u Burundi (Rundi)/
République du Burundi

CAPITAL Bujumbura
AREA 27,834 km² (10,747 sq. mi.)
POPULATION 5.287 million (1989)
POPULATION GROWTH 2.9% p.a.
GDP PER CAPITA $214 (1988)
CURRENCY 1 Burundi franc = 100 centimes
LIFE EXPECTANCY 47 (male) 51 (female)
POPULATION UNDER 15 YEARS 45.6%
LITERACY RATE 33.8% (1982)
RELIGION Roman Catholic 62.0%; traditional beliefs 32.0%; Protestant 5.0%; Muslim 1.0%
ETHNIC GROUPS Rundi 96.4% (Hutu 81.9%; Tutsi 13.5%; Twa Pygmy 1.0%)
LANGUAGE Rundi, French (both official); Swahili
NUCLEAR CAPACITY No
LABOUR FORCE IN AGRICULTURE 91.5% (1988)
MAIN INTERNATIONAL ORGANIZATIONS UN; OAU

Burundi is a landlocked military republic. It became independent from Belgium in 1962. Power is in the hands of the minority Tutsi

group, but there have been attempts to bring more Hutu into government to ease tension. The economy depends heavily on coffee exports, with cotton and tea as subsidiary exports. The biggest sector of employment is subsistence agriculture. There are large unexploited nickel deposits, and uranium, vanadium, and gold. Industry is limited. Thousands of Burundians have fled endemic ethnic violence and are refugees in Rwanda.

Cambodia (Kampuchea)

Roat Kampuchea

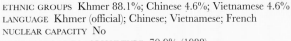

CAPITAL Phnom Penh
AREA 181,035 km² (69,898 sq. mi.)
POPULATION 8.055 million (1989)
POPULATION GROWTH 2.9% p.a.
GDP PER CAPITA $83 (1988)
CURRENCY 1 riel = 100 sen
LIFE EXPECTANCY 47 (male) 58 (female)
POPULATION UNDER 15 YEARS 34.9%
LITERACY RATE 48.0% (1980)
RELIGION Buddhist 88.4%; Muslim 2.4%
ETHNIC GROUPS Khmer 88.1%; Chinese 4.6%; Vietnamese 4.6%
LANGUAGE Khmer (official); Chinese; Vietnamese; French
NUCLEAR CAPACITY No
LABOUR FORCE IN AGRICULTURE 70.9% (1988)
MAIN INTERNATIONAL ORGANIZATIONS UN; Colombo Plan

Cambodia was a one-party socialist republic until 1991, when its 13-year civil war was ended by a UN-brokered peace accord which installed an interim Supreme National Council. The Council represents the former government, which had Vietnamese military backing until 1989, and the three former guerrilla movements: that led by Prince Sihanouk; the Khmer People's National Liberation Front; and the former Khmer Rouge government. Multiparty elections are scheduled for 1993, and a UN peacekeeping force has been installed to supervise the process, and the repatriation of an estimated 345,000 refugees from Thailand and a further 170,000 internally displaced people. Cambodia's economy is overwhelmingly agricultural, and rubber was the main export in the mid-1980s. There is limited light industry. The prolonged civil war and the Khmer Rouge regime's policies of enforced resettlement have decimated agriculture, causing a sharp drop in productivity of rice, the staple crop.

Cameroon

Republic of Cameroon/
République du Cameroun

CAPITAL Yaoundé
AREA 475,458 km² (179,714 sq. mi.)
POPULATION 11.407 million (1989)
POPULATION GROWTH 3.0% p.a.
GDP PER CAPITA $1,135 (1988)
CURRENCY 1 CFA franc = 100 centimes
LIFE EXPECTANCY 49 (male) 53 (female)
POPULATION UNDER 15 YEARS 43.5%
LITERACY RATE 55.2% (1980)
RELIGION Roman Catholic 35.0%; traditional religions 25.0%; Muslim 22.0%; Protestant 18.0%
ETHNIC GROUPS Bamileke 27.0%; Beti-Pahonin 18.0%; Kirdi 15.0%; Fulani 9.5%; Bassa Bakoko 8.0%; Baya Mbum 6.0%
LANGUAGE French, English (both official); Bati-Pahonin, Bamileke, and almost one hundred other languages and dialects
NUCLEAR CAPACITY No
LABOUR FORCE IN AGRICULTURE 62.9% (1988)
MAIN INTERNATIONAL ORGANIZATIONS UN; OAU; Non-Aligned Movement; Franc Zone

Cameroon is a multiparty republic. Following the independence in 1960 of French- and British-mandated territories, it became a one-party republic ruled by the Cameroon People's Democratic Movement until political parties were legalized in 1990. The first multiparty elections, held in 1992, were boycotted by leading opposition parties. Crude oil is the largest export, followed by cocoa and coffee. Mineral deposits include oil and natural gas, gold, uranium, bauxite, nickel, and cobalt. Industries include aluminium smelting (from imported bauxite and alumina), food-processing, and brewing. Fifty per cent of land is under forest, but poor transportation has restricted its development.

Canada

Canada

CAPITAL Ottawa
AREA 9,970,610 km² (3,849,675 sq. mi.)
POPULATION 26.189 million (1989)
POPULATION GROWTH 1.0% p.a.
GDP PER CAPITA $18,834 (1988)
CURRENCY 1 Canadian dollar = 100 cents
LIFE EXPECTANCY 73 (male) 80 (female)
POPULATION UNDER 15 YEARS 20.9%
LITERACY RATE 95.6% (1975)
RELIGION Roman Catholic 46.5%; Protestant 41.2%; non-religious 7.4%; Eastern Orthodox 1.5%; Jewish 1.2%; Muslim 0.4%; Hindu 0.3%; Sikh 0.3%;
ETHNIC GROUPS (by origin) British 34.4%; French 25.7%; German 3.6%; Italian 2.8%; Ukrainian 1.7%; Amerindian and Inuit (Eskimo) 1.5%; Chinese 1.4%; Dutch 1.4%
LANGUAGE English, French (both official)
NUCLEAR CAPACITY Civil and research (32 reactors) uranium producer
LABOUR FORCE IN AGRICULTURE 3.6% (1988)
MAIN INTERNATIONAL ORGANIZATIONS UN; Commonwealth; OECD; NATO; Colombo Plan; OAS; CSCE

Canada is a parliamentary and federal monarchy, with a governor-general appointed by the British monarch. The governor-general in turn appoints members of the federal senate and a lieutenant-governor for each province, acting on the advice of the prime minister. The ten provinces each have a separate legislature and bureaucracy, and a large degree of autonomy in matters such as direct taxation, health, education, highways, and labour law. A separatist movement is strong in French-speaking Quebec. Until 1992 Canada had armed forces stationed in Europe as part of its commitments to NATO. In area the second-largest country in the world and a leading industrial nation, Canada depends on the neighbouring USA, with whom it signed a free-trade agreement in 1989, for about 75 per cent of its trade. Major exports include motor vehicles (assembled from imported components), machinery, crude oil, timber, natural gas, non-ferrous metals, chemicals, and newsprint. Canada is the world's largest producer of zinc, nickel, and uranium and is rich in many other minerals. A little more than half the country's electricity comes from hydroelectric generation. Canadian agriculture is diverse, with extensive grain, dairy, and fruit-farming as well as ranching and fur-farming. Of Canada's native peoples there are half a million Amerindians, about two-thirds of whom live on 2,283 reserves (lands set aside for their use) spread across the country, and some 27,000 Inuit, who live in the far north.

Cape Verde

República de Cabo Verde

CAPITAL Praia
AREA 4,033 km² (1,557 sq. mi.)
POPULATION 359,000
POPULATION GROWTH 2.0% p.a.
GNP PER CAPITA $460 (1986) (GDP n.a.)
CURRENCY Escudo Caboverdiano
LIFE EXPECTANCY 60 (male) 64 (female)
POPULATION UNDER 15 YEARS 45.6%
LITERACY RATE 49.3%
RELIGION Roman Catholic 80.0%; Protestant and other 2.2%
ETHNIC GROUPS Mixed 71.0%; Black 28.0%; White 1.0%
LANGUAGE Portuguese (official); Portuguese creole (crioulo)
NUCLEAR CAPACITY No
LABOUR FORCE IN AGRICULTURE 33.1%
MAIN INTERNATIONAL ORGANIZATIONS UN; OAU; ECOWAS; Non-Aligned Movement

The Cape Verde Islands are a republic which became independent from Portugal in 1975. There was a one-party system until 1991

when free elections were held. Agriculture and fishing are the main productive sectors, with fish and salt dominating exports. The domestic economy relies heavily on remittances from Cape Verdeans working overseas.

Cayman Islands

Colony of Cayman Islands

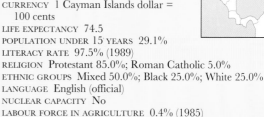

CAPITAL George Town
AREA 264 km² (102 sq. mi.)
POPULATION 25,300 (1989)
POPULATION GROWTH 4.9% p.a.
GDP PER CAPITA $17,390 (1987)
CURRENCY 1 Cayman Islands dollar = 100 cents
LIFE EXPECTANCY 74.5
POPULATION UNDER 15 YEARS 29.1%
LITERACY RATE 97.5% (1989)
RELIGION Protestant 85.0%; Roman Catholic 5.0%
ETHNIC GROUPS Mixed 50.0%; Black 25.0%; White 25.0%
LANGUAGE English (official)
NUCLEAR CAPACITY No
LABOUR FORCE IN AGRICULTURE 0.4% (1985)
MAIN INTERNATIONAL ORGANIZATIONS Commonwealth

Cayman Islands is a UK colony which is largely self-governing. The soil is unable to sustain agriculture, and the main economic activities are tourism and finance, which flourishes in the absence of direct taxation. In 1988 over 16,000 companies were registered in the islands.

Central African Republic

République Centrafricaine

CAPITAL Bangui
AREA 622,436 km² (240,324 sq. mi.)
POPULATION 2.813 million (1989)
POPULATION GROWTH 2.7% p.a.
GDP PER CAPITA $388 (1988)
CURRENCY 1 CFA franc = 100 centimes
LIFE EXPECTANCY 44 (male) 47 (female)
POPULATION UNDER 15 YEARS 43.2%
LITERACY RATE 40.2% (1985)
RELIGION Traditional beliefs 60.0%; Roman Catholic 25.0%; Muslim 9.0%; Protestant 6.0%
ETHNIC GROUPS Banda 31.0%; Baya 29.0%; Mandjia 8.5%
LANGUAGE French (official); Banda; Baya; Sango; local languages
NUCLEAR CAPACITY No
LABOUR FORCE IN AGRICULTURE 64.7% (1988)
MAIN INTERNATIONAL ORGANIZATIONS UN; OAU; Non-Aligned Movement; Franc Zone

The Central African Republic is a landlocked one-party republic where the Rassemblement Démocratique Centrafricain is the sole legal party. It became independent from France in 1960. It is one of Africa's poorer countries, with a largely agricultural economy. There are export crops of coffee, cotton, and hardwood timber, and subsistence crops such as maize, bananas, and cassava, which are often adversely affected by drought. Diamonds, followed by coffee and cotton, constitute the largest export commodity; some gold is mined and uranium extraction is planned. Light industry includes food-processing and the manufacture of cotton fabrics, footwear, and motorcycles.

Chad

République du Tchad

CAPITAL Ndjamena
AREA 1,284,000 km² (495,755 sq. mi.)
POPULATION 5.538 million (1989)
POPULATION GROWTH 2.5% p.a.
GDP PER CAPITA $159 (1988)
CURRENCY 1 CFA franc = 100 centimes
LIFE EXPECTANCY 44 (male) 47 (female)
POPULATION UNDER 15 YEARS 42.8%

LITERACY RATE 17.8% (1980)
RELIGION Muslim 50.0%; traditional beliefs 45.0%; Christian 5.0%
ETHNIC GROUPS Arabic (Hassauna and Djoheina) 46.0%; Sudanic 28.0%; Nilotic 8.0%; Saharan 7.0%
LANGUAGE Arabic, French (both official); Sara; Nilotic; Saharan
NUCLEAR CAPACITY No
LABOUR FORCE IN AGRICULTURE 76.6% (1988)
MAIN INTERNATIONAL ORGANIZATIONS UN; OAU; Non-Aligned Movement; Franc Zone

Chad is a landlocked one-party republic ruled by the Union Nationale pour l'Indépendence et la Révolution. Since independence from France in 1960, there have been frequent civil wars between north and south; Libya's support of the north and virtual annexation of huge areas of territory was defeated only with French and US support (1987). Libya occupies the disputed Aozou strip in the north, which has uranium deposits. Mainly desert, the  north is populated by Arabic-speaking Muslims, while the people of the more economically developed and fertile south are Christian or follow traditional beliefs. Chad is one of the poorest countries in Africa, with a mainly agricultural economy which is vulnerable to drought. Major exports include cotton and livestock products. The industrial sector is small, mostly comprising textiles and food-processing.

Channel Islands

The Channel Islands are dependencies of the British Crown, the two largest islands being Jersey and Guernsey, which have elected parliaments called 'states'. The islands have a *de facto* customs union with the UK. Tourism and international finance are important, favourable tax rates making the islands attractive as a tax haven. The official language is English, although each island has a distinct local French patois.

Chile

República de Chile
CAPITAL Santiago
AREA 756,626 km² (292,135 sq. mi.)
POPULATION 12.961 million (1989)
POPULATION GROWTH 1.7% p.a.
GDP PER CAPITA $1,732 (1988)
CURRENCY 1 peso
LIFE EXPECTANCY 68 (male) 75 (female)
POPULATION UNDER 15 YEARS 30.6%
LITERACY RATE 94.3% (1988)
RELIGION Roman Catholic 80.7%; atheist and non-religious 12.8%; Protestant 6.1%; Jewish 0.2%
ETHNIC GROUPS Mestizo 91.6%; Amerindian (mostly Araucarian) 6.8%; others (mainly European) 1.6%
LANGUAGE Spanish (official); also Amerindian languages (mostly Araucarian)
NUCLEAR CAPACITY Research (2 reactors)
LABOUR FORCE IN AGRICULTURE 13.2% (1988)
MAIN INTERNATIONAL ORGANIZATIONS UN; OAS

Chile is a multiparty republic. Although it has a long history of democratic politics and strong political parties, Chile suffered an extended period of military government from 1973 to 1989, and some restrictions on political activity persist. There is a territorial dispute with Argentina over the status of Tierra del Fuego and the Beagle Channel, now in abeyance. The economy is based largely on exploitation of substantial mineral reserves, and agriculture. Copper accounts for almost half of exports, with other minerals and fruit, fishmeal, and timber products of secondary importance. About 80 per cent of electricity is generated by hydroelectric power, and domestic oil production accounts for about half of total requirements. Manufacturing industry

includes chemicals, brewing, wood-pulping, and tyre manufacture. The country has one of the best public education and social service systems in Latin America, although these suffered under military rule in the 1980s.

China

Zhōnghuá Rénmín Gònghéguó
CAPITAL Beijing
AREA 9,572,900 km² (3,696,100 sq. mi.)
POPULATION 1,133.682 million (1990)
POPULATION GROWTH 1.3% p.a.
GDP PER CAPITA $301 (1988)
CURRENCY 1 Renminbi (yuan) = 10 jiao = 100 fen
LIFE EXPECTANCY 68 (male) 71 (female)
POPULATION UNDER 15 YEARS 26.2%
LITERACY RATE 72.6% (1982)
RELIGION Non-religious 59.2%; Chinese traditional religions 20.1%; atheist 12.0%; Buddhist 6.0%; Muslim 2.4%; Christian 0.2%
ETHNIC GROUPS Han (Chinese) 93.3%; Chuang 1.33%; Hui 0.72%; Uighur 0.59%; Yi 0.54%; Miao 0.5%; Manchu 0.43%; Tibetan 0.39%; Mongolian 0.34%; Tuchia 0.28%; Puyi 0.21%; Korean 0.18%; Tung 0.14%; Yao 0.14%; Pai 0.11%; Hani 0.11%; Kazakh 0.09%; Tai 0.08%; Li 0.08%
LANGUAGE Mandarin Chinese (official); six other dialects of Chinese; at least 41 other minority languages
NUCLEAR CAPACITY Defence, civil under construction, and research (12 reactors)
LABOUR FORCE IN AGRICULTURE 60.1% (1988)
MAIN INTERNATIONAL ORGANIZATIONS UN

China is a communist republic with power vested in the National People's Congress, effectively controlled by the Communist Party. A student-led movement calling for greater political freedom and democratic elections was brutally crushed by the army in 1989, an event which coincided with a power struggle within the Communist Party over the political direction of the country. The world's most populous country, China has a highly centralized political system with twenty-two provinces, five autonomous regions with large ethnic minorities, including *Tibet, and three government-controlled municipalities. China claims *Hong Kong, *Macao, and *Taiwan; by treaty with the British Government, Hong Kong reverts to China in 1997. Since the late 1970s China has adopted pragmatic policies of liberalizing the economy. Four Special Economic Zones were established to attract foreign investment, direct state control of factories has been loosened, stockmarkets have been set up, and responsibility for agriculture switched from collective farms to individual households. China's economy is predominantly agricultural, with rice, wheat, and pigs the main products. Agriculture prospers, although there is a need for investment in irrigation and fertilizers. Mineral extraction is important: crude oil is refined and exported, there are large coal, tin, and iron ore deposits, and China leads the world in tungsten ore production. Several nuclear energy plants are under construction. Industry is targeted for expansion, and major industrial products include textiles and clothing, cement, chemicals, steel, and consumer electrical goods. Japan is the main trading partner. Tourism is also of increasing economic importance. There has been an attempt to restrict population growth by limiting couples to one child each; China faces severe ecological problems, such as soil erosion caused by demographic pressure, and degradation of the environment by state enterprises.

Colombia

República de Colombia
CAPITAL Bogotá
AREA 1,141,748 km² (440,831 sq. mi.)
POPULATION 32.317 million (1989)
POPULATION GROWTH 2.1% p.a.
GDP PER CAPITA $1,316 (1988)
CURRENCY 1 peso = 100 centavos
LIFE EXPECTANCY 63 (male) 67 (female)
POPULATION UNDER 15 YEARS 36.2%
LITERACY RATE 69.1% (1985)

RELIGION Roman Catholic 95%
ETHNIC GROUPS Mestizo 58.0%; White 20.0%; Mulatto 14.0%;
 Black 4.0%; mixed Black-Indian 3.0%; Amerindian 1.0%
LANGUAGE Spanish (official); Amerindian languages
NUCLEAR CAPACITY Research (1 reactor)
LABOUR FORCE IN AGRICULTURE 28.9% (1988)
MAIN INTERNATIONAL ORGANIZATIONS UN; OAS; Andean Group

Colombia is a multiparty republic, divided into twenty-three departments, four intendencies, and six commissaries, each with a directly elected legislature and governor appointed by the President. There has been endemic violence from a long-standing guerrilla movement, the most important groups being the FARC (Revolutionary Armed Forces of Colombia) and M-19, which has partly demobilized to join mainstream politics. The illegal production and trade of the drugs cocaine and heroin are major political problems for the government. Colombia has a wide range of agricultural crops and is virtually self-sufficient in food production. Considerable mineral reserves, such as crude oil, coal, natural gas, gold, platinum (one of the world's richest deposits), and precious stones, are substantially under-exploited. Coffee accounts for half of exports, and industrial products such as textiles, iron, chemicals, and petroleum products are also exported. Political instability has deterred much-needed foreign investment, and disrupted agriculture.

Comoros

Jumhurīyat al-Qumur al-Ittihādīyah
 al- Islāmīyah/République Fédéral
 Islamique des Comores

CAPITAL Moroni
AREA 1,862 km² (719 sq. mi.)
POPULATION 448,000 (1989)
POPULATION GROWTH 3.4% p.a.
GNP PER CAPITA $380 (1987) (GDP n.a.)
CURRENCY 1 Comorian franc = 100
 centimes
LIFE EXPECTANCY 53 (male) 57 (female)
POPULATION UNDER 15 YEARS 46.0%
LITERACY RATE 46.3% (1980)
RELIGION Sunnī Muslim 99.7%; Christian 0.2%; Bahā'ī 0.1%
ETHNIC GROUPS Comorian (a mixture of Bantu, Arab, and Malagasy
 peoples) 96.9%; Makua 1.6%; French 0.4%
LANGUAGE Arabic, French (both official); Comoran
NUCLEAR CAPACITY No
LABOUR FORCE IN AGRICULTURE 53.3% (1985)
MAIN INTERNATIONAL ORGANIZATIONS UN; Non-Aligned Movement;
 Franc Zone; OAU

Comoros has been a multiparty federal republic since 1990. Three of its four islands became independent from France in 1975, but Mayotte remains under French administration. Exports are dominated by cloves, vanilla, and essential oils for perfume. Most foodstuffs are imported. France, the main trading partner, provides economic aid, while tourism is being developed by South African investors. There is high unemployment and the country suffers from lack of energy resources. Most of the population speak Comoran, an Arabic version of Swahili.

Congo

République Populaire du Congo
CAPITAL Brazzaville
AREA 342,000 km² (132,047 sq. mi.)
POPULATION 2.245 million (1989)
POPULATION GROWTH 3.6% p.a.
GDP PER CAPITA $1,175 (1988)
CURRENCY 1 CFA franc = 100 centimes
LIFE EXPECTANCY 47 (male) 50 (female)
POPULATION UNDER 15 YEARS 44.0%
LITERACY RATE 62.9% (1985)

RELIGION Traditional religions 47.0%; Roman Catholic 33.0%;
 Protestant 17.0%; Muslim 2.0%
ETHNIC GROUPS Kongo 51.5%; Teke 17.3%; Mboshi 11.5%; Mbete
 7.0%; Sanga 5.0%

LANGUAGE French (official); Kongo; Teke; local languages
NUCLEAR CAPACITY No
LABOUR FORCE IN AGRICULTURE 60.0% (1988)
MAIN INTERNATIONAL ORGANIZATIONS UN; OAU; Non-Aligned
 Movement; Franc Zone

Congo is a socialist republic. It gained independence from France in 1960. The Parti Congolais du Travail was the sole political party until other political parties were legalized in 1991. Crude oil is the principal export, and oil revenues have funded a growing manufacturing base which includes food-processing, textiles, chemicals, and metalwork. Lead, copper, zinc, and gold ore are mined. Cassava, sugar-cane, and pineapples are the chief agricultural crops, and timber is an important export.

Costa Rica

República de Costa Rica

CAPITAL San José
AREA 51,100 km² (19,730 sq. mi.)
POPULATION 2.941 million (1989)
POPULATION GROWTH 2.8% p.a.
GDP PER CAPITA $1,638 (1988)
CURRENCY 1 Costa Rican colón = 100
 céntimos
LIFE EXPECTANCY 72 (male) 77 (female)
POPULATION UNDER 15 YEARS 36.2%
LITERACY RATE 92.6% (1984)
RELIGION Roman Catholic 88.6%; other (mostly Protestant) 11.4%
ETHNIC GROUPS European 87.0%; Mestizo 7.0%; Black/Mulatto
 3.0%; East Asian (mostly Chinese) 2.0%; Amerindian 1.0%
LANGUAGE Spanish (official); other minority languages
NUCLEAR CAPACITY No
LABOUR FORCE IN AGRICULTURE 25.1% (1988)
MAIN INTERNATIONAL ORGANIZATIONS UN; OAS

Costa Rica is a multiparty republic whose constitution forbids the creation of an army. It has a long history of stable, democratic government unusual in Central America; the literacy rate is the highest in Latin America, and Costa Rica does not suffer from the same extremes of poverty and wealth as many of its neighbours. The economy is primarily agricultural, with bananas and coffee the major exports. The chemical and textile industries and cattle-rearing also contribute to the economy. Costa Rica has played an important role in the OAS in attempting to resolve regional conflicts.

Côte d'Ivoire (Ivory Coast)

République de la Côte d'Ivoire
CAPITAL Abidjan (capital designate,
 Yamoussoukvo)
AREA 322,463 km² (124,471 sq. mi.)
POPULATION 12.135 million (1989)
POPULATION GROWTH 4.0% p.a.
GDP PER CAPITA $856 (1988)
CURRENCY 1 CFA franc = 100 centimes
LIFE EXPECTANCY 51 (male) 54 (female)
POPULATION UNDER 15 YEARS 49.4%
LITERACY RATE 57.3% (1985)
RELIGION Traditional beliefs 65.0%; Muslim 23.0%; Christian
 12.0%
ETHNIC GROUPS Akan 27.0%; Mande 24.0%; Kru 18.0%; Senufo
 12.0%; Lagoon 8.0%; Lobi 5.0%
LANGUAGE French (official); Akan; Kru; local languages
NUCLEAR CAPACITY No
LABOUR FORCE IN AGRICULTURE 57.7% (1988)
MAIN INTERNATIONAL ORGANIZATIONS ECOWAS; Non-Aligned
 Movement; OAU; UN; Franc Zone

Côte d'Ivoire is a multiparty republic where the Parti Démocratique de la Côte d'Ivoire, which has dominated politics since independence from France in 1960, held power in the first multiparty elections in 1990. The economy is primarily agricultural, with main exports including cocoa, coffee, cotton, tropical timber, and vegetable oils. Offshore oil reserves are exploited, but output does not meet domestic require-

In the **Côte d'Ivoire** the rainforest is threatened as the search for hardwoods such as ebony and mahogany intensifies. Export of wood has earned valuable foreign exchange since the world price for the country's main exports, cocoa and coffee, plummeted in the late 1970s.

ments. Industries such as oil-refining, food-processing, textiles, and chemicals are well established, and there is a well-developed system of hydraulic electricity production from dams. Mineral deposits include iron, cobalt, bauxite, nickel, manganese, and diamonds.

Croatia

Republika Hrvatska

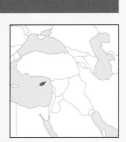

CAPITAL Zagreb
AREA 56,537 km² (21,829 sq. mi.)
POPULATION 4.68 million
CURRENCY Croatian dinar
RELIGION Roman Catholic 75.0%; Eastern Orthodox 12 0%
ETHNIC GROUPS Croat 75.0%; Serb 12 0%
LANGUAGE Serbo-Croat (official)
NUCLEAR CAPACITY Civil
MAIN INTERNATIONAL ORGANIZATIONS CSCE

Croatia is a republic which gained independence from *Yugoslavia in early 1992 following a bitter civil war. The majority of the population are Roman Catholic Croats, but there is a large Eastern Orthodox Serbian minority. The government has offered Serb-dominated regions, such as the enclave of Krajina, a degree of autonomy, but they have refused to accept any Croat control. Conflict between Serbs and Croats became acute in World War II, especially in the Nazi-sponsored puppet state of Croatia, and again in the civil war between Croat separatists and the Serb-dominated Yugoslav federal army, which occupies parts of Croatia. A UN peacekeeping force was installed in early 1992. Croatia has an industrialized economy in which mining, petroleum production, shipbuilding, and other heavy industry are important. Mineral resources include bauxite, petroleum, and natural gas. The civil war has inflicted great damage on·tourism, the principal earner of foreign exchange. The main agricultural products are grains, sugar-beet, and potatoes.

Cuba

República de Cuba

CAPITAL Havana
AREA 110,861 km² (42,804 sq. mi.)

POPULATION 10.54 million (1989)
POPULATION GROWTH 1.0% p.a.
GDP PER CAPITA $2,509 (1988)
CURRENCY 1 Cuban peso = 100 centavos
LIFE EXPECTANCY 72 (male) 76 (female)
POPULATION UNDER 15 YEARS 21.8%
LITERACY RATE 96.0% (1985)
RELIGION Non-religious 48.7%; Roman Catholic 39.6%; atheist 6.4%; Protestant 3.3%; Afro-Cuban syncretist 1.6%
ETHNIC GROUPS White 66.0%; Mixed 21.9%; Black 12.0%
LANGUAGE Spanish (official)
NUCLEAR CAPACITY Civil under construction (2 reactors)
LABOUR FORCE IN AGRICULTURE 20.1% (1988)
MAIN INTERNATIONAL ORGANIZATIONS UN; Non-Aligned Movement; suspended member of OAS

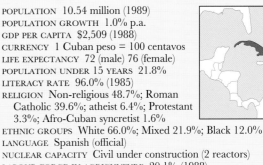

Cuba is a one-party communist republic, dominated since the 1959 revolution by Fidel Castro. Aid from the former Soviet Union enabled Cuba to develop rapidly, but the loss of Soviet aid and trade since the Soviet Union's disintegration in 1991 has had serious consequences on the economy. Since 1959 relations with the USA have been strained. Cuba has the largest military force in Latin America, and has played a role in conflicts in Africa, notably in Angola. Compared to its neighbours, Cuba has a sizeable industrial sector and high standards of social services. The world's second largest producer of sugar, Cuba has a centrally planned economy. Exports have been heavily dependent on sugar (75 per cent in 1975, mainly to the Soviet Union), though nickel and petroleum products (based on the resale of imported Soviet crude oil) have also been important. Agriculture is highly mechanized, and most farms are co-operatively run on state-owned land.

Cyprus

Kipriaki Demokratia (Greek)/Küzey Kibris Türk Cumhuryeti (Turkish)

CAPITAL Nicosia
AREA 9,251 km² (3,572 sq. mi.) (south: 5,896 km² (2,276 sq. mi.)) (north: 3,355 km² (1,295 sq. mi.))
POPULATION 733,000 (combined) 564,000 (south) 169,000 (north)
POPULATION GROWTH 1.0% p.a. (1988)
GDP PER CAPITÀ $7,709 (1988)
CURRENCY south: 1 Cyprus pound = 100 cents; north: 1 Turkish lira = 100 kurush
LIFE EXPECTANCY south: 73 (male) 78 (female); north: n.a.
POPULATION UNDER 15 YEARS 25.4%
LITERACY RATE 94.5% (1987)
RELIGION south: predominantly Greek Orthodox; north: predominantly Muslim
ETHNIC GROUPS south: Greek 99.2%; north: Turkish 98.7%
LANGUAGE south: Greek; north: Turkish (both official)
NUCLEAR CAPACITY No
LABOUR FORCE IN AGRICULTURE south: 13.8%; north: 33.6%
MAIN INTERNATIONAL ORGANIZATIONS south: Council of Europe; UN; Commonwealth; Non-Aligned Movement; CSCE; the north is recognized only by Turkey

Cyprus is a multiparty republic, created in 1960. It has been divided since the Turkish invasion (1974) into the Greek 'Republic of Cyprus' in the south, and the Turkish 'Turkish Republic of Northern Cyprus' in the north. There is a UN peacekeeping force and talks continue under the aegis of the UN to encourage the formation of a federal state. Some 200,000 Greek Cypriots have fled as refugees from the north to the south. In the south, exports of manufactured goods such as clothing, and agricultural products, together with the successful development of tourism, contribute to a thriving economy. The north, by contrast, is primarily agricultural and is dependent on Turkish aid.

Czecho-Slovakia

Česka a Slovenská Federativní Republika (Czech)/Česka a Slovenská Federativna Republika (Slovak)

CAPITAL Prague
AREA 127,900 km² (49,382 sq. mi.)
POPULATION 15.636 million (1989)
POPULATION GROWTH 0.3% p.a.
GDP PER CAPITA $2,737 (1988)
CURRENCY 1 koruna = 100 halura
LIFE EXPECTANCY 68 (male) 75 (female)
POPULATION UNDER 15 YEARS 23.3%
LITERACY RATE virtually 100% (1987)
RELIGION Roman Catholic 65.6%; atheist
  20.1%; Protestant 5.8%
ETHNIC GROUPS Czech 63.0%; Slovak 31.6%; Hungarian 3.8%;
  Polish 0.5%; German 0.4%; Ukrainian 0.3%; Russian 0.1%
LANGUAGE Czech, Slovak (both official); Hungarian; Romany; other
  minority languages
NUCLEAR CAPACITY Civil and research (11 reactors; 8 under
  construction)
LABOUR FORCE IN AGRICULTURE 10.0% (1988)
MAIN INTERNATIONAL ORGANIZATIONS UN; CSCE; Council of
  Europe; North Atlantic Co-operation Council

Czecho-Slovakia is a multiparty federal republic which was a Soviet-dominated communist republic until 1989. The two federal states, the Czech and Slovak republics, each have National Councils, with a degree of autonomy, although the federal assembly retains control over foreign policy, defence, constitutional, and major economic matters. In the economically less developed Slovak republic, there have been calls for secession. IMF resources have been made available to stabilize the transition to a market economy. In 1991, state-owned shops were the first concerns to be privatized, followed by large-scale privatization using a vouchers system, which made enterprises available to both domestic and foreign purchasers. The main mineral resources are brown coal, lignite, copper, and zinc, and large gold deposits have been found. Agriculturally, Czecho-Slovakia is to some extent reliant on imports, although wheat, barley, sugar-beet, and hops are grown, and there is an extensive timber industry. Industry is in urgent need of modernization, and is hampered by the need to import energy, as the potential for hydroelectric power has not yet been exploited. Motor vehicles, glass, beer, ceramics, footwear, and textiles are the main exports.

Denmark

Kongeriget Danmark
CAPITAL Copenhagen
AREA 43,092 km² (16,638 sq. mi.)
POPULATION 5.135 million (1989)
POPULATION GROWTH 0.1% p.a.
GDP PER CAPITA $20,988 (1988)
CURRENCY 1 krone = 100 øre
LIFE EXPECTANCY 73 (male) 78 (female)
POPULATION UNDER 15 YEARS 17.0%
LITERACY RATE Virtually 100% (1986)
RELIGION Evangelical Lutheran 90.6%; Roman Catholic 0.5%;
  Jewish 0.1%
ETHNIC GROUPS Danish 97.2%; Turkish 0.5%; other Scandinavian
  0.4%; British 0.2%; Yugoslav 0.2%
LANGUAGE Danish (official); Turkish; other minority languages
NUCLEAR CAPACITY Research (2 reactors)
LABOUR FORCE IN AGRICULTURE 5.1% (1988)
MAIN INTERNATIONAL ORGANIZATIONS UN; NATO; OECD; EC;
  Council of Europe; CSCE

Denmark is a parliamentary monarchy which includes the outlying territories of the Faeroe Islands and Greenland, both of which have autonomy except in foreign affairs. Denmark has a highly developed system of social security, but, at the same time, has severe balance-of-payments problems and budgetary deficits. Both industry and agriculture are important: agricultural products account for about a quarter of exports, with machinery and chemicals taking another third. Engineering, shipbuilding, petroleum-refining, and furniture manufacture are important industries. In the Faeroe Islands and Greenland fishing is the primary economic activity.

Djibouti

Jumhūrīyah Jībūtī/République
  de Djibouti
CAPITAL Djibouti City
AREA 23,200 km² (8,950 sq. mi.)
POPULATION 390,000 (1989)
POPULATION GROWTH 4.8% p.a.
GNP PER CAPITA $740 per capita (1984)
  (GDP n.a.)
CURRENCY 1 Djibouti franc = 100 centimes
LIFE EXPECTANCY 45 (male) 49 (female)
POPULATION UNDER 15 YEARS 38.4%
LITERACY RATE 33.7% (1987)
RELIGION Sunnī Muslim 94%; Roman Catholic 4%; Protestant 1%;
  Orthodox 1%
ETHNIC GROUPS Somali (Issa 33.4%;; Gadaboursi 15.0%; Issaq
  13.3%;) 61.7%; Afar 20.0%; Arab (mostly Yemeni) 6.0%;
  European 4.0%; other (refugees) 8.3%
LANGUAGE Arabic, French (both official); Somali; minority languages
NUCLEAR CAPACITY No
LABOUR FORCE IN AGRICULTURE 77.5% (1985)
MAIN INTERNATIONAL ORGANIZATIONS UN; OAU; Arab League;
  Non-Aligned Movement

Djibouti is a republic whose sole legal party is the Rassemblement Populaire pour le Progrès. It became independent from France in 1977. The Issa (Somali) majority dominates the government. Trade is the mainstay of the economy; Djibouti City, the capital, is a free port and through its rail link to Addis Ababa handles trade for Ethiopia and other neighbouring African states. The main exports are livestock and foodstuffs. Agriculture is limited to livestock-rearing by the nomadic population, with market-gardening at the Ambouli oasis and near urban areas. In late 1991, there were an estimated 93,000 refugees from Ethiopia and Somalia in Djibouti.

Dominica

Commonwealth of Dominica
CAPITAL Roseau
AREA 750 km² (290 sq. mi.)
POPULATION 82,800 (1989)
POPULATION GROWTH 1.4% p.a.
GNP PER CAPITA $1,440 (GDP n.a.)
CURRENCY 1 East Caribbean dollar = 100
  cents
LIFE EXPECTANCY 64 (male) 69 (female)
POPULATION UNDER 15 YEARS 39.8%
LITERACY RATE 94.9%
RELIGION Roman Catholic 76.9%; Methodist 5.0%; Seventh-day
  Adventist 3.2%; Pentecostal 2.9%
ETHNIC GROUPS Black 91.2%; mixed 6.0%; Amerindian 1.5%; White
  and other 1.3%
LANGUAGE English (official); French creole
NUCLEAR CAPACITY No
LABOUR FORCE IN AGRICULTURE 31% (1981)
MAIN INTERNATIONAL ORGANIZATIONS UN; OAS; CARICOM;
  Commonwealth

Dominica is a multiparty island republic. It became independent from the UK in 1978. The economy is primarily agricultural, with bananas the leading export crop. Other crops include root crops, coconuts, and citrus, but much land is still under forest. Tourism is being developed, while industry is limited to food-processing and soap-making.

Dominican Republic

República Dominicana
CAPITAL Santo Domingo
AREA 48,443 km² (18,704 sq. mi.)
POPULATION 7.01 million (1989)
POPULATION GROWTH 2.0% p.a.

GDP PER CAPITA $671 (1988)
CURRENCY 1 Dominican peso = 100
  centavos
LIFE EXPECTANCY 64 (male) 68 (female)
POPULATION UNDER 15 YEARS 37.9%
LITERACY RATE 77.3% (1985)
RELIGION Roman Catholic 91.9%; other
  (mostly evangelical Protestant and
  followers of voodoo) 8.1%
ETHNIC GROUPS Mulatto 73.0%; Black
  11.0%; White 10.0%
LANGUAGE Spanish (official); Haitian creole
NUCLEAR CAPACITY No
LABOUR FORCE IN AGRICULTURE 37.8% (1988)
MAIN INTERNATIONAL ORGANIZATIONS UN; OAS

The Dominican Republic is a multiparty republic comprising the eastern two-thirds of the island of Hispaniola which it shares with Haiti. Light industry, expansion of duty-free industrial zones, and tourism are being fostered to diversify a primarily agricultural economy which exports sugar, cocoa, and coffee. Nickel is the chief export, and gold is also important.

East Timor

East Timor is a former Portuguese colony which was seized by Indonesia in 1975. It is claimed as a province by Indonesia, but not recognized as such by the UN. There is an independence movement, and strict restrictions on travel to the territory. The economy is largely agricultural, with coffee the major export. Traditional religions prevail, and Indonesian, Portuguese, and local languages are spoken.

Easter Island *Polynesia.

Ecuador

República del Ecuador

CAPITAL Quito
AREA 269,178 km² (103,930 sq. mi.)
POPULATION 10.49 million (1989)
POPULATION GROWTH 2.9% p.a.
GDP PER CAPITA $691 (1988)
CURRENCY 1 sucre = 100 centavos
LIFE EXPECTANCY 63 (male) 68 (female)
POPULATION UNDER 15 YEARS 40.6%
LITERACY RATE 69.1% (1982)
RELIGION Roman Catholic 93.5%
ETHNIC GROUPS Quechua 49.9%; Mestizo 40.0%; White 8.5%; other
  Amerindian 1.6%
LANGUAGE Spanish (official); Quechuan; other Amerindian languages
NUCLEAR CAPACITY No
LABOUR FORCE IN AGRICULTURE 31.9% (1988)
MAIN INTERNATIONAL ORGANIZATIONS UN; OAS; Andean Group;
  Non-Aligned Movement; OPEC

Ecuador is a multiparty republic. There is a disputed border with Peru. The oil industry, nationalized since 1988, produces the country's chief export, but otherwise the economy is primarily agricultural with bananas (of which Ecuador is the world's leading exporter), coffee, and, increasingly, fish the other exports of importance. Oil revenues have been invested to develop some manufacturing industry. There are plentiful supplies of natural gas and hydroelectric power to meet domestic energy requirements, and also mineral deposits of lignite, gold, and silver. The coastal plains support tropical agriculture, while the Andean highlands, where most of the Quechua population live, are temperate.

Egypt

Jumhūrīyah Miṣr al-'Arabīyah

CAPITAL Cairo
AREA 997,739 km² (385,229 sq. mi.)
POPULATION 51.748 million (1989)
POPULATION GROWTH 2.7% p.a.
GDP PER CAPITA $568 (1988)
CURRENCY 1 Egyptian pound = 100
  piastres = 1,000 millièmes
LIFE EXPECTANCY 59 (male) 62 (female)
POPULATION UNDER 15 YEARS 40.9%
LITERACY RATE 44.9% (1986)
RELIGION Sunnī Muslim 90.0%; Christian (mostly Coptic) 10.0%
ETHNIC GROUPS Egyptian 99.8%
LANGUAGE Arabic (official)
NUCLEAR CAPACITY Research (1 reactor)
LABOUR FORCE IN AGRICULTURE 41.5% (1988)
MAIN INTERNATIONAL ORGANIZATIONS UN; OAU; Arab League;
  OAPEC; Non-Aligned Movement

Egypt is a republic dominated by the National Democratic Party, which held multiparty elections in the 1980s. The main opposition coalition, including the Muslim Brotherhood, which advocates government by the *sharī'ah* (Islamic law) has boycotted recent elections. Main exports are of crude oil, petroleum products, and cotton. Agriculture is the main economic activity, but Egypt is no longer self-sufficient in food, due partly to swift population growth and partly to the neglect of agriculture. The Aswan High Dam regulates the flow of the Nile essential for most crop irrigation, but has had a deleterious effect on soil fertility; it also produces hydroelectric power. Foreign-exchange earnings from the Suez Canal, from the estimated 3 million Egyptians working abroad, and from tourism, make an important contribution to the economy, which also depends on high levels of US aid and loans. Islam is the state religion. Following a period of cool relations with other Arab states at the time of the Israeli–Egyptian peace agreement in 1979, Egypt has re-emerged as a leading Arab voice in the region.

El Salvador

República de El Salvador

CAPITAL San Salvador
AREA 21,041 km² (8,124 sq. mi.)
POPULATION 5.138 million (1989)
POPULATION GROWTH 1.6% p.a.
GDP PER CAPITA $1,090 (1988)
CURRENCY 1 colón = 100 centavos
LIFE EXPECTANCY 58 (male) 67 (female)
POPULATION UNDER 15 YEARS 44.5%
LITERACY RATE 69.0% (1980)

Although the land of the Nile delta is rich agriculturally, **Egypt** is unable to produce sufficient food for its population. Much of the agricultural work is done by women, as shown here in a lucerne field in Fayuum.

RELIGION Roman Catholic 92.4%
ETHNIC GROUPS Mestizo 90.0%; Amerindian (mostly Pipil) 5.0%;
   White 5.0%
LANGUAGE Spanish (official)
NUCLEAR CAPACITY No
LABOUR FORCE IN AGRICULTURE 37.8% (1988)
MAIN INTERNATIONAL ORGANIZATIONS UN; OAS

El Salvador is a multiparty republic. The 12-year civil war between
the left-wing Farabundo Marti National Liberation Front (FMLN) and
the military-backed right-wing ruling party Arena, ended in early 1992
with a ceasefire under the supervision of a UN peacekeeping force. Full
elections are scheduled for 1994. In the 1980s the civil war became a
major focus of confrontation between the USA and the former Soviet
Union. The most densely populated Central American state, El Salvador has been devastated by internal strife, with an estimated 75,000
dead, some 400,000 displaced persons (1990), and an increasing rate of
illiteracy. The economy is primarily agricultural, with coffee and cotton important exports. There is some manufacturing industry, principally textiles, chemicals, food-processing, and paper.

Equatorial Guinea

República de Guinea Ecuatorial

CAPITAL Malabo
AREA 28,051 km² (10,831 sq. mi.)
POPULATION 373,000 (1987)
POPULATION GROWTH 2.3% p.a.
GDP PER CAPITA $430 (1988)
CURRENCY 1 CFA franc = 100 centimes
LIFE EXPECTANCY 45 (male) 48 (female)
POPULATION UNDER 15 YEARS 38.1%
LITERACY RATE c.31% (c.1985)
RELIGION Christian (mostly Roman Catholic) 88.8%; traditional
   beliefs 4.6%; atheist 1.4%; Muslim 0.5%
ETHNIC GROUPS Fang 72.0%; Bubi 14.7%; Duala 2.7%; Ibibio 1.3%;
   Maka 1.3%
LANGUAGE Spanish (official); Fang, Bubi, and local languages
NUCLEAR CAPACITY No
LABOUR FORCE IN AGRICULTURE 85.7% (1983)
MAIN INTERNATIONAL ORGANIZATIONS UN; OAU; Non-Aligned
   Movement; Franc Zone

Equatorial Guinea is a one-party republic ruled by a supreme military council. It became independent from Spain in 1968. It has a
mainly agricultural economy, the main exports being timber and
cocoa. Offshore oil and gold are exploited, and there are deposits of
iron ore, copper, manganese, uranium, silica, and titanium. Equatorial
Guinea is one of Africa's poorest countries; political upheaval has led
to extensive emigration and agricultural neglect, with widespread food
shortages. The economy is heavily dependent on foreign aid, largely
from Spain.

Estonia

Eesti Vabariik

CAPITAL Tallin
AREA 45,111 km² (17,413 sq. mi.)
POPULATION 1.6 million
CURRENCY rouble (kroon to be introduced)
RELIGION Lutheran Church
ETHNIC GROUPS Estonian 62.0%; Russian
   30.0%
LANGUAGE Estonian (official); Russian
MAIN INTERNATIONAL ORGANIZATIONS UN;
   CSCE; North Atlantic Co-operation Council

Estonia is a multiparty republic. A former Soviet republic, it declared
sovereignty of its laws over those of the Soviet Union in 1988 and in
1989 annulled its 1940 vote to join the Soviet Union, restoring its 1938
constitution in 1990. One of the Baltic states (with Latvia and Lithuania), Estonia in 1990 re-established the Baltic Council. The principal
mineral resource is bituminous shale, together with peat; industries uti-
lizing oil shale to produce artificial gas and electricity produce much of
the power of the north-west region of the former Soviet Union, but at

serious environmental cost. Other industries include machinery, chemicals, timber, and textiles. Agriculture concentrates on animal husbandry.

Ethiopia

Ye Etiyop'iya Hezbawi Dimokrasīyawā
   Republēk

CAPITAL Addis Ababa
AREA 1,223,500 km² (472,400 sq. mi.)
POPULATION 48.898 million (1989)
POPULATION GROWTH 2.9% p.a.
GDP PER CAPITA $114 (1988)
CURRENCY 1 Ethiopian Birr = 100 cents
LIFE EXPECTANCY 39.5 (male) 43 (female)
POPULATION UNDER 15 YEARS 44.9%
LITERACY RATE 15% (1980)
RELIGION Ethiopian Orthodox 40.0%; Muslim 40.0%; traditional
   beliefs 15.0%; other Christian 4.5%
ETHNIC GROUPS Galla 40.0%; Amhara-Tigre 32.0%; Kafa Sidano
   9.0%; Somali 6.0%; Nilotic 6.0%; Afar 5.0%
LANGUAGE Amharic (official); Gallinya; local languages
NUCLEAR CAPACITY No
LABOUR FORCE IN AGRICULTURE 75.7% (1988)
MAIN INTERNATIONAL ORGANIZATIONS UN; OAU; Non-Aligned
   Movement

Ethiopia is a republic under the interim rule of a Council of Representatives drawn from the Ethiopian People's Revolutionary Democratic Front, which ousted the Soviet-backed Marxist military regime
in 1991. Eritrea and Tigre have separatist movements, the Tigrean
People's Liberation Front and the Eritrean People's Liberation Front,
both of which played an important part in overthrowing the former
government. A referendum on Eritrean independence is scheduled for
1993; meanwhile the interim government favours regional devolution
and redrawing provincial boundaries along the lines of ethnic divisions.
Somalia has supported the Western Somalia Liberation Front in claiming the Ogaden region. Prolonged civil war, combined with natural
disasters, has led to extreme poverty and recurrent famines. About a
million refugees have fled to Sudan, Djibouti, and Somalia. The economy has been centrally planned and has been based on collectivized
agriculture. Coffee, hides, and skins are the main exports. Ethiopia has
an oil refinery, but derives most of its energy from firewood, charcoal,
and dung. Industry is limited.

Falkland Islands

The Falkland Islands (Malvinas) is a
UK colony comprising two main islands
and some 100 smaller islands. A dispute
over its sovereignty led to war between the
UK and Argentina in 1982. Britain continues to have a significant, but scaled-down,
military presence. Wool is the dominant
export, though fishing is the largest source
of revenue since the declaration of a
241-km (150-mile) fishing zone around the
islands in 1987. It is believed that there are
offshore oil reserves.

Fiji

Republic of Fiji

CAPITAL Suva
AREA 18,274 km² (7,056 sq. mi.)
POPULATION 734,000 (1989)
POPULATION GROWTH 1.4% p.a.
GDP PER CAPITA $1,431 (1988)
CURRENCY 1 Fiji dollar = 100 cents
LIFE EXPECTANCY 68 (male) 73 (female)
POPULATION UNDER 15 YEARS 36.7%
LITERACY RATE 85.5% (1985)

RELIGION Christian 52.9%; Hindu 38.1%; Muslim 7.8%; Sikh 0.7%
ETHNIC GROUPS Indian 48.6%; Fijian 46.3%
LANGUAGE English (official); Fijian; Hindi; local languages
NUCLEAR CAPACITY No
LABOUR FORCE IN AGRICULTURE 44.1% (1986)
MAIN INTERNATIONAL ORGANIZATIONS UN; Colombo Plan; South
Pacific Commission

Fiji is a republic consisting of about 840 islands. Following a period of military rule (1987–92), multi-party government was restored. Commonwealth membership lapsed at the time of the military coup in 1987. The economy is agricultural, with sugar the chief crop and export. Other trade is in re-exported petroleum products, coconut oil, fish, and gold. Tourism provides substantial additional revenue. Food-processing is the main industry.

Finland

Suomen Tasavalta (Finnish)/Republiken
Finland (Swedish)

CAPITAL Helsinki
AREA 338,145 km² (130,559 sq. mi.)
POPULATION 4.96 million (1989)
POPULATION GROWTH 0.4% p.a.
GDP PER CAPITA $21,156 (1988)
CURRENCY 1 Markka = 100 pennia
LIFE EXPECTANCY 71 (male) 79 (female)
POPULATION UNDER 15 YEARS 19.3%
LITERACY RATE Virtually 100% (1987)
RELIGION Evangelical Lutheran 88.9%; Finnish (Greek) Eastern
Orthodox 1.1%
ETHNIC GROUPS Finnish 93.6%; Swedish 6.1%; Lapp minority
LANGUAGE Finnish, Swedish (both official); Lapp
NUCLEAR CAPACITY Civil and research (5 reactors)
LABOUR FORCE IN AGRICULTURE 8.8% (1988)
MAIN INTERNATIONAL ORGANIZATIONS UN; OECD; EFTA; Council
of Europe; CSCE

Finland is a neutral multiparty republic. The size and composition of its armed forces are no longer limited by the 1947 peace treaty, but Finland has committed itself not to acquire nuclear weapons. The treaty of friendship, co-operation, and mutual assistance with the former Soviet Union, once its most important trading partner, has been replaced by a new trade and co-operation treaty with Russia, and Finland applied for EC membership in 1992. Finland is an industrialized country with little agriculture, since 76 per cent of land is under forest; paper, timber, and wood-pulp are significant exports. Other industry includes shipbuilding, and the manufacture of machinery, steel, clothing, and chemicals. The only significant mineral resources are chromium and copper. A minority Lapp population lives in the north.

France

République Française

CAPITAL Paris
AREA 543,965 km² (210,026 sq. mi.)
POPULATION 56.107 million (1989)
POPULATION GROWTH 0.4% p.a.
GDP PER CAPITA $17,004 (1988)
CURRENCY 1 franc = 100 centimes
LIFE EXPECTANCY 72 (male) 80 (female)
POPULATION UNDER 15 YEARS 20.2%
LITERACY RATE 98.8% (1980)
RELIGION Roman Catholic 76.4%; other Christian 3.7%; atheist
3.4%; Muslim 3.0%
ETHNIC GROUPS French 86.8%; Occitan 2.7%; Arab 2.6%; Alsatian
2.3%; Breton 1.0%; Catalan 0.4%
LANGUAGE French (official); minority languages
NUCLEAR CAPACITY Defence, civil, and research (75 reactors, 9 under
construction), uranium producer
LABOUR FORCE IN AGRICULTURE 5.8% (1988)
MAIN INTERNATIONAL ORGANIZATIONS UN; NATO; EC; OECD;
South Pacific Commission; Council of Europe; CSCE

France is a multiparty republic. The directly elected President has significant powers. A national assembly is elected by direct suffrage, while senators are elected indirectly by the ninety-six metropolitan departments and eleven overseas departments and territories. France is divided into twenty-two regions with directly elected councils. A founding member of the EC, France is a full member of NATO but remains outside the integrated military structure. The armed forces have a nuclear component. There are rich mineral deposits of iron, potash, bauxite, zinc, lead, and gold, but France also imports raw materials such as oil for processing. The leading agricultural nation of Western Europe, France is also the fourth most industrialized Western country, with a wide range of manufacturing industry. Services account for some three-fifths of GNP, and principal exports are chemicals, machinery, motor vehicles, iron, steel, and textiles, as well as foodstuffs and wines. Major agricultural crops include wheat, barley, maize, sugar-beet, and fruit-growing. Dairy and poultry farming are also substantial. Nuclear power supplies some 70 per cent of electricity, with considerable hydroelectric capacity. The population is concentrated in the north, in the conurbations of Paris and Lyons, and in the south-east. French overseas departments and dependencies include French Guyana, French Polynesia, *Guadeloupe, *Martinique, Mayotte, New Caledonia, and *Réunion.

French Polynesia   *Polynesia.

Gabon

République Gabonaise

CAPITAL Libreville
AREA 267,667 km² (103,347 sq. mi.)
POPULATION 1.245 million (1989)
POPULATION GROWTH 3.9% p.a.
GDP PER CAPITA $2,733 (1988)
CURRENCY 1 CFA franc = 100 centimes
LIFE EXPECTANCY 50 (male) 53 (female)
POPULATION UNDER 15 YEARS 42.3%
LITERACY RATE 77.0% (1978)
RELIGION Roman Catholic 65.2%; Protestant 18.8%; African
indigenous Christian 12.1%; traditional religions 2.9%; Muslim
0.8%
ETHNIC GROUPS Fang 30.0%; Eshura 20.0%; Mbete 15.0%; Kota
13.0%; Omyene 15.0%
LANGUAGE French (official); Fang; Eshura; local languages
NUCLEAR CAPACITY No
LABOUR FORCE IN AGRICULTURE 69.4% (1988)
MAIN INTERNATIONAL ORGANIZATIONS UN; OAU; OPEC; Non-
Aligned Movement; Franc Zone

Gabon is a multiparty republic where the ruling Parti Démocratique Gabonais retained power in the first multiparty elections held in 1990. It became independent from France in 1960. Gabon is the wealthiest mainland African country, with substantial, albeit falling, revenues from offshore oilfields. Mineral deposits also include gold and diamonds. Exports are petroleum, timber, manganese, and uranium. Sugar-cane, cassava, and plantains are the chief agricultural crops.

Gambia

Republic of The Gambia

CAPITAL Banjul
AREA 10,689 km² (4,127 sq. mi.)
POPULATION 835,000 (1989)
POPULATION GROWTH 3.0% p.a.
GNP PER CAPITA $220 (1987)
CURRENCY 1 dalasi = 100 butut
LIFE EXPECTANCY 41 (male) 45 (female)
POPULATION UNDER 15 YEARS 44.6%
LITERACY RATE 24.9% (1985)
RELIGION Muslim 95.4%; Christian 3.7%; traditional beliefs 0.9%;
ETHNIC GROUPS Mandingo 40.4%; Fulani 18.7%; Wolof 14.6%;
Dyola 10.3%; Serahuli 6.5%
LANGUAGE English (official); Mandingo; Fulani; local languages
NUCLEAR CAPACITY No

LABOUR FORCE IN AGRICULTURE 73.7% (1983)
MAIN INTERNATIONAL ORGANIZATIONS UN; OAU; Commonwealth;
ECOWAS; Non-Aligned Movement

The Gambia is a multiparty republic. It became fully independent
from the UK in 1970. The confederation of Senegambia with Senegal,
for closer military and economic co-operation, collapsed in 1989, but
a Treaty of Friendship (1991) provides a basis for renewed links. The
economy is heavily dependent on ground-nuts, with fish, the re-export-
ing of imports, mainly to Senegal, and tourism providing additional
revenue. Gambia imports about a third of its food requirements.

Georgia

Sakartvelos Respublika

CAPITAL Tblisi
AREA 69,700 km² (26,900 sq. mi.)
POPULATION 5.4 million (1989)
CURRENCY rouble
RELIGION Georgian Eastern Orthodox
Church
ETHNIC GROUPS Georgian 80.0%;
Armenian 8.0%; Russian 6.0%; Azeri
6.0%; Abkhazian and Ossete minorities
LANGUAGE Georgian (official); Russian; minority languages
MAIN INTERNATIONAL ORGANIZATIONS CSCE

Georgia is a republic governed by an interim State Council. A former Soviet republic, Georgia became fully independent following the
disintegration of the Soviet Union in late 1991. A period of civil war
when the elected president was ousted precluded its membership of the
Commonwealth of Independent States and other international organizations. Georgia retains a degree of economic interdependence with
the other former Soviet republics. Mineral resources include coal,
petroleum, and manganese. Industry is based on the exploitation of
these resources; there is also some machinery production and other
light industry. About one-third of the land is forest. Agriculture
includes viticulture, and tea, tobacco, and citrus are the main crops.

Germany

Bundesrepublik Deutschland

CAPITAL Bonn (capital-designate is Berlin)
AREA 356,954 km² (137,820 sq. mi.)
POPULATION 78.934 million
POPULATION GROWTH FRG: −0.1% p.a.
(negative) GDR: 0.0% p.a.
GDP PER CAPITA FRG: $19,743 (1988)
GDR: $5,256 (1988)
CURRENCY 1 Deutsche Mark = 100
Pfennige
LIFE EXPECTANCY FRG: 72 (male) 78 (female); GDR: 70 (male) 76
(female)
POPULATION UNDER 15 YEARS FRG: 14.9%; GDR: 19.8%
LITERACY RATE Virtually 100%
RELIGION FRG: Roman Catholic 42.9%; Lutheran 41.6%; Muslim
2.7%; GDR: Protestant 47.0%; unaffiliated 46.0%; Roman
Catholic 7.0%
ETHNIC GROUPS FRG: (nationality) German 93.2%; Turkish 2.3%;
Yugoslav 0.9%; Italian 0.8%; GDR: German 99.7%
LANGUAGE German (official); minority languages
NUCLEAR CAPACITY Civil and research (54 reactors; 8 under
construction)
LABOUR FORCE IN AGRICULTURE FRG: 3.9%; GDR: 8.6% (1988)
MAIN INTERNATIONAL ORGANIZATIONS UN; EC; OECD; NATO;
Council of Europe; CSCE

Germany is a multiparty federal republic of sixteen states (*Länder*). It
was divided into the Federal Republic of Germany (FRG; West Germany) and the German Democratic Republic (GDR; East Germany)
until reunification on 3 October 1990. Concerns about the balance of
power in Europe, were addressed at talks held by the World War II
allies (USA, UK, France, and the former Soviet Union), and also
attended by Poland, which resulted in the united Germany's continued
membership of NATO and full sovereignty. In exchange for Soviet

compliance, Germany provided aid towards the cost of the withdrawal
of Soviet troops from the GDR. Following monetary union, FRG systems of welfare, wage-bargaining, labour laws, banking, and land ownership were adopted in the FDR, and privatization of state-owned
industries was begun. The costs of reunification and population movement from east to west are expected to cause further economic and
social tensions. West Germany has one of the world's most successful
industrial economies, excellent labour relations, and a high degree of
worker participation in management. Industry includes mechanical
and electrical engineering, electronics, vehicles, chemicals, and food-
processing, with machinery and transport equipment the principal
exports. Mineral resources include coal, lignite, salt, and some natural
gas. The main agricultural crops are potatoes, sugar-beet, wheat, and
barley. East Germany, by contrast, faces rising unemployment, a high
level of bankruptcies, higher prices as subsidies are removed, and lower
wages than in West Germany. Industry, which concentrates on chemicals, metal products, and textiles, is badly in need of modernization
and has caused severe environmental degradation because of its dependence on lignite as the main source of energy. Other than lignite, mineral resources are meagre. Agriculture, with main crops of potatoes,
sugar-beet, barley, and wheat, is unproductive and overmanned. Following reunification, there are many unresolved land disputes.

Ghana

Republic of Ghana

CAPITAL Accra
AREA 238,533 km² (92,098 sq. mi.)
POPULATION 14.566 million (1989)
POPULATION GROWTH 3.5% p.a.
GDP PER CAPITA $369 (1988)
CURRENCY 1 cedi = 100 pesewas
LIFE EXPECTANCY 52 (male) 56 (female)
POPULATION UNDER 15 YEARS 45.4%
LITERACY RATE 53.2% (1985)
RELIGION Protestant 27.9%; traditional beliefs 21.4%; Roman
Catholic 18.7%; African indigenous churches 16.0%; Muslim
15.7% (of which Ahmadīyah 7.9%)
ETHNIC GROUPS Akan 52.4%; Mossi 15.8%; Ewe 11.9%;
Ga-Adangme 7.8%
LANGUAGE English (official); Akan; Mole Dagbani; local languages
NUCLEAR CAPACITY No
LABOUR FORCE IN AGRICULTURE 51.1% (1988)
MAIN INTERNATIONAL ORGANIZATIONS Commonwealth; ECOWAS;
Non-Aligned Movement; OAU; UN

Ghana is a one-party republic under military rule. It became independent from the UK in 1957. A new constitution has been approved
as part of the planned transition to multiparty government. The economy is mainly agricultural. Exports are cocoa, gold, and timber. Offshore oil deposits await development; other mineral extraction includes
gold, manganese, diamonds, and bauxite. There is some light industry
and manufacturing of aluminium. Hydraulic power accounts for much
of elecricity production.

Gibraltar

Gibraltar is a UK colony whose sovereignty is contested by Spain. The economy
is based on tourism, defence expenditure,
and shipping. Gibraltar is a naval and air-
force base of strategic importance to the
UK, and there is a resident British army
battalion. There is also a commercial ship
and yacht repair-yard. Financial services
are being developed.

Greece

Ellinikí Dimokratiá

CAPITAL Athens
AREA 131,957 km² (50,949 sq. mi.)

POPULATION 10.096 million (1989)
POPULATION GROWTH 0.3% p.a.
GDP PER CAPITA $5,244 (1988)
CURRENCY 1 drachma = 100 lepta
LIFE EXPECTANCY 74 (male) 78 (female)
POPULATION UNDER 15 YEARS 19.7%
LITERACY RATE 93.8% (1985)
RELIGION Greek Orthodox 97.6%; Roman
   Catholic 0.4%; Protestant 0.1%; Muslim
   1.5%
ETHNIC GROUPS Greek 95.5%; Macedonian
   1.5%; Turkish 0.9%; Albanian 0.6%
LANGUAGE Greek (official); minority languages
NUCLEAR CAPACITY Research (2 reactors)
LABOUR FORCE IN AGRICULTURE 25.5% (1988)
MAIN INTERNATIONAL ORGANIZATIONS UN; EC; NATO; OECD;
   Council of Europe; CSCE

Greece is a multiparty republic. Considerable diplomatic tension exists with Turkey over the status of Cyprus, the disputed continental shelf in the Aegean, and the Turkish minority in Thrace. Both agriculture and industry are important, and the manufacturing sector experienced large growth in the 1980s. Important exports include fruit and vegetables, clothing, petroleum products, textiles, and yarns. Shipping and tourism are substantial earners of foreign exchange. About one-third of the population is concentrated in the region of greater Athens.

Grenada

Grenada
CAPITAL St George's
AREA 345 km² (133 sq. mi.)
POPULATION 96,600
POPULATION GROWTH 0.8% p.a.
GNP PER CAPITA $1,340 (GDP n.a.)
CURRENCY East Caribbean dollar
LIFE EXPECTANCY 65 (male) 69 (female)
POPULATION UNDER 15 YEARS 35.1%
LITERACY RATE 85.0%
RELIGION Roman Catholic 64.4%; Anglican 20.7%; Seventh-day
   Adventist 3.1%; Methodist 2.1%
ETHNIC GROUPS Black 84.0%; mixed 12.0%; East Indian 3.0%;
   White 1.0%
LANGUAGE English (official)
NUCLEAR CAPACITY No
LABOUR FORCE IN AGRICULTURE 28.7% (1981)
MAIN INTERNATIONAL ORGANIZATIONS UN; OAS; CARICOM;
   Commonwealth

Grenada is an island parliamentary monarchy whose head of state is the UK monarch; the islands of the Southern Grenadines are its dependency. It became independent from the UK in 1974. The economy is primarily agricultural, although there is limited manufacturing industry, mostly food-processing, and tourism is a growing source of revenue. The principal exports are nutmeg, bananas, cocoa, and mace. Other crops include coconuts, sugar-cane, and citrus. There is a high level of foreign debt, and political life has been slow to recover from the left-wing coup attempt in 1983 which led to US military intervention.

Guadeloupe

Département de Guadeloupe
CAPITAL Basse-Terre
AREA 1,780 km² (687 sq. mi.)
POPULATION 341,000 (1989)
POPULATION GROWTH 0.5% p.a.
GNP PER CAPITA $3,490 (1985) (GDP n.a.)
CURRENCY 1 French franc = 100 centimes
LIFE EXPECTANCY 69 (male) 76 (female)
POPULATION UNDER 15 YEARS 31.1%
LITERACY RATE 90.1% (1982)
RELIGION Roman Catholic 90.7%
ETHNIC GROUPS Mixed 77.0%; Black 10.0%; Indochinese 10.0%;
   European 2.0%

LANGUAGE French (official); French creole
NUCLEAR CAPACITY No
LABOUR FORCE IN AGRICULTURE 7.2% (1986)

Guadeloupe is a seven-island French overseas department. Tourism and agriculture are the mainstays of the economy, with principal exports of sugar, rum, and bananas. The economy is dependent on food imports and French aid, which enables a relatively high standard of living. A number of political groupings, the most radical of which is the Revolutionary Caribbean Alliance, favour independence.

Guam *Micronesia.

Guatemala

República de Guatemala
CAPITAL Guatemala City
AREA 108,889 km² (42,042 sq. mi.)
POPULATION 8.935 million (1989)
POPULATION GROWTH 2.9% p.a.
GDP PER CAPITA $858 (1988)
CURRENCY 1 Guatemalan quetzal = 100
   centavos
LIFE EXPECTANCY 60 (male) 64 (female)
POPULATION UNDER 15 YEARS 45.5%
LITERACY RATE 55.0%
RELIGION Roman Catholic 75.0% (of which Catholic/traditional
   syncretist 25.0%) Protestant (mostly fundamentalist) 25.0%
ETHNIC GROUPS Amerindian 55.0%; Ladino (Hispanic/Amerindian)
   42.0%
LANGUAGE Spanish (official); Mayan languages
NUCLEAR CAPACITY No
LABOUR FORCE IN AGRICULTURE 52.4% (1988)
MAIN INTERNATIONAL ORGANIZATIONS UN; OAS

Guatemala is a multiparty republic which returned to civilian rule in 1985 after a period of military rule. Guatemala has a history of political violence and military intervention in politics, with frequent reports of human rights violations, particularly against the Maya population, and bitter disputes over land reform. Guatemala has a primarily agricultural economy, the largest in Central America, with coffee, cotton, sugar, and bananas accounting for half of exports. Crude oil was discovered in the 1970s, and revenues from oil production have been used to develop manufacturing industry. Guatemala has not recognized the independence of its neighbour Belize, and claims part of its territory.

Guinea

République de Guinée
CAPITAL Conakry
AREA 245,857 km² (94,926 sq. mi.)
POPULATION 6.705 million (1989)
POPULATION GROWTH 2.4% p.a.
GDP PER CAPITA $416 (1988)
CURRENCY 1 Guinean franc = 100
   centimes
LIFE EXPECTANCY 41 (male) 44 (female)
POPULATION UNDER 15 YEARS 43.7%
LITERACY RATE 28.3% (1985)
RELIGION Muslim 85.0%; traditional beliefs 5.0%; Christian 1.5%
ETHNIC GROUPS Mande 48.0%; Peul 28.0%; Mande-fu 11.0%
LANGUAGE French (official); Malinke; Poulor; local languages
NUCLEAR CAPACITY No
LABOUR FORCE IN AGRICULTURE 75.6% (1988)
MAIN INTERNATIONAL ORGANIZATIONS UN; OAU; ECOWAS; Non-
   Aligned Movement

Guinea is a one-party republic under military rule. It became independent from France in 1958. A new constitution provides for the end of military rule and a transition to a two-party system. It is linked with Liberia and Sierra Leone in the Mano River Union. It has a broadly based agricultural economy: the chief crops include cassava, rice, pineapples, coffee, and palm oil. The major exports are bauxite, alumina, gold, and diamonds. Iron-ore mining is being developed.

Guinea-Bissau

República da Guiné-Bissau

CAPITAL Bissau
AREA 36,125 km² (13,948 sq. mi.)
POPULATION 953,000 (1989)
POPULATION GROWTH 2.2% p.a.
GNP PER CAPITA $170 (1987) (GDP n.a.)
CURRENCY 1 Guinea-Bissau peso = 100
    centavos
LIFE EXPECTANCY 43 (male) 47 (female)
POPULATION UNDER 15 YEARS 43.7%
LITERACY RATE 31.4% (1985)
RELIGION Traditional beliefs 65.0%; Muslim 30.0%; Christian 5.0%
ETHNIC GROUPS Senegambian 60.0%; Peul 20.0%; Manding 13.0%
LANGUAGE Portuguese (official); Balante; Fulani; local languages
NUCLEAR CAPACITY No
LABOUR FORCE IN AGRICULTURE 71.9% (1979)
MAIN INTERNATIONAL ORGANIZATIONS UN; OAU; Non-Aligned
    Movement; ECOWAS

Guinea-Bissau is a one-party republic. It became independent from Portugal in 1974. The introduction of a multiparty system is in progress. Guinea-Bissau has a mainly agricultural economy, whose significant exports are cashews, fish, ground-nuts, and palm kernels. Further cash crops are being developed. Bauxite and phosphate reserves are yet to be exploited. Offshore oil deposits have not been developed because of boundary disputes with Guinea and Senegal.

Guyana

Co-operative Republic of Guyana

CAPITAL Georgetown
AREA 215,083 km² (83,044 sq. mi.)
POPULATION 754,000 (1989)
POPULATION GROWTH 1.9% p.a.
GDP PER CAPITA $356 (1988)
CURRENCY 1 Guyana dollar = 100 cents
LIFE EXPECTANCY 67 (male) 72 (female)
POPULATION UNDER 15 YEARS 34.6%
LITERACY RATE 95.9% (1985)
RELIGION Protestant 30.5%; Hindu 37.1%; Roman Catholic 11.4%;
    Muslim 8.7%; non-religious 3.7%
ETHNIC GROUPS East Indian 51.4%; Black (African Negro and Bush
    Negro) 30.5%; Mixed 11.0%; Amerindian 5.3%; Chinese 0.2%
LANGUAGE English (official); English creole; also Caribbean, Hindi,
    and Amerindian languages
NUCLEAR CAPACITY No
LABOUR FORCE IN AGRICULTURE 23.2% (1988)
MAIN INTERNATIONAL ORGANIZATIONS UN; Commonwealth;
    CARICOM; Non-Aligned Movement; OAS

Guyana is a multiparty republic where democratic rights have been restricted in recent years. It became independent from the UK in 1966. The two main political parties are both left-wing, but are distinguished by the support of different ethnic groups. The economy is based on agriculture and mining. Major exports are bauxite and alumina, sugar, and rice. There are rich mineral deposits and huge timber reserves, but these are largely unexploited, and lack of foreign exchange has led to food shortages. There is potential for hydroelectricity which would reduce its dependence on imported oil.

Haiti

République d'Haïti (French)/Republik
    Dayti (Haitian creole)

CAPITAL Port-au-Prince
AREA 27,400 km² (10,579 sq. mi.)
POPULATION 5.52 million (1989)
POPULATION GROWTH 1.5% p.a.
GDP PER CAPITA $440 (1988)
CURRENCY 1 gourde = 100 centimes
LIFE EXPECTANCY 53 (male) 56 (female)

POPULATION UNDER 15 YEARS 39.2%
LITERACY RATE 41.5% (1986)
RELIGION Roman Catholic 80.3% (of whom about 90% also practise
    voodoo); Protestant 15.8% (of which Baptist 9.7%); Pentecostal
    3.6%; non-religious 1.2%
ETHNIC GROUPS Black 95.0%; Mulatto 4.9%; White 0.1%
LANGUAGE Haitian (French) creole, French (both official)
NUCLEAR CAPACITY No
LABOUR FORCE IN AGRICULTURE 65.0% (1988)
MAIN INTERNATIONAL ORGANIZATIONS UN; OAS

Haiti is a republic with strong military influence. Thirty years of dictatorship by the Duvalier family were ended by popular unrest in 1986, but the President elected in 1990 was overthrown in a military coup the following year. Extreme poverty and inequality in the distribution of wealth have been exacerbated by years of corrupt government, and reliance on US and other foreign aid has created further problems. Haiti has a predominantly agricultural economy, with coffee the most important agricultural export; bauxite is also an important export. Tourism has been a major source of foreign exchange. There is some light industry, especially textiles and the assembly or finishing of imported goods.

Honduras

República de Honduras

CAPITAL Tegucigalpa
AREA 112,088 km² (43,277 sq. mi.)
POPULATION 4.53 million (1989)
POPULATION GROWTH 3.3% p.a.
GDP PER CAPITA $917 (1988)
CURRENCY 1 Honduran lempira = 100
    centavos
LIFE EXPECTANCY 62 (male) 66 (female)
POPULATION UNDER 15 YEARS 44.6%
LITERACY RATE 59.5% (1985)
RELIGION Roman Catholic 94.6%; other (mostly Protestant) 5.4%
ETHNIC GROUPS Mestizo 89.9%; Amerindian 6.7%; Black (including
    Black Carib) 2.1%; White 1.3%
LANGUAGE Spanish (official); Black Carib (Garifuna); minority
    languages
NUCLEAR CAPACITY No
LABOUR FORCE IN AGRICULTURE 56.2% (1988)
MAIN INTERNATIONAL ORGANIZATIONS UN; OAS

Honduras is a multiparty republic, which returned to civilian rule following a period of military government from 1972 to 1981. During the 1980s the USA provided Honduras with substantial military support, and US-backed 'contra' guerrillas operated from bases in Honduras in the Nicaraguan civil war. Honduras has an agricultural economy with bananas and coffee the principal exports; there are extensive forests (45 per cent of land area) and timber is also exported. Zinc, lead, and silver are mined, and there is limited light industry.

Hong Kong

Hsiang Kang (Chinese) Hong Kong
    (English)

AREA 1,044.6 km² (403.3 sq. mi.)
POPULATION 5.754 million (1989)
POPULATION GROWTH 1.3% p.a.
GDP PER CAPITA $9,613 (1988)
CURRENCY 1 HK dollar = 100 cents
LIFE EXPECTANCY 74 (male) 80 (female)
POPULATION UNDER 15 YEARS 22.1%
LITERACY RATE 88.1% (1985)
RELIGION Predominantly Buddhist and Daoist; also about 0.5 million
    Christians, 50,000 Muslims, and 12,000 Hindus
ETHNIC GROUPS Chinese 97.0%; Filipino 0.7%; British 0.3%
LANGUAGE Chinese (Cantonese), English (both official); minority
    languages
NUCLEAR CAPACITY No
LABOUR FORCE IN AGRICULTURE 1.3% (1988)
MAIN INTERNATIONAL ORGANIZATIONS Commonwealth

A geothermal power plant in the Svartsengi ('black field') area of **Iceland**. Underground hot water, a legacy of the country's volcanic origin, is used to generate electricity. It is also popular with bathers, and alleviates skin complaints.

Hong Kong is a UK colony administered by a governor appointed by the British Crown. Direct elections were introduced in 1991 to a limited number of seats on the Legislative Council (Legco). Hong Kong is on a ninety-nine year lease from China, which expires in 1997. An agreement with China in 1984 ensured the colony's return to China as a 'special administrative region', with guarantees for the existing social and economic systems lasting for a further fifty years. There has been a significant increase in joint industrial ventures with China since then, especially with the adjacent Shenzen Special Economic Zone. Hong Kong's prosperity was initially based on its excellent harbour (it is the world's largest container port) and trading, but manufacturing industry, especially textiles and electronics, now predominates. Hong Kong is a flourishing financial services centre, and tourism is also an important source of revenue.

Hungary

Magyar Köztársaság

CAPITAL Budapest
AREA 93,033 km² (35,920 sq. mi.)
POPULATION 10.58 million (1989)
POPULATION GROWTH −0.2% p.a.
GDP PER CAPITA $2,625 (1988)
CURRENCY 1 forint = 100 filler
LIFE EXPECTANCY 67 (male) 74 (female)
POPULATION UNDER 15 YEARS 19.9%
LITERACY RATE 98.9% (1984)
RELIGION Roman Catholic 62.4%; Protestant 23.4%; atheist and non-religious 12.9%; Orthodox 0.5%; Jewish 0.8%
ETHNIC GROUPS Magyar 96.6%; German 1.6%; Slovak 1.1%; Romanian and gypsy 0.7%

LANGUAGE Hungarian (official); minority languages
NUCLEAR CAPACITY Civil and research (7 reactors)
LABOUR FORCE IN AGRICULTURE 12.7% (1988)
MAIN INTERNATIONAL ORGANIZATIONS UN; CSCE; Council of Europe; North Atlantic Co-operation Council

Hungary is a multiparty republic. It was formerly a Soviet-dominated communist republic, which held elections in 1990 following mass popular demonstrations. In 1990, the Hungarian stock exchange was opened and legislation passed allowing for privatization of collectively owned businesses and farms. Some state-owned farms remain, but most agricultural land is now in private hands. The high cost of imported petroleum, following the ending of low-cost Soviet oil imports, has caused shortages and inflation. IMF-backed economic reforms include cuts in industrial subsidies which are expected to lead to further price rises. In an attempt to compensate for the resulting economic hardship, expanded social services and welfare payments have been introduced. Principal crops are wheat, maize, barley, sugar-beet, potatoes, and grapes, while mineral resources include bauxite, brown coal, lignite, and copper. Increases in Western joint ventures, new management techniques, and the replacement of outdated machinery are measures which aim to revive industrial profitability. Hungary's main exports are machinery and transport equipment, agricultural produce, and computer software. Tourism is an expanding source of revenue. Hungary has significant Slovak and gypsy minorities; its relations with Czecho-Slovakia, Yugoslavia, and Romania are strained because of their discrimination against Hungarian minorities.

Iceland

Lýdhveldidh Ísland

CAPITAL Reykjavík
AREA 103,000 km² (39,769 sq. mi.)
POPULATION 252,000
POPULATION GROWTH 0.8% p.a.
GDP PER CAPITA $23,640 (1988)
CURRENCY 1 krona = 100 aurar

LIFE EXPECTANCY 75 (male) 80 (female)
POPULATION UNDER 15 YEARS 25.1%
LITERACY RATE 99.9% (1985)
RELIGION Evangelical Lutheran 92.9%;
    other Lutheran 3.4%; non-religious
    1.3%; Roman Catholic 0.9%
ETHNIC GROUPS (Place of birth, 1988):
    Iceland 96.3%; Denmark 0.9%; USA
    0.5%; Sweden 0.4%; Germany 0.3%
LANGUAGE Icelandic (official)
NUCLEAR CAPACITY No
LABOUR FORCE IN AGRICULTURE 7.4% (1988)
MAIN INTERNATIONAL ORGANIZATIONS UN; EFTA; OECD; NATO;
    Council of Europe; CSCE

Iceland is a multiparty republic which has been independent from Denmark since 1944. The Parliament, the oldest in the world, has a higher proportion of women representatives than in any other country. Iceland has neither an army nor navy, though US forces constitute the Iceland Defence Force. Hydroelectric power stations provide over three-quarters of the country's electricity needs and geothermal energy is abundant. Six-sevenths of the land area is agriculturally unproductive. The fishing industry is of vital importance to the economy, accounting for three-quarters of exports; other exports are aluminium (produced from imported alumina) and ferro-silicon. Iceland has had high rates of inflation, ranging from 40 to 100 per cent in recent years.

India

Bhārat (Hindi)/Republic of India
CAPITAL New Delhi
AREA 3,166,414 km² (1,222,559 sq. mi.)
POPULATION 843.931 million (1991)
POPULATION GROWTH 2.0% p.a.
GDP PER CAPITA $335 (1988)
CURRENCY 1 Indian rupee = 100 paisa
LIFE EXPECTANCY 58 (male) 59 (female)
POPULATION UNDER 15 YEARS 36.5%
LITERACY RATE 40.8% (1981)

RELIGION Hindu 82.64%; Muslim 11.35%; Christian 2.43%; Sikh
    1.97%; Buddhist 0.71%; Jain 0.48%; Parsee 0.01%
ETHNIC GROUPS (based on language) Hindi 28.1%; Telugu 8.2%;
    Bengali 8.1%; Marathi 7.6%; Tamil 6.9%; Urdu 5.2%; Gujarati
    4.7%; Malayalam 4.0%; Kannada 3.9%; Oriya 3.6%; Bhojpuri
    2.6%; Punjabi 2.5%; Assamese 1.6%; Chhattisgarhi 1.2%;
    Magadhi 1.2%; Maithili 1.1%
LANGUAGE Hindi, English (both official); Gujarati, Bengali, Marathi,
    Telugu, Tamil, Urdu, Oriya, Malayalam, Kannada, Punjabi and
    Bhojpuri are each spoken by over 20 million people
NUCLEAR CAPACITY Civil and research (11 reactors, 8 under
    construction)
LABOUR FORCE IN AGRICULTURE 67.1% (1988)
MAIN INTERNATIONAL ORGANIZATIONS UN; Commonwealth;
    Colombo Plan; Non-Aligned Movement

India is a multiparty federal republic formed by the union of twenty-five states and seven union territories. It is the world's largest democracy. Each state has a legislature, but the national government retains considerable powers. A land of great diversity, India is subject to endemic intercommunal strife between the many different ethnic and religious groups. In Jammu and Kashmir, the only state with a Muslim majority, the Kashmir National Liberation Front is one of a number of groups fighting for independence or union with Pakistan, a dispute which exacerbates strained relations between India and neighbouring Pakistan. In Punjab there are violent clashes between government forces and Sikh militants, who want an independent Sikh state; other violent separatist movements in recent years have been those of the Bodos in Assam, the Gurkhas in West Bengal, and the Tribal National Volunteers (TNP) in Tripura. India is a founding member who has played an important role in the Non-Aligned Movement. There were close ties with the former Soviet Union, which was a major supplier of economic and military aid; relations with the USA are cordial, although the degree of US military aid to Pakistan has caused concern in India. China and India dispute an area on the Himalayan border. India's economy is largely agrarian, and India has become self-sufficient in food, although agricultural yields are comparatively low

and malnutrition is a perennial problem. Manufacturing industry has been developed since independence in 1947, with considerable state investment and control. The state also controls most mining, of which coal and iron ore are the most important products. Electricity is produced by thermal, hydroelectric, and a minority of nuclear power plants. The principal exports are gems, engineering products, garments, and leather goods. The main crops are rice, sugar-cane, tea, cotton, and jute, and the chief industrial products are steel, transport equipment and machinery, textiles, and cement. India is the world's second most populous country, and active government promotion of family planning has scarcely reduced population growth. The entrenched caste system is backed up by constitutional safeguards for certain groups; attempts to amend these have met with widespread resistance.

Indonesia

Republik Indonesia
CAPITAL Jakarta
AREA 1,919,443 km² (741,101 sq. mi.)
POPULATION 177.046 million (1989)
POPULATION GROWTH 2.3% p.a.
GDP PER CAPITA $473 (1988)
CURRENCY 1 Indonesian rupiah = 100 sen
LIFE EXPECTANCY 55 (male) 57 (female)
POPULATION UNDER 15 YEARS 35.0%
LITERACY RATE 74.1% (1985)

RELIGION Muslim 86.9%; Christian 9.6% (of which Roman Catholic
    3.1%;) Hindu 1.9%; Buddhist 1.0%
ETHNIC GROUPS Javanese 40.1%; Sundanese 15.3%; Bahasa
    Indonesian 12.0%; Madurese 4.8%; Chinese minority
LANGUAGE Bahasa Indonesian (official); also Javanese, Sundanese,
    and many others
NUCLEAR CAPACITY Research (3 reactors) (1989)
LABOUR FORCE IN AGRICULTURE 50.2% (1988)
MAIN INTERNATIONAL ORGANIZATIONS UN; OPEC; ASEAN; Non-
    Aligned Movement; Colombo Plan

The Land Dayaks of the rainforest of Sarawak are one of the distinct ethnic groups making up the population of **Indonesia**. Their way of life—hunting, gathering fruit, and clearing small patches of jungle to grow rice—is threatened by commercial exploitation of rainforest timber.

Indonesia is a multiparty republic with strong military influence. It consists of 13,677 islands, including Sumatra, Java, and parts of New Guinea and Borneo. In 1975 Indonesia occupied the former Portuguese colony of *East Timor, which was declared the 27th province in 1976, although the UN does not recognize it as such. Here, as in Irian Jaya (West New Guinea), local independence movements are active. Government policies of 'transmigration' aim to exert control over tribal areas by forcibly resettling people from Indonesia's heavily populated inner islands in the tribal areas. Agriculture is important, principal exports being timber, coffee, rubber, shrimps, pepper, and palm oil, and Indonesia is the most important oil producer of the region. Other mining products include nickel, bauxite, copper, iron, and tin. There is some light industry, and manufacturing is increasing in importance. Indonesia has approximately 250 different ethnic groups, and as many different languages. A disproportionate share of the country's wealth is controlled by the Chinese minority.

Iran

Jomhūrī-ye Eslamī-ye Irān

CAPITAL Tehrān
AREA 1,648,196 km² (636,372 sq. mi.)
POPULATION 54.333 million (1989)
POPULATION GROWTH 3.5% p.a.
GDP PER CAPITA $1,222 (1988)
CURRENCY 1 toman = 10 rials
LIFE EXPECTANCY 65 (male) 66 (female)
POPULATION UNDER 15 YEARS 43.9%
LITERACY RATE 61.8% (1986)
RELIGION Shī'ī Muslim 91.0%; Sunnī Muslim 7.8%; Christian 0.7%; Jewish 0.3%; Bahā'ī minority
ETHNIC GROUPS Persian 45.6%; Azeri 16.8%; Kurdish 9.1%; Gīlanī 5.3%; Luri 4.3%; Māzandarānī 3.6%; Baluch 2.3%; Arab 2.2%; Bakhtiari 1.7%
LANGUAGE Farsi (Persian) (official); Azeri Turkish; Kurdish; Arabic and other minority languages
NUCLEAR CAPACITY Research (1 reactor, 2 civil reactors under construction) (1989)
LABOUR FORCE IN AGRICULTURE 29.1% (1988)
MAIN INTERNATIONAL ORGANIZATIONS UN; OPEC; Colombo Plan; Non-Aligned Movement

Iran has been an Islamic republic since 1979, when the Shah's monarchy was overthrown by a revolution with massive popular support. Islam is the state religion, and the constitution vests supreme authority in a religious leader elected by the clergy. Executive power is held by the elected president. All legislation must be in accordance with the *sharī'ah* (Islamic law). Iran's Islamic revolution has inspired Muslims throughout the world, and especially in the Middle East, and Iran has actively supported Shī'ī militants in the region, notably in Lebanon. Since the revolution, Iran's relations with the West, especially the USA, have been strained, but there are indications that the government is ready to cultivate closer links. The Iran–Iraq War (1980–9) resulted in huge loss of life and much destruction on both sides. Iran's economy is based on its huge reserves of oil, which accounts for some 95 per cent of exports; however, oil and gas production are restricted due to war damage. Substantial mineral deposits of coal, copper, and iron ore are relatively undeveloped, and ambitious industrial and infrastructural projects embarked on under the Shah have been curtailed. Banks, insurance, and most industries have been nationalized since the revolution. The chief industries are mining, machinery production, and textiles. The neglect of agriculture, which focuses on producing grains and rice, and rearing sheep and cattle, has not yet been successfully reversed, and there is food rationing. Political opposition within Iran is strictly repressed, but there are opposition groups in exile. The Bahā'ī minority has been severely persecuted.

Iraq

al-Jumhūrīyah al-'Irāqīyah

CAPITAL Baghdād
AREA 435,052 km² (167,975 sq. mi.)
POPULATION 17.215 million (1989)
POPULATION GROWTH 3.1% p.a.

GDP PER CAPITA $3,090 (1988)
CURRENCY 1 Iraqi dinar = 20 dirhams = 1,000 fils
LIFE EXPECTANCY 63 (male) 65 (female)
POPULATION UNDER 15 YEARS 36.4%
LITERACY RATE 45.9% (1984)
RELIGION Shī'ī Muslim 53.5%; Sunnī Muslim 42.3%; Christian 3.5%
ETHNIC GROUPS Arab 77.1%; Kurdish 19.0%; Turkmen 1.4%; Persian 0.8%; Assyrian 0.8%
LANGUAGE Arabic (official); Kurdish and minority languages
NUCLEAR CAPACITY Research (2 reactors) (1989)
LABOUR FORCE IN AGRICULTURE 21.9% (1988)
MAIN INTERNATIONAL ORGANIZATIONS UN; Arab League; Non-Aligned Movement; OAPEC; OPEC

Iraq is a one-party republic dominated by the Ba'ath party headed by Saddam Hussein. Facing a period of economic recovery following its war with Iran (1980–9) over the sovereignty of the Shatt al-Arab waterway, Iraq invaded Kuwait in August 1990 and declared the emirate its thirteenth province. A US-led coalition defeated Iraq after a brief campaign (1991), destroying much of Iraq's infrastructure by systematic bombing raids. Income from Iraq's oil exports, on which the economy is based, had enabled an unprecedented build-up of weaponry (supplied principally by the former Soviet Union and Western Europe), and substantial investments in welfare facilities. Following the war a UN team has attempted to locate and destroy Iraq's nuclear and weapons installations, and an international trade embargo was enforced, with a provision, not accepted by Iraq, for oil revenues to be administered by the UN for humanitarian purposes. Rigid state control, political oppression, the trade embargo, and war have taken their toll of the civilian population, agriculture, and industry. The main industries are petroleum products and chemicals. Iraq relies on imports of foodstuffs, its main agricultural products being grains, livestock, and dates. The population of Iraq is divided on religious and ethnic grounds; the Sunnī-dominated ruling Ba'ath party has employed brutal methods to enforce its rule in the north, where the Kurds seek autonomy and are protected by a UN presence, and the south, where Shī'ī Muslims predominate.

Ireland

Éire (Irish)/Ireland (English)

CAPITAL Dublin
AREA 70,285 km² (27,137 sq. mi.)
POPULATION 3.515 million (1989)
POPULATION GROWTH 0.2% p.a.
GDP PER CAPITA $9,181 (1988)
CURRENCY 1 Irish pound = 100 new pence
LIFE EXPECTANCY 72 (male) 77 (female)
POPULATION UNDER 15 YEARS 27.7%
LITERACY RATE Virtually 100% (1987)
RELIGION Roman Catholic 93.1%; Church of Ireland (Anglican) 2.8%; Presbyterian 0.4%
ETHNIC GROUPS Over 94.0% Irish nationality
LANGUAGE English, Irish (both official)
NUCLEAR CAPACITY No
LABOUR FORCE IN AGRICULTURE 14.4% (1988)
MAIN INTERNATIONAL ORGANIZATIONS EC; OECD; UN; Council of Europe; CSCE

Ireland is a neutral multiparty republic, whose constitution looks to the eventual unification of the island of Ireland to include the six counties of Northern Ireland, which are currently part of the *UK. In 1985 Ireland signed the Anglo-Irish Agreement with the UK, thereby obtaining a consultative role in Northern Ireland. Ireland has a diversified economy in which agriculture predominates, although industry has become increasingly important; the chief exports are foodstuffs (especially beef), electrical machinery, and chemicals. Other industries include textiles, and tourism is also important. The country generates 15 per cent of its electricity by burning peat, of which there are extensive reserves. Ireland has a higher rate of emigration than any other member of the EC, which it joined in 1973. Irish citizens have had the right to reside, work, and vote in the UK since independence.

Israel

Medinat Yisra'el (Hebrew)/Isrā'īl (Arabic)

CAPITAL Jerusalem
AREA 20,700 km² (7,992 sq. mi.) (excluding occupied territories)
POPULATION 4.563 million (1989)
POPULATION GROWTH 1.5% p.a.
GDP PER CAPITA $9,368 (1988)
CURRENCY 1 New (Israeli) sheqel = 100 agorot
LIFE EXPECTANCY 74 (male) 77 (female)
POPULATION UNDER 15 YEARS 30.9%
LITERACY RATE 91.8% (1983)
RELIGION Jewish 82.0%; Muslim (mostly Sunnī) 13.9%; Christian 2.3%; Druze and other 1.8%
ETHNIC GROUPS Jewish 83.0%; Arab 16.8%
LANGUAGE Hebrew, Arabic (both official); Yiddish; Russian; Romanian; English
NUCLEAR CAPACITY Research (2 reactors) (1989)
LABOUR FORCE IN AGRICULTURE 4.6% (1988)
MAIN INTERNATIONAL ORGANIZATIONS UN

Israel is a multiparty republic established in 1948 as an independent state for the Jewish people. According to the Law of Return (1950) all Jews have the right of immigration to Israel; between 1987 and 1992 some 350,000 Soviet Jews have emigrated to Israel. A system of proportional representation leads to a preponderance of coalition governments, in which ultra-conservative parties have held much influence in recent years. Israel relies on financial and political support from the USA, where a strong Jewish lobby has influenced foreign policy. Since Israel's foundation, it has been in continual tension with its Arab neighbours, with full-scale war in 1956, 1967, 1973, and 1982. The US-brokered Camp David peace agreement was signed with Egypt in 1979, making Egypt the first Arab nation to grant Israel full diplomatic recognition (1980). In 1991 an international peace conference on the Arab–Israeli conflict was convened. Israel occupies former Jordanian land on the West Bank of the River Jordan, Egyptian land in the Gaza Strip, and Syrian land in the Golan Heights; the status of these occupied territories and of Jerusalem, which Israel has declared its capital, is disputed. It consolidates its hold on the occupied territories by a programme of Jewish settlement. However, the USA has warned Israel that future US aid will depend on its willingness to negotiate, and must not be used to finance further settlements in the occupied territories. Israel's Palestinian minority is discriminated against, and the Palestinians of the West Bank and Gaza Strip are deprived of civil and political rights. Since the late 1980s the Palestinians in the occupied territories have engaged in a violent uprising, or *intifāda*. The Israeli economy has a well-developed manufacturing base, the main products being chemicals and small metal manufactures. However, high military expenditure and reliance on imported fuels and minerals have resulted in a high rate of inflation and dependence on foreign, mostly US, aid. Agriculture, largely carried out by communes (kibbutzim) and co-operatives (moshavim), has been successfully developed by irrigation, and Israel is self-sufficient in food. Exports include diamonds, chemicals, small metal manufactures, and fruit. (See also entry on the Palestinians in main section.)

Italy

Repubblica Italiana

CAPITAL Rome
AREA 301,277 km² (116,324 sq. mi.)
POPULATION 57.436 million (1989)
POPULATION GROWTH 0.2% p.a.
GDP PER CAPITA $14,432 (1988)
CURRENCY 1 lira = 100 centesimi
LIFE EXPECTANCY 72 (male) 79 (female)
POPULATION UNDER 15 YEARS 17.1%
LITERACY RATE 97.0% (1985)
RELIGION Roman Catholic 83.2%; non-religious 13.6%; atheist 2.6%
ETHNIC GROUPS Italian 94.1%; Sardinian 2.7%; Rhaetian 1.3%
LANGUAGE Italian (official); Sardinian; minority languages
NUCLEAR CAPACITY Civil and research (8 reactors) (1989)
LABOUR FORCE IN AGRICULTURE 7.9% (1988)

MAIN INTERNATIONAL ORGANIZATIONS EC; NATO; OECD; UN; Council of Europe; CSCE

Italy is a multiparty republic. Coalitions and frequent changes of government have been the norm, although the Christian Democrats are dominant in government. The fifteen regional parliaments have a measure of self-government; the five autonomous regions of Valle d'Aosta, Trentino-Alto Adige, Friuli-Venezia Giulia, Sicily, and Sardinia have more extensive powers. With a developed industrial economy, Italy's main exports include electrical machinery (especially office equipment), chemicals, clothing, motor vehicles, textiles, and footwear. The public sector is significant, and industry is concentrated in north and central Italy with the south remaining predominantly agricultural and relatively poor. There are few large mineral deposits, excepting sulphur, mercury, and some oil in Sicily; crude oil accounts for some 15 per cent of imports. The tourist industry is significant. There are over 3 million agricultural holdings, with only a small degree of mechanization compared with other European countries. The chief agricultural products are sugar-beet, grains, tomatoes, citrus, and olives.

Jamaica

Jamaica

CAPITAL Kingston
AREA 10,991 km² (4,244 sq. mi.)
POPULATION 2.376 million (1989)
POPULATION GROWTH 1.8% p.a.
GDP PER CAPITA $1,298 (1988)
CURRENCY 1 Jamaican dollar = 100 cents
LIFE EXPECTANCY 71 (male) 77 (female)
POPULATION UNDER 15 YEARS 34.4%
LITERACY RATE 88.6% (1980)
RELIGION Church of God 18.4%; non-religious or atheist 17.7%; Baptist 10.0%; Anglican 7.1%; Seventh-day Adventist 6.9%; Pentecostal 5.2%; Roman Catholic 5.0%; Rastafarian 5.0%
ETHNIC GROUPS Black 76.3%; Afro-European 15.1%; East Indian and Afro-East Indian 3.4%; White 3.2%; Chinese and Lebanese minorities
LANGUAGE English (official); English creole; Hindi; Chinese
NUCLEAR CAPACITY Research (1 reactor) (1989)
LABOUR FORCE IN AGRICULTURE 27.9% (1988)
MAIN INTERNATIONAL ORGANIZATIONS CARICOM; Commonwealth; Non-Aligned Movement; OAS; UN

Jamaica is a parliamentary monarchy whose head of state is the UK monarch. It became independent from the UK in 1962. Jamaica is the world's fourth largest producer of bauxite, and bauxite and alumina dominate exports. Both agriculture and industry are important, with sugar, bananas, and coffee the principal agricultural exports, and a developing manufacturing industry. Tourism is an important source of foreign exchange. A high level of debt, sporadic violence, and hurricane damage in 1988 have damaged the economy.

Japan

Nihon or Nippon

CAPITAL Tokyo
AREA 377,835 km² (145,883 sq. mi.)
POPULATION 123.12 million (1989)
POPULATION GROWTH 0.5% p.a.
GDP PER CAPITA $23,325 (1988)
CURRENCY Yen
LIFE EXPECTANCY 75 (male) 81 (female)
POPULATION UNDER 15 YEARS 18.5%
LITERACY RATE Virtually 100% (1989)
RELIGION Joint adherents of Shinto and Buddhism 80.0%; Christian 1.2%
ETHNIC GROUPS Japanese 99.4%; Korean 0.5%; Chinese and other 0.1%
LANGUAGE Japanese (official)
NUCLEAR CAPACITY Civil and research (56 reactors, 12 under construction) (1989)
LABOUR FORCE IN AGRICULTURE 7.2% (1988)
MAIN INTERNATIONAL ORGANIZATIONS OECD; UN; Colombo Plan

The world's first computerized restaurant order system in a *sushi* shop in **Japan**. The system, designed for use in fast food outlets, is an example of Japanese excellence in applying technological innovation.

Japan is a multiparty parliamentary monarchy under a titular emperor. The USA guarantees defence under the US–Japan security agreement, and Japanese defence spending is comparatively low as a proportion of the budget. Japan claims from Russia the four Kurile islands occupied by Stalin at the end of World War II. The Japanese economy is the second largest in the world and is still growing rapidly. Economic growth has been built on a huge level of exports, and Japan has export surpluses with all its major trading partners, which include developed economies such as the USA and Germany, as well as the developing economies of its neighbours such as China and the ASEAN states of South-east Asia. Japan leads the world in the manufacture of electrical appliances and electronic equipment, which, along with motor vehicles, iron, and steel, make up most of the country's exports. The shipping and chemicals industries are also important. Japan is under pressure to facilitate access to its domestic markets for imports of foreign manufactured goods. Japan is a leading financial market, and the Tokyo stock market is one of the world's foremost financial centres. There are gas fields around the main island of Honshu, but Japan is short of mineral and energy resources, being the world's largest importer of oil. It has a substantial nuclear energy capacity. Only one-sixth of Japan's land can be farmed or is habitable; agriculture is dominated by rice cultivation, and a quarter of food needs must be met by imports. With the rise in the value of the yen since the mid-1980s, Japan has invested heavily overseas, and contributed increasing amounts of aid, often in the form of Japanese goods and services, to developing countries.

Jordan

al-Mamlakah al-Urdunnīyah al-
  Hāshimīyah

CAPITAL Amman
AREA 88,947 km² (34,342 sq. mi.)
POPULATION 3.059 million (1989)
POPULATION GROWTH 3.9% p.a.
GDP PER CAPITA $1,162 (1988)
CURRENCY 1 Jordanian dinar = 1,000 fils
LIFE EXPECTANCY 64 (male) 68 (female)
POPULATION UNDER 15 YEARS 47.9%
LITERACY RATE 79.4% (1986)
RELIGION Sunnī Muslim 93.0%; Christian 4.9%
ETHNIC GROUPS Arab (including Palestinian and Bedouin) 99.2%;
  Circassian 0.5%; Armenian 0.1%; Turkish 0.1%; Kurdish 0.1%
LANGUAGE Arabic (official); minority languages
NUCLEAR CAPACITY No
LABOUR FORCE IN AGRICULTURE 6.5% (1988)
MAIN INTERNATIONAL ORGANIZATIONS UN; Arab League; Non-
  Aligned Movement

Jordan is a constitutional monarchy. Political parties are banned, but general elections, the first in which women have voted, were held in 1989, for the first time since 1967. Supporters of the Muslim Brotherhood won over one-third of the votes. At least 60 per cent of Jordan's

population is Palestinian, and there are about half a million Palestinian refugees in camps on the East Bank of the River Jordan. In 1988 Jordan relinquished its claim to the Israeli-occupied West Bank and asserted the Palestine Liberation Organization's (PLO) status as sole representative of the Palestinians. Jordan's economy is dependent on foreign aid and remittances from Jordanian workers abroad, particularly the Gulf states; the loss of income caused by the 1991 Gulf War was disastrous and compounded by the fact that Iraq had been the major trading partner. Phosphates and agricultural produce are the mainstay of the economy.

Kazakhstan

Kazakh Respublikasy

CAPITAL Alma Ata
AREA 2,717,300 km² (1,048,877 sq. mi.)
POPULATION 16.691 million
CURRENCY rouble
RELIGION Sunnī Muslim; Eastern Orthodox
ETHNIC GROUPS Kazakh 40.0%; Russian
  38.0%; Ukrainian 5.0%; Tatar,
  Armenian, Azeri, German, Greek, and
  Korean minorities
LANGUAGE Kazakh (official); Russian; minority languages
NUCLEAR CAPACITY Defence; uranium producer
MAIN INTERNATIONAL ORGANIZATIONS UN; CSCE; Commonwealth
  of Independent States; North Atlantic Co-operation Council

Kazakhstan is a republic. Formerly a Soviet republic, it became fully independent on the dissolution of the Soviet Union in late 1991. It retains a degree of economic interdependence with the other former Soviet republics. The forced settlement of other ethnic groups and skilled workers from other parts of the former Soviet Union under Stalin and during the process of industrialization in the 1950s, has created an ethnically mixed republic, where some groups, such as the Germans and Black Sea Greeks, are attempting to return to their original homelands, and others, such as the Kazakhs of Mongolia, to return to Kazakhstan. Kazakhstan has rich and varied mineral deposits, including tungsten, copper, lead, uranium, diamonds, coal, iron ore, natural gas, and petroleum. Industry is largely based on the exploitation of these reserves. There is also some light and manufacturing industry. Grain production and sheep-rearing dominate agriculture.

Kenya

Jamhuri ya Kenya (Swahili)/Republic
  of Kenya

CAPITAL Nairobi
AREA 582,646 km² (224,961 sq. mi.)
POPULATION 23.883 million
POPULATION GROWTH 3.8% p.a.
GDP PER CAPITA $309 (1988)
CURRENCY 1 Kenya shilling = 100 cents
LIFE EXPECTANCY 57 (male) 61 (female)
POPULATION UNDER 15 YEARS 52.1%
LITERACY RATE 59.2% (1985)
RELIGION Protestant 26.5%; Roman Catholic 26.4%; traditional
  beliefs 18.9%; African Indigenous 17.6%; Muslim 6.0%; Orthodox
  2.5%
ETHNIC GROUPS Kikuyu 20.9%; Luhya 13.8%; Luo 12.8%; Kamba
  11.3%; Kalenjin 10.8%; other African 29.2%; other including
  Asian 1.2%
LANGUAGE Swahili (official); English; local languages
NUCLEAR CAPACITY No
LABOUR FORCE IN AGRICULTURE 77.8% (1988)
MAIN INTERNATIONAL ORGANIZATIONS Non-Aligned Movement;
  OAU; UN; Commonwealth

Kenya is a one-party republic ruled by the Kenyan African National Union. It became independent from the UK in 1963. Kenya has a record of political stability and freedom of speech despite recent authoritarian policies. The government has resisted calls for multiparty politics, on the grounds that this would lead to divisive ethnic politics, but in 1991 it legalized other political parties, in response to international pressure. Kenya has an agricultural economy with a developing industrial sector. Main exports are coffee, tea, and petroleum products (from imported crude oil) from the Mombasa oil refinery. Tourism is an important sector of the economy, while the textiles, chemical, and vehicle-assembly industries are also significant. There is a developed financial services sector, and a flourishing informal sector. Kenya obtains some two-thirds of its electricity from hydroelectric dams. There are mineral deposits of soda ash, fluorspar, salt, and gold. Agriculture is diverse: the highlands produce maize, coffee, tea, and sisal, while lowland crops include coconuts, cashew-nuts, and cotton.

Kiribati *Micronesia.

'Korea, North

Choso‾n Minjujuu‾i In'min Konghwaguk

CAPITAL Pyongyang
AREA 122,400 km² (47,300 sq. mi.)
POPULATION 22.418 million (1989)
POPULATION GROWTH 1.9% p.a.
GDP PER CAPITA $858 (1988)
CURRENCY 1 won = 100 chon
LIFE EXPECTANCY 66 (male) 73 (female)
POPULATION UNDER 15 YEARS 37.0%
LITERACY RATE 90.0% (1979)
RELIGION Atheist or non-religious 67.9%; traditional beliefs 15.6%; Ch'o‾ndogyo 13.9%; Buddhist 1.7%; Christian 0.9%
ETHNIC GROUPS Korean 99.8%; Chinese 0.2%
LANGUAGE Korean (official); Chinese
NUCLEAR CAPACITY Research (2 reactors)
LABOUR FORCE IN AGRICULTURE 35.3% (1988)
MAIN INTERNATIONAL ORGANIZATIONS UN

North Korea is a one-party communist republic ruled by the Korean Workers' Party. North Korea has held talks on reunification with South Korea since 1972, but these have been blocked by its refusal to allow UN inspection of its alleged nuclear weapons facilities. North Korea is rich in metal deposits such as iron ore, magnesite, phosphate, sulphur, zinc, and copper, which are major exports. Industries include textiles, metal-refining, and chemical fertilizers. Ninety per cent of cultivated land is owned by co-operatives producing the principal crops of rice, maize, and potatoes. The main trading partners have been the former Soviet Union and China; North Korea received substantial aid from the former. It is believed that a quarter of GNP is spent on the armed forces, which are thought to be amongst the world's largest. North Korea remains a closed society, politically and economically, although there have been limited attempts at liberalization.

Korea, South

Taehan Min'guk

CAPITAL Seoul
AREA 99,237 km² (38,316 sq. mi.)
POPULATION 42.38 million (1989)
POPULATION GROWTH 1.0% p.a.
GDP PER CAPITA $4,081 (1988)
CURRENCY 1 South Korean won = 100 jeon
LIFE EXPECTANCY 66 (male) 73 (female)
POPULATION UNDER 15 YEARS 26.5%
LITERACY RATE 92.7% (1981)
RELIGION Atheist or non-religious 57.4%; Buddhist 19.9%; Protestant 16.1%; Roman Catholic 4.6%; Confucian 1.2%
ETHNIC GROUPS Korean 99.9%
LANGUAGE Korean (official)
NUCLEAR CAPACITY Civil and research (11 reactors, 1 under construction)
LABOUR FORCE IN AGRICULTURE 26.8%;
MAIN INTERNATIONAL ORGANIZATIONS UN; Colombo Plan

South Korea is a multiparty republic which returned to full democracy in 1988 following a period of military rule. Talks on reunification with North Korea are in progress, but have been hampered by North

Korea's refusal to allow UN inspection of its alleged nuclear weapons facilities.. South Korea has a mixed economy with a rapidly expanding and successful export-based industrial sector, and an agricultural sector which provides self-sufficiency in food and high yields in rice production. The principal manufacturing industries are petrochemicals, shipbuilding, textiles, and electronics. The chief exports are transport equipment, electrical machinery, footwear, and textiles. South Korea has few minerals except for large tungsten deposits. South Korea is regarded as a successful example of a newly industrializing country, and it plays an increasingly important role in world-wide investment.

Kuwait

Dawlat al-Kuwayt

CAPITAL Kuwait City
AREA 17,818 km² (6,880 sq. mi.)
POPULATION 2.048 million (1989)
POPULATION GROWTH 4.5% p.a.
GDP PER CAPITA $10,189 (1988)
CURRENCY 1 Kuwaiti dinar = 1,000 fils
LIFE EXPECTANCY 71 (male) 75 (female)
POPULATION UNDER 15 YEARS 48.7%
LITERACY RATE 74.5%
RELIGION Sunnī Muslim 63.0%; Shī'ī Muslim 27.0%; Christian 8.0%; Hindu 2.0%
ETHNIC GROUPS Kuwaiti Arab 40.1%; non-Kuwaiti Arab 37.9%; Asian 21.0%; European 0.7%
LANGUAGE Arabic (official); minority languages
NUCLEAR CAPACITY No
LABOUR FORCE IN AGRICULTURE 1.9%
MAIN INTERNATIONAL ORGANIZATIONS UN; Arab League; Gulf Co-operation Council; OPEC; OAPEC

Kuwait is an emirate with a non-legislative national assembly. Political parties are banned. The family of the emir dominates political and economic life, although he has undertaken to introduce a democratic system by 1993. Only males whose forebears were residents before 1920 have the right to vote, excluding all women and most migrant workers. Kuwait was invaded and occupied by Iraq in 1990–1, with far-reaching consequences on its economic and political life. With an estimated 10 per cent of the world's petroleum reserves, Kuwait's economy is based on petroleum extraction, refining, and petrochemical industries; there is also an entrepôt trade, and income from overseas investments is believed to equal that from oil production before the Iraqi occupation. Iraq's pillage and firing of Kuwaiti oil wells destroyed billions of dollars of infrastructure and petroleum reserves, and caused incalculable environmental damage. Kuwait has made substantial investment in welfare, and healthcare and education are free. About 60 per cent of the population are migrant workers, including a high proportion of Palestinians, who were subjected to reprisals for alleged support of the Iraqis during the occupation and are gradually being expelled.

Kyrgyzstan

Kyrgyz Respublikasy

CAPITAL Bishkek
AREA 198,500 km² (76,460 sq. mi.)
POPULATION 4.367 million
CURRENCY rouble
RELIGION Sunnī Muslim; Eastern Orthodox
ETHNIC GROUPS Kirghiz 52.0%; Russian 22.0%; Uzbek 12.0%; Ukrainian and Tatar minorities
LANGUAGE Kirghiz (official); Russian; minority languages
MAIN INTERNATIONAL ORGANIZATIONS CSCE; UN; Commonwealth of Independent States; North Atlantic Co-operation Council

Kyrgyzstan is a republic. Formerly a Soviet republic, it became fully independent following the dissolution of the Soviet Union in 1991. A process of speedy privatization of agriculture and housing has been introduced. There are substantial mineral reserves, including coal, petroleum, and natural gas, but other than coal-mining these have not

Peasant farmers selling their produce at a typical Lao market in the capital Vientiane. Known throughout history as *Lane Xang*, 'the land of a million elephants', **Laos** is one of Asia's smallest, poorest, and least developed countries.

been fully prospected or exploited. Industry is based on mineral extraction and processing, and there is also some light industry such as food-processing and textile manufacture. Agriculture is based on livestock-raising and crops such as fruit, cereals, cotton, sugar-beet, tobacco, and opium poppies.

Laos

Sathalahat Paxathipatai Paxaxôn Lao

CAPITAL   Vientiane
AREA   236,800 km² (91,400 sq. mi.)
POPULATION   3.936 million (1989)
POPULATION GROWTH   2.5% p.a.
GDP PER CAPITA $129 (1988)
CURRENCY   1 kip = 100 at
LIFE EXPECTANCY   47 (male) 50 (female)
POPULATION UNDER 15 YEARS   42.6%
LITERACY RATE   83.9%
RELIGION   Buddhist 57.8%; tribal religions 33.6%; Christian 1.8%; Muslim 1.0%; atheist 1.0%
ETHNIC GROUPS   Lao 67.1%; Palaung-wa 11.9%; Tai 7.9%; Miao (Hmong) and Man (Yao) 5.2%; Mon-Khmer 4.6%
LANGUAGE   Lao (official); minority languages
NUCLEAR CAPACITY   No
LABOUR FORCE IN AGRICULTURE   72.4%
MAIN INTERNATIONAL ORGANIZATIONS   UN

Laos is a landlocked one-party republic, controlled by the People's Revolutionary Party through a politburo and central committee. A new constitution omits references to socialism, and the New Economic Mechanism charts a transition to a market economy. Laos has close ties with Vietnam; much-needed foreign aid has come from Vietnam and the former Soviet Union, and investment from China, Japan, Thailand, and the USA is being encouraged. The Lao economy is mainly agricultural, rice being the chief crop and coffee an export crop. The forests are rich in teak wood, a major export to Thailand at the cost of the destruction of much forest land. High-grade tin is mined. The development of hydroelectric power has made exports of electricity to Thailand the largest export. Limited industry includes food-processing and textiles.

Latvia

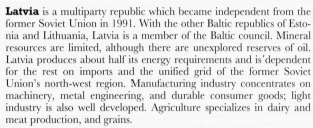

Latvijas Respublika

CAPITAL   Riga
AREA   63,718 km² (24,595 sq. mi.)
POPULATION   2.7 million
CURRENCY   rouble (lat to be introduced)
RELIGION   Lutheran; Eastern Orthodox, Roman Catholic
ETHNIC GROUPS   Latvian 52.0%; Russian 35.0%; Belorussian, Polish, and Ukrainian minorities
LANGUAGE   Latvian (official); Russian; minority languages
MAIN INTERNATIONAL ORGANIZATIONS   UN; CSCE; North Atlantic Co-operation Council

Latvia is a multiparty republic which became independent from the former Soviet Union in 1991. With the other Baltic republics of Estonia and Lithuania, Latvia is a member of the Baltic council. Mineral resources are limited, although there are unexplored reserves of oil. Latvia produces about half its energy requirements and is dependent for the rest on imports and the unified grid of the former Soviet Union's north-west region. Manufacturing industry concentrates on machinery, metal engineering, and durable consumer goods; light industry is also well developed. Agriculture specializes in dairy and meat production, and grains.

Lebanon

al-Jumhūrīyah al-Lubnānīyah

CAPITAL   Beirut
AREA   10,230 km² (3,950 sq. mi.)
POPULATION   2.897 million
POPULATION GROWTH   1.4% p.a.
GDP PER CAPITA $1,887 (1988)
CURRENCY   1 Lebanese pound = 100 piastres
LIFE EXPECTANCY   65 (male) 69 (female)
POPULATION UNDER 15 YEARS   35.3%
LITERACY RATE   78.0%
RELIGION   Shī'ī Muslim 32.0–41.0%; Sunnī Muslim 21.0–27.0%; Maronite Christian 16.0–24.5%; Druze 7.0%; Armenian Christian 4.0%; Greek Catholic 3.0–4.0%; Greek Orthodox 5.0–6.5%
ETHNIC GROUPS   Lebanese Arab 82.6%; Palestinian Arab 9.6%; Armenian 4.9%; Syrian, Kurdish, and other 2.9%
LANGUAGE   Arabic (official); Armenian; French; Kurdish
NUCLEAR CAPACITY   No
LABOUR FORCE IN AGRICULTURE   9.7%
MAIN INTERNATIONAL ORGANIZATIONS   UN; Arab League

Lebanon is a republic under a Syrian-backed government of national unity, which includes the leaders of seven former militias. Its 15-year civil war between rival militias representing the different religious and ethnic communities and their foreign backers was ended in 1990 when Syrian forces, assisted by the Lebanese army, expelled Christian forces from power. This paved the way for the implementation of the 1989 Taif accord, which provides for the disbandment of the militias, a new constitution redressing the balance of power between Muslims and Christians, and the withdrawal of foreign troops. Syrian troops are scheduled to withdraw from Beirut in late 1992; meantime Israel controls part of southern Lebanon through its proxy militia the South Lebanon Army, and the Iran-backed Hizbollah militia, the only mili-

Soldiers clear the debris of war from a street in Beirut, **Lebanon**, in December 1990. Lebanese troops were able to take control of the city for the first time in 15 years after the last remaining Christian militia left it.

tia to refuse to be disarmed under the Taif accord, continues to operate in the south. The Palestine Liberation Organization (PLO) retains a military presence in Sidon despite the expulsion of its headquarters following Israel's 1982 invasion. There are an estimated 300,000 Palestinian refugees in Lebanon. Agriculture, industry, and commerce have been devastated by the civil war; Beirut, formerly the Middle East's leading centre of finance, trade, and tourism, faces a period of reconstruction.

Lesotho

Lesotho (Sotho)/Kingdom of Lesotho

CAPITAL Maseru
AREA 30,355 km² (11,720 sq. mi.)
POPULATION 1.715 million (1989)
POPULATION GROWTH 2.7% p.a.
GDP PER CAPITA $420 (1988)
CURRENCY 1 loti = 100 lisente
LIFE EXPECTANCY 52 (male) 61 (female)
POPULATION UNDER 15 YEARS 43.1%
LITERACY RATE 73.0%
RELIGION Roman Catholic 43.5%; Protestant (mainly Lesotho Evangelical) 29.8%; Anglican 11.5%; other Christian 8.0%; tribal 6.2%
ETHNIC GROUPS Sotho 99.7%
LANGUAGE Sotho, English (both official)
NUCLEAR CAPACITY No
LABOUR FORCE IN AGRICULTURE 81.1%
MAIN INTERNATIONAL ORGANIZATIONS UN; OAU; Commonwealth

Lesotho is a landlocked monarchy under military rule. It gained independence from the UK in 1966. Lesotho is surrounded by South Africa, which dominates the economy, being the principal trading partner. Almost half Lesotho's adult male population work as migrant workers in South Africa, and their remittances are an important source

of revenue. The major exports are manufactures, wool and mohair, food, and livestock. Erosion caused by over-grazing makes soil conservation an urgent priority; droughts are also recurrent. The South African firm de Beers owns 75 per cent of the currently non-operative diamond mines; the Highlands water and power project will supply water to South Africa and hydroelectricity to Lesotho. Tourism is an expanding source of income. Limited industry includes food-processing, textiles, and metal-processing. Lesotho is a member of the Southern African Customs Union.

Liberia

Republic of Liberia

CAPITAL Monrovia
AREA 111,400 km² (43,000 sq. mi.)
POPULATION 2.508 million (1989)
POPULATION GROWTH 3.2% p.a.
GDP PER CAPITA $426 (1988)
CURRENCY 1 Liberian dollar = 100 cents
LIFE EXPECTANCY 53 (male) 56 (female)
POPULATION UNDER 15 YEARS 45.7%
LITERACY RATE 35.0%
RELIGION Christian 67.7%; Muslim 13.8%; traditional beliefs and other 18.5%
ETHNIC GROUPS Kpelle 19.4%; Bassa 13.8%; Grebo 9.0%; Gio 7.8%; Kru 7.3%; Mano 7.1%
LANGUAGE English (official); Mande; Kru-Bassa
NUCLEAR CAPACITY No
LABOUR FORCE IN AGRICULTURE 70.7% (1988)
MAIN INTERNATIONAL ORGANIZATIONS UN; OAU; ECOWAS

Liberia is a republic ruled by an interim government following a short but bloody civil war in 1990. There are links with Guinea and Sierra Leone through the Mano River Union. Iron ore is Liberia's chief export. Rubber, diamonds, timber, and coffee are the other main exports. Cassava, rice, and sugar-cane are important crops. Industry is

The kingdom of **Lesotho** is entirely surrounded by South Africa, and its economy is heavily dependent on its powerful neighbour. The country's poor soil, most suitable for grazing sheep, cannot support the population, many of whom migrate to work in South African mines.

limited to food-processing. Shipping registration fees contribute substantial revenues; ships are registered in Liberia because of its low taxation and lenient inspection policies. Monrovia is a free port. The civil war and low world commodity prices have contributed to economic decline.

Libya

al-Jamāhīrīyah al-'Arabīyah al-Lībīyah
ash- Sha'bīyah al-Ishtilākīyah

CAPITAL Tripoli
AREA 1,757,000 km² (678,400 sq. mi.)
POPULATION 4.080 million (1989)
POPULATION GROWTH 4.0% p.a.
GDP PER CAPITA $5,853 (1988)
CURRENCY 1 Libyan dinar = 1,000 dirhams
LIFE EXPECTANCY 59 (male) 63 (female)
POPULATION UNDER 15 YEARS 45.8%
LITERACY RATE 75.0%
RELIGION Sunnī Muslim 97.0%
ETHNIC GROUPS Libyan Arab and Berber 89.0%
LANGUAGE Arabic (official)
NUCLEAR CAPACITY Research (1 reactor)
LABOUR FORCE IN AGRICULTURE 14.4% (1988)
MAIN INTERNATIONAL ORGANIZATIONS UN; OAU; OAPEC; OPEC;
    Maghreb Union; Arab League

Libya is a one-party republic under military government, with authority at the local level vested in people's congresses. Colonel Muammar Qaddafi, whose current title is Leader of the Revolution, is effective head of state and stifles all opposition. Libya's alleged support for international terrorist groups led to a US bombing raid in 1986, embargo on specialized equipment, and severe deterioration in relations. In 1992 Libya's refusal to hand over two Libyans accused of organizing the bombing of a PanAm aircraft over Lockerbie in 1988 resulted in UN sanctions. The status of the Aozou Strip in northern Chad is disputed with Chad. The economy and exports are dominated by crude oil. Attempts at diversification and infrastructural development, such as the ambitious project (Great Man-Made River) to bring water from the Mediterranean to the south, have been slowed by declining oil revenues. Industry is limited mainly to petroleum by-products and agriculture is limited by the arid nature of most of the country.

Liechtenstein

Liechtenstein/Fürstentum

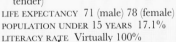

CAPITAL Vaduz
AREA 160 km² (61.8 sq. mi.)
POPULATION 28,300 (1989)
POPULATION GROWTH n/a
GNP PER CAPITA $16,500 (1985) (GDP n.a.)
CURRENCY 1 Swiss franc = 100 rappen (or
    centimes)
LIFE EXPECTANCY 78 (male) 83 (female)
POPULATION UNDER 15 YEARS 19.5%
LITERACY RATE Virtually 100%
RELIGION Roman Catholic 87.0%; Protestant 9.0%
ETHNIC GROUPS Liechtensteiner 63.9%; Swiss 15.7%; Austrian 7.7%;
    German 3.7%
LANGUAGE German (official); Italian; French
NUCLEAR CAPACITY No
LABOUR FORCE IN AGRICULTURE 2.5%
MAIN INTERNATIONAL ORGANIZATIONS CSCE; EFTA; Council of
    Europe

Liechtenstein is a landlocked constitutional principality with no army. Any 900 persons or three communes may initiate legislation in the Diet (parliament). Women were given the right to vote on national, but not local, issues in 1984. There is a customs and monetary union with Switzerland. The economy is based on manufacturing industry; tourism and agriculture play a role, and the registration of foreign holding companies provides a source of tax income and stimulus to financial activity. The main exports are machinery and metal and chemical products.

Lithuania

Lietuvos Respublika

CAPITAL Vilnius
AREA 65,207 km² (25,170 sq. mi.)
POPULATION 3.7 million
CURRENCY rouble (litas to be introduced)
RELIGION Roman Catholic; Eastern
    Orthodox; Lutheran
ETHNIC GROUPS Lithuanian 80.0%;
    Russian 9.0%; Polish 7.0%
LANGUAGE Lithuanian (official); Russian;
    minority languages
NUCLEAR CAPACITY Civil
MAIN INTERNATIONAL ORGANIZATIONS UN; CSCE; North Atlantic
    Co-operation Council

Lithuania is a multiparty republic which became independent from the former Soviet Union in 1991. With the other Baltic states of Estonia and Latvia, Lithuania is a member of the Baltic Council. Lithuania is agriculturally self-sufficient, specializing in meat and milk production, but it depends on imports for supplies of energy and raw materials. There is some electricity production, but Lithuania relies on the unified grid of the north-west former Soviet Union for much of its electricity supply. Mineral resources are varied, including various chemicals, iron ore, and unexploited offshore oil deposits. Lithuania's main industries are machinery, shipbuilding, electronics, chemicals, and oil-refining, together with light industries such as food-processing.

Luxemburg

Grand-Duché de Luxembourg (French)
    Grossherzogtum Luxemburg (German)

CAPITAL Luxemburg
AREA 2,586 km² (999 sq. mi.)
POPULATION 377,000 (1989)
POPULATION GROWTH 0.0% p.a.
GDP PER CAPITA $18,000 (1988)
CURRENCY 1 Luxemburg franc = 100
    centimes (Belgian currency also legal
    tender)
LIFE EXPECTANCY 71 (male) 78 (female)
POPULATION UNDER 15 YEARS 17.1%
LITERACY RATE Virtually 100%
RELIGION Roman Catholic 93.0%; Protestant 1.3%
ETHNIC GROUPS Luxemburger 73.8%; Portuguese 8.1%; Italian
    5.4%; French 3.3%; German 2.3%; Belgian 2.3%
LANGUAGE French, German (both official); Letzeburgesch; minority
    languages
NUCLEAR CAPACITY No
LABOUR FORCE IN AGRICULTURE 3.2%
MAIN INTERNATIONAL ORGANIZATIONS UN; EC; OECD; NATO;
    Council of Europe; CSCE

Luxemburg is a landlocked, neutral constitutional grand duchy. The Benelux economic union with Belgium and The Netherlands came into force in 1960. Although steel is a major industry (iron ore being abundant), and chemicals and machine manufacture are significant, attractive conditions including banking secrecy have made international financial services increasingly important. There is concern that EC fiscal harmonization may jeopardize Luxemburg's status as a leading financial centre.

Macau

Aomen (Chinese)/Macau (Portuguese)

CAPITAL Macau
AREA 16.9 km² (6.5 sq. mi.)
POPULATION 484,000
POPULATION GROWTH 5.9% p.a.
GDP PER CAPITA $5,909 (1988)
CURRENCY 1 pataca = 100 avos
LIFE EXPECTANCY 75 (male) 80 (female)

POPULATION UNDER 15 YEARS 22.0%
LITERACY RATE 61.3%;
RELIGION Non-religious 45.8%; Buddhist
45.1%; Roman Catholic 7.4%;
Protestant 1.3%
ETHNIC GROUPS Chinese 73.5%;
Portuguese 20.3%; British 0.9%
LANGUAGE Portuguese, Chinese
(Cantonese) (both official)
NUCLEAR CAPACITY No
LABOUR FORCE IN AGRICULTURE 5.9%

Macau is a Portuguese special territory which occupies a peninsula on the coast of southern mainland China. There is considerable independence in economic and administrative affairs. Following negotiations between the Chinese and Portuguese governments, it was agreed that Macau would become a special administrative region of the People's Republic of China in 1999. Agriculture is limited and there are few natural resources other than fish. Macau lacks an airport and deepwater harbour, but the economy is based on trading and manufacturing industry, with tourism and gambling important sources of revenue. Manufacturing includes clothing and textiles, electrical goods, and paper, and these products form the principal exports.

Macedonia

Republika Macedonia

CAPITAL Skopje
AREA 25,713 km² (9,928 sq. mi.)
POPULATION 2.3 million
CURRENCY dinar
RELIGION Eastern Orthodox
ETHNIC GROUPS Macedonian 65.0%;
Albanian 21.0%; Turkish, Serb, gypsy,
and Vlach minorities
LANGUAGE Macedonian; Serbo-Croat;
minority languages

Macedonia is a republic which declared independence from Yugoslavia in 1991. International recognition has been blocked by Greece, which fears Macedonian claims on the neighbouring Greek province of Macedonia. Macedonian is linguistically close to Bulgarian, and there is a Macedonian minority in neighbouring Bulgaria. In eastern Macedonia, the large Albanian minority has voted for autonomy which is expected to lead towards ultimate reunification with Albania. Mineral resources include iron ore, lead, zinc, and nickel. Macedonia is almost agriculturally self-sufficient, the chief crops being cereals, rice, and tobacco. Industry comprises steel, chemicals, and textiles production. An estimated 100,000 Macedonians are migrant workers in Germany and Switzerland.

Madagascar

Repoblika Demokratika Malagasy
(Malagasy)/République Démocratique
de Madagascar (French)

CAPITAL Antananarivo
AREA 587,041 km² (226,658 sq. mi.)
POPULATION 11.602 million (1989)
POPULATION GROWTH 2.8% p.a.
GDP PER CAPITA $190 (1988)
CURRENCY 1 Malagasy franc = 100
centimes
LIFE EXPECTANCY 52 (male) 55 (female)
POPULATION UNDER 15 YEARS 44.2%
LITERACY RATE 68.0%
RELIGION Roman Catholic 26.0%; Protestant 22.8%; traditional
beliefs 47.0%; Muslim 1.7%
ETHNIC GROUPS Malagasy 98.9% (Merina 26.6%; Betsimisaraka
14.9%; Betsileo 11.7%; Tsimihety 7.4%; Sakalava 6.4%;
Antandroy 5.3%; Comorian 0.3%; Indian and Pakistani 0.2%;
French 0.2%; Chinese 0.1%)
LANGUAGE Malagasy, French (both official)
NUCLEAR CAPACITY No

LABOUR FORCE IN AGRICULTURE 77.5% (1988)
MAIN INTERNATIONAL ORGANIZATIONS UN; OAU

Madagascar is a multiparty republic. It became independent from France in 1960. The ruling Arena party was returned in elections in 1989, but popular demonstrations forced a coalition with the opposition in 1991. Tension between the majority coastal tribes (côtiers) and the highland people (Merina) underpins politics. Economic activity is mainly agricultural: coffee, vanilla, and cloves are major exports. Rice, cassava, and sweet potatoes are the chief food crops; cattle-breeding is extensive. Mining of chrome ore is significant, and there are bauxite deposits. An oil refinery produces petroleum-based products. Industry is limited mostly to food-processing.

Malawi

Republic of Malaŵi

CAPITAL Lilongwe
AREA 118,484 km² (45,747 sq. mi.)
POPULATION 8.515 million (1989)
POPULATION GROWTH 3.2% p.a.
GDP PER CAPITA $186 (1988)
CURRENCY 1 kwacha = 100 tambala
LIFE EXPECTANCY 46 (male) 48 (female)
POPULATION UNDER 15 YEARS 46.1%
LITERACY RATE 42.0%
RELIGION Protestant 33.7%; Roman Catholic 27.6%; traditional
beliefs 19.0%; Muslim 16.2%
ETHNIC GROUPS Chewa 46.0%; Lomwe 19.0%; Yao 14.0%; Ngoni
9.0%; Tumbuka 6.0%
LANGUAGE English, Chichewa (both official); Lomwe; local languages
NUCLEAR CAPACITY No
LABOUR FORCE IN AGRICULTURE 76.9% (1988)
MAIN INTERNATIONAL ORGANIZATIONS UN; Commonwealth Non-
Aligned Movement; OAU; SADCC

Malawi is a one-party republic ruled by the Malawi Congress Party. President Hastings Banda, who has dominated politics since before independence from the UK in 1964, is president for life. Malawi's policies have been pragmatic, and include the unusual step of recognizing South Africa, where many Malawians find employment. The economy is mainly agricultural, exports being dominated by tobacco, sugar, and tea. Ground-nuts, cotton, and maize are also grown. Industrial development is being financed through foreign aid. Light industries include beer, cement, and cigarette manufacture. Electricity is generated mainly from hydroelectric sources. There are an estimated 1 million refugees from Mozambique.

Malaysia

Malaysia

CAPITAL Kuala Lumpur
AREA 330,442 km² (127,584 sq. mi.)
POPULATION 17.421 million (1989)
POPULATION GROWTH 2.8% p.a.
GDP PER CAPITA $2,045
CURRENCY 1 ringgit = 100 sen
LIFE EXPECTANCY 68 (male) 72 (female)
POPULATION UNDER 15 YEARS 36.2%
LITERACY RATE 69.6%
RELIGION Muslim 52.9%; Buddhist 17.3%; Chinese popular religions
11.6%; Hindu 7%; Christian 6.4%
ETHNIC GROUPS Malay, Orang Asli, Iban, Land Dayak, Bajan, and
Kadazan 60.0%; Chinese 31.0%; Indian, Pakistani, and
Bangladeshi 8.0%
LANGUAGE Malay (official); English; Chinese; Tamil; minority
languages
NUCLEAR CAPACITY Research (1 reactor) (1989)
LABOUR FORCE IN AGRICULTURE 33.9% (1988)
MAIN INTERNATIONAL ORGANIZATIONS UN; Commonwealth; Non-
Aligned Movement; Colombo Plan; ASEAN

Malaysia is a multiparty parliamentary monarchy with a federal structure comprising the eleven states of peninsular Malaya, Sabah, Sarawak, and the federal territory of Kuala Lumpur. The supreme head of the federation is one of the nine Malay rulers elected by the conference of (hereditary) rulers. Manufacturing industry produces automobiles, electronics, cigarettes, tyres, sawn logs, and cement. Crude oil is an important export. Agriculture, with rice the principal subsistence crop, remains the mainstay of the economy, despite high industrial growth in recent years. Malaysia is the world's largest producer of rubber, palm oil, and tin; timber is also an important export. Other mineral resources include bauxite, iron ore, and copper. The New Economic Policy (NEP), initiated after ethnic riots in 1970, introduced ethnic quotas in an attempt to promote economic growth and eradicate the association of race with occupation.

Maldives

Divehi Jumhuriyya

CAPITAL Male
AREA 298 km² (115 sq. mi.)
POPULATION 202,000 (1988)
POPULATION GROWTH 3.4% p.a.
GNP PER CAPITA $310 (1986) (GDP n.a.)
CURRENCY 1 Maldivian rufiyaa = 100 laaris
LIFE EXPECTANCY 58 (male) 59 (female)
POPULATION UNDER 15 YEARS 44.4%
LITERACY RATE n.a.
RELIGION Virtually 100% Sunnī Muslim
ETHNIC GROUPS Majority Sinhalese and Dravidian; Arab, African, and Negrito minorities
LANGUAGE Divehi (official)
NUCLEAR CAPACITY No
LABOUR FORCE IN AGRICULTURE 45.5%;
MAIN INTERNATIONAL ORGANIZATIONS UN; Commonwealth; Colombo Plan

The Maldives is a republic of about 2,000 islands where political parties are forbidden. The head of state is the president, who is nominated by a Citizen's Council. The economy is based on fishing, clothing, shipping, and tourism. Islam is the state religion. Ecological change threatens the future of the country, since many of its islands are a mere 1.8 m (6 feet) above sea level.

Mali

République du Mali

CAPITAL Bamako
AREA 1,240,192 km² (478,841 sq. mi.)
POPULATION 7.911 million (1989)
POPULATION GROWTH 2.4% p.a.
GDP PER CAPITA $217 (1988)
CURRENCY 1 CFA franc = 100 centimes
LIFE EXPECTANCY 42 (male) 46 (female)
POPULATION UNDER 15 YEARS 46.6%
LITERACY RATE 17.0%
RELIGION Muslim 90.0%; traditional beliefs 9.0%; Christian 1.0%
ETHNIC GROUPS Bambara 31.9%; Fulani 13.9%; Senufo 12.0%; Soninke 8.8%; Tuareg 7.3%; Songhai 7.2%; Malinke 6.6%; Dogon 4.0%; Dyula 2.9%; Bobo 2.4%; Arab 1.2%
LANGUAGE French (official); Bambara; Fulani; local languages
NUCLEAR CAPACITY No
LABOUR FORCE IN AGRICULTURE 81.9%
MAIN INTERNATIONAL ORGANIZATIONS UN; OAU; Franc Zone

Mali is a one-party republic ruled by the Union Démocratique du Peuple Malien. It is moving towards a multiparty system: new parties were registered in 1991 and free presidential elections were held in 1992. Landlocked, Mali is amongst the world's poorest countries. The economy is agricultural, with livestock-rearing predominant in the drought-ridden north, and cotton cultivation in the southern savannah. Cotton, livestock, and gold are the chief exports. Millet, sorghum, and rice are also important subsistence crops. Light industry is based on clothing and food-processing. Hydroelectric power contributes substantially to electricity supplies. There are deposits of gold, marble, limestone, salt, and phosphates. Enhanced Tuareg control over local affairs is intended to end fighting in the north between Tuareg rebels and the government.

Malta

Republic of Malta/Repubblika ta' Malta (Maltese)

CAPITAL Valletta
AREA 316 km² (122 sq. mi.)
POPULATION 349,000 (1989)
POPULATION GROWTH 1.0% p.a.
GDP PER CAPITA $5,057 (1988)
CURRENCY 1 Maltese lira = 100 cents = 1,000 mils
LIFE EXPECTANCY 71 (male) 75 (female)
POPULATION UNDER 15 YEARS 23.1%
LITERACY RATE 84.1%
RELIGION Roman Catholic 97.0%; Anglican 1.0%
ETHNIC GROUPS Maltese (of Italian, British, and Phoenician origin) 96.0%; British 2.0%
LANGUAGE Maltese, English (both official)
NUCLEAR CAPACITY No
LABOUR FORCE IN AGRICULTURE 2.5%
MAIN INTERNATIONAL ORGANIZATIONS UN; Commonwealth; Council of Europe; CSCE

Malta is a multiparty republic. It became independent from the UK in 1954, and applied for EC membership in 1990. Major exports include clothing, machinery, and instruments; ship repair is significant and an offshore financial sector is being developed. Offshore oil exploration is being undertaken, and tourism is an important economic activity intended to replace loss of income from UK defence expenditure after the UK base was removed in 1979. Malta is the most densely populated country in Europe, with two-thirds of the population under 40.

Marshall Islands   *Micronesia.

Martinique

Département de Martinique

CAPITAL Fort-de-France
AREA 1,100 km² (424.6 sq. mi.)
POPULATION 340,000
POPULATION GROWTH n.a.
GDP PER CAPITA $5,280
CURRENCY 1 French franc = 100 centimes
LIFE EXPECTANCY 71 (male) 77 (female)
POPULATION UNDER 15 YEARS
LITERACY RATE 92.0%
RELIGION Roman Catholic 87.9%
ETHNIC GROUPS Mulatto 93.7%; French 2.6%; East Indian 1.7%
LANGUAGE French (official)
NUCLEAR CAPACITY No
LABOUR FORCE IN AGRICULTURE n.a.

Martinique is a one-island French overseas department. Tourism and agriculture are the main economic activities. The principal exports are bananas, refined petroleum, rum, and fertilizer. Limited industry includes food-processing and textiles. Martinique is dependent on food imports and French aid.

Mauritania

République Islamique de Mauritanie (French)/al-Jumhūrīyah al-Islāmīyah al-Mūrītānīyah (Arabic)

CAPITAL Nouakchott
AREA 1,030,700 km² (398,000 sq. mi.)
POPULATION 1.946 million (1989)
POPULATION GROWTH 2.8% p.a.
GDP PER CAPITA $521 (1988)
CURRENCY 1 ouguiya = 5 khoums
LIFE EXPECTANCY 44 (male) 48 (female)
POPULATION UNDER 15 YEARS 44.6%
LITERACY RATE 17.0%

RELIGION Muslim 99.0%; Christian 0.5%
ETHNIC GROUPS Moor (Arab-Berber and African-Sudanic) 81.5%; Tukulor 8.0%; Fulani 5.0%
LANGUAGE French, Arabic (both official); ethnic languages
NUCLEAR CAPACITY No
LABOUR FORCE IN AGRICULTURE 65.5% (1988)
MAIN INTERNATIONAL ORGANIZATIONS UN; OAU; Arab League; Maghreb Union

Mauritania is a republic. Multiparty elections in 1992 were boycotted by opposition parties, and power was retained by the ruling Social and Democratic Republican Party. In 1980 it was one of the last countries to abolish slavery. Government policies of arabization have caused resentment among the black Mauritanians of the south. Exports are dominated by iron ore and fish. Agriculture, confined mainly to the Senegal River valley in the south, despite attempts to extend irrigation by constructing dams, includes the growing of millet, dates, and rice. Around one-quarter of the population consists of nomadic Berbers, but nomadic livestock-rearing has declined with periodic droughts and the expansion of mining. Apart from mining, industrial activity involves a small amount of light manufacturing. There are deposits of copper, gypsum, phosphates, sulphur, gold, and uranium. Relations with Senegal have deteriorated in recent years with outbreaks of violence along the common border.

Mauritius

Mauritius

CAPITAL Port Louis
AREA 2,040 km² (788 sq. mi.)
POPULATION 1.049 million (1989)
POPULATION GROWTH 1.0% p.a.
GNP PER CAPITA $1,800 (GDP n.a.)
CURRENCY 1 Mauritian rupee = 100 cents
LIFE EXPECTANCY 64 (male) 71 (female)
POPULATION UNDER 15 YEARS 31.3%
LITERACY RATE 81.8%
RELIGION Hindu 52.5%; Roman Catholic 25.7%; Muslim 12.9%; Protestant 4.4%; Buddhist 0.4%
ETHNIC GROUPS Creole 55.5%; Indian 39.6%; European 3.8%; Chinese 0.6%
LANGUAGE English (official); French creole; Bhojpuri; Hindi; other Indian languages
NUCLEAR CAPACITY No

As well as being the country's most important export, sugar has also shaped the demography of **Mauritius**, one of the Indian Ocean Islands. Two-thirds of the population are descended from slaves brought to the island from Madagascar and East Africa to work the sugar plantations.

LABOUR FORCE IN AGRICULTURE 19.0%
MAIN INTERNATIONAL ORGANIZATIONS Non-Aligned Movement; UN; Commonwealth; OAU

Mauritius is an island republic. It has had a multiparty democracy since independence from the UK in 1968. The main exports are textiles and sugar. Tourism is an important source of revenue. Tea, fruit, and vegetables are important agricultural crops. There are no significant minerals.

Mayotte *Comoros.

Melanesia

Melanesia is a group of islands in the south-western Pacific. All have Christian majorities and are members of the South Pacific Commission and, except New Caledonia, the South Pacific Forum. **New Caledonia** is a French Overseas Territory, re-affirmed as a French possession by referendum in 1987 despite a separatist movement. Agriculture and mining are important, with exports dominated by nickel and its alloys. There is violent tension between aboriginal Kanaks and the majority French settlers. **The Solomon Islands** are a parliamentary monarchy, whose head of state is the UK monarch. It is a member of the Commonwealth, and an ACP state of the EC. Agriculture and fishing are important, and fish and wood products the chief exports. Land ownership is determined largely by kinship and clan membership. As well as English the islands include speakers of eighty-seven languages of the Austronesian family. **Vanuatu** is a multiparty republic, a member of the Commonwealth, and an ACP state of the EC. The economy is predominantly agricultural, tuna fish and copra being the main exports. The official language, Bislama, is an English-based pidgin; English and French are also spoken. Most of the islanders are Christian, but animist beliefs are prevalent.

Mexico

Estados Unidos Mexicanos

CAPITAL Mexico City
AREA 1,958,201 km² (756,066 sq. mi.)
POPULATION 84.275 million (1989)
POPULATION GROWTH 2.1% p.a.
GDP PER CAPITA $2,102 (1988)
CURRENCY 1 peso = 100 centavos
LIFE EXPECTANCY 66 (male) 72 (female)
POPULATION UNDER 15 YEARS 37.2
LITERACY RATE 90.3%
RELIGION Roman Catholic 92.6%; Protestant (incl. Evangelical) 3.3%; Jewish 0.1%
ETHNIC GROUPS Mestizo 55.0%; Amerindian 30.0%; European 15.0%
LANGUAGE Spanish (official); Amerindian languages
NUCLEAR CAPACITY Research (3 reactors, 2 civil reactors under construction) (1989)
LABOUR FORCE IN AGRICULTURE 31.2% (1988)
MAIN INTERNATIONAL ORGANIZATIONS UN; OAS

Mexico is a multiparty federal republic comprising thirty-one states and one federal district (Mexico City). Although formally democratic, the political system has been dominated by the Party of the Institutionalized Revolution (PRI). The party has been discredited in recent years by charges of corruption and election-rigging and by its difficulties in controlling the economy. Crude oil accounts for a majority of Mexico's foreign earnings, and oil revenues have been used to develop an industrial base. However, the economy has suffered from a massive external debt ($81 billion in 1988), with high unemployment. There is considerable other mineral wealth, particularly silver and zinc, which has not been fully exploited. The main exports are chemicals, non-ferrous ores, motor vehicles, and petroleum products. Agriculture relies on irrigation. The main food crop is maize, and export crops include fruit, vegetables, shrimps, and coffee. Large numbers of illegal emigrants enter the USA annually across the northern border in search of work, and there is a line of assembly plants along this border. Mexico City is the world's largest urban centre, with severe problems of pollution, infrastructure, and overcrowding.

Micronesia

Micronesia is a group of western Pacific islands, all members of the South Pacific Commission. The four **US Territories** formerly comprised the US Trust Territory of the Pacific Islands. There is limited fertile land, and agriculture is based on coconut oil, copra, and fishing. Tourism is being developed. The islands are populated mainly by Micronesians and Chamorrans (of mixed Indonesian, Spanish, and Filipino origin). **Guam** is a self-governing US Outlying Territory, with a large US naval and air base. It is a free trade zone. **Kiribati** is a republic, a member of the Commonwealth and the South Pacific Forum, and an ACP state of the EC. The international date-line runs through the country. **The Marshall Islands** comprise a republic in free association with the USA, with a US missile-testing range and airfield. It is a member of the UN. English is the official language. **The Federated States of Micronesia** are a federal republic of four states, Kosrae, Truk, Yap, and Pohnpei. It is a member of the UN. English is the official language, though each state has its own language of the Austronesian family. **Nauru** is a republic and member of the Commonwealth and the South Pacific Forum. Phosphate mining, which dominates the economy and employs many immigrant workers, is expected to exhaust reserves by the end of the century. Nauru is reputed to have the world's deepest offshore moorings. **The North Mariana Islands** comprise a commonwealth in union with the USA. English is the official language, but over half the population speak Chamorro, an Austronesian language.

Moldova

Republica Moldoveneasca

CAPITAL Chisinau
AREA 33,700 km² (13,000 sq. mi.)
POPULATION 4.3 million
CURRENCY rouble
RELIGION Eastern Orthodox
ETHNIC GROUPS Moldovan (Romanian) 65.0%; Ukrainian 14.0%; Russian 13.0%; Gagauz, Jewish, and Bulgarian minorities
LANGUAGE Romanian (official); Russian; minority languages
MAIN INTERNATIONAL ORGANIZATIONS UN; CSCE; Commonwealth of Independent States; North Atlantic Co-operation Council

Moldova is a republic which became independent from the former Soviet Union in 1991. The majority of the population is Romanian, and further moves towards reunification with Romania are expected. There is conflict between the government, and Russian and Ukrainian minorities in the Slavic region of Dnestr, where most industry is concentrated, which has declared its independence from Moldova. Mineral resources are meagre, but the soil is fertile and agriculture prospers, with viticulture, fruits and vegetables, tobacco, grains, and industrial crops, such as sunflower seeds, of importance. Industry concentrates on food-processing, machinery, and other light industry.

Monaco

Principauté de Monaco

AREA 1.95 km² (0.75 sq. mi.)
POPULATION 29,300 (1990)
GNP PER CAPITA $11,350 (GDP n.a.)

CURRENCY 1 French franc = 100 centimes
LIFE EXPECTANCY 72 (male) 80 (female)
LITERACY RATE Virtually 100%
RELIGION Roman Catholic 90.0%
ETHNIC GROUPS French 46.8%; Monégasque 16.6%; Italian 16.5%
LANGUAGE French (official); Italian; Monégasque
NUCLEAR CAPACITY No
MAIN INTERNATIONAL ORGANIZATIONS CSCE

Monaco is a sovereign principality with elected national and communal councils. There is a customs union with France, which is responsible for its defence. Tourism is the major industry, with gambling the chief attraction. Postage stamps also provide an important source of government revenue. Light industry includes electronics and pharmaceuticals. Financial and trading interests are a growing sector. Mineral resources are lacking, and agriculture is very limited.

Mongolia

Bügd Nayramdah Mongol Ard Uls

CAPITAL Ulan Bator
AREA 1,566,500 km² (604,800 sq. mi.)
POPULATION 2.096 million (1989)
POPULATION GROWTH 3.0% p.a.
GDP PER CAPITA $1,053 (1988)
CURRENCY 1 tugrik = 100 mongo
LIFE EXPECTANCY 62 (male) 66 (female)
POPULATION UNDER 15 YEARS 41.8%
LITERACY RATE 89.5% (1979)
RELIGION Buddhism; Shamanism; Islam
ETHNIC GROUPS Khalkha 77.5%; Kazakh 5.3%; Dorbed 2.8%; Bayad 2.0%; Buryat Mongol 1.9%; Draiganga Mongol 1.5%
LANGUAGE Khalkha Mongolian (official); minority languages and dialects
NUCLEAR CAPACITY No
LABOUR FORCE IN AGRICULTURE 32.2% (1988)
MAIN INTERNATIONAL ORGANIZATIONS UN

Mongolia is a multiparty republic which held free elections in 1990 after a long period of one-party rule by the communist Mongolian People's Revolutionary Party. It is making the transition from a planned economy to a free-market economy. Aid from the former Soviet Union enabled infrastructural and limited industrial development, but has left Mongolia with a large foreign debt, and dependent on trade with the former Soviet Union, including imports of Soviet fuel, equipment, and spare parts. The predominantly nomadic pastoral economy is based on animal-breeding, with meat, livestock, and wool the main exports. However, agriculture, particularly cereal production, is being extended. Mineral resources such as fluorite and copper are exploited.

Morocco

al-Mamlakah al-Maghribīyah

CAPITAL Rabat
AREA 458,730 km² (177,117 sq. mi.)
POPULATION 24.530 million (1989)
POPULATION GROWTH 2.7% p.a.
GDP PER CAPITA $775 (1988)
CURRENCY 1 dirham = 100 francs
LIFE EXPECTANCY 59 (male) 63 (female)
POPULATION UNDER 15 YEARS 40.7%
LITERACY RATE 44.0%
RELIGION Muslim (mostly Sunnī) 98.7%; Christian 1.1%
ETHNIC GROUPS Arab-Berber 99.5%
LANGUAGE Arabic (official); Berber; Spanish; French
NUCLEAR CAPACITY No
LABOUR FORCE IN AGRICULTURE 38.4% (1988)
MAIN INTERNATIONAL ORGANIZATIONS UN; Non-Aligned Movement; Arab League; Maghreb Union

Morocco is a constitutional monarchy whose monarch is both head of government and the highest religious authority. The legal system is

A camel ride on Agadir beach gives an artificial taste of the desert. Like many developing countries, **Morocco** has learned to exploit its natural advantages of sun and scenery to create a tourist industry which caters for those seeking a more exotic destination.

based on a mixture of French law and the *sharī'ah* (Islamic law). King Hassan II exerts stringent control over the political process. Since 1976 Morocco has occupied the Western Sahara, a former Spanish colony, against the opposition of the Algerian-backed Polisario Front. A UN-brokered peace plan, signed by both sides in 1991, has not yet been implemented. The Western Saharan government-in-exile, the Sahrawi Arab Democratic Republic (SADR), has been admitted as a member of the OAU, prompting Morocco to withdraw from the OAU. Morocco claims the two Spanish coastal enclaves of Ceuta and Melilla. Morocco's main export is phosphates, of which it has the world's largest reserves; other minerals extracted include anthracite, iron, lead, and manganese. Morocco is dependent on imported fuel for most of its energy needs, and also relies on imports to meet food requirements. Other than phosphate production, industry concentrates on textiles and motor vehicles. Tourism is regarded as an expanding source of revenue. Traditional methods of farming keep yields of crops such as grains, citrus fruit, and grapes low.

Mozambique

Republica Popular de Moçambique
CAPITAL Maputo
AREA 802,000 km² (309,572 sq. mi.)
POPULATION 15.293 million (1989)
POPULATION GROWTH 2.6% p.a.
GDP PER CAPITA $78 (1988)
CURRENCY 1 metical = 100 centavos
LIFE EXPECTANCY 45 (male) 48 (female)
POPULATION UNDER 15 YEARS 44.1
LITERACY RATE 27.2%

RELIGION Traditional beliefs 47.8%; Christian (mostly Roman Catholic) 38.9%; Muslim 13.0%
ETHNIC GROUPS Makua 47.3%; Tsonga 23.3%; Malawi 12.0%; Shona 11.3%; Yao 3.8%; Swahili 0.8%; Makonde 0.6%; Portuguese 0.2%
LANGUAGE Portuguese (official); Makua; Tsonga; local languages
NUCLEAR CAPACITY No
LABOUR FORCE IN AGRICULTURE 82.2% (1988)
MAIN INTERNATIONAL ORGANIZATIONS UN; OAU; SADCC

Mozambique is a republic moving towards a multiparty system and free-market economy after adopting a new constitution in 1990. Since independence from Portugal in 1975, it has been governed by the Frelimo (Mozambique Liberation Front) Party, which has in recent years rejected its former Marxist–Leninist policies. There has been civil war between the government and Renamo guerrillas; peace talks in Rome have as yet proved inconclusive, and South Africa is believed to continue its support for the guerrillas. Civil war, compounded by drought and floods, has made the economy dependent on foreign aid, and displaced some 5.6 million persons. Mineral resources include large reserves of coal, iron ore, tantalite, and unknown reserves of natural gas and precious stones. The Cabora Bassa dam is one of Africa's largest hydroelectric dams, and electricity is exported to South Africa. Much of agriculture has been collectivized; the main crops are cassava, maize, coconuts, and sugar-cane. Shrimps and cashew-nuts are the main exports. Industry consists primarily of the processing of local raw materials; an oil-refinery processes imported petroleum.

Myanmar (Burma)

Pyidaungzu Myanma Naingngandaw
CAPITAL Yangon (formerly Rangoon)
AREA 676,577 km² (261,228 sq. mi.)
POPULATION 40.810 million (1989)
POPULATION GROWTH 2.1% p.a.
GNP PER CAPITA $200 (1986) (GDP n.a.)

CURRENCY 1 kyat = 100 pyas
LIFE EXPECTANCY 59 (male) 62 (female)
POPULATION UNDER 15 YEARS 41.2%
LITERACY RATE 78.5%
RELIGION Buddhist 75.2%; Christian 4.9%;
    Muslim 16.0%; traditional beliefs 1.1%;
    Hindu 0.5%
ETHNIC GROUPS Burman 69.0%; Shan
    8.5%; Karen 6.2%; Rakhine 4.5%; Mon
    2.4%; Chin 2.2%; Kachin 1.4%
LANGUAGE Burmese (official); minority languages; English
NUCLEAR CAPACITY No
LABOUR FORCE IN AGRICULTURE 65.1%
MAIN INTERNATIONAL ORGANIZATIONS UN; Colombo Plan

Myanmar is a republic under military rule. Multiparty elections held in 1988 and 1990 were won by the National League for Democracy, but it has not been allowed to take office, and its leader has been held under house arrest since 1989. The country has a broadly based agricultural economy. Crops include sugar-cane, pulses, ground-nuts, and maize. Major exports are timber, especially teak, whose production is in the state sector, rice, minerals, and gems. Crude oil is extracted, and production of natural gas is increasing. The small industrial sector includes oil-refining, food-processing, and textiles. Mineral resources include copper, zinc, lead, tin, and silver. Minority populations, the Karen and Nagas, control the opium-producing parts of Myanmar and are fighting for independence and the pro-democracy movement. In the Muslim-majority state of Arakan, Rohingya rebels are fighting for an independent homeland. An estimated 200,000 Rohingya Muslims fled to neighbouring Bangladesh in 1992.

Namibia

Republic of Namibia
CAPITAL Windhoek
AREA 824,292 km² (317,818 sq. mi.)
POPULATION 1.252 million (est. 1988)
POPULATION GROWTH 3.2% p.a.
GDP PER CAPITA $938 (1988)
CURRENCY 1 South African rand = 100
    cents
LIFE EXPECTANCY 55 (male) 58 (female)
POPULATION UNDER 15 YEARS 45.8%
LITERACY RATE 72.5%
RELIGION Lutheran 51.2%; Roman Catholic 19.8%; Dutch
    Reformed 6.1%; Anglican 5.0%
ETHNIC GROUPS Ovambo 49.8%; Kavango 9.3%; Herero 7.5%;
    Damara 7.5%; White 6.4%; Nama 4.8%
LANGUAGE Afrikaans; English; German (official); Ambo; Herero;
    local languages
NUCLEAR CAPACITY No (uranium producer)
LABOUR FORCE IN AGRICULTURE 36.6% (1988)
MAIN INTERNATIONAL ORGANIZATIONS Commonwealth; UN; OAS

Namibia is a multiparty republic which gained independence from South Africa in 1990. The South West African People's Association (SWAPO), which led the struggle for independence, now holds power. Poor rainfall limits agriculture to livestock-raising, although fishing, millet, maize, and wheat are also important. Exports are dominated by uranium and diamonds. There are also deposits of tungsten, vanadium, tin, copper, and lead. There is a shortage of skilled labour, and manufacturing industry is limited. The economy has not recovered from the devastation of the war for independence, and is still highly dependent on South Africa and multinational companies.

Nauru   *Micronesia.

Nepal

Nepāl Adhirājya
CAPITAL Kathmandu
AREA 147,181 km² (56,827 sq. mi.)
POPULATION 18.452 million (1989)

POPULATION GROWTH 2.6% p.a.
GDP PER CAPITA $160 (1988)
CURRENCY 1 Nepalese rupee = 100 paisa
    (or pice)
LIFE EXPECTANCY 52 (male) 50 (female)
POPULATION UNDER 15 YEARS 42.2%
LITERACY RATE 21.6%
RELIGION Hindu 89.5%; Buddhist 5.3%;
    Muslim 2.7%; Jain 0.1%
ETHNIC GROUPS Nepalese 58.4%; Bihari
    18.7%; Tharu 3.6%; Tamang 3.5%; Newar 3.0%
LANGUAGE Nepali (official); Bihari; Tamang
NUCLEAR CAPACITY No
LABOUR FORCE IN AGRICULTURE 92.0% (1988)
MAIN INTERNATIONAL ORGANIZATIONS UN; Colombo Plan

Nepal is a monarchy with executive power vested in the crown. The indirectly elected *Rashtriya Panchayat* was replaced by a multiparty parliamentary form of government in early 1990. Much of the land is not cultivable and deforestation is a major problem. However, the economy is primarily agrarian, with principal crops of rice, sugar-cane, maize, and wheat. Industry is limited mainly to agricultural processing. Tourism is an increasing source of revenue. Foreign aid supports 60 per cent of the development budget.

The Netherlands

Koninkrijk der Nederlanden

CAPITAL Amsterdam
AREA 41,863 km² (16,163 sq. mi.)
POPULATION 14.846 million (1989)
POPULATION GROWTH 0.6% p.a.
GDP PER CAPITA $15,421 (1988)
CURRENCY 1 guilder (florin) = 100 cents
LIFE EXPECTANCY 74 (male) 80 (female)
POPULATION UNDER 15 YEARS 17.8%
LITERACY RATE Virtually 100%
RELIGION Roman Catholic 36.0%; non-religious 32.6%; Dutch
    Reformed Church 18.5%; Reformed Churches 8.4%
ETHNIC GROUPS Netherlander 96.0%; Turkish 1.0%; Moroccan
    1.0%
LANGUAGE Dutch (official); minority languages
NUCLEAR CAPACITY Civil and research (4 reactors)
LABOUR FORCE IN AGRICULTURE 4.0% (1988)
MAIN INTERNATIONAL ORGANIZATIONS UN; OECD; NATO; EC;
    Council of Europe; CSCE

The Netherlands is a constitutional monarchy. The religious division of Protestant and Catholic is strongly reflected in the composition of the political parties. Each of the eleven provinces has its own representative body, the Provincial States. The International Court of Justice has its seat at The Hague, which is the seat of the court, government, and Parliament. Trade, banking, and shipping have traditionally been important to the economy, which is now primarily industrial. Many raw materials are imported; petroleum products and chemicals are the principal exports. The manufacturing base includes electrical and other machinery, textiles, and food-processing. Of native minerals, natural gas extraction is substantial and a major source of domestic energy. An ongoing programme of maritime land reclamation has increased total land area.

Netherlands Antilles

Nederlandse Antillen

CAPITAL Willemstad
AREA 800 km² (308 sq. mi.)
POPULATION 183,000 (1989)
POPULATION GROWTH 2.2% p.a.
GDP PER CAPITA $7,895 (1988)
CURRENCY 1 Netherlands Antilles guilder =
    100 cents
LIFE EXPECTANCY 71 (male) 76 (female)
POPULATION UNDER 15 YEARS 30.0%
LITERACY RATE 83.8%

RELIGION Roman Catholic 83.8%; Reformed tradition 3.3%;
Methodist 3.2%; non-religious 2.6%; Seventh-day Adventist 1.5%;
Jewish 0.3%
ETHNIC GROUPS Mixed 84.0%; White 6.0%
LANGUAGE Dutch (official); English; Papiamento
NUCLEAR CAPACITY No
LABOUR FORCE IN AGRICULTURE 0.6%

The Netherlands Antilles is an overseas territory of The Netherlands, comprising two groups of islands, the Leeward and the Windward Islands, which have internal self-government. Calcium
phosphate is the chief mineral extracted. Curaçao Island, a Leeward
Island, has an oil refinery and large dry docks. The islands cannot support much agriculture, and rely on imports for most of their needs.
Tourism and finance are important, but the economies are supported
by Dutch aid. Papiamento (a French-based creole) is spoken in the Leeward Islands, English in the Windward Islands.

New Caledonia *Melanesia.

New Zealand

New Zealand/Aotearoa (Maori)

CAPITAL Wellington
AREA 267,844 km² (103,415 sq. mi.)
POPULATION 3.371 million (1989)
POPULATION GROWTH 0.6% p.a.
GDP PER CAPITA $11,544 (1988)
CURRENCY 1 New Zealand dollar = 100 cents
LIFE EXPECTANCY 72 (male) 80 (female)

In **The Netherlands**, the area of Rotterdam known as Europoort was built
in the 1960s and designed for the unloading and storing of petroleum. The
city's initial expansion resulted from its monopolization of the trade with
Germany's industrial Ruhr district in the 19th century.

POPULATION UNDER 15 YEARS 22.5%
LITERACY RATE Virtually 100%
RELIGION Anglican 24.3%; Presbyterian
18.0%; non-religious 16.4%; Roman
Catholic 15.2%; Methodist 4.7%
ETHNIC GROUPS European origin 82.2%;
Maori 9.2%; Pacific Island Polynesian
2.9%
LANGUAGE English, Maori (both official)
NUCLEAR CAPACITY No (nuclear-free zone)
LABOUR FORCE IN AGRICULTURE 9.5% (1988)
MAIN INTERNATIONAL ORGANIZATIONS UN; Commonwealth; OECD;
South Pacific Forum; Colombo Plan

New Zealand is a multiparty parliamentary monarchy whose head
of state is the UK monarch. New Zealand has twenty-two regions, of
which Auckland and Wellington have directly elected regional councils, while twenty are governed by united councils appointed by the
lower tier of government. Membership of the Anzus Treaty was suspended in 1986, after New Zealand declared itself a nuclear-free zone.
A treaty for closer economic relations aiming at the gradual introduction of a free market has been signed with Australia. New Zealand has
a largely agricultural economy with major exports of meat, wool, and
butter. The economy has still not fully recovered from the loss of preferential treatment by the UK, once the chief trading partner, when the
UK joined the EC. New Zealand imports most manufactured goods
and suffers from a balance of payments deficit. Most indigenous woodlands are protected by National Parks, though commercial forestry is a
thriving industry. Hydroelectricity is the basis of power generation, and
supplies a large bauxite smelter. There is also some geothermal electricity production. Limited mineral deposits of iron, gold, salt, clay, and
pumice are exploited. An oil refinery manufactures petrochemicals and
there is some light industry.

New Zealand Self-Governing Territories Overseas are territories sharing a head of state (the UK monarch) and citizenship with
New Zealand while having full internal self-government. The territories are the Cook Islands and Niue. Both are members of the South

The Apapa Docks in the modern seaport of Lagos, the capital of **Nigeria**. The city is on an island in a coastal lagoon and became a seaport only after a shipping channel was dredged to the open sea.

Pacific Forum. Niue's exports include coconuts, honey, limes, and root-crops, while the Cook Islands also export copra and clothing. Both territories have their own Congregationalist churches.

Nicaragua

República de Nicaragua

CAPITAL Managua
AREA 130,700 km² (50,464 sq. mi.)
POPULATION 3.745 million (1989)
POPULATION GROWTH 3.4% p.a.
GDP PER CAPITA $550 (1988)
CURRENCY 1 cordoba = 100 centavos
LIFE EXPECTANCY 62 (male) 65 (female)
POPULATION UNDER 15 YEARS 45.8%
LITERACY RATE 88.0%
RELIGION Roman Catholic 88.3%; other (mostly Baptist, Moravian, and Pentecostal) 11.7%
ETHNIC GROUPS Mestizo 77.0%; White 10.0%; Black 9.0%; Amerindian 4.0%
LANGUAGE Spanish (official); Amerindian languages
NUCLEAR CAPACITY No
LABOUR FORCE IN AGRICULTURE 40.0% (1988)
MAIN INTERNATIONAL ORGANIZATIONS UN; OAS

Nicaragua is a multiparty republic. Free elections were held in 1990 in which the Sandinistas, who had held power since their overthrow of the dictator Anastasio Somoza in 1979, were defeated by a centre-right coalition. The USA had opposed the democratically elected Sandinista government, supporting the 'contra' guerrillas. The civil war has devastated the economy, which has also suffered from US attempts to enact a trade blockade and suspend foreign aid. There have been shortages of most goods and very high inflation. The economy is principally agricultural, with coffee, cotton, beef, and bananas the principal exports. There is also some gold-mining. Manufacturing industry includes food-processing, petroleum-refining, textiles, and cement.

Niger

République du Niger

CAPITAL Niamey
AREA 1,267,000 km² (489,062 sq. mi.)
POPULATION 7.523 million (1989)
POPULATION GROWTH 3.5% p.a.
GDP PER CAPITA $359 (1988)
CURRENCY 1 CFA franc = 100 centimes
LIFE EXPECTANCY 43 (male) 46 (female)
POPULATION UNDER 15 YEARS 47.3%
LITERACY RATE 14.0%
RELIGION Sunnī Muslim 80.0%; traditional beliefs 20.0%
ETHNIC GROUPS Hausa 54.1%; Songhai, Zerma, and Dendi 21.7%; Fulani 10.1%; Tuareg 8.4%; Kanuri 4.2%; Teda 0.2%
LANGUAGE French (official); Hausa; Songhai; local languages
NUCLEAR CAPACITY No (uranium producer)
LABOUR FORCE IN AGRICULTURE 89.6% (1985)
MAIN INTERNATIONAL ORGANIZATIONS UN; OAU; Franc Zone

Niger is a landlocked republic where the military government was replaced by an interim government in 1991. It became independent from France in 1960. A new constitution (1989) and the legalization of political parties (1991) are moves towards multiparty elections, scheduled by the end of 1992. Agriculture is the principal economic activity, concentrating on livestock (the second-largest export) and the cultivation of millet, ground-nuts, sorghum, and other arable staples. Drought is a continuing problem. Uranium accounts for almost three-quarters of exports, with livestock and vegetables also exported; other mineral reserves are phosphates, tin, and coal, and unexploited reserves of iron, oil, gold, and copper. Industry is mainly textiles, cement, and mining.

Nigeria

Federal Republic of Nigeria

CAPITAL Lagos
AREA 923,768 km² (356,669 sq. mi.)
POPULATION 88.5 million (1991)
POPULATION GROWTH 3.3% p.a.
GDP PER CAPITA $350 (1991)
CURRENCY 1 naira = 100 kobo
LIFE EXPECTANCY 49 (male) 52 (female)
POPULATION UNDER 15 YEARS 48.4%
LITERACY RATE 43.0%
RELIGION Muslim 45.0%; Protestant 26.3%; African indigenous and traditional 17.2%; Roman Catholic 12.1%
ETHNIC GROUPS Hausa 21.3%; Yoruba 21.3%; Ibo 18.0%; Fulani 11.2%; Ibibio 5.6%; Kanuri 4.2%; Edo 3.4%; Tiv 2.2%; Ijaw 1.8%; Bura 1.7%; Nupe 1.2%
LANGUAGE English (official); Hausa; Yoruba; Ibo; local languages
NUCLEAR CAPACITY No
LABOUR FORCE IN AGRICULTURE 65.5% (1988)
MAIN INTERNATIONAL ORGANIZATIONS UN; Commonwealth; ECOWAS; OAU; OPEC

Nigeria is a twenty-one-state federal republic which has been under military rule since 1982. It became independent from the UK in 1960. The lifting of the ban on political parties in 1989 is part of the transition to civilian two-party rule planned for 1992, despite fears of ethnic violence. Oil accounts for 95 per cent of Nigeria's exports (1989); other minerals include abundant supplies of natural gas, iron ore, coal, lead, and zinc. Heavy investment in petroleum and other industries such as steel, cement, and vehicles was halted by the drop in world oil prices in the mid-1980s, but led to a massive foreign debt ($41 billion in 1989) and the neglect of agriculture. IMF-backed austerity measures include cuts in subsidies and the development of traditional cash crops such as cocoa, cotton, and ground-nuts, and staple crops such as millet, sorghum, plantains, and cassava to reduce dependence on food imports. The north is predominantly Muslim and dominated by the Hausa–Fulani people, while the south is Christian, populated by Yoruba and Ibo peoples. Christian fears of Muslim domination were expressed in a coup attempt in 1990.

North Mariana Islands *Micronesia.

Norway

Kongeriket Norge

CAPITAL Oslo
AREA 323,878 km² (125,050 sq. mi.)
POPULATION 4.228 million (1989)
POPULATION GROWTH 0.3% p.a.
GDP PER CAPITA $21,724 (1988)
CURRENCY 1 krone = 100 ore
LIFE EXPECTANCY 74 (male) 80 (female)
POPULATION UNDER 15 YEARS 18.8%
LITERACY RATE Virtually 100%
RELIGION Church of Norway (Evangelical Lutheran) 88.0%; Pentecostalist 1.0%
ETHNIC GROUPS Norwegian 98.0%; Danish 0.3%; US 0.3%; British 0.2%; Swedish 0.2%; Pakistani 0.2%
LANGUAGE Norwegian (official)
NUCLEAR CAPACITY Research (2 reactors)
LABOUR FORCE IN AGRICULTURE 5.8%
MAIN INTERNATIONAL ORGANIZATIONS UN; NATO; EFTA; OECD; Council of Europe; CSCE

Norway is a parliamentary monarchy. The extraction of North Sea oil and natural gas increased sharply in the 1970s and 1980s, and they make up about half of exports. Most electricity is generated by hydro-electric sources. Norway's annual fish catch is the second highest in Europe after that of the former Soviet Union. Norway has an industrial economy, exporting aluminium and ferrous metals, machinery, ships, chemicals, and paper. Fur production and conifer forestry are significant. Mineral resources include iron ore, copper, zinc, and lead. Agriculture is limited since only 3 per cent of land area is cultivable.

Oman

Salṭanat 'Umān

CAPITAL Muscat
AREA 300,000 km² (120,000 sq. mi.)
POPULATION 1.422 million (1989)
POPULATION GROWTH 3.9% p.a.
GDP PER CAPITA $5,500 (1988)
CURRENCY 1 Omani rial = 1,000 baiza
LIFE EXPECTANCY 54 (male) 57 (female)
POPULATION UNDER 15 YEARS 45.8%
LITERACY RATE 30.0%
RELIGION Muslim 86.0%; Hindu 13.0%
ETHNIC GROUPS Omani Arab 77.0%; Indian 15.0%; Pakistani (mostly Baluchi) 3.5%; Bengali 2.5%
LANGUAGE Arabic (official); minority languages
NUCLEAR CAPACITY No
LABOUR FORCE IN AGRICULTURE 42.0% (1988)
MAIN INTERNATIONAL ORGANIZATIONS UN; Arab League; GCC

Oman is an absolute sultanate with a consultative council appointed by the sultan. There are strong diplomatic links with the UK. Crude oil and natural gas are important exports and sources of government revenue. Oman is not a member of OPEC. The manufacturing base includes oil-refining, copper-smelting, and the manufacture of cement and motor vehicles. Agricultural crops include dates and bananas.

Pacific Islands *Melanesia, *Micronesia, *Polynesia.

Pakistan

Islāmī Jamhurīya-e-Pākistān

CAPITAL Islāmābād
AREA 796,095 km² (307,374 sq. mi.)
POPULATION 118.820 million (1989) (includes Afghan refugees and Jammu and Kashmir residents)
POPULATION GROWTH 3.1% p.a.
GDP PER CAPITA $384 (1988)
CURRENCY 1 Pakistan rupee = 100 paisa
LIFE EXPECTANCY 57 (male) 57 (female)
POPULATION UNDER 15 YEARS 45.7%
LITERACY RATE 26.2%
RELIGION Muslim 96.7%; Christian 1.6%; Hindu 1.5%;
ETHNIC GROUPS Punjabi 48.2%; Pashto 13.1%; Sindhi 11.8%; Saraiki 9.8%; Urdu 7.6%
LANGUAGE Urdu (official); Punjabi; Sindhi; Pashtu; English
NUCLEAR CAPACITY Unverified research reactor
LABOUR FORCE IN AGRICULTURE 50.7% (1988)
MAIN INTERNATIONAL ORGANIZATIONS UN; Commonwealth; Colombo Plan

Pakistan is a multiparty federal Islamic republic where the military has played a significant political role. Although it was established as a unitary Muslim state, Pakistan is subject to strong ethnic pressures. The Federal Sharia Court, an Islamic court, reviews laws in the context of Islam. Jammu and Kashmir is claimed by both India and Pakistan and is currently divided between the two. Pakistan has a mainly agricultural economy, the main exports being raw and processed cotton, cotton fabrics, and rice. However, Pakistani workers abroad earn more foreign currency than do exports. Other crops include sugar-cane, wheat, and maize. Livestock-raising is also substantial. Textiles are an important part of industry and contribute substantially to exports. Other industry includes cement, fertilizer, chemicals, and food-processing. In 1986 only half of all villages had access to electricity. Since the Soviet invasion of Afghanistan in 1979, Pakistan has been host to an estimated 3.6 million Afghan refugees.

Panama

República de Panamá

CAPITAL Panama City
AREA 77,082 km² (29,762 sq. mi.)

POPULATION 2.370 million (1989)
POPULATION GROWTH 2.1% p.a.
GDP PER CAPITA $1,918 (1988)
CURRENCY 1 balboa = 100 centesimos
(US $ also in circulation)
LIFE EXPECTANCY 70 (male) 74 (female)
POPULATION UNDER 15 YEARS 34.9%
LITERACY RATE 88.2%
RELIGION Roman Catholic 84.0%;
Protestant 4.8%; Muslim 4.5%; Bahā'ī
1.1%; Hindu 0.3%
ETHNIC GROUPS Mestizo 62.0%; Black and mixed 19.0%; White
10.0%; Amerindian 6.0%; Asian 2.0%
LANGUAGE Spanish (official); English creole; Amerindian languages
NUCLEAR CAPACITY No
LABOUR FORCE IN AGRICULTURE 26.3%
MAIN INTERNATIONAL ORGANIZATIONS UN; OAS; Non-Aligned
Movement

Panama is a multiparty republic. In 1989 US troops invaded, and General Manuel Noriega, the then head of state, was captured and imprisoned in the USA on drugs charges. In 1979, Panama assumed sovereignty over the Panama Canal area, though the USA retains a military presence and considerable influence, with a controlling interest in the canal until 1999. International finance and shipping are of importance due to Panama's position as a world trade centre. The principal agricultural exports are bananas, shrimps, and coffee; there are substantial, as yet unexploited, copper reserves, and some light industry, mostly food-processing. There is a petroleum refinery, but its products are of declining importance.

Papua New Guinea

Independent State of Papua New Guinea

CAPITAL Port Moresby
AREA 462,840 km² (178,704 sq. mi.)
POPULATION 3.592 million (1989)
POPULATION GROWTH 2.3% p.a.
GDP PER CAPITA $733 (1988)
CURRENCY 1 kina = 100 toea
LIFE EXPECTANCY 53 (male) 55 (female)
POPULATION UNDER 15 YEARS 42.0%
LITERACY RATE 45.0%
RELIGION Protestant 58.4%; Roman Catholic 32.8%; Anglican
5.4%; traditional beliefs 2.5%; Bahā'ī 0.6%
ETHNIC GROUPS Papuan 83.0%; Melanesian 15.0%
LANGUAGE English (official); Tok Pisin; about 700 Melanesian and
Papuan languages and dialects
NUCLEAR CAPACITY No
LABOUR FORCE IN AGRICULTURE 77.0% (1980)
MAIN INTERNATIONAL ORGANIZATIONS UN; Commonwealth;
Colombo Plan; South Pacific Forum; Observer status at ASEAN

Papua New Guinea is a parliamentary monarchy which consists of a number of islands. In 1990 the island of Bougainville declared independence, not recognized by Papua New Guinea. Papua New Guinea exploits extensive copper and substantial gold deposits, and together these account for half of exports. There are also petroleum reserves. Coffee, timber, cocoa, and palm oil are significant exports, and tropical fruits grow in abundance. Tuna-fishing is also important. Other agriculture includes bananas, coconuts, yams, and sugar-cane. Industry is limited mainly to food-processing. Australia contributes one-fifth of the annual budget in direct aid. High unemployment is a long-term problem.

Paraguay

República del Paraguay

CAPITAL Asunción
AREA 406,752 km² (157,048 sq. mi.)
POPULATION 4.157 million (1989)
POPULATION GROWTH 3.1% p.a.
GDP PER CAPITA $1,545
CURRENCY 1 guaraní = 100 céntimos

A distinct ethnic group descended from the Incas, the Quechua population of **Peru** face racial prejudice and live mainly as poor peasants or *campesinos*. Their oppression has led some to join the Maoist terrorist group Shining Path in violent rebellion against the state.

LIFE EXPECTANCY 65 (male) 69 (female)
POPULATION UNDER 15 YEARS 40.4%
LITERACY RATE 87.5%
RELIGION Roman Catholic 96.0%;
Protestant 2.0%
ETHNIC GROUPS Mestizo 90.0%;
Amerindian 3.0%; German 1.7%
LANGUAGE Spanish (official); Guarani
NUCLEAR CAPACITY No
LABOUR FORCE IN AGRICULTURE 46.7%
MAIN INTERNATIONAL ORGANIZATIONS UN; OAS

Paraguay is a landlocked multiparty republic. Elections were held in 1989 after years of dictatorship by General Stroessner and his right-wing Colorado Party. With a weak and divided opposition, the Colorado Party was once more returned to power in 1989. Paraguay has suffered from long-standing political repression and mistreatment of its Amerindian minority. It has a primarily agricultural economy, with cotton and soya beans the principal exports, and subsistence crops of cassava and maize. The construction of the Itaipu dam (1985), the world's largest hydroelectric project, benefited the economy, but high inflation and debt remain a problem. Industry is restricted to textiles, food-processing, and cement. Mineral resources are limited.

Peru

República del Perú

CAPITAL Lima
AREA 1,285,216 km² (496,225 sq. mi.)
POPULATION 21.792 million (1989)
POPULATION GROWTH 2.6% p.a.
GDP PER CAPITA $1,432 (1988)

CURRENCY 1 inti = 100 centimos
LIFE EXPECTANCY 60 (male) 63 (female)
POPULATION UNDER 15 YEARS 39.2%
LITERACY RATE 81.9%
RELIGION Roman Catholic 92.4%
ETHNIC GROUPS Quechua 47.0%; Mestizo
   32.0%; European 12.0%; Aymara 5.0%
LANGUAGE Spanish, Quechua (both
   official); Aymara
NUCLEAR CAPACITY Research (1 reactor)
LABOUR FORCE IN AGRICULTURE 35.7% (1988)
MAIN INTERNATIONAL ORGANIZATIONS UN; OAS; Andean Group

Peru was a multiparty republic until 1992 when the President dissolved Congress and formed a government of national reconstruction. A powerful Maoist insurgency group, the Sendero Luminoso or 'Shining Path', is active in the department of Ayacucho and in Lima itself. High inflation and a large foreign debt ($12 billion in 1988) have caused economic problems. Exports include copper, zinc, lead, and silver. There is a wide range of agriculture, and Peru is almost self-sufficient in food, with crops such as potatoes, rice, and sugar. One of the world's leading producers of fishmeal, Peru has a well-established manufacturing sector which includes petroleum products, although oil production is declining. There is widespread illegal cultivation of coca, which is sent to Colombia for processing into cocaine.

Philippines

Republic of the Philippines/Republika
ng Pilipinas (Pilipino)

CAPITAL Manila
AREA 300,000 km² (115,800 sq. mi.)
POPULATION 59.906 million (1989)
POPULATION GROWTH 2.4% p.a.
GDP PER CAPITA $662 (1988)
CURRENCY 1 Philippine peso = 100
   centavos
LIFE EXPECTANCY 62 (male) 65 (female)
POPULATION UNDER 15 YEARS 40.1%
LITERACY RATE 83.3%
RELIGION Roman Catholic 84.1%; Aglipayan Philippine
   Independent Church 6.2%; Muslim 4.3%; Protestant 3.9%
ETHNIC GROUPS Tagalog 29.7%; Cebuano 24.2%; Ilocano 10.3%;
   Hiligaynon Ilongo 9.2%; Bicol 5.6%; Samar-Leyte 4.0%;
   Pampango 2.8%; Pangasinan 1.8%
LANGUAGE English, Pilipino (based on Tagalog) (both official);
   Cebuano; Ilocano; local languages
NUCLEAR CAPACITY Civil (suspended) and research (2 reactors)
LABOUR FORCE IN AGRICULTURE 47.7% (1988)
MAIN INTERNATIONAL ORGANIZATIONS UN; Colombo Plan

The Philippines is a multiparty republic comprising over 7,000 islands. There is strong military influence, and there have been six failed coup attempts since President Aquino came to power in 1986, following the ousting of the dictator Ferdinand Marcos. The Moro National Liberation Front, a Muslim insurgent group, and the Communist New People's Army are fighting the state for control of a number of the islands. The USA has an influential relationship with the Philippines, but the status of several large American bases is under review. The economy is predominantly agricultural, but manufacturing industry such as textiles, chemicals, electric machinery, and food-processing is expanding. Mineral resources include nickel ore, copper, chromite, silver, and gold. The principal exports are electronics and clothing, while sugar, rice, and timber are important crops. There is widespread poverty, and land reform is an important issue.

Pitcairn Island   *Polynesia.

Poland

Polska Rzeczpospolita
CAPITAL Warsaw
AREA 312,683 km² (120,727 sq. mi.)

POPULATION 37.875 million (1989)
POPULATION GROWTH 0.7% p.a.
GDP PER CAPITA $1,719 (1988)
CURRENCY 1 zloty = 100 groszy
LIFE EXPECTANCY 68 (male) 76 (female)
POPULATION UNDER 15 YEARS 25.2%
LITERACY RATE 99.2%
RELIGION Roman Catholic 95.0%
ETHNIC GROUPS Polish 98.7%; Ukrainian
   0.6%; German and other 0.7%
LANGUAGE Polish (official); minority languages
NUCLEAR CAPACITY Research (3 reactors, 2 civil under construction)
LABOUR FORCE IN AGRICULTURE 22.2% (1988)
MAIN INTERNATIONAL ORGANIZATIONS UN; CSCE; Council of
   Europe; North Atlantic Co-operation Council

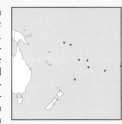

Poland is a multiparty republic. It was controlled by the Soviet-dominated communist Polish United Workers' Party, until demonstrations by the free trade union Solidarity forced free partial elections in 1989 and full elections in 1990, in which the Solidarity leader Lech Walesa was elected president. Poland is moving towards a market economy; its economic problems include high inflation, a large budget deficit, and high foreign debt. In late 1989, an economic reform package, introduced to gain IMF support, reduced wages and removed price subsidies. The Polish stock exchange was opened in late 1989, and privatization is under way. The majority of agricultural land is in private hands, wheat, rye, barley, oats, potatoes, and sugar-beet being the main crops. Mineral resources include coal, copper, silver, sulphur, and natural gas. Industry is hampered by power shortages and high fuel prices, and financial problems have delayed the nuclear energy programme. Loss-making industries, such as steel, and ship-building, have been heavily subsidized at the expense of other areas. Coal, clothing, iron and steel products, metals and agricultural products are the main exports.

Polynesia

Polynesia is a group of Pacific islands in Oceania. The larger islands are volcanic while the smaller islands are mainly coral. The region's economy has experienced little industrialization. Staple foods include yams, sweet potatoes, breadfruit, and bananas. The islands' religions are predominantly Christian. The native languages are part of the Austronesian language group. **American Samoa** is an unincorporated US Outlying Territory and member of the South Pacific Commission. Fagatogo is the seat of government. The main export of a largely agricultural economy is canned fish. Tourism is important, and economic expansion is being promoted by the USA. **Easter Island** is a dependency of Chile and is under the administration of Valparaiso province. **French Polynesia** is a French Overseas Territory of some 150 islands, including the nuclear test sites of the Mururoa and Fangotauga Atolls. There have been moves towards independence. Tourism is substantial. Copra and coconut oil are important crops, while pearls are a major export. There is a small Chinese community. **Pitcairn Island** is a UK colony, founded by mutineers from HMS *Bounty*, and a member of the South Pacific Commission. Postage stamps, fruit, vegetables, and fishing are the mainstays of the economy. There has been significant emigration to New Zealand. **Tuvalu** is a parliamentary monarchy, a member of the Commonwealth, the South Pacific Forum, the South Pacific Commission, and an ACP state of the EC. Copra is the principal export. **The Wallis and Futuna Islands** are a French Overseas Territory; the country is a member of the South Pacific Commission. The agricultural economy is supplemented by remittances from some 12,000 migrant workers. **Tonga** is a parliamentary monarchy of 169 islands, a member of the Commonwealth and the South Pacific Forum. The economy is mainly agricultural, with exports of coconut products, vanilla, and bananas. **Western Samoa** is a parliamentary monarchy which is a member of the Commonwealth and South Pacific Forum, and is an ACP state of the EC. Cocoa and coconuts are the main exports of a predominantly agricultural economy to which tourism makes an important contribution.

Portugal

República Portuguesa

CAPITAL Lisbon
AREA 92,389 km² (35,672 sq. mi.)
POPULATION 10.372 million
POPULATION GROWTH 0.8% p.a.
GDP PER CAPITA $4,017 (1988)
CURRENCY 1 escudo = 100 centavos
LIFE EXPECTANCY 70 (male) 77 (female)
POPULATION UNDER 15 YEARS 21.2%
LITERACY RATE 84.0%
RELIGION Roman Catholic 95.0%; Protestant 1.0%; Jewish 0.1%
ETHNIC GROUPS Portuguese 99.0%; Angolan 0.2%; Cape Verdean 0.2%
LANGUAGE Portuguese (official)
NUCLEAR CAPACITY Research (1 reactor, uranium producer)
LABOUR FORCE IN AGRICULTURE 17.5% (1988)
MAIN INTERNATIONAL ORGANIZATIONS UN; OECD; NATO; Council of Europe; EC; CSCE

Portugal is a multiparty republic. It includes the Atlantic archipelagos of Madeira and the Azores, which have a large measure of self-government. One of the poorest countries in Western Europe, Portugal has a mixed economy, with a large agricultural sector. Fishing is important, with a substantial annual sardine catch; Portugal is the world's largest producer of cork. Manufacturing industries include the principal exports of clothing, machinery, footwear, textiles, and chemicals. Tourism is important, and Portuguese workers abroad contribute substantially to foreign earnings. Portugal has also benefited from EC development aid.

Puerto Rico

Commonwealth of Puerto Rico/Estado Libre Associado de Puerto Rico (Spanish)

CAPITAL San Juan
AREA 9,104 km² (3,515 sq. mi.)
POPULATION 3.270 million (1984 est.)
POPULATION GROWTH 0.4% p.a.
GNP PER CAPITA $5,520 (1987) (GDP n.a.)
CURRENCY 1 US dollar = 100 cents
LIFE EXPECTANCY 72 (male) 78 (female)
POPULATION UNDER 15 YEARS 31.6%
LITERACY RATE 89.1% (1980)
RELIGION Roman Catholic 85.0%; Protestant 5.0%
ETHNIC GROUPS Hispanic 75.0%; Black 15.0%; mixed 10.0%
LANGUAGE Spanish; English (both official)
NUCLEAR CAPACITY No
LABOUR FORCE IN AGRICULTURE 3.2% (1988)

Puerto Rico is a self-governing commonwealth associated with the USA. The mainstays of the economy are tourism and manufacturing industry, the major products being chemicals, food products, electrical goods, and machinery. Chemicals, metals, and foodstuffs are the main exports, almost all to the USA. Agriculture is of declining importance, with dairy, livestock, and cereals the principal products. Mineral resources are scanty.

Qatar

Dawlat Qatar

CAPITAL Doha
AREA 11,337 km² (4,377 sq. mi.)
POPULATION 427,000 (1989)
POPULATION GROWTH 4.1% p.a.
GDP PER CAPITA $15,909 (1988)
CURRENCY 1 Qatar riyal = 100 dirhams
LIFE EXPECTANCY 67 (male) 72 (female)
POPULATION UNDER 15 YEARS 35.1%
LITERACY RATE 75.7%
RELIGION Muslim (mainly Sunnī) 92%; Christian 6.0%; Hindu 1.0%; Bahā'ī 0.2%
ETHNIC GROUPS South Asian 34.0%; Qatari Arab 20.0%; other Arab 25.0%; Iranian 16.0%
LANGUAGE Arabic (official); South Asian languages; Persian
NUCLEAR CAPACITY No
LABOUR FORCE IN AGRICULTURE 3.1%
MAIN INTERNATIONAL ORGANIZATIONS UN; Arab League; OAPEC

Qatar is an absolute emirate. Its economy and exports are dominated by crude oil. Industries include oil-refining, gas liquefaction, fertilizers, cement, and steel. Due to its oil wealth the country has one of the highest per capita incomes in the world. In 1987, native Qataris constituted less than a quarter of the total population, the remainder being immigrant workers.

Réunion

Réunion

CAPITAL Saint-Denis
AREA 2,500 km² (965 sq. mi.)
POPULATION 604,000
POPULATION GROWTH 1.6% p.a.
GNP PER CAPITA $3,580 (1984) (GDP n.a.)
CURRENCY 1 French franc = 100 centimes
LIFE EXPECTANCY 65 (male) 73 (female)
LITERACY RATE 92%
RELIGION Roman Catholic 85.0%; Muslim 5.0%
ETHNIC GROUPS Mixed 80.0%; White 5.0%; Chinese 4.0%
LANGUAGE French (official); Reyone
NUCLEAR CAPACITY No

Réunion is a French department. There is no significant pressure for independence. The main exports are sugar and rum, and the chief agricultural products are tobacco, spices, and livestock. Fishing is also important. Tourism is a major source of revenue, and French aid is a significant factor in sustaining a relatively high level of income.

Romania

România

CAPITAL Bucharest
AREA 237,500 km² (91,699 sq. mi.)
POPULATION 23.168 million (1989)
POPULATION GROWTH 0.4% p.a.
GDP PER CAPITA $1,374 (1988)
CURRENCY 1 leu = 100 bani
LIFE EXPECTANCY 68 (male) 73 (female)
POPULATION UNDER 15 YEARS 23.4%
LITERACY RATE 95.8%
RELIGION Romanian Orthodox 70.0%; Greek Orthodox 10.0%; Muslim 1.0%
ETHNIC GROUPS Romanian 86.0%; Hungarian 9.0%; gypsy 4.0%; German and other 1.0%
LANGUAGE Romanian (official); Hungarian; Romany
NUCLEAR CAPACITY Research (2 reactors, 5 civil under construction) (1989)
LABOUR FORCE IN AGRICULTURE 22.1%
MAIN INTERNATIONAL ORGANIZATIONS UN; CSCE; North Atlantic Co-operation Council

Romania is a multiparty republic. The repressive communist regime of Nicolae Ceausescu was ousted in a bloody revolution in December 1989, and free elections were held in 1990 amidst charges of irregularity. The policy of promoting exports regardless of domestic needs to pay off foreign debt has caused massive hardship. Ceausescu's 'systematization' programme, which forced resettlement in towns, ostensibly to free land for agricultural use, has been reversed, and collective and state farms have been privatized in the hope of boosting food supplies. Romania is moving towards a market economy, and small businesses have also been freed from state control. Principal crops are maize, wheat, rye, potatoes, sugar-beet, plums, and apples, while mineral resources include coal, iron ore, petroleum, and natural gas. Despite heavy subsidies at the expense of agriculture, industry is in great need of modernization. Major industries are metallurgical, mechanical engineering, and chemicals, with mineral fuels, machinery, and transport

The plight of these children in an orphanage in **Romania**, shows the human consequences of Ceausescu's regime, which sought to force people to have unwanted children for whom they were unable to care.

equipment the principal exports. Social conditions were poor under the previous regime, and remain bleak. The Hungarian minority's demands for enhanced cultural autonomy have led to ethnic clashes and strained relations with Hungary. Romania has the world's largest gypsy population, but victimization is rife.

Russia

Rossiiskaya Federatsiya

CAPITAL Moscow
AREA 17,075,000 km² (6,590,950 sq. mi.)
POPULATION 147.021 million
CURRENCY 1 rouble = 100 kopeks
RELIGION Eastern Orthodox; Jewish, Muslim, and other minorities
ETHNIC GROUPS Russian 82.0%; Tatar 4.0%; Ukrainian, Mordvin, Lapp, Chuvash, Bashkir, Polish, German, Udmurt, Mari, Yakut, and Ossete minorities
LANGUAGE Russian (official); minority languages
NUCLEAR CAPACITY Civil, defence and research; uranium producer
MAIN INTERNATIONAL ORGANIZATIONS UN; CSCE; Commonwealth of Independent States; North Atlantic Co-operation Council

Russia is a federal republic. The largest of the former Soviet republics, and the core of the former Soviet Union, it became an independent sovereign state in late 1991 following the dissolution of the Soviet Union. A new constitution is in preparation. It includes twenty autonomous republics and regions, of which eighteen have signed a new federal treaty. Chechen-Ingushetia and the oil-producing region of Tatarstan seek independence. Russia has agreed to restore a German republic for its ethnic German citizens. In June 1991 Boris Yeltsin was elected president with wide-ranging emergency powers in Russia's first presidential elections. Russia controls the former Soviet Central Bank, and has taken the seat of the Soviet Union in international organizations such as the UN and Security Council, but it shares responsibility for the Soviet Union's foreign debt with other former Soviet republics. The ownership of certain Soviet assets such as foreign exchange and gold is disputed. Russia has announced plans to set up its own army, but the control of Soviet weapons and military equipment is yet to be allocated between the former Soviet republics. Control of the Soviet Black Sea fleet is also disputed between Russia and Ukraine. Some 25 million Russians live in the other former Soviet

republics, half of them in eastern Ukraine and northern Kazakhstan. Ukraine's sovereignty over the predominantly Russian Crimea, which was transferred to it in 1954, is challenged by Russia. Russia has embarked on a difficult transition to a free-market economy by freeing prices and introducing measures for privatization and land reform. However, chronic food shortages have been worsened by the disintegration of distribution systems and lack of confidence in the monetary system. Potentially of enormous wealth, Russia has rich mineral resources, with huge deposits of coal, iron ore, gold, platinum, copper, diamonds, and other metals, and, in Siberia, the world's largest reserves of petroleum and natural gas. Heavy industry, such as machinery, automobile production, paper and wood industries, and chemicals, dominates the economy, with mining and oil refineries also of importance. There is also light industry such as textiles and food-processing. Half the agricultural produce of the former Soviet Union was grown in Russia: the principal crops are grain and livestock, as well as commercial crops such as sunflower seeds, sugar-beet, and flax.

Rwanda

Republika y'u Rwanda (Rwanda)/
   République Rwandaise (French)

CAPITAL Kigali
AREA 26,338 km² (10,169 sq. mi.)
POPULATION 6.989 million (1989)
POPULATION GROWTH 3.2% p.a.
GDP PER CAPITA $338 (1988)
CURRENCY 1 Rwanda franc = 100 centimes
LIFE EXPECTANCY 47 (male) 50 (female)
POPULATION UNDER 15 YEARS 48.9%
LITERACY RATE 47%
RELIGION Roman Catholic 65.0%; traditional beliefs 17.0%; Protestant 9.0%; Muslim 9.0%
ETHNIC GROUPS Hutu 90.0%; Tutsi 9.0%; Twa 1.0%
LANGUAGE Rwanda, French (both official); Swahili
NUCLEAR CAPACITY No
LABOUR FORCE IN AGRICULTURE 91.6% (1988)
MAIN INTERNATIONAL ORGANIZATIONS UN; OAU

Rwanda is a landlocked one-party republic dominated by the military. It was under a Belgian mandate until 1962. The political system is under review, and in 1991 political parties were legalized. One of the poorest countries in the world, subject to drought and famine and with a high incidence of parasitic and other diseases, Rwanda has one of the highest population densities in Africa and a high birth-rate. Coffee and tea are the main exports, and plantains, sweet potatoes, and cassava are staple crops. The principal mineral resource is cassiterite (a tin ore), but exports are at a standstill since the collapse in world tin prices. Unexploited natural gas reserves are believed to be amongst the world's largest. Limited manufacturing industry comprises mostly food-processing. There have been border clashes with some of the 70,000 Rwandan exiles in Uganda, most of whom are from the formerly dominant minority Tutsi population.

Saint Helena   *Atlantic Islands.

Saint Kitts and Nevis

Federation of Saint Christopher and
   Nevis

CAPITAL Basseterre
AREA 269.4 km² (104.0 sq. mi.)
POPULATION 44,100
POPULATION GROWTH −0.9% p.a.
GNP PER CAPITA $1,700 (1987) (GDP n.a.)
CURRENCY East Caribbean dollar
LIFE EXPECTANCY 63 (male) 67 (female)
POPULATION UNDER 15 YEARS 34.3%
LITERACY RATE 90.0% (1985)
RELIGION Anglican 32.6%; Methodist 28.8%; Moravian 8.7%; Roman Catholic 7.2%
ETHNIC GROUPS Black 90.5%; mixed 5.0%; East Indian 3.0%; White 1.5%

LANGUAGE English (official)
NUCLEAR CAPACITY No
LABOUR FORCE IN AGRICULTURE 29.6%
MAIN INTERNATIONAL ORGANIZATIONS UN; OAS; Commonwealth

Saint Kitts and Nevis is a federation of two islands. After becoming independent from the UK in 1979, it became a parliamentary monarchy whose head of state is the UK monarch. Agriculture has been replaced by tourism as the main source of revenue, and both manufacturing and service industries are developing. The chief crops are sugar-cane, coconuts, and fruit, and the leading industries are food-processing, electronics, and clothing. Foodstuffs and machinery are the leading exports.

Saint Lucia

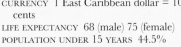

Saint Lucia

CAPITAL Castries
AREA 617.4 km² (238.4 sq. mi.)
POPULATION 150,000 (1989)
POPULATION GROWTH 2.0% p.a.
GNP PER CAPITA $1,810 (1989) (GDP n.a.)
CURRENCY 1 East Caribbean dollar = 100 cents
LIFE EXPECTANCY 68 (male) 75 (female)
POPULATION UNDER 15 YEARS 44.5%
LITERACY RATE 90.0%
RELIGION Roman Catholic 85.6%; Seventh-day Adventist 4.3%; Anglican 2.7%
ETHNIC GROUPS Black 87.0%; mixed 9.1%; East Indian 2.6%; White 1.3%
LANGUAGE English (official); English and French creoles
NUCLEAR CAPACITY No
LABOUR FORCE IN AGRICULTURE 29.7% (1983)
MAIN INTERNATIONAL ORGANIZATIONS UN; OAS; CARICOM; Commonwealth

Saint Lucia is an island parliamentary monarchy which became independent from the UK in 1979. The head of state is the UK monarch. Tourism is an important source of revenue, but agriculture is still predominant, with bananas the largest export. Manufacturing industry includes paper products and clothing, both exported, and food-processing.

Saint Vincent and the Grenadines

Saint Vincent and the Grenadines

CAPITAL Kingstown
AREA 389.3 km² (150.3 sq. mi.)
POPULATION 114,000
POPULATION GROWTH 1.1% p.a.
GNP PER CAPITA $1,070 (1987) (GDP n.a.)
CURRENCY 1 East Caribbean dollar = 100 cents
LIFE EXPECTANCY 68 (male) 74 (female)
POPULATION UNDER 15 YEARS 37.4%
LITERACY RATE 85.0%
RELIGION Anglican 36.0%; Methodist 20.4%; Roman Catholic 19.3%; Seventh-day Adventist 4.1%; Plymouth Brethren 3.9%
ETHNIC GROUPS Black 74.0%; mixed 19.0%; White 3.0%; Amerindian 2.0%; East Indian 2.0%
LANGUAGE English (official); English creole
NUCLEAR CAPACITY No
LABOUR FORCE IN AGRICULTURE 25.7% (1980)
MAIN INTERNATIONAL ORGANIZATIONS UN; OAS; CARICOM; Commonwealth

Saint Vincent and the Grenadines is a parliamentary monarchy which became independent from the UK in 1979. The head of state is the UK monarch. It consists of the island of Saint Vincent and the smaller islands of the Grenadines. Luxury tourism is an important source of revenue, with exports headed by agricultural products such as bananas and vegetables. Manufacturing industry includes food-processing and electronics.

San Marino

Serenissima Repubblica di San Marino

CAPITAL San Marino
AREA 61.19 km² (23.63 sq. mi.)
POPULATION 22,860 (1989)
POPULATION GROWTH 0.2% p.a.
GDP PER CAPITA $200 (estimate) (1985)
CURRENCY 1 San Marino lira = 100 centesimi
LIFE EXPECTANCY 71 (male) 76 (female)
POPULATION UNDER 15 YEARS 17.0%
LITERACY RATE 98.0%
RELIGION Roman Catholic 95.0%
ETHNIC GROUPS Sammarinesi 85.8%; Italian 13.8%
LANGUAGE Italian (official)
NUCLEAR CAPACITY No
LABOUR FORCE IN AGRICULTURE 3.0%
MAIN INTERNATIONAL ORGANIZATIONS UN; CSCE; Council of Europe

San Marino is a neutral landlocked multiparty republic. There is a treaty of friendship and co-operation and a *de facto* customs union with Italy, the major trading partner. The economy is dominated by tourism and agriculture, with postage stamps an important source of foreign currency.

São Tomé and Príncipe

República Democrática de São Tomé é Príncipe

CAPITAL São Tomé
AREA 1,001 km² (386 sq. mi.)
POPULATION 118,000 (1989)
POPULATION GROWTH 1.9% p.a.
GNP PER CAPITA $360 (1986) (GDP n.a.)
CURRENCY 1 dobra = 100 centimos
LIFE EXPECTANCY 63 (male) 67 (female)
POPULATION UNDER 15 YEARS 46.3%
LITERACY RATE 54.2%
RELIGION Roman Catholic 84.0%; remainder mainly Seventh-day Adventist and indigenous Evangelical Church
ETHNIC GROUPS Mixed 43.0%; African 51.0%
LANGUAGE Portuguese (official); Portuguese creole
NUCLEAR CAPACITY No
LABOUR FORCE IN AGRICULTURE 40.4% (1987)
MAIN INTERNATIONAL ORGANIZATIONS UN; OAU

São Tomé and Príncipe is an island multiparty republic, where the former ruling party was defeated in multiparty elections held in 1991. The economy was centrally planned until the mid-1980s, when severe drought and worsening economic conditions, including a drop in world cocoa prices, prompted the government to seek Western aid and reduce state controls. The main export is cocoa, followed by copra. Industry is restricted to food-processing. Since agriculture concentrates on cash crops for exports, most food is imported.

Saudi Arabia

al-Mamlakah al-'Arabīyah as-Sa'ūdīyah

CAPITAL Riyadh (royal); Jiddah (administrative); Mecca (religious)
AREA 2,240,000 km² (865,000 sq. mi.)
POPULATION 13.592 million (1989)
POPULATION GROWTH 5.6% p.a.
GDP PER CAPITA $5,311 (1988)
CURRENCY 1 Saudi riyal = 100 halalah
LIFE EXPECTANCY 62 (male) 65 (female)
POPULATION UNDER 15 YEARS 45.4%
LITERACY RATE 51.1%
RELIGION Muslim (mostly Sunnī) 98.8%; Christian 0.8%
ETHNIC GROUPS Saudi Arab (including Bedouin 27.0%) 82.0%; Yemeni Arab 9.6%; other Arab 3.4%

LANGUAGE Arabic (official)
NUCLEAR CAPACITY No
LABOUR FORCE IN AGRICULTURE 40.9% (1988)
MAIN INTERNATIONAL ORGANIZATIONS UN; Arab League; GCC; OAPEC; OPEC

Saudi Arabia is an absolute monarchy based on Islamic principles. Political reforms in 1992 provided for the establishment of a Consultative Council and a basic law giving constitutional rights and freedom from arbitrary arrest. The natural resources of the former Neutral Zone with Kuwait are shared. With a quarter of the world's oil reserves, the Saudi economy and exports are dominated by crude oil, extracted mainly by the state-owned Aramco company. Oil-refining, and the manufacture of cement, fertilizers, and steel, are the main areas of industry. Agriculture suffers from poor rainfall and moving sands, but investment in irrigation and livestock production has resulted in self-sufficiency in some foodstuffs. Islam is the state religion, with an emphasis on the strict conservative values of the Wahhabī sect in public life, and the legal code is entirely based on Islamic law. There is a large population of immigrant workers.

Senegal

République du Sénégal

CAPITAL Dakar
AREA 196,722 km² (75,955 sq. mi.)
POPULATION 7.400 million (1989)
POPULATION GROWTH 3.0% p.a.
GDP PER CAPITA $717 (1988)
CURRENCY 1 CFA franc = 100 centimes
LIFE EXPECTANCY 44 (male) 47 (female)
POPULATION UNDER 15 YEARS 44.5%
LITERACY RATE 28.0%
RELIGION Sunnī Muslim 91.0%; Roman Catholic 5.6%; traditional beliefs 3.2%
ETHNIC GROUPS Wolof 38.0%; Fulani-(Peul-)Tukulor 22.0%; Serer 19.0%; Diola 7.0%; Mande 7.0%
LANGUAGE French (official); Wolof; other local languages
NUCLEAR CAPACITY No
LABOUR FORCE IN AGRICULTURE 78.9% (1988)
MAIN INTERNATIONAL ORGANIZATIONS UN; OAU; Franc Zone

Senegal is a multiparty republic. However, the same party has remained in power since independence from France in 1960. The Confederation of Senegambia between Senegal and The Gambia was disbanded in 1989, but a treaty of friendship in 1991 forms the basis for new formal links. The predominantly agricultural economy has been weakened by drought and low world prices for agricultural exports. The principal exports are fish, ground-nuts, and phosphates. Other crops include sugar-cane, millet, rice, and cotton. Mineral resources include phosphates, and unexploited reserves of iron ore, and gold. Industry includes ship repair and oil-refining in Dakar, and food-processing. Relations with neighbouring Mauritania are strained for both economic and ethnic reasons; and there is a dispute with Guinea-Bissau over the sovereignty of a maritime zone. There is a separatist movement in the southern province of Casamance.

Seychelles

Repiblik Sesel (creole)/République des Seychelles (French)/Republic of Seychelles

CAPITAL Victoria
AREA 453 km² (175 sq. mi.)
POPULATION 66,900 (1988)
POPULATION GROWTH 1.5% p.a.
GNP PER CAPITA $3,800 (1988) (GDP n.a.)
CURRENCY 1 Seychelles rupee = 100 cents
LIFE EXPECTANCY 66 (male) 74 (female)
POPULATION UNDER 15 YEARS 36.5%
LITERACY RATE 57.3% (1971)
RELIGION Roman Catholic 90.9%; other Christian (mostly Anglican) 7.5%; Hindu 0.7%
ETHNIC GROUPS Seychellois creole (mixture of Asian, African, and

European) 89.1%; Indian 4.7%; Malagasy 3.1%; Chinese 1.6%; British 1.5%
LANGUAGE Creole, English, French (all official)
NUCLEAR CAPACITY No
LABOUR FORCE IN AGRICULTURE 9.5%
MAIN INTERNATIONAL ORGANIZATIONS UN; Commonwealth; OAU

The Seychelles has been a one-party socialist republic since 1979. It consists of ninety-two islands which became independent from the UK in 1975. The introduction of a multiparty system is under consideration. Exclusive tourism is the mainstay of the economy. The main exports are fish and copra.

Sierra Leone

Republic of Sierra Leone

CAPITAL Freetown
AREA 71,740 km² (27,699 sq. mi.)
POPULATION 3.957 million (1989)
POPULATION GROWTH 2.5% p.a.
GDP PER CAPITA $233 (1988)
CURRENCY 1 leone = 100 cents
LIFE EXPECTANCY 39 (male) 43 (female)
POPULATION UNDER 15 YEARS 44.5%
LITERACY RATE 30.0%
RELIGION Traditional beliefs 51.5%; Sunnī Muslim 39.4%; Protestant 4.7%; Roman Catholic 2.2%; Anglican 1.2%
ETHNIC GROUPS Mende 46.0%; Temne 45.0%
LANGUAGE English (official); Krio (English creole); Mende; Temne; other local languages
NUCLEAR CAPACITY No
LABOUR FORCE IN AGRICULTURE 63.8%
MAIN INTERNATIONAL ORGANIZATIONS UN; OAU; ECOWAS; Commonwealth

Sierra Leone was a one-party republic until a military coup in 1992. The introduction of a multiparty system is under review. It became independent from the UK in 1961. The leading exports are rutile, diamonds, bauxite, cocoa, and coffee; smuggling of gold and diamonds is widespread. Iron-ore mines are inactive due to lack of financing. In agriculture, the main cash crops are cocoa and coffee, and the main staple crops are cassava, rice, and plantains. Industry is confined to food-processing and other light industry. In the north, the Temne are mostly Muslim, while in the centre and south the Mende follow traditional beliefs. The economic strength of the Lebanese minority has caused much tension. Sierra Leone is host to many Liberian refugees.

An iron-ore mine in **Sierra Leone**, where exploitation of natural resources, particularly diamonds, earns valuable foreign exchange. Unlike many African countries, who grow cash crops for export, this enables Sierra Leone to devote agricultural effort to the production of food for domestic needs.

Singapore

Hsin-chia-p'o Kung-ho-kuo (Mandarin
   Chinese)/Republik Singapura (Malay)/
   Singapore Kudiyarasu (Tamil)/
   Republic of Singapore (English)

CAPITAL Singapore
AREA 622 km² (240 sq. mi.)
POPULATION 2.674 million (1989)
POPULATION GROWTH 1.2% p.a.
GNP PER CAPITA $7,940 (GDP n.a.)
CURRENCY 1 Singapore dollar = 100 cents
LIFE EXPECTANCY 70 (male) 76 (female)
POPULATION UNDER 15 YEARS 26.5%
LITERACY RATE 82.9%
RELIGION Buddhist 28.3%; Christian 18.7%; Muslim 16.0%; Taoist
   13.4%; Hindu 4.9%
ETHNIC GROUPS Chinese 77.0%; Malay 15.0%; Indian and Sri
   Lankan 6.0%
LANGUAGE Malay, Mandarin, Tamil, English (all official); Chinese
   dialects
NUCLEAR CAPACITY No
LABOUR FORCE IN AGRICULTURE 1.1%;
MAIN INTERNATIONAL ORGANIZATIONS UN; Colombo Plan;
   Commonwealth; ASEAN

Singapore is a multiparty island republic whose presidential council guarantees the rights of minorities. The port of Singapore is one of the largest in the world and entrepôt trade has long been important. Manufacturing industry, including shipbuilding, electronics, and refining of imported crude oil, has also been developed, and Singapore is a leading financial centre. Tourism is significant, and although agriculture is relatively unimportant, rare orchids and exotic fish are valuable exports. The principal exports are machinery, petroleum products, communications equipment, and clothing. Singapore has among the world's largest capital reserves; and there is high government spending on social services, with some 20 per cent of the budget earmarked for education.

Slovenia

Republika Slovenija

CAPITAL Ljubljana
AREA 20,251 km² (7,897 sq. mi.)
POPULATION 1.94 million
CURRENCY tolar
LIFE EXPECTANCY 70 (male) 76 (female)
RELIGION Roman Catholic 90.0%
ETHNIC GROUPS Slovene 90.0%
LANGUAGE Slovenian (official)
NUCLEAR CAPACITY Civil
MAIN INTERNATIONAL ORGANIZATIONS CSCE

Slovenia is a republic which became independent from *Yugoslavia in 1992. Its geographic and historical links with Western Europe, its relatively homogeneous population, and its comparatively peaceful secession from Yugoslavia provide a favourable foundation for its new status. Industry is well developed, including iron, steel, and textiles. Deposits of coal, lead, zinc, aluminium, and mercury are exploited. Agriculture includes livestock-rearing, viticulture, and crops such as cereals, sugar-beet, and potatoes. Tourism is an important source of foreign exchange.

Solomon Islands *Melanesia.

Somalia

Jamhuuriyadda Dimuqraadiga Soomaaliya (Somali)/Jumhūrīyah aṣ-
   Ṣūmāl ad-Dīmuqrāṭīyah (Arabic)

CAPITAL Mogadishu
AREA 637,000 km² (246,000 sq. mi.)
POPULATION 7.339 million (1989)
POPULATION GROWTH 3.5% p.a.

GDP PER CAPITA $241 (1988)
CURRENCY 1 Somali shilling = 100 cents
LIFE EXPECTANCY 43 (male) 47 (female)
POPULATION UNDER 15 YEARS 47.6%
LITERACY RATE 39.0%
RELIGION Sunnī Muslim 99.8%; Christian
   0.1%
ETHNIC GROUPS Somali 98.3%; Arab
   1.2%; Bantu 0.4%
LANGUAGE Somali, Arabic, English
   (official); Italian; Swahili
NUCLEAR CAPACITY No
LABOUR FORCE IN AGRICULTURE 72.1%
MAIN INTERNATIONAL ORGANIZATIONS UN; OAU; Arab League

Somalia is a republic in a state of civil war between rival clans following the overthrow of President Muhammad Siyad Barrah's military-dominated one-party socialist state in 1991. The Somali republic was formed in 1960 from British and Italian protectorates. One of Africa's poorest countries and heavily dependent on foreign aid, Somalia has suffered from drought, flooding, famine, civil war, and high foreign debt in recent years. The main exports are livestock and bananas; other crops are sugar-cane, maize, and sorghum. Industry is confined mainly to processing agricultural products, although imported petroleum is refined. Mineral resources include lead, gold, zircon, coal, and kyanite, but most of these are not fully exploited. Somalia has had a long-running conflict with Ethiopia over its claims to the Ethiopian province of Ogaden, and has also claimed Kenya's north-eastern province. There were an estimated 700,000 Ethiopian refugees in Somalia in 1990, and many Somalis had fled to Ethiopia and Kenya.

South Africa

Republic of South Africa (English)/
   Republiek van Suid-Afrika (Afrikaans)

CAPITAL Pretoria (executive) Bloemfontein
   (judicial) Cape Town (legislative)
AREA 1,123,226 km² (433,680 sq. mi.)
POPULATION 34 million (1988)
POPULATION GROWTH 2.3% p.a.
GDP PER CAPITA $2,290 (1988)
CURRENCY 1 rand = 100 cents
LIFE EXPECTANCY 58 (male) 64 (female)
POPULATION UNDER 15 YEARS 37.0%
LITERACY RATE White 93.0%; Asian 69.0%; Coloured 62.0%; Black
   32.0%
RELIGION Christian 59.0%; Bantu Churches 17.0%; Hindu 2.0%;
   Muslim 1.0%; Jewish 1.0%
ETHNIC GROUPS Zulu 23.8%; White 18.0%; Coloured 10.5%; North
   Sotho 9.8%; Xhosa 9.7%; South Sotho 7.3%; Tswana 5.7%;
   Asian 3.3%
LANGUAGE Afrikaans, English (both official); Zulu; Sotho; Xhosa;
   other local languages
NUCLEAR CAPACITY Civil and research (3 reactors)
LABOUR FORCE IN AGRICULTURE 14.6%
MAIN INTERNATIONAL ORGANIZATIONS UN

South Africa is a republic of four provinces and ten Bantu 'homelands' (nominally independent states which are in practice dependent on South Africa). It is making the transition to a fully democratic and equal society from the apartheid system, which became law in 1948 but operated well before. Apartheid separated political, social, and economic life on racial lines, and put all effective political power in the hands of the white minority, which owns most of the land and industry. The legislation for apartheid was repealed in 1991, and the Convention for a Democratic South Africa (Codesa), in which nineteen political groups are represented, is attempting to reach agreement on a new constitution. A Whites-only referendum in 1992 backed constitutional reform. Opposition groups, including the African National Congress (ANC), were legalized in 1990, but there is continuing violence between the Zulu Inkatha Movement, and Xhosa and other ANC supporters; and between the police and military and Black protesters and ultra-right White vigilante groups. South Africa's economy profits from plentiful natural resources and cheap Black labour. Mineral resources, among the world's richest, include gold, platinum, coal, diamonds, iron ore, lime, uranium, and natural gas. Gold and other metal products are the chief exports. Industry is highly developed, and includes metal production, chemicals, engineering, and food-processing. Arms production is also important. Agriculture is vulnerable to droughts and inadequate irrigation; the main crops are cereals, sugar, and fruit, and livestock-raising is also important. International trade and sporting sanctions were imposed in protest against apartheid; sporting and EC sanctions were lifted in 1991 and 1992 respectively, but US trade sanctions remain, as do UN arms and oil embargoes. World recession and low commodity prices have also had adverse effects. There is endemic poverty and high unemployment among Blacks, who have been deprived of access to social services such as health care and education. The Southern African Customs Union links South Africa to Botswana, Lesotho, and Swaziland.

South Georgia and the South Sandwich Islands   *Atlantic Islands.

Spain

Reino de España

CAPITAL Madrid
AREA 504,750 km² (194,885 sq. mi.)
POPULATION 39.159 million (1989)
POPULATION GROWTH 0.5% p.a.
GDP PER CAPITA $8,668
CURRENCY peseta
LIFE EXPECTANCY 74 (male) 80 (female)
POPULATION UNDER 15 YEARS 20.4%
LITERACY RATE 92.9%
RELIGION Roman Catholic 97.0%
ETHNIC GROUPS Spanish 73.0%; Catalan 16.0%; Galician 8.0%; Basque 2.0%
LANGUAGE Spanish (Castilian) (official); Catalan; Galician; Basque
NUCLEAR CAPACITY Civil (10 reactors) (1989)
LABOUR FORCE IN AGRICULTURE 11.8% (1988)
MAIN INTERNATIONAL ORGANIZATIONS UN; EC; NATO; OECD; Council of Europe; CSCE

Spain is a parliamentary monarchy with a semi-federal system of seventeen autonomous regions, each with an assembly and government. In the Basque and Catalan regions local nationalist parties have formed governments, but there are continuing internal tensions caused by demands for greater autonomy. The Basque terrorist organization Euzkadi ta Azkatasnn'a (ETA) conducts a sporadic campaign of violence. Spanish territory includes Ceuta, Melilla, Alhucemas, Chafarinas, and Peñón de Vélez in North Africa, which are the subject of territorial disputes with Morocco, and the Canary and Balearic Islands. The sovereignty of *Gibraltar is disputed with the UK. Spain has a broadly based manufacturing sector, which has experienced rapid growth in recent years. Tourism makes a substantial contribution to the economy. Exports include motor vehicles, iron and steel, zinc, petroleum products, and chemicals. Agriculture remains important and concentrates on grains, tomatoes, citrus, and livestock-raising. Mineral resources include iron ore, zinc, and lead. Spain has had a consistently high level of unemployment and a weak system of social security.

Sri Lanka

Sri Lanka Prajathanthrika Samajavadi Janarajaya (Sinhalese)/Ilangai Jananayaka Socialisa Kudiarasu (Tamil)

CAPITAL Colombo (president and judiciary); Sri Jayewardenepura Kotte (prime minister and legislature)
AREA 65,610 km² (25,332 sq. mi.)
POPULATION 16.855 million (1989)
POPULATION GROWTH 1.5% p.a.
GDP PER CAPITA $423 (1988)
CURRENCY 1 Sri Lankan rupee = 100 cents
LIFE EXPECTANCY 68 (male) 73 (female)
POPULATION UNDER 15 YEARS 32.5%
LITERACY RATE 86.8%

RELIGION Buddhist 70.0%; Hindu 15.0%; Christian 8.0%; Muslim 7.0%
ETHNIC GROUPS Sinhalese 74.0%; Tamil 18.0%; Moor 7.0%
LANGUAGE Sinhalese, Tamil (both official); English
NUCLEAR CAPACITY No
LABOUR FORCE IN AGRICULTURE 52.0% (1988)
MAIN INTERNATIONAL ORGANIZATIONS UN; Commonwealth; Non-Aligned Movement; Colombo Plan

Sri Lanka is a multiparty island republic. Political stability is threatened by conflict between the Buddhist Sinhalese majority and the Hindu Tamil minority. Indian troops, who intervened in the conflict, withdrew in 1990. The main separatist group is the Tamil Tigers, which received Indian backing until 1991. The economy is largely agrarian, with exports of tea, rubber, precious stones, and coconut products. Manufacturing industry includes textiles, cement, and petroleum-refining. Remittances from emigrant workers are significant, as was tourism until it was disrupted by the civil war. There are an estimated 200,000 Tamil refugees in India's Tamil Nadu state.

Sudan

Jamhūrīyat as-Sūdān

CAPITAL Khartoum
AREA 2,503,890 km² (966,757 sq. mi.)
POPULATION 23.8 million (1988)
POPULATION GROWTH 3.0% p.a.
GDP PER CAPITA $467 (1988)
CURRENCY 1 Sudanese pound = 100 piastres = 1,000 millimes
LIFE EXPECTANCY 47 (male) 51 (female)
POPULATION UNDER 15 YEARS 45.3%
LITERACY RATE 33.0%
RELIGION Sunnī Muslim 73.0%; traditional beliefs 16.7%; Roman Catholic 5.6%; Anglican 2.3%
ETHNIC GROUPS Sudanese Arab 49.1%; Dinka 11.5%; Nuba 8.1%; Beja 6.4%; Nuer 4.9%; Azande 2.7%; Bari 2.5%; Fur 2.1%; Shilluk 1.7%; Lotuko 1.5%
LANGUAGE Arabic (official); Dinka; Nuba; other local languages
NUCLEAR CAPACITY No
LABOUR FORCE IN AGRICULTURE 62.5% (1988)
MAIN INTERNATIONAL ORGANIZATIONS UN; OAU; Arab League

Sudan is a military republic which has been in a state of civil war since 1983. The conflict reflects the racial and religious differences between the Arab Muslim north and the Black African south, and focuses on the imposition in 1983 of strict Islamic law, which is opposed by the Sudan People's Liberation Movement (SPLM). The war, drought, and flooding have devastated the economy, which is also crippled by massive foreign debt ($13.5 billion in 1990), and have led to famine in the south among both Sudanese and the several million refugees from Ethiopia and Chad. The distribution of food aid has been seriously hampered by the war. Agriculture is the principal economic activity, with cotton, gum arabic, sorghum, and sesame the main exports. Sugar-cane, sorghum, and livestock are the other main products. The war has stopped exploitation of oil reserves; other resources include silver, chromite, lead, mica, asbestos, talc, tungsten, diamonds, uranium, copper, zinc, iron ore, and gold. Industry is limited to oil-refining and processing agricultural products such as sugar and cotton.

Suriname

Republiek Suriname

CAPITAL Paramaribo
AREA 163,820 km² (63,251 sq. mi.)
POPULATION 405,000 (1989)
POPULATION GROWTH n/a
GNP PER CAPITA $2,360 (1987) (GDP n.a.)
CURRENCY 1 Suriname guilder = 100 cents
LIFE EXPECTANCY 67 (male) 72 (female)
POPULATION UNDER 15 YEARS 40.2%
LITERACY RATE 79.2% (1980)
RELIGION Hindu 27.0%; Roman Catholic 23.0%; Muslim 20.0%; Protestant (mostly Moravian) 19.0%

Sweden's economic success depends heavily on its industrial output, half of which is exported. The Volvo company, one of whose car-assembly plants is shown here, is a major component in that success: foreign sales represent 75 per cent of corporate revenue.

ETHNIC GROUPS East Indian 35.0%; Creole 32.0%; Indonesian 15.0%; African (bush negro) 10.0%; Amerindian 3.0%; Chinese 3.0%; European 1.0%
LANGUAGE Dutch (official); English; Sronan Tongo; Spanish; Hindi; Javanese; Chinese; local Amerindian and pidgin languages
NUCLEAR CAPACITY No
LABOUR FORCE IN AGRICULTURE 16.8% (1985)
MAIN INTERNATIONAL ORGANIZATIONS UN; OAS

Suriname is a multiparty republic, restored to civilian from military rule in 1988. Political unrest has continued in the interior. Dutch aid, on which the economy depends, was restored after the elections. Suriname's exports are dominated by bauxite and its aluminium products but production has been disrupted by civil war. Bauxite-smelting and food-processing are the main industries. There are considerable mineral reserves, especially iron ore and gold. Agriculture is restricted to the alluvial coastal area, rice being the main crop. Sronan Tongo, or Surinamese, a Dutch-based creole, is used as the lingua franca, though Spanish is planned to be the official language.

Swaziland

Kingdom of Swaziland / Umbuso weSwatini (Swazi)

CAPITAL Mbabane (administrative) Lobamba (royal and executive)
AREA 17,364 km² (6,704 sq. mi.)
POPULATION 746,000 (1989)
POPULATION GROWTH 3.4% p.a.
GNP PER CAPITA $810 (1988) (GDP n.a.)
CURRENCY 1 lilangeni = 100 cents
LIFE EXPECTANCY 54 (male) 57 (female)
POPULATION UNDER 15 YEARS 47.3%
LITERACY RATE 67.0%
RELIGION Protestant 37.3%; African indigenous churches 28.9%; traditional beliefs 20.9%; Roman Catholic 10.8%;
ETHNIC GROUPS Swazi 84.3%; Zulu 9.9%; Tsonga 2.5%; Indian 0.8%; Pakistani 0.8%; Portuguese 0.2%
LANGUAGE English, Swazi (both official); Zulu; local languages
NUCLEAR CAPACITY No
LABOUR FORCE IN AGRICULTURE 30.2% (1986)
MAIN INTERNATIONAL ORGANIZATIONS UN; OAU; Commonwealth; SADCC

Swaziland is a landlocked absolute monarchy. The economy is heavily dependent on South Africa; many Swazis find work in South

African mines, and much of Swaziland's electricity is imported from South Africa. The land is fertile, and sugar, citrus fruit, pineapples, and cotton are grown for export. Maize and livestock are important locally, and the forestry industry produces wood-pulp for export. Tourism is increasing. Industry concentrates on processing agricultural products. Coal, diamonds, gold, and asbestos are mined and exported, but the falling world market for asbestos has led to unemployment. Swaziland is a member of the Southern African Customs Union.

Sweden

Konungariket Sverige

CAPITAL Stockholm
AREA 449,964 km² (173,732 sq. mi.)
POPULATION 8.498 million (1989)
POPULATION GROWTH 0.3% p.a.
GDP PER CAPITA $21,155 (1988)
CURRENCY 1 Swedish krona = 100 ore
LIFE EXPECTANCY 74 (male) 80 (female)
POPULATION UNDER 15 YEARS 16.5%
LITERACY RATE Virtually 100%
RELIGION Church of Sweden (Evangelical Lutheran) 90.0%
ETHNIC GROUPS Swedish 90.0%; Finnish 3.1%; Lapp minority
LANGUAGE Swedish (official); minority languages
NUCLEAR CAPACITY Civil and research (14 reactors, 1989)
LABOUR FORCE IN AGRICULTURE 4.2%
MAIN INTERNATIONAL ORGANIZATIONS UN; EFTA; Council of Europe; CSCE

Sweden is a constitutional monarchy. It maintained a policy of non-alignment and neutrality in the two world wars, with a system known as total defence, which includes compulsory national service for males. Sweden applied for EC membership in 1991. It has an industrial economy based on the exploitation of abundant natural and mineral resources. Major exports include machinery, motor vehicles, paper, iron, and steel. A leading producer of iron ore, the country also has deposits of copper, lead, and zinc. Commercial forestry is important, though threatened by acid rain, as are the wood-pulp, sawmill, and paper industries. Electricity is generated almost entirely from nuclear and hydroelectric sources, but it is planned that the nuclear programme be discontinued by 2010. Agriculture has declined in importance, although livestock and dairy-farming are still substantial. Sweden has a large immigrant population, largely as a result of its willingness to provide asylum for refugees. A high level of government expenditure has provided one of the world's best systems of social welfare.

Switzerland

Schweizerische Eidgenossenschaft (German)/Confédération Suisse (French)/Confederazione Svizzera (Italian)

CAPITAL Berne
AREA 41,293 km² (15,943 sq. mi.)
POPULATION 6.689 million (1989)
POPULATION GROWTH 0.4% p.a.
GDP PER CAPITA $27,748 (1988)
CURRENCY 1 Swiss franc = 100 centimes
LIFE EXPECTANCY 74 (male) 80 (female)
POPULATION UNDER 15 YEARS 16.4%
LITERACY RATE Virtually 100%
RELIGION Roman Catholic 48.0%; Protestant 44.0%; Jewish 0.3%
ETHNIC GROUPS German 65.0%; French 18.4%; Italian 9.8%; Spanish 1.6%; Romansch 0.8%; Turkish 0.6%
LANGUAGE French, German, Italian (all official); minority languages
NUCLEAR CAPACITY Civil and research (9 reactors)
LABOUR FORCE IN AGRICULTURE 4.4%
MAIN INTERNATIONAL ORGANIZATIONS OECD; EFTA; Council of Europe; CSCE

Switzerland is a multiparty landlocked federal republic comprising twenty-six cantons (or regions), each with its own parliament and sovereignty, within the limits of the federal constitution. Nationally, government is by a permanent coalition of the four leading political parties. Referenda are commonly used, for example on membership of the UN in 1986, which went against joining. Switzerland applied for EC membership in 1991. Women were not granted suffrage till 1971. Switzerland is neutral and is the headquarters of international organizations such as the Red Cross. It is a prosperous country with the highest GDP per capita in the world. Major exports include machinery, electrical goods, instruments, watches, textiles, and pharmaceuticals. Tourism and international finance and banking are important. Agriculture is mainly livestock- and dairy-farming.

Syria

al-Jumhūrīyah al-'Arabīyah as-Sūrīyah

CAPITAL Damascus
AREA 185,180 km² (71,498 sq. mi.)
POPULATION 11.719 million (1989)
POPULATION GROWTH 3.4% p.a.
GDP PER CAPITA $1,314 (1988)
CURRENCY 1 Syrian pound = 100 piastres
LIFE EXPECTANCY 63 (male) 67 (female)
POPULATION UNDER 15 YEARS 48.1%
LITERACY RATE 60.0%;
RELIGION Sunnī Muslim 72.0%; Alawi (Shī'ī) 11.0%; Druze 3.0%; Christian 9.0%
ETHNIC GROUPS Arab 89.0%; Kurdish 6.0%; Armenian and other 4.0%
LANGUAGE Arabic (official); minority languages
NUCLEAR CAPACITY No
LABOUR FORCE IN AGRICULTURE 25.3% (1988)
MAIN INTERNATIONAL ORGANIZATIONS UN; Arab League; OAPEC

Syria is a republic controlled by the National Progressive Front, a coalition of five socialist parties, including the Ba'ath Party. The ruling élite, headed by President Hafez al-Assad, is from the Alawi minority; political opposition is severely restricted. The Golan Heights area has been occupied by Israel since 1967. Host to some 270,000 Palestinian refugees in 1985, Syria has played a major role in Lebanon, with the aim of fostering unity and preventing its rivals from establishing power bases there. Although still largely agricultural, with sheep- and goat-raising the primary agricultural activities, Syria is becoming more industrialized and has benefited in recent years from rising oil exports. Other exports are textiles, clothing, and chemicals. Mineral resources include petroleum, phosphates, salt, and gypsum, and manufacturing industry includes textiles, cement, and chemicals. The judicial system is based on the Code Napoléon and the *sharī'ah* (Islamic law).

Taiwan

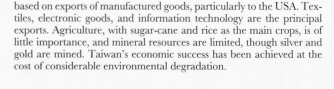

Chung-hua Min-kuo

CAPITAL Taipei
AREA 36,000 km² (13,900 sq. mi.)
POPULATION 20.024 million (1989)
POPULATION GROWTH 1.1% p.a.
GDP PER CAPITA $5,975 (1988)
CURRENCY 1 New Taiwan dollar = 100 cents
LIFE EXPECTANCY 71 (male) 76 (female)
POPULATION UNDER 15 YEARS 28.7%
LITERACY RATE 91.2% (1987)
RELIGION Buddhist 43.0%; Daoist 21.0%; Christian 7.0%; Muslim 0.5%
ETHNIC GROUPS Taiwanese 84.0%; Mainland Chinese 14.0%; Aborigine (Indonesian) 2.0%
LANGUAGE Mandarin Chinese (official); Chinese dialects
NUCLEAR CAPACITY Civil and research (11 reactors, 1989)
LABOUR FORCE IN AGRICULTURE 15.3% (1988)

Taiwan is a multiparty republic which held elections in 1989 after a long period of one-party nationalist government. Taiwan is regarded as a province by the People's Republic of China over which it, in turn, claims jurisdiction. It has had no seat at the UN since 1971, when the People's Republic gained membership and took up the Chinese seat. Taiwan is a newly industrializing country with very high growth rates

based on exports of manufactured goods, particularly to the USA. Textiles, electronic goods, and information technology are the principal exports. Agriculture, with sugar-cane and rice as the main crops, is of little importance, and mineral resources are limited, though silver and gold are mined. Taiwan's economic success has been achieved at the cost of considerable environmental degradation.

Tajikistan

Respublika i Tojikiston

CAPITAL Dushanbe
AREA 143,100 km² (55,240 sq. mi.)
POPULATION 5.1 million
CURRENCY rouble
RELIGION Sunnī Muslim; Eastern Orthodox; Ismā'īlī minority
ETHNIC GROUPS Tajik 62.0%; Uzbek 23.0%; Russian 7.0%
LANGUAGE Tajik (Persian) (official); Russian; minority languages
MAIN INTERNATIONAL ORGANIZATIONS UN; CSCE; Commonwealth of Independent States; North Atlantic Co-operation Council

Tajikistan is a former Soviet republic which became fully independent in 1991 following the disintegration of the Soviet Union. There is a territorial dispute with neighbouring Kyrgyzstan. The poorest of the former Soviet republics, Tajikistan has considerable mineral resources, including coal, zinc, lead, molybdenum, petroleum, and natural gas; mining and extraction of these are the principal heavy industries. Light industry includes a number of textile mills to process cotton, which is the chief agricultural crop. Silk, fruit, wheat, and natural oils are also produced, and cattle are raised. Thousands of Afghan refugees have settled in Tajikistan.

Tanzania

United Republic of Tanzania/Jamhuri ya Muungano wa Tanzania (Swahili)

CAPITAL Dar es Salaam
AREA 945,037 km² (364,881 sq. mi.)
POPULATION 23.729 million (1989)
POPULATION GROWTH 2.9% p.a.
GDP PER CAPITA $160 (1988)
CURRENCY 1 Tanzanian shilling = 100 cents
LIFE EXPECTANCY 51 (male) 55 (female)

Primary sorting of coffee beans in **Tanzania**, where the economy is heavily dependent on this cash crop. The rapid fall in the price of coffee on world markets in the late 1970s undermined the country's economic planning and stifled attempts to improve social conditions.

POPULATION UNDER 15 YEARS 49.1%
LITERACY RATE 85.0%
RELIGION Christian 34.0%; Muslim 33.0%; traditional beliefs and other 33.0%
ETHNIC GROUPS Nyamwezi and Sukuma 21.1%; Swahili 8.8%; Hehet and Bena 6.9%; Makonde 5.9%; Haya 5.9%
LANGUAGE Swahili, English (both official); Sukuma; local languages
NUCLEAR CAPACITY No
LABOUR FORCE IN AGRICULTURE 81.9% (1988)
MAIN INTERNATIONAL ORGANIZATIONS UN; OAU; Commonwealth; Non-Aligned Movement; SADCC

Tanzania is a one-party republic which includes the offshore islands of Pemba and Zanzibar, which have a degree of autonomy. The former British protectorates of Tanganyika and Zanzibar united to form Tanzania in 1964. In recent years Tanzania has shifted from socialist principles in economic planning to IMF-backed liberalization policies, and is making the transition to a multiparty system. Agriculture is the mainstay of the economy, which is dependent on foreign aid, but export cash crops of coffee, cotton, tea, sisal, cashew-nuts, and cloves have all been adversely affected by drought and falling commodity prices. Cassava and maize are the main staple crops. Mineral resources include diamonds, gold, iron ore, coal, and phosphates; there are unexploited natural gas reserves. Industry, mostly state-owned, is limited, with food-processing, textiles, oil- and metal-refining the principal sectors.

Thailand

Prathet Thai/Muang Thai

CAPITAL Bangkok
AREA 513,115 km² (198,115 sq. mi.)
POPULATION 55.258 million (1989)
POPULATION GROWTH 1.9% p.a.
GDP PER CAPITA $1,063
CURRENCY 1 baht = 100 satang
LIFE EXPECTANCY 63 (male) 67 (female)
POPULATION UNDER 15 YEARS 32.7%
LITERACY RATE 88.0%
RELIGION Buddhist 95.0%; Muslim 4.0%; Christian 1.0%
ETHNIC GROUPS Siamese 54.0%; Lao 28.0%; Chinese 11.0%; Malay 4.0%; Khmer 3.0%
LANGUAGE Thai (official); Lao; Chinese; Malay; Mon-Khmer languages
NUCLEAR CAPACITY Research (1 reactor)
LABOUR FORCE IN AGRICULTURE 65.7% (1988)
MAIN INTERNATIONAL ORGANIZATIONS UN; ASEAN; Colombo Plan

Thailand is a parliamentary monarchy with strong military influence. A military coup in 1991 was followed by a new constitution giving the military significant powers, and elections in 1992, which were dominated by parties linked to the military. A newly industrializing country, Thailand has experienced high economic growth in recent years, based on exports of textiles and machinery and agricultural products such as rice, tapioca, and rubber. Mining and industry are replacing agriculture as the leading economic activities. Mineral resources include tin, lead, iron ore, and petroleum. Rice, once the leading export, dominates agricultural production; other crops include sugar-cane, cassava, maize, and rubber. Teak production is also important and tourism a significant earner of foreign exchange. Rapid industrial growth concentrated around Bangkok has strained Thailand's infrastructure.

Tibet

Tibet has been an autonomous region of China since 1965, although it is not recognized as such by the UN. It lost its independence in 1950 when it became a Chinese province. Traditionally, Tibetans were primarily agriculturalists, many of whom were tenant farmers, although some nomadic and semi-nomadic groups of yak-herders also existed. Society was stratified according to occupation, and life was dominated by Tibetan Buddhism. As many as 20 per cent of the population, men and women, were members of religious orders. China has imposed socialism and a variety of changes to traditional Tibetan economy and society, which are fiercely resisted by the local inhabitants. Industrial

development has been promoted, hydroelectric dams have been constructed, and gold, iron ore, and coal are among the minerals mined. The Tibetan language was reinstated in 1988 as a major official language, and more liberal policies towards Tibetan culture were briefly experimented with before a violent clampdown in 1989. The Dalai Lama, Tibet's spiritual and former political leader, is in exile in northern India, together with many Tibetan refugees.

Togo

République Togolaise

CAPITAL Lomé
AREA 56,785 km² (21,925 sq. mi.)
POPULATION 3.622 million (1989)
POPULATION GROWTH 3.5% p.a.
GDP PER CAPITA $370 (1988)
CURRENCY 1 CFA franc = 100 centimes
LIFE EXPECTANCY 51 (male) 55 (female)
POPULATION UNDER 15 YEARS 45.3%
LITERACY RATE 31.4%
RELIGION Traditional beliefs 58.8%; Roman Catholic 21.5%; Muslim 12.0%; Protestant 6.8%
ETHNIC GROUPS Ewé-Adja 43.1%; Tem-Kabre 26.7%; Gurma 5.0%; Kebu-Akposo 3.8%; Ana-Ife (Yoruba) 3.2%; non-African 0.3%
LANGUAGE French (official); Ewé; Kabre; local languages
NUCLEAR CAPACITY No
LABOUR FORCE IN AGRICULTURE 70.3% (1988)
MAIN INTERNATIONAL ORGANIZATIONS UN; OAU; ECOWAS; Franc Zone

Togo is a one-party republic. It became independent in 1960 from its status as a UN mandate under French administration. A new constitution is expected to allow for a multiparty system. Drought and falling world commodity prices adversely affect the economy and loss of income has been exacerbated by a high foreign debt. Agricultural crops for export include cocoa, coffee, and cotton, and staple crops include cassava, maize, and sorghum. Livestock-raising is also of importance. Mining includes phosphates, the principal export, salt, and marble, while industry concentrates on food-processing and cement production. Relations with neighbouring Ghana and Benin have been strained because of political activity by exiles; the Ewé people of the south are divided between Ghana and Togo.

Tonga *Polynesia.

Trinidad and Tobago

Republic of Trinidad and Tobago

CAPITAL Port of Spain
AREA 5,128.4 km² (1,980.1 sq. mi.)
POPULATION 1.285 million (1989)
POPULATION GROWTH 1.7% p.a.
GDP PER CAPITA $3,379 (1988)
CURRENCY 1 Trinidad and Tobago dollar = 100 cents
LIFE EXPECTANCY 68 (male) 73 (female)
POPULATION UNDER 15 YEARS 32.0
LITERACY RATE 94.9%
RELIGION Roman Catholic 32.2%; Hindu 24.3%; Anglican 14.4%; Muslim 5.9%; Presbyterian 3.7%; Pentecostal 3.4%
ETHNIC GROUPS Black 40.8%; East Indian 40.7%; mixed 16.3%; White 0.9%; Chinese 0.5%; Lebanese 0.1%
LANGUAGE English (official)
NUCLEAR CAPACITY No
LABOUR FORCE IN AGRICULTURE 8.0% (1988)
MAIN INTERNATIONAL ORGANIZATIONS UN; Commonwealth; OAS; CARICOM

Trinidad and Tobago is a two-island multiparty republic. It became independent from the UK in 1962. The island of Tobago has its own House of Assembly with a degree of self-government. The economy is dominated by oil, which, with petroleum products, accounts for the majority of exports. There are also large reserves of natural gas. The industrial sector includes an oil refinery, steelworks, and chemicals. With declining oil revenues, tourism, which is comparatively undeveloped, is being encouraged as an alternative source of foreign exchange. Agriculture has been neglected and many staples are imported, although cocoa, sugar, and citrus are grown.

Tunisia

Al-Jumhūrīyah at-Tūnisīyah

CAPITAL Tunis
AREA 154,530 km² (59,664 sq. mi.)
POPULATION 7.973 million (1989)
POPULATION GROWTH 2.7% p.a.
GDP PER CAPITA $1,287 (1988)
CURRENCY 1 Tunisian dinar = 1,000 millimes
LIFE EXPECTANCY 65 (male) 66 (female)
POPULATION UNDER 15 YEARS 37.8%
LITERACY RATE 50.7%
RELIGION Sunnī Muslim 99.4%; Christian 0.3%; Jewish 0.1%
ETHNIC GROUPS Arab 98.2%; Berber 1.2%; French 0.2%; Italian 0.1%
LANGUAGE Arabic (official); French
NUCLEAR CAPACITY No
LABOUR FORCE IN AGRICULTURE 26.1% (1988)
MAIN INTERNATIONAL ORGANIZATIONS UN; OAU; Arab League; Maghreb Union

Tunisia is a republic. A French protectorate until 1956, it became fully independent in that year. Multiparty elections were held after the downfall of President-for-life Bourguiba in 1987, but political life is still dominated by his party, the Rassemblement Constitutionnel Démocratique. The Hizb al-Nahdah, or Party of the Renaissance, an Islamic party, is not legally recognized, but is the principal opposition party. Improved relations with neighbouring Libya have led to renewed interest in developing a Union of the Arab Maghreb composed of Algeria, Libya, Mauritania, Morocco, and Tunisia. Since 1980 Tunisia has provided a temporary headquarters for the Palestine Liberation Organization (PLO). Crude oil is the mainstay of Tunisia's economy, but falling production has caused economic problems. Other mineral resources include phosphate, iron ore, zinc, and lead. Agriculture, though adversely affected by drought and locust plagues in recent years, is well developed, producing cereals, olives, and citrus. Food-processing, oil, and phosphates are the chief manufacturing industries. Tourism also plays an important part in the economy.

Turkey

Türkiye Cumhuriyeti

CAPITAL Ankara
AREA 779,452 km² (300,948 sq. mi.)
POPULATION 55.541 million (1989)
POPULATION GROWTH 2.1% p.a.
GDP PER CAPITA $1,382 (1988)
CURRENCY 1 Turkish lira = 100 kurush
LIFE EXPECTANCY 63 (male) 66 (female)
POPULATION UNDER 15 YEARS 34.3%
LITERACY RATE 74.2%
RELIGION Muslim (principally Sunnī) 99.0%; Eastern Orthodox 0.3%; other Christian and Jewish 0.5%
ETHNIC GROUPS Turkish 85.7%; Kurdish 10.6%; Arab 1.6%; Greek, Armenian, and other 2.1%
LANGUAGE Turkish (official); Kurdish; Arabic
NUCLEAR CAPACITY Research (2 reactors, 1989)
LABOUR FORCE IN AGRICULTURE 50.1% (1988)
MAIN INTERNATIONAL ORGANIZATIONS UN; OECD; NATO; Council of Europe; CSCE

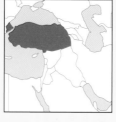

Turkey is a secular multiparty republic, which has been subject to military intervention and the repression of political dissent. A member of NATO, Turkey has associate membership of the EC, and has made an adjourned application for full membership. The status of *Cyprus and the Aegean continental shelf is disputed with Greece. Turkey has an expanding industrial sector and prospering agriculture. Although exports, which include textiles, fruit, vegetables, and metals, have risen, high inflation has threatened economic stability as has rapid population growth and rural exodus to the towns. One of the world's four largest chrome producers, Turkey has rich mineral deposits of coal, antimony, copper, iron ore, sulphur, lead, and zinc. Tourism is expanding, and remittances from Turkish workers abroad are an important source of foreign exchange. The Kurdish insurgent group PKK (Kurdish Workers' Party) is fighting government forces in southeast Turkey, where the Kurdish minority predominates, and Armenian terrorists make sporadic strikes, mainly against Turkish officials abroad.

Turkmenistan

Turkmenostan Respublikasy

CAPITAL Ashkhabad
AREA 488,100 km² (186,400 sq. mi.)
POPULATION 3.522 million
CURRENCY rouble
RELIGION Sunnī Muslim; Eastern Orthodox; Bahā'ī
ETHNIC GROUPS Turkmen 72.0%; Russian 9.0%; Uzbek 9.0%; Kazakh minority
LANGUAGE Turkmen (official); Russian; minority languages
MAIN INTERNATIONAL ORGANIZATIONS UN; CSCE; Commonwealth of Independent States; North Atlantic Co-operation Council;

Turkmenistan is a former Soviet republic which became fully independent in 1991 following the disintegration of the former Soviet Union. Four-fifths of the republic is desert, but it is rich in mineral resources, including chemicals, high-grade petroleum, and natural gas. Other heavy industry concentrates on chemicals, engineering, and metal-processing; light industry includes carpet-making and food- and textile-processing. Agriculture is largely dependent on irrigation; cotton is the chief crop, and karakul sheep, horses, and camels are raised. Silk is also an important product.

Tuvalu *Polynesia.

Uganda

Republic of Uganda

CAPITAL Kampala
AREA 241,040 km² (93,070 sq. mi.)
POPULATION 16.452 million (1989)
POPULATION GROWTH 3.2% p.a.
GDP PER CAPITA $280 (1988)
CURRENCY 1 Uganda shilling = 100 cents
LIFE EXPECTANCY 49 (male) 53 (female)
POPULATION UNDER 15 YEARS 48.5%
LITERACY RATE 68.0%
RELIGION Roman Catholic 49.6%; Protestant 28.7%; traditional beliefs 15.0%; Muslim 6.6%
ETHNIC GROUPS Ganda 17.8%; Teso 8.9%; Nkole 8.2%; Soga 8.2%; Gisu 7.2%; Chiga 6.8%; Lango 6.0%; Rwanda 5.8%; Acholi 4.6%
LANGUAGE English (official); Swahili; Ganda; local languages
NUCLEAR CAPACITY No
LABOUR FORCE IN AGRICULTURE 82.0% (1988)
MAIN INTERNATIONAL ORGANIZATIONS UN; OAU; Non-Aligned Movement; Commonwealth

Uganda is a landlocked republic under the military rule of the National Resistance Movement. It became independent from the UK in 1962. Civil war and repeated coups have disrupted all aspects of national life, leaving about 1 million dead and some 2 million refugees. An Aids epidemic has further crippled the population. High inflation and a thriving unofficial economy create economic problems exacerbated by falling world prices for coffee, which accounts for about 95 per cent of exports. Other cash crops are cotton, tea, and maize, and there are livestock-raising, fishing, and subsistence crops of cassava, cereals, plantains, and yams. Mineral resources include copper, mining

The waters of Lake Victoria, the world's second largest inland fresh water lake, flow through the Owen Falls in **Uganda** into the Victoria Nile River. The Owen Falls dam, shown here, provides hydroelectric power.

of which has ceased, apatite, tin, tungsten, and unexploited iron-ore reserves. Industry concentrates on agricultural processing.

Ukraine

Ukraina

CAPITAL Kiev
AREA 603,700 km² (171,700 sq. mi.)
POPULATION 51.452 million
CURRENCY coupons; grivna to be introduced
RELIGION Eastern Orthodox; Ukrainian Catholic; Jewish minority
ETHNIC GROUPS Ukrainian 73.0%; Russian 22.0%; Belorussian, Moldavan, and Polish minorities
LANGUAGE Ukrainian (official); Russian; minority languages
NUCLEAR CAPACITY civil, defence, and research
MAIN INTERNATIONAL ORGANIZATIONS UN; CSCE; Commonwealth of Independent States; North Atlantic Co-operation Council

Ukraine is a former Soviet republic which became fully independent following the disintegration of the Soviet Union in 1991. Ukraine has granted a degree of autonomy to the predominantly Russian Crimea, which also has large Tatar and German communitiies, but there is a strong independence movement. Control of the former Soviet Black Sea fleet is disputed with Russia. Ukraine has taken measures to reduce its economic interdependence with Russia and the other former Soviet republics, including the introduction of a Ukrainian currency and an agreement to import Iranian oil and natural gas to replace Russian supplies. The largest and most populous of the Soviet republics after the Russian Federation, the Ukraine produced over a fifth of all Soviet agricultural and industrial goods. Mineral resources are abundant and varied, including iron ore, coal, manganese, and some petroleum. Other than mining, heavy industry includes iron and steel production, machinery and transport equipment, aircraft, chemicals, and consumer goods. Food-processing, notably sugar, sunflower oil and wine, and textiles are important light industries. Grain is the most important agricultural product, followed by potatoes, vegetables, fruit, and grapes; industrial crops are sunflower seeds, sugar-beet, and flax. The effects of the Chernobyl nuclear accident have not yet been fully measured, but Ukraine has pledged that it will become a nuclear-free zone.

United Arab Emirates

Ittiḥād al-Imārāt al-ʿArabīyah
CAPITAL Abu Dhabi
AREA 77,700 km² (30,000 sq. mi.)

POPULATION 1.827 million
POPULATION GROWTH 4.4% p.a.
GDP PER CAPITA $15,560 (1988)
CURRENCY 1 UAE dirham = 100 fils
LIFE EXPECTANCY 69 (male) 73 (female)
POPULATION UNDER 15 YEARS 31.1%
LITERACY RATE 73.0% (1986)
RELIGION Sunnī Muslim 80.0%; Shīʿī Muslim 20.0%; Christian minority
ETHNIC GROUPS UAE Arab 30.7%; other Arab 56.4%; Pakistani and Indian 10.0%; Iranian 1.7%
LANGUAGE Arabic (official); other immigrant languages
NUCLEAR CAPACITY No
LABOUR FORCE IN AGRICULTURE 2.9% (1988)
MAIN INTERNATIONAL ORGANIZATIONS UN; GCC; Arab League; OAPEC

The United Arab Emirates (UAE) is a federation of the emirates of Abu Dhabi, Ajman, Dubai, al-Fujayrah, Raʾs al-Khaymah, ash-Shariqah, and Umm al-Qaywayn, each of the seven rulers having autonomy in his own state. The economy of the UAE is based largely on crude oil, which, with natural gas, dominates exports. In addition, Dubai has a substantial entrepôt trade. Industries include petroleum products, cement, and aluminium-smelting. Agriculture suffers from arid conditions and poor irrigation. The judicial system is based on the *sharīʿah* (Islamic law). There is a large immigrant workforce, mainly of Pakistanis, Indians, and Iranians.

United Kingdom

United Kingdom of Great Britain and Northern Ireland

CAPITAL London
AREA 244,110 km² (94,251 sq. mi.)
POPULATION 57.218 million (1989)
POPULATION GROWTH 0.3% p.a.
GDP PER CAPITA $14,477
CURRENCY 1 pound sterling = 100 pence
LIFE EXPECTANCY 72 (male) 78 (female)
POPULATION UNDER 15 YEARS 18.9%
LITERACY RATE Virtually 100%
RELIGION Church of England 50.0%; Roman Catholic 13.0%; Church of Scotland 4.0%; Methodist 2.0%; Baptist 1.0%; Muslim 2.0%; Jewish 0.8%; Hindu 0.75%; Sikh 0.5%
ETHNIC GROUPS White 94.4%; Asian Indian 1.3%; West Indian 1.0%; Pakistani 0.7%; Chinese 0.2%; African 0.2%; Bangladeshi 0.2%; Arab 0.1%
LANGUAGE English (official); Welsh; Scots-Gaelic; other minority languages
NUCLEAR CAPACITY Civil, defence, and research (40 operable, 15 research, 2 under construction)
LABOUR FORCE IN AGRICULTURE 2.1% (1988)
MAIN INTERNATIONAL ORGANIZATIONS UN; EC; Commonwealth; OECD; NATO; Colombo Plan; Council of Europe; CSCE

The United Kingdom (UK) is a parliamentary monarchy, whose Crown is also head of the Commonwealth. Legislative power rests with Parliament, consisting of a directly elected House of Commons and a House of Lords comprised of hereditary peers, life peers, and bishops. Executive power is vested in a cabinet of ministers chosen by the leader of the majority party in the House of Commons, who becomes Prime Minister. The UK is one of the world's most densely populated countries, and the presence of immigrant minorities, especially from former colonies in the Commonwealth, has been a source of tension. There is pressure for further devolution in Wales and Scotland and a revival of Celtic languages in these areas. Scotland has a separate legal system based on Roman law, and a separatist Scottish Nationalist Party, while in Wales, Welsh is the official language, with English. There is incessant political violence in Northern Ireland. The UK has a heavily industrialized economy with substantial, though declining, offshore oil production in the North Sea; main exports include machinery, chemicals, electrical equipment, petroleum, and steel. The UK is one of the world's ten largest steel producers, but its wide range of manufacturing industry has declined in recent years. There is a growing service sector and high-technology industries are being developed. London is an expanding finance and banking centre. The large state sector has shrunk during the 1980s owing to policies of privatization. Coal is mined for domestic consumption and electricity generation. Other mineral resources include iron ore, zinc, tin, and lead. Agricultural productivity has been boosted by mechanization and intensive-farming methods. The UK has a number of colonies and dependencies across the globe. These include *Gibraltar, the *Falkland Islands, British Antarctic Territory, Ascension Island, and South Georgia, British Virgin Islands, *Hong Kong, Isle of Man, and the *Channel Islands.

Northern Ireland comprises the six north-eastern counties of Ireland. The constitution provides for a degree of devolved government, though a policy of direct rule from Westminster has been in force since 1968. There is a Protestant majority, and discrimination against the Roman Catholic minority has led to continuing violent conflict. There has been extensive terrorist violence by the Irish Republican Army (IRA), who are fighting against continuing British rule, and by extremist Protestant groups, who wish to retain the connection with the UK. In 1985, the Anglo-Irish (Hillsborough) Agreement between the UK and Republic of *Ireland was drawn up, giving the Republic a consultative role in the government of the province. Considerably more industrialized than the Republic of Ireland, Northern Ireland is heavily subsidized by the UK, and has a substantial manufacturing base, whose industries include engineering, shipbuilding, construction, electronics, textiles, and chemicals.

United States of America

United States of America

CAPITAL Washington DC
AREA 9,529,063 km² (3,679,192 sq. mi.)
POPULATION 248.777 million (1989)
POPULATION GROWTH 1.0% p.a.
GDP PER CAPITA $19,815
CURRENCY 1 dollar = 100 cents
LIFE EXPECTANCY 72 (male) 79 (female)
POPULATION UNDER 15 YEARS 21.5%
LITERACY RATE 96.0%

RELIGION Protestant 49.1%; Roman Catholic 29.6%; other Christian 8.4%; Jewish 2.7%; Muslim 1.9%; Hindu 0.2%; non-religious and atheist 6.8%
ETHNIC GROUPS European origin (White, of whom Hispanic 6.4%) 83.2%; Black 12.4%; Asian and Pacific Islander 1.5%; Amerindian 0.6%
LANGUAGE English (official); Spanish; numerous minority or immigrant languages
NUCLEAR CAPACITY Civil, defence, and research (108 operable, 92 research, 7 under construction)
LABOUR FORCE IN AGRICULTURE 2.5% (1988)
MAIN INTERNATIONAL ORGANIZATIONS UN; OAS; NATO; OECD; Colombo Plan; Anzus; CSCE

The United States of America (USA) is a multiparty federal republic of fifty states. The constitution provides for the strict separation of the executive, legislative, and judicial branches of the states. Executive power is vested in the President and Vice-President, elected through an electoral college by universal suffrage. Legislative authority lies with Congress, which has two chambers: the Senate, which has two elected members from each state; and the House of Representatives, comprised of members elected from each state, the numbers being linked to the state's population. Each state has its own constitution and a degree of self-government. Voting systems vary among the states, which each have an elected governor and two chambers (except Nebraska, which only has one). Politics have traditionally been dominated by two main parties, Republicans and Democrats. The economy benefits from abundant natural resources and a large internal market. A free-trade treaty was signed with Canada in 1989, and a free-trade region is planned with Canada and Mexico (the North America Free Trade Agreement). Exports, at only 7 per cent of gross domestic product in 1988, show the economy to be largely self-sufficient and comparatively unaffected by global economic trends. However, a surge in imports in the 1980s, particularly from Japan, and the uncompetitiveness of exports have caused a trade deficit which, together with the large federal budget deficit, has aroused world-wide concern. Major exports are electrical goods, machinery, chemicals, motor vehicles, cereals, and aircraft. The USA has a wealth of mineral deposits, including coal, oil, gold, silver, lead, copper, iron ore, zinc, uranium, and phosphates. Regional climatic differences enable agricultural diversity: the main crops are maize and wheat, soya beans, cotton, and tobacco. Fishing, forestry, and livestock are also substantial. Although the open immigration policies of the 19th century have been considerably restricted, the USA still takes more immigrants than any other country, and the ethnic and religious diversity of the population reflects its different cultural origins. A powerful lobbying system operates whereby ethnic or other interest groups may substantially influence policies, as, for example, in the Jewish community's influence of US policy on the Arab–Israeli question, or the farming sector's influence on agricultural policy. Against its historical tradition of isolationism, the USA came to play a dominant role in post-war world politics: first, as a result of the cold war confrontation with the former Soviet Union, which led to the growth of high levels of military power, and which involved the assumption by the US of global commitments and, on occasions, direct intervention; second, as a result of the extent of US economic power, its leading role in the creation of international economic institutions such as the GATT, the IMF, and the World Bank, and the extensive activities of its multinational banks and companies. This position is currently undergoing significant change as a result of the collapse of communist power in Eastern Europe, the disintegration of the Soviet Union, and the economic strength of Germany and Japan. Internally the USA faces serious social problems created by lack of educational opportunity, drug abuse, and rising crime rates, particularly in deprived urban areas.

United States Outlying Territories and Freely Associating States are overseas possessions of the USA. They include the 'unincorporated territories' of Guam (in *Micronesia), and American Samoa (in *Polynesia), the Trust Territory of Palau, the Commonwealths of *Puerto Rico and the Northern Mariana Islands, and the Freely Associating States of the Marshall Islands and the Federated States of Micronesia. Other Pacific territories, all with populations of under 500 in 1980, are Johnston Atoll, the Midway Islands, and Wake Island.

Uruguay

República Oriental del Uruguay

CAPITAL Montevideo
AREA 176,215 km² (68,037 sq. mi.)
POPULATION 3.017 million (1989)
POPULATION GROWTH 0.6% p.a.
GDP PER CAPITA $2,595 (1988)
CURRENCY 1 Uruguayan new peso = 100 centésimos
LIFE EXPECTANCY 68 (male) 74 (female)
POPULATION UNDER 15 YEARS 26.2%
LITERACY RATE 95.0%

RELIGION Roman Catholic 60.0%; Jewish 2.0%; Protestant 2.0%
ETHNIC GROUPS European (Spanish/Italian) 90.0%; Mestizo 3.0%; Jewish 2.0%; mixed 2.0%
LANGUAGE Spanish (official)
NUCLEAR CAPACITY No
LABOUR FORCE IN AGRICULTURE 14.0% (1988)
MAIN INTERNATIONAL ORGANIZATIONS UN; OAS

Uruguay has been a multiparty republic since a period of military domination ended in 1985. Politics have traditionally been dominated by two main parties, the Colorados (Reds) and the Blancos (Whites). Uruguay has a predominantly agricultural economy dominated by livestock-rearing. Textiles, wool, and meat are the major exports. Arable crops, particularly cereals and rice, occupy only 10 per cent of agricultural land. Mineral deposits are insignificant, but hydroelectricity is exported to Brazil, and accounts for some 90 per cent of domestic consumption. Food-processing and textiles are the principal industries.

Uzbekistan

Ozbekiston Respublikasy

CAPITAL Tashkent
AREA 447,400 km² (172,741 sq. mi.)

Oil rigs on Lake Maracaibo, on the Caribbean coast of **Venezuela**. The city of Maracaibo is the capital of Zulia state, which produces 60 per cent of the country's oil. Venezuela has the world's fourth largest oil reserves.

POPULATION 20.3 million
CURRENCY rouble
RELIGION Sunnī Muslim; Eastern Orthodox; Jewish and minority faiths
ETHNIC GROUPS Uzbek 71.0%; Russian 8.0%; Tatar, Tajik, Ukrainian, and Armenian minorities
LANGUAGE Uzbek (official) Russian; minority languages
NUCLEAR CAPACITY uranium producer
MAIN INTERNATIONAL ORGANIZATIONS UN; Commonwealth of Independent States; CSCE; North Atlantic Co-operation Council

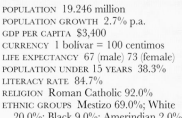

Uzbekistan is a former Soviet republic which became fully independent following the disintegration of the Soviet Union in 1991. It retains a degree of interdependence with other former Soviet republics. The principal mineral reserves are natural gas, petroleum, coal, and metal ores, all of which are extracted. Heavy industry focuses on machinery production, particularly for the cultivation and processing of cotton, of which Uzbekistan is the third largest producer in the world. Other agricultural products are silkworms, fruit, grapes, and livestock, particularly karakul sheep. The increased mechanization of cotton cultivation has cut employment dramatically, and the use of defoliants and pesticides has caused health problems and environmental degradation. The waters of the inland Aral Sea have subsided due to excessive use in agriculture and industry.

Vanuatu *Melanesia.

Venezuela

República de Venezuela
CAPITAL Caracas
AREA 912,050 km² (352,144 sq. mi.)

POPULATION 19.246 million
POPULATION GROWTH 2.7% p.a.
GDP PER CAPITA $3,400
CURRENCY 1 bolívar = 100 centimos
LIFE EXPECTANCY 67 (male) 73 (female)
POPULATION UNDER 15 YEARS 38.3%
LITERACY RATE 84.7%
RELIGION Roman Catholic 92.0%
ETHNIC GROUPS Mestizo 69.0%; White 20.0%; Black 9.0%; Amerindian 2.0%
LANGUAGE Spanish (official); Amerindian languages
NUCLEAR CAPACITY Research (2 reactors)
LABOUR FORCE IN AGRICULTURE 11.9% (1988)
MAIN INTERNATIONAL ORGANIZATIONS UN; OAS; OPEC; Andean Group

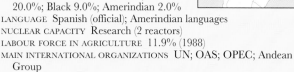

Venezuela is a multiparty republic. Democracy, dominated by the two main parties, Accion Democratica (Democratic Action) and Christian Democrat Copei (Christian Democrat), has been stable since 1958, despite a failed coup by rebel soldiers in 1992. The economy is dominated by state-owned oil production and associated industries, but production has fallen due to a policy of conservation. There are substantial mineral deposits, including bauxite and iron ore, refined by the government-owned steel industry. Although agriculture is potentially rich, Venezuela imports about 60 per cent of its food. The economy has suffered from its over-dependence on oil, high rates of inflation, and foreign debt, and recent austerity measures have caused unrest.

Vietnam

Cong Hoa Xa Hoi Chu Nghia Viet Nam
CAPITAL Hanoi
AREA 331,688 km² (128,065 sq. mi.)
POPULATION 64.747 million (1989)
POPULATION GROWTH 2.3% p.a.
GDP PER CAPITA $154 (1988)
CURRENCY 1 dong = 10 hao = 100 xu
LIFE EXPECTANCY 61 (male) 64 (female)
POPULATION UNDER 15 YEARS 39.2%

LITERACY RATE n.a.
RELIGION Buddhist 55.3%; Roman Catholic 7.0%; Muslim 1.0%
ETHNIC GROUPS Vietnamese (Kinh) 88.0%; Chinese (Hoa) 2.0%; Tai 2.0%; Khmer 1.0%; Muong 1.0%; Thai 1.0%; Nung 1.0%
LANGUAGE Vietnamese (official); minority languages
NUCLEAR CAPACITY Research (1 reactor)
LABOUR FORCE IN AGRICULTURE 62.0% (1988)
MAIN INTERNATIONAL ORGANIZATIONS UN

Vietnam is a one-party communist republic. It was partitioned in 1954 into North and South Vietnam, but following a bitter civil war, which with US military intervention in 1964 became the Vietnam War (1964–75), the south fell to the communist north in 1975. Despite policies of economic liberalization and a decision in 1986 to switch to a free-market economy, the government maintains its adherence to communism. Primarily agricultural, the Vietnamese economy has been badly damaged by war, poor climatic conditions, and a US embargo and veto on Western aid. Once-substantial Soviet aid has ceased, and many of the Vietnamese migrant workers in the former Eastern bloc have returned home. The chief agricultural crops are rice, sugar-cane, and fruits, but Vietnam depends on imports to meet its food requirements. There are large coal and other mineral reserves, including off-shore oil fields. Political change, economic hardship, and ethnic discrimination, particularly against the Chinese minority, have led to the exodus of 'boat people' as refugees from Vietnam.

Wallis and Futuna Islands *Polynesia.

Western Sahara *Morocco.

Western Samoa *Polynesia.

Yemen

al-Jumhūrīyah al-Yamanīyah

CAPITAL San'ā' (political) Aden (economic)
AREA 472,099 km² (182,336 sq. mi.)
POPULATION 11.546 million (1990)
POPULATION GROWTH 3.5% p.a. (1990)
GNP PER CAPITA $640 (1989) (GDP n.a.)
CURRENCY 1 Yemeni dinar = 1,000 fils
    1 Yemeni rial = 100 fils
LIFE EXPECTANCY 50 (male) 53 (female) (S. Yemen); 46 (male) 50 (female) (N. Yemen)
POPULATION UNDER 15 YEARS 49.9%
LITERACY RATE 38.9% (S. Yemen); 18.9% (N. Yemen) (1986)
RELIGION Sunnī Muslim 53.0%; Shī'ī Muslim (mainly in north) 46.9%
ETHNIC GROUPS Arab 97.0%; Indian and Pakistani 1.5%; Somali 1.5%
LANGUAGE Arabic (official)
NUCLEAR CAPACITY No
LABOUR FORCE IN AGRICULTURE 46.6% (S. Yemen); 59.9% (N. Yemen)
MAIN INTERNATIONAL ORGANIZATIONS UN; Arab League

Yemen is a multiparty republic formed by the union in 1990 of the former Yemen Arab Republic (North Yemen) and the former People's Democratic Republic of Yemen (South Yemen). Free elections and a plebiscite on the draft constitution are planned for 1992. In the north, agriculture, mainly sheep- and goat-raising, cotton, coffee, the narcotic *qat*, and other food crops, was the mainstay of the economy until oil production began in 1986. However, further oil exploration is jeopardized by a border dispute with Saudi Arabia. In the south, which was formerly a one-party communist republic with a centrally planned economy heavily dependent on Soviet aid, agriculture is the principal economic activity. Production of the chief crops (cotton, millet, and wheat) is limited by lack of arable land and irrigation. Other than the oil refinery in the south, industry is limited to food-processing. Yemen is heavily dependent on the remittances of migrant workers, and the economy was severely affected by Saudi Arabia's repatriation of some 1 million Yemeni workers following Yemen's neutral stance in the 1991 Gulf War.

Yugoslavia

Federativna Republika
    Jugoslavija

CAPITAL Belgrade
AREA 127,886 km² (49,359 sq. mi.)
POPULATION 12.785 million
POPULATION GROWTH 0.7% p.a.
GDP PER CAPITA $2,279 (1988)
CURRENCY Yugoslav dinar
LIFE EXPECTANCY 69 (male) 75 (female)
POPULATION UNDER 15 YEARS 22.9%
LITERACY RATE 89.6%
RELIGION Serbian Orthodox; Roman Catholic; Muslim; Protestant minority
ETHNIC GROUPS Serb; Croat; Muslim Slav; Slovene; Shiptar (Albanian); Macedonian; Montenegrin; Hungarian; Romany
LANGUAGE Serbo-Croat, Macedonian (official); minority languages
NUCLEAR CAPACITY Civil and research (4 reactors)
LABOUR FORCE IN AGRICULTURE 23.6% (1988)
MAIN INTERNATIONAL ORGANIZATIONS UN; special relationship with OECD; Non-Aligned Movement; CSCE

Yugoslavia is a federal republic. Until 1990 the six republics (Croatia, Slovenia, Macedonia, Bosnia-Herzegovina, Montenegro, and Serbia) and two autonomous provinces within the republic of Serbia (Kosovo and Voyvodina) were united under a one-party communist government, but the transition to multiparty democracy and a free-market economy unleashed powerful secessionist movements, leading to civil war and heavy casualties. *Croatia and *Slovenia, followed by *Bosnia-Herzegovina, achieved independence in early 1992, despite opposition from Serbia, the largest republic, and from the Serb-dominated federal army and government. In 1992 a UN-peacekeeping force was installed in Croatia, where Serbian enclaves seek independence. *Macedonia declared independence at the end of 1991. Kosovo, where there has been long-standing conflict between the Albanian majority and the federal government, seeks independence and is expected, against Serbian opposition, to move towards union with Albania. With Montenegro, Serbia declared a new Yugoslav state in 1992. Under Marshal Tito, Yugoslavia split with Soviet communism in 1948, and played an important role in the Non-Aligned Movement. Policies of 'self-management' led to a lesser degree of centralized control than in other planned economies and an intermediate form of market socialism. However, economic subsidies for the poorer southern republics caused much resentment in the more economically developed northern republics, playing a large part in the latter's search for independence. Common ownership, once widespread, is being displaced by policies of privatization and liberalization. A high level of foreign debt ($13 billion in 1988) and inflation have restricted economic growth. The principal exports are machinery, chemicals, electrical equipment, and food products. Mineral resources include coal, copper, iron ore, lead and zinc ore, and bauxite. Manufacturing industry is well developed, the main industries being steel, chemicals, electronics, and textiles. Agriculture remains significant, the principal products being cereals, livestock, sugar-beet, fruit, and wine. Tourism, which once earned substantial foreign exchange, has been crippled by civil war.

Zaire

République du Zaïre

CAPITAL Kinshasa
AREA 2,345,000 km² (905,446 sq. mi.)
POPULATION 33.336 million
POPULATION GROWTH 3.1% p.a.
GDP PER CAPITA $193 (1988)
CURRENCY 1 zaïre = 100 makuta
LIFE EXPECTANCY 51 (male) 54 (female)
POPULATION UNDER 15 YEARS 46.2%
LITERACY RATE 62.0%
RELIGION Roman Catholic 48.4%; Protestant 29.0%; indigenous Christian 17.1%; traditional beliefs 3.4%; Muslim 1.4%
ETHNIC GROUPS Luba 18.0%; Kongo 16.1%; Mongo 13.5%; Rwanda 10.3%; Azande 6.1%; Bangi and Ngale 5.8%; Rundi 3.8%; Teke 2.7%; Boa 2.3%; Chokwe 1.8%; Lugbara 1.6%; Banda 1.4%

Paddlers on the River Zambesi at Kymboka, in western **Zambia**. This traditional ceremony is performed each year following the floods, when the chief or *Litunga* of the Lozi people is carried upriver to his summer palace.

LANGUAGE French (official); Lingala; Kongo; Swahili; local languages
NUCLEAR CAPACITY Research (1 reactor)
LABOUR FORCE IN AGRICULTURE 66.9% (1988)
MAIN INTERNATIONAL ORGANIZATIONS UN; OAU

Zaire is a republic under the authoritarian rule of President Mobuto. It became independent from Belgium as the Congo Republic in 1960. Opposition parties were allowed in 1990, and the next elections are expected to be multiparty. Africa's third largest country in area, Zaire has substantial agricultural, mineral, and energy resources, whose development is impeded by corruption, smuggling, lack of infrastructure and investment, and falling world commodity prices. The main exports are copper, coffee, diamonds, crude petroleum, and cobalt. Other mineral resources include manganese, zinc, uranium, tin, and gold. Other than coffee, agriculture includes cash crops such as palm kernels, sugar, tea, cocoa, rubber, and cotton, livestock, forestry, and subsistence crops such as plantains and cassava. Coffee production is threatened by fungal disease. Industry includes textiles, cement, engineering, and food-processing. Although its own population is subject to recurrent abuses of human rights, Zaire is host to large numbers of refugees, mainly from Angola.

Zambia

Republic of Zambia

CAPITAL Lusaka
AREA 752,614 km² (290,586 sq. mi.)
POPULATION 7.6 million (1988)
POPULATION GROWTH 3.8% p.a.
GDP PER CAPITA $290 (1988)
CURRENCY 1 Zambian kwacha = 100 ngwee
LIFE EXPECTANCY 52 (male) 55 (female)
POPULATION UNDER 15 YEARS 49.1%
LITERACY RATE 76.0%
RELIGION Protestant 34.2%; Roman Catholic 26.2%; African Christian 8.3%; traditional beliefs 27.0%; Muslim 0.3%
ETHNIC GROUPS Bemba 36.2%; Nyanja 15%; Tonga 19%; Mambwe 8.0%; Barotze 7.0%
LANGUAGE English (official); Bemba; Tonga; local languages
NUCLEAR CAPACITY No
LABOUR FORCE IN AGRICULTURE 69.8% (1988)
MAIN INTERNATIONAL ORGANIZATIONS UN; Commonwealth; SADCC; OAU

Zambia was a one-party republic until multiparty elections were held in 1991 and the ruling party since independence from the UK in 1964 was ousted. With the fourth largest copper reserves in the world, landlocked Zambia has rich mineral resources, including coal, lead, zinc, manganese, cobalt, and gemstones; copper accounts for 91 per cent of exports, followed by cobalt and zinc. However, economic development has been restricted by fluctuating world commodity prices, lack of investment in infrastructure, especially in the mining sector, a large foreign debt, and drought. Industry includes vehicle assembly, petroleum-refining, cement, and chemicals. Neglect of agriculture has led to dependence on food imports; staple crops include maize, cassava and millet, and cattle-rearing is also important.

Zimbabwe

Republic of Zimbabwe

CAPITAL Harare
AREA 390,759 km² (150,873 sq. mi.)
POPULATION 9.122 million (1989)
POPULATION GROWTH 3.7% p.a.
GDP PER CAPITA $650 (1988)
CURRENCY 1 Zimbabwe dollar = 100 cents
LIFE EXPECTANCY 57 (male) 60 (female)
POPULATION UNDER 15 YEARS 44.8%
LITERACY RATE 74.0%;
RELIGION Protestant 17.5%; African indigenous 13.6%; Roman Catholic 11.7%; traditional beliefs 40.0%
ETHNIC GROUPS Shona 70.8%; Ndebele Nguni 15.8%; Nyanja 5.0%; European 2.0%; Asian 0.1%
LANGUAGE English (official); Shona; Ndebele
NUCLEAR CAPACITY No
LABOUR FORCE IN AGRICULTURE 69.1% (1988)
MAIN INTERNATIONAL ORGANIZATIONS UN; Commonwealth; OAU; SADCC; Non-Aligned Movement

Zimbabwe is a landlocked republic. As Rhodesia, it declared unilateral independence from the UK in 1965, and was recognized as the independent state of Zimbabwe under Black majority rule in 1979, following a guerrilla campaign. The commitment of the ruling Zimbabwe African National Union-Patriotic Front (ZANU-PF) to Marxist–Leninist principles and a one-party state is under review. Plans to redistribute White-owned land are in progress. The main exports are tobacco, gold, metal alloys, and cotton. Mineral resources include gold, nickel, copper, tin, chrome, gems, and coal. The main cash crops are tobacco, maize (the main staple), cotton, coffee, and sugar. Beef production is also important. Agriculture has substantially recovered from the devastation of the liberation war, despite recurrent drought. Fluctuations in international commodity prices have restricted the foreign-exchange investment necessary to expand industry, which concentrates on food-processing, metal-refining, chemicals, and textiles. Zimbabwe is subject to ethnic tensions between Shona and Ndebele, and is host to about 150,000 refugees from Mozambique.

Acknowledgements

Photographs

Abbreviations: *u* = upper; *l* = lower/left; *r* = right

AHRTAG, H. Hughes 9; WHO 196

Allsport, David Leah 37; David Cannon 77; 272; Vandystadt 334

Amnesty International, 313

Andes Press Agency, Carlos Reyes 258; Carlos Reyes-Manzo 343

Anglo American Corporation of South Africa, 58

Associated Press, 157; 300 *ul*; Ahmed Azakir 364 *ul*

Axel Poignant Archive, 51

Building Research Establishment Crown Copyright, 2

Camerapix, 167

Camera Press London, Tom Lanser 96; 120

Colorific, Mirella Ricciardi 188

Douglas Dickins Photo Library, 302, 358

Mary Evans Picture Library, Sigmund Freud Copyrights 127

Werner Forman Archive, 94; James Hooper Collection, Watersfield 295

Sally and Richard Greenhill, 110; 193; 262

Greenpeace Communications, Morgan 90

Hammacher Schlemmer, 132

Robert Harding Picture Library, 36; F. Jackson 85; 170; Sassoon 230; J. H. C. Wilson 251; 284; 317; 387; 389

The Hutchison Library, Jeremy Horner 4; Disappearing World/Granada TV 12; Anna Tullis 18; R. Ian Lloyd 20; Leslie Woodhead 28; 29; Michael Macintyre 30; Philip Wolmuth 41; Liba Taylor 44; J. G. Fuller 54; Michael Macintyre 65; Nancy Durrell/Mo Kenna 116; Sarah Errington 128; National Museum Lagos 151 *ll*; 201; Christine Pemberton 226; 286; 292; Leslie Woodhead 308; Bernard Regent 349; Robert Francis 357; Wright Errington 363; 368; 373; 375; 380; 384; 391

Impact Photos, Steve Connors 60; Piers Cavendish 225; Piers Cavendish 240; Steve Connors 267; Ben Edwards 280

Index on Censorship, 43

Intermediate Technology Development Group, 70 *ul*

Islamic Relief, 218

Jerrican, Desplanches 139 *ur*

C. J. Jung Institute, Zurich, 173

Katz Pictures, Jeremy Nicholl 211; J B Pictures/Peter Charlesworth 219

Kobal Collection, 281

Liverpool Daily Post and Echo, 180

Lynx, PO Box 300, Nottingham, UK, 13

Magnum Photos, Martine Franck 82 *ul*; Fred Mayer 126; Gilles Peress 200; Raghu Rai 204; DJG 249; Abbas 329

National Portrait Gallery, London, 176

Jim Meads, 150

M. Mitchell, 268

National Grid, 151 *ur*

Network, Mike Abrahams 139 *u*; Sturrock 146; Mike Abrahams 288; Roger Hutchings 320; Mike Abrahams 332

Norsk Folkemuseum, 210

Novosti Press Agency, 275

Christine Osborne Pictures, 45; 70 *lr*; 177; 271; 351

Oxfam, S. Noble 190

Pacemaker Press, 114

Panos Pictures, Tom Learmonth 6

Ann and Bury Peerless Slide Resources and Picture Library, 142

Popperfoto, Peter Skingley 68; Reuter 84; Agence France Presse 163; 206; 223; A. Durand/Agence France Presse 264; Joel Robine/Agence France Presse 378

Refugee Studies Programme, Oxford, 260

Rex Features, Unimedia 24; 61; Sipa/Win McNamee 72; Sipa/Morvan 74; Sipa/Patrick Durand 118 *lr*; Sipa/Ozturk 130; 154;

Sipa/Torregano 184; Sipa/Keiichi Toyoizumi 227; 245; 309; Sipa/B. Rosen 327; Today 340

Roger-Viollet, 274

SAAB, 383

Science Photo Library, Simon Fraser 140

Spectrum Colour Library, 186; 266; 364 *lr*; 370

Frank Spooner Pictures, Gamma/Marc Deville 32; Gamma/Xavier Zimbardo 55; Gamma/Mitsuhiro Wada 71; Gamma/Gyorgy Sugar 104; Gamma/Pascal Maitre 118 *ul*; Gamma/Art Zanur 137; Gamma/Eric Sander 149; Gamma/Esaias Baitel 152; Gamma/Sidali 168; Gamma/J. Barr 189; Gamma/Utsumi 199; Gamma/Rafael Wollman 248; Gamma/Novosti 297; Gamma/Eric Rouvet 310; Gamma/Kaku Kurita 314; Fujino/Kurita 361

Topham Picture Source, Press Association 17; Associated Press 89; Associated Press 216; Associated Press 239

Turner Broadcasting International, 38

UN, Photo 157804/John Isaac, 231

UNESCO, 93; B. Herzog 321

UNRWA, George Nehmeh 322

US AID, 82 *lr*

Wantok Newspaper, 236

WHO, P. Sharma 333

ZEFA, H. Sunak 49; R. Issing 194; A. Liesecke 283; Spichtinger 311; Aerocamera 372

Illustrations

Russell Birkett and Paul Hazell/Information Design Unit

Picture researcher: Sandra Assersohn

The publishers have made every attempt to contact the owners of material appearing in this book. In the few instances where they have been unsuccessful they invite the copyright holders to contact them direct.

Religions of the world

Muslim

Sunni

Shi'a

Christian

Protestant

Roman Catholic

Orthodox

Minority religions/Non-religious

African traditional beliefs

Daoism

Buddhism

Hinduism

Jewish

Shinto

Shamanism

Chinese or other popular religion

Countries are coloured with the predominant
religion according to available statistics.
Where there are significant minorities, the
proportions are shown by coloured bands.